Writings
Franklin, Benjamin

23585
973.2 FRA

Daniels County Library

DATE DUE

FEB 0 8 2018	

	D0016356

BRODART, INC.   Cat. No. 23-221

BENJAMIN FRANKLIN

BENJAMIN FRANKLIN

WRITINGS

Boston and London, 1722–1726
Philadelphia, 1726–1757
London, 1757–1775
Paris, 1776–1785
Philadelphia, 1785–1790
Poor Richard's Almanack, 1733–1758
The Autobiography

THE LIBRARY OF AMERICA

Volume arrangement, notes, and chronology copyright © 1987 by
Literary Classics of the United States, Inc., New York, N.Y.
All rights reserved.
No part of this book may be reproduced commercially
by offset-lithographic or equivalent copying devices without
the permission of the publisher.

Some of the material in this volume is reprinted by
permission of the holders of copyright and publication rights.
Acknowledgments will be found in the Note on the Texts.

The paper used in this publication meets the minimum
requirements of the American National Standard
for Information Sciences—Permanence of Paper for
Printed Library Materials, ANSI Z39.48–1984.

Distributed to the trade in the United States
and Canada by the Viking Press.

Library of Congress Catalog Card Number: 87–3303
For cataloging information, see end of the index.
ISBN 0-940450-29-1

Second Printing
The Library of America—37

Manufactured in the United States of America

J. A. Leo Lemay
WROTE THE NOTES AND SELECTED THE
TEXTS FOR THIS VOLUME

Grateful acknowledgment is made to the National Endowment for the Humanities, the Ford Foundation, and the Andrew W. Mellon Foundation for their generous support of this series.

The publishers wish to thank the Library Company of Philadelphia, Historical Society of Pennsylvania, American Philosophical Society, The Papers of Benjamin Franklin, Yale University Library, New-York Historical Society, Columbia University Library, New York Public Library, and Massachusetts Historical Society for the use of archival materials.

Contents

Each section has its own table of contents.

BOSTON AND LONDON
1722 – 1726

Contents

Silence Dogood, No. 1

To the Author of the New-England Courant.

Sir,

It may not be improper in the first Place to inform your Readers, that I intend once a Fortnight to present them, by the Help of this Paper, with a short Epistle, which I presume will add somewhat to their Entertainment.

And since it is observed, that the Generality of People, now a days, are unwilling either to commend or dispraise what they read, until they are in some measure informed who or what the Author of it is, whether he be *poor* or *rich*, *old* or *young*, a *Schollar* or a *Leather Apron Man*, &c. and give their Opinion of the Performance, according to the Knowledge which they have of the Author's Circumstances, it may not be amiss to begin with a short Account of my past Life and present Condition, that the Reader may not be at a Loss to judge whether or no my Lucubrations are worth his reading.

At the time of my Birth, my Parents were on Ship-board in their Way from *London* to *N. England*. My Entrance into this troublesome World was attended with the Death of my Father, a Misfortune, which tho' I was not then capable of knowing, I shall never be able to forget; for as he, poor Man, stood upon the Deck rejoycing at my Birth, a merciless Wave entred the Ship, and in one Moment carry'd him beyond Reprieve. Thus was the *first Day* which I saw, the *last* that was seen by my Father; and thus was my disconsolate Mother at once made both a *Parent* and a *Widow*.

When we arrived at *Boston* (which was not long after) I was put to Nurse in a Country Place, at a small Distance from the Town, where I went to School, and past my Infancy and Childhood in Vanity and Idleness, until I was bound out Apprentice, that I might no longer be a Charge to my Indigent Mother, who was put to hard Shifts for a Living.

My Master was a Country Minister, a pious good-natur'd young Man, & a Batchelor: He labour'd with all his Might to instil vertuous and godly Principles into my tender Soul, well knowing that it was the most suitable Time to make deep and lasting Impressions on the Mind, while it was yet untainted with Vice, free and unbiass'd. He endeavour'd that I might be instructed in all that Knowledge and Learning which is necessary for our Sex, and deny'd me no Accomplishment that could possibly be attained in a Country Place; such as all Sorts of Needle-Work, Writing, Arithmetick, &c. and observing that I took a more than ordinary Delight in reading ingenious Books, he gave me the free Use of his Library, which tho' it was but small, yet it was well chose, to inform the Understanding rightly, and enable the Mind to frame great and noble Ideas.

Before I had liv'd quite two Years with this Reverend Gentleman, my indulgent Mother departed this Life, leaving me as it were by my self, having no Relation on Earth within my Knowledge.

I will not abuse your Patience with a tedious Recital of all the frivolous Accidents of my Life, that happened from this Time until I arrived to Years of Discretion, only inform you that I liv'd a chearful Country Life, spending my leisure Time either in some innocent Diversion with the neighbouring Females, or in some shady Retirement, with the best of Company, *Books.* Thus I past away the Time with a Mixture of Profit and Pleasure, having no Affliction but what was imaginary, and created in my own Fancy; as nothing is more common with us Women, than to be grieving for nothing, when we have nothing else to grieve for.

As I would not engross too much of your Paper at once, I will defer the Remainder of my Story until my next Letter; in the mean time desiring your Readers to exercise their Patience, and bear with my Humours now and then, because I shall trouble them but seldom. I am not insensible of the Impossibility of pleasing all, but I would not willingly displease any; and for those who will take Offence where none is intended, they are beneath the Notice of

Your Humble Servant,
SILENCE DOGOOD.

The New-England Courant, April 2, 1722

Silence Dogood, No. 2

To the Author of the New-England Courant.

SIR,   [No 2

Histories of Lives are seldom entertaining, unless they contain something either admirable or exemplar: And since there is little or nothing of this Nature in my own Adventures, I will not tire your Readers with tedious Particulars of no Consequence, but will briefly, and in as few Words as possible, relate the most material Occurrences of my Life, and according to my Promise, confine all to this Letter.

My Reverend Master who had hitherto remained a Batchelor, (after much Meditation on the Eighteenth verse of the Second Chapter of *Genesis*,) took up a Resolution to marry; and having made several unsuccessful fruitless Attempts on the more topping Sort of our Sex, and being tir'd with making troublesome Journeys and Visits to no Purpose, he began unexpectedly to cast a loving Eye upon Me, whom he had brought up cleverly to his Hand.

There is certainly scarce any Part of a Man's Life in which he appears more silly and ridiculous, than when he makes his first Onset in Courtship. The aukward Manner in which my Master first discover'd his Intentions, made me, in spite of my Reverence to his Person, burst out into an unmannerly Laughter: However, having ask'd his Pardon, and with much ado compos'd my Countenance, I promis'd him I would take his Proposal into serious Consideration, and speedily give him an Answer.

As he had been a great Benefactor (and in a Manner a Father to me) I could not well deny his Request, when I once perceived he was in earnest. Whether it was Love, or Gratitude, or Pride, or all Three that made me consent, I know not; but it is certain, he found it no hard Matter, by the Help of his Rhetorick, to conquer my Heart, and perswade me to marry him.

This unexpected Match was very astonishing to all the Country round about, and served to furnish them with Discourse for a long Time after; some approving it, others disliking it, as they were led by their various Fancies and Inclinations.

We lived happily together in the Heighth of conjugal Love and mutual Endearments, for near Seven Years, in which Time we added Two likely Girls and a Boy to the Family of the *Dogoods*: But alas! When my Sun was in its meridian Altitude, inexorable unrelenting Death, as if he had envy'd my Happiness and Tranquility, and resolv'd to make me entirely miserable by the Loss of so good an Husband, hastened his Flight to the Heavenly World, by a sudden unexpected Departure from this.

I have now remained in a State of Widowhood for several Years, but it is a State I never much admir'd, and I am apt to fancy that I could be easily perswaded to marry again, provided I was sure of a good-humour'd, sober, agreeable Companion: But one, even with these few good Qualities, being hard to find, I have lately relinquish'd all Thoughts of that Nature.

At present I pass away my leisure Hours in Conversation, either with my honest Neighbour *Rusticus* and his Family, or with the ingenious Minister of our Town, who now lodges at my House, and by whose Assistance I intend now and then to beautify my Writings with a Sentence or two in the learned Languages, which will not only be fashionable, and pleasing to those who do not understand it, but will likewise be very ornamental.

I shall conclude this with my own Character, which (one would think) I should be best able to give. *Know then*, That I am an Enemy to Vice, and a Friend to Vertue. I am one of an extensive Charity, and a great Forgiver of *private* Injuries: A hearty Lover of the Clergy and all good Men, and a mortal Enemy to arbitrary Government & unlimited Power. I am naturally very jealous for the Rights and Liberties of my Country; & the least appearance of an Incroachment on those invaluable Priviledges, is apt to make my Blood boil exceedingly. I have likewise a natural Inclination to observe and reprove the Faults of others, at which I have an excellent Faculty. I speak this by Way of Warning to all such whose Offences shall come under my Cognizance, for I never intend to wrap my Talent in a Napkin. To be brief; I am courteous and affable, good-humour'd (unless I am first provok'd,) and handsome, and sometimes witty, but always,

SIR,

> Your Friend, and Humble Servant,
> SILENCE DOGOOD.

The New-England Courant, April 16, 1722

Silence Dogood, No. 3

To the Author of the New-England Courant.

SIR,   [No 3

It is undoubtedly the Duty of all Persons to serve the Country they live in, according to their Abilities; yet I sincerely acknowledge, that I have hitherto been very deficient in this Particular; whether it was for want of Will or Opportunity, I will not at present stand to determine: Let it suffice, that I now take up a Resolution, to do for the future all that *lies in my Way* for the Service of my Countrymen.

I have from my Youth been indefatigably studious to gain and treasure up in my Mind all useful and desireable Knowledge, especially such as tends to improve the Mind, and enlarge the Understanding: And as I have found it very beneficial to me, I am not without Hopes, that communicating my small Stock in this Manner, by Peace-meal to the Publick, may be at least in some Measure useful.

I am very sensible that it is impossible for me, or indeed any *one* Writer to please *all* Readers at once. Various Persons have different Sentiments; and that which is pleasant and delightful to one, gives another a Disgust. He that would (in this Way of Writing) please all, is under a Necessity to make his Themes almost as numerous as his Letters. He must one while be merry and diverting, then more solid and serious; one while sharp and satyrical, then (to mollify that) be sober and religious; at one Time let the Subject be Politicks, then let the next Theme be Love: Thus will every one, one Time or other find some thing agreeable to his own Fancy, and in his Turn be delighted.

According to this Method I intend to proceed, bestowing now and then a few gentle Reproofs on those who deserve them, not forgetting at the same time to applaud those whose Actions merit Commendation. And here I must not forget to invite the ingenious Part of your Readers, particularly those of my own Sex to enter into a Correspondence with me, assuring them, that their Condescension in this Particular shall be received as a Favour, and accordingly acknowledged.

I think I have now finish'd the Foundation, and I intend in my next to begin to raise the Building. Having nothing more to write at present, I must make the usual excuse in such Cases, of *being in haste*, assuring you that I speak from my Heart when I call my self, The most humble and obedient of all the Servants your Merits have acquir'd,

SILENCE DOGOOD.

The New-England Courant, April 30, 1722

Silence Dogood, No. 4

An sum etiam nunc vel Græcè loqui vel Latinè docendus?   Cicero.

To the Author of the New-England Courant.

Sir,   [No 4

Discoursing the other Day at Dinner with my Reverend Boarder, formerly mention'd, (whom for Distinction sake we will call by the Name of *Clericus,*) concerning the Education of Children, I ask'd his Advice about my young Son *William,* whether or no I had best bestow upon him Academical Learning, or (as our Phrase is) *bring him up at our College*: He perswaded me to do it by all Means, using many weighty Arguments with me, and answering all the Objections that I could form against it; telling me withal, that he did not doubt but that the Lad would take his Learning very well, and not idle away his Time as too many there now-a-days do. These Words of *Clericus* gave me a Curiosity to inquire a little more strictly into the present Circumstances of that famous Seminary of Learning; but the Information which he gave me, was neither pleasant, nor such as I expected.

As soon as Dinner was over, I took a solitary Walk into my Orchard, still ruminating on *Clericus*'s Discourse with much Consideration, until I came to my usual Place of Retirement under the *Great Apple-Tree*; where having seated my self, and carelesly laid my Head on a verdant Bank, I fell by Degrees into a soft and undisturbed Slumber. My waking Thoughts remained with me in my Sleep, and before I awak'd again, I dreamt the following DREAM.

I fancy'd I was travelling over pleasant and delightful Fields and Meadows, and thro' many small Country Towns and Villages; and as I pass'd along, all Places resounded with the Fame of the Temple of LEARNING: Every Peasant, who had wherewithal, was preparing to send one of his Children at least to this famous Place; and in this Case most of them consulted their own Purses instead of their Childrens Capacities: So that I observed, a great many, yea, the most part of those who were travelling thither, were little better than Dunces and Blockheads. Alas! alas!

At length I entred upon a spacious Plain, in the Midst of which was erected a large and stately Edifice: It was to this that a great Company of Youths from all Parts of the Country were going; so stepping in among the Crowd, I passed on with them, and presently arrived at the Gate.

The Passage was kept by two sturdy Porters named *Riches* and *Poverty*, and the latter obstinately refused to give Entrance to any who had not first gain'd the Favour of the former; so that I observed, many who came even to the very Gate, were obliged to travel back again as ignorant as they came, for want of this necessary Qualification. However, as a Spectator I gain'd Admittance, and with the rest entred directly into the Temple.

In the Middle of the great Hall stood a stately and magnificent Throne, which was ascended to by two high and difficult Steps. On the Top of it sat LEARNING in awful State; she was apparelled wholly in Black, and surrounded almost on every Side with innumerable Volumes in all Languages. She seem'd very busily employ'd in writing something on half a Sheet of Paper, and upon Enquiry, I understood she was preparing a Paper, call'd, *The New-England Courant*. On her Right Hand sat *English*, with a pleasant smiling Countenance, and handsomely attir'd; and on her left were seated several *Antique Figures* with their Faces vail'd. I was considerably puzzl'd to guess who they were, until one informed me, (who stood beside me,) that those Figures on her left Hand were *Latin*, *Greek*, *Hebrew*, &c. and that they were very much reserv'd, and seldom or never unvail'd their Faces here, and then to few or none, tho' most of those who have in this Place acquir'd so much Learning as to distinguish them from *English*, pretended to an intimate Acquaintance with them. I then enquir'd of him, what could be the Reason why they continued vail'd, in this Place especially: He pointed to the Foot of the Throne, where I saw *Idleness*, attended with *Ignorance*, and these (he informed me) were they, who first vail'd them, and still kept them so.

Now I observed, that the whole Tribe who entred into the Temple with me, began to climb the Throne; but the Work proving troublesome and difficult to most of them, they withdrew their Hands from the Plow, and contented themselves to sit at the Foot, with Madam *Idleness* and her Maid *Ignorance*, until those who were assisted by Diligence and a docible Temper, had well nigh got up the first Step: But the Time drawing nigh in which they could no way avoid ascending, they were fain to crave the Assistance of those who had got up before them, and who, for the Reward perhaps of a *Pint of Milk*, or a *Piece of Plumb-Cake*, lent the Lubbers a helping Hand, and sat them in the Eye of the World, upon a Level with themselves.

The other Step being in the same Manner ascended, and the usual Ceremonies at an End, every Beetle-Scull seem'd well satisfy'd with his own Portion of Learning, tho' perhaps he was *e'en just* as ignorant as ever. And now the Time of their Departure being come, they march'd out of Doors to make Room for another Company, who waited for Entrance: And I, having seen all that was to be seen, quitted the Hall likewise, and went to make my Observations on those who were just gone out before me.

Some I perceiv'd took to Merchandizing, others to Travelling, some to one Thing, some to another, and some to Nothing; and many of them from henceforth, for want of

Patrimony, liv'd as poor as Church Mice, being unable to dig, and asham'd to beg, and to live by their Wits it was impossible. But the most Part of the Crowd went along a large beaten Path, which led to a Temple at the further End of the Plain, call'd, *The Temple of Theology.* The Business of those who were employ'd in this Temple being laborious and painful, I wonder'd exceedingly to see so many go towards it; but while I was pondering this Matter in my Mind, I spy'd *Pecunia* behind a Curtain, beckoning to them with her Hand, which Sight immediately satisfy'd me for whose Sake it was, that a great Part of them (I will not say all) travel'd that Road. In this Temple I saw nothing worth mentioning, except the ambitious and fraudulent Contrivances of *Plagius*, who (notwithstanding he had been severely reprehended for such Practices before) was diligently transcribing some eloquent Paragraphs out of *Tillotson's Works, &c.* to embellish his own.

Now I bethought my self in my Sleep, that it was Time to be at Home, and as I fancy'd I was travelling back thither, I reflected in my Mind on the extream Folly of those Parents, who, blind to their Childrens Dulness, and insensible of the Solidity of their Skulls, because they think their Purses can afford it, will needs send them to the Temple of Learning, where, for want of a suitable Genius, they learn little more than how to carry themselves handsomely, and enter a Room genteely, (which might as well be acquir'd at a Dancing-School,) and from whence they return, after Abundance of Trouble and Charge, as great Blockheads as ever, only more proud and self-conceited.

While I was in the midst of these unpleasant Reflections, *Clericus* (who with a Book in his Hand was walking under the Trees) accidentally awak'd me; to him I related my Dream with all its Particulars, and he, without much Study, presently interpreted it, assuring me, *That it was a lively Representation of* HARVARD COLLEGE, *Etcetera.*

> *I remain, Sir,*
> *Your Humble Servant,*
> SILENCE DOGOOD.

The New-England Courant, May 14, 1722

Silence Dogood, No. 5

———*Mulier Mulieri magis congruet.*   Ter.

To the Author of the New-England Courant.

Sir,   [No V.

I shall here present your Readers with a Letter from one, who informs me that I have begun at the wrong End of my Business, and that I ought to begin at Home, and censure the Vices and Follies of my own Sex, before I venture to meddle with your's: Nevertheless, I am resolved to dedicate this Speculation to the Fair Tribe, and endeavour to show, that Mr. *Ephraim* charges Women with being particularly guilty of Pride, Idleness, *&c.* wrongfully, inasmuch as the Men have not only as great a Share in those Vices as the Women, but are likewise in a great Measure the Cause of that which the Women are guilty of. I think it will be best to produce my Antagonist, before I encounter him.

To Mrs. DOGOOD.

'*Madam,*

'My Design in troubling you with this Letter is, to desire you would begin with your own Sex first: Let the first Volley of your Resentments be directed against *Female* Vice; let Female Idleness, Ignorance and Folly, (which are Vices more peculiar to your Sex than to our's,) be the Subject of your Satyrs, but more especially Female Pride, which I think is intollerable. Here is a large Field that wants Cultivation, and which I believe you are able (if willing) to improve with Advantage; and when you have once reformed the Women, you will find it a much easier Task to reform the Men, because Women are the prime Causes of a great many Male Enormities. This is all at present from

Your Friendly Wellwisher,
Ephraim Censorious.'

After Thanks to my Correspondent for his Kindness in cutting out Work for me, I must assure him, that I find it a very difficult Matter to reprove Women separate from the Men; for what Vice is there in which the Men have not as great a Share as the Women? and in some have they not a far greater, as in Drunkenness, Swearing, *&c.*? And if they have, then it follows, that when a Vice is to be reproved, Men, who are most culpable, deserve the most Reprehension, and certainly therefore, ought to have it. But we will wave this Point at present, and proceed to a particular Consideration of what my Correspondent calls *Female Vice*.

As for Idleness, if I should Quære, Where are the greatest Number of its Votaries to be found, with us or the Men? it might I believe be easily and truly answer'd, *With the latter*. For notwithstanding the Men are commonly complaining how hard they are forc'd to labour, only to maintain their Wives in Pomp and Idleness, yet if you go among the Women, you will learn, that *they have always more Work upon their Hands than they are able to do*, and that *a Woman's Work is never done*, &c. But however, Suppose we should grant for once, that we are generally more idle than the Men, (without making any Allowance for the *Weakness of the Sex*,) I desire to know whose Fault it is? Are not the Men to blame for their Folly in maintaining us in Idleness? Who is there that can be handsomely supported in Affluence, Ease and Pleasure by another, that will chuse rather to earn his Bread by the Sweat of his own Brows? And if a Man will be so fond and so foolish, as to labour hard himself for a Livelihood, and suffer his Wife in the mean Time to sit in Ease and Idleness, let him not blame her if she does so, for it is in a great Measure his own Fault.

And now for the Ignorance and Folly which he reproaches us with, let us see (if we are Fools and Ignoramus's) whose is the Fault, the Men's or our's. An ingenious Writer, having this Subject in Hand, has the following Words, wherein he lays the Fault wholly on the Men, for not allowing Women the Advantages of Education.

"I have (says he) often thought of it as one of the most barbarous Customs in the World, considering us as a civiliz'd and Christian Country, that we deny the Advantages of Learning to Women. We reproach the Sex every Day with Folly and Impertinence, while I am confident, had they the Advantages of Education equal to us, they would be guilty of less than our selves. One would wonder indeed how it should happen that Women are conversible at all, since they are only beholding to natural Parts for all their Knowledge. Their

Youth is spent to teach them to stitch and sow, or make Bau-bles: They are taught to read indeed, and perhaps to write their Names, or so; and that is the Heigth of a Woman's Ed-ucation. And I would but ask any who slight the Sex for their Understanding, What is a Man (a Gentleman, I mean) good for that is taught no more? If Knowlege and Understanding had been useless Additions to the Sex, God Almighty would never have given them Capacities, for he made nothing Need-less. What has the Woman done to forfeit the Priviledge of being taught? Does she plague us with her Pride and Imper-tinence? Why did we not let her learn, that she might have had more Wit? Shall we upbraid Women with Folly, when 'tis only the Error of this inhumane Custom that hindred them being made wiser."

So much for Female Ignorance and Folly; and now let us a little consider the Pride which my Correspondent thinks is *intollerable*. By this Expression of his, one would think he is some dejected Swain, tyranniz'd over by some cruel haughty Nymph, who (perhaps he thinks) has no more Reason to be proud than himself. *Alas-a-day!* What shall we say in this Case! Why truly, if Women are proud, it is certainly owing to the Men still; for if they will be such *Simpletons* as to humble themselves at their Feet, and fill their credulous Ears with ex-travagant Praises of their Wit, Beauty, and other Accomplish-ments (perhaps where there are none too,) and when Women are by this Means perswaded that they are Something more than humane, what Wonder is it, if they carry themselves haughtily, and live extravagantly. Notwithstanding, I believe there are more Instances of extravagant Pride to be found among Men than among Women, and this Fault is certainly more hainous in the former than in the latter.

Upon the whole, I conclude, that it will be impossible to lash any Vice, of which the Men are not equally guilty with the Women, and consequently deserve an equal (if not a greater) Share in the Censure. However, I exhort both to amend, where both are culpable, otherwise they may expect to be severely handled by

> *Sir,*
> *Your Humble Servant,*
> SILENCE DOGOOD.

N. B. *Mrs.* Dogood *has lately left her Seat in the Country, and come to* Boston, *where she intends to tarry for the Summer Season, in order to compleat her Observations of the present reigning Vices of the Town.*

The New-England Courant, May 28, 1722

Silence Dogood, No. 6

Quem Dies videt veniens Superbum,
Hunc Dies vidit fugiens jacentem.
                                        Seneca.

To the Author of the New-England Courant.

Sir,   [No VI.

Among the many reigning Vices of the Town which may at any Time come under my Consideration and Reprehension, there is none which I am more inclin'd to expose than that of *Pride.* It is acknowledg'd by all to be a Vice the most hateful to God and Man. Even those who nourish it in themselves, hate to see it in others. The proud Man aspires after Nothing less than an unlimited Superiority over his Fellow-Creatures. He has made himself a King in *Soliloquy;* fancies himself conquering the World; and the Inhabitants thereof consulting on proper Methods to acknowledge his Merit. I speak it to my Shame, I my self was a Queen from the Fourteenth to the Eighteenth Year of my Age, and govern'd the World all the Time of my being govern'd by my Master. But this speculative Pride may be the Subject of another Letter: I shall at present confine my Thoughts to what we call *Pride of Apparel.* This Sort of Pride has been growing upon us ever since we parted with our Homespun Cloaths for *Fourteen Penny Stuffs,* &c. And the *Pride of Apparel* has begot and nourish'd in us a *Pride of Heart,* which portends the Ruin of Church and State. *Pride goeth before Destruction, and a haughty Spirit before a Fall*: And I remember my late Reverend Husband would often say upon this Text, That a Fall was the *natural Consequence,* as well as *Punishment* of Pride. Daily Experience is sufficient to evince the Truth of this Obser-

vation. Persons of small Fortune under the Dominion of this
Vice, seldom consider their Inability to maintain themselves
in it, but strive to imitate their Superiors in Estate, or Equals
in Folly, until one Misfortune comes upon the Neck of
another, and every Step they take is a Step backwards. By
striving to appear rich they become really poor, and deprive
themselves of that Pity and Charity which is due to the
humble poor Man, who is made so more immediately by
Providence.

This Pride of Apparel will appear the more foolish, if we
consider, that those airy Mortals, who have no other Way of
making themselves considerable but by gorgeous Apparel,
draw after them Crowds of Imitators, who hate each other
while they endeavour after a Similitude of Manners. They
destroy by Example, and envy one another's Destruction.

I cannot dismiss this Subject without some Observations
on a particular Fashion now reigning among my own Sex,
the most immodest and inconvenient of any the Art of
Woman has invented, namely, that of *Hoop-Petticoats*. By
these they are incommoded in their General and Particular
Calling, and therefore they cannot answer the Ends of either
necessary or ornamental Apparel. These monstrous topsy-
turvy *Mortar-Pieces*, are neither fit for the Church, the Hall,
or the Kitchen; and if a Number of them were well mounted
on *Noddles-Island*, they would look more like Engines of War
for bombarding the Town, than Ornaments of the Fair Sex.
An honest Neighbour of mine, happening to be in Town
some time since on a publick Day, inform'd me, that he saw
four Gentlewomen with their Hoops half mounted in a Bal-
cony, as they withdrew to the Wall, to the great Terror of
the Militia, who (he thinks) might attribute their irregular
Volleys to the formidable Appearance of the Ladies Petti-
coats.

I assure you, Sir, I have but little Hopes of perswading my
Sex, by this Letter, utterly to relinquish the extravagant Fool-
ery, and Indication of Immodesty, in this monstrous Garb of
their's; but I would at least desire them to lessen the Circumference of their Hoops, and leave it with them to consider,
Whether they, who pay no Rates or Taxes, ought to take up

more Room in the King's High-Way, than the Men, who yearly contribute to the Support of the Government.

> *I am, Sir,*
> *Your Humble Servant,*
> SILENCE DOGOOD.

The New-England Courant, June 11, 1722

Silence Dogood, No. 7

> *Give me the Muse, whose generous Force,*
> *Impatient of the Reins,*
> *Pursues an unattempted Course,*
> *Breaks all the Criticks Iron Chains.*
> Watts.

To the Author of the New-England Courant.

Sir,   No VII.

It has been the Complaint of many Ingenious Foreigners, who have travell'd amongst us, *That good Poetry is not to be expected in* New-England. I am apt to Fancy, the Reason is, not because our Countreymen are altogether void of a Poetical Genius, nor yet because we have not those Advantages of Education which other Countries have, but purely because we do not afford that Praise and Encouragement which is merited, when any thing extraordinary of this Kind is produc'd among us: Upon which Consideration I have determined, when I meet with a Good Piece of *New-England* Poetry, to give it a suitable Encomium, and thereby endeavour to discover to the World some of its Beautys, in order to encourage the Author to go on, and bless the World with more, and more Excellent Productions.

There has lately appear'd among us a most Excellent Piece of Poetry, entituled, *An Elegy upon the much Lamented Death of Mrs.* Mehitebell Kitel, *Wife of Mr.* John Kitel *of* Salem, *&c.* It may justly be said in its Praise, without Flattery to the Author, that it is the most *Extraordinary* Piece that ever was wrote in *New-England*. The Language is so soft and Easy, the Expression so moving and pathetick, but above all, the Verse and Numbers so Charming and Natural, that it is almost beyond Comparison,

> * The Muse *disdains*
> *Those Links and Chains,*
> *Measures and Rules of vulgar Strains,*
> *And o'er the Laws of Harmony a Sovereign Queen she reigns.*

I find no English Author, Ancient or Modern, whose Elegies may be compar'd with this, in respect to the Elegance of Stile, or Smoothness of Rhime; and for the affecting Part, I will leave your Readers to judge, if ever they read any Lines, that would sooner make them *draw their Breath* and Sigh, if not shed Tears, than these following.

> *Come let us mourn, for we have lost a Wife, a Daughter,*
>   *and a Sister,*
> *Who has lately taken Flight, and greatly we have mist her.*

In another Place,

> Some little Time *before she yielded up her Breath,*
> *She said, I ne'er shall hear one Sermon more on Earth.*
> *She kist her Husband* some little Time *before she expir'd,*
> *Then lean'd her Head the Pillow on, just out of Breath*
>   *and tir'd.*

But the Threefold Appellation in the first Line

> —— *a Wife, a Daughter, and a Sister,*

must not pass unobserved. That Line in the celebrated *Watts,*

> *GUNSTON the Just, the Generous, and the Young,*

is nothing Comparable to it. The latter only mentions three Qualifications of *one* Person who was deceased, which therefore could raise Grief and Compassion but for *One.* Whereas the former, (*our most excellent Poet*) gives his Reader a Sort of an Idea of the Death of *Three Persons,* viz.

> —— *a Wife, a Daughter, and a Sister,*

which is *Three Times* as great a Loss as the Death of *One,*

*Watts.

and consequently must raise *Three Times* as much Grief and Compassion in the Reader.

I should be very much straitned for Room, if I should attempt to discover even half the Excellencies of this Elegy which are obvious to me. Yet I cannot omit one Observation, which is, that the Author has (to his Honour) invented a new Species of Poetry, which wants a Name, and was never before known. His Muse scorns to be confin'd to the old Measures and Limits, or to observe the dull Rules of Criticks;

> *Nor* Rapin *gives her Rules to fly, nor* Purcell *Notes to Sing.*
>   Watts.

Now 'tis Pity that such an Excellent Piece should not be dignify'd with a particular Name; and seeing it cannot justly be called, either *Epic, Sapphic, Lyric,* or *Pindaric,* nor any other Name yet invented, I presume it may, (in Honour and Remembrance of the Dead) be called the *KITELIC.* Thus much in the Praise of *Kitelic Poetry.*

It is certain, that those Elegies which are of our own Growth, (and our Soil seldom produces any other sort of Poetry) are by far the greatest part, wretchedly Dull and Ridiculous. Now since it is imagin'd by many, that our Poets are honest, well-meaning Fellows, who do their best, and that if they had but some Instructions how to govern Fancy with Judgment, they would make indifferent good Elegies; I shall here subjoin a Receipt for that purpose, which was left me as a Legacy, (among other valuable Rarities) by my Reverend Husband. It is as follows,

A RECEIPT to make a New-England *Funeral ELEGY.*

For the Title of your Elegy. *Of these you may have enough ready made to your Hands; but if you should chuse to make it your self, you must be sure not to omit the Words* Ætatis Suæ, *which will Beautify it exceedingly.*

For the Subject of your Elegy. *Take one of your Neighbours who has lately departed this Life; it is no great matter at what Age the Party dy'd, but it will be best if he went away suddenly, being* Kill'd, Drown'd, *or* Froze to Death.

Having chose the Person, take all his Virtues, Excellencies, &c.

and if he have not enough, you may borrow some to make up a sufficient Quantity: To these add his last Words, dying Expressions, &c. *if they are to be had; mix all these together, and be sure you* strain *them well. Then season all with a Handful or two of Melancholly Expressions, such as,* Dreadful, Deadly, cruel cold Death, unhappy Fate, weeping Eyes, *&c. Have mixed all these Ingredients well, put them into the empty Scull of some* young Harvard; (*but in Case you have ne'er a One at Hand, you may use your own,*) *there let them Ferment for the Space of a Fort-night, and by that Time they will be incorporated into a Body, which take out, and having prepared a sufficient Quantity of double Rhimes, such as,* Power, Flower; Quiver, Shiver; Grieve us, Leave us; tell you, excel you; Expeditions, Physicians; Fatigue him, Intrigue him; *&c. you must spread all upon Paper, and if you can procure a Scrap of Latin to put at the End, it will garnish it mightily; then having affixed your Name at the Bottom, with a* Mæstus Composuit, *you will have an Excellent Elegy.*

N. B. *This Receipt will serve when a Female is the Subject of your Elegy, provided you borrow a greater Quantity of Virtues, Excellencies,* &c.

SIR,

Your Servant,

SILENCE DOGOOD.

P. S. I shall make no other Answer to *Hypercarpus*'s Criticism on my last Letter than this, *Mater me genuit, peperit mox filia matrem.*

The following Lines coming to Hand soon after I had receiv'd the above Letter from Mrs. *Dogood*, I think it proper to insert them in this Paper, that the *Dr.* may at once be paid for his Physical Rhimes administred to the Dead.

To the Sage and Immortal Doctor H———k, *on his Incomparable*
ELEGY, upon the Death of Mrs. Mehitebell Kitel, *&c.*

pressing writing
on Speech

A PANEGYRICK.

Thou hast, great Bard, in thy Mysterious Ode,
Gone in a Path which ne'er before was trod,
And freed the World from the vexatious Toil,
Of Numbers, Metaphors, of Wit and Stile,
Those Childish Ornaments, and gravely chose
The middle Way between good Verse and Prose.
Well might the Rhiming Tribe the Work decline,
Since 'twas too great for every Pen but thine.
What Scribbling Mortal dare the Bayes divide?
Thou shalt alone in Fame's bright Chariot ride;
For thou with matchless Skill and Judgment fraught,
Hast, Learned Doggrell, to Perfection brought.
The Loftyest Piece renowned LAW can show,
Deserves less Wonder, than to thine we owe.
No more shall TOM's, but henceforth thine shall be,
The Standard of Eleg'ac Poetry.
The healing Race thy Genius shall admire,
And thee to imitate in vain aspire:
For if by Chance a Patient you should kill,
You can Embalm his Mem'ry with your Quill.
What tho' some captious Criticks discommend
What they with all their Wit, can't comprehend,
And boldly doom to some Ignoble Use,
The Shining Product of thy Fertile Muse?
From your exhaustless Magazine of Sence
To their Confusion keen Replies dispence;
And them behold with a Contemptuous Mien,
Since not a Bard can boast of such a Strain.
By none but you cou'd *Kitel's* Worth be shown;
And none but your great Self can tell your Own;
Then least what is your due should not be said,
Write your own Elegy against you're Dead.

PHILOMUSUS.

The New-England Courant, June 25, 1722

Silence Dogood, No. 8

To the Author of the New-England Courant.

SIR,   No VIII.

I prefer the following Abstract from the London Journal to any Thing of my own, and therefore shall present it to your Readers this week without any further Preface.

'Without Freedom of Thought, there can be no such Thing as Wisdom; and no such Thing as publick Liberty, without Freedom of Speech; which is the Right of every Man, as far as by it, he does not hurt or controul the Right of another: And this is the only Check it ought to suffer, and the only Bounds it ought to know.

'This sacred Privilege is so essential to free Governments, that the Security of Property, and the Freedom of Speech always go together; and in those wretched Countries where a Man cannot call his Tongue his own, he can scarce call any Thing else his own. Whoever would overthrow the Liberty of a Nation, must begin by subduing the Freeness of Speech; a *Thing* terrible to Publick Traytors.

'This Secret was so well known to the Court of *King Charles the First*, that his wicked Ministry procured a Proclamation, to forbid the People to talk of Parliaments, which those Traytors had laid aside. To assert the undoubted Right of the Subject, and defend his Majesty's legal Prerogative, was called Disaffection, and punished as Sedition. Nay, People were forbid to talk of Religion in their Families: For the Priests had combined with the Ministers to cook up Tyranny, and suppress Truth and the Law, while the late *King James*, when *Duke of York*, went avowedly to Mass, Men were fined, imprisoned and undone, for saying he was a Papist: And that *King Charles the Second* might live more securely a Papist, there was an Act of Parliament made, declaring it Treason to say that he was one.

'That Men ought to speak well of *their Governours* is true, while *their Governours* deserve to be well spoken of; but to do publick Mischief, without hearing of it, is only the Prerogative and Felicity of Tyranny: A free People will be shewing that they are *so*, by their Freedom of Speech.

'The Administration of Government, is nothing else but the Attendance of the *Trustees of the People* upon the Interest and Affairs of the People: And as it is the Part and Business of the People, for whose Sake alone all publick Matters are, or ought to be transacted, to see whether they be well or ill transacted; so it is the Interest, and ought to be the Ambition, of all honest Magistrates, to have their Deeds openly examined, and publickly scann'd: Only the *wicked Governours* of Men dread what is said of them; *Audivit* Tiberius *probra queis lacerabitur, atque* perculsus est. The publick Censure was true, else he had not felt it bitter.

'Freedom of Speech is ever the Symptom, as well as the Effect of a good Government. In old *Rome*, all was left to the Judgment and Pleasure of the People, who examined the publick Proceedings with such Discretion, & censured those who administred them with such Equity and Mildness, that in the space of Three Hundred Years, not five publick Ministers suffered unjustly. Indeed whenever the *Commons* proceeded to Violence, the great Ones had been the Agressors.

'*GUILT* only dreads Liberty of Speech, which drags it out of its lurking Holes, and exposes its Deformity and Horrour to Day-light. *Horatius, Valerius, Cincinnatus,* and other vertuous and undesigning Magistrates of the Roman Commonwealth, had nothing to fear from Liberty of Speech. *Their virtuous* Administration, the more it was examin'd, the more it brightned and gain'd by Enquiry. When *Valerius* in particular, was accused upon some slight Grounds of affecting the Diadem; he, who was the first Minister of *Rome*, does not accuse the People for examining his Conduct, but approved his Innocence in a Speech to them; and gave such Satisfaction to them, and gained such Popularity to himself, that they gave him a new Name; *inde cognomen factum Publicolæ est*; to denote that he was their Favourite and their Friend.—*Latæ deinde leges—Ante omnes de provocatione* ADVERSUS MAGISTRATUS AD POPULUM, Livii, lib. 2. Cap. 8.

'But Things afterwards took another Turn. *Rome*, with the Loss of its Liberty, lost also its Freedom of Speech; then Mens Words began to be feared and watched; and then first began the *poysonous Race of Informers*, banished indeed under the righteous Administration of *Titus, Narva, Trajan, Aure-*

lius, &c. but encouraged and enriched under the *vile Ministry* of *Sejanus, Tigillinus, Pallas,* and *Cleander: Queri libet, quod in secreta nostra non inquirant principes, nisi quos Odimus,* says *Pliny* to *Trajan*.

'The best Princes have ever encouraged and promoted Freedom of Speech; they know that upright Measures would defend themselves, and that all upright Men would defend them. *Tacitus,* speaking of the Reign of some of the Princes abovemention'd, says with Extasy, *Rara Temporum felicitate, ubi sentire quæ velis, & quæ sentias dicere licet.* A blessed Time when you might think what you would, and speak what you thought.

'I doubt not but old *Spencer* and his *Son,* who were the *Chief Ministers* and *Betrayers* of *Edward the Second,* would have been very glad to have stopped the Mouths of all the honest Men in *England.* They dreaded to be called *Traytors,* because they were *Traytors.* And I dare say, Queen *Elizabeth's Walsingham,* who deserved no Reproaches, feared none. Misrepresentation of publick Measures is easily overthrown, by representing publick Measures truly; when they are honest, they ought to be publickly known, that they may be publickly commended; but if they are knavish or pernicious, they ought to be publickly exposed, in order to be publickly detested.'

> *Yours, &c.,*
> SILENCE DOGOOD.

The New-England Courant, July 9, 1722

Silence Dogood, No. 9

Corruptio optimi est pessima.

To the Author of the New-England Courant.

Sir,

It has been for some Time a Question with me, Whether a Commonwealth suffers more by hypocritical Pretenders to Religion, or by the openly Profane? But some late Thoughts of this Nature, have inclined me to think, that the Hypocrite is the most dangerous Person of the Two, especially if he sustains a Post in the Government, and we consider his Conduct as it regards the Publick. The first Artifice of a *State Hypocrite* is, by a few savoury Expressions which cost him Nothing, to betray the best Men in his Country into an Opinion of his Goodness; and if the Country wherein he lives is noted for the Purity of Religion, he the more easily gains his End, and consequently may more justly be expos'd and detested. A notoriously profane Person in a private Capacity, ruins himself, and perhaps forwards the Destruction of a few of his Equals; but a publick Hypocrite every day deceives his betters, and makes them the Ignorant Trumpeters of his supposed Godliness: They take him for a Saint, and pass him for one, without considering that they are (as it were) the Instruments of publick Mischief out of Conscince, and ruin their Country for God's sake.

This Political Description of a Hypocrite, may (for ought I know) be taken for a new Doctrine by some of your Readers; but let them consider, that *a little Religion, and a little Honesty, goes a great way in Courts.* 'Tis not inconsistent with Charity to distrust a Religious Man in Power, tho' he may be a good Man; he has many Temptations "to propagate *publick Destruction* for *Personal Advantages* and Security:" And if his Natural Temper be covetous, and his Actions often contradict his pious Discourse, we may with great Reason conclude, that he has some other Design in his Religion besides barely getting to Heaven. But the most dangerous Hypocrite in a Common-Wealth, is one who *leaves the Gospel for the sake of the Law*: A Man compounded of Law and Gospel, is able to cheat a whole Country with his Religion, and then destroy them under *Colour of Law*: And here the Clergy are in great Danger of being deceiv'd, and the People of being deceiv'd by the Clergy, until the Monster arrives to such Power and Wealth, that he is out of the reach of both, and can oppress the People without their own blind Assistance. And it is a sad Observation, that when the People too late see their Error, yet the Clergy still persist in their Encomiums on the Hypocrite; and when he happens to die *for the Good of his Country*, without leaving behind him the Memory of *one good Action*, he shall be sure to have his Funeral Sermon stuff'd with *Pious Expressions* which he dropt at such a Time, and at such a Place, and on such an Occasion; than which nothing can be more prejudicial to the Interest of Religion, nor indeed to the Memory of the Person deceas'd. The Reason of this Blindness in the Clergy is, because they are honourably supported (as they ought to be) by their People, and see nor feel nothing of the Oppression which is obvious and burdensome to every one else.

But this Subject raises in me an Indignation not to be born; and if we have had, or are like to have any Instances of this Nature in *New England*, we cannot better manifest our Love to Religion and the Country, than by setting the Deceivers in a true Light, and undeceiving the Deceived, however such Discoveries may be represented by the ignorant or designing Enemies of our Peace and Safety.

I shall conclude with a Paragraph or two from an ingenious Political Writer in the *London Journal*, the better to convince your Readers, that Publick Destruction may be easily carry'd on by *hypocritical Pretenders to Religion*.

"A raging Passion for immoderate Gain had made Men universally and intensely hard-hearted: They were every where devouring one another. And yet the Directors and their Accomplices, who were the acting Instruments of all this outrageous Madness and Mischief, set up for wonderful pious Persons, while they were defying Almighty God, and plundering Men; and they set apart a Fund of Subscriptions for charitable Uses; that is, they mercilesly made a whole People Beggars, and charitably supported a few *necessitous* and *worthless FAVOURITES*. I doubt not, but if the Villany had gone on with Success, they would have had their Names handed down to Posterity with Encomiums; as the Names of other *publick Robbers* have been! We have *Historians* and *ODE MAKERS* now living, very proper for such a Task. It is certain, that most People did, at one Time, believe the *Directors* to be *great and worthy Persons*. And an honest Country Clergyman told me last Summer, upon the Road, that *Sir John* was an excellent publick-spirited Person, for that he had beautified his Chancel.

"Upon the whole we must not judge of one another by their best Actions; since the worst Men do some Good, and all Men make fine Professions: But we must judge of Men by the whole of their Conduct, and the Effects of it. Thorough

Honesty requires great and long Proof, since many a Man, long thought honest, has at length proved a Knave. And it is from judging without Proof, or false Proof, that Mankind continue Unhappy."

I am, SIR,
Your humble Servant,
SILENCE DOGOOD.

The New-England Courant, July 23, 1722

Silence Dogood, No. 10

Optimè societas hominum servabitur.   Cic.

To the Author of the New-England Courant.

Sir,   [No X.

Discoursing lately with an intimate Friend of mine of the lamentable Condition of Widows, he put into my Hands a Book, wherein the ingenious Author proposes (I think) a certain Method for their Relief. I have often thought of some such Project for their Benefit my self, and intended to communicate my Thoughts to the Publick; but to prefer my own Proposals to what follows, would be rather an Argument of Vanity in me than Good Will to the many Hundreds of my Fellow-Sufferers now in *New-England*.

"We have (says he) abundance of Women, who have been Bred well, and Liv'd well, Ruin'd in a few Years, and perhaps, left Young, with a House full of Children, and nothing to Support them; which falls generally upon the Wives of the Inferior Clergy, or of Shopkeepers and Artificers.

"They marry Wives with perhaps 300*l.* to 1000*l.* Portion, and can settle no Jointure upon them; either they are Extravagant and Idle, and Waste it, or Trade decays, or Losses, or a Thousand Contingences happen to bring a Tradesman to Poverty, and he Breaks; the Poor Young Woman, it may be, has Three or Four Children, and is driven to a thousand shifts, while he lies in the *Mint* or *Fryars* under the *Dilemma* of a Statute of Bankrupt; but if he Dies, then she is absolutely Undone, unless she has Friends to go to.

"Suppose an Office to be Erected, to be call'd *An Office of Ensurance for Widows*, upon the following Conditions;

"Two thousand Women, or their Husbands for them, Enter their Names into a Register to be kept for that purpose, with the Names, Age, and Trade of their Husbands, with the Place of their abode, Paying at the Time of their Entring 5s. down with 1s. 4d. *per* Quarter, which is to the setting up and support of an Office with Clerks, and all proper Officers for the same; *for there is no maintaining such without Charge*; they receive every one of them a Certificate, Seal'd by the Secretary of the Office, and Sign'd by the Governors, for the Articles hereafter mentioned.

"If any one of the Women becomes a Widow, at any Time after Six Months from the Date of her Subscription, upon due Notice given, and Claim made at the Office in form, as shall be directed, she shall receive within Six Months after such Claim made, the Sum of 500l. in Money, without any Deductions, saving some small Fees to the Officers, which the Trustees must settle, that they may be known.

"In Consideration of this, every Woman so Subscribing, Obliges her self to Pay as often as any Member of the Society becomes a Widow, the due Proportion or Share allotted to her to Pay, towards the 500l. for the said Widow, provided her Share does not exceed the Sum of 5s.

"No Seamen or Soldiers Wives to be accepted into such a Proposal as this, on the Account before mention'd, because the Contingences of their Lives are not equal to others, unless they will admit this general Exception, supposing they do not Die out of the Kingdom.

"It might also be an Exception, That if the Widow, that Claim'd, had really, *bona fide*, left her by her Husband to her own use, clear of all Debts and Legacies, 2000l. she shou'd have no Claim; the Intent being to Aid the Poor, not add to the Rich. But there lies a great many Objections against such an Article: As

"1. It may tempt some to forswear themselves.

"2. People will Order their Wills so as to defraud the Exception.

"One Exception must be made; and that is, Either very un-equal Matches, as when a Woman of Nineteen Marries an old

Man of Seventy; or Women who have infirm Husbands, I mean known and publickly so. To remedy which, Two things are to be done.

'The Office must have moving Officers without doors, who shall inform themselves of such matters, and if any such Circumstances appear, the Office should have 14 days time to return their Money, and declare their Subscriptions Void.

'2. No Woman whose Husband had any visible Distemper, should claim under a Year after her Subscription.

'One grand Objection against this Proposal, is, How you will oblige People to pay either their Subscription, or their Quarteridge.

'To this I answer, *By no Compulsion* (tho' that might be perform'd too) but altogether voluntary; only with this Argument to move it, that if they do not continue their Payments, they lose the Benefit of their past Contributions.

'I know it lies as a fair Objection against such a Project as this, That the number of Claims are so uncertain, That no Body knows what they engage in, when they Subscribe, for so many may die Annually out of Two Thousand, as may perhaps make my Payment 20 or 25 *l. per Ann*, and if a Woman happen to Pay that for Twenty Years, though she receives the 500 *l.* at last she is a great Loser; but if she dies before her Husband, she has lessened his Estate considerably, and brought a great Loss upon him.

'*First*, I say to this, That I wou'd have such a Proposal as this be so fair and easy, that if any Person who had Subscrib'd found the Payments too high, and the Claims fall too often, it shou'd be at their Liberty at any Time, upon Notice given, to be released and stand Oblig'd no longer; and if so, *Volenti non fit Injuria*; every one knows best what their own Circumstances will bear.

'In the next Place, because Death is a Contingency, no Man can directly Calculate, and all that Subscribe must take the Hazard; yet that a Prejudice against this Notion may not be built on wrong Grounds, let's examine a little the Probable hazard, and see how many shall die Annually out of 2000 Subscribers, accounting by the common proportion of Burials, to the number of the Living.

'Sir *William Petty* in his *Political Arithmetick*, by a very Ingenious Calculation, brings the Account of Burials in *London*, to be 1 in 40 Annually, and proves it by all the proper Rules of proportion'd Computation; and I'le take my Scheme from thence. If then One in Forty of all the People in *England* should Die, that supposes Fifty to Die every Year out of our Two Thousand Subscribers; and for a Woman to Contribute 5 *s.* to every one, would certainly be to agree to Pay 12 *l.* 10 *s. per Ann.* upon her Husband's Life, to receive 500 *l.* when he Di'd, and lose it if she Di'd first; and yet this wou'd not be a hazard beyond reason too great for the Gain.

'But I shall offer some Reasons to prove this to be impossible in our Case; First, Sir *William Petty* allows the City of *London* to contain about a Million of People, and our Yearly Bill of Mortality never yet amounted to 25000 in the most Sickly Years we have had, Plague Years excepted, sometimes but to 20000, which is but One in Fifty: Now it is to be consider'd here, that Children and Ancient People make up, one time with another, at least one third of our Bills of Mortality; and our *Assurances* lies upon none but the Midling Age of the People, which is the only age wherein Life is any thing steady; and if that be allow'd, there cannot Die by his Computation, above One in Eighty of such People, every Year; but because I would be sure to leave Room for Casualty, I'le allow one in Fifty shall Die out of our Number Subscrib'd.

'Secondly, It must be allow'd, that our Payments falling due only on the Death of Husbands, this One in Fifty must not be reckoned upon the Two thousand; for 'tis to be suppos'd at least as many Women shall die as Men, and then there is nothing to Pay; so that One in Fifty upon One Thousand, is the most that I can suppose shall claim the Contribution in a Year, which is Twenty Claims a Year at 5 *s.* each, and is 5 *l. per Ann.* and if a Woman pays this for Twenty Year, and claims at last, she is Gainer enough, and no extraordinary Loser if she never claims at all: And I verily believe any Office might undertake to demand at all Adventures not above 6 *l. per Ann.* and secure the Subscriber 500 *l.* in case she come to claim as a Widow.'

I would leave this to the Consideration of all who are concern'd for their own or their Neighbour's Temporal Happiness; and I am humbly of Opinion, that the Country is ripe for many such *Friendly Societies*, whereby every Man might help another, without any Disservice to himself. We have many charitable Gentlemen who Yearly give liberally to the Poor, and where can they better bestow their Charity than on those who become so by Providence, and for ought they know on themselves. But above all, the Clergy have the most need of coming into some such Project as this. They as well as poor Men (according to the Proverb) generally abound in Children; and how many Clergymen themselves in the Country are forc'd to labour in their Fields, to keep themselves in a Condition above Want? How then shall they be able to leave any thing to their forsaken, dejected, & almost forgotten Wives and Children. For my own Part, I have nothing left to live on, but Contentment and a few Cows; and tho' I cannot expect to be reliev'd by this Project, yet it would be no small Satisfaction to me to see it put in Practice for the Benefit of others.

I am, SIR, &c.
SILENCE DOGOOD.

The New-England Courant, August 13, 1722

Silence Dogood, No. II

Neque licitum interea est meam amicam visere.

To the Author of the New-England Courant.
Sir,   [No XI.

From a natural Compassion to my Fellow-Creatures, I have sometimes been betray'd into Tears at the Sight of an Object of Charity, who by a bear Relation of his Circumstances, seem'd to demand the Assistance of those about him. The following Petition represents in so lively a Manner the forlorn State of a Virgin well stricken in Years and Repentance, that I cannot forbear publishing it at this Time, with some Advice to the Petitioner.

To Mrs. Silence Dogood.
The Humble Petition of Margaret Aftercast,
    SHEWETH,
    "1. That your Petitioner being puff'd up in her younger

Years with a numerous Train of Humble Servants, had the Vanity to think, that her extraordinary Wit and Beauty would continually recommend her to the Esteem of the Gallants; and therefore as soon as it came to be publickly known that any Gentleman address'd her, he was immediately discarded.

"2. That several of your Petitioners Humble Servants, who upon their being rejected by her, were, to all Appearance in a dying Condition, have since recover'd their Health, and been several Years married, to the great Surprize and Grief of your Petitioner, who parted with them upon no other Conditions, but that they should die or run distracted for her, as several of them faithfully promis'd to do.

"3. That your Petitioner finding her self disappointed in and neglected by her former Adorers, and no new Offers appearing for some Years past, she has been industriously contracting Acquaintance with several Families in Town and Country, where any young Gentlemen or Widowers have resided, and endeavour'd to appear as conversable as possible before them: She has likewise been a strict Observer of the Fashion, and always appear'd well dress'd. And the better to restore her decay'd Beauty, she has consum'd above Fifty Pound's Worth of the most approved *Cosmeticks*. But all won't do.

"Your Petitioner therefore most humbly prays, That you would be pleased to form a Project for the Relief of all those penitent Mortals of the fair Sex, that are like to be punish'd with their Virginity until old Age, for the Pride and Insolence of their Youth.

"And your Petitioner (as in Duty bound) shall ever pray, *&c.*
Margaret Aftercast."

Were I endow'd with the Faculty of Match-making, it should be improv'd for the Benefit of Mrs. *Margaret*, and others in her Condition: But since my extream Modesty and Taciturnity, forbids an Attempt of this Nature, I would advise them to relieve themselves in a Method of *Friendly Society*; and that already publish'd for Widows, I conceive would be a very proper Proposal for them, whereby every single Woman, upon full Proof given of her continuing a Virgin for the Space of Eighteen Years, (dating her Virginity from the Age of Twelve,) should be entituled to 500*l.* in ready Cash.

I doubt not but *moderate Drinking* has been improv'd for the Diffusion of Knowledge among the ingenious Part of Mankind, who want the Talent of a ready Utterance, in order to discover the Conceptions of their Minds in an entertaining and intelligible Manner. 'Tis true, drinking does not *improve* our Faculties, but it enables us to *use* them; and therefore I conclude, that much Study and Experience, and a little Liquor, are of absolute Necessity for some Tempers, in order to make them accomplish'd Orators. *Dic. Ponder* discovers an excellent Judgment when he is inspir'd with a Glass or two of *Claret*, but he passes for a Fool among those of small Observation, who never saw him the better for Drink. And here it will not be improper to observe, That the moderate Use of Liquor, and a well plac'd and well regulated Anger, often produce this same Effect; and some who cannot ordinarily talk but in broken Sentences and false Grammar, do in the Heat of Passion express themselves with as much Eloquence as Warmth. Hence it is that my own Sex are generally the most eloquent, because the most passionate. "It has been said in the Praise of some Men, (says an ingenious Author,) that they could talk whole Hours together upon any thing; but it must be owned to the Honour of the other Sex, that there are many among them who can talk whole Hours together upon Nothing. I have known a Woman branch out into a long extempore Dissertation on the Edging of a Petticoat, and chide her Servant for breaking a China Cup, in all the Figures of Rhetorick."

But after all it must be consider'd, that no Pleasure can give Satisfaction or prove advantageous to a *reasonable Mind*, which is not attended with the *Restraints of Reason*. Enjoyment is not to be found by Excess in any sensual Gratification; but on the contrary, the immoderate Cravings of the Voluptuary, are always succeeded with Loathing and a palled Appetite. What Pleasure can the Drunkard have in the Reflection, that, while in his Cups, he retain'd only the Shape of a Man, and acted the Part of a Beast; or that from reasonable Discourse a few Minutes before, he descended to Impertinence and Nonsense?

I cannot pretend to account for the different Effects of Liquor on Persons of different Dispositions, who are guilty of Excess in the Use of it. 'Tis strange to see Men of a regular Conversation become rakish and profane when intoxicated with Drink, and yet more surprizing to observe, that some who appear to be the most profligate Wretches when sober, become mighty religious in their Cups, and will then, and at no other Time address their Maker, but when they are destitute of Reason, and actually affronting him. Some shrink in the Wetting, and others swell to such an unusual Bulk in their Imaginations, that they can in an Instant understand all Arts and Sciences, by the liberal Education of a little vivifying *Punch*, or a sufficient Quantity of other exhilerating Liquor.

And as the Effects of Liquor are various, so are the Characters given to its Devourers. It argues some Shame in the Drunkards themselves, in that they have invented numberless Words and Phrases to cover their Folly, whose proper Significations are harmless, or have no Signification at all. They are seldom known to be *drunk*, tho they are very often *boozey*, *cogey*, *tipsey*, *fox'd*, *merry*, *mellow*, *fuddl'd*, *groatable*, *Confoundedly cut*, *See two Moons*, are *Among the Philistines*, *In a very good Humour*, *See the Sun*, or, *The Sun has shone upon them*; they *Clip the King's English*, are *Almost froze*, *Feavourish*, *In their Altitudes*, *Pretty well enter'd*, &c. In short, every Day produces some new Word or Phrase which might be added to the Vocabulary of the *Tiplers*: But I have chose to mention these few, because if at any Time a Man of Sobriety and Temperance happens to *cut himself confoundedly*, or is *almost froze*, or *feavourish*, or accidentally *sees the Sun*, &c. he may escape the Imputation of being *drunk*, when his Misfortune comes to be related.

> *I am SIR,*
> *Your Humble Servant,*
> SILENCE DOGOOD.

The New-England Courant, September 10, 1722

Silence Dogood, No. 13

To the Author of the New-England Courant.

Sir,   [No XIII.

In Persons of a contemplative Disposition, the most indifferent Things provoke the Exercise of the Imagination; and the Satisfactions which often arise to them thereby, are a certain Relief to the Labour of the Mind (when it has been intensely fix'd on more substantial Subjects) as well as to that of the Body.

In one of the late pleasant Moon-light Evenings, I so far indulg'd in my self the Humour of the Town in walking abroad, as to continue from my Lodgings two or three Hours later than usual, & was pleas'd beyond Expectation before my Return. Here I found various Company to observe, and various Discourse to attend to. I met indeed with the common Fate of *Listeners*, (who *hear no good of themselves*,) but from a Consciousness of my Innocence, receiv'd it with a Satisfaction beyond what the Love of Flattery and the Daubings of a Parasite could produce. The Company who rally'd me were about Twenty in Number, of both Sexes; and tho' the *Confusion of Tongues* (like that of *Babel*) which always happens among so many impetuous Talkers, render'd their Discourse not so intelligible as I could wish, I learnt thus much, That one of the Females pretended to know me, from some Discourse she had heard at a certain House before the Publication of one of my Letters; adding, *That I was a Person of an ill Character, and kept a criminal Correspondence with a Gentleman who assisted me in Writing.* One of the Gallants clear'd me of this random Charge, by saying, *That tho' I wrote in the Character of a Woman, he knew me to be a Man; But,* continu'd he, *he has more need of endeavouring a Reformation in himself, than spending his Wit in satyrizing others.*

I had no sooner left this Set of Ramblers, but I met a Crowd of *Tarpolins* and their Doxies, link'd to each other by the Arms, who ran (by their own Account) after the Rate of *Six Knots an Hour*, and bent their Course towards the *Common*. Their eager and amorous Emotions of Body, occasion'd by taking their Mistresses *in Tow*, they call'd *wild Steerage*: And as a Pair of them happen'd to trip and come to the Ground, the Company were call'd upon to *bring to*, for that *Jack* and *Betty* were *founder'd*. But this Fleet were not less comical or irregular in their Progress than a Company of Females I soon after came up with, who, by throwing their Heads to the Right and Left, at every one who pass'd by them, I concluded came out with no other Design than to

pointment appears unavoidable, when their easy Proselytes too suddenly start into Extreams, and are immediately fill'd with Arguments to invalidate their former Practice. This creates a Suspicion in the more considerate Part of Mankind, that those who are thus *given to Change*, neither *fear God*, nor *honour the King*. In Matters of Religion, he that alters his Opinion on a *religious Account*, must certainly go thro' much Reading, hear many Arguments on both Sides, and undergo many Struggles in his Conscience, before he can come to a full Resolution: Secular Interest will indeed make quick Work with an immoral Man, especially if, notwithstanding the Alteration of his Opinion, he can with any Appearance of Credit retain his Immorality. But, by this Turn of Thought I would not be suspected of Uncharitableness to those Clergymen at *Connecticut*, who have lately embrac'd the Establish'd Religion of our Nation, some of whom I hear made their Professions with a Seriousness becoming their Order: However, since they have deny'd the Validity of *Ordination* by the Hands of *Presbyters*, and consequently their Power of Administring the *Sacraments*, &c. we may justly expect a suitable Manifestation of their Repentance for invading the *Priests* Office, and living so long in a *Corah*-like Rebellion. All I would endeavour to shew is, That an indiscreet Zeal for spreading an Opinion, hurts the Cause of the Zealot. There are too many blind Zealots among every Denomination of Christians; and he that propagates the Gospel among *Rakes* and *Beaus* without reforming them in their Morals, is every whit as ridiculous and impolitick as a Statesman who makes Tools of Ideots and Tale-Bearers.

Much to my present Purpose are the Words of two Ingenious Authors of the *Church of England*, tho' in all Probability they were tainted with *Whiggish* Principles; and with these I shall conclude this Letter.

'I would (says one) have every zealous Man examine his Heart thoroughly, and, I believe, he will often find that what he calls a Zeal for his Religion, is either Pride, Interest or Illnature. A Man who differs from another in Opinion sets himself above him in his own Judgment, and in several Particulars pretends to be the wiser Person. This is a great Provocation to the Proud Man, and gives a keen Edge to what he calls his

Zeal. And that this is the Case very often, we may observe
from the Behaviour of some of the most Zealous for Orthodoxy, who have often great Friendships and Intimacies with
vicious immoral Men, provided they do but agree with them
in the same Scheme of Belief. The Reason is, because the
vicious Believer gives the Precedency to the virtuous Man,
and allows the good Christian to be the worthier Person, at
the same Time that he cannot come up to his Perfections.
This we find exemplified in that trite Passage which we see
quoted in almost every System of Ethicks, tho' upon another
Occasion;

> ——*Video meliore proboque*
> *Deteriora sequor*——

On the contrary, it is certain if our Zeal were true and genuine, we should be much more angry with a Sinner than a
Heretick, since there are several Cases which may excuse the
latter before his great Judge, but none which can excuse the
former.'

'I have (says another) found by Experience, that it is impossible to talk distinctly without defining the Words of
which we make use. There is not a Term in our Language
which wants Explanation so much as the Word *Church*. One
would think when People utter it, they should have in their
Minds Ideas of Virtue and Religion; but that important
Monosyllable drags all the other Words in the Language after
it, and it is made use of to express both Praise and Blame,
according to the Character of him who speaks it. By this
means it happens, that no one knows what his Neighbour
means when he says such a one is for or against the Church.
It has happen'd that he who is seen every Day at Church, has
not been counted in the Eye of the World a Churchman; and
he who is very zealous to oblige every one to frequent it but
himself, has been a very good Son of the Church. This
Præpossession is the best Handle imaginable for Politicians to
make use of, for managing the Loves and Hatreds of Mankind to the Purposes to which they would lead them. But this
is not a Thing for Fools to meddle with, for they only bring
Disesteem upon those whom they attempt to serve, when
they unskilfully pronounce Terms of Art. I have observed

Hugo Grim on Silence Dogood

Mr. *Couranto*,

Since Mrs. Dogood has kept SILENCE for so long a Time, you have no doubt lost a very valuable Correspondent, and the Publick been depriv'd of many profitable Amusements, for which reason I desire you to convey the following Lines to Her, that so if she be in the Land of the Living we may know the Occasion of her *Silence*.

Mrs. *Dogood*.

I Greatly wonder why you have so soon done exercising your Gifts, and *hid your Talent in a Napkin*. You told us at first that you intended to favour the Publick with a Speculation *once a Fortnight*, but how comes it to pass that you have laid aside so *Good* a Design? Why have you so soon *withdrawn your Hand from the Plough* (with which you tax'd some of the Scholars) and grown weary of *Doing Good*?

Is your Common-Place Wit all Exhausted, your stock of matter all spent? We thought you were well stor'd with that by your striking your first blow at the *College*. You say (in your No 2.) that you *have an Excellent Faculty at observing and reproving the Faults of others*, and are the Vices of the Times all mended? Is there not Whoring, Drinking, Swearing, Lying, Gaming, Cheating and Oppression, and many other Sins prevailing in the Land? Can you *observe* no faults in others (or your self) to *reprove*? Or are you married and remov'd to some distant Clime, that we hear nothing from you? Are you (as the Prophet supposed *Baal* that sottish Deity) *asleep*, or *on a journey*, and cannot write? Or has the Sleep of *inexorable unrelenting Death* procur'd your *Silence*? and if so you ought to have told us of it, and appointed your Successor. But if you are still in Being, and design to amuse the Publick any more, proceed in your usual Course; or if not, let us know it, that some other hand may take up your Pen.

Your Friend,
HUGO GRIM.

ADVERTISEMENT.

||*|| *If any Person or Persons will give a true Account of Mrs.*

Silence Dogood, *whether Dead or Alive, Married or unmarried, in Town or Countrey, that so, (if living) she may be spoke with, or Letters convey'd to her, they shall have Thanks for their Pains.*

The New-England Courant, December 3, 1722

Rules for The New-England Courant

Vide quam rem agas.

To the Author of the New-England Courant.

Sir,

Seeing your Courant is a Paper which (like the Primitive Christians) begins to be *every where spoken against,* It is our *humble Opinion* that it is high Time for you to think of some Method wherein to carry it on without ministring just occasion of Offence to any, especially to the polite and *pious* People, of whom there are considerable numbers in this Land.

It is a common saying; *that it is a bad thing to have a Bad Name*; when a Man has once got a bad Name, people are apt to misrepresent, and misconstrue whatever he says or does, tho' it be Innocent, nay, good and laudable in it self, and tho' it proceed from a good Intention, which is absolutely necessary to denominate any Action Good.

Hence it is that so many good people, have entertain'd strong prejudices against your Courant, because, say they, *there can no good thing come out of that Paper*; let a Discourse be ever so good, instructive, and Edifying in it self, and strengthen'd by many Texts of Scripture, and quotations from the Works of the most *Eminent Divines*, who have *great Names* in all the Universities of Europe;—yet, they say, it is base and vile, and has a wicked Tendency, it is written with a bad intention, with a design to mock and deride Religion, and the serious, consciencious professors of it.

Now, tho' we are of Opinion that this matter has been strain'd a little too far, by persons whose Zeal is not sufficiently poiz'd with Knowledge and Prudence, yet, it may be very proper to lay before you some Rules, which if duly observ'd will render your Paper not only inoffensive, but pleasant and agreeable. Our present purpose therefore is, to suggest several things to you by way of Direction, which may conduce to so desireable an end.

1. In the first place then, Whatever you do, be very tender of the *Religion of the Country*, which you were brought up in and Profess. The Honour of Religion ought ever to ly near our Hearts; nor should any thing grieve us so much as to see That reflected on, and brought into contempt. Religion is our safety and security, and if we lose the Honour of that, no small part of our strength and Glory will be lost with it.

2. Take great care that you do not cast injurious Reflections on the *Reverend and Faithful Ministers of the Gospel*, or any of them. We think New-England may boast of almost an unparallel'd Happiness in its MINISTERS; take them in general, there is scarce a more *Candid, Learned, Pious* and *Laborious* Set of Men under Heaven. But tho' they are the *Best of Men*, yet they are but Men at the best, and by consequence subject to like *Frailties* and *Passions* as other Men; And when we hear of the *Imprudencies* of any of them, we should cover them with the mantle of Love and Charity, and not profanely expose and Aggravate them. *Charity covers a multitude of Sins.* Besides, when you abuse the Clergy you do not consult your own Interest, for you may be sure they will improve their influence to the uttermost, to suppress your Paper.

3. Be very careful of the reputation of the People of this Land in general. Indeed, it must be confess'd that there is a visible Declension and Apostacy among us, from the good ways of our Fore-Fathers, but yet we hope there is a great number of serious Christians, many more then *Seven Thousand* who have not bowed the Knee of the Image of *Baal*: And therefore you ought to take great care that you are not *too general* in your reflections. Here it may be you will say, there has been more said and printed in some Sermons on this Head, than ever you published. To this we Answer, that there are many things good and proper in the *Pulpit*, which would be vile and wicked in a *Courant*. And what if all men are not moulded according to your Humour? must you presently stigmatize them as Knaves and Hypocrites? Certainly on no Account whatsoever.

4. By no means cast any Reflections on the *Civil Government*, under the Care and Protection of which you live. Blessed be God, we sit under the Administration of Wise and Good Rulers; let us prize them and be thankful for them. But if you will be so Fool-hardy as to cast scurrilous and unjust Reflections on them, we think you ought to smart for it without any pity: And here we would caution you to avoid with care those Rocks, on which you have once and again almost suffered Shipwrack. Furthermore, when you abuse and villify Rulers, you do in some sense resist a *Divine Ordinance*, and *he that resisteth shall receive to himself Damnation*. Princes, Magistrates, and Grandees, can by no means endure their Conduct should be scann'd by the meanest of their Subjects; and such may justly be offended when private Men, of as private parts, presume to intermeddle with their *Arcana*, and fault their Administration.

5. We advise you to avoid Quotations from prophane and scandalous Authors, which will be but like so many *dead Flies* in your Courant; And in particular, we think it by no means proper to Introduce your Speculations with Lines out of *Butler's Hudibras*, for he was no *Pious Author*, but a profane Wit, who set himself up to Burlesque the *Brethren* and Lampoon the *Saints* that liv'd in his Time. On the other hand, we think it very unsuitable to bring in Texts of *Sacred Scripture* into your Paper, (unless on extraordinary Occasions) for hereby Men lose that Reverence & Veneration which is due to the Divine Oracles, nay, sometimes they come to be profanely droll'd on in *Taverns* and *Coffee-Houses*, which ought not to be.

6. In writing your Courants, we advise you carefully to avoid the Form and Method of Sermons, for that is vile and impious in such a Paper as yours. Here, perhaps you will say, you do not set up for a *Preacher*; to which we Answer, that to print your Paper *Sermon-wise* is as bad as if you preach'd. And besides, for a private Man to Exhort and Admonish in such a method, is *boldly to invade the Province of others*, and comes little short of a *Corah-like* Usurpation. Nor is it suitable, as we conceive, to fill your Paper with Religious Exhortations of any kind; or to conclude your Letters with *the words of the Psalmist*, or any other sacred writer.

7. Be very general in your Writings, and when you condemn any Vice, do not point out particular Persons; for that has offended many Good People, and may occasion great disturbances in Families and Neighbourhoods.

8. *And Lastly*, BEWARE of casting dirty Reflections on that worthy Society of *Gentlemen*, scoffingly call'd, *The CANVAS CLUB*. Truly, they are Gentlemen of as good Credit and Reputation as any we have; and some of them are Men of Power and Influence, and (if you offend them) may contribute not a little to the crushing of your Paper.

Thus we have offered you some plain Directions, which if you wisely follow, we doubt not but you will steer clear of Rocks, Shelves and Quick-sands; This will render your Performances at once both pleasant and profitable, even to Persons of the most Different Apprehensions among us, and your own Innocence and Vertue will protect and secure you in so good a Work.

We are your hearty Friends and Wellwishers,
A, B, C, &c.

The New-England Courant, January 28, 1722/3

To "*your Honour*":
Defense of James Franklin to Samuel Sewall

SIR,
I am inform'd that your Honour was a leading Man in the late Extraordinary procedure against *F———n* the Printer: And inasmuch as it cannot be long before you must appear at *Christ's* enlightned Tribunal, where every Man's work shall be tryed, I humbly beseech you, in the Fear of GOD, to consider & Examine, whether that Procedure be according to *the strict Rules of Justice and Equity?* It is manifest, that this Man had broke no *Law*; and you know, Sir, that where there is no Law, there can be no Transgression: And, Sir, methinks you cannot but know, that it is highly *unjust* to punish a Man by a *Law*, to which the Fact committed is *Antecedent*. The Law ever looks *forward*, but never *backward*; but if once we come

to punish Men, by vertue of Laws *Ex post Facto*, Farewel *Magna Charta*, and *English Liberties*, for no Man can ever be *safe*, but may be punished for every Action he does by Laws made afterwards. This in my humble Opinion, both the Light of Nature and Laws of Justice abhor, and is what ought to be detested by all Good Men.

Summum jus, est summa injuria.

Moreover, this is not according to the procedure of the *supream Judge of all the Earth*, (who cannot but do right) which is the most perfect Rule for *Humane Gods* to copy after. You know, Sir, that he will Judge and punish Men, according to that *Light and Law* they were favour'd with; And that he will not punish the *Heathen* for disobeying the Gospel, of which they were intirely ignorant.

The end of Humane Law is to fix the boundaries within which Men ought to keep themselves; But if any are so hardy and presumptuous as to break through them, doubtless they deserve punishment. Now, If this *Printer* had transgress'd any Law, he ought to have been presented by a Grand Jury, and a fair Tryal brought on.

I would further observe to your Honour the danger of ill Precedents, and that this Precedent *will not sleep*; And, Sir, can you bear to think that Posterity will have Reason to Curse you on the Account hereof! By this our Religion may suffer extreamly hereafter; for, whatever those Ministers (if any such there were) who have push'd on this matter, may think of it, they have made a Rod for themselves in times to come, Blessed be God, we have a good King at present; but if it should please him for our Sins to punish us with a bad one, we may have a S——y that will so *Supervise* our Ministers Sermons, as to suffer them to print none at all.

I would also humbly remind your Honour, that you were formerly led into an Error, which you afterwards Publickly and Solemnly (and I doubt not, Sincerely) Confess'd and repented of; and Sir, ought not this to make you the more Cautious & Circumspect in your Actions which relate to the publick all your Days?

The New-England Courant, February 4, 1722/3

On Titles of Honour

Mero meridie si dixerit illi tenebras esse, credit.

There is nothing in which Mankind reproach themselves more than in their Diversity of Opinions. Every Man sets himself above another in his own Opinion, and there are not two Men in the World whose Sentiments are alike in every thing. Hence it comes to pass, that the same Passages in the Holy Scriptures or the Works of the Learned, are wrested to the meaning of two opposite Parties, of contrary Opinions, as if the Passages they recite were like our Master *Janus*, looking *two ways at once*, or like Lawyers, who with equal Force of Argument, can plead either for the *Plaintiff* or *Defendant*.

The most absurd and ridiculous Opinions, are sometimes spread by the least colour of Argument: But if they stop at the first Broachers, *they* have still the Pleasure of being wiser (in their own Conceits) than the rest of the World, and can with the greatest Confidence pass a Sentence of Condemnation upon the Reason of all Mankind, who dissent from the peculiar Whims of their troubled Brains.

We were easily led into these Reflections at the last Meeting of our Club, when one of the Company read to us some Passages from a zealous Author against *Hatt-Honour*, *Titular Respects*, &c. which we will communicate to the Reader for the Diversion of this Week, if he is dispos'd to be merry with the Folly of his Fellow-Creature.

'*Honour*, Friend, *says he*, properly ascends, & not descends; yet the Hat, when the Head is uncover'd, *descends*, and therefore there can be no Honour in it. Besides, Honour was from the *Beginning*, but Hats are an Invention of a *late Time*, and consequently true Honour standeth not therein.

'In old Time it was no disrespect for Men and Women to be call'd by their own Names: *Adam*, was never called *Master* Adam; we never read of Noah *Esquire*, Lot *Knight* and *Baronet*, nor the *Right Honourable* Abraham, *Viscount* Mesopotamia, *Baron of* Carran; no, no, they were plain Men, honest Country Grasiers, that took Care of their Families and their Flocks. *Moses* was a great Prophet, and *Aaron* a Priest of the Lord; but we never read of the *Reverend* Moses, nor the

Right Reverend Father in God, Aaron, by Divine Providence, *Lord Arch-Bishop of* Israel: Thou never sawest *Madam* Rebecca in the Bible, my *Lady* Rachel, nor *Mary*, tho' a Princess of the Blood after the Death of *Joseph,* call'd the *Princess Dowager of* Nazareth; no, plain *Rebecca*, *Rachel*, *Mary*, or the *Widow* Mary, or the like: It was no Incivility then to mention their naked Names as they were expressed.'

If common civility, and a generous Deportment among Mankind, be not put out of Countenance by the profound Reasoning of this Author, we hope they will continue to treat one another handsomely to the end of the World. We will not pretend an Answer to these Arguments against *modern Decency* and *Titles of Honour*; yet one of our Club will undertake to prove, that tho' *Abraham* was not styl'd *Right Honourable*, yet he had the Title of *Lord* given him by his Wife *Sarah*, which he thinks entitles her to the Honour of *My Lady* Sarah; and *Rachel* being married into the same Family, he concludes she may deserve the Title of *My Lady* Rachel. But this is but the Opinion of one Man; it was never put to Vote in the Society.

P.S. At the last Meeting of our Club, it was unanimously agreed, That all Letters to be inserted in this Paper, should come directed to old *Janus*; whereof our Correspondents are to take Notice, and conform themselves accordingly.

The New-England Courant, February 18, 1722/3

High Tide in Boston

Boston, March 4.

On Lord's Day, the 24th past, we were surprized with the extraordinary Heighth of the Tide, which fill'd most of the Streets as well as Cellars near the Water, insomuch that many People living in Drawbridge-Street, Union-Street, and some other Places, were carry'd to their Houses in Canooes, after the Morning Service was over. In some Houses the Water rose so high in their lower Rooms as that they were oblig'd to run away with their Meat half dress'd upon their Spits and in their Potts into some of their Neighbours, or into their upper Rooms, their Fire being all put out, and the Wood floating about the Rooms. The Cordwood, Shingles, Staves, &c. were all wash'd off the Wharffs and carry'd into the Harbour, or left in the Streets after the Tide was down. The Water rose so high in the Ship Carpenters Yards, that they fear'd the Vessels would be carried off the Stocks, and made them fast with Ropes to the Tops of the Houses. The Loss sustain'd by this Tide (in Town and Country) is reckon'd by some to be as great as that by the Fire in 1711. Charlestown likewise suffer'd very much; and we hear a great Number of Whaleboats have been carry'd from the shore towards Cape Codd, where the Tide was never known to come before. They write from Newport on Rhode-Island, that the Tide has entirely wash'd away several Wharffs, and done great Damage in several Warehouses and Dwelling Houses near the Water. By an Article in the Boston News-Letter of Thursday last, we are told, that, *The many great Wharffs which since the last overflowing Tides have been run out into the Harbour, and fill'd so great a Part of the* Bason, *have methinks contributed something not inconsiderable to the Rise of the Water upon us.* And upon the Authority of this News Letter, some begin to blame the Dutch for damming out the Sea, and sending the Tide over the Atlantick upon us: Some more reasonably conclude, that a large Fleet of Ships have been sunk in the Storm upon our Coast, (the Wind blowing hard at North East,) which occasion'd the rising of the Tide. Others have upon this Account, framed a new Hypothesis to solve the Phænomena of Noah's Flood, and very rationally suppose, that the Antediluvians brought the Deluge upon themselves by running too many Great Wharffs out into their Harbours. So that the Notions (*which were not without their Probabilities*) of *Burnet*, *Warren*, *Whiston*, &c. who were troubled with the Distemper call'd *Hypothesimania*, seem now less probable than ever.

The New-England Courant, March 4, 1722/3

Timothy Wagstaff

Quô semel est imbuta recens, servabit odorem Testa din.——

To old Master JANUS.

Sir,

The extravagant Notions which some Men entertain from the Influence of Education and Custom, may be thought worth Notice in your Paper, if we consider only, that the Sufferings of its late Publisher were owing in a great measure to his carrying it on in an *unusual Method.* Had he staid till some Gentlemen of the best Reputation in our Country had run the venture of being witty, and wrote a competent Number of *Joco-Serious Dialogues*, he might have continu'd his Paper without incurring the charge of *Shocking and Heaven-rending Blasphemy!* I must ask Mr. *Symmes*'s Pardon, if I improve his late *Joco-Serious* Discourse concerning Regular Singing, in Vindication of the *Courant*: And if I am as merry with the *Anti-Couranteers* as he is with the scrupulous Consciences of his *Anti-Regular-Singers*, I may yet hope to find Five able Hands in Town and Country, who will (at least) approve of the *Substance* and *Design* of this Letter.

And now, you Gentlemen, who are the avowed Enemies of the *Courant*, let me beseech you to beware of a certain *Joco-Serious Dialogue*, wrote by a Clergyman, (Heaven forgive him!) which *inevitably tends to the Subversion of your Religion.* Have you not often said, that the *Courant* offended GOD because it offended *good People*? And has not *he* (think you) offended many a weak Brother, almost as weak as your selves, by declaring against the *good old Way* of Singing? Are not the Select-Men of *Milton* good Men, who have the *Protestant Religion* so much at heart as to forbid the teaching of Regular Singing in their *Borders*, lest it should infect the whole Town with *Popery*; and will not they (think you) be offended with this abominable *Joco-Serious Confabulation*? You make a grievous Complaint against the *Courant*, because (you say) it *exposes the Failings of particular Persons.* And does not Mr. *Symmes* (not to mention all his broad Hints) in Scorn call one of his Neighbours a *good Man* who is *shy of his Bible*, &c. Nay does he not say of one whom he calls a *Reverend Brother*, that *whatever he is for a Christian, he is but a poor Tool of a Scholar*, and ridicule him both in *English* and *Latin*? Phy upon him! Has he never heard of the Fate of Mr. *Turner* (a Gentleman of the Law) who was indicted by the Grand-Jury of *Plymouth* County for *prophaning the Name of Justice* O——s, for which he was oblig'd to stand at the Bar and plead *Not Guilty* before the whole Court? And does he not know, that a famous Country Justice sent a Warrant after poor *Jeremiah Levett* of *Rochester*, because he (*being of no good Name and Fame*) *did upon the 19th Day of* March, 1717,18. *give out and utter reviling and blasphemous Words against a Justice of the Peace*? I can assure him this is true, for I have a Copy of the Warrant now in my Hands. And is it not a greater Crime to *write Blasphemy against a Minister of the Gospel*, than to *give out and utter reviling and blasphemous Words against a Justice of the Peace*? But further Gentlemen, I desire you to consider how intollerably he has abus'd your *Ancestors*, by saying, that *some of your Fathers and Grandfathers could not read*, and that *they are gone to Heaven the wrong way*. The Reverend Mr. *Alsop* indeed says, that some Men are *sent to Heaven upon pain of Death*; but shou'd you meet with such a Phrase in the *Courant*, wou'd you not presently affirm it to be *against the* Principles *of Religion*? I have but one thing more to observe to you, Gentlemen, and that is, that you bitterly inveigh against the *Courant* when you find things *serious* and *comical* inserted in the same Paper, tho' in different Pieces: But has not Mr. *Symmes* quoted Texts of Scripture in the same Page wherein he reproaches the Anti-Regular-Singers with their Ignorance of the *Gun-Powder-Plot*? And has he not mixt the *Faithful Servants of Jesus Christ, Learning and Wisdom and Piety, Family Religion*, &c. in the same Page with *Barns, Ploughs*, and *Carts*, and whole *Barrels of Herring*? Is he not often very witty and good humour'd at the proper Cost and Charge of *Solomon*, the Prophets and Apostles? *&c.* What else can you make of his saying, (*p.* 34.) 'In Plain English Neighbour, a *broad Laugh*, is all the Answer such *whymsical* Objections deserve: or rather, a hearty *Scoul* or deep *Sigh*, to observe the doleful Effects of Man's Apostacy. To be oppress'd with such Objections would *make a wise man mad*, Eccl. 7.7.?'

Upon the whole, Friend *Janus*, we may conclude, that the

Anti-Couranteers are a sort of *Precisians*, who mistaking Religion for the peculiar Whims of their own distemper'd Brain, are for cutting or stretching all Men to their own Standard of Thinking. I wish Mr. *Symmes*'s Character may secure him from the Woes and Curses they are so free of dispensing among their dissenting Neighbours, who are so unfortunate as to discover a Chearfulness becoming Christianity. Sir *Thomas Pope Blount* in his *Essays*, has said enough to convince us of the Unreasonableness of this sour Temper among Christians, and with his Words I shall conclude.

'Certainly (*says he*) of all Sorts of Men, none do more mistake the Divine Nature, and by consequence do greater mischief to Religion, than those who would perswade us, That to be truly Religious, is to renounce all the Pleasures of Humane Life; As if Religion were a *Caput Mortuum*, a heavy, dull, insipid thing; that has neither Heat, Life, nor motion in it: Or were intended for a *Medusa*'s Head to transform Men into Monuments of Stone. Whereas (really) Religion is of an Active Principle, it not only elevates the Mind, and invigorates the Fancy; but it admits of Mirth, and pleasantness of Conversation, and indulges us in our Christian Liberties; and for this reason, says the Lord *Bacon*, *It is no less impious to shut where God Almighty has open'd, than to open where God Almighty has shut*. But, I say, if Men will suffer themselves to be thus impos'd upon, as to Believe, That Religion requires any such unnecessary Rigours and Austerities, all that can be said, is, The fault does not lye in Religion, but in their Understandings; Nor is this to paint Religion like her self, but rather like one of the Furies with nothing but Whips and Snakes about her. And so, they Worship *God* just as the *Indians* do the *Devil*, not as they love him, but because they are afraid of him. It is not therefore to be wonder'd, that since their Notions of God are such, their Way of Worship is agreeable thereunto; And hence it is, That these Men serve our God, just as some Idolaters Worship theirs; with painful Convulsions of Body, and unnatural Distortions of Face, and all the dismal solemnities of a gloomy Soul, and a dejected Countenance. Now these are the Men, who upon all Occasions are so apt to condemn their Brethren, and, as if they were of God's Cabinet Council, pretend to know the Final

Decrees of the *Almighty*. But alas! who is sufficient for these Things? Certainly, no Man can render himself more foolishly ridiculous, than by meddling with these *Secrets* of *Heaven*.'

I am, Sir, Your Humble Servant,
Timothy Wagstaff.

The New-England Courant, April 15, 1723

Abigail Twitterfield

To assert, That because Posterity is a Blessing, therefore those who want it are cursed, is a meer Platonick Dream.

Honest Doctor JANUS,

Seeing you have ever manifested a Readiness to assist the fair Sex as there has been Occasion, we flatter our selves that what we have now to offer, will by your next Paper be convey'd to the Publick, that so all the World may see to what a Pitch our Resentments are rais'd, and judge whether there be not just Occasion!

Know then, Sir, (and we would have it known to all Christian People) that we have not long since been intollerably affronted in the publick Assembly: Our Spiritual Guide taking Occasion to exclaim at an high Rate against the *Sin of Barrenness*, we Nine (now met together) thought our selves particularly singled out, and pointed at in his Discourse.

We readily confess, it is a great Blessing to have Posterity, but can by no means think the Want of it so heavy a Curse as was represented; and we think it was prov'd to be so in a very lame and sophistical manner: For, by this manner of *Ratiocination*, one may as well argue thus: *Earthly Riches, the Confluence of outward good things, is a Blessing*; Ergo, *Poverty is a Judgment and heavy Curse. Desirable Friends are a Blessing*; Ergo, *He that is bereft of them is cursed*, &c.

For our own parts, tho' Children are witheld from us, and we see not the lovely *Olive Plants* around our *Tables*, yet (we speak for our selves respectively) we live a chearful, thankful Life, rejoycing in the other outward Blessings which we have;

nor do we envy (for *Envy* is no *Vertue*, tho' falsly so call'd by some) those who enjoy the Blessing of Children. And seeing we are no more the *blameable Cause* of this our Unhappiness, than Persons who are born blind, or Ideots, we are far from thinking such a *humbling Curse* and *Reproach* belongs to us, as we have been told: For which reason we think it the more intollerable, to be insulted with the bitter Names of *dry Sticks*, *sapless Trees*, *unfruitful Vines*, &c. Job.24.21. *He evil entreateth the barren that beareth not*.

Who could hear themselves *tantaliz'd* at such a Rate, and not be vext intollerably, beyond Measure!

> *We went to Church to hear the Word,*
> *But to our Grief we found*
> *Our Ears oppress'd with things absurd;*
> *A vain and empty sound.*

But we were the more surpriz'd at this Entertainment, when we reckon'd up no less than Fourteen Persons (from the greatest to the least) below Stairs, besides a considerable Number above Stairs, who were call'd upon to be *humbled under the Reproach and Curse of Barrenness*; and when we consider'd, that Four of our Reverend Pastors in this Town are deny'd the Blessing of Children.

Upon the whole, we conclude, That if Ministers would deliver nothing but the plain substantial Truths of the Gospel, they would best *magnify their Office*, and edify their Hearers. They ought not to calculate their Discourses to the Circumstances of themselves and Families, when they are *marryed*, *bereav'd of near Relations*, or have *Children born to them*, &c. but should study *to know the State of their Flocks in general*, and acquit themselves in their Office accordingly.

> *Sign'd,*
> Abigail Twitterfield,
> *In the Name of the rest.*

P. S.   It is reported, that there are nineteen *Virgins* who are resolv'd to lead a Single Life, least they should incur the *Reproach and Curse of Barrenness*.

The New-England Courant, July 8, 1723

A Dissertation on Liberty and Necessity, Pleasure and Pain

Whatever is, is in its Causes just
Since all Things are by Fate; but purblind Man
Sees but a part o' th' Chain, the nearest Link,
His Eyes not carrying to the equal Beam
That poises all above.

Dryd.

To Mr. *J. R.*

SIR,

I have here, according to your Request, given you my *present* Thoughts of the *general State of Things* in the Universe. Such as they are, you have them, and are welcome to 'em; and if they yield you any Pleasure or Satisfaction, I shall think my Trouble sufficiently compensated. I know my Scheme will be liable to many Objections from a less discerning Reader than your self; but it is not design'd for those who can't understand it. I need not give you any Caution to distinguish the hypothetical Parts of the Argument from the conclusive: You will easily perceive what I design for Demonstration, and what for Probability only. The whole I leave entirely to you, and shall value my self more or less on this account, in proportion to your Esteem and Approbation.

SECT. I. *Of* Liberty *and* Necessity.

I. *There is said to be a* First Mover, *who is called* GOD, *Maker of the Universe.*

II. *He is said to be all-wise, all-good, all powerful.*

These two Propositions being allow'd and asserted by People of almost every Sect and Opinion; I have here suppos'd them granted, and laid them down as the Foundation of my Argument; What follows then, being a Chain of Consequences truly drawn from them, will stand or fall as they are true or false.

III. *If He is all-good, whatsoever He doth must be good.*

IV. *If He is all-wise, whatsoever He doth must be wise.*

The Truth of these Propositions, with relation to the two first, I think may be justly call'd evident; since, either that infinite Goodness will act what is ill, or infinite Wisdom what is not wise, is too glaring a Contradiction not to be perceiv'd by any Man of common Sense, and deny'd as soon as understood.

V. *If He is all-powerful, there can be nothing either existing or acting in the Universe* against *or* without *his Consent; and what He consents to must be good, because He is good; therefore Evil doth not exist.* Doesn't follow

Unde Malum? has been long a Question, and many of the Learned have perplex'd themselves and Readers to little Purpose in Answer to it. That there are both Things and Actions to which we give the Name of *Evil*, is not here deny'd, as *Pain, Sickness, Want, Theft, Murder*, &c. but that these and the like are not in reality *Evils, Ills*, or *Defects* in the Order of the Universe, is demonstrated in the next Section, as well as by this and the following Proposition. Indeed, to suppose any Thing to exist or be done, *contrary* to the Will of the Almighty, is to suppose him not almighty; or that Something (the Cause of *Evil*) is more mighty than the Almighty; an Inconsistence that I think no One will defend: And to deny any Thing or Action, which he consents to the existence of, to be good, is entirely to destroy his two Attributes of *Wisdom* and *Goodness.*

There is nothing done in the Universe, say the Philosophers, *but what God either does, or* permits *to be done.* This, as He is Almighty, is certainly true: But what need of this Distinction between *doing* and *permitting*? Why, first they take it for granted that many Things in the Universe exist in such a Manner as is not for the best, and that many Actions are done which ought not to be done, or would be better undone;

these Things or Actions they cannot ascribe to God as His, because they have already attributed to Him infinite Wisdom and Goodness; Here then is the Use of the Word *Permit*; He *permits* them to be done, *say they*. But we will reason thus: If God permits an Action to be done, it is because he wants either *Power* or *Inclination* to hinder it; in saying he wants *Power*, we deny Him to be *almighty*; and if we say He wants *Inclination* or *Will*, it must be, either because He is not Good, or the Action is not *evil*, (for all Evil is contrary to the Essence of *infinite Goodness*.) The former is inconsistent with his before-given Attribute of Goodness, therefore the latter must be true.

It will be said, perhaps, that *God permits evil Actions to be done, for* wise *Ends and Purposes*. But this Objection destroys itself; for whatever an infinitely good God hath wise Ends in suffering to *be*, must be good, is thereby made good, and cannot be otherwise.

VI. *If a Creature is made by God, it must depend upon God, and receive all its Power from Him; with which Power the Creature can do nothing contrary to the Will of God, because God is Almighty; what is not contrary to His Will, must be agreeable to it; what is agreeable to it, must be good, because He is Good; therefore a Creature can do nothing but what is good.*

This Proposition is much to the same Purpose with the former, but more particular; and its Conclusion is as just and evident. Tho' a Creature may do many Actions which by his Fellow Creatures will be nam'd *Evil*, and which will naturally and necessarily cause or bring upon the Doer, certain *Pains* (which will likewise be call'd *Punishments*;) yet this Proposition proves, that he cannot act what will be in itself really Ill, or displeasing to God. And that the painful Consequences of his evil Actions (*so call'd*) are not, as indeed they ought not to be, *Punishments* or Unhappinesses, will be shewn hereafter.

Nevertheless, the late learned Author of *The Religion of Nature*, (which I send you herewith) has given us a Rule or Scheme, whereby to discover which of our Actions ought to be esteem'd and denominated *good*, and which *evil*: It is in short this, "Every Action which is done according to *Truth*, is good; and every Action contrary to Truth, is evil: To act according to Truth is to use and esteem every Thing as what it is, *&c*. Thus if *A* steals a Horse from *B*, and rides away upon him, he uses him not as what he is in Truth, *viz*. the Property of another, but as his own, which is contrary to Truth, and therefore *evil*". But, as this Gentleman himself says, (Sect. I. Prop. VI.) "In order to judge rightly what any Thing is, it must be consider'd, not only what it is in one Respect, but also what it may be in any other Respect; and the whole Description of the Thing ought to be taken in:" So in this Case it ought to be consider'd, that *A* is naturally a *covetous* Being, feeling an Uneasiness in the want of *B*'s Horse, which produces an Inclination for stealing him, stronger than his Fear of Punishment for so doing. This is *Truth* likewise, and *A* acts according to it when he steals the Horse. Besides, if it is prov'd to be a *Truth*, that *A* has not Power over his own Actions, it will be indisputable that he acts according to Truth, and impossible he should do otherwise.

I would not be understood by this to encourage or defend Theft; 'tis only for the sake of the Argument, and will certainly have no *ill Effect*. The Order and Course of Things will not be affected by Reasoning of this Kind; and 'tis as just and necessary, and as much according to Truth, for *B* to dislike and punish the Theft of his Horse, as it is for *A* to steal him.

(not Limited!)

VII. *If the Creature is thus limited in his Actions, being able to do only such Things as God would have him to do, and not being able to refuse doing what God would have done; then he can have no such Thing as Liberty, Free-will or Power to do or refrain an Action.*

By *Liberty* is sometimes understood the Absence of Opposition; and in this Sense, indeed, all our Actions may be said to be the Effects of our Liberty: But it is a Liberty of the same Nature with the Fall of a heavy Body to the Ground; it has Liberty to fall, that is, it meets with nothing to hinder its Fall, but at the same Time it is necessitated to fall, and has no Power or Liberty to remain suspended.

But let us take the Argument in another View, and suppose

ourselves to be, in the common sense of the Word, *Free Agents*. As Man is a Part of this great Machine, the Universe, his regular Acting is requisite to the regular moving of the whole. Among the many Things which lie before him to be done, he may, as he is at Liberty and his Choice influenc'd by nothing, (for so it must be, or he is not at Liberty) chuse any one, and refuse the rest. Now there is every Moment something *best* to be done, which is alone then *good*, and with respect to which, every Thing else is at that Time *evil*. In order to know which is best to be done, and which not, it is requisite that we should have at one View all the intricate Consequences of every Action with respect to the general Order and Scheme of the Universe, both present and future; but they are innumerable and incomprehensible by any Thing but Omniscience. As we cannot know these, we have but as one Chance to ten thousand, to hit on the right Action; we should then be perpetually blundering about in the Dark, and putting the Scheme in Disorder; for every wrong Action of a Part, is a Defect or Blemish in the Order of the Whole. Is it not necessary then, that our Actions should be over-rul'd and govern'd by an all-wise Providence?—How exact and regular is every Thing in the *natural* World! How wisely in every Part contriv'd! We cannot here find the least Defect! Those who have study'd the mere animal and vegetable Creation, demonstrate that nothing can be more harmonious and beautiful! All the heavenly Bodies, the Stars and Planets, are regulated with the utmost Wisdom! And can we suppose less Care to be taken in the Order of the *moral* than in the *natural* System? It is as if an ingenious Artificer, having fram'd a curious Machine or Clock, and put its many intricate Wheels and Powers in such a Dependance on one another, that the whole might move in the most exact Order and Regularity, had nevertheless plac'd in it several other Wheels endu'd with an independent *Self-Motion*, but ignorant of the general Interest of the Clock; and these would every now and then be moving wrong, disordering the true Movement, and making continual Work for the Mender; which might better be prevented, by depriving them of that Power of Self-Motion, and placing them in a Dependance on the regular Part of the Clock.

VIII. *If there is no such Thing as Free-Will in Creatures, there can be neither Merit nor Demerit in Creatures.*

IX. *And therefore every Creature must be equally esteem'd by the Creator.*

These Propositions appear to be the necessary Consequences of the former. And certainly no Reason can be given, why the Creator should prefer in his Esteem one Part of His Works to another, if with equal Wisdom and Goodness he design'd and created them all, since all Ill or Defect, as contrary to his Nature, is excluded by his Power. We will sum up the Argument thus, When the Creator first design'd the Universe, either it was His Will and Intention that all Things should exist and be in the Manner they are at this Time; or it was his Will they should *be* otherwise *i.e.* in a different Manner: To say it was His Will Things should be otherwise than they are, is to say Somewhat hath contradicted His Will, and broken His Measures, which is impossible because inconsistent with his Power; therefore we must allow that all Things exist now in a Manner agreeable to His Will, and in consequence of that are all equally Good, and therefore equally esteem'd by Him.

I proceed now to shew, that as all the Works of the Creator are equally esteem'd by Him, so they are, as in Justice they ought to be, equally us'd.

SECT. II. *Of* Pleasure *and* Pain.

I. *When a Creature is form'd and endu'd with Life, 'tis suppos'd to receive a Capacity of the Sensation of* Uneasiness *or* Pain.

It is this distinguishes Life and Consciousness from unactive unconscious Matter. To know or be sensible of Suffering or being acted upon is *to live*; and whatsoever is not so, among created Things, is properly and truly *dead*.

All *Pain* and *Uneasiness* proceeds at first from and is caus'd by Somewhat without and distinct from the Mind itself. The

Soul must first be acted upon before it can re-act. In the Beginning of Infancy it is as if it were not; it is not conscious of its own Existence, till it has receiv'd the first Sensation of *Pain*; then, and not before, it begins to feel itself, is rous'd, and put into Action; then it discovers its Powers and Faculties, and exerts them to expel the Uneasiness. Thus is the Machine set on work; this is Life. We are first mov'd by *Pain*, and the whole succeeding Course of our Lives is but one continu'd Series of Action with a View to be freed from it. As fast as we have excluded one Uneasiness another appears, otherwise the Motion would cease. If a continual Weight is not apply'd, the Clock will stop. And as soon as the Avenues of Uneasiness to the Soul are choak'd up or cut off, we are dead, we think and act no more.

II. *This Uneasiness, whenever felt, produces* Desire *to be freed from it, great in exact proportion to the Uneasiness.*

Thus is *Uneasiness* the first Spring and Cause of all Action; for till we are uneasy in Rest, we can have no Desire to move, and without Desire of moving there can be no voluntary Motion. The Experience of every Man who has observ'd his own Actions will evince the Truth of this; and I think nothing need be said to prove that the *Desire* will be equal to the *Uneasiness*, for the very Thing implies as much: It is not *Uneasiness* unless we desire to be freed from it, nor a great *Uneasiness* unless the consequent Desire is great.

I might here observe, how necessary a Thing in the Order and Design of the Universe this *Pain* or *Uneasiness* is, and how beautiful in its Place! Let us but suppose it just now banish'd the World entirely, and consider the Consequence of it: All the Animal Creation would immediately stand stock still, exactly in the Posture they were in the Moment Uneasiness departed; not a Limb, not a Finger would henceforth move; we should all be reduc'd to the Condition of Statues, dull and unactive: Here I should continue to sit motionless with the Pen in my Hand thus —— and neither leave my Seat nor write one Letter more. This may appear odd at first View, but a little Consideration will make it evident; for 'tis impossible to assign any other Cause for the voluntary

Motion of an Animal than its *uneasiness* in Rest. What a different Appearance then would the Face of Nature make, without it! How necessary is it! And how unlikely that the Inhabitants of the World ever were, or that the Creator ever design'd they should be, exempt from it!

I would likewise observe here, that the VIIIth Proposition in the preceding Section, viz. *That there is neither Merit nor Demerit*, &c. is here again demonstrated, as infallibly, tho' in another manner: For since *Freedom from Uneasiness* is the End of all our Actions, how is it possible for us to do any Thing disinterested? — How can any Action be meritorious of Praise or Dispraise, Reward or Punishment, when the natural Principle of *Self-Love* is the only and the irresistible Motive to it?

III. *This* Desire *is always fulfill'd or satisfy'd,*

In the *Design* or *End* of it, tho' not in the *Manner*: The first is requisite, the latter not. To exemplify this, let us make a Supposition; A Person is confin'd in a House which appears to be in imminent Danger of Falling, this, as soon as perceiv'd, creates a violent *Uneasiness*, and that instantly produces an equal strong *Desire*, the *End* of which is *freedom from the Uneasiness*, and the *Manner* or Way propos'd to gain this *End*, is *to get out of the House*. Now if he is convinc'd by any Means, that he is mistaken, and the House is not likely to fall, he is immediately freed from his *Uneasiness*, and the *End* of his Desire is attain'd as well as if it had been in the *Manner* desir'd, viz. *leaving the House*.

All our different Desires and Passions proceed from and are reducible to this one Point, *Uneasiness*, tho' the Means we propose to ourselves for expelling of it are infinite. One proposes *Fame*, another *Wealth*, a third *Power*, &c. as the Means to gain this *End*; but tho' these are never attain'd, if the Uneasiness be remov'd by some other Means, the *Desire* is satisfy'd. Now during the Course of Life we are ourselves continually removing successive Uneasinesses as they arise, and the *last* we suffer is remov'd by the *sweet Sleep* of Death.

IV. *The fulfilling or Satisfaction of this* Desire, *produces the Sensation of* Pleasure, *great or small in exact proportion to the* Desire.

Pleasure is that Satisfaction which arises in the Mind upon, and is caus'd by, the accomplishment of our *Desires*, and by no other Means at all; and those Desires being above shewn to be caus'd by our *Pains* or *Uneasinesses*, it follows that *Pleasure* is wholly caus'd by *Pain*, and by no other Thing at all.

V. *Therefore the Sensation of* Pleasure *is equal, or in exact proportion to the Sensation of* Pain.

As the *Desire* of being freed from Uneasiness is equal to the *Uneasiness*, and the *Pleasure* of satisfying that Desire equal to the *Desire*, the *Pleasure* thereby produc'd must necessarily be equal to the *Uneasiness* or *Pain* which produces it: Of three Lines, *A*, *B*, and *C*, if *A* is equal to *B*, and *B* to *C*, *C* must be equal to *A*. And as our *Uneasinesses* are always remov'd by some Means or other, it follows that *Pleasure* and *Pain* are in their Nature inseparable: So many Degrees as one Scale of the Ballance descends, so many exactly the other ascends; and one cannot rise or fall without the Fall or Rise of the other: 'Tis impossible to taste of *Pleasure*, without feeling its preceding proportionate *Pain*; or to be sensible of *Pain*, without having its necessary Consequent *Pleasure*: The *highest Pleasure* is only Consciousness of Freedom from the *deepest Pain*, and Pain is not Pain to us unless we ourselves are sensible of it. They go Hand in Hand; they cannot be divided.

You have a View of the whole Argument in a few familiar Examples: The *Pain* of Abstinence from Food, as it is greater or less, produces a greater or less *Desire* of Eating, the Accomplishment of this *Desire* produces a greater or less *Pleasure* proportionate to it. The *Pain* of Confinement causes the *Desire* of Liberty, which accomplish'd, yields a *Pleasure* equal to that *Pain* of Confinement. The *Pain* of Labour and Fatigue causes the *Pleasure* of Rest, equal to that *Pain*. The *Pain* of Absence from Friends, produces the *Pleasure* of Meeting in exact proportion. *&c.*

This is the *fixt Nature* of Pleasure and Pain, and will always be found to be so by those who examine it.

One of the most common Arguments for the future Existence of the Soul, is taken from the generally suppos'd Inequality of Pain and Pleasure in the present; and this, notwithstanding the Difficulty by outward Appearances to make a Judgment of another's Happiness, has been look'd upon as almost unanswerable: but since *Pain* naturally and infallibly produces a *Pleasure* in proportion to it, every individual Creature must, in any State of *Life*, have an equal Quantity of each, so that there is not, on that Account, any Occasion for a future Adjustment.

Thus are all the Works of the Creator *equally* us'd by him; And no Condition of Life or Being is in itself better or preferable to another: The Monarch is not more happy than the Slave, nor the Beggar more miserable than *Cræsus*. Suppose *A*, *B*, and *C*, three distinct Beings; *A* and *B*, animate, capable of *Pleasure* and *Pain*, *C* an inanimate Piece of Matter, insensible of either. *A* receives ten Degrees of *Pain*, which are necessarily succeeded by ten Degrees of *Pleasure*: *B* receives fifteen of *Pain*, and the consequent equal Number of *Pleasure*: *C* all the while lies unconcern'd, and as he has not suffer'd the former, has no right to the latter. What can be more equal and just than this? When the Accounts come to be adjusted, *A* has no Reason to complain that his Portion of *Pleasure* was five Degrees less than that of *B*, for his Portion of *Pain* was five Degrees less likewise: Nor has *B* any Reason to boast that his *Pleasure* was five Degrees greater than that of *A*, for his *Pain* was proportionate: They are then both on the same Foot with *C*, that is, they are neither Gainers nor Losers.

It will possibly be objected here, that even common Experience shews us, there is not in Fact this Equality: "Some we see hearty, brisk and chearful perpetually, while others are constantly burden'd with a heavy Load of Maladies and Misfortunes, remaining for Years perhaps in Poverty, Disgrace, or Pain, and die at last without any Appearance of Recompence." Now tho' 'tis not necessary, when a Proposition is demonstrated to be a general Truth, to shew in what manner it agrees with the particular Circumstances of Persons, and indeed ought not to be requir'd; yet, as this is a common Objection, some Notice may be taken of it: And here let it be observ'd, that we cannot be proper Judges of the good or bad Fortune of Others; we are apt to imagine, that what would give us a great Uneasiness or a great Satisfaction, has the same

Effect upon others: we think, for Instance, those unhappy, who must depend upon Charity for a mean Subsistence, who go in Rags, fare hardly, and are despis'd and scorn'd by all; not considering that Custom renders all these Things easy, familiar, and even pleasant. When we see Riches, Grandeur and a chearful Countenance, we easily imagine Happiness accompanies them, when oftentimes 'tis quite otherwise: Nor is a constantly sorrowful Look, attended with continual Complaints, an infallible Indication of Unhappiness. In short, we can judge by nothing but Appearances, and they are very apt to deceive us. Some put on a gay chearful Outside, and appear to the World perfectly at Ease, tho' even then, some inward Sting, some secret Pain imbitters all their Joys, and makes the Ballance even: Others appear continually dejected and full of Sorrow; but even Grief itself is sometimes *pleasant*, and Tears are not always without their Sweetness: Besides, Some take a Satisfaction in being thought unhappy, (as others take a Pride in being thought humble,) these will paint their Misfortunes to others in the strongest Colours, and leave no Means unus'd to make you think them thoroughly miserable; so great a *Pleasure* it is to them *to be pitied*; Others retain the Form and outside Shew of Sorrow, long after the Thing itself, with its Cause, is remov'd from the Mind; it is a Habit they have acquir'd and cannot leave. These, with many others that might be given, are Reasons why we cannot make a true Estimate of the *Equality* of the Happiness and Unhappiness of others; and unless we could, Matter of Fact cannot be opposed to this Hypothesis. Indeed, we are sometimes apt to think, that the Uneasinesses we ourselves have had, outweigh our Pleasures; but the Reason is this, the Mind takes no Account of the latter, they slip away un-remark'd, when the former leave more lasting Impressions on the Memory. But suppose we pass the greatest part of Life in Pain and Sorrow, suppose we die by Torments and *think no more*, 'tis no Diminution to the Truth of what is here advanc'd; for the *Pain*, tho' exquisite, is not so to the *last* Moments of Life, the Senses are soon benumm'd, and render'd incapable of transmitting it so sharply to the Soul as at first; She perceives it cannot hold long, and 'tis an *exquisite Pleasure* to behold the immediate Approaches of Rest. This makes an Equivalent tho' Annihilation should follow: For the Quantity of *Pleasure* and *Pain* is not to be measur'd by its Duration, any more than the Quantity of Matter by its Extension; and as one cubic Inch may be made to contain, by Condensation, as much Matter as would fill then thousand cubic Feet, being more expanded, so one single Moment of *Pleasure* may outweigh and compensate an Age of *Pain*.

It was owing to their Ignorance of the Nature of Pleasure and Pain that the Antient Heathens believ'd the idle Fable of their *Elizium*, that State of uninterrupted Ease and Happiness! The Thing is intirely impossible in Nature! Are not the Pleasures of the Spring made such by the Disagreeableness of the Winter? Is not the Pleasure of fair Weather owing to the Unpleasantness of foul? Certainly. Were it then always Spring, were the Fields always green and flourishing, and the Weather constantly serene and fair, the Pleasure would pall and die upon our Hands; it would cease to be Pleasure to us, when it is not usher'd in by Uneasiness. Could the Philosopher visit, in reality, every Star and Planet with as much Ease and Swiftness as he can now visit their Ideas, and pass from one to another of them in the Imagination; it would be a *Pleasure* I grant; but it would be only in proportion to the *Desire* of accomplishing it, and that would be no greater than the *Uneasiness* suffer'd in the Want of it. The Accomplishment of a long and difficult Journey yields a great *Pleasure;* but if we could take a Trip to the Moon and back again, as frequently and with as much Ease as we can go and come from Market, the Satisfaction would be just the same.

The *Immateriality* of the Soul has been frequently made use of as an Argument for its *Immortality*; but let us consider, that tho' it should be allow'd to be immaterial, and consequently its Parts incapable of Separation or Destruction by any Thing material, yet by Experience we find, that it is not incapable of Cessation of *Thought*, which is its Action. When the Body is but a little indispos'd it has an evident Effect upon the Mind; and a right Disposition of the Organs is requisite to a right Manner of Thinking. In a sound Sleep sometimes, or in a Swoon, we cease to think at all; tho' the Soul is not therefore then annihilated, but *exists* all the while tho' it does not *act*; and may not this probably be the Case after

Death? All our Ideas are first admitted by the Senses and imprinted on the Brain, increasing in Number by Observation and Experience; there they become the Subjects of the Soul's Action. The Soul is a mere Power or Faculty of *contemplating* on, and *comparing* those Ideas when it has them; hence springs Reason: But as it can *think* on nothing but Ideas, it must have them before it can *think* at all. Therefore as it may exist before it has receiv'd any Ideas, it may exist before it *thinks*. To remember a Thing, is to have the Idea of it still plainly imprinted on the Brain, which the Soul can turn to and contemplate on Occasion. To forget a Thing, is to have the Idea of it defac'd and destroy'd by some Accident, or the crouding in and imprinting of great variety of other Ideas upon it, so that the Soul cannot find out its Traces and distinguish it. When we have thus lost the Idea of any one Thing, we can *think* no more, or *cease to think*, on that Thing; and as we can lose the Idea of one Thing, so we may of ten, twenty, a hundred, *&c.* and even of all Things, because they are not in their Nature permanent; and often during Life we see that some Men, (by an Accident or Distemper affecting the Brain,) lose the greatest Part of their Ideas, and remember very little of their past Actions and Circumstances. Now upon *Death*, and the Destruction of the Body, the Ideas contain'd in the Brain, (which are alone the Subjects of the Soul's Action) being then likewise necessarily destroy'd, the Soul, tho' incapable of Destruction itself, must then necessarily *cease to think* or *act*, having nothing left to think or act upon. It is reduc'd to its first inconscious State before it receiv'd any Ideas. And to cease to *think* is but little different from *ceasing to be*.

Nevertheless, 'tis not impossible that this same *Faculty* of contemplating Ideas may be hereafter united to a new Body, and receive a new Set of Ideas; but that will no way concern us who are now living; for the Identity will be lost, it is no longer that same *Self* but a new Being.

I shall here subjoin a short Recapitulation of the Whole, that it may with all its Parts be comprehended at one View.

1. *It is suppos'd that God the Maker and Governour of the Universe, is infinitely wise, good, and powerful.*

2. *In consequence of His infinite Wisdom and Goodness, it is asserted, that whatever He doth must be infinitely wise and good;*

3. *Unless He be interrupted, and His Measures broken by some other Being, which is impossible because He is Almighty.*

4. *In consequence of His infinite Power, it is asserted, that nothing can exist or be done in the Universe which is not agreeable to His Will, and therefore good.*

5. *Evil is hereby excluded, with all Merit and Demerit; and likewise all preference in the Esteem of God, of one Part of the Creation to another.* This is the Summary of the first Part.

Now our common Notions of Justice will tell us, that if all created Things are equally esteem'd by the Creator, they ought to be equally us'd by Him; and that they are therefore equally us'd, we might embrace for Truth upon the Credit, and as the true consequence of the foregoing Argument. Nevertheless we proceed to confirm it, by shewing *how* they are equally us'd, and that in the following Manner.

1. *A Creature when endu'd with Life or Consciousness, is made capable of Uneasiness or Pain.*

2. *This Pain produces Desire to be freed from it, in exact proportion to itself.*

3. *The Accomplishment of this Desire produces an equal Pleasure.*

4. *Pleasure is consequently equal to Pain.*

From these Propositions it is observ'd,

1. *That every Creature hath as much Pleasure as Pain.*

2. *That Life is not preferable to Insensibility; for Pleasure and Pain destroy one another: That Being which has ten Degrees of Pain subtracted from ten of Pleasure, has nothing remaining, and is upon an equality with that Being which is insensible of both.*

3. *As the first Part proves that all Things must be equally us'd by the Creator because equally esteem'd; so this second Part demonstrates that they are equally esteem'd because equally us'd.*

4. *Since every Action is the Effect of Self-Uneasiness, the Distinction of Virtue and Vice is excluded; and* Prop. VIII. *in* Sect. I. *again demonstrated.*

5. *No State of Life can be happier than the present, because Pleasure and Pain are inseparable.*

Thus both Parts of this Argument agree with and confirm one another, and the Demonstration is reciprocal.

I am sensible that the Doctrine here advanc'd, if it were to be publish'd, would meet with but an indifferent Reception. Mankind naturally and generally love to be flatter'd: Whatever sooths our Pride, and tends to exalt our Species above the rest of the Creation, we are pleas'd with and easily believe, when ungrateful Truths shall be with the utmost Indignation rejected. "What! bring ourselves down to an Equality with the Beasts of the Field! with the *meanest* part of the Creation! 'Tis insufferable!" But, (to use a Piece of *common* Sense) our *Geese* are but *Geese* tho' we may think 'em *Swans*; and Truth will be Truth tho' it sometimes prove mortifying and distasteful.

London, 1725

Plan of Conduct

Those who write of the art of poetry teach us that if we would write what may be worth the reading, we ought always, before we begin, to form a regular plan and design of our piece: otherwise, we shall be in danger of incongruity. I am apt to think it is the same as to life. I have never fixed a regular design in life; by which means it has been a confused variety of different scenes. I am now entering upon a new one: let me, therefore, make some resolutions, and form some scheme of action, that, henceforth, I may live in all respects like a rational creature.

1. It is necessary for me to be extremely frugal for some time, till I have paid what I owe.

2. To endeavour to speak truth in every instance; to give nobody expectations that are not likely to be answered, but aim at sincerity in every word and action—the most amiable excellence in a rational being.

3. To apply myself industriously to whatever business I take in hand, and not divert my mind from my business by any foolish project of growing suddenly rich; for industry and patience are the surest means of plenty.

4. I resolve to speak ill of no man whatever, not even in a matter of truth; but rather by some means excuse the faults I hear charged upon others, and upon proper occasions speak all the good I know of every body.

1726

PHILADELPHIA
1726 – 1757

Contents

LETTERS

Articles of Belief and Acts of Religion

IN TWO PARTS.

Here will I hold—If there is a Pow'r above us
(And that there is, all Nature cries aloud,
Thro' all her Works), He must delight in Virtue
And that which he delights in must be Happy.   Cato.

Part I.

Philada.
Nov. 20 1728.

First Principles

I believe there is one Supreme most perfect Being, Author and Father of the Gods themselves.

For I believe that Man is not the most perfect Being but One, rather that as there are many Degrees of Beings his Inferiors, so there are many Degrees of Beings superior to him.

Also, when I stretch my Imagination thro' and beyond our System of Planets, beyond the visible fix'd Stars themselves, into that Space that is every Way infinite, and conceive it fill'd with Suns like ours, each with a Chorus of Worlds for ever moving round him, then this little Ball on which we move, seems, even in my narrow Imagination, to be almost Nothing, and my self less than nothing, and of no sort of Consequence.

When I think thus, I imagine it great Vanity in me to suppose, that the *Supremely Perfect*, does in the least regard such an inconsiderable Nothing as Man. More especially, since it is impossible for me to have any positive clear Idea of that which is infinite and incomprehensible, I cannot conceive otherwise, than that He, *the Infinite Father*, expects or requires no Worship or Praise from us, but that he is even INFINITELY ABOVE IT.

But since there is in all Men something like a natural Principle which enclines them to DEVOTION or the Worship of some unseen Power;

And since Men are endued with Reason superior to all other Animals that we are in our World acquainted with;

Therefore I think it seems required of me, and my Duty, as a Man, to pay Divine Regards to SOMETHING.

I CONCEIVE then, that the INFINITE has created many Beings or Gods, vastly superior to Man, who can better conceive his Perfections than we, and return him a more rational and glorious Praise. As among Men, the Praise of the Ignorant or of Children, is not regarded by the ingenious Painter or Architect, who is rather honour'd and pleas'd with the Approbation of Wise men and Artists.

It may be that these created Gods, are immortal, or it may be that after many Ages, they are changed, and Others supply their Places.

Howbeit, I conceive that each of these is exceeding wise, and good, and very powerful; and that Each has made for himself, one glorious Sun, attended with a beautiful and admirable System of Planets.

It is that particular wise and good God, who is the Author and Owner of our System, that I propose for the Object of my Praise and Adoration.

For I conceive that he has in himself some of those Passions he has planted in us, and that, since he has given us Reason whereby we are capable of observing his Wisdom in the Creation, he is not above caring for us, being pleas'd with our Praise, and offended when we slight Him, or neglect his Glory.

I conceive for many Reasons that he is a *good Being*, and as I should be happy to have so wise, good and powerful a Being my Friend, let me consider in what Manner I shall make myself most acceptable to him.

Next to the Praise due, to his Wisdom, I believe he is pleased and delights in the Happiness of those he has created; and since without Virtue Man* can have no Happiness in this World, I firmly believe he delights to see me Virtuous, because he is pleas'd when he sees me Happy.

And since he has created many Things which seem purely design'd for the Delight of Man, I believe he is not offended when he sees his Children solace themselves in any manner of

*See Junto Paper of Good and Evil, &c.

pleasant Exercises and innocent Delights, and I think no Pleasure innocent that is to Man hurtful.

I *love* him therefore for his Goodness and I *adore* him for his Wisdom.

Let me then not fail to praise my God continually, for it is his Due, and it is all I can return for his many Favours and great Goodness to me; and let me resolve to be virtuous, that I may be happy, that I may please Him, who is delighted to see me happy. Amen.

   I. Adoration.   ♄2. Petition.   ♄3. Thanks.

Prel.   Being mindful that before I address the DEITY, my Soul ought to be calm and Serene, free from Passion and Perturbation, or otherwise elevated with Rational Joy and Pleasure, I ought to use a Countenance that expresses a filial Respect, mixt with a kind of Smiling, that signifies inward Joy, and Satisfaction, and Admiration.

O wise God,
   My good Father,
Thou beholdest the Sincerity of my Heart,
   And of my Devotion;
Grant me a Continuance of thy Favour!

(1)

Powerful Goodness, &c.

O Creator, O Father, I believe that thou art Good, and that thou art *pleas'd with the Pleasure* of thy Children.

                Praised be thy Name for Ever.

(2)

By thy Power hast thou made the glorious Sun, with his attending Worlds; from the Energy of thy mighty Will they first received their prodigious Motion, and by thy Wisdom hast thou prescribed the wondrous Laws by which they move.

                Praised be thy Name for ever.

(3)

By thy Wisdom hast thou formed all Things, Thou hast

created Man, bestowing Life and Reason, and plac'd him in Dignity superior to thy other earthly Creatures.

Praised be thy Name for ever.

(4)

Thy Wisdom, thy Power, and thy GOODNESS are every where clearly seen; in the Air and in the Water, in the Heavens and on the Earth; Thou providest for the various winged Fowl, and the innumerable Inhabitants of the Water; Thou givest Cold and Heat, Rain and Sunshine in their Season, and to the Fruits of the Earth Increase.

Praised be thy Name for ever.

(5)

I believe thou hast given Life to thy Creatures that they might Live, and art not delighted with violent Death and bloody Sacrifices.   Praised be thy Name for Ever.

(6)

Thou abhorrest in thy Creatures Treachery and Deceit, Malice, Revenge, Intemperance and every other hurtful Vice; but Thou art a Lover of Justice and Sincerity, of Friendship, Benevolence and every Virtue. Thou art my Friend, my Father, and my Benefactor.

Praised be thy Name, O God, for Ever.

Amen.

After this, it will not be improper to read part of some such Book as Ray's Wisdom of God in the Creation or Blacmore on the Creation, or the Archbishop of Cambray's Demonstration of the Being of a God; &c. or else spend some Minutes in a serious Silence, contemplating on those Subjects.

Then Sing
Milton's Hymn to the Creator

These are thy Glorious Works, Parent of Good!
Almighty: Thine this Universal Frame,
Thus wondrous fair! Thy self how wondrous then!
Speak ye who best can tell, Ye Sons of Light,
Angels, for ye behold him, and with Songs,

And Choral Symphonies, Day without Night
Circle his Throne rejoicing. You in Heav'n,
On Earth, join all Ye Creatures to extol
Him first, him last, him midst and without End.
   Fairest of Stars, last in the Train of Night,
If rather thou belongst not to the Dawn,
Sure Pledge of Day! That crown'st the smiling Morn
With thy bright Circlet; Praise him in thy Sphere
While Day arises, that sweet Hour of Prime.
   Thou Sun, of this Great World both Eye and Soul
Acknowledge Him thy Greater, Sound his Praise
In thy Eternal Course; both when thou climb'st,
And when high Noon hast gain'd, and when thou fall'st.
Moon! that now meet'st the orient Sun, now fly'st
With the fix'd Stars, fix'd in their Orb that flies,
And ye five other Wandring Fires, that move
In mystic Dance, not without Song, resound
His Praise, that out of Darkness call'd up Light.
Air! and ye Elements! the Eldest Birth
Of Nature's Womb, that in Quaternion run
Perpetual Circle, multiform; and mix
And nourish all Things, let your ceaseless Change
Vary to our great Maker still new Praise.
Ye Mists and Exhalations! that now rise
From Hill or steaming Lake, dusky or grey,
Till the Sun paint your fleecy Skirts with Gold,
In Honour to the World's Great Author rise.
Whether to deck with Clouds th' uncolour'd Sky
Or wet the thirsty Earth with falling Show'rs,
Rising or falling still advance his Praise.
His Praise, ye Winds! that from 4 Quarters blow,
Breathe soft or loud; and wave your Tops ye Pines!
With every Plant, in Sign of Worship wave.
Fountains! and ye that warble as ye flow
Melodious Murmurs, warbling tune his Praise.
Join Voices all ye living Souls, ye Birds!
That singing, up to Heav'n's high Gate ascend,
Bear on your Wings, and in your Notes his Praise.
Ye that in Waters glide! and ye that walk
The Earth! and stately Tread, or lowly Creep;

Witness *if I be silent*, Ev'n or Morn,
To Hill or Valley, Fountain or Fresh Shade,
Made Vocal by my Song, and taught his Praise.

{ Here follows the Reading of some Book or part of a Book
{ Discoursing on and exciting to MORAL VIRTUE

Petition.

Prel. {

In as much as by Reason of our Ignorance We
cannot be Certain that many Things Which we often hear mentioned in the Petitions of Men to the
Deity, would prove REAL GOODS if they were in our
Possession, and as I have Reason to hope and believe that the Goodness of my Heavenly Father will
not withold from me a suitable Share of Temporal
Blessings, if by a VIRTUOUS and HOLY Life I merit
his Favour and Kindness, Therefore I presume not
to ask such Things, but rather Humbly, and with a
sincere Heart express my earnest Desires that he
would graciously assist my Continual Endeavours
and Resolutions of eschewing Vice and embracing
Virtue; Which kind of Supplications will at least be
thus far beneficial, as they remind me in a solemn
manner of my Extensive   DUTY.

That I may be preserved from Atheism and Infidelity, Impiety and Profaneness, and in my Addresses to Thee carefully
avoid Irreverence and Ostentation, Formality and odious
Hypocrisy,   Help me, O Father

That I may be loyal to my Prince, and faithful to my Country,
careful for its Good, valiant in its Defence, and obedient to
its Laws, abhorring Treason as much as Tyranny,
                                        Help me, O Father

That I may to those above me be dutiful, humble, and submissive, avoiding Pride, Disrespect and Contumacy,
                                        Help me, O Father

That I may to those below me, be gracious, Condescending
and Forgiving, using Clemency, protecting *Innocent Distress*,

avoiding Cruelty, Harshness and Oppression, Insolence and unreasonable Severity,   Help me, O Father

That I may refrain from Calumny and Detraction; that I may avoid and abhor Deceit and Envy, Fraud, Flattery and Hatred, Malice, Lying and Ingratitude,

Help me, O Father

That I may be sincere in Friendship, faithful in Trust, and impartial in Judgment, watchful against Pride, and against Anger (that momentary Madness),   Help me, O Father

That I may be just in all my Dealings and temperate in my Pleasures, full of Candour and Ingenuity, Humanity and Benevolence,   Help me, O Father

That I may be grateful to my Benefactors and generous to my Friends, exerting Charity and Liberality to the Poor, and Pity to the Miserable,   Help me, O Father

That I may avoid Avarice, Ambition, and Intemperance, Luxury and Lasciviousness,   Help me, O Father

That I may possess Integrity and Evenness of Mind, Resolution in Difficulties, and Fortitude under Affliction; that I may be punctual in performing my Promises, peaceable and prudent in my Behaviour,   Help me, O Father

That I may have Tenderness for the Weak, and a reverent Respect for the Ancient; That I may be kind to my Neighbours, good-natured to my Companions, and hospitable to Strangers,   Help me, O Father

That I may be averse to Craft and Overreaching, abhor Extortion, Perjury, and every kind of Wickedness,

Help me, O Father

That I may be honest and Openhearted, gentle, merciful and Good, chearful in Spirit, rejoicing in the Good of Others,

Help me, O Father

That I may have a constant Regard to Honour and Probity;

That I may possess a perfect Innocence and a good Conscience, and at length become Truly Virtuous and Magnanimous,   Help me, Good God,
                                                        Help me, O Father

And forasmuch as Ingratitude is one of the most odious of Vices, let me not be unmindful gratefully to acknoledge the Favours I receive from Heaven.

Thanks.

For Peace and Liberty, for Food and Raiment, for Corn and Wine, and Milk, and every kind of Healthful Nourishment,   *Good God, I Thank thee.*

For the Common Benefits of Air and Light, for useful Fire and delicious Water,   *Good God, I Thank thee.*

For Knowledge and Literature and every useful Art; for my Friends and their Prosperity, and for the fewness of my Enemies,   *Good God, I Thank thee.*

For all thy innumerable Benefits; For Life and Reason, and the Use of Speech, for Health and Joy and every Pleasant Hour,   *my Good God, I thank thee.*

End of the first Part.

The Busy-Body, No. 1

Mr. *Andrew Bradford*,

I design this to acquaint you, that I, who have long been one of your *Courteous Readers*, have lately entertain'd some Thoughts of setting up for an Author my Self; not out of the least Vanity, I assure you, or Desire of showing my Parts, but purely for the Good of my Country.

I have often observ'd with Concern, that your *Mercury* is not always equally entertaining. The Delay of Ships expected in, and want of fresh Advices from *Europe*, make it frequently very Dull; and I find the Freezing of our River has the same Effect on News as on Trade.—With more Concern have I continually observ'd the growing Vices and Follies of my Country-folk. And tho' Reformation is properly the concern of every Man; that is, *Every one ought to mend One*; yet 'tis too true in this Case, that *what is every Body's Business is no Body's Business*, and the Business is done accordingly. I, therefore, upon mature Deliberation, think fit to take *no Body's Business* wholly into my own Hands; and, out of Zeal for the Publick Good, design to erect my Self into a Kind of *Censor Morum*; proposing with your Allowance, to make Use of the *Weekly Mercury* as a Vehicle in which my Remonstrances shall be convey'd to the World.

I am sensible I have, in this Particular, undertaken a very unthankful Office, and expect little besides my Labour for my Pains. Nay, 'tis probable I may displease a great Number of your Readers, who will not very well like to pay 10 s a Year for being told of their Faults. But as most People delight in Censure when they themselves are not the Objects of it, if any are offended at my publickly exposing their private Vices, I promise they shall have the Satisfaction, in a very little Time, of seeing their good Friends and Neighbours in the same Circumstances.

However, let the Fair Sex be assur'd, that I shall always treat them and their Affairs with the utmost *Decency* and Respect. I intend now and then to dedicate a Chapter wholly to their Service; and if my Lectures any Way contribute to the

Embellishment of their Minds, and Brightning of their Understandings, without offending their *Modesty*, I doubt not of having their Favour and Encouragement.

'Tis certain, that no Country in the World produces naturally finer Spirits than ours, Men of Genius for every kind of Science, and capable of acquiring to Perfection every Qualification that is in Esteem among Mankind. But as few here have the Advantage of good Books, for want of which, good Conversation is still more scarce, it would doubtless have been very acceptable to your Readers, if, instead of an old out-of-date Article from *Muscovy* or *Hungary*, you had entertained them with some well-chosen Extract from a good Author. This I shall sometimes do, *when I happen to have nothing of my own to say that I think of more Consequence*. Sometimes, I propose to deliver Lectures of Morality or Philosophy, and (because I am naturally enclin'd to be meddling with Things that don't concern me) perhaps I may sometimes talk Politicks. And if I can by any means furnish out a Weekly Entertainment for the Publick, that will give a rational Diversion, and at the same Time be instructive to the Readers, I shall think my Leisure Hours well employ'd: And if you publish this I hereby invite all ingenious Gentlemen and others, (that approve of such an Undertaking) to my Assistance and Correspondence.

'Tis like by this Time you have a Curiosity to be acquainted with my Name and Character. As I do not aim at publick Praise I design to remain concealed; and there are such Numbers of our Family and Relations at this Time in the Country, that tho' I've sign'd my Name at full Length, I am not under the least Apprehension of being distinguish'd and discover'd by it. My Character indeed I would favour you with, but that I am cautious of praising my Self, lest I should be told *my Trumpeter's dead*: And I cannot find in my Heart, at present, to say any Thing to my own Disadvantage.

It is very common with Authors in their First Performances to talk to their Readers thus, *If this meets with a SUITABLE Reception*; Or, *If this should meet with DUE Encouragement, I shall hereafter publish, &c.* This only manifests the Value they put on their own Writings, since they think to frighten the

Publick into their Applause, by threatning, that unless you approve what they have already wrote, they intend never to write again; when perhaps, it mayn't be a Pin Matter whether they ever do or no. As I have not observ'd the Criticks to be more favourable on this Account, I shall always avoid saying any Thing of the Kind; and conclude with telling you, that if you send me a Bottle of Ink and a Quire of Paper by the Bearer, you may depend on hearing further from

SIR,

Your most humble Servant
The Busy Body.

No 1.

The American Weekly Mercury, February 4, 1728/9

The Busy-Body, No. 2

All Fools have still an Itching to deride;
And fain would be upon the laughing Side.   Pope.

Monsieur *Rochefocaut* tells us somewhere in his Memoirs, that the Prince of *Conde* delighted much in Ridicule; and us'd frequently to shut himself up for Half a Day together in his Chamber with a Gentleman that was his Favourite, purposely to divert himself with examining what was the Foible or ridiculous side of every Noted Person in the Court. That Gentleman said afterwards in some Company, that he thought nothing was more ridiculous in any Body, than this same Humour in the Prince; and I am somewhat inclin'd to be of his Opinion. The General Tendency there is among us to this Embellishment, (which I fear has too often been grossly imposed upon my loving Countrymen instead of Wit) and the Applause it meets with from a rising Generation, fill me with fearful Apprehensions for the future Reputation of my Country: A young Man of Modesty (which is the most certain Indication of large Capacities) is hereby discourag'd from attempting to make any Figure in Life: His Apprehensions of being out-laugh'd, will force him to continue in a restless Obscurity, without having an Opportunity of knowing his own Merit himself, or discovering it to the World, rather than venture to expose himself in a Place where a Pun or a Sneer shall pass for Wit, Noise for Reason, and the Strength of the Argument be judg'd by that of the Lungs. Among these witty Gentlemen let us take a View of *Ridentius*: What a contemptible Figure does he make with his Train of paultry Admirers? This Wight shall give himself an Hours Diversion with the Cock of a Man's Hat, the Heels of his Shoes, an unguarded Expression in his Discourse, or even some Personal Defect; and the Height of his low Ambition is to put some One of the Company to the Blush, who perhaps must pay an equal Share of the Reckoning with himself. If such a Fellow makes Laughing the sole End and Purpose of his Life, if it is necessary to his Constitution, or if he has a great Desire of growing suddenly fat, let him treat; let him give publick Notice where any dull stupid Rogues may get a Quart of Four-penny for being laugh'd at; but 'tis barbarously unhandsome, when Friends meet for the Benefit of Conversation, and a proper Relaxation from Business, that one should be the *Butt* of the Company, and Four Men made merry at the Cost of the Fifth.

How different from this Character is that of the good-natur'd gay *Eugenius*? who never spoke yet but with a Design to divert and please; and who was never yet baulk'd in his Intention. *Eugenius* takes more Delight in applying the Wit of his Friends, than in being admir'd himself: And if any one of the Company is so unfortunate as to be touch'd a little too nearly, he will make Use of some ingenious Artifice to turn the Edge of Ridicule another Way, chusing rather to make even himself a publick Jest, than be at the Pain of seeing his Friend in Confusion.

Among the Tribe of Laughers I reckon the *pretty Gentlemen* that write *Satyrs*, and carry them about in their Pockets, reading them themselves in all Company they happen into; taking an Advantage of the ill Taste of the Town, to make themselves famous for a Pack of paultry low Nonsense, for which they deserve to be kick'd, rather than admir'd, by all who have the least Tincture of Politeness. These I take to be the most incorrigible of all my Readers; nay I expect they will be squibbing at the *BUSY-BODY* himself: However the only Favour he begs of them is this; that if they cannot controul their over-bearing Itch of *Scribbling*, let him be attack'd in down right *BITING LYRICKS*; for there is no *Satyr* he Dreads half so much as an Attempt towards a Panegyrick.

The American Weekly Mercury, February 11, 1728/9

The Busy-Body, No. 3

Non vultus instantis Tyranni
Mente quatit solida —neque Auster
Dux inquieti turbidus Adriæ,
Nec fulminantis magna Jovis manus.   Hor.

It is said that the *Persians* in their ancient Constitution, had publick Schools in which Virtue was taught as a Liberal Art or Science; and it is certainly of more Consequence to a Man that he has learnt to govern his Passions; in spite of Temptation to be just in his Dealings, to be Temperate in his Pleasures, to support himself with Fortitude under his Misfortunes, to behave with Prudence in all Affairs and in every Circumstance of Life; I say, it is of much more real Advantage to him to be thus qualified, than to be a Master of all the Arts and Sciences in the World beside.

Virtue alone is sufficient to make a Man Great, Glorious and Happy.—He that is acquainted with *CATO*, as I am, cannot help thinking as I do now, and will acknowledge he deserves the Name without being honour'd by it. *Cato* is a Man whom Fortune has plac'd in the most obscure Part of the Country. His Circumstances are such as only put him above Necessity, without affording him many Superfluities; Yet who is greater than *Cato*?—I happened but the other Day to be at a House in Town, where among others were met Men of the most Note in this Place: *Cato* had Business with some of them, and knock'd at the Door. The most trifling Actions of a Man, in my Opinion, as well as the smallest Features and Lineaments of the Face, give a nice Observer some Notion of his Mind. Methought he rapp'd in such a peculiar Manner, as seem'd of itself to express, there was One who deserv'd as well as desir'd Admission. He appear'd in the plainest Country Garb; his Great Coat was coarse and looked old and thread-bare; his Linnen was homespun; his Beard perhaps of Seven Days Growth, his Shoes thick and heavy, and every Part of his Dress corresponding. Why was this Man receiv'd with such concurring Respect from every Person in the Room, even from those who had never known him or seen him before? It was not an exquisite Form of Person, or Grandeur of Dress that struck us with Admiration. I believe long Habits of Virtue have a sensible Effect on the Countenance: There was something in the Air of his Face that manifested the true Greatness of his Mind; which likewise appear'd in all he said, and in every Part of his Behaviour, obliging us to regard him with a Kind of Veneration. His Aspect is sweetned with Humanity and Benevolence, and at the same Time emboldned with Resolution, equally free from a diffident Bashfulness and an unbecoming Assurance. The Consciousness of his own innate Worth and unshaken Integrity renders him calm and undaunted in the Presence of the most Great and Powerful, and upon the most extraordinary Occasions. His strict Justice and known Impartiality make him the Arbitrator and Decider of all Differences that arise for many Miles around him, without putting his Neighbours to the Charge, Perplexity and Uncertainty of Law-Suits. He always speaks the Thing he means, which he is never afraid or asham'd to do, because he knows he always means well; and therefore is never oblig'd to blush and feel the Confusion of finding himself detected in the Meanness of a Falshood. He never contrives Ill against his Neighbour, and therefore is never seen with a lowring suspicious Aspect. A mixture of Innocence and Wisdom makes him ever seriously chearful. His generous Hospitality to Strangers according to his Ability, his Goodness, his Charity, his Courage in the Cause of the Oppressed, his Fidelity in Friendship, his Humility, his Honesty and Sincerity, his Moderation and his Loyalty to the Government, his Piety, his Temperance, his Love to Mankind, his Magnanimity, his Publick-spiritedness, and in fine, his *Consummate Virtue*, make him justly deserve to be esteem'd the Glory of his Country.

—— The Brave do never shun the Light,
Just are their Thoughts and open are their Tempers;
Freely without Disguise they love and hate;
Still are they found in the fair Face of Day,
And Heaven and Men are Judges of their Actions.

Rowe.

Who would not rather chuse, if it were in his Choice, to merit the above Character, than be the richest, the most learned, or the most powerful Man in the Province without it?

Almost every Man has a strong natural Desire of being valu'd and esteem'd by the rest of his Species; but I am concern'd and griev'd to see how few fall into the Right and only infallible Method of becoming so. That laudable Ambition is too commonly misapply'd and often ill employ'd. Some to make themselves considerable pursue Learning, others grasp at Wealth, some aim at being thought witty, and others are only careful to make the most of an handsome Person; But what is Wit, or Wealth, or Form, or Learning when compar'd with Virtue? 'Tis true, we love the handsome, we applaud the Learned, and we fear the Rich and Powerful; but we even Worship and adore the Virtuous.—Nor is it strange; since Men of Virtue, are so rare, so very rare to be found. If we were as industrious to become Good, as to make ourselves Great, we should become really Great by being Good, and the Number of valuable Men would be much increased; but it is a Grand Mistake to think of being Great without Goodness; and I pronounce it as certain, *that there was never yet a truly Great Man that was not at the same Time truly Virtuous.*

O *Cretico!* Thou sowre Philosopher! Thou cunning Statesman! Thou art crafty, but far from being Wise. When wilt thou be esteem'd, regarded and belov'd like *Cato?* When wilt thou, among thy Creatures meet with that unfeign'd Respect and warm Good-will that all Men have for him? Wilt thou never understand that the cringing, mean, submissive Deportment of thy Dependants, is (like the Worship paid by *Indians* to the Devil) rather thro' Fear of the Harm thou may'st do to them, than out of Gratitude for the Favours they have receiv'd of thee?—Thou art not wholly void of Virtue; there are many good Things in thee, and many good Actions reported of thee. Be advised by thy Friend: Neglect those musty Authors; let them be cover'd with Dust, and moulder on their proper Shelves; and do thou apply thy self to a Study much more profitable, The Knowledge of Mankind, and of thy Self.

This is to give Notice that the BUSY-BODY strictly forbids all Persons, from this Time forward, of what Age, Sex, Rank, Quality, Degree or Denomination soever, on any Pretence to enquire who is the Author of this Paper, on Pain of his Displeasure, (his own near and Dear Relations only excepted).

'Tis to be observ'd that if any bad Characters happen to be drawn in the Course of these Papers, they mean no particular Person, if they are not particularly apply'd.

Likewise that the Author is no Partyman, but a general Meddler.

N. B. Cretico *lives in a neighbouring Province.*

The American Weekly Mercury, February 18, 1728/9

The Busy-Body, No. 4

Nequid nimis.

In my first Paper I invited the Learned and the Ingenious to join with me in this Undertaking; and I now repeat that Invitation. I would have such Gentlemen take this Opportunity, (by trying their Talent in Writing) of diverting themselves and their Friends, and improving the Taste of the Town. And because I would encourage all Wit of our own Growth and Produce, I hereby promise, that whoever shall send me a little Essay on some moral or other Subject, that is fit for publick View in this Manner (and not basely borrow'd from any other Author) I shall receive it with Candour, and take Care to place it to the best Advantage. It will be hard if we cannot muster up in the whole Country, a sufficient Stock of Sense to supply the *Busy-Body* at least for a Twelvemonth. For my own Part, I have already profess'd that I have the Good of my Country wholly at Heart in this Design, without the least sinister View; my chief Purpose being to inculcate the noble Principles of Virtue, and depreciate Vice of every kind. But as I know the Mob hate Instruction, and the Generality would never read beyond the first Line of my Lectures, if they were usually fill'd with nothing but wholesome Precepts and Advice; I must therefore sometimes humour them in their own Way. There are a Set of Great Names in the Province, who are the common Objects of Popular Dislike. If I can now and then overcome my Reluctance, and prevail with my self to Satyrize a little, one of these Gentlemen, the Expectation of meeting with such a Gratification, will induce many to read me through, who would otherwise proceed immediately to the Foreign News. As I am very well assured that the greatest Men among us have a sincere Love for their Country, notwithstanding its Ingratitude, and the Insinuations of the Envious and Malicious to the contrary, so I doubt not but they will chearfully tolerate me in the Liberty I design to take for the End above mentioned.

As yet I have but few Correspondents, tho' they begin now to increase. The following Letter, left for me at the Printers, is one of the first I have receiv'd, which I regard the more for that it comes from one of the Fair Sex, and because I have my self oftentimes suffer'd under the Grievance therein complain'd of.

To the Busy-Body.

Sir,

'You having set your self up for a *Censuror Morum* (as I think you call it) which is said to mean a *Reformer of Manners*, I know no Person more proper to be apply'd to for Redress in all the Grievances we suffer from *Want of Manners* in some People. You must know I am a single Woman, and keep a Shop in this Town for a Livelyhood. There is a certain Neighbour of mine, who is really agreeable Company enough, and with whom I have had an Intimacy of some Time standing; But of late she makes her Visits so excessively often, and stays so very long every Visit, that I am tir'd out of all Patience. I have no Manner of Time at all to my self; and you, who seem to be a wise Man, must needs be sensible that every Person

has little Secrets and Privacies that are not proper to be expos'd even to the nearest Friend. Now I cannot do the least
Thing in the World, but she must know all about it; and it is
a Wonder I have found an Opportunity to write you this Letter. My Misfortune is, that I respect her very well, and know
not how to disoblige her so much as to tell her I should be
glad to have less of her Company; for if I should once hint
such a Thing, I am afraid she would resent it so as never to
darken my Door again.—But, alas, Sir, I have not yet told
you half my Afflictions. She has two Children that are just
big enough to run about and do pretty Mischief: These are
continually along with *Mamma*, either in my Room or Shop,
if I have never so many Customers or People with me about
Business. Sometimes they pull the Goods off my low Shelves
down to the Ground, and perhaps where one of them has just
been making Water; My Friend takes up the Stuff, and cries,
*Eh! thou little wicked mischievous Rogue!—But however, it has
done no great Damage; 'tis only wet a little*; and so puts it up
upon the Shelf again. Sometimes they get to my Cask of Nails
behind the Counter, and divert themselves, to my great Vexation, with mixing my Ten-penny and Eight-penny and Four-
penny together. I Endeavour to conceal my Uneasiness as
much as possible, and with a grave Look go to Sorting them
out. She cries, *Don't thee trouble thy self, Neighbour: Let them
play a little; I'll put all to rights my self before I go*. But Things
are never so put to rights but that I find a great deal of Work
to do after they are gone. Thus, Sir, I have all the Trouble
and Pesterment of Children, without the Pleasure of—calling
them my own; and they are now so us'd to being here that
they will be content no where else. If she would have been so
kind as to have moderated her Visits to ten times a Day, and
stay'd but half an hour at a Time, I should have been contented, and I believe never have given you this Trouble: But
this very Morning they have so tormented me that I could
bear no longer; For while the Mother was asking me twenty
impertinent Questions, the youngest got to my Nails, and
with great Delight rattled them by handfuls all over the
Floor; and the other at the same Time made such a terrible
Din upon my Counter with a Hammer, that I grew half distracted. I was just then about to make my self a new Suit of

Pinners, but in the Fret and Confusion I cut it quite out of all Manner of Shape, and utterly spoil'd a Piece of the first Muslin. Pray, Sir, tell me what I shall do. And talk a little against such unreasonable Visiting in your next Paper: Tho' I would not have her affronted with me for a great Deal, for sincerely I love her and her Children as well I think, as a Neighbour can, and she buys a great many Things in a Year at my Shop. But I would beg her to consider that she uses me unmercifully; Tho' I believe it is only for want of Thought.—But I have twenty Things more to tell you besides all this; There is a handsome Gentleman that has a Mind (I don't question) to make love to me, but he can't get the least Opportunity to—: O dear, here she comes again;—I must conclude

Yours, &c.
Patience.'

Indeed, 'tis well enough, as it happens, that *she is come*, to shorten this Complaint which I think is full long enough already, and probably would otherwise have been as long again. However, I must confess I cannot help pitying my Correspondent's Case, and in her Behalf exhort the Visitor to remember and consider the Words of the Wise Man, *Withdraw thy Foot from the House of thy Neighbour least he grow weary of thee, and so hate thee*. It is, I believe, a nice thing and very difficult, to regulate our Visits in such a Manner, as never to give Offence by coming too seldom, or too often, or departing too abruptly, or staying too long. However, in my Opinion, it is safest for most People, in a general way, who are unwilling to disoblige, to visit seldom, and tarry but a little while in a Place; notwithstanding pressing Invitations, which are many times insincere. And tho' more of your Company should be really desir'd; yet in this Case, too much Reservedness is a Fault more easily excus'd than the Contrary.

Men are subjected to various Inconveniences meerly through lack of a small Share of Courage, which is a Quality very necessary in the common Occurences of Life, as well as in a Battle. How many Impertinences do we daily suffer with great Uneasiness, because we have not Courage enough to discover our Dislike? And why may not a Man use the Boldness and Freedom of telling his Friends that their long Visits sometimes incommode him?—On this Occasion, it may be entertaining to some of my Readers, if I acquaint them with the *Turkish* Manner of entertaining Visitors, which I have from an Author of unquestionable Veracity; who assures us, that even the Turks are not so ignorant of Civility, and the Arts of Endearment, but that they can practice them with as much Exactness as any other Nation, whenever they have a Mind to shew themselves obliging.

'When you visit a Person of Quality, (says he) and have talk'd over your Business, or the Complements, or whatever Concern brought you thither, he makes a Sign to have Things serv'd in for the Entertainment, which is generally, a little Sweetmeat, a Dish of Sherbet, and another of Coffee; all which are immediately brought in by the Servants, and tender'd to all the Guests in Order, with the greatest Care and Awfulness imaginable. At last comes the finishing Part of your Entertainment, which is, Perfuming the Beards of the Company; a Ceremony which is perform'd in this Manner. They have for the Purpose a small Silver Chaffing-Dish, cover'd with a Lid full of Holes, and fixed upon a handsome Plate. In this they put some fresh Coals, and upon them a piece of *Lignum Aloes*, and shutting it up, the Smoak immediately ascends with a grateful Odour thro' the Holes of the Cover. This Smoak is held under every one's Chin, and offer'd as it were a Sacrifice to his Beard. The bristly Idol soon receives the Reverence done to it, and so greedily takes in and incorporates the gummy Steam, that it retains the Savour of it, and may serve for a Nosegay a good while after.

'This Ceremony may perhaps seem ridiculous at first hearing; but it passes among the *Turks* for an high Gratification. And I will say this in its Vindication, that it's Design is very wise and useful. For it is understood to give a civil Dismission to the Visitants; intimating to them, that the Master of the House has Business to do, or some other Avocation, that permits them to go away as soon as they please; and the sooner after this Ceremony the better. By this Means you may, at any Time, without Offence, deliver your self from being detain'd from your Affairs by tedious and unseasonable Visits; and from being constrain'd to use that Piece of

Hypocrisy so common in the World, of pressing those to stay longer with you, whom perhaps in your Heart you wish a great Way off for having troubled you so long already.'

Thus far my Author. For my own Part, I have taken such a Fancy to this Turkish Custom, that for the future I shall put something like it in Practice. I have provided a Bottle of right French Brandy for the Men, and Citron-Water for the Ladies. After I have treated with a Dram, and presented a Pinch of my best Snuff, I expect all Company will retire, and leave me to pursue my Studies for the Good of the Publick.

Advertisement.

I give Notice that I am now actually compiling, and design to publish in a short Time, the true History of the Rise, Growth and Progress of the renowned Tiff-Club. *All Persons who are acquainted with any Facts, Circumstances, Characters, Transactions,* &c. *which will be requisite to the Perfecting and Embellishment of the said Work, are desired to communicate the same to the Author, and direct their Letters to be left with the Printer hereof.*

The Letter sign'd *Would-be-something* is come to hand.

The American Weekly Mercury, February 25, 1728/9

The Busy-Body, No. 5

*Vos, O Patricius sanguis, quos vivere fas est
Occipiti cæco, posticæ occurrite sannæ.* Persius.

This Paper being design'd for a Terror to Evil-Doers, as well as a Praise to them that do well, I am lifted up with secret Joy to find that my Undertaking is approved, and encourag'd by the Just and Good, and that few are against me but those who have Reason to fear me.

There are little Follies in the Behaviour of most Men, which their best Friends are too tender to acquaint them with: There are little Vices and small Crimes which the Law has no Regard to, or Remedy for: There are likewise great Pieces of Villany sometimes so craftily accomplish'd, and so circumspectly guarded, that the Law can take no Hold of the Actors. All these Things, and all Things of this Nature, come within my Province as *CENSOR*, and I am determined not to be negligent of the Trust I have reposed in my self, but resolve to execute my Office diligently and Faithfully.

And that all the World may judge with how much Humanity as well as Justice I shall behave in this Office; and that even my Enemies may be convinc'd I take no Delight to rake into the Dunghill Lives of vicious Men; and to the End that certain Persons may be a little eas'd of their Fears, and reliev'd from the terrible Palpitations they have lately felt and suffer'd, and do still suffer; I hereby graciously pass an Act of general Oblivion, for all Offences, Crimes and Misdemeanors of what Kind soever, committed from the Beginning of Year sixteen hundred and eighty one, until the Day of the Date of my first Paper; and promise only to concern my self with such as have been since and shall hereafter be committed. I shall take no Notice who has, (heretofore) rais'd a Fortune by Fraud and Oppression, nor who by Deceit and Hypocrisy: What Woman has been false to her good Husband's Bed; nor what Man has, by barbarous Usage or Neglect, broke the Heart of a faithful Wife, and wasted his Health and Substance in Debauchery: What base Wretch has betray'd his Friend, and sold his Honesty for Gold, nor what yet baser Wretch, first corrupted him and then bought the Bargain: All this, and much more of the same Kind I shall forget and pass over in Silence;—but then it is to be observed that I expect and require a sudden and general Amendment.

These Threatnings of mine I hope will have a good Effect, and, if regarded, may prevent abundance of Folly and Wickedness in others, and at the same Time save me abundance of Trouble. And that People may not flatter themselves with the Hopes of concealing their Misdemeanours from my Knowledge, and in that View persist in Evil-doing, I must acquaint them, that I have lately enter'd into an Intimacy with the extraordinary Person who some Time since wrote me the following Letter; and who, having a Wonderful Faculty that enables him to discover the most secret Iniquity, is capable of giving me great Assistance in my designed Work of Reformation.

Mr. Busy-Body.

'I rejoice Sir, at the Opportunity you have given me to be serviceable to you, and by your Means to this Province. You must know, that such have been the Circumstances of my Life, and such were the marvellous Concurrences of my Birth, that I have not only a Faculty of discovering the Actions of Persons that are absent or asleep; but even of the Devil himself in many of his secret Workings, in the various Shapes, Habits and Names of Men and Women. And having travel'd and conversed much and met but with a very few of the same Perceptions and Qualifications, I can recommend my Self to you as the most useful Man you can correspond with. My Father's Father's Father (for we had no Grandfathers in our Family) was the same *John Bunyan* that writ that memorable Book *The Pilgrim's Progress*, who had in some Degree a natural Faculty of *Second Sight*. This Faculty (how derived to him, our Family Memoirs are not very clear) was enjoy'd by all his Descendants, but not by equal Talents—'Twas very dim in several of my first Cousins, and probably had been nearly extinct in our particular Branch, had not my Father been a Traveller—He lived in his youthful Days in *New-England*. There he married, and there was born my elder Brother, who had so much of this Faculty, as to discover Witches in some of their occult Performances. My Parents transporting themselves to *Great Britain* my second Brother's Birth was in that Kingdom—He shared but a small Portion of this Virtue, being only able to discern Transactions about the Time, and for the most Part after their happening. My good Father, who delighted in the *Pilgrim's Progress*, and mountainous Places, took Shipping with his Wife for *Scotland*, and inhabited in the Highlands, where my Self was born; and whether the Soil, Climate or Astral Influences, of which are preserved divers Prognosticks, restored our Ancestors Natural Faculty of *Second Sight*, in a greater Lustre to me than it had shined in thro' several Generations, I will not here discuss. But so it is, that I am possess'd largely of it, and design if you encourage the Proposal, to take this Opportunity of doing good with it, which I question not will be accepted of in a grateful Way, by many of your honest Readers, Tho' the Discovery of my Extraction bodes me no Deference from your great Scholars and modern Philosophers. This my Father was long ago aware of, and lest the Name alone should hurt the Fortunes of his Children; he in his Shiftings from one Country to another wisely changed it.

'Sir, I have only this further to say, how I may be useful to you & as a Reason for my not making my Self more known in the World: By Virtue of this Great Gift of Nature *Second-Sightedness*. I do continually see Numbers of Men, Women and Children of all Ranks, and what they are doing, while I am sitting in my Closet; which is too great a Burthen for the Mind, and makes me also conceit even against Reason, that all this Host of People can see and observe me, which strongly inclines me to Solitude and an obscure Living; and on the other Hand, it will be an Ease to me to disburthen my Thoughts and Observations in the Way proposed to you by, Sir, your Friend, and humble Servant.——'

I conceal this Correspondent's Name in my Care for his Life and Safety, and cannot but approve his Prudence in chusing to live obscurely. I remember the Fate of my poor Monkey: He had an ill-natur'd Trick of grinning and chattering at every Thing he saw in Pettycoats. My ignorant Country Neighbours got a Notion that *Pugg* snarl'd by instinct at every Female who had lost her Virginity. This was no sooner generally believ'd than he was condemn'd to Death; By whom I could never learn, but he was assassinated in the Night, barbarously stabb'd and mangled in a Thousand Places, and left hanging dead on one of my Gate posts, where I found him the next Morning.

The Censor *observing that the* Itch of Scribbling *begins to spread exceedingly, and being carefully tender of the Reputation of his Country in Point of* Wit *and* Good Sense, *has determined to take all manner of Writings, in Verse or Prose, that pretend to either, under his immediate Cognizance; and accordingly hereby prohibits the Publishing any such for the future, 'till they have first pass'd his Examination, and receiv'd his* Imprimatur. *For which he demands as a Fee only* 6 d. *per Sheet.*

N. B. *He nevertheless permits to be published all Satyrical Remarks on the* Busy-Body, *the above Prohibition notwithstanding, and without Examination, or requiring the said Fees: which Indulgence the small Wits in and about this City are advised gratefully to accept and acknowledge.*

The Gentleman who calls himself Sirronio, *is directed, on the Receipt of this, to burn his great Book of* Crudities.

P. S. *In Compassion to that young Man on Account of the great Pains he has taken; in Consideration of the Character I have just receiv'd of him, that he is really* Good-*natured; and on Condition he shows it to no Foreigner or Stranger of Sense, I have thought fit to reprieve his said* great Book of Crudities *from the Flames, 'till further Order.*

Noli me tangere.

I had resolved when I first commenc'd this Design, on no Account to enter into a publick Dispute with any Man; for I judg'd it would be equally unpleasant to me and my Readers, to see this Paper fill'd with contentious Wrangling, Answers, Replies, *&c.* which is a Way of Writing that is Endless, and at the same time seldom contains any Thing that is either edifying or entertaining. Yet when such a considerable Man as Mr. —— finds himself concern'd so warmly to accuse and condemn me, as he has done in *Keimer's* last *Instructor*, I cannot forbear endeavouring to say something in my own Defence, from one of the worst of Characters that could be given of me by a Man of Worth. But as I have many Things of more Consequence to offer the Publick, I declare that I will never, after this Time, take Notice of any Accusations not better supported with Truth and Reason; much less may every little Scribbler, that shall attack me, expect an Answer from the *Busy-Body.*

The Sum of the *Charge deliver'd* against me, either directly or indirectly in the said Paper, is this. Not to mention the first weighty Sentence concerning *Vanity and Ill-Nature,* and the shrew'd Intimation *that I am without Charity, and therefore can have no Pretence to Religion,* I am represented as guilty of *Defamation and Scandal, the Odiousness of which is apparent*

to every good Man, and the Practice of it opposite to Christianity,
Morality, and common Justice, and in some Cases so far below all
these as to be inhumane. As a *Blaster of Reputations.* As *attempt-*
ing by a Pretence to screen my Self from the Imputation of Malice
and Prejudice. As *using a Weapon which the Wiser and better*
Part of Mankind hold in Abhorrence: And as *giving Treatment*
which the wiser and better Part of Mankind dislike on the same
Principles, and for the same Reason as they do Assassination. &c,
And all this, is infer'd and concluded from a Character I
wrote in my Number 3.

In order to examine the Justice and Truth of this heavy
Charge, let us recur to that Character.—And here we may be
surpriz'd to find what a Trifle has rais'd this mighty Clamour
and Complaint, this Grievous Accusation!—The worst Thing
said of the Person, in what is called my gross Description, (be
he who he will to whom my Accuser has apply'd the Character of *Cretico*) is, that he is a *sower Philosopher, crafty, but*
not wise: Few Humane Characters can be drawn that will not
fit some body, in so large a Country as this; But one would
think, supposing I meant *Cretico* a real Person, I had sufficiently manifested my impartiality, when I said in that very
Paragraph, *That* Cretico *is not without Virtue; that there are*
MANY good Things in him, and MANY good Actions reported
of him; Which must be allow'd in all Reason, very much to
overballance in his Favour those worst Words, *sowre Temper'd*
and *cunning.* Nay my very Enemy and Accuser must have
been sensible of this, when he freely acknowledges, *that he*
has been seriously considering, and cannot yet determine, which he
would chuse to be, the Cato *or* Cretico *of that Paper*: Since my
Cato is one of the best of Characters.

Thus much in my own Vindication. As to the *only reasons*
there given why I ought not to continue drawing Characters,
viz. *Why should any Man's Picture be published which he never*
sat for; or his good Name taken from him any more than his
Money or Possessions at the arbitrary Will of another, &c? I have
but this to answer. The Money or Possessions I presume are
nothing to the Purpose, since no Man can claim a Right either to those or a good Name, if he has acted so as to forfeit
them. And are not the Publick the only Judges what Share of
Reputation they think proper to allow any Man?—Sup-

posing I was capable, and had an Inclination to draw all the good and bad Characters in *America*; Why should a good Man be offended with me for drawing good Characters? And if I draw Ill Ones, can they fit any but those that deserve them? And ought any *but such* to be concern'd that they have their Deserts? I have as great an Aversion and Abhorrence from Defamation and Scandal as any Man, and would with the utmost Care avoid being guilty of such base Things: Besides I am very sensible and certain, that if I should make use of this Paper to defame any Person, my Reputation would be sooner hurt by it than his, and the *Busy-Body* would quickly become detestable; because in such a Case, as is justly observ'd, *The Pleasure arising from a Taste of Wit and Novelty soon dies away in generous and Honest Minds, and is follow'd with a secret Grief to see their Neighbours calumniated.* But if I my self was actually the worst Man in the Province, and any one should draw my true Character, would it not be ridiculous in me to say, *he had defam'd and scandaliz'd me*; unless added, *in a Matter of Truth?* — If any Thing is meant by asking, *Why any Man's Picture should be publish'd which he never sate for?* It must be, that we should give no Character without the Owner's Consent. If I discern the Wolf disguis'd in harmless Wool, and contriving the Destruction of my Neighbour's Sheep, must I have his Permission before I am allow'd to discover and prevent him? If I know a Man to be a designing Knave, must I ask his Consent to bid my Friends beware of him? If so, Then by the same Rule, supposing the *Busy-Body* had really merited all his Enemy has charg'd him with, his Consent likewise ought to have been obtain'd before so terrible an Accusation was published against him.

I shall conclude with observing, that in the last Paragraph save one of the Piece now examin'd, much *ILL-NATURE* and some Good Sense are *Co-inhabitants*, (as he expresses it.) The *Ill Nature* appears, in his endeavouring to discover Satyr, where I intended no such Thing, but quite the Reverse: The good Sense is this, *that drawing too good a Character of any one, is a refined Manner of Satyr that may be as injurious to him as the contrary, by bringing on an Examination that undresses the Person, and in the Haste of doing it, he may happen to be stript of what he really owns and deserves.* As I am *Censor*, I might punish the first, but I forgive it. Yet I will not leave the latter unrewarded; but assure my Adversary, that in Consideration of the Merit of those four Lines, I am resolved to forbear *injuring* him on any Account in that *refined Manner.*

I thank my Neighbour P—w—l *for his kind Letter.* The Lions complain'd of shall be muzzled.

The American Weekly Mercury, March 4, 1728/9

The Busy-Body, No. 8

——*Quid non mortalia Pectora cogis
Auri sacra Fames!*   Virgil.

One of the greatest Pleasures an Author can have is certainly the Hearing his Works applauded. The hiding from the World our Names while we publish our Thoughts, is so absolutely necessary to this Self-Gratification, that I hope my Well-wishers will congratulate me on my Escape from the many diligent, but fruitless Enquires that have of late been made after me. Every Man will own, That an Author, as such, ought to be try'd by the Merit of his Productions only; but Pride, Party, and Prejudice at this Time run so very high, that Experience shews we form our Notions of a Piece by the Character of the Author. Nay there are some very humble Politicians in and about this City, who will ask on which Side the Writer is, before they presume to give their Opinion of the Thing wrote. This ungenerous Way of Proceeding I was well aware of before I publish'd my first Speculation; and therefore concealed my Name. And I appeal to the more generous Part of the World, if I have since I appear'd in the Character of the *Busy-Body* given an Instance of my siding with any Party more than another, in the unhappy Divisions of my Country; and I have above all, this Satisfaction in my Self, That neither Affection, Aversion or Interest, have byass'd me to use any Partiality towards any Man, or Sett of Men; but whatsoever I find nonsensically ridiculous, or immorally dishonest, I have, and shall continue openly to attack with the Freedom of an honest Man, and a Lover of my Country.

I profess I can hardly contain my Self, or preserve the Gravity and Dignity that should attend the *Censorial-Office*, when I hear the odd and unaccountable Expositions that are put upon some of my Works, thro' the malicious Ignorance of some, and the vain Pride of more than ordinary Penetration in others; one Instance of which many of my Readers are acquainted with. A certain Gentleman has taken a great Deal of Pains to write a *KEY* to the Letter in my *No.* 4. wherein he has ingeniously converted a gentle Satyr upon tedious and impertinent Visitants into a Libel on some in the Government: This I mention only as a Specimen of the Taste of the Gentlemen, I am forsooth, bound to please in my Speculations, not that I suppose my Impartiality will ever be called in Question upon that Account. Injustices of this Nature I could complain of in many Instancies; but I am at present diverted by the Reception of a Letter, which tho' it regards me only in my Private Capacity, as an Adept, yet I venture to publish it for the Entertainment of my Readers.

To CENSOR MORUM, *Esq*; *Busy-Body* General of the Province of *Pennsylvania*, and the Counties of *Newcastle, Kent,* and *Sussex,* upon *Delaware.*

Honourable Sir,
'I judge by your Lucubrations, that you are not only a Lover of Truth and Equity, but a Man of Parts and Learning, and a Master of Science; as such I honour you. Know then, *Most profound Sir,* That I have from my Youth up, been a very indefatigable Student in, and Admirer of that Divine Science, *Astrology.* I have read over *Scot, Albertus Magnus,* and *Cornelius Agrippa* above 300 Times; and was in hopes by my Knowledge and Industry, to gain enough to have recompenced me for my Money expended, and Time lost in the Pursuit of this Learning. You cannot be ignorant *Sir,* (for your intimate *Second sighted* Correspondent knows all Things) that there are large Sums of Money hidden under Ground in divers Places about this Town, and in many Parts of the

Country; But alas, Sir, Notwithstanding I have used all the Means laid down in the *immortal Authors* before-mentioned, and when they fail'd, the ingenious Mr. *P—d—l* with his *Mercurial Wand* and *Magnet*, I have still fail'd in my Purpose. This therefore I send to Propose and desire an Acquaintance with you, and I do not doubt, notwithstanding my repeated Ill-Fortune, but we may be exceedingly serviceable to each other in our Discoveries; and that if we use our united Endeavours, the Time will come when the *Busy-Body*, his *Second-sighted Correspondent*, and *your very humble Servant*, will be Three of the richest Men in the Province: And then Sir, what may not we do?—*A Word to the Wise is sufficient*,

I conclude with all demonstrable Respect,

Yours, and *Urania*'s Votary,

Titan Pleiades.'

In the Evening after I had received this Letter, I made a Visit to my *Second-sighted* Friend, and communicated to him the Proposal. When he had read it, he assur'd me, that to his certain Knowledge there is not at this Time so much as one Ounce of Silver or Gold hid under Ground in any Part of this Province, For that the late and present Scarcity of Money had obliged those who were living, and knew where they had formerly hid any, to take it up, and use it in their own necessary Affairs: And as to all the Rest which was buried by Pyrates and others in old Times, who were never like to come for it, he himself had long since dug it all up and applied it to charitable Uses, And this he desired me to publish for general Good. For, as he acquainted me, There are among us great Numbers of honest Artificers and labouring People, who fed with a vain Hope of growing suddenly rich, neglect their Business, almost to the ruining of themselves and Families, and voluntarily endure abundance of Fatigue in a fruitless Search after Imaginary hidden Treasure. They wander thro' the Woods and Bushes by Day, to discover the Marks and Signs; at Midnight they repair to the hopeful Spot with Spades and Pickaxes; full of Expectation they labour violently, trembling at the same Time in every Joint, thro' Fear of certain malicious Demons who are said to haunt and guard such Places. At length a mighty hole is dug, and perhaps several

Cart-loads of Earth thrown out, but alas, no Cag or Iron Pot is found! no Seaman's Chest cram'd with Spanish Pistoles, or weighty Pieces of Eight! Then they conclude, that thro' some Mistake in the Procedure, some rash Word spoke, or some Rule of Art neglected, the Guardian Spirit had Power to sink it deeper into the Earth and convey it out of their Reach. Yet when a Man is once thus infatuated, he is so far from being discouraged by ill Success, that he is rather animated to double his Industry, and will try again and again in a Hundred Different Places, in Hopes at last of meeting with some lucky Hit, that shall at once Sufficiently reward him for all his Expence of Time and Labour.

This odd Humour of Digging for Money thro' a Belief that much has been hid by Pirates formerly frequenting the River, has for several Years been mighty prevalent among us; insomuch that you can hardly walk half a Mile out of Town on any Side, without observing several Pits dug with that Design, and perhaps some lately opened. Men, otherwise of very good Sense, have been drawn into this Practice thro' an overweening Desire of sudden Wealth, and an easy Credulity of what they so earnestly wish'd might be true. While the rational and almost certain Methods of acquiring Riches by Industry and Frugality are neglected or forgotten. There seems to be some peculiar Charm in the conceit of *finding* Money; and if the Sands of *Schuylkil* were so much mixed with small Grains of Gold, that a Man might in a Day's Time with Care and Application get together to the Value of half a Crown, I make no Question but we should find several People employ'd there, that can with Ease earn Five Shillings a Day at their proper Trades.

Many are the idle Stories told of the private Success of some People, by which others are encouraged to proceed; and the Astrologers, with whom the Country swarms at this Time, are either in the Belief of these things themselves, or find their Advantage in persuading others to believe them; for they are often consulted about the critical Times for Digging, the Methods of laying the Spirit, and the like Whimseys, which renders them very necessary to and very much caress'd by the poor deluded *Money-hunters*.

There is certainly something very bewitching in the Pursuit

after Mines of Gold and Silver, and other valuable Metals; And many have been ruined by it. A Sea Captain of my Acquaintance used to blame the *English* for envying *Spain* their Mines of Silver; and too much despising or overlooking the Advantages of their own Industry and Manufactures. For my Part, says he, I esteem the Banks of *Newfoundland* to be a more valuable Possession than the Mountains of *Potosi*; and when I have been there on the Fishing Account, have look'd upon every Cod puli'd up into the Vessel as a certain Quantity of Silver Ore, which required only carrying to the next *Spanish* Port to be coin'd into Pieces of Eight; not to mention the *National Profit* of fitting out and Employing such a Number of Ships and Seamen. Let honest *Peter Buckrum*, who has long without Success been a Searcher after hidden Money, reflect on this, and be reclaimed from that unaccountable Folly. Let him consider that every Stitch he takes when he is on his Shop-board, is picking up part of a Grain of Gold that will in a few Days Time amount to a Pistole; And let *Faber* think the same of every Nail he drives, or every Stroke with his Plain. Such Thoughts may make them industrious, and of consequence in Time they may be Wealthy. But how absurd is it to neglect a certain Profit for such a ridiculous Whimsey: To spend whole Days at the *George*, in company with an idle Pretender to Astrology, contriving Schemes to discover what was never hidden, and forgetful how carelessly Business is managed at Home in their Absence: To leave their Wives and a warm Bed at Midnight (no matter if it rain, hail, snow or blow a Hurricane, provided that be the critical Hour) and fatigue themselves with the Violent Exercise of Digging for what they shall never find, and perhaps getting a Cold that may cost their Lives, or at least disordering themselves so as to be fit for no Business beside for some Days after. Surely this is nothing less than the most egregious Folly and Madness.

I shall conclude with the Words of my discreet Friend *Agricola*, of *Chester*-County, when he gave his Son a Good Plantation, *My Son,* says he, *I give thee now a Valuable Parcel of Land; I assure thee I have found a considerable Quantity of Gold by Digging there; —Thee mayst do the same. —But thee must carefully observe this, Never to dig more than Plow-deep.*

Monday Night, March 24.

I have received Letters lately from several considerable Men, earnestly urging me to write on the Subject of *Paper-Money*; and containing very severe Reflections on some Gentlemen, who are said to be Opposers of that Currency. I must desire to be excus'd if I decline publishing any Thing lent to me at this Juncture, that may add Fuel to the Flame, or aggravate that Management that has already sufficiently exasperated the Minds of the People. The Subject of *Paper Currency* is in it self very intricate, and I believe, understood by Few; I mean as to its Consequences *in Futurum*: And tho' much might be said on that Head, I apprehend it to be the less necessary for me to handle it at this Time, because *EXPERIENCE*, (more prevalent than all the *Logic* in the World) has fully convinced us all, that it has been, and is now of the greatest Advantage to the Country: Not only those who were once doubtful are intirely of this Opinion, but the very Gentlemen who were at first most violent Enemies to that *Currency*, have lately, (particularly about the Time of the last Election) declared, freely, both in private Conversation, and publickly in Print, *That they now are heartily for it; that they are sensible it has been a great Benefit to the Country; and that it has not now one Opponent that they know of.* They have likewise assured us, *That the Governour is a zealous Friend to it*; and I do not understand that any material Reason is given for the Additional Bill's not passing, but this. *That it is contrary to the Constituents Orders from Home.* If this be the Case, I see nothing further in it but this; that those Gentlemen who in their Zeal for the Good of their Country, formerly oppos'd *Paper-Money*, when they thought it would prove hurtful, and by their powerful Representations procured those Orders from Home, but now being better acquainted with its Usefulness, and sensible how much it is to our Advantage to have such a Currency, are become hearty Friends to it; I say, nothing remains, but that those Gentlemen join as heartily with the Representative Body of the Country to endeavour, by different Representations, a Revocation of those Orders: And in the mean Time, as it is certain They would be pleased at Home to see this Province in Prosperity, so without Doubt there is no Man so unreasonable among them, supposing that Act should now pass, as to imagine, that the whole Country united is entirely ignorant of its own true Interest. And the Interest of the Country is the same, I presume, with that of the Proprietary.

'Tis true indeed, I am not satisfied that it is for our Advantage to rest contented with *Paper-Money* for ever, without endeavouring to recover our Silver and Gold; which may be done without much Difficulty, (as I shall shew in some future Papers) if those who have the Management of Publick Affairs should have no Interests to pursue separate from those of their Country. Yet at this Time it seems absolutely necessary to have a large Additional Sum struck for the Relief of the People in their present miserable Circumstances, and until such Methods of Trade are thought on, and put in Practice, as will make that Currency needless; which I hope the Legislature will as soon as possible take into their Consideration. And in the mean Time I cannot but think it commendable in every honest *Thinking* Man, to publish his Sentiments on this Head, to the End such Methods may be chose and fallen upon as will appear most conducive.

Unhappy is the Case of that good Gentleman, our Governor, who sees a flourishing Province sinking under his Administration into the most wretched and deplorable Circumstances; and while no Good-will is wanting in him to wards us and our Welfare, finds his Hands are tyed, and that without deviating from his Instructions, it is not in his Power to help us. The whole Country is at this Instant filled with the greatest Heat and Animosity; and if there are yet among us any Opposers of a *Paper-Currency*, it is probable the Resentments of the People point at them; and tho' I must earnestly exhort my Countrymen to Peace and Quietness, for that publick Disturbances are seldom known to be attended with any good Consequence; yet I cannot but think it would be highly prudent in those Gentlemen with all Expedition to publish such Vindications of themselves and their Actions, as will sufficiently clear them in the Eyes of all reasonable Men, from the Imputation of having a Design to engross the Property of the Country, and make themselves and their Posterity Lords, and the Bulk of the Inhabitants their Tenants and Vassals; which Design they are everywhere openly accused of. And such a Vindication is the more necessary at this Time,

A Modest Enquiry into the Nature and Necessity of a Paper-Currency

——*Quid asper*
Utile Nummus habet; patriæ, charisq; propinquis
Quantum elargiri deceat. ——

Pers.

There is no Science, the Study of which is more useful and commendable than the Knowledge of the true Interest of one's Country; and perhaps there is no Kind of Learning more abstruse and intricate, more difficult to acquire in any Degree of Perfection than This, and therefore none more generally neglected. Hence it is, that we every Day find Men in Conversation contending warmly on some Point in Politicks, which, altho' it may nearly concern them both, neither of them understand any more than they do each other.

Thus much by way of Apology for this present *Enquiry into the Nature and Necessity of a Paper Currency*. And if any Thing I shall say, may be a Means of fixing a Subject that is now the chief Concern of my Countrymen, in a clearer Light, I shall have the Satisfaction of thinking my Time and Pains well employed.

To proceed, then,

There is a certain proportionate Quantity of Money requisite to carry on the Trade of a Country freely and currently; More than which would be of no Advantage in Trade, and Less, if much less, exceedingly detrimental to it.

This leads us to the following general Considerations.

First, *A great Want of Money in any Trading Country, occasions Interest to be at a very high Rate*. And here it may be observed, that it is impossible by any Laws to restrain Men from giving and receiving exorbitant Interest, where Money is suitably scarce: For he that wants Money will find out Ways to give 10 *per Cent.* when he cannot have it for less, altho' the Law forbids to take more than 6 *per Cent.* Now the Interest of Money being high is prejudicial to a Country several Ways: It makes Land bear a low Price, because few Men will lay out their Money in Land, when they can make a much greater Profit by lending it out upon Interest: And much less will

Men be inclined to venture their Money at Sea, when they can, without Risque or Hazard, have a great and certain Profit by keeping it at home; thus Trade is discouraged. And if in two Neigbouring Countries the Traders of one, by Reason of a greater Plenty of Money, can borrow it to trade with at a lower Rate than the Traders of the other, they will infallibly have the Advantage, and get the greatest Part of that Trade into their own Hands; For he that trades with Money he hath borrowed at 8 or 10 *per Cent.* cannot hold Market with him that borrows his Money at 6 or 4.—On the contrary, *A plentiful Currency will occasion Interest to be low:* And this will be an Inducement to many to lay out their Money in Lands, rather than put it out to Use, by which means Land will begin to rise in Value and bear a better Price: And at the same Time it will tend to enliven Trade exceedingly, because People will find more Profit in employing their Money that Way than in Usury; and many that understand Business very well, but have not a Stock sufficient of their own, will be encouraged to borrow Money to trade with, when they can have it at moderate Interest.

Secondly, *Want of Money in a Country reduces the Price of that Part of its Produce which is used in Trade:* Because Trade being discouraged by it as above, there is a much less Demand for that Produce. And this is another Reason why Land in such a Case will be low, especially where the Staple Commodity of the Country is the immediate Produce of the Land, because that Produce being low, fewer People find an Advantage in Husbandry, or the Improvement of Land.—On the contrary, *A Plentiful Currency will occasion the Trading Produce to bear a good Price:* Because Trade being encouraged and advanced by it, there will be a much greater Demand for that Produce; which will be a great Encouragement of Husbandry and Tillage, and consequently make Land more valuable, for that many People would apply themselves to Husbandry, who probably might otherwise have sought some more profitable Employment.

As we have already experienced how much the Increase of our Currency by what Paper Money has been made, has encouraged our Trade; particularly to instance only in one Article, *Ship-Building*; it may not be amiss to observe under this

Head, what a great Advantage it must be to us as a Trading Country, that has Workmen and all the Materials proper for that Business within itself, to have *Ship-Building* as much as possible advanced: For every Ship that is built here for the *English* Merchants, gains the Province her clear Value in Gold and Silver, which must otherwise have been sent Home for Returns in her Stead; and likewise, every Ship built in and belonging to the Province, not only saves the Province her first Cost, but all the Freight, Wages and Provisions she ever makes or requires as long as she lasts; provided Care is taken to make This her *Pay Port*, and that she always takes Provisions with her for the whole Voyage, which may easily be done. And how considerable an Article this is yearly in our Favour, every one, the least acquainted with mercantile Affairs, must needs be sensible; for if we could not Build our selves, we must either purchase so many Vessels as we want from other Countries, or else Hire them to carry our Produce to Market, which would be more expensive than Purchasing, and on many other Accounts exceedingly to our Loss. Now as Trade in general will decline where there is not a plentiful Currency, so *Ship-Building* must certainly of Consequence decline where Trade is declining.

Thirdly, *Want of Money in a Country discourages Labouring and Handicrafts Men (which are the chief Strength and Support of a People) from coming to settle in it, and induces many that were settled to leave the Country, and seek Entertainment and Employment in other Places, where they can be better paid.* For what can be more disheartning to an industrious labouring Man, than this, that after he hath earned his Bread with the Sweat of his Brows, he must spend as much Time, and have near as much Fatigue in getting it, as he had to earn it. *And nothing makes more bad Paymasters than a general Scarcity of Money.* And here again is a Third Reason for Land's bearing a low Price in such a Country, because Land always increases in Value in Proportion with the Increase of the People settling on it, there being so many more Buyers; and its Value will infallibly be diminished, if the Number of its Inhabitants diminish.—On the contrary, *A Plentiful Currency will encourage great Numbers of Labouring and Handicrafts Men to come and Settle in the Country*, by the same Reason that a Want of it will discourage and drive them out. Now the more Inhabitants, the greater Demand for Land (as is said above) upon which it must necessarily rise in Value, and bear a better Price. The same may be said of the Value of House-Rent, which will be advanced for the same Reasons; and by the Increase of Trade and Riches People will be enabled to pay greater Rents. Now the Value of House-Rent rising, and Interest becoming low, many that in a Scarcity of Money practised Usury, will probably be more inclined to Building; which will likewise sensibly enliven Business in any Place; it being an Advantage not only to *Brickmakers*, *Bricklayers*, *Masons*, *Carpenters*, *Joiners*, *Glaziers*, and several other Trades immediately employ'd by Building, but likewise to *Farmers*, *Brewers*, *Bakers*, *Taylors*, *Shoemakers*, *Shop-keepers*, and in short to every one that they lay their Money out with.

Fourthly, *Want of Money in such a Country as ours, occasions a greater Consumption of* English *and* European *Goods, in Proportion to the Number of the People, than there would otherwise be*. Because Merchants and Traders, by whom abundance of Artificers and labouring Men are employed, finding their other Affairs require what Money they can get into their hands, oblige those who work for them to take one half, or perhaps two thirds Goods in Pay. By this Means a greater Quantity of Goods are disposed of, and to a greater Value; because Working Men and their Families are thereby induced to be more profuse and extravagant in fine Apparel and the like, than they would be if they were obliged to pay ready Money for such Things after they had earn'd and received it, or if such Goods were not imposed upon them, of which they can make no other Use: For such People cannot send the Goods they are paid with to a Foreign Market, without losing considerably by having them sold for less than they stand 'em in here; neither can they easily dispose of them at Home, because their Neighbours are generally supplied in the same Manner; But how unreasonable would it be, if some of those very Men who *have been a Means* of thus forcing People into unnecessary Expence, should be the first and most earnest in accusing them of *Pride and Prodigality*. Now tho' this extraordinary Consumption of Foreign Commodities may be a Profit to particular Men, yet the Country in general grows poorer by it apace.—On the contrary, As *A plentiful Currency will occasion a less Consumption of* European *Goods, in Proportion to the Number of the People,* so it will be a means of making the Balance of our Trade more equal than it now is, if it does not give it in our Favour; because our own Produce will be encouraged at the same Time. And it is to be observed, that tho' less Foreign Commodities are consumed in Proportion to the Number of People, yet this will be no Disadvantage to the Merchant, because the Number of People increasing, will occasion an increasing Demand of more Foreign Goods in the Whole.

Thus we have seen some of the many heavy Disadvantages a Country (especially such a Country as ours) must labour under, when it has not a sufficient Stock of running Cash to manage its Trade currently. And we have likewise seen some of the Advantages which accrue from having Money sufficient, or a Plentiful Currency.

The foregoing Paragraphs being well considered, we shall naturally be led to draw the following Conclusions with Regard to what Persons will probably be for or against Emitting a large Additional Sum of Paper Bills in this Province.

1. Since Men will always be powerfully influenced in their Opinions and Actions by what appears to be their particular Interest: Therefore all those, who wanting Courage to venture in Trade, now practise Lending Money on Security for exorbitant Interest, which in a Scarcity of Money will be done notwithstanding the Law, I say all such will probably be against a large Addition to our present Stock of Paper-Money; because a plentiful Currency will lower Interest, and make it common to lend on less Security.

2. All those who are Possessors of large Sums of Money, and are disposed to purchase Land, which is attended with a great and sure Advantage in a growing Country as this is; I say, the Interest of all such Men will encline them to oppose a large Addition to our Money. Because their Wealth is now continually increasing by the large Interest they receive, which will enable them (if they can keep Land from rising) to purchase More some time hence than they can at present; and in the mean time all Trade being discouraged, not only those who borrow of them, but the Common People in

general will be impoverished, and consequently obliged to sell More Land for less Money than they will do at present. And yet, after such Men are possessed of as much Land as they can purchase, it will then be their Interest to have Money made Plentiful, because that will immediately make Land rise in Value in *their* Hands. Now it ought not to be wonder'd at, if People from the Knowledge of a Man's Interest do sometimes make a true Guess at his Designs; for, *Interest*, they say, *will not Lie*.

3. Lawyers, and others concerned in Court Business, will probably many of them be against a plentiful Currency; because People in that Case will have less Occasion to run in Debt, and consequently less Occasion to go to Law and Sue one another for their Debts. Tho' I know some even among these Gentlemen, that regard the Publick Good before their own apparent private Interest.

4. All those who are any way Dependants on such Persons as are above mentioned, whether as holding Offices, as Tenants, or as Debtors, must at least *appear* to be against a large Addition; because if they do not, they must sensibly feel their present Interest hurt. And besides these, there are, doubtless, many well-meaning Gentlemen and Others, who, without any immediate private Interest of their own in View, are against making such an Addition, thro' an Opinion they may have of the Honesty and sound Judgment of some of their Friends that oppose it, (perhaps for the Ends aforesaid) without having given it any thorough Consideration themselves. And thus it is no Wonder if there is a *powerful* Party on that Side.

On the other Hand, Those who are Lovers of Trade, and delight to see Manufactures encouraged, will be for having a large Addition to our Currency: For they very well know, that People will have little Heart to advance Money in Trade, when what they can get is scarce sufficient to purchase Necessaries, and supply their Families with Provision. Much less will they lay it out in advancing new Manufactures; nor is it possible new Manufactures should turn to any Account, where there is not Money to pay the Workmen, who are discouraged by being paid in Goods, because it is a great Disadvantage to them.

Again, Those who are truly for the Proprietor's Interest

(and have no separate Views of their own that are predominant) will be heartily for a large Addition: Because, as I have shewn above, Plenty of Money will for several Reasons make Land rise in Value exceedingly: And I appeal to those immediately concerned for the Proprietor in the Sale of his Lands, whether Land has not risen very much since the first Emission of what Paper Currency we now have, and even by its Means. Now we all know the Proprietary has great Quantities to sell.

And since a Plentiful Currency will be so great a Cause of advancing this Province in Trade and Riches, and increasing the Number of its People; which, tho' it will not sensibly lessen the Inhabitants of *Great Britain*, will occasion a much greater Vent and Demand for their Commodities here; and allowing that the Crown is the more powerful for its Subjects increasing in Wealth and Number, I cannot think it the Interest of *England* to oppose us in making as great a Sum of Paper Money here, as we, who are the best Judges of our own Necessities, find convenient. And if I were not sensible that the Gentlemen of Trade in *England*, to whom we have already parted with our Silver and Gold, are misinformed of our Circumstances, and therefore endeavour to have our Currency stinted to what it now is, I should think the Government at Home had some Reasons for discouraging and impoverishing this Province, which we are not acquainted with.

It remains now that we enquire, *Whether a large Addition to our Paper Currency will not make it sink in Value very much;* And here it will be requisite that we first form just Notions of the Nature and Value of Money in general.

As Providence has so ordered it, that not only different Countries, but even different Parts of the same Country, have their peculiar most suitable Productions; and likewise that different Men have Genius's adapted to Variety of different Arts and Manufactures, Therefore *Commerce*, or the Exchange of one Commodity or Manufacture for another, is highly convenient and beneficial to Mankind. As for Instance, *A* may be skilful in the Art of making Cloth, and *B* understand the raising of Corn; *A* wants Corn, and *B* Cloth; upon which they make an Exchange with each other for as much as each has Occasion, to the mutual Advantage and Satisfaction of both.

But as it would be very tedious, if there were no other Way of general Dealing, but by an immediate Exchange of Commodities; because a Man that had Corn to dispose of, and wanted Cloth for it, might perhaps in his Search for a Chapman to deal with, meet with twenty People that had Cloth to dispose of, but wanted no Corn; and with twenty others that wanted his Corn, but had no Cloth to suit him with. To remedy such Inconveniences, and facilitate Exchange, Men have invented MONEY, properly called a *Medium of Exchange*, because through or by its Means Labour is exchanged for Labour, or one Commodity for another. And whatever particular Thing Men have agreed to make this Medium of, whether Gold, Silver, Copper, or Tobacco; it is, to those who possess it (if they want any Thing) that very Thing which they want, because it will immediately procure it for them. It is Cloth to him that wants Cloth, and Corn to those that want Corn; and so of all other Necessaries, it *is* whatsoever it will procure. Thus he who had Corn to dispose of, and wanted to purchase Cloth with it, might sell his Corn for its Value in this general Medium, to one who wanted Corn but had no Cloth; and with this Medium he might purchase Cloth of him that wanted no Corn, but perhaps some other Thing, as Iron it may be, which this Medium will immediately procure, and so he may be said to have exchanged his Cloth for Iron; and thus the general Exchange is soon performed, to the Satisfaction of all Parties, with abundance of Facility.

For many Ages, those Parts of the World which are engaged in Commerce, have fixed upon Gold and Silver as the chief and most proper Materials for this Medium; they being in themselves valuable Metals for their Fineness, Beauty, and Scarcity. By these, particularly by Silver, it has been usual to value all Things else: But as Silver it self is of no certain permanent Value, being worth more or less according to its Scarcity or Plenty, therefore it seems requisite to fix upon Something else, more proper to be made a *Measure of Values*, and this I take to be *Labour*.

By Labour may the Value of Silver be measured as well as other Things. As, Suppose one Man employed to raise Corn, while another is digging and refining Silver; at the Year's End, or at any other Period of Time, the compleat Produce of Corn, and that of Silver, are the natural Price of each other; and if one be twenty Bushels, and the other twenty Ounces, then an Ounce of that Silver is worth the Labour of raising a Bushel of that Corn. Now if by the Discovery of some nearer, more easy or plentiful Mines, a Man may get Forty Ounces of Silver as easily as formerly he did Twenty, and the same Labour is still required to raise Twenty Bushels of Corn, then Two Ounces of Silver will be worth no more than the same Labour of raising One Bushel of Corn, and that Bushel of Corn will be as cheap at two Ounces, as it was before at one; *cæteris paribus.*

Thus the Riches of a Country are to be valued by the Quantity of Labour its Inhabitants are able to purchase, and not by the Quantity of Silver and Gold they possess; which will purchase more or less Labour, and therefore is more or less valuable, as is said before, according to its Scarcity or Plenty. As those Metals have grown much more plentiful in *Europe* since the Discovery of *America*, so they have sunk in Value exceedingly; for, to instance in *England*, formerly one Penny of Silver was worth a Days Labour, but now it is hardly worth the sixth Part of a Days Labour; because not less than Six-pence will purchase the Labour of a Man for a Day in any Part of that Kingdom; which is wholly to be attributed to the much greater Plenty of Money now in *England* than formerly. And yet perhaps *England* is in Effect no richer now than at that Time; because as much Labour might be purchas'd, or Work got done of almost any kind, for 100 *l.* then, as will now require or is now worth 600 *l.*

In the next Place let us consider the Nature of *Banks* emitting *Bills of Credit*, as they are at this Time used in *Hamburgh*, *Amsterdam*, *London* and *Venice*.

Those Places being Seats of vast Trade, and the Payment of great Sums being for that Reason frequent, *Bills of Credit* are found very convenient in Business; because a great Sum is more easily counted in Them, lighter in Carriage, concealed in less Room, and therefore safer in Travelling or Laying up, and on many other Accounts they are very much valued. The Banks are the general Cashiers of all Gentlemen, Merchants and great Traders in and about those Cities; there they deposite their Money, and may take out Bills to the Value, for which they can be certain to have Money again at the Bank at any Time: This gives the Bills a Credit; so that in *England* they are never less valuable than Money, and in *Venice* and *Amsterdam* they are generally worth more. And the Bankers always reserving Money in hand to answer more than the common Run of Demands (and some People constantly putting in while others are taking out) are able besides to lend large Sums, on good Security, to the Government or others, for a reasonable Interest, by which they are paid for their Care and Trouble; and the Money which otherwise would have lain dead in their Hands, is made to circulate again thereby among the People: And thus the Running Cash of the Nation is as it were doubled; for all great Payments being made in Bills, Money in lower Trade becomes much more plentiful: And this is an exceeding great Advantage to a Trading Country, that is not over-stock'd with Gold and Silver.

As those who take Bills out of the Banks in *Europe*, put in Money for Security; so here, and in some of the neighbouring Provinces, we engage our Land. Which of these Methods will most effectually secure the Bills from actually sinking in Value, comes next to be considered.

Trade in general being nothing else but the Exchange of Labour for Labour, the Value of all Things is, as I have said before, most justly measured by Labour. Now suppose I put my Money into a Bank, and take out a Bill for the Value; if this Bill at the Time of my receiving it, would purchase me the Labour of one hundred Men for twenty Days; but some time after will only purchase the Labour of the same Number of Men for fifteen Days; it is plain the Bill has sunk in Value one fourth Part. Now Silver and Gold being of no permanent Value; and as this Bill is founded on Money, and therefore to be esteemed as such, it may be that the Occasion of this Fall is the increasing Plenty of Gold and Silver, by which Money is one fourth Part less valuable than before, and therefore one fourth more is given of it for the same Quantity of Labour; and if Land is not become more plentiful by some proportionate Decrease of the People, one fourth Part more of Money is given for the same Quantity of Land; whereby it appears that it would have been more profitable to me to have laid that Money out in Land which I put into the Bank, than to place it there and take a Bill for it. And it is certain that the Value of Money has been continually sinking in *England* for several Ages past, because it has been continually increasing in Quantity. But if Bills could be taken out of a Bank in *Europe* on a Land Security, it is probable the Value of such Bills would be more certain and steady, because the Number of Inhabitants continue to be near the same in those Countries from Age to Age.

For as Bills issued upon Money Security are Money, so Bills issued upon Land, are in Effect *Coined Land*.

Therefore (to apply the Above to our own Circumstances) If Land in this Province was falling, or any way likely to fall, it would behove the Legislature most carefully to contrive how to prevent the Bills issued upon Land from falling with it. But as our People increase exceedingly, and will be further increased, as I have before shewn, by the Help of a large Addition to our Currency; and as Land in consequence is continually rising, So, in case no Bills are emitted but what are upon Land Security, the Money-Acts in every Part punctually enforced and executed, the Payments of Principal and Interest being duly and strictly required, and the Principal *bona fide* sunk according to Law, it is absolutely impossible such Bills should ever sink below their first Value, or below the Value of the Land on which they are founded. In short, there is so little Danger of their sinking, that they would certainly rise as the Land rises, if they were not emitted in a proper Manner for preventing it; That is, by providing in the Act *That Payment may be made, either in those Bills, or in any other Bills made current by any Act of the Legislature of this Province;* and that the Interest, as it is received, may be again emitted in Discharge of Publick Debts; whereby circulating it returns again into the Hands of the Borrowers, and becomes Part of their future Payments; and thus as it is likely there will not be any Difficulty for want of Bills to pay the Office, they are hereby kept from rising above their first Value: For else, supposing there should be emitted upon mortgaged Land its full present Value in Bills; as in the Banks in *Europe* the full Value of the Money deposited is given out in Bills; and supposing the Office would take nothing but the same Sum in those Bills in Discharge of the Land; as in the Banks aforesaid, the same

Sum in their Bills must be brought in, in order to receive out
the Money: In such Case the Bills would most surely rise in
Value as the Land rises; as certainly as the Bank Bills founded
on Money would fall if that Money was falling. Thus if I were
to mortgage to a Loan-Office, or Bank, a Parcel of Land now
valued at 100 *l.* in Silver, and receive for it the like Sum in
Bills, to be paid in again at the Expiration of a certain Term
of Years; before which, my Land rising in Value, becomes
worth 150 *l.* in Silver: 'Tis plain, that if I have not these Bills
in Possession, and the Office will take nothing but these Bills,
or else what it is now become worth in Silver, in Discharge
of my Land; I say it appears plain, that those Bills will now
be worth 150 *l.* in Silver to the Possessor; and if I can purchase them for less, in order to redeem my Land, I shall by
so much be a Gainer.

I need not say any Thing to convince the Judicious that our
Bills have not yet sunk, tho' there is and has been some Difference between them and Silver; because it is evident that
that Difference is occasioned by the Scarcity of the latter,
which is now become a Merchandize, rising and falling, like
other Commodities, as there is a greater or less Demand for
it, or as it is more or less Plenty.

Yet farther, in order to make a true Estimate of the Value
of Money, we must distinguish between Money as it is Bullion, which is Merchandize, and as by being coin'd it is made
a Currency: For its Value as a Merchandize, and its Value as
a Currency, are two distinct Things; and each may possibly
rise and fall in some Degree independent of the other. Thus
if the Quantity of Bullion increases in a Country, it will proportionably decrease in Value; but if at the same Time the
Quantity of current Coin should decrease, (supposing Payments may not be made in Bullion) what Coin there is will
rise in Value as a Currency, *i. e.* People will give more Labour
in Manufactures for a certain Sum of ready Money.

In the same Manner must we consider a *Paper Currency*
founded on Land; as it is Land, and as it is a Currency.

*Money as Bullion, or as Land, is valuable by so much Labour
as it costs to procure that Bullion or Land.*

*Money, as a Currency, has an Additional Value by so much
Time and Labour as it saves in the Exchange of Commodities.*

If, as a Currency, it saves one Fourth Part of the Time and Labour of a Country; it has, on that Account, one Fourth added to its original Value.

When there is no Money in a Country, all Commerce must be by Exchange. Now if it takes one fourth Part of the Time and Labour of a Country, to exchange or get their Commodities exchanged; then, in computing their Value, that Labour of Exchanging must be added to the Labour of manufacturing those Commodities: But if that Time or Labour is saved by introducing Money sufficient, then the additional Value on Account of the Labour of Exchanging may be abated, and Things sold for only the Value of the Labour in making them; because the People may now in the same Time make one Fourth more in Quantity of Manufactures than they could before.

From these Considerations it may be gathered, that in all the Degrees between having no Money in a Country, and Money sufficient for the Trade, it will rise and fall in Value as a Currency, in Proportion to the Decrease or Increase of its Quantity: And if there may be at some Time more than enough, the Overplus will have no Effect towards making the Currency, as a Currency, of less Value than when there was but enough; because such Overplus will not be used in Trade, but be some other way disposed of.

If we enquire, *How much* per Cent. *Interest ought to be required upon the Loan of these Bills;* we must consider what is the Natural Standard of Usury: And this appears to be, where the Security is undoubted, at least the Rent of so much Land as the Money lent will buy: For it cannot be expected that any Man will lend his Money for less than it would fetch him in as Rent if he laid it out in Land, which is the most secure Property in the World. But if the Security is casual, then a kind of Ensurance must be enterwoven with the simple natural Interest, which may advance the Usury very conscionably to any height below the Principal it self. Now among us, if the Value of Land is twenty Years Purchase, Five *per Cent*. is the just Rate of Interest for Money lent on undoubted Security. Yet if Money grows scarce in a Country, it becomes more difficult for People to make punctual Payments of what they borrow, Money being hard to be raised; likewise Trade being discouraged, and Business impeded for want of a Currency, abundance of People must be in declining Circumstances, and by these Means Security is more precarious than where Money is plenty. On such Accounts it is no wonder if People ask a greater Interest for their Money than the natural Interest; and what is above is to be look'd upon as a kind of *Præmium* for the Ensurance of those Uncertainties, as they are greater or less. Thus we always see, that where Money is scarce, Interest is high, and low where it is plenty. Now it is certainly the Advantage of a Country to make Interest as low as possible, as I have already shewn; and this can be done no other way than by making Money plentiful. And since, in Emitting Paper Money among us, the Office has the best of Security, the Titles to the Land being all skilfully and strictly examined and ascertained; and as it is only permitting the People by Law to coin their own Land, which costs the Government nothing, the Interest being more than enough to pay the Charges of Printing, Officers Fees, *&c.* I cannot see any good Reason why Four *per Cent.* to the Loan-Office should not be thought fully sufficient. As a low Interest may incline more to take Money out, it will become more plentiful in Trade; and this may bring down the common Usury, in which Security is more dubious, to the Pitch it is determined at by Law.

If it should be objected, *That Emitting It at so low an Interest, and on such easy Terms, will occasion more to be taken out than the Trade of the Country really requires:* It may be answered, That, as has already been shewn, there can never be so much of it emitted as to make it fall below the Land it is founded on; because no Man in his Senses will mortgage his Estate for what is of no more Value to him than That he has mortgaged, especially if the Possession of what he receives is more precarious than of what he mortgages, as that of Paper Money is when compared to Land: And if it should ever become so plenty by indiscreet Persons continuing to take out a large Overplus, above what is necessary in Trade, so as to make People imagine it would become by that Means of less Value than their mortgaged Lands, they would immediately of Course begin to pay it in again to the Office to redeem their Land, and continue to do so till there was no more left in Trade than was absolutely necessary. And thus the Proportion would find it self, (tho' there were a Million too much in the Office to be let out) without giving any one the Trouble of Calculation.

It may perhaps be objected to what I have written concerning the Advantages of a large Addition to our Currency, *That if the People of this Province increase, and Husbandry is more followed, we shall overstock the Markets with our Produce of Flower,* &c. To this it may be answered, that we can never have too many People (nor too much Money) For when one Branch of Trade or Business is overstocked with Hands, there are the more to spare to be employed in another. So if raising Wheat proves dull, more may (if there is Money to support and carry on new Manufactures) proceed to the raising and manufacturing of *Hemp, Silk, Iron,* and many other Things the Country is very capable of, for which we only want People to work, and Money to pay them with.

Upon the Whole it may be observed, That it is the highest Interest of a Trading Country in general to make Money plentiful; and that it can be a Disadvantage to none that have honest Designs. It cannot hurt even the Usurers, tho' it should sink what they receive as Interest; because they will be proportionably more secure in what they lend; or they will have an Opportunity of employing their Money to greater Advantage, to themselves as well as to the Country. Neither can it hurt those Merchants who have great Sums out-standing in Debts in the Country, and seem on that Account to have the most plausible Reason to fear it; *to wit,* because a large Addition being made to our Currency, will increase the Demand of our Exporting Produce, and by that Means raise the Price of it, so that they will not be able to purchase so much Bread or Flower with 100 *l.* when they shall receive it after such an Addition, as they now can, and may if there is no Addition: I say it cannot hurt even such, because they will get in their Debts just in exact Proportion so much the easier and sooner as the Money becomes plentier; and therefore, considering the Interest and Trouble saved, they will not be Losers; because it only sinks in Value as a Currency, proportionally as it becomes more plenty. It cannot hurt the Interest of *Great Britain*, as has been shewn; and it will greatly advance the Interest of the Proprietor. It will be an Advantage to every industrious Tradesman, *&c.* because his Business will be carried on more freely, and Trade be universally enlivened by it. And as more Business in all Manufactures will be done, by so much as the Labour and Time spent in Exchange is saved, the Country in general will grow so much the richer.

It is nothing to the Purpose to object the wretched Fall of the Bills in *New-England* and *South-Carolina*, unless it might be made evident that their Currency was emitted with the same Prudence, and on such good Security as ours is; and it certainly was not.

As this Essay is wrote and published in Haste, and the Subject in it self intricate, I hope I shall be censured with Candour, if, for want of Time carefully to revise what I have written, in some Places I should appear to have express'd my self too obscurely, and in others am liable to Objections I did not foresee. I sincerely desire to be acquainted with the Truth, and on that Account shall think my self obliged to any one, who will take the Pains to shew me, or the Publick, where I am mistaken in my Conclusions, And as we all know there are among us several Gentlemen of acute Parts and profound Learning, who are very much against any Addition to our Money, it were to be wished that they would favour the Country with their Sentiments on this Head in Print; which, supported with Truth and good Reasoning, may probably be very convincing. And this is to be desired the rather, because many People knowing the Abilities of those Gentlemen to manage a good Cause, are apt to construe their Silence in This, as an Argument of a bad One. Had any Thing of that Kind ever yet appeared, perhaps I should not have given the Publick this Trouble: But as those ingenious Gentlemen have not yet (and I doubt never will) think it worth their Concern to enlighten the Minds of their erring Countrymen in this Particular, I think it would be highly commendable in every one of us, more fully to bend our Minds to the Study of *What is the true Interest of PENNSYLVANIA;* whereby we may be enabled, not only to reason pertinently with one another; but, if Occasion requires, to transmit Home such clear Representations, as must inevitably convince our Superiors of the Reasonableness and Integrity of our Designs.

B. B.

Philadelphia, April 3. 1729.

Philadelphia, New Printing-Office, 1729

The Printer to the Reader

The *Pennsylvania Gazette* being now to be carry'd on by other Hands, the Reader may expect some Account of the Method we design to proceed in.

Upon a View of *Chambers*'s great Dictionaries, from whence were taken the Materials of the *Universal Instructor in all Arts and Sciences*, which usually made the First Part of this Paper, we find that besides their containing many Things abstruse or insignificant to us, it will probably be fifty Years before the Whole can be gone thro' in this Manner of Publication. There are likewise in those Books continual References from Things under one Letter of the Alphabet to those under another, which relate to the same Subject, and are necessary to explain and compleat it; these taken in their Turn may perhaps be Ten Years distant; and since it is likely that they who desire to acquaint themselves with any particular Art or Science, would gladly have the whole before them in a much less Time, we believe our Readers will not think such a Method of communicating Knowledge to be a proper One.

However, tho' we do not intend to continue the Publication of those Dictionaries in a regular Alphabetical Method, as has hitherto been done; yet as several Things exhibited from them in the Course of these Papers, have been entertaining to such of the Curious, who never had and cannot have the Advantage of good Libraries; and as there are many Things still behind, which being in this Manner made generally known, may perhaps become of considerable Use, by giving such Hints to the excellent natural Genius's of our Country, as may contribute either to the Improvement of our present Manufactures, or towards the Invention of new Ones; we propose from Time to Time to communicate such particular Parts as appear to be of the most general Consequence.

As to the *Religious Courtship*, Part of which has been retal'd to the Publick in these Papers, the Reader may be inform'd, that the whole Book will probably in a little Time be printed and bound up by it self; and those who approve of it, will doubtless be better pleas'd to have it entire, than in this broken interrupted Manner.

There are many who have long desired to see a good News-

Paper in *Pennsylvania*; and we hope those Gentlemen who are able, will contribute towards the making This such. We ask Assistance, because we are fully sensible, that to publish a good News-Paper is not so easy an Undertaking as many People imagine it to be. The Author of a *Gazette* (in the Opinion of the Learned) ought to be qualified with an extensive Acquaintance with Languages, a great Easiness and Command of Writing and Relating Things cleanly and intelligibly, and in few Words; he should be able to speak of War both by Land and Sea; be well acquainted with Geography, with the History of the Time, with the several Interests of Princes and States, the Secrets of Courts, and the Manners and Customs of all Nations. Men thus accomplish'd are very rare in this remote Part of the World; and it would be well if the Writer of these Papers could make up among his Friends what is wanting in himself.

Upon the Whole, we may assure the Publick, that as far as the Encouragement we meet with will enable us, no Care and Pains shall be omitted, that may make the *Pennsylvania Gazette* as agreeable and useful an Entertainment as the Nature of the Thing will allow.

The Pennsylvania Gazette, October 2, 1729

"One Piles a Fidler"

And sometime last Week, we are informed, that one Piles a Fidler, with his Wife, were overset in a Canoo near Newtown Creek. The good Man, 'tis said, prudently secur'd his Fiddle, and let his Wife go to the Bottom.

The Pennsylvania Gazette, October 16, 1729

Fire and the Nature of Horses

We hear from Trenton, that on Friday the 5th Instant, a good new Stable belonging to Mr. John Severn, was burnt down to the Ground, in which was consumed five Load of English

Hay, and seven Horses were burnt to Death; occasioned by the Carelessness of a Servant, who let a Candle fall among the Hay.

About the same Time a Barn and Stable was burnt near Allen's-Town: The Owner attempting to save a good Horse he had in the Stable, very narrowly escap'd with his own Life; 'tis observed as something unaccountable in the Nature of Horses, that they are so far from endeavouring to avoid the Danger of Fire, as to stand obstinately and suffer themselves to be burnt; nor will they be led from it unless first made blindfold.

The Pennsylvania Gazette, December 16, 1729

The Trial and Reprieve of Prouse and Mitchel

Last Week at a Court of Oyer and Terminer held in this City, two Servants, James Prouse and James Mitchel (the same who broke Prison some time since, and were retaken at Amboy) were tried for Burglary. It appeared by the King's Evidence, that *Prouse* entred the House of Mr. *Sheed*, Barber, in Front-street, (being admitted by a Servant of the Family) and there broke open a Desk, from whence he took *Seven Pounds Ten Shillings* in Paper Money, and some Copper Half-pence; and that *Mitchel* in the mean time waited without to watch. It was proved that the Money lost was found upon *Prouse* when he was taken; who only said in his Defence at the Bar, that it was given him by Mr. *Sheed*'s Man to keep. *Mitchel* in his Defence said, that tho' he had been in Company with *Prouse* and other Servants drinking *Rum* out of Town in the Day Time, being Sunday, yet that he heard nothing of any Contrivance to Rob, or the like; and that he was in Bed when the Fact was committed, from whence *Prouse* afterwards call'd him to go and drink, but did not acquaint with what had been done. The Jury brought them both in Guilty; and *Prouse* being asked what he had to say why Sentence of Death should not pass against him, answered, that he had nothing to say in his own Behalf, but declared that *Mitchel* was wholly innocent, and knew nothing of the Fact. The Court passed Sentence on them both, but directed *Mitchel* to apply to His Honour the Governour for Mercy.

Mr. *Sheed*'s Servant (who in the above Trial was Evidence for the King) is hereafter to be tried for Robbery; the Law not making it Burglary in a Servant to open a Door in the Night time, tho' it be to admit Thieves, *&c.*

The Pennsylvania Gazette, December 23, 1729

We hear to Morrow is appointed for the Execution of *Prouse* and *Mitchel*.

The Pennsylvania Gazette, January 13, 1729/30

We think our Readers will not be displeased to have the following remarkable Transaction related to them in this particular Manner.

Wednesday the 14th Instant, being the Day appointed for the Execution of *James Prouse* and *James Mitchel* for Burglary, suitable Preparations were accordingly made. The tender Youth of one of them (who was but about 19) and the supposed Innocence of the other as to the Fact for which they were condemned, had induced the Judges (upon the Application of some compassionate People) to recommend them to His Honour's known Clemency: But several Malefactors having been already pardoned, and every Body being sensible, that, considering the great Increase of Vagrants and idle Persons, by the late large Importation of such from several Parts of *Europe*, it was become necessary for the common Good to make some Examples, there was but little Reason to hope that either, and less that both of them might escape the Punishment justly due to Crimes of that enormous Nature. About 11 o'Clock the Bell began to Toll, and a numerous Croud of People was gathered near the Prison, to see these unhappy young Men brought forth to suffer. While their Irons were taken off, and their Arms were binding, *Prouse* cry'd immoderately; but *Mitchel* (who had himself all along behaved with unusual Fortitude) endeavoured in a friendly tender Manner to comfort him: *Do not cry, Jemmy;* (says he) *In an Hour or two it will be over with us, and we shall both be easy.* They were then placed in a Cart, together with a Coffin for each of them, and led thro' the Town to the Place of Execution: *Prouse* appear'd extreamly dejected, but *Mitchel* seemed to support himself with a becoming manly Constancy: When they arriv'd at the fatal Tree, they were told that it was expected they should make some Confession of their Crimes, and say something by Way of Exhortation to the People. *Prouse* was at length with some Difficulty prevailed on to speak; he said, his Confession had been taken in Writing the Evening before; he acknowledged the Fact for which he was to die, but said, That *Greyer* who had sworn against him was the Person that persuaded him to it; and declared that he had never wronged any Man beside Mr. *Sheed*, and his Master. *Mitchel* being desired to speak, reply'd with a sober compos'd Countenance, *What would you have me to say? I am innocent of the Fact*. He was then told, that it did not appear well in him to persist in asserting his Innocence; that he had had a fair Trial, and was found guilty by twelve honest and good Men. He only answer'd, *I am innocent; and it will appear so before God;* and sat down. Then they were both bid to stand up, and the Ropes were order'd to be thrown over the Beam; when the Sheriff took a Paper out of his Pocket and began to read. The poor Wretches, whose Souls were at that Time fill'd with the immediate Terrors of approaching Death, having nothing else before their Eyes, and being without the least Apprehension or Hope of a Reprieve, took but little Notice of what was read; or it seems imagined it to be some previous Matter of Form, as a Warrant for their Execution or the like, 'till they heard the Words PITY and MERCY [*And whereas the said* James Prouse *and* James Mitchel *have been recommended to me as proper Objects of Pity and Mercy.*] Immediately *Mitchel* fell into the most violent Agony; and having only said, *God bless the Governor*, he swooned away in the Cart. Suitable Means were used to recover him; and when he came a little to himself, he added; *I have been a great Sinner; I have been guilty of almost every Crime; Sabbath-breaking in particular, which led me into ill Company; but Theft I never was guilty of. God bless the Governor; and God Almighty's Name be praised;* and then swooned again. *Prouse* likewise seemed to be overwhelmed with Joy, but did not swoon. All the Way back to the Prison,

Mitchel lean'd on his Coffin, being unable to support himself, and shed Tears in abundance. He who went out to die with a large Share of Resolution and Fortitude, returned in the most dispirited Manner imaginable; being utterly over-power'd by the Force of that sudden Turn of excessive Joy, for which he had been no Way prepared. The Concern that appeared in every Face while these Criminals were leading to Execution, and the Joy that diffused it self thro' the whole Multitude, so visible in their Countenances upon the mention of a Reprieve, seems to be a pleasing Instance, and no small Argument of the general laudable Humanity even of our common People, who were unanimous in their loud Acclamations of *God bless the Governor for his Mercy.*

The following are Copies of the Papers delivered out by *Prouse* and *Mitchel* the Evening before, with little or no Alteration from their own Words.

"I *James Prouse* was born in the Town of *Brentford* in *Middlesex* County in *Old England*, of honest Parents, who gave me but little Education. My Father was a Corporal in the late Lord *Oxford*'s Regiment of Horse, (then named the said Lord's Blues) and I was for some Time in the Care of an Uncle who lived at *Eling* near *Brentford* aforesaid, and who would have given me good Learning; but I being young would not take his good Counsel, and in the 12th Year of my Age came into *Philadelphia*, where I was recommended to one of the best of Masters, who never let me want for any Thing: But I minding the evil Insinuations of wicked People, more than the good Dictates of my Master, and having not the Fear of God before my Eyes, am deservedly brought to this wretched and shameful End. I acknowledge I justly merit Death for the Fact which condemns me; but I never had the least Design or Thought of the like, until often press'd, and at length seduced to it by *John Greyer*, who was the only Person that ruined me. He often solicited me to be guilty of other Crimes of the like Nature, but I never was guilty of any such, neither with him or any one else; neither did I ever wrong any Man before, save my too indulgent Master; from whom I now and then pilfer'd a Yard or the like of Cloth, in

order to make Money to spend with the said *Greyer*. As for
James Mitchel who dies for the same Fact with me, as I hope
to receive Mercy at the great Tribunal, he the said *James
Mitchel* is intirely innocent,* and knew nothing of the Fact
until apprehended and taken. I am about Nineteen Years of
Age and die a Protestant.

JAMES PROUSE."

The Speech or Declaration of James Mitchel
written with his own Hand.

"I *James Mitchel*, was born, at *Antrim* in the Kingdom of
Ireland, of good and honest Parents, and brought up with
them until the Age of 13 Years, and had a suitable Education
given me, such as being taught to read and write *English*,
with some *Latin*; and might have been further instructed, but
at my earnest Request was bound Apprentice to a Bookbinder, and served 4 Years to that Trade; after which I left
the Kingdom and went for *England* in order to be further
improved in my Business; but there had the Misfortune to be
press'd on board the *Berwick* Man of War, commanded by the
Honorable *George Gordon*, and having been at several Parts
abroad, returned to *England* in *Octob.* 1728. where I was by
Sickness reduced to a very sad Condition, through which I
came over to this Country a Servant; here I was it seems unfortunately led into bad Company, and one Evening by *James
Prouse* was raised out of my Bed to go and drink with him
and one *Greyer*, the which *Greyer* after parting gave to the
said *James Prouse* Six-pence, which was all the Money I saw
that Night and till next Morning, and then *James Prouse* took
out of his Pocket a 15 Shilling Bill, and desired me to get it
changed for him, in order to spend some of it; but coming
unto Town I was apprehended for the robbing of Mr. *George
Sheed*, and now am to die for the same. I die a Protestant.

JAMES MITCHEL."

N. B. He declared the same Thing at the Bar just before he received Sentence.

A Gallant Duel and an Unhappy Man

Saturday last, about nine o'Clock in the Morning two young *Hibernian* Gentlemen met on *Society Hill*, and fought a gallant Duel before a Number of Spectators not very usual on such Occasions. The Cause of their Quarrel is it seems unknown; and as they were parted without much Difficulty, and neither of them received any considerable Hurt, it is generally looked upon to be only a Piece of *Theatrical Representation*.

The same Day an unhappy Man one *Sturgis*, upon some Difference with his Wife, determined to drown himself in the River; and she, (kind Wife) went with him, it seems, to see it faithfully performed, and accordingly stood by silent and unconcerned during the whole Transaction: He jump'd in near *Carpenter*'s Wharff, but was timely taken out again, before what he came about was thoroughly effected, so that they were both obliged to return home as they came, and put up for that Time with the Disappointment.

The Pennsylvania Gazette, February 10, 1729/30

Printer's Errors

To the Publisher of the Pennsylvania Gazette.

Printerum est errare.

SIR,

As your last Paper was reading in some Company where I was present, these Words were taken Notice of in the Article concerning Governor *Belcher*, [*After which his Excellency, with the Gentlemen trading to New-England,* died *elegantly at Pontack's*]. The Word *died* should doubtless have been *dined, Pontack*'s being a noted Tavern and Eating-house in *London* for Gentlemen of Condition; but this Omission of the letter (*n*) in that Word, gave us as much Entertainment as any Part of your Paper. One took the Opportunity of telling us, that in a certain Edition of the Bible, the Printer had, where *David* says *I am fearfully and wonderfully made*, omitted the Letter (*e*) in the last Word, so that it was, *I am fearfully and wonder-fully mad*; which occasion'd an ignorant Preacher, who took that Text, to harangue his Audience for half an hour on the Subject of *Spiritual Madness*. Another related to us, that when the Company of Stationers in *England* had the Printing of the Bible in their Hands, the Word (*not*) was left out in the Seventh Commandment, and the whole Edition was printed off with *Thou shalt commit Adultery*, instead of *Thou shalt not*, &c. This material *Erratum* induc'd the Crown to take the Patent from them which is now held by the King's Printer. The *Spectator*'s Remark upon this Story is, that he doubts many of our modern Gentlemen have this faulty Edition by 'em, and are not made sensible of the Mistake. A Third Person in the Company acquainted us with an unlucky Fault that went through a whole Impression of Common-Prayer-Books; in the Funeral Service, where these Words are, *We shall all be changed in a moment, in the twinkling of an Eye*, &c. the Printer had omitted the (*c*) in *changed*, and it read thus, *We shall all be hanged*, &c. And lastly, a Mistake of your Brother News-Printer was mentioned, in *The Speech of* James Prouse *written the Night before he was to have been executed*, instead of *I die a Protestant*, he has put it, *I died a Protestant*. Upon the whole you came off with the more favourable Censure, because your Paper is most commonly very correct, and yet you were never known to triumph upon it, by publickly ridiculing and exposing the continual Blunders of your Contemporary. Which Observation was concluded by a good old Gentleman in Company, with this general just Remark, That whoever accustoms himself to pass over in Silence the Faults of his Neighbours, shall meet with much better Quarter from the World when he happens to fall into a Mistake himself; for the Satyrical and Censorious, whose Hand is against every Man, shall upon such Occasions have every Man's Hand against him.

I am, SIR, your Friend, &c.

J. T.

The Pennsylvania Gazette, March 13, 1729/30

Letter of the Drum

To the Publisher of the GAZETTE.

SIR,

I know well that the Age in which we live, abounds in *Spinosists*, *Hobbists*, and *most impious Free-Thinkers*, who despise *Revelation*, and treat the *most sacred Truths* with *Ridicule* and *Contempt*: Nay, to such an Height of Iniquity are they arrived, that they not only deny the *Existence* of the *Devil*, and of *Spirits* in general, but would also persuade the World, that the Story of *Saul* and the *Witch of Endor* is an Imposture; and which is still worse, that no Credit is to be given to the so well-attested One of the *Drummer* of *Tedsworth*. I do, indeed, confess that the Arguments of some of these unbelieving Gentlemen, with whom I have heretofore conversed on the Subject of *Spirits*, *Apparitions*, *Witches*, &c. carried with them a great Shew of Reason, and were so specious, that I was strongly inclined to think them in the Right; and for several Years past have lived without any Fear or Apprehensions of *Dæmons* or *Hobgoblins*; but the Case is quite alter'd with me now; and I who used to sleep without drawing my Curtains, am now so fearful, that I pin them every Night I go to Bed with corking Pins, and cover my self Head over Ears with the Clothes. Now this Change is not owing, as you would imagine, to any frightful Apparition I have seen, or uncommon Noise I have heard; but to a most amazing Account I received the other Day from a Reverend Gentleman, of a certain House's being haunted with the *D——l* of a Drummer, not a whit less obstreperous, than the *Tedsworthian* Tympanist: This Gentleman, whose Veracity few People presume to call in Question, told me, that he was not long since obliged to meet some of his Brethren, at a certain Town about fifteen Miles below *Philadelphia*, in order to settle some Affairs of the Church, and to consult on proper Measures to prevent the *Growth of Atheism*; that he was there joined by four of his Brethren; who insisting that it was unpresidented to proceed to Business at their first Meeting, they thereupon unanimously agreed to defer their Consultations 'till the next Day; that they spent the Evening chearfully, yet soberly; that about ten at Night they retired to repose themselves, but lodged in separate Rooms; that he, with his Companion, were no sooner warm in their Bed, than they heard a Drum beating very loud, now on the one Side of their Bed, then on the other, and in a Moment after on the Teaster; that sometimes they distinctly heard the *Scots Traveller*, and at other Times the *Grenadiers March*; that the Noise continued all Night, frighted them almost to Death, and yet, which is the most surprizing and unaccountable Part of the Relation, disturbed no Mortal in the House save themselves; that early in the Morning they went into the next Room, where they found two of their Brethren sleeping soundly; that they were amazed to find them so fast asleep after such a terrible Night; that having awakened them, they asked whether they had not been disturbed with the Noise of a Drum? that they replied, They had rested well, and were surprized to hear them ask such a Question, and hinted that they believed them to be out of their Senses; upon which he related to them the Adventure of the Night, so full of Horror, with all the Particulars I have mentioned, and many more which I have omitted; That at first they seemed to give little Credit to what he said; but upon his Bedfellow's affirming it to be true, they appeared to be satisfied of the Reality of the Fact. Then the Gentleman went on with his Story in this wise: That the next Night he with his Companion went to Bed in the same Room, in which they had been so terribly frighten'd; that they had not taken their first Nap, before they heard an uncouth Noise under them; that his Companion was shortly after seized violently and forcibly by the great Toe, and in great Danger of being pulled out of the Bed; but that upon the Beating of the Drum, which happen'd at the same Instant, his Toe was released; and that to prevent any future Attacks, they hoisted their Knees up to their very Noses; the Noise still growing louder, they felt a most prodigious Weight on them, heavier, as he said, than the *Night-Mare*; that by his Voice they presently discovered it to be one of their Brethren, who had come into their Room on purpose to scare them; either believing that they had told him a Fib, or that they were under such potent Influences the Night before, as made them imagine they heard a Drum, when in Reality they did not; But mark, said the Relater to me; according to the old Proverb, *Harm watch Harm catch*; for he was so frighted himself, that he would not have ventured back to his own Room, though he were sure to be made a Bishop; so that we were obliged to share our Bed with him, in which we lay sweating, and almost dead with Fear, 'till Morning. Thus he concluded his surprizing Relation, which wrought so strongly on me, that I could no longer Doubt of the *D*——*l*'s having plaid them this Prank; and to this Story only my Timorousness is owing. Now, I know well enough, that some Folks will be apt to say; it is all a Lye, a meer Forgery; in short, they will raise an infinite Number of Objections to destroy its Credit; for when I told it to a certain Person, he swore it could not be true; because in a Piece of the learned *Greutzius*, which he had read, *De examine Sagarum*, he found that all the Divines in *Germany* were clearly of Opinion, that the Devil never begins to play his Pranks 'till after Midnight, and that no Spectres were seen before that Time; and this Noise beginning between ten and eleven both Nights, he was assured, for that Reason, that the Devil was no Way concern'd in it; but he had almost staggered me, when he told me this Story: *A certain Curate lived in the Island of* Jamaica, *who loved his Bottle, no Curate better; he chanced to be drinking in a Tavern, when he was called upon to do the last Offices to a Brother departed; upon which with great Reluctance he leaves his Company, but told them he would return immediately: away he hies to the Place of Burial, and, as is usual, reads over the Service for the Dead, 'till he came to the Words,* I heard a Voice from Heaven, saying, blessed, *&c. at which he was interrupted by one of his Companions, who had followed him from the Ale-house, with a 'By* G—— *that's a d*——'d Lye, *for I have been drinking with you all Day at Mother* ——'s, *and if you had heard the Voice, I should have heard it too, for my Ears are as good as yours.'* The Gentleman left me to apply the Story.

Now, Sir, as I take you to be a Person of profound Learning and Judgment, I desire you will set me to rights, by giving me your Opinion candidly, whether I ought to give

Credit to the above Relation or not, altho' it be attested by
two Reverend Fathers,

I am, Sir, yours, &c.

The Pennsylvania Gazette, April 23, 1730

On that Odd Letter of the Drum

To the Author of the Pennsylvania Gazette.

SIR,   *Burlington, April* 27. 1730.
   As I am your sincere Friend and Well-wisher, it is with a
great deal of Pleasure I have observed your prudent Management of the News-Paper, in which, till last Week, there has
been no one Thing seen that might justly give Offence either
to Church or State, or to any private Person: But when I
reflect how good a Judge you are of what is or is not proper
to be published in that manner, I am puzzled to think what
could induce you to insert that odd Letter of the *Drum* in
your last *Gazette*. I am satisfied you know better than to
imagine that such a Thing would please the Generality of
your Readers, or that it might be instrumental in doing Good
to any one Creature living; I believe you have had no Reason
to be piqu'd against the Gentlemen there reflected on; and as
to the Wit and Humour which some Persons of reputed Taste
pretend to discern in it, I protest I can see none, and I think
that true Wit and Humour cannot be employ'd in ridiculing
Things serious and sacred. Whoever was the Writer of it, notwithstanding his seeming Reflection on *Spinosists, Hobbists,
and most impious Freethinkers*, his Design is apparent, To bring
the Dispensers of Religion among us into Contempt, and to
weaken our Belief of the Divine Writings; a Design, in my
Opinion, very unworthy an honest Man and a good Subject,
even tho' he was of no Religion at all. His depreciating the
Holy Scriptures, by insinuating that the Story of the Drummer of *Tedsworth* is a better attested One than that of *Saul*
and the Witch of *Endor*, as also his satyrical Sneer at the
Meeting of those Reverend Gentlemen *to prevent the Growth*

of Atheism, I pass over at present without any further Remark; and as I apprehend that Arguments drawn from the Truth of our Religion, will have but little Weight with this Writer, in dissuading him from such a Way of indulging his satyrical Humour, I would only request him to consider these Things seriously, *to wit*, That wise Men have in all Ages thought Government necessary for the Good of Mankind; and, that wise Governments have always thought Religion necessary for the well ordering and well-being of Society, and accordingly have been ever careful to encourage and protect the Ministers of it, paying them the highest publick Honours, that their Doctrines might thereby meet with the greater Respect among the common People; And that if there were no Truth in Religion, or the Salvation of Men's Souls not worth regarding, yet, in consideration of the inestimable Service done to Mankind by the Clergy, as they are the Teachers and Supporters of Virtue and Morality, without which no Society could long subsist, prudent Men should be very cautious how they say or write any thing that might bring them into Contempt, and thereby weaken their Hands and render their Labours ineffectual. If this Writer is a Man of good Sense, as I am willing to think he is, I am persuaded this single Consideration will be sufficient to prevail with him never more to employ his Pen in so unjustifiable a manner.

For my Part, I am entirely unacquainted with the Fact, the Relation of which this Writer pretends to have at first believ'd, till the Story of the *Jamaica* Curate stagger'd his Faith. If he really believ'd the Relation at first, I cannot see why that Story should stagger his Faith in the least: For tho' one Man's Ears may be as good as another's when both are awake and in Company, it does not thence follow that one Man may not sleep sounder than another when in Bed. Besides, as far as we know, *there is nothing absolutely impossible in the Thing it self:* We cannot be certain there are no Spirits existing; it is rather highly probable that there are: But we are sure that if Spirits do exist, we are very ignorant of their Natures, and know neither their Motives nor Methods of Acting, nor can we tell by what Means they may render themselves perceptible to our Senses. Those who have contemplated the Nature of Animals seem to be convinced that Spirit can act upon Matter, for they ascribe the Motion of the Body to the Will and Power of the Mind. Anatomists also tell us, that there are Nerves of Communication from all Parts of the Body to the Brain: And Philosophers assure us, that the Vibrations of the Air striking on the Auditory Nerves, give to the Brain the Sensation of what we call Sound; and that the Rays of Light striking on the optic Nerves, communicate a Motion to the Brain which forms there the Image of that Thing from which those Rays were reflected: We find that a sudden Blow upon the Eye shakes the visual Nerve in the same Manner as when Light strikes it, and therefore we think we see a Light, when there is no such Thing at that Time visible without us, and no one standing by can see it, but the Person that is struck alone. Now, how can we be assur'd that it is not in the Power of a Spirit *without* the body to operate in a like manner on the Nerves of Sight, and give them the same Vibrations as when a certain Object appears before the Eye, (tho' no such Object is really present) and accordingly make a particular Man see the Apparition of any Person or Thing at Pleasure, when no One else in Company can see it? May not such a Spirit likewise occasion the same Vibrations in the auditory Nerves as when the Sound of a Drum, or any other Sound, is heard, and thereby affect the Party in the same manner as a real Drum beating in the Room would do, tho' no one hears it but himself. Perhaps I need not have said all this to a Person who believes *the well-attested Story of the Drummer of Tedsworth*, since there are many other Stories, equally incontestible with that, by which reasonable Men are convinc'd that Spirits do not only actually exist, but are able to make themselves sometimes both seen and heard.

In the Close of his Letter, after paying a Complement to your *profound Learning and Judgment*, he requests *your Opinion, whether he ought to give Credit to the said Relation, tho' it be attested by two Reverend Fathers*. Since you have not thought proper to say any thing to it, I beg Leave to give the Gentleman my Opinion, which is, *That he may very safely believe it*, and that for the following Reasons.

1. Because, as I have shewn above, there is nothing absolutely impossible in the Thing it self.

2. Because they were Men of Probity, Learning and sound

good Sense, who related this Fact to him upon their own Knowledge. If they were not such, 'tis presum'd they would not have been thought proper Persons to be made publick Instructors.

3. Because they both concur'd in the same Testimony; and it cannot be imagin'd what Interest they should have in contriving together to impose a Falshood of that Nature upon him; since they could expect Nothing but to be ridicul'd for their Pains, both by him and every other unthinking Sceptic in the Country.

If you insert this Epistle in your next Gazette, I shall believe you did not approve of That I have been writing against, and shall continue,

SIR,

Your real Friend and constant Reader,

PHILOCLERUS.

The Pennsylvania Gazette, May 7, 1730

An Unlucky She-Wrestler

We have here an unlucky She-Wrestler who has lately thrown a young Weaver, and broke his Leg, so that tis thought he will not be able to tread the Treadles these two Months. In the mean Time, however, he may employ himself in winding Quills.

The Pennsylvania Gazette, July 23, 1730

Rules and Maxims for Promoting Matrimonial Happiness

Ver novum, ver jam canorum, vere natus Orbis est:
Vere concordant amores, vere nubent alites—Catul.

Fælices ter, & amplius,
　Quos irrupta tenet Copula: nec malis
Divulsis Querimoniis
　Suprema citius solvet amor die.　　Horat.

The happy State of Matrimony is, undoubtedly, the surest
and most lasting Foundation of Comfort and Love; the
Source of all that endearing Tenderness and Affection which
arises from Relation and Affinity; the grand Point of Property; the Cause of all good Order in the World, and what
alone preserves it from the utmost Confusion; and, to sum up
all, the Appointment of infinite Wisdom for these great and
good Purposes. Notwithstanding, such is the Perverseness of
human Nature, and so easy is it to misuse the best of Things,
that by the Folly and Ill-behaviour of those who enter into
it, this is very often made a State of the most exquisite
Wretchedness and Misery; which gives the wild and vicious
Part of Mankind but too much reason to rail against it, and
treat it with Contempt. Wherefore, it highly becomes the virtuous of both Sexes, by the Prudence of their Conduct, to
redeem this noble Institution from those unjust Reproaches
which it at present labours under, and restore it to the Honour and Esteem it merits, by endeavouring to make each
other as happy as they can.

I am now about to lay down such Rules and Maxims as I
think most practicable and conducive towards the End and
Happiness of Matrimony. And these I address to all Females
that would be married, or are already so; not that I suppose
their Sex more faulty than the other, and most to want Advice, for I assure them, upon my Honour, I believe the quite
contrary; but the Reason is, because I esteem them better disposed to receive and practice it, and therefore am willing to
begin, where I may promise myself the best Success. Besides,
if there is any Truth in Proverbs, *Good Wives* usually make *Good
Husbands*.

RULES and MAXIMS for promoting Matrimonial
Happiness. *Address'd to all* Widows, Wives, *and* Spinsters.

The likeliest Way, either to obtain a *good Husband*, or to
keep one *so*, is to be *Good* yourself.

Never use a *Lover* ill whom you design to make your *Husband*, lest he either upbraid you with it, or return it afterwards: and if you find, at any Time, an Inclination to play the Tyrant, remember these two Lines of Truth and Justice.

> *Gently shall those be* rul'd, *who* gently *sway'd;*
> Abject *shall those* obey, *who* haughty *were* obey'd.

Avoid, both before and after Marriage, all Thoughts of *managing* your Husband. Never endeavour to deceive or impose on his Understanding: nor give him *Uneasiness* (as some do very foolishly) to *try* his Temper; but treat him always beforehand with *Sincerity*, and afterwards with *Affection* and *Respect*.

Be not over sanguine before Marriage, nor promise your self Felicity without Alloy, for that's impossible to be attain'd in this present State of Things. Consider beforehand, that the Person you are going to spend your Days with, is a Man, and not an Angel; and if, when you come together, you discover any Thing in his Humour or Behaviour that is not altogether so agreeable as you expected, *pass it over as a humane Frailty*: smooth your Brow; compose your Temper; and try to amend it by *Cheerfulness* and Good-nature.

Remember always, that whatever Misfortunes may happen to either, they are not to be charg'd to the Account of *Matrimony*, but to the Accidents and Infirmities of humane Life, a Burthen which each has engaged to assist the other in supporting, and to which both Parties are equally expos'd. Therefore, instead of *Murmurs*, *Reflections*, and *Disagreement*, whereby the *Weight* is rendred abundantly more *grievous*, readily put your Shoulders to the Yoke, and make it easier to both.

Resolve every Morning to be *good-natur'd* and CHEERFUL that Day: and if any Accident should happen to break that Resolution, suffer it not to put you out of Temper with every Thing besides, and especially with your Husband.

Dispute not with him, be the Occasion what it will; but much rather deny yourself the trivial Satisfaction of having your own Will, or gaining the better of an Argument, than risk a Quarrel or create an Heart-burning, which it's impossible to know the End of.

Be assured, a Woman's Power, as well as Happiness, has no other Foundation but her Husband's Esteem and Love, which consequently it is her undoubted Interest by all Means possible to preserve and increase. Do you, therefore, study his Temper, and command your own; enjoy his Satisfaction with him, share and sooth his Cares, and with the utmost Diligence conceal his Infirmities.

Read frequently with due Attention the Matrimonial Service; and take care in doing so, not to overlook the Word *Obey*.

In your Prayers be sure to add a Clause for Grace to make you a good Wife; and at the same Time, resolve to do your utmost endeavour towards it.

Always wear your Wedding Ring, for therein lies more Virtue than usually is imagined. If you are ruffled unawares, assaulted with improper Thoughts, or tempted in any kind against your Duty, cast your Eyes upon it, and call to Mind, who gave it you, where it was received, and what passed at that solemn Time.

Let the Tenderness of your conjugal Love be expressed with such Decency, Delicacy and Prudence, as that it may appear plainly and thorowly distinct from the designing Fondness of an Harlot.

Have you any Concern for your own Ease, or for your Husband's Esteem? then, have a due Regard to his Income and Circumstances in all your Expences and Desires: For if Necessity should follow, you run the greatest Hazard of being deprived of both.

Let not many Days pass together without a serious Examination how you have behaved as a Wife, and if upon Reflection you find your self guilty of any Foibles or Omissions, the best Attonement is, to be exactly careful of your future Conduct.

I am fully persuaded, that a strict Adherence to the foregoing Rules would equally advance the Honour of Matrimony, and the *Glory* of the *Fair Sex*: And since the greatest Part of them, with a very little Alteration, are as proper for Husbands as for Wives to practice, I recommend them accordingly to their Consideration, and hope, in a short time, to receive Acknowledgments from *married Persons* of *both Sexes* for the Benefit they receive thereby.

And now, in behalf of my *unlearned Readers*, I beg Leave of my *learned Ones*, to conclude this Discourse with Mr. *Creech*'s Translation of that Part of *Horace* which I have taken for the *Motto* of this Paper.

> *Thrice happy* They, *that free from* Strife,
> *Maintain a* Love *as long as Life:*
>   *Whose fixt and binding Vows,*
> *No intervening* Jealousy,
> *No* Fears *and no* Debates *untye;*
>   *And* Death *alone can loose.*

The Pennsylvania Gazette, October 8, 1730

A Witch Trial at Mount Holly

Burlington, Oct. 12. Saturday last at *Mount-Holly*, about 8 Miles from this Place, near 300 People were gathered together to see an Experiment or two tried on some Persons accused of Witchcraft. It seems the Accused had been charged with making their Neighbours Sheep dance in an uncommon Manner, and with causing Hogs to speak, and sing Psalms, &c. to the great Terror and Amazement of the King's good and peaceable Subjects in this Province; and the Accusers being very positive that if the Accused were weighed in Scales against a Bible, the Bible would prove too heavy for them; or that, if they were bound and put into the River, they would swim; the said Accused desirous to make their Innocence appear, voluntarily offered to undergo the said Trials, if 2 of the most violent of their Accusers would be tried with them. Accordingly the Time and Place was agreed on, and advertised about the Country; The Accusers were 1 Man and 1 Woman; and the Accused the same. The Parties being met, and the People got together, a grand Consultation was held, before they proceeded to Trial; in which it was agreed to use the

Scales first; and a Committee of Men were appointed to search the Men, and a Committee of Women to search the Women, to see if they had any Thing of Weight about them, particularly Pins. After the Scrutiny was over, a huge great Bible belonging to the Justice of the Place was provided, and a Lane through the Populace was made from the Justices House to the Scales, which were fixed on a Gallows erected for that Purpose opposite to the House, that the Justice's Wife and the rest of the Ladies might see the Trial, without coming amongst the Mob; and after the Manner of *Moor-fields*, a large Ring was also made. Then came out of the House a grave tall Man carrying the Holy Writ before the supposed Wizard, &c. (as solemnly as the Sword-bearer of *London* before the Lord Mayor) the Wizard was first put in the Scale, and over him was read a Chapter out of the Books of *Moses*, and then the Bible was put in the other Scale, (which being kept down before) was immediately let go; but to the great Surprize of the Spectators, Flesh and Bones came down plump, and outweighed that great good Book by abundance. After the same Manner, the others were served, and their Lumps of Mortality severally were too heavy for *Moses* and all the Prophets and Apostles. This being over, the Accusers and the rest of the Mob, not satisfied with this Experiment, would have the Trial by Water; accordingly a most solemn Procession was made to the Mill-pond; where both Accused and Accusers being stripp'd (saving only to the Women their Shifts) were bound Hand and Foot, and severally placed in the Water, lengthways, from the Side of a Barge or Flat, having for Security only a Rope about the Middle of each, which was held by some in the Flat. The Accuser Man being thin and spare, with some Difficulty began to sink at last; but the rest every one of them swam very light upon the Water. A Sailor in the Flat jump'd out upon the Back of the Man accused, thinking to drive him down to the Bottom; but the Person bound, without any Help, came up some time before the other. The Woman Accuser, being told that she did not sink, would be duck'd a second Time; when she swam again as light as before. Upon which she declared, That she believed the Accused had bewitched her to make her so light, and that she would be duck'd again a Hundred Times, but she would duck the Devil out of her. The accused Man, being surpriz'd at his own Swimming, was not so confident of his Innocence as before, but said, *If I am a Witch, it is more than I know*. The more thinking Part of the Spectators were of Opinion, that any Person so bound and plac'd in the Water (unless they were mere Skin and Bones) would swim till their Breath was gone, and their Lungs fill'd with Water. But it being the general Belief of the Populace, that the Womens Shifts, and the Garters with which they were bound help'd to support them; it is said they are to be tried again the next warm Weather, naked.

The Pennsylvania Gazette, October 22, 1730

The Aurora Borealis

Last Thursday Evening there was seen throughout this Province in the N. East, a very bright Appearance of the *Aurora Borealis*, or Northern Twilight. It seems this kind of Meteor never appears near the Equator, and has therefore obtained the above Name. In 1716, March 6. there was one visible to the West of *Ireland*, Confines of *Russia*, and to the East of *Poland*; extending at least near 30 deg. of Longitude, and 50 deg. in Latitude, that is, over almost all the North of *Europe*; it continued three Nights successively, and in all Places at the same time it exhibited the like wondrous Circumstances. In the Years 1707 and 1708, five small ones were observ'd in little more than eighteen Months. But a sufficient Number of Observations have not yet been made by the Curious, to enable them to assign the Cause of this Phænomenon with any Certainty.

The Pennsylvania Gazette, October 29, 1730

The Earliest New-England Immigrants

Sometime since, the following Lines were found stuck on the outside of the Door of the Council Chamber.

> *Our Fathers pass'd the wide* Atlantick *Sea,*
> *And bless'd themselves when in the Desert Free:*
> *And shall their Sons thro' Treachery and Fear,*
> *Give up that Freedom which has cost so dear?*
> *Whate'er Pretence our Enemies may frame,*
> *The Man is alter'd, but the Cause the same.*
> *From* Cæsar's *Court should* Cato *fawning come,*
> *Be sure that* Cato *is no Friend to* Rome.

To which a Gentleman in *New-York* has wrote the following Answer.

> *Their Fathers crost the wide* Atlantick Sea,
> *To be in Desarts from their* Deserts *free;*
> *And shall their Sons with glaring Insolence*
> *Support a Cause so void of common Sense?*
> *What-e'er Pretence this stubborn People frame,*
> *The Case is alter'd, but the Men the same.*
> *From* Cæsar's *Court should a new Ruler come,*
> *Be sure they'll starve him, as they've others done.*

Whatever Wit there may be in this Answer, it contains one Reflection not altogether just: Since 'tis certain, that the greatest Part of the Settlers of New-England removed thither on no other Account than for the sake of enjoying their Liberty, especially their religious Liberties, in greater Security: Being persecuted at home, as *Puritans* in the Reign of *James* I. and among all other Dissenters in the Reign of *Charles* II.

The Pennsylvania Gazette, November 5, 1730

Lying Shopkeepers

Veritas Luce clarior.

A Friend of mine was the other Day cheapening some Trifles at a Shopkeepers, and after a few Words, they agreed on a Price; at the lapping up this Purchase, the Mistress of the Shop told him, People were grown very hard, for she actually lost by every thing she sold: How then is it possible, replied my Friend, that you can keep on your Business? Indeed, Sir, answer'd she, I must of Necessity shut my Doors, had I not a very great Trade. The Reason, said my Friend, with a Sneer, is admirable.

There are a great many Retailers, who falsly imagine that being *Historical* (the modern Phrase for *Lying*) is much for their Advantage; and some of them have a Saying, *That 'tis a Pity Lying is a Sin, it is so useful in Trade*; tho', if they would examine into the Reason why a Number of Shopkeepers raise considerable Estates, while others, who have set out with better Fortunes have become Bankrupts; they will find, that the former made up with Truth, Diligence and Probity, what they wanted in Stock, and the latter have been guilty of imposing on such Customers as they found had no Skill in their Goods. The former's Character raises a Credit which supplies the Want of Fortune, and their fair Dealing, brings them Custom; whereas none will return to buy of him, by whom he has been once defrauded. If People in Trade would judge rightly, we might buy blindfold, and they would save, both to themselves and Customers, the uneasiness of Haggling.

Though there are Numbers of Shopkeepers, who scorn that mean Vice of *Lying*, and whose Word may very safely be relied on; yet there are too many, who will endeavour to deceive, and, backing their Falsities with Asseverations, pawn their Salvation to raise their Price. As Example works more than Precept, and my sole View being the Good and Interest of my Countrymen, whom I could wish without Vice or Folly, I shall shew the Esteem of *Truth*, and the Abbhorrence of *Falsity* among the Antients.

Augustus triumphing over *Mark Anthony* and *Cleopatra*, among other Captives, brought to *Rome* a Priest about 60 Years old. The Senate being inform'd that this Man was never detected in a *Lie*, and thought never to have been guilty of one, not only restored him to his Liberty, but made him a High Priest, and raised him a Statue. This Priest thus honoured, was an *Ægyptian*, and an Enemy to *Rome*, but this Virtue cover'd all Obstacles: Whereas *Pamphilus* was a *Roman* Citizen, whose Body was deny'd Burial, his Estate confiscated, his House raz'd, and his Wife and Children banished the *Roman* Territories, for his having been a noted and irreclaimable *Liar*. Can there be a greater Demonstration of Respect to Truth than this of the *Romans*, who raised an Enemy to the greatest Honour, and exposed a Citizen's Family to the greatest Contumely!

There is no Excuse for *Lying*, neither is there any equally despicable and dangerous with a *Liar*, no Man being in Safety who frequents his Company; for who will *lie* (says the *English* Proverb) will *swear*; and such an one may take away my Life, turn my Family a begging, and ruin my Reputation, whenever he shall find it for his Interest: For if a Man will *lie* and *swear* in his Shop to get a Trifle, why should we question his doing of it, when he may hope to make his Fortune by his *Perjury*! the Crime is in itself so mean, that to call a Man a *Liar*, is every where esteem'd an Affront not to be forgiven. If any have Lenity enough to allow the *Dealer*'s Excuse for this base Practice, yet I believe they will allow none for the *Gentleman* who is addicted to this Vice, and must look upon him as a Wretch undeserving the Name; and that the World does so, is visible, by the Contempt with which he is mentioned whenever there is Occasion to name him.

Epimenides the Philosopher, gave the *Rhodians* this Definition of Truth, That she was Companion of the Gods, the Joy of Heaven, the Light of the Earth, the Basis of Justice, and the Foundation of good Policy. *Eschines* told the same People, that Truth was a Virtue, without which, Force was enfeebled, Justice corrupted; Humility was Dissimulation, Patience intolerable, Chastity dissembled, Liberty lost, and Pity superfluous. *Pharmacus* the Philosopher; told the *Romans*, that Truth was the Centre in which all Things rested; a Chart to sail by, a Remedy for all Evils, and a Light to the whole World. *Anaxarchus* speaking of *Truth*, to the *Lacedemonians*, said, It was Health incapable of Sickness; Life not subject to Death; an Elixir which healeth all; a Sun not to be obscur'd; a Moon without Eclipse; an Herb which never withereth; a Gate that is never closed, and a Path which never fatigues the Traveller.

But if we are blind to the Beauties of *Truth*, it's astonishing that we should not open our Eyes to the Inconveniencies of Falsities; for a Man given to Romance, must be always on his Guard, for Fear of contradicting, and exposing himself to

the Derision of his Hearers: For the most *Historical* would
avoid the odious Character; tho' 'tis impossible for any, with
all their Circumspection, to travel long in this Road, without
being discover'd; and then what Shame, what Confusion follows! he is continually anxious to hide himself from the
Knowledge of the World, and loads his Memory with Trifles,
for fear of being taken with his own Words. Whereas, who is
a Votary to *Truth*, never hesitates for an Answer, never
wrecks his Invention, to make the Sequel quadrate with the
foregoing Part of his Discourse; is not obliged to burden his
Memory with minute Circumstances, since Truth easily recol-
lects them, speaks openly, and will repeat the same Things
often, without varying; which a *Liar* can hardly do, without
that necessary Gift, a good Memory.

The Pennsylvania Gazette, November 19, 1730

Replies by "Betty Diligent" and "Mercator"

*As a Nail sticketh fast between the Joinings of the Stones, so doth
Sin stick close between Buying and Selling.*   Apocrypha.

We have received the two following Letters, relating to our
Gazette of the 19th past. The first is from a *Shopkeeper*, and
the other from a *Merchant*.

To the Author of the GAZETTE.

SIR,
'I am a Shopkeeper in this City, and I suppose am the Person
at whom some Reflections are aimed in one of your late Papers. It is an easy Matter for Gentlemen that can write, to say
a great deal upon any Subject, and to censure Faults of which
perhaps they are as guilty as other People. I cannot help
thinking that Paper is wrote with much Partiality, and is a
very unfair Representation of Things. Shopkeepers are
therein accus'd of *Lying*, as if they were the only Persons culpable, without the least Notice being taken of the general

Lying practis'd by *Customers. I am sure 'tis very ordinary at that Price; I have bought much better at such a one's Shop for less Money;* are very common Falsities repeated on this Occasion, almost worn threadbare; but some have even the Confidence to aver, *that they have bought cheaper of me;* when I know the Price they mention is less than the Goods cost me. In short, they will tell a hundred Lies to undervalue our Goods, and make our Demands appear extravagant: So that the Blame of all the Lying properly belongs to the Customers that come to buy; because if the Shopkeepers strain the Truth a little now and then, they are forc'd to do it in their own Defence. In hopes you will do us Justice in this Affair, I remain,

Your Friend and Servant,

Betty Diligent.'

Mr. *Gazetteer,*

'You have in a late Paper very justly taken Notice of, and censur'd the too common Practice of Lying used by Shopkeepers in *selling* their Goods; but you have omitted just one half the Story, *viz.* their Lying when they come to the Stores to *buy.* I believe they think Lying full as convenient and beneficial in *buying* their Goods as selling them; for to my Knowledge some of them are most egregiously guilty in this Particular.

I am, Sir, Yours, &c.

Mercator.'

The Pennsylvania Gazette, December 3, 1730

On the Providence of God in the Government of the World

When I consider my own Weakness, and the discerning Judgment of those who are to be my Audience, I cannot help blaming my self considerably, for this rash Undertaking of mine, it being a Thing I am altogether ill practis'd in and very much unqualified for; I am especially discouraged when I reflect that you are all my intimate Pot Companions who have heard me say a 1000 silly Things in Conversations, and therefore have not that laudable Partiality and Veneration for whatever I shall deliver that Good People commonly have for their Spiritual Guides; that You have no Reverence for my Habit, nor for the Sanctity of my Countenance; that you do not believe me inspir'd or divinely assisted, and therefore will think your Selves at Liberty to assent or dissent approve or disapprove of any Thing I advance, canvassing and sifting it as the private Opinion of one of your Acquaintance. These are great Disadvantages and Discouragements but I am enter'd and must proceed, humbly requesting your Patience and Attention.

I propose at this Time to discourse on the Subject of our last Conversation: the Providence of God in the Government of the World. I shall not attempt to amuse you with Flourishes of Rhetorick, were I master of that deceitful Science because I know ye are Men of substantial Reason and can easily discern between sound Argument and the false Glosses of Oratory; nor shall I endeavour to impose on your Ears, by a musical Accent in delivery, in the Tone of one violently affected with what he says; for well I know that ye are far from being superstitious or fond of unmeaning Noise, and that ye believe a Thing to be no more true for being sung than said. I intend to offer you nothing but plain Reasoning, devoid of Art and Ornament; unsupported by the Authority of any Books or Men how sacred soever; because I know that no Authority is more convincing to Men of Reason than the Authority of Reason itself. It might be judg'd an Affront to your Understandings should I go about to prove this first Principle, the Existence of a Deity and that he is the Creator of the

Universe, for that would suppose you ignorant of what all Mankind in all Ages have agreed in. I shall therefore proceed to observe: 1. That he must be a Being of great Wisdom; 2. That he must be a Being of great Goodness and 3. That he must be a Being of great Power. That he must be a Being of infinite Wisdom, appears in his admirable Order and Disposition of Things, whether we consider the heavenly Bodies, the Stars and Planets, and their wonderful regular Motions, or this Earth compounded of such an Excellent mixture of all the Elements; or the admirable Structure of Animal Bodies of such infinite Variety, and yet every one adapted to its Nature, and the Way of Life it is to be placed in, whether on Earth, in the Air or in the Waters, and so exactly that the highest and most exquisite human Reason, cannot find a fault and say this would have been better so or in another Manner, which whoever considers attentively and thoroughly will be astonish'd and swallow'd up in Admiration.

2. That the Deity is a Being of great Goodness, appears in his giving Life to so many Creatures, each of which acknowledge it a Benefit by their Unwillingness to leave it; in his providing plentiful Sustenance for them all, and making those Things that are most useful, most common and easy to be had; such as Water necessary for almost every Creature's Drink; Air without which few could subsist, the inexpressible Benefits of Light and Sunshine to almost all Animals in general; and to Men the most useful Vegetables, such as Corn, the most useful of Metals as Iron, and the most useful Animals, as Horses, Oxen and Sheep, he has made easiest to raise, or procure in Quantity or Numbers: each of which particulars if considered seriously and carefully would fill us with the highest Love and Affection. 3. That he is a Being of infinite Power appears, in his being able to form and compound such Vast Masses of Matter as this Earth and the Sun and innumerable Planets and Stars, and give them such prodigious Motion, and yet so to govern them in their greatest Velocity as that they shall not flie off out of their appointed Bounds nor dash one against another, to their mutual Destruction; but 'tis easy to conceive his Power, when we are convinc'd of his infinite Knowledge and Wisdom; for if weak and foolish Creatures as we are, by knowing the Nature of a

few Things can produce such wonderful Effects; such as for instance by knowing the Nature only of Nitre and Sea Salt mix'd we can make a Water which will dissolve the hardest Iron and by adding one Ingredient more, can make another Water which will dissolve Gold and render the most Solid Bodies fluid—and by knowing the Nature of Salt Peter Sulphur and Charcoal those mean Ingredients mix'd we can shake the Air in the most terrible Manner, destroy Ships Houses and Men at a Distance and in an Instant, overthrow Cities, rend Rocks into a Thousand Pieces, and level the highest Mountains. What Power must he possess who not only knows the Nature of every Thing in the Universe, but can make Things of new Natures with the greatest Ease and at his Pleasure!

Agreeing then that the World was at first made by a Being of infinite Wisdom, Goodness and Power, which Being we call God; The State of Things ever since and at this Time must be in one of these four following manners, viz.

1. Either he unchangeably decreed and appointed every Thing that comes to pass; and left nothing to the Course of Nature, nor allow'd any Creature free agency. or

2. Without decreeing any thing, he left all to general Nature and the Events of Free Agency in his Creatures, which he never alters or interrupts. or

3. He decreed some Things unchangeably, and left others to general Nature and the Events of Free agency, which also he never alters or interrupts; or

4. He sometimes interferes by his particular Providence and sets aside the Effects which would otherwise have been produced by any of the Above Causes.

I shall endeavour to shew the first 3 Suppositions to be inconsistent with the common Light of Reason; and that the 4th is most agreeable to it, and therefore most probably true.

In the 1. place. If you say he has in the Beginning unchangeably decreed all Things and left Nothing to Nature or free Agency. These Strange Conclusions will necessarily follow; 1. That he is now no more a God. 'Tis true indeed, before he had made such unchangeable Decree, he was a Being of Power, Almighty; but now having determin'd every Thing, he has divested himself of all further Power, he has done and has no more to do, he has ty'd up his Hands, and has now no greater Power than an Idol of Wood or Stone; nor can there be any more Reason for praying to him or worshipping of him, than of such an Idol for the Worshippers can be never the better for such Worship. Then 2. he has decreed some things contrary to the very Notion of a wise and good Being; Such as that some of his Creatures or Children shall do all Manner of Injury to others and bring every kind of Evil upon them without Cause; that some of them shall even blaspheme him their Creator in the most horrible manner; and, which is still more highly absurd that he has decreed the greatest Part of Mankind, shall in all Ages, put up their earnest Prayers to him both in private and publickly in great Assemblies, when all the while he had so determin'd their Fate that he could not possibly grant them any Benefits on that Account, nor could such Prayers be any way available. Why then should he ordain them to make such Prayers? It cannot be imagined they are of any Service to him. Surely it is not more difficult to believe the World was made by a God of Wood or Stone, than that the God who made the World should be such a God as this.

In the 2. Place. If you say he has decreed nothing but left all things to general Nature, and the Events of Free Agency, which he never alters or interrupts. Then these Conclusions will follow; He must either utterly hide him self from the Works of his Hands, and take no Notice at all of their Proceedings natural or moral; or he must be as undoubtedly he is, a Spectator of every thing; for there can be no Reason or Ground to suppose the first—I say there can be no Reason to imagine he would make so glorious a Universe meerly to abandon it. In this Case imagine the Deity looking on and beholding the Ways of his Creatures; some Hero's in Virtue he sees are incessantly indeavouring the Good of others, they labour thro vast difficulties, they suffer incredible Hardships and Miseries to accomplish this End, in hopes to please a Good God, and obtain his Favour, which they earnestly Pray for; what Answer can he make them within himself but this; *take the Reward Chance may give you, I do not intermeddle in these Affairs;* he sees others continually doing all manner of Evil, and bringing by their Actions Misery and Destruction among Mankind: What can he say here but this, *if Chance rewards you I shall not punish you, I am not to be concerned*. He sees the just, the innocent and the Beneficent in the Hands of the wicked and violent Oppressor; and when the good are at the Brink of Destruction they pray to him, *thou, O God, art mighty and powerful to save; help us we beseech thee:* He answers, *I cannot help you, 'tis none of my Business nor do I at all regard these things*. How is it possible to believe a wise and an infinitely Good Being can be delighted in this Circumstance; and be utterly unconcern'd what becomes of the Beings and Things he has created; for thus, we must believe him idle and unactive, and that his glorious Attributes of Power, Wisdom and Goodness are no more to be made use of.

In the Third Place. If you say he has decreed some things and left others to the Events of Nature and Free Agency, Which he never alters or interrupts; Still you unGod him, if I may be allow'd the Expression; he has nothing to do; he can cause us neither Good nor Harm; he is no more to be regarded than a lifeless Image, than Dagon, or Baall, or Bell and the Dragon; and as in both the other Suppositions foregoing, that Being which from its Power is most able to Act, from its Wisdom knows best how to act, and from its Goodness would always certainly act best, is in this Opinion supposed to become the most unactive of all Beings and remain everlastingly Idle; an Absurdity, which when considered or but barely seen, cannot be swallowed without doing the greatest Violence to common Reason, and all the Faculties of the Understanding.

We are then necessarily driven into the fourth Supposition, That the Deity sometimes interferes by his particular Providence, and sets aside the Events which would otherwise have been produc'd in the Course of Nature, or by the Free Agency of Men; and this is perfectly agreeable with what we can know of his Attributes and Perfections: But as some may doubt whether 'tis possible there should be such a Thing as free Agency in Creatures; I shall just offer one Short Argument on that Account and proceed to shew how the Duties of Religion necessary follow the Belief of a Providence. You acknowledge that God is infinitely Powerful, Wise and Good, and also a free Agent; and you will not deny that he has communicated to us part of his Wisdom, Power and Goodness; i.e. he has made us in some Degree Wise, potent and good; and is it then impossible for him to communicate any Part of his Freedom, and make us also in some Degree Free? Is not even his *infinite* Power sufficient for this? I should be glad to hear what Reason any Man can give for thinking in that Manner; 'tis sufficient for me to shew tis not impossible, and no Man I think can shew 'tis improbable, but much more might be offer'd to demonstrate clearly that Men are in some Degree free Agents, and accountable for their Actions; however, this I may possibly reserve for another separate Discourse hereafter if I find Occasion.

Lastly If God does not sometimes interfere by his Providence tis either because he cannot, or because he will not; which of these Positions will you chuse? There is a righteous Nation grievously oppress'd by a cruel Tyrant, they earnestly intreat God to deliver them; If you say he cannot, you deny his infinite Power, which you at first acknowledg'd; if you say he will not, you must directly deny his infinite Goodness. You are then of necessity oblig'd to allow, that 'tis highly reasonable to believe a Providence because tis highly absurd to believe otherwise.

Now if tis unreasonable to suppose it out of the Power of the Deity to help and favour us particularly or that we are out of his Hearing or Notice or that Good Actions do not procure more of his Favour than ill Ones. Then I conclude, that believing a Providence we have the Foundation of all true Religion; for we should love and revere that Deity for his Goodness and thank him for his Benefits; we should adore him for his Wisdom, fear him for his Power, and pray to him for his Favour and Protection; and this Religion will be a Powerful Regulater of our Actions, give us Peace and Tranquility within our own Minds, and render us Benevolent, Useful and Beneficial to others.

1730

Compassion and Regard for the Sick

————— *Mors sola fatetur*
Quantula sunt hominum corpuscula—— Juv.
Post obitum bene facta manent, æternaq; virtus
Non metuit Stygiis nec rapiatur aquis.

Among all the innumerable Species of Animals which inhabit the Air, Earth and Water, so exceedingly different in their Production, their Properties, and the Manner of their Existence, and so varied in Form, that even of the same Kind it can scarce be said there are two Individuals in all Respects alike; it is remarkable there are none, within our Observation, distinguish'd from the rest by this Particular, *that they are by Nature incapable of DISEASES*. The old Poets, how extravagant soever in their Fictions, durst never offend so far against Nature and Probability, as even to feign such a Thing; and though they made *Achilles* invulnerable from Head to Foot, and clad him beside in impenetrable Armour forg'd by the Immortals, yet they were oblig'd to leave one soft Place in his Heel, how small soever, for Destruction to enter at. But though every Animal that hath Life is liable to Death, Man of all other Creatures has the greatest Number of *Diseases* to his Share; whether they are the Effects of our Intemperance and Vice, or are given us that we may have a greater Opportunity of exercising towards each other that Virtue which most of all recommends us to the Deity, I mean *CHARITY*.

The great Author of our Faith, whose Life should be the constant Object of our Imitation, as far as it is not inimitable, always shew'd the greatest Compassion and Regard for the *SICK*; he disdain'd not to Visit and minister Comfort and Health to the meanest of the People, and he frequently inculcated the same Disposition in his Doctrine and Precepts to his Disciples. For this one Thing (in that beautiful Parable of the Traveller wounded by Thieves) the *Samaritan*, (who was esteemed no better than an Heretick or an Infidel by the Orthodox of those Times) is prefer'd to the *Priest* and the *Levite*; because he did not, like them, pass by regardless of the Distress of his Brother Mortal, but when he came to the Place where the half-dead Traveller lay, he *had Compassion on him, and WENT TO HIM, and bound up his Wounds, pouring in Oyl and Wine, and set him on his own Beast, and brought him to an Inn, and TOOK CARE OF HIM.* The Rich Man also is represented as being excluded from the Happiness of Heaven, because he fared sumptuously every Day, and had Plenty of all Things, and yet neglected to comfort and assist his poor Neighbour who was helpless and *full of Sores*, and might perhaps have been revived and restored with small Care, *with the Crums that fell from his Table.* — *I was SICK and ye VISITED me*, is one of the Terms of Admission into Bliss, and the contrary a Cause of Exclusion: That is, as our Saviour himself explains it, *Ye have visited, or ye have not visited, assisted and comforted those who stood in need of it, even tho' they were the least or meanest of Mankind.* This Branch of *Charity* seems essential to the true Spirit of Christianity; and it should be extended to all in general, whether deserving or undeserving, as far as our Power reaches. Of the ten Lepers that were cleansed, nine seem to have been much more unworthy than the tenth, yet in respect of their Disease they equally shared the Goodness of God. And when the great Physician sent forth his Disciples, he always gave them a particular Charge, *that into whatsoever City they entred, they should heal* all *the Sick*, without distinction.

Now tho' in these Days we cannot work Miracles, and are not all Physicians; yet in this time of general Distress by Sickness, there are few Persons that have their Health, but what have Opportunity enough of exercising that humane and Christian Virtue, which teaches a tender Regard for the Afflicted. It is thought by some, that in the present Distemper, a greater Number have been heretofore lost for want of suitable Care and Attendance, than thro' the natural Malignity of the Disease. The Rich have Visitors enough, and Advice enough; but perhaps there may be some poor Families, where not only those few that are well, have their Health endanger'd by the constant Fatigue of Watching Night and Day, but the Sick suffer much for want of Friends to offer their Assistance. The good *Samaritan* gave *Money* to the Host where he had lodg'd his Patient, and said, *TAKE CARE OF HIM, and what thou spendest more, I will repay thee.* If our Circumstances will not afford This, we may at least be helpful in Visiting, Watching, and doing many other kind Things, which the Poor have almost as much in their Power as the Wealthy.

Now if the Considerations of Religion and Humanity have not the Effect they ought to have on the Minds of some, perhaps this Observation, which generally holds true, may have its weight with the Self-interested, *That there are no Kindnesses done by one Man to another, which are remembred so long, and so frequently return'd with Gratitude, as those received in Sickness, whether they are only present Comforts, or assist in restoring Health.*

The Pennsylvania Gazette, March 25, 1731

English Officials for America

We hear from *North-Carolina*, That Governor *Burrington* is arrived there, accompanied by several Gentlemen, who are to have the chief Places of Profit and Trust in that Government.

The Pennsylvania Gazette, May 27, 1731

Apology for Printers

Being frequently censur'd and condemn'd by different Persons for printing Things which they say ought not to be printed, I have sometimes thought it might be necessary to make a standing Apology for my self, and publish it once a Year, to be read upon all Occasions of that Nature. Much Business has hitherto hindered the execution of this Design; but having very lately given extraordinary Offence by printing an Advertisement with a certain *N. B.* at the End of it, I find an Apology more particularly requisite at this Juncture, tho' it happens when I have not yet Leisure to write such a thing in the proper Form, and can only in a loose manner throw those Considerations together which should have been the Substance of it.

I request all who are angry with me on the Account of printing things they don't like, calmly to consider these following Particulars

1. That the Opinions of Men are almost as various as their Faces; an Observation general enough to become a common Proverb, *So many Men so many Minds*.

2. That the Business of Printing has chiefly to do with Mens Opinions; most things that are printed tending to promote some, or oppose others.

3. That hence arises the peculiar Unhappiness of that Business, which other Callings are no way liable to; they who follow Printing being scarce able to do any thing in their way of getting a Living, which shall not probably give Offence to some, and perhaps to many; whereas the Smith, the Shoemaker, the Carpenter, or the Man of any other Trade, may work indifferently for People of all Persuasions, without offending any of them: and the Merchant may buy and sell with Jews, Turks, Hereticks, and Infidels of all sorts, and get Money by every one of them, without giving Offence to the most orthodox, of any sort; or suffering the least Censure or Ill-will on the Account from any Man whatever.

4. That it is as unreasonable in any one Man or Set of Men to expect to be pleas'd with every thing that is printed, as to think that nobody ought to be pleas'd but themselves.

5. Printers are educated in the Belief, that when Men differ in Opinion, both Sides ought equally to have the Advantage of being heard by the Publick; and that when Truth and Error have fair Play, the former is always an overmatch for the latter: Hence they chearfully serve all contending Writers that pay them well, without regarding on which side they are of the Question in Dispute.

6. Being thus continually employ'd in serving all Parties, Printers naturally acquire a vast Unconcernedness as to the right or wrong Opinions contain'd in what they print; regarding it only as the Matter of their daily labour: They print things full of Spleen and Animosity, with the utmost Calmness and Indifference, and without the least Ill-will to the Persons reflected on; who nevertheless unjustly think the Printer

as much their Enemy as the Author, and join both together in their Resentment.

7. That it is unreasonable to imagine Printers approve of every thing they print, and to censure them on any particular thing accordingly; since in the way of their Business they print such great variety of things opposite and contradictory. It is likewise as unreasonable what some assert, *That Printers ought not to print any Thing but what they approve;* since if all of that Business should make such a Resolution, and abide by it, an End would thereby be put to Free Writing, and the World would afterwards have nothing to read but what happen'd to be the Opinions of Printers.

8. That if all Printers were determin'd not to print any thing till they were sure it would offend no body, there would be very little printed.

9. That if they sometimes print vicious or silly things not worth reading, it may not be because they approve such things themselves, but because the People are so viciously and corruptly educated that good things are not encouraged. I have known a very numerous Impression of *Robin Hood's Songs* go off in this Province at 2 s. per Book, in less than a Twelvemonth; when a small Quantity of *David's Psalms* (an excellent Version) have lain upon my Hands above twice the Time.

10. That notwithstanding what might be urg'd in behalf of a Man's being allow'd to do in the Way of his Business whatever he is paid for, yet Printers do continually discourage the Printing of great Numbers of bad things, and stifle them in the Birth. I my self have constantly refused to print any thing that might countenance Vice, or promote Immorality; tho' by complying in such Cases with the corrupt Taste of the Majority, I might have got much Money. I have also always refus'd to print such things as might do real Injury to any Person, how much soever I have been solicited, and tempted with Offers of great Pay; and how much soever I have by refusing got the Ill-will of those who would have employ'd me. I have heretofore fallen under the Resentment of large Bodies of Men, for refusing absolutely to print any of their Party or Personal Reflections. In this Manner I have made my self many Enemies, and the constant Fatigue of denying is

almost insupportable. But the Publick being unacquainted with all this, whenever the poor Printer happens either through Ignorance or much Persuasion, to do any thing that is generally thought worthy of Blame, he meets with no more Friendship or Favour on the above Account, than if there were no Merit in't at all. Thus, as *Waller* says,

> *Poets loose half the Praise they would have got*
> *Were it but known what they discreetly blot;*

Yet are censur'd for every bad Line found in their Works with the utmost Severity.

I come now to the particular Case of the *N. B.* above-mention'd, about which there has been more Clamour against me, than ever before on any other Account.—In the Hurry of other Business an Advertisement was brought to me to be printed; it signified that such a Ship lying at such a Wharff, would sail for *Barbadoes* in such a Time, and that Freighters and Passengers might agree with the Captain at such a Place; so far is what's common: But at the Bottom this odd Thing was added, N. B. *No Sea Hens nor Black Gowns will be admitted on any Terms.* I printed it, and receiv'd my Money; and the Advertisement was stuck up round the Town as usual. I had not so much Curiosity at that time as to enquire the Meaning of it, nor did I in the least imagine it would give so much Offence. Several good Men are very angry with me on this Occasion; they are pleas'd to say I have too much Sense to do such things ignorantly; that if they were Printers they would not have done such a thing on any Consideration; that it could proceed from nothing but my abundant Malice against Religion and the Clergy: They therefore declare they will not take any more of my Papers, nor have any farther Dealings with me; but will hinder me of all the Custom they can. All this is very hard!

I believe it had been better if I had refused to print the said Advertisement. However, 'tis done and cannot be revok'd. I have only the following few Particulars to offer, some of them in my Behalf, by way of Mitigation, and some not much to the Purpose; but I desire none of them may be read when the Reader is not in a very good Humour.

1. That I really did it without the least Malice, and imagin'd the *N. B.* was plac'd there only to make the Advertisement star'd at, and more generally read.

2. That I never saw the Word *Sea-Hens* before in my Life; nor have I yet ask'd the meaning of it; and tho' I had certainly known that *Black Gowns* in that Place signified the Clergy of the Church of *England*, yet I have that confidence in the generous good Temper of such of them as I know, as to be well satisfied such a trifling mention of their Habit gives them no Disturbance.

3. That most of the Clergy in this and the neighbouring Provinces, are my Customers, and some of them my very good Friends; and I must be very malicious indeed, or very stupid, to print this thing for a small Profit, if I had thought it would have given them just Cause of Offence.

4. That if I have much Malice against the Clergy, and withal much Sense; 'tis strange I never write or talk against the Clergy my self. Some have observed that 'tis a fruitful Topic, and the easiest to be witty upon of all others. I can print any thing I write at less Charge than others; yet I appeal to the Publick that I am never guilty this way, and to all my Acquaintance as to my Conversation.

5. That if a Man of Sense had Malice enough to desire to injure the Clergy, this is the foolishest Thing he could possibly contrive for that Purpose.

6. That I got Five Shillings by it.

7. That none who are angry with me would have given me so much to let it alone.

8. That if all the People of different Opinions in this Province would engage to give me as much for not printing things they don't like, as I can get by printing them, I should probably live a very easy Life; and if all Printers were every where so dealt by, there would be very little printed.

9. That I am oblig'd to all who take my Paper, and am willing to think they do it out of meer Friendship. I only desire they would think the same when I deal with them. I thank those who leave off, that they have taken it so long. But I beg they would not endeavour to dissuade others, for that will look like Malice.

10. That 'tis impossible any Man should know what he would do if he was a Printer.

11. That notwithstanding the Rashness and Inexperience of Youth, which is most likely to be prevail'd with to do things that ought not to be done; yet I have avoided printing such Things as usually give Offence either to Church or State, more than any Printer that has followed the Business in this Province before.

12. And lastly, That I have printed above a Thousand Advertisements which made not the least mention of *Sea-Hens* or *Black Gowns*; and this being the first Offence, I have the more Reason to expect Forgiveness.

I take leave to conclude with an old Fable, which some of my Readers have heard before, and some have not.

"A certain well-meaning Man and his Son, were travelling towards a Market Town, with an Ass which they had to sell. The Road was bad; and the old Man therefore rid, but the Son went a-foot. The first Passenger they met, asked the Father if he was not ashamed to ride by himself, and suffer the poor Lad to wade along thro' the Mire; this induced him to take up his Son behind him: He had not travelled far, when he met others, who said, they were two unmerciful Lubbers to get both on the Back of that poor Ass, in such a deep Road. Upon this the old Man gets off, and let his Son ride alone. The next they met called the Lad a graceless, rascally young Jackanapes, to ride in that Manner thro' the Dirt, while his aged Father trudged along on Foot; and they said the old Man was a Fool, for suffering it. He then bid his Son come down, and walk with him, and they travell'd on leading the Ass by the Halter; 'till they met another Company, who called them a Couple of sensless Blockheads, for going both on Foot in such a dirty Way, when they had an empty Ass with them, which they might ride upon. The old Man could bear no longer; My Son, said he, it grieves me much that we cannot please all these People: Let us throw the Ass over the next Bridge, and be no farther troubled with him."

Had the old Man been seen acting this last Resolution, he would probably have been call'd a Fool for troubling himself about the different Opinions of all that were pleas'd to find Fault with him: Therefore, tho' I have a Temper almost as complying as his, I intend not to imitate him in this last Particular. I consider the Variety of Humours among Men, and despair of pleasing every Body; yet I shall not therefore leave off Printing. I shall continue my Business. I shall not burn my Press and melt my Letters.

The Pennsylvania Gazette, June 10, 1731

"A certain St-n-c-tt-r"

Friday Night last, a certain St-n-c-tt-r was, it seems, in a fair way of dying the Death of a Nobleman; for being caught Napping with another Man's Wife, the injur'd Husband took the Advantage of his being fast asleep, and with a Knife began very diligently to cut off his Head. But the Instrument not being equal to the intended Operation, much Struggling prevented Success; and he was oblig'd to content himself for the present with bestowing on the Aggressor a sound Drubbing. The Gap made in the Side of the St-n-c-tt-r's Neck, tho' deep, is not thought dangerous; but some People admire, that when the Person offended had so fair and suitable an Opportunity, it did not enter into his Head to turn St-n-c-tt-r himself.

The Pennsylvania Gazette, June 17, 1731

The Molasses Bill

By way of Boston there is Advice, That a Bill for prohibiting the Importation of Rum, Sugar and Mellasses from the French and Dutch Plantations into the Northern Colonies in America, has pass'd both Houses of Parliament, pursuant to a Petition from the Island of Barbadoes. What Effect this will have, as to raising or falling the Prices of those Commodities and of our Flour, &c. is left to the Judicious to consider.

The Pennsylvania Gazette, June 17, 1731

"A certain C-n-table"

Sure some unauspicious cross-grain'd Planet, in Opposition to *Venus*, presides over the Affairs of Love about this Time. For we hear, that on Tuesday last, a certain C-n-table having made an Agreement with a neighbouring Female, to *Watch* with her that Night; she promised to leave a Window open for him to come in at; but he going his Rounds in the dark, unluckily mistook the Window, and got into a Room where another Woman was in bed, and her Husband it seems lying on a Couch not far distant. The good Woman perceiving presently by the extraordinary Fondness of her Bedfellow that it could not possibly be her Husband, made so much Disturbance as to wake the good Man; who finding somebody had got into his Place without his Leave, began to lay about him unmercifully; and 'twas thought, that had not our poor mistaken Galant, call'd out manfully for Help (as if he were commanding Assistance in the King's Name) and thereby raised the Family, he would have stood no more Chance for his Life between the Wife and Husband, than a captive L—— between two Thumb Nails.

The Pennsylvania Gazette, June 24, 1731

"George is as good as de best"

We are credibly inform'd, that the young Woman who not long since petitioned the Governor, and the Assembly to be divorced from her Husband, and at times industriously solicited most of the Magistrates on that Account, has at last concluded to cohabit with him again. It is said the Report of the Physicians (who in Form examined his *Abilities*, and allowed him to be in every respect *sufficient*,) gave her but small Satisfaction; Whether any Experiments *more satisfactory* have been try'd, we cannot say; but it seems she now declares it as her Opinion, That *George is as good as de best*.

The Pennsylvania Gazette, July 29, 1731

Fighting Bucks

We hear from Hopewell in the Jerseys, that on the 4th past, two Bucks were observed fighting near the new Meeting House there; one of them extraordinary large, supposed to be a Roe-buck; the other small and of the common sort. In company with them was a black Doe, who stood by to see the Engagement. The small Buck proved a full match for the great one, giving him many violent Punches in the Ribs, but in the height of the Battle, they fastned their Horns so strongly together, that they were not able with all their Strength to disengage; and in that condition they were taken. The Doe retreated into the Woods, but being pursued with several Beagle Hounds, she was taken also alive, and they have put her and the large Buck into a boarded Pasture together, in hopes to have a Breed, if the Sizes are not too unsuitable. This is the second Brace of Bucks that have been caught by the Horns this Fall. *Had they not better put 'em up quietly in their Pockets?*

The Pennsylvania Gazette, October 14, 1731

Doctrine to be Preached

Doct. to be preached

That there is one God Father of the Universe.

That he is infinitely good, Powerful and wise.

That he is omnipresent.

That he ought to be worshipped, by Adoration Prayer and Thanksgiving both in publick and private.

That he loves such of his Creatures as love and do good to others: and will reward them either in this World or hereafter.

That Men's Minds do not die with their Bodies, but are made more happy or miserable after this Life according to their Actions.

That Virtuous Men ought to league together to strengthen the Interest of Virtue, in the World: and so strengthen themselves in Virtue.

That Knowledge and Learning is to be cultivated, and Ignnorance dissipated.

That none but the Virtuous are wise.

That Man's Perfection is in Virtue.

1731

Death of a Lion

Boston, Jan. 3. Last Saturday Night, The LYON, King of Beasts, who had travelled all over North America by Sea and Land, died here in a Tan-yard. Like other Kings, his Death was often reported, long before it happened.

The Pennsylvania Gazette, January 25, 1731/2

A Burnt-Offering

We hear from the Jersey side, that a Man near Sahaukan being disordred in his Senses, protested to his Wife that he would kill her immediately, if she did not put her Tongue into his Mouth: She through Fear complying, he bit off a large Piece of it; and taking it between his Fingers threw it into the Fire with these Words, *Let this be for a Burnt-Offering.*

The Pennsylvania Gazette, February 15, 1731/2

Lost Money

Lost last Saturday Night, in Market Street, about 40 or 50 s. if the Finder will bring it to the Printer hereof, who will describe the Marks, he shall have 10 s. Reward.

The Pennsylvania Gazette, March 30, 1732

On Simplicity

There is in Humane Nature a certain charming Quality, innate and original to it, which is called SIMPLICITY. In latter Ages, this has been almost universally exploded, and banished from amongst Men, as the Characteristic of Folly; whilst *Cunning* and *Artifice* have prevailed in its stead, and with equal Justice been dignified with the Titles of Wisdom and Understanding. But I believe the juster Account of the Matter is, that Simplicity is the homespun Dress of Honesty, and Chicanery and Craft are the Tinsel Habits and the false Elegance which are worn to cover the Deformity of Vice and Knavery.

In the first Ages of the World, when Men had no Wants but what were purely natural, before they had refin'd upon their Necessities, and Luxury and Ambition had introduced a Thousand fantastick Forms of Happiness, Simplicity was the Dress and Language of the World, as Nature was its Law. The little Cunning which was then in use, only taught them to ensnare, or to make tame such Animals as were necessary to their Support or their Convenience, and were otherwise too swift or too strong for them; but since these Arts have attain'd their utmost Perfection, Men have practised the same low Stratagems upon one another, and by an infinite Variety of Disguises and well-covered Treacheries, have long since instituted those little Basenesses among the necessary Arts and Knowledges of Life, and practised without Scruple, that which they have long owned without Shame.

But if we look into the History of the World, and into the Characters of those who have had the greatest Names in it, we shall find, that this original Simplicity of Mind has gradually been worn off in every Age, down to the present Time, when there is hardly any Characters of it remaining undefaced. The old Greeks and Romans, whose unperishable Writings have preserved to us the Actions and Manners of their Countrymen, and who were so well studied in all the Forms and reasonable Happinesses of Life, are so full of that just and beautiful Stile and Sentiment, as seems to have been the only proper Method of transcribing the frank and open

Characters of the Heroes they celebrate, and of making them and their Writers immortal.

To prove the natural Charm and Beauty there is in this Simplicity, we need only, at this Day, as false as the World is grown, retire but far enough from great Cities, the Scenes of all worldly Business and Action; and, I believe; the most cunning Man will be obliged to own, the high and sincere Pleasure there is in conversing from the Heart, and without Design. What Relief do we find in the simple and unaffected Dialogues of uncorrupted Peasants, after the tiresome Grimace of the Town! The veriest Double-Dealer in the World is ever hankering after an Opportunity to open his own Heart, tho' perhaps he curses himself after he has done it. We are all forward enough to protest and complain against the Falshood and Treachery of Mankind, tho' the Remedy be always in our own Power, and each is at Liberty to reform himself.

But perhaps we need not be forced always to go into the Country in search of this amiable Complexion of Mind, Simplicity; for I believe it will be found sometimes, that the Men of the truest Genius and highest Characters in the Conduct of the World, (as few of them as rise in any Age) are observed to possess this Quality in the highest Degree. They are Pretenders only, to Policy and Business, who have recourse to Cunning, and the little Chicaneries thereof: for Cunning is but the Ape of Wisdom, as Sheepishness is of Modesty, Impudence of Courage, and Pedantry of Learning.—Cunning, says my Lord *Bacon*, is a sinister or crooked Wisdom, and Dissimulation but a faint kind of Policy; for it asks a strong Wit and a strong Heart, to know when to tell Truth and to do it; therefore they are the weaker sort of Politicians, that are the greatest Dissemblers. And certainly there is a great Difference between a cunning Man and a wise One, not only in point of Honesty but in point of Ability; as there are those that can pack the Cards, who cannot play the Game well.

Cunning is a Vice purely personal, and is with the greatest Difficulty practised in free and mixed Assemblies. A cunning Man is obliged to hunt his Game alone, and to live in the dark; he is uncapable of Counsel and Advice, for his dishonest Purpose dies upon Discovery. A vertuous and an honourable Action only, will bear a Conference and Freedom of Debate. And this is the Part of true Wisdom, to be busy and assistant in a fair and worthy Design. None but Fools are Knaves, for wise Men cannot help being honest. Cunning therefore is the Wisdom of a Fool; one who has Designs that he dare not own.

To draw these loose Thoughts towards an End. If Cunning were any real Excellence in Human Nature, how comes it that the greatest and ablest, the most amiable and worthy of Mankind, are often entirely without it, and vastly above it; while Numbers of the weaker Part are observed to be very expert therein; sordid and ignorant Servants, and dishonest idle Vagabonds, often attain to the highest Perfection in it. Simplicity we are sure is natural, and the highest Beauty of Nature; and all that is excellent in Arts which Men have invented, is either to demonstrate this native Simplicity and Truth in Nature, or to teach us to transcribe and copy in every Thing from it. Simplicity of Speech and Manners is the highest Happiness as well as the greatest Ornament of Life; whereas nothing is so tiresome to one's self, as well as so odious to others, as Disguise and Affectation. Who was ever cunning enough to conceal his being so? No Mask ever hid it self. In a Word, those cunning Men, tho' they are not declared Enemies to the World, yet they are really Spies upon it, and ought in the Justice of Things to be considered and treated as such, whenever they are caught. And to what purpose is all this Craft? To make themselves suspected and avoided by the World in return, and to have never a Friend in it. A Knave cannot have a Friend, any more than he can be one: An honest Man must discover him, a Rascal will betray him. And by this Time I hope my Reader and I are agreed, that Wisdom and Vertue are the same Thing, as Knavery and Cunning are generally so too; and that for the future, we shall resolve to be what we would seem, which is the only sure way not to be afraid to seem what we really are.

Perhaps it is not necessary to add here, that by Simplicity is not at all meant the Pretences to it, which are made now a-days, by many good People, who I believe very honestly mistake the Thing, and while they aim at Simplicity are guilty of very gross Affectation. The Plainness and Integrity of Mind, which is here recommended, is very little concerned in any Quaintness of Habit, or Oddness of Behaviour: Nor is it at all of Importance to Vertue and Simplicity, that great care is taken to appear unfashionable. Again, on the other side, I know very well that the Word *Cunning* did in the ancient Sense of it imply Knowledge. The Word Ken may perhaps be akin to it; it is of Saxon Original, and we are told the Word King is derived from it. I have no Quarrel to this Construction of it; but only against (what it now comes to signify) the little Subtilty of base Minds, who are incapable of great and honest Actions; in which Sense the Word is now commonly used.

After all, I am sensible this crooked Wisdom has established itself by the Force of an unhappy Fashion, too firmly to be immediately exploded; and though I could wish my Reader would be ashamed to live in the World by such a wretched Method, yet I would warn him to be well aware of those that do; and to be sure to arm against them, not with the same Weapons, but those which are of much better Proof, the Integrity of a wise Man, and the Wisdom of an honest one.

The Pennsylvania Gazette, April 13, 1732

"To melt the Pewter Button"

From New-York, we hear, that on Saturday se'nnight, in the Afternoon, they had there most terrible Thunder and Lightning, but no great Damage done. The same Day we had some very hard Claps in these Parts; and 'tis said, that in Bucks County, one Flash came so near a Lad, as, without hurting him, to melt the Pewter Button off the Wasteband of his Breeches. 'Tis well nothing else thereabouts, was made of Pewter.

The Pennsylvania Gazette, June 19, 1732

Anthony Afterwit

Mr. Gazetteer,

I am an honest Tradesman, who never meant Harm to any Body. My Affairs went on smoothly while a Batchelor; but of late I have met with some Difficulties, of which I take the Freedom to give you an Account.

About the Time I first address'd my present Spouse, her Father gave out in Speeches, that if she married a Man he liked, he would give with her 200 *l.* on the Day of Marriage. 'Tis true he never said so to me, but he always receiv'd me very kindly at his House, and openly countenanc'd my Courtship. I form'd several fine Schemes, what to do with this same 200 *l.* and in some Measure neglected my Business on that Account: But unluckily it came to pass, that when the old Gentleman saw I was pretty well engag'd, and that the Match was too far gone to be easily broke off; he, without any Reason given, grew very angry, forbid me the House, and told his Daughter that if she married me he would not give her a Farthing. However (as he foresaw) we were not to be disappointed in that Manner; but having stole a Wedding, I took her home to my House; where we were not in quite so poor a Condition as the Couple describ'd in the Scotch Song, who had

> *Neither Pot nor Pan,*
> *But four bare Legs together;*

for I had a House tolerably furnished, for an ordinary Man, before. No thanks to Dad, who I understand was very much pleased with his politick Management. And I have since learn'd that there are old Curmudgeons (*so called*) besides him, who have this Trick, to marry their Daughters, and yet keep what they might well spare, till they can keep it no longer: But this by way of Digression; *A Word to the Wise is enough*.

I soon saw that with Care and Industry we might live tolerably easy, and in Credit with our Neighbours: But my Wife had a strong Inclination to be a *Gentlewoman*. In Consequence of this, my old-fashioned Looking-Glass was one Day broke, as she said, *No Mortal could tell which way*. However, since we could not be without a Glass in the Room, *My Dear,* says she, *we may as well buy a large fashionable One that Mr.* Such-a-one *has to sell; it will cost but little more than a common Glass, and will be much handsomer and more creditable.* Accordingly the Glass was bought, and hung against the Wall: But in a Week's time, I was made sensible by little and little, *that the Table was by no Means sutable to such a Glass.* And a more proper Table being procur'd, my Spouse, who was an excellent Contriver, inform'd me where we might have very handsome Chairs *in the Way*: And thus, by Degrees, I found all my old Furniture stow'd up into the Garret, and every thing below alter'd for the better.

Had we stopp'd here, we might have done well enough; but my Wife being entertain'd with *Tea* by the Good Women she visited, we could do no less than the like when they visited us; and so we got a *Tea-Table* with all its Appurtenances of *China* and *Silver.* Then my Spouse unfortunately overwork'd herself in washing the House, so that we could do no longer without a *Maid.* Besides this, it happened frequently, that when I came home at *One*, the Dinner was but just put in the Pot; for, *My Dear thought really it had been but Eleven:* At other Times when I came at the same Hour, *She wondered I would stay so long, for Dinner was ready and had waited for me these two Hours.* These Irregularities, occasioned by mistaking the Time, convinced me, that it was absolutely necessary *to buy a Clock*; which my Spouse observ'd, *was a great Ornament to the Room!* And lastly, to my Grief, she was frequently troubled with some Ailment or other, and nothing did her so much Good as *Riding*; And *these Hackney Horses were such wretched ugly Creatures, that*—I bought a very fine pacing Mare, which cost 20 *l.* And hereabouts Affairs have stood for some Months past.

I could see all along, that this Way of Living was utterly inconsistent with my Circumstances, but had not Resolution enough to help it. Till lately, receiving a very severe Dun, which mention'd the next Court, I began in earnest to project Relief. Last Monday my Dear went over the River, to see a Relation, and stay a Fortnight, because *she could not bear the Heat of the Town.* In the Interim, I have taken my Turn to make Alterations, *viz.* I have turn'd away the Maid, Bag and

Baggage (for what should we do with a Maid, who have (except my Boy) none but our selves.) I have sold the fine Pacing Mare, and bought a good Milch Cow, with 3 *l.* of the Money. I have dispos'd of the Tea-Table, and put a Spinning Wheel in its Place, which methinks *looks very pretty*: Nine empty Canisters I have stuff'd with Flax; and with some of the Money of the Tea-Furniture, I have bought a Set of Knitting-Needles; for to tell you a Truth, which I would have go no farther, *I begin to want Stockings.* The stately Clock I have transform'd into an Hour-Glass, by which I gain'd a good round Sum; and one of the Pieces of the old Looking-Glass, squar'd and fram'd, supplies the Place of the Great One, which I have convey'd into a Closet, where it may possibly remain some years. In short, the Face of Things is quite changed; and I am mightily pleased when I look at my Hour-Glass, *what an Ornament it is to the Room.* I have paid my Debts, and find Money in my Pocket. I expect my Dame home next Friday, and as your Paper is taken in at the House where she is, I hope the Reading of this will prepare her Mind for the above surprizing Revolutions. If she can conform to this new Scheme of Living, we shall be the happiest Couple perhaps in the Province, and, by the Blessing of God, may soon be in thriving Circumstances. I have reserv'd the great Glass, because I know her Heart is set upon it. I will allow her when she comes in, to be taken suddenly ill with the *Headach*, the *Stomach-ach*, *Fainting-Fits*, or whatever other Disorder she may think more proper; and she may retire to Bed as soon as she pleases: But if I do not find her in perfect Health both of Body and Mind the next Morning, away goes the aforesaid Great Glass, with several other Trinkets I have no Occasion for, to the Vendue that very Day. Which is the irrevocable Resolution of, Sir,

> *Her loving Husband,* and
> *Your very humble Servant,*
> ANTHONY AFTERWIT.

Postscript, *You know we can return to our former Way of Living, when we please, if* Dad *will be at the Expence of it.*

The Pennsylvania Gazette, July 10, 1732

Celia Single

My Correspondent Mrs. Celia, *must excuse my omitting those Circumstances of her Letter, which point at People* too plainly; *and content herself that I insert the rest as follows.*

Mr. *Gazetteer,*

I must needs tell you, that some of the Things you print do more Harm than Good; particularly I think so of my Neighbour the Tradesman's Letter in one of your late Papers, which has broken the Peace of several Families, by causing Difference between Men and their Wives: I shall give you here one Instance, of which I was an Eye and Ear Witness.

Happening last *Wednesday* Morning to be in at Mrs. *C——ss*'s, when her Husband return'd from Market, among other Things which he had bought, he show'd her some Balls of Thread. *My Dear,* says he, *I like mightily those Stockings which I yesterday saw Neighbour* Afterwit *knitting for her Husband, of Thread of her own Spinning: I should be glad to have some such Stockins my self: I understand that your Maid* Mary *is a very good Knitter, and seeing this Thread in Market, I have bought it, that the Girl may make a Pair or two for me.* Mrs. *Careless* was just then at the Glass, dressing her Head; and turning about with the Pins in her Mouth, *Lord, Child,* says she, *are you crazy? What Time has* Mary *to knit? Who must do the Work, I wonder, if you set her to Knitting?* Perhaps, my Dear, *says he,* you have a mind to knit 'em yourself; I remember, when I courted you, I once heard you say you had learn'd to knit of your Mother. *I knit Stockins for you,* says she, *not I truly; There are poor Women enough in Town, that can knit; if you please you may employ them.* Well, but my Dear, *says he,* you know a penny sav'd is a penny got, a pin a day is a groat a year, every little makes a mickle, and there is neither Sin nor Shame in Knitting a pair of Stockins; why should you express such a mighty Aversion to it? As to *poor* Women, you know we are not People of Quality, we have no Income to maintain us, but what arises from my Labour and Industry; methinks you should not be at all displeas'd, if you have an Opportunity to get something as well as my self. *I wonder,* says she, *how you can propose such a thing to me; did not you always tell me you would maintain me like a Gentlewoman? If I had married* Capt. ——, *he would have scorn'd even to mention Knitting of Stockins.* Prithee, *says he*, (*a little nettled*) what do you tell me of your Captains? If you could have had him, I suppose you would; or perhaps you did not very well like him: If I did promise to maintain you like a Gentlewoman, I suppose 'tis time enough for that when you know how to behave like one; mean while 'tis your Duty to help make me able. How long d'ye think I can maintain you at your present Rate of Living? *Pray*, says she, (somewhat fiercely, and dashing the Puff into the Powder-Box) *don't use me after this Manner, for I assure you I won't bear it. This is the Fruit of your poison* News-papers; *there shall come no more here, I promise you.* Bless us, *says he*, what an unaccountable thing is this! Must a Tradesman's Daughter, and the Wife of a Tradesman, necessarily and instantly be a Gentlewoman? You had no Portion; I am forc'd to work for a Living; if you are too great to do the like, there's the Door, go and live upon your Estate, if you can find it; in short, I don't desire to be troubled w'ye. — What Answer she made, I cannot tell; for knowing that a Man and his Wife are apt to quarrel more violently when before Strangers, than when by themselves, I got up and went out hastily: But I understood from *Mary*, who came to me of an Errand in the Evening, that they dined together pretty peaceably, (the Balls of Thread that had caused the Difference, being thrown into the Kitchen Fire) of which I was very glad to hear.

I have several times in your Paper seen severe Reflections upon us Women, for Idleness and Extravagance, but I do not remember to have once seen any such Animadversions upon the Men. If I were dispos'd to be censorious, I could furnish you with Instances enough: I might mention Mr. *Billiard*, who spends more than he earns, at the Green Table; and would have been in Jail long since, were it not for his industrious Wife: Mr. *Husselcap*, who often all day long leaves his Business for the rattling of Halfpence in a certain Alley: Mr. *Finikin*, who has seven different Suits of fine Cloaths, and wears a Change every Day, while his Wife and Children sit at home half naked: Mr. *Crownhim*, who is always dreaming over the Checquer-board, and cares not how the World goes, so he gets the Game: Mr. *T'otherpot* the Tavern-haunter; Mr. *Bookish*, the everlasting Reader; Mr. *Tweedledum*, Mr. *Toot-a-toot*, and several others, who are mighty diligent at any thing beside their Business. I say, if I were dispos'd to be censorious, I might mention all these, and more; but I hate to be thought a Scandalizer of my Neighbours, and therefore forbear. And for your part, I would advise you, for the future, to entertain your Readers with something else besides People's Reflections upon one another; for remember, that there are Holes enough to be pick'd in your Coat as well as others; and those that are affronted by the Satyrs you may publish, will not consider so much who *wrote*, as who *printed*: Take not this Freedom amiss, from

> *Your Friend and Reader*,
> CELIA SINGLE.

The Pennsylvania Gazette, July 24, 1732

Praise for William Penn

Philadelphia, August 12. Yesterday Afternoon, our Governor having received by Express the agreeable News of the Arrival of the Honourable *THOMAS PENN*, Esq; our Proprietary, at *Chester*, immediately dispatch'd his Secretary thither with his Compliments of Congratulation; and next Morning, attended by the Council, and many other Gentlemen, His Honour our Governor set out for *Chester*, where great Numbers of People from the neighbouring Parts of the Country were flocking together. After Dinner, our Honourable Proprietor, with his Company which was now grown very numerous, set out for *Philadelphia*, and passing the Ferry at *Skuylkill*, was met by the Mayor, Recorder and Aldermen of this City, in whose Name *Andrew Hamilton*, Esq; the Recorder, made the following congratulatory Speech.

May it please our Honourable Proprietor,
The Mayor and Commonalty of the City of Philadelphia, *do most*

joyfully congratulate You, on your safe Arrival into your Province of Pennsylvania.

You are now entring into the Liberties of the City of Philadelphia, *the Capital of your Province, where You have been long and impatiently expected: Be pleased, Sir, to accept from this Corporation, the Acknowledgements due to a Son of its Honourable Founder.*

That generous Charter which he gave this City, those wise and just Laws which he gave to the People of Pennsylvania, *and above all his religious Care in securing to all its Inhabitants that natural Right* Liberty of Conscience, *and Freedom from* Spiritual Tyranny, *will ever continue a Testimony of his great Wisdom and Goodness, in framing a Constitution every way fitted to make a happy People, and be a lasting Monument of his Benevolence to Mankind.*

But he is gone!— and to whom can we so properly own these Obligations, as to the Descendants of that good Man, under whom, next to our gracious Sovereign, the Inhabitants of Philadelphia *derive and enjoy so many valuable Privileges.*

We are indeed strongly prejudiced in favour of a Son *of the great Mr. PENN; We know you have the same Powers of Government, and if You shall imitate his excellent Example, in using them for the Good of the People, as that made his Memory dear to all who lived under his Influence, so this will give you a peculiar Claim to Our Duty and Affections, and lay the Citizens of* Philadelphia *under the strongest Obligations of doing you the most acceptable Services in their Power.*

To which our Honourable Proprietor gave the following Answer.

"I am oblig'd to the City of *Philadelphia*, for this Mark of their Affection to me, and Regard for the Memory of my Father; and shall be pleased with every Opportunity of doing your Corporation any agreeable Service."

The *Proprietor* then proceeding forwards, was welcomed to this City with the Discharge of many Guns from the Ships in our River, and the joyful Acclamations of a Multitude of People, who lined all the Streets through which the Cavalcade (consisting of between Seven and Eight Hundred Horse) passed; and alighting at our Governour's House, was saluted with the Discharge of a large Battery of Cannon on *Society*

Hill. The universal Joy and Satisfaction which appeared on this Occasion, seems a just Tribute to a worthy Son of the Great and Good Mr. *PENN*, whose Memory must ever remain dear to all those who set a just Value on the ample Privileges and Liberties granted by him, and at this Time fully enjoyed by all the Inhabitants of this flourishing Colony.

The Pennsylvania Gazette, August 14, 1732

On Censure or Backbiting

Impia sub dulci melle venena latent.   Ovid.
Naturam expellas furcâ licet, usq; recurret.   Hor.

There is scarce any one Thing so generally spoke against, and at the same time so universally practis'd, as *Censure* or *Backbiting*. All Divines have condemn'd it, all Religions have forbid it, all Writers of Morality have endeavour'd to discountenance it, and all Men hate it at all Times, except only when they have Occasion to make use of it. For my part, after having frankly declar'd it as my Opinion, that the general Condemnation it meets with, proceeds only from a Consciousness in most People that they have highly incurr'd and deserv'd it, I shall in a very fearless impudent Manner take upon me to oppose the universal Vogue of Mankind in all Ages, and say as much in Behalf and Vindication of this decry'd Virtue, as the usual Vacancy in your Paper will admit.

I have call'd it a Virtue, and shall take the same Method to prove it such, as we commonly use to demonstrate any other Action or Habit to be a Virtue, that is, by shewing its Usefulness, and the great Good it does to Society. What can be said to the contrary, has already been said by every body; and indeed it is so little to the purpose, that any body may easily say it: But the Path I mean to tread, has hitherto been trod by no body; if therefore I should meet with the Difficulties usual in tracing new Roads, and be in some Places a little at loss, the Candour of the Reader will the more readily excuse me.

The first Advantage I shall mention, arising from the free Practice of *Censure* or *Backbiting*, is, that it is frequently the Means of preventing powerful, politick, ill-designing Men, from growing too popular for the Safety of a State. Such Men are always setting their best Actions to view, in order to obtain Confidence and Trust, and establish a Party: They endeavour to shine with false or borrow'd Merit, and carefully conceal their real Demerit: (that they fear to be evil spoken of is evident from their striving to cover every Ill with a specious Pretence;) But all-examining CENSURE, with her hundred Eyes and her thousand Tongues, soon discovers and as speedily divulges in all Quarters, every the least Crime or Foible that is a part of their true Character. This clips the Wings of their Ambition, weakens their Cause and Party, and reduces them to the necessity of dropping their pernicious Designs, springing from a violent Thirst of Honour and Power; or, if that Thirst is unquenchable, they are oblig'd to enter into a Course of true Virtue, without which real Grandeur is not to be attained.

Again, the common Practice of *Censure* is a mighty Restraint upon the Actions of every private Man; it greatly assists our otherwise weak Resolutions of living virtuously. *What will the World say of me, if I act thus?* is often a Reflection strong enough to enable us to resist the most powerful Temptation to Vice or Folly. This preserves the Integrity of the Wavering, the Honesty of the Covetous, the Sanctity of some of the Religious, and the Chastity of all Virgins. And, indeed, when People once become regardless of *Censure*, they are arrived to a Pitch of Impudence little inferior to the Contempt of all Laws humane and divine.

The common Practice of *Censure* is also exceedingly serviceable, in helping a Man to *the Knowledge of himself*; a piece of Knowledge highly necessary for all, but acquired by very few, because very few sufficiently regard and value the Censure past by others on their Actions. There is hardly such a Thing as a Friend, sincere or rash enough to acquaint us freely with our Faults; nor will any but an Enemy tell us of what we have done amiss, *to our Faces*; and Enemies meet with little Credit in such Cases, for we believe they speak from Malice and Ill-will: Thus we might always live in the blindest Ignorance of our own Folly, and, while every body reproach'd us in their Hearts, might think our Conduct irreproachable: But Thanks be to Providence, (that has given every Man a natural Inclination to backbite his Neighbour) we now hear of many Things said *of* us, that we shall never hear said *to* us; (for out of Goodwill to us, or Illwill to those that have spoken ill of us, every one is willing enough to tell us how we are censur'd by others,) and we have the Advantage of mending our Manners accordingly.

Another vast Benefit arising from the common Practice of *Backbiting*, is, that it helps exceedingly to a thorough *Knowledge of Mankind*, a Science the most useful of all Sciences. Could we come to know no Man of whom we had not a particular Experience, our Sphere of Knowledge of this Sort would certainly be narrow and confined, and yet at the same Time must probably have cost us very dear. For the crafty tricking Villain would have a vast Advantage over the honest undesigning Part of Men, when he might cheat and abuse almost every one he dealt with, if none would take the Liberty to characterize him among their Acquaintance behind his Back.

Without saying any more in its Behalf, I am able to challenge all the Orators or Writers in the World, to show (with solid Reason) that the few trifling Inconveniencies attending it, bear any Proportion to these vast Benefits! And I will venture to assert to their Noses, that nothing would be more absurd or pernicious than a Law against Backbiting, if such a Law could possibly take Effect; since it would undoubtedly be the greatest Encouragement to Vice that ever Vice met with, and do more towards the encreasing it, than would the Abolishing of all other Laws whatsoever.

I might likewise have mentioned the Usefulness of *Censure* in Society, as it is a certain and an equal Punishment for such Follies and Vices as the common Laws either do not sufficiently punish, or have provided no Punishment for. I might have observed, that were it not for this, we should find the Number of some Sorts of Criminals increased to a Degree sufficient not only to infest, but even to overthrow all good and civil Conversation: But it is endless to enumerate every particular Advantage arising from this glorious Virtue! A

Virtue, which whoever exerts, must have the largest Share of Publick Spirit and Self-denial, the highest Benevolence and Regard to the Good of others; since in This he entirely sacrifices his own Interest, making not only the Persons he accuses, but all that hear him, his Enemies; for all that deserve Censure (which are by far the greatest Number) hate the Censorious;

> *That dangerous Weapon, Wit,*
> *Frightens a Million when a few you hit:*
> *Whip but a Cur as you ride thro' a Town,*
> *And strait his Fellow Curs the Quarrel own:*
> *Each Knave or Fool that's conscious of a Crime,*
> *Tho' he scapes now, looks for't another time.*

A Virtue! decry'd by all that fear it, but a strong Presumption of the Innocence of them that practise it; for they cannot be encouraged to offend, from the least Prospect of Favour or Impunity; their Faults or Failings will certainly meet with no Quarter from others. And whoever practises the Contrary, always endeavouring to excuse and palliate the Crimes of others, may rationally be suspected to have some secret darling Vice, which he hopes will be excused him in return. A Virtue! which however ill People may load it with the opprobrious Names of *Calumny*, *Scandal*, and *Detraction*, and I know not what; will still remain a Virtue, a bright, shining, solid Virtue, of more real Use to Mankind than all the other Virtues put together; and indeed, is the Mother or the Protectress of them all, as well as the Enemy, the Destructress of all kinds of Vice. A Virtue, innately, necessarily, and essentially so; for—— But, dear Reader, large Folio Volumes closely written, would scarce be sufficient to contain all the Praises due to it. I shall offer you at present only one more convincing Argument in its Behalf, *viz.* that you would not have had the Satisfaction of seeing this Discourse so agreeably short as I shall make it, were it not for the just Fear I have of incurring your *Censure*, should I continue to be troublesome by extending it to a greater Length.

The Pennsylvania Gazette, September 7, 1732

Alice Addertongue

Mr. Gazetteer,

I was highly pleased with your last Week's Paper upon SCANDAL, as the uncommon Doctrine therein preach'd is agreeable both to my Principles and Practice, and as it was published very seasonably to reprove the Impertinence of a Writer in the foregoing Thursdays *Mercury*, who at the Conclusion of one of his silly Paragraphs, laments, forsooth, that the *Fair Sex* are so peculiarly guilty of this enormous Crime: Every Blockhead ancient and modern, that could handle a Pen, has I think taken upon him to cant in the same senseless Strain. If to *scandalize* be really a *Crime*, what do these Puppies mean? They describe it, they dress it up in the most odious frightful and detestable Colours, they represent it as the worst of Crimes, and then roundly and charitably charge the whole Race of Womankind with it. Are they not then guilty of what they condemn, at the same time that they condemn it? If they accuse us of any other Crime, they must necessarily *scandalize* while they do it: But to *scandalize* us with being guilty of *Scandal*, is in itself an egregious Absurdity, and can proceed from nothing but the most consummate Impudence in Conjunction with the most profound Stupidity.

This, supposing, as they do, that to scandalize is a Crime; which you have convinc'd all reasonable People, is an Opinion absolutely erroneous. Let us leave then these Ideot Mock-Moralists, while I entertain you with some Account of my Life and Manners.

I am a young Girl of about thirty-five, and live at present with my Mother. I have no Care upon my Head of getting a Living, and therefore find it my Duty as well as Inclination, to exercise my Talent at *CENSURE*, for the Good of my Country folks. There was, I am told, a certain generous Emperor, who if a Day had passed over his Head, in which he had conferred no Benefit on any Man, used to say to his Friends, in Latin, *Diem perdidi*, that is, it seems, *I have lost a Day*. I believe I should make use of the same Expression, if it were possible for a Day to pass in which I had not, or miss'd, an Opportunity to scandalize somebody: But, Thanks be praised, no such Misfortune has befel me these dozen Years.

Yet, whatever Good I may do, I cannot pretend that I first entred into the Practice of this Virtue from a Principle of Publick Spirit; for I remember that when a Child, I had a violent Inclination to be ever talking in my own Praise, and being continually told that it was ill Manners, and once severely whipt for it, the confin'd Stream form'd itself a new Channel, and I began to speak for the future in the Dispraise of others. This I found more agreable to Company, and almost as much so to my self: For what great Difference can there be, between putting your self up, or putting your Neighbour down? *Scandal*, like other Virtues, is in part its own Reward, as it gives us the Satisfaction of making our selves appear better than others, or others no better than ourselves.

My Mother, good Woman, and I, have heretofore differ'd upon this Account. She argu'd that Scandal spoilt all good Conversation, and I insisted that without it there could be no such Thing. Our Disputes once rose so high, that we parted Tea-Table, and I concluded to entertain my Acquaintance in the Kitchin. The first Day of this Separation we both drank Tea at the same Time, but she with her Visitors in the Parlor. She would not hear of the least Objection to any one's Character, but began a new sort of Discourse in some such queer philosophical Manner as this; *I am mightily pleas'd sometimes,* says she, *when I observe and consider that the World is not so bad as People out of humour imagine it to be. There is something amiable, some good Quality or other in every body. If we were only to speak of People that are least respected, there is* such a one *is very dutiful to her Father, and methinks has a fine Set of Teeth;* such a one *is very respectful to her Husband;* such a one *is very kind to her poor Neighbours, and besides has a very handsome Shape;* such a one *is always ready to serve a Friend, and in my Opinion there is not a Woman in Town that has a more agreeable Air and Gait.* This fine kind of Talk, which lasted near half an Hour, she concluded by saying, *I do not doubt but every one of you have made the like Observations, and I should be glad to have the Conversation continu'd upon this Subject.* Just at that Juncture I peep'd in at the Door, and never in my Life before saw such a Set of simple vacant Countenances; they looked somehow neither glad, nor sorry, nor angry, nor pleas'd, nor indifferent, nor attentive; but, (excuse the Simile) like so many blue wooden Images of Rie Doe. I in the Kitchin had already begun a ridiculous Story of Mr. ——'s Intrigue with his Maid, and his Wife's Behaviour upon the Discovery; at some Passages we laugh'd heartily, and one of the gravest of Mama's Company, without making any Answer to her Discourse, got up *to go and see what the Girls were so merry about:* She was follow'd by a Second, and shortly after by a Third, till at last the old Gentlewoman found herself quite alone, and being convinc'd that her Project was impracticable, came her self and finish'd her Tea with us; ever since which *Saul also has been among the Prophets*, and our Disputes lie dormant.

By Industry and Application, I have made my self the Center of all the *Scandal* in the Province, there is little stirring but I hear of it. I began the World with this Maxim, *That no Trade can subsist without Returns*; and accordingly, whenever I receiv'd a good Story, I endeavour'd to give two or a better in the Room of it. My Punctuality in this Way of Dealing gave such Encouragement, that it has procur'd me an incredible deal of Business, which without Diligence and good Method it would be impossible for me to go through. For besides the Stock of Defamation thus naturally flowing in upon me, I practice an Art by which I can pump Scandal out of People that are the least enclin'd that way. Shall I discover my Secret? Yes; to let it die with me would be inhuman.—If I have never heard Ill of some Person, I always impute it to defective Intelligence; *for there are none without their Faults, no not one.* If she is a Woman, I take the first Opportunity to let all her Acquaintance know I have heard that one of the handsomest or best Men in Town has said something in Praise either of her Beauty, her Wit, her Virtue, or her good Management. If you know any thing of Humane Nature, you perceive that this naturally introduces a Conversation turning upon all her Failings, past, present, and to come. To the same purpose, and with the same Success, I cause every Man of Reputation to be praised before his Competitors in Love, Business, or Esteem on Account of any particular Qualification. Near the Times of *Election*, if I find it necessary, I commend every Candidate before some of the opposite Party, listning attentively to what is said of him in answer: (But

Commendations in this latter Case are not always necessary, and should be used judiciously;) of late Years I needed only observe what they said of one another freely; and having for the Help of Memory taken Account of all Information & Accusations received, whoever peruses my Writings after my Death, may happen to think, that during a certain Term, the People of *Pennsylvania* chose into all their Offices of Honour and Trust, the veriest Knaves, Fools and Rascals in the whole Province. The Time of Election used to be a busy Time with me, but this Year, with Concern I speak it, People are grown so good natur'd, so intent upon mutual Feasting and friendly Entertainment, that I see no Prospect of much Employment from that Quarter.

I mention'd above, that without good Method I could not go thro' my Business: In my Father's Life-time I had some Instruction in Accompts, which I now apply with Advantage to my own Affairs. I keep a regular Set of Books, and can tell at an Hour's Warning how it stands between me and the World. In my *Daybook* I enter every Article of Defamation as it is transacted; for Scandals *receiv'd in*, I give Credit; and when I pay them out again, I make the Persons to whom they respectively relate *Debtor*. In my *Journal*, I add to each Story by Way of Improvement, such probable Circumstances as I think it will bear, and in my *Ledger* the whole is regularly posted.

I suppose the Reader already condemns me in his Heart, for this particular of *adding Circumstances*; but I justify that part of my Practice thus. 'Tis a Principle with me, that none ought to have a greater Share of Reputation than they really deserve; if they have, 'tis an Imposition upon the Publick: I know it is every one's Interest, and therefore believe they endeavour, to conceal *all* their Vices and Follies; and I hold, that those People are *extraordinary* foolish or careless who suffer a *Fourth* of their Failings to come to publick Knowledge: Taking then the common Prudence and Imprudence of Mankind in a Lump, I suppose none suffer above *one Fifth* to be discovered: Therefore when I hear of any Person's Misdoing, I think I keep within Bounds if in relating it I only make it *three times* worse than it is; and I reserve to my self the Privilege of charging them with one Fault in four, which, for aught I know, they may be entirely innocent of. You see there are but few so careful of doing Justice as my self; what Reason then have Mankind to complain of *Scandal*? In a general way, the worst that is said of us is only half what *might* be said, if all our Faults were seen.

But alas, two great Evils have lately befaln me at the same time; an extream Cold that I can scarce speak, and a most terrible Toothach that I dare hardly open my Mouth: For some Days past I have receiv'd ten Stories for one I have paid; and I am not able to ballance my Accounts without your Assistance. I have long thought that if you would make your Paper a Vehicle of Scandal, you would double the Number of your Subscribers. I send you herewith Account of 4 *Knavish Tricks*, 2 *crackt M—n–ds*, 5 *Cu–ld-ms*, 3 *drub'd Wives*, and 4 *Henpeck'd Husbands*, all within this Fortnight; which you may, as Articles of News, deliver to the Publick; and if my Toothach continues, shall send you more; being, in the mean time,   *Your constant Reader,*
                           ALICE ADDERTONGUE.

I thank my Correspondent Mrs. Addertongue *for her Good-Will; but desire to be excus'd inserting the Articles of News she has sent me; such Things being in Reality* no News at all.

The Pennsylvania Gazette, September 12, 1732

Men are Naturally Benevolent
as Well as Selfish

To the Printer of the GAZETTE.

SIR,

It is the Opinion of some People, that Man is a Creature altogether selfish, and that all our Actions have at Bottom a View to private Interest; If we do good to others, it is, say they, because there is a certain Pleasure attending virtuous Actions. But how Pleasure comes to attend a virtuous Action, these Philosophers are puzzled to shew, without contradicting their first Principles, and acknowledging that Men are *naturally* benevolent as well as selfish. For whence can arise the Pleasure you feel after having done a good-natured Thing, if not hence, that you had *before* strong humane and kind Inclinations in your Nature, which are by such Actions in some Measure gratified?

I am told that a late ingenious Author, enquiring why we approve and disapprove of Actions done many Ages since, which can no way be suppos'd to affect our present Interest, conceives that we have a certain internal *Moral Sense*, which tastes the Beauty of a rational benevolent Action, and the Deformity of an ill-natured cruel one; and that our consequent Judgment is as involuntary as when the Tongue is apply'd to Aloes, and we can by no Act of the Will prevail with the Mind to acknowledge it tastes like Honey. However this be, the Fact is certain, that we do approve and disapprove of Actions which cannot in the least influence our present Affairs. How could this happen, if we did not in contemplating such Actions, find something agreeable or disagreeable to our natural Inclinations as Men, that is, to our benevolent Inclinations?

Let this serve as an Introduction to a short Story, which I have translated from the French, for the Pleasure of your Readers, who will therein find wherewith to exercise their *moral Sense* of Tasting, if such a Sense they have. The Writer delivers it as a known Affair, transacted but a few Years since. It is as follows.

'A certain French Merchant, remarkable for his Honesty and Uprightness, which had procured him the Confidence of the greatest Traders in *Europe*, having suffered very considerable Losses at Sea, followed by the Bankrupcy of several who were deeply in his Debt, fell at length into so great Necessity, that he resolved to visit *Paris* in quest of Succours. He addressed himself to all his old Correspondents, acquainted them with his Misfortunes, and prayed them to help him in beginning the World again; assuring those to whom he owed any thing, that he had no greater Desire than to pay them, and that he should die contented if he might be so happy as to accomplish it. All equally affected with his Condition, promised to assist him.

'One only inexorable, to whom he owed 1000 Crowns, took him precisely in these Circumstances, and threw him into Prison, absolutely resolved there to let him rot, rather than risque longer what was his due.

'The Son of this Merchant, aged about two and twenty Years, informed of the sorrowful Situation of his Father, arrives at *Paris*, goes and throws himself at the Feet of the pitiless Creditor, and there dissolving in Tears, intreats him by every Thing that is most touching, to restore him his Father; protesting solemnly, that if he would not thus make himself an Obstacle to their Hopes of being re-establish'd in their Affairs, he should certainly be the first payed.

'But if this fail'd to move, he conjures him to have Pity of his Youth, and to be sensible to the Unhappinesses of a Mother, charg'd with seven or eight young Children, who are reduc'd to Beggary, and perish: And in fine, if nothing was capable to touch him, at least that he would permit him to put himself in his Father's Place, who by his greater Skill in Business would probably sooner come to give him entire Satisfaction. In uttering these last Words, he so tenderly press'd his Knees in hope the Request would be granted, that this Man, so hard and inflexible, struck with the Sight of so much Virtue at his Feet, raised the young Man and embrac'd him in his Turn, with Eyes all bathed in Tears: Ah! my Son, said he, your Father shall come out. So much Love, and so much Respect for him, makes me even die with Shame. I have resisted too long; let me efface forever the Remembrance of it. I have one only Daughter, and she is worthy of you. She would do as much for me as you for your Father. I give her to you with all my Wealth, accept her; and let us run to your Father, and demand his Consent.

'This tender Scene finished through all that the purest Generosity might inspire on such Occasions, they ran to renew it at the Dungeon of the poor Prisoner. But what was his Joy and his Surprize! He saw his Son, of whose Arrival at *Paris* he had not known; and in the same Moment he saw him at the Top of Fortune and Happiness. The Day of Marriage was fixed, all the Creditors were payed by the Father-in-law, and the Merchant even in these so delicate Circumstances, found himself free enough to take their Receipts. In fine, they live

for the Reckoning; Mr. *R. Brockden*, Master of the House, suspecting it to be a Counterfeit, went with it immediately to *A. Hamilton*, Esq; (under Pretence of going out to get Change) who caused them presently to be apprehended. Upon Examination, two of them appeared innocent, and were discharged; the third, who offer'd to pass the Bill, being ask'd how he came by it, answer'd that he brought Hogs to Town to sell, and had taken it of a Woman unknown in the Market: Upon searching him, two more of the same sort were found in his Pocket-book, all which he said he had taken for Pork. From the Indian Prince he was carried over to another Tavern, where he had put up his Horse, in order to see if he had any Bags wherein more Bills might be found: While the Examination was continuing there, a Woman Stranger in the outer Room was observed to appear somewhat concern'd; upon which she was call'd in, and ask'd, if she knew that Man? she answer'd Yes, he was her Brother; being ask'd if she had any Money about her, the Man was seen to wink at her, and she answer'd, No; but attempting to slide her Hand into her Pocket, they prevented her, and brought the Woman of the House to search her, who found in her Pocket twenty-three 20 *s.* Bills of the same Sort. The Fellow finding the Story of the Hogs would not answer, nor any other Shuffles avail him any thing, betook himself at last to make an ingenuous Confession. He said that one *Grindal* who arrived this Summer in Capt. Blair from *Ireland*, got 600 20 *s.* Bills printed there from a Pattern he carried home last Year; that when he came here, he admitted one *Watt* into the Secret, and gave him a Number of the Bills to pass and exchange in *Pennsylvania*, while he went into the Jersies on the same Account, altering his Name to *Thomson* lest a Wife he had married at New-Garden should hear of him; and that they were to meet next Christmas at *Philadelphia*, and divide the Profits: That *Watt* had communicated the Thing to him, and given him Twenty-seven Bills to pass, of which he was to have a Share for himself; telling him, to persuade him to it, that it was no Sin, for it would make Money plentier among poor People. He said he had as yet pass'd but one, of which the Change 19 *s.* was found in his Pocket. He could not tell where *Grindal* might be at this Time in the Jersies, but he inform'd that *Watt* was at Eastown in Chester County. Officers were immediately dispatch'd in quest of him, who rid all Night, surpriz'd him in his Bed about Day-break, and guarded him to Town. After Examination he was committed to Prison, to keep company with his Friend the Pork-seller, who it seems has *brought his Hogs to a fine Market*. Tis hoped that by Christmas we shall see *Grindal* here also, that he may (according to Agreement) *share the Profits with 'em*. The Bills they have attempted to counterfeit are of the last Impression; the Counterfeits might pass with many People who do not take much Notice, but they have imitated the Paper very ill, that of the new Bills being thick and stiff, and the Counterfeits soft and flimsy. What is most surprising is, that the Counterfeiters, with all their care and exactness, have entirely omitted numbering their Bills; at least none of those are number'd which are seiz'd. Was this Infatuation, or were they afraid they should not number them right?

The Pennsylvania Gazette, December 19, 1732

Yesterday, being Market Day, Watt who was concern'd in the Counterfeit Money, as mentioned in one of our late Papers, receiv'd part of his Punishment, being whipt, pilloried and cropt. He behaved so as to touch the Compassion of the Mob, and they did not fling at him (as was expected) neither Snow-balls nor any Thing else. We hear that Grindal, the Importer of the Bills, and chief Person concern'd, was taken in the Jersies, but afterwards made his Escape. In his Pocket-Book was found the Account of Charge, so much to the Printer, so much for engraving the Plates, so much for Paper, &c.

The Pennsylvania Gazette, January 11, 1732/3

Rules for a Club Formerly Established in Philadelphia

Previous question, to be answer'd at every meeting.

Have you read over these queries this morning, in order to

consider what you might have to offer the Junto touching any one of them? viz.

'1. Have you met with any thing in the author you last read, remarkable, or suitable to be communicated to the Junto? particularly in history, morality, poetry, physic, travels, mechanic arts, or other parts of knowledge.

'2. What new story have you lately heard agreeable for telling in conversation?

'3. Hath any citizen in your knowledge failed in his business lately, and what have you heard of the cause?

'4. Have you lately heard of any citizen's thriving well, and by what means?

'5. Have you lately heard how any present rich man, here or elsewhere, got his estate?

'6. Do you know of any fellow citizen, who has lately done a worthy action, deserving praise and imitation? or who has committed an error proper for us to be warned against and avoid?

'7. What unhappy effects of intemperance have you lately observed or heard? of imprudence? of passion? or of any other vice or folly?

'8. What happy effects of temperance? of prudence? of moderation? or of any other virtue?

'9. Have you or any of your acquaintance been lately sick or wounded? If so, what remedies were used, and what were their effects?

'10. Who do you know that are shortly going voyages or journies, if one should have occasion to send by them?

'11. Do you think of any thing at present, in which the Junto may be serviceable to *mankind*? to their country, to their friends, or to themselves?

'12. Hath any deserving stranger arrived in town since last meeting, that you heard of? and what have you heard or observed of his character or merits? and whether think you, it lies in the power of the Junto to oblige him, or encourage him as he deserves?

'13. Do you know of any deserving young beginner lately set up, whom it lies in the power of the Junto any way to encourage?

'14. Have you lately observed any defect in the laws of your *country*, of which it would be proper to move the legislature for an amendment? Or do you know of any beneficial law that is wanting?

'15. Have you lately observed any encroachment on the just liberties of the people?

'16. Hath any body attacked your reputation lately? and what can the Junto do towards securing it?

'17. Is there any man whose friendship you want, and which the Junto or any of them, can procure for you?

'18. Have you lately heard any member's character attacked, and how have you defended it?

'19. Hath any man injured you, from whom it is in the power of the Junto to procure redress?

'20. In what manner can the Junto, or any of them, assist you in any of your honourable designs?

'21. Have you any weighty affair in hand, in which you think the advice of the Junto may be of service?

'22. What benefits have you lately received from any man not present?

'23. Is there any difficulty in matters of opinion, of justice, and injustice, which you would gladly have discussed at this time?

'24. Do you see any thing amiss in the present customs or proceedings of the Junto, which might be amended?'

————————

Any person to be qualified, to stand up, and lay his hand on his breast, and be asked these questions; viz.

'1. Have you any particular disrespect to any present members?—*Answer.* I have not.

'2. Do you sincerely declare that you love mankind in general; of what profession or religion soever?—*Answ.* I do.

'3. Do you think any person ought to be harmed in his body, name or goods, for mere speculative opinions, or his external way of worship?—*Ans.* No.

'4. Do you love truth for truth's sake, and will you endeavour impartially to find and receive it yourself and communicate it to others?—*Answ.* Yes.'

1732

Proposals and Queries to be Asked the Junto

Proposals

That P S and A N be immediately invited into the Junto.

That all New Members be qualified by the 4 qualifications and all the old ones take it.

That these Queries be copied at the beginning of a Book and be read distinctly each Meeting with a Pause between each while one might fill and drink a Glass of Wine.

That if they cannot all be gone thro' in one Night we begin the next where we left off, only such as particularly regard the Junto to be read every Night.

That it be not hereafter the Duty of any Member to bring Queries but left to his Discretion.

That an old Declamation be without fail read every Night when there is no New One.

That Mr. Brientnals Poem on the Junto be read once a Month, and hum'd in Consort, by as many as can hum it.

That once a Month in Spring, Summer and Fall the Junto meet of a Sunday in the Afternoon in some proper Place cross the River for Bodily Exercise.

That in the aforesaid Book be kept Minutes thus

Fryday June 30. 1732.

Present ABCDEF &c.

1. HP read this Maxim viz. or this Experiment viz or &c.
5. Lately arriv'd one —— of such a Profession or such a Science &c.
7. XY grew rich by this Means &c.

That these Minutes be read once a Year at the Anniversary.

That all Fines due be immediately paid in, and that penal Laws for Queries and Declamations be abolish'd only he who is absent above ten Times in the Year, to pay 10s. towards the Anniversary Entertainment.

That the Secretary for keeping the Minutes be allow'd one Shilling per Night, to be paid out of the Money already in his Hands.

That after the Queries are begun reading, all Discourse foreign to them shall be deem'd impertinent.

When any thing from Reading an Author is mention'd, if

it excead   lines and the Junto require it; The Person shall
bring the Passage, or an Abstract of it, in Writing, the next
Night, if he has it not with him.

When the Books of the Library come: Every Member shall
undertake some Author, that he may not be without Observations to communicate.

Queries to be ask'd the Junto

Whence comes the Dew that stands on the Outside of a
Tankard that has cold Water in it in the Summer Time?

Does the Importation of Servants increase or advance the
Wealth of our Country?

Would not an Office of Insurance for Servants be of Service, and what Methods are proper for the erecting such an
Office?

Qu. Whence does it proceed, that the Proselytes to any
Sect or Persuasion generally appear more zealous than those
who are bred up in it?

Answ. I Suppose that People *bred* in different Persuasions
are nearly zealous alike. He that changes his Party is either
sincere, or not sincere; that is he either does it for the sake of
the Opinions merely, or with a View of Interest. If he is sincere and has no View of Interest; and considers before he
declares himself, how much Ill will he shall have from those
he leaves, and that those he is about to go among will be apt
to suspect his Sincerity: if he is not really zealous he will not
declare; and therefore must be zealous if he does declare. If
he is not sincere, He is oblig'd at least to put on an Appearance of great Zeal, to convince the better, his New Friends
that he is heartily in earnest, for his old ones he knows dislike
him. And as few Acts of Zeal will be more taken Notice of
than such as are done against the Party he has left, he is
inclin'd to injure or malign them, because he knows they
contemn and despise him. Hence one Renegade is (as the
Proverb says) worse than 10 Turks.

Qu. Can a Man arrive at Perfection in this Life as some
Believe; or is it impossible as others believe?

A. Perhaps they differ in the meaning of the Word Perfection.

I suppose the Perfection of any Thing to be only the greatest the Nature of that Thing is capable of;

different Things have different Degrees of Perfection; and the same thing at different Times.

Thus an Horse is more perfect than an Oyster yet the Oyster may be a perfect Oyster as well as the Horse a perfect Horse.

And an Egg is not so perfect as a Chicken, nor a Chicken as a Hen; for the Hen has more Strength than the Chicken, and the Chicken more Life than the Egg: Yet it may be a perfect Egg, Chicken and Hen.

If they mean, a Man cannot in this Life be so perfect as an Angel, it may be true; for an Angel by being incorporeal is allow'd some Perfections we are at present incapable of, and less liable to some Imperfections that we are liable to.

If they mean a Man is not capable of being so perfect here as he is capable of being in Heaven, that may be true likewise. But that a Man is not capable of being so perfect here, as he is capable of being here; is not Sense; it is as if I should say, a Chicken in the State of a Chicken is not capable of being so perfect as a Chicken is capable of being in that State. In the above Sense if there may be a perfect Oyster, a perfect Horse, a perfect Ship, why not a perfect Man? that is as perfect as his present Nature and Circumstances admit?

Quest. Wherein consists the Happiness of a rational Creature?

Ans. In having a Sound Mind and a healthy Body, a Sufficiency of the Necessaries and Conveniencies of Life, together with the Favour of God, and the Love of Mankind.

Qu. What do you mean by a sound Mind?

A. A Faculty of reasoning justly and truly in searching after and discovering such Truths as relate to my Happiness. Which Faculty is the Gift of God, capable of being improv'd by Experience and Instruction, into Wisdom.

Q. What is Wisdom?

A. The Knowledge of what will be best for us on all Occasions and of the best Ways of attaining it.

Q. Is any Man wise at all Times, and in all Things?

A. No; but some are much more frequently wise than others.

Q. What do you mean by the Necessaries of Life?

A. Having wholesome Food and Drink wherewith to satis-fie Hunger and Thirst, Cloathing and a Place of Habitation fit to secure against the inclemencies of the Weather.

Q. What do you mean by the Conveniencies of Life?

A. Such a Plenty [   ]

And if in the Conduct of your Affairs you have been de-ceived by others, or have committed any Error your self, it will be a Discretion in you to observe and note the same, and the Defailance, with the Means or Expedient to repair it.

No Man truly wise but who hath been deceived.

Let all your observations be committed to writing every Night before you go to Sleep.

Query, Whether it is worth a Rational Man's While to forego the Pleasure arising from the present Luxury of the Age in Eating and Drinking and artful Cookery, studying to gratify the Appetite for the Sake of enjoying healthy Old Age, a Sound Mind and a Sound Body, which are the Advantages reasonably to be expected from a more simple and temperate Diet.

Whether those Meats and Drinks are not the best, that con-tain nothing in their natural Tastes, nor have any Thing added by Art so pleasing as to induce us to Eat or Drink when we are not athirst or Hungry or after Thirst and Hunger are sat-isfied; Water for Instance for Drink and Bread or the Like for Meat?

Is there any Difference between Knowledge and Prudence?

If there is any, which of the two is most Eligible?

Is it justifiable to put private Men to Death for the Sake of publick Safety or Tranquility, who have committed no Crime?

As in the Case of the Plague to stop Infection, or as in the Case of the Welshmen here Executed.

Whether Men ought to be denominated Good or ill Men from their Actions or their Inclinations?

If the Sovereign Power attempts to deprive a Subject of his Right, (or which is the same Thing, of what he thinks his Right) is it justifiable in him to resist if he is able?

What general Conduct of Life is most suitable for Men in such Circumstances as most of the Members of the Junto are; Or, of the many Schemes of Living which are in our Power to pursue, which will be most probably conducive to our Happiness.

Which is best to make a Friend of, a wise and good Man that is poor; or a Rich Man that is neither wise nor good? Which of the two is the greatest Loss to a Country, if they both die?

Which of the two is happiest in Life?

Does it not in a general Way require great Study and intense Application for a Poor Man to become rich and Powerful, if he would do it, without the Forfeiture of his Honesty?

Does it not require as much Pains, Study and Application to become truly Wise and strictly Good and Virtuous as to become rich?

Can a Man of common Capacity pursue both Views with Success at the same Time?

If not, which of the two is it best for him to make his whole Application to?

1732

On Drunkenness

To the Printer of the GAZETTE.

I was much pleas'd with the short Caution you gave in one of your late Papers, on Occasion of a Woman whose sudden Death the Coroner's Inquest ascrib'd to the violent Effect of strong Drink; and being my self related in the nearest manner to one, on whom that Caution seem'd to have some good Effect, I could wish you would pursue it further, in which perhaps you may oblige others beside me: For it is now become the Practice of some otherwise discreet Women, instead of a Draught of Beer and a Toast, or a Hunk of Bread and Cheese, or a wooden Noggin of good Porridge and Bread, as our good old English Custom is, or Milk and Bread boiled, or Tea and Bread and Butter, or Milk-Coffee, &c. they must have their two or three DRAMS in a Morning; by which, as I believe, their Appetite for wholesome Food is taken away, and their Minds stupified, so that they have no longer that prudent Care for their Family, to manage well the Business of their Station, nor that regard for Reputation, which good Women ought to have. And tho' they find their Husband's Affairs every Day going backward thro' their Negligence, and themselves want Necessaries; tho' there be no Bread in the House, and the Children almost barefoot this cold Weather, yet, as if Drinking Rum were part of their Religious Worship, they never fail their constant daily Sacrifice. It is not long since I was present at the following Scene. Enters one who was once a handsome Woman, but now with bloated Face and swollen Legs, *How do you do, Neighbour?* Indifferent. *Bless me, it's very cold, and I've no Wood at home; but I'll go down to ——, and they'll help me to Wood; for they have a penny to spend, and a penny to lend, and a penny to lay up. Come, can't you give us a Dram?* No, I wish I had one. *Come, I've got a Penny.* And I've got but a Penny, if more would save my Life I ha'nt it. *Come then, I've got two pence, and your Penny will fetch half a Pint of Rum; and you shall be two-pence another time.* So away goes the half-pint Bottle. *And you shall find Sugar, and a little Bit of Butter, and that's pure good this cold Weather.* Judge you how finely things are like to be carried on in the Families over which such Women are placed. I for any part shall never more speak against TEA; let those that like it enjoy it for ever: Tea will not take away their Sense of Shame and of Duty, nor their Fear of Censure: Their Pride in this Particular, may make them careful, and industrious, and frugal in other Respects, that they may have wherewith to support their Rank and Credit in the World. They may still preserve their Modesty, and their natural Affection; But Drunkenness is utterly inconsistent with any one of those Virtues which make Women amiable or valuable to Men. *I am your Friend and Reader,* &c.

Altho' it has happened, that of the four unfortunate Wretches, who within these few Weeks have died suddenly in this County, by excessive Drinking of strong Liquor, two were indeed Women; yet it must be acknowledged, that this Kind of Intemperance is by far more frequent among the Men than among them: And perhaps 'tis owing to the general Moderation of Women in the Use of strong Drink, that the present Race of Englishmen retain any considerable Degree of the Health, Robustness, and Activity of their Ancestors. There are, however, some, it seems, who, directly contrary to the Advice given by the Angel to the Mother of the strongest Man, instead of refraining all Drink that may intoxicate, are determin'd to drink nothing else. Their Fault will be its own Punishment: But what Crimes have their unhappy Offspring committed, that they are condemn'd to bring Misery into the World with them, to be born with the Seeds of many future Diseases in their Constitution.

The Practice of Drinking Drams is so general, and so well establish'd in the World at present, that some People are apt to wonder, and scarce think it possible, when they are told, that Men formerly lived and performed their Labour without it; and that 'tis scarce 50 Years since distill'd Spirits have been commonly used in England. They were first only to be found in the Apothecary's Shop, and prescrib'd by Physicians in extraordinary Cases, a *Drachm* at a time, whence we have the present Word *Dram*, but it signifies now much more than the *eighth part of an Ounce*. Our Forefathers, 'tis true, have had Beer many Ages; but within the Memory of Men, Temperance in Drinking was so universal amongst them, especially in the inland Country Places, that a good old Man not long since dead with us, could speak it as an extraordinary Thing, *Verily I tell thee, Friend, I knew a Smith in ooer Toon, who would sometimes go to th' Alehouse, when he had no other Business there, but to drink!* Observe, it was *a Smith*, which is allow'd to be a thirsty Trade, *and but one Smith!* I am afraid we have never a modern Miracle on the other side to match it; that is to say, *A Smith*, or indeed any other Tradesman, *in our Town, who never goes to the Tavern* but when he has other Business there *beside Drinking*.

That decrying of *Drams* may not be thought the Fancy of whimsical particular Men, who love Singularity, and to talk against every thing that is in Fashion; see the united Wisdom of the British Nation, King, Lords, and Commons in Parliament assembled, condemning that Practice, in the Act made 1729, for restraining it. The Preamble is worth transcribing. *Whereas the Drinking of Spirits and strong Waters is become very common amongst the People of Inferior Rank, and the constant Use thereof tends greatly to the Destruction of their Healths, enervating them, and rendring them unfit for useful Labour, intoxicating them, and debauching their Morals, and leading them into all manner of Vices and Wickedness, the Prevention whereof would be of the greatest publick Good and Benefit,* &c. 'Tis pity that Act had not fully its desired Effect.

I might cite the Opinions of our most famous Physicians, who are universally against the Practice we are speaking of: but I have not Room, and can only at present give a Paragraph or two from Dr. *Allen*'s *Synopsis of Physick*, lately published with considerable Applause. In his Chapter of *POISONS*, having treated of mineral, vegetable, and animal *Poisons*, he concludes with this.

DISTILLED POISONS.

'There is yet another Family of Poisons, to wit, *Vinous Spirits* and *distilled intoxicating Liquors*; for the too frequent and plentiful devouring of these (as the ill Custom obtains) hath killed as many Thousands of Men as there are Stars in the Skie; nay, ten times ten hundred Thousands have died by these, more than by all the rest of Poisons whatever, which is not in the least to be doubted of; wherefore I usually call this pernicious Mischief, by way excellence, THE HARM, whether in jest or earnest I need not say. It not only occasions violent Distempers in a great many, but also sometimes *sudden Death* in some; for which Reason, if it does not deserve the Name of *Poison*, what else it should be called I can neither learn nor conjecture.

'An ungrateful Burthen lies upon generous Physicians. Those who guzzle burning Spirits Night and Day, according to their detestable Custom, perpetually tippling *liquid Fire*, when they have extinguished all Concoctions, enervated all the Solids, and corrupted the Liquids; and the Fabrick a long while staggering is now ready to fall, then they seek our Help. What is to be done? The Office of a Scavenger is to be performed; and perhaps when the Drain is made, and by chance the Matter retrieved, they presently return to the same Practice again, as a Dog to the Vomit, or a Sow to the Mire; and prodigal of their Lives, they shorten the remaining part of their Days. What must Physicians, or what can Divines do? Medicines can be of no Service, and they will not hearken to Counsel. All Things will be in vain, they rush into the Embraces of the wicked Poison, they become stupid and blind, deafer to Reason and Counsel than *Marpassus's Rocks*, they thirst forever, and drink as if bit by the *Dipsas*, and the more they drink the more they covet of the *deadly distilled Water*, with which, in as much Haste as they can, they close the Scene, even at the Point of Death calling for the Bottle. Most miserable! and deplorable!

'O happy Temperance! never too much to be praised! of the *first*, which thou mad'st the *golden* Age, *the Ornament and Safeguard!* thy own Persuasive and Value! sometimes to be seen in the joyful Times of *Saturn*! worshipped and adored by all pure and pious Souls in all Ages. Thou art, if any thing in the Earth, *the true Composer of Archæus*, and the Preserver of a sound Mind in a sound Body. Thou lead'st thy Adorers right on the way to a long and happy old Age, with a pleasant and youthful, graceful and lovely Countenance. To conclude, thou art adorned with the Praises even of thy Enemies, and art counted lovely by them, with whom, when thou art cast off, there remains the Curse of *Satyricus*, *Let them see this Virtue, and waste away, since they have forsaken it.*'

The Pennsylvania Gazette, February 1, 1732/3

A Meditation on a Quart Mugg

Wretched, miserable, and unhappy Mug! I pity thy luckless Lot, I commiserate thy Misfortunes, thy Griefs fill me with Compassion, and because of thee are Tears made frequently to burst from my Eyes.

How often have I seen him compell'd to hold up his Handle at the Bar, for no other Crime than that of being empty; then snatch'd away by a surly Officer, and plung'd suddenly into a Tub of cold Water: Sad Spectacle, and Emblem of human Penury, oppress'd by arbitrary Power! How often is he hurry'd down into a dismal Vault, sent up fully laden in a cold Sweat, and by a rude Hand thrust into the Fire! How often have I seen it obliged to undergo the Indignities of a dirty Wench; to have melting Candles dropt on its naked Sides, and sometimes in its Mouth, to risque being broken into a thousand Pieces, for Actions which itself was not guilty of! How often is he forced into the Company of boisterous Sots, who lay all their Nonsense, Noise, profane Swearing, Cursing, and Quarreling, on the harmless Mug, which speaks not a Word! They overset him, maim him, and sometimes turn him to Arms offensive or defensive, as they please; when of himself he would not be of either Party, but would as willingly stand still. Alas! what Power, or Place, is provided, where this poor Mug, this unpitied Slave, can have Redress of his Wrongs and Sufferings? Or where shall he have a Word of Praise bestow'd on him for his Well-doings, and faithful Services? If he prove of a large size, his Owner curses him, and says he will devour more than he'll earn: If his Size be small, those whom his Master appoints him to serve will curse him as much, and perhaps threaten him with the Inquisition of the Standard. Poor Mug, unfortunate is thy Condition! Of thy self thou wouldst do no Harm, but much Harm is done with thee! Thou art accused of many Mischiefs; thou art said to administer Drunkenness, Poison, and broken Heads: But none praise thee for the good Things thou yieldest! Shouldest thou produce double Beer, nappy Ale, stallcop Cyder, or Cyder mull'd, fine Punch, or cordial Tiff; yet for all these shouldst thou not be prais'd, but the rich Liquors themselves, which tho' within thee, twill be said to be foreign to thee! And yet, so unhappy is thy Destiny, thou must bear all their Faults and Abominations! Hast thou been industriously serving thy Employers with Tiff or Punch, and instantly they dispatch thee for Cyder, then must thou be abused for smelling of Rum. Hast thou been steaming their Noses gratefully, with mull'd Cyder or butter'd Ale, and then offerest to refresh their

Palates with the best of Beer, they will curse thee for thy Greasiness. And how, alas! can thy Service be rendered more tolerable to thee? If thou submittest thy self to a Scouring in the Kitchen, what must thou undergo from sharp Sand, hot Ashes, and a coarse Dishclout; besides the Danger of having thy Lips rudely torn, thy Countenance disfigured, thy Arms dismantled, and thy whole Frame shatter'd, with violent Concussions in an Iron Pot or Brass Kettle! And yet, O Mug! if these Dangers thou escapest, with little Injury, thou must at last untimely fall, be broken to Pieces, and cast away, never more to be recollected and form'd into a Quart Mug. Whether by the Fire, or in a Battle, or choak'd with a Dishclout, or by a Stroke against a Stone, thy Dissolution happens; 'tis all alike to thy avaritious Owner; he grieves not for thee, but for the Shilling with which he purchased thee! If thy Bottom-Part should chance to survive, it may be preserv'd to hold Bits of Candles, or Blacking for Shoes, or Salve for kibed Heels; but all thy other Members will be for ever buried in some miry Hole; or less carefully disposed of, so that little Children, who have not yet arrived to Acts of Cruelty, may gather them up to furnish out their Baby-Houses: Or, being cast upon the Dunghill, they will therewith be carted into Meadow Grounds; where, being spread abroad and discovered, they must be thrown to the Heap of Stones, Bones, and Rubbish; or being left until the Mower finds them with his Scythe, they will with bitter Curses be tossed over the Hedge; and so serve for unlucky Boys to throw at Birds and Dogs; until by Length of Time and numerous Casualties, they shall be press'd into their Mother Earth, and be converted to their original Principles.

The Pennsylvania Gazette, July 19, 1733

Blackamore, on Molatto Gentlemen

Set a Beggar on Horseback, &c.   Chesh.

Mr. *Gazetteer,*

It is observed concerning the Generation of *Molattoes,* that they are seldom well belov'd either by the Whites or the

Blacks. Their Approach towards Whiteness, makes them look back with some kind of Scorn upon the Colour they seem to have left, while the Negroes, who do not think them better than themselves, return their Contempt with Interest: And the Whites, who respect them no Whit the more for the nearer Affinity in Colour, are apt to regard their Behaviour as too bold and assuming, and bordering upon Impudence. As they are next to Negroes, and but just above 'em, they are terribly afraid of being thought Negroes, and therefore avoid as much as possible their Company or Commerce: and White-folks are as little fond of the Company of *Molattoes*.

When People by their Industry or good Fortune, from mean Beginnings find themselves in Circumstances a little more easy, there is an Ambition seizes many of them imme-diately to become *Gentlefolks*: But 'tis no easy Thing for a Clown or a Labourer, on a sudden to hit in all respects, the natural and easy Manner of those who have been genteely educated: And 'tis the Curse of *Imitation*, that it almost al-ways either under-does or over-does.

The *true Gentleman*, who is well known to be such, can take a Walk, or drink a Glass, and converse freely, if there be occasion, with honest Men of any Degree below him, with-out degrading or fearing to degrade himself in the least. For my Part, I am an ordinary Mechanick, and I pray I may al-ways have the Grace to know my self and my Station. As little as I have learnt of the World, whenever I find a Man well dress'd whom I do not know, and observe him mighty cau-tious how he mixes in Company, or converses, or engages in any kind of equal Affair with such as appear to be his Inferi-ors; I always judge him, and I generally find him, to be some *new Gentleman*, or rather *half Gentleman*, or *Mungrel*, an un-natural Compound of Earth and *Brass* like the Feet of *Nebu-chadnezzar*'s Image. And if in the Way of my Business, I find some young Woman Mistress of a newly fine furnished House, treating me with a kind of Superiority, a distant sort of Freedom, and a high Manner of Condescension that might become a Governor's Lady, I cannot help imagining her to be some poor Girl that is but lately well married: Or if I see something in her very haughty and imperious, I conclude that 'tis not long since she was somebody's Servant Maid.

With Regard to the Respect shown them by the *true Gentry* and the *no Gentry*, our *half Gentry* are exactly in the Case of the *Mulattoes* abovementioned. They are the Ridicule and Contempt of both sides.

There is my former Acquaintance (but now he cannot speak to me) the lumpish stupid *Jack Chopstick*, while he kept in his natural Sphere, which (as that of all heavy Bodies) is the lowest, the Figure he made among Acquaintance of his own Rank was well enough; none of us envy'd him, 'tis true, nor none of us despis'd him: But now he has got a little Money, the Case is exceedingly alter'd. Without Experience of Men or Knowledge of Books, or even common Wit, the vain Fool thrusts himself into Conversation with People of the best Sense and the most polite. All his Absurdities, which were scarcely taken Notice of among us, stand evident among them, and afford them continual Matter of Diversion. At the same time, we below cannot help considering him as a Monkey that climbs a Tree, the higher he goes, the more he shows his Arse.

To conclude with the Thought I began; there are perhaps *Molattoes* in Religion, in Politicks, in Love, and in several other Things; but of all sorts of *Molattoes*, none appear to me so monstrously ridiculous as the *Molatto Gentleman*.

I am Yours, &c.
BLACKAMORE.

The *Pennsylvania Gazette*, August 30, 1733

Brave Men at Fires

To the Publisher of the GAZETTE.

An experienc'd Writer has said, there was never a great Man that was not an industrious Man, and I believe that there never was a good Man that was a lazy Man. This may serve to introduce a few Thoughts I have had while meditating on the Circumstances of Buildings on Fire, and the Persons there gather'd. Accidental Fires in Houses are most frequent in the

Winter and in the Night Time: But neither Cold nor Darkness will deter good People, who are able, from hastening to the dreadful Place, and giving their best Assistance to quench the Flames; nor wicked People from making as much Haste to pilfer; nor others to be idle Spectators. The two latter Sort are not to be easily instructed and made good; and as it is not in my Power to punish them otherwise than by despising them, as all good People do, I shall here neglect to characterize them further.

The brave Men who at Fires are active and speedy with their best Advice and Example, or the Labour of their Hands, are uppermost in my Thoughts. This kind of Industry seems to me a great Virtue. He that is afraid to leave a warm Bed, and to walk in the Dark, and to dawb or tear his Clothes or his Skin; He that makes no Difference between Virtue and Vice, and takes no Pleasure in Hospitality; and He that cares not who suffers, if he himself gains by it, or suffers not; will not any one of them, be industriously concern'd (if their own Dwellings are out of Danger) in preserving from devouring Flames either private or publick Buildings.

But how pleasing must it be to a thinking Man to observe, that not a Fire happens in this Town, but soon after it is seen and cry'd out, the Place is crowded by active Men of different Ages, Professions and Titles; who, as of one Mind and Rank, apply themselves with all Vigilance and Resolution, according to their Abilities, to the hard Work of conquering the increasing Fire. Some of the chiefest in Authority, and numbers of good Housekeepers, are ever ready, not only to direct but to labour, and are not seen to shun Parts or Places the most hazardous; and Others who having scarce a Coat in the World besides that on their Backs, will venture that, and their Limbs, in saving of Goods surrounded with Fire, and in rending off flaming Shingles. They do it not for Sake of Reward of Money or Fame: There is no Provision of either made for them. But they have a Reward in themselves, and they love one another. If it were prudent to mention Names, and could Virtue be prais'd without Danger of Envy and Calumny rising against her, I should rejoyce to know a skilful Pen employ'd, to distinguish, in lively Expressions and significant Language, Men so deserving.

This poor Paper shall praise them altogether; and while neither its Author nor they are nam'd, Virtue will be its own Reward, and Envy and Calumny have no Body to point at. Ye Men of Courage, Industry, and Goodness, continue thus in well doing; and if you grow not ostentatious, it will be thought by every good Man who sees your Performances; here are brave Men, Men of Spirit and Humanity, good Citizens, or Neighbours, capable and worthy of civil Society, and the Enjoyment of a happy Government. We see where these Men are, and what they are busy about; they are not snoring in their Beds after a Debauch; they are not employ'd in any Crimes for Concealment whereof the Vicious chuse the Night Season, nor do they prefer their own Ease at Home to the Safety of other Peoples Fortunes or Lives. See there a gallant Man who has rescu'd Children from the Flames!—Another receives in his Arms a poor scorch'd Creature escaping out at a Window!—Another is loaded with Papers and the best Furniture, and secures them for the Owner.—What daring Souls are cutting away the flaming Roof to stop the Fires Progress to others!—How vigorously do these brave Fellows hand along the Water and work the Engines, and assist the Ladders; and with what Presence of Mind, Readiness and Clearness, do these fine Men observe, advise and direct. Here are Heroes and effective Men fit to compose the Prime of an Army, and to either lay or defend a Siege or Storm.

This little City, but esteem'd great of its Age, owes not more at this Day for its long Streets and fair Stories, to Architects of any kind, than to those worthy Inhabitants, who have always started at the first Warning, to oppose and vanquish the Rage of Fire.

Besides the Pains freely taken by a great many good People in putting out Fires, some are at the Expence of Buckets and Ladders; without which the Business could not be done. And if it be a Duty incumbent on all that can afford it, to provide such useful Implements, I am of Opinion that it is most so on those, who being decrepid or infirm, cannot assist in Person; or who wearing costly Clothes, would not risque their being spoil'd. But such as can neither advise nor labour, should not stand in the Way of others who can, and are willing.

It is true indeed, as well among Men as Bees, that some Drones are in every Hive or Swarm; but I hope there are few so void of Consideration, and Regard to private and publick Safety, as a vagabond Fellow at the late Fire, who, being smartly ask'd by an industrious young Man, why he did not lend a Hand to the Buckets, answer'd, He car'd not if all the Houses in Town were o' Fire: For which he receiv'd a Bucket of Water on his impudent Face. This was a fit Reward, as it was near at Hand and took up a little Time to give it, but I doubt not a large Majority of People think with me, that he deserves a Punishment much greater and more exemplary.

December 1. 1733.   *Pennsilvanus.*

The Pennsylvania Gazette, December 20, 1733

Queries on a Pennsylvania Militia

B. Franklin,
> *Thee art desired to insert the following Queries in the* Gazette, *for the Consideration of People.*

Whether it is not a great Disadvantage to the *French*, and a great Discouragement to their Colonies on this Continent, that from the Mouth of *Missisipi* to St. *Lawrence* they have no Ports to the Sea, for the Benefit of Trade; but see them all in the Hands of the *English*, for 1500 Miles; tho' they possess a fine Country back of the same Extent?

Whether the Possession of the Governments of N. Y. J. *and* P. would not be very convenient for them, as well on Account of the Plenty of Provisions raised here, as for our Rivers which run far back towards their present Settlements?

Whether it is not possible for our Pilots to be compell'd to bring armed Vessels up this River?

Whether Vessels do not oftentimes turn the Point in Sight of this Town, before we hear of their being in the River?

Whether if this Town could be surpriz'd, there is not Plate, Clocks, Watches and other rich Goods in it, sufficient to make it worth their While that attempt?

Whether, considering our present Circumstances, any great Number of Men would be necessary for such an Enterprize, or whether a moderate Number would run any great Risque in it?

Whether they who are against fortifying their Country against an Enemy, ought not, by the same Principle to be against shutting and locking their Doors a Nights?

Whether it be not as just to shoot an Enemy who comes to destroy my Country, and deprive the People of their Substance, Lives and Liberties, as to sit (being either Judge or Juryman) and condemn a Man to Death for breaking open a House, or taking a Purse?

Whether there was not formerly a People, who possessed a large and good Land, where there was plenty of every Thing; and who lived *after the Manner of the Zidonians, careless, quiet, and secure*? Whether this was not an Invitation to an Enemy? And what was the Consequence? See Judges 18.

Whether the *French* Soldiers are a good, friendly, harmless Sort of People; or whether they are not composed of the Scum, the most profligate, wicked, and abandoned of the Nation?

Whether, if they were in Possession of these Governments, and quarter'd upon the Inhabitants, they would out of Honesty and Scruple of Conscience, forbear to take any Thing which was not their own? And out of Modesty and Bashfulness, forbear to ravish any of our Wives and Daughters? Or whether they would not do as they did, when they overrun *Holland* in 1675?

Whether we are sure that if they should attempt to abuse our Women, our Men could be quiet and peaceable Witnesses of it; and that Attempts to rescue and prevent, would not occasion frequent and daily Murders here, as well as in *Holland* aforesaid?

Whether they would not take as much Pride in deflouring *Quaker* Girls, as the *English* did in the Nuns of the Town they took in *Spain*?

Whether from the Purity of our Lives and the Sanctity of our Manners, we have any more Reason to expect the immediate Protection of Heaven than the rest of our Neighbours?

Whether the ancient Story of the Man, who sat down and prayed his Gods to lift his Cart out of the Mire, hath not a very good Moral?

Whether 500 disciplined Men well armed, are not able to beat an unarm'd, unheaded, undisciplined, and affrighted Mob of 5000?

Whether, if it were known that we fortifyed and exercised ourselves, it would not contribute towards discouraging an Enemy from attacking us?

The Pennsylvania Gazette, March 6, 1733/4

On Constancy

———*Hi mores hæc duri immota* Catonis
Secta fuit, servare modum, finemque tenere,
Naturamque sequi, patriæque impendere vitam.   Lucan.

When I have sometimes observ'd Men of Wit and Learning, in Spite of their excellent natural and acquir'd Qualifications, fail of obtaining that Regard and Esteem with Mankind, which their Inferiors in point of Understanding frequently arrive at, I have, upon a slight Reflection, been apt to think, that it was owing to the ill Judgment, Malice, or Envy of their Acquaintance: But of late two or three flagrant Instances of this kind have put me upon thinking and deliberating more maturely, and I find within the Compass of my Observation the greatest part of those fine Men have been ruined for want of *CONSTANCY*, a Virtue never too highly priz'd, and whose true Worth is by few rightly understood.

A Man remarkably wavering and inconstant, who goes through with no Enterprize, adheres to no Purpose that he has resolv'd on, whose Courage is surmounted by the most trifling Obstacles, whose Judgment is at any time byass'd by his Fears, whose trembling and disturb'd Imagination will at every Turn suggest to him Difficulties and Dangers that actually have no Existence, and enlarge those that have; A Man, I say, of this Stamp, whatever natural and acquir'd Qualities he may have, can never be a truly useful Member of a Common-wealth, a sincere or amiable Friend, or a formidable

Enemy; and when he is once incapable of bearing either of these Characters, 'tis no Wonder he is contemn'd and disregarded by Men of all Ranks and Conditions.

Without Steadiness or Perseverance no Virtue can long subsist; and however honest and well-meaning a Man's Principles may be, the Want of this is sufficient to render them ineffectual, and useless to himself or others. Nor can a Man pretend to enjoy or impart the lasting Sweets of a strict and glorious Friendship, who has not Solidity enough to despise the malicious Misrepresentations frequently made use of to disturb it, and which never fail of Success where a mutual Esteem is not founded upon the solid Basis of Constancy and Virtue. An Intimacy of this sort, contracted by chance, or the Caprice of an unstable Man, is liable to the most violent Shocks, and even an intire Ruin, from very trifling Causes. Such a Man's Incapacity for Friendship, makes all that know his Character absolutely indifferent to him: His known Fickleness of Temper renders him too inconsiderable to be fear'd as a Foe, or caress'd as a Friend.

I may venture to say there never was a Man eminently famous but what was distinguish'd by this very Qualification; and few if any can live comfortably even in a private Life without it; for a Man who has no End in View, no Design to pursue, is like an irresolute Master of a Ship at Sea, that can fix upon no one Port to steer her to, and consequently can call not one Wind favourable to his Wishes.

'Tis by his firm and unshaken Adherence to his Country's Cause, his constant Bravery in her Defence, and his burying himself but in her Ruins, that the rigid and severe *Cato* shines thro' those admirable Lines of *Lucan*, of which my Motto is a part, superior to the learn'd and eloquent *Cicero*, the great and majestick *Pompey*, or the mighty and invincible *Cæsar* himself. This is alone what could move the Poet to set him in Competition with the Gods themselves, and will transmit him down to latest Posterity with the highest Veneration and Honour.

To come nearer to our own Times; 'Tis the extraordinary Constancy of *Charles* XII. of *Sweden*, which makes up the most admirable and inimitable Part of his Character: His severe and impartial Distribution of Justice in his Army, and that fierce and resolute Speech with which he broke up his

Council, *Gentlemen, I have resolved never to engage in an unjust War, but never to finish one that is founded upon Justice and Right, but by the Destruction of my Enemies:* these and such like Instances of his Steadiness and Perseverance in the Pursuit of Justice, have deservedly made him esteem'd the Wonder of his Age.

King *Charles* II. of *England*, was doubtless a Man of great Understanding: His acquir'd Qualities far surpass'd those of *Cromwell*, and his natural Talents at least equal'd them: He came to rule over a People, formidable to all *Europe* for their Bravery, and exceedingly prepossessed in his Favour; he had learn'd to bear Misfortune by many Years Exile, and numerous Hazards and Difficulties: With these Advantages how great and glorious might he have made his Reign, by the Happiness, Content and Security of his People! 'Tis however undeniable, that the *English* never were less happy, or less regarded by their Neighbours, than during his Reign. The Reason is obvious; his Inconstancy and Indolence laid him open to every trifling Project, every self-interested Scheme, that an avaritious or revengeful Minister or Mistress could suggest to him for their own sinister Ends. 'Tis this has given many Occasion to think, that he acted thro'out his whole Reign upon no Principles and Maxims, and had no one Design in View.

Cromwel came to the supreme Authority with few of these Advantages, and against the Will of the whole Nation, except a few Fanaticks in the Army; but his constant and resolute Carriage, which was the Effect of his keeping one principal End in view, surmounted all Obstacles: 'Twas this, and this alone, which rais'd him so far above the Malice of his Enemies, or the Expectation of his Friends; and gain'd him that high Character from a judicious Historian, *That never Man chose his Party with more Judgment, and executed his Designs with more Constancy and Vigour*. By virtue of this Constancy the *English* Nation under him arriv'd to that Pitch of Grandeur, as to become a Terror and Dread to their Enemies, and the greatest Protection to their Allies. 'Tis this steady Perseverance that render'd him the Center of the different Factions and Interests in which *England* was at that time embroil'd, that secur'd his former Friends and Adherents to his Interest, and deter'd his Foes from attempting to undermine his Authority.

The Pennsylvania Gazette, April 4, 1734

The Death of Infants

Ostendunt Terris hunc tantum Fata, neque ultra
Esse sinunt.————   Virgil.

It has been observ'd Sir *William Petty* in his *Political Arith-metick*, that one half of Mankind, which are born into this World, die, before they arrive to the age of *Sixteen*, and that an half of the remaining part never measure out the short Term of *Thirty* Years. That this Observation is pretty just, every inquisitive Person may be satisfied by comparing the several Bills of Mortality, published in *Europe*, for some Years past; even a cursory View of any common Burial-place may, in a great measure evidence the Truth of it.

Many Arguments, to prove a *Future State*, have been drawn from the unequal Lot of good and bad Men upon Earth, but no one seems to carry a greater Degree of Proba-bility in it, than the foregoing Observation.—, To see Virtue languish and repine, to see Vice prosperous and triumphant, to see a *Dives* faring deliciously every Day, and rioting in all the Excess of Luxury and Wantonness; to see a *Lazarus* poor, hungry, naked, and full of Sores, lying at his Door, and denied even the Crumbs that fall from his Table, the Portion of his Dogs, which Dogs are more charitable, more human than their Master: Such a View, I confess, raises in us a violent Presumption that there is another State of Retribution, where the Just and the Unjust will be equally punished or rewarded by an impartial Judge. On the other hand, when we reflect on the vast Numbers of Infants, that just struggle into Life, then weep and die, and at the same time consider, that it can be in no wise consistent with the Justice and Wisdom of an infinite Being, to create to no end, we may very reasonably conclude, that those animated Machines, those *Men* in *miniature*, who know no Difference between Good and Evil, who are incapable of any good Offices towards their Fellow-Creatures, or of serving their Maker, were made for good and wise Designs and Purposes, which Purposes, and Designs transcend all the Limits of our Ideas and all our present Capacities to conceive. Should an able and expert Artificer employ all his Time and his Skill in contriving and framing an exquisite Piece of *Clock-work*, which, when he had brought it to the utmost Perfection Wit and Art were capable of, and just set it a-going, he should suddenly dash it to pieces; would not every wise Man naturally infer, that his intense Application had disturb'd his Brain and impair'd his Reason?

Let us now contemplate the Body of an Infant, that curious Engine of Divine Workmanship. What a rich and artful Structure of Flesh upon the solid and well compacted Foundation of Bones! What curious Joints and Hinges, on which the Limbs are moved to and fro! What an inconceivable Variety of Nerves, Veins, Arteries, Fibres and little invisible parts are found in every Member! What various Fluids, Blood and Juices run thro' and agitate the innumerable slender Tubes, the hollow Strings and Strainers of the Body! What millions of folding Doors are fixed within, to stop those red or transparent Rivulets in their course, either to prevent their Return backwards, or else as a Means to swell the Muscles and move the Limbs! What endless contrivances to secure Life, to nourish Nature, and to propagate the same to future Animals! Can we now imagine after such a Survey, that so wise, so good and merciful a Creator should produce *Myriads* of such exquisite Machines to no other End or Purpose, but to be deposited in the dark Chambers of the Grave, where each of the Dead lie in their cold Mansions, in Beds of Darkness and Dust. The Shadows of a long Evening are stretch'd over them, the Curtains of a deep Midnight are drawn around them, *The Worm lies under them, and the Worm covers them.* No! the Notion of Annihilation has in it something so shocking and absurd, Reason should despise it; rather let us believe, that when they drop this earthly Vehicle they assume an Ætherial one, and become the Inhabitants of some more glorious Region. May they not help to people that infinite Number of *Starry* and *Planetary* Worlds that roll above us:

may they not become our better *Genii*, our Guardian Angels, watch round our Bed and our Couch, direct our wandring Paths thro' the Maze and Labyrinth of Life, and at length conduct us safe, even us, who were the Instruments of their passing thro' this *Valley* of Sorrow and Death, to a Land of Peace and the Mountains of *Paradise*?—But these are things that belong to the Provinces of Light and immortality, and lie far beyond our mortal Ken.—

I was led into this Train of thinking by the Death of a desireable Child, whose Beauty is now turning a-pace into Corruption, and all the Loveliness of its Countenance fled for ever. Death sits heavy upon it, and the Sprightliness and Vigour of Life is perished in every Feature and in every Limb. If the foregoing Reflections should urge any one forward in the Paths of Vertue, or yield any Consolation to those in the like Circumstances, and help to divert the Stream of their Sorow into a better Channel, I shall hope my Thoughts have been employ'd to good Purpose. When Nature gave us Tears, she gave us leave to weep. A long Separation from those who are so near a-kin to us in Flesh and Blood, will touch the Heart in a painful Place, and awaken the tenderest Springs of Sorrow. The Sluices must be allowed to be held open a little; *Nature* seems to demand it as a Debt to *Love*. When *Lazarus* died, *Jesus* groaned and wept.

I shall only add by way of Conclusion an *Epitaph* upon an Infant: It is taken from a Tombstone in a little obscure Village in *England*, that seems to have very little Title to any thing so elegantly poetical, which renders it the more remarkable.

> *Read this and weep—but not for me;*
> *Lament thy longer Misery:*
> *My Life was short, my Grief the less;*
> *Blame not my Hast to Happiness!*

The Pennsylvania Gazette, June 20, 1734

Parody and Reply to a Religious Meditation

By being too nice in the Choice of the little Pieces sent me by my Correspondents to be printed, I had almost discouraged them

from writing to me any more. For the Time to come, and that my
Paper may become still more generally agreeable, I have resolved
not to regard my own Humour so much in what I print; and
thereupon I give my Readers the two following Letters.

Mr. *Franklin*,
You gave us in your last a melancholy Account of Human
Life, in the Meditation upon that Subject. The gloomy and
splenetick Part of your Readers like it much; but as for me, I
do not love to see the dark Side of Things; and besides, I do
not think such Reflections upon Life altogether just. The
World is a very good World, and if we behave our selves well,
we shall doubtless do very well in it. I never thought even *Job*
in the right, when he repin'd that the Days of a Man are *few*
and *full of Trouble*; for certainly both these Things cannot be
together just Causes of Complaint; if our Days are full of
Trouble, the fewer of 'em the better. But as for the Author of
the Meditation above-mention'd, besides what he says in
common with *Job*, he seems to complain in several respects
very weakly, and without the least shadow of Reason; in particular, That he cannot be alive now, and ten Years ago, and
ten Years hence, at the same time: With very little Variation,
as you shall see, his elegant Expressions will serve for a Child
who laments that he cannot eat his Cake and have his Cake.

All the few days we live are full of Vanity; and our choicest
Pleasures sprinkled with bitterness:

All the few Cakes we have are puffed up with Yeast; and
the nicest Gingerbread is spotted with Flyshits!

The time that's past is vanish'd like a dream; and that which
is to come is not yet at all:

The Cakes that we have eaten are no more to be seen; and
those which are to come are not yet baked.

The present we are in stays but for a moment, and then flies
away, and returns no more:

The present Mouthful is chewed but a little while, and then
is swallowed down, and comes up no more.

Already we are dead to the years we have liv'd; and shall never
live them over again:

Already we have digested the Cakes we have eaten, and
shall never eat them over again.

But the longer we live, the shorter is our life; and in the end we become a little lump of clay.

And the more we eat, the less is the Piece remaining; and in the end the whole will become Sir-reverence!

O vain, and miserable world! how sadly true is all this story!

O vain and miserable Cake-shop! *&c.*

Away with all such insignificant Meditations. I am for taking *Solomon*'s Advice, *eating Bread with Joy, and drinking Wine with a merry Heart.* Let us rejoice and bless God, that we are neither Oysters, Hogs, nor Dray-Horses; and not stand repining that He has not made us Angels; lest we be found unworthy of that share of Happiness He has thought fit to allow us.   *I am, Yours,* &c.

S. M.

SIR,

Seeing a very *melancholy* Piece in your Paper of last Week, asking your Pardon, I think we have enough of that Humour in the World already, without your Addition: I have therefore written the following few Lines in order to palliate it. And as that may be very acceptable to some of your Readers, this may to some others, if you think fit to give it a Place in your next.

I am, Yours, &c.

J. Anonymous.

Most happy are we, the sons of men, above all other creatures, who are born to behold the glorious rays of the sun, and to enjoy the pleasant fruits of the earth.

With what pleasure did our parents first receive us, first to hear us cry, then to see us smile, and afterwards to behold us growing up and thriving in the world.

By their good examples and a vertuous education, they put us in the right path to happiness, as all good parents do;

Then we, by making a right use of that share of reason with which God hath endued us, spend our days in gaining and enjoying the blessings of life, which are innumerable.

If we meet with crosses and disappointments, they are but as sowr sauce to the sweet meats we enjoy, and the one hath not a right relish without the other.

As time passes away, it carries our past pains with it, and returns no more; and the longer we live the fewer misfortunes we have to go through.

If death takes us off in the heighth of our prosperity, it takes us from the pains which may ensue.

And a great blessing attends old age, for by that we are naturally wean'd from the pleasures of youth, and a more solid pleasure takes place, The thoughts of our having so far escaped all the hazards that attend mankind, and a contemplation on all our former good actions.

And if we have done all the good we could, we have done all that we ought, and death is no terror to a good man.

And after we are far declined, with hearty praises and thanks we recommend our soul to God, the eternal Being from whom we received it.

Then comes the grave, and the sweet sleep of death, pleasant as a bed to a weary traveller after a long journey.

The Pennsylvania Gazette, August 8, 1734

A Thunderstorm

Sunday last between 7 and 8 in the Evening we had the most terrible Gust of Wind and Rain accompanied with Thunder and Lightning, that can be remembred in these Parts: It blew down several Stacks of Chimneys, uncovered several Houses, some wholly and others in Part; and quite demolished some weak Buildings. The Violence of it did not continue long, but the Storm was of wide Extent, for we have heard of it from *Conestogoe*, from the Mouth of the Bay, and from *New-York*: At *Conestogoe* it was about half an hour before it arrived here, but in the Bay it was at near Midnight.

The Pennsylvania Gazette, September 25, 1734

The Murder of a Daughter

Saturday last, at a Court of Oyer and Terminer held here, came on the Tryal of a Man and his Wife, who were indicted for the Murder of a Daughter which he had by a former Wife, (a Girl of about 14 Years of Age) by turning her out of Doors, and thereby exposing her to such Hardships, as afterwards produced grievous Sickness and Lameness; during which, instead of supplying her with Necessaries and due Attendance, they treated her with the utmost Cruelty and Barbarity, suffering her to lie and rot in her Nastiness, and when she cried for Bread giving her into her Mouth with a Iron Ladle, her own Excrements to eat, with a great Number of other Circumstances of the like Nature, so that she languished and at length died. The Evidence against them was numerous, and in many Particulars positive; but the Opinion of the Physician who had visited the Child, that whatever Usage might be given her, the Distemper she laboured under was such, as would of itself in all Probability have ended her Life about the Time she died, it is thought weighed so much with the Jury, that they brought in their Verdict only *Man-slaughter*. A Verdict which the Judge, (in a short but pathetic Speech to the Prisoners before the Sentence) told them was *extreamly favourable*; and that, as the Relation of their hitherto unheard-of Barbarity had in the highest Manner shocked all that were present; so, if they were not perfectly stupified, the inward Reflection upon their own enormous Crimes, must be more terrible and shocking to them, than the Punishment they were to undergo: For that they had not only acted contrary to the particular Laws of all Nations, but had even broken the Universal Law of Nature; since there are no Creatures known, how savage, wild, and fierce soever, that have not implanted in them a natural Love and Care of their tender Offspring, and that will not even hazard Life in its Protection and Defence.—But this is not the only Instance the present Age has afforded, of the incomprehensible Insensibility 𝔇ram-𝔡rinking is capable of producing.—They were sentenced to be burnt in the Hand, which was accordingly executed in Court, upon them both, but first upon the Man, who offer'd to receive another Burning if so be his Wife might be excused; but was told the Law would not allow it.

The Pennsylvania Gazette, October 24, 1734

Variant Accounts of a Battle

As there is nothing more partial than the Accounts given of Battles, all of them lessening or magnifying the Loss or Gain on either Side, just as the Writers are affected; we find it necessary to publish several Accounts on both Sides, when there has been any important Action, that so the Reader may be the better enabled to form a true Judgment: And therefore to the Relations we have already publish'd of the late important Battle in Italy, *we shall add the following.*

Guastalla, Sept. 18. Long had the brave Count Koningsegg meditated Revenge for the fatal Battle of Parma, and Relief for the Honour of the Imperial Arms, by giving the Allies some desperate Blow. He had made several Attempts, but was constantly betrayed; his Designs always took Air, and he could never discover the Traitors: At last, however, he has carried them into Execution. There is an old Saying in Lombardy, That if a Man would execute any Grand Design, he must take Care to possess himself of the Seraglio, (a Spot of Ground between Mantua and the Po). Count Merci neglected this Advice; but Count Koningsegg thought it very just and solid, and posted the 4000 Croatians there, supported by three Regiments of Horse under the Command of General Berlinger, whom he ordered to act along the Oglio as Opportunity should offer. On the 4th, Count Koningsegg ordered the whole Army to be upon its Guard, and every Man in his Post, as if he had received Notice that he should be attacked by the Allies. About Five o'Clock in the Evening, he gave Orders, at the same time that he discovered to them the Design he was going to execute. The Guards were doubled, and Notice was given, that no Person should stir out of the Camp without Leave. The Retreat was beat, as usual, that they might hear it in the Enemy's Camp; and the Trumpets having flourished as at other times, every one retired. At Midnight the Army began its March in three Columns, and in Order of Battle, the Soldiers only in their Wastecoats, without Coats or Knapsacks; *We shall find enough in the Enemy's Camp,* said their Officers to them, *if you have any Hearts.*

13,000 Foot and 6 Regiments of Horse advanced first towards
the Secchia above Quistello, and forded it, there not being
above three Foot Water. The Count de Waldebeck staid with
his Brigade facing Quistello, to make a faint Attack there, as
soon as he should hear that they had surprized the Head-
Quarters at Bondanello. The French had at Quistello, (which
they had well retrenched) 1000 Men and nine Pieces of Cannon; and they had at that time above sixty Officers there. As
soon as the Germans had passed the Secchia, they fell upon
the Marshal de Broglio's Quarters, who was so sound asleep,
that our Granadiers were in his Court-Yard, before he was
well awake: Fifty Men and the Officers of the Guard made
some Resistance, to give him Time to make his Escape at the
back Door in his Shirt, with his Breeches in one Hand, and
his two Sons in the other. The Guard then surrendered; and
we advanced to the Bridge over-against Quistello, and carried
that Quarter; but here the Count de Waldebeck was killed,
greatly lamented. During these Preliminaries, the Army advanced apace, and fell upon the Count de Broglio's Body,
which consisted of 28 or 30 Battalions, who fled in their Shirts
and left their very Arms behind them. The brave Regiments
of the King and Picardie were among these; every Man made
the best Shift he could for himself, and carried the Alarm to
the Right. The Marshal de Coigny made the Troops under
his Command take Arms, all in a Hurry and Disorder, and
was advancing to the Right; but perceiving that the Imperial
Army was marching towards him in three Columns, he halted
and called a Council of War; and the Imperialists just then
moving towards their Left, it was imagined that they would
endeavour to cut off the Army's Retreat towards the Bridge
of Guastalla; and therefore it was instantly resolved to make
a Retreat that way in the best Order they could. Some Battalions were left with Artillery in the neighbouring Cassines,
to stop the Enemy; but those Troops made but a very slender
Resistance, and were obliged to yield themselves Prisoners of
War. Count Koningsegg seeing the Enemy's Disorder on all
Sides, sent 10,000 Men this way, under the Command of
Prince Lewis of Wirtemberg, and advanced towards San Be-
nedetto, where were the Head-Quarters of the Savoyards:
The King of Sardinia made his Escape in his Night-Gown

and Slippers; but two Regiments of his Troops were cut off from the rest and taken. Some Squadrons of Dragoons and the Hussars broke and put into Disorder the Enemy's Rear-Guard, who are divided into Bodies of 2 or 3000 Men each, most of them without Arms, Baggage or Artillery, which we hope to cut off and take one after the other; for we are still pursuing them. The Booty already taken, amounts to upwards of 15 Millions of Livres; for we have taken the Arms of one Third of the Gallo-Sardinick Army, all the Artillery, 12 or 1500 Waggons, all the Baggage, heavy and light, all the Tents; and between 6 and 8000 Prisoners. There were doubtless 1000 or 1200 of the Enemy killed. Never was seen such Confusion. But the Generals who suffered themselves to be thus surprized, how will they come off.

Next here follows a more particular Account of the Second Battle between the same Armies, which happened on the 19th of Sept. viz.

Mantua, Sept. 24. We have here the following Particulars of the Battle fought the 19th near Guastalla. Count Konigsegg broke up from Luzara the 16th about Nine in the Morning, and at Ten he ordered the Enemy, who were posted under Guastalla, to be attack'd by seven Battalions of Foot and 12 Companies of General Valpereve and Colmenero, who made the Onset in a very brave and intrepid Manner. The Enemy pour'd on fresh Troops continually; whereupon our Troops were reinforc'd with 17 Companies of Grenadiers and 19 Battallions of Foot: Then the Action became general in a Moment, and thereupon we order'd 50 Squadrons to engage: The Enemy's Horse were then on a Plain, where they were, most advantageously posted behind the Cassines, very deep Ditches, and a great many Bushes, from whence they made a terrible and constant Fire upon our Men, which prevented our knowing their Number. The Generals Valpareve and Colmenero were killed in the Beginning of this Attack, as were all the Field Officers; so that only one Lieutenant-Colonel was at the Head of the seven Battalions who began the Attack. The Prince of Wirtemberg was killed in the Middle of this Action, when his Presence was most necessary to lead on the Foot. Count Koningsegg then seeing that it was impossible for him to break the Enemy's Cavalry, after a continual Fire of about six Hours, order'd his Army to retire, which they did in so good Order, that the Enemy durst not pursue him; and he went and encamped at Luzara, where his Army was encamped the Day before. Notwithstanding the great Loss of Officers above-mentioned, whereby the Attack was something slackened, and our Troops brought into some disorder, our Men did not retire or lose one Inch of Ground, till they were ordered to draw off from the Field of Battle. The Number of our killed and wounded Men amounts to between 4 and 6000. For six or seven Hours nothing was to be seen but Fire and Sword, Dead and Wounded, and Rivulets of Blood. The Field of Battle was indeed left to the Enemy, where they could find nothing to give them Occasion to boast of a Victory; for as the Fire on both Sides was equally strong and continual, we judge their Loss must be equal to ours.

The Velt Marshal Konnigsegg has been join'd since the last Battle by 4000 Croatians and three Regiments of Horse. His Excellency is actually making new Dispositions for another Combat.

The Retreat of the Imperial Army was owing to the unhappy Loss of the Prince of Wirtemberg, and the Wounds receiv'd by the Generals Valpariso and Watchtendonck; most of the prime Officers were also disabled, by which means none but Lieutenant-Colonel de Uhlenfeld was left to command the seven Battalions engag'd in the heat of Action. Our Loss amounts to between 4 or 5000 Men; that of the Enemy must be as considerable, if not larger.

Paris, Octo. 6. By our last Account from Italy the Battle of the 19th past was very bloody; for during the Combat wherein the Enemy had between 12 and 13000 kill'd and wounded, they sent away 200 Waggons full of wounded Men; but towards the End, being press'd closely, were oblig'd to leave 900 wounded in the Field, whom our General had remov'd in order to be taken care of. We reckon between 6 and 7000 killed and wounded on our Side. After the Battle the Enemy intrench'd themselves on the Banks of the Po, overagainst Burgo-Fort, where they have a Bridge to retire over into the Mantuan in case of Occasion.

On the 3d Te Deum was sung in the Church of Notre Dame for the signal Victory in Italy.

London, Octo. 5. Letters from Paris intimate, that his Most Christian Majesty has been pleas'd to order 100,000 Crowns to be distributed among the Officers who lost their Equipages, when Count Koninsegg surpriz'd the Marshal de Broglio's Quarters; and at the same Time sent Instructions to Marshal Coigny, to inform him of the Number of Officers who had been kill'd in the Surprize, as well as at the Battle, in order to settle Pensions upon their Widows and Children.

A private Letter from Paris, dated the 29th, tells us, that the Germans, on the 19th being Sunday, with uncommon Valour attack'd the Allies in their Intrenchment at Guastalla. At 10 the whole Armies were engaged, Sword in Hand. The Fight lasted till 5 in the Afternoon, when the Germans retired, without being pursued, to Luzara, and left behind them some Pieces of Cannon, and a few Colours and Standards. That 15000 Men were kill'd on both Sides, among them 800 Officers. That Marshal de Coigny was wounded, M. d'Harcourt lost one Arm. 'Tis agreed on all Hands, that the Allies were much superior in Number, notwithstanding which, putting the two Actions together, the Loss on both Sides was supposed to be equal.

The Pennsylvania Gazette, December 19, 1734

On Protection of Towns from Fire

Mr. Franklin,

Being old and lame of my Hands, and thereby uncapable of assisting my Fellow Citizens, when their Houses are on Fire; I must beg them to take in good Part the following Hints on the Subject of Fires.

In the first Place, as *an Ounce of Prevention is worth a Pound of Cure,* I would advise 'em to take Care how they suffer living Brands-ends, or Coals in a full Shovel, to be carried out of one Room into another, or up or down Stairs, unless in a

Warmingpan shut; for Scraps of Fire may fall into Chinks, and make no Appearance till Midnight; when your Stairs being in Flames, you may be forced, (as I once was) to leap out of your Windows, and hazard your Necks to avoid being over-roasted.

And now we talk of Prevention, where would be the Damage, if, to the Act for preventing Fires, by regulating Bake-houses and Coopers Shops, a Clause were added to regulate all other Houses in the particulars of too shallow Hearths, and the detestable Practice of putting wooden Mouldings on each side the Fire Place, which being commonly of Heart-of-Pine and full of Turpentine, stand ready to flame as soon as a Coal or a small Brand shall roul against them.

Once more; If Chimneys were more frequently and more carefully clean'd, some Fires might thereby be prevented. I have known foul Chimneys burn most furiously a few Days after they were swept: People in Confidence that they are clean, making large Fires. Every Body among us is allow'd to sweep Chimneys, that please to undertake that Business; and if a Chimney fires thro' fault of the Sweeper, the Owner pays the Fine, and the Sweeper goes free. This Thing is not right. Those who undertake Sweeping of Chimneys, and employ Servants for that Purpose, ought to be licensed by the Mayor; and if any Chimney fires and flames out 15 Days after Sweeping, the Fine should be paid by the Sweeper; for it is his Fault.

We have at present got Engines enough in the Town, but I question, whether in many Parts of the Town, Water enough can be had to keep them going for half an Hour together. It seems to me some Publick Pumps are wanting; but that I submit to better Judgments.

As to our Conduct in the Affair of Extinguishing Fires, tho' we do not want Hands or Good-will, yet we seem to want Order and Method, and therefore I believe I cannot do better than to offer for our Imitation, the Example of a City in a Neigbouring Province. There is, as I am well inform'd, a Club or Society of active Men belonging to each Fire Engine; whose Business is to attend all Fires with it whenever they happen; and to work it once a Quarter, and see it kept in order: Some of these are to handle the Firehooks, and others the Axes, which are always kept with the Engine; and for this Service they are consider'd in an Abatement or Exemption in the Taxes. In Time of Fire, they are commanded by Officers appointed by Law, called *Firewards*, who are distinguish'd by a Red Staff of five Feet long, headed with a Brass Flame of 6 Inches; And being Men of Prudence and Authority, they direct the opening and stripping of Roofs by the Ax-Men, the pulling down burning Timbers by the Hook-men, and the playing of the Engines, and command the making of Lanes, &c. and they are impowered to require Assistance for the Removing of Goods out of Houses on fire or in Danger of Fire, and to appoint Guards for securing such Goods; and Disobedience, to these Officers in any, at such Times, is punished by a Fine of 40 s. or Ten Days Imprisonment. These Officers, with the Men belonging to the Engine, at their Quarterly Meetings, discourse of Fires, of the Faults committed at some, the good Management in some Cases at others, and thus communicating their Thoughts and Experience they grow wise in the Thing, and know how to command and to execute in the best manner upon every Emergency. Since the Establishment of this Regulation, it seems there has been no extraordinary Fire in that Place; and I wish there never may be any here. But they suffer'd before they made such a Regulation, and so must we; for *Englishmen* feel but cannot see; as the *Italian* says of us. And it has pleased God, that in the Fires we have hitherto had, all the bad Circumstances have never happened together, such as dry Season, high Wind, narrow Street, and little or low Water: which perhaps tends to make us secure in our own Minds; but if a Fire with those Circumstances, which God forbid, should happen, we should afterwards be careful enough.

Let me say one thing more, and I will be silent. I could wish, that either Tiles would come in use for a Covering to Buildings; or else that those who build, would make their Roofs more safe to walk upon, by carrying the Wall above the Eves, in the Manner of the new Buildings in *London*, and as Mr. *Turner's* House in *Front-Street*, or Mr. *Nichols's* in *Chesnut-Street*, are built; which I conceive would tend considerably to their Preservation.

Let others communicate their Thoughts as freely as I have

done mine, and perhaps something useful may be drawn from the Whole.

I am yours, &c.

A. A.

The Pennsylvania Gazette, February 4, 1734/5

Self-Denial Not the Essence of Virtue

To the Printer of the Gazette.

That SELF-DENIAL is not the ESSENCE of VIRTUE.

It is commonly asserted, that without *Self-Denial* there is no Virtue, and that the greater the *Self-Denial* the greater the Virtue.

If it were said, that he who cannot deny himself in any Thing he inclines to, tho' he knows it will be to his Hurt, has not the Virtue of *Resolution* or *Fortitude*, it would be intelligible enough; but as it stands it seems obscure or erroneous.

Let us consider some of the Virtues singly.

If a Man has no inclination to *wrong* People in his Dealings, if he feels no Temptation to it, and therefore never does it; can it be said that he is not a just Man? If he is a just Man, has he not the Virtue of Justice?

If to a certain Man, idle Diversions have nothing in them that is tempting, and therefore he never relaxes his Application to Business for their Sake; is he not an Industrious Man? Or has he not the Virtue of Industry?

I might in like manner instance in all the rest of the Virtues: But to make the Thing short, As it is certain, that the more we strive against the Temptation to any Vice, and practise the contrary Virtue, the weaker will that Temptation be, and the stronger will be that Habit; 'till at length the Temptation has no Force, or entirely vanishes: Does it follow from thence, that in our Endeavours to overcome Vice, we grow continually less and less Virtuous; till at length we have no Virtue at all?

If Self-Denial be the Essence of Virtue, then it follows, that the Man who is naturally temperate, just, &c. is not virtuous; but that in order to be virtuous, he must, in spight of his natural Inclinations, wrong his Neighbours, and eat and drink, &c. to excess.

But perhaps it may be said, that by the Word *Virtue* in the above Assertion, is meant, *Merit*; and so it should stand thus; Without Self-Denial there is no Merit; and the greater the Self-Denial the greater the Merit.

The Self-denial here meant, must be when our Inclinations are towards Vice, or else it would still be Nonsense.

By Merit is understood, Desert; and when we say a Man merits, we mean that he deserves Praise or Reward.

We do not pretend to merit any thing of God, for he is above our Services; and the Benefits he confers on us, are the Effects of his Goodness and Bounty.

All our Merit then is with regard to one another, and from one to another.

Taking then the Assertion as it last stands,

If a Man does me a Service from a natural benevolent Inclination, does he deserve less of me than another who does me the like Kindness against his Inclination?

If I have two Journeymen, one naturally industrious, the other idle, but both perform a Days Work equally good, ought I to give the latter the most Wages?

Indeed, lazy Workmen are commonly observ'd to be more extravagant in their Demands than the Industrious; for if they have not more for their Work, they cannot live so well: But tho' it be true to a Proverb, *That Lazy Folks take the most Pains*, does it follow that they deserve the most Money?

If you were to employ Servants in Affairs of Trust, would you not bid more for one you knew was naturally honest, than for one naturally roguish, but who had lately acted honestly? For Currents whose natural Channel is damm'd up, (till the new Course is by Time worn sufficiently deep and become natural,) are apt to break their Banks. If one Servant is more valuable than another, has he not more Merit than the other? And yet this is not on Account of Superior Self-denial.

Is a Patriot not praise-worthy, if Publick Spirit is natural to him?

Is a Pacing-Horse less valuable for being a natural Pacer?

Nor in my Opinion has any Man less Merit for having in general natural virtuous Inclinations.

The Truth is, that Temperance, Justice, Charity, &c. are Virtues, whether practis'd with or against our Inclinations; and the Man who practises them, merits our Love and Esteem: And Self-denial is neither good nor bad, but as 'tis apply'd: He that denies a Vicious Inclination is Virtuous in proportion to his Resolution, but the most perfect Virtue is above all Temptation, such as the Virtue of the Saints in Heaven: And he who does a foolish, indecent or wicked Thing, meerly because 'tis contrary to his Inclination, (like some mad Enthusiasts I have read of, who ran about naked, under the Notion of taking up the Cross) is not practising the reasonable Science of Virtue, but is lunatick.

New-Castle, Feb. 5. 1734,5.

The Pennsylvania Gazette, February 18, 1734/5

A Man of Sense

Mr. Franklin,

'Being the other Day near the Meeting-House Corner with some Gentlemen, in the open Street, I heard the following Piece of Conversation; and penn'd it down as soon as I came home. I am confident it varies scarce any thing from what really passed; and as it pleased the By-standers, it may possibly please the Publick, if you give it a Place in your Paper.

'It not being proper to name the Persons discoursing, I shall call one of them *Socrates*, his manner of Arguing being in my Opinion, somewhat like that of *Socrates*: And, if you please, the other may be *Crito*.'

I am Yours, &c.

A. A.

Socrates. Who is that well-dress'd Man that passed by just now?

Crito. He is a Gentleman of this City, esteem'd a *Man of Sense*, but not very honest.

S. The Appellation of *a Man of Sense* is of late frequently given, and seems to come naturally into the Character of every Man we are about to praise: But I am at some Loss to know whether a Man who *is not honest* can deserve it.

C. Yes, doubtless; There are many vicious Men who are nevertheless Men of very good Sense.

S. You are of Opinion, perhaps, that a Man of Knowledge is *a Man of Sense.*

C. I am really of that Opinion.

S. Is the Knowledge of Push-pin, or of the Game at Nine-pins, or of Cards and Dice, or even of Musick and Dancing, sufficient to constitute the Character of a Man of Sense?

C. No certainly; there are many silly People that understand these Things tolerably well.

S. Will the Knowledge of Languages, or of Logic and Rhetoric serve to make a Man of Sense.

C. I think not; for I have known very senseless Fellows to be Masters of two or three Languages; and mighty full of their Logic, or their Rhetoric.

S. Perhaps some Men may understand all the Forms and Terms of Logic, or all the Figures of Rhetoric, and yet be no more able to convince or to perswade, than others who have not learnt those Things?

C. Indeed I believe they may.

S. Will not the Knowledge of the Mathematicks, Astronomy, and Natural Philosophy, those sublime Sciences, give a Right to the Character of *a Man of Sense.*

C. At first Sight I should have thought they might: But upon Recollection I must own I have known some Men, Masters of those Sciences, who, in the Management of their Affairs, and *Conduct of their Lives*, have acted very weakly, I do not mean viciously but foolishly; and therefore I cannot find in my Heart to allow 'em the Character of *Men of Sense.*

S. It seems then, that no Knowledge will serve to give this Character, but the Knowledge of our *true Interest*; that is, of what is best to be done in all the Circumstances of Humane Life, in order to arrive at our main End in View, HAPPINESS.

C. I am of the same Opinion. And now, as to the Point in Hand, I suppose you will no longer doubt whether a vicious

Man may deserve the Character of a Man of Sense, since 'tis certain that there are many Men who *know* their true Interest, &c. and are therefore *Men of Sense*, but are nevertheless vicious and dishonest Men, as appears from the whole Tenour of their Conduct in Life.

S. Can Vice consist with any Man's true Interest, or contribute to his Happiness.

C. No certainly; for in Proportion as a Man is vicious he loses the Favour of God and Man, and brings upon himself many Inconveniences, the least of which is capable of marring and demolishing his Happiness.

S. How then does it appear that those vicious Men have the Knowledge we have been speaking of, which constitutes *a Man of Sense*, since they act directly contrary?

C. It appears by their Discoursing perfectly well upon the Subjects of Vice and Virtue, when they occur in Conversation, and by the just Manner in which they express their Thoughts of the pernicious Consequences of the one, and the happy Effects of the other.

S. Is it the Knowledge of all the Terms and Expressions proper to be used in Discoursing well upon the Subject of making a good Shoe, that constitutes a Shoemaker; or is it the Knowing how to go about it and do it?

C. I own it is the latter, and not the former.

S. And if one who could only *talk finely* about Shoemaking, were to be set to work, would he not presently discover his Ignorance in that Art?

C. He would, I confess.

S. Can the Man who is only able to talk justly of Virtue and Vice, and to say that "Drunkenness, Gluttony and Lewdness destroy a Man's Constitution; waste his Time and Substance, and bring him under many Misfortunes, (to the Destruction of his Happiness) which the contrary Virtues would enable him to avoid;" but notwithstanding his talking thus, continues in those Vices; can such a Man deserve the Character of a Temperate and Chaste Man? Or does not that Man rather deserve it, who having *a thorough Sense* that what the other has said is true, *knows* also *how* to resist the Temptation to those Vices, and embrace Virtue with a hearty and steady Affection?

C. The latter, I acknowledge. And since Virtue is really the true Interest of all Men; and some of those who talk well of it, do not put it in Practice, I am now inclined to believe they speak only by rote, retailing to us what they have pick'd out of the Books or Conversation of wise and virtuous Men; but what having never enter'd or made any Impression on their Hearts, has therefore no Influence on the Conduct of their Lives.

S. Vicious Men, then, do not appear to have that Knowledge which constitutes *the Man of Sense.*

C. No, I am convinced they do not deserve the Name. However, I am afraid, that instead of *defining* a Man of Sense we have now entirely *annihilated* him: For if the Knowlege of his true Interest in all Parts of the Conduct of Life, and a constant Course of Practice agreeable to it, are essential to his Character, I do not know where we shall find him.

S. There seems no necessity that to be a Man of Sense, he should never make a Slip in the Path of Virtue, or in Point of Morality; provided he is sensible of his Failing and diligently applys himself to rectify what is done amiss, and to prevent the like for the future. The best Arithmetician may err in casting up a long Account; but having found that Error, he *knows how* to mend it, and immediately does so; and is notwithstanding that Error, an Arithmetician; But he who *always* blunders, and cannot correct his Faults in Accounting, is no Arithmetician; nor is the habitually-vicious Man *a Man of Sense.*

C. But methinks 'twill look hard, that all other Arts and Sciences put together, and possess'd by one Man in the greatest Perfection, are not able to dignify him with the Title of *a Man of Sense*, unless he be also a Man of Virtue.

S. We shall agree, perhaps, that one who is *a Man of Sense*, will not spend his Time in learning such Sciences as, if not useless in themselves, will probably be useless to him?

C. I grant it.

S. And of those which may be useful to him, that is, may contribute to his Happiness, he ought, if he is a Man of Sense to know how to make them so.

C. To be sure.

S. And of those which may be useful, he will not (if he is a Man of Sense) acquire all, except that One only which is the most useful of all, to wit, the Science of Virtue.

C. It would, I own, be inconsistent with his Character to do so.

S. It seems to follow then, that the vicious Man, tho' Master of many Sciences, must needs be an ignorant and foolish Man; for being, as he is vicious, of consequence unhappy, either he has acquired only the useless Sciences, or having acquired such as might be useful, he knows not how to make them contribute to his Happiness; and tho' he may have every other Science, he is ignorant that the SCIENCE OF VIRTUE is of more worth, and of more consequence to his Happiness than all the rest put together. And since he is ignorant of what *principally* concerns him, tho' it has been told him a thousand Times from Parents, Press, and Pulpit, the Vicious Man however learned, cannot be *a Man of Sense*, but is a Fool, a Dunce, and a Blockhead.

The Pennsylvania Gazette, February 11, 1734/5

Reply to a Piece of Advice

Mr. Franklin,

In your Paper of the 18th past, some Verses were inserted, said to be design'd as a PIECE OF ADVICE to a good Friend. As this *Piece of Advice,* if it had been intended for a particular Friend alone, might have been as well convey'd to him privately; I suppose the Author by getting it publish'd, thinks it may be of Use to great Numbers of others, in his Friend's Circumstances. The import of it is, "That 'tis mighty silly for a single Man to change his State; for assoon as his Wishes are crown'd, his expected Bliss dissolves into Cares in Bondage, which is a compleat Curse; That only Fools in Life wed, for every Woman is a Tyrant: That he who marries, acts contrary to his Interest, loses his Liberty and his Friends, and will soon perceive himself undone; and that the best of the Sex are no better than a Plague." So ill-natur'd a Thing must have been written, either by some forlorn old Batchelor, or some cast-away Widower, that has got the Knack of drowning all his softer Inclinations in his Bowl or his Bottle. I am grown old and have made abundance of Observations, and I have had three Wives my self; so that from both Experience and Observation I can say, that this Advice is wrong and untrue in every Particular. It is wrong to assert *that tis silly in a single Man to change his State*: For what old Batchelor can die without Regret and Remorse, when he reflects upon his Death-bed, that the inestimable Blessing of Life and Being has been communicated by Father to Son through all Generations from *Adam* down to him, but in him it stops and is extinguished; and that *the Humane Race divine* would be no more, for any Thing he has done to continue it; he having, like the wicked Servant, *wrapt up and hid his Talent in a Napkin*, (i. e. his Shirt Tail,) while his Neighbours the Good and Faithful Servants, had some of them produced *Five* and some *Ten*. I say such an one shall not only die with Regret, but he may justly fear a severe Punishment. Nor is it true that *assoon as a Man weds, his expected Bliss dissolves into slavish Cares and Bondage*. Every Man that is really a Man is Master of his own Family; and it cannot be *Bondage* to have another submit to one's Government. If there be any Bondage in the Case, 'tis the Woman enters into it, and not the Man. And as to the *Cares*, they are chiefly what attend the bringing up of Children; and I would ask any Man who has experienced it, if they are not the most delightful Cares in the World; and if from that Particular alone, he does not find the *Bliss* of a double State much greater, instead of being less than he expected. In short this *Bondage* and these *Cares* are like the Bondage of having a beautiful and fertile Garden, which a Man takes great Delight in; and the Cares are the Pleasure he finds in cultivating it, and raising as many beautiful and useful Plants from it as he can. And if common Planting and Gardening be an Honourable Employment, (as 'tis generally allow'd, since the greatest Heroes have practic'd it without any Diminution to their Glory) I think *Human Planting* must be more Honourable, as the Plants to be raised are more excellent in their Nature, and to bring them to Perfection requires the greater Skill and Wisdom.

As to the Adviser's next Insinuation, that *only Fools wed, and every Woman is a Tyrant*; 'tis a very severe and undutiful Reflection upon his own Father and Mother; and since he is most likely to know best the Affairs of his own Family, I shall not contradict him in that particular, so far as relates to his own Relations: for perhaps his Aversion to a Wife arises from observing how his Mamma treated his Daddy; for she might be a *Xantippe* tho' he was no *Socrates*; it being probable that a wise Man would have instill'd sounder Principles into his Son. But in general I utterly dissent from him, and declare, that I scarce ever knew a Man who knew how to command in a proper Manner, but his Wife knew as well how to show a becoming Obedience. And there are in the World infinitely more He-Tyrants than She-Ones.

In the next Place he insinuates, that *a Man by marrying, acts contrary to his Interest, loses his Liberty and his Friends, and soon finds himself undone*. In which he is as much mistaken as in any of the rest. A Man does not act contrary to his Interest by Marrying; for I and Thousands more know very well that we could never thrive till we were married; and have done well ever since; What we get, the Women save; a Man being fixt in Life minds his Business better and more steadily; and he that cannot thrive married, could never have throve better single; for the Idleness and Negligence of Men is more frequently fatal to Families, than the Extravagance of Women. Nor does a Man *lose his Liberty* but encrease it; for when he has no Wife to take Care of his Affairs at Home, if he carries on any Business there, he cannot go Abroad without a Detriment to that; but having a Wife, that he can confide in, he may with much more Freedom be abroad, and for a longer Time; thus the Business goes on comfortably, and the good Couple relieve one another by turns, like a faithful Pair of Doves. Nor does he *lose Friends* but gain them, by prudently marrying; for there are all the Woman's Relations added to his own, ready to assist and encourage the new-married Couple; and a Man that has a Wife and Children, is sooner trusted in Business, and can have Credit longer and for larger Sums than if he was single, inasmuch as he is look'd upon to be more firmly settled, and under greater Obligations to behave honestly, for his Family's Sake.

I have almost done with our *Adviser*, for he says but one

thing more; to wit, *that the best of the Sex are no better than Plagues*. Very hard again upon his poor Mother, who tho' she might be the best Woman in the World, was, it seems, in her graceless Son's Opinion, no better than a Pestilence. Certainly this Versifyer never knew what a Woman is! He must be, as I conjectur'd at first, some forlorn old Batchelor. And if I could conjure, I believe I should discover, that his Case is like that of many other old He-Maids I have heard of. Such senseless Advice as this can have no Effect upon them; 'tis nothing like this, that deters them from marrying. But having in some of their first Attempts upon the kinder Sort of the Fair Sex, come off with Shame and Disgrace, they persuade themselves that they are, (and perhaps they are) really Impotent: And so durst not marry, for fear of those dishonourable Decorations of the Head, which they think it the inevitable Fate of a Fumbler to wear. Then, like the Fox who could not use his Tail, (but the Fox had really lost it) they set up for *Advisers*, as the Gentleman I have been dealing with; and would fain persuade others, that the Use of their own Tails is more mischievous than beneficial. But I shall leave him to Repentance; and endeavour to make the Reader some Amends for my Scribble, by adding the following Verses from the two best English Poets that ever were; only hinting, that by the first two Lines 'tis plain from whence our Poetical Adviser had his Inspiration.

> Our Maker bids increase; who bids abstain,
> But our *Destroyer*, foe to GOD and Man?
> Hail wedded Love! mysterious Law, true source
> Of human Offspring, sole propriety
> In Paradise! of all Things common else.
> By thee adult'rous Lust was driv'n from Men,
> Among the bestial Herds to range; by thee,
> (Founded in Reason, loyal, just, and pure)
> Relations dear, and all the Charities
> Of Father, Son, and Brother, first were known.
> Perpetual Fountain of domestic Sweets!
> Whose Bed is undefil'd, and chaste, pronounc'd.
> Here, Love his golden shafts employs; here lights
> His constant Lamp; and waves his purple Wings;

Reigns here, and revels: not in the bought smile
Of harlots; loveless, joyless, un-endear'd;
Casual fruition!   *Milton.*

BUT happy they! the happiest of their Kind!
Whom gentler Stars unite, and in one Fate
Their Hearts, their Fortunes, and their Beings blend.
'Tis not the courser Tie of human Laws,
Unnatural oft, and foreign to the Mind,
Which binds their Peace, but Harmony itself,
Attuning all their Passions into Love;
Where Friendship full-exerts his softest Power,
Perfect Esteem enliven'd by Desire
Ineffable, and Sympathy of Soul,
Thought meeting Thought, and Will preventing Will,
With boundless Confidence; for nought but Love
Can answer Love, and render Bliss secure.
——those whom Love cements, in holy Faith,
And equal Transport, free as Nature, live,
Disdaining Fear; for what's the World to them,
It's Pomp, it's Pleasure, and it's Nonsense all!
Who in each other clasp whatever fair
High Fancy forms, and lavish Heart can wish,
Something than Beauty dearer, should they look
Or on the Mind, or mind-illumin'd Face;
Truth, Goodness, Honour, Harmony and Love,
The richest Bounty of indulgent *Heaven.*
Mean-time a smiling Offspring rises round,
And mingles both their Graces. By degrees,
The human Blossom blows; and every Day,
Soft as it rolls along, shows some new Charm,
The Father's Lustre, and the Mother's Bloom.
Then infant Reason grows apace, and calls
For the kind Hand of an assiduous Care;
Delightful Task! to rear the tender Thought,
To teach the young Idea how to shoot,
To pour the fresh Instruction o'er the Mind,
To breathe th' inspiring Spirit, and to plant
The generous Purpose in the glowing Breast.
Oh speak the Joy! You, whom the sudden Tear

Surprizes often, while you look around,
And nothing strikes your Eye but Sights of Bliss,
All various Nature pressing on the Heart,
Obedient Fortune, and approving *Heaven*.
These are the Blessings of diviner Love;
And thus their Moments fly; the *Seasons* thus,
As ceaseless round a jarring World they roll,
Still find them happy; and consenting SPRING
Sheds her own rosy Garland on their Head:
Till Evening comes at last, cool, gentle, calm;
When after the long vernal Day of Life,
Enamour'd more, as Soul approaches Soul,
Together, down they sink in social Sleep.   *Thomson*.

I am, Sir,
Your most humble Servant,
A. A.

The Pennsylvania Gazette, March 4, 1734/5

On a Pertinacious Obstinacy in Opinion

As a *pertinacious Obstinacy* in Opinion, and confident *Self-Sufficiency*, is possibly one of the greatest Vices, as well as Weaknesses, that the human Mind is capable of; so on the contrary a Readiness to give up a *loved Opinion*, upon due Conviction, is as great a Glory, as well as Happiness, as we are here capable of attaining: For as *Solomon* justly observes, a *wise Man* feareth; he, conscious of his own Imperfections, and sensible of the numberless Mistakes and Errors we are here subject and liable to, submits to the Dictates of Truth and Wisdom, where-ever he finds them, and thereby avoids the Evil, and attains the Glory. But the *Fool*, the self-sufficient Man, who proudly arrogates all Knowledge and Science to himself, rageth at Contradiction, and will not suffer his Knowledge to be questioned; what wonder is it then, if he *fall into Evil* when he is thus *confident*?

It is a just Observation, that a love of Truth and Goodness is not more essential to an honest Man than a Readiness to change his Mind and Practice, upon Conviction that he is in the wrong: And indeed, these two are inseparably connected in our present fallible Condition; possibly those who are arrived at a better State, may get clear of all their Mistakes, as well as their ill Habits immediately, and yet be capable of an endless Improvement in Knowledge, by having their Minds extended still to discover further Objects and new Relations of Things which they had no Notions of before. Upon this Supposition they may receive continual Additions to their Store, and yet have no Occasion to change their former Sentiments, because they were right as far as they went: But I am sure in this Life we find frequent Reason *to give up mistaken Opinions*, as well as to take in additional Light. We cannot but perceive ourselves liable to innumerable Errors, even when we are most careful to avoid them, either from our Ignorance in the Nature of Things, or in the Use and Meaning of Words. We take up Opinions, or engage in Parties, thro' the influence of Education, Friendship, and Alliances, or in the Heat of Opposition and Prejudice, which cannot be maintained upon more exact Enquiries, or in cool impartial Thoughts. *Prevailing Opinions* insensibly gain the Possession of our Minds, and have commonly the Advantage of being Firstcomers: and yet are very often no better than *prevailing Falshoods*, directly the Reverse of Truth. We are all apt to be misled, where the Safety of our Interest, or Peace with our Neighbours appear to depend upon a particular Sett of Principles, or upon falling in with a Party. A Man can hardly forbear wishing those Things to be true and right, which he apprehends would be for his Conveniency to find so: And many Perswasions, when they are looked into, plainly appear to have no better a Foundation.

It must therefore be highly reasonable, to examine our Sentiments, and always to *lie open to Conviction* and farther Light upon better Consideration of a Case, and to be willing to profit by the Diligence and Enquiries, as well of other Men, as ourselves. Without this, *Reason* would be given us in vain, *Study* and *Converse* wou'd be useless and unprofitable Things. It would be much happier for us to have no Advantages for better Instruction, or no Capacity to improve by them, if we must necessarily be staked down to those Apprehensions of

Things, either in *Religion* or *Politicks*, which we have happened to light upon.

That Man only, who is ready to change his Mind upon proper Conviction, is in the Way to come at the Knowledge of Truth. He who is neither *ashamed* of his own Ignorance, nor *unwilling* to receive Help from any Quarter towards the better Information of his Mind, or *afraid* to discard an old and *favoured* Opinion, upon better Evidence; he, I say, will find Truth kindly open before him, and freely offer it self to him: He will be surprized with the noble Pleasure of a new Discovery, and his Knowledge will be always progressive as long as he lives. But a Man *tenacious* of his *first Thoughts* is necessarily concluded in Error, if ever he happens to mistake: For when People once arrive to an Opinion of Infallibility, they can never grow wiser than they already are.

It is an Argument indeed of *Levity* and *Weakness* of Mind, to change our Opinion upon every slight Appearance, or to give it up to the Authority of others: But it argues a *real Greatness* of Soul, to have always a regard for Truth, superiour to every other Consideration, and to feel an undissembled Pleasure upon the Discovery of it.

If Truth is *Divine* and *Eternal*, 'tis the natural Homage of a Reasonable Mind to yield to its powerful Light, and embrace its lovely Form wherever it appears; 'tis *Superstition* to be fond of an old Opinion not supported by it; It is *Idolatry* to adore the Image and false Appearance of it: But it is open *Prophaness*, to neglect and contemn it. The only acceptable Sacrifice here, is that of our *darling Prejudice*, and the Offering of an upright Mind is like the Perfume of Incense.

But a sincere and hearty Lover of Truth will not content himself with a meer Change of his Sentiments upon Conviction, concealed within his own Breast; but will ingenuously acknowledge his Mistake, as freely and as publickly as he avowed it. The same Frankness and Sincerity which make me declare myself of one Opinion at one Time, will oblige me to declare myself of another afterwards, if my Sentiments are really altered. We owe this Justice to Mankind as well as Truth.

VERIDICUS.

The Pennsylvania Gazette, March 27, 1735

Dialogue Between Two Presbyterians

Mr. FRANKLIN,

You are desired by several of your Readers to print the following DIALOGUE. *It is between Two of the Presbyterian Meeting in this City. We cannot tell whether it may not be contrary to your Sentiments, but hope, if it should, you will not refuse publishing it on that Account: nor shall we be offended if you print any thing in Answer to it. We are yours, &c.*   A.B.C.D.

S. Good Morrow! I am glad to find you well and abroad; for not having seen you at Meeting lately, I concluded you were indispos'd.

T. Tis true I have not been much at Meeting lately, but that was not occasion'd by any Indisposition. In short, I stay at home, or else go to Church, because I do not like Mr. H. your new-fangled Preacher.

S. I am sorry we should differ in Opinion upon any Account; but let us reason the Point calmly; what Offence does Mr. *H.* give you?

T. Tis his Preaching disturbs me: He talks of nothing but the Duties of Morality: I do not love to hear so much of Morality: I am sure it will carry no Man to Heaven, and I do not think it fit to be preached in a Christian Congregation.

S. I suppose you think no Doctrine fit to be preached in a Christian Congregation, but such as Christ and his Apostles used to preach.

T. To be sure I think so.

S. I do not conceive then how you can dislike the Preaching of Morality, when you consider, that Morality made the principal Part of their Preaching as well as of Mr. *H*'s. What is Christ's Sermon on the Mount but an excellent moral Discourse, towards the End of which, (as foreseeing that People might in time come to depend more upon their *Faith* in him, than upon *Good Works*, for their Salvation) he tells the Hearers plainly, that their saying to him, *Lord, Lord*, (that is, professing themselves his Disciples or *Christians*) should give them no Title to Salvation, but their *Doing* the Will of his Father; and that tho' they have prophesied in his Name, yet he will declare to them, as Neglecters of Morality, that he never knew them.

T. *But what do you understand by that Expression of Christ's, Doing the Will of my Father.*

S. I understand it to be the Will of God, that we should live virtuous, upright, and good-doing Lives; as the Prophet understood it, when he said, *What doth the Lord require of thee, O Man, but to do justly, love Mercy, and walk humbly with the Lord thy God.*

T. *But is not Faith recommended in the New Testament as well as Morality?*

S. Tis true, it is. Faith is recommended as a Means of producing Morality: Our Saviour was a Teacher of Morality or Virtue, and they that were deficient and desired to be taught, ought first to *believe* in him as an able and faithful Teacher. Thus Faith would be a Means of producing Morality, and Morality of Salvation. But that from such Faith alone Salvation may be expected, appears to me to be neither a Christian Doctrine nor a reasonable one. And I should as soon expect, that my bare Believing Mr. *Grew* to be an excellent Teacher of the Mathematicks, would make me a Mathematician, as that Believing in Christ would of it self make a Man a Christian.

T. *Perhaps you may think, that tho' Faith alone cannot save a Man, Morality or Virtue alone, may.*

S. Morality or Virtue is the End, Faith only a Means to obtain that End: And if the End be obtained, it is no matter by what Means. What think you of these Sayings of Christ, when he was reproached for conversing chiefly with gross Sinners, *The whole,* says he, *need not a Physician, but they that are sick;* and, *I come not to call the Righteous, but Sinners, to Repentance:* Does not this imply, that there were good Men, who, without Faith in him, were in a State of Salvation? And moreover, did he not say of *Nathanael,* while he was yet an Unbeliever in him, and thought no Good could possibly come out of Nazareth, *Behold an Israelite indeed, in whom there is no Guile!* that is, *behold a virtuous upright Man.* Faith in Christ, however, may be and is of great Use to produce a good Life, but that it can conduce nothing towards Salvation where it does not conduce to Virtue, is, I suppose, plain from the Instance of the Devils, who are far from being Infidels, *they believe*, says the Scripture, *and tremble*. There were some indeed, even in the Apostles' Days, that set a great Value upon Faith, distinct from Good Works, they meerly idolized it, and thought that a Man ever so righteous could not be saved without it: But one of the Apostles, to show his Dislike of such Notions, tells them, that not only those heinous Sins of Theft, Murder, and Blasphemy, but even *Idleness*, or the Neglect of a Man's Business, was more pernicious than meer harmless Infidelity, *He that neglects to provide for them of his own House, says he, is WORSE than an Infidel*. St. *James*, in his second Chapter, is very zealous against these Cryers-up of Faith, and maintains that Faith without Virtue is useless, *Wilt thou know, O vain Man, says he, that Faith without Works is dead; and, shew me your Faith without your Works, and I will shew you mine by my Works*. Our Saviour, when describing the last Judgment, and declaring what shall give Admission into Bliss, or exclude from it, says nothing of *Faith* but what he says against it, that is, that those who cry *Lord, Lord*, and profess to have *believed* in his Name, have no Favour to expect on that Account; but declares that 'tis the Practice, or the omitting the Practice of the Duties of Morality, *Feeding the Hungry, cloathing the Naked, visiting the Sick*, &c. in short, 'tis the Doing or not Doing all the Good that lies in our Power, that will render us the Heirs of Happiness or Misery.

T. *But if Faith is of great Use to produce a good Life, why does not Mr.* H. *preach up Faith as well as Morality?*

S. Perhaps it may be this, that as the good Physician suits his Physick to the Disease he finds in the Patient, so Mr. *H.* may possibly think, that though Faith in Christ be properly first preach'd to Heathens and such as are ignorant of the Gospel, yet since he knows that we have been baptized in the Name of Christ, and educated in his Religion, and call'd after his Name, it may not be so immediately necessary to preach *Faith* to us who abound in it, as *Morality* in which we are evidently deficient: For our late Want of Charity to each other, our Heart-burnings and Bickerings are notorious. St. *James* says, *Where Envying and Strife is, there is Confusion and every evil Work*: and where Confusion and every evil Work is, *Morality* and Good-will to Men, can, I think, be no unsuitable

Doctrine. But surely *Morality* can do us no harm. Upon a Supposition that we all have Faith in Christ already, as I think we have, where can be the Damage of being exhorted to Good Works? Is Virtue Heresy; and Universal Benevolence False Doctrine, that any of us should keep away from Meeting because it is preached there.

T. *Well, I do not like it, and I hope we shall not long be troubled with it. A Commission of the Synod will sit in a short Time, and try this Sort of Preaching.*

S. I am glad to hear that the Synod are to take it into Consideration. There are Men of unquestionable Good Sense as well as Piety among them, and I doubt not but they will, by their Decision, deliver our Profession from the satyrical Reflection, which a few uneasy People of our Congregation have of late given Occasion for, *to wit*, That the *Presbyterians* are going to persecute, silence and condemn a good Preacher, for exhorting them to be honest and charitable to one another and the rest of Mankind.

T. *If Mr. H. is a Presbyterian Teacher, he ought to preach as Presbyterians use to preach; or else he may justly be condemn'd and silenc'd by our Church Authority. We ought to abide by the* Westminster *Confession of Faith; and he that does not, ought not to preach in our Meetings.*

S. The Apostacy of the Church from the primitive Simplicity of the Gospel, came on by Degrees; and do you think that the Reformation was of a sudden perfect, and that the first Reformers knew at once all that was right or wrong in Religion? Did not *Luther* at first preach only against selling of Pardons, allowing all the other Practices of the *Romish* Church for good. He afterwards went further, and *Calvin*, some think, yet further. The Church of *England* made a Stop, and fix'd her Faith and Doctrine by 39 Articles; with which the Presbyterians not satisfied, went yet farther; but being too self-confident to think, that as their Fathers were mistaken in some Things, they also might be in some others; and fancying themselves infallible in *their* Interpretations, they also ty'd themselves down by the *Westminster Confession*. But has not a Synod that meets in King GEORGE the Second's Reign, as much Right to interpret Scripture, as one that met in *Oliver*'s Time? And if any Doctrine then maintain'd, is, or shall hereafter be found not altogether orthodox, why must we be for ever confin'd to that, or to any, *Confession*?

T. But if the Majority of the Synod be against any Innovation, they may justly hinder the Innovator from Preaching.

S. That is as much as to say, if the Majority of the Preachers be in the wrong, they may justly hinder any Man from setting the People right; for a *Majority* may be in the wrong as well as the *Minority*, and frequently are. In the beginning of the Reformation, the *Majority* was vastly against the Reformers, and continues so to this Day; and, if, according to your Opinion, they had a Right to silence the *Minority*, I am sure the *Minority* ought to have been silent. But tell me, if the *Presbyterians* in this Country, being charitably enclin'd, should send a Missionary into *Turky*, to propagate the Gospel, would it not be unreasonable in the *Turks* to prohibit his Preaching?

T. It would, to be sure, because he comes to them for their good.

S. And if the *Turks*, believing us in the wrong, as we think them, should out of the same charitable Disposition, send a Missionary to preach *Mahometanism* to us, ought we not in the same manner to give him free Liberty of preaching his Doctrine?

T. It may be so; but what would you infer from that?

S. I would only infer, that if it would be thought reasonable to suffer a *Turk* to preach among us a Doctrine diametrically opposite to *Christianity*, it cannot be reasonable to silence one of our own Preachers, for preaching a Doctrine exactly agreeable to *Christianity*, only because he does not perhaps zealously propagate all the Doctrines of an old *Confession*. And upon the whole, though the *Majority* of the Synod should not in all respects approve of Mr. *H*'s Doctrine, I do not however think they will find it proper to condemn him. We have justly deny'd the Infallibility of the *Pope* and his *Councils* and *Synods* in their Interpretations of Scripture, and can we modestly claim *Infallibility* for our selves or our *Synods* in our way of Interpreting? Peace, Unity and Virtue in any Church are more to be regarded than Orthodoxy. In the present weak State of humane Nature, surrounded as we are on all sides with Ignorance and Error, it little becomes poor fallible Man to be positive and dogmatical in his Opinions.

No Point of Faith is so plain, as that *Morality* is our Duty, for all Sides agree in that. A virtuous Heretick shall be saved before a wicked Christian: for there is no such Thing as voluntary Error. Therefore, since 'tis an Uncertainty till we get to Heaven what true Orthodoxy in all points is, and since our Congregation is rather too small to be divided, I hope this Misunderstanding will soon be got over, and that we shall as heretofore unite again in mutual *Christian Charity*.

T. *I wish we may. I'll consider of what you've said, and wish you well.*

S. Farewell.

The Pennsylvania Gazette, April 10, 1735

Women's Court

We hear from Chester County, that last Week at a Vendue held there, a Man being unreasonably abusive to his Wife upon some trifling Occasion, the Women form'd themselves into a Court, and order'd him to be apprehended by their Officers and brought to Tryal: Being found guilty he was condemn'd to be duck'd 3 times in a neighbouring Pond, and to have one half cut off, of his Hair and Beard (which it seems he wore at full length) and the Sentence was accordingly executed, to the great Diversion of the Spectators.

The Pennsylvania Gazette, April 17, 1735

Advice to a Pretty Creature and Replies

Mr. *Franklin*,

"Pray let the prettiest Creature in this Place know, (by publishing this) That if it was not for her Affectation, she would be absolutely irresistible."

The Pennsylvania Gazette, November 20, 1735

The little Epistle in our last, has produced no less than six, which follow in the order we receiv'd 'em.

Mr. *Franklin*,

'I cannot conceive who your Correspondent means by *the prettiest Creature* in this Place; but I can assure either him or her, that she who is truly so, has no Affectation at all.'

SIR,

'Since your last Week's Paper I have look'd in my Glass a thousand Times, I believe, in one Day; and if it was not for the Charge of Affectation I might, without Partiality, believe myself the Person meant.'

Mr. *Franklin*,

'I must own that several have told me, I am the prettiest Creature in this Place; but I believe I shou'd not have been tax'd with Affectation if I cou'd have thought as well of them as they do of themselves.'

SIR,

'Your Sex calls me pretty; my own affected. Is it from Judgment in the one, or Envy in the other?'

Mr. *Franklin*,

'They that call me affected are greatly mistaken; for I don't know that I ever refus'd a Kiss to any Body but a Fool.'

Friend Benjamin,

'I am not at all displeased at being charged with Affectation. Thou know'st the vain People call Decency of Behaviour by that Name.'

The Pennsylvania Gazette, November 27, 1735

A Sea Monster

From Bermuda, they write, that a Sea Monster has been lately seen there, the upper part of whose Body was in the Shape and about the Bigness of a Boy of 12 Years old, with long black Hair; the lower Part resembled a Fish. He was first seen on shore, and taking to the Water, was pursu'd by People in a Boat, who intended to strike him with a Fishgig; but approaching him, the human Likeness surpris'd them into Compassion, and they had not the Power to do it.

The Pennsylvania Gazette, April 29, 1736

The Art of Saying Little in Much

Amplification, or the Art of saying *Little in Much*, seems to be principally studied by the Gentlemen Retainers to the Law. 'Tis highly useful when they are to speak at the Bar; for by its Help, they talk a great while, and appear to say a great deal, when they have really very little to say. But 'tis principally us'd in Deeds and every thing they write. You must abridge their Performances to understand them; and when you find how little there is in a Writing of vast Bulk, you will be as much surpriz'd as a Stranger at the Opening of a *Pumpkin*.

It is said, that in the Reign of *William* the Conqueror, the Conveyance of a large Estate, might be made in about half a dozen short Lines; which was nevertheless in every Respect sufficiently authentick. For several Hundred Years past, Conveyances and Writings in the Law have been continually encreasing in Bulk, and when they will come to their full Growth, no Man knows: For the Rule, *That every thing past and present ought to be express'd, and every thing future provided for*, (tho' one would think a large Writing might be made by it) does not serve to confine us at present; since all those things are not only to be express'd, but may (by the Modern License) be express'd by all the *different Words* we can think of. Probably the Invention of Printing, which took from the Scribes great Part of their former Employment, put them on the Contrivance of making up by a Multitude of Words, what they wanted in real Business; hence the plain and strong Expression, *shall be his own*, is now swoln into, *shall and may at all Times hereafter forever, and so from time to time, freely, quietly and peaceably, have, hold and enjoy, &c*. The Lawyer, in one of *Steele*'s Comedies, instructs his Pupil, that *Tautology* is the first, second, and third Parts of his Profession, that is to say, *the whole of it*: And adds, *That he hopes to see the Time, when it will require as much Parchment to convey a Piece of Land as will cover it.* That time perhaps is not far off: For I am told, that the Deeds belonging to the Title of some small Lotts, (which have gone thro' several Hands) are nearly sufficient for the Purpose.

But of all the Writings I have ever seen, for the Multiplicity, Variety, Particularity, and prodigious Flow of Expression, none come up to the Petition of *Dermond O Folivey*, an Attorney of the Kingdom of *Ireland*: As the Petition is curious in itself, and may serve as a Precedent for young Clerks, when they would acquire a proper Stile in their Performances, I shall give it to the Publick entire, as follows.

To the Right Honourable *Sir William Asten*, Knight, and
Lord Judge of Assize of the *Munster* Circuit.
The humble Petition *of* Dermond O Folivey *a well
and most accomplished Gentleman.*

'Most humbly, and most submissively, and most obediently, and most dutifully, by shewing, and expressing, and declaring to your Lordship, that whereby, and whereas, and wherein, the most major, and most greater, and most bigger, and the most stronger Part of the most best, and the most ablest, and the most mightiest Sort of the People of the Barony of *Torrough* and County of *Kerry*, finding, and knowing, and certifying themselves, both hereafter, and the Time past, and now, and then, and at the present time, to be very much oppressed, and distressed, and overcharged in all Taxes, and Quit-rents, and other Levies, and accidental Applotments, and Collections, and Gatherings-together in the Barony of *Torrough* and County of *Kerry* aforesaid, And for the future Prevention of all, and every such, henceforth, hereafter, heretofore, and for the time to come, and now, and then, and at this time, and forever, the aforesaid most major, and most bigger, and most better, and most stronger Part of the most best, and most ablest, and most mightiest Sort of the People of *Torrough* and County of *Kerry* aforesaid, HATH appointed, nominated, constituted, ordained, declared, elected, and made me Mr. *Dermond O Folivey* to solicite, and make mention to your Lordship, looking upon me now, and then, and there, and here, the said Mr. *Dermond O Folivey*, to be the fittest, the most mightiest, and the most ablest, and the most best, and the most accomplished, and the most eloquentest Spokesman within the said Barony and County, their granded, and well beloved, and well bestowed, and better merited Agent and Sollicitor, to represent Oppression, and Suppression, and Extortion, for all such, and for all much, and whereof, and whereby, and whereupon, your Petitioner fairly, and finely, and honestly, and ingeniously, and deservedly appointed, nominated, constituted, and ordained, and elected, and approved, and made choice of me the said Mr. *Dermond O Folivey* as an Agent and Sollicitor, to undergo, and overgo, and under-run, and over-run, and manage this much, big, and mighty Service.

'These are therefore to will, and to shall be, now, and then, and there, and at this time, and at the time past, and heretofore, and formerly, and at the present, and forever, the humble, and special, and important, and mighty, and irrefatigable Request of me, your Petitioner and Sollicitor-General aforesaid; THAT your Lordship will be pleased, and satisfied, and resolved, to grant, and give, and deliver, and bestow, upon me Mr. *Dermond O Folivey*, your before recited, and nominated Petitioner and Sollicitor-General aforesaid, an Order and Judgment, and Warrant, and Authority of Preference to my Lord *Kerry*, and Mr. *Henry Punceby*, Esq; and Justice of the Peace and Quorum, or to any four or five or more or less, or either or neither of them, now, and then, and there, and here, and any where, and every where, and somewhere, and no-where, to call and bring, and fetch, and carry, before him, or them, or either of them, or neither, or both, such Party or Parties as they shall imagine, and conceive, and consider, and suppose, and assent, and esteem, and think fit, and meet, and necessary, and decent, and convenient, all, and every, and either, or neither of them, to call, to examine, and call to a strict Account; and that Part, and most Part, Extortion; and then, and there, when, and where, and whether, to establish, and elect, and direct, and impower, and authorize all such, and all much, Bailiffs, and under Receivers, and Collectors and Gatherers-together of Money, as your Petitioner did, or do, or have, or had, or shall, or will, or may, or might, or should, or could, or ought to chuse, or pitch upon with, and punctually to desire my self Mr. *Dermond O Folivey* that they, them, and these, and every, and either, and neither of them, that shall, and did, and have, and do, and will him in Peace, and Unity, and Amity, and Concord, and Tranquility, henceforth, and for the time to come, and hereafter, and for the time past, and not past, and the time present, and now, and for everlasting; and especially not to molest, or trouble, or hinder, or disturb, or hurt, or meddle with the Petitioner, my self, Mr. *Dermond O Folivey*, in his Possession of 72 Acres of Land in *Gertogolinmore* in the Barony of *Torrough* and County of *Kerry*.'

Given, and granted, and dated, and signed, and sealed by my own Hand and with my own Hand, and for my own Hand, and under my own Hand and Seal this — Day of — Anno Dom. —— } Mr. *Dermond O Folivey*.

The Pennsylvania Gazette, June 17, 1736

The Drinker's Dictionary

Nothing more like a Fool than a drunken Man.
Poor Richard.

'Tis an old Remark, that Vice always endeavours to assume the Appearance of Virtue: Thus Covetousness calls itself *Prudence*; *Prodigality* would be thought *Generosity*; and so of others. This perhaps arises hence, that Mankind naturally and universally approve Virtue in their Hearts, and detest Vice; and therefore, whenever thro' Temptation they fall into a Practice of the latter, they would if possible conceal it from themselves as well as others, under some other Name than that which properly belongs to it.

But DRUNKENNESS is a very unfortunate Vice in this respect. It bears no kind of Similitude with any sort of Virtue, from which it might possibly borrow a Name; and is therefore reduc'd to the wretched Necessity of being express'd by distant round-about Phrases, and of perpetually varying those Phrases, as often as they come to be well understood to signify plainly that A MAN IS DRUNK.

Tho' every one may possibly recollect a Dozen at least of the Expressions us'd on this Occasion, yet I think no one who has not much frequented Taverns would imagine the number of them so great as it really is. It may therefore surprize as well as divert the sober Reader, to have the Sight of a new Piece, lately communicated to me, entitled

The DRINKERS DICTIONARY.

A

He is Addled,
He's casting up his Accounts,
He's Afflicted,
He's in his Airs.

B

He's Biggy,
  Bewitch'd,
  Block and Block,
  Boozy,
  Bowz'd,
  Been at Barbadoes,
  Piss'd in the Brook,
  Drunk as a Wheel-Barrow,
  Burdock'd,
  Buskey,
  Buzzey,
Has Stole a Manchet out of the Brewer's Basket,
His Head is full of Bees,
Has been in the Bibbing Plot,
Has drank more than he has bled,
He's Bungey,
  As Drunk as a Beggar,
He sees the Bears,

He's kiss'd black Betty,
He's had a Thump over the Head with Sampson's Jawbone,
He's Bridgey.

C

He's Cat,
  Cagrin'd,
  Capable,
  Cramp'd,
  Cherubimical,
  Cherry Merry,
  Wamble Crop'd,
  Crack'd,
  Concern'd,
  Half Way to Concord,
Has taken a Chirriping-Glass,
  Got Corns in his Head,
  A Cup to much,
  Coguy,
  Copey,
He's heat his Copper,
He's Crocus,
  Catch'd,
He cuts his Capers,
He's been in the Cellar,

He's in his Cups,
  Non Compos,
  Cock'd,
  Curv'd,
  Cut,
  Chipper,
  Chickery,
  Loaded his Cart,
He's been too free with the
    Creature,
Sir Richard has taken off his
    Considering Cap,
He's Chap-fallen,

D
He's Disguiz'd,
He's got a Dish,
  Kill'd his Dog,
  Took his Drops,
It is a Dark Day with him,
He's a Dead Man,
Has Dipp'd his Bill,
He's Dagg'd,
He's seen the Devil,

E
He's Prince Eugene,
  Enter'd,
  Wet both Eyes,
  Cock Ey'd,
  Got the Pole Evil,
  Got a brass Eye,
  Made an Example,
He's Eat a Toad & half for
    Breakfast.
  In his Element,

F
He's Fishey,
  Fox'd,
  Fuddled,
  Sore Footed,
  Frozen,

Well in for't,
Owes no Man a Farthing,
Fears no Man,
Crump Footed,
Been to France,
Flush'd,
Froze his Mouth,
Fetter'd,
Been to a Funeral,
His Flag is out,
Fuzl'd,
Spoke with his Friend,
Been at an Indian Feast.

G
He's Glad,
  Groatable,
  Gold-headed,
  Glaiz'd,
  Generous,
  Booz'd the Gage,
  As Dizzy as a Goose,
  Been before George,
  Got the Gout,
  Had a Kick in the Guts,
  Been with Sir John Goa,
  Been at Geneva,
  Globular,
  Got the Glanders.

H
Half and Half,
Hardy,
Top Heavy,
Got by the Head,
Hiddey,
Got on his little Hat,
Hammerish,
Loose in the Hilts,
Knows not the way Home,
Got the Hornson,
Haunted with Evil Spirits,

Has Taken Hippocrates
  grand Elixir,

I

He's Intoxicated,
  Jolly,
  Jagg'd,
  Jambled,
  Going to Jerusalem,
  Jocular,
  Been to Jerico,
  Juicy.

K

He's a King,
  Clips the King's English,
  Seen the French King,
  The King is his Cousin,
  Got Kib'd Heels,
  Knapt,
  Het his Kettle.

L

He's in Liquor,
  Lordly,
  He makes Indentures with
    his Leggs,
  Well to Live,
  Light,
  Lappy,
  Limber,

M

He sees two Moons,
  Merry,
  Middling,
  Moon-Ey'd,
  Muddled,
  Seen a Flock of Moons,
  Maudlin,
  Mountous,
  Muddy,
  Rais'd his Monuments,
  Mellow,

N

He's eat the Cocoa Nut,
  Nimptopsical,
  Got the Night Mare,

O

He's Oil'd,
  Eat Opium,
  Smelt of an Onion,
  Oxycrocium,
  Overset,

P

He drank till he gave up his
    Half-Penny,
  Pidgeon Ey'd,
  Pungey,
  Priddy,
  As good conditioned as a
    Puppy,
Has scalt his Head Pan,
  Been among the
    Philistines,
  In his Prosperity,
He's been among the
    Philippians,
He's contending with
    Pharaoh,
  Wasted his Paunch,
He's Polite,
  Eat a Pudding
    Bagg,

Q

He's Quarrelsome,

R

He's Rocky,
  Raddled,
  Rich,
  Religious,
  Lost his Rudder,
  Ragged,
  Rais'd,

Been too free with Sir
   Richard,
Like a Rat in Trouble.

S

He's Stitch'd,
   Seafaring,
   In the Sudds,
   Strong,
   Been in the Sun,
   As Drunk as David's Sow,
   Swampt,
His Skin is full,
He's Steady,
He's Stiff,
He's burnt his Shoulder,
He's got his Top Gallant Sails
   out,
   Seen the yellow Star,
   As Stiff as a Ring-bolt,
   Half Seas over,
   His Shoe pinches him,
   Staggerish,
   It is Star-light with him,
   He carries too much Sail,
   Stew'd
   Stubb'd,
   Soak'd,
   Soft,
Been too free with Sir John
   Strawberry,

He's right before the Wind
   with all his Studding
   Sails out,
Has Sold his Senses.

T

He's Top'd,
   Tongue-ty'd,
   Tann'd,
   Tipium Grove,
   Double Tongu'd,
   Topsy Turvey,
   Tipsey,
Has Swallow'd a Tavern
   Token,
He's Thaw'd,
He's in a Trance,
He's Trammel'd,

V

He makes Virginia Fence,
   Valiant,
   Got the Indian Vapours,

W

The Malt is above the
   Water,
He's Wise,
He's Wet,
He's been to the Salt Water,
He's Water-soaken,
He's very Weary,
   Out of the Way.

The Phrases in this Dictionary are not (like most of our
Terms of Art) borrow'd from Foreign Languages, neither are
they collected from the Writings of the Learned in our own,
but gather'd wholly from the modern Tavern-Conversation of
Tiplers. I do not doubt but that there are many more in use;
and I was even tempted to add a new one my self under
the Letter B, to wit, *Brutify'd*: But upon Consideration, I
fear'd being guilty of Injustice to the Brute Creation, if I
represented Drunkenness as a beastly Vice, since, 'tis well-

known, that the Brutes are in general a very sober sort of People.

The Pennsylvania Gazette, January 13, 1736/7

Captain Farra

The same Day arrived Capt. Farra, who has long been given over for lost. In his Voyage from Jamaica hither, he was cast away in Palachee Bay within Cape Florida, among the Cannibal Indians, who were extreamly kind and assisted in saving the Cargo, Rigging, &c. And News of the Wreck coming to Augustine, the Spaniards sent Periagua's and other small Vessels round to take in what was sav'd, and bring it to that Port; where Capt. Farra hir'd a Rhode-Island Sloop to bring it hither. Had this English Vessel been forc'd ashore on the civil, polite, hospitable, christian, protestant Coast of Great-Britain, Query, *Might they have expected kinder Treatment from their own Countrymen?*

The Pennsylvania Gazette, June 2, 1737

Upon the Talents Requisite in an Almanack-Writer

To the Author of the Pennsylvania Gazette.

SIR,

As I am a great Lover of all Works of Ingenuity, and the Authors of them, so more especially am I a great Reader and Admirer of those *Labours of the Learned*, called *ALMA-NACKS*.

As I am a considerable Proficient in this Sort of Learning; and as at this time of the Year, Copies of Almanacks for the next Year usually come to the Press, long before they are wanted: And as I have laid out many a Six-pence among your Customers, the Profit whereof has in a great Measure redounded to you: So I may reasonably hope to be look'd on as a good Customer, and claim a favourable Place in your Paper.

I have a large Volume in Manuscript by me, on the Important Subject of *Almanack-making*, which I may in time communicate to the Publick; but at present I am willing to oblige them, with only a Taste of my Skill, which (if I have any Title to the Art of Prognostication) will certainly make them long for the whole.

My present Design, is to give to you and the Publick, *a short Essay*, upon the Talents requisite in *an Almanack-Writer*, by which it will plainly appear, how much the Community is indebted to Men of such *great and uncommon Parts and Sagacity*.

An *Almanack-Writer*, Sir, should be born one like a Poet; for as I read among the Works of the learned, *Poeta nascitur non fit*; so it is a Maxim with me, that *Almanackorum scriptor nascitur not fit*. Gifts of Nature, Sir, compleated by Rules of Art, are indispensably Necessary to make a great Man this way, as well as any other.

The first Thing requisite in an *Almanack-Writer*, is, *That he should be descended of a great Family, and bear a Coat of Arms*, this gives Lustre and Authority to what a Man writes, and makes the common People to believe, that *certainly this is a great Man*. I have known Almanack-Writers so curious and exact in this particular, that they have been at the Expence and Charge of a Wooden Cut in the Frontispiece, with their Arms emblazon'd, and surrounded with a Label, expressing the Name of the Family. This, Sir, made a great Impression, I confess, upon myself and others, and made those Works to go off well.

If the Author who was *born to be an Almanack-maker*, has the Misfortune to be meanly descended, but yet, has a true Genius; if he has by him, or can borrow a Book, entitul'd the Peerage of *England*, he may safely borrow a Coat, (if there happens to be a Peer of his own Name) by reason, we are so great a Way distant from the Earl Marshal of that Part of *Great-Britain* call'd *England*.

The next Talent requisite in the forming of *a compleat Almanack-Writer*, is a Sort of Gravity, which keeps a due medium between Dulness and Nonsense, and yet has a Mixture of both. Now you know, Sir, that grave Men are taken by the common People always for wise Men. Gravity is just as good a Picture of Wisdom, as Pertness is of Wit, and therefore very taking. And to compleat an Almanack-maker, in this particular, he shou'd write Sentences, and throw out Hints, that neither himself, nor any Body else can understand or know the Meaning of. And this is also a necessary Talent. I will give you some Instances of this Way of Writing, which are almost inimitable, such as these, *Leeds, Jan.* 23. 1736. *Beware, the Design is suspected.* Feb. 23. *The World is bad with somebody.* Mar. 27. *Crimes not remitted.* April 10. *Cully Mully puff appears.* May 21 *The Sword of Satan is drawn.* June 7. *The Cat eat the Candle.* Now, Sir, Why should the Sword of Satan be drawn to kill the Cat on the 21st Day of *May*, when it plainly appears in Print, that the Cat did not eat the Candle till the 7th of *June* following? This Question no Man but an Astrologer can possibly answer.

In the next Place, I lay it down as a certain Maxim or Position, that *an Almanack-Writer show'd not be a finish'd Poet, but a Piece of one*, and qualify'd to write, what we vulgarly call Doggerel; and that his Poetry shou'd bear a near Resemblance to his Prose. I must beg *Horace's* and my Lord *Roscommon's* Pardon, if I dissent from them in this one particular. I will give you their Rule in my Lord's English Translation, and save myself the Trouble of transcribing the Latin of *Horace*.

> *"But no Authority of Gods nor Men*
> *Allow of any Mean in Poesy."*

This might for all I know be a Rule for Poetry among the Ancients, but the Moderns have found it troublesome, and the most of them, have wholly neglected it for that Reason. Witness the Authors Verses, whose Praise I am now celebrating, *December* 1736.

> *Now is my 12 Months Task come to conclusion,*
> *Lord free us from Hatred, Envy and Confusion.*
> *All are not pleas'd, nor never will i'th' main.*
> *Fewds and Discords among us will remain.*
> *Be that as 'twill, however I'm glad to see,*
> *Envy disappointed both at Land and Sea.*

I do not pretend to say, that this is like the Poetry of *Horace*, or Lord *Roscommon*, but it is the Poesy of an Astrologer; it is his own and not borrowed; It is occult and mysterious. It has a due Degree of that Sort of Gravity, which I have mentioned: In short, it is form'd upon the Rules which I have laid down in this short Essay.

I could further prove to you, if I was to go about it, That *an Almanack-Writer* ought not only to be a Piece of a Wit, but a very Wag; and that he shou'd have the Art also to make People believe, that he is almost a Conjurer, &c. But these Things I reserve for my greater Work, and in the mean time, until that appears, I desire to remain,

Sir,

Sept. 27. 1737.   *Your very humble Servant,*

PHILOMATH.

The Pennsylvania Gazette, October 20, 1737

The Compassion of Captain Croak

On the 3d Inst. arrived here the *Rose*, of *London*, Capt. *Croak* Commander, from whom we have the following Relation, viz.

That on the 17th of *June* last, being on his Voyage from *Newfoundland* to this Port, and in the Latitude of 41 Deg. N. and 48 Deg. of Longitude, he espied a Sail that made Signals of Distress; whereupon he came up to her, and found her so near Sinking, that he had only just Time to save the Persons belonging to her, (who were to the Number of 61) for he had no sooner taken them on board his own Vessel, but the other foundered in the Sea. The Persons thus providentially saved, informed him:

That they were for the most part indented Servants and set Sail from *Cork* for *Boston*, the 29th of *March* last, on board the said Vessel, which was called the Speedwell, of which *William Stockdale* had been Master. That about the 7th of *May*, their Water and Bread beginning to fall short, they were obliged to touch at the Island of St. *Michael's*, and having lain there at Anchor, about 5 Days, a boisterous and violent

Wind, blowing S W (while the Captain and Super-Cargo, and several others belonging to the Vessel were on Shore) forced her out to Sea, leaving her Anchor and Cable behind. That it was 21 Days before she could recover the Island, and being arrived there, which was on a Friday, those on board were informed, that the Master and those before mentioned, to have been left ashore, had set Sail for *Lisbon* the Friday before, on Board one Capt. *Gillegan*. That thereupon the Persons, who had then the Care of the Vessel, put to Sea in order to proceed on their Voyage to *Boston*. That having met with a hard Gale of Wind, which caused the Vessel's Larboard Quarter to give way, they were obliged to keep two Pumps a going without Intermission, during the Space of three Days, when they most providentially met with the *Rose*, that saved their Lives, which otherwise were inevitably lost. *As it was running a Risque, which few others have cared to do, it was therefore a more remarkable Act of Humanity, in the Commander of the* Rose*, to take so many additional Mouths on Board, when he had only Provisions for his own Company. This is such an Instance of a laudable Compassion, that it is to be wished it may not be more admired than imitated on the like Occasions.*

The Pennsylvania Gazette, August 10, 1738

Octuplets

Aug. 5. We hear that the Wife of a Peasant in the District of *Boisleduc* was brought to Bed of eight Children, seven Girls and one Boy, who were all living.

The Pennsylvania Gazette, November 24, 1738

Obadiah Plainman Defends the Meaner Sort

To the Author of the Letter in the last Pennsylvania *Gazette.*
SIR,
On my first hearing of the Outcry that was raised against the Paragraph, that related to the shutting up of the Concert

Room, &c. I immediately called for the *Gazette*; but, tho' I read the Article over and over with the greatest Attention, I was not able to discover in it the least injurious Reflection on the Characters of the Gentlemen concerned. My ill Success, I then attributed to my Stupidity, and concluded that the Abuse, tho' I could not see it, must nevertheless be very perspicuous to the BETTER SORT, otherwise, they would not have made so loud a Complaint against it, as it is publickly known they did, *since it was in the publick Street*.

I comforted myself with the Hopes, that, on the Appearance of your Letter, the Mist would have been dispelled from my Eyes. But, I can't help declaring, that, notwithstanding all the Assistance you have furnished me with, the Injury complained of, still remains to me as great a Secret as ever.

You tell us *the Paragraph manifestly carries in it an Insinuation,* that *the Persons concerned in the Concert declin'd meeting, as thinking it inconsistent with the Doctrine of the Christian Religion.* But, with Submission, I think the Paragraph manifestly insinuates the quite contrary. It mentions, that the Gentlemen concerned in the Concert, &c. caused the Door to be *broke open*, which was the strongest Evidence that could be given of their Dislike to the Principles on which it had been shut up. Therefore, tho' it immediately follows, that no Company came the last Assembly Night, it was *most unnatural* to suppose they should so *suddenly* have changed their Sentiments, and declined their Diversions on any religious Consideration.

Let us admit for Argument's Sake (which, otherwise, can by no Means be admitted) that the Words are guilty of the Insinuation, which you are so fond it should be thought they are. Yet, how does it appear that the Characters of the Gentlemen are injured by it? You tell us, *They think so.* But, is that a Reason to induce *Us* to believe it is *really* so? Since you have appealed to the *Mob* as *Judges* of this IMPORTANT Controversy, I must inform you, that the Assertion (and much less, *the Belief*) of any Man, never passes for Argument at *Our* impartial Tribunal. For my own Part (I speak with an humble Deference to the rest of my Brethren) I cannot conceive how any Person's Reputation can be prejudiced, tho' it should be reported, that he has left off making of Legs, or cutting of Capers.

Perhaps you will object, *that it is not the Fact, but the Motive, which is controverted; That you admit the Company did not meet; but deny, they declined meeting, for the Reason, which,* as you pretend, *is insinuated in the Gazette.* If this be the true State of the Question, *we* unanimously pronounce the Accusation to be groundless. In Matters of such a Nature, no Man can judge of your Thoughts but yourself: Therefore, your Denial of the Charge was a sufficient, and indeed the *only* proper Defence you could make.

But you were not contented to stop here, but must needs tell *us* incoherent Stories of Mr. *Whitefield* and Mr. *Seward*, and, under Pretence of a Vindication, foist into the News-Paper Invectives against those two Gentlemen. You might with equal Propriety have entertained *Us* with the History of *Romulus* and *Remus*, and entituled it "an Argument to prove, that you did not *think* Dancing, or *idle* Capering an unchristian Diversion."

I hope, Sir, from what I have said, you are now convinced, that you have brought before *Us* a most *ridiculous* Complaint against an *imaginary* Abuse, and consequently you have been all this Time doing nothing more than beating the Air, and *fighting without an Adversary.*

In the next Place, I am to reprimand you, Sir, for your disrespectful Behaviour to *Us*, whom you had chosen for your Judges. *We* take Notice, that you have ranked yourself under the Denomination of the BETTER SORT of People, which is an Expression always made use of in Contradistinction to the *meaner Sort, i.e.* the Mob, or the Rabble. Tho' *We* are not displeased with such Appellations when bestowed on *Us* by our Friends, yet *We* have ever regarded them as Terms of outrageous Reproach, when applied to *Us* by our Enemies; for in this (and so it is in many other Cases) the Words are to receive their Construction from the *known* Mind of the Speaker: Your *Demosthenes'* and *Ciceroes*, your *Sidneys* and *Trenchards* never approached *Us* but with Reverence: *The High and Mighty Mob, The Majesty of the Rabble, The Honour and Dignity of the Populace, Or* such *like* Terms of Respect, were frequent in their Orations; and what a high Opinion they entertained of the Accuracy of *Our* Judgment, appears from those elaborate Compositions they addressed to *Us*.

They never took upon them to make a Difference of Persons, but as they were distinguished by their Virtues or their Vices. But now our present Scriblers expect our Applause for reviling us to our Faces. They consider us as a stupid Herd, in whom the Light of Reason is extinguished. Hence every impertinent Babler thinks himself qualified to harangue us, without Style, Argument or Justness of Sentiment. Your gross Deficiency in the two latter Particulars I have already given Instances of; and as to your Skill in Language you have furnished *Us* with the following notable Example: You affirm *That Mr.* Whitefield's *Tenets are mischievous*: Therefore, on that Supposition, it is impossible they should be contemptible; yet, with the same Breath *you assure* Us*, that you have them in the utmost Contempt*. This is the merriest Gibberish I ever met with. Surely, you have not published it as a Sample of the Stile of those polite Folks, who by their own Authority, *"contrary to Law and Justice, without any previous Application to or Consent first had"* of their Fellow-Citizens, have usurped the Title of the BETTER SORT.

Under these *gentle* Reprehensions *We* now dismiss you, hoping you will make a proper Use of them, when you shall judge it *convenient* to appeal to *Us* again.

   I am,   *On Behalf of myself and the Rest of my*
                            Brethren of the Meaner Sort,
                                Yours, *&c.*
                                OBADIAH PLAINMAN.

The Pennsylvania Gazette, May 15, 1740

Obadiah Plainman to Tom Trueman

To TOM TRUEMAN.

Dear Tommy,

Tho' there are two Letters addressed to me, one in the *Gazette*, and the other in the *Mercury*; yet, from the near

Conformity they bear to one another in Sentiment, Reasoning, and *Similes*, I am apt to conclude they were wrote by the same Hand, *Or*, if by different Persons, that they communicated their Thoughts to one another, and then club'd them together for the Service of the *Public*. On the latter Supposition, it would be unnecessary in my Reply, to regard them as distinct Performances of several Writers; I therefore address myself to you as the Author of both.

You tell me you have found out by my Letter, that I imagine myself the Prince and Leader of a mighty People. I wonder how a Genius so penetrating as yours could be led into so gross an Error: For, alas! I am but a poor ordinary Mechanick of this City, obliged to work hard for the Maintenance of myself, my Wife, and several small Children. When my daily Labour is over, instead of going to the Alehouse, I amuse myself with the Books of the Library Company, of which I am an *unworthy* Member. This Account of my Circumstances, the Meanness of my Education, and my innocent Manner of Life, I hope, will effectually remove those *groundless* Suspicions, which you seemed to entertain, of my being in a Plot against the State.

You are pleased to inform me, that *you are* But *a young Man, Country-born*. In Return for such an *important* Discovery, I will let you into another Secret of as great Consequence.—"Hark in your Ear," *I am* But *an old Man not Country-born*. In Respect of Soil, I presume neither of us will pretend to any Superiority; but the Pre-eminence being on my Side in Regard to my Age, I shall make Use of that Privilege to *Document* you a little.

I shall first consider the argumentative Part of your Letter in the Gazette. You there assert, *that from the first Facts alledged in the Paragraph, supposing nothing more said, a Stranger would unquestionably imagine that the Rooms were shut up by the Owners*. This Assertion is granted you, *because* you are so kind to allow that It is absolutely *destroyed* by the Remainder of the Article; which says, *the Gentlemen caused the Door to be broke open again*. Thus far we have travelled, thro' the Construction of the Paragraph, with a mutual Agreement, and a wonderful Satisfaction on both Sides. But now you ask, *What does the Author mean by informing the World that no*

Company came the, then, *last Assembly Night?* Ay, what does he mean? This is the "plaguy" Difficulty that has so *strangely puzzled,* and which still seems to *continue* to puzzle the *Better Sort.* You are however sure, for your Part, that his Words must be intended to signify *Something* or NOTHING. As I shall always be ready to gratify you, when I can do it safely, I agree to your latter Alternative. But then, how can those Words which, on your own Concession, mean NOTHING, carry in them the *Insinuation* you contend for, or any Insinuation at all. This notwithstanding, you think yourself so absolutely certain of the Truth of your Consequence, that one would imagine you were ready to take your corporal Oath of it, when required, tho' you acknowledge there is not the *least Shadow* of any Premises from which it can be deduced. This is such strange Reasoning, that *doubtless, it has been reserved to this Time, solely,* dear *Tommy,* for a Head so singularly clear and logical as yours. You desire I would show the World the Interpretation the Words will bear. Your Request, my dear Child, is contrary to all Laws of Argument, and therefore (tho' I am heartily sorry it should happen so) I cannot comply with your Desire. If you advance an Assertion, it is at your own Peril to support it with Proofs, which if you fail in, every one has a Right to *reject it as false.*

In my first I did not give any Construction of the Paragraph, for my Business was to defend it from the Insinuation with which it unjustly stood accused; and therefore, from the Gentlemen's declared Dislike of Mr. *Whitefield*'s Principles, I inferred it was unnatural to suppose they should so suddenly have changed their Sentiments. Against this Defence you object, *that the* Followers of Mr. *Whitefield* would naturally believe so sudden a Conversion. Now, that They should be capable of *Thinking* so, whom, in the first Colume of the *Gazette,* you regard as *irrational* Creatures, and, consequently, destitute of the Faculty of *Thinking,* is to me quite incomprehensible.

I now proceed to your Complaint of the gross Misrepresentation, as you imagine, of the Meaning of the Words, *Better Sort,* in your first Letter. That *notable* Epistle was published as the Sentiments of the whole Company concerned in the Concert. Therefore (whether the Fact be so or not; for that is entirely out of the Question) I had NO RIGHT to consider it, but as Theirs, nor Them in any other Light than as they there appeared, namely as Part of the *People*, which always signifies the Governed, or *private Persons*. Tho' the Stile be in the third Person, yet, without any Prejudice to the Sense, it may be changed to the first, and then it will run thus, *We think our Characters injured by the Paragraph, as tho' Mr.* Whitefield *had met with great Success among us the* BETTER SORT *of People of Pennsilvania*. This Case has no Manner of Resemblance to those which you have put, of Boys at Bandy-Wicket, young Fellows at Foot-Ball, Magistrates on the Bench, Quakers with their Hats on, or the Library Company with their Hats off or on, for all those Persons are said to be OF the *Better Sort*, which does not exclude others from the same Rank. But the Denomination of *Better Sort* in your first Letter (where the Particle *of*, as applied in the latter Cases, cannot be found) is evidently engrossed by Those who, with such a commendable Modesty, bestowed it on themselves. Now when private Persons publickly stile themselves, exclusively of all others, the BETTER SORT of People of the Province, can it be doubted but that they look on the Rest of their Fellow Subjects in the same Government with Contempt, and consequently regard them as Mob and Rabble. For so gross an Insult on the People in general, I endeavoured (but without respecting any Party in particular, as you groundlessly insinuate) to turn the Writer into Ridicule; and therefore made Use of the Words Mob and Rabble, to expose him more effectually; but with very different Ideas annexed to them in my Mind (of which I was careful to give Notice) from those they receive, when deduced from that extraordinary Epistle. In my Animadversions on it I personated the Public, which you charge as a Crime, tho' it is an allowed Figure in Speech, frequently used, and particularly by those great Assertors of *Public Liberty*, whose Names I mentioned at the Time.

I imagined my Design lay so apparently on the Surface, that you could not have overlooked it. However, I am far from imitating the Example you have set me, and shall not attribute your Mistake of my Intentions, to an impenetrable Stupidity; but I fairly place it on the Obscurity of my Stile.

This, dear *Tommy*, will be esteem'd a very liberal Concession, by those who consider your Unskilfulness in Language.
You have not, by your Answer, mended the Blunder I remarked in your first: Your saying, that the same Person may
be both mischievous and contemptible, is nothing to the Purpose; for you must regard him in different Views before you
can properly affirm so differently of him: But Mr. *Whitefield's*
Doctrine you represented simply as mischievous, and, under
that Appearance only, you pronounced it the Object of your
Contempt. It seems as if you would rather have it believed a
Fault in Sentiment than Language: So you admit you understood the Word, but charge the wrong Application of it, to
the Defect of your Judgment. In my poor Opinion, you gain
nothing by the Change, to furnish Matter of Triumph.

Tho' your Absurdities and Mistakes are such, that no
Writer was ever guilty of before; yet, I question not, but you
will inform the World in your next, as you did in your last,
that my Animadversions on them are only *Extracts out of other
Men's Works,* viz. *those of the Party-Writers in* England. I have,
more than once, told you, that no Man has a Right to bring
an Accusation before the Publick, without bringing his *Proofs*
along with it. You have confined your Evidence, which is to
support this Charge, to the Party-Writers of *Great Britain.* I
will not limit you to them, but shall admit, that there is a
Possibility of its being true, if you can produce any Author, of
any Age or Country, that ever was engaged in a Controversy
of the like Nature with Ours. The Paragraph in Dispute contains but five Lines. The Insinuation, deduced from it in your
first, is also comprized within five; in your second it takes up
fifteen; I *hope* I shall live to see the Day, when It shall have
swelled to a large Volume in Folio: For so useful and edifying
a Work, as that is likely to be, must redound to the immortal
Honour of that IMPORTANT Article of News, in the Reputation and Defence of which I am so *deeply* interested.

As to the PERSONAL SCANDAL, in both your Letters,
it is a Commodity I never deal in; and therefore, cannot make
you any Return for those *flagrant* UNMERITED *Civilities,*
which I have received from your *polite* Hand. However, if
you think that such delicate *genteel* Touches of Raillery will
be of any Service to you, in the farther Prosecution of this

worthy Argument, I shall be far from objecting against your Use of them.

> And so, *my dear* Tommy, *for the present,*
> *I bid you heartily Farewell.*
> OBADIAH PLAINMAN.

The Pennsylvania Gazette, May 29, 1740

Religious Mood in Philadelphia

During the Session of the *Presbyterian* Synod, which began on the 28th of the last Month, and continued to the third of this Instant, there were no less than 14 Sermons preached on *Society-Hill* to large Audiences, by the Rev. Messrs. the *Tennents*, Mr. *Davenport*, Mr. *Rowland* and Mr. *Blair*, besides what were deliver'd at the *Presbyterian* and *Baptist* Meetings, and Expoundings and Exhortations in private Houses. The Alteration in the Face of Religion here is altogether surprizing. Never did the People show so great a Willingness to attend Sermons, nor the Preachers greater Zeal and Diligence in performing the Duties of their Function. Religion is become the Subject of most Conversations. No Books are in Request but those of Piety and Devotion; and instead of idle Songs and Ballads, the People are every where entertaining themselves with Psalms, Hymns and Spiritual Songs. All which, under God, is owing to the successful Labours of the Reverend Mr. *Whitefield*.

The Pennsylvania Gazette, June 12, 1740

Statement of Editorial Policy

It is a Principle among Printers, that when Truth has fair Play, it will always prevail over Falshood; therefore, though they have an undoubted Property in their own Press, yet they willingly allow, that any one is entitled to the Use of it, who thinks it necessary to offer his Sentiments on disputable Points to the Publick, and will be at the Expence of it. If what is thus publish'd be good, Mankind has the Benefit of it: If it be bad (I speak now in general without any design'd Application to any particular Piece whatever) the more 'tis made publick, the more its Weakness is expos'd, and the greater Disgrace falls upon the Author, whoever he be; who is at the same Time depriv'd of an Advantage he would otherwise without fail make use of, *viz.* of Complaining, *that Truth is suppress'd, and that he could say MIGHTY MATTERS, had he but the Opportunity of being heard.*

The Printers of this City have been unjustly reflected on, as if they were under some undue Influence, and guilty of great Partiality in favour of the Preaching lately admir'd among us, so as to refuse Printing any Thing in Opposition to it, how just or necessary soever. A Reflection entirely false and groundless, and without the least Colour of Fact to support it; which all will be convinc'd of when they see the following Piece from one Press, and the Rev. Mr. *Cummings*'s Sermons against the Doctrines themselves, from the other.

Englishmen thought it an intolerable Hardship, when (tho' by an Act of their own Parliament) Thoughts, which should be free, were fetter'd and confin'd, and an Officer was erected over the Nation, call'd *a Licenser of the Press*, without whose Consent no Writing could be publish'd. Care might indeed be taken in the Choice of this Officer, that he should be a Man of great Understanding, profound Learning, and extraordinary Piety; yet, as the greatest and best of Men may have *some* Errors, and have been often found averse to *some* Truths, it was justly esteem'd a National Grievance, that the People should have Nothing to read but the Opinions, or what was agreeable to the Opinions of *ONE MAN*. But should every petty Printer (who, if he can read his Hornbook, may be thought to have Learning enough to qualify him for his own Sphere) presume to erect himself into an Officer of this kind, and arbitrarily decide what ought and what ought not to be published, much more justly might the World complain. 'Tis true, where Invectives are contain'd in any Piece, there is no good-natur'd Printer but had much rather be employ'd in Work of another kind: However, tho' many personal Reflections be interwoven in the following Performance, yet as the Author (*who has subscrib'd his Name*) thought them necessary, to vindicate his own Conduct and Character, it is therefore hoped, on that Consideration, the Reader will excuse the Printer for publishing them.

The Pennsylvania Gazette, July 24, 1740

Essay on Paper-Currency, Proposing a New Method for Fixing Its Value

To the Author of the General Magazine.

It appears by the Resolutions of the Honourable the House of Commons of *Great Britain*, that it is their Opinion, that the Issuing Paper Currencies in the *American* Colonies hath been prejudicial to the Trade of *Great Britain*, by causing a Confusion in Dealings, and lessening of Credit in those Parts; and that there is Reason to apprehend, that some Measures will be fallen upon, to hinder or restrain any future Emissions of such Currencies, when those that are now extant shall be called in and sunk. But if any Scheme could be formed, for fixing and ascertaining the Value of Paper Bills of Credit, in all future Emissions, it may be presumed such Restraints will be taken off, as the Confusion complained of in Dealings would thereby be avoided. Something of this Kind is here attempted, in hopes that it may be improved into a useful Project. But I shall first set down a few plain Remarks touching the Fluctuation of Exchange, and the Value of Gold and Silver in the Colonies; with some Observations on the Ballance of Trade; in order to render what follows the more clear and intelligible.

I. Every particular Man, that is concerned in Trade, whose Imports and Exports are not exactly equal, must either *draw* Bills of Exchange on other Countries, or *buy* Bills to send abroad to ballance his Accounts.

II. The Exports and Imports in any Colony, may be managed by different Hands, and the Number of those chiefly imployed in the latter may greatly exceed the Number of those imployed in the former.

Hence it is evident there may sometimes be many Buyers and few Sellers of Bills of Exchange, even whilst the Exports may exceed in Value the Imports: And it is easy to conceive, that in this Case, Exchange may rise.

III. The *British* Merchants, who trade to the Colonies, are often unacquainted with the Advantages that may be made by building of Ships there, or by the Commodities of those Colonies carried to the *West-Indies*, or to Foreign Markets: And for that Reason, frequently order all their Remittances in Bills of Exchange, tho' less advantageous; which must encrease the Demand for Bills, and enhance the Price of them.

IV. A great Demand in *Europe* for any of the Commodities of the Colonies, and large Orders for those Commodities from the *British* Merchants to their Factors here, with Directions to draw for the Value, may occasion Exchange to fall for a Time, even tho' the Imports should be greater than the Exports.

V. Hence it appears, that a sudden great Demand for Bills in the Colonies, may, at any time, advance the Exchange; and a sudden great Demand abroad for their Commodities may fall the Exchange.

VI. Gold and Silver will always rise and fall, very near in Proportion as Exchange rises and falls; being only wanted, in those Colonies that have a Paper Currency, for the same Use as Bills of Exchange, *viz.* for Remittances to *England*.

VII. When few People can draw on *England*, or furnish those who want Remittances with Gold or Silver, Paper Currency may fall with respect to Sterling-Money and Gold and Silver, (by which the *British* Merchants always judge of it) and yet keep up to its original Value in Respect to all other Things.

VIII. From all these Considerations, I think, it appears that the Rising or Falling of the Exchange can be no sure Rule for Discovering on which Side the Ballance of Trade lies; because that Exchange may be affected by various Accidents independent thereof. But in order to determine this Point with more Certainty, it should be considered;

IX. That whatever is imported, must, first or last, be paid for in the Produce or Manufactures of the Country: If the Commodities exported in one Year be not sufficient to pay for what is imported, the Deficiency must be made up by exporting more in succeeding Years; otherwise the Colony becomes Debtor for so much as the Deficiency is; which at last must be discharged (if it is ever discharged) by their Lands.

X. If this has been the Case with any Colony; or if the Debt of the Colony to *Great Britain* has been increasing for several Years successively, it is a Demonstration that the Ballance of Trade is against them: But on the Contrary, if the Debt to *Great Britain* is lessening yearly, or not increasing, it is as evident, that the Ballance of Trade is not against them; notwithstanding the Currency of that Colony may be falling gradually all the while.

I shall now proceed to the Scheme for fixing the Value of a Paper Currency, *viz.*

XI. Let it be supposed, that in some one of the Colonies the Sum of 110,000 in Bills of Credit was proposed to be struck, and all other Currencies to be called in and destroyed; and that 133 *l.* 6 *s.* 8 *d.* in these Bills should be equivalent to 100 *l.* Sterling; which likewise would make the said Bills equal to Foreign Coins, at the Rates settled by the Act of Parliament made in the Sixth Year of Queen ANNE. At which Rate, according to this Scheme, it may be as well settled as at any other.

XII. Let *One Hundred Thousand Pounds* be emitted on Loan, upon good Securities, either in Land or Plate, according to the Method used in *Pensylvania*, the Borrowers to pay *Five per Cent per Annum* Interest, together with a *Twentieth* Part of the Principal, which would give the Government an Opportunity of sinking it by Degrees, if any Alteration in the Circumstances of the Province should make it necessary: But if no such Necessity appeared, so much of the Principal as should be paid in, might be re-emitted on the same Terms as before.

XIII. The other *Ten Thousand* Pounds to be laid out in such Commodities as should be most likely to yield a Profit at Foreign Markets, to be ship'd off on Account of the Colony, in order to raise a Fund or Bank in *England*: Which Sum, so laid out, would in two Years time, be returned into the Office again by the Interest Money.

XIV. The Trustees or Managers of this Bank to be impowered and directed to supply all Persons that should apply to them, with Bills of Exchange, to be drawn on the Colony's Banker in *London*, at the aforesaid Rate of 133 *l.* 6 *s.* 8 *d.* of the said Bills of Credit for 100 *l.* Sterling. The Monies thus brought in, to be laid out again as before, and replaced in *England* in the said Bank with all convenient Speed: And as these provincial Bills would have, at least, as good a Credit as those of any private Person; every Man, who had occasion to draw, would, of Course, be obliged to dispose of his Bills at the same Rate.

XV. It is by Means of this Bank, that it is proposed to regulate the Rate of Exchange; and therefore it would be necessary to make it so large, or procure the Trustees such a Credit in *London*, as should discourage and prevent any mischievous Combinations for draining it and rendering the Design useless. I know of no Inconvenience that could arise by allotting double the proposed Sum for that Service, but that the annual Interest would be lessen'd; which in some Governments has been found a useful Engine for defraying the publick Expence. But if only a Credit should be thought needful, over and above the said Sum, and upon some Emergency Recourse should be had to it, the Interest-Money would soon afford sufficient Means for answering that Credit.

XVI. The Trustees might further be impowered and directed, to take in Foreign Coins, at the Rates prescribed by the Act of Parliament, from those who wanted to change them for Paper Currency, and to exchange for those who wanted Gold and Silver. This, it is imagined, might reduce those Coins again to a Currency, which now are only bought and sold as a Commodity. Or, if it should be judged more advantageous to the Credit of the Paper-Currency, Part of the Proceeds of what should be sent abroad, might be returned to the Province in Gold and Silver, for creating a Fund here.

XVII. I hope it will appear upon examining into the Circumstances of the Paper-Money-Colonies, by the Rule proposed above, that the Ballance of Trade has not been so much against them as is commonly imagined; but that the Fall of their Currencies, with Respect to Sterling, and to Gold and Silver, has been chiefly occasioned either by some such Accidents as are above shewed to influence it; which by this Scheme will be all prevented: Or to their being issued without any good Foundation for supporting their Credit, such as a Land Security, *&c.* However that be, I think, there can be no room, upon our Plan, to fear, that the Credit of the Paper-Currency can be injur'd, even though the Ballance of Trade were against the Colony, while their Bank in *London* can be duely supported.

From the sad Consequence of a losing Trade, *viz.* that of having the Property of the Lands transferr'd to another Country, it appears absolutely necessary for every Colony, that finds or suspects that to be its own Case, to think timely of all proper Means for preventing it; such as encouraging Iron-Works, Ship-building, raising and manufacturing of Hemp and Flax, and all other Manufactures not prohibited by their Mother Country. They might likewise save considerable Sums, which are now sent to *England*, by setting up and establishing an Insurance-Office. This, I think, might effectually be done by an Act of Assembly for impowering the Trustees of the Loan-Office to subscribe all Policies that should be brought to them, on such Terms as should be settled by the said Trustees jointly with a Committee of Assembly, at a Meeting for that Purpose, once a Month, or oftner if necessary. Besides the saving to the Country in the Article of Trade, it would probably yield a considerable yearly Income towards the Support of Government; it being evident, that most prudent Insurers are great Gainers upon the Whole of their Insurances, after all Losses are deducted.

Upon the Execution of this Scheme, I am persuaded, two very great Advantages must accrue; *First*, That the Export would be increased, and consequently bring the Ballance of Trade more in favour of the Province: And, *Secondly*, that the Rate of Exchange would be fixed and ascertained; which, 'tis hoped, would effectually remove the Prejudices which the Merchants in *England* seem to have conceived against a Paper Currency in the Colonies.

The General Magazine, February, 1741

Letter from Theophilus, Relating to the Divine Prescience

To the Author of the General MAGAZINE.

SIR,

There is a Question in the Schools, and I think generally resolved in the Affirmative; *Whether God concurs with all human Actions or not?* That is, Whether he be the principal efficient Cause of every Action we produce? This Question, I say, is generally resolved in the Affirmative: And the *Reason* they give is this; *Because,* say they, *if God did not concur with every Action that's produc'd, then there would be an Action, and consequently some Being, independent of God, which is absurd: Therefore,* &c.

It hath been the Opinion of many great and learned Men, that second Causes have no proper Activity of their own; but that God acts directly and immediately in them and by them; that he produces all the Acts of Thinking, and all the Volitions or Acts of Willing; and that he has from all Eternity decreed, *That he will do with such and such a Creature, at such a Time, such and such Acts;* which shall *infallibly* come to pass, the contrary whereof could not fall out from any Principle in the Creature; that the Creature neither can nor ought to have any thing real, nor positively do any Act but what God produces in it.

There is no Possibility, they think, of defending the Doctrine of the *Divine Prescience,* if this be deny'd. For nothing can be foreknown that is contingent in its own Nature; but every Action depending upon the Will of an Agent, left at Liberty to do as it pleases, is contingent, *i. e.* it may or may not happen, and therefore cannot be foreknown: For when any Being knows that a Thing will be, it must be, otherwise it could not be an Object of Knowledge: It is absolutely impossible to know, that any Event *will* come to pass, that *may not* come to pass.

So that whoever denies God's immediate Concourse with every Action we produce, must of Consequence deny God's Foreknowledge.

I should be glad therefore to see some Remarks made upon this Subject; and knowing of no better Method to invite some proper Person to undertake it, I make bold to desire you to insert the Contents hereof in the *General Magazine* for the Month of *March*, and you will oblige

Your constant Reader, and
most humble Servant,
THEOPHILUS.

The General Magazine, March, 1741

Obituary of Andrew Hamilton

On the 4th Instant, died ANDREW HAMILTON, Esq; and was the next Day inter'd at *Bush-Hill*, his Country Seat. His Corps was attended to the Grave by a great Number of his Friends, deeply affected with their own, but more with their Country's Loss. He lived not without Enemies: For, as he was himself open and honest, he took pains to unmask the Hypocrite, and boldly censured the Knave, without regard to Station and Profession. Such, therefore, may exult at his Death. He steadily maintained the Cause of Liberty; and the Laws made, during the time he was Speaker of the Assembly, which was many Years, will be a lasting Monument of his Affection to the People, and of his Concern for the welfare of this Province. He was no Friend to Power, as he had observed an ill use had been frequently made of it in the Colonies; and therefore was seldom upon good Terms with Governors. This Prejudice, however, did not always determine his Conduct towards them; for where he saw they meant well, he was for supporting them honourably, and was indefatigable in endeavouring to remove the Prejudices of others. He was long at the Top of his Profession here, and had he been as griping as he was knowing and active, he might have left a much greater Fortune to his Family than he has done: But he spent more Time in hearing and reconciling Differences in private, to the Loss of his Fees, than he did in pleading Causes at the Bar. He was just, where he sat as a Judge; and tho' he was stern and severe in his Manner, he was compassionate in his Nature, and very slow to punish. He was the Poor Man's Friend, and was never known to with-hold his Purse or Service from the Indigent or Oppressed. He was a tender Husband and a fond Parent: But—these are Virtues which Fools and Knaves have sometimes in common with the Wise and the Honest. His free Manner of treating Religious Subjects, gave Offence to many, who, if a Man may judge by their Actions, were not themselves much in earnest. He feared God, loved Mercy, and did Justice: If he could not subscribe to the Creed of any particular Church, it was not for want of considering them All; for he had read much on Religious Subjects. He went through a tedious

Sickness with uncommon Chearfulness, Constancy and Courage. Nothing of affected Bravery or Ostentation appeared; But such a Composure and Tranquility of Mind, as results from the Reflection of a Life spent agreeable to the best of a Man's Judgment. He preserved his Understanding and his Regard for his Friends to the last Moment. What was given as a Rule for a Poet, upon another Occasion, may be justly apply'd to Him upon this,

> —— *Servetur ad imum*
> *Qualis ab incepto processerit, & sibi constet.*

The Pennsylvania Gazette, August 6, 1741

Obituary of James Merrewether

On Sunday last died after a short Illness, JAMES MERREWETHER, a Person somewhat obscure, and of an unpromising Appearance, but esteem'd by those few who enjoy'd an Intimacy with him, to be one of the honestest, best, and wisest Men in Philadelphia.

The Pennsylvania Gazette, April 22, 1742

I Sing My Plain Country Joan

Poor RICHARD's Description of his
Country WIFE JOAN.

A SONG—TUNE, *The Hounds are all out.*

1. Of their *Chloes* and *Phyllises* Poets may prate,
    I will sing my plain COUNTRY JOAN;
Twice twelve Years my Wife, still the Joy of my Life:
    Bless'd Day that I made her my own,
                                My dear Friends.
Bless'd Day that I made her my own.

2. Not a Word of her Shape, or her Face, or her Eyes,
     Of Flames or of Darts shall you hear:
   Though I BEAUTY admire, 'tis VIRTUE I prize,
     Which fades not in seventy Years.

3. In Health a Companion delightful and gay,
     Still easy, engaging, and free;
   In Sickness no less than the faithfullest Nurse,
     As tender as tender can be.

4. In Peace and good Order my Houshold she guides,
     Right careful to save what I gain;
   Yet chearfully spends, and smiles on the Friends
     I've the Pleasure to entertain.

5. Am I laden with Care, she takes off a large Share,
     That the Burden ne'er makes me to reel;
   Does good Fortune arrive, the Joy of my Wife
     Quite doubles the Pleasure I feel.

6. She defends my good Name, even when I'm to blame,
     Friend firmer to Man ne'er was given:
   Her compassionate Breast feels for all the distress'd,
     Which draws down the Blessings of Heaven.

7. In Raptures the giddy Rake talks of his Fair,
     Enjoyment will make him despise.
   I speak my cool Sense, which long Exper'ence
     And Acquaintance has chang'd in no Wise.

8. The Best have some Faults, and so has My JOAN,
     But then they're exceedingly small,
   And, now I'm us'd to 'em, they're so like my own,
     I scarcely can feel them at all.

9. Was the fairest young Princess, with Millions in Purse,
     To be had in Exchange for My JOAN,
   She could not be a better Wife, might be a worse,
     So I'll stick to My JUGGY alone,

c. 1742

A Proposal for Promoting Useful Knowledge Among the British Plantations in America

The *English* are possess'd of a long Tract of Continent, from *Nova Scotia* to *Georgia*, extending North and South thro' different Climates, having different Soils, producing different Plants, Mines and Minerals, and capable of different Improvements, Manufactures, *&c.*

The first Drudgery of Settling new Colonies, which confines the Attention of People to mere Necessaries, is now pretty well over; and there are many in every Province in Circumstances that set them at Ease, and afford Leisure to cultivate the finer Arts, and improve the common Stock of Knowledge. To such of these who are Men of Speculation, many Hints must from time to time arise, many Observations occur, which if well-examined, pursued and improved, might produce Discoveries to the Advantage of some or all of the *British* Plantations, or to the Benefit of Mankind in general.

But as from the Extent of the Country such Persons are widely separated, and seldom can see and converse or be acquainted with each other, so that many useful Particulars remain uncommunicated, die with the Discoverers, and are lost to Mankind; it is, to remedy this Inconvenience for the future, proposed,

That One Society be formed of Virtuosi or ingenious Men residing in the several Colonies, to be called *The American Philosophical Society*; who are to maintain a constant Correspondence.

That *Philadelphia* being the City nearest the Centre of the Continent-Colonies, communicating with all of them northward and southward by Post, and with all the Islands by Sea, and having the Advantage of a good growing Library, be the Centre of the Society.

That at *Philadelphia* there be always at least seven Members, *viz.* a Physician, a Botanist, a Mathematician, a Chemist, a Mechanician, a Geographer, and a general Natural Philosopher, besides a President, Treasurer and Secretary.

That these Members meet once a Month, or oftner, at their own Expence, to communicate to each other their Observations, Experiments, &c. to receive, read and consider such Letters, Communications, or Queries as shall be sent from distant Members; to direct the Dispersing of Copies of such Communications as are valuable, to other distant Members, in order to procure their Sentiments thereupon, &c.

That the Subjects of the Correspondence be, All new-discovered Plants, Herbs, Trees, Roots, &c. their Virtues, Uses, &c. Methods of Propagating them, and making such as are useful, but particular to some Plantations, more general. Improvements of vegetable Juices, as Cyders, Wines, &c. New Methods of Curing or Preventing Diseases. All new-discovered Fossils in different Countries, as Mines, Minerals, Quarries, &c. New and useful Improvements in any Branch of Mathematicks. New Discoveries in Chemistry, such as Improvements in Distillation, Brewing, Assaying of Ores, &c. New Mechanical Inventions for saving Labour; as Mills, Carriages, &c. and for Raising and Conveying of Water, Draining of Meadows, &c. All new Arts, Trades, Manufactures, &c. that may be proposed or thought of. Surveys, Maps and Charts of particular Parts of the Sea-coasts, or Inland Countries; Course and Junction of Rivers and great Roads, Situation of Lakes and Mountains, Nature of the Soil and Productions, &c. New Methods of Improving the Breed of useful Animals; Introducing other Sorts from foreign Countries. New Improvements in Planting, Gardening, Clearing Land, &c. And all philosophical Experiments that let Light into the Nature of Things, tend to increase the Power of Man over Matter, and multiply the Conveniencies or Pleasures of Life.

That a Correspondence already begun by some intended Members, shall be kept up by this Society with the ROYAL SOCIETY of *London*, and with the DUBLIN SOCIETY.

That every Member shall have Abstracts sent him Quarterly, of every Thing valuable communicated to the Society's Secretary at *Philadelphia*; free of all Charge except the Yearly Payment hereafter mentioned.

That by Permission of the Postmaster-General, such Communications pass between the Secretary of the Society and the Members, Postage-free.

That for defraying the Expence of such Experiments as the Society shall judge proper to cause to be made, and other contingent Charges for the common Good, every Member send a Piece of Eight *per Annum* to the Treasurer, at *Philadelphia*, to form a Common Stock, to be disburs'd by Order of the President with the Consent of the Majority of the Members that can conveniently be consulted thereupon, to such Persons and Places where and by whom the Experiments are to be made, and otherwise as there shall be Occasion; of which Disbursements an exact Account shall be kept, and communicated yearly to every Member.

That at the first Meetings of the Members at *Philadelphia*, such Rules be formed for Regulating their Meetings and Transactions for the General Benefit, as shall be convenient and necessary; to be afterwards changed and improv'd as there shall be Occasion, wherein due Regard is to be had to the Advice of distant Members.

That at the End of every Year, Collections be made and printed, of such Experiments, Discoveries, Improvements, *&c.* as may be thought of publick Advantage: And that every Member have a Copy sent him.

That the Business and Duty of the Secretary be, To receive all Letters intended for the Society, and lay them before the President and Members at their Meetings; to abstract, correct and methodize such Papers, *&c.* as require it, and as he shall be directed to do by the President, after they have been considered, debated and digested in the Society; to enter Copies thereof in the Society's Books, and make out Copies for distant Members; to answer their Letters by Direction of the President, and keep Records of all material Transactions of the Society, *&c.*

Benjamin Franklin, the Writer of this Proposal, offers himself to serve the Society as their Secretary, 'till they shall be provided with one more capable.

Philadelphia, May 14. 1743.

Philadelphia, broadside, 1743

Apology for the Young Man in Goal

An Apology *for the young Man in Goal, and in Shackles, for ravishing an old Woman of* 85 *at* Whitemarsh, *who had only one Eye, and that a red one.*

Unhappy Youth, that could not longer stay,
Till by old Age thy Choice had dy'd away;
A few Days more had given to thy Arms,
Free from the Laws, her aged Lump of Charms,
Which, tho' defunct, might feel not less alive
Than we imagine Maids of Eighty-five;
Or hadst thou staid till t'other Eye was gone,
Thou mightst have lov'd and jogg'd securely on.
Yet may thy Council urge this prudent Plea,
That by one Crime, thou has avoided three;
For had a Mare or Sow attack'd thy Love,
No human Form to save thy Life would move;
Or had thy Lust been offer'd to a Male,
All Vindications would and ought to fail;
Or hadst thou sought a blooming Virgin's Rape,
Thou shouldst not from the Penalty escape:
But when the Object is long past her Flow'r,
And brings no County-Charge, and wants no Dow'r;
Who, slighted all her Life, would fain be ravish'd,
Thou shouldst be pity'd for thy Love so lavish'd.

The American Weekly Mercury, September 15, 1743

An Over-Masted Privateer

Sunday last the Tartar, Capt. Mackey, sail'd down the Bay in order to proceed on his Cruise, but being (as 'tis said) over-masted, and not well ballasted, she was unfortunately overset, by a slight Flaw of Wind, near the Capes, and sunk immediately in about 8 Fathom Water. The Captain with about 60 Officers and Seamen were saved in her Long-boat, and went

ashore at the Cape; 14 were taken up by Capt. Plasket in a
Pilot Boat; and Capt. Claes, who was coming in from Barbadoes, ran his Vessel near the Ship, and took up 47. The rest
perished. 'Tis expected she will soon be weigh'd, and with
some Alterations, fitted out again, as she is a most extraordinary Sailor; so that we hope our Enemies will hardly hear of
the Misfortune, before they find they have no great Reason
to rejoice at it.

The Pennsylvania Gazette, July 5, 1744

American Privateers

'Tis computed that there are and will be before Winter 113
Sail of Privateers at Sea, from the *British American* Colonies;
most of them stout Vessels and abundantly well mann'd. A
Naval Force, equal (some say) to that of the Crown of *Great-
Britain* in the Time of Queen *Elizabeth*.

The Pennsylvania Gazette, August 30, 1744

Account of Louisburgh

As the *CAPE-BRETON* Expedition is at present the Subject
of most Conversations, we hope the following Draught
(rough as it is, for want of good Engravers here) will be acceptable to our Readers; as it may serve to give them an Idea
of the Strength and Situation of the Town now besieged by
our Forces, and render the News we receive from thence
more intelligible.

EXPLANATION.

1. The Island Battery, at the Mouth of the Harbour, mounting 34 Guns, —— Pounders. This Battery can rake Ships

PLAN of the Town and Harbour of *LOUISBURGH*.

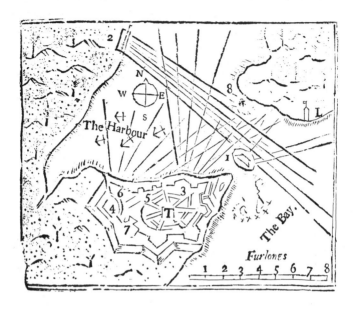

fore and aft before they come to the Harbour's Mouth, and take them in the Side as they are passing in.

2. The Grand Battery, of 36 Forty-two Pounders, planted right against the Mouth of the Harbour, and can rake Ships fore and aft as they enter.

3. The Town N. East Battery, which mounts 18 Twenty-four Pounders on two Faces, which can play on the Ships as soon as they have entered the Harbour.

4. The Circular Battery, which mounts 16 Twenty four Pounders, stands on high Ground, and overlooks all the Works. This Battery can also gaul Ships, as soon as they enter the Harbour.

5. Three Flanks, mounting 2 Eighteen Pounders each.

6. A small Battery, which mounts 8 Nine Pounders. All these Guns command any Ship in the Harbour.

7. The Fort or Citadel, fortified distinctly from the Town, in which the Governor lives.

8. A Rock, called the Barrel.

T   The Center of the Town.   L   The Light-House.

Every Bastion of the Town Wall has Embrasures or Ports for a Number of Guns to defend the Land Side.

The black Strokes drawn from the several Batteries, shew the Lines in which the Shot may be directed.

CAPE-BRETON Island, on which *Louisburgh* is built, lies on the South of the Gulph of *St. Lawrence*, and commands the Entrance into that River, and the Country of *Canada*. It is reckon'd 140 Leagues in Circuit, full of fine Bays and Harbours, extreamly convenient for Fishing Stages. It was always reckon'd a Part of *Nova-Scotia*. For the Importance of this Place see our *Gazette*, No. 858. As soon as the French King had begun the present unjust War against the English, the People of *Louisburgh* attack'd the *New-England* Town of *Canso*, consisting of about 150 Houses and a Fort, took it, burnt it to the Ground, and carried away the People, Men, Women and Children, Prisoners. They then laid Siege to *Annapolis Royal*, and would have taken it, if seasonable Assistance had not been sent from *Boston*. Mr. *Duvivier* went home to *France* last Fall for more Soldiers, *&c.* to renew that Attempt, and for Stores for Privateers, of which they proposed to fit out a great Number this Summer, being the last Year unprovided: Yet one of their Cruisers only, took 4 Sail in a few Days, off our Capes, to a very considerable Value. What might we have expected from a dozen Sail, making each 3 or 4 Cruises a Year? They boasted that during the War they should have no Occasion to cut Fire-Wood, for that the Jackstaves of English Vessels would be a Supply sufficient. It is therefore in their own NECESSARY DEFENCE, as well as that of all the other *British* Colonies, that the People of *New-England* have undertaken the present Expedition against that Place, to which may the *GOD OF HOSTS* grant Success. *Amen*.

The Pennsylvania Gazette, June 6, 1745

Old Mistresses Apologue

My dear Friend,   June 25. 1745

I know of no Medicine fit to diminish the violent natural Inclinations you mention; and if I did, I think I should not communicate it to you. Marriage is the proper Remedy. It is the most natural State of Man, and therefore the State in which you are most likely to find solid Happiness. Your Reasons against entring into it at present, appear to me not well-founded. The circumstantial Advantages you have in View by postponing it, are not only uncertain, but they are small in comparison with that of the Thing itself, the being *married and settled*. It is the Man and Woman united that make the compleat human Being. Separate, she wants his Force of Body and Strength of Reason; he, her Softness, Sensibility and acute Discernment. Together they are more likely to succeed in the World. A single Man has not nearly the Value he would have in that State of Union. He is an incomplete Animal. He resembles the odd Half of a Pair of Scissars. If you get a prudent healthy Wife, your Industry in your Profession, with her good Œconomy, will be a Fortune sufficient.

But if you will not take this Counsel, and persist in thinking a Commerce with the Sex inevitable, then I repeat my former Advice, that in all your Amours you should *prefer old Women to young ones*. You call this a Paradox, and demand my Reasons. They are these:

1. Because as they have more Knowledge of the World and their Minds are better stor'd with Observations, their Conversation is more improving and more lastingly agreable.

2. Because when Women cease to be handsome, they study to be good. To maintain their Influence over Men, they supply the Diminution of Beauty by an Augmentation of Utility. They learn to do a 1000 Services small and great, and are the most tender and useful of all Friends when you are sick. Thus they continue amiable. And hence there is hardly such a thing to be found as an old Woman who is not a good Woman.

3. Because there is no hazard of Children, which irregularly produc'd may be attended with much Inconvenience.

4. Because thro' more Experience, they are more prudent

and discreet in conducting an Intrigue to prevent Suspicion. The Commerce with them is therefore safer with regard to your Reputation. And with regard to theirs, if the Affair should happen to be known, considerate People might be rather inclin'd to excuse an old Woman who would kindly take care of a young Man, form his Manners by her good Counsels, and prevent his ruining his Health and Fortune among mercenary Prostitutes.

5. Because in every Animal that walks upright, the Deficiency of the Fluids that fill the Muscles appears first in the highest Part: The Face first grows lank and wrinkled; then the Neck; then the Breast and Arms; the lower Parts continuing to the last as plump as ever: So that covering all above with a Basket, and regarding only what is below the Girdle, it is impossible of two Women to know an old from a young one. And as in the dark all Cats are grey, the Pleasure of corporal Enjoyment with an old Woman is at least equal, and frequently superior, every Knack being by Practice capable of Improvement.

6. Because the Sin is less. The debauching a Virgin may be her Ruin, and make her for Life unhappy.

7. Because the Compunction is less. The having made a young Girl *miserable* may give you frequent bitter Reflections; none of which can attend the making an old Woman *happy*.

8thly and Lastly   They are *so grateful!!*

Thus much for my Paradox. But still I advise you to marry directly; being sincerely Your affectionate Friend.

The Antediluvians Were All Very Sober

The Antediluvians were all very sober
For they had no Wine, and they brew'd no October;
All wicked, bad Livers, on Mischief still thinking,
For there can't be good Living where there is not
    good Drinking.
                                    Derry down

'Twas honest old Noah first planted the Vine,
And mended his Morals by drinking its Wine;
He justly the drinking of Water decry'd;
For he knew that all Mankind, by drinking it, dy'd.

          Derry down.

From this Piece of History plainly we find
That Water's good neither for Body or Mind;
That Virtue and Safety in Wine-bibbing's found
While all that drink Water deserve to be drown'd.

          Derry down

So For Safety and Honesty put the Glass round.

c. 1745

Appreciation of George Whitefield

On Sunday the 20th Instant, the Rev. Mr. *Whitefield* preach'd twice, tho' apparently much indispos'd, to large Congregations in the New-Building in this City, and the next Day set out for New-York. When we seriously consider how incessantly this faithful Servant (not yet 32 Years old) has, for about 10 Years past, laboured in his great Master's Vineyard, with an Alacrity and fervent Zeal, which an infirm Constitution, still daily declining, cannot abate; and which have triumphed over the most vigorous Opposition from whole Armies of invidious Preachers and Pamphleteers; under whose Performances, the Pulpits and Presses, of *Great-Britain* and *America*, have groaned; We may reasonably think with the learned Dr. WATTS, "That he is a Man raised up by Providence in an uncommon Way, to awaken a stupid and ungodly World, to a Sense of the important Affairs of Religion and Eternity:" And the Lines of Mr. *Wesley*, concerning another young Methodist, may justly be applied to his dear Friend *Whitefield*—

> *Wise in his Prime, he waited not for Noon,*
> *Convinc'd that Mortals never liv'd too soon;*
> *As if foreboding here his little Stay,*
> *He makes his Morning bear the Heat of Day.*

Fifth Time, Gentlemen, that I have been dragg'd before your Courts on the same Account; twice I have paid heavy Fines, and twice have been brought to public Punishment, for want of Money to pay those Fines. This may have been agreeable to the Laws; I do not dispute it: But since Laws are sometimes unreasonable in themselves, and therefore repealed; and others bear too hard on the Subject in particular Circumstances; and therefore there is left a Power somewhere to dispense with the Execution of them; I take the Liberty to say, that I think this Law, by which I am punished, is both unreasonable in itself, and particularly severe with regard to me, who have always lived an inoffensive Life in the Neighbourhood where I was born, and defy my Enemies (if I have any) to say I ever wrong'd Man, Woman, or Child. Abstracted from the Law, I cannot conceive (may it please your Honours) what the Nature of my Offence is. I have brought Five fine Children into the World, at the Risque of my Life: I have maintained them well by my own Industry, without burthening the Township, and could have done it better, if it had not been for the heavy Charges and Fines I have paid. Can it be a Crime (in the Nature of Things I mean) to add to the Number of the King's Subjects, in a new Country that really wants People? I own I should think it rather a Praise worthy, than a Punishable Action. I have debauch'd no other Woman's Husband, nor inticed any innocent Youth: These Things I never was charged with; nor has any one the least cause of Complaint against me, unless, perhaps the Minister, or the Justice, because I have had Children without being Married, by which they have miss'd a Wedding Fee. But, can even this be a Fault of mine? I appeal to your Honours. You are pleased to allow I don't want Sense; but I must be stupid to the last Degree, not to prefer the honourable State of Wedlock, to the Condition I have lived in. I always was, and still am, willing to enter into it; I doubt not my Behaving well in it, having all the Industry, Frugality, Fertility, and Skill in Oeconomy, appertaining to a good Wife's Character. I defy any Person to say I ever Refused an Offer of that Sort: On the contrary, I readily Consented to the only Proposal of Marriage that ever was made me, which was when I was a Virgin; but too easily confiding in the Person's Sincerity that made it, I unhappily lost my own Honour, by trusting to his; for he got me with Child, and then forsook me: That very Person you all know; he is now become a Magistrate of this County; and I had hopes he would have appeared this Day on the Bench, and have endeavoured to moderate the Court in my Favour; then I should have scorn'd to have mention'd it; but I must Complain of it as unjust and unequal, that my Betrayer and Undoer, the first Cause of all my Faults and Miscarriages (if they must be deemed such) should be advanced to Honour and Power, in the same Government that punishes my Misfortunes with Stripes and Infamy. I shall be told, 'tis like, that were there no Act of Assembly in the Case, the Precepts of Religion are violated by my Transgressions. If mine, then, is a religious Offence, leave it, Gentlemen, to religious Punishments. You have already excluded me from all the Comforts of your Church Communion: Is not that sufficient? You believe I have offended Heaven, and must suffer eternal Fire: Will not that be sufficient? What need is there, then, of your additional Fines and Whippings? I own, I do not think as you do; for, if I thought, what you call a Sin, was really such, I would not presumptuously commit it. But how can it be believed, that Heaven is angry at my having Children, when, to the little done by me towards it, God has been pleased to add his divine Skill and admirable Workmanship in the Formation of their Bodies, and crown'd it by furnishing them with rational and immortal Souls? Forgive me Gentlemen, if I talk a little extravagantly on these Matters; I am no Divine: But if you, great Men, * must be making Laws, do not turn natural and useful Actions into Crimes, by your Prohibitions. Reflect a little on the horrid Consequences of this Law in particular: What Numbers of procur'd Abortions! and how many distress'd Mothers have been driven, by the Terror of Punishment and public Shame, to imbrue, contrary to Nature, their own trembling Hands in the Blood of their helpless Offspring! Nature would have induc'd them to nurse it up with a Parent's Fondness. 'Tis the Law therefore, 'tis the Law itself that is guilty of all these Barbarities and Murders. Repeal it then, Gentlemen; let it be expung'd for

* *Turning to some Gentlemen of the Assembly, then in Court.*

ever from your Books: And on the other hand, take into your wise Consideration, the great and growing Number of Batchelors in the Country, many of whom, from the mean Fear of the Expence of a Family, have never sincerely and honourably Courted a Woman in their Lives; and by their Manner of Living, leave unproduced (which I think is little better than Murder) Hundreds of their Posterity to the Thousandth Generation. Is not theirs a greater Offence against the Public Good, than mine? Compel them then, by a Law, either to Marry, or pay double the Fine of Fornication every Year. What must poor young Women do, whom Custom has forbid to sollicit the Men, and who cannot force themselves upon Husbands, when the Laws take no Care to provide them any, and yet severely punish if they do their Duty without them? Yes, Gentlemen, I venture to call it a Duty; 'tis the Duty of the first and great Command of Nature, and of Nature's God, *Increase and multiply*: A Duty, from the steady Performance of which nothing has ever been able to deter me; but for it's Sake, I have hazarded the Loss of the public Esteem, and frequently incurr'd public Disgrace and Punishment; and therefore ought, in my humble Opinion, instead of a Whipping, to have a Statue erected to my Memory.

The Maryland Gazette, August 11, 1747; first printed April 15, 1747

Whitefield's Accounts

Extract of a Letter from the Reverend Mr. Smith, *of* Charles-Town, South-Carolina, *dated* March 2. 1746–7.

"Mr. WHITEFIELD's excellent Parts, fine Elocution, and masterly Address; His admirable Talent of opening the Scriptures, and enforcing the most weighty Subjects upon the Conscience; His polite and serious Behaviour; His unaffected and superior Piety; His Prudence, Humility, and Catholick Spirit, are Things which must silence and disarm Prejudice itself. By these Qualifications of the *Orator*, the *Divine*, and the *Christian*, He has not only fixed himself deeper in the Affections of his former Friends, but greatly increased the

Number wherever he has preached; and made his Way into the Hearts of several, who, till this Visit, had said all the severe Things against him that *Enmity* itself seemed capable of. He now seems to *reign* over his Hearers, among whom are Gentlemen of the best Figure and Estate we have, and has gained some, whose former Prejudices one would have thought insuperable. As an Instance of our Affection and Esteem, no sooner was the Motion started by some particular Gentlemen, but, with the greatest Alacrity, and in a *very short* Time, we subscribed, and gave him, much above *Two Hundred Pounds* STERLING; which we should not have done, but upon a firm Persuasion of the Sincerity of his Intentions. We hope we have laid an effectual Scheme for *tying* him faster to *America*, which will give us the Satisfaction of seeing a Man we so highly esteem the oftener. These Things are so universally known in *this Town*, that you have free Leave to publish them, and to affix the Name of,

> *Dear Sir,*
> *Your affectionate Friend and Servant,*
> *JOSIAH SMITH.*"

Extract of another Letter from South-Carolina, dated March 11th. 1746—7.

"It is with Pleasure I can now assure you, that the Rev. Mr. *Whitefield* has more Friends in *Charlestown* among Gentlemen, especially of Distinction and Substance, than ever heretofore. The Orator in the Pulpit, and the Gentleman and the Christian, happily united in Conversation, has triumph'd over a thousand Prejudices, and is become the Admiration of several, who before had conceiv'd the worst Idea of him imaginable. And since Actions are the best Expositors of the Heart, we have not been content to court his Company only, but, as a further Expression of our Esteem, have given him between two and three hundred Pounds Sterling."

The above Extracts will, we doubt not, at once please the Friends of the Reverend Mr. *Whitefield*, and convince every candid Reader, that his Accounts of the Disposition of the Sums of Money heretofore collected for the Use of his *Orphan House* in *Georgia* are just; since it cannot be conceived that Gentlemen, who live so near to that House as *Charles-Town, South-Carolina*, and have daily Opportunities of knowing how the Affair is conducted, should contribute so generously to Mr. *Whitefield*, if they thought his former Collections were not duly applied.

The Pennsylvania Gazette, April 23, 1747

Verses on the Virginia Capitol Fire

Mr. Printer,

   It may entertain the curious and learned Part of your Subscribers, if you give them the following genuine *Speech* and *Address*, which, for the *Importance* of the *Subject*, *Grandeur* of *Sentiment*, and *Elegance* of *Expression*, perhaps exceed Any they have hitherto seen. For the Benefit of more common Readers, I have turn'd them, with some Paraphrase, into *plain English Verse*. I am told by Friends, that my Performance is excellent: But I claim no other Praise than what regards my *Rhyme*, and my *Perspicuity*. All the other Beauties I acknowledge, are owing to the *Original*, whose true Sense I have every where follow'd with a scrupulous Exactness. If envious Critics should observe, that some of my Lines are *too short* in their Number of Feet, I own it; but then, to make ample Amends, I have given *very good Measure* in most of the others.

I am, Sir,
your constant Reader,
NED. TYPE.

*   *   *   *   *

The SPEECH *Versyfied*.

L—d have Mercy on us!—the CAPITOL! the CAPITOL!
   is burnt down!
O astonishing Fate!—which occasions this Meeting in
   Town.
And this *Fate* proves a *Loss*, to be deplored the more,
The said *Fate* being th'*Effect* of Malice and *Design*, to be
   sure.

And yet 'tis hard to comprehend how a Crime of so
  flagitious a Nature,
Should be committed, or even *imagined*, by any but an
  irrational Creature.
But when you consider, that the first *Emission of Smoke* was
  not from below,
And that Fires kindled by Accident *always burn slow*,
And not with half the Fury as when they *burn on Purpose*
  you know
You'll be forced to ascribe it (with Hearts full of Sadness)
To the horrid Machinations of desperate Villains, instigated
  by infernal Madness.
  God forbid I should accuse or excuse any without just
  Foundation,
Yet I may venture to assert,—for our own Reputation,
That such superlative Wickedness never entred the Hearts of
  Virginians, who are the CREAM of the *British* Nation.
  The Clerks have been examin'd, and clear'd by the May'r,
Yet are willing to be examin'd again by you, and that's fair.
And will prove in the Face of the Country, if requir'd,
That it was not by their *Conduct* our Capitol was fir'd.
I must add, to do 'em Justice, that the Comfort we have,
In enjoying our authentic Registers, which those Clerks did
  save,
Is owing to their Activity, Resolution and Diligence,
Together with Divine Providence.
All which would have been in vain, I protest,
If the Wind, at the bursting out of the Flames, had not
  changed from *East* to *Northwest*.
  Our Treasury being low, and my Infirmities great,
I would have kept you prorogu'd till the Revisal of the Laws
  was compleat;
But this Misfortune befalling the *Capitol* of the Capital of
  our Nation
Require your immediate Care and Assistance for its
  Instauration.
  To press you in a Point of such Usefulness manifest,
Would shew a Diffidence of your sincere Zeal for the public
  Interest
For which you and I always make such a laudable Pother,

And for which we've so often *applauded one Another*.
  The same public Spirit which within these Walls us'd to
    direct you all,
Will determine you (as Fathers of your Country) to apply
    Means effectual
For restoring the ROYAL FABRIC to its former Beauty
And Magnificence, according to your Duty;
With the like Apartments, elegant and spacious
For all the *weighty* purposes of Government, so capacious.
  Mean time the College and Court of Hustings our *Weight*
    may sustain,
But pray let us speedily have our CAPITOL, our *important*
    CAPITOL again.

The COUNCIL's Answer.

We the King's *best Subjects*, the Council of this
    Dominion,
Are deeply affected (as is every true *Virginian*)
With the unhappy Occasion of our present Meeting:
  ——In Troth we have but a sorry Greeting.
  We are also not a little touch'd (in the Head) with the
    same *Weakness* as your Honour's,
And therefore think this raging Fire which consum'd our
    Capitol, should incite us to reform our Manners:
The best *Expedient* at present to avert the Indignation
    divine,
And *nobly* to express our *Gratitude* for the *Justice*, which
    (temper'd with Mercy) doth shine,
In *preserving* our Records, tho' Red hot,
And like Brands pluck'd out of the Flames, in which they
    were going to pot,
Without this *Expedient* we shall be ruin'd quite.——
Besides, This FIRE puts us in Mind of NEW-LIGHT;
And we think it Heav'n's Judgment on us for tolerating the
    Presbyterians,
Whose Forefathers drubb'd ours, about a hundred Year-
    hence.
We therefore resolve to abate a little of our Drinking,
    Gaming, Cursing and Swearing,

And make up for the rest, by persecuting some itinerant
    Presbyterian.
  An *active Discharge* of our *important* Trusts, according to
    your Honour's Desire,
Is the wisest *Project of Insurance* that can be, of the Public
    Safety, from the Attempts of such as would *set it
    on fire*.
'Tis *a Project* also for advancing the Honour and Interest of
    our King and Nation,
And *a Project* for engaging Heaven's Protection from
    Generation to Generation.
  We take this Opportunity, that we may not be suspected
    of Malignity,
To congratulate you, Sir, on your Promotion to the
    Baronet's Dignity;
A fresh Instance of just Regard to your long and faithful
    Services we say,
Because from *Carthagena* your Honour came safe away,
And you lent and sent such * *great Assistance* for reducing
    CANADA.

The BARONET's Reply.

The just Sense you express for the Loss of our CAP-
    ITOL, which to be sure was a fatal Mishap,
Your affectionate Concern for the *Infirmities of my Honour*,
And Joy at my new Title, of which our good K—g is the
    Donor,
Claim sincere Acknowledgments of Thankfulness,
And Gratitude, for this obliging Address.
  And, (lest here and hereafter we're left in the Lurch)
To promote *true Religion*, (I mean our own Church)
I'll heartily concur with you, and lend a few Knocks
To suppress these confounding New Light Heterodox.
Then if from our Sins, we also refrain,
Perhaps we may have our CAPITOL! our dear CAPITOL!
    our glorious ROYAL CAPITOL again.

*One WHOLE Company.

The New-York Gazette, June 1, 1747, supplement

The Necessity of Self-Defence

Mr. *FRANKLIN*,

The absolute and obvious Necessity of Self-Defence, in the present Conjuncture, occasioned me to consider attentively several Passages in the New Testament, from whence some have endeavoured to shew the Unlawfulness of Christians bearing Arms on any Account, wherein I had made a small Progress before hearing Mr. *Tennent*'s Sermon last *Thursday* on that Occasion, which is so full and clear on the Subject, so well supported by Strength of Argument, and carried on with such masterly Judgment and Address, that I am of Opinion, the Publication thereof may sufficiently answer the most material Purposes in my View; wherefore I only now present you a few Thoughts which lay ready, on one particular Passage, as an Amusement to your Readers, till the above Sermon appears in Print, as I hear it soon will.

When it is considered that some Kinds of War were held lawful amongst the primitive Christians, as appears evidently from many of the ancient Martyrs, who suffered Torture and Death, for their Faith in Jesus, and Constancy to the Christian Religion, being at the Time of such Martyrdom, actually in the Station of Soldiers, and this in the early Ages of Christianity, while the Streams flow'd pure from the Fountain, 'ere the Apostacy had crept in, or the holy Doctrines of Jesus and his Apostles, were exchanged for the corrupt Traditions of Men, being only a few Centuries from Christ, it may seem strange that any Christians should now deny the Lawfulness of defensive War, and attempt to infer from our Saviour's Answer and Command to the Disciple who drew a Sword in his Defence, that the Use of Arms is in all Cases forbid by Christ. For the better understanding this Matter, observe what the several Evangelists say theron.

Mark is very short: *One of them that stood by, drew a Sword, and smote a Servant of the High Priest, and cut off his Ear,* chap. xiv. 47.

Luke only says; *When they which were about him saw what would follow, they said unto him, Lord, shall we smite with the Sword? And one of them smote the Servant of the High Priest, and cut off his right Ear. And Jesus answered and said, Suffer ye thus far, and he touched his Ear, and healed him,* Chap. xx. 49–51.

This is all the Notice taken by *Mark* and *Luke*, which implies not so much as a Prohibition of Arms, even on this Occasion.

John xviii. 10. writes; *Then Simon Peter having a Sword, drew it, and smote the High Priest's Servant, and cut off his right Ear. The Servant's Name was Malchus. Then said Jesus unto Peter, Put up thy Sword into the Sheath:* The Reason follows, not that the Use of Arms is unlawful, but *The Cup which my Father hath given me, shall I not drink it?*

Matthew is most full on the Passage, Chap. xxvi. 51,–54. *And behold one of them which were with Jesus, stretched out his Hand, and drew a Sword, and struck a Servant of the High Priest's, and smote off his Ear. Then said Jesus unto him, Put up again thy Sword into his Place; for all they that take the Sword, shall perish with the Sword. Thinkest thou that I cannot now pray to my Father, and he shall presently give me more than twelve Legions of Angels? But how then shall the Scripture be fulfilled, that thus it must be?*

From whence neither will it follow, that the Use of Arms is prohibited, since it must be granted, the Words, *All they that take the Sword, shall perish with the Sword*, cannot be understood in an absolute literal Sense, as to Individuals; it being evident that all Men who have taken the Sword, have not perished by the Sword, but many of them died in the common Course of Nature, by Diseases, or old Age: Nor will any, 'tis presum'd, be so uncharitable to suppose, this can be meant of the Souls of all those who have taken the Sword. The Passage therefore by no Means determines this Point, whether to use a Sword on any Occasion, be right or wrong; altho' it might have warned People against attempting to propagate the Christian Religion by Fire or Sword, and apparently tends to convince the *Jews* of their great Mistake, in expecting the Messiah with outward Pomp and Regal Authority; also may be easily understood to illustrate the great Difference between Christ's Kingdom and those of Princes. If Force had been necessary to the former, an invincible Army of Angels would assuredly have conquered all Opposition, the Disciples poor Help had been quite needless: But the Defence of Christ's Kingdom not depending on Men or Angels, could have no Support from their Assistance, being neither liable to Change, or subject to Dissolution. *The Word of the Lord endureth for ever; and this is the Word which by the Gospel is preached unto you,* 1 Pet. i. 24, 25. On the other Hand, the above quoted Words of Christ may either generally relate to the Revolutions and Periods of States, or in a more limited Sense (as in this Case of the Disciples) only signify, that all who persist in opposing their Swords, as private Men against the legal Authority of the Magistracy, shall perish with the Sword. Other Explications may be given, all *agreeing* to demonstrate no Inconsistency in the Passage, unless taken in an absolute literal Sense, and without which, a total Prohibition or Discouragement of bearing Arms will not follow. The Words, *Put up again thy Sword into his Place,* convey an Idea very different to laying it aside for ever as unlawful; do they not rather hint, The Sword, when in its proper Place, is ready against a suitable Occasion. The Passage might be enlarged upon; but, in my Apprehension, no Construction appears more clear and easy, than the Text simply pointing out a Contradistinction between the Kingdom of Christ, and those of temporal Princes; carnal Weapons, tho' useful and necessary in the latter, are not only unlawful, but improper and ineffectual for establishing the former; and if Liberty may be taken to vary the concise, comprehensive Stile of Scripture into a familiar Way of Speech, the Sense of those Verses appears much the same as if Christ had said, "*Peter,* put up thy Sword on this Occasion, it is no Time now to use carnal Weapons; My Kingdom is not of this World, is neither capable of being supported, or liable to be subverted by the Sword, to the Dangers of which all earthly Kingdoms are continually exposed: Mine stands on a more sure Foundation, in the Defence whereof, if Force availed, a most powerful Army of Angels would now descend to my Assistance." But in the 54th Verse an immediate Reason is given why our Saviour did not admit any kind of Defence to be made in his Behalf: It would frustrate the End of his Coming, and prevent the fulfilling of the Scriptures, which agrees with that given by St. *John*; and the whole Passage appears plainly to have no Relation to the Lawfulness or Unlawfulness of using the Sword in any other Case than on the Score of Religion, but most particularly in

preventing Christ being delivered to the *Jews*. From whence
follows this most obvious Remark, That since Swords were
by Christ commanded to be procured, yet forbidden to be
used on this Occasion, they were certainly intended for some
other Purpose: For the Injunction of providing them will
presently be shewn in the strongest Terms; and we may here
well use an Expression of *Cicero* with redoubled Energy, *Quid
Gladii volunt? quos habere certi non liceret, si uti illis nullo pacto
liceret**. But in St. *Luke*, xxii. 35. we find very plainly Christ's
Opinion of the Necessity of having Swords in these Words,
*When I sent you without Purse, and Scrip, and Shoes, lacked ye any
Thing? And they said, Nothing.* This was when our Lord sent
his Disciples, Chapter x. 1. *Before his Face, into every City, and
Place, whither he himself would come.* But now, when the Lord
is about to be offered up, and his Disciples are to remain in
the World, it seems they are not to expect a miraculous Support and Defence: For Christ says, Chapter xxii. 36. *But now,
he that hath a Purse, let him take it, and likewise his Scrip, and
he that hath no Sword, let him sell his Garment, and buy one.*

(*He that hath a Purse, let him take it*) Money, it seems, in
the tedious Journey of human Life was lawful and necessary
(*and likewise his Scrip*) Provisions or Food were also; (*And he
that hath no Sword, let him sell his Garment, and buy one*) But
a Sword was lawful, and still more necessary, even of greater
Consequence than our very Clothes; and the Experience of
Christians from that Time down to the present, may be appealed to, Whether Money and Provisions have not been
found very useful, and, in many Cases, the Defence of Mens
Lives and Liberties of greater Consequence than Food or
Raiment; agreeable to our Saviour's Words in another Place,
Is not the Life more than Meat, and the Body than Raiment?
Matth. vi. 25.

Yet how punctually do some Christians perform the first
and second Parts of this Injunction? Very diligently they provide Purse, and Scrip, yet neglect that most necessary Provision, the Sword, notwithstanding Food and Raiment are
represented by Christ of so much less Consequence than Life,
which, under Providence, is protected and defended by the

*In Oratione pro T. Annio Milone.

Sword, and (on Account of its signal Use, no Doubt) is commanded to be purchased at the Expence of our Garments: Wherefor it is most plain some Use was to be made of Swords; but it has been already shewn that Christianity was not to be forced upon People by the Sword: What better Use then remains, than the Defence of our Country, and the Protection of the Helpless and Innocent? If any can be shewn more consistent with Christianity, or beneficial to Mankind, it would be kind in the *Quakers* to inform those, whose present Measures of using Arms they condemn. Should some object, that on the Answer, Verse 38. *Lord, Behold here are two Swords*, Christ said, *It is enough*. Let them remember, that the same Proportion which was adjusted for the Disciples, is enough in most well peopled Countries.

I am Yours, &c.

The Pennsylvania Gazette, December 29, 1747, supplement

Devices and Mottoes of the Associators

DEVICES and MOTTOES painted on some of the Silk Colours of the Regiments of ASSOCIATORS, in and near *Philadelphia*.

I. A Lion erect, a naked Scymeter in one Paw, the other holding the *Pennsylvania* Scutcheon. Motto, PRO PATRIA.

II. Three Arms, wearing different Linnen, ruffled, plain and chequed; the Hands joined by grasping each the other's Wrist, denoting the Union of all Ranks. Motto, UNITA VIRTUS VALET.

III. An Eagle, the Emblem of Victory, descending from the Skies. Motto, A DEO VICTORIA.

IV. The Figure of LIBERTY, sitting on a Cube, holding a Spear with the Cap of Freedom on its Point. Motto, INESTIMABILIS.

V. An armed Arm, with a naked Faulchion in its Hand. Motto, DEUS ADJUVAT FORTES.

VI. An Elephant, being the Emblem of a Warrior always on his Guard, as that Creature is said never to lie down, and hath his Arms ever in Readiness. Motto, SEMPER PARATUS.

VII. A City walled round. Motto, SALUS PATRIÆ, SUMMA LEX.

VIII. A Soldier, with his Piece recover'd, ready to present. Motto, SIC PACEM QUERIMUS.

IX. A Coronet and Plume of Feathers. Motto, IN GOD WE TRUST.

X. A Man with a Sword drawn. Motto, PRO ARIS ET FOCIS. &c. &c.

Most of the above Colours, together with the Officers Half-Pikes and Spontons, and even the Halberts, Drums, &c. have been given by the good Ladies of this City, who raised Money by Subscription among themselves for that Purpose.

The Pennsylvania Gazette, January 12, 1747/8

Continuation of Devices and Mottoes painted on some of the Silk Colours of the Regiments of Associators in this City and Country adjacent.

XI. Three of the Associators marching with their Muskets shoulder'd, and dressed in different Clothes, intimating the Unanimity of the different Sorts of People in the Association; Motto, Vis Unita Fortior.

XII. A Musket and Sword crossing each other; Motto, Pro Rege & Grege.

XIII. Representation of a Glory, in the Middle of which is wrote *Jehovah Nissi*, in English, The Lord our Banner.

XIV. A Castle, at the Gate of which a Soldier stands Centinel; Motto, Cavendo Tutus.

XV. David, as he advanced against Goliah, and slung the Stone; Motto, In Nomine Domini.

XVI. A Lion rampant, one Paw holding up a Scymiter, another on a Sheaf of Wheat; Motto, Domine Protege Alimentum.

XVII. A sleeping Lion; Motto, Rouze me if you dare.

XVIII. Hope, represented by a Woman standing cloathed in blue, holding one Hand on an Anchor; Motto, Spero per Deum vincere.

XIX. The Duke of Cumberland as a General; Motto, Pro Deo & Georgio Rege.

XX. A Soldier on Horseback; Motto, Pro Libertate Patriæ.

The Pennsylvania Gazette, April 16, 1748

Advice to a Young Tradesman, Written by an Old One

To my Friend *A. B.*

As you have desired it of me, I write the following Hints, which have been of Service to me, and may, if observed, be so to you.

Remember that TIME is Money. He that can earn Ten Shillings a Day by his Labour, and goes abroad, or sits idle one half of that Day, tho' he spends but Sixpence during his Diversion or Idleness, ought not to reckon That the only Expence; he has really spent or rather thrown away Five Shillings besides.

Remember that CREDIT is Money. If a Man lets his Money lie in my Hands after it is due, he gives me the Interest, or so much as I can make of it during that Time. This amounts to a considerable Sum where a Man has good and large Credit, and makes good Use of it.

Remember that Money is of a prolific generating Nature. Money can beget Money, and its Offspring can beget more, and so on. Five Shillings turn'd, is *Six*: Turn'd again, 'tis Seven and Three Pence; and so on 'til it becomes an Hundred Pound. The more there is of it, the more it produces every Turning, so that the Profits rise quicker and quicker. He that kills a breeding Sow, destroys all her Offspring to the thousandth Generation. He that murders a Crown, destroys all it might have produc'd, even Scores of Pounds.

Remember that Six Pounds a Year is but a Groat a Day. For this little Sum (which may be daily wasted either in Time or Expence unperceiv'd) a Man of Credit may on his own Security have the constant Possession and Use of an Hundred Pounds. So much in Stock briskly turn'd by an industrious Man, produces great Advantage.

Remember this Saying, *That the good Paymaster is Lord of another Man's Purse*. He that is known to pay punctually and exactly to the Time he promises, may at any Time, and on any Occasion, raise all the Money his Friends can spare. This is sometimes of great Use: Therefore never keep borrow'd

Money an Hour beyond the Time you promis'd, lest a Disappointment shuts up your Friends Purse forever.

The most trifling Actions that affect a Man's Credit, are to be regarded. The Sound of your Hammer at Five in the Morning or Nine at Night, heard by a Creditor, makes him easy Six Months longer. But if he sees you at a Billiard Table, or hears your Voice in a Tavern, when you should be at Work, he sends for his Money the next Day. Finer Cloaths than he or his Wife wears, or greater Expence in any particular than he affords himself, shocks his Pride, and he duns you to humble you. Creditors are a kind of People, that have the sharpest Eyes and Ears, as well as the best Memories of any in the World.

Good-natur'd Creditors (and such one would always chuse to deal with if one could) feel Pain when they are oblig'd to ask for Money. Spare 'em that Pain, and they will love you. When you receive a Sum of Money, divide it among 'em in Proportion to your Debts. Don't be asham'd of paying a small Sum because you owe a greater. Money, more or less, is always welcome; and your Creditor had rather be at the Trouble of receiving Ten Pounds voluntarily brought him, tho' at ten different Times or Payments, than be oblig'd to go ten Times to demand it before he can receive it in a Lump. It shews, besides, that you are mindful of what you owe; it makes you appear a careful as well as an honest Man; and that still encreases your Credit.

Beware of thinking all your own that you possess, and of living accordingly. 'Tis a mistake that many People who have Credit fall into. To prevent this, keep an exact Account for some Time of both your Expences and your Incomes. If you take the Pains at first to mention Particulars, it will have this good Effect; you will discover how wonderfully small trifling Expences mount up to large Sums, and will discern what might have been, and may for the future be saved, without occasioning any great Inconvenience.

In short, the Way to Wealth, if you desire it, is as plain as the Way to Market. It depends chiefly on two Words, INDUSTRY and FRUGALITY; *i. e.* Waste neither Time nor Money, but make the best Use of both. He that gets all he can honestly,

Proposals Relating to the Education of Youth in Pensilvania

Advertisement to the Reader.

It has long been regretted as a Misfortune to the Youth of this Province, that we have no ACADEMY, *in which they might receive the Accomplishments of a regular Education.*

The following Paper of Hints *towards forming a Plan for that Purpose, is so far approv'd by some publick-spirited Gentlemen, to whom it has been privately communicated, that they have directed a Number of Copies to be made by the Press, and properly distributed, in order to obtain the Sentiments and Advice of Men of Learning, Understanding, and Experience in these Matters; and have determin'd to use their Interest and best Endeavours, to have the Scheme, when compleated, carried gradually into Execution; in which they have Reason to believe they shall have the hearty Concurrence and Assistance of many who are Wellwishers to their Country.*

Those who incline to favour the Design with their Advice, either as to the Parts of Learning to be taught, the Order of Study, the Method of Teaching, the Oeconomy of the School, or any other Matter of Importance to the Success of the Undertaking, are desired to communicate their Sentiments as soon as may be, by Letter directed to B. Franklin, *Printer, in* Philadelphia.

AUTHORS *quoted in this* PAPER.

1. The famous *Milton*, whose Learning and Abilities are well known, and who had practised some Time the Education of Youth, so could speak from Experience.

2. The great Mr. *Locke*, who wrote a Treatise on Education, well known, and much esteemed, being translated into most of the modern Languages of *Europe*.

3. *Dialogues on Education*, 2 Vols. Octavo, that are much esteem'd, having had two Editions in 3 Years. Suppos'd to be wrote by the ingenious Mr. *Hutcheson* (Author of *A Treatise on the Passions*, and another on the *Ideas of Beauty and Virtue*)

who has had much Experience in Educating of Youth, being a Professor in the College at *Glasgow*, &c.

4. The learned Mr. *Obadiah Walker*, who had been many Years a Tutor to young Noblemen, and wrote a Treatise *on the Education of a young Gentleman*; of which the Fifth Edition was printed 1687.

5. The much admired Mons. *Rollin*, whose whole Life was spent in a College; and wrote 4 Vols. on Education, under the Title of, *The Method of Teaching and Studying the Belles Lettres*; which are translated into *English*, *Italian*, and most of the modern Languages.

6. The learned and ingenious Dr. *George Turnbull*, Chaplain to the present Prince of *Wales*; who has had much Experience in the Educating of Youth, and publish'd a Book, Octavo, intituled, *Observations on Liberal Education, in all its Branches*, 1742.

With some others.

The good Education of Youth has been esteemed by wise Men in all Ages, as the surest Foundation of the Happiness both of private Families and of Common-wealths. Almost all Governments have therefore made it a principal Object of their Attention, to establish and endow with proper Revenues, such Seminaries of Learning, as might supply the succeeding Age with Men qualified to serve the Publick with Honour to themselves, and to their Country.

Many of the first Settlers of these Provinces, were Men who had received a good Education in *Europe*, and to their Wisdom and good Management we owe much of our present Prosperity. But their Hands were full, and they could not do

---

As some Things here propos'd may be found to differ a little from the Forms of Education in common Use, the following Quotations are to shew the Opinions of several learned Men, who have carefully considered and wrote expresly on the Subject; such as *Milton, Locke, Rollin, Turnbull*, and others. They generally complain, that the *old Method* is in many Respects wrong; but long settled Forms are not easily changed. For us, who are now to make a Beginning, 'tis, at least, as easy to set out right as wrong; and therefore their Sentiments are on this Occasion well worth our Consideration.

Mr. *Rollin* says (*Belles Lett. p.* 249. speaking of the Manner of Educating Youth) "Though it be generally a very wise and judicious Rule to avoid all

all Things. The present Race are not thought to be generally of equal Ability: For though the *American* Youth are allow'd not to want Capacity; yet the best Capacities require Cultivation, it being truly with them, as with the best Ground, which unless well tilled and sowed with profitable Seed, produces only ranker Weeds.

That we may obtain the Advantages arising from an Increase of Knowledge, and prevent as much as may be the mischievous Consequences that would attend a general Ignorance among us, the following *Hints* are offered towards forming a Plan for the Education of the Youth of *Pennsylvania*, viz.

It is propos'd,

THAT some Persons of Leisure and publick Spirit, apply for a CHARTER, by which they may be incorporated, with Power to erect an ACADEMY for the Education of Youth, to govern the same, provide Masters, make Rules, receive Donations, purchase Lands, &c. and to add to their Number, from Time to Time such other Persons as they shall judge suitable.

That the Members of the Corporation make it their Pleasure, and in some Degree their Business, to visit the Academy often, encourage and * countenance the Youth, countenance and assist the Masters, and by all Means in their Power ad-

---

Singularity, and to follow the received Customs, yet I question whether, in the Point we now treat of, this Principle does not admit of some Exception, and whether we ought not to apprehend the Dangers and Inconveniencies of blindly following the Footsteps of those who have gone before us, so as to consult *Custom* more than *Reason*, and the governing our Actions rather by what others *do*, than by what they *should do*; from whence it often happens, that an Error once established is handed down from Age to Age, and becomes almost a certain Law, from a Notion, that we ought to act like the rest of Mankind, and follow the Example of the greatest Number. But human Nature is not so happy as to have the greatest Number always make the best Choice, and we too frequently observe the contrary."

Rollin, Vol. 2. p. 371. mentions a *French* Gentleman, Mons. *Hersan*, who, "at his own Expence, built a School for the Use of poor Children, one of the finest in the Kingdom; and left a Stipend for the Master. That he himself taught them very often, and generally had some of them at his Table. He clothed several of them; and distributed Rewards among them from Time to Time, in order to encourage them to study."

vance the Usefulness and Reputation of the Design; that they look on the Students as in some Sort their Children, treat them with Familiarity and Affection, and when they have behav'd well, and gone through their Studies, and are to enter the World, zealously unite, and make all the Interest that can be made to establish them *, whether in Business, Offices, Marriages, or any other Thing for their Advantage, preferably to all other Persons whatsoever even of equal Merit.

And if Men may, and frequently do, catch such a Taste for cultivating Flowers, for Planting, Grafting, Inoculating, and the like, as to despise all other Amusements for their Sake, why may not we expect they should acquire a Relish for that *more useful* Culture of young Minds. *Thompson* says,

> *'Tis Joy to see the human Blossoms blow,*
> *When infant Reason grows apace, and calls*
> *For the kind Hand of an assiduous Care;*
> *Delightful Task! to rear the tender Thought,*
> *To teach the young Idea how to shoot,*
> *To pour the fresh Instruction o'er the Mind,*
> *To breathe th' enliv'ning Spirit, and to fix*
> *The generous Purpose in the glowing Breast.*

That a House be provided for the ACADEMY, if not in the Town, not many Miles from it; the Situation high and dry, and if it may be, not far from a River, having a Garden, Orchard, Meadow, and a Field or two.

That the House be furnished with a Library (if in the Country, if in the Town, the Town † Libraries may serve)

*Something seems wanting in *America* to incite and stimulate Youth to Study. In *Europe* the Encouragements to Learning are of themselves much greater than can be given here. Whoever distinguishes himself there, in either of the three learned Professions, gains Fame, and often Wealth and Power: A poor Man's Son has a Chance, if he studies hard, to rise, either in the Law or the Church, to gainful Offices or Benefices; to an extraordinary Pitch of Grandeur; to have a Voice in Parliament, a Seat among the Peers; as a Statesman or first Minister to govern Nations, and even to mix his Blood with Princes.

†Besides the *English* Library begun and carried on by Subscription in *Philadelphia*, we may expect the Benefit of another much more valuable in the Learned Languages, which has been many Years collecting with the greatest Care, by a Gentleman distinguish'd for his universal Knowledge, no less than

with Maps of all Countries, Globes, some mathematical Instruments, and Apparatus for Experiments in Natural Philosophy, and for Mechanics; Prints, of all Kinds, Prospects, Buildings, Machines, &c.*

That the RECTOR be a Man of good Understanding, good Morals, diligent and patient, learn'd in the Languages and Sciences, and a correct pure Speaker and Writer of the *English* Tongue; to have such Tutors under him as shall be necessary.

That the boarding Scholars diet † together, plainly, temperately, and frugally.

That to keep them in Health, and to strengthen and render

---

for his Judgment in Books. It contains many hundred Volumes of the best Authors in the best Editions, among which are the *Polyglot* Bible, and *Castel*'s Lexicon on it, in 8 large Vols. *Aldus*'s Septuagint, Apocrypha and New Testament, in *Greek*, and some other Editions of the same; most of the Fathers; almost all the *Greek* Authors from *Homer* himself, in divers Editions (and one of them in that of *Rome*, with *Eustathius*'s Commentaries, in 4 Vols.) to near the End of the 4th Century, with divers later, as *Photius*, *Suidas*, divers of the *Byzantine* Historians; all the old Mathematicians, as *Archimedes*, *Apollonius*, *Euclid*, *Ptolomy*'s Geography and Almagest, with *Theon*'s Commentaries and *Diophantus*, in the whole above 100 Vols. in *Greek* Folio's. All the old *Roman* Classics without Exception, and some of them in several Editions (as all *Tully*'s Works in four Editions). All *Grævius*, *Gronovius*, *Salengre*'s and *Poleni*'s Collections of *Roman* and *Greek* Antiquities, containing above Five Hundred distinct Discourses in 33 Tomes, with some Hundreds of late Authors in *Latin*, as *Vossius*, *Lipsius*, *Grotius*, &c. A good Collection of Mathematical Pieces, as *Newton* in all the three Editions, *Wallis*, *Huygens*, *Tacquet*, *Dechales*, &c. in near 100 Vols. in all Sizes, with some *Orientals*, *French* and *Italian* Authors, and many more *English*, &c. A handsome Building above 60 Feet in front, is now erected in this City, at the private Expence of that Gentleman, for the Reception of this Library, where it is soon to be deposited, and remain for the publick Use, with a valuable yearly Income duly to enlarge it; and I have his Permission to mention it as an Encouragement to the propos'd Academy; to which this noble Benefaction will doubtless be of the greatest Advantage, as not only the Students, but even the Masters themselves, may very much improve by it.

*See in *Turnbull*, p. 415. the Description of the Furniture of the School called the *Instituto* at *Bologna*, procur'd by the Care and Direction of Count *Marsigli*, and originally at his private Expence.

†Perhaps it would be best if none of the Scholars were to diet abroad. *Milton* is of that Opinion (*Tractate of Education*) for that much Time would else be lost, and many ill Habits got.

active their Bodies, they be frequently * exercis'd in Running, Leaping, Wrestling, and Swimming †, &c.

*Milton proposes, that an Hour and Half before Dinner should be allow'd for Exercise, and recommends among other Exercises, the handling of Arms, but perhaps this may not be thought necessary here. *Turnbull*, p. 318. says, "Corporal Exercise invigorates the Soul as well as the Body; let one be kept closely to Reading, without allowing him any Respite from Thinking, or any Exercise to his Body, and were it possible to preserve long, by such a Method, his Liking to Study and Knowledge, yet we should soon find such an one become no less soft in his Mind than in his outward Man. Both Mind and Body would thus become gradually too relaxed, too much unbraced for the Fatigues and Duties of active Life. Such is the Union between Soul and Body, that the same Exercises which are conducive, when rightly managed, to consolidate or strengthen the former, are likewise equally necessary and fit to produce Courage, Firmness, and manly Vigour, in the latter. For this, and other Reasons, certain hardy Exercises were reckoned by the Antients an essential Part in the Formation of a liberal Character; and ought to have their Place in Schools where Youth are taught the Languages and Sciences." See p. 318 to 323.

†'Tis suppos'd that every Parent would be glad to have their Children skill'd in *Swimming*, if it might be learnt in a Place chosen for its Safety, and under the Eye of a careful Person. Mr. *Locke* says, p. 9. in his *Treatise of Education*; " 'Tis that saves many a Man's Life; and the *Romans* thought it so necessary, that they rank'd it with Letters; and it was the common Phrase to mark one ill educated, and good for nothing, that he had neither learnt to read nor to swim; *Nec Literas didicit nec Natare*. But besides the gaining a Skill which may serve him at Need, the Advantages to Health by often Bathing in cold Water during the Heat of the Summer, are so many, that I think nothing need be said to encourage it."

'Tis some Advantage besides, to be free from the slavish Terrors many of those feel who cannot swim, when they are oblig'd to be on the Water even in crossing a Ferry.

Mr. *Hutchinson*, in his *Dialogues concerning Education*, 2 Vols. Octavo, lately publish'd, says, Vol. 2. p. 297. "I would have the Youth accustomed to such Exercises as will harden their Constitution, as Riding, Running, Swimming, Shooting, and the like."

Charlemagne, Founder of the *German* Empire, brought up his Sons hardily, and even his Daughters were inur'd to Industry. *Henry* the Great of *France*, saith Mons. *Rhodez*, " was not permitted by his Grand-father to be brought up with Delicacy, who well knew that *seldom lodgeth other than a mean and feeble Spirit in an effeminate and tender Body*. He commanded that the Boy should be accustomed to run, to leap, to climb the Rocks and Mountains; that by such Means he might be inured to Labour, &c. His ordinary Food also was of coarse Bread, Beef, Cheese and Garlick; his Cloathing plain and coarse, and often he went barefoot and bareheaded." *Walker* of Education, p. 17, 18.

That they have peculiar Habits to distinguish them from other Youth, if the Academy be in or near the Town; for this, among other Reasons, that their Behaviour may be the better observed.

As to their STUDIES, it would be well if they could be taught *every Thing* that is useful, and *every Thing* that is ornamental: But Art is long, and their Time is short. It is therefore propos'd that they learn those Things that are likely to be *most useful* and *most ornamental*. Regard being had to the several Professions for which they are intended.

All should be taught to write a *fair Hand*, and swift, as that is useful to All. And with it may be learnt something of * *Drawing*, by Imitation of Prints, and some of the first Principles of Perspective.

Drawing is a kind of Universal Language, understood by all Nations. A Man may often express his Ideas, even to his own Countrymen, more clearly with a Lead Pencil, or Bit of Chalk, than with his Tongue. And many can understand a Figure, that do not comprehend a Description in Words, tho' ever so properly chosen. All Boys have an early Inclination to this Improvement, and begin to make Figures of Animals, Ships, Machines, *&c.* as soon as they can use a Pen: But for want of a little Instruction at that Time, generally are discouraged, and quit the Pursuit.

Mr. *Locke* says, p. 234. "When your Son can write well and quick, I think it may be convenient not only to continue the Exercise of his Hand in Writing, but also to improve the Use of it further in *Drawing*; a Thing very useful to a Gentleman on several Occasions; but especially if he travel; as that which helps a Man often to express in a *few Lines* well put together, what a *whole Sheet of Paper in Writing* would not be able to represent and make intelligible. How many Buildings may a Man see, how many *Machines* and Habits meet with, the Ideas whereof would be easily retain'd, and communicated by a little Skill in Drawing; which being committed to Words, are in Danger to be lost, or at best but ill retained in the most exact Descriptions? I do not mean that I would have him a perfect Painter; to be that to any tolerable Degree, will require more Time than he can spare from his other Improvements of greater Moment. But so much Insight into Perspective and Skill in Drawing, as will enable him to represent tolerably on Paper any Thing he sees, except Faces, may, I think, be got in a little Time."

Drawing is no less useful to a *Mechanic* than to a Gentleman. Several Handicrafts seem to require it; as the Carpenter's, Shipwright's, Engraver's, Painter's, Carver's, Cabinet-maker's, Gardiner's, and other Businesses. By a little Skill of this kind, the Workman may perfect his own Idea of the Thing to be done, before he begins to work; and show a Draft for the Encouragement and Satisfaction of his Employer.

* *Arithmetick*, *Accounts*, and some of the first Principles of *Geometry* and *Astronomy*.

The † *English* Language might be taught by Grammar; in

*Mr. *Locke* is of Opinion, p. 269. that a Child should be early enter'd in Arithmetick, Geography, Chronology, History and Geometry. "Merchants Accounts, he says, if it is not necessary to help a Gentleman to *get* an Estate, yet there is nothing of more Use and Efficacy to make him *preserve* the Estate he has. 'Tis seldom observ'd that he who keeps an Account of his Income and Expences, and thereby has constantly under View the Course of his Domestic Affairs, lets them run to Ruin: And I doubt not but many a Man gets behind-hand before he is aware, or runs farther on when he is once in, for want of this Care, or the Skill to do it. I would therefore advise all Gentlemen to learn perfectly *Merchants Accounts*; and not to think 'tis a Skill that belongs not to them, because it has received its Name, and has been chiefly practis'd by Men of Traffick." p. 316.

Not only the *Skill*, but the *Habit* of keeping Accounts, should be acquir'd by all, as being necessary to all.

†Mr. *Locke*, speaking of *Grammar*, p. 252. says, "That to those the greatest Part of whose Business in this World is to be done with their Tongues, and with their Pens, it is convenient, if not necessary, that they should speak properly and correctly, whereby they may let their Thoughts into other Mens Minds the more easily, and with the greater Impression. Upon this Account it is, that any sort of Speaking, so as will make him be understood, is not thought enough for a Gentleman. He ought to study *Grammar*, among the other Helps of Speaking well, but it *must be* THE GRAMMAR OF HIS OWN TONGUE, of the Language he uses, that he may understand his own Country Speech nicely, and speak it properly, without shocking the Ears of those it is addressed to with Solecisms and offensive Irregularities. And to this Purpose *Grammar is necessary*; but it is the Grammar *only* of *their own proper Tongues*, and to those who would take Pains in cultivating their Language, and perfecting their Stiles. Whether all Gentlemen should not do this, I leave to be considered, since the Want of Propriety and Grammatical Exactness is thought very misbecoming one of that Rank, and usually draws on one guilty of such Faults, the Imputation of having had a lower Breeding and worse Company than suits with his Quality. If this be so (as I suppose it is) it will be Matter of Wonder, why young Gentlemen are forc'd to learn the Grammars of foreign and dead Languages, and are never once told of the Grammar of their own Tongues. They do not so much as know there is any such Thing, much less is it made their Business to be instructed in it. Nor is their own Language ever propos'd to them as worthy their Care and Cultivating, tho' they have *daily Use* of it, and are not seldom, in the future Course of their Lives, judg'd of by their handsome or awkward Way of expressing themselves in it. Whereas the Languages whose Grammars they have been so much employed in, are such as probably they shall scarce ever speak or write; or if upon Occasion this should happen, they should be excused for the Mistakes and Faults they make in it. Would not a *Chinese*, who took Notice of

which some of our best Writers, as *Tillotson*, *Addison*, *Pope*, *Algernoon Sidney*, *Cato*'s Letters, *&c.* should be Classicks: The *Stiles* principally to be cultivated, being the *clear* and the

---

this Way of Breeding, be apt to imagine, that all our young Gentlemen were designed to be Teachers and Professors of the dead Languages of foreign Countries, and not to be Men of Business in their own." Page 255. the same Author adds, "That if Grammar ought to be taught at any Time, it must be to one that can speak the Language already; how else can he be taught the Grammar of it? This at least is evident from the Practice of the wise and learned Nations among the Antients. They made it a *Part of Education* to cultivate *their own*, not foreign Tongues. The *Greeks* counted all other Nations barbarous, and had a Contempt for their Languages. And though *Greek* Learning grew in Credit amongst the *Romans* towards the End of their Commonwealth, yet it was the *Roman* Tongue that was made the Study of their Youth: *Their own* Language they were to make Use of, and therefore it was *their own* Language they were *instructed* and *exercised* in." And p. 281. "There can scarce be a greater Defect (says he) in a Gentleman, than not to express himself well either in Writing or Speaking. But yet I think I may ask the Reader, whether he doth not know a great many, who live upon their Estates, and so, with the Name, should have the Qualities of Gentlemen, who cannot so much as tell a Story as they should, much less speak clearly and persuasively in any Business. This I think not to be so much their Fault as the *Fault of their Education*." Thus far *Locke*.

Mons. *Rollin*, reckons the Neglect of Teaching their own Tongue a great Fault in the *French* Universities. He spends great Part of his first Vol. of *Belles Lettres*, on that Subject; and lays down some excellent Rules or Methods of Teaching *French* to *Frenchmen* grammatically, and making them Masters therein, which are very applicable to our Language, but too long to be inserted here. He practis'd them on the Youth under his Care with great Success.

Mr. *Hutchinson*, Dial. p. 297. says, "To perfect them in the Knowledge of their Mother Tongue, they should learn it in the Grammatical Way, that they may not only speak it purely, but be able both to correct their own Idiom, and afterwards enrich the Language on the same Foundation."

Dr. *Turnbull*, in his Observations on a liberal Education, says, p. 262. "The *Greeks*, perhaps, made more early Advances in the most useful Sciences than any Youth have done since, chiefly on this Account, that they studied no other Language but their own. This no Doubt saved them very much Time; but they *applied themselves carefully* to the Study of *their own* Language, and were *early* able to speak and write it in *the greatest Perfection*. The *Roman* Youth, though they learned the *Greek*, did not neglect their own Tongue, but studied it more carefully than we now do *Greek* and *Latin*, without giving ourselves any Trouble about our own Tongue."

Mons. *Simon*, in an elegant Discourse of his among the Memoirs of the Academy of *Belles Lettres* at *Paris*, speaking of the Stress the *Romans* laid on Purity of Language and graceful Pronunciation, adds, "May I here make a

concise. Reading should also be taught, and pronouncing, properly, distinctly, emphatically; not with an even Tone, which *under-does*, nor a theatrical, which *over-does* Nature.

To form their Stile, they should be put on Writing * Letters

Reflection on the Education we commonly give our Children? It is very re-mote from the Precepts I have mentioned. Hath the Child arrived to six or seven Years of Age, he mixes with a Herd of ill-bred Boys at School, where under the Pretext of Teaching him *Latin*, no Regard is had to his *Mother Tongue*. And what happens? What we see every Day. A young Gentleman of eighteen, who has had this Education, CANNOT READ. For to articulate the Words, and join them together, I do not call *Reading*, unless one can pro-nounce well, observe all the proper Stops, vary the Voice, express the Senti-ments, and read with a delicate Intelligence. Nor can he speak a Jot better. A Proof of this is, that he cannot write ten Lines without committing gross Faults; and because he did not learn his own Language well in his early Years, he will never know it well. I except a few, who being afterwards engaged by their Profession, or their natural Taste, cultivate their Minds by Study. And yet even they, if they attempt to write, will find by the *Labour* Composition costs them, what a *Loss it is*, not to have learned their Language in the proper Season. Education among the *Romans* was upon a quite different Footing. Masters of Rhetoric taught them early the Principles, the Difficulties, the Beauties, the Subtleties, the Depths, the Riches of their own Language. When they went from these Schools, they were perfect Masters of it, they were never at a Loss for proper Expressions; and I am much deceived if it was not owing to this, that they produced such excellent Works with so *mar-vellous Facility*."

Pliny, in his Letter to a Lady on chusing a Tutor for her Son, speaks of it as the most material Thing in his Education, that he should have a good *Latin* Master of Rhetoric, and recommends *Julius Genitor* for his *eloquent, open and plain Faculty of Speaking*. He does not advise her to a *Greek* Master of Rhetoric, tho' the *Greeks* were famous for that Science; but to a *Latin* Master, because *Latin* was the Boy's Mother Tongue. In the above Quota-tion from Mons. *Simon*, we see what was the Office and Duty of the Master of Rhetoric.

*This Mr. *Locke* recommends, *Educ. p.* 284. and says, "The Writing of Letters has so much to do in all the Occurrences of human Life, that no Gentleman can avoid shewing himself in this Kind of Writing. Occasions will daily force him to make this Use of his Pen, which, besides the Consequences that, in his Affairs, the well or ill managing it often draws after it, always lays him open to a severer Examination of his Breeding, Sense and Abilities, than oral Discourses, whose transient Faults dying for the most Part with the Sound that gives them Life, and so not subject to a strict Review, more easily escape Observation and Censure." He adds,

"Had the Methods of Education been directed to their right End, one would have thought this so necessary a Part could not have been neglected,

to each other, making Abstracts of what they read; or writing the same Things in their own Words; telling or writing

---

whilst Themes and Verses in *Latin*, of no Use at all, were so constantly every where pressed, to the Racking of Childrens Inventions beyond their Strength, and hindring their chearful Progress by unnatural Difficulties. But Custom has so ordained it, and who dares disobey? And would it not be very unreasonable to require of a learned Country Schoolmaster (who has all the Tropes and Figures in *Farnaby*'s Rhetorick at his Finger's Ends) to teach his Scholar to express himself handsomely in *English*, when it appears to be so little his Business or Thought, that the Boy's Mother (despised, 'tis like, as illiterate for not having read a System of Logic or Rhetoric) outdoes him in it?

"To speak and write correctly, gives a Grace, and gains a favourable Attention to what one has to say: And since 'tis *English* that an *Englishman* will have constant Use of, that is the Language he should chiefly cultivate, and wherein most Care should be taken to polish and perfect his Stile. To speak or write better *Latin* than *English*, may make a Man be talk'd of, but he will find it more to his Purpose to express himself well in his own Tongue, that he uses every Moment, than to have the vain Commendation of others for a very insignificant Quality. This I find universally neglected, nor no Care taken any where to improve young Men in their own Language, that they may thoroughly understand and be Masters of it. If any one among us have a Facility or Purity more than ordinary in his Mother Tongue, it is owing to Chance, or his Genius, or any Thing, rather than to his Education, or any Care of his Teacher. To mind what *English* his Pupil speaks or writes, is below the Dignity of one bred up among *Greek* and *Latin*, tho' he have but little of them himself. These are the Learned Languages, fit only for Learned Men to meddle with and teach: *English* is the Language of the illiterate Vulgar. Though the Great Men among the *Romans* were daily exercising themselves in their own Language; and we find yet upon Record the Names of Orators who taught some of their Emperors *Latin*, tho' it were their Mother Tongue. 'Tis plain the *Greeks* were yet more nice in theirs. All other Speech was barbarous to them but their own, and no foreign Language appears to have been studied or valued amongst that learned and acute People; tho' it be past Doubt, that they borrowed their Learning and Philosophy from abroad.

"I am not here speaking against *Greek* and *Latin*. I think *Latin* at least ought to be well understood by every Gentleman. But whatever foreign Languages a young Man meddles with, that which he should critically study, and labour to get a Facility, Clearness and Elegancy to express himself in, should be *his own*; and to this Purpose *he should daily be* EXERCISED in it."

To the same Purpose writes a Person of eminent Learning in a Letter to Dr. *Turnbull*: "Nothing certainly (says he) can be of more Service to Mankind than a right Method of Educating the Youth, and I should be glad to hear —— —— to give an Example of the great Advantage it would be to

Stories lately read, in their own Expressions. All to be revis'd and corrected by the Tutor, who should give his Reasons, explain the Force and Import of Words, &c.

To form their * Pronunciation, they may be put on making Declamations, repeating Speeches, delivering Orations, &c. The Tutor assisting at the Rehearsals, teaching, advising, correcting their Accent, &c.

But if † HISTORY be made a constant Part of their Reading,

---

the *rising Age*, and to our Nation. When our publick Schools were first established, the Knowledge of *Latin* was thought Learning; and he that had a tolerable Skill in two or three Languages, tho' his Mind was not enlightened by any *real Knowledge*, was a profound Scholar. But it is not so at present; and People confess, that Men may have obtained a Perfection in these, and yet continue *deeply ignorant*. The *Greek* Education was of another Kind [which he describes in several Particulars, and adds] They studied to write their *own Tongue* more accurately than we do *Latin* and *Greek*. But where is *English* taught at present? Who thinks it of Use to study correctly *that Language* which he is to use *every Day* in his Life, be his Station ever so high, or ever so insignificant. It is in *this* the Nobility and Gentry defend their Country, and serve their Prince in Parliament; in *this* the Lawyers plead, the Divines instruct, and all Ranks of People write their Letters, and transact all their Affairs; and yet who thinks it worth his learning to write *this* even accurately, not to say politely? Every one is suffer'd to form his Stile by Chance; to imitate the first wretched Model which falls in his Way, before he knows what is faulty, or can relish the Beauties of a just Simplicity. Few think their Children qualified for a Trade till they have been whipt at a *Latin* School for five or six Years, to learn a little of that which they are oblig'd to forget; when in those Years right Education would have improv'd their Minds, and taught them to acquire Habits of Writing *their own Language* easily under right Direction; and this would have been useful to them as long as they lived." *Introd. p.* 3, 4, 5.

Since Mr. *Locke*'s Time, several good Grammars have been wrote and publish'd for the Use of Schools; as *Brightland*'s, *Greenwood*'s, &c.

*By Pronunciation is here meant, the proper Modulation of the Voice, to suit the Subject with due Emphasis, Action, &c. In delivering a Discourse in Publick, design'd to persuade, the *Manner*, perhaps, contributes more to Success, than either the *Matter* or *Method*. Yet the two latter seem to engross the Attention of most Preachers and other Publick Speakers, and the former to be almost totally neglected.

†As nothing *teaches* (saith Mr. *Locke*) so nothing *delights* more than HISTORY. The first of these recommends it to the Study of grown Men, the latter makes me think it the *fittest* for a young Lad, who as soon as he is instructed in Chronology, and acquainted with the several Epochas in Use in this Part

such as the Translations of the *Greek* and *Roman* Historians, and the modern Histories of antient *Greece* and *Rome*, &c. may not almost all Kinds of useful Knowledge be that Way introduc'd to Advantage, and with Pleasure to the Student? As

GEOGRAPHY, by reading with Maps, and being required to point out the Places *where* the greatest Actions were done, to give their old and new Names, with the Bounds, Situation, Extent of the Countries concern'd, *&c.*

CHRONOLOGY, by the Help of *Helvicus* or some other Writer of the Kind, who will enable them to tell *when* those Events happened; what Princes were Cotemporaries, what States or famous Men flourish'd about that Time, *&c.* The several principal Epochas to be first well fix'd in their Memories.

ANTIENT CUSTOMS, religious and civil, being frequently mentioned in History, will give Occasion for explaining them; in which the * Prints of Medals, Basso Relievo's, and antient Monuments will greatly assist.

MORALITY, † by descanting and making continual Observations on the Causes of the Rise or Fall of any Man's Character, Fortune, Power, *&c.* mention'd in History; the

---

of the World, and can reduce them to the *Julian* Period, should then have some History put into his Hand. *Educ. p.* 276.

Mons. *Rollin* complains, that the College Education in *France* is defective in Teaching *History*, which he thinks may be made of great Advantage to Youth. This he demonstrates largely in his *Belles Lettres*, to the Satisfaction of all that read the Book. He lays down the following Rules for Studying History, *viz.* 1. To reduce the Study to Order and Method. 2. To observe what relates to Usages and Customs. 3. To enquire particularly, and above all Things, after the Truth. 4. To endeavour to find out the Causes of the Rise and Fall of States, of the Gaining or Losing of Battles, and other Events of Importance. 5. To study the Character of the Nations and great Men mentioned in History. 6. To be attentive to such Instructions as concern MORAL EXCELLENCY and the CONDUCT OF LIFE. 7. Carefully to note every Thing that relates to RELIGION: *Vol.* 3. *p.* 146.

*Plenty of these are to be met with in *Montfaucon*; and other Books of Antiquities.

†For the Importance and Necessity of moral Instructions to Youth, see the latter Notes.

Advantages of Temperance, Order, Frugality, Industry, Perseverance, &c. &c. * Indeed the general natural Tendency of Reading good History, must be, to fix in the Minds of Youth deep Impressions of the Beauty and Usefulness of Virtue of all Kinds, Publick Spirit, Fortitude, &c.

History will show the wonderful Effects of ORATORY, in governing, turning and leading great Bodies of Mankind, Armies, Cities, Nations. When the Minds of Youth are struck with Admiration at this, † then is the Time to give them the Principles of that Art, which they will study with Taste and Application. Then they may be made acquainted with the best Models among the Antients, their Beauties being particularly pointed out to them. Modern Political Oratory being chiefly performed by the Pen and Press, its Advantages over the Antient in some Respects are to be shown; as that its Effects are more extensive, more lasting, &c.

History will also afford frequent Opportunities of showing the Necessity of a *Publick Religion*, from its Usefulness to the Publick; the Advantage of a Religious Character among private Persons; the Mischiefs of Superstition, &c. and the

*Dr. *Turnbull*, Liberal Education, *p.* 371, says, "That the useful Lessons which ought to be inculcated upon Youth, are much better taught and enforced from *Characters*, *Actions*, and *Events*, developing the inward Springs of human Conduct, and the different Consequences of Actions, whether with Respect to private or publick Good, than by abstract Philosophical Lectures. History points out in Examples, as in a Glass, all the Passions of the human Heart, and all their various Workings in different Circumstances, all the Virtues and all the Vices human Nature is capable of; all the Snares, all the Temptations, all the Vicissitudes and Incidents of human Life; and gives Occasion for Explaining all the Rules of Prudence, Decency, Justice and Integrity, in private Oeconomy, and in short all the Laws of natural Reason."

†"Rules are best understood, when Examples that confirm them, and point out their Fitness or Necessity, naturally lead one, as it were by the Hand, to take Notice of them. One who is persuaded and moved by a Speech, and heartily admires its Force and Beauty, will with Pleasure enter into a critical Examination of its Excellencies; and willingly lay up in his Mind the Rules of Rhetoric such an Example of Eloquence plainly suggests. But to teach Rules abstractly, or without Examples, and before the agreeable Effects the Observance of them tends to produce (which are in Reality their Reason or Foundation) have been felt, *is exceedingly preposterous.*" *Turnbull*, p. 410.

"I have seldom or never observed any one to get the Skill of Speaking handsomely, by Studying the Rules which pretend to teach Rhetoric." *Locke*, p. 279.

Excellency of the CHRISTIAN RELIGION above all others antient or modern*.

History will also give Occasion to expatiate on the Advantage of Civil Orders and Constitutions, how Men and their Properties are protected by joining in Societies and establishing Government; their Industry encouraged and rewarded, Arts invented, and Life made more comfortable: The Advantages of *Liberty*, Mischiefs of *Licentiousness*, Benefits arising from good Laws and a due Execution of Justice, *&c*. Thus may the first Principles of sound † *Politicks* be fix'd in the Minds of Youth.

On *Historical* Occasions, Questions of Right and Wrong, Justice and Injustice, will naturally arise, and may be put to Youth, which they may debate in Conversation and in Writing ‡. When they ardently desire Victory, for the Sake of the Praise attending it, they will begin to feel the Want, and be sensible of the Use of *Logic*, or the Art of Reasoning to *discover* Truth, and of Arguing to *defend* it, and *convince*

---

*See *Turnbull* on this Head, from p. 386 to 390. very much to the Purpose, but too long to be transcribed here.

†Thus, as *Milton* says, *Educ.* p. 381. should they be instructed in the Beginning, End and Reasons of political Societies; that they may not, in a dangerous Fit of the Commonwealth, be such poor, shaken, uncertain Reeds, of such a tottering Conscience, as many of our great Councellors have lately shewn themselves, but stedfast Pillars of the State.

‡After this, they are to dive into the Grounds of Law and legal Justice; deliver'd first and with best Warrant by *Moses*; and as far as human Prudence can be trusted, in those celebrated Remains of the antient *Grecian* and *Roman* Lawgivers, *&c*. p. 382.

"When he has pretty well digested *Tully*'s Offices, says Mr. *Locke*, p. 277. and added to it *Puffendorff de Officio Hominis & Civis*, it may be seasonable to set him upon *Grotius, de Jure Belli & Pacis*, or which perhaps is the better of the two, *Puffendorff de Jure naturali & Gentium*; wherein he will be instructed in the natural Rights of Men, and the Original and Foundations of Society, and the Duties resulting from thence. This *general Part of Civil Law* and History are Studies which a Gentleman should not barely touch at, but constantly dwell upon, and never have done with. A virtuous and well-behaved young Man, that is well versed in the *general Part of the Civil Law* (which concerns not the Chicane of private Cases, but the Affairs and Intercourse of civilized Nations in general, grounded upon Principles of Reason) understands *Latin* well, and can write a good Hand, one may turn loose into the World, with great Assurance that he will find Employment and Esteem every where."

Adversaries. This would be the Time to acquaint them with the Principles of that Art. *Grotius, Puffendorff,* and some other Writers of the same Kind, may be used on these Occasions to decide their Disputes. * Publick Disputes warm the Imagination, whet the Industry, and strengthen the natural Abilities.

When Youth are told, that the Great Men whose Lives and Actions they read in History, spoke two of the best Languages that ever were, the most expressive, copious, beautiful; and that the finest Writings, the most correct Compositions, the most perfect Productions of human Wit and Wisdom, are in those Languages, which have endured Ages, and will endure while there are Men; that no Translation can do them Justice, or give the Pleasure found in Reading the Originals; that those Languages contain all Science; that one of them is become almost universal, being the Language of Learned Men in all Countries; that to understand them is a distinguishing Ornament, *&c.* they may be thereby made desirous of learning those Languages, and their Industry sharpen'd in the Acquisition of them. All intended for Divinity should be taught the *Latin* and *Greek*; for Physick, the *Latin*, *Greek* and *French*; for Law, the *Latin* and *French*; Merchants, the

*Mr. *Walker,* in his excellent Treatise of the Education of young Gentlemen, speaking of *Publick and open Argumentation pro and con,* says p. 124, 125. "*This is it* which brings a Question to a Point, and discovers the very Center and Knot of the Difficulty. *This* warms and *activates* the Spirit in the Search of Truth, excites Notions, and by replying and frequent Beating upon it, *cleanseth* it from the Ashes, and makes it shine and flame out the clearer. Besides, it puts them upon a continual *Stretch* of their Wits to defend their Cause, it makes them quick in Replies, intentive upon their Subject; where the *Opponent* useth all Means to drive his Adversary from his Hold; and the *Answerer* defends himself *sometimes* with the Force of Truth, *sometimes* with the Subtilty of his Wit; and *sometimes* also he escapes in a Mist of Words, and the Doubles of a Distinction, whilst he seeks all Holes and Recesses to shelter his persecuted Opinion and Reputation. This properly belongeth to the Disputations which are Exercises of young Students, who are by these Velitations and in this Palæstra brought up to a more serious Search of Truth. And in them I think it not a Fault *to dispute for Victory,* and to endeavour to save their Reputation; nor that their Questions and Subjects are concerning Things of small Moment and little Reality; yea, I have known some Governors that have absolutely forbidden such Questions, where the Truth was of Concernment, on purpose that the Youth might have the Liberty of exerting their Parts to the uttermost, and that there might be no Stint to their Emulation."

French, *German*, and *Spanish*: And though all should not be compell'd to learn *Latin*, *Greek*, or the modern foreign Languages; yet none that have an ardent Desire to learn them should be refused; their *English*, Arithmetick, and other Studies absolutely necessary, being at the same Time not neglected.

If the new *Universal History* were also read, it would give a *connected* Idea of human Affairs, so far as it goes, which should be follow'd by the best modern Histories, particularly of our Mother Country; then of these Colonies; which should be accompanied with Observations on their Rise, Encrease, Use to *Great-Britain*, Encouragements, Discouragements, *&c.* the Means to make them flourish, secure their Liberties, *&c.*

With the History of Men, Times and Nations, should be read at proper Hours or Days, some of the best *Histories of Nature* *, which would not only be delightful to Youth, and furnish them with Matter for their Letters, *&c.* as well as

---

Rollin, *Vol.* 4. *p.* 211. speaking of *Natural Philosophy*, says, "That much of it falls within the Capacity of all Sorts of Persons, even of Children. It consists in attending to the Objects with which nature presents us, in considering them with Care, and admiring their different Beauties, *&c.* Searching out their secret Causes indeed more properly belongs to the Learned.

"I say that even Children are capable of Studying Nature, for they have Eyes, and don't want Curiosity; they ask Questions, and love to be informed; and here we need only awaken and keep up in them the Desire of Learning and Knowing, which is natural to all Mankind. Besides this Study, if it is to be called a Study, instead of being painful and tedious, is pleasant and agreeable; it may be used as a Recreation, and should usually be made a Diversion. It is inconceivable, how many Things Children are capable of, if all the Opportunities of Instructing them were laid hold of, with which they themselves supply us.

"A Garden, a Country, a Plantation, are all so many Books which lie open to them; but they must have been taught and accustomed to read in them. Nothing is more common amongst us than the Use of Bread and Linnen. How seldom do Children know how either of them are prepared, through how many Operations and Hands the Corn and Flax must pass, before they are turned into Bread and Linnen? The same may be said of Cloth, which bears no Resemblance to the Wool whereof it is formed, any more than Paper to the Rags which are picked up in the Streets: And why should not Children be instructed in these wonderful Works of Nature and Art which they every Day make Use of without reflecting upon them?

"He adds, that a careful Master may in this Way enrich the Mind of his

other History; but afterwards of great Use to them, whether they are Merchants, Handicrafts, or Divines; enabling the first the better to understand many Commodities, Drugs, &c. the second to improve his Trade or Handicraft by new Mixtures, Materials, &c. and the last to adorn his Discourses by beautiful Comparisons, and strengthen them by new Proofs of Divine Providence. The Conversation of all will be improved by it, as Occasions frequently occur of making Natural Observations, which are instructive, agreeable, and entertaining in almost all Companies. *Natural History* will also afford Opportunities of introducing many Observations, relating to the Preservation of Health, which may be afterwards of great Use. *Arbuthnot* on Air and *Aliment, Sanctorius* on Perspiration, *Lemery* on Foods, and some others, may now be read, and a very little Explanation will make them sufficiently intelligible to Youth.

While they are reading Natural History, might not a little *Gardening, Planting, Grafting, Inoculating,* &c. be taught and practised; and now and then Excursions made to the neighbouring Plantations of the best Farmers, their Methods observ'd and reason'd upon for the Information of Youth. The Improvement of Agriculture being useful to all *, and Skill in it no Disparagement to any.

Disciple with a great Number of useful and agreeable Ideas, and by a proper Mixture of short Reflections, will at the same Time take Care to form his Heart, and lead him by Nature to Religion."

Milton also recommends the Study of *Natural Philosophy* to Youth, *Educ. p.* 380. "In this, says he, they may proceed leisurely from the History of Meteors, Minerals, Plants and living Creatures, as far as Anatomy; Then also in Course might be read to them out of some not tedious Writer, the Institution of Physick; that they may know the Tempers, the Humours, the Seasons, and how to manage a Crudity; which he who can wisely and timely do, is not only a great Physician to himself, and to his Friends, but also may at some Time or other save an Army by this frugal and expenseless Means only; and not let the healthy and stout Bodies of young Men rot away under him for want of this Discipline, which is a great Pity, and no less a Shame to the Commander."

Proper Books may be, *Ray*'s *Wisdom of God in the Creation, Derham*'s *Physico-Theology, Spectacle de la Nature,* &c.

Milton would have the *Latin* Authors on Agriculture taught at School, as *Cato, Varro* and *Columella*; "for the Matter, says he, is most easy, and if

The History of *Commerce*, of the Invention of Arts, Rise of Manufactures, Progress of Trade, Change of its Seats, with the Reasons, Causes, *&c.* may also be made entertaining to Youth, and will be useful to all. And this, with the Accounts in other History of the prodigious Force and Effect of Engines and Machines used in War, will naturally introduce a Desire to be instructed in * *Mechanicks*, and to be inform'd of the Principles of that Art by which weak Men perform such Wonders, Labour is sav'd, Manufactures expedited, *&c.* *&c.* This will be the Time to show them Prints of antient and modern Machines, to explain them, to let them be † copied, and to give Lectures in Mechanical Philosophy.

With the whole should be constantly inculcated and culti-

---

the Language be difficult, yet it may be master'd. And here will be an Occasion of *inciting* and *enabling* them hereafter to improve the Tillage of their Country, to recover the bad Soil, and to remedy the Waste that is made of Good; for this was one of *Hercules'* Praises." *Educ. p.* 379.

Hutcheson (Dialogues on Educ. 303, 2d Vol.) says, "Nor should I think it below the Dignity or Regard of an University, to descend even to the general Precepts of *Agriculture* and *Gardening*. *Virgil*, *Varro*, and others eminent in Learning, tho't it not below their Pen—and why should we think meanly of that Art, which was the Mother of Heroes, and of the Masters of the World."

Locke also recommends the Study of Husbandry and Gardening, as well as gaining an Insight in several of the manual Arts; *Educ. p.* 309, 314, 315. It would be a Pleasure and Diversion to Boys to be led now and then to the Shops of Artificers, and suffer'd to spend some Time there in observing their Manner of Working. For the Usefulness of Mechanic Skill, even to Gentlemen, see the Pages above cited, to which much might be added.

*How many Mills are built and Machines constructed, at great and fruitless Expence, which a little Knowledge in the Principles of Mechanics would have prevented?

†We are often told in the Journals of Travellers, that such and such Things are done in foreign Countries, by which Labour is sav'd, and Manufactures expedited, *&c.* but their Description of the Machines or Instruments used, are quite unintelligible for want of good Drafts. Copying Prints of Machines is of Use to fix the Attention on the several Parts, their Proportions, Reasons, Effects, *&c.* A Man that has been us'd to this Practice, is not only better able to make a Draft when the Machine is before him, but takes so much better Notice of its Appearance, that he can carry it off by Memory when he has not the Opportunity of Drawing it on the Spot. Thus may a Traveller bring home Things of great Use to his Country.

vated, that *Benignity of Mind* *, which shows itself in *searching for* and *seizing* every Opportunity *to serve* and *to oblige*; and is the Foundation of what is called GOOD BREEDING; highly useful to the Possessor, and most agreeable to all†.

The Idea of what is *true Merit*, should also be often presented to Youth, explain'd and impress'd on their Minds, as consisting in an *Inclination* join'd with an *Ability* to serve Mankind, one's Country, Friends and Family; which *Ability* is (with the Blessing of God) to be acquir'd or greatly encreas'd by *true Learning*; and should indeed be the great *Aim* and ‡ *End* of all Learning.

*"Upon this excellent Disposition (says *Turnbull*, p. 326.) it will be *easy to build* that amiable Quality commonly called GOOD BREEDING, and upon *no other Foundation* can it be raised. For whence else can it spring, but from a general Good-will and Regard for all People, deeply rooted in the Heart, which makes any one that has it, careful not to shew in his Carriage, any Contempt, Disrespect, or Neglect of them, but to express a Value and Respect for them according to their Rank and Condition, suitable to the Fashion and Way of their Country? 'Tis a Disposition to make all we converse with easy and well pleased."

†"It is this lovely Quality which gives true Beauty to all other Accomplishments, or renders them useful to their Possessor, in procuring him the Esteem and Good-will of all that he comes near. Without it, his other Qualities, however good in themselves, make him but pass for proud, conceited, vain or foolish. Courage, says an excellent Writer, in an ill-bred Man has the Air, and escapes not the Opinion of Brutality; Learning becomes Pedantry; Wit, Buffoonery; Plainness, Rusticity; and there cannot be a good Quality in him which Ill-breeding will not warp and disfigure to his Disadvantage." *Turnbull*, p. 327.

‡To have in View the *Glory* and *Service of God*, as some express themselves, is only the same Thing in other Words. For *Doing Good to Men* is the *only Service of God* in our Power; and to *imitate his Beneficence* is to *glorify him*. Hence *Milton* says, "The *End* of Learning is to repair the Ruins of our first Parents, by regaining to *know God aright*, and out of that Knowledge to *love him*, to *imitate* him, to be *like him*, as we may the nearest by possessing our Souls of true Virtue." *Educ. p.* 373. Mr. *Hutcheson* says, *Dial.* v. 2. *p.* 97. "The *principal End* of Education is, to *form us wise and good Creatures, useful to others, and happy ourselves.* The whole Art of Education lies within a narrow Compass, and is reducible to a very simple Practice; namely, *To assist in unfolding those Natural and Moral Powers with which Man is endowed, by presenting proper Objects and Occasions; to watch their Growth that they be not diverted from their End, or disturbed in their Operation by any foreign Violence; and gently to conduct and apply them to all the Purposes of private and of public Life.*" And Mr. *Locke* (p. 84. Educ.) says, " 'Tis VIRTUE, then, direct VIRTUE, which is to be *aim'd at* in Education. All other Considerations and Accomplishments are

nothing in Comparison to this. This is the *solid* and *substantial* Good, which Tutors should not only read Lectures and talk of, but the *Labour* and *Art of Education* should furnish the Mind with, and *fasten* there, and never cease till the young Man had a true Relish of it, and plac'd his *Strength*, his *Glory*, and his *Pleasure*, in it." And Mons. *Rollin*, *Belles Lettres*, Vol. 4. p. 249. to the same Purpose, "If we consult our Reason ever so little, it is easy to discern that the END which Masters should have in View, is not barely to teach their Scholars *Greek* and *Latin*, to learn them to make Exercises and Verses, to charge their Memory with Facts and historical Dates, to draw up Syllogisms in Form, or to trace Lines and Figures upon Paper. These Branches of Learning I own are useful and valuable, but as *Means*, and not as the *End*; when they conduct us to other Things, and not when we stop at them; when they serve us as Preparatives and Instruments for better Knowledge, without which the rest would be useless. Youth would have Cause to complain, if they were condemned to spend eight or ten of the best Years of their Life in learning, at a great Expence, and with incredible Pains, one or two Languages, and some other Matters of a like Nature, which perhaps they would seldom have Occasion to use. The End of Masters, in the long Course of their Studies, is to habituate their Scholars to serious Application of Mind, to make them love and value the Sciences, and to cultivate in them such a Taste, as shall make them thirst after them when they are gone from School; to point out the Method of attaining them; and make them thoroughly sensible of their Use and Value; and by that Means dispose them for the different Employments to which it shall please God to call them. Besides this, the *End* of Masters should be, *to improve their Hearts* and Understandings, to protect their Innocence, to *inspire* them with Principles of *Honour* and *Probity*, to train them up to good Habits; to correct and subdue in them by gentle Means, the ill Inclinations they shall be observed to have, such as Pride, Insolence, an high Opinion of themselves, and a saucy Vanity continually employed in lessening others; a blind Self-love solely attentive to its own Advantage; a Spirit of Raillery which is pleased with offending and insulting others; an Indolence and Sloth, which renders all the good Qualities of the Mind useless."

Dr. *Turnbull* has the same Sentiments, with which we shall conclude this Note. If, says he, there be any such Thing as DUTY, or any such Thing as HAPPINESS; if there be any Difference between right and wrong Conduct; any Distinction between Virtue and Vice, or Wisdom and Folly; in fine, if there be any such Thing as Perfection or Imperfection belonging to the rational Powers which constitute moral Agents; or if Enjoyments and Pursuits admit of Comparison; *Good Education* must of Necessity be acknowledged to mean, *proper Care* to instruct early in the Science of Happiness and Duty, or in the Art of Judging and *Acting aright* in Life. Whatever else one may have learned, if he comes into the World from his Schooling and Masters, quite unacquainted with the Nature, Rank and Condition, of Mankind, and the *Duties of human Life* (in its more ordinary Circumstances at least) he hath lost his Time; *he is not educated*; he is not prepared for the World; he is not qualified for Society; he is not fitted for discharging the *proper Business of Man*. The Way therefore to judge whether Education be on a right Footing

Rules Proper to be Observed in Trade

I. Endeavour to be perfect in the calling you are engaged in; and be assiduous in every part thereof; INDUSTRY being the natural means of acquiring *wealth*, *honour*, and *reputation*; as *idleness* is of *poverty*, *shame*, and *disgrace*.

II. Lay a good foundation in regard to principle: Be sure not wilfully to over-reach, or deceive your neighbour; but keep always in your eye the golden rule of *doing as you would be done unto*.

III. Be strict in discharging all legal debts: Do not evade your creditors by any shuffling arts, in giving notes under your hand, only to defer payment; but, if you have it in your power, discharge all debts when they become due. Above all, when you are straitened for want of money, be cautious of taking it up at an high interest. This has been the ruin of many, therefore endeavour to avoid it.

IV. Endeavour to be as much in your shop, or warehouse, or in whatever place your business properly lies, as possibly you can: Leave it not to servants to transact, for customers will not regard them as yourself; they generally think they shall not be so well served: Besides, mistakes may arise by the negligence, or inexperience, of servants; and therefore, your presence will prevent, probably, the loss of a good customer.

V. Be complaisant to the *meanest*, as well as greatest: You are as much obliged to use good manners for a farthing, as a pound; the one demands it from you, as well as the other.

VI. Be not too talkative, but speak as much as is necessary to recommend your goods, and always observe to keep within the rules of decency. If customers slight your goods, and under-value them, endeavour to convince them of their mistake, if you can, but not affront them: Do not be pert in your answers, but with patience hear, and with meekness give an answer; for if you affront in a small matter, it may probably hinder you from a future good customer. They may think that you are dear in the articles they want; but, by going to another, may find it not so, and probably may return again; but if you behave rude and affronting, there is no hope either of returning, or their future custom.

VII. Take great care in keeping your accounts well: Enter

every thing necessary in your books with neatness and exactness; often state your accounts, and examine whether you gain, or lose; and carefully survey your stock, and inspect into every particular of your affairs.

VIII. Take care, as much as you can, whom you trust: Neither take nor give long credit; but, at the farthest, annually settle your accounts. Deal at the fountain head for as many articles as you can; and, if it lies in your power, for ready money: This method you will find to be the most profitable in the end. Endeavour to keep a proper assortment in your way, but not over-stock yourself. Aim not at making a great figure in your shop, in unnecessary ornaments, but let it be neat and useful: Too great an appearance may rather prevent, than engage customers. Make your *business* your pleasure, and other entertainments will only appear necessary for relaxation therefrom.

IX. Strive to maintain a *fair character* in the world: That will be the best means for advancing your credit, gaining you the most flourishing trade, and enlarging your fortune. Condescend to no mean action, but add a lustre to trade, by keeping up to the dignity of your nature.

The Pennsylvania Gazette, February 20, 1749/50

Rules for Making Oneself a Disagreeable Companion

RULES, *by the Observation of which, a Man of Wit and Learning may nevertheless make himself a* disagreeable *Companion*.

Your Business is to *shine*; therefore you must by all means prevent the shining of others, for their Brightness may make yours the less distinguish'd. To this End,

1. If possible engross the whole Discourse; and when other Matter fails, talk much of your-self, your Education, your Knowledge, your Circumstances, your Successes in Business, your Victories in Disputes, your own wise Sayings and Observations on particular Occasions, &c. &c. &c.

2. If when you are out of Breath, one of the Company should seize the Opportunity of saying something; watch his Words, and, if possible, find somewhat either in his Sentiment or Expression, immediately to contradict and raise a Dispute upon. Rather than fail, criticise even his Grammar.

3. If another should be saying an indisputably good Thing; either give no Attention to it; or interrupt him; or draw away the Attention of others; or, if you can guess what he would be at, be quick and say it before him; or, if he gets it said, and you perceive the Company pleas'd with it, own it to be a good Thing, and withal remark that it had been said by *Bacon*, *Locke*, *Bayle*, or some other eminent Writer; thus you deprive him of the Reputation he might have gain'd by it, and gain some yourself, as you hereby show your great Reading and Memory.

4. When modest Men have been thus treated by you a few times, they will chuse ever after to be silent in your Company; then you may shine on without Fear of a Rival; rallying them at the same time for their Dullness, which will be to you a new Fund of Wit.

Thus you will be sure to please *yourself*. The polite Man aims at pleasing *others*, but you shall go beyond him even in that. A Man can be present only in one Company, but may at the same time be absent in twenty. He can please only where he *is*, you where-ever you are *not*.

The Pennsylvania Gazette, November 15, 1750

Idea of the English School

Sketch'd out for the Consideration of the TRUSTEES *of the*
PHILADELPHIA ACADEMY.

It is expected that every Scholar to be admitted into this
School, be at least able to pronounce and divide the Syllables
in Reading, and to write a legible Hand. None to be receiv'd
that are under   Years of Age.

First or lowest CLASS.

Let the first Class learn the *English Grammar* Rules, and at
the same time let particular Care be taken to improve them in
Orthography. Perhaps the latter is best done by *Pairing* the
Scholars, two of those nearest equal in their Spelling to be
put together; let these strive for Victory, each propounding
Ten Words every Day to the other to be spelt. He that spells
truly most of the other's Words, is Victor for that Day; he
that is Victor most Days in a Month, to obtain a Prize, a
pretty neat Book of some Kind useful in their future Studies.
This Method fixes the Attention of Children extreamly to the
Orthography of Words, and makes them good Spellers very
early. 'Tis a Shame for a Man to be so ignorant of this little
Art, in his own Language, as to be perpetually confounding
Words of like Sound and different Significations; the Consciousness of which Defect, makes some Men, otherwise of
good Learning and Understanding, averse to Writing even a
common Letter.

Let the Pieces read by the Scholars in this Class be short,
such as *Croxall*'s Fables, and little Stories. In giving the Lesson, let it be read to them; let the Meaning of the difficult
Words in it be explained to them, and let them con it over by
themselves before they are called to read to the Master, or
Usher; who is to take particular Care that they do not read
too fast, and that they duly observe the Stops and Pauses. A
Vocabulary of the most usual difficult Words might be formed
for their Use, with Explanations; and they might daily get a
few of those Words and Explanations by Heart, which would
a little exercise their Memories; or at least they might write a
Number of them in a small Book for the Purpose, which

would help to fix the Meaning of those Words in their Minds, and at the same Time furnish every one with a little Dictionary for his future Use.

The Second CLASS *to be taught*

Reading with Attention, and with proper Modulations of the Voice according to the Sentiments and Subject.

Some short Pieces, not exceeding the Length of a *Spectator*, to be given this Class as Lessons (and some of the easier *Spectators* would be very suitable for the Purpose.) These Lessons might be given over Night as Tasks, the Scholars to study them against the Morning. Let it then be required of them to give an Account, first of the Parts of Speech, and Construction of one or two Sentences; this will oblige them to recur frequently to their Grammar, and fix its principal Rules in their Memory. Next of the *Intention* of the Writer, or the *Scope* of the Piece; the Meaning of each Sentence, and of every uncommon Word. This would early acquaint them with the Meaning and Force of Words, and give them that most necessary Habit, of Reading with Attention.

The Master then to read the Piece with the proper Modulations of Voice, due Emphasis, and suitable Action, where Action is required; and put the Youth on imitating his Manner.

Where the Author has us'd an Expression not the best, let it be pointed out; and let his Beauties be particularly remarked to the Youth.

Let the Lessons for Reading be varied, that the Youth may be made acquainted with good Stiles of all Kinds in Prose and Verse, and the proper Manner of reading each Kind. Sometimes a well-told Story, a Piece of a Sermon, a General's Speech to his Soldiers, a Speech in a Tragedy, some Part of a Comedy, an Ode, a Satyr, a Letter, Blank Verse, Hudibrastick, Heroic, &c. But let such Lessons for Reading be chosen, as contain some useful Instruction, whereby the Understandings or Morals of the Youth, may at the same Time be improv'd.

It is requir'd that they should first study and understand the Lessons, before they are put upon reading them properly, to which End each Boy should have an *English* Dictionary to help him over Difficulties. When our Boys read *English* to us, we are apt to imagine *they* understand what *they* read because *we* do, and because 'tis their Mother Tongue. But they often read as Parrots speak, knowing little or nothing of the Meaning. And it is impossible a Reader should give the due Modulation to his Voice, and pronounce properly, unless his Understanding goes before his Tongue, and makes him Master of the Sentiment. Accustoming Boys to read aloud what they do not first understand, is the Cause of those even set Tones so common among Readers, which when they have once got a Habit of using, they find so difficult to correct: By which Means, among Fifty Readers we scarcely find a good One. For want of good Reading, Pieces publish'd with a View to influence the Minds of Men for their own or the publick Benefit, lose Half their Force. Were there but one good Reader in a Neighbourhood, a publick Orator might be heard throughout a Nation with the same Advantages, and have the same Effect on his Audience, as if they stood within the Reach of his Voice.

The Third CLASS *to be taught*

Speaking properly and gracefully, which is near of Kin to good Reading, and naturally follows it in the Studies of Youth. Let the Scholars of this Class begin with learning the Elements of Rhetoric from some short System, so as to be able to give an Account of the most usual Tropes and Figures. Let all their bad Habits of Speaking, all Offences against good Grammar, all corrupt or foreign Accents, and all improper Phrases, be pointed out to them. Short Speeches from the *Roman* or other History, or from our *Parliamentary Debates*, might be got by heart, and deliver'd with the proper Action, *&c.* Speeches and Scenes in our best Tragedies and Comedies (avoiding every Thing that could injure the Morals of Youth) might likewise be got by Rote, and the Boys exercis'd in delivering or acting them; great Care being taken to form their Manner after the truest Models.

For their farther Improvement, and a little to vary their Studies, let them now begin to read *History*, after having got by Heart a short Table of the principal Epochas in Chronology. They may begin with *Rollin's Antient and Roman Histories*, and proceed at proper Hours as they go thro' the subsequent Classes, with the best Histories of our own Nation and Colonies. Let Emulation be excited among the Boys by giving, Weekly, little Prizes, or other small Encouragements to those who are able to give the best Account of what they have read, as to Times, Places, Names of Persons, *&c.* This will make them read with Attention, and imprint the History well in their Memories. In remarking on the History, the Master will have fine Opportunities of instilling Instruction of various Kinds, and improving the Morals as well as the Understandings of Youth.

The Natural and Mechanic History contain'd in *Spectacle de la Nature*, might also be begun in this Class, and continued thro' the subsequent Classes by other Books of the same Kind: For next to the Knowledge of *Duty*, this Kind of Knowledge is certainly the most useful, as well as the most entertaining. The Merchant may thereby be enabled better to understand many Commodities in Trade; the Handicraftsman to improve his Business by new Instruments, Mixtures and Materials; and frequently Hints are given of new Manufactures, or new Methods of improving Land, that may be set on foot greatly to the Advantage of a Country.

The Fourth CLASS *to be taught*

Composition. Writing one's own Language well, is the next necessary Accomplishment after good Speaking. 'Tis the Writing-Master's Business to take Care that the Boys make fair Characters, and place them straight and even in the Lines: But to *form their Stile*, and even to take Care that the Stops and Capitals are properly disposed, is the Part of the *English* Master. The Boys should be put on Writing Letters to each other on any common Occurrences, and on various Subjects, imaginary Business, *&c.* containing little Stories, Accounts of their late Reading, what Parts of Authors please them, and why. Letters of Congratulation, of Compliment, of Request, of Thanks, of Recommendation, of Admonition, of Consolation, of Expostulation, Excuse, *&c.* In these they should be taught to express themselves clearly, concisely, and naturally, without affected Words, or high-flown Phrases. All their Letters to pass through the Master's Hand, who is to point out the Faults, advise the Corrections, and commend what he finds right. Some of the best Letters published in our own Language, as Sir *William Temple*'s, those of *Pope*, and his Friends, and some others, might be set before the Youth as Models, their Beauties pointed out and explained by the Master, the Letters themselves transcrib'd by the Scholar.

Dr. Johnson's *Ethices Elementa*, or first Principles of Morality, may now be read by the Scholars, and explain'd by the Master, to lay a solid Foundation of Virtue and Piety in their Minds. And as this Class continues the Reading of History, let them now at proper Hours receive some farther Instructions in Chronology, and in that Part of Geography (from the Mathematical Master) which is necessary to understand the Maps and Globes. They should also be acquainted with the modern Names of the Places they find mention'd in antient Writers. The Exercises of good Reading and proper Speaking still continued at suitable Times.

Fifth CLASS.

To improve the Youth in *Composition*, they may now, besides continuing to write Letters, begin to write little Essays in Prose; and sometimes in Verse, not to make them Poets, but for this Reason, that nothing acquaints a Lad so speedily with Variety of Expression, as the Necessity of finding such Words and Phrases as will suit with the Measure, Sound and Rhime of Verse, and at the same Time well express the Sentiment. These Essays should all pass under the Master's Eye, who will point out their Faults, and put the Writer on correcting them. Where the Judgment is not ripe enough for forming new Essays, let the Sentiments of a *Spectator* be given, and requir'd to be cloath'd in a Scholar's own Words; or the Circumstances of some good Story, the Scholar to find Expression. Let them be put sometimes on abridging a Paragraph of a diffuse Author, sometimes on dilating or amplifying what is wrote more closely. And now let Dr. *Johnson*'s

Noetica, or first Principles of human Knowledge, containing a Logic, or Art of Reasoning, *&c.* be read by the Youth, and the Difficulties that may occur to them be explained by the Master. The Reading of History, and the Exercises of good Reading and just Speaking still continued.

Sixth CLASS.

In this Class, besides continuing the Studies of the preceding, in History, Rhetoric, Logic, Moral and Natural Philosophy, the best *English* Authors may be read and explain'd; as *Tillotson*, *Milton*, *Locke*, *Addison*, *Pope*, *Swift*, the higher Papers in the *Spectator* and *Guardian*, the best Translations of *Homer*, *Virgil* and *Horace*, of *Telemachus*, *Travels of Cyrus*, &c.

Once a Year, let there be publick Exercises in the Hall, the Trustees and Citizens present. Then let fine gilt Books be given as Prizes to such Boys as distinguish themselves, and excel the others in any Branch of Learning; making three Degrees of Comparison; giving the best Prize to him that performs best; a less valuable One to him that comes up next to the best; and another to the third. Commendations, Encouragement and Advice to the rest; keeping up their Hopes that by Industry they may excel another Time. The Names of those that obtain the Prizes, to be yearly printed in a List.

The Hours of each Day are to be divided and dispos'd in such a Manner, as that some Classes may be with the Writing-Master, improving their Hands, others with the Mathematical Master, learning Arithmetick, Accompts, Geography, Use of the Globes, Drawing, Mechanicks, *&c.* while the rest are in the *English* School, under the *English* Master's Care.

Thus instructed, Youth will come out of this School fitted for learning any Business, Calling or Profession, except such wherein Languages are required; and tho' unaquainted with any antient or foreign Tongue, they will be Masters of their own, which is of more immediate and general Use; and withal will have attain'd many other valuable Accomplishments; the Time usually spent in acquiring those Languages, often without Success, being here employ'd in laying such a

Foundation of Knowledge and Ability, as, properly improv'd, may qualify them to pass thro' and execute the several Offices of civil Life, with Advantage and Reputation to themselves and Country.

Philadelphia, B. Franklin and D. Hall, at the Post-Office, 1751

Course of Experiments

Philadelphia, April 11, 1751.

Notice is hereby given to the CURIOUS, That on *Wednesday* next, Mr. *Kinnersley* proposes to begin a Course of Experiments on the newly-discovered ELECTRICAL FIRE, containing not only the most curious of those that have been made and published in *Europe*, but a considerable Number of new Ones lately made in this City; to be accompanied with methodical LECTURES on the Nature and Properties of that wonderful Element, *viz.*

LECTURE I.

I. Of Electricity in General, giving some Account of the Discovery of it.

II. That the Electric Fire is a real Element, and different from those heretofore known and named, and *collected* out of other Matter (not created) by the Friction of Glass, *&c.*

III. That it is an extreamly subtile Fluid.

IV. That it doth not take up any perceptible Time in passing thro' large Portions of Space.

V. That it is intimately mixed with the Substance of all the other Fluids and Solids of our Globe.

VI. That our Bodies at all Times contain enough of it to set a House on Fire.

VII. That tho' it will fire inflammable Matters, itself has no sensible Heat.

VIII. That it differs from common Matter in this; Its Parts do not mutually attract, but mutually repel each other.

IX. That it is strongly attracted by all other Matter.

X. An artificial Spider, animated by the Electric Fire, so as to act like a live One.

XI. A perpetual Shower of Sand, which rises again as fast as it falls.

XII. That common Matter in the form of Points attracts this Fire more strongly than in any other Form.

XIII. A Leaf of the most weighty of Metals suspended in the Air, as is said of *Mahomet*'s Tomb.

XIV. An Appearance like Fishes swimming in the Air.

XV. That this Fire will live in Water, a River not being sufficient to quench the smallest Spark of it.

XVI. A Representation of the Sensitive Plant.

XVII. A Representation of the seven Planets, shewing a probable Cause of their keeping their due Distances from each other, and from the Sun in the Center.

XVIII. The Salute repulsed by the Ladies Fire; or Fire darting from a Lady's Lips, so that she may defy any Person to salute her.

XIX. Eight musical Bells rung by an electrified Phial of Water.

XX. A Battery of eleven Guns discharged by Fire issuing out of a Person's Finger.

LECTURE II.

I. A Description and Explanation of Mr. *Muschenbroek*'s wonderful Bottle.

II. The amazing Force of the Electric Fire in passing thro' a Number of Bodies at the same Instant.

III. An Electric Mine sprung.

IV. Electrified Money, which scarce any Body will take when offer'd to them.

V. A Piece of Money drawn out of a Persons Mouth in spite of his Teeth; yet without touching it, or offering him the least Violence.

VI. Spirits kindled by Fire darting from a Lady's Eyes (without a Metaphor.)

VII. Various Representations of Lightning, the Cause and Effects of which will be explained by a more probable Hypothesis than has hitherto appeared, and some useful Instructions given how to avoid the Danger of it: How to secure Houses, Ships, &c. from being hurt by its destructive Violence.

VIII. The Force of the Electric Spark making a fair Hole thro' a Quire of Paper.

IX. Metal melted by it (tho' without any Heat) in less than the thousandth Part of a Minute.

X. Animals killed by it instantaneously (if any of the Company desire it, and will be pleased to send some for that Purpose.)

XI. Air issuing out of a Bladder set on Fire by a Spark from a Person's Finger, and burning like a Volcano.

XII. A few Drops of electrified cold Water let fall on a Person's Hand, supplying him with Fire sufficient to kindle a burning Flame with one of the Fingers of his other Hand.

XIII. A Sulphureous Vapour kindled into Flame by Fire issuing out of a cold Apple.

XIV. A curious Machine acting by means of the Electric Fire, and playing Variety of Tunes on eight musical Bells.

XV. A Battery of eleven Guns discharged by a Spark, after it has passed thro' ten Foot of Water.

As the Knowledge of Nature tends to enlarge the human Mind, and give us more noble, more grand and exalted Ideas of the AUTHOR of Nature, and if well pursu'd seldom fails producing something *useful* to Man, 'tis hoped these Lectures may be thought worthy of Regard and Encouragement.

Tickets to be had at Mr. *Kinnersley's* House in *Arch-street*, Price *Seven Shillings* and *Six-pence* for each Person to go thro' the Course. The Lectures to begin precisely at 4 in the Afternoon of each Day, in the same Room Mr. *Dove* lately used for his Course of Natural Philosophy.

Note, the Experiments succeed best when the Air is dry.

The Pennsylvania Gazette, April 11, 1751

On Transported Felons

From *Virginia* we hear, that six Convicts, who were transported for fourteen Years, and shipp'd at *Liverpool*, rose at Sea, shot the Captain, overcame and confin'd the Seamen, and kept Possession of the Vessel 19 Days; that coming in Sight of *Cape Hatteras*, they hoisted out the Boat to go on shore; when a Vessel passing by, a Boy they had not confin'd, hail'd her, and attempted to tell their Condition, but was prevented; and then the Villains drove a Spike up thro' his under and upper Jaws, and wound Spunyarn round the End that came out near his Nose, to prevent his getting it out: They then cut away the Sails from the Yards, left the Ship, and went ashore. But a *New-England* Sloop coming by soon after, and seeing a Ship driving in the Sea in that Manner, boarded her, found Things as above mentioned, and carried her into *North-Carolina*; from whence a Hue and Cry went after the Villains, who had stroll'd along to *Virginia*; they were taken at *Norfolk*, and one of them confess'd the Fact; upon which they were order'd up, about two Weeks since, to *Williamsburgh*, for Trial as Pyrates.

From *Maryland* we hear, that a Convict Servant, about three Weeks since, went into his Master's House, with an Ax in his Hand, determin'd to kill his Mistress; but changing his Purpose on seeing, as he expressed it, *how d——d innocent she look'd*, he laid his Left-hand on a Block, cut it off, and threw it at her, saying, *Now make me work, if you can.*

> N. B. *'Tis said this desperate Villain is now begging in* Pennsylvania, *and 'tis thought has been seen in this City; he pretends to have lost his Hand by an Accident: The Publick are therefore caution'd to beware of him.*

From *Bucks* County we hear, that a Convict Servant, one *John McCaulefd*, imported here last Fall, has broke open and robb'd several Houses, of Goods to a considerable Value; but being apprehended at a Ferry, is committed to Prison.

Yesterday the Trial of *Samuel Saunders*, for the Murder of *Simon Girtie*, came on at the Supream Court, when the Jury return'd their Verdict *Manslaughter*.

"When we see our Papers fill'd continually with Accounts of the most audacious Robberies, the most cruel Murders, and infinite other Villainies perpetrated by Convicts transported from *Europe*, what melancholly, what terrible Reflections must it occasion! What will become of our Posterity!— These are some of thy Favours, BRITAIN! Thou art called our MOTHER COUNTRY; but what good *Mother* ever sent *Thieves* and *Villains* to accompany her *Children*; to corrupt some with their infectious Vices, and murder the rest? What *Father* ever endeavour'd to spread the *Plague* in his Family!—We do not ask Fish, but thou givest us *Serpents*, and worse than Serpents!—In what can *Britain* show a more Sovereign Contempt for us, than by emptying their *Jails* into our Settlements; unless they would likewise empty their *Jakes* on our Tables?—What must we think of that B——d, which has advis'd the Repeal of every Law we have hitherto made to prevent this Deluge of Wickedness overwhelming us; and with this *cruel* Sarcasm, *That these Laws were against the* Publick Utility*, for they tended to prevent the* IMPROVEMENT *and* WELL-PEOPLING *of the Colonies!*—And what must we think of those Merchants, who for the sake of a little paltry Gain, will be concern'd in importing and disposing of these abominable Cargoes?"

The Pennsylvania Gazette, April 11, 1751

Rattle-Snakes for Felons

To the Printers of the Gazette.

By a Passage in one of your late Papers, I understand that the Government at home will not suffer our mistaken Assemblies to make any Law for preventing or discouraging the Importation of Convicts from Great Britain, for this kind Reason, *'That such Laws are against the Publick Utility, as they tend to prevent the* IMPROVEMENT *and* WELL PEOPLING *of the Colonies.'*

Such a tender *parental* Concern in our *Mother Country* for the *Welfare* of her Children, calls aloud for the highest *Returns* of Gratitude and Duty. This every one must be sensible of: But 'tis said, that in our present Circumstances it is absolutely impossible for us to make *such* as are adequate to the Favour. I own it; but nevertheless let us do our Endeavour. 'Tis something to show a grateful Disposition.

In some of the uninhabited Parts of these Provinces, there are Numbers of these venomous Reptiles we call RATTLE-SNAKES; Felons-convict from the Beginning of the World: These, whenever we meet with them, we put to Death, by Virtue of an old Law, *Thou shalt bruise his Head.* But as this is a sanguinary Law, and may seem too cruel; and as however mischievous those Creatures are with us, they may possibly change their Natures, if they were to change the Climate; I would humbly propose, that this general Sentence of *Death* be changed for *Transportation.*

In the Spring of the Year, when they first creep out of their Holes, they are feeble, heavy, slow, and easily taken; and if a small Bounty were allow'd *per* Head, some Thousands might be collected annually, and *transported* to Britain. There I would propose to have them carefully distributed in *St. James's Park*, in the *Spring-Gardens* and other Places of Pleasure about *London*; in the Gardens of all the Nobility and Gentry throughout the Nation; but particularly in the Gardens of the *Prime Ministers*, the *Lords of Trade* and *Members of Parliament*; for to them we are *most particularly* obliged.

There is no human Scheme so perfect, but some Inconveniencies may be objected to it: Yet when the Conveniencies far exceed, the Scheme is judg'd rational, and fit to be executed. Thus Inconveniencies have been objected to that *good* and *wise* Act of Parliament, by virtue of which all the *Newgates* and *Dungeons* in *Britain* are emptied into the Colonies. It has been said, that these Thieves and Villains introduc'd among us, spoil the Morals of Youth in the Neighbourhoods that entertain them, and perpetrate many horrid Crimes: But let not *private Interests* obstruct *publick Utility*. Our *Mother* knows what is best for us. What is a little *Housebreaking*, *Shoplifting*, or *Highway Robbing*; what is a *Son* now and then *corrupted* and *hang'd*, a Daughter *debauch'd* and *pox'd*, a Wife *stabb'd*, a Husband's *Throat cut*, or a Child's *Brains beat out* with an Axe, compar'd with this 'IMPROVEMENT and WELL PEOPLING of the Colonies!'

Thus it may perhaps be objected to my Scheme, that the *Rattle-Snake* is a mischievous Creature, and that his changing his Nature with the Clime is a mere Supposition, not yet confirm'd by sufficient Facts. What then? Is not Example more prevalent than Precept? And may not the honest rough British Gentry, by a Familiarity with these Reptiles, learn to *creep*, and to *insinuate*, and to *slaver*, and to *wriggle* into Place (and perhaps to *poison* such as stand in their Way) Qualities of no small Advantage to Courtiers! In comparison of which '*Improvement* and *Publick Utility*,' what is a *Child* now and then kill'd by their venomous Bite,—or even a favourite *Lap-Dog*?

I would only add, That this Exporting of Felons to the Colonies, may be consider'd as a *Trade*, as well as in the Light of a *Favour*. Now all Commerce implies *Returns*:

Justice requires them: There can be no Trade without them. And *Rattle-Snakes* seem the most *suitable Returns* for the *Human Serpents* sent us by our *Mother* Country. In this, however, as in every other Branch of Trade, she will have the Advantage of us. She will reap *equal* Benefits without equal Risque of the Inconveniencies and Dangers. For the *Rattle-Snake* gives Warning before he attempts his Mischief; which the Convict does not. I am

Yours, &c.

ΑΜΕΡΙCANUS.

The Pennsylvania Gazette, May 9, 1751

Appeal for the Hospital

Post obitum benefacta manent, æternaque Virtus
Non metuit Stygiis, nec rapiatur Aquis.

I was sick, and ye visited me.   Matth. xxv.

Among all the innumerable Species of Animals which inhabit the Air, Earth and Water, so exceedingly different in their Production, their Properties, and the Manner of their Existence, and so varied in Form, that even of the same Kind, it can scarce be said there are two Individuals in all Respects alike; it is remarkable, there are none within our Observation, distinguish'd from the rest by this Particular, *that they are by Nature incapable of* DISEASES. The old Poets, how extravagant soever in their Fictions, durst never offend so far against Nature and Probability, as even to feign such a Thing; and therefore, tho' they made their *Achilles* invulnerable from Head to Foot, and clad him beside in impenetrable Armour, forg'd by the Immortals, they were obliged to leave one soft unguarded Place in his Heel, how small soever, for Destruction to enter at.—But tho' every Animal that hath Life is liable to Death, Man, of all other Creatures, has the greatest Number of *Diseases* to his Share; whether they are the Effects of our Intemperance and Vice, or are given us, that we may have a greater Opportunity of exercising towards each other that Virtue, which most of all recommends us to the Deity, I mean CHARITY.

The great Author of our Faith, whose Life should be the constant Object of our Imitation, as far as it is not inimitable, always shew'd the greatest Compassion and Regard for the SICK; he disdain'd not to visit and minister Comfort and Health to the meanest of the People; and he frequently inculcated the same Disposition in his Doctrine and Precepts to his Disciples. For this one Thing, (in that beautiful Parable of the Traveller wounded by Thieves) the *Samaritan* (who was esteemed no better than a *Heretick*, or an *Infidel* by the *Orthodox* of those Times) is preferred to the *Priest* and the *Levite*; because he did not, like them, pass by, regardless of the Distress of his Brother Mortal; but when he came to the Place where the half-dead Traveller lay, *he had Compassion on him, and went to him, and bound up his Wounds, pouring in Oil and Wine, and set him on his own Beast, and brought him to an Inn, and took Care of him.* — *Dives*, also, the rich Man, is represented as being excluded from the Happiness of Heaven, because he fared sumptuously every Day, and had Plenty of all Things, and yet neglected to comfort and assist his poor Neighbour, who was helpless and *full of Sores*, and might perhaps have been revived and restored with small Care, *by the Crumbs that fell from his Table*, or, as we say, *with his loose Corns.* — *I was Sick, and ye Visited me*, is one of the Terms of Admission into Bliss, and the Contrary, a Cause of Exclusion: That is, as our Saviour himself explains it, *Ye have visited, or ye have not visited, assisted and comforted those who stood in need of it, even tho' they were the least, or meanest of Mankind*. This Branch of *Charity* seems essential to the true Spirit of Christianity; and should be extended to all in general, whether Deserving or Undeserving, as far as our Power reaches. Of the ten Lepers who were cleansed, *nine* seem to have been much more unworthy than the *tenth*, yet in respect to the Cure of their Disease, they equally shared the Goodness of God. And the great Physician in sending forth his Disciples, always gave them a particular Charge, *that into whatsoever City they entered, they should heal* ALL *the Sick*, without Distinction.

When the good *Samaritan* left his Patient at the Inn, *he gave Money to the Host, and said,* TAKE CARE OF HIM, *and what thou spendest more, I will repay thee.* We are in this World mutual Hosts to each other; the Circumstances and Fortunes of Men and Families are continually changing; in the Course of a few Years we have seen the Rich become Poor, and the Poor Rich; the Children of the Wealthy languishing in Want and Misery, and those of their Servants lifted into Estates, and abounding in the good Things of this Life. Since then, our present State, how prosperous soever, hath no Stability, but what depends on the good Providence of God, how careful should we be not to *harden our Hearts* against the Distresses of our Fellow Creatures, lest He who owns and governs all, should punish our Inhumanity, deprive us of a Stewardship in which we have so unworthily behaved, *laugh at our Calamity, and mock when our Fear cometh.* Methinks when Objects of Charity, and Opportunities of relieving them, present themselves, we should hear the Voice of this *Samaritan,* as if it were the Voice of God sounding in our Ears, TAKE CARE OF THEM, *and whatsoever thou spendest, I will repay thee.*

But the Good particular Men may do separately, in relieving the Sick, is small, compared with what they may do collectively, or by a joint Endeavour and Interest. Hence the Erecting of Hospitals or Infirmaries by Subscription, for the Reception, Entertainment, and Cure of the Sick Poor, has been found by Experience exceedingly beneficial, as they turn out annually great Numbers of Patients perfectly cured, who might otherwise have been lost to their Families, and to Society. Hence Infirmaries spread more and more in Europe, new Ones being continually erected in large Cities and populous Towns, where generally the most skilful Physicians and Surgeons inhabit. And the Subscribers have had the Satisfaction in a few Years of seeing the Good they proposed to do, become much more extensive than was at first expected; for the Multitude and Variety of Cases continually treated in those Infirmaries, not only render the Physicians and Surgeons who attend them, still more expert and skilful, for the Benefit of others, but afford such speedy and effectual Instruction to the young Students of both Professions, who come from different and remote Parts of the Country for Improvement, that they return with a more ample Stock of

Knowledge in their Art, and become Blessings to the Neighbourhoods in which they fix their Residence.

It is therefore a great Pleasure to all the Benevolent and
Charitable, who have been acquainted with these Things in
other Countries, to observe, that an Institution of the same
Kind has met with such Encouragement in *Pensilvania*, and is
in such Forwardness, that there is reason to expect it may be
carried into Execution the ensuing Year. May the Father of
Mercies grant it his Blessing, and Thousands of our unhappy
Fellow Creatures, yet unborn, will have Cause to bless him,
for putting it into the Hearts of the generous Contributors,
and enabling them thus to provide for their Relief.

The Pennsylvania Gazette, August 8, 1751

*Homines ad Deos, nulla re propius accedunt, quam Salutem
    Hominibus dando.*   CICER. ORAT.

This Motto, taken from a *Pagan* Author, expresses the general Sense of Mankind, even in the earliest Ages, concerning
that great Duty and extensive Charity, the *administring Comfort and Relief to the Sick*. If Men without any other Assistance
than the Dictates of natural Reason, had so high an Opinion
of it, what may be expected from Christians, to whom it has
been so warmly recommended by the best Example of human
Conduct. To visit the Sick, to feed the Hungry, to clothe the
Naked, and comfort the Afflicted, are the inseparable Duties
of a christian Life.

Accordingly 'tis observable, that the Christian Doctrine
hath had a real Effect on the Conduct of Mankind, which the
mere Knowledge of Duty without the Sanctions Revelation
affords, never produc'd among the *Heathens*: For History
shows, that from the earliest Times of Christianity, in all well-
regulated States where Christians obtain'd sufficient Influence, publick Funds and private Charities have been appropriated to the building of Hospitals, for receiving, supporting
and curing those unhappy Creatures, whose Poverty is aggravated by the additional Load of bodily Pain. But of these
Kind of Institutions among the *Pagans*, there is no Trace in
the History of their Times.

That good Prince *Edward* VI. was so affected at the

Miseries of his poor diseas'd Subjects, represented in a charity Sermon preach'd to him on the Occasion, that he soon after laid the Foundation of four of the largest Hospitals now in *London*, which the Citizens finished, and have ever since maintain'd.

In *Hidepark*, at *Bath*, in *Edinburgh*, *Liverpool*, *Winchester*, and in the County of *Devon*, and sundry other Places in *Great-Britain*, large and commodious Infirmaries have been lately erected, from trifling Beginnings of private Charities: And so wonderfully does Providence favour these pious Institutions, that there is not an Instance of any One's failing for want of necessary charitable Contributions. *

Extract from the Tour thro' Great Britain, Vol. III. Pag. 293.

In the Year 1740, on the Promotion of Dr. Gilbert, Dean of this Church, to the Bishoprick of Landaff, his Majesty was pleas'd to confer the Deanery on Dr. Alured Clarke, who was installed in the Month of January, in that Year; and if we may be allowed to judge from the pious Acts he began with in that Station, a more worthy Man could not have been preferr'd thereto.

The House, an antient Building, belonging to that Dignity, had, thro' the Remissness of its former Possessors, been too long neglected; wherefore his First Work was to set about altering and repairing that, which he did within Nine Months of his Instalment, at an Expence of about 800l.

Before this was perfected, viz. in the Spring 1741, he drew up and published Proposals for founding an Hospital in this City, for Lodging, Dieting, and Curing the Sick and Lame Poor thereof, and of the County of Devon, on the like Plan of that which he had before founded at Winchester, for the Benefit of that City, and County of Hants. A Design so good, recommended by the pious Eloquence of a Divine so learned and judicious, on Views so visibly disinterested, and so clearly abstracted from all Party Schemes or Intentions, met with the general Applause and Assistance of the Gentry and Clergy of all Parties, Sects and Denominations; who, however different in Religion and Politicks, unanimously join'd in this pious Undertaking: And a Subscription being opened in March, hath already (November 1741) brought in about 2000l. of which near 1500l. are annual Engagements, which, 'tis highly probable, will be not only continued, but much augmented, so that 'tis hoped, that 200 Patients at a Time may be provided for. John Tuckfield, of Raddon, Esq; was pleased to accommodate the Governors with a Plot of Ground near Southernhay, without the City-walls, at a very moderate Price, and to give 100l. towards carrying on the Building for the intended Hospital, the Plan of which was commodiously designed by the Direction of the Dean, and the first Stone thereof laid by him, assisted by the Bishop of Exon, Sir William Courtenay, Knight of the Shire, Sir Henry Northcote and Humphry Sydenham, Esquires, the Citizens in Parliament, the Honourable Henry Rolle, and John Tuckfield Esq; attended by a great Number of Clergy and Gentry, that are Subscribers, and Thousands of joyful Spectators, on the 27th of August 1741. The Building contains upwards of 300 Feet in Length, and is already in a good Forwardness.

The Increase of poor diseas'd Foreigners and others, settled in the distant Parts of this Province, where regular Advice and Assistance cannot be procured, but at an Expence that neither they nor their Townships can afford, has awaken'd the Attention of sundry humane and well dispos'd Minds, to procure some more certain, effectual and easy Methods for their Relief than have hitherto been provided, and having represented the Affair to the Assembly, a Law was pass'd, without one dissenting Voice, giving *Two Thousand Pounds* for building and furnishing a Provincial Hospital, on Condition that *Two Thousand Pounds* more should be rais'd by private Donations, to be put out to Interest as Part of a perpetual Fund for supporting it; and the Contributors were made a Body Corporate, with all the Powers necessary on the Occasion. Since which, People of all Ranks in this City have united zealously and heartily in promoting this pious and excellent Design, and more than the Sum stipulated was subscribed in a few Days only, and a much larger Sum will probably be rais'd here if the Country chearfully contributes to the capital Stock, which 'tis not to be doubted they will do, when they consider how much they are interested in it.

The Difference between nursing and curing the Sick in an Hospital, and separately in private Lodgings, with Regard to the Expence, is at least as ten to one. For Instance, suppose a Person under the Necessity of having a Limb amputated, he must have the constant Attendance of a Nurse, a Room, Fire, &c. which cannot for the first three or four Weeks be procured at less Expence than *Fifteen Shillings* a Week, and never after at less than *Ten*. If he continues two Months his Nursing will be *Five Pounds*, his Surgeons Fee, and other accidental Charges, commonly amounts to *Three Pounds*, in the whole near *Ten Pounds*; whereas in an Hospital, one Nurse, one Fire, &c. will be sufficient for ten Patients, the extra Expences will be inconsiderable, and the Surgeon's Fees taken off, which will bring the above Calculation within the Limits of Truth.

But the Difference with Regard to the unhappy Sufferer is still greater. In an Hospital his Case will be treated according to the best Rules of Art, by Men of Experience and known Abilities in their Profession. His Lodgings will be commodious, clean and neat, in an healthy and open Situation, his Diet will be well chosen, and properly administred: He will have many other necessary Conveniencies for his Relief, such as hot and cold Baths, sweating Rooms, chirurgic Machines, Bandage, &c. which can rarely be procured in the best private Lodgings, much less in those miserable loathsome Holes, which are the common Receptacles of the diseas'd Poor that are brought to this City.—In short a Beggar in a well regulated Hospital, stands an equal Chance with a Prince in his Palace, for a comfortable Subsistence, and an expeditious and effectual Cure of his Diseases.

It is hoped therefore, that whoever will maturely consider the inestimable Blessings that are connected to a proper Execution of the present Hospital Scheme in this City, can never be so void of Humanity and the essential Duties of Religion, as to turn a deaf Ear to the numberless Cries of the Poor and Needy, and refuse for their Assistance, a little of that Superfluity, which a bountiful Providence has so liberally bestowed on them.

The Pennsylvania Gazette, August 15, 1751

Observations Concerning the Increase of Mankind, Peopling of Countries, &c.

1. Tables of the Proportion of Marriages to Births, of Deaths to Births, of Marriages to the Numbers of Inhabitants, &c. form'd on Observations made upon the Bills of Mortality, Christnings, &c. of populous Cities, will not suit Countries; nor will Tables form'd on Observations made on full settled old Countries, as *Europe*, suit new Countries, as *America*.

2. For People increase in Proportion to the Number of Marriages, and that is greater in Proportion to the Ease and Convenience of supporting a Family. When Families can be easily supported, more Persons marry, and earlier in Life.

3. In Cities, where all Trades, Occupations and Offices are full, many delay marrying, till they can see how to bear the Charges of a Family; which Charges are greater in Cities, as Luxury is more common: many live single during Life, and

continue Servants to Families, Journeymen to Trades, &c. hence Cities do not by natural Generation supply themselves with Inhabitants; the Deaths are more than the Births.

4. In Countries full settled, the Case must be nearly the same; all Lands being occupied and improved to the Heighth; those who cannot get Land, must Labour for others that have it; when Labourers are plenty, their Wages will be low; by low Wages a Family is supported with Difficulty; this Difficulty deters many from Marriage, who therefore long continue Servants and single.—Only as the Cities take Supplies of People from the Country, and thereby make a little more Room in the Country; Marriage is a little more incourag'd there, and the Births exceed the Deaths.

5. *Europe* is generally full settled with Husbandmen, Manufacturers, &c. and therefore cannot now much increase in People: *America* is chiefly occupied by Indians, who subsist mostly by Hunting.—But as the Hunter, of all Men, requires the greatest Quantity of Land from whence to draw his Subsistence, (the Husbandman subsisting on much less, the Gardner on still less, and the Manufacturer requiring least of all), The *Europeans* found *America* as fully settled as it well could be by Hunters; yet these having large Tracks, were easily prevail'd on to part with Portions of Territory to the new Comers, who did not much interfere with the Natives in Hunting, and furnish'd them with many Things they wanted.

6. Land being thus plenty in *America*, and so cheap as that a labouring Man, that understands Husbandry, can in a short Time save Money enough to purchase a Piece of new Land sufficient for a Plantation, whereon he may subsist a Family; such are not afraid to marry; for if they even look far enough forward to consider how their Children when grown up are to be provided for, they see that more Land is to be had at Rates equally easy, all Circumstances considered.

7. Hence Marriages in *America* are more general, and more generally early, than in *Europe*. And if it is reckoned there, that there is but one Marriage per Annum among 100 Persons, perhaps we may here reckon two; and if in *Europe* they have but 4 Births to a Marriage (many of their Marriages being late) we may here reckon 8, of which if one half grow up, and our Marriages are made, reckoning one with another

at 20 Years of Age, our People must at least be doubled every 20 Years.

8. But notwithstanding this Increase, so vast is the Territory of *North-America*, that it will require many Ages to settle it fully; and till it is fully settled, Labour will never be cheap here, where no Man continues long a Labourer for others, but gets a Plantation of his own, no Man continues long a Journeyman to a Trade, but goes among those new Settlers, and sets up for himself, &c. Hence Labour is no cheaper now, in *Pennsylvania*, than it was 30 Years ago, tho' so many Thousand labouring People have been imported.

9. The Danger therefore of these Colonies interfering with their Mother Country in Trades that depend on Labour, Manufactures, &c. is too remote to require the Attention of *Great-Britain*.

10. But in Proportion to the Increase of the Colonies, a vast Demand is growing for British Manufactures, a glorious Market wholly in the Power of *Britain*, in which Foreigners cannot interfere, which will increase in a short Time even beyond her Power of supplying, tho' her whole Trade should be to her Colonies: Therefore *Britain* should not too much restrain Manufactures in her Colonies. A wise and good Mother will not do it. To distress, is to weaken, and weakening the Children, weakens the whole Family.

11. Besides if the Manufactures of *Britain* (by Reason of the *American* Demands) should rise too high in Price, Foreigners who can sell cheaper will drive her Merchants out of Foreign Markets; Foreign Manufactures will thereby be encouraged and increased, and consequently foreign Nations, perhaps her Rivals in Power, grow more populous and more powerful; while her own Colonies, kept too low, are unable to assist her, or add to her Strength.

12. 'Tis an ill-grounded Opinion that by the Labour of Slaves, *America* may possibly vie in Cheapness of Manufactures with *Britain*. The Labour of Slaves can never be so cheap here as the Labour of working Men is in *Britain*. Any one may compute it. Interest of Money is in the Colonies from 6 to 10 per Cent. Slaves one with another cost 30 £. Sterling per Head. Reckon then the Interest of the first Purchase of a Slave, the Insurance or Risque on his Life, his

Cloathing and Diet, Expences in his Sickness and Loss of
Time, Loss by his Neglect of Business (Neglect is natural to
the Man who is not to be benefited by his own Care or Diligence), Expence of a Driver to keep him at Work, and his
Pilfering from Time to Time, almost every Slave being *by Nature* a Thief, and compare the whole Amount with the Wages
of a Manufacturer of Iron or Wool in *England*, you will see
that Labour is much cheaper there than it ever can be by
Negroes here. Why then will *Americans* purchase Slaves? Because Slaves may be kept as long as a Man pleases, or has
Occasion for their Labour; while hired Men are continually
leaving their Master (often in the midst of his Business,) and
setting up for themselves. §. 8.

13. As the Increase of People depends on the Encouragement of Marriages, the following Things must diminish a
Nation, *viz.* 1. The being conquered; for the Conquerors will
engross as many Offices, and exact as much Tribute or Profit
on the Labour of the conquered, as will maintain them in
their new Establishment, and this diminishing the Subsistence
of the Natives discourages their Marriages, & so gradually
diminishes them, while the Foreigners increase. 2. Loss of
Territory. Thus the *Britons* being driven into *Wales*, and
crowded together in a barren Country insufficient to support
such great Numbers, diminished 'till the People bore a Proportion to the Produce, while the *Saxons* increas'd on their
abandoned Lands; 'till the Island became full of *English*. And
were the *English* now driven into *Wales* by some foreign Nation, there would in a few Years be no more Englishmen in
Britain, than there are now People in *Wales*. 3. Loss of Trade.
Manufactures exported, draw Subsistence from Foreign
Countries for Numbers; who are thereby enabled to marry
and raise Families. If the Nation be deprived of any Branch
of Trade, and no new Employment is found for the People
occupy'd in that Branch, it will also be soon deprived of so
many People. 4. Loss of Food. Suppose a Nation has a Fishery, which not only employs great Numbers, but makes the
Food and Subsistence of the People cheaper: If another Nation becomes Master of the Seas, and prevents the Fishery,
the People will diminish in Proportion as the Loss of Employ,
and Dearness of Provision, makes it more difficult to subsist

a Family. 5. Bad Government and insecure Property. People not only leave such a Country, and settling Abroad incorporate with other Nations, lose their native Language, and become Foreigners; but the Industry of those that remain being discourag'd, the Quantity of Subsistence in the Country is lessen'd, and the Support of a Family becomes more difficult. So heavy Taxes tend to diminish a People. 6. The Introduction of Slaves. The Negroes brought into the *English* Sugar *Islands*, have greatly diminish'd the Whites there; the Poor are by this Means depriv'd of Employment, while a few Families acquire vast Estates; which they spend on Foreign Luxuries, and educating their Children in the Habit of those Luxuries; the same Income is needed for the Support of one that might have maintain'd 100. The Whites who have Slaves, not labouring, are enfeebled, and therefore not so generally prolific; the Slaves being work'd too hard, and ill fed, their Constitutions are broken, and the Deaths among them are more than the Births; so that a continual Supply is needed from *Africa*. The Northern Colonies having few Slaves increase in Whites. Slaves also pejorate the Families that use them; the white Children become proud, disgusted with Labour, and being educated in Idleness, are rendered unfit to get a Living by Industry.

14. Hence the Prince that acquires new Territory, if he finds it vacant, or removes the Natives to give his own People Room; the Legislator that makes effectual Laws for promoting of Trade, increasing Employment, improving Land by more or better Tillage; providing more Food by Fisheries; securing Property, &c. and the Man that invents new Trades, Arts or Manufactures, or new Improvements in Husbandry, may be properly called *Fathers* of their Nation, as they are the Cause of the Generation of Multitudes, by the Encouragement they afford to Marriage.

15. As to Privileges granted to the married, (such as the *Jus trium Liberorum* among the *Romans*), they may hasten the filling of a Country that has been thinned by War or Pestilence, or that has otherwise vacant Territory; but cannot increase a People beyond the Means provided for their Subsistence.

16. Foreign Luxuries & needless Manufactures imported and used in a Nation, do, by the same Reasoning, increase

the People of the Nation that furnishes them, and diminish the People of the Nation that uses them.—Laws therefore that prevent such Importations, and on the contrary promote the Exportation of Manufactures to be consumed in Foreign Countries, may be called (with Respect to the People that make them) *generative Laws*, as by increasing Subsistence they encourage Marriage. Such Laws likewise strengthen a Country, doubly, by increasing its own People and diminishing its Neighbours.

17. Some *European* Nations prudently refuse to consume the Manufactures of *East-India*:—They should likewise forbid them to their Colonies; for the Gain to the Merchant, is not to be compar'd with the Loss by this Means of People to the Nation.

18. Home Luxury in the Great, increases the Nation's Manufacturers employ'd by it, who are many, and only tends to diminish the Families that indulge in it, who are few. The greater the common fashionable Expence of any Rank of People, the more cautious they are of Marriage. Therefore Luxury should never be suffer'd to become common.

19. The great Increase of Offspring in particular Families, is not always owing to greater Fecundity of Nature, but sometimes to Examples of Industry in the Heads, and industrious Education; by which the Children are enabled to provide better for themselves, and their marrying early, is encouraged from the Prospect of good Subsistence.

20. If there be a Sect therefore, in our Nation, that regard Frugality and Industry as religious Duties, and educate their Children therein, more than others commonly do; such Sect must consequently increase more by natural Generation, than any other Sect in *Britain*.—

21. The Importation of Foreigners into a Country that has as many Inhabitants as the present Employments and Provisions for Subsistence will bear; will be in the End no Increase of People; unless the New Comers have more Industry and Frugality than the Natives, and then they will provide more Subsistence, and increase in the Country; but they will gradually eat the Natives out.—Nor is it necessary to bring in Foreigners to fill up any occasional Vacancy in a Country; for such Vacancy (if the Laws are good, § 14, 16) will soon be

filled by natural Generation. Who can now find the Vacancy made in *Sweden*, *France* or other Warlike Nations, by the Plague of Heroism 40 Years ago; in *France*, by the Expulsion of the Protestants; in *England*, by the Settlement of her Colonies; or in *Guinea*, by 100 Years Exportation of Slaves, that has blacken'd half *America*?—The thinness of Inhabitants in *Spain*, is owing to National Pride and Idleness, and other Causes, rather than to the Expulsion of the *Moors*, or to the making of new Settlements.

22. There is in short, no Bound to the prolific Nature of Plants or Animals, but what is made by their crowding and interfering with each others Means of Subsistence. Was the Face of the Earth vacant of other Plants, it might be gradually sowed and overspread with one Kind only; as, for Instance, with Fennel; and were it empty of other Inhabitants, it might in a few Ages be replenish'd from one Nation only; as, for Instance, with *Englishmen*. Thus there are suppos'd to be now upwards of One Million *English* Souls in *North-America*, (tho' 'tis thought scarce 80,000 have been brought over Sea) and yet perhaps there is not one the fewer in *Britain*, but rather many more, on Account of the Employment the Colonies afford to Manufacturers at Home. This Million doubling, suppose but once in 25 Years, will in another Century be more than the People of *England*, and the greatest Number of *Englishmen* will be on this Side the Water. What an Accession of Power to the *British* Empire by Sea as well as Land! What Increase of Trade and Navigation! What Numbers of Ships and Seamen! We have been here but little more than 100 Years, and yet the Force of our Privateers in the late War, united, was greater, both in Men and Guns, than that of the whole *British* Navy in Queen *Elizabeth*'s Time.—How important an Affair then to *Britain*, is the present Treaty for settling the Bounds between her Colonies and the *French*, and how careful should she be to secure Room enough, since on the Room depends so much the Increase of her People?

23. In fine, A Nation well regulated is like a Polypus; take away a Limb, its Place is soon supply'd; cut it in two, and each deficient Part shall speedily grow out of the Part remaining. Thus if you have Room and Subsistence enough, as you may by dividing, make ten Polypes out of one, you may of

one make ten Nations, equally populous and powerful; or rather, increase a Nation ten fold in Numbers and Strength.

And since Detachments of *English* from *Britain* sent to *America*, will have their Places at Home so soon supply'd and increase so largely here; why should the *Palatine Boors* be suffered to swarm into our Settlements, and by herding together establish their Language and Manners to the Exclusion of ours? Why should *Pennsylvania*, founded by the *English*, become a Colony of *Aliens*, who will shortly be so numerous as to Germanize us instead of our Anglifying them, and will never adopt our Language or Customs, any more than they can acquire our Complexion.

24. Which leads me to add one Remark: That the Number of purely white People in the World is proportionably very small. All *Africa* is black or tawny. *Asia* chiefly tawny. *America* (exclusive of the new Comers) wholly so. And in *Europe*, the *Spaniards*, *Italians*, *French*, *Russians* and *Swedes*, are generally of what we call a swarthy Complexion; as are the *Germans* also, the *Saxons* only excepted, who with the *English*, make the principal Body of White People on the Face of the Earth. I could wish their Numbers were increased. And while we are, as I may call it, *Scouring* our Planet, by clearing *America* of Woods, and so making this Side of our Globe reflect a brighter Light to the Eyes of Inhabitants in *Mars* or *Venus*, why should we in the Sight of Superior Beings, darken its People? why increase the Sons of *Africa*, by Planting them in *America*, where we have so fair an Opportunity, by excluding all Blacks and Tawneys, of increasing the lovely White and Red? But perhaps I am partial to the Complexion of my Country, for such Kind of Partiality is natural to Mankind.

1751

The Kite Experiment

As frequent Mention is made in the News Papers from *Europe*, of the Success of the *Philadelphia* Experiment for drawing the Electric Fire from Clouds by Means of pointed Rods of Iron erected on high Buildings, *&c.* it may be agreeable to the Curious to be inform'd, that the same Experiment has succeeded in *Philadelphia*, tho' made in a different and more easy Manner, which any one may try, as follows.

Make a small Cross of two light Strips of Cedar, the Arms so long as to reach to the four Corners of a large thin Silk Handkerchief when extended; tie the Corners of the Handkerchief to the Extremities of the Cross, so you have the Body of a Kite; which being properly accommodated with a Tail, Loop and String, will rise in the Air, like those made of Paper; but this being of Silk is fitter to bear the Wet and Wind of a Thunder Gust without tearing. To the Top of the upright Stick of the Cross is to be fixed a very sharp pointed Wire, rising a Foot or more above the Wood. To the End of the Twine, next the Hand, is to be tied a silk Ribbon, and where the Twine and the silk join, a Key may be fastened. This Kite is to be raised when a Thunder Gust appears to be coming on, and the Person who holds the String must stand within a Door, or Window, or under some Cover, so that the Silk Ribbon may not be wet; and Care must be taken that the Twine does not touch the Frame of the Door or Window. As soon as any of the Thunder Clouds come over the Kite, the pointed Wire will draw the Electric Fire from them, and the Kite, with all the Twine, will be electrified, and the loose Filaments of the Twine will stand out every Way, and be attracted by an approaching Finger. And when the Rain has wet the Kite and Twine, so that it can conduct the Electric Fire freely, you will find it stream out plentifully from the Key on the Approach of your Knuckle. At this Key the Phial may be charg'd; and from Electric Fire thus obtain'd, Spirits may be kindled, and all the other Electric Experiments be perform'd, which are usually done by the Help of a rubbed Glass Globe or Tube; and thereby the *Sameness* of the Electric Matter with that of Lightning compleatly demonstrated.

The Pennsylvania Gazette, October 19, 1752

Join or Die

Friday last an Express arrived here from Major Washington, with Advice, that Mr. Ward, Ensign of Capt. Trent's Company, was compelled to surrender his small Fort in the Forks of Monongahela to the French, on the 17th past; who fell down from Venango with a Fleet of 360 Battoes and Canoes, upwards of 1000 Men, and 18 Pieces of Artillery, which they planted against the Fort; and Mr. Ward having but 44 Men, and no Cannon to make a proper Defence, was obliged to surrender on Summons, capitulating to march out with their Arms, &c. and they had accordingly joined Major Washington, who was advanced with three Companies of the Virginia Forces, as far as the New Store near the Allegheny Mountains, where the Men were employed in clearing a Road for the Cannon, which were every Day expected with Col. Fry, and the Remainder of the Regiment.—We hear farther, that some few of the English Traders on the Ohio escaped, but 'tis supposed the greatest Part are taken, with all their Goods, and Skins, to the Amount of near 20,000£. The Indian Chiefs, however, have dispatch'd Messages to Pennsylvania, and Virginia, desiring that the English would not be discouraged, but send out their Warriors to join them, and drive the French out of the Country before they fortify; otherwise the Trade will be lost, and, to their great Grief, an eternal Separation made between the Indians and their Brethren the English. 'Tis farther said, that besides the French that came down from Venango, another Body of near 400, is coming up the Ohio; and that 600 French Indians, of the Chippaways and Ottaways, are coming down Siota River, from the Lake, to join them; and many more French are expected from Canada; the Design being to establish themselves, settle their Indians, and build Forts just on the Back of our Settlements in all our Colonies; from which Forts, as they did from Crown-Point, they may send out their Parties to kill and scalp the Inhabitants, and ruin the Frontier Counties. Accordingly we hear, that the Back Settlers in Virginia, are so terrify'd by the Murdering and Scalping of the Family last Winter, and the Taking of this Fort, that they begin already to abandon their Plantations, and remove to Places of more Safety.—The Confidence of the French in this Undertaking seems well-grounded on the present disunited State of the British Colonies, and the extreme Difficulty of bringing so many different Governments and Assemblies to agree in any speedy and effectual Measures for our common Defence and Security; while our Enemies have the very great Advantage of being under one Direction, with one Council, and one Purse. Hence, and from the great Distance of Britain, they presume that they may with Impunity violate the most solemn Treaties subsisting between the two Crowns, kill, seize and imprison our Traders, and confiscate their Effects at Pleasure (as they have done for several Years past) murder and scalp our Farmers, with their Wives and Children, and take an easy Possession of such Parts of the British Territory as they find most convenient for them; which if they are permitted to do, must end in the Destruction of the British Interest, Trade and Plantations in America.

The Pennsylvania Gazette, May 9, 1754

The Albany Plan of Union

Plan of a Proposed Union of the Several Colonies of Masachusets-bay, New Hampshire, Coneticut, Rhode Island, New York, New Jerseys, Pensilvania, Maryland, Virginia, North Carolina, and South Carolina, For their Mutual Defence and Security, and for Extending the British Settlements in North America.

That humble Application be made for an Act of the Parliament of Great Britain, by Virtue of which, one General Government may be formed in America, including all the said Colonies, within and under which Government, each Colony may retain its present Constitution, except in the Particulars wherein a Change may be directed by the said Act, as hereafter follows.

President
General

Grand Council.

That the said General Government be administred by a President General, To be appointed and Supported by the Crown, and a Grand Council to be Chosen by the Representatives of the People of the Several Colonies, met in their respective Assemblies.

Election of
Members.

That within   Months after the passing of such Act, The House of Representatives in the Several Assemblies, that Happen to be Sitting within that time or that shall be Specially for that purpose Convened, may and Shall Choose Members for the Grand Council in the following Proportions, that is to say.

Masachusets-Bay	7.
New Hampshire	2.
Conecticut	5.
Rhode-Island	2.
New-York	4.
New-Jerseys	3.
Pensilvania	6.
Maryland	4.
Virginia	7.
North-Carolina	4.
South-Carolina	4.
	48.

Place of first
meeting.

Who shall meet for the first time at the City of Philadelphia, in Pensilvania, being called by the President General as soon as conveniently may be, after his Appointment.

New Election.

That there shall be a New Election of Members for the Grand Council every three years; And on the Death or Resignation of any Member his Place shall be Supplyed by a New Choice at the next Sitting of the Assembly of the Colony he represented.

Proportion of
Members after
first 3 years.

That after the first three years, when the Proportion of Money arising out of each Colony to the General Treasury can be known, The Number of Members to be Chosen, for each Colony shall from time to time in all ensuing Elections be regulated by that proportion (yet so as that the Number to be Chosen by any one Province be not more than Seven nor less than Two).

Meetings of
Grand Council.

Call.

That the Grand Council shall meet once in every Year, and oftner if Occasion require, at such Time and place as they shall adjourn to at the last preceeding meeting, or as they shall be called to meet at by the President General, on any Emergency, he having first obtained in Writing the Consent of seven of the Members to such call, and sent due and timely Notice to the whole.

Speaker.

Continuance.

That the Grand Council have Power to Chuse their Speaker, and shall neither be Dissolved, prorogued nor Continue Sitting longer than Six Weeks at one Time without their own Consent, or the Special Command of the Crown.

Member's
Allowance

That the Members of the Grand Council shall be Allowed for their Service ten shillings Sterling per Diem, during their Sessions or Journey to and from the Place of Meeting; Twenty miles to be reckoned a days Journey.

Assent of President General. His Duty.

That the Assent of the President General be requisite, to all Acts of the Grand Council, and that it be His Office, and Duty to cause them to be carried into Execution.

Power of President and Grand Council. Peace and War.

Indian Purchases.

New Settlements.

Laws to Govern them.

That the President General with the Advice of the Grand Council, hold or Direct all Indian Treaties in which the General Interest or Welfare of the Colony's may be Concerned; And make Peace or Declare War with the Indian Nations. That they make such Laws as they Judge Necessary for regulating all Indian Trade. That they make all Purchases from Indians for the Crown, of Lands not within the Bounds of Particular Colonies, or that shall not be within their Bounds when some of them are reduced to more Convenient Dimensions. That they make New Settlements on such Purchases, by Granting Lands in the Kings Name, reserving a Quit Rent to the Crown, for the use of the General Treasury. That they make Laws for regulating and Governing such new Settlements, till the Crown shall think fit to form them into Particular Governments.

Raise Soldiers &c.

Lakes.
Not to Impress

Power to make Laws Duties &c.

That they raise and pay Soldiers, and build Forts for the Defence of any of the Colonies, and equip Vessels of Force to Guard the Coasts and Protect the Trade on the Ocean, Lakes, or Great Rivers; But they shall not Impress Men in any Colonies, without the Consent of its Legislature. That for these purposes they have Power to make Laws And lay and Levy such General Duties, Imposts, or Taxes, as to them shall appear most equal and Just, Considering the Ability and other Circumstances of the Inhabitants in the Several Colonies, and such as may be Collected with the least Inconvenience to the People, rather discouraging Luxury, than

Treasurer.

Money how
to Issue.

Accounts.

Quorum.

Laws to be
Transmitted.

Death of
President
General.

Officers how
Appointed.

Loading Industry with unnecessary Burthens. That they may Appoint a General Treasurer and a Particular Treasurer in each Government, when Necessary, And from Time to Time may Order the Sums in the Treasuries of each Government, into the General Treasury, or draw on them for Special payments as they find most Convenient; Yet no money to Issue, but by joint Orders of the President General and Grand Council Except where Sums have been Appropriated to particular Purposes, And the President General is previously impowered By an Act to draw for such Sums.

That the General Accounts shall be yearly Settled and Reported to the Several Assembly's.

That a Quorum of the Grand Council impower'd to Act with the President General, do consist of Twenty-five Members, among whom there shall be one, or more from a Majority of the Colonies. That the Laws made by them for the Purposes aforesaid, shall not be repugnant but as near as may be agreeable to the Laws of England, and Shall be transmitted to the King in Council for Approbation, as Soon as may be after their Passing and if not disapproved within Three years after Presentation to remain in Force.

That in case of the Death of the President General The Speaker of the Grand Council for the Time Being shall Succeed, and be Vested with the Same Powers, and Authority, to Continue until the King's Pleasure be known.

That all Military Commission Officers Whether for Land or Sea Service, to Act under this General Constitution, shall be Nominated by the President General But the

Approbation of the Grand Council, is to be Obtained before they receive their Commissions, And all Civil Officers are to be Nominated, by the Grand Council, and to receive the President General's Approbation, before

Vacancies how Supplied. they Officiate; But in Case of Vacancy by Death or removal of any Officer Civil or Military under this Constitution, The Governor of the Province, in which such Vacancy happens, may Appoint till the Pleasure of the President General and Grand Council can be known. That the Particular Military as well as Civil Establishments in each Colony remain in their present State, this General Constitution Notwithstanding. And that on

Each Colony may defend itself on Emergency. Sudden Emergencies any Colony may Defend itself, and lay the Accounts of Expence thence Arisen, before the President General and Grand Council, who may allow and order payment of the same As far as they Judge such Accounts Just and reasonable.

July 10, 1754

Reasons and Motives for the Albany Plan of Union

I. Reasons and Motives on which the Plan of Union was formed.

The Commissioners from a number of the northern colonies being met at *Albany*, and considering the difficulties that have always attended the most necessary general measures for the common defence, or for the annoyance of the enemy, when they were to be carried through the several particular assemblies of all the colonies; some assemblies being before at variance with their governors or councils, and the several branches of the government not on terms of doing business with each other; others taking the opportunity, when their concurrence is wanted, to push for favourite laws, powers, or points that they think could not at other times be obtained, and so *creating* disputes and quarrels; one assembly waiting to see what another will do, being afraid of doing more than its share, or desirous of doing less; or refusing to do any thing, because its country is not at present so much exposed as others, or because another will reap more immediate advantage; from one or other of which causes, the assemblies of six (out of seven) colonies applied to, had granted no assistance to *Virginia*, when lately invaded by the *French*, though purposely convened, and the importance of the occasion earnestly urged upon them: Considering moreover, that one principal encouragement to the French, in invading and insulting the British American dominions, was their knowledge of our disunited state, and of our weakness arising from such want of union; and that from hence different colonies were, at different times, extremely harassed, and put to great expence both of blood and treasure, who would have remained in peace, if the enemy had had cause to fear the drawing on themselves the resentment and power of the whole; the said Commissioners, considering also the present incroachments of the French, and the mischievous consequences that may be expected from them, if not opposed with our force, came to an unanimous resolution,— *That an union of the colonies is absolutely necessary for their preservation.*

The *manner* of forming and establishing this union was the

next point. When it was considered that the colonies were seldom all in equal danger at the same time, or equally near the danger, or equally sensible of it; that some of them had particular interests to manage, with which an union might interfere; and that they were extremely jealous of each other;—it was thought impracticable to obtain a joint agreement of all the colonies to an union, in which the expence and burthen of defending any of them should be divided among them all; and if ever acts of assembly in all the colonies could be obtained for that purpose, yet as any colony, on the least dissatisfaction, might repeal its own act and thereby withdraw itself from the union, it would not be a stable one, or such as could be depended on: for if only one colony should, on any disgust withdraw itself, others might think it unjust and unequal that they, by continuing in the union, should be at the expence of defending a colony which refused to bear its proportionable part, and would therefore one after another, withdraw, till the whole crumbled into its original parts.—Therefore the commissioners came to another previous resolution, viz. *That it was necessary the union should be established by act of parliament.*

They then proceeded to sketch out a *plan of union*, which they did in a plain and concise manner, just sufficient to shew their sentiments of the kind of union that would best suit the circumstances of the colonies, be most agreeable to the people, and most effectually promote his Majesty's service and the general interest of the British empire.—This was respectfully sent to the assemblies of the several colonies for their consideration, and to receive such alterations and improvements as they should think fit and necessary; after which it was proposed to be transmitted to *England* to be perfected, and the establishment of it there humbly solicited.

This was as much as the commissioners could do. [   ]

II. *Reasons against partial Unions.*

It was proposed by some of the Commissioners to form the colonies into two or three distinct unions; but for these reasons that proposal was dropped even by those that made it; *viz.*

1. In all cases where the strength of the whole was necessary

to be used against the enemy, there would be the same difficulty in degree, to bring the several unions to unite together, as now the several colonies; and consequently the same delays on our part and advantage to the enemy.

2. Each union would separately be weaker than when joined by the whole, obliged to exert more force, be more oppressed by the expence, and the enemy less deterred from attacking it.

3. Where particular colonies have *selfish views*, as New York with regard to Indian trade and lands; or are *less exposed*, being covered by others, as New Jersey, Rhode Island, Connecticut, Maryland; or have *particular whims and prejudices* against warlike measures in general, as Pensylvania, where the Quakers predominate; such colonies would have more weight in a partial union, and be better able to oppose and obstruct the measures necessary for the general good, than where they are swallowed up in the general union.

4. The *Indian* trade would be better regulated by the union of the whole than by partial unions. And as *Canada* is chiefly supported by that trade, if it could be drawn into the hands of the *English*, (as it might be if the Indians were supplied on moderate terms, and by honest traders appointed by and acting for the public) that alone would contribute greatly to the weakening of our enemies.

5. The establishing of new colonies westward on the *Ohio* and the lakes, (a matter of considerable importance to the increase of *British* trade and power, to the breaking that of the *French*, and to the protection and security of our present colonies,) would best be carried on by a joint union.

6. It was also thought, that by the frequent meetings-together of commissioners or representatives from all the colonies, the circumstances of the whole would be better known, and the good of the whole better provided for; and that the colonies would by this connection learn to consider themselves, not as so many independent states, but as members of the same body; and thence be more ready to afford assistance and support to each other, and to make diversions in favour even of the most distant, and to join cordially in any expedition for the benefit of all against the common enemy.

These were the principal reasons and motives for forming the plan of union as it stands. To which may be added this, that as the union of the [   ]

III. *Plan of a proposed Union of the several Colonies of* Massachusett's Bay, New Hampshire, Connecticut, Rhode Island, New York, New Jersey, Pensylvania, Maryland, Virginia, North Carolina, *and* South Carolina *for their mutual Defence and Security, and for extending the* British *Settlements in* North America, *with the Reasons and Motives for each Article of the Plan as far as could be remembered.*

It is proposed.—That humble application be made for an act of parliament of *Great Britain*, by virtue of which one general government may be formed in *America* including all the said colonies, within and under which government each colony may retain its present constitution, except in the particulars wherein a change may be directed by the said act as hereafter follows.

President General, and Grand Council.

That the said general government be administered by a President General to be appointed and supported by the crown; and a Grand Council to be chosen by the representatives of the people of the several colonies met in their respective assemblies.

It was thought that it would be best the President General should be supported as well as appointed by the crown; that so all disputes between him and the Grand Council concerning his salary might be prevented; as such disputes have been frequently of mischievous consequence in particular colonies, especially in time of public danger. The quit-rents of crown-lands in America, might in a short time be sufficient for this purpose.—The choice of members for the grand council is placed in the house of representatives of each government, in order to give the people a share in this new general government, as the crown has its share by the appointment of the President General.

But it being proposed by the gentlemen of the council of *New York*, and some other counsellors among the commissioners, to alter the plan in this particular, and to give the governors and council of the several provinces a share in the choice of the grand council, or at least a power of approving and confirming or of disallowing the choice made by the house of representatives, it was said:

"That the government or constitution proposed to be formed by the plan, consists of two branches; a President General appointed by the crown, and a council chosen by the people, or by the people's representatives, which is the same thing.

"That by a subsequent article, the council chosen by the people can effect nothing without the consent of the President General appointed by the crown; the crown possesses therefore full one half of the power of this constitution.

"That in the British constitution, the crown is supposed to possess but one third, the Lords having their share.

"That this constitution seemed rather more favourable for the crown.

"That it is essential to English liberty, that the subject should not be taxed but by his own consent or the consent of his elected representatives.

"That taxes to be laid and levied by this proposed constitution will be proposed and agreed to by the representatives of the people, if the plan in this particular be preserved:

"But if the proposed alteration should take place, it seemed as if matters may be so managed as that the crown shall finally have the appointment not only of the President General, but of a majority of the grand council; for, seven out of eleven governors and councils are appointed by the crown:

"And so the people in all the colonies would in effect be taxed by their governors.

"It was therefore apprehended that such alterations of the plan would give great dissatisfaction, and that the colonies could not be easy under such a power in governors, and such an infringement of what they take to be *English* liberty.

"Besides, the giving a share in the choice of the grand council would not be equal with respect to all the colonies, as their constitutions differ. In some, both governor and council are appointed by the crown. In others, they are both appointed by the proprietors. In some, the people have a share in the choice of the council; in others, both government and council are wholly chosen by the people. But the house of representatives is every where chosen by the people; and therefore placing the right of choosing the grand council in the representatives, is equal with respect to all.

"That the grand council is intended to represent all the several houses of representatives of the colonies, as a house of representatives doth the several towns or counties of a colony. Could all the people of a colony be consulted and unite in public measures, a house of representatives would be needless: and could all the assemblies conveniently consult and unite in general measures, the grand council would be unnecessary.

"That a house of commons or the house of representatives, and the grand council, are thus alike in their nature and intention. And as it would seem improper that the King or house of Lords should have a power of disallowing or appointing members of the house of commons;—so likewise that a governor and council appointed by the crown should have a power of disallowing or appointing members of the grand council, (who, in this constitution, are to be the representatives of the people.)

"If the governors and councils therefore were to have a share in the choice of any that are to conduct this general government, it should seem more proper that they chose the President General. But this being an office of great trust and importance to the nation, it was thought better to be filled by the immediate appointment of the crown.

"The power proposed to be given by the plan to the grand council is only a concentration of the powers of the several assemblies in certain points for the general welfare; as the power of the President General is of the powers of the several governors in the same points.

"And as the choice therefore of the grand council by the representatives of the people, neither gives the people any new powers, nor diminishes the power of the crown, it was thought and hoped the crown would not disapprove of it."

Upon the whole, the commissioners were of opinion, that

the choice was most properly placed in the representatives of the people.

Election of Members.

That within   months after the passing such act, the house of representatives that happen to be sitting within that time, or that shall be especially for that purpose convened, may and shall choose members for the grand council, in the following proportion, that is to say,

Massachussett's Bay	7
New Hampshire	2
Connecticut	5
Rhode Island.	2
New York.	4
New Jerseys	3
Pensylvania	6
Maryland.	4
Virginia	7
North Carolina.	4
South Carolina.	4
	48

It was thought that if the least colony was allowed two, and the others in proportion, the number would be very great and the expence heavy; and that less than two would not be convenient, as a single person, being by any accident prevented appearing at the meeting, the colony he ought to appear for would not be represented. That as the choice was not immediately popular, they would be generally men of good abilities for business, and men of reputation for integrity; and that forty-eight such men might be a number sufficient. But, though it was thought reasonable that each colony should have a share in the representative body in some degree, according to the proportion it contributed to the general treasury; yet the proportion of wealth or power of the colonies is not to be judged by the proportion here fixed; because it was at first agreed that the greatest colony should not have more than seven members, nor the least less than two: and the settling these proportions between these two extremes was not nicely attended to, as it would find itself, after the first election from the sums brought into the treasury, as by a subsequent article.

Place of first Meeting.

—who shall meet for the first time at the city of *Philadelphia* in Pensylvania, being called by the President General as soon as conveniently may be after his appointment.

Philadelphia was named as being near the center of the colonies and where the Commissioners would be well and cheaply accommodated. The high-roads through the whole extent, are for the most part very good, in which forty or fifty miles a day may very well be and frequently are travelled. Great part of the way may likewise be gone by water.—In summer-time the passages are frequently performed in a week from *Charles Town* to Philadelphia and New York; and from *Rhode Island* to New York through the Sound in two or three days; and from *New York* to Philadelphia by water and land in two days, by stage-boats and wheel-carriages that set out every other day. The journey from *Charles Town* to Philadelphia may likewise be facilitated by boats running up Chesapeak Bay three hundred miles.—But if the whole journey be performed on horseback, the most distant members, (*viz.* the two from *New Hampshire* and from *South Carolina*) may probably render themselves at Philadelphia in fifteen or twenty-days;—the majority may be there in much less time.

New Election.

That there shall be a new election of the members of the Grand Council every three years; and on the death or resignation of any member, his place shall be supplied by a new choice at the next sitting of the assembly of the colony he represented.

Some colonies have annual assemblies, some continue during a governor's pleasure; three years was thought a reasonable medium, as affording a new member time to improve himself in the business, and to act after such improvement; and yet giving opportunities, frequent enough, to change him if he has misbehaved.

Proportion of Members after the first three Years.

That after the first three years, when the proportion of money arising out of each colony to the general treasury can be known, the number of members to be chosen for each colony shall from time to time, in all ensuing elections, be regulated by that proportion (yet so as that the number to be chosen by any one province be not more than seven, nor less than two).

By a subsequent article it is proposed, that the general council shall lay and levy such general duties as to them may appear most equal and least burthensome, &c. Suppose, for instance, they lay a small duty or excise on some commodity imported into or made in the colonies, and pretty generally and equally used in all of them; as rum perhaps, or wine: the yearly produce of this duty or excise, if fairly collected, would be in some colonies greater, in others less, as the colonies are greater or smaller. When the collectors accounts are brought in, the proportions will appear; and from them it is proposed to regulate the proportion of representatives to be chosen at the next general election, within the limits however of seven and two. These numbers may therefore vary in course of years, as the colonies may in the growth and increase of people. And thus the quota of tax from each colony would naturally vary with its circumstances; thereby preventing all disputes and dissatisfactions about the just proportions due from each; which might otherwise produce pernicious consequences, and destroy the harmony and good agreement that ought to subsist between the several parts of the union.

Meetings of the Grand Council, and Call.

That the Grand Council shall meet once in every year and oftener if occasion require, at such time and place as they shall adjourn to at the last preceding meeting, or as they shall be called to meet at by the President General on any emergency; he having first obtained in writing the consent of seven of the members to such call, and sent due and timely notice to the whole.

It was thought, in establishing and governing new colonies or settlements, regulating *Indian* trade, *Indian* treaties, &c. there would be every year sufficient business arise to require at least one meeting, and at such meeting many things might be suggested for the benefit of all the colonies. This annual meeting may either be at a time or place certain, to be fixed by the President General and grand council at their first meeting; or left at liberty, to be at such time and place as they shall adjourn to, or be called to meet at by the President General.

In *time of war* it seems convenient, that the meeting should be in that colony, which is nearest the seat of action.

The power of calling them on any emergency seemed necessary to be vested in the President General; but that such power might not be wantonly used to harass the members, and oblige them to make frequent long journies to little purpose, the consent of seven at least to such call was supposed a convenient guard.

Continuance.

That the Grand Council have power to choose their speaker; and shall neither be dissolved, prorogued, nor continued sitting longer than six weeks at one time; without their own consent or the special command of the crown.

The speaker should be presented for approbation; it being convenient, to prevent misunderstandings and disgusts, that the mouth of the council should be a person agreeable, if possible, both to the council and the President General.

Governors have sometimes wantonly exercised the power of proroguing or continuing the sessions of assemblies, merely to harass the members and compel a compliance; and sometimes dissolve them on slight disgusts. This it was feared might be done by the President General, if not provided against: and the inconvenience and hardship would be greater in the general government than in particular colonies, in proportion to the distance the members must be from home, during sittings, and the long journies some of them must necessarily take.

Members' Allowance.

That the members of the Grand Council shall be allowed for their service ten shillings sterling *per diem*, during their session and journey to and from the place of meeting; twenty miles to be reckoned a day's journey.

It was thought proper to allow *some* wages, lest the expence might deter some suitable persons from the service;—and not to allow *too great* wages, lest unsuitable persons should be tempted to cabal for the employment for the sake of gain.—Twenty miles was set down as a day's journey to allow for accidental hinderances on the road, and the greater expences of travelling than residing at the place of meeting.

Assent of President General and his Duty.

That the assent of the President General be requisite to all acts of the Grand Council; and that it be his office and duty to cause them to be carried into execution.

The assent of the President General to all acts of the grand council was made necessary, in order to give the crown its due share of influence in this government, and connect it with that of *Great Britain*. The President General, besides one half of the legislative power, hath in his hands the whole executive power.

Power of President General and Grand Council.
Treaties of Peace and War.

That the President General, with the advice of the Grand Council, hold or direct all *Indian* treaties in which the general interest of the colonies may be concerned; and make peace or declare war with Indian nations.

The power of making peace or war with *Indian* nations is at present supposed to be in every colony, and is expressly granted to some by charter, so that no new power is hereby intended to be granted to the colonies.—But as, in consequence of this power, one colony might make peace with a nation that another was justly engaged in war with; or make war on slight occasions without the concurrence or approbation of neighbouring colonies, greatly endangered by it; or make particular treaties of neutrality in case of a general war, to their own private advantage in trade, by supplying the common enemy; of all which there have been instances—it was thought better to have all treaties of a general nature under a general direction; that so the good of the whole may be consulted and provided for.

Indian Trade.

That they make such laws as they judge necessary for regulating all Indian trade.

Many quarrels and wars have arisen between the colonies and Indian nations, through the bad conduct of traders; who cheat the Indians after making them drunk, &c. to the great expence of the colonies both in blood and treasure. Particular colonies are so interested in the trade as not to be willing to admit such a regulation as might be best for the whole; and therefore it was thought best under a general direction.

Indian Purchases.

That they make all purchases from Indians for the crown, of lands not now within the bounds of particular colonies or that shall not be within their bounds when some of them are reduced to more convenient dimensions.

Purchases from the Indians made by private persons, have been attended with many inconveniences. They have frequently interfered, and occasioned uncertainty of titles, many disputes and expensive law-suits, and hindered the settlement of the land so disputed. Then the Indians have been cheated by such private purchases, and discontent and wars have been the consequence. These would be prevented by public fair purchases.

Several of the colony charters in America extend their bounds to the *South Sea*, which may be perhaps three or four thousand miles in length to one or two hundred miles in breadth. It is supposed they must in time be reduced to dimensions more convenient for the common purposes of government.

Very little of the land in those grants is yet purchased of the Indians.

It is much cheaper to purchase of them, than to take and maintain the possession by force: for they are generally very reasonable in their demands for land; and the expence of guarding a large frontier against their incursions is vastly great; because all must be guarded and always guarded, as we know not where or when *to expect them*.

New Settlements.

That they make new settlements on such purchases by granting lands in the King's name, reserving a quit-rent to the crown for the use of the general treasury.

It is supposed better that there should be one purchaser than many; and that the crown should be that purchaser, or the union in the name of the crown. By this means the bargains may be more easily made, the price not inhanced by numerous bidders, future disputes about private Indian purchases, and monopolies of vast tracts to particular persons (which are prejudicial to the settlement and peopling of a country) prevented; and the land being again granted in small tracts to the settlers, the quit-rents reserved may in time become a fund for support of government, for defence of the country, ease of taxes, &c.

Strong forts on the lakes, the Ohio, &c. may at the same time they secure our present frontiers, serve to defend new colonies settled under their protection; and such colonies would also mutually defend and support such forts, and better secure the friendship of the far Indians.

A particular colony has scarce strength enough to extend itself by new settlements, at so great a distance from the old: but the joint force of the union might suddenly establish a new colony or two in those parts, or extend an old colony to particular passes, greatly to the security of our present frontiers, increase of trade and people, breaking off the French communication between *Canada* and *Louisiana*, and speedy settlement of the intermediate lands.

The power of settling new colonies is therefore thought a valuable part of the plan; and what cannot so well be executed by two unions as by one.

Laws to govern them.

That they make laws for regulating and governing such new settlements, till the crown shall think fit to form them into particular governments.

The making of laws suitable for the new colonies, it was thought would be properly vested in the President General and grand council; under whose protection they will at first necessarily be, and who would be well acquainted with their circumstances, as having settled them. When they are become sufficiently populous, they may by the crown, be formed into compleat and distinct governments.

The appointment of a Sub-president by the crown, to take place in case of the death or absence of the President General, would perhaps be an improvement of the plan; and if all the governors of particular provinces were to be formed into a standing council of state, for the advice and assistance of the President General, it might be another considerable improvement.

Raise Soldiers and equip Vessels, &c.

That they raise and pay soldiers and build forts for the defence of any of the colonies, and equip vessels of force to guard the coasts and protect the trade on the ocean, lakes, or great rivers; but they shall not impress men in any colony without the consent of the legislature.

It was thought, that quotas of men to be raised and paid by the several colonies, and joined for any public service, could not always be got together with the necessary expedition. For instance, suppose one thousand men should be wanted in *New Hampshire* on any emergency; to fetch them by fifties and hundreds out of every colony as far as *South Carolina*, would be inconvenient, the transportation chargeable, and the occasion perhaps passed before they could be assembled; and therefore that it would be best to raise them (by offering bounty-money and pay) near the place where they would be wanted, to be discharged again when the service should be over.

Particular colonies are at present backward to build forts at their own expence, which they say will be equally useful to their neighbouring colonies; who refuse to join, on a presumption that such forts *will* be built and kept up, though they contribute nothing. This unjust conduct weakens the whole; but the forts being for the good of the whole, it was thought best they should be built and maintained by the whole, out of the common treasury.

In the time of war, small vessels of force are sometimes necessary in the colonies to scour the coast of small privateers. These being provided by the Union, will be an advantage in turn to the colonies which are situated on the sea, and whose frontiers on the land-side, being covered by other colonies, reap but little immediate benefit from the advanced forts.

Power to make Laws, lay Duties, &c.

That for these purposes they have power to make laws, and lay and levy such general duties, imports, or taxes, as to them shall appear most equal and just, (considering the ability and other circumstances of the inhabitants in the several colonies,) and such as may be collected with the least inconvenience to the people; rather discouraging luxury, than loading industry with unnecessary burthens.

The laws which the President General and grand council are impowered to make, *are such only* as shall be necessary for the government of the settlements; the raising, regulating and paying soldiers for the general service; the regulating of Indian trade; and laying and collecting the general duties and taxes. (They should also have a power to restrain the exportation of provisions to the enemy from any of the colonies, on particular occasions, in time of war.) But it is not intended that they may interfere with the constitution and government of the particular colonies; who are to be left to their own laws, and to lay, levy, and apply their own taxes as before.

General Treasurer and Particular Treasurer.

That they may appoint a General Treasurer and Particular Treasurer in each government when necessary; and from time to time may order the sums in the treasuries of each government into the general treasury; or draw on them for special payments, as they find most convenient.

The treasurers here meant are only for the general funds; and not for the particular funds of each colony, which remain in the hands of their own treasurers at their own disposal.

Money how to issue.

Yet no money to issue but by joint orders of the President General and Grand Council; except where sums have been appropriated to particular purposes, and the President General is previously impowered by an act to draw for such sums.

To prevent misapplication of the money, or even application that might be dissatisfactory to the crown or the people, it was thought necessary to join the President General and grand council in all issues of money.

Accounts.

That the general Accounts shall be yearly settled and reported to the several assemblies.

By communicating the accounts yearly to each assembly, they will be satisfied of the prudent and honest conduct of their representatives in the grand council.

Quorum.

That a quorum of the Grand Council impowered to act with the President General, do consist of twenty-five members; among whom there shall be one or more from a majority of the colonies.

The quorum seems large, but it was thought it would not be satisfactory to the colonies in general, to have matters of importance to the whole transacted by a smaller number, or even by this number of twenty-five, unless there were among them one at least from a majority of the colonies; because otherwise the whole quorum being made up of members from three or four colonies at one end of the union, something might be done that would not be equal with respect to the rest, and thence dissatisfactions and discords might rise to the prejudice of the whole.

Laws to be transmitted.

That the laws made by them for the purposes aforesaid shall not be repugnant, but, as near as may be, agreeable to the laws of *England*, and shall be transmitted to the King in council for approbation as soon as may be after their passing; and if not disapproved within three years after presentation, to remain in force.

This was thought necessary for the satisfaction of the crown, to preserve the connection of the parts of the *British* empire with the whole, of the members with the head, and to induce greater care and circumspection in making of the laws, that they be good in themselves and for the general benefit.

Death of the President General.

That in case of the death of the President General, the speaker of the Grand Council for the time being shall succeed, and be vested with the same powers and authorities, to continue till the King's pleasure be known.

It might be better, perhaps, as was said before, if the crown appointed a Vice President, to take place on the death or absence of the President General; for so we should be more sure of a suitable person at the head of the colonies. On the death or absence of both, the speaker to take place (or rather the eldest King's-governor) till his Majesty's pleasure be known.

Officers how appointed.

That all military commission officers, whether for land or sea service, to act under this general constitution, shall be nominated by the President General; but the approbation of the Grand Council is to be obtained, before they receive their commissions. And all civil officers are to be nominated by the Grand Council, and to receive the President General's approbation before they officiate.

It was thought it might be very prejudicial to the service, to have officers appointed unknown to the people, or unacceptable; the generality of Americans serving willingly under officers they know; and not caring to engage in the service under strangers, or such as are often appointed by governors through favour or interest. The service here meant, is not the stated settled service in standing troops; but any sudden and short service, either for defence of our own colonies, or invading the enemies country; (such as, the expedition to *Cape Breton* in the last war; in which many substantial farmers and tradesmen engaged as common soldiers under officers of their own country, for whom they had an esteem and affection; who would not have engaged in a standing army, or under officers from England.)—It was therefore thought best to give the council the power of approving the officers, which the people will look upon as a great security of their being good men. And without some such provision as this, it was thought the expence of engaging men in the service on any emergency would be much greater, and the number who could be induced to engage much less; and that therefore it would be most for the King's service and general benefit of the nation, that the prerogative should relax a little in this particular throughout all the colonies in America; as it had already done much more in the charters of some particular colonies, viz. *Connecticut* and *Rhode Island.*

The civil officers will be chiefly treasurers and collectors of taxes; and the suitable persons are most likely to be known by the council.

Vacancies how supplied.

But in case of vacancy by death, or removal of any officer civil or military under this constitution, the governor of the province in which such vacancy happens, may appoint till the pleasure of the President General and Grand Council can be known.

The vacancies were thought best supplied by the governors in each province, till a new appointment can be regularly made; otherwise the service might suffer before the meeting of the President General and grand council.

Each Colony may defend itself on Emergency, &c.

That the particular military as well as civil establishments in each colony remain in their present state, the general constitution notwithstanding; and that on sudden

emergencies any colony may defend itself and lay the accounts of expence thence arising before the President General and general council, who may allow and order payment of the same as far as they judge such accounts just and reasonable.

Otherwise the Union of the whole would weaken the parts, contrary to the design of the union. The accounts are to be judged of by the President General and grand council, and allowed if found reasonable: this was thought necessary to encourage colonies to defend themselves, as the expence would be light when borne by the whole; and also to check imprudent and lavish expence in such defences.

Remark, Feb. 9. 1789.

On Reflection it now seems probable, that if the foregoing Plan or some thing like it, had been adopted and carried into Execution, the subsequent Separation of the Colonies from the Mother Country might not so soon have happened, nor the Mischiefs suffered on both sides have occurred, perhaps during another Century. For the Colonies, if so united, would have really been, as they then thought themselves, sufficient to their own Defence, and being trusted with it, as by the Plan, an Army from Britain, for that purpose would have been unnecessary: The Pretences for framing the Stamp-Act would then not have existed, nor the other Projects for drawing a Revenue from America to Britain by Acts of Parliament, which were the Cause of the Breach, and attended with such terrible Expence of Blood and Treasure: so that the different Parts of the Empire might still have remained in Peace and Union. But the Fate of this Plan was singular. For tho' after many Days thorough Discussion of all its Parts in Congress it was unanimously agreed to, and Copies ordered to be sent to the Assembly of each Province for Concurrence, and one to the Ministry in England for the Approbation of the Crown. The Crown disapprov'd it, as having plac'd too much Weight in the democratic Part of the Constitution; and every Assembly as having allow'd too much to Prerogative. So it was totally rejected.

July, 1754; February 9, 1789

No Taxation Without Representation: Three Letters of *1754* to Governor *William Shirley*, with a Preface of *1766*

To the PRINTER *of the* LONDON CHRONICLE.

SIR,

In July 1754, when from the encroachments of the French in America on the lands of the crown, and the interruption they gave to the commerce of this country among the Indians, a war was apprehended, commissioners from a number of the colonies met at Albany, to form a PLAN of UNION for their common defence. The plan they agreed to was in short this; 'That a grand council should be formed, of members to be chosen by the assemblies and sent from all the colonies; which council, together with a governor general to be appointed by the crown, should be empowered to make general laws to raise money in all the colonies for the defence of the whole.' This plan was sent to the government here for approbation: had it been approved and established by authority from hence, English America thought itself sufficiently able to cope with the French, without other assistance; several of the colonies having alone in former wars withstood the whole power of the enemy, unassisted not only by the mother country, but by any of the neighbouring provinces. The plan however was not approved here: but a new one was formed instead of it, by which it was proposed, that 'the Governors of all the colonies, attended by one or two members of their respective councils, should assemble, concert measures for the defence of the whole, erect forts where they judged proper, and raise what troops they thought necessary, with power to draw on the treasury here for the sums that should be wanted; and the treasury to be reimbursed by a tax laid on the colonies by act of parliament.' This new plan being communicated by Governor *Shirley* to a gentleman of Philadelphia, then in Boston, (who hath very eminently distinguished himself, before and since that time, in the literary world, and whose judgment, penetration and candor, as well as his readiness and ability to suggest, forward, or carry into execution every scheme of publick utility, hath most deservedly endeared him not only to our fellow subjects throughout the whole continent of North-America, but to his numberless friends on this side the Atlantic) occasioned the following remarks from him, which perhaps may contribute in some degree to its being laid aside. As they very particularly show the then sentiments of the Americans on the subject of a parliamentary tax, *before* the French power in that country was subdued, and *before* the late restraints on their commerce, they satisfy me, and I hope they will convince your readers, contrary to what has been advanced by some of your correspondents, that those particulars have had no share in producing the present opposition to such a tax, nor in the disturbances occasioned by it; which these papers indeed do almost prophetically foretell. For this purpose, having accidentally fallen into my hands, they are communicated to you by one who is, not *partially*, but in the *most enlarged sense*,

A LOVER OF BRITAIN.

SIR,   *Tuesday Morning.*
    "I return the loose sheets of the plan, with thanks to your Excellency for communicating them.
    "I apprehend, that excluding the *People* of the Colonies from all share in the choice of the Grand Council, will give extreme dissatisfaction, as well as the taxing them by Act of Parliament, where they have no Representative. It is very possible, that this general Government might be as well and faithfully administer'd without the people, as with them; but where heavy burthens are to be laid on them, it has been found useful to make it, as much as possible, their own act; for they bear better when they have, or think they have some share in the direction; and when any public measures are generally grievous or even distasteful to the people, the wheels of Government must move more heavily."

December 3, 1754

Sir,   Boston. December 4. 1754
    I mention'd it Yesterday to your Excellency as my Opinion, that Excluding the People of the Colonies from all Share in

the Choice of the Grand Council would probably give extreme Dissatisfaction, as well as the Taxing them by Act of Parliament where they have no Representative. In Matters of General Concern to the People, and especially where Burthens are to be laid upon them, it is of Use to consider as well what they will *be apt* to think and say, as what they *ought* to think: I shall, therefore, as your Excellency requires it of me, briefly mention what of either Kind occurs at present, on this Occasion.

First, they will say, and perhaps with Justice, that the Body of the People in the Colonies are as loyal, and as firmly attach'd to the present Constitution and reigning Family, as any Subjects in the King's Dominions; that there is no Reason to doubt the Readiness and Willingness of their Representatives to grant, from Time to Time, such Supplies, for the Defence of the Country, as shall be judg'd necessary, so far as their Abilities will allow: That the People in the Colonies, who are to feel the immediate Mischiefs of Invasion and Conquest by an Enemy, in the Loss of their Estates, Lives and Liberties, are likely to be better Judges of the Quantity of Forces necessary to be raised and maintain'd, Forts to be built and supported, and of their own Abilities to bear the Expence, than the Parliament of England at so great a Distance. That Governors often come to the Colonies meerly to make Fortunes, with which they intend to return to Britain, are not always Men of the best Abilities and Integrity, have no Estates here, nor any natural Connections with us, that should make them heartily concern'd for our Welfare; and might possibly be sometimes fond of raising and keeping up more Forces than necessary, from the Profits accruing to themselves, and to make Provision for their Friends and Dependents. That the Councellors in most of the Colonies, being appointed by the Crown, on the Recommendation of Governors, are often of small Estates, frequently dependant on the Governors for Offices, and therefore too much under Influence. That there is therefore great Reason to be jealous of a Power in such Governors and Councils, to raise such Sums as they shall judge necessary, by Draft on the Lords of the Treasury, to be afterwards laid on the Colonies by Act of Parliament, and paid by the

People here; since they might abuse it, by projecting useless Expeditions, harrassing the People, and taking them from their Labour to execute such Projects, and meerly to create Offices and Employments, gratify their Dependants and divide Profits. That the Parliament of England is at a great Distance, subject to be misinform'd by such Governors and Councils, whose united Interests might probably secure them against the Effect of any Complaints from hence. That it is suppos'd an undoubted Right of Englishmen not to be taxed but by their own Consent given thro' their Representatives. That the Colonies have no Representatives in Parliament. That to propose taxing them by Parliament, and refusing them the Liberty of chusing a Representative Council, to meet in the Colonies, and consider and judge of the Necessity of any General Tax and the Quantum, shews a Suspicion of their Loyalty to the Crown, or Regard for their Country, or of their Common Sense and Understanding, which they have not deserv'd. That compelling the Colonies to pay Money without their Consent would be rather like raising Contributions in an Enemy's Country, than taxing of Englishmen for their own publick Benefit. That it would be treating them as a conquer'd People, and not as true British Subjects. That a Tax laid by the Representatives of the Colonies might easily be lessened as the Occasions should lessen, but being once laid by Parliament, under the Influence of the Representations made by Governors, would probably be kept up and continued, for the Benefit of Governors, to the grievous Burthen and Discouragement of the Colonies, and preventing their Growth and Increase. That a Power in Governors to march the Inhabitants from one End of the British and French Colonies to the other, being a Country of at least 1500 Miles square, without the Approbation or Consent of their Representatives first obtain'd to such Expeditions, might be grievous and ruinous to the People, and would put them on a Footing with the Subjects of France in Canada, that now groan under such Oppression from their Governor, who for two Years past has harrass'd them with long and destructive Marches to the Ohio. That if the Colonies in a Body may be well governed by Governors and Councils appointed by the Crown, without Representatives, particular Colonies may as well or better be so governed; a Tax may be laid on them all by Act of Parliament, for Support of Government, and their Assemblies be dismiss'd as a useless Part of their Constitution. That the Powers propos'd, by the Albany Plan of Union to be vested in a Grand Council representative of the People, even with Regard to Military Matters, are not so great as those the Colonies of Rhode-Island and Connecticut are intrusted with, and have never abused; for by this Plan the President-General is appointed by the Crown, and controlls all by his Negative; but in those Governments the People chuse the Governor, and yet allow him no Negative. That the British Colonies, bordering on the French, are properly Frontiers of the British Empire; and that the Frontiers of an Empire are properly defended at the joint Expence of the Body of People in such Empire. It would now be thought hard, by Act of Parliament, to oblige the Cinque Ports or Sea Coasts of Britain to maintain the whole Navy, because they are more immediately defended by it, not allowing them, at the same Time, a Vote in chusing Members of Parliament: And if the Frontiers in America must bear the Expence of their own Defence, it seems hard to allow them no Share in Voting the Money, judging of the Necessity and Sum, or advising the Measures. That besides the Taxes necessary for the Defence of the Frontiers, the Colonies pay yearly great Sums to the Mother Country unnotic'd: For Taxes, paid in Britain by the Land holder or Artificer, must enter into and increase the Price of the Produce of Land, and of Manufactures made of it; and great Part of this is paid by Consumers in the Colonies, who thereby pay a considerable Part of the British Taxes. We are restrain'd in our Trade with Foreign Nations, and where we could be supplied with any Manufactures cheaper from them, but must buy the same dearer from Britain, the Difference of Price is a clear Tax to Britain. We are oblig'd to carry great Part of our Produce directly to Britain, and where the Duties there laid upon it lessens its Price to the Planter, or it sells for less than it would in Foreign Markets, the Difference is a Tax paid to Britain. Some Manufactures we could make, but are forbid, and must take them of British Merchants; the whole Price of these is a Tax paid to

Britain. By our greatly increasing the *Consumption* and *Demand* of British Manufactures, their Price is considerably rais'd of late Years; the Advance is clear Profit to Britain, and enables its People better to pay great Taxes; and much of it being paid by us is clear Tax to Britain. In short, as we are not suffer'd to regulate our Trade, and restrain the Importation and Consumption of British Superfluities, (as Britain can the Consumption of Foreign Superfluities) our whole Wealth centers finally among the Merchants and Inhabitants of Britain, and if we make them richer, and enable them better to pay their Taxes, it is nearly the same as being taxed ourselves, and equally beneficial to the Crown. These Kind of Secondary Taxes, however, we do not complain of, tho' we have no Share in the Laying or Disposing of them; but to pay immediate heavy Taxes, in the Laying Appropriation or Disposition of which, we have no Part, and which perhaps we may know to be as unnecessary as grievous, must seem hard Measure to Englishmen, who cannot conceive, that by hazarding their Lives and Fortunes in subduing and settling new Countries, extending the Dominion and encreasing the Commerce of their Mother Nation, they have forfeited the native Rights of Britons, which they think ought rather to have been given them, as due to such Merit, if they had been before in a State of Slavery.

These, and such Kind of Things as these, I apprehend will be thought and said by the People, if the propos'd Alteration of the Albany Plan should take Place. Then, the Administration of the Board of Governors and Council so appointed, not having any Representative Body of the People to approve and unite in its Measures, and conciliate the Minds of the People to them, will probably become suspected and odious. Animosities and dangerous Feuds will arise between the Governors and Governed, and every Thing go into confusion. Perhaps I am too apprehensive in this Matter, but having freely given my Opinion and Reasons, your Excellency can better judge whether there be any Weight in them. And the Shortness of the Time allow'd me will I hope, in some Degree, excuse the Imperfections of this Scrawl.

With the greatest Respect and Fidelity, I am, Your Excellency's most obedient and most humble Servant.

SIR,   *Boston, Dec.* 22, 1754.

"Since the conversation your Excellency was pleased to honour me with, on the subject of uniting the Colonies more intimately with Great Britain, by allowing them Representatives in Parliament, I have something further considered that matter, and am of opinion, that such an Union would be very acceptable to the Colonies, provided they had a reasonable number of Representatives allowed them; and that all the old Acts of Parliament restraining the trade or cramping the manufactures of the Colonies, be at the same time repealed, and the British Subjects on this side the water put, in those respects, on the same footing with those in Great Britain, 'till the new Parliament, representing the whole, shall think it for the interest of the whole to reenact some or all of them: It is not that I imagine so many Representatives will be allowed the Colonies, as to have any great weight by their numbers; but I think there might be sufficient to occasion those laws to be better and more impartially considered, and perhaps to overcome the private interest of a petty corporation, or of any particular set of artificers or traders in England, who heretofore seem, in some instances, to have been more regarded than all the Colonies, or than was consistent with the general interest, or best national good. I think too, that the government of the Colonies by a Parliament, in which they are fairly represented, would be vastly more agreeable to the people, than the method lately attempted to be introduced by Royal Instructions, as well as more agreeable to the nature of an English Constitution, and to English Liberty; and that such laws as now seem to bear hard on the Colonies, would (when judged by such a Parliament for the best interest of the whole) be more chearfully submitted to, and more easily executed.

"I should hope too, that by such an union, the people of Great Britain and the people of the Colonies would learn to consider themselves, not as belonging to different Communities with different Interests, but to one Community with one Interest, which I imagine would contribute to strengthen the whole, and greatly lessen the danger of future separations.

"It is, I suppose, agreed to be the general interest of any state, that it's people be numerous and rich; men enow to fight in its defence, and enow to pay sufficient taxes to defray the charge; for these circumstances tend to the security of the state, and its protection from foreign power: But it seems not of so much importance whether the fighting be done by John or Thomas, or the tax paid by William or Charles: The iron manufacture employs and enriches British Subjects, but is it of any importance to the state, whether the manufacturers live at Birmingham or Sheffield, or both, since they are still within its bounds, and their wealth and persons at its command? Could the Goodwin Sands be laid dry by banks, and land equal to a large country thereby gain'd to England, and presently filled with English Inhabitants, would it be right to deprive such Inhabitants of the common privileges enjoyed by other Englishmen, the right of vending their produce in the same ports, or of making their own shoes, because a merchant, or a shoemaker, living on the old land, might fancy it more for his advantage to trade or make shoes for them? Would this be right, even if the land were gained at the expence of the state? And would it not seem less right, if the charge and labour of gaining the additional territory to Britain had been borne by the settlers themselves? And would not the hardship appear yet greater, if the people of the new country should be allowed no Representatives in the Parliament enacting such impositions? Now I look on the Colonies as so many Counties gained to Great Britain, and more advantageous to it than if they had been gained out of the sea around its coasts, and joined to its land: For being in different climates, they afford greater variety of produce, and materials for more manufactures; and being separated by the ocean, they increase much more its shipping and seamen; and since they are all included in the British Empire, which has only extended itself by their means; and the strength and wealth of the parts is the strength and wealth of the whole; what imports it to the general state, whether a merchant, a smith, or a hatter, grow rich in *Old* or *New* England? And if, through increase of people, two smiths are wanted for one employed before, why may not the *new* smith be allowed to live and thrive in the *new Country*, as well as the *old* one in the *Old*? In fine, why should the countenance of a state be *partially* afforded to its people, unless it be most in favour of

Y. What are those Words you mention?

X. Here is the Act itself, I'll read that Part of it. "From and after the Publication of this Act, it shall and may be lawful for the Freemen of this Province to form themselves into Companies, *as heretofore they have used in time of War without Law*, and for each Company, by Majority of Votes, in the Way of Ballot, to chuse its own Officers, *&c.*" The Words I meant are these, *as heretofore they have used in Time of War*. Now I suppose we have none of us forgot the Association in the Time of the last War; 'tis not so long since, but that we may well enough remember the Method we took to form ourselves into Companies, chuse our Officers, and present them to the Governor for Approbation and Commissions; and the Act in question says plainly, we may now *lawfully do* in this Affair, what we then did *without Law.*

Y. I did not before take so much Notice of those Words, but to be sure the Thing is easy enough; for I remember very well how we managed at that Time; and indeed 'tis easier to effect it now than it was then: For the Companies and Regiments, and their Districts, *&c.* were then all to form and settle; but now, why may not the Officers of the old Companies call the old Associators together, with such others in the District of each Company as incline to be concerned, and proceed immediately to a new Choice by Virtue of the Act? Other new Companies may in other Places be formed as the associated Companies were.

Z. You say right. And if this were all the Objection to the Act, no Doubt they would do so immediately. But 'tis said there are other Faults in it.

X. What are they?

Z. The Act is so loose, that Persons who never intend to engage in the Militia, even *Quakers* may meet and vote in the Choice of the Officers.

X. Possibly;—but was any such thing observed in the Association Elections?

Z. Not that I remember.

X. Why should it be more apprehended now, than it was at that Time? Can they have any Motives to such a Conduct now, which they had not then?

Z. I cannot say.

X. Nor can I. If a Militia be necessary for the Safety of the Province, I hope we shall not boggle at this little Difficulty. What else is objected?

Z. I have heard this objected, That it were better the Governor should appoint the Officers; for the Choice being in the People, a Man very unworthy to be an Officer, may happen to be popular enough to get himself chosen by the undiscerning Mob.

X. 'Tis possible. And if all Officers appointed by Governors were always Men of Merit, and fully qualified for their Posts, it would be wrong ever to hazard a popular Election. It is reasonable, I allow, that the Commander in Chief should not have Officers absolutely forced upon him, in whom, from his Knowledge of their Incapacity, he can place no Confidence. And, on the other Hand, it seems likely that the People will engage more readily in the Service, and face Danger with more Intrepidity, when they are commanded by a Man they know and esteem, and on whose Prudence and Courage, as well as Good-will and Integrity, they can have Reliance, than they would under a Man they either did not know, or did not like. For supposing Governors ever so judicious and upright in the Distribution of Offices, they cannot know every Body, in every Part of the Province, and are liable to be imposed on by partial Recommendations; but the People generally know their Neighbours. And to me, the Act in question seems to have hit a proper Medium, between the two Modes of appointing: The People chuse, and if the Governor approves, he grants the Commission; if not, they are to chuse a second, and even a third Time. Out of three Choices, 'tis probable one may be right; and where an Officer is approved both by Superiors and Inferiors, there is the greater Prospect of those Advantages that attend a good Agreement in the Service. This Mode of Choice is moreover agreeable to the Liberty and Genius of our Constitution. 'Tis similar to the Manner in which by our Laws Sheriffs and Coroners are chosen and approved. And yet it has more Regard to the Prerogative than the Mode of Choice in some Colonies, where the military Officers are either chosen absolutely by the Companies themselves, or by the House of Representatives, without any Negative on that Choice, or any Approbation necessary from the Governor.

Υ. But is that agreeable to the *English* Constitution?

X. Considered in this Light, I think it is; *British* Subjects, by removing into *America*, cultivating a Wilderness, extending the Dominion, and increasing the Wealth, Commerce and Power of their Mother Country, at the Hazard of their Lives and Fortunes, ought not, and in Fact do not thereby lose their native Rights. There is a Power in the Crown to grant a Continuance of those Rights to such Subjects, in any Part of the World, and to their Posterity born in such new Country; and for the farther Encouragement and Reward of such Merit, to grant *additional* Liberties and Privileges, not used in *England*, but suited to the different Circumstances of different Colonies. If then the Grants of those additional Liberties and Privileges may be regularly made under an *English* Constitution, they may be enjoyed agreeable to that Constitution.

Υ. But the Act is very short, there are numberless Circumstances and Occasions pertaining to a Body of armed Men, which are not as they ought to have been expressly provided for in the Act.

X. 'Tis true, there are not express Provisions in the Act for all Circumstances; but there is a Power lodged by the Act in the Governor and Field Officers of the Regiments, to make all such Provisions, in the Articles of War, which they may form and establish.

Υ. But can it be right in the Legislature by any Act to delegate their Power of making Laws to others?

X. I believe not, generally; but certainly in particular Cases it may. Legislatures may, and frequently do give to Corporations, Power to make By-Laws for their own Government. And in this Case, the Act of Parliament gives the Power of making Articles of War for the Government of the Army to the King alone, and there is no Doubt but the Parliament understand the Rights of Government.

Υ. Are you sure the Act of Parliament gives such Power?

X. This is the Act. The Power I mention is here in Section LV. "Provided always, That it shall and may be lawful to and

for his Majesty, to form, make and establish Articles of War
for the better Government of his Majesty's Forces, and for
bringing Offenders against the same to Justice; and to erect
and constitute Courts Martial, with Power to try, hear, and
determine any Crimes or Offences by such Articles of War,
and inflict Penalties by Sentence or Judgment of the same."
And here you see bound up with the Act, the Articles of War,
made by his Majesty in Pursuance of the Act, and providing
for every Circumstance.

Z. It is so, sure enough. I had been told that our Act of
Assembly was impertinently singular in this Particular.

X. The G——r himself, in a Message to the House,
expresly recommended this Act of Parliament for their Imitation, in forming the Militia Bill.

Z. I never heard that before.

X. But it is true.—The Assembly, however (considering
that this Militia would consist chiefly of Freeholders) have
varied a little from that Part of the Act of Parliament, in Favour of Liberty; they have not given the sole Power of making those Articles of War *to the Governor*, as that Act does *to
the King*; but have joined with the Governor, for that Purpose, a Number of Officers to be chosen by the People. The
Articles moreover are not to be general Laws, binding on all
the Province, nor on any Man who has not first approved of
them, and voluntarily engaged to observe them.

Z. Is there no Danger that the Governor and Officers may
make those Articles too severe?

X. Not without you can suppose them Enemies to the Service, and to their Country: For if they should make such as
are unfit for Freemen and *Englishmen* to be subjected to, they
will get no Soldiers; no body will engage. In some Cases,
however, if you and I were in actual Service, I believe we
should both think it necessary for our own Safety that the
Articles should be pretty severe.

Z. What Cases are they?

X. Suppose a Centinel should betray his Trust, give Intelligence to the Enemy, or conduct them into our Quarters.

Z. To be sure there should be severe Punishments for such
Crimes, or we might all be ruined.

X. Chuse reasonable Men for your Officers, and you need

not fear their making reasonable Laws; and if they make such, I hope reasonable Men will not refuse to engage under them.

Y. But here is a Thing I don't like. By this Act of Assembly, the *Quakers* are neither compelled to muster, nor to pay a Fine if they don't.

X. It is true; nor could they be compelled either to muster or pay a Fine of that Kind by any Militia Law made here. They are exempted by the Charter and fundamental Laws of the Province.

Y. How so?

X. See here; it is the first Clause in the Charter. I'll read it. "Because no People can be truly happy, though under the greatest Enjoyment of civil Liberties, if abridged of the Freedom of their Consciences, as to their *Religous Profession* and Worship: And Almighty God being the only Lord of Conscience, Father of Lights and Spirits, and the Author as well as Object of all divine Knowledge, Faith and Worship, who only doth enlighten the Minds, and persuade and convince the Understandings of People, I do hereby grant and declare, That no Person or Persons inhabiting in this Province or Territories, who shall confess and acknowledge one Almighty God, the Creator, Upholder and Ruler of the World; and profess him or themselves obliged to live quietly under the civil Government, shall be, IN ANY CASE, MOLESTED or PREJUDICED in his or their PERSON or ESTATE, because of his or their *conscientious Persuasion* or Practice, nor be compelled to frequent or maintain any religious Worship, Place or Ministry, contrary to his or their Mind, or to DO or SUFFER any OTHER ACT or THING, contrary to their religious Persuasion." And in the eighth Section of the same Charter, you see a Declaration, that "neither the Proprietor, nor his Heirs or Assigns, shall procure or do any Thing or Things, whereby the Liberties in this Charter contained or expressed, nor any Part thereof, shall be infringed or broken; and if any Thing shall be procured or done by *any Person or Persons*, contrary to these Presents, it shall be held of NO FORCE OR EFFECT." This Liberty of Conscience granted by Charter, is also established by the first Law in our Book, and confirmed by the Crown.—And moreover, the Governor has an express Instruction from the Proprietaries, that in case of making any

Militia Law, he shall take especial Care that the Charter be not infringed in this Respect. Besides, most of our Petitions for a Militia from the moderate Part of the People, requested particularly that due Regard might be had to scrupulous and tender Consciences. When Taxes are raised however, for the King's Service, the *Quakers* and *Menonists* pay their Part of them, and a great Part; for as their Frugality and Industry makes them generally wealthy, their Proportion is the greater compared with their Numbers. And out of these Taxes those Men are paid who go into actual Service. As for Mustering and Training, no Militia are any where paid for that. It is by many justly delighted in as a manly Exercise. But those who are engaged in actual Service for any Time, ought undoubtedly to have Pay.

Y. There is no Provision in this Militia Act to pay them.

X. There is a Provision that no Regiment, Company, or Party, though engaged in the Militia, shall be obliged "to more than three Days March, *&c.* without an Express Engagement for that Purpose first voluntarily entred into and subscribed by every Man so to march or remain in Garrison." And 'tis to be supposed that no Man will subscribe such particular Engagement without reasonable Pay, or other Encouragement.

Y. But where is that Pay to come from?

X. From the Government to be sure; and out of the Money struck by the Act for granting £ 60,000.

Z. Yes; but those who serve must pay their Share of the Tax, as well as those who don't.

X. Perhaps not. 'Tis to be supposed that those who engage in the Service for any Time, upon Pay, will be chiefly single Men, and they are expresly exempted from the Tax by the £ 60,000 Act. Consequently those who do not serve, must pay the more; for the Sum granted must be made up.

Z. I never heard before that they were exempted by that Act.

X. It is so, I assure you.

Y. But there is no Provision in the Militia Act for the Maimed.

X. If they are poor, they are provided for by the Laws of their Country. There is no other Provision by any Militia Law that I know of. If they have behaved well, and suffered in their Country's Cause, they deserve moreover some grateful Notice of their Service, and some Assistance from the common Treasury; and if any particular Township should happen to be overburthened, they may, on Application to the Government, reasonably expect Relief.

Z. Though the *Quakers* and others conscientiously scrupulous of bearing Arms, are exempted, as you say, by Charter; they might, being a Majority in the Assembly, have made the Law compulsory on others. At present, 'tis so loose, that no body is obliged by it, who does not voluntarily engage.

X. They might indeed have made the Law compulsory on all others. But it seems they thought it more equitable and generous to leave to all as much Liberty as they enjoy themselves, and not lay even a seeming Hardship on others, which they themselves declined to bear. They have however granted all we asked of them. Our Petitions set forth, that " we were freely willing and ready to defend ourselves and Country, and all we wanted was legal Authority, Order and Discipline." These are now afforded by the Law, if we think fit to make use of them. And indeed I do not see the Advantage of compelling People of any Sect into martial Service merely for the Sake of raising Numbers. I have been myself in some Service of Danger, and I always thought Cowards rather *weakened*, than *strengthened*, the Party. Fear is contagious, and a Pannick once begun spreads like Wildfire, and infects the stoutest Heart. All Men are not by Nature brave: And a few who are so, will do more effectual Service by themselves, than when accompanied by, and mixed with, a Multitude of Poltroons, who only create Confusion, and give Advantage to the Enemy.

Z. What signifies what *you thought* or think? Others think differently. And all the wise Legislatures in the other Colonies have thought fit to compel all Sorts of Persons to bear Arms, or suffer heavy Penalties.

X. As you say, what I *thought* or *think* is not of much Consequence. But a wiser Legislator than all those you mention put together, and who better knew the Nature of Mankind, made his military Law very different from theirs in that Respect.

Z. What Legislator do you mean?

X. I mean God himself, who would have no Man led to Battle that might rather wish to be at home, either from Fear or other Causes.

Z. Where do you find that Law?

X. 'Tis in the 20th Chapter of *Deuteronomy*, where are these Words, *When thou goest out to Battle against thine Enemies,—the Officers shall speak unto the People, saying, What Man is there that hath built a new House, and hath not dedicated it? let him go and return to his House, lest he die in the Battle, and another Man dedicate it. And what Man is he that hath planted a Vineyard, and hath not yet eaten of it? let him also go, and return unto his House, lest he die in the Battle, and another Man eat of it. And what Man is there that hath betrothed a Wife, and hath not taken her? let him go and return unto his House, lest he die in Battle, and another Man take her.—And—*

Z. These all together could not be many; and this has no Relation to Cowardice.

X. If you had not interrupted me, I was coming to that Part, Verse 8. *And the Officers shall speak farther unto the People, and they shall say, What Man is there that is* FEARFUL *and* FAINTHEARTED? *let him go and return unto his House; lest his Brethrens Heart faint as well as his Heart;* that is, lest he communicate his Fears, and his brave Brethren catch the Contagion, to the Ruin of the whole Army. Accordingly we find, that under this military Law, no People in the World fought more gallantly, or performed greater Actions than the *Hebrew* Soldiery.—And if you would be informed what Proportion of the People would be discharged by such a Proclamation, you will find that Matter determined by an actual Experiment made by General *Gideon*, as related in the seventh Chapter of *Judges*: For he having assembled 32,000 Men against the *Midianites*, proclaimed, according to Law (Verse the third) *Whosoever is* FEARFUL *and* AFRAID, *let him return and depart early from* Mount Gilead.

Z. And pray how many departed?

X. The Text says, there departed 22,000, and there remained but 10,000. A very great Sifting! and yet on that particular Occasion a farther Sifting was required. Now it seems to me, that this Militia Law of ours, which gives the Brave all the Advantages they can desire, of Order, Authority,

Discipline, and the like, and compels no Cowards into their Company, is such a Kind of Sieve, as the *Mosaic* Proclamation. For with us, not only every Man who has built a House, or planted a Vineyard, or betrothed a Wife, or is afraid of his Flesh; but the narrow Bigot, filled with *Sectarian* Malice (if such there be) who hates *Quakers* more than he loves his Country, his Friends, his Wife or Family, may say: *I won't engage, for I don't like the Act;* or, *I don't like the Officers that are chosen;* or, *I don't like the Articles of War;* and so we shall not be troubled with them, but all that engage will be hearty.

Z. For my Part, I am no Coward; but hang me if I'll fight to save the *Quakers.*

X. That is to say, you won't pump Ship, because 'twill save the Rats,—as well as yourself.

Y. You have answered most of the Objections I have heard against the Act, to my Satisfaction; but there is one remaining. The Method of carrying it into Execution seems so round about, I am afraid we cannot have the Benefit of it in any reasonable Time.

X. I cannot see much in that Objection. The several Neighbourhoods out of which Companies are formed may meet and chuse their Company-Officers in one and the same Day; and the Regiments may be formed, and the Field Officers chosen in a Week or ten Days after, who may immediately proceed to consider the several Militia Laws of *Britain* and the Colonies, and (with the Governor) form out of them such Articles, as will appear most suitable for the Freemen of this Province, who incline to bear Arms voluntarily; and the Whole may be in Order in a Month from the first Elections, if common Diligence be used.—And indeed, as the Colonies are at present the Prize contended for between *Britain* and *France*, and the latter, by the last Advices, seems to be meditating some grand Blow, Part of which may probably fall on *Pennsylvania*, either by Land or Sea, or both, it behoves us, I think, to make the best Use we can of this Act, and carry it immediately into Execution both in Town and Country. If there are material Defects in it, Experience will best discover them, and show what is proper or necessary to amend them.—The approaching Winter will afford us some Time to arm and prepare, and more Leisure than other Seasons for Exercising and Improving in good Discipline.

Z. But if this Act should be carried into Execution, prove a good One, and answer the End; what shall we have to say against the *Quakers* at the next Election?

X. O my Friends, let us on this Occasion cast from us all these little Party Views, and consider ourselves as *Englishmen* and *Pennsylvanians*. Let us think only of the Service of our King, the Honour and Safety of our Country, and Vengeance on its Murdering Enemies.—If Good be done, what imports it by whom 'tis done?—The Glory of serving and saving others, is superior to the Advantage of being served or secured. Let us resolutely and generously unite in our Country's Cause (in which to die is the sweetest of all Deaths) and may the God of Armies bless our honest Endeavours.

The Pennsylvania Gazette, December 18, 1755

A Parable Against Persecution

CHAP. XXVII

1. And it came to pass after these Things, that Abraham sat in the Door of his Tent, about the going down of the Sun.

2. And behold a Man, bowed with Age, came from the Way of the Wilderness, leaning on a Staff.

3. And Abraham arose and met him, and said unto him, Turn in, I pray thee, and wash thy Feet, and tarry all Night, and thou shalt arise early on the Morrow, and go on thy Way.

4. And the Man said, Nay, for I will abide under this Tree.

5. But Abraham pressed him greatly; so he turned, and they went into the Tent; and Abraham baked unleavend Bread, and they did eat.

6. And when Abraham saw that the Man blessed not God, he said unto him, Wherefore dost thou not worship the most high God, Creator of Heaven and Earth?

7. And the Man answered and said, I do not worship the God thou speakest of; neither do I call upon his Name; for I

have made to myself a God, which abideth alway in mine House, and provideth me with all Things.

8. And Abraham's Zeal was kindled against the Man; and he arose, and fell upon him, and drove him forth with Blows into the Wilderness.

9. And at Midnight God called unto Abraham, saying, Abraham, where is the Stranger?

10. And Abraham answered and said, Lord, he would not worship thee, neither would he call upon thy Name; therefore have I driven him out from before my Face into the Wilderness.

11. And God said, Have I born with him these hundred ninety and eight Years, and nourished him, and cloathed him, notwithstanding his Rebellion against me, and couldst not thou, that art thyself a Sinner, bear with him one Night?

12. And Abraham said, Let not the Anger of my Lord wax hot against his Servant. Lo, I have sinned; forgive me, I pray Thee:

13. And Abraham arose and went forth into the Wilderness, and sought diligently for the Man, and found him, and returned with him to his Tent; and when he had entreated him kindly, he sent him away on the Morrow with Gifts.

14. And God spake again unto Abraham, saying, For this thy Sin shall thy Seed be afflicted four Hundred Years in a strange Land:

15. But for thy Repentance will I deliver them; and they shall come forth with Power, and with Gladness of Heart, and with much Substance.

1755

A Parable on Brotherly Love

1 In those days there was no Worker of Iron in all the Land, And the Merchants of Midian passed by with their Camels, bearing Spices, and Myrrh, and Balm, and Wares of Iron. And Reuben bought an Ax from the Ishmaelite Merchants,

which he prized highly, for there were none in his Father's house.

2 And Simeon said unto Reuben his Brother, lend me I pray thee, thine Ax: But he refused, and would not.

3 And Levi also said unto him, My Brother, lend me thine Ax. And he refused him also.

4 Then came Judah unto Reuben and entreated him, saying, Lo, thou lovest me, and I have always loved thee do not refuse me the use of thine Ax, for I desire it earnestly.

5 But Reuben turned from him, and refused him Likewise.

6 Now it came to pass that Reuben hewed Timber on the Bank of the River, and the Ax fell therein, and he could by no means find it.

7 But Simeon, Levi and Judah, had sent a Mesenger after the Ishmaelites with money and had bought for each of them an Ax also.

8 Then came Reuben unto Simeon, and said unto him, Lo, I have lost mine Ax, and my work is unfinished, lend me thine I pray thee.

9 And Simeon answered, saying, Thou wouldst not lend me thine Ax, therefore will I not lend thee mine.

10 Then went he unto Levi, and said unto him, My Brother, thou knowest my Loss and my Necessity; lend me, I pray thee, thine Ax.

11 And Levi reproached him, saying, Thou wouldest not lend me thine when I desired it, but I will be better than thee, and will lend thee mine.

12 And Reuben was grieved at the Rebuke of Levi; and being ashamed, turned from him, and took not the Ax; but sought his Brother Judah.

13 And as he drew near, Judah beheld his Countenance as it were confused with Grief and shame; and he prevented him, saying, My Brother, I know thy Loss, but why should it grieve thee? Lo, have I not an Ax that will serve both thee and me? take it I pray thee, and use it as thine own.

14 And Reuben fell on his Neck, and kissed him with Tears, saying, Thy Kindness is great, but thy Goodness in forgiving me is greater. Lo thou art indeed a Brother, and whilst I live will I surely love thee.

15 And Judah said, Let us also love our other Brethren; Behold, are we not all of one Blood.

16 And Joseph saw these Things, and reported them to his Father Jacob.

17 And Jacob said, Reuben did wrong but he repented, Simeon also did wrong, and Levi was not altogether blameless.

18 But the Heart of Judah is princely. Judah hath the Soul of a King. His Fathers Children shall bow down before him, and he shall rule over his Brethren, nor shall the Sceptre depart from his house, nor a Lawgiver from between his Feet, until Shiloh come.

1755

LETTERS

"I CONCLUDED TO SEND YOU A SPINNING WHEEL"

To Jane Franklin

DEAR SISTER, *Philadelphia, January 6, 1726-7.*

I am highly pleased with the account captain Freeman gives me of you. I always judged by your behaviour when a child that you would make a good, agreeable woman, and you know you were ever my peculiar favourite. I have been thinking what would be a suitable present for me to make, and for you to receive, as I hear you are grown a celebrated beauty. I had almost determined on a tea table, but when I considered that the character of a good housewife was far preferable to that of being only a pretty gentlewoman, I concluded to send you a *spinning wheel*, which I hope you will accept as a small token of my sincere love and affection.

Sister, farewell, and remember that modesty, as it makes the most homely virgin amiable and charming, so the want of it infallibly renders the most perfect beauty disagreeable and odious. But when that brightest of female virtues shines among other perfections of body and mind in the same person, it makes the woman more lovely than an angel. Excuse this freedom, and use the same with me. I am, dear Jenny, your loving brother,

"TOO SEVERE UPON HOBBES"

To James Logan

Having read the Chapter on Moral Good or Virtue, with all the Attention I am Capable of, amidst the many little Cares that Continually infest me, I shall, as the Author Condescends to desire, give my Opinion of it, and that with all Sincerity and Freedom, neither apprehending the Imputation of Flattery on the one hand, nor that of Ill Manners on the other.

I think the Design excellent—and the Management of it in the Main, good; a short Summary of the Chapter plac'd at the Beginning, and little Summaries of each Paragraph in the Margin being only necessary, and what will in my Opinion sufficiently remove any Disgust that the Authors dilate Manner of Writing may give to some Readers; And the whole is so curious and entertaining, that I know not where any thing can be spared.

It seems to me that the Author is a little too severe upon Hobbes, whose Notion, I imagine, is somewhat nearer the Truth than that which makes the State of Nature a State of Love: But the Truth perhaps lies between both Extreams.

I think what is said upon Musick, might be enlarg'd to Advantage by showing that what principally makes a Tune agreeable, is the Conformity between its Air or Genius, and some Motion, Passion or Affection of the Mind, which the Tune imitates.

I should have been glad to have seen the Virtues enumerated, distinguish'd, and the proper Ideas affix'd to each Name; which I have not yet seen, scarce two Authors agreeing therein, some annexing more, others fewer and different Ideas to the Same Name. But I think there is some Incorrectness of Sentiment in what the Author has said of Temperance concerning which I have not time to explain myself in writing.

1737?

"OPINIONS SHOULD BE JUDG'D OF BY THEIR INFLUENCES"

To Josiah and Abiah Franklin

Honour'd Father and Mother   April 13. 1738

I have your Favour of the 21st of March in which you both seem concern'd lest I have imbib'd some erroneous Opinions. Doubtless I have my Share, and when the natural Weakness and Imperfection of Human Understanding is considered, with the unavoidable Influences of Education, Custom, Books and Company, upon our Ways of thinking, I imagine a Man must have a good deal of Vanity who believes, and a good deal of Boldness who affirms, that all the Doctrines he holds, are true; and all he rejects, are false. And perhaps the same may be justly said of every Sect, Church and Society of men when they assume to themselves that Infallibility which they deny to the Popes and Councils. I think Opinions should be judg'd of by their Influences and Effects; and if a Man holds none that tend to make him less Virtuous or more vicious, it may be concluded he holds none that are dangerous; which I hope is the Case with me. I am sorry you should have any Uneasiness on my Account, and if it were a thing possible for one to alter his Opinions in order to please others, I know none whom I ought more willingly to oblige in that respect than your selves: But since it is no more in a Man's Power *to think* than *to look* like another, methinks all that should be expected from me is to keep my Mind open to Conviction, to hear patiently and examine attentively whatever is offered me for that end; and if after all I continue in the same Errors, I believe your usual Charity will induce you rather to pity and excuse than blame me. In the mean time your Care and Concern for me is what I am very thankful for.

As to the Freemasons, unless she will believe me when I assure her that they are in general a very harmless sort of People; and have no principles or Practices that are inconsistent with Religion or good Manners, I know no Way of giving my Mother a better Opinion of them than she seems to have at present, (since it is not allow'd that Women should be admitted into that secret Society). She has, I must confess, on that Account, some reason to be displeas'd with it; but for any thing else, I must entreat her to suspend her Judgment till she is better inform'd, and in the mean time exercise her Charity.

My Mother grieves that one of her Sons is an Arian, another an Arminian. What an Arminian or an Arian is, I cannot say that I very well know; the Truth is, I make such Distinctions very little my Study; I think vital Religion has always suffer'd, when Orthodoxy is more regarded than Virtue. And the Scripture assures me, that at the last Day, we shall not be examin'd what we *thought*, but what we *did*; and our Recommendation will not be that we said *Lord, Lord*, but that we did GOOD to our Fellow Creatures. See Matth. 26.

We have had great Rains here lately, which with the Thawing of Snow in the Mountains back of our Country has made vast Floods in our Rivers, and by carrying away

Bridges, Boats, &c. made travelling almost impracticable for
a Week past, so that our Post has entirely mist making one
Trip.

I know nothing of Dr. Crook, nor can I learn that any such
Person has ever been here.

I hope my Sister Janey's Child is by this time recovered. I
am Your dutiful Son

READING JONATHAN EDWARDS

To Jane Mecom

Dearest Sister Jenny   Philada. July 28. 1743

I took your Admonition very kindly, and was far from
being offended at you for it. If I say any thing about it to
you, 'tis only to rectify some wrong Opinions you seem to
have entertain'd of me, and that I do only because they give
you some Uneasiness, which I am unwilling to be the Occasion of. You express yourself as if you thought I was against
Worshipping of God, and believed Good Works would merit
Heaven; which are both Fancies of your own, I think, without Foundation. I am so far from thinking that God is not to
be worshipped, that I have compos'd and wrote a whole
Book of Devotions for my own Use: And I imagine there are
few, if any, in the World, so weake as to imagine, that the
little Good we can do here, can *merit* so vast a Reward hereafter. There are some Things in your New England Doctrines
and Worship, which I do not agree with, but I do not therefore condemn them, or desire to shake your Belief or Practice
of them. We may dislike things that are nevertheless right in
themselves. I would only have you make me the same Allow-
ances, and have a better Opinion both of Morality and your
Brother. Read the Pages of Mr. Edward's late Book entitled
SOME THOUGHTS CONCERNING THE PRESENT REVIVAL OF
RELIGION IN NE. from 367 to 375; and when you judge of
others, if you can perceive the Fruit to be good, don't terrify
your self that the Tree may be evil, but be assur'd it is not
so; for you know who has said, *Men do not gather Grapes of*

Thorns or Figs of Thistles. I have not time to add but that I shall always be Your affectionate Brother

P S. It was not kind in you to imagine when your Sister commended Good Works, she intended it a Reproach to you. 'Twas very far from her Thoughts.

"MORE DEPENDENCE ON WORKS, THAN ON FAITH"

To John Franklin

Philadelphia, 1745.

—Our people are extremely impatient to hear of your success at Cape Breton. My shop is filled with thirty inquiries at the coming in of every post. Some wonder the place is not yet taken. I tell them I shall be glad to hear that news three months hence. Fortified towns are hard nuts to crack; and your teeth have not been accustomed to it. Taking strong places is a particular trade, which you have taken up without serving an apprenticeship to it. Armies and veterans need skilful engineers to direct them in their attack. Have you any? But some seem to think forts are as easy taken as snuff. Father Moody's prayers look tolerably modest. You have a fast and prayer day for that purpose; in which I compute five hundred thousand petitions were offered up to the same effect in New England, which added to the petitions of every family morning and evening, multiplied by the number of days since January 25th, make forty-five millions of prayers; which, set against the prayers of a few priests in the garrison, to the Virgin Mary, give a vast balance in your favor.

If you do not succeed, I fear I shall have but an indifferent opinion of Presbyterian prayers in such cases, as long as I live. Indeed, in attacking strong towns I should have more dependence on *works*, than on *faith*; for, like the kingdom of heaven, they are to be taken by force and violence; and in a French garrison I suppose there are devils of that kind, that they are not to be cast out by prayers and fasting, unless it be by their own fasting for want of provisions. I believe there is Scripture in what I have wrote, but I cannot adorn the

margin with quotations, having a bad memory, and no Con-
cordance at hand; besides no more time than to subscribe
myself, &c.

May? 1745

To James Read

DEAR J——,   *Saturday morning, Aug.* 17. '45.
   I have been reading your letter over again, and since you desire an answer, I sit me down to write you one; yet, as I write
in the market, will, I believe, be but a short one, tho' I may be
long about it. I approve of your method of writing one's mind,
when one is too warm to speak it with temper: but being
myself quite cool in this affair, I might as well speak as write,
if I had an opportunity. Your copy of *Kempis*, must be a corrupt one, if it has that passage as you quote it, *in omnibus
requiem quæsivi, sed non inveni, nisi in angulo cum libello.* The
good father understood pleasure (requiem) better, and wrote,
in angulo cum puella. Correct it thus, without hesitation.
I know there is another reading, *in angulo puellæ*; but this
reject, tho' more *to the point*, as an expression too indelicate.
   Are you an attorney by profession, and do you know no
better, how to chuse a proper court in which to bring your
action? Would you submit to the decision of a husband, a
cause between you and his wife? Don't you know, that all
wives are in the right? It may be you don't, for you are yet
but a young husband. But see, on this head, the learned
Coke, that oracle of the law, in his chapter *De Jus Marit.
Angl.* I advise you not to bring it to trial; for if you do, you'll
certainly be cast.
   Frequent interruptions make it impossible for me to go
thro' all your letter. I have only time to remind you of the
saying of that excellent old philosopher, Socrates, *that in differences among friends, they that make the first concessions are the
WISEST*; and to hint to you, that you are in danger of losing
that honour in the present case, if you are not very speedy in

your acknowledgments; which I persuade myself you will be, when you consider the sex of your adversary.

Your visits never had but one thing disagreeable in them, that is, they were always too short. I shall exceedingly regret the loss of them, unless you continue, as you have begun, to make it up to me by long letters. I am dear J——, with sincerest love to our dearest Suky,

Your very affectionate friend and cousin,

ATLANTIC SHIP CROSSINGS AND THE MOTION OF THE EARTH

To Cadwallader Colden

Sir

I receiv'd yours with others enclos'd for Mr. Bertram and Mr. Armit, to which I suppose the enclos'd are Answers. The Person who brought yours said he would call for Answers, but did not; or, if he did, I did not see him.

I understand Parker has begun upon your Piece. A long Sitting of our Assembly has hitherto hinder'd me from beginning the Miscellany. I shall write to Dr. Gronovius as you desire.

I wish I had Mathematics enough to satisfy my self, Whether the much shorter Voyages made by Ships bound hence to England, than by those from England hither, are not in some Degree owing to the Diurnal Motion of the Earth; and if so, in what Degree? 'Tis a Notion that has lately entred my Mind; I know not if ever any other's. Ships in a Calm at the Equator move with the Sea 15 Miles per minute; at our Capes suppose 12 Miles per Minute; in the British Channel suppose 10 Miles per Minute: Here is a Difference of 2 Miles Velocity per Minute between Cape Hinlopen and the Lizard! no small Matter in so Weighty a Body as a laden Ship swimming in a Fluid! How is this Velocity lost in the Voyage thither, if not by the Resistance of the Water? and if so, then the Water, which resisted in part, must have given Way in part to the Ship, from time to time as she proceeded continually

out of Parallels of Latitude where the Earths Motion or Rotation was quicker into others where it was slower. And thus
as her Velocity tends eastward with the Earth's Motion, she
perhaps makes her Easting sooner. Suppose a Vessel lying still
in a Calm at our Cape, could be taken up and the same Instant set down in an equal Calm in the English Channel,
would not the Difference of Velocity between her and the Sea
she was plac'd in, appear plainly by a violent Motion of the
Ship thro' the Water eastward? I have not Time to explain my
self farther, the Post waiting, but believe have said enough for
you to comprehend my Meaning. If the Reasons hinted at
should encline you to think there is any Thing in this Notion,
I should be glad of an Answer to this Question, (if it be
capable of a precise Answer) viz.

Suppose a Ship sails on a N. East Line from Lat. 39 to Lat.
52 in 30 Days, how long will she be returning on the same
Line, Winds, Currents, &c. being equal?

Just so much as the East Motion of the Earth helps her
Easting, I suppose it will hinder her Westing.

Perhaps the Weight and Dimensions or Shape of the Vessel
should be taken into the Consideration, as the Water resists
Bodies of different Shapes differently.

I must beg you to excuse the incorrectness of this Scrawl
as I have not time to transcribe. I am Sir Your most humble
Servant

February, 1746

REFUTATION OF ANDREW BAXTER'S "ENQUIRY INTO THE NATURE OF THE HUMAN SOUL"

To [*Thomas Hopkinson?*]

According to my Promise I send you *in Writing* my Observations on your Book. You will be the better able to consider
them; which I desire you to do at your Leisure, and to set
me right where I am wrong.

I stumble at the Threshold of the Building, and therefore
have not read farther. The Author's *Vis Inertiae essential to*

Matter, upon which the whole Work is founded, I have not been able to comprehend. And I do not think he demonstrates at all clearly (at least to me he does not) that there is really any such Property in Matter.

He says, No. 2. "Let a given Body or Mass of Matter be called A, and let any given Celerity be called C: That Celerity doubled, tripled, &c. or halved, thirded, &c. will be 2C, 3C &c. or ½C, ⅓C &c. respectively. Also the Body doubled, tripled or halved, thirded; will be 2A, 3A, or ½A, ½A, respectively." Thus far is clear. But he adds, "Now to move the Body A with the Celerity C, requires a certain Force to be impressed upon it; and to move it with a Celerity as 2C, requires twice that Force to be impressed upon it, &c." Here I suspect some Mistake creeps in occasioned by the Author's not distinguishing between a *great* Force apply'd *at once*, and a *small* one *continually* apply'd, to a Mass of Matter, in order to move it. I think 'tis generally allow'd by the Philosophers, and for aught we know is certainly true, That there is no Mass of Matter how great soever, but may be moved by any Force how small soever (taking Friction out of the Question) and this small Force continued will in Time bring the Mass to move with any Velocity whatsoever. Our Author himself seems to allow this towards the End of the same No. 2 when he is subdividing his Celerities and Forces: For as in continuing the Division to Eternity by his Method of ½C, ⅓C, ¼C, ⅕C, &c. you can never come to a Fraction of Celerity that is equal to oC, or no Celerity at all; so dividing the Force in the same Manner, you can never come to a Fraction of Force that will not produce an equal Fraction of Celerity. Where then is the mighty *Vis Inertiae*, and what is its Strength when the greatest assignable Mass of Matter will give way to or be moved by the least assignable Force? Suppose two Globes each equal to the Sun and to one another, exactly equipoised in Jove's Ballance: Suppose no Friction in the Center of Motion in the Beam or elsewhere: If a Musketo then were to light on one of them, would he not give Motion to them both, causing one to descend and the other to rise? If 'tis objected, that the Force of Gravity helps one Globe to descend: I answer, The same Force opposes the other's Rising: Here is an Equality, that leaves the whole Motion to be produc'd by the Musketo, without whom those Globes would not be moved at all. What then does Vis Inertiae do in this Case? And what other Effect could we expect if there were no such Thing? Surely if it was any Thing more than a Phantom, there might be enough of it in such vast Bodies to annihilate, by its Opposition to Motion, so trifling a Force?

Our Author would have reason'd more clearly, I think, if, as he has us'd the Letter A for a certain Quantity of Matter, and C for a certain Degree of Celerity, he had employ'd one Letter more, and put F (perhaps) for a certain Quantity of Force. This let us suppose to be done; and then, as it is a Maxim that the Force of Bodies in Motion is equal to the Quantity of Matter multiply'd by the Celerity, or $F = C \times A$; and as the Force received by and subsisting in Matter when it is put in Motion, can never exceed the Force given; so if F move A with C, there must needs be required (See No. 3) 2F to move A with 2C; for A moving with 2C would have a Force equal to 2F, which it could not receive from 1F; and this, not because there is such a Thing as Vis Inertiae, for the Case would be the same if that had no Existence; but, *because nothing can give more than it hath*. And now again, if a Thing can give what it hath; if 1F can to 1A give 1C, which is the same thing as giving it 1F; i.e. if Force apply'd to Matter at Rest, can put it in Motion, and give it *equal* Force; Where then is Vis Inertiae? If it existed at all in Matter, should we not find the Quantity of its Resistance subtracted from the Force given?

In No. 4. our Author goes on and says, "The Body A requires a certain Force to be impressed on it, to be moved with a Celerity as C, or such a Force is necessary; and therefore it makes a certain Resistance, &c. A Body as 2A, requires *twice* that Force to be moved with the same Celerity, or it makes *twice* that Resistance, and so on." This I think is not true, but that the Body 2A moved by the Force 1F, (tho' the Eye may judge otherwise of it) does really move with the same Celerity as 1A did when impell'd by the same Force: For 2A is compounded of 1A + 1A; And if each of the 1A's or each Part of the Compound were made to move with 1C, (as they might be by 2F) then the whole would move with 2C, and not with 1C as our Author Supposes. But 1F apply'd to 2A makes each A move with ½C, and so the Whole moves with 1C, exactly the same as 1A was made to do by 1F before. What is *equal Celerity* but a Measuring of the same Space by moving Bodies in the same Time? Now if 1A impell'd by 1F measures 100 Yards in a Minute; and in 2A impell'd by 1F, each A measures 50 Yards in a Minute, which added make 100, are not the Celerities as well as the Forces equal? And since Force and Celerity in the same Quantity of Matter are always in *Proportion* to each other, why should we, when the Quantity of Matter is doubled, allow the Force to continue unimpair'd, and yet suppose one Half of the Celerity to be lost? I wonder the more at our Author's Mistake in this Point, since in the same No. I find him observing, "We may easily conceive that a Body as 3A, 4A, &c. would make 3 or 4 Bodies equal to once A, each of which would require once the first Force to be moved with the Celerity C." If then in 3A, each A require once the first Force F to be moved with the Celerity C, would not each move with the Force F, and Celerity C; and consequently the whole be 3A moving with 3F, and 3C? After so distinct an Observation, how could he miss of the Consequence, and imagine that 1C and 3C were the same? Thus as our Author's Abatement of Celerity in the Case of 2A moved by 1F, is imaginary, so must be his additional Resistance. And here again I am at a Loss to discover any Effect of the Vis Inertiae.

In No. 6 he tells us, "That all this is likewise certain when taken the contrary way, viz. from Motion to Rest; For the Body A moving with a certain Velocity as C requires a certain Degree of Force or Resistance to stop that Motion, &c. &c." That is, in other Words, equal Force is necessary to destroy Force. It may be so; but how does that discover a Vis Inertiae? Would not the Effect be the same if there were no such Thing? A Force 1F strikes a Body 1A, and moves it with the Celerity 1C, i.e. with the Force 1F. It requires, even according to our Author, only an opposing 1F to stop it. But ought it not, (if there were a Vis Inertiae) to have not only the Force 1F, but an additional Force equal to the Force of Vis Inertiae, that *obstinate Power, by which a Body endeavours with all its Might to continue in its present State, whether of Motion or Rest?* I say, ought there not to be an opposing Force equal to the

Sum of these? The Truth however is, that there is no Body how large soever, moving with any Velocity how great soever, but may be stopped by any opposing Force how small soever, continually apply'd. At least all our modern Philosophers agree to tell us so.

Let me turn the Thing in what Light I please, I cannot discover the Vis Inertiae nor any Effect of it. Tis allowed by all that a Body 1A, moving with a Velocity 1C, and a Force 1F, striking another Body 1A at Rest, they will afterwards move on together, each with ½C, and ½F; which, as I said before, is equal in the Whole to 1C and 1F. If Vis Inertiae as in this Case neither abates the Force nor the Velocity of Bodies, What does it, or how does it discover itself?

I imagine I may venture to conclude my Observations on this Piece, almost in the Words of the Author, "That if the Doctrines of the Immateriality of the Soul, and the Existence of God, and of Divine Providence are demonstrable from *no plainer* Principles, the *Deist* hath a desperate Cause in Hand." I oppose my *Theist* to his *Atheist*, because I think they are diametrically opposite and not near of kin, as Mr. Whitefield seems to suppose where (in his Journal) he tells us, *Mr. B. was a Deist, I had almost said an Atheist*. That is, *Chalk*, I had almost said *Charcoal*.

Shall I hazard a Thought to you that for aught I know is new, viz. If God was before all Things, and fill'd all Space; then, when he form'd what we call Matter, he must have done it out of his own Thinking immaterial Substance. The same, tho' he had not fill'd all Space; if it be true that *Ex nihilo nihil fit*. From hence may we not draw this Conclusion, That if any Part of Matter does not at present act and think, 'tis not from an Incapacity in its Nature but from a positive Restraint. I know not yet what other Consequences may follow the admitting of this position and therefore I will not be oblig'd to defend it. [   ] 'tis with some Reluctance that I either [   ] in the metaphysical Way. The great Uncertainty I have found in that Science; the wide Contradictions and endless Disputes it affords; and the horrible Errors I led my self into when a young Man, by drawing a Chain of plain Consequences as I thought them, from true Principles, have given me a Disgust to what I was once extreamly fond of.

The Din of the Market encreases upon me, and that, with frequent Interruptions, has, I find, made me say some things twice over, and I suppose forget some others I intended to say. It has, however, one good Effect, as it obliges me to come to the Relief of your Patience, with Your Humble Servant

October 16, 1746

"THE NATURE OF BOYS"

To Jane Mecom

DEAR SISTER,   Philadelphia,
I received your letter, with one for Benny, and one for Mr. Parker, and also two of Benny's letters of complaint, which, as you observe, do not amount to much. I should have had a very bad opinion of him, if he had written to you those accusations of his master, which you mention; because, from long acquaintance with his master, who lived some years in my house, I know him to be a sober, pious, and conscientious man; so that Newport, to whom you seem to have given too much credit, must have wronged Mr. Parker very much in his accounts, and have wronged Benny too, if he says Benny told him such things, for I am confident he never did.

As to the bad attendance afforded him in the smallpox, I believe, if the negro woman did not do her duty, her master or mistress would, if they had known it, have had that matter mended. But Mrs. Parker was herself, if I am not mistaken, sick at that time, and her child also. And though he gives the woman a bad character in general, all he charges her with in particular, is, that she never brought him what he called for directly, and sometimes not at all. He had the distemper favorably, and yet I suppose was bad enough to be, like other sick people, a little impatient, and perhaps might think a short time long, and sometimes call for things not proper for one in his condition.

As to clothes, I am frequently at New York, and I never saw him unprovided with what was good, decent, and sufficient. I was there no longer ago than March last, and he was then well clothed, and made no complaint to me of any kind. I heard both his master and mistress call upon him on Sunday morning to get ready to go to meeting, and tell him of his frequently delaying and shuffling till it was too late, and he made not the least objection about clothes. I did not think it any thing extraordinary, that he should be sometimes willing to evade going to meeting, for I believe it is the case with all boys, or almost all. I have brought up four or five myself, and have frequently observed, that if their shoes were bad, they would say nothing of a new pair till Sunday morning, just as the bell rung, when, if you asked them why they did not get ready, the answer was prepared, "I have no shoes," and so of other things, hats and the like; or if they knew of any thing that wanted mending, it was a secret till Sunday morning, and sometimes I believe they would rather tear a little, than be without the excuse.

As to going on petty errands, no boys love it, but all must do it. As soon as they become fit for better business, they naturally get rid of that, for the master's interest comes in to their relief. I make no doubt but Mr. Parker will take another apprentice, as soon as he can meet with a likely one. In the mean time I should be glad if Benny would exercise a little patience. There is a negro woman that does a great many of those errands.

I do not think his going on board the privateer arose from any difference between him and his master, or any ill usage he had received. When boys see prizes brought in, and quantities of money shared among the men, and their gay living, it fills their heads with notions, that half distract them, and put them quite out of conceit with trades, and the dull ways of getting money by working. This I suppose was Ben's case, the Catherine being just before arrived with three rich prizes; and that the glory of having taken a privateer of the enemy, for which both officers and men were highly extolled, treated, presented, &c. worked strongly upon his imagination, you will see, by his answer to my letter, is not unlikely. I send it to you enclosed. I wrote him largely on the occasion; and though he might possibly, to excuse that slip to others, complain of his place, you may see he says not a syllable of any such thing to me. My only son, before I permitted him to go to Albany,

left my house unknown to us all, and got on board a privateer, from whence I fetched him. No one imagined it was hard
usage at home, that made him do this. Every one, that knows
me, thinks I am too indulgent a parent, as well as master.

I shall tire you, perhaps, with the length of this letter; but
I am the more particular, in order, if possible, to satisfy your
mind about your son's situation. His master has, by a letter
this post, desired me to write to him about his staying out of
nights, sometimes all night, and refusing to give an account
where he spends his time, or in what company. This I had
not heard of before, though I perceive you have. I do not
wonder at his correcting him for that. If he was my own son,
I should think his master did not do his duty by him, if he
omitted it, for to be sure it is the high road to destruction.
And I think the correction very light, and not likely to be very
effectual, if the strokes left no marks.

His master says farther, as follows; —"I think I can't charge
my conscience with being much short of my duty to him. I
shall now desire you, if you have not done it already, to invite
him to lay his complaints before you, that I may know how
to remedy them." Thus far the words of his letter, which
giving me a fair opening to inquire into the affair, I shall accordingly do it, and I hope settle every thing to all your
satisfactions. In the mean time, I have laid by your letters
both to Mr. Parker and Benny, and shall not send them till I
hear again from you, because I think your appearing to give
ear to such groundless stories may give offence, and create a
greater misunderstanding, and because I think what you write
to Benny, about getting him discharged, may tend to unsettle
his mind, and therefore improper at this time.

I have a very good opinion of Benny in the main, and have
great hopes of his becoming a worthy man, his faults being
only such as are commonly incident to boys of his years, and
he has many good qualities, for which I love him. I never
knew an apprentice contented with the clothes allowed him
by his master, let them be what they would. Jemmy Franklin,
when with me, was always dissatisfied and grumbling. When
I was last in Boston, his aunt bid him go to a shop and please
himself, which the gentleman did, and bought a suit of
clothes on my account dearer by one half, than any I ever

afforded myself, one suit excepted; which I don't mention by way of complaint of Jemmy, for he and I are good friends, but only to show you the nature of boys.

The letters to Mr. Vanhorne were sent by Mr. Whitfield, under my cover.

I am, with love to brother and all yours, and duty to mother, to whom I have not time now to write, your affectionate brother,

June, 1748

THE EXAMPLE OF CONFUCIUS

To George Whitefield

Dear Sir,   *Philadelphia, July* 6, 1749.

Since your being in England, I have received two of your favours, and a box of books to be disposed of. It gives me great pleasure to hear of your welfare, and that you purpose soon to return to America.

We have no kind of news here worth writing to you. The affair of the building remains in *statu quo*, there having been no new application to the Assembly about it, nor any thing done in consequence of the former.

I have received no money on your account from Mr. Thanklin, or from Boston. Mrs. Read, and your other friends here in general, are well, and will rejoice to see you again.

I am glad to hear that you have frequent opportunities of preaching among the great. If you can gain them to a good and exemplary life, wonderful changes will follow in the manners of the lower ranks; for, *ad Exemplum Regis, &c.* On this principle Confucius, the famous eastern reformer, proceeded. When he saw his country sunk in vice, and wickedness of all kinds triumphant, he applied himself first to the grandees; and having by his doctrine won them to the cause of virtue, the commons followed in multitudes. The mode has a wonderful influence on mankind; and there are numbers that perhaps fear less the being in Hell, than out of the fashion! Our more western reformations began with the ignorant mob; and when numbers of them were gained, interest and party-views drew in the wise and great. Where both methods can be used, reformations are like to be more speedy. O that some method could be found to make them lasting! He that shall discover that, will, in my opinion, deserve more, ten thousand times, than the inventor of the longitude.

My wife and family join in the most cordial salutations to you and good Mrs. Whitefield. I am, dear Sir, your very affectionate friend, and most obliged humble servant,

MOVEMENT OF HURRICANES

To Jared Eliot

Dear Sir   Philada. Feb. 13. 1749,50

You desire to know my Thoughts about the N.E. Storms beginning to Leeward. Some Years since there was an Eclipse of the Moon at 9 in the Evening, which I intended to observe, but before 8 a Storm blew up at N E. and continued violent all Night and all next Day, the Sky thick clouded, dark and rainy, so that neither Moon nor Stars could be seen. The Storm did a great deal of Damage all along the Coast, for we had Accounts of it in the News Papers from Boston, Newport, New York, Maryland and Virginia. But what surpriz'd me, was to find in the Boston Newspapers an Account of an Observation of that Eclipse made there: For I thought, as the Storm came from the N E. it must have begun sooner at Boston than with us, and consequently have prevented such Observation. I wrote to my Brother about it, and he inform'd me, that the Eclipse was over there, an hour before the Storm began. Since which I have made Enquiries from time to time of Travellers, and of my Correspondents N Eastward and S. Westward, and observ'd the Accounts in the Newspapers from N England, N York, Maryland, Virginia and South Carolina, and I find it to be a constant Fact, that N East Storms begin to Leeward; and are often more violent there than farther to Windward. Thus the last October Storm, which with you was on the 8th. began on the 7th in Virginia and N

Carolina, and was most violent there. As to the Reason of this, I can only give you my Conjectures. Suppose a great Tract of Country, Land and Sea, to wit Florida and the Bay of Mexico, to have clear Weather for several Days, and to be heated by the Sun and its Air thereby exceedingly rarified; Suppose the Country North Eastward, as Pensilvania, New England, Nova Scotia, Newfoundland, &c. to be at the same time cover'd with Clouds, and its Air chill'd and condens'd. The rarified Air being lighter must rise, and the Dense Air next to it will press into its Place; that will be follow'd by the next denser Air, that by the next, and so on. Thus when I have a Fire in my Chimney, there is a Current of Air constantly flowing from the Door to the Chimney: but the beginning of the Motion was at the Chimney, where the Air being rarified by the Fire, rising, its Place was supply'd by the cooler Air that was next to it, and the Place of that by the next, and so on to the Door. So the Water in a long Sluice or Mill Race, being stop'd by a Gate, is at Rest like the Air in a Calm; but as soon as you open the Gate at one End to let it out, the Water next the Gate begins first to move, that which is next to it follows; and so tho' the Water proceeds forward to the Gate, the Motion which began there runs backwards, if one may so speak, to the upper End of the Race, where the Water is last in Motion. We have on this Continent a long Ridge of Mountains running from N East to S. West; and the Coast runs the same Course. These may, perhaps, contribute towards the Direction of the winds or at least influence them in some Degree, [   ]. If these Conjectures do not satisfy you, I wish to have yours on the Subject.

I doubt not but those Mountains which you mention contain valuable mines which Time will discover. I know of but one valuable Mine in this country which is that of Schuyler's in the Jerseys. This yields good Copper, and has turn'd out vast Wealth to the Owners. I was at it last Fall; but they were not then at Work; the Water is grown too hard for them; and they waited for a Fire Engine from England to drain their Pits; I suppose they will have that at Work next Summer; it costs them £1000 Sterling.

Col. John Schuyler, one of the Owners, has a Deer Park 5 Miles round, fenc'd with Cedar Logs, 5 Logs high, with chocks of Wood between; it contains variety of Land high and Low, woodland and clear. There are a great many Deer in it; and he expects in a few Years to be able to kill 200 head a Year, which will be a profitable Thing. He has likewise 600 Acres of Meadow, all within Bank. The Mine is not far from Passaic Falls, which I went also to see. They are very curious: the Water falls 70 foot perpendicular, as we were told; but we had nothing to measure with. It gives me great Pleasure that your Sentiments are in accord with mine. I like your Notion [   ]ming; and tho' perhaps it [   ]n prudent, as we are circumstanced [   ] them in the Proposals; I doubt not that they will in time become Part of the [   ]. It will be agreable to you to hear, and therefore I inform you, that our Subscription goes on with great Success, and we suppose will exceed £5000 of our Currency: We have bought for the Academy, the House that was built for Itinerant Preaching, which stands on a large Lot of Ground capable of receiving more Buildings to lodge the Scholars, if it should come to be a regular Colledge. The House is 100 foot long and 70 wide, built of Brick; very strong; and sufficiently high for three lofty Stories: I suppose it did not cost less than £2000 building; but we bought it for £775 18s. 11¾d: tho' it will cost us 3 or perhaps 400 more to make the Partitions and Floors, and fit up the Rooms. I send you enclos'd a Copy of our present Constitutions; but we expect a Charter from our Proprietaries this Summer, when they may prob'ly receive considerable Alterations. The Paper admonishes me that 'tis Time to conclude. I am, Sir, Your obliged humble Servant

"SECURING THE FRIENDSHIP OF THE INDIANS"

To James Parker

Dear Mr. *Parker*,   Philadelphia, March 20, 1750,1.

I have, as you desire, read the Manuscript you sent me; and am of Opinion, with the publick-spirited Author, that securing the Friendship of the *Indians* is of the greatest Consequence to these Colonies; and that the surest Means of doing it, are, to regulate the *Indian* Trade, so as to convince them, by Experience, that they may have the best and cheapest Goods, and the fairest Dealing from the *English*; and to unite the several Governments, so as to form a Strength that the *Indians* may depend on for Protection, in Case of a Rupture with the *French*; or apprehend great Danger from, if they should break with us.

This Union of the Colonies, however necessary, I apprehend is not to be brought about by the Means that have hitherto been used for that Purpose. A Governor of one Colony, who happens from some Circumstances in his own Government, to see the Necessity of such an Union, writes his Sentiments of the Matter to the other Governors, and desires them to recommend it to their respective Assemblies. They accordingly lay the Letters before those Assemblies, and perhaps recommend the Proposal in general Words. But Governors are often on ill Terms with their Assemblies, and seldom are the Men that have the most Influence among them. And perhaps some Governors, tho' they openly recommend the Scheme, may privately throw cold Water on it, as thinking additional publick Charges will make their People less able, or less willing to give to them. Or perhaps they do not clearly see the Necessity of it, and therefore do not very earnestly press the Consideration of it: And no one being present that has the Affair at Heart, to back it, to answer and remove Objections, *&c.* 'tis easily dropt, and nothing is done.—Such an Union is certainly necessary to us all, but more immediately so to your Government. Now, if you were to pick out half a Dozen Men of good Understanding and Address, and furnish them with a reasonable Scheme and proper Instructions, and send them in the Nature of Ambassadors to the other Colonies, where they might apply particularly to all the leading Men, and by proper Management get them to engage in promoting the Scheme; where, by being present, they would have the Opportunity of pressing the Affair both in publick and private, obviating Difficulties as they arise, answering Objections as soon as they are made, before they spread and gather Strength in the Minds of the People, *&c.* *&c.* I imagine such an Union might thereby be made and established: For reasonable sensible Men, can always make a reasonable Scheme appear such to other reasonable Men, if they take Pains, and have Time and Opportunity for it; unless from some Circumstances their Honesty and good Intentions are suspected. A voluntary Union entered into by the Colonies themselves, I think, would be preferable to one impos'd by Parliament; for it would be perhaps not much more difficult to procure, and more easy to alter and improve, as Circumstances should require, and Experience direct. It would be a very strange Thing, if six Nations of ignorant Savages should be capable of forming a Scheme for such an Union, and be able to execute it in such a Manner, as that it has subsisted Ages, and appears indissoluble; and yet that a like Union should be impracticable for ten or a Dozen *English* Colonies, to whom it is more necessary, and must be more advantageous; and who cannot be supposed to want an equal Understanding of their Interests.

Were there a general Council form'd by all the Colonies, and a general Governor appointed by the Crown to preside in that Council, or in some Manner to concur with and confirm their Acts, and take Care of the Execution; every Thing relating to Indian Affairs and the Defence of the Colonies, might be properly put under their Management. Each Colony should be represented by as many Members as it pays Sums of   Hundred Pounds into the common Treasury for the common Expence; which Treasury would perhaps be best and most equitably supply'd, by an equal Excise on strong Liquors in all the Colonies, the Produce never to be apply'd to the private Use of any Colony, but to the general Service. Perhaps if the Council were to meet successively at the Capitals of the several Colonies, they might thereby become better acquainted with the Circumstances, Interests, Strength or Weakness, &c. of all, and thence be able to judge better of Measures propos'd from time to time: At least it might be more satisfactory to the Colonies, if this were propos'd as a Part of the Scheme; for a Preference might create Jealousy and Dislike.

I believe the Place mention'd is a very suitable one to build a Fort on. In Times of Peace, Parties of the Garrisons of all Frontier Forts might be allowed to go out on Hunting Expeditions, with or without Indians, and have the Profit to themselves of the Skins they get: By this Means a Number of

Wood-Runners would be form'd, well acquainted with the Country, and of great Use in War Time, as Guides of Parties and Scouts, *&c.*—Every Indian is a Hunter; and as their Manner of making War, *viz.* by Skulking, Surprizing and Killing particular Persons and Families, is just the same as their Manner of Hunting, only changing the Object, Every Indian is a disciplin'd Soldier. Soldiers of this Kind are always wanted in the Colonies in an Indian War; for the *European* Military Discipline is of little Use in these Woods.

Publick Trading Houses would certainly have a good Effect towards regulating the private Trade; and preventing the Impositions of the private Traders; and therefore such should be established in suitable Places all along the Frontiers; and the Superintendant of the Trade, propos'd by the Author, would, I think, be a useful Officer.

The Observation concerning the Importation of *Germans* in too great Numbers into *Pennsylvania*, is, I believe, a very just one. This will in a few Years become a *German* Colony: Instead of their Learning our Language, we must learn their's, or live as in a foreign Country. Already the *English* begin to quit particular Neighbourhoods surrounded by *Dutch*, being made uneasy by the Disagreeableness of dissonant Manners; and in Time, Numbers will probably quit the Province for the same Reason. Besides, the *Dutch* under-live, and are thereby enabled to under-work and under-sell the *English*; who are thereby extreamly incommoded, and consequently disgusted, so that there can be no cordial Affection or Unity between the two Nations. How good Subjects they may make, and how faithful to the *British* Interest, is a Question worth considering. And in my Opinion, equal Numbers might have been spared from the *British* Islands without being miss'd there, and on proper Encouragement would have come over. I say without being miss'd, perhaps I might say without lessening the Number of People at Home. I question indeed, whether there be a Man the less in *Britain* for the Establishment of the Colonies. An Island can support but a certain Number of People: When all Employments are full, Multitudes refrain Marriage, 'till they can see how to maintain a Family. The Number of Englishmen in *England*, cannot by their present common Increase be doubled in a Thousand

Years; but if half of them were taken away and planted in *America*, where there is Room for them to encrease, and sufficient Employment and Subsistance; the Number of *Englishmen* would be doubled in 100 *Years*: For those left at home, would multiply in that Time so as to fill up the Vacancy, and those here would at least keep Pace with them.

Every one must approve the Proposal of encouraging a Number of sober discreet Smiths to reside among the *Indians*. They would doubtless be of great Service. The whole Subsistance of *Indians*, depends on keeping their Guns in order; and if they are obliged to make a Journey of two or three hundred Miles to an English Settlement to get a Lock mended; it may, besides the Trouble, occasion the Loss of their Hunting Season. They are People that think much of their temporal, but little of their spiritual Interests; and therefore, as he would be a most useful and necessary Man to them, a Smith is more likely to influence them than a Jesuit; provided he has a good common Understanding, and is from time to time well instructed.

I wish I could offer any Thing for the Improvement of the Author's Piece, but I have little Knowledge, and less Experience in these Matters. I think it ought to be printed; and should be glad there were a more general Communication of the Sentiments of judicious Men, on Subjects so generally interesting; it would certainly produce good Effects. Please to present my Respects to the Gentleman, and thank him for the Perusal of his Manuscript.

> I am,
> Yours affectionately.

A FLEXIBLE CATHETER

To John Franklin

Dear Brother   Philada. Dec. 8. 1752

Reflecting yesterday on your Desire to have a flexible Catheter, a Thought struck into my Mind how one might possibly be made: And lest you should not readily conceive it by any

Description of mine, I went immediately to the Silversmith's, and gave Directions for making one, (sitting by 'till it was finish'd), that it might be ready for this Post. But now it is done I have some Apprehensions that it may be too large to be easy: if so, a Silversmith can easily make it less, by twisting it on a smaller Wire, and putting a smaller Pipe to the End, if the Pipe be really necessary. This Machine may either be cover'd with a small fine Gut first clean'd and soak'd a Night in a Solution of Alum and Salt in Water, then rubb'd dry which will preserve it longer from Putrefaction: then wet again, and drawn on, and ty'd to the Pipes at each End where little Hollows are made for the Thread to bind in and the Surface greas'd: Or perhaps it may be used without the Gut, having only a little Tallow rubb'd over it, to smooth it and fill the Joints. I think it is as flexible as could be expected in a thing of the kind, and I imagine will readily comply with the Turns of the Passage, yet has Stiffness enough to be protruded; if not, the enclos'd Wire may be us'd to stiffen the hinder Part of the Pipe while the fore Part is push'd forward; and as it proceeds the Wire may be gradually withdrawn. The Tube is of such a Nature, that when you have Occasion to withdraw it its Diameter will lessen, whereby it will move more easily. It is also a kind of Scrue, and may be both withdrawn and introduc'd by turning. Experience is necessary for the right using of all new Tools or Instruments, and that will perhaps suggest some Improvements to this Instrument as well as better direct the Manner of Using it.

I have read Whytt on Lime Water. You desire my Thoughts on what he says. But what can I say? He relates Facts and Experiments; and they must be allow'd good, if not contradicted by other Facts and Experiments. May not one guess by holding Lime Water some time in one's Mouth, whether it is likely to injure the Bladder?

I know not what to advise, either as to the Injection, or the Operation. I can only pray God to direct you for the best, and to grant Success.

I am, my dear Brother Yours most affectionately

I find Whytt's Experiments are approv'd and recommended by Dr. Mead.

To Peter Collinson

SIR,

According to your request, I now send you the Arithmetical Curiosity, of which this is the history.

Being one day in the country, at the house of our common friend, the late learned Mr. *Logan*, he shewed me a folio *French* book, filled with magic squares, wrote, if I forget not, by one M. *Frenicle*, in which he said the author had discovered great ingenuity and dexterity in the management of numbers; and, though several other foreigners had distinguished themselves in the same way, he did not recollect that any one *Englishman* had done any thing of the kind remarkable.

I said, it was, perhaps, a mark of the good sense of our *English* mathematicians, that they would not spend their time in things that were merely *difficiles nugæ*, incapable of any useful application. He answered, that many of the arithmetical or mathematical questions, publickly proposed and answered in *England*, were equally trifling and useless. Perhaps the considering and answering such questions, I replied, may not be altogether useless, if it produces by practice an habitual readiness and exactness in mathematical disquisitions, which readiness may, on many occasions, be of real use. In the same way, says he, may the making of these squares be of use. I then confessed to him, that in my younger days, having once some leisure, (which I still think I might have employed more usefully) I had amused myself in making these kind of magic squares, and, at length, had acquired such a knack at it, that I could fill the cells of any magic square, of reasonable size, with a series of numbers as fast as I could write them, disposed in such a manner, as that the sums of every row, horizontal, perpendicular, or diagonal, should be equal; but not being satisfied with these, which I looked on as common and easy things, I had imposed on myself more difficult tasks, and succeeded in making other magic squares, with a variety of properties, and much more curious. He then shewed me several in the same book, of an uncommon and more curious

kind; but as I thought none of them equal to some I remembered to have made, he desired me to let him see them; and
accordingly, the next time I visited him, I carried him a
square of 8, which I found among my old papers, and which
I will now give you, with an account of its properties. (*See
Plate.*)

The properties are,

1. That every strait row (horizontal or vertical) of 8 numbers added together, makes 260, and half each row half 260.

2. That the bent row of 8 numbers, ascending and descending diagonally, *viz.* from 16 ascending to 10, and from 23 descending to 17; and every one of its parallel bent rows of 8
numbers, make 260.—Also the bent row from 52, descending
to 54, and from 43 ascending to 45; and every one of its parallel bent rows of 8 numbers, make 260.—Also the bent row
from 45 to 43 descending to the left, and from 23 to 17 descending to the right, and every one of its parallel bent rows
of 8 numbers make 260.—Also the bent row from 52 to 54
descending to the right, and from 10 to 16 descending to the
left, and every one of its parallel bent rows of 8 numbers make
260.—Also the parallel bent rows next to the above-mentioned, which are shortened to 3 numbers ascending, and 3
descending, *&c.* as from 53 to 4 ascending, and from 29 to 44
descending, make, with the 2 corner numbers, 260.—Also the
2 numbers 14, 61 ascending, and 36, 19 descending, with the
lower 4 numbers situated like them, *viz.* 50, 1, descending,
and 32, 47, ascending, make 260.—And, lastly, the 4 corner
numbers, with the 4 middle numbers, make 260.

So this magical square seems perfect in its kind. But these
are not all its properties; there are 5 other curious ones,
which, at some other time, I will explain to you.

Mr. *Logan* then shewed me an old arithmetical book, in
quarto, wrote, I think, by one *Stifelius*, which contained a
square of 16, that he said he should imagine must have been
a work of great labour; but if I forget not, it had only the
common properties of making the same sum, *viz.* 2056, in
every row, horizontal, vertical, and diagonal. Not willing to
be out-done by Mr *Stifelius*, even in the size of my square, I
went home, and made, that evening, the following magical
square of 16, which, besides having all the properties of the

A Magic Square of Squares.

200	217	232	249	8	25	40	57	72	89	104	121	136	153	168	181
58	39	26	7	250	231	218	199	186	167	154	135	122	103	90	71
198	219	230	251	6	27	38	59	70	91	102	123	134	155	166	187
60	37	28	5	252	229	220	197	188	165	156	133	124	101	92	69
201	216	233	248	9	24	41	56	73	88	105	120	137	152	169	184
55	42	23	10	247	234	215	202	183	170	151	138	119	106	87	74
203	214	235	246	11	22	43	54	75	86	107	118	139	150	171	182
53	44	21	12	245	236	213	204	181	172	149	140	117	108	85	76
205	212	237	244	13	20	45	52	77	84	109	116	141	148	173	180
51	46	19	14	243	238	211	206	179	174	147	142	115	110	83	78
207	210	239	242	15	18	47	50	79	82	111	114	143	146	175	178
49	48	17	16	241	240	209	208	177	176	145	144	113	112	81	80
196	221	228	253	4	29	36	61	68	93	100	125	132	157	164	189
62	35	30	3	254	227	222	195	190	163	158	131	126	99	94	67
194	223	226	255	2	31	34	63	66	95	98	127	130	159	162	191
64	33	32	1	256	225	224	193	192	161	160	129	128	97	96	65

S. Skillett Sculp.

foregoing square of 8, *i.e.* it would make the 2056 in all the same rows and diagonals, had this added, that a four square hole being cut in a piece of paper of such a size as to take in and shew through it, just 16 of the little squares, when laid on the greater square, the sum of the 16 numbers so appearing through the hole, wherever it was placed on the greater square, should likewise make 2056. This I sent to our friend the next morning, who, after some days, sent it back in a letter, with these words:—"I return to thee thy astonishing or most stupendous piece of the magical square, in which"— but the compliment is too extravagant, and therefore, for his sake, as well as my own, I ought not to repeat it. Nor is it necessary; for I make no question but you will readily allow this square of 16 to be the most magically magical of any magic square ever made by any magician. (*See the Plate.*)

I did not, however, end with squares, but composed also a magick circle, consisting of 8 concentric circles, and 8 radial rows, filled with a series of numbers, from 12 to 75, inclusive, so disposed as that the numbers of each circle, or each radial row, being added to the central number 12, they made exactly 360, the number of degrees in a circle; and this circle had, moreover, all the properties of the square of 8. If you desire it, I will send it; but at present, I believe, you have enough on this subject.

I am, &c.

1752?

"I NOW SEND YOU THE MAGICAL CIRCLE"

To Peter Collinson

SIR,

I am glad the perusal of the magical squares afforded you any amusement. I now send you the magical circle.

Its properties, besides those mentioned in my former, are these.

Half the number in any radial row, added with half the

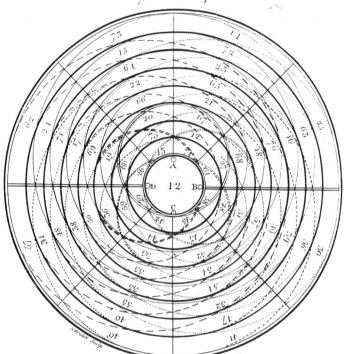

1. Magic Circle of Circles.

central number, make 180, equal to the number of degrees in a semi-circle.

Also half the numbers in any one of the concentric circles, taken either above or below the horizontal double line, with half the central number, make 180.

And if any four adjoining numbers, standing nearly in a square, be taken from any part, and added with half the central number, they make 180.

There are, moreover, included four other sets of circular spaces, excentric with respect to the first, each of these sets containing five spaces. The centers of the circles that bound them, are at A, B, C, and D. Each set, for the more easy distinguishing them from the first, are drawn with a different colour'd ink, red, blue, green, and yellow*.

These sets of excentric circular spaces intersect those of the concentric, and each other; and yet the numbers contained in each of the twenty excentric spaces, taken all around, make, with the central number, the same sum as those in each of the 8 concentric, *viz.* 360. The halves, also, of those drawn from the centers A and C, taken above or below the double horizontal line, and of those drawn from centers B and D, taken to the right or left of the vertical line, do, with half the central number, make just 180.

It may be observed, that there is not one of the numbers but what belongs at least to two of the different circular spaces; some to three, some to four, some to five; and yet they are all so placed as never to break the required number 360, in any of the 28 circular spaces within the primitive circle.

These interwoven circles make so perplexed an appearance, that it is not easy for the eye to trace every circle of numbers one would examine, through all the maze of circles intersected by it; but if you fix one foot of the compasses in either of the centers, and extend the other to any number in the circle you would examine belonging to that center, the moving foot will point the others out, by passing round over all the numbers of that circle successively.

I am, &c.

*In the plate they are distinguished by dashed or dotted lines, as different as the engraver could well make them.

1752?

SPOUTS AND WHIRLWINDS

To John Perkins

Dear Sir   Philada. Feb. 4. 1753

I ought to have wrote to you long since, in Answer to yours of Oct. 16. concerning the Water Spout: But Business partly, and partly a Desire of procuring further Information by Inquiry among my Seafaring Acquaintance, induc'd me to postpone Writing from time to time, till I am now almost asham'd to resume the Subject, not knowing but you may have forgot what has been said upon it.

Nothing certainly can be more improving to a Searcher into Nature, than Objections judiciously made to his Opinions, taken up perhaps too hastily: For such Objections oblige him to restudy the Point, consider every Circumstance carefully, compare Facts, make Experiments, weigh Arguments, and be slow in drawing Conclusions. And hence a sure Advantage results; for he either confirms a Truth, before too slightly supported; or discovers an Error and receives Instruction from the Objector.

In this View I consider the Objections and Remarks you sent me, and thank you for them sincerely: But how much soever my Inclinations lead me to philosophical Inquiries, I am so engag'd in Business public and private, that those more pleasing pursuits are frequently interrupted, and the Chain of Thought necessary to be closely continu'd in such Disquisitions, so broken and disjointed, that it is with Difficulty I satisfy myself in any of them. And I am now not much nearer a Conclusion in this Matter of the Spout, than when I first read your Letter.

Yet hoping we may in time sift out the Truth between us, I will send you my present Thoughts with some Observations on your Reasons, on the Accounts in the Transactions, and other Relations I have met with. Perhaps while I am writing some new Light may strike me—for I shall now be oblig'd to consider the Subject with a little more Attention. I agree with you, that by means of a Vacuum in a Whirlwind, Water cannot be suppos'd to rise in large Masses to the Region of the Clouds: For the Pressure of the surrounding Atmosphere could not force it up in a continu'd Body or Column to a much greater Height than thirty feet: But if there really is a Vacuum in the Center or near the Axis of Whirlwinds, then I think Water may rise in such Vacuum to that Height or to less Height as the Vacuum may be less perfect.

I had not read Stuart's Account in the Transactions for many Years before the receipt of your Letter and had quite forgot it; but now, on Viewing his Drafts, and considering his Descriptions, I think they seem to favour *my Hypothesis*; For he describes and draws Columns of Water of various Heights, terminating abruptly at the Top, exactly as Water would do when forc'd up by the Pressure of the Atmosphere into an exhausted Tube.

I must, however, no longer call it *my Hypothesis*, since I find Stuart had the same Thought tho' somewhat obscurely express'd, where he says, "he imagines this Phaenomenon may be solv'd by Suction (improperly so call'd) or rather Pulsion, as in the Application of a Cupping Glass to the Flesh, the Air being first voided by the kindled Flax."

In my Paper, I supposed a Whirlwind and a Spout, to be the same Thing, and to proceed from the same Cause; the only Difference between them being, that the one passes over Land, the other over Water. I find also, in the Transactions, that Mr. de la Pryme was of the same Opinion; for he there describes two Spouts as he calls them, which were seen at different Times at Hatfield in Yorkshire, whose Appearances in the Air were the same with those of the Spouts at Sea, and Effects the same with those of real Whirlwinds.

Whirlwinds have generally a progressive as well as a circular Motion; so had what is called the Spout at Topsham; See the Account of it in the Transactions; which also appears by its Effects described to have been a real Whirlwind. Water Spouts have likewise a progressive Motion. Tho' this is sometimes greater and sometimes less, in some violent, in others barely perceivable. The Whirlwind at Warrington continu'd long in Acrement Close.

Whirlwinds generally arise after Calms and great Heats: The same is observ'd of Water Spouts, which are therefore most frequent in the warm Latitudes. The Spout that happen'd in Cold Weather in the Downs, describ'd by Mr.

Gordon, in the Transactions, was for that reason thought extraordinary, but he remarks withal, that the Weather tho' cold when the Spout appeared, was soon after much colder; as we find it commonly less warm after a Whirlwind.

You agree that the Wind blows every way towards a Whirlwind from a large Space round; An intelligent Whaleman of Nantucket, informed me, that three of their Vessels which were out in search of Whales, happening to be becalmed lay in Sight of each other at about a League distance if I remember right nearly forming a Triangle; after some time a Water Spout appeared near the Middle of the Triangle, when a brisk Breeze of Wind also sprang up; and every Vessel made Sail and then it appeared to them all by the Setting of the Sails and the Course each Vessel stood, that the Spout was to Leeward of every one of them, and they all declar'd it to have been so when they happen'd afterwards in Company and came to confer about it. So that in this Particular likewise, Whirlwinds and Waterspouts agree.

But if that which appears a Water Spout at Sea, does sometimes in its progressive Motion, meet with and pass over Land, and there produce all the Phenomena and Effects of a Whirlwind, it should thence seem still more evident that a Whirlwind and Spout are the same. I send you herewith a Letter from an ingenious Physician of my Acquaintance, which gives one Instance of this, that fell within his Observation.

A Fluid moving from all Points horizontally towards a Center, must at that Center either ascend or descend. Water being in a Tub, if a Hole be open'd in the Middle of the Bottom, will flow from all Sides to the Center, and there descend in a Whirl. But Air flowing on and near the Surface of Land or Water from all Sides toward a Center, must at that Center ascend; the Land or Water hindering its Descent.

If these concentring Currents of Air be in the upper Region, they may indeed descend in the Spout or Whirlwind; but then when the united Current reach'd the Earth or Water it would spread and probably blow every way *from* the Center: There may be Whirlwinds of both kinds, but from the common observ'd Effects, I suspect the Rising one to be the

most common; and that when the upper Air descends, tis perhaps in a greater Body, extending wider and without much
whirling as in our Thunder Gusts. When Air descends in a
Spout or Whirlwind, I should rather expect it would press
the Roof of a House inwards, or force in the Tiles, Shingles
or Thatch; force a Boat down into the Water, or a Piece of
Timber into the Earth than that it would lift them up and
carry them away.

It has so happen'd that I have not met with any Accounts
of Spouts, that certainly descended. I suspect they are not
frequent. Please to communicate those you mention. The apparent dropping of a Pipe from the Clouds towards the Earth
or Sea, I will endeavour to explain hereafter.

The Augmentation of the Cloud, which, as I am inform'd
is generally if not always the case during a Spout, seems to
show an Ascent rather than a Descent of the Matter of which
such Cloud is composed. For a descending Spout one would
expect should diminish a Cloud. I own, however, that descending cold Air, may by Condensing the Vapours of a lower
Region form and increase Clouds, which I think is generally
the Case in our common Thunder Gusts, and therefore do
not lay great Stress on this Argument.

Whirlwinds and Spouts are not always tho' most commonly in the Day-time. The terrible Whirlwind which
damag'd a great Part of Rome June 11. 1749 happen'd in the
Night of that Day. The same was supposed to have been first
a Spout, for it is said to be beyond doubt that it gathered in
the neighbouring Sea, as it could be tracked from Ostia to
Rome. I find this in Pere Boschovich's Account of it, as
abridg'd in the Monthly Review for December 1750.

In that Account the Whirlwind is said to have appear'd as
a very black long and lofty Cloud, (discoverable notwithstanding the Darkness of the Night by its continually lightning or emitting Flashes on all Sides) pushing along with a
surprizing Swiftness, and within 3 or 4 feet of the Ground.
Its general Effects on Houses, were stripping off the Roofs,
blowing away Chimneys, breaking Doors and Windows,
forcing up the Floors, and unpaving the Rooms: [Some of these
Effects seem to agree well with a supposed Vacuum in the

Center of the Whirlwind;] and the very Rafters of the Houses were broke and dispersed, and even hurled against Houses at a considerable Distance, &c.

It seems by an Expression of Pere Boschovich's as if the Wind blew from all sides towards this Whirlwind for having carefully observ'd its Effects he concludes of all Whirlwinds "that their Motion is circular, and their Action *attractive*."

He observes on a Number of Histories of Whirlwinds &c. "that a common Effect of them is to carry up into the Air, Tiles, Stones and Animals themselves, which happen to be in their Course, and all kinds of Bodies unexceptionally, throwing them to a considerable Distance, with great Impetuosity." Such Effects seem to show a rising Current of Air.

I will endeavour to explain my Conceptions of this Matter, by Figures, representing a Plan and an Elevation of a Spout or Whirlwind.

I would only first beg to be allowed two or three Positions mentioned in my former Paper.

1st. That the lower Region of Air is often more heated and so more rarified, than the upper; consequently specifically lighter. The Coldness of the upper Region is manifested by the Hail which sometimes falls from it in a hot Day:

2dly. That heated Air may be very moist, and yet the Moisture so equally diffus'd and rarified, as not to be visible, till colder Air mixes with it, when it condenses and becomes visible. Thus our Breath, invisible in Summer, becomes visible in Winter.

Now let us suppose a Tract of Land or Sea of perhaps 60 Miles square unscreen'd by Clouds and unfann'd by Winds during great Part of a Summer's Day, or it may be for several Days successively till 'tis violently heated, together with the lower Region of Air in Contact with it, so that the said lower Air becomes specifically lighter than the superincumbent higher Region of the Atmosphere, in which the Clouds commonly float. Let us suppose also, that the Air surrounding this Tract has not been so much heated during those Days, and therefore remains heavier. The Consequence of this should be, as I imagine that the heated lighter Air being press'd on all Sides must ascend, and the heavier descend; and as this Rising cannot be in all Parts or the whole Area of the

Tract at once, for that would leave too extensive a Vacuum, the Rising will begin precisely in that Column that happens to be the lightest or most rarified; and the warm Air will flow horizontally from all Points to this Column, where the several Currents meeting and joining to rise, a Whirl is naturally formed, in the same Manner as a Whirl is formed in the Tub of Water by the descending Fluid flowing from all Sides of the Tub to the Hole in the Center.

And as the several Currents arrive at this central rising Column with a considerable Degree of horizontal Motion, they cannot suddenly change it to a vertical Motion, therefore as they gradually in approaching the Whirl decline from right to curve or circular Lines, so having join'd the Whirl they *ascend* by a spiral Motion; in the same Manner as the Water *descends* spirally thro' the Hole in the Tub before-mentioned.

Lastly, as the lower Air and nearest the Surface, is most rarified by the Heat of the Sun, that Air is most acted on by the Pressure of the surrounding cold and heavy Air which is to take its Place, consequently its Motion towards the Whirl is swiftest, and so the force of the lower Part of the Whirl or Trump strongest, and the Centrifugal Force of its Particles greatest; and hence the Vacuum round the Axis of the Whirl should be greatest near the Earth or Sea, and be gradually diminish'd as it approaches the Region of the Clouds, till it ends in a Point, as at A in Fig II. forming a long and sharp Cone.

In Fig I. which is a Plan or Ground Plot of a Whirlwind, the Circle V represents the central Vacuum.

Between aaaa and bbbb I suppose a Body of Air condens'd strongly by the Pressure of the Currents moving towards it from all sides without, and by its Centrifugal Force from within; moving round with prodigious Swiftness, (having as it were the Momenta of all the Currents $\rightarrow \rightarrow \rightarrow \rightarrow$ united in itself) and with a Power equal to its Swiftness and Density.

It is this whirling Body of Air between aaaa and bbbb that rises spirally. By its Force it tears Buildings to Pieces, twists up great Trees by the Roots, &c. and by its spiral Motion raises the Fragments so high till the Pressure of the surrounding and approaching Currents diminishing can no longer confine them to the Circle, or their own centrifugal Force

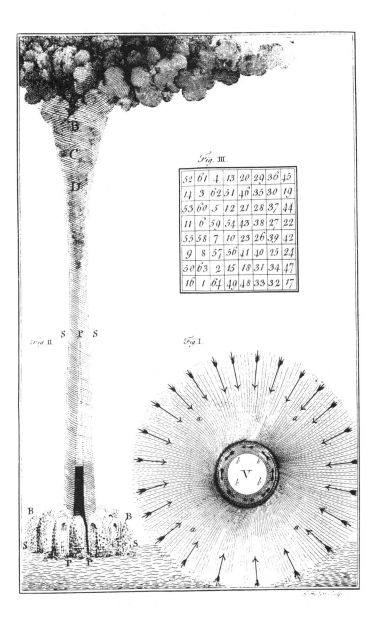

Fig. III.

52	61	4	13	20	29	36	45
14	3	62	51	46	35	30	19
53	60	5	12	21	28	37	44
11	6	59	54	43	38	27	22
55	58	7	10	23	26	39	42
9	8	57	56	41	40	25	24
50	63	2	15	18	31	34	47
16	1	64	49	48	33	32	17

Fig. II.

Fig. I.

encreasing grows too strong for such Pressure, when they fly off in Tangent Lines as Stones out of a Sling, and fall on all Sides and at great Distances.

If it happens at Sea, the Water between aaaa and bbbb will be violently agitated and driven about, and parts of it raised with the spiral Current, and thrown about so as to form a Bushlike Appearance.

This Circle is of various Diameters, sometimes very large.

If the Vacuum passes over Water the Water may rise in it in a Body or Column to near the Height of 32 feet. If it passes over Houses, it may burst their Windows or Walls outwards, pluck off the Roofs and blow up the Floors, by the Sudden Rarefaction of the Air contain'd within such Buildings, the outward Pressure of the Atmosphere being suddenly taken off; So the stop'd Bottle of Air bursts under the exhausted Receiver of the Air Pump.

Fig II. is to represent the Elevation of a Water Spout; wherein I suppose PPP to be the Cone, at first a Vacuum till WW the rising Column of Water has fill'd so much of it. SSSS the Spiral Whirl of Air surrounding the Vacuum and continu'd higher in a close Column after the Vacuum ends in the Point P. till it reach the cool Region of the Air. B.B. the Bush describ'd by Stuart, surrounding the Foot of the Column of Water.

Now I suppose this Whirl of Air will at first be as invisible as the Air itself tho' reaching in reality from the Water to the Region of cool Air in which our low Summer Thunder Clouds commonly float; but presently it will become visible at its Extremities. *At its lower End* by the Agitation of the Water, under the Whirling Part of the Circle, between P and S. forming Stuart's Bush, and by the Swelling and Rising of the Water in the beginning Vacuum, which is at first a small low broad Cone whose Top gradually rises and sharpens as the Force of the Whirl increases. *At its upper End*, it becomes visible by the Warm Air brought up to the cooler Region, where its Moisture begins to be condens'd into thick Vapour by the Cold, and is seen first at A. the highest Parts, which being now cool'd, condenses what rises next at B. which condenses that at C; and that condenses what is rising at D. The Cold operating by the Contact of the Vapours faster in a right

Line downwards, than the Vapours themselves can climb in a spiral Line upwards; they climb however, and as by continual Addition they grow denser and consequently their centrifugal Force greater, and being risen above the concentrating Currents that compose the Whirl, they flie off, spread and form a Cloud.

It seems easy to conceive, how by this successive Condensation from above the Spout appears to drop or descend from the Cloud, tho' the Materials of which it is composed are all the while ascending.

The Condensation of the Moisture contain'd in so great a Quantity of warm Air as may be suppos'd to rise in a short Time in this prodigiously rapid Whirl, is perhaps sufficient to form a great Extent of Cloud, tho' the Spout should be over Land as those at Hatfield; and if the Land happens not to be very dusty, perhaps the lower Part of the Spout will scarce become visible at all; Tho' the upper or what is commonly call'd the descending Part be very distinctly seen.

The same may happen at Sea, in case the Whirl is not violent enough to make a high Vacuum and raise the Column, &c. In such Case the upper Part ABCD only will be visible, and the Bush perhaps below.

But if the Whirl be strong, and there be much Dust on the Land, or the Column WW be rais'd from the Water; then the lower Part becomes visible, and sometimes even united to the upper Part. For the Dust may be carried up in the Spiral Whirl till it reach the Region where the Vapour is condens'd, and rise with that even to the Clouds. And the Friction of the Whirling Air on the Sides of the Column WW may detach great Quantities of its Water, break it into Drops and carry them up in the Spiral Whirl mix'd with the Air; the heavier Drops may indeed fly off, and fall in a Shower round the Spout; but much of it will be broken into Vapour, yet visible; and thus in both Cases, by Dust at Land, and by Water at Sea, the whole Tube may be darkned and render'd visible.

As the Whirl weakens, the Tube may (in Appearance) separate in the Middle; the Column of Water subsiding, and the superior condens'd Part drawing up to the Cloud. Yet still the Tube or Whirl of Air may remain entire, the middle only becoming invisible, as not containing visible Matter.

Dr. Stuart says, "it was observable of all the Spouts he saw, but more perceptible of the great One; that towards the End it began to appear like a hollow Canal, only black in the Borders but white in the Middle, and tho' at first it was altogether black and opaque, yet now one could very distinctly perceive the Sea Water to fly up along the Middle of this Canal, as Smoak up a Chimney." And Dr. Mather describing a Whirlwind says, "a thick dark small Cloud arose, with a Pillar of Light in it, of about 8 or 10 foot Diameter and passed along the Ground in a Tract not wider than a Street, horribly tearing up Trees by the Roots, blowing them up in the Air like Feathers, and throwing up Stones of great Weight to a considerable Height in the Air, &c."

These Accounts, the one of Water Spouts, the other of a Whirlwind, seem in this particular to agree; what one Gentleman describes as a Tube black in the Borders, and white in the middle; the other calls a black Cloud with a Pillar of Light in it; the latter Expression has only a little more of the marvellous, but the Thing is the same. And it seems not very difficult to understand. When Dr. Stuarts Spouts were full charg'd; that is, when the whirling Pipe of Air was filled, between aaaa and bbbb [Fig. I], with Quantities of Drops and Vapour torn off from the Column WW [Fig. II], the whole was render'd so dark as that it could not be seen thro', nor the spiral ascending Motion discover'd; but when the Quantity ascending lessen'd, the Pipe became more transparent, and the ascending Motion visible. For by Inspection of this Figure in the Margin representing a Section of our Spout with the Vacuum in the Middle, it is plain, that if we look at such a hollow Pipe in the Direction of the Arrows, and suppose opacous Particles to be equally mix'd in the Space between the two circular Lines, both the Part between the Arrows a and b and that between the Arrows c and d, will appear much darker than that between b and c; as there must be many more of those opaque Particles in the Line of Vision across the Sides than across the Middle. It is thus, that a Hair in a Microscope evidently appears to be a Pipe, the Sides shewing darker than the Middle. Dr. Mather's Whirl was probably fill'd with Dust; the Sides were very dark, but the Vacuum within rendering the Middle more transparent he

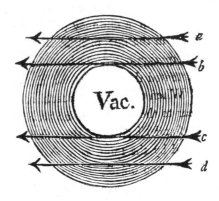

calls it a Pillar of Light. It was in this more transparent Part between b and c that Stuart could see the spiral Motion of the Vapours, whose Lines on the nearest and farthest Side of this transparent Part crossing each other, represented Smoke ascending in a Chimney; for the Quantity being still too great in the Line of Sight thro' the Sides of the Tube, the Motion could not be discover'd there, and so they represented the solid Sides of the Chimney.

When the Vapours reach in the Pipe from the Clouds near to the Earth, it is no Wonder now to those who understand Electricity, that Flashes of Lightning should descend by the Spout, as in that at Rome.

But you object, If Water may be thus carried into the Clouds, why have we no salt Rains? The Objection is strong and reasonable; and I know not whether I can answer it to your Satisfaction. I never heard but of one Salt Rain, and that was where a Spout passed pretty near a Ship, so I suppose it to be only the Drops thrown off from the Spout by the centrifugal Force, (as the Birds were at Hatfield) when they had been carried so high as to be above or to be too strongly centrifugal for the Pressure of the concurring Winds surrounding it. And indeed I believe there can be no other kind of Salt Rain; for it has pleased the Goodness of God so to order it, that the Particles of Air will not attract the Particles of Salt; tho' they strongly attract Water. Hence tho' all Metals, even Gold, may be united with Air and render'd volatile,

Salt remains fix'd in the Fire, and no Heat can force it up to any considerable Height or oblige the Air to hold it; Hence when Salt rises as it will a little Way into Air with Water, there is instantly a Separation made; the Particles of Water adhere to the Air, and the Particles of Salt fall down again, as if repell'd and forc'd off from the Water by some Power in the Air: Or as some Metals dissolv'd in a proper Menstruum will quit the Solvent when other matter approaches, and adhere to that, so the Water quits the Salt and embraces the Air but Air will not embrace the Salt and quit the Water. Otherwise, our Rains would indeed be salt, and every Tree and Plant on the Face of the Earth be destroy'd, with all the Animals that depend on them for Subsistence. He who hath proportioned and given proper Qualities to all Things, was not unmindful of this. Let us adore him with Praise and Thanksgiving!

By some Accounts of Seamen, it seems the Column of Water WW sometimes falls suddenly, and if it be as some say 15 or 20 Yards Diameter it must fall with great Force, and they may well fear for their Ships. By one Account in the Transactions of a Spout that fell at Coln in Lancashire one would think the Column is sometimes lifted off from the Water, and carried over Land, and there let fall in a Body; but this I suppose happens rarely.

Stuart describes his Spouts as appearing no bigger than a Mast! and sometimes less: but they were at a League and half Distance.

I think I formerly read in Dampier, or some other Voyager, that a Spout in its progressive Motion went over a Ship becalmed on the Coast of Guinea: and first threw her down on one Side, carrying away her Foremast; then suddenly, whipt her up, and threw her down on the other Side, carrying away her Mizen Mast; and the whole was over in an Instant. I suppose the first Mischief was done by the foreside of the Whirl, the latter by the hinder Side, their Motion being contrary.

I suppose a Whirlwind or Spout may be stationary when the concurring Winds are equal; but if unequal, the Whirl acquires a progressive Motion, in the direction of the Strongest Pressure.

Where the Wind that gives the progressive Motion becomes stronger below than above, or above than below, the Spout will be bent, and the Cause ceasing, straiten again.

Your Queries towards the End of your Paper, appear judicious and worth considering. At present I am not furnish'd with Facts sufficient to make any pertinent Answer to them. And this Paper has already a sufficient Quantity of Conjecture.

Your manner of accommodating the Accounts to your Hypothesis, of descending Spouts, is I own ingenious; and perhaps that Hypothesis may be true: I will consider it farther; but as yet I am not satisfy'd with it, tho' hereafter I may be. Here you have my Method of Accounting for the principal Phaenomena, which I submit to your candid Examination. If my Hypothesis is not the Truth itself, it is least as naked: For I have not with some of our learned Moderns disguis'd my Nonsense in Greek, cloth'd it in Algebra, or adorn'd it with Fluxions. And as I now seem to have almost written a Book instead of a Letter, you will think it high time I should conclude, which I beg Leave to do with assuring you that I am most sincerely, Dear Sir Your obliged Friend and humble Servant.

ELECTRICITY, THE TRANSIT OF MERCURY, AND A NORTHWEST PASSAGE

To Cadwallader Colden

Dear Sir   Philada. Feb. 28. 1753

I return you herewith Professor Kanster's Remarks. As far as I am able to judge, the Translation is just, and your Answer a good one. I am pleas'd with the Omission of that part of a Paragraph relating to the German and Pensilvanian Electricians, and have corrected the Copy as you direct. I have but one other Alteration to propose, which is, to omit some Part of the last Paragraph, and read the rest thus;—"After all, Mr. Colden must think himself obliged to the Professor, for exposing the Difficulties his Treatise lies under in the Opinion of others, as thereby an Opportunity is given of explaining his Doctrine more fully to their Satisfaction." For it seems to me not so proper to make Acknowledgement for his Translating your Piece, as if it were a Favour, when he tells the World he did it by Command: And I apprehend it unnecessary, and that it may look like too great a Fondness for Complement, to draw one from him by Consequence; viz. *That he did not think it a trifling Performance, or he would not have taken the Trouble, &c.* since he himself freely says, *that the many new, good and just Thoughts contain'd in it, made him willingly undertake the Task enjoin'd him.* Besides that it is not clear he could have refus'd to obey the Command he received, whatever might have been his private Sentiments. The Ship I intended to forward these Papers by to Mr. Collinson, has stay'd much longer than I expected, and now I am told will not sail before the End of next Month, so that I may possibly receive your Directions concerning this propos'd Alteration before she sails.

I find I was not wrong in my Apprehensions that your Book would be incorrectly printed. I hope however, that the Errata will be in England time enough to be published with the Work; and I thank you for sending them to me. I have corrected the Book accordingly, and given it one Reading; but it is not a Piece to make sudden Remarks on, as one might of a Poem or other Performance on common Subjects. I must read and consider it yet more attentively; at present I can only tell you, that some Things in it please me exceedingly; some I do not yet clearly understand; and one or two Positions I think wrong; of all which you shall hear more fully in my next. On the whole it gives me great Satisfaction, when I consider it as a Work that will not only improve Philosophy, but do Honour to America.

I am sorry I have not, as you expect, anything new to communicate to you on the Subject of Electricity. My Time and Thoughts have of late been much engag'd in other Matters: And ever since I heard of your being furnish'd with an Apparatus, I have hoped rather to receive Information of new Discoveries from you, than expected to send you any. If your other philosophical Pursuits do not prevent your Application to the Experiments you propos'd to make on various Salts, &c. I shall still hope it. Your Skill and Expertness in Mathematical Computations, will afford you an Advantage in these

Disquisitions, that I lament the want of, who am like a Man searching for something in a dark Room, where I can only grope and guess; while you proceed with a Candle in your Hand.

We are preparing here to make accurate Observations on the approaching Transit of Mercury over the Sun. You will oblige us much by sending the Account you have received from Lord Macclesfield of his great mural Quadrant. I congratulate you on your Discovery of a new Motion in the Earth's Axis: You will, I see, render your Name immortal.

I believe I have not before told you, that I have procur'd a Subscription here of £1500 to fit out a Vessel in Search of a NWest Passage: she sails in a few Days, and is called the Argo, commanded by Mr. Swaine, who was in the last Expedition in the California, Author of a Journal of that Voyage in two Volumes. We think the Attempt laudable, whatever may be the Success: if he fails, *Magnis tamen excidit ausis.*

With great Esteem, I am, Dear Sir, Your most humble Servant

THE SUPPORT OF THE POOR

To Peter Collinson

Sir   Philadelphia May 9th. 1753

I received your Favour of the 29th. August last and thank you for the kind and judicious remarks you have made on my little Piece. Whatever further occurs to you on the same subject, you will much oblige me in communicating it.

I have often observed with wonder, that Temper of the poor English Manufacturers and day Labourers which you mention, and acknowledge it to be pretty general. When any of them happen to come here, where Labour is much better paid than in England, their Industry seems to diminish in equal proportion. But it is not so with the German Labourers; They retain the habitual Industry and Frugality they bring with them, and now receiving higher Wages an accumulation arises that makes them all rich.

When I consider, that the English are the Offspring of Germans, that the Climate they live in is much of the same Temperature; when I can see nothing in Nature that should create this Difference, I am apt to suspect it must arise from Institution, and I have sometimes doubted, whether the Laws peculiar to England which compel the Rich to maintain the Poor, have not given the latter, a Dependance that very much lessens the care of providing against the wants of old Age.

I have heard it remarked that the Poor in Protestant Countries on the Continent of Europe, are generally more industrious than those of Popish Countries, may not the more numerous foundations in the latter for the relief of the poor have some effect towards rendering them less provident. To relieve the misfortunes of our fellow creatures is concurring with the Deity, 'tis Godlike, but if we provide encouragements for Laziness, and supports for Folly, may it not be found fighting against the order of God and Nature, which perhaps has appointed Want and Misery as the proper Punishments for, and Cautions against as well as necessary consequences of Idleness and Extravagancy.

Whenever we attempt to mend the scheme of Providence and to interfere in the Government of the World, we had need be very circumspect lest we do more harm than Good. In New England they once thought Black-birds useless and mischievous to their corn, they made Laws to destroy them, the consequence was, the Black-birds were diminished but a kind of Worms which devoured their Grass, and which the Black-birds had been used to feed on encreased prodigiously; Then finding their Loss in Grass much greater than their saving in corn they wished again for their Black-birds.

We had here some years since a Transylvanian Tartar, who had travelled much in the East, and came hither merely to see the West, intending to go home thro' the spanish West Indies, China &c. He asked me one day what I thought might be the Reason that so many and such numerous nations, as the Tartars in Europe and Asia, the Indians in America, and the Negroes in Africa, continued a wandring careless Life, and refused to live in Cities, and to cultivate the arts they saw practiced by the civilized part of Mankind. While I was considering what answer to make him; I'll tell you, says he in his broken English, God make man for Paradise, he make him for to live lazy; man make God angry, God turn him out of Paradise, and bid him work; man no love work; he want to go to Paradise again, he want to live lazy; so all mankind love lazy. Howe'er this may be it seems certain, that the hope of becoming at some time of Life free from the necessity of care and Labour, together with fear of penury, are the main-springs of most peoples industry.

To those indeed who have been educated in elegant plenty, even the provision made for the poor may appear misery, but to those who have scarce ever been better provided for, such provision may seem quite good and sufficient, these latter have then nothing to fear worse than their present Conditions, and scarce hope for any thing better than a Parish maintainance; so that there is only the difficulty of getting that maintainance allowed while they are able to work, or a little shame they suppose attending it, that can induce them to work at all, and what they do will only be from hand to mouth.

The proneness of human Nature to a life of ease, of freedom from care and labour appears strongly in the little success that has hitherto attended every attempt to civilize our American Indians, in their present way of living, almost all their Wants are supplied by the spontaneous Productions of Nature, with the addition of very little labour, if hunting and fishing may indeed be called labour when Game is so plenty, they visit us frequently, and see the advantages that Arts, Sciences, and compact Society procure us, they are not deficient in natural understanding and yet they have never shewn any Inclination to change their manner of life for ours, or to learn any of our Arts; When an Indian Child has been brought up among us, taught our language and habituated to our Customs, yet if he goes to see his relations and make one Indian Ramble with them, there is no perswading him ever to return, and that this is not natural to them merely as Indians, but as men, is plain from this, that when white persons of either sex have been taken prisoners young by the Indians, and lived a while among them, tho' ransomed by their Friends, and treated with all imaginable tenderness to prevail with them to stay among the English, yet in a Short time they become disgusted with our manner of life, and the care and pains that are necessary to support it, and take the first good Opportunity of escaping again into the Woods, from whence there is no reclaiming them. One instance I remember to have heard, where the person was brought home to possess a good Estate; but finding some care necessary to keep it together, he relinquished it to a younger Brother, reserving to himself nothing but a gun and a match-Coat, with which he took his way again to the Wilderness.

Though they have few but natural wants and those easily supplied. But with us are infinite Artificial wants, no less craving than those of Nature, and much more difficult to satisfy; so that I am apt to imagine that close Societies subsisting by Labour and Arts, arose first not from choice, but from necessity: When numbers being driven by war from their hunting grounds and prevented by seas or by other nations were crowded together into some narrow Territories, which without labour would not afford them Food. However as matters now stand with us, care and industry seem absolutely necessary to our well being; they should therefore have every Encouragement we can invent, and not one Motive to diligence be subtracted, and the support of the Poor should not be by maintaining them in Idleness, But by employing them in some kind of labour suited to their Abilities of body &c. as I am informed of late begins to be the practice in many parts of England, where work houses are erected for that purpose. If these were general I should think the Poor would be more careful and work voluntarily and lay up something for themselves against a rainy day, rather than run the risque of being obliged to work at the pleasure of others for a bare subsistence and that too under confinement. The little value Indians set on what we prize so highly under the name of Learning appears from a pleasant passage that happened some years since at a Treaty between one of our Colonies and the Six Nations; when every thing had been settled to the Satisfaction of both sides, and nothing remained but a mutual exchange of civilities, the English Commissioners told the Indians, they had in their Country a College for the instruction of Youth who were there taught various languages, Arts, and Sciences; that there was a particular foundation in favour of the Indians to defray the expense of the Education of any of their sons who should desire to take the Benefit of it. And now if the Indians would accept of the Offer, the English would take half a dozen of their brightest lads and bring them up in the Best manner; The Indians after consulting on the proposal replied that it was remembered some of their Youths had formerly been educated in that College, but it had been observed that for a long time after they returned to their Friends, they were absolutely good for nothing being neither acquainted with the true methods of killing deer, catching Beaver or surprizing an enemy. The Proposition however, they looked on as a mark of the kindness and good will of the English to the Indian Nations which merited a grateful return; and therefore if the English Gentlemen would send a dozen or two of their Children to Onondago the great Council would take care of their Education, bring them up in really what was the best manner and make men of them.

I am perfectly of your mind, that measures of great Temper are necessary with the Germans: and am not without Apprehensions, that thro' their indiscretion or Ours, or both, great disorders and inconveniences may one day arise among us; Those who come hither are generally of the most ignorant Stupid Sort of their own Nation, and as Ignorance is often attended with Credulity when Knavery would mislead it, and with Suspicion when Honesty would set it right; and as few of the English understand the German Language, and so cannot address them either from the Press or Pulpit, 'tis almost impossible to remove any prejudices they once entertain. Their own Clergy have very little influence over the people; who seem to take an uncommon pleasure in abusing and discharging the Minister on every trivial occasion. Not being used to Liberty, they know not how to make a modest use of it; and as Kolben says of the young Hottentots, that they are not esteemed men till they have shewn their manhood by beating their mothers, so these seem to think themselves not free, till they can feel their liberty in abusing and insulting their Teachers. Thus they are under no restraint of Ecclesiastical Government; They behave, however, submissively enough at present to the Civil Government which I wish they may continue to do: For I remember when they modestly declined intermeddling in our Elections, but now they come in droves, and carry all before them, except in one or two Counties; Few of their children in the Country learn English; they import many Books from Germany; and of the six printing houses in the Province, two are entirely German, two half German half English, and but two entirely English; They have one German News-paper, and one half German. Advertisments intended to be general are now printed in Dutch and English; the Signs in our Streets have inscriptions in both languages, and in some places only German: They begin of late to make all their Bonds and other legal Writings in their own Language, which (though I think it ought not to be) are allowed good in our Courts, where the German Business so encreases that there is continual need of Interpreters; and I suppose in a few years they will be also necessary in the Assembly, to tell one half of our Legislators what the other half say; In short unless the stream of their importation could be turned from this to other Colonies, as you very judiciously propose, they will soon so out number us, that all the advantages we have will not in My Opinion be able to preserve our language, and even our Government will become precarious. The French who watch all advantages, are now themselves making a German settlement back of us in the Ilinoes Country, and by means of those Germans they may in time come to an understanding with ours, and indeed in the last war our Germans shewed a general disposition that seems to bode us no good; for when the English who were not Quakers, alarmed by the danger arising from the defenceless state of our Country entered unanimously into an Association within this Government and the lower Countries raised armed and Disciplined near 10,000 men, the Germans except a very few in proportion to their numbers refused to engage in it, giving out one among another, and even in print, that if they were quiet the French should they take the Country would not molest them; at the same time abusing the Philadelphians for fitting out Privateers against the Enemy; and representing the trouble hazard and Expence of defending the Province, as a greater inconvenience than any that might be expected from a change of Government. Yet I am not for refusing entirely to admit them into our Colonies: all that seems to be necessary is, to distribute them more equally, mix them with the English, establish English Schools where they are now too thick settled, and take some care to prevent the practice lately fallen into by some of the Ship Owners, of sweeping the German Goals to make up the number of their Passengers. I say I am not against the Admission of Germans in general, for they have their Virtues, their industry and frugality is exemplary; They are excellent husbandmen and contribute greatly to the improvement of a Country.

I pray God long to preserve to Great Britain the English Laws, Manners, Liberties and Religion notwithstanding the complaints so frequent in Your public papers, of the prevailing corruption and degeneracy of your People; I know you have a great deal of Virtue still subsisting among you, and I hope the Constitution is not so near a dissolution, as some seem to apprehend; I do not think you are generally become such Slaves to your Vices, as to draw down that *Justice* Milton speaks of when he says that

> ——sometimes Nations will descend so low
> From reason, which is virtue, that no Wrong,
> But Justice, and some fatal curse annex'd
> Deprives them of their *outward* liberty,
> Their *inward* lost.   Parad: lost.

In history we find that Piety, Public Spirit and military Prowess have their Flows, as well as their ebbs, in every nation, and that the Tide is never so low but it may rise again; But should this dreaded fatal change happen in my time, how should I even in the midst of the Affliction rejoice, if we have been able to preserve those invaluable treasures, and can invite the good among you to come and partake of them! O let not Britain seek to oppress us, but like an affectionate parent endeavour to secure freedom to her children; they may be able one day to assist her in defending her own—Whereas a Mortification begun in the Foot may spread upwards to the destruction of the nobler parts of the Body.

I fear I have already extended this rambling letter beyond your patience, and therefore conclude with requesting your acceptance of the inclosed Pamphlet from Sir Your most humble servant

DOING GOOD AND RELIGIOUS BIGOTS

To Joseph Huey

Sir,   Philada. June 6. 1753

I received your kind Letter of the 2d Inst. and am glad to hear that you increase in Strength; I hope you will continue mending till you recover your former Health and Firmness. Let me know whether you still use the cold Bath, and what Effect it has.

As to the Kindness you mention, I wish it could have been of more Service to you. But if it had, the only Thanks I should desire is, that you would always be equally ready to serve any other Person that may need your Assistance, and so let good Offices go round, for Mankind are all of a Family.

For my own Part, when I am employed in serving others, I do not look upon my self as conferring Favours, but as paying Debts. In my Travels and since my Settlement I have received much Kindness from Men, to whom I shall never have any Opportunity of making the least direct Return. And numberless Mercies from God, who is infinitely above being benefited by our Services. These Kindnesses from Men I can therefore only return on their Fellow-Men; and I can only show my Gratitude for those Mercies from God, by a Readiness to help his other Children and my Brethren. For I do not think that Thanks, and Compliments, tho' repeated Weekly, can discharge our real Obligations to each other, and much less those to our Creator.

You will see in this my Notion of Good Works, that I am far from expecting (as you suppose) that I shall merit Heaven by them. By Heaven we understand, a State of Happiness, infinite in Degree, and eternal in Duration: I can do nothing to deserve such Reward: He that for giving a Draught of Water to a thirsty Person should expect to be paid with a good Plantation, would be modest in his Demands, compar'd with those who think they deserve Heaven for the little Good they do on Earth. Even the mix'd imperfect Pleasures we enjoy in this World are rather from God's Goodness than our Merit; how much more such Happiness of Heaven. For my own part, I have not the Vanity to think I deserve it, the Folly to expect it, nor the Ambition to desire it; but content myself in submitting to the Will and Disposal of that God who made me, who has hitherto preserv'd and bless'd me, and in whose fatherly Goodness I may well confide, that he will never make me miserable, and that even the Afflictions I may at any time suffer shall tend to my Benefit.

The Faith you mention has doubtless its use in the World; I do not desire to see it diminished, nor would I endeavour to lessen it in any Man. But I wish it were more productive of Good Works than I have generally seen it: I mean real good Works, Works of Kindness, Charity, Mercy, and Publick Spirit; not Holiday-keeping, Sermon-Reading or Hearing, performing Church Ceremonies, or making long Prayers, fill'd with Flatteries and Compliments, despis'd even by wise Men, and much less capable of pleasing the Deity. The Worship of God is a Duty, the hearing and reading of Sermons may be useful; but if Men rest in Hearing and Praying, as too many do, it is as if a Tree should value itself on being water'd and putting forth Leaves, tho' it never produc'd any Fruit.

Your great Master tho't much less of these outward Appearances and Professions than many of his modern Disciples. He prefer'd the Doers of the Word to the meer Hearers; the Son that seemingly refus'd to obey his Father and yet perform'd his Commands, to him that profess'd his Readiness but neglected the Works; the heretical but charitable Samaritan, to the uncharitable tho' orthodox Priest and sanctified Levite: and those who gave Food to the hungry, Drink to the Thirsty, Raiment to the Naked, Entertainment to the Stranger, and Relief to the Sick, &c. tho' they never heard of his Name, he declares shall in the last Day be accepted, when those who cry Lord, Lord; who value themselves on their Faith tho' great enough to perform Miracles but have neglected good Works shall be rejected. He profess'd that he came not to call the Righteous but Sinners to Repentance; which imply'd his modest Opinion that there were some in his Time so good that they need not hear even him for Improvement; but now a days we have scarce a little Parson, that does not think it the Duty of every Man within his Reach to sit under his petty Ministrations, and that whoever omits them offends God. I wish to such more Humility, and to you Health and Happiness, being Your Friend and Servant

"KISSES IN THAT WIND"

To Catharine Ray

Dear Katy,   Philada. March 4. 1755

Your kind Letter of January 20. is but just come to hand, and I take this first Opportunity of acknowledging the Favour.

It gives me great Pleasure to hear that you got home safe and well that Day. I thought too much was hazarded, when I saw you put off to Sea in that very little Skiff, toss'd by every Wave. But the Call was strong and just, a sick Parent. I stood on the Shore, and look'd after you, till I could no longer distinguish you, even with my Glass; then returned to your Sister's, praying for your safe Passage. Towards Evening all agreed that you must certainly be arriv'd before that time, the Weather having been so favourable; which made me more easy and chearful, for I had been truly concern'd for you.

I left New England slowly, and with great Reluctance: Short Days Journeys, and loitering Visits on the Road, for three or four Weeks, manifested my Unwillingness to quit a Country in which I drew my first Breath, spent my earliest and most pleasant Days, and had now received so many fresh Marks of the People's Goodness and Benevolence, in the kind and affectionate Treatment I had every where met with. I almost forgot I had a Home; till I was more than half-way towards it; till I had, one by one, parted with all my New England Friends, and was got into the western Borders of Connecticut, among meer Strangers: then, like an old Man, who, having buried all he lov'd in this World, begins to think of Heaven, I begun to think of and wish for Home; and as I drew nearer, I found the Attraction stronger and stronger, my Diligence and Speed increas'd with my Impatience, I drove on violently, and made such long Stretches that a very few Days brought me to my own House, and to the Arms of my good old Wife and Children, where I remain, Thanks to God, at present well and happy.

Persons subject to the Hyp, complain of the North East Wind as increasing their Malady. But since you promis'd to send me Kisses in that Wind, and I find you as good as your Word, 'tis to me the gayest Wind that blows, and gives me the best Spirits. I write this during a N. East Storm of Snow, the greatest we have had this Winter: Your Favours come mixd with the Snowy Fleeces which are pure as your Virgin Innocence, white as your lovely Bosom,—and as cold:—But let it warm towards some worthy young Man, and may Heaven bless you both with every kind of Happiness.

I desired Miss Anna Ward, to send you over a little Book I left with her; for your Amusement in that lonely Island. My Respects to your good Father and Mother, and Sister unknown. Let me often hear of your Welfare, since it is not likely I shall ever again have the Pleasure of seeing you. Accept mine, and my Wife's sincere Thanks for the many Civilities I receiv'd from you and your Relations; and do me the Justice to believe me, Dear Girl, Your affectionate faithful Friend and humble Servant

My respectful Compliments to your good Brother Ward, and Sister; and to the agreable Family of the Wards at Newport when you see them. Adieu.

"ONE OF GODS NOBILITY"

To Joshua Babcock

Dear Sir   Philada. Sept. 1. 1755

I beg Leave to introduce to you the Revd. Mr. Allison Rector of our Academy; a Person of great Ingenuity and Learning, a catholic Divine, and what is more, an *Honest Man*; For as Pope says

> A Wit's a Feather, and a Chief's a Rod;
> An honest Man's the *noblest* Work of God.

By Entertaining then this Gent. with your accustomed Hospitality and Benevolence, you will Entertain one of the

Nobility. I mean one of *Gods* Nobility; for as to the *Kings*, there are many of them not worthy your Notice.

Do me the Favour to make my Compliments acceptable to your good Lady, Sisters and Children in whose most agreeable Company I passed those Chearful Winter Evenings, which I remember with high Pleasure. I am, with the greatest Esteem and Respect, Dear Sir Your most Obedient and Most humble Servant

ADDITION, SUBTRACTION, AND MULTIPLICATION

To Catharine Ray

Dear Katy   Philadelphia Oct. 16. 1755

Your Favour of the 28th of June came to hand but the 28th of September, just 3 Months after it was written. I had, two Weeks before, wrote you a long Chat, and sent it to the Care of your Brother Ward. I hear you are now in Boston, gay and lovely as usual. Let me give you some fatherly Advice. Kill no more Pigeons than you can eat. Be a good Girl, and don't forget your Catechise. Go constantly to Meeting—or Church—till you get a good Husband; then stay at home, and nurse the Children, and live like a Christian. Spend your spare Hours, in sober Whisk, Prayers, or learning to cypher. You must practise *Addition* to your Husband's Estate, by Industry and Frugality; *Subtraction* of all unnecessary Expences; *Multiplication* (I would gladly have taught you that myself, but you thought it was time enough, and wou'dn't learn) he will soon make you a Mistress of it. As to *Division*, I say with Brother Paul, *Let there be no Divisions among ye*. But as your good Sister Hubbard (my Love to her) is well acquainted with *The Rule of Two*, I hope you will become as expert in the *Rule of Three*; that when I have again the Pleasure of seeing you, I may find you like my Grape Vine, surrounded with Clusters, plump, juicy, blushing, pretty little rogues, like their Mama. Adieu. The Bell rings, and I must go among the Grave ones, and talk Politicks. Your affectionate Friend p.s. The Plums came safe, and were so sweet from the Cause you mention'd, that I could scarce taste the Sugar.

"THE QUANTITY OF HUMAN IGNORANCE"

To William Shipley

Philada. Nov. 27. 1755.

I have just received your very obliging Favour of the 13th. September last; and as this Ship sails immediately, have little more time than to thank you cordially for communicating to me the Papers relating to your most laudable Undertaking, and to assure you, that I should esteem the being admitted into such a Society as a corresponding Member, a very great Honour, which I should be glad I could in the least deserve, by promoting in any Degree so useful an Institution. But tho' you do not require your Correspondents to bear any Part of your Expence, you will I hope permit me to throw my Mite into your Fund, and accept of 20 Guineas I purpose to send you shortly, to be apply'd in Premiums for some Improvement *in Britain*, as a grateful, tho' small, Return for your most kind and generous Intentions of Encouraging Improvements *in America*. I flatter myself, from that Part of your Plan, that those Jealousies of her Colonies, which were formerly entertained by the Mother Country, begin to subside. I once wrote a little Paper, tending to show that such Jealousies with Regard to Manufactures were ill-founded. It was lately printed in Boston at the End of a Pamphlet which I take the Liberty to send you. Never be discouraged by any Apprehension that Arts are come to such Perfection in England, as to be incapable of farther Improvement. As yet, the Quantity of Human Knowledge bears no Proportion to the Quantity of Human Ignorance. The Improvements made within these 2000 Years, considerable as they are, would have been much more so, if the Ancients had possess'd one or two Arts now in common Use, I mean those of Copper Plate- and Letter-Printing. Whatever is now exactly delineated and describ'd by those, can scarcely (from the Multitude of Copies) be lost to Posterity. And the Knowledge of small Matters being preserv'd, gives the Hint and is sometimes the Occasion of great Discoveries, perhaps Ages after.

The French War, which came on in 1744, took off our Thoughts from the Prosecution of my Proposal for Promoting useful Knowledge in America; and I have ever since the Peace been so engag'd in other Schemes of various kinds and in publick Affairs, as not to find Leisure to revive that useful and very practicable Project. But if I live to see our present Disturbances over in this Part of the World, I shall apply my self to it with fresh Spirit, as beside the Good that may be done, I hope to make myself thereby a more valuable Correspondent.

You will greatly oblige me by the Communication of the Inventions and Improvements you mention. And as it is a Maxim in Commerce, That there is no Trade without Returns, I shall be always endeavouring to ballance Accounts with you, tho' probably never able to accomplish it.

I am, Sir, Your most obedient humble Servant

"WE ARE SPIRITS"

To Elizabeth Hubbart

DEAR CHILD, PHILADELPHIA, February 22, 1756.

I condole with you, we have lost a most dear and valuable relation, but it is the will of God and Nature that these mortal bodies be laid aside, when the soul is to enter into real life; 'tis rather an embrio state, a preparation for living; a man is not completely born until he be dead: Why then should we grieve that a new child is born among the immortals? A new member added to their happy society? We are spirits. That bodies should be lent us, while they can afford us pleasure, assist us in acquiring knowledge, or doing good to our fellow creatures, is a kind and benevolent act of God—when they become unfit for these purposes and afford us pain instead of pleasure—instead of an aid, become an incumbrance and answer none of the intentions for which they were given, it is equally kind and benevolent that a way is provided by which we may get rid of them. Death is that way. We ourselves prudently choose a partial death. In some cases a mangled painful limb, which cannot be restored, we willingly cut off—He who plucks out a tooth, parts with it freely since the pain goes with it, and he that quits the whole body, parts at once with all pains and possibilities of pains and diseases it was liable to, or capable of making him suffer.

Our friend and we are invited abroad on a party of pleasure—that is to last forever—His chair was first ready and he is gone before us—we could not all conveniently start together, and why should you and I be grieved at this, since we are soon to follow, and we know where to find him.   Adieu,

HEAT AND COLD

To John Lining

Sir,   New-York, April 14. 1757.

It is a long Time since I had the Pleasure of a Line from you. And indeed the Troubles of our Country, with the Hurry of Business, I have been engag'd in on that Account, have made me so bad a Correspondent, that I ought not to expect Punctuality in others.

But being just taking Passage for England, I could not leave the Continent, without paying my Respects to you, and at the same Time taking Leave to introduce to your Acquaintance a Gentleman of Learning and Merit, Col. Henry Bouquet, who does me the Favour to present you this Letter, and with whom I am sure you will be much pleased.

Mr. Professor Simpson of Glasgow, lately communicated to me some curious Experiments of a Physician of his Acquaintance, by which it appeared that an extraordinary Degree of Cold, even to Freezing, might be produced by Evaporation. I have not had Leisure to repeat and examine more than the first and easiest of them, viz. Wet the Ball of a Thermometer by a Feather dipt in Spirit of Wine, which has been kept in the same Room, and has of Course the same Degree of Heat or Cold. The Mercury sinks presently 3 or 4

Degrees, and the quicker if during the Evaporation you blow on the Ball with Bellows; a second Wetting and Blowing when the Mercury is down, carries it yet lower. I think I did not get it lower than 5 or 6 Degrees from where it naturally stood, which was at that time 60. But it is said, that a Vessel of Water being plac'd in another somewhat larger containing Spirit, in such a Manner that the Vessel of Water is surrounded with the Spirit, and both plac'd under the Receiver of an Air-pump, on Exhausting the Air, the Spirit evaporating leaves such a Degree of Cold as to freeze the Water, tho' the Thermometer in the open Air stands many Degrees above the Freezing Point.

I know not how this Phenomenon is to be accounted for, but it gives me Occasion to mention some loose Notions relating to Heat and Cold, which I have for some Time entertain'd, but not yet reduc'd into any Form. Allowing common Fire as well as the Electrical, to be a Fluid, capable of permeating other Bodies, and seeking an Equilibrium, I imagine some Bodies are better fitted by Nature to be Conductors of that Fluid than others; and that generally those which are the best Conductors of the Electrical Fluid, are also the best Conductors of this; and e contra. Thus a Body which is a good Conductor of Fire readily receives it into its Substance, and conducts it thro' the Whole to all the Parts; as Metals and Water do; and if two Bodies, both good Conductors, one heated, the other in its common State, are brought into Contact with each other, the Body which has most Fire, readily communicates of it to that which had least; and that which had least readily receives it, till an Equilibrium is produced. Thus, if you take a Dollar between your Fingers with one Hand, and a Piece of Wood of the same Dimensions with the other, and bring both at the same Time to the Flame of a Candle, you will find yourself obliged to drop the Dollar before you drop the Wood, because it conducts the Heat of the Candle sooner to your Flesh. Thus, if a Silver Teapot had a Handle of the same Metal, it would conduct the Heat from the Water to the Hand, and become too hot to be used; we therefore give to a Metal Teapot a Handle of Wood, which is not so good a Conductor as Metal. But a China or Stone Teapot being in some Degree of the Nature of Glass, which is not a good Conductor of Heat, may have a Handle of the same Stuff. Thus also a damp moist Air shall make a Man more sensible of Cold, or chill him more than a dry Air that is colder, because a moist Air is fitter to receive and conduct away the Heat of his Body. This Fluid entring Bodies in great Quantity, first expands them by separating their Parts a little, afterwards by farther separating their Parts, it renders solids fluid, and at length dissipates their Parts in Air. Take this Fluid from melted Lead, or from Water, the Parts cohere again, the first grows solid, the latter becomes Ice. And this is soonest done by the Means of good Conductors. Thus, if you take (as I have done) a square Bar of Lead, 4 Inches long, and 1 Inch thick, together with 3 Pieces of Wood planed to the same Dimensions, and lay them as in the Margin, on a

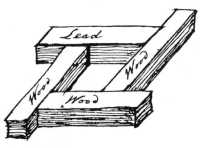

smooth Board, fix'd so as not to be easily separated or moved, and pour into the square Cavity they form as much melted Lead as will fill it, you will see the melted Lead chill and become firm on the Side next the Leaden Bar, some Time before it chills on the other three Sides in Contact with the Wooden Bars; tho' before the Lead was poured in, they might all be supposed to have the same Degree of Heat or Coldness, as they had been exposed in the same Room to the same Air. You will likewise observe, that the leaden Bar, as it has cooled the melted Lead more than the wooden Bars have done, so it is itself more heated by the melted Lead. There is a certain Quantity of this Fluid, called Fire, in every living human Body, which Fluid, being in due Proportion, keeps the Parts of the Flesh and Blood at such a just Distance from each other, as that the Flesh and Nerves are suple, and the Blood fit for Circulation. If Part of this due Proportion of Fire be

conducted away by Means of a Contact with other Bodies, as
Air, Water, or Metals, the Parts of our Skin and Flesh that
come into such Contact, first draw more near together than
is agreeable, and give that Sensation which we call Cold, and
if too much be conveyed away, the Body stiffens, the Blood
ceases to flow, and Death ensues. On the other Hand, if too
much of this Fluid be communicated to the Flesh, the Parts
are separated too far, and Pain ensues as when they are separated by a Pin or Lancet. The Sensation that the Separation
by Fire occasions, we call Heat, or Burning. My Desk, on
which I now write, and the Lock of my Desk, are both expos'd to the same Temperature of the Air, and have therefore
the same Degree of Heat and Cold; yet if I lay my Hand
successively on the Wood and on the Metal, the latter feels
much the Coldest; not that it is really so, but being a better
Conductor, it more readily than the Wood takes away and
draws into it self the Fire that was in my Skin. Accordingly,
if I lay one Hand, Part on the Lock, and Part on the Wood,
and after it has lain so some Time I feel both Parts with my
other Hand, I find the Part that has been in Contact with the
Lock, very sensibly colder to the Touch than the Part that lay
on the Wood. How a living Animal obtains its Quantity of
this Fluid called Fire, is a curious Question. I have shown
that some Bodies (as Metals) have a Power of Attracting it
stronger than others, and I have sometimes suspected that a
living Body had some Power of Attracting out of the Air or
other Bodies the Heat it wanted. Thus Metal hammer'd or
repeatedly bent, grows hot in the bent or hammered Part. But
when I consider'd that Air in contact with the Body cools it;
that the surrounding Air is rather heated by its Contact with
the Body; that every Breath of cooler Air drawn in, carries
off Part of the Body's Heat when it passes out again: That
therefore there must be in the Body a Fund for producing it,
or otherwise the Animal would soon grow cold: I have been
rather enclin'd to think that the Fluid, *Fire*, as well as the
Fluid, *Air*, is attracted by Plants in their Growth, and becomes consolidated with the other Materials of which they
are formed, and makes a great Part of their Substance. That
when they come to be digested, and to suffer in the Vessels a
Kind of Fermentation, Part of the Fire as well as Part of the

Air, recovers its fluid Active State again, and diffuses itself in the Body digesting and separating it. That the Fire so reproduc'd by Digestion and Separation, continually leaving the Body, its Place is supply'd by fresh Quantities arising from the continual Separation. That whatever quickens the Motion of the Fluids in an Animal, quickens the Separation, and reproduces more of the Fire, as Exercise. That all the Fire emitted by Wood and other Combustibles when burning, existed in them before in a solid State, being only discovered when separating. That some Fossils, as Sulphur, Seacoal, &c. contain a great deal of solid Fire; that Gunpowder is almost all solid Fire: And that, in short, what escapes and is dissipated in the Burning of Bodies, besides Water and Earth, is generally the Air and Fire that before made Parts of the solid. Thus I imagin that Animal Heat arises by or from a Kind of Fermentation in the Juices of the Body, in the same Manner as Heat arises in the Liquors preparing for Distillation; wherein there is a Separation of the spirituous from the watry and earthy Parts. And it is remarkable, that the Liquor in a Distiller's Vat, when in its highest and best State of Fermentation, shows by the Thermometer, as I have been informed, the same Degree of Heat with the human Body, that is about 94 or 96. Thus, as by a constant Supply of Fuel in a Chimney, you keep a warm Room, so by a constant Supply of Food in the Stomach, you keep a warm Body. Only where little Exercise is used, the Heat may possibly be conducted away too fast, in which Case such Materials are to be used for Cloathing and Bedding, against the Effect of an immediate Contact of the Air, as are in themselves bad Conductors of Heat, and consequently prevent its being communicated thro' their Substance to the Air. Hence what is called *Warmth* in Wool, and its Preference on that Account to Linen; Wool not being so good a Conductor. And hence all the natural Coverings of Animals to keep them warm, are such, as retain and confine the natural Heat in the Body, by being bad Conductors; such as Wool, Hair, Feathers, and the Silk by which the Silk-worm in its tender embrio State is first cloathed. Cloathing, thus considered, does not make a Man warm, by *giving* Warmth, but by preventing the too quick Dissipation of the Heat produc'd in his Body, and so occasioning an Accumulation.

There is another curious Question I will just venture to touch upon, viz. Whence arises the sudden extraordinary Degree of Cold, perceptible on mixing some Chymical Liquors, and even on mixing Salt and Snow, where the Composition appears colder than the coldest of the Ingredients? I have never seen the chymical Mixtures made, but Salt and Snow I have often mixed myself, and am fully satisfied that the Composition feels much colder to the Touch, and lowers the Mercury in the Thermometer more than either Ingredient would do separately. I suppose with others, that Cold is nothing more than an Absence of Heat or Fire. Now if the Quantity of Fire before contain'd or diffus'd in the Snow and Salt, was expell'd in the Uniting of the two Matters, it must be driven away either thro' the Air or the Vessel containing them. If it is driven off thro' the Air, it must warm the Air, and a Thermometer held over the Mixture without touching it, would discover the Heat by the Rising of the Mercury, as it must and always does in warmer Air. This indeed I have not try'd; but I should guess it would rather be driven off thro' the Vessel, especially if the Vessel be Metal, as being a better Conductor than Air, and so one should find the Bason warmer after such Mixture. But on the contrary the Vessel grows cold, and even Water in which the Vessel is sometimes plac'd for the Experiment, freezes into hard Ice on the Bason. Now I know not how to account for this otherwise than by supposing, that the Composition is a better Conductor of Fire than the Ingredients separately, and like the Lock compar'd with the Wood, has a stronger Power of Attracting Fire, and does accordingly attract it suddenly from the Fingers or a Thermometer put into it, from the Bason that contains it, and from the Water in contact with the Outside of the Bason, so that the Fingers have the Sensation of extream Cold, by being depriv'd of much of their natural Fire; the Thermometer sinks, by having part of its Fire drawn out of the Mercury; the Bason grows colder to the Touch, as by having its Fire drawn into the Mixture, it is become more capable of drawing and receiving it from the Hand; and thro' the Bason the Water loses its Fire that kept it fluid, so it becomes Ice. One would expect, That from all this attracted Acquisition of Fire to the Composition, it should become warmer; and in fact, the Snow and Salt dissolves at the same Time into Water without freezing.

I doubt whether in all this I have talked intelligibly; and indeed how should a Man do so, that does not himself clearly understand the Thing he talks of. This I confess to be my present Case. I intended to amuse you, but I fear I have done more, and tired you. Be so good as to excuse it, and believe me, with sincere Esteem and Respect, Sir, Your most obedient humble Servant

"OLD FOLKS AND OLD TREES"

To Jane Mecom

Dear Sister   New York, April 19. 1757

I wrote a few Lines to you yesterday, but omitted to answer yours relating to Sister Douse: As *having their own Way*, is one of the greatest Comforts of Life, to old People, I think their Friends should endeavour to accommodate them in that, as well as in any thing else. When they have long liv'd in a House, it becomes natural to them, they are almost as closely connected with it as the Tortoise with his Shell, they die if you tear them out of it. Old Folks and old Trees, if you remove them, tis ten to one that you kill them. So let our good old Sister be no more importun'd on that head. We are growing old fast ourselves, and shall expect the same kind of Indulgencies. If we give them, we shall have a Right to receive them in our Turn.

And as to her few fine Things, I think she is in the right not to sell them, and for the Reason she gives, that they will fetch but little. When that little is spent, they would be of no farther use to her; but perhaps the Expectation of Possessing them at her Death, may make that Person tender and careful of her, and helpful to her, to the amount of ten times their Value. If so, they are put to the best Use they possibly can be.

I hope you visit Sister as often as your Affairs will permit, and afford her what Assistance and Comfort you can, in her present Situation. *Old Age*, *Infirmities*, and *Poverty*, join'd, are

Afflictions enough; the *Neglect and Slight* of Friends and near Relations, should never be added. People in her Circumstances are apt to suspect this sometimes without Cause; *Appearances* should therefore be attended to, in our Conduct towards them, as well as *Realities*.

I write by this Post to Cousin Williams, to continue his Care, which I doubt not he will do.

We expect to sail in about a Week, so that I can hardly hear from you again on this Side the Water. But let me have a Line from you now and then while I am in London. I expect to stay there at least a 12 month. Direct your Letters to be left for me at the Pensilvania Coffee House in Birchin Lane London. My Love to all, from Dear Sister, Your affectionate Brother

PS. April 25. We are still here, and perhaps may be here a Week longer, Once more Adieu my dear Sister.

"THEY EXPECT TOO MUCH OF ME"

To Jane Mecom

DEAR SISTER,   *New York, May 30, 1757.*

I have before me yours of the 9th and 16th instant: I am glad you have resolved to visit sister Dowse oftener; it will be a great comfort to her, to find she is not neglected by you, and your example may, perhaps, be followed by some other of her relations.

As Neddy is yet a young man, I hope he may get over the disorder he complains of, and in time wear it out. My love to him and his wife and the rest of your children. It gives me pleasure to hear that Eben is likely to get into business at his trade. If he will be industrious and frugal, 'tis ten to one but he gets rich, for he seems to have spirit and activity.

I am glad that Peter is acquainted with the crown soap business, so as to make what is good of the kind. I hope he will always take care to make it faithfully, never slight manufacture, or attempt to deceive by appearances. Then he may boldly put his name and mark, and in a little time it will acquire as good a character as that made by his late uncle, or any other person whatever. I believe his aunt at Philadelphia, can help him to sell a good deal of it; and I doubt not of her doing every thing in her power to promote his interest in that way. Let a box be sent to her (but not unless it be right good) and she will immediately return the ready money for it. It was beginning once to be in vogue in Philadelphia, but brother John sent me one box, an ordinary sort, which checked its progress. I would not have him put the Franklin arms on it; but the soapboilers arms he has a right to use, if he thinks fit. The other would look too much like an attempt to counterfeit. In his advertisements, he may value himself on serving his time with the original maker, but put his own mark or device on the papers, or any thing he may be advised to as proper; only on the soap, as it is called by the name of crown soap, it seems necessary to use a stamp of that sort, and perhaps no soapboiler in the king's dominions has a better right to the crown than himself.

Nobody has wrote a syllable to me concerning his making use of the hammer, or made the least complaint of him or you. I am sorry however that he took it without leave. It was irregular, and if you had not approved of his doing it, I should have thought it indiscreet. *Leave* they say is *light*, and it seems to me a piece of respect that was due to his aunt to ask it, and I can scarce think she would have refused him the favour.

I am glad to hear Jamey is so good and diligent a workman; if he ever sets up at the goldsmith's business, he must remember that there is one accomplishment without which he cannot possibly thrive in that trade, (i. e. *to be perfectly honest*). It is a business that though ever so uprightly managed, is always liable to suspicion; and if a man is once detected in the smallest fraud it soon becomes public, and every one is put upon their guard against him; no one will venture to try his hands, or trust him to make up their plate; so at once he is ruined. I hope my nephew will therefore establish a character as an *honest* and faithful, as well as *skilful* workman, and then he need not fear employment.

And now as to what you propose for Benny I believe he may be, as you say, well enough qualified for it, and when he appears to be settled, if a vacancy should happen, it is very probable he may be thought of to supply it; but it is a rule with me, not to remove any officer that behaves well, keeps regular accounts, and pays duly; and I think the rule is founded on reason and justice. I have not shown any backwardness to assist Benny, where it could be done without injuring another. But if my friends require of me to gratify not only their inclinations, but their resentments, they expect too much of me. Above all things I dislike family quarrels, and when they happen among my relations, nothing gives me more pain. If I were to set myself up as a judge of those subsisting between you and brother's widow and children, how unqualified must I be, at this distance, to determine rightly, especially having heard but one side. They always treated me with friendly and affectionate regard, you have done the same. What can I say between you, but that I wish you were reconciled, and that I will love that side best that is most ready to forgive and oblige the other. You will be angry with me here, for putting you and them too much upon a footing, but I shall nevertheless be,

Dear sister, your truly
Affectionate brother,

LONDON
1757–1775

Contents

LETTERS

William Franklin to the Printer of the Citizen: A Defense of the Quakers and the Pennsylvania Assembly

Some Account of the late Disputes between the Assembly of Pensylvania, *and their present Governor* William Denny, *Esq;*

In our *Magazine, Vol.* xxv. p. 87 *Vol.* xxvi. *p.* 28. we have given a very particular account of the disputes between the assembly of *Pensylvania* and the late Governor *Morris*, which had exactly the same cause, and produced exactly the same effects, as the late dispute between this assembly and Mr *Denny.*

The acting governor, who is only lieutenant governor, besides the royal instructions, receives instructions from the proprietaries. By these proprietary instructions the governor is required not to pass any bill for taxing their quit rents, their located unimproved lands, and their purchase money at interest, but the assembly have ever been determined to frame no money bill, in which these quit rents, lands, and money shall be exempted, for the following reasons.

1st, Because they conceive that neither the proprietaries nor any other power on earth, ought to interfere between them and their sovereign, either to modify or refuse their free gifts and grants for his majesty's service.

2d, Because though the governor may be under obligations to the proprietaries, yet he is under greater to the crown, and to the people he is appointed to govern, to promote the service of his majesty, and preserve the rights of his subjects, and protect them from their cruel enemies.

3d. Because a tax laid comformable to the proprietary instructions, could not possibly produce the necessary supply. By these instructions all the proprietors estate, except a trifle, and all located unimproved lands, to whomsoever belonging, are to be exempted. There remains then to be taxed, only the improved lands, houses, and personal estates of the people. Now it is well known, from the tax books, that there are not in the province more than 20,000 houses, including those of the towns with those on plantations. If these, with the improved lands annexed to them, and the personal estate of those that inhabit them, are worth, one with another, 250*l.* each, it may, we think, be reckoned their full value; then multiply 20,000 the number of houses, by 250*l.* the value of each estate, and the produce is 5,000,000*l.* for the full value of all our estates, real and personal, the unimproved lands excepted. Now three *per cent.* on five millions is but one hundred and fifty thousand pounds; and four shillings in the pound on one hundred and fifty thousand pounds, being but a fifth part, is no more than thirty thousand pounds; so that we ought to have near seventeen millions to produce, by such a tax, one hundred thousand pounds.

4th. Because the bill * which they have prepared, without the exceptions required in the proprietaries instructions, is exactly conformable to an act lately passed by a former governor, and allowed by the crown.

It is indeed matter of equal astonishment and concern, that in this time of danger and distress, when the utmost unanimity and dispatch is necessary to the preservation of life, liberty, and estate, a governor should be sent to our colonies with such instructions as must inevitably produce endless dispute and delay, and prevent the assembly from effectually opposing the *French* upon any other condition, than the giving up their rights as *Englishmen.*

The assembly, indeed, have been stigmatized as obstinate, fanatical, and disaffected; and reproached as the authors of every calamity under which they suffer. A paragraph in one of the public papers, which lately ecchoed the charge that has been long urged against them, has been answered by Mr *William Franklin* of *Philadelphia*, who is now in *England.* We shall insert the paragraph and reply at large, as we cannot exhibit any other representation with equal authority.

In the bill which passed in March *last, the proprietary estate was not taxed, that matter being intended to be referred to the determination of superior authority in* England.

To the Printer of the CITIZEN.

SIR,

In your Paper of the 9th Instant, I observe the following Paragraph, viz. 'The last Letters from Philadelphia bring Accounts of the Scalping the Inhabitants of the Back Provinces by the Indians: At the same Time the Disputes between the Governor and the Assembly are carried to as great a Height as ever, and the Messages sent from the Assembly to the Governor, and from the Governor to the Assembly, are expressed in Terms which give very little Hopes of a Reconciliation. The Bill to raise Money is clogged, so as to prevent the Governor from giving his Consent to it; and the Obstinacy of the Quakers in the Assembly is such, that they will in no Shape alter it: So that, while the Enemy is in the Heart of the Country, Cavils prevent any Thing being done for its Relief.—Mr. Denny is the third Governor with whom the Assembly has had these Disputes within a few Years.'

As this Paragraph, like many others heretofore published in the Papers, is not founded on Truth, but calculated to prejudice the Public against the Quakers and People of Pennsylvania, you are desired to do that injured Province some Justice, in publishing the following Remarks; which would have been sent you sooner, had the Paper come sooner to my Hands.

1. That the Scalping of the Frontier Inhabitants by the Indians is not peculiar to Pennsylvania, but common to all the Colonies, in Proportion as their Frontiers are more or less extended and exposed to the Enemy. That the Colony of Virginia, in which there are very few, if any Quakers, and none in the Assembly, has lost more Inhabitants and Territory by the War than Pennsylvannia. That even the Colony of New York, with all its own Forces, a great Body of New-England Troops encamp'd on its Frontier, and the regular Army under Lord Loudoun, posted in different Places, has not been able to secure its Inhabitants from Scalping by the Indians; who coming secretly in very small Parties skulking in the Woods, must sometimes have it in their Power to surprize and destroy Travellers, or single Families settled in scattered Plantations, notwithstanding all the Care that can possibly be taken by any Government for their Protection. Centinels posted round an Army, while standing on their Guard, with Arms in their

Hands, are often kill'd and scalp'd by Indians. How much easier must it be for such an Enemy to destroy a Ploughman at Work in his Field?

2. That the Inhabitants of the Frontiers of Pennsylvania are not Quakers, were in the Beginning of the War supplied with Arms and Ammunition by the Assembly, and have frequently defended themselves, and repelled the Enemy, being withheld by no Principle from Fighting; and the Losses they have suffer'd were owing entirely to their Situation, and the loose scattered Manner in which they had settled their Plantations and Families in the Woods, remote from each other, in Confidence of lasting Peace.

3. That the Disputes between the late and present Governors, and the Assembly of Pennsylvania, were occasioned, and are continued, chiefly by *new* Instructions from the Proprietors to those Governors, forbidding them to pass any Laws to raise Money for the Defence of the Country, unless the proprietary Estate, or much the greatest Part of it, was exempted from the Tax to be raised by Virtue of such Laws, and other Clauses inserted in them, by which the Privileges long enjoyed by the People, and which they think they have a Right to, not only as Pennsylvanians, but as Englishmen, were to be extorted from them, under their present Distresses. The Quakers, who, tho' the first Settlers, are now but a small Part of the People of Pennsylvania, were concerned in those Disputes only as Inhabitants of the Province, and not as Quakers; and all the other Inhabitants join in opposing those Instructions, and contending for their Rights, the Proprietary Officers and Dependants only excepted, with a few of such as they can influence.

4. That though some Quakers have Scruples against bearing Arms, they have when most numerous in the Assembly, granted large Sums for the King's Use (as they expressed it) which have been applied to the Defence of the Province; for Instance, in 1755, and 1756, they granted the Sum of 55,000l. to be raised by a Tax on Estates real and personal, and 30,000l. to be raised by Excise on Spirituous Liquors; besides near 10,000l. in Flour, &c. to General Braddock and for cutting his Roads, and 10,000l. to General Shirley in Provisions for the New England and New-York Forces, then on the

Frontiers of New-York; at the same Time that the Contingent Expences of Government to be otherwise provided for, were greatly and necessarily enhanced. That however, to remove all Pretence for Reflection on their Sect, as obstructing military Measures in Time of War, a Number of them voluntarily quitted their Seats in Assembly, in 1756; others requested their Friends not to chuse them in the ensuing Election, nor did any of that Profession stand as Candidates, or request a Vote for themselves at that Election, many Quakers refusing even to vote at all, and others voting for such Men as would, and did, make a considerable Majority in the House, who were not Quakers; and yet four of the Quakers, who were nevertheless chosen, refused to serve, and Writs were issued for new Elections, when four others, not Quakers, were chosen in their Places; that of 36 Members, the Number of which the House consists, there are not at the most above 12 of that Denomination, and those such as are well known to be for supporting the Government in Defence of the Country, but are too few, if they were against such a Measure, to prevent it.

5. That the Bill to raise Money said in the above Article of News, to be so clogged as to prevent the Governor from giving his Assent, was drawn in the same Form, and with the same Freedom from all Clogs, as that for granting 60,000l. which had been passed by the Governor in 1755, and received the Royal Approbation; that the real Clogs or Obstructions to its passing were not in the Bill, but in the above-mentioned proprietary Instructions; that the Governor having long refused his Assent to the Bill, did in Excuse of his Conduct, on Lord Loudoun's Arrival at Philadelphia, in March last, lay his Reasons before his Lordship, who was pleased to communicate them to one of the Members of the House, and patiently to hear what that Member had to say in Answer, the Governor himself being present; and that his Lordship did finally declare himself fully satisfied with the Answers made to those Reasons, and to give it as his Opinion to the Governor, that he ought immediately to pass the Bill, any Instructions he might have to the contrary from the Proprietors notwithstanding, which the Governor accordingly complied with, passed the Bill on the 22d of March, and the Money, being 100,000l. for the Service of the current Year, has been ever

since actually expending in the Defence of the Province; so
that the whole Story of the Bill's not passing, the clogging of
the Bill by the Assembly, and the Obstinacy of the Quakers
preventing its Passage, is absolutely a malicious and notorious
Falshood.

6. The Assertion of the News-Writers, 'That while the Enemy is in the Heart of the Country, Cavils prevent any Thing
being done for its Relief,' is so far from being true: That
First, the Enemy is not, nor ever was, in the Heart of the
Country, having only molested the Frontier Settlements by
their Parties. Secondly, More is done for the Relief and Defence of the Country, without any Assistance from the Crown,
than is done perhaps by any other Colony in America; there
having been, soon after the War broke out, the following
Forts erected at the Province Expence, in a Line to cover the
Frontier, viz. Henshaw's Fort on Delaware, Fort Hamilton,
Fort Norris, Fort Allen, Fort Franklin, Fort Lebanon, Fort
William Henry, Fort Augustus, Fort Halifax, Fort Granville,
Fort Shirley, Fort Littleton, and Shippensburg Fort, besides
several smaller Stockades and Places of Defence, garrisoned
by Troops in the Pay of the Province, under whose Protection
the Inhabitants, who at first abandoned their Frontier Settlements, returned generally to their Habitations, and many
yet continue, though not without some Danger, to cultivate
their Lands: By these Pennsylvanian Troops, under Col. Armstrong, the greatest Blow was given to the Enemy last Year
on the Ohio that they have received during the War: in burning and destroying the Indian Town of Kittanning, and killing their great Captain Jacobs, with many other Indians, and
recovering a Number of Captives of their own and the neighbouring Provinces: Besides the Garrisons, in the Forts, 1100
Soldiers are maintained on the Frontiers in Pay, being armed
and accoutred by the Province, as ranging Companies.

And at Philadelphia, 15 Iron Cannon, 18 Pounders, were last
Year purchased in England, and added to the 50 they had
before, either mounted on their Batteries, or ready to be
mounted, besides a Train of Artillery, being new Brass Field
Pieces, 12 and 6 Pounders, with all their Appurtenances in
extreme good Order, and a Magazine stored with Ammunition, a Quantity of large Bomb-shells, and above 2000 new

Small Arms lately procured, exclusive of those in the Hands of the People. They have likewise this Summer fitted out a 20 Gun Province Ship of War, to scour the Coast of Privateers, and protect the Trade of that and the neighbouring Provinces, which is more than any other Colony to the Southward of New England has done. Pennsylvania also, by its Situation, covers the greatest Part of New Jersey, all the Government of the Delaware Countries, and great Part of Maryland, from the Invasions of the Indians, without receiving any Contribution from those Colonies, or the Mother-Country, towards the Expence.

The above are Facts, consistent with the Knowledge of the Subscriber, who but lately left Philadelphia, is now in London, is not, nor ever was, a Quaker, nor writes this at the Request of any Quaker, but purely to do Justice to a Province and People, of late frequently abused in nameless Papers and Pamphlets published in England. And he hereby calls upon the Writer of that Article of News to produce the Letters out of which, he says, he has drawn those Calumnies and Falshoods, or to take the Shame to himself.

WILLIAM FRANKLIN.

Pensylvania Coffee-house
London, Sept. 16, 1757.

The London Chronicle, September 20, 1757

A Letter from Father Abraham, to His Beloved Son

Dear Isaac,

You frequently desire me to give you some *Advice*, in Writing. There is, perhaps, no other valuable Thing in the World, of which so great a Quantity is *given*, and so little *taken*. Men do not generally err in their Conduct so much through Ignorance of their Duty, as thrô Inattention to their own Faults, or thrô strong Passions and bad Habits; and, therefore, till that Inattention is cured, or those Passions reduced under the Government of Reason, *Advice* is rather resented as a Reproach, than gratefully acknowledged and followed.

Supposing then, that from the many good Sermons you have heard, good Books read, and good Admonitions received from your Parents and others, your Conscience is by this Time pretty well informed, and capable of advising you, if you attentively listen to it, I shall not fill this Letter with Lessons or Precepts of Morality and Religion; but rather recommend to you, that in order to obtain a *clear* Sight and *constant* Sense of your Errors, you would set apart a Portion of every Day for the Purpose of *Self-Examination*, and trying your daily Actions by that Rule of Rectitude implanted by GOD in your Breast. The properest Time for this, is when you are retiring to Rest; then carefully review the Transactions of the past Day; and consider how far they have agreed with *what you know* of your Duty to God and to Man, in the several Relations you stand in of a Subject to the Government, Servant to your Master, a Son, a Neighbour, a Friend, *&c.* When, by this Means, you have discovered the Faults of the Day, acknowledge them to God, and humbly beg of him not only Pardon for what is past, but Strength to fulfil your solemn Resolutions of guarding against them for the Future. Observing this Course steadily for some Time, you will find (through God's Grace assisting) that your Faults are continually diminishing, and your Stock of Virtue encreasing; in Consequence of which you will grow in Favour both with GOD and Man.

I repeat it, that for the Acquirement of solid, uniform, steady Virtue, nothing contributes more, than a daily strict SELF-EXAMINATION, by the Lights of Reason, Conscience, and the Word of GOD; joined with firm Resolutions of amending what you find amiss, and fervent Prayer for Grace and Strength to execute those Resolutions.—This Method is very antient. 'Twas recommended by *Pythagoras*, in his truly *Golden Verses*, and practised since in every Age, with Success, by Men of all Religions. Those golden Verses, as translated by *Rowe*, are well worth your Reading, and even getting by Heart. The Part relating to this Matter I have transcribed, to give you a Taste of them, *viz.*

> Let not the stealing God of Sleep surprize,
> Nor creep in Slumbers on thy weary Eyes,

Ere ev'ry Action of the former Day,
Strictly thou dost, and *righteously* survey.
With Rev'rence at thy own Tribunal stand,
And answer justly to thy own Demand.
Where have I been? In what have I transgrest?
What Good or Ill has this Day's Life exprest?
Where have I fail'd in what I ought to do?
In what to GOD, to Man, or to myself I owe?
Inquire severe whate'er from first to last,
From Morning's Dawn till Ev'nings Gloom has past.
If Evil were thy Deeds, repenting mourn,
And let thy Soul with strong Remorse be torn:
If Good, the Good with Peace of Mind repay,⎫
And to thy secret Self with Pleasure say,⎬
Rejoice, my Heart, for all went well to Day.⎭

And that no Passage to your Improvement in Virtue may be kept secret, it is not sufficient that you make Use of *Self-Examination* alone; therefore I have also added a *golden Extract* from *a favourite* OLD BOOK, to instruct you in the prudent and deliberate Choice of some disinterested Friend, to remind you of such Misconduct as must necessarily escape your severest Inquiry: Which is as follows;

Every prudent Man ought to be jealous and fearful of himself, lest he run away too hastily with a Likelihood instead of Truth; and abound too much in his own Understanding. All Conditions are equal, that is, Men may be contented in every Condition: For Security is equal to Splendor; Health to Pleasure, *&c.* Every Condition of Life has its Enemies, for *Deus posuit duo & duo, unum contra unum.* A rich Man hath Enemies sometimes for no other Reason than because he is rich; the poor Man hath as poor Neighbours, or rich Ones that gape after that small Profit which he enjoys. The Poor very often subsist merely by Knavery and Rapine among each other. Beware, therefore, how you offend any Man, for he that is displeased at your Words or Actions, commonly joins against you, without putting the *best* Construction on (or endeavouring to find out a reasonable Excuse for) them. And be sure you *hate* no Man, though you think him a worthless or unjust Person. Never *envy* any one above you: You have

Enemies enough by the common Course of Human Nature; be cautious not to encrease the Number; and rather procure as many Friends as you can, to countenance and strengthen you. Every Man has also an Enemy within himself. Every Man is choleric and covetous, or gentle and generous by Nature. Man is naturally a beneficent Creature: But there are many external Objects and Accidents, met with as we go through Life, which *seem* to make great Alterations in our natural Dispositions and Desires. A Man naturally passionate and greedy, may, to all Appearance, become complaisant and hospitable, merely by Force of Instruction and Discipline; and so the Contrary. 'Tis in vain for a passionate Man to say, *I am pardonable* because *it is natural to me*, when we can perhaps point out to him an Example in his next Neighbour, who was *once* affected in the very same Manner, and could say as much to defend himself, who is now exceedingly *different* in his Behaviour, and quite free from those unhappy Affections which disturbed his Repose so often, not long ago, and become a chearful, facetious, and profitable Companion to his Friends, and a Pattern of Humility to all around him.

Nothing was ever well done or said *in a Passion*. One Man's Infirmities and bad Inclinations may be harder to conquer than another Man's, according to the various and *secret* Circumstances that attend them; but they are capable of being conquered, or very much improved for the better, except they have been suffered to *take Root in* OLD *Age*; in this Case it is most convenient to let them *have their* OWN *Way*, as the Phrase is.

The strongest of our natural Passions are seldom perceived by us; a choleric Man does not always discover when he is angry, nor an envious Man when he is invidious; at most they think they commit no great Faults.

Therefore it is necessary that you should have a MONITOR. Most Men are very indifferent Judges of themselves, and often think they do well when they sin; and imagine they commit only small Errors, when they are guilty of Crimes. It is in Human Life as in the Arts and Sciences; their plainest Doctrines are easily comprehended, but the finest Points cannot be discovered without the closest Attention; of these Parts only the wise and skilful in the Art or Science, can be deemed competent Judges. Many Vices and Follies resemble their opposite Virtues and Prudence; they border upon, and seem to mix with each other; and therefore the exact Line of Division betwixt them is hard to ascertain. Pride resembles a generous Spirit; Superstition and Enthusiasm frequently resemble true Religion; a laudable worthy Ambition resembles an unworthy Self-Sufficiency; Government resembles Tyranny; Liberty resembles Licentiousness; Subjection resembles Slavery; Covetousness resembles Frugality; Prodigality resembles Generosity; and so of the Rest. Prudence chiefly consists in that Excellence of Judgment, which is capable of discerning the MEDIUM; or of acting so as not to intermingle the one with the other; and in being able to assign to every Cause its *proper* Actions and Effects. It is therefore necessary for every Person who desires to be a wise Man, to *take particular Notice of* HIS OWN *Actions*, and of HIS OWN *Thoughts and Intentions* which are the Original of his Actions; with great Care and Circumspection; otherwise he can never arrive to that Degree of Perfection which constitutes the amiable Character he aspires after. And, lest all this Diligence should be insufficient, as Partiality to himself will certainly render it, it is very requisite for him to *chuse a* FRIEND, or MONITOR, who must be allowed the greatest Freedom to advertise and remind him of his Failings, and to point out Remedies. Such a One, I mean, as is a discreet and virtuous Person; but especially One that does not creep after the Acquaintance of, or play the Spaniel to, *great* Men; One who does not covet Employments which are known to be scandalous for Opportunities of Injustice: One who can bridle his Tongue and curb his Wit; One that can converse with himself, and industriously attends upon his Affairs whatever they be. Find out such a *Man*; insinuate yourself into a Confidence with him; and desire him to observe your Conversation and Behaviour; intreat him to admonish you of what he thinks amiss, in a serious and friendly Manner; importune his Modesty till he condescends to grant your Request.—Do not imagine that you live one Day without Faults, or that those Faults are undiscovered. Most Men see that in another, which they can not or will not see in themselves: And he is happiest, who through the whole Course of his Life, can attain to a reasonable Freedom from Sin and Folly, even by the Help of *Old Age*, that great Mortifier and Extinguisher of our Lusts and Passions. If such a Monitor informs you of any Misconduct, whether you know his Interpretations to be true or false, take it not only *patiently*, but *thankfully*; and be careful to reform. Thus you get and keep a Friend, break the inordinate mischievous Affection you bore towards your Frailities, and advance yourself in Wisdom and Virtue. When you consider that you must give an Account of your Actions to your vigilant Reprover; that other Men see the same Imperfections in you as he does; and that it is impossible for a good Man to enjoy the Advantages of Friendship, except he first puts off those Qualities which render him subject to Flattery, that is, except he first cease to flatter himself. A good, a generous *Christian* Minister, or worthy sensible Parents, may be suitable Persons for a difficult Office; difficult, though it should be performed by *familiar* Conversation. And how much more meritorious of Entertainment are People of such a Character, than those who come to your Table to *make Faces*, talk Nonsense, devour your Substance, censure their Neighbours, flatter and deride you? Remember that if a Friend tells you of a Fault, always imagine that he does not tell you the whole, which is commonly the Truth; for he desires your Reformation, but is loth to offend you. And *nunquam sine querela ægra tanguntur*.

> I know, dear Son, *Ambition* fills your Mind,
> And in Life's Voyage, is th' impelling Wind;
> But, at the Helm, let sober Reason stand,
> To steer the Bark with Heav'n directed Hand:
> So shall you safe *Ambition*'s Gales receive,
> And ride securely, though the Billows heave;
> So shall you shun the giddy Hero's Fate,
> And by her Influence be both good and great.
>
> She bids you first, in Life's soft vernal Hours,
> With active Industry wake Nature's Pow'rs;
> With rising Years still rising Arts display,
> With new-born Graces mark each new-born Day.
> 'Tis now the Time *young Passion* to command,
> While yet the pliant Stem obeys the Hand;

Guide now the Courser with a steady Rein,
E'er yet he bounds o'er Pleasure's flowry Plain;
In Passion's Strife no Medium you can have;
You rule, a Master; or submit, a Slave.

To conclude.—You are just entering into the World: Beware of the *first Acts* of Dishonesty: They present themselves to the Mind under *specious Disguises*, and *plausible Reasons* of Right and Equity: But being admitted, they open the Way for admitting others, that are *but a little* more dishonest, which are followed by others *a little* more knavish than they, till by Degrees, however slow, a Man becomes an *habitual* Sharper, and at length a *consummate Rascal* and Villain. Then farewel all Peace of Mind, and inward Satisfaction; all Esteem, Confidence, and Reputation among Mankind. And indeed if *outward* Reputation could be preserved, what Pleasure can it afford to a Man that must *inwardly* despise himself, whose own Baseness will, in Spite of his Endeavours to forget it, be ever presenting itself to his View. If you have a *Sir-Reverence* in your Breeches, what signifies it if you *appear* to Others neat and clean and genteel, when you *know* and *feel* yourself to be b——t. I make no Apology for the Comparison, however coarse, since none can be too much so for a defiled and foul Conscience. But never flatter yourself with *Concealment*; 'tis impossible to last long. One Man may be too cunning for another Man, but not for *all Men*: Some Body or other will smell you out, or some Accident will discover you; or who can be sure that he shall never be heard to talk in his Sleep, or be delirious in a Fever, when the working Mind usually throws out Hints of what has inwardly affected it? Of this there have been many Instances; some of which are within the Compass of your own Knowledge.

Whether you chuse to act in a public or a private Station, if you would maintain the personal Character of a Man of Sincerity, Integrity and Virtue, there is a Necessity of becoming *really good*, if you would *do good*: For the thin Disguises of *pretended* private Virtue and Public Spirit, are easily seen through; the Hypocrite detected and exposed. For this Reason then, *My dear* ISAAC, as well as for many others, be sincere, candid, honest, well-meaning, and upright, in all you do and say; be *really* good, if you would *appear* so: Your Life then shall give Strength to your *Counsels*; and though you should be found out an indifferent *Speaker* or *Writer*, you shall not be without Praise for the Benevolence of your Intention.

But, again, suppose it possible for a Knave to preserve a fair Character among Men, and even to approve his own Actions, what is that to the Certainty of his being discovered and detested by the all-seeing Eye of *that righteous* BEING, who made and governs the World, whose just Hand never fails to do right and to punish Iniquity, and whose Approbation, Favour, and Friendship, is worth the Universe?

Heartily wishing you every Accomplishment that can make a Man amiable and valuable, to HIS Protection I commit you, being, with sincere Affection, *dear Son*,

Your very loving Father,
Abraham.

The New-England Magazine, August, 1758

A New Englandman to the Printer of the London Chronicle: A Defense of the Americans

To the Printer of the CHRONICLE.

SIR,

While the public attention is so much turned towards *America*, every letter from thence that promises new information, is pretty generally read; it seems therefore the more necessary that care should be taken to disabuse the Public, when those letters contain facts false in themselves, and representations injurious to bodies of people, or even to private persons.

In your paper, No. 310. I find an extract of a letter, said to be from a gentleman in General *Abercrombie*'s army. As there are several strokes in it tending to render the colonies despicable, and even odious to the mother country, which may have ill consequences; and no notice having been taken of the injuries contained in that letter, other letters of the same nature have since been published, permit me to make a few observations on it.

The writer says, 'New England was settled by Presbyterians and Independents, who took shelter there from the persecutions of Archbishop Laud;—they still retain their original character, they generally hate the Church of England,' says he. If it were true, that some resentment still remained for the hardships their fathers suffer'd, it might perhaps be not much wondered at; but the fact is, that the moderation of the present church of England towards Dissenters in Old as well as New England, has quite effaced those impressions; the Dissenters too are become less rigid and scrupulous, and the good-will between those different bodies in that country is now both mutual and equal.

He goes on: 'They came out with a levelling spirit, and they retain it. They cannot bear to think that one man should be exorbitantly rich and another poor, so that, except in the seaport towns, there are few great estates among them. This equality produces also a rusticity of manners; for in their language, dress, and in all their behaviour, they are more boorish than any thing you ever saw in a certain Northern latitude.' One would imagine from this account, that those who were growing poor, plundered those who were growing rich to preserve this equality, and that property had no protection; whereas in fact, it is no where more secure than in the New England colonies, the law is no where better executed, or justice obtain'd at less expence. The equality he speaks of, arises first from a more equal distribution of lands by the assemblies in the first settlement than has been practised in the other colonies, where favourites of governors have obtained enormous tracts for trifling considerations, to the prejudice both of the crown revenues and the public good; and secondly, from the nature of their occupation; husbandmen with small tracts of land, though they may by industry maintain themselves and families in mediocrity, having few means of acquiring great wealth, especially in a young colony that is to be supplied with its cloathing, and many other expensive articles of consumption from the mother country. Their dress the gentleman may be a more critical judge of than I can pretend to be; all I know of it is, that they wear the manufactures of Britain, and follow its fashions perhaps too closely, every remarkable change in the mode making its appearance there within a few months after its invention here; a natural effect of their constant intercourse with *England*, by ships arriving almost every week from the capital, their respect for the mother country, and admiration of every thing that is *British*. But as to their language, I must beg this gentleman's pardon if I differ from him. His ear, accustomed perhaps to the dialect practised in the *certain northern latitude* he mentions, may not be qualified to judge so nicely in what relates to *pure English*. And I appeal to all Englishmen here, who have been acquainted with the Colonists, whether it is not a common remark, that they speak the language with such an exactness both of expression and accent, that though you may know the natives of several of the counties of *England*, by peculiarities in their dialect, you cannot by that means distinguish a *North American*. All the new books and pamphlets worth reading, that are published here, in a few weeks are transmitted and found there, where there is not a man or woman born in the country but what can read: and it must, I should think, be a pleasing reflection to those who write either for the benefit of the present age or of posterity, to find their audience increasing with the increase of our colonies; and their language extending itself beyond the narrow bounds of these islands to a continent, larger than all *Europe*, and to a future empire as fully peopled, which *Britain* may probably one day possess in those vast western regions.

But the Gentleman makes more injurious comparisons than these: '*That latitude*, he says, has this advantage over them, that it has produced sharp, acute men, fit for war or learning, whereas the other are remarkably simple or silly, and blunder eternally. We have 6000 of their militia, which the General would willingly exchange for 2000 regulars. They are for ever marring some one or other of our plans when sent to execute them. They can, indeed, some of them at least, range in the woods; but 300 Indians with their yell, throw 3000 of them into a panick, and then they will leave nothing to the enemy to do, for they will shoot one another; and in the woods our regulars are afraid to be on a command with them *on that very account.*' I doubt, Mr. Chronicle, that this paragraph, when it comes to be read in *America*, will have no good effect, and rather increase that inconvenient disgust that is too apt to arise between the troops of different corps, or countries, who are obliged to serve together. Will not a *New England Officer* be apt to retort and say, What foundation have you for this odious distinction in favour of the officers from your *certain northern latitude*? They may, as you say, be *fit for learning*, but, surely, the return of your first General, with a well-appointed and sufficient force from his expedition against *Louisbourg*, is not the most shining proof of his *talents for war*. And no one will say his plan was *marred by us*, for we were not with him.—Was his successor, who conducted the blundering attack and inglorious retreat from *Ticonderoga*, a New England man, or one of *that certain latitude*?—Then as to the comparison between *Regulars* and *Provincials*, will not the latter remark, That it was 2000 New England *Provincials*, with but about 150 *Regulars*, that took the strong fort of *Beausejour* in the beginning of the war, though in the accounts transmitted to the English Gazette, the honour was claimed by the regulars, and little or no notice taken of the others.—That it was the *Provincials* who beat General *Dieskau*, with his *Regulars, Canadians*, and '*yelling*' *Indians*, and sent him prisoner to *England.*—That it was a *Provincial-born* Officer *, with *American* battoemen, that beat the *French* and *Indians* on *Oswego* river.—That it was the same Officer, *with Provincials*, who made that long and admirable march into the enemies country, took and destroyed Fort *Frontenac*, with the whole French fleet on the lakes, and struck terror into the heart of *Canada*. That it was a *Provincial* Officer †, *with Provincials* only, who made another extraordinary march into the enemy's country, surprised and destroyed the *Indian* town of *Kittanning*, bringing off the scalps of their chiefs. That one ranging Captain of a few *Provincials, Rogers*, has harrassed the enemy *more* on the frontiers of *Canada*, and destroyed *more* of their men, than the *whole* army of *Regulars.*—That it was the *Regulars* who surrendered themselves,

*Colonel *Bradstreet.*
†Colonel *Armstrong* of *Pensilvania.*

with the Provincials under their command, prisoners of war, almost as soon as they were besieged, with the forts, fleet, and all the provisions and stores that had been provided and amassed at so immense an expence, at *Oswego*. That it was the *Regulars* who surrendered Fort *William Henry*, and suffered themselves to be butchered and scalped with arms in their hands. That it was the *Regulars*, under *Braddock*, who were thrown into a panick by the '*yells* of 3 or 400 Indians,' in their confusion shot one another, and, with five times the force of the enemy, fled before them, destroying all their own stores, ammunition, and provisions!—These *Regular Gentlemen*, will the *Provincial rangers* add, may possibly be *afraid*, as they say they are, *to be on a command with us* in the woods; but when it is considered, that from all past experience the chance of our shooting them is not as one to an hundred, compared with that of their being shot by the enemy, may it not be suspected, that what they give as the *very account* of their fear and unwillingness to venture out with us, is only the *very excuse*; and that a concern for their scalps weighs more with them than a regard for their honour.

Such as these, Sir, I imagine may be the reflections *extorted* by such provocations from the Provincials in general. But the *New England Men* in particular will have reason to resent the remarks on their reduction of *Louisbourg*. Your writer proceeds, 'Indeed they are all very ready to make their boast of taking *Louisbourg*, in 1745; but if people were to be acquitted or condemned according to the propriety and wisdom of their plans, and not according to their success, the persons that undertook that siege merited little praise: for I have heard officers, who assisted at it, say, never was any thing more rash; for had one single part of their plan failed, or had the French made the fortieth part of the resistance then that they have made now, every soul of the New Englanders must have fallen in the trenches. The garrison was weak, sickly, destitute of provisions, and disgusted, and therefore became a ready prey; and, when they returned to France were decimated for their gallant defence. Where then is the glory arising from thence?'—After denying his facts, 'that the garrison was weak, wanted provisions, made not a fortieth part of the resistance, were decimated,' &c. the *New England* men will ask this regular gentleman, If the place was well fortified, and had (as it really had) a numerous garrison, was it not at least *brave* to attack it with a handful of raw undisciplined militia? If the garrison was, as you say, 'sickly, disgusted, destitute of provisions, and ready to become a prey,' was it not *prudent* to seize that opportunity, and put the nation in possession of so important a fortress at so small an expence? So that if you will not allow the enterprize to be, as we think it was, both *brave* and *prudent*, ought you not at least to grant it was *either one* or *the other*? But is there no merit on this score in the people, who, tho' at first so greatly divided, as to the making or forbearing the attempt, that it was carried in the affirmative, by the small majority of *one* vote only; yet when it was once resolved on, *unanimously* prosecuted the design *, and prepared the means with the greatest zeal and diligence; so that the whole equipment was completely ready before the season would permit the execution? Is there no merit of praise in laying and executing their plan so well, that, as you have confessed, not a *single part* of it failed? If the plan was destitute of 'propriety and wisdom,' would it not have required the *sharp acute* men of the *northern latitude* to execute it, that by supplying its deficiencies they might give it some chance of success? But if such 'remarkably silly, simple, blundering *Mar-plans*,' as you say we are, could execute *this plan*, so that not a *single part* of it failed, does it not at least show that the plan itself must be laid with *some* ' wisdom and propriety?'—Is there no merit in the ardour with which all degrees and ranks of people quitted their private affairs, and ranged themselves under the banners of their King, for the honour, safety, and advantage of their country †? Is there no

*'As the Massachuset's assembly at first entered into the expedition upon the *coolest deliberation*, so did they on the other hand exert themselves with *uncommon vigour* in the persecution of it. As soon as the point was carried for undertaking it, EVERY MEMBER which had opposed it *gave up his own private judgment* to the public voice, and *vied* with those who had voted for the expedition, in encouraging the enlistment of the troops, and forwarding the preparations for the attempt.' *Memoirs of the last War*, p. 41.

†'The bounty, pay, and other encouragements, allowed by the Massachuset's government to both officers and men, especially the former, was but small; but the *spirit* which reigned thro' the province supplied the want of that; the complement of troops was soon inlisted; not only the officers, who

merit in the profound secrecy guarded by a whole people, so that the enemy had not the least intelligence of the design, till they saw the fleet of transports cover the sea before their port?—Is there none in the indefatigable labour the troops went thro' during the siege, performing the duty both of men and horses; the hardships they patiently suffered for want of tents and other necessaries; the readiness with which they learnt to move, direct, and manage cannon, raise batteries, and form approaches *; the bravery with which they sus-

---

served in this enterprize, were gentlemen of considerable property, but most of the non-commission'd officers, and many of the private men, had valuable freeholds, and entered into the service upon the same principles that the old *Roman* citizens in the first Consular armies used to do.' *Memoirs of the last War*, p. 41.

To which I may add, that instances of the same noble spirit are not uncommon in all the other colonies; where men have entered into the service not for the sake of the pay, for their own affairs in their absence suffer more by far than its value; not in hopes of preferment in the army, for the Provincials are shut out from such expectations, their own forces being always disbanded on a peace, and the vacancies among the Regulars filled with *Europeans*; but merely from *public spirit* and a sense of duty. Among many others, give me leave to name Col. PETER SCHUYLER of *New Jersey*; who, though a gentleman of a considerable independent fortune, has, both in the last and present war, quitted that domestic ease and quiet which such affluence afforded, to take upon him the command of his country's forces, and by his example animated the soldiery to undergo the greatest fatigues and hardships: And who when a prisoner in *Canada* for fifteen months, did, during the whole time, generously make use of his own credit to relieve such *British* subjects as unhappily fell into the hands of the enemy.—Not to mention his advancing his own private fortune towards paying the forces, raised during last war in *America* by order of the crown; when, by the continued delays in sending the money from *England* for that purpose, it was generally doubted whether it would ever be sent, and the common soldiers were therefore, from necessity, on the point of quitting his Majesty's service in a body. An event which must at that time have been attended with very fatal consequences; and would not have been prevented, had not he risqued so considerable a part of his substance.

*'The *New England* troops, within the compass of 23 days from the time of their first landing, erected five fascine batteries against the town, mounted with cannon of 42 lb. 22 lb. and 18 lb. shot, mortars of 13, 11, and 9 inches diameter, with some cohorns; all which were transported *by hand*, with incredible labour and difficulty, most of them above two miles; all the ground over which they were drawn, except small patches or hills of rocks, was a *deep morass*, in which, whilst the cannon were upon wheels, they several times

tained sallies; and finally in their consenting to stay and garrison the place after it was taken, absent from their business and families, till troops could be brought from England for that purpose, tho' they undertook the service on a promise of being discharged as soon as it was over, were unprovided for so long an absence, and actually suffered ten times more loss by mortal sickness, thro' want of necessaries, than they suffered from the arms of the enemy? The nation, however, had a sense of this undertaking different from the unkind one of this gentleman. At the treaty of peace, the possession of *Louisbourg* was found of great advantage to our affairs in *Europe*; and if the brave men that made the acquisition for us were not *rewarded*, at least they were *praised*. Envy may continue a while to cavil and detract, but *public virtue* will in the end obtain esteem; and honest impartiality in this and future ages will not fail doing justice to merit.

Your *gentleman writer* thus *decently* goes on. 'The most substantial men of most of the provinces are children or grandchildren of those that came here at the King's expence, that is, thieves, highwaymen, and robbers.' Being probably a military gentleman, this, and therefore a person of nice honour, if any one should tell him in the *plainest* language, that what he here says is an absolute falsehood, challenges and cutting of throats might immediately ensue. I shall therefore only refer him to *his own account in this same letter*, of the *peopling* of *New England*, which he says, with more truth, was by *Puritans* who fled thither for shelter from the persecutions of Archbishop *Laud*. Is there not a wide difference between

---

sunk so deep, as not only to bury the carriages, but their whole bodies. Horses and oxen could not be employed in this service, but all must be drawn by men, up to the knees in mud; the nights, in which the work was done, were cold and foggy, their tents bad, there being no proper materials for tents to be had in New England at the outset of the expedition. But notwithstanding these difficulties, and many of the men's being taken down with fluxes, so that at one time there were 1500 incapable of duty, they went on *without being discouraged or murmuring*, and transported the cannon over those ways, which the French had always thought impassable for such heavy weights; and besides this, they had all their provisions and heavy ammunition, which they daily made use of, to bring from the camp over the same way upon their backs.' *Memoirs of the last war in America*, page 52.

removing to a distant country to enjoy the exercise of religion
according to a man's conscience, and his being transported
thither by law as a punishment for his crimes? This contradiction we therefore leave the *gentleman* and *himself* to settle as
well as they can between them. One would think from his
account, that the provinces were so many colonies from
Newgate. The truth is, not only *Laud*'s persecution, but the
other publick troubles in the following reigns, induc'd many
thousand families to leave *England*, and settle in the plantations. During the predominance of the parliament, many royalists removed or were banished to *Virginia* and *Barbadoes*,
who afterwards spread into the other settlements: The Catholics shelter'd themselves in *Maryland*. At the restoration,
many of the depriv'd nonconformist ministers with their
families, friends and hearers, went over. Towards the end of
Charles the Second's reign and during *James* the Second's, the
dissenters again flocked into *America*, driven by persecution,
and dreading the introduction of popery at home. Then the
high price or reward of labour in the colonies, and want of
Artisans there, drew over many, as well as the occasion of
commerce; and when once people begin to migrate, every one
has his little sphere of acquaintance and connections, which
he draws after him, by invitation, motives of interest, praising
his new settlement, and other encouragements. The 'most
substantial men' are descendants of those early settlers; new
comers not having yet had time to raise estates. The practice
of sending convicts thither, is modern; and the same indolence of temper and habits of idleness that make people poor
and tempt them to steal in *England*, continue with them
when they are sent to *America*, and must there have the same
effects, where all who live well owe their subsistence to labour
and business, and where it is a thousand times more difficult
than here to acquire wealth without industry. Hence the instances of transported thieves advancing their fortunes in the
colonies are extreamly rare, if there *really is* a single instance
of it, which I very much doubt; but of their being advanc'd
there to the gallows the instances are plenty. Might they not
as well have been hang'd at home?—We call *Britain* the
mother country; but what good mother besides, would introduce thieves and criminals into the company of her children,

to corrupt and disgrace them?—And how cruel is it, to force, by the high hand of power, a particular country of your subjects, who have not deserv'd such usage, to receive your outcasts, repealing all the laws they make to prevent their admission, and then reproach them with the detested mixture you have made. 'The emptying their jails into our settlements (says a writer of that country) is an insult and contempt, the cruellest perhaps that ever one people offered another; and would not be equal'd even by emptying their jakes on our tables.'

The letter I have been considering, Mr. *Chronicle*, is follow'd by another, in your paper of Tuesday the 17th past, said to be *from an officer who attended Brigadier General* Forbes *in his march from* Philadelphia *to* Fort Duquesne; but wrote probably by the same gentleman who wrote the former, as it seems calculated to raise the character of the officers of the *certain northern latitude*, at the expence of the reputation of the colonies, and the provincial forces. According to this letter-writer, if the *Pensilvanians* granted large supplies, and raised a great body of troops for the last campaign, it was not obedience to his Majesty's commands, signified by his minister Mr. *Pitt*, zeal for the King's service, or even a regard for their own safety; but it was owing to the 'General's proper management of the Quakers and other parties in the province.' The withdrawing of the Indians from the French interest by negotiating a peace, is all ascribed to the General, and not a word said to the honour of the poor *Quakers* who first set those negotiations on foot, or of honest *Frederic Post* that compleated them with so much ability and success. Even the little merit of the Assembly's making a law to regulate carriages, is imputed to the General's 'multitude of letters.' Then he tells us, 'innumerable scouting parties had been sent out during a long period, both by the General and Colonel *Bouquet*, towards Fort *Duquesne*, to catch a prisoner, if possible, for intelligence, but never got any.'—How happened that?— Why, 'It was the *Provincial troops* that were constantly employed in that service,' and they, it seems, never do any thing they are ordered to do.—*That*, however, one would think, might be easily remedied, by sending *Regulars* with them, who of course must command them, and may see that they do their duty. *No; The Regulars are afraid of being shot by the Provincials in a Panick.*—Then send all Regulars.—*Aye; That was what the Colonel* resolved *upon.*—'Intelligence was now wanted. (says the letter-writer) Col. *Bouquet*, whose attention to business was [only] very considerable [that is, *not quite so great* as the General's, for he was not of the *northern latitude*] was *determined* to send NO MORE Provincials a scouting.'— And how did he execute this determination? Why, by sending 'Major *Grant* of the Highlanders, with *seven* hundred men, *three* hundred of them Highlanders, THE REST *Americans, Virginians*, and *Pensilvanians*!' No *blunder* this, in our writer; but a *misfortune*; and he is nevertheless one of those '*acute sharp*' men who are '*fit for learning!*'—And how did this Major and seven hundred men succeed in catching the prisoner?—Why, their 'march to Fort Duquesne was *so conducted* that the *surprize* was *compleat*.'—Perhaps you may imagine, gentle reader, that this was a surprize of the enemy.—No such matter. They knew every step of his motions, and had, every man of them, left their fires and huts in the fields, and retired into the fort.—But the Major and his 700 men, *they* were *surprized*; first to find no body there at night; and next to find themselves surrounded and cut to pieces in the morning; two or three hundred being killed, drowned, or taken prisoners, and among the latter the Major himself. Those who escaped were also *surprized* at their own good fortune; and the whole army was *surprized* at the Major's bad management. Thus the *surprize* was indeed *compleat*;—but not the disgrace; for *Provincials were there* to lay the blame on. The *misfortune* (we must not call it *misconduct*) of the Major was owing, it seems, to an un-named and perhaps unknown *Provincial* officer, who, it is said, 'disobeyed his orders and quitted his post.' Whence a formal conclusion is drawn, 'That a Planter is not to be taken from the plow and made an officer in a day.'—Unhappy *Provincials*! If *success* attends where you are joined with the Regulars, they claim all the honour, tho' not a tenth part of your number. If *disgrace*, it is all yours, though you happen to be but a small part of the whole, and have not the command; as if Regulars were in their nature invincible, when not mix'd with Provincials, and Provincials of no kind of value without Regulars! Happy is it for you that you were present neither at *Preston-Pans* nor *Falkirk*, at the faint attempt against *Rochfort*, the route of *St. Cas*, or the hasty retreat from *Martinico*. Every thing that went wrong, or did not go right, would have been ascribed to you. Our commanders would have been saved the labour of writing long apologies for their conduct. It might have been sufficient to say, *Provincials were with us!*

But these remarks, which we only suppose may be made by the provok'd provincials, are probably too severe. The generals, even those who have been recall'd, had in several respects great merit, as well as many of the officers of the same nation that remain, which the cool discreet part of the provincials will readily allow. They are not insensible of the worth and bravery of the *British* troops in general, honour them for the amazing valour they manifested at the landing on *Cape Breton*, the prudence and military skill they show'd in the siege and reduction of *Louisburg*, and their good conduct on other occasions; and can make due allowance for mistakes naturally arising where even the best men are engag'd in a new kind of war, with a new and strange enemy, and in a country different from any they had before experienc'd. Lord Howe was their darling *, and others might be nam'd who are growing daily in their esteem and admiration.—There are also among the regular officers, men of sentiments, concerning the colonies, more generous and more just than those express'd by these letter-writers; who can see faults even in their own corps, and who can allow the Provincials their share of merit; who feel pleasure as *Britons*, in observing that the *children* of *Britain* retain their native intrepidity to the third and fourth generation in the regions of *America*; together with that ardent love of liberty and zeal in its defence, which in every age has distinguish'd their progenitors among the rest of mankind.—To conclude, in all countries, all nations, and all armies, there is, and will be a mixture of characters, a medley of brave men, fools, wise-men and cowards. National reflections being general,

*The assembly of the *Massachusets-Bay* have voted a sum of money for erecting a monument in *Westminster-Abbey*, to the memory of that Nobleman, as a testimony of their veneration for his virtues.—A proof that their sense of merit is not narrow'd to a country.

are therefore unjust. But panegyrics, tho' they should be too
general, cannot offend the subjects of them. I shall therefore
boldly say, that the *English* are brave and wise; the *Scotch* are
brave and wise; and the people of the *British* colonies, proceeding from both nations—I would say the same of them,
if it might not be thought vanity in

Your humble servant,

May 9, 1759.   *A New Englandman.*

A Description of Those, Who, at Any Rate, Would Have a Peace with France

The two prevailing motives among us, which strongly bias
great numbers of people, at this time, to wish for a peace with
France, let the terms be ever so dishonourable, ever so disadvantageous, or likely to prove of ever so short a duration, are
Power and Self-interest.

As to the First, there is a set of men, who have been so
long used to Power, that it is become part of their constitution; and if they cannot preserve it, they and their Dependants must linger and pine away. They find plainly, that
whatever they have undertaken has succeeded so ill, that, instead of their gaining the people's Applause and Confidence,
They become every day more and more Obnoxious and Contemptible: And they perceive, on the other hand, that such
part of the Administration, in which they have had no share,
has been so well understood and conducted, that such general
Satisfaction has been given throughout the whole kingdom,
as reflects highly on the want of Integrity and Capacity in
those who have gone before. No wonder therefore, if such
men should be desirous of peace at any rate, so it lasts their
time; that the frequent scenes of Honour to others, and Dishonour to themselves, may not haunt them any more: And,
especially being sensible the National Credit has been strained

to such a degree by their extravagant plan of Dissipation, as to render it necessary for the Publick Accounts being taken, as was so frequently and honestly done during the reigns of King William and Queen Anne, even at the Minister's own desire.

The latter are those who are engaged in our Public Funds, and are impatient to have them rise, AND THOSE (IN NO SMALL NUMBER) WHO HAVE SO INFAMOUSLY LENT THEIR MONEY TO THE FRENCH GOVERNMENT: Merchants who are concerned in branches of Commerce and of Business, which they imagine will improve upon their hands, in case of a Peace: other Mercantile People, who have their prospects of advantage, upon the conclusion of a Peace; such for example, who think we shall hold some of our conquests, which of course will give room for new Settlements; and some who have prospects of Places in such new Settlements: Some who have formed to themselves agreeable plans, for striking into new Branches of Trade: Many Country Gentlemen and others, who wouldn't perhaps be sorry for a Peace, in hopes of being eas'd in their taxes: And lastly, there are very few Roman Catholicks in the Kingdom, but would rejoice at a Peace, at any rate.

It is a melancholy Reflection, that there should be among us such selfish wretches, and such enemies to their Country, who had rather see it sink, a while hence, and its bitterest enemies triumph, than that their present lust for Power, and their sordid Views, should not be gratified; And that there should be those, who are striving to diminish the Importance of every conquest we make, that the people mayn't grow too fond of keeping them; and even go so far, as to propagate the very Nonsensical Language of MAUBERT; viz. THE ENGLISH *will persevere in their conquests till they draw all the Powers of Europe upon their backs.*

Such is the true Picture of those, who, on such infamous Terms, wou'd sell advantages their Country has obtained, at the expence of so much blood and treasure, over their most Inveterate and most Treacherous enemies.

London, Nov. 24.

The London Chronicle, November 24, 1759

Humourous Reasons for Restoring Canada

Mr. Chronicle,

We Britons are a nation of statesmen and politicians; we are privy councellors by birthright; and therefore take it much amiss when we are told by some of your correspondents, 'that it is not proper to expose to public view the many good reasons there are for restoring Canada,' (*if we reduce it.*)

I have, with great industry, been able to procure a full account of those reasons, and shall make no secret of them among ourselves. Here they are.—Give them to all your readers; that is, to all that can read, in the King's dominions.

1. We should restore Canada; because an uninterrupted trade with the Indians throughout a vast country, where the communication by water is so easy, would encrease our commerce, *already too great*, and occasion a large additional demand for our manufactures, * *already too dear*.

2. We should restore it, lest, thro' a greater plenty of beaver, broad-brimmed hats become cheaper to that unmannerly sect, the Quakers.

3. We should restore Canada, that we may *soon* have a new war, and another opportunity of spending two or three millions a year in America; there being great danger of our growing too rich, our European expences not being sufficient to drain our immense treasures.

4. We should restore it, that we may have occasion constantly to employ, in time of war, a fleet and army in those parts; for otherwise we might be too strong at home.

5. We should restore it, that the French may, by means of their Indians, carry on, (as they have done for these 100 years past even in times of peace between the two crowns) a constant scalping war against our colonies, and thereby stint their growth; for, otherwise, the children might in time be as tall as their mother †.

---

*Every Indian now wears a woollen blanket, a linnen shirt, and cloth stockings; besides a knife, a hatchet and a gun; and they use a variety of other European and Indian goods, which they pay for in skins and furs.

†This reason is seriously given by some who do not wish well to the Colonies: But, is it not too like the Egyptian Politics practised by Pharoah, destroying the young males to prevent the increase of the children of Israel?

6. What tho' the blood of thousands of unarmed English farmers, surprized and assassinated in their fields; of harmless women and children murdered in their beds; doth at length call for vengeance;—what tho' the Canadian measure of iniquity be full, and if ever any country did, that country now certainly does, deserve the judgment of *extirpation*;—yet let not us be the executioners of Divine justice;—it will look as if Englishmen were revengeful.

7. Our colonies, 'tis true, have exerted themselves beyond their strength, on the expectations we gave them of driving the French from Canada; but tho' we ought to keep faith with our Allies, it is not necessary with our children. That might teach them (against Scripture) to *put their trust in Princes*: Let 'em learn to trust in God.

8. Should we not restore Canada, it would look as if our statesmen had *courage* as well as our soldiers; but what have statesmen to do with *courage*? Their proper character is *wisdom*.

9. What can be *braver*, than to show all Europe we can afford to lavish our best blood as well as our treasure, in conquests we do not intend to keep? Have we not plenty of *Howe's*, and *Wolfe's*, &c. &c. &c. in every regiment?

10. The French * have long since openly declar'd, *'que les Anglois & les François sont incompatible dans cette partie de l'Amerique;'* 'that our people and theirs were incompatible in that part of the continent of America:' *'que rien n'etoit plus important à l'etat, que de delivrer leur colonie du facheux voisinage des Anglois;'* 'that nothing was of more importance to France, than delivering its colony from the troublesome neighbourhood of the English;' to which end, there was an avowed project on foot *'pour chasser premierement les Anglois de la Nouvelle York;'* 'to drive the English in the first place out of the province of New York;' *'& apres la prise de la capitale, il falloit* (says the scheme) *la* BRULER *&* RUINER *le pays jusqu' à Orange;'* 'and after taking the capital, to *burn it*, and *ruin* (that is, *make a desart* of) the whole country, quite up to Albany.' Now, if we do not fairly leave the French in Canada, till they have a favourable opportunity of putting their

*Histoire Generale de la Nouvelle France, par Charlevoix. Liv. XII.

burning and *ruining* schemes in execution, will it not look
as if we were afraid of them?

11. Their historian, Charlevoix, in his IVth book, also tells
us, that when Canada was formerly taken by the English, it
was a question at the court of France, whether they should
endeavour to recover it; for, says he, *'bien de gens douterent si
l'on avoit fait une veritable perte;'* 'many thought it was not
really a loss.' But tho' various reasons were given why it was
scarce worth recovering, *'le seul motive* (says he) *d'empecher les
Anglois de se rendre trop puissans—étoit plus que suffissant pour
nous engager a recouvrer Quebec, a quelque prix que ce fût;'* 'the
single motive of preventing the increase of *English* power,
was more than sufficient to engage us in recovering Quebec,
what price soever it might cost us.' Here we see the high value
they put on that country, and the reason of their valuing it
so highly. Let us then, *oblige them* in this (to them) so important an article, and be assured they will *never prove ungrateful.*

I will not dissemble, Mr. *Chronicle*; that in answer to all
these reasons and motives for restoring Canada, I have heard
one that appears to have some weight on the other side of
the question. It is said, that nations, as well as private persons, should, for their honour's sake, take care to preserve a
consistence of character: that it has always been the character of
the English to fight strongly, and negotiate weakly; generally
agreeing to restore, at a peace, what they ought to have kept,
and to keep what they had better have restored: then, if it
would really, according to the preceding reasons, be prudent
and right to restore Canada, we ought, say these objectors, to
keep it; otherwise *we shall be inconsistent with ourselves.* I shall
not take upon myself to weigh these different reasons, but
offer the whole to the consideration of the public. Only permit me to suggest, that there is one method of avoiding fairly
all future dispute about the propriety of *keeping* or *restoring*
Canada; and that is, *let us never take it.* The French still hold
out at Montreal and Trois Rivieres, in hopes of succour from
France. Let us be but *a little too late* with our ships in the
river St. Laurence, so that the enemy may get their supplies
up next spring, as they did the last, with reinforcements

may so speak, some of its smaller limbes and members, that, being remote therefrom, are not easilie defended; to wit, our islands and colonies in the Indies; thereby however depriving the bodie of its wonted nourishment, so that it must thenceforthe languish and grow weake, if those parts be not recovered, which possibly may, by continuance of warre, be found unlikely to be done. And the enemie, puffed up with their successes, and hoping still for more, may not be disposed to peace on such termes as would be suitable to the honour of your Majestie, and to the welfare of your State and Subjectes. In such case, the following meanes may have good effect.

'It is well known, that these northerne people, though hardie of bodie, and bold in fight, be neverthelesse, through over-much eating and other intemperance, slowe of wit and dull in understanding, so that they be oftimes more easilie to be governed and turned by skille than by force. There is therefore always hope, that by wise counsel and dextrous management, those advantages which through cross accidents in warre have been lost, may again with honour be recovered. In this place I shall say little of the power of money secretly distributed amongst grandees or their friends or mistresses, that method being in all ages known and practised. If the *minds* of enemies can be *changed*, they may be brought to grant willingly and for nothing, what much golde would scarcelie have otherwise prevailed to obtaine. Yet as the procuring this change is to be by fitte instruments, some few doublones will not unprofitablie be disbursed by your Majestie; the manner whereof I shall now brieflie recite.

'In those countries, and particularly in England, there are not wanting men of learning, ingenious speakers and writers, who are neverthelesse in lowe estate and pinched by fortune; these being privatelie gained by proper meanes, must be instructed in their sermons, discourses, writings, poems and songs, to handle and specially inculcate points like these which followe. Let them magnify the blessings of peace and enlarge mightily thereon, which is not unbecoming grave Divines and other Christian men; let them expatiate on the miseries of warre, the waste of Christian bloode, the growing scarcitie of labourers and workmen, the dearness of all foreign wares and merchandises, the interruption of commerce by the captures or delay of ships, the increase and great burthen of taxes, and the impossibilitie of supplying much longer the expence of the contest;—let them represent the warre as an unmeasurable advantage to particulars, and to particulars only (thereby to excite envie against those that manage and provide for the same) while so prejudicial to the Commonweale and people in general: let them represent the advantages gained against us as trivial and of little import; the places taken from us as of small trade or produce, inconvenient for situation, unwholesome for ayre and climate, useless to their nations, and greatly chargeable to keepe, draining the home Countries both of men and money: let them urge, that if a peace be forced on us, and those places withheld, it will nourishe secret griefe and malice in the King and Grandees of Spain, which will ere long breake forthe in new warres, wherein those places may again be retaken, and lost without the merit and grace of restoring them willingly for peacesake:—let them represent the making and continuance of warres from view of gaine, to be base and unworthie a brave people; as those made from view of ambition are mad and wicked; and let them insinuate that the continuance of the present warre on their parte, when peace is offered, hath these ingredients strongly in its nature. Then let them magnifie the great power of your Majestie, and the strength of your kingdome, the inexhaustible wealthe of your mines, the greatness of your incomes, and thence your abilitie of continuing the warre; hinting withal, the new alliances you may possibly make; at the same time setting forth the sincere disposition you have for peace, and that it is only a concerne for your honour and the honour of your realme, that induceth you to insist on the restitution of the places taken.—If with all this they shrewdly intimate and cause it to be understood by artefull words, and beleeved, that their own Prince is himself in heart for peace on your Majesties termes, and grieved at the obstinacie and perverseness of those among his people that be for continuing the warre, a marvellous effect shall by these discourses and writings be produced; and a wonderful strong party shall your Majestie raise among your enemies in favour of the peace you desire; insomuch that their own Princes and wisest Councellours will in a sort be constrained to yeeld thereto. For in this warre of words, the avarice and ambition, the hopes and fears, and all the croud of human passions, will, in the minds of your enemies, be raised, armed, and put in array, to fight for your interests, against the reall and substantiall interest of their own countries. The simple and undiscerning many, shall be carried away by the plausibilitie and well-seeming of these discourses; and the opinions becoming popular, all the rich men, who have great possessions, and fear the continuance of taxes, and hope peace will end them, shall be imboldened thereby to cry aloud for peace;—their dependents who are many, must do the same: all marchants, fearing loss of ships and greater burthens on trade by farther duties and subsidies, and hoping greater profittes by the ending of the warre, shall join in the cry for peace: All the usurers and lenders of monies to the State, who on a peace hope great profit from their bargaines, and fear if the warre be continued, the State shall become bankeroute, and unable to pay them; these, who have no small weight, shall joine the cry for peace:—All the gowne and booke-statesmen, who maligne the bold conductors of the warre, and envie the glorie they may have thereby obtained; these shall cry aloud for peace; hoping, that when the Warre shall cease, such men becoming less necessarie shall be more lightelie esteemed, and themselves more sought after:—All the officers of the enemies armies and fleets, who wish for repose, and to enjoy their spoiles, salaries, or rewards, in quietness, and without peril, these, and their friends and families, who desire their safetie, and the solace of their societie, shall all cry for peace:—All those who be timorous by nature, amongst whom be reckoned men of learning that lead sedentarie lives, using little exercise of bodie, and thence obtaining but few and weake spirits; great Statesmen, whose natural spirits be exhausted by much thinking, or depress'd by over-much feasting; together with all women, whose power, weake as they are, is not a little among such men; these shall incessantly speake for peace: And finallie, all Courtiers, who suppose they conforme thereby to the inclinations of the Prince *; all who are *in* places of profit, and fear to lose them, or hope for better; all

*Ad Exemplum Regis, &c.

who are *out* of places, and hope to obtain them; all the worldly-minded clergie, who seeke preferment; these, with all the weight of their character and influence, shall joine the cry for peace, till it becomes one universal clamour, and no sound but that of *Peace, Peace, Peace,* shall be heard from every quarter. Then shall your Majesties termes of peace be listened to with much readiness, the places taken from you be willingly restored, and your kingdome, recovering its strength, shall only need to waite a few years for more favourable occasions, when the advantages to your power proposed by beginning the warre, but lost by its bad successe, shall, with better fortune, be finallie obtained.'

What effect the artifices here recommended might have had in the times when this Jesuit wrote, I cannot pretend to say; but I believe, the present age being more enlightened, and our people better acquainted than formerly with our true national interests, such arts can now hardly prove so generally successful: For we may with pleasure observe, and to the honour of the British people, that though writings and discourses like these have lately not been wanting, yet few in any of the classes he particularises seem to be affected by them; but all ranks and degrees among us persist hitherto in declaring for a vigorous prosecution of the war, in preference to an unsafe, disadvantageous peace.

Yet, as a little change of fortune may make such writings more attended to, and give them greater weight, I think the publication of this piece, as it shows the spring from whence these scribblers draw their poisoned waters, may be of publick utility. I am, Sir, yours, &c.

A Briton.

The London Chronicle, August 13, 1761

A Narrative of the Late Massacres, in Lancaster County, of a Number of Indians, Friends of this Province, by Persons Unknown

WITH SOME OBSERVATIONS ON THE SAME

These *Indians* were the Remains of a Tribe of the *Six Nations*, settled at *Conestogoe*, and thence called *Conestogoe Indians*. On the first Arrival of the *English* in *Pennsylvania*, Messengers from this Tribe came to welcome them, with Presents of Venison, Corn and Skins; and the whole Tribe entered into a Treaty of Friendship with the first Proprietor, WILLIAM PENN, which was to last "as long as the Sun should shine, or the Waters run in the Rivers."

This Treaty has been since frequently renewed, and the *Chain brightened*, as they express it, from time to time. It has never been violated, on their Part or ours, till now. As their Lands by Degrees were mostly purchased, and the Settlements of the White People began to surround them, the Proprietor assigned them Lands on the Manor of *Conestogoe*, which they might not part with; there they have lived many Years in Friendship with their White Neighbours, who loved them for their peaceable inoffensive Behaviour.

It has always been observed, that *Indians*, settled in the Neighbourhood of White People, do not increase, but diminish continually. This Tribe accordingly went on diminishing, till there remained in their Town on the Manor, but 20 Persons, *viz.* 7 Men, 5 Women, and 8 Children, Boys and Girls.

Of these, *Shehaes* was a very old Man, having assisted at the second Treaty held with them, by Mr. PENN, in 1701, and ever since continued a faithful and affectionate Friend to the *English*; he is said to have been an exceeding good Man, considering his Education, being naturally of a most kind benevolent Temper.

Peggy was *Shehaes*'s Daughter; she worked for her aged Father, continuing to live with him, though married, and attended him with filial Duty and Tenderness.

John was another good old Man; his Son *Harry* helped to support him.

George and *Will Soc* were two Brothers, both young Men.

John Smith, a valuable young Man, of the *Cayuga* Nation, who became acquainted with *Peggy*, *Shehaes*'s Daughter, some few Years since, married her, and settled in that Family. They had one Child, about three Years old.

Betty, a harmless old Woman; and her Son *Peter*, a likely young Lad.

Sally, whose *Indian* Name was *Wyanjoy*, a Woman much esteemed by all that knew her, for her prudent and good Behaviour in some very trying Situations of Life. She was a truly good and an amiable Woman, had no Children of her own, but a distant Relation dying, she had taken a Child of that Relation's, to bring up as her own, and performed towards it all the Duties of an affectionate Parent.

The Reader will observe, that many of their Names are *English*. It is common with the *Indians* that have an Affection for the *English*, to give themselves, and their Children, the Names of such *English* Persons as they particularly esteem.

This little Society continued the Custom they had begun, when more numerous, of addressing every new Governor, and every Descendant of the first Proprietor, welcoming him to the Province, assuring him of their Fidelity, and praying a Continuance of that Favour and Protection they had hitherto experienced. They had accordingly sent up an Address of this Kind to our present Governor, on his Arrival; but the same was scarce delivered, when the unfortunate Catastrophe happened, which we are about to relate.

On *Wednesday*, the 14th of *December*, 1763, Fifty-seven Men, from some of our Frontier Townships, who had projected the Destruction of this little Common-wealth, came, all well-mounted, and armed with Firelocks, Hangers and Hatchets, having travelled through the Country in the Night, to *Conestogoe* Manor. There they surrounded the small Village of *Indian* Huts, and just at Break of Day broke into them all at once. Only three Men, two Women, and a young Boy, were found at home, the rest being out among the neighbouring White People, some to sell the Baskets, Brooms and Bowls they manufactured, and others on other Occasions. These poor defenceless Creatures were immediately fired upon, stabbed and hatcheted to Death! The good *Shehaes*, among the rest, cut to Pieces in his Bed. All of them were scalped, and otherwise horribly mangled. Then their Huts were set on Fire, and most of them burnt down. When the Troop, pleased with their own Conduct and Bravery, but enraged that any of the poor *Indians* had escaped the Massacre, rode off, and in small Parties, by different Roads, went home.

The universal Concern of the neighbouring White People on hearing of this Event, and the Lamentations of the younger *Indians*, when they returned and saw the Desolation, and the butchered half-burnt Bodies of their murdered Parents, and other Relations, cannot well be expressed.

The Magistrates of *Lancaster* sent out to collect the remaining *Indians*, brought them into the Town for their better Security against any farther Attempt; and it is said condoled with them on the Misfortune that had happened, took them by the Hand, comforted and *promised them Protection.*—They were all put into the Workhouse, a strong Building, as the Place of greatest Safety.

When the shocking News arrived in Town, a Proclamation was issued by the Governor, in the following Terms, *viz.*

"WHEREAS I have received Information, That on *Wednesday*, the Fourteenth Day of this Month, a Number of People, armed, and mounted on Horseback, unlawfully assembled together, and went to the *Indian* Town in the *Conestogoe* Manor, in *Lancaster* County, and without the least Reason or Provocation, in cool Blood, barbarously killed six of the *Indians* settled there, and burnt and destroyed all their Houses and Effects: And whereas so cruel and inhuman an Act, committed in the Heart of this Province on the said *Indians*, who have lived peaceably and inoffensively among us, during all our late Troubles, and for many Years before, and were justly considered as under the Protection of this Government and its Laws, calls loudly for the vigorous Exertion of the civil Authority, to detect the Offenders, and bring them to condign Punishment; I have therefore, by and with the Advice and Consent of the Council, thought fit to issue this Proclamation, and do hereby strictly charge and enjoin all

Judges, Justices, Sheriffs, Constables, Officers Civil and Military, and all other His Majesty's liege Subjects within this Province, to make diligent Search and Enquiry after the Authors and Perpetrators of the said Crime, their Abettors and Accomplices, and to use all possible Means to apprehend and secure them in some of the publick Goals of this Province, that they may be brought to their Trials, and be proceeded against according to Law.

"And whereas a Number of other *Indians*, who lately lived on or near the Frontiers of this Province, being willing and desirous to preserve and continue the ancient Friendship which heretofore subsisted between them and the good People of this Province, have, at their own earnest Request, been removed from their Habitations, and brought into the County of *Philadelphia*, and seated, for the present, for their better Security, on the *Province-Island*, and in other Places in the Neighbourhood of the City of *Philadelphia*, where Provision is made for them at the public Expence; I do therefore hereby strictly forbid all Persons whatsoever, to molest or injure any of the said *Indians*, as they will answer the contrary at their Peril.

> *GIVEN under my Hand, and the Great Seal of the said Province, at* Philadelphia, *the Twenty-second Day of* December, *Anno Domini* One Thousand Seven Hundred and Sixty-three, *and in the Fourth Year of His Majesty's Reign.*
> JOHN PENN."

By His Honour's Command,
JOSEPH SHIPPEN, *jun. Secretary.*
GOD Save the KING.

Notwithstanding this Proclamation, those cruel Men again assembled themselves, and hearing that the remaining fourteen *Indians* were in the Work-house at *Lancaster*, they suddenly appeared in that Town, on the 27th of *December*. Fifty of them, armed as before, dismounting, went directly to the Work-house, and by Violence broke open the Door, and entered with the utmost Fury in their Countenances.—When the poor Wretches saw they had *no Protection* nigh, nor could possibly escape, and being without the least Weapon for

Defence, they divided into their little Families, the Children clinging to the Parents; they fell on their Knees, protested their Innocence, declared their Love to the *English*, and that, in their whole Lives, they had never done them Injury; and in this Posture they all received the Hatchet!—Men, Women and little Children—were every one inhumanly murdered!—in cold Blood!

The barbarous Men who committed the atrocious Fact, in Defiance of Government, of all Laws human and divine, and to the eternal Disgrace of their Country and Colour, then mounted their Horses, huzza'd in Triumph, as if they had gained a Victory, and rode off— *unmolested!*

The Bodies of the Murdered were then brought out and exposed in the Street, till a Hole could be made in the Earth, to receive and cover them.

But the Wickedness cannot be covered, the Guilt will lie on the whole Land, till Justice is done on the Murderers. THE BLOOD OF THE INNOCENT WILL CRY TO HEAVEN FOR VENGEANCE.

It is said that *Shehaes*, being before told, that it was to be feared some *English* might come from the Frontier into the Country, and murder him and his People; he replied, "It is impossible: There are *Indians*, indeed, in the Woods, who would kill me and mine, if they could get at us, for my Friendship to the *English*; but the *English* will wrap me in their Matchcoat, and secure me from all Danger." How unfortunately was he mistaken!

Another Proclamation has been issued, offering a great Reward for apprehending the Murderers, in the following Terms, *viz.*

"WHEREAS on the Twenty-second Day of *December* last, I issued a Proclamation for the apprehending and bringing to Justice, a Number of Persons, who, in Violation of the Public Faith, and in Defiance of all Law, had inhumanly killed six of the *Indians*, who had lived in *Conestogoe* Manor, for the Course of many Years, peaceably and inoffensively, under the Protection of this Government, on Lands assigned to them for their Habitation; notwithstanding which, I have received

Information, that on the Twenty-seventh of the same Month, a large Party of armed Men again assembled and met together in a riotous and tumultuous Manner, in the County of *Lancaster*, and proceeded to the Town of *Lancaster*, where they violently broke open the Work-house, and butchered and put to Death fourteen of the said *Conestogoe Indians*, Men, Women and Children, who had been taken under the immediate Care and Protection of the Magistrates of the said County, and lodged for their better Security in the said Work-house, till they should be more effectually provided for by Order of the Government. And whereas common Justice loudly demands, and the Laws of the Land (upon the Preservation of which not only the Liberty and Security of every Individual, but the Being of the Government itself depend) require that the above Offenders should be brought to condign Punishment; I have therefore, by and with the Advice of the Council, published this Proclamation, and do hereby strictly charge and command all Judges, Justices, Sheriffs, Constables, Officers Civil and Military, and all other His Majesty's faithful and liege Subjects within this Province, to make diligent Search and Enquiry after the Authors and Perpetrators of the said last mentioned Offence, their Abettors and Accomplices, and that they use all possible Means to apprehend and secure them in some of the public Goals of this Province, to be dealt with according to Law.

"And I do hereby further promise and engage, that any Person or Persons, who shall apprehend and secure, or cause to be apprehended and secured, any Three of the Ringleaders of the said Party, and prosecute them to Conviction, shall have and receive for each, the public Reward of *Two Hundred Pounds*; and any Accomplice, not concerned in the immediate shedding the Blood of the said *Indians*, who shall make Discovery of any or either of the said Ringleaders, and apprehend and prosecute them to Conviction, shall, over and above the said Reward, have all the Weight and Influence of the Government, for obtaining His Majesty's Pardon for his Offence.

GIVEN under my Hand, and the Great Seal of the said Province, at Philadelphia, *the Second Day of* January, *in the*

Fourth Year of His Majesty's Reign, and in the Year of our Lord One Thousand Seven Hundred and Sixty-four.

JOHN PENN."

By His Honour's Command,
JOSEPH SHIPPEN, *jun. Secretary.*

GOD Save the KING.

These Proclamations have as yet produced no Discovery; the Murderers having given out such Threatenings against those that disapprove their Proceedings, that the whole County seems to be in Terror, and no one durst speak what he knows; even the Letters from thence are unsigned, in which any Dislike is expressed of the Rioters.

There are some (I am ashamed to hear it) who would extenuate the enormous Wickedness of these Actions, by saying, "The Inhabitants of the Frontiers are exasperated with the Murder of their Relations, by the Enemy *Indians*, in the present War." It is possible;—but though this might justify their going out into the Woods, to seek for those Enemies, and avenge upon them those Murders; it can never justify their turning in to the Heart of the Country, to murder their Friends.

If an *Indian* injures me, does it follow that I may revenge that Injury on all *Indians*? It is well known that *Indians* are of different Tribes, Nations and Languages, as well as the White People. In *Europe*, if the *French*, who are White People, should injure the *Dutch*, are they to revenge it on the *English*, because they too are White People? The only Crime of these poor Wretches seems to have been, that they had a reddish brown Skin, and black Hair; and some People of that Sort, it seems, had murdered some of our Relations. If it be right to kill Men for such a Reason, then, should any Man, with a freckled Face and red Hair, kill a Wife or Child of mine, it would be right for me to revenge it, by killing all the freckled red-haired Men, Women and Children, I could afterwards any where meet with.

But it seems these People think they have a better Justification; nothing less than the *Word of God*. With the Scriptures in their Hands and Mouths, they can set at nought that express Command, *Thou shalt do no Murder*; and justify their

Wickedness, by the Command given *Joshua* to destroy the Heathen. Horrid Perversion of Scripture and of Religion! to father the worst of Crimes on the God of Peace and Love!— Even the *Jews*, to whom that particular Commission was directed, spared the *Gibeonites*, on Account of their Faith once given. The Faith of this Government has been frequently given to those *Indians*;—but that did not avail them with People who despise Government.

We pretend to be *Christians*, and, from the superior Light we enjoy, ought to exceed *Heathens*, *Turks*, *Saracens*, *Moors*, *Negroes* and *Indians*, in the Knowledge and Practice of what is right. I will endeavour to show, by a few Examples from Books and History, the Sense those People have had of such Actions.

HOMER wrote his Poem, called the *Odyssey*, some Hundred Years before the Birth of Christ. He frequently speaks of what he calls not only *the Duties*, but *the sacred Rites of Hospitality*, (exercised towards Strangers, while in our House or Territory) as including, besides all the common Circumstances of Entertainment, full Safety and Protection of Person, from all Danger of Life, from all Injuries, and even Insults. The Rites of Hospitality were called *sacred*, because the Stranger, the Poor and the Weak, when they applied for Protection and Relief, were, from the Religion of those Times, supposed to be sent by the Deity to try the Goodness of Men, and that he would avenge the Injuries they might receive, where they ought to have been protected.—These Sentiments therefore influenced the Manners of all Ranks of People, even the meanest; for we find that when *Ulysses* came, as a poor Stranger, to the Hut of *Eumæus*, the Swineherd, and his great Dogs ran out to tear the ragged Man, *Eumæus* drave them away with Stones; and

> *Unhappy Stranger! (thus the faithful Swain*
> *Began, with Accent gracious and humane)*
> *What Sorrow had been mine, if at* my *Gate*
> *Thy rev'rend Age had met a shameful Fate?*
> *——But enter this my homely Roof, and see*
> *Our Woods not void of Hospitality.*
> *He said, and seconding the kind Request,*

With friendly Step precedes the unknown Guest.
A shaggy Goat's soft Hide beneath him spread,
And with fresh Rushes heap'd an ample Bed.
Joy touch'd the Hero's tender Soul, to find
So just *Reception from a Heart so kind:*
And oh, ye Gods! with all your Blessings grace
(He thus broke forth) this Friend of human Race!
    The Swain reply'd. It never was our guise
To slight the Poor, or aught humane despise.
For Jove *unfolds the hospitable Door,*
Tis Jove *that sends the Stranger and the Poor.*

These Heathen People thought, that after a Breach of the Rites of Hospitality, a Curse from Heaven would attend them in every thing they did, and even their honest Industry in their Callings would fail of Success.—Thus when *Ulysses* tells *Eumæus*, who doubted the Truth of what he related, *If I deceive you in this, I should deserve Death, and I consent that you should put me to Death*; *Eumæus* rejects the Proposal as what would be attended with both Infamy and Misfortune, saying ironically,

Doubtless, oh Guest! great Laud and Praise were mine,
If, after social Rites and Gifts bestow'd,
I stain'd my Hospitable Hearth with Blood.
How would the Gods my righteous Toils succeed,
And bless the Hand that made a Stranger bleed?
No more. —

Even an open Enemy, in the Heat of Battle, throwing down his Arms, submitting to his Foe, and asking Life and Protection, was supposed to acquire an immediate Right to that Protection. Thus one describes his being saved, when his Party was defeated.

We turn'd to Flight; the gath'ring Vengeance spread
On all Parts round, and Heaps on Heaps lie dead.
—The radiant Helmet from my Brows unlac'd,
And lo on Earth my Shield and Jav'lin cast,
I meet the Monarch with a Suppliant's Face,
Approach his Chariot, and his Knees embrace.
He heard, he sav'd, he plac'd me at his Side;

My State he pity'd, and my Tears he dry'd;
Restrain'd the Rage the vengeful Foe express'd,
And turn'd the deadly Weapons from my Breast.
Pious to guard the Hospitable Rite,
And fearing Jove, *whom Mercy's Works delight.*

The Suitors of *Penelope* are by the same ancient Poet described as a Sett of lawless Men, who were *regardless of the sacred Rites of Hospitality.* And therefore when the Queen was informed they were slain, and that by *Ulysses*, she, not believing that *Ulysses* was returned, says,

Ah no!—some God the Suitors Deaths decreed,
Some God descends, and by his Hand they bleed:
Blind, to contemn the Stranger's righteous Cause,
And violate all hospitable Laws!
——————*The Powers they defy'd;*
But Heav'n is just, and by a God they dy'd.

Thus much for the Sentiments of the ancient *Heathens.*— As for the *Turks*, it is recorded in the Life of *Mahomet*, the Founder of their Religion, that *Khaled*, one of his Captains, having divided a Number of Prisoners between himself and those that were with him, he commanded the Hands of his own Prisoners to be tied behind them, and then, in a most cruel and brutal Manner, put them to the Sword; but he could not prevail on his Men to massacre *their* Captives, because in Fight they had laid down their Arms, submitted, and demanded Protection. *Mahomet*, when the Account was brought to him, applauded the Men for their Humanity; but said to *Khaled*, with great Indignation, *Oh* Khaled, *thou Butcher, cease to molest me with thy Wickedness.*—*If thou possessedst a Heap of Gold as large as Mount* Obod, *and shouldst expend it all in God's Cause, thy Merit would not efface the Guilt incurred by the Murder of the meanest of those poor Captives.*

Among the *Arabs* or *Saracens*, though it was lawful to put to Death a Prisoner taken in Battle, if he had made himself obnoxious by his former Wickedness, yet this could not be done after he had once eaten Bread, or drank Water, while in their Hands. Hence we read in the History of the Wars of the *Holy Land*, that when the *Franks* had suffered a great Defeat from *Saladin*, and among the Prisoners were the King of *Je-rusalem*, and *Arnold*, a famous Christian Captain, who had been very cruel to the *Saracens*; these two being brought before the Soltan, he placed the King on his right Hand, and *Arnold* on his left; and then presented the King with a Cup of Water, who immediately drank to *Arnold*; but when *Arnold* was about to receive the Cup, the Soltan interrupted, saying, *I will not suffer this wicked Man to drink, as that, according to the laudable and generous Custom of the* Arabs, *would secure him his Life.*

That the same laudable and generous Custom still prevails among the *Mahometans*, appears from the Account but last Year published of his Travels by Mr. *Bell* of *Antermony*, who accompanied the Czar *Peter* the Great, in his Journey to *Der-bent* through *Daggestan.* "The Religion of the *Daggestans*, says he, is generally *Mahometan*, some following the Sect of *Osman*, others that of *Haly*. Their Language for the most Part is *Turkish*, or rather a Dialect of the *Arabic*, though many of them speak also the *Persian* Language. One Article I cannot omit concerning their Laws of Hospitality, which is, if their greatest Enemy comes under their Roof for Protection, the Landlord, of what Condition soever, is obliged to keep him safe, from all Manner of Harm or Violence, during his Abode with him, and even to conduct him safely through his Territories to a Place of Security."—

From the *Saracens* this same Custom obtained among the *Moors* of *Africa*; was by them brought into *Spain*, and there long sacredly observed. The *Spanish* Historians record with Applause one famous Instance of it. While the *Moors* governed there, and the *Spaniards* were mixed with them, a *Span-ish* Cavalier, in a sudden Quarrel, slew a young *Moorish* Gentleman, and fled. His Pursuers soon lost Sight of him, for he had, unperceived, thrown himself over a Garden Wall. The Owner, a *Moor*, happening to be in his Garden, was addressed by the *Spaniard* on his Knees, who acquainted him with his Case, and implored Concealment. *Eat this,* said the *Moor*, giving him Half a Peach; *you now know that you may confide in my Protection.* He then locked him up in his Garden Apartment, telling him, that as soon as it was Night he would provide for his Escape to a Place of more Safety.—The *Moor* then went into his House, where he had scarce seated himself, when a great Croud, with loud Lamentations, came to his Gate, bringing the Corps of his Son, that had just been killed by a *Spaniard*. When the first Shock of Surprize was a little over, he learnt, from the Description given, that the fatal Deed was done by the Person then in his Power. He mentioned this to no One; but as soon as it was dark, retired to his Garden Apartment, as if to grieve alone, giving Orders that none should follow him. There accosting the *Spaniard*, he said, *Christian, the Person you have killed, is my Son: His Body is now in my House. You ought to suffer; but you have eaten with me, and I have given you my Faith, which must not be broken. Follow me.* — He then led the astonished *Spaniard* to his Stables, mounted him on one of his fleetest Horses, and said, *Fly far while the Night can cover you. You will be safe in the Morning. You are indeed guilty of my Son's Blood, but God is just and good, and I thank him that I am innocent of yours, and that my Faith given is preserved.*

The *Spaniards* caught from the *Moors* this *Punto* of Honour, the Effects of which remain, in a great Degree, to this Day. So that when there is Fear of a War about to break out between *England* and *Spain*, an *English* Merchant there, who apprehends the Confiscation of his Goods as the Goods of an Enemy, thinks them safe, if he can get a *Spaniard* to take Charge of them; for the *Spaniard* secures them as his own, and faithfully redelivers them, or pays the Value, whenever the *Englishman* can safely demand it.

Justice to that Nation, though lately our Enemies, and hardly yet our cordial Friends, obliges me, on this Occasion, not to omit mentioning an Instance of *Spanish* Honour, which cannot but be still fresh in the Memory of many yet living. In 1746, when we were in hot War with *Spain*, the *Elizabeth*, of *London*, Captain *William Edwards*, coming through the Gulph from *Jamaica*, richly laden, met with a most violent Storm, in which the Ship sprung a Leak, that obliged them, for the Saving of their Lives, to run her into the *Havannah*. The Captain went on Shore, directly waited on the Governor, told the Occasion of his putting in, and that he surrendered his Ship as a Prize, and himself and his Men as Prisoners of War, only requesting good Quarter. *No, Sir,* replied the *Spanish* Governor, *If we had taken you in fair War at Sea, or approaching our Coast with hostile Intentions, your Ship would then have been a Prize, and your People Prisoners. But when distressed by a Tempest, you come into our Ports for the Safety of your Lives, we, though Enemies, being Men, are bound as such, by the Laws of Humanity, to afford Relief to distressed Men, who ask it of us. We cannot, even against our Enemies, take Advantage of an Act of God. You have Leave therefore to unload your Ship, if that be necessary, to stop the Leak; you may refit here, and traffick so far as shall be necessary to pay the Charges; you may then depart, and I will give you a Pass, to be in Force till you are beyond* Bermuda. *If after that you are taken, you will then be a Prize, but now you are only a Stranger, and have a Stranger's Right to Safety and Protection.* — The Ship accordingly departed, and arrived safe in *London*.

Will it be permitted me to adduce, on this Occasion, an Instance of the like Honour in a poor unenlightened *African Negroe*. I find it in Capt. *Seagrave*'s Account of his Voyage to *Guinea*. He relates that a *New-England* Sloop, trading there in 1752, left their second Mate, *William Murray*, sick on Shore, and sailed without him. *Murray* was at the House of a Black, named *Cudjoe*, with whom he had contracted an Acquaintance during their Trade. He recovered, and the Sloop being gone, he continued with his black Friend, till some other Opportunity should offer of his getting home. In the mean while, a *Dutch* Ship came into the Road, and some of the Blacks going on board her, were treacherously seized, and carried off as Slaves. Their Relations and Friends, transported with sudden Rage, ran to the House of *Cudjoe* to take Revenge, by killing *Murray*. *Cudjoe* stopt them at the Door, and demanded what they wanted? The White Men, said they, have carried away our Brothers and Sons, and we will kill all White Men;—give us the White Man that you keep in your House, for we will kill him. *Nay,* said *Cudjoe; the White Men that carried away your Brothers are bad Men, kill them when you can catch them; but this White Man is a good Man, and you must not kill him.* —But he is a White Man, they cried; the White Men are all bad; we will kill them all.—*Nay,* says he, *you must not kill a Man, that has done no Harm, only for being white. This Man is my Friend, my House is his Fort, and I am his Soldier. I must fight for him. You must kill me, before you can kill him.—What good Man will ever come again under my Roof, if I let my Floor be stained with a good Man's Blood!*—The *Negroes* seeing his Resolution, and being convinced by his Discourse that they were wrong, went away ashamed. In a few Days *Murray* ventured abroad again with *Cudjoe*, when several of them took him by the Hand, and told him they were glad they had not killed him; for as he was a good (meaning an innocent) Man, *their God would have been angry, and would have spoiled their Fishing.*—I relate this, says Captain *Seagrave*, to show, that some among these dark People have a strong Sense of Justice and Honour, and that even the most brutal among them are capable of feeling the Force of Reason, and of being influenced by a Fear of God (if the Knowledge of the true God could be introduced among them) since even the Fear of a false God, when their Rage subsided, was not without its good Effect.

Now I am about to mention something of *Indians*, I beg that I may not be understood as framing Apologies for *all Indians*. I am far from desiring to lessen the laudable Spirit of Resentment in my Countrymen against those now at War with us, so far as it is justified by their Perfidy and Inhumanity.—I would only observe that the *Six Nations*, as a Body, have kept Faith with the *English* ever since we knew them, now near an Hundred Years; and that the governing Part of those People have had Notions of Honour, whatever may be the Case with the Rum-debauched, Trader-corrupted Vagabonds and Thieves on *Sasquehannah* and the *Ohio*, at present in Arms against us.—As a Proof of that Honour, I shall only mention one well-known recent Fact. When six *Catawba* Deputies, under the Care of Colonel *Bull*, of *Charlestown*, went by Permission into the *Mohawks* Country, to sue for and treat of Peace for their Nation, they soon found the *Six Nations* highly exasperated, and the Peace at that Time impracticable: They were therefore in Fear for their own Persons, and apprehended that they should be killed in their Way back to *New-York*; which being made known to the *Mohawk* Chiefs, by Colonel *Bull*, one of them, by Order of the Council, made this Speech to the *Catawbas*:—

"*Strangers and Enemies,*

"While you are in this Country, blow away all Fear out of your Breasts; change the black Streak of Paint on your Cheek for a red One, and let your Faces shine with Bear's-Grease: You are safer here than if you were at home. The *Six Nations* will not defile their own Land with the Blood of Men that come unarmed to ask for Peace. We shall send a Guard with you, to see you safe out of our Territories. So far you shall have Peace, but no farther. Get home to your own Country, and there take Care of yourselves, for there we intend to come and kill you."

The *Catawbas* came away unhurt accordingly.

It is also well known, that just before the late War broke out, when our Traders first went among the *Piankeshaw Indians*, a Tribe of the *Twightwees*, they found the Principle of *giving Protection to Strangers* in full Force; for the *French* coming with their *Indians* to the *Piankeshaw* Town, and demanding that those Traders and their Goods should be delivered up;—the *Piankeshaws* replied, the *English* were come there upon their Invitation, and they could not do so base a Thing. But the *French* insisting on it, the *Piankeshaws* took Arms in Defence of their Guests, and a Number of them, with their old Chief, lost their Lives in the Cause; the *French* at last prevailing by superior Force only.

I will not dissemble that numberless Stories have been raised and spread abroad, against not only the poor Wretches that are murdered, but also against the Hundred and Forty christianized *Indians*, still threatned to be murdered; all which Stories are well known, by those who know the *Indians* best, to be pure Inventions, contrived by bad People, either to excite each other to join in the Murder, or since it was committed, to justify it; and believed only by the Weak and Credulous. I call thus publickly on the Makers and Venders of these Accusations to produce their Evidence. Let them satisfy the Public that even *Will Soc*, the most obnoxious of all that Tribe, was really guilty of those Offences against us which they lay to his Charge. But if he was, ought he not to have been fairly tried? He lived under our Laws, and was subject to them; he was in our Hands, and might easily have been prosecuted; was it *English Justice* to condemn and execute him unheard? Conscious of his own Innocence, he did not endeavour to hide himself when the Door of the Workhouse, his Sanctuary, was breaking open; *I will meet them,* says he, *for they are my Brothers.* These Brothers of his shot him down at the Door, while the Word Brothers was still between his Teeth!—But if *Will Soc* was a bad Man, what had poor old *Shehaes* done? what could he or the other poor old Men and Women do? What had little Boys and Girls done; what could Children of a Year old, Babes at the Breast, what could they do, that they too must be shot and hatcheted?—Horrid to relate!—and in their Parents Arms! This is done by no civilized Nation in *Europe.* Do we come to *America* to learn and practise the Manners of *Barbarians*? But this, *Barbarians* as they are, they practise against their Enemies only, not against their Friends.—

These poor People have been always our Friends. Their Fathers received ours, when Strangers here, with Kindness and Hospitality. Behold the Return we have made them!—When we grew more numerous and powerful, they put themselves under our *Protection.* See, in the mangled Corpses of the last Remains of the Tribe, how effectually we have afforded it to them!—

Unhappy People! to have lived in such Times, and by such Neighbours!—We have seen, that they would have been safer among the ancient *Heathens,* with whom the Rites of Hospitality were *sacred.*—They would have been considered as *Guests* of the Publick, and the Religion of the Country would have operated in their Favour. But our Frontier People call themselves *Christians*!—They would have been safer, if they had submitted to the *Turks*; for ever since *Mahomet's* Reproof to *Khaled,* even the *cruel Turks,* never kill Prisoners in cold Blood. These were not even Prisoners:—But what is the Example of *Turks* to Scripture *Christians*?—They would have been safer, though they had been taken in actual War against the *Saracens,* if they had once drank Water with them. These were not taken in War against us, and have drank with us, and we with them, for Fourscore Years.—But shall we compare *Saracens* to *Christians*?—They would have been safer among the *Moors* in *Spain,* though they had been *Murderers of Sons*; if Faith had once been pledged to them, and a

Promise of Protection given. But these have had the Faith of the *English* given to them many Times by the Government, and, in Reliance on that Faith, they lived among us, and gave us the Opportunity of murdering them.—However, what was honourable in *Moors*, may not be a Rule to us; for we are *Christians!*—They would have been safer it seems among *Popish Spaniards*, even if Enemies, and delivered into their Hands by a Tempest. These were not Enemies; they were born among us, and yet we have killed them all.—But shall we imitate *idolatrous Papists*, we that are *enlightened Protestants?*—They would even have been safer among the *Negroes* of *Africa*, where at least one manly Soul would have been found, with Sense, Spirit and Humanity enough, to stand in their Defence:—But shall *Whitemen* and *Christians* act like a *Pagan Negroe?*—In short it appears, that they would have been safe in any Part of the known World,—except in the Neighbourhood of the CHRISTIAN WHITE SAVAGES of *Peckstang* and *Donegall!*—

O ye unhappy Perpetrators of this horrid Wickedness! Reflect a Moment on the Mischief ye have done, the Disgrace ye have brought on your Country, on your Religion, and your Bible, on your Families and Children! Think on the Destruction of your captivated Country-folks (now among the wild *Indians*) which probably may follow, in Resentment of your Barbarity! Think on the Wrath of the United *Five Nations*, hitherto our Friends, but now provoked by your murdering one of their Tribes, in Danger of becoming our bitter Enemies.—Think of the mild and good Government you have so audaciously insulted; the Laws of your King, your Country, and your GOD, that you have broken; the infamous Death that hangs over your Heads:—For JUSTICE, though slow, will come at last.—All good People every where detest your Actions.—You have imbrued your Hands in innocent Blood; how will you make them clean?—The dying Shrieks and Groans of the Murdered, will often sound in your Ears: Their Spectres will sometimes attend you, and affright even your innocent Children!—Fly where you will, your Consciences will go with you:—Talking in your Sleep shall betray you, in the Delirium of a Fever you yourselves shall make your own Wickedness known.

One Hundred and Forty peaceable *Indians* yet remain in this Government. They have, by Christian Missionaries, been brought over to a *Liking*, at least, of our Religion; some of them lately left their Nation which is now at War with us, because they did not chuse to join with them in their Depredations; and to shew their Confidence in us, and to give us an equal Confidence in them, they have brought and put into our Hands their Wives and Children. Others have lived long among us in *Northampton* County, and most of their Children have been born there. These are all now trembling for their Lives. They have been hurried from Place to Place for Safety, now concealed in Corners, then sent out of the Province, refused a Passage through a neighbouring Colony, and returned, not unkindly perhaps, but disgracefully, on our Hands. O *Pennsylvania*! once renowned for Kindness to Strangers, shall the Clamours of a few mean Niggards about the Expence of this *Publick Hospitality*, an Expence that will not cost the noisy Wretches *Sixpence* a Piece (and what is the Expence of the poor Maintenance we afford them, compared to the Expence they might occasion if in Arms against us) shall so senseless a Clamour, I say, force you to turn out of your Doors these unhappy Guests, who have offended their own Country-folks by their Affection for you, who, confiding in your Goodness, have put themselves under your Protection? Those whom you have disarmed to satisfy groundless Suspicions, will you leave them exposed to the armed Madmen of your Country?—Unmanly Men! who are not ashamed to come with Weapons against the Unarmed, to use the Sword against Women, and the Bayonet against young Children; and who have already given such bloody Proofs of their Inhumanity and Cruelty.—Let us rouze ourselves, for Shame, and redeem the Honour of our Province from the Contempt of its Neighbours; let all good Men join heartily and unanimously in Support of the Laws, and in strengthening the Hands of Government; that JUSTICE may be done, the Wicked punished, and the Innocent protected; otherwise we can, as a People, expect no Blessing from Heaven, there will be no Security for our Persons or Properties; Anarchy and Confusion will prevail over all, and Violence, without Judgment, dispose of every Thing.

When I mention the Baseness of the Murderers, in the Use they made of Arms, I cannot, I ought not to forget, the very different Behaviour of *brave Men* and *true Soldiers*, of which this melancholy Occasion has afforded us fresh Instances. The *Royal Highlanders* have, in the Course of this War, suffered as much as any other Corps, and have frequently had their Ranks thinn'd by an *Indian* Enemy; yet they did not for this retain a brutal undistinguishing Resentment against *all Indians*, Friends as well as Foes. But a Company of them happening to be here, when the 140 poor *Indians* above mentioned were thought in too much Danger to stay longer in the Province, chearfully undertook to protect and escort them to *New-York*, which they executed (as far as that Government would permit the *Indians* to come) with Fidelity and Honour; and their Captain *Robinson*, is justly applauded and honoured by all sensible and good People, for the Care, Tenderness and Humanity, with which he treated those unhappy Fugitives, during their March in this severe Season. General *Gage*, too, has approved of his Officer's Conduct, and, as I hear, ordered him to remain with the *Indians* at *Amboy*, and continue his Protection to them, till another Body of the King's Forces could be sent to relieve his Company, and escort their Charge back in Safety to *Philadelphia*, where his Excellency has had the Goodness to direct those Forces to remain for some Time, under the Orders of our Governor, for the Security of the *Indians*; the Troops of this Province being at present necessarily posted on the Frontier. Such just and generous Actions endear the Military to the Civil Power, and impress the Minds of all the Discerning with a still greater Respect for our national Government.—I shall conclude with observing, that *Cowards* can handle Arms, can strike where they are sure to meet with no Return, can wound, mangle and murder; but it belongs to *brave* Men to spare, and to protect; for, as the Poet says,

——*Mercy still sways the Brave.*

Philadelphia, 1764

The Duke of York's Travels

To the Printer of the Public Advertiser.

SIR,

I have observed all the News-papers have of late taken great Liberties with a noble Personage nearly allied to his Majesty. They have one Day made him Commander of a Fleet in the Mediterranean; again in the Channel; then to hoist his Flag on board a Yatcht, and go on a grand Commission to Copenhagen; then to take a Tour to Brunswick, and so parade all over Germany to our unsatisfied Ally the King of Prussia; then he is said to commence Admiral again, and go with a large Fleet to America; first for a little Amusement to go a Cod Fishing with Monsieurs, and then to range the Continent, and I suppose they mean to go a Wood-hunting with the Cherokee Kings; these are the Peregrinations, Mr. Woodfall, that our noble Duke is to be sent upon; but indeed I am much surprised in all their high-flown Schemes they have never thought of sending him with a grand Squadron to East India up the Ganges to call upon the Nabob, and then advance and pay a Visit to the Great Mogul, and afterwards sail for China, and go up to see the Grandeur of the Court of Pekin: This would have been a fine Subject to have enlarged upon, and they might have thrown in how many sumptuous Barges were building to be sent on board the Squadron to be put together in India, and advance up the River with the utmost Magnificence. If these Hints will be any ways instructive to the News-writers, I shall be happy to have pleased so useful a Body of Men in this great City; and am

Mr. Woodfall's most humble Servant,

Pimlico, May 10.   The SPECTATOR.

The Public Advertiser, May 15, 1765

The Grand Leap of the Whale

To the Printer of the Public Advertiser.

SIR,

In your Paper of Wednesday last, an ingenious Correspondent that calls himself *the* SPECTATOR, and dates from *Pim-lico*, under the Guise of Good-Will to the News-Writers, whom he allows to be "an useful Body of Men in this great City," has, in my Opinion artfully attempted to turn them and their Works into Ridicule; wherein, if he could succeed, great Injury might be done to the Public, as well as to those good People.

Supposing, Sir, that the *We hears* they give us of this and t'other intended Voyage, or Tour of this and t'other great Personage, were mere Inventions, yet they at least afford us an innocent Amusement while we read, and useful Matter of Conversation when we are disposed to converse. Englishmen, Sir, are too apt to be silent when they have nothing to say; too apt to be sullen when they are silent, and when they are sullen to h—g themselves. But by these *We Hears* we are supplied with abundant Fund of Discourse: We discuss the Motives to such Voyages, the Probability of their being undertaken, and the Practicability of their Execution. Here we can display our Judgment in Politics, our Knowledge of the Interests of Princes, and our Skill in Geography; and (if we have it) shew our Dexterity moreover in Argumentation. In the mean time, the tedious Hours is killed; we go home pleased with the Applauses we have received from others, or at least with those we secretly give to ourselves; we sleep soundly, and live on, to the Comfort of our Families.

But, Sir, I beg leave to say, that all the Articles of News, that seem improbable, are not mere Inventions. Some of them, I can assure you on the Faith of a Traveller, are serious Truths. And here, quitting Mr. Spectator of Pimlico, give me Leave to instance the various numberless Accounts the News-Writers have given us (with so much honest Zeal for the Welfare of Poor Old England!) of the establishing Manufactures in the Colonies to the Prejudice of those of this Kingdom. It is objected by superficial Readers, who yet pretend to some Knowledge of those Countries, that such Establishments are not only improbable but impossible; for that their Sheep have but little Wool, not in the whole sufficient for a Pair of Stockings a Year to each Inhabitants; and that, from the universal Dearness of Labour among them, the working of Iron and other Materials, except in some few coarse Instances, is impracticable to any Advantage. Dear Sir, do not let us suffer ourselves to be amused with such groundless Objections. The very Tails of the American Sheep are so laden with Wool, that each has a Car or Waggon on four little Wheels to support and keep it from trailing on the Ground. Would they caulk their Ships? would they fill their Beds? would they even litter their Horses with Wool, if it was not both plenty and cheap? And what signifies Dearness of Labour, where an English Shilling passes for Five-and-twenty? Their engaging three hundred Silk Throwsters here in one Week for New York was treated as a Fable, because, forsooth, they have "no Silk there to throw." Those who made this Objection perhaps did not know, that at the same Time the Agents from the King of Spain were at Quebec contracting for 1000 Pieces of Cannon to be made there for the Fortifications of Mexico, with 25,000 Axes for their industrious Logwood-Cutters; and at New-York engaging an annual Supply of warm Floor-Carpets for their West-India Houses *; other Agents from the Emperor of China were at Boston in New-England treating about an Exchange of Raw-Silk for Wool, to be carried on in Chinese Jonks through the Straits of Magellan. And yet all this is as certainly true as the Account, said to be from Quebec, in the Papers of last Week, that the Inhabitants of Canada are making Preparations for a Cod and Whale Fishery this Summer in the Upper Lakes. Ignorant People may object that the Upper Lakes are fresh, and that Cod and Whale are Salt-water Fish: But let them know, Sir, that Cod, like other Fish, when attacked by their Enemies, fly into any Water where they think they can be safest; that Whales, when they have a Mind to eat Cod, pursue them wherever they fly; and that the grand Leap of the Whale in that Chace up the Fall of Niagara is esteemed by all who have seen it, as one of the finest Spectacles in Nature!—Really, Sir, the World is grown too incredulous: Pendulum-like, it is ever swinging from one Extream to another. Formerly every Thing printed was believed, because it was in Print: Now Things seem to be disbelieved for just the very same Reason. Wise Men wonder at the present Growth of Infidelity! They should have consider'd, when they taught

---

* See the late Papers.

People to doubt the Authority of News-papers, and the Truth of Predictions in Almanacs, that the next Step might be a Disbelief in the well-vouch'd Accounts of Ghosts and Witches, and Doubts even of the Truth of the A——n Creed.

Thus much I thought it necessary to say in favour of an honest Set of Writers, whose comfortable Living depends on collecting and supplying the Printers with News, at the small Price of Six-pence an Article; and who always show their Regard to Truth, by contradicting such as are wrong in a subsequent Article—for another Six-pence, to the great Satisfaction and Improvement of us Coffee-house Students in History and Politics, and the infinite Advantage of all future Livies, Rapins, Robertsons, Humes, Smollets, and Macaulays, who may be sincerely inclin'd to furnish the World with that *rara Avis*, a true History.

> I am, SIR,
> Your humble Servant,
> A TRAVELLER.

The Public Advertiser, May 22, 1765

Invectives Against the Americans

To the PRINTER.

I would fain know what good purpose can be answered, by the frequent invectives published in your and other papers against the Americans. Do these small writers hope to provoke the nation by their oratory, to embrue its hands in the blood of its, perhaps mistaken children? And if this should be done, do they imagine it could be of any advantage to this country? Do they expect to convince the Americans, and reduce them to submission, by their flimsey arguments of *virtual represen-tation*, and of *Englishmen by fiction of law only*, mixed with insolence, contempt and abuse? Can it be supposed that such treatment will make them rest satisfied with the unlimited claim set up, of a power to tax them *ad libitum*, without their consent; while they are to work only for us, and our profit; restrained in their foreign trade by our laws, however profit-able it might be to them; forbidden to manufacture their own produce, and obliged to purchase the work of our artificers at our own prices? Is this the state we wish to keep them in? And can it be thought such writings (which are unfortunately reprinted in all *their* papers) will induce them to bear it with greater patience, and during a longer period of time?

The gentle terms of *republican race*, *mixed rabble of Scotch*, *Irish and foreign vagabonds*, *descendants of convicts*, *ungrateful rebels*, &c. are some of the sweet flowers of English rhetorick, with which our colonists have of late been regaled. Surely, if we are so much their superiors, we should shew the superiority of our breeding by our better manners! Our slaves they may be thought: But every master of slaves ought to know, that though all the slave possesses is the property of the master, his *goodwill* is his own, he bestows it where he pleases; and it is of *some importance* to the master's *profit*, if he can obtain that *good-will* at the cheap rate of a few kind words, with fair and gentle usage.

These people, however, are not, never were, nor ever will be our slaves. The first settlers of New England particularly, were English gentlemen of fortune, who, being Puritans, left this country with their families and followers, in times of persecution, for the sake of enjoying, though in a wilderness, the blessings of civil and religious liberty; of which they retain to this day, as high a sense as any Briton whatsoever; and possess as much virtue, humanity, civility, and, let me add, *loyalty to their Prince*, as is to be found among the like number of people in any part of the world; and the other colonies merit and maintain the same character. They should then be treated with *decency* and with *candour*.

Your correspondent VINDEX PATRIÆ, who is indeed more of a reasoner than a railer, has nevertheless thought fit to assert, that "their refusing submission to the stamp act, proceeds *only* from their *ambition* of becoming *independent*; and that it is plain the colonies have no other aim but a *total enfranchisement* from obedience to our Parliament." These are strong charges; but the proofs of such ambitious and rebellious views no where appear in his paper. He has, however, condescended to give us his proofs of another point, viz. "That the colonies have no tenderness for their mother country;" (and of course I suppose, the mother country is to have none for them.) "The sugar, teas, and other commodities, says he, which they daily buy from St. Eustatia and Monte Christi, in particular, are too *convincing proofs*, that they have *no tenderness* for their mother country." May one ask this profound writer; are sugar and teas the produce of the mother country? does not she herself buy her teas from strangers? were the north americans to buy all the sugars they consume, even of our own Islands, would not that raise the price of such sugars upon us here in England? is not then their buying them of Foreigners, if it proves any thing, a Proof rather of their tenderness for their mother country? but the grocerly argument of tea and sugar, is not inferior to the lawyerly argument with which he demonstrates, that, "by a *fiction* between us and the colonists, Connecticut is in England, and therefore represented in the British parliament." I am afraid the common Americans will be as much at a loss as I am, to understand what he means by his *estoppers*, and his *averments*, and therefore not in the least convinced by his demonstration. They will only find out upon the whole, that he is not their friend; and perhaps conclude from that and his learning in the law, that he is one of their *virtual representatives* by *fiction* in P—t:

I hope, however, to see prudent measures taken by our rulers, such as may heal and not widen our breaches. The Americans, I am sure, for I know them, have not the least desire of independence; they submit, in general, to all the laws we make for them; they desire only a continuance of what they think a *right*, the privilege of manifesting their loyalty by granting their own money, when the occasions of their prince shall call for it. This right they say they have always enjoyed and exercised, and never misused; and they think it wrong that any body of men whatever, should claim a power of giving what is not their own, and make to themselves a merit with the sovereign and their own constituents, by granting away the property of others who have no representatives in that body, and therefore make no part of the *common consent in parliament*, by which alone, according to *magna charta* and the *petition of right*, taxes can be legally laid upon the subject. These are their notions. They may be errors; 'tis a part of our common constitution perhaps not hitherto sufficiently considered. 'Tis fit for the discussion of wise and learned men, who will, I doubt not, settle it wisely and benevolently. Cowardice and cruelty are indeed almost inseparable companions, and none are more ready to propose sending out fleets and armies, and to expose friends and foes to one common carnage, than such pusilanimous men as would tremble at a sword drawn in their presence tho' with the most peaceable Intention. But Britons, as a people, are equally brave and generous; prodigal of their blood and treasure where there are just calls for its expence; and by no means niggards of those rights, liberties and privileges, that make the subjects of Britain the envy and admiration of the universe.   N. N.

The Gazetteer and New Daily Advertiser, December 28, 1765

The Mother Country

A SONG

We have an old Mother that peevish is grown,
She snubs us like Children that scarce walk alone;
She forgets we're grown up and have Sense of our own;
> *Which nobody can deny, deny,*
> *Which no body can deny.*

If we don't obey Orders, whatever the Case;
She frowns, and she chides, and she loses all Patience, and sometimes she hits us a Slap in the Face,
> *Which nobody can deny, &c.*

Her Orders so odd are, we often suspect
That Age has impaired her sound Intellect:
But still an old Mother should have due Respect,
> *Which nobody can deny, &c.*

Let's bear with her Humours as well as we can:
But why should we bear the Abuse of her Man?
When Servants make Mischief, they earn the Rattan,
> *Which nobody should deny, &c.*

Know too, ye bad Neighbours, who aim to divide
The Sons from the Mother, that still she's our Pride;
And if ye attack her we're all of her side,
>   *Which nobody can deny,* &c.

We'll join in her Lawsuits, to baffle all those,
Who, to get what she has, will be often her Foes:
For we know it must all be our own, when she goes,
>   *Which nobody can deny, deny,*
>   *Which nobody can deny.*

c. 1765

On the Prospects of War in America

To the Printer of the Public Advertiser.

SIR,

PACIFICUS, in your Paper of Friday last, tells us, that the Inhabitants of New England are "descended from the Stiff-Rumps in Oliver's Time;" and he accounts for their being "so tenacious of what they call their Rights and Liberties," from the "independent Principles handed down to them by their Forefathers, and that Spirit of Contradiction, which, he says, is the distinguishing Characteristic of Fanaticism." But it seems the Inhabitants of Virginia and Maryland, who are descended from the Royalists of the Church of England, driven hence by those very Oliverian Stiff-Rumps, and never tinctured with Fanaticism, are, in the present Case as stiff-rump'd as the others, and even led the Way in asserting what "they call their Rights." So that his Hypothesis of Fanaticism appears insufficient to account for the Opposition universally given to the Stamp-Act in America; and I fancy the Gentleman thought so himself, as he mends it a little after, by lumping all the Americans under the general Character of "House-breakers and Felons."

Supposing them such, his Proposal of "vacating all their Charters, taking away the Power of their Assemblies, and sending an armed Force among them, to reduce them all to a military Government, in which the Order of a commanding Officer is to be their Law," will certainly be a very *justifiable*

Measure. I have only some Doubts as to the Expediency of it, and the Facility of carrying it into Execution. For I apprehend 'tis not unlikely they may set their Rumps more stiffly against this Method of Government, than ever they did against that by Act of Parliament. But, on second Thoughts, I conceive it may possibly do very well: For though there should be, as 'tis said there are, at least 250,000 fighting Men among them, many of whom have lately seen Service; yet, as one Englishman is to be sure as good as five Americans, I suppose it will not require Armies of above 50,000 Men in the whole, sent over to the different Parts of that extensive Continent, for reducing them; and that a three or four Years Civil War, at perhaps a less Expence than ten or twelve Millions a Year, Transports and Carriages included, will be sufficient to compleat *Pacificus*'s Pacification, notwithstanding any Disturbance our restless Enemies in Europe might think fit to give us while engaged in this necessary Work. I mention three or four Years only; for I can never believe the Americans will be able to spin it out to seventy, as the Hollanders did the War for their Liberties against Spain, how much soever it may be found the Interest of our own numerous Commissaries, Contractors, and Officers afraid of Half Pay, to continue and protract it.

It may be objected, that by ruining the Colonies, killing one half the People, and driving the rest over the Mountains, we may deprive ourselves of their Custom for our Manufactures: But a Moment's Consideration will satisfy us, that since we have lost so much of our European Trade, it can only be the Demand in America that keeps up, and has of late so greatly enhanced the Price of those Manufactures, and therefore a Stop put to that Demand will be an Advantage to us all, as we may thereafter buy our own Goods cheaper for our own Use at home. I can think of but one Objection more, which is, that Multitudes of our Poor may starve for want of Employment. But our wise Laws have provided a Remedy for that. The Rich are to maintain them.

I am, SIR,

Your humble Servant,

PACIFICUS SECUNDUS.

The Public Advertiser, January 2, 1766

"Homespun" Celebrates Indian Corn

To the PRINTER.

VINDEX PATRIÆ, a writer in your paper, comforts himself, and the India Company, with the fancy, that the Americans, should they resolve to drink no more tea, can by no means keep that resolution, their Indian corn not affording "an agreeable, or easy digestible breakfast." Pray let me, an American, inform the gentleman, who seems quite ignorant of the matter, that Indian corn, take it for *all in all*, is one of the most agreeable and wholesome grains in the world; that its green ears roasted are a delicacy beyond expression; that *samp, hominy, succatash,* and *nokehock,* made of it, are so many pleasing varieties; and that a *johny,* or *hoe-cake,* hot from the fire, is better than a Yorkshire muffin—But if Indian corn were as *disagreeable* and *indigestible* as the Stamp Act, does he imagine we can get nothing else for breakfast?—Did he never hear that we have oatmeal in plenty, for water-gruel or burgoo; as good wheat, rye, and barley as the world affords, to make frumenty; or toast and ale; that there is every where plenty of milk, butter, and cheese; that rice is one of our staple commodities; that for tea, we have sage and bawm in our gardens, the young leaves of the sweet white hickery or walnut, and, above all, the buds of our pine, infinitely preferable to any tea from the Indies; while the islands yield us plenty of coffee and chocolate?—Let the gentleman do us the honour of a visit in America, and I will engage to breakfast him every day in the month with a fresh variety, without offering him either tea or Indian corn.—As to the Americans using no more of the former, I am not sure they will take such a resolution; but if they do, I fancy they will not lightly break it. I question whether the army proposed to be sent among them, would oblige them to swallow a drop more of tea than they chuse to swallow; for, as the proverb says, though one man may *lead* a horse to the water, ten can't *make him drink.* Their resolutions have hitherto been pretty steadily kept. They resolved to wear no more mourning;—and it is now totally out of fashion with near two millions of people; and yet nobody sighs for Norwich crapes, or any other of the expensive, flimsey, rotten, black stuffs and cloths you used to send us for that purpose, with the frippery gauses, loves, rib-bands, gloves, &c. thereunto belonging.—They resolved last spring to eat no more lamb; and not a joint of lamb has since been seen on any of their tables, throughout a country of 1500 miles extent, but the sweet little creatures are all alive to this day, with the prettiest fleeces on their backs imaginable. Mr. VINDEX's very civil letter will, I dare say, be printed in all our provincial news papers, from Nova Scotia to Georgia; and together with the other *kind, polite,* and *humane* epistles of your correspondents PACIFICUS, TOM HINT, &c. &c. contribute not a little to strengthen us in every resolution that may be of advantage, to *our* country at least, if not to *yours.*

HOMESPUN.

The Gazetteer and New Daily Advertiser, January 2, 1766

On the Paving of Chancery Lane

To the PRINTER.

By an advertisement in your paper of Wednesday last, I find, "the inhabitants of Chancery-lane are desired to meet at the Crown and Rolls, to consider about new paving the said street." I hope and pray they may not agree to it. *Chancery lane* is in every respect so like a *Chancery suit*; it is so very *long* a lane, so subject to *obstructions* and *delays*, one is so *unwilling* to enter into it, so *uneasy* and *unsafe* all the while one is going through it, and so *glad* to get out of it, that the very reflection on this similarity has often, to my great advantage, deterred me from law, and inclined me rather to end a dispute by arbitration. I therefore wish to see the lane contin-ued in its present state (even after all the rest of the city shall be new paved) as a standing *memento* that may be beneficial to my fellow citizens.

F. B.

The Gazetteer and New Daily Advertiser, January 4, 1766

On the Tenure of the Manor
of East Greenwich

To the PRINTER.

I did not think to have given you any farther trouble, having already exprest my sentiments pretty fully, on the *impropriety* and *imprudence* of angry reflections on the Americans in the public papers, as more than half the trade of this country is with them; and that trade depends greatly on the regard they have for us, and in consequence for our fashions and fineries, which are by no means necessary to their subsistence; the Northern colonies having among themselves the natural means of furnishing, by a little additional industry, every convenience and ornament of life; and to that industry I apprehended a resentment of harsh and contemptuous treatment might naturally provoke them.

But I cannot take leave of my antagonist VINDEX PATRIÆ, without a few remarks on his letter of Friday last. All the mad proceedings of the mobs in America, however disapproved of by the sober and prudent part of the inhabitants, are charged to the account of the country in general, and the people are all involved in one common accusation. He remembers that your papers have informed us of the riots at Boston, but forgets that they likewise informed us, some of the rioters were apprehended and imprisoned, in order to be brought to justice; and that the body of the people detested these violences. It is true, they universally deem the stamp act an infringement of their rights, but then their assemblies have taken no violent measures to oppose it; they have only entered into resolutions among themselves, declaring their sense of these rights; and joined, as we are well assured, in dutiful petitions to the King and Parliament here, that the act may be repealed, and those rights preserved to them. Can more be expected from any subjects, how loyal soever, that think themselves aggrieved?—Is it right to abuse all England as rebellious, because it has sometimes mobs of weavers, coal-diggers, &c.? Candour then should distinguish in this case fairly, between the proceedings of the assemblies there, and the actions of mobs; the latter are *certainly* wrong, the former *may* be so; but if they are, it is a mistaken judgment only of what they think their right;—of this mistake they may possibly be convinced by reason;—but I still doubt the argument of your correspondent, proving, or attempting to prove, "that they are represented in parliament, because the manor of East Greenwich in Kent is represented there, and they all live in that manor;" will hardly appear so intelligible, so clear, so satisfactory, and so convincing to the Americans, as it seems it does to himself.

I own it does not appear so to me; and that my plain understanding, unaccustomed to the subtile refinements of law, cannot easily conceive, that in the King's grants of territory in America to the colonists, the words, "to be holden of us, our heirs and successors, as *of* the manor of East Greenwich, in our county of Kent, in free and common soccage, and not *in capite*, or by knight's service;" do truly imply, that the lands so granted really lie *in* East Greenwich. I should rather have thought those words meant only to express, that the tenure should be of the *same kind* with that of the manor of East Greenwich. The countries held by this tenure, Sir, are perhaps as big as all Europe; and East Greenwich, in the county of Kent, in England, is at most but of a few miles circumference. I have read that the whale swallowed Jonah; and as that is in Holy Writ, to be sure I ought to believe it. But if I were told, that, in fact, it was Jonah that swallowed the whale, I fancy I could myself as easily swallow the whale as the story.

If *"New England lies within England,"* as your correspondent would have the New England men beleive, and particularly in the manor of East Greenwich, a few questions must thence naturally arise, to which his law knowledge will probably furnish ready answers. As, What have these inhabitants of East Greenwich in Kent done, that they, more than any other inhabitants of Kent, should be curbed in their manufactures and commerce? Why are they restrained in making hats of their own beaver, nail rods and steel of their own iron, and cloth of their own wool? Why may not ships from East Greenwich carry its commodities to any part of Europe, and thence bring back others in exchange, with the same freedom that ships may go from any other part of Kent, or of England? And since it is agreed, that by our constitution, the

King can raise no money *in England* but by act of parliament, how has it come to pass, that in consequence of requisitions from the crown, large sums have been raised for its service on these inhabitants of East Greenwich, in the county of Kent, *unauthorized by any such act*, particularly between three and four millions during the last war? And if this money was illegally taken, whether it ought not to be refunded, and the ministers impeached that advised the measure? These seem questions of some importance, and may possibly admit of satisfactory answers; but to that end I doubt it will be found necessary, that these new inhabitants of East Greenwich in Kent, planted there by your correspondent, should be all sent back, and replaced in their native America.

In considering of these questions, perhaps it may be of use to recollect; that the colonies were planted in times when the powers of parliament were not supposed so extensive, as they are become since the Revolution:—That they were planted in lands and countries where the parliament had not then the least jurisdiction:—That, excepting the yet infant colonies of Georgia and Nova Scotia, *none of them* were settled at the expence of *any money* granted by parliament:—That the people went from hence by permission from the crown, purchased or conquered the territory, at the expence of their own private treasure and blood:—That these territories thus became *new* dominions *of the crown*, settled under royal charters, that formed their several governments and constitutions, on which the parliament was *never consulted*; or had the *least participation*.—The people there have had, from the beginning, like Ireland, their separate parliaments, called modestly assemblies: by these chiefly our Kings have governed them. How far, and in what particulars, they are *subordinate* and *subject* to the British parliament; or whether they may not, if the King pleases, be governed as *domains of the crown*, without that parliament, are points newly agitated, never yet, but probably soon will be, thoroughly considered and settled. Different opinions are now entertained concerning them; and till such settlement is made by due authority, it is not criminal to think differently. Therefore, I wish the American opinion may, in the mean time, be treated with less acrimony.

As to VINDEX's accusation of the Americans, "that they run into their country divers commodities of the manufacture of France, to the *ruin* of Great Britain;" I fancy, they will be apt to answer, *Look at home*;—and perhaps it will be found, that in this ruinous trade, the rest of the people of Kent, are not a whit behind-hand with the inhabitants of East Greenwich.

Jan. 6, 1766.   N. N.

The Gazetteer and New Daily Advertiser, January 11, 1766

"Two Taylors"

To the PRINTER.

TOM HINT's virulence against the people of New York, has been in some sort accounted for by himself, in one of his former letters. It seems, tho' he lived several years in that country, they never extended to him any of that civility they generally shew to strangers. He now tells us, in your paper of Saturday, by way of fresh abuse on that *whole people*, that "he admires their wonderful sagacity in distinguishing the *gentleman* from the *scoundrel*; for in serious truth, it would be a difficult matter for an *old-country* man to make that distinction among *them*, after living with them for many years." This will excuse my remarking, that it appears this *old-country* man has little of that sagacity himself, and, from the difficulty he supposed in making *such distinction*, might naturally conceive an opinion when he arrived there, that he should be able easily to pass upon those ignorant *new-country* men, as a *gentleman*. The event, it seems, did not answer his expectations; and hence he *had reason* to admire *their* sagacity, but still continues to be angry at its consequences.—It puts me in mind of a short story, which, in return for his scraps of plays, I will take the liberty of telling him. Two journeymen *Snips*, during the season of little business, agreed to make a trip to Paris, with each a fine lac'd waistcoat, in which they promised themselves the great pleasure of being received and treated as *gentlemen*. On the road from Calais, at every inn, when they called for any thing hastily, they were answered, *Tout a l'heure, Tout a l'heure*; which not a little surprized them. At length, D— these French scoundrels, says one, how *shrewd* they are! I find it won't do;—e'en let us go back again to London.—Aye, says 'tother, they must certainly deal with the devil, or, dress'd as we are dress'd, they could not possibly all at first sight have known us to be *two taylors*.

F. B.

The Gazetteer and New Daily Advertiser, January 14, 1766

"Homespun's" Further Defense of Indian Corn

To the PRINTER.

JOHN BULL shews in nothing more his great veneration for good eating, and how much he is always thinking of his belly, than in his making it the constant topic of his contempt for other nations, that *they do not eat so well as himself*. The *roast beef of Old England* he is always exulting in, as if no other country had beef to roast;—reproaching, on every occasion, the *Welsh* with their leeks and toasted cheese, the *Irish* with their potatoes, and the *Scotch* with their oatmeal. And now that we are a little out of favour with him, he has begun, by his attorney VINDEX PATRIÆ, to examine our eating and drinking, in order, I apprehend, to fix some horrible scandal of the same kind upon us poor *Americans*.

I did but say a word or two in favour of *Indian corn*, which he had treated as "disagreable and indigestible," and this vindictive gentleman grows angry. "Let him tell the world, IF HE DARES (says he) that the Americans prefer it to a place at their own tables." Ah, Sir, I see the dilemma you have prepared for me. If I should not *dare* to say, that we do prefer it to a place at our tables, then you demonstrate, that we must come to England for tea, or go without our breakfasts: and if I do *dare* to say it, you fix upon me and my countrymen for ever, the indelible disgrace of being *Indian corn-eaters*.

I am afraid, Mr. Printer, that you will think this too trifling a dispute to deserve a place in your paper: but pray, good Sir, consider, as you are yourself an Englishman, that we Americans, who are allowed even by Mr. VINDEX to have some English blood in our veins, may think it a very serious thing to have the honour of our eating impeached in any particular whatsoever.

"Why doth he not deny the fact (says VINDEX) that it is assigned to the slaves for their food? To proclaim the *wholesomeness* of this corn, without assigning a reason why white men give it to their slaves, when they can get other food, is only satirizing the good sense of their brethren in America." In truth I cannot deny the fact, though it should reflect ever so much on the *good sense* of my countrymen. I own we do give food made of Indian corn to our slaves, as well as eat it ourselves; not, as you suppose, because it is *"indigestible* and *unwholesome;"* but because it keeps them healthy, strong and hearty, and fit to go through all the labour we require of them. Our slaves, Sir, cost us money, and we buy them to make money by their labour. If they are sick, they are not only unprofitable, but expensive. Where then was your *English good sense*, when you imagined we gave the slaves our Indian corn, because we knew it to be *unwholesome*?

In short, this is only another of Mr. VINDEX's paradoxes, in which he is a great dealer. The first endeavoured to persuade us, that we were represented in the British Parliament *virtually*, and by *fiction*:—Then that we were *really* represented there, because the Manor of East Greenwich in Kent is represented there, and all the Americans live in East Greenwich. And now he undertakes to prove to us, that taxes are the most profitable things in the world to those that pay them; for that Scotland is grown rich since the Union, by paying English taxes. I wish he would accommodate himself a little better to our dull capacities. We Americans have a great many heavy taxes of our own, to support our several governments, and pay off the enormous debt contracted by the war; we never conceived ourselves the richer for paying taxes, and are willing to leave all new ones to those that like them. At least, if we must with Scotland, participate in your taxes, let us likewise, with Scotland, participate in the Union, and in all the privileges and advantages of commerce that accompanied it.

VINDEX, however, will never consent to this. He has made

us partakers in all the odium with which he thinks fit to load Scotland:—"They resemble the Scots in sentiments (says he) their religion is Scottish; their customs and *laws* are Scottish; like the Scotch they Judaically observe what *they call* the Sabbath, persecute old women for witches, are intolerant to other sects, &c." But we must not, like the Scots, be admitted into Parliament; for that, he thinks, would increase "the Scotch interest in England, which is equally hostile to the cause of liberty, and the cause of our church."

Pray, Sir, who informed you that our "*laws* are Scottish?" The same, I suppose, that told you our Indian corn is unwholesome. Indeed, Sir, your information is very imperfect. The common law of England, is, I assure you, the common law of the colonies: and if the civil law is what you mean by the Scottish law, we have none of it but what is forced upon us by England, in its courts of Admiralty, depriving us of that inestimable part of the common law, trials by juries. And do you look upon keeping the *Sabbath*, as part of the Scottish law? "The Americans, like the Scots, (you say,) observe what *they call* the Sabbath." Pray, Sir, you who are so zealous for your church (in abusing other Christians) what *do you call* it? and where the harm of their *observing* it? If you look into your prayer-book, or over your altars, you will find these words written, *Remember to keep holy the* SABBATH *Day*. This law, tho' it may be observed in Scotland, and has been *countenanced* by some of your statutes, is, Sir, originally one of *God's Commandments*: a body of laws still in force in America, tho' they may have become *obsolete* in *some other* countries.

Give me leave, Master JOHN BULL, to remind you, that you are *related to all mankind*; and therefore it less becomes you than any body, to affront and abuse other nations. But you have mixed with your many virtues, a pride, a haughtiness, and an insolent contempt for all but yourself, that, I am afraid, will, if not abated, procure you one day or other a handsome drubbing. Besides your rudeness to foreigners, you are far from being civil even to your own family. The Welch you have always despised for submitting to your government: But why despise your own English, who conquered and settled Ireland for you; who conquered and settled America for you? Yet these you now think you may treat as you please, because, forsooth, they are a *conquered* people. Why dispise the Scotch, who fight and die for you all over the world? Remember, you courted Scotland for one hundred years, and would fain have had your *wicked will* of her. She virtuously resisted all your importunities, but at length kindly consented to become your lawful wife. You then solemnly promised to *love*, *cherish*, and *honour* her, as long as you both should live; and yet you have ever since treated her with the utmost contumely, which you now begin to extend to your common children. But, pray, when your enemies are uniting in a *Family Compact* against you, can it be discreet in you to kick up in your own house a *Family Quarrel*? And at the very time you are inviting foreigners to settle on your lands, and when you have more to settle than ever you had before, is it prudent to suffer your lawyer, VINDEX, to abuse those who have settled there already, because they cannot yet speak "Plain English?"—It is my opinion, Master BULL, that the Scotch and Irish, as well as the colonists, are capable of speaking much *plainer English* than they have ever yet spoke, but which I hope they will never be provoked to speak.

To be brief, Mr. VINDEX, I pass over your other accusations of the Americans, and of the Scotch, that we "Persecute old women for witches, and are intolerant to other sects," observing only, that we were wise enough to leave off both those foolish tricks, long before Old England made the act of toleration, or repealed the statute against witchcraft; so that even *you yourself* may safely travel through all Scotland and the Colonies, without the least danger of being persecuted as a churchman, or taken (up) for a conjurer. And yet I own myself so far of an intolerant spirit, that though I thank you for the box-in-the-ear you have given TOM HINT, as being, what you justly call him, "a futile calumniator," I cannot but wish he would give you another—for the same reason.

One word more, however, about the *Indian corn*, which I began and must end with, even though I should hazard your remarking, that it is certainly "indigestible," as it plainly appears to *stick in my stomach*. "Let him tell the world, IF HE DARES, (you say) that the Americans prefer it to a place at their tables."—And, pray, if I should DARE,—what then?— Why then—"You will enter upon a discussion of its salubrity

and pleasant taste."—Really?—Would you venture to write
on the salubrity and *pleasant taste* of Indian corn, when you
never in your life have tasted a *single grain* of it?—But why
should that hinder your writing on it? Have you not written
even on *politics*?   Your's,

                                                    HOMESPUN.

The Gazetteer and New Daily Advertiser, January 15, 1766

Pax Quæritur Bello

To the Printer of the Public Advertiser.
Pax quæritur Bello.

SIR,

The very important Controversy being next Tuesday to be
finally determined between the Mother Country and their rebellious American Children, I shall think myself happy if I can
furnish any Hints that may be of public Utility.

There are some Persons besides the Americans so amazingly
stupid, as to distinguish in this Dispute between *Power* and
Right, as tho' the former did not always imply the latter. The
Right of Conquest invests the Conqueror with Authority to
establish what Laws he pleases, however contrary to the Laws
of Nature, and the common Rights of Mankind. Examine
every Form of Government at this Day subsisting on the Face
of the Globe, from the absolute Despotism of the Grand Sul-
tan to the Democratic Government of the City of Geneva,
and it will be found that the Exertion of Power in those
Hands with whom it is lodged, however unconstitutional, is
always justified. The Reign of the *Stuarts* might serve to exemplify this Observation. Happy it was for the Nation that,
upon Trial, the superior Power was found to be in the People.
The American Plea of *Right*, their Appeal to Magna Charta,
must of course be set aside; and I make no Doubt but the
Grand Council of the Nation will at all Hazards insist upon
an absolute Submission to the Tax imposed upon them. But
that they will comply without coercive Measures, is to me a
Matter of very great Doubt: For when we consider, that these
People, especially the more Northern Colonies, are the De-

scendants of your Pymms, Hampdens, and others of the like Stamp, those outrageous Assertors of Civil and Religious Liberties; that they have been nursed up in the same Old English Principles; that a little more than a Century ago their Forefathers, many of them of Family and Fortune, left their native Land, and endured all the Distresses and Hardships which are the necessary Consequences of an Establishment in a new uncultivated Country, surrounded with a cruel Bloodthirsty Enemy, oftentimes severely pinched with Cold and Hunger; and all this to enjoy unmolested that Liberty which they thought was infringed: I say, however these People may be mistaken, they will not tamely give up what they call their natural, their constitutional Rights. Force must therefore be made use of.

Now in order to bring these People to a proper Temper, I have a Plan to propose, which I think cannot fail, and which will be entirely consistent with the Oeconomy at present so much in Vogue. It is so cheap a Way of going to work, that even Mr. G—— G——, that great Oeconomist, could have no reasonable Objection to it.

Let Directions be given, that Two Thousand Highlanders be immediately raised, under proper Officers of their own. It ought to be no Objection, that they were in the Rebellion in Forty-five: If Roman Catholics, the better. The C——l at present in the P——ze Service may be at their Head. Transport them early in the Spring to Quebec: There with the Canadians, natural Enemies to our Colonists, who would voluntarily engage, might make a Body of Five or Six Thousand Men; and I doubt not, by artful Management, and the Value of two or three Thousand Pounds in Presents, with the Hopes of Plunder, as likewise a Gratuity for every Scalp, the Savages on the Frontiers might be engaged to join, at least they would make a Diversion, which could not fail of being useful. I could point out a very proper General to command the Expedition; he is of a very sanguine Disposition, and has an inordinate Thirst for Fame, and besides has the Hearts of the Canadians. He might march from Canada, cross the Lakes, and fall upon these People without their expecting or being prepared for him, and with very little Difficulty overrun the whole Country.

The Business might be done without employing any of the
Regular Troops quartered in the Country, and I think it
would be best they should remain neuter, as it is to be feared
they would be rather backward in embruing their Hands in
the Blood of their Brethren and Fellow Subjects.

I would propose, that all the Capitals of the several Provinces should be burnt to the Ground, and that they cut the
Throats of all the Inhabitants, Men, Women, and Children,
and scalp them, to serve as an Example; that all the Shipping
should be destroyed, which will effectually prevent Smuggling, and save the Expence of Guarda Costas.

No Man in his Wits, after such terrible Military Execution,
will refuse to purchase stamp'd Paper. If any one should hesitate, five or six Hundred Lashes in a cold frosty Morning
would soon bring him to Reason.

If the Massacre should be objected to, as it would too
much depopulate the Country, it may be replied, that the
Interruption this Method would occasion to Commerce,
would cause so many Bankruptcies, such Numbers of Manufacturers and Labourers would be unemployed, that, together with the Felons from our Gaols, we should soon be
enabled to transport such Numbers to repeople the Colonies, as to make up for any Deficiency which Example made
it necessary to sacrifice for the Public Good. Great Britain
might then reign over a loyal and submissive People, and be
morally certain, that no Act of Parliament would ever after
be disputed.

Your's,

Jan. 23, 1766.   PACIFICUS

The Public Advertiser, January 26, 1766

On Chastising the Colonies

To the PRINTER.

A Certain Judge, at an Assize, declared it from the Bench,
as his Opinion, that every man had a *legal* right to chastise
his wife, if she was stubborn and obstinate; but then he

observed, that his right ought to be exercised with great lenity and moderation.

It seems our Lawyers are of opinion, that England has an indisputable right to correct her refractory children of North America. But then, as the Judge observed, it ought to be done with temper and moderation; lest, like an unskilful Surgeon, we should *exasperate* and *inflame* the wound we ought to *mollify*. It is an old maxim, but not the less true, that it is much easier to *lead* than to *drive*. If the Duke d'Alva had treated the people of the Netherlands with gentleness and humanity, they would never have revolted. Thank God, we have no Duke d'Alva in England.

The Great Commoner is, at least in the present instance, a *Friend to Peace*, and for *healing measures*: So are the late King's *old and faithful servants*. The same Apostle who says, *Children, obey your Parents*; says also, *Fathers, provoke not your Children to wrath*.

PACIFICUS.

The London Chronicle, February 13, 1766

The Frenchman and the Poker

To the PRINTER.

It is reported, I know not with what Foundation, that there is an Intention of obliging the Americans to pay for all the Stamps they ought to have used, between the Commencement of the Act, and the Day on which the Repeal takes Place, *viz.* from the first of November 1765, to the first of *May* 1766; that this is to make Part of an Act, which is to give Validity to the Writings and Law Proceedings, that contrary to Law have been executed without Stamps, and is to be the Condition on which they are to receive that Validity. Shall we then keep up for a Trifle the Heats and Animosities that have been occasioned by the Stamp-Act? and lose all the Benefit of Harmony and good Understanding between the different Parts of the Empire, which were expected from a generous total Repeal? Is this Pittance likely to be a Whit more easily collected than the whole Duty? Where are Officers to be found who will undertake to collect it? Who is to protect them while they are about it? In my Opinion, it will meet with the same Opposition, and be attended with the same Mischiefs that would have attended an Enforcement of the Act entire.

But I hear, that this is thought necessary, to raise a Fund for defraying the Expence that has been incurred by stamping so much Paper and Parchment for the Use of America, which they have refused to take and turn'd upon our Hands; and that since they are highly favour'd by the Repeal, they cannot with any Face of Decency refuse to make good the Charges we have been at on their Account. The whole Proceeding would put one in Mind of the Frenchman that used to accost English and other Strangers on the *Pont-Neuf* *, with many Compliments, and a red hot Iron in his Hand; *Pray Monsieur Anglois,* says he, *Do me the Favour to let me have the Honour of thrusting this hot Iron into your Backside?* Zoons, what does the Fellow mean! Begone with your Iron, or I'll break your Head! *Nay, Monsieur,* replies he, *if you do not chuse it, I do not insist upon it. But at least, you will in Justice have the Goodness to pay me something for the heating of my Iron.*

F. B.

*A Bridge over the River Siene, leading to Paris.

February–March, 1766; reprinted in *The Pennsylvania Chronicle*, March 23, 1767

A Mock Petition to the House of Commons

To the honourable the Knights Citizens and Burgesses of Great Britain in Parliament assembled,

The Petition of BF. Agent for the Province of Pensilvania, Most humbly Sheweth,

That the Transporting of Felons from England to the Plantations in America, is and hath long been a great Grievance to the said Plantations in general.

That the said Felons being landed in America, not only continue their evil Practices, to the Annoyance of his Majesty's good Subjects there, but contribute greatly to corrupt the Morals of the Servants and poorer People among whom they are mixed.

That many of the said Felons escape from the Servitude to which they were destined, into other Colonies, where their Condition is not known and wandering at large from one populous Town to another commit many Burglaries Robberies and Murders, to the great Terror of the People, and occasioning heavy Charges for the apprehending and securing such Felons, and bringing them to Justice.

That your Petitioner humbly conceives the Easing one Part of the British Dominions of their Felons by burthening another Part with the same Felons, cannot increase the common Happiness of his Majesty's Subjects; and that therefore the Trouble and Expence of transporting them is upon the whole altogether useless.

That your Petitioner nevertheless observes with extream Concern, in the Votes of Friday last, that Leave is given to bring in a Bill, for extending to Scotland the Act made in the 4th. Year of the Reign of King George the First, whereby the aforesaid Grievances are (as he understands) to be greatly increas'd by allowing Scotland also to transport its Felons to America.

Your Petitioner therefore humbly prays, in behalf of Pensilvania and the other Plantations in America that the House wou'd take the Premisses into Consideration, and in their great Wisdom and Goodness repeal all Acts and Clauses of Acts for Transporting of Felons; or if this may not at present be done, that they would at least reject the propos'd Bill for extending of the said Acts to Scotland; or, if it be thought fit to allow of such Extension, that then the said Extension may be carried farther, and the Plantations be also by an equitable Clause in the same Bill permitted to transport their Felons to Scotland.

And your Petitioner, as in Duty bound shall pray, &c.

April 12–15, 1766

Contempt for the Thames

To the Printer of the Public Advertiser.

SIR,

I am an American Gentleman, and as yet not entirely acquainted with the Customs of my dear Mother Country, and therefore apply to the Public for Information what to do as a Redress of a Grievance I lately met with.

Being fond of the Water, I took a Pair of Oars at Westminster Bridge to go to the Temple, thinking to save Ground, but to my great Surprise the Waterman landed me two thirds across the River at the End of what he called a Causeway, and called that landing me at the Temple, taking Sixpence for his Fare. Now, Sir, what vexed me was, that I had near as far to walk to get to the natural Shore as if I had walked all the Way. At first I thought of applying to the Benchers of the Temple; but I remember an old Friend of mine, Mr. Gulliver, a great Traveller, told me that the Lawyers of this Country understood nothing else but Law; in other Respects they were of no real Use to Mankind. I then thought it my Duty to wait upon the Trinity House, or the City Conservators, to know why I was not properly landed according to Agreement, but was advised to apply to the Public.

We Americans have the same Contempt for the Thames as the Inhabitants of Gravesend have for Fleet Ditch, and much wonder that as the Thames is so mean a River, any Causeways, Shoals, or accumulated Points should be suffered, as the Preservation of the City entirely depends upon it's Navigation.

I am, Sir,

Your humble Servant,
AMERICANUS.

The Public Advertiser, August 22, 1766

On the Price of Corn, and Management of the Poor

For the LONDON CHRONICLE.

To Messieurs the PUBLIC *and* Co.

I am one of that class of people that feeds you all, and at present is abus'd by you all;—in short I am a *Farmer*.

By your News-papers we are told, that God had sent a very short harvest to some other countries of Europe. I thought this might be in favour to Old England; and that now we should get a good price for our grain, which would bring in millions among us, and make us flow in money, that to be sure is scarce enough.

But the wisdom of Government forbad the exportation.

Well, says I, then we must be content with the market price at home.

No, says my Lords the mob, you sha'n't have that. Bring your corn to market if you dare;—we'll sell it for you, for less money, or take it for nothing.

Being thus attack'd by both ends *of the Constitution*, the head and the tail *of Government*, what am I to do?

Must I keep my corn in barn to feed and increase the breed of rats?—be it so;—they cannot be less thankful than those I have been used to feed.

Are we Farmers the only people to be grudged the profits of honest labour?—And why?—One of the late scribblers against us gives a bill of fare of the provisions at my daughter's wedding, and proclaims to all the world that we had the insolence to eat beef and pudding!—Has he never read that precept in the good book, *Thou shalt not muzzle the mouth of the ox that treadeth out the corn*; or does he think us less worthy of good living than our oxen?

O, but the Manufacturers! the Manufacturers! they are to be favour'd, and they must have bread at a cheap rate!

Hark-ye, Mr. Oaf;—The Farmers live splendidly, you say. And pray, would you have them hoard the money they get? —Their fine cloaths and furniture, do they make them themselves, or for one another, and so keep the money among them? Or do they employ these your darling Manufacturers, and so scatter it again all over the nation?

My wool would produce me a better price if it were suffer'd to go to foreign markets. But that, Messieurs the Public, your laws will not permit. It must be kept all at home, that our *dear* Manufacturers may have it the cheaper. And then, having yourselves thus lessened our encouragement for raising sheep, you curse us for the scarcity of mutton!

I have heard my grandfather say, that the Farmers submitted to the prohibition on the exportation of wool, being made to expect and believe, that when the Manufacturer bought his wool cheaper, they should have their cloth cheaper. But the deuce a bit. It has been growing dearer and dearer from that day to this. How so? why truly the cloth is exported; and that keeps up the price.

Now if it be a good principle, that the exportation of a commodity is to be restrain'd, that so our own people at home may have it the cheaper, stick to that principle, and go thorough stitch with it. Prohibit the exportation of your cloth, your leather and shoes, your iron ware, and your manufactures of all sorts, to make them all cheaper at home. And cheap enough they will be, I'll warrant you—till people leave off making them.

Some folks seem to think they ought never to be easy, till *England* becomes another *Lubberland*, where 'tis fancied the streets are paved with penny rolls, the houses tiled with pancakes, and chickens ready roasted cry, come eat me.

I say, when you are sure you have got a good principle, stick to it, and carry it thorough.—I hear 'tis said, that though it was *necessary and right* for the M——y to advise a prohibition of the exportation of corn, yet it was *contrary to law*: And also, that though it was *contrary to law* for the mob to obstruct the waggons, yet it was *necessary and right*.—Just the same thing, to a tittle. Now they tell me, an act of indemnity ought to pass in favour of the M——y, to secure them from the consequences of having acted illegally.—If so, pass another in favour of the mob. Others say, some of the mob ought to be hanged, by way of example.—If so,—— but I say no more than I have said before, *when you are sure that you have got a good principle, go thorough with it.*

You say, poor labourers cannot afford to buy bread at a high price, unless they had higher wages.—Possibly.—But how shall we Farmers be able to afford our labourers higher wages, if you will not allow us to get, when we might have it, a higher price for our corn?

By all I can learn, we should at least have had a guinea a quarter more if the exportation had been allowed. And this money England would have got from foreigners.

But, it seems, we Farmers must take so much less, that the poor may have it so much cheaper.

This operates then as a tax for the maintenance of the poor.—A very good thing, you will say. But I ask, Why a partial tax? Why laid on us Farmers only?—If it be a good thing, pray, Messrs. the Public, take your share of it, by in-demnifying us a little out of your public treasury. In doing a good thing there is both honour and pleasure;—you are wel-come to your part of both.

For my own part, I am not so well satisfied of the goodness of this thing. I am for doing good to the poor, but I differ in opinion of the means.—I think the best way of doing good to the poor, is not making them easy *in* poverty, but leading or driving them *out* of it. In my youth I travelled much, and I observed in different countries, that the more public provi-sions were made for the poor, the less they provided for themselves, and of course became poorer. And, on the con-trary, the less was done for them, the more they did for them-selves, and became richer. There is no country in the world where so many provisions are established for them; so many hospitals to receive them when they are sick or lame, founded and maintained by voluntary charities; so many alms-houses for the aged of both sexes, together with a solemn general law made by the rich to subject their estates to a heavy tax for the support of the poor. Under all these obligations, are our poor modest, humble, and thankful; and do they use their best endeavours to maintain themselves, and lighten our shoulders of this burthen?—On the contrary, I affirm that there is no country in the world in which the poor are more idle, dissolute, drunken, and insolent. The day you passed that act, you took away from before their eyes the greatest of all inducements to industry, frugality, and sobriety, by giving

them a dependance on somewhat else than a careful accumulation during youth and health, for support in age or sickness.
In short, you offered a premium for the encouragement of
idleness, and you should not now wonder that it has had its
effect in the increase of poverty. Repeal that law, and you will
soon see a change in their manners. St. *Monday*, and St. *Tuesday*, will cease to be holidays. SIX *days shalt thou labour*,
though one of the old commandments long treated as out of
date, will again be looked upon as a respectable precept; industry will increase, and with it plenty among the lower people; their circumstances will mend, and more will be done for
their happiness by inuring them to provide for themselves,
than could be done by dividing all your estates among them.

Excuse me, Messrs. the Public, if upon this *interesting* subject, I put you to the trouble of reading a little of *my* nonsense. I am sure I have lately read a great deal of *yours*; and
therefore from you (at least from those of you who are writers) I deserve a little indulgence.

I am, your's, &c.
ARATOR.

The London Chronicle, November 29, 1766

The Misrepresentation of America

To the PRINTER *of the* LONDON CHRONICLE.

SIR,

As the *bare letter* of a Governor of one of our provinces,
accusing his People of rebellious *intentions*, is by many here
thought sufficient ground for inflicting penalties on such
province, *unheard,* without *farther evidence*, and without
knowing what it may have to say in its justification: I wish
you would give the Public the following Extract of a Letter,
in which, Accusations of the Colonies from Officers of Government residing there, are set in a light *very different* from
that they have usually been considered in.—It was written
here at the time of our last year's disputes, by one who had
lived long in America, knew the people and their affairs

extremely well—and was equally well acquainted with the temper and practices of government officers. Speaking of the opinion entertained in Britain of the Americans, he says,

"Much has been said of a *virtual representation*, which the colonies are supposed to have here. Of that I understand nothing. But I know what kind of *actual representation*, or rather *misrepresentation*, is continually made of them, by those from whom ministers chiefly have their information. Governors and other officers of the crown, even the little officers of the revenue sent from hence, have all at times some account to give of their own loyal and faithful conduct, with which they mix some contrary character of the people that tends to place that conduct in a more advantageous light. Every good thing done there in the assemblies, for promoting his Majesty's service, was obtained by the Governor's influence: He proposed, he urged strongly, he managed parties;—there was a great opposition;—the assembly were refractory and disaffected;—but his zeal and dexterity overcame all difficulties. And if thro' his own imprudence, or real want of capacity, any thing goes wrong; he is never in fault; the assembly and the people are to bear all the blame;—they are factious, they are turbulent, disloyal, impatient of government, disrespectful to his *Majesty's Representative.*—Then the Custom-house Officer represents the people as all inclined to *smuggling*. Dutch and French goods (by his account) swarm in the country; nothing else would be used if it were not for his *extream vigilance*; which, indeed, as it takes up all his time, he hopes will be considered in the allowance of a *larger salary.*—Even the Missionary Clergy, to whom all credit is due, cannot forbear acquainting the Bishops, and their other superiors here from whom they receive their stipends, that they are indeed very diligent in their respective missions; but that they meet with great difficulties from the adverse disposition of the people:—Quakers oppose them in one place, Presbyterians in another:—*this* country swarms with thwarting hereticks; *t'other* with malevolent sectaries:—Infidelity gains ground *here*, Popery is countenanced *there*. Their unwearied endeavours, which are never wanting, scarce suffice to prevent the colonists being overwhelmed with vice, irreligion, ignorance, and error!—Then the Military Officer, who has served in the

scribes, timid by nature, or from their little bodily exercise deficient in those spirits that give real courage, are ever bawling for war on the most trifling occasions, and seem the most blood-thirsty of mankind.

At this present juncture, when we have scarce had time to breathe, after a war the most general and the most expensive both of blood and treasure Europe was ever involv'd in, we have three sets of orators, who are labouring, by exasperating us against our friends to engage us in three new wars, viz. a war with Portugal, a war with Holland, and a war with our own colonies. As to the two first of these wars, I shall not dispute the prudence or the justice of them. I suppose no Englishman can doubt, that if the Hollanders did our grandfathers an injury 150 years ago, whatever friendship there has been between us since, we may, whenever we think fit, revenge it; and that if the Portuguese buy cloth cheaper of the French than they can of us, we have a right to drub them till they are willing to give us the preference. Allowing then that we are strong enough to beat both Holland and Portugal, cause or no cause, with all the friends and allies they can both muster, and all the enemies such a conduct may draw upon our hands, and that the Dutch too will probably lend us money enough to pay the expence, I would only humbly submit it to consideration whether there may not be some small convenience in being the mean while at peace with ourselves, and finding some other way of settling matters between our late ministers and colonists than cutting of throats.

Every step is now taking to enrage us against *America*. Pamphlets and news-papers flie about, and coffee-houses ring with lying reports of its being in rebellion. Force is call'd for. Fleets and troops should be sent. Those already there should be called in from the distant posts, and quartered on the capital towns. The principal people should be brought here and hang'd, &c.—And why?

Why!—Do you ask why?

Yes. I beg leave to ask why?

Why they are going to throw off the government of *this country*, and set up for themselves.

Pray how does that appear?

Why, are they not all in arms?

No. They are all in peace.

Have they not refused to make the compensation to the sufferers by the late riots, that was requir'd of them by government here?

No. They have made ample satisfaction. Which, by the way, has not been done here to the sufferers by your own riots.

Have they not burnt the custom-house?

No. That story is an absolute invented lie, without the least foundation.

Have they not refus'd to comply with an act of parliament for quartering of troops? And have they not sent a petition to government for taking off the restraint on their trade, and so to overthrow the navigation-act?

Allowing that the assembly of *one* colony, New York, has refus'd to comply with that act, and that some merchants of that one colony have dared to petition, and that refusing and petitioning are high treason; are *five and twenty* colonies to be punished for the crime of *one*?

But let us consider cooly the nature of this act, of this refusal, and of this petition.

The act was a production of the same administration that made the stamp-act, and was probably intended to facilitate the awing the colonies into a submission to it. For that purpose there was in the bill, when first brought in, a clause to impower the officers of the army to quarter soldiers on private houses in America. This clause being strongly oppos'd, was omitted; and the act only requir'd the hiring of empty houses, barns, &c. for the troops, where they were to be furnish'd with firing, candles, bedding, utensils to dress victuals, five pints of small beer or cyder, or half a pint of rum per man per diem, and some other articles, without paying any thing for the same, but the expence to be borne by the province.

There is no other way to raise money in a province, but by the assembly's making an act or law for that purpose. This is therefore to be considered as a law made here, directing that the assembly in America should make another law. The propriety of this proceeding has by some been doubted, they having been of opinion that an assembly is a kind of little parliament in America, not an *executive* officer of government, and as such oblig'd to obey and execute orders; that it is in its nature a *deliberative* body; its members are to consider such matters as come before them; and when a law is proposed, they are to weigh well its utility, necessity, propriety, possibility or practicability, and determine on the whole according to their judgments. If they were oblig'd to make laws right or wrong in obedience to a law made by a superior legislature, they would be of no use as a parliament, their nature would be changed, their constitution destroyed. Indeed the act of parliament itself seems sensible of this;—for in other acts where a duty is enjoin'd to be perform'd by any person, it has always been usual to appoint a penalty on neglect or refusal, and direct the mode of recovering or inflicting that penalty. But nothing of this kind is, or indeed well could be, in this act of parliament, with respect to what is required of the assemblies. It was therefore look'd upon in America merely as a requisition, which the assemblies were to consider, and comply with or decline, in the whole or in part, as it might happen to suit the different circumstances and abilities of different colonies. Accordingly Pensylvania, where but few troops generally are, comply'd readily with the whole. But New York, thro' which all the troops usually pass and repass between Britain and the French conquests, conceiv'd the burthen of the whole would be too great for them, and therefore comply'd only with a part of the requisition, and in an address to their governor gave their reasons couch'd in the most decent and respectful terms.

To many persons, indeed, the principle of the act seems wrong. It is hard, say they, to assign a good reason why soldiers should, in any part of the King's dominions, be furnished with any thing for nothing. There is always a paymaster with them. Why should they not pay for all they have? 'Tis otherwise a partial burthen on the places where they happen to be, and therefore unjust. In Britain this burthen is only thrown on inn-keepers, and may be considered as a tax on that employment, which they however can exonerate themselves of, by higher bills on their customers, and so spread the tax more equally. But one colony that happens to be so opprest, has no means of laying part of their burthen on another colony, that from its situation is generally exempted.

Our coffee-house orators, however, would have it declared, that this refusal of full compliance with the act, is REBEL-LION, and to be punished accordingly. A rare proceeding this would be, to make a law requiring something to be done that is new, not expressing what the offence shall be of refusing to comply with it, or what the punishment; and after the offence is committed, then to name the one, and declare the other! The first instance, I believe, of this kind, in legislation; and would look not so much like making of *laws*, as making of *traps* for the subject. This is, besides, a new kind of *Rebellion*. It used to be thought that Rebellion consisted in *doing* something; but this is a Rebellion that consists in *not doing* something, or in doing nothing. If every man who neglects or refuses to comply with an act of parliament is a rebel, I am afraid we have many more rebels among us than we were aware: Among others, they that have not registered the weight of their plate, and paid the duty, are all rebels; and these, I think, are not a few: To whom may be added the acting rebels that wear French silks and cambricks.

As to the petition mentioned above, it is, I have been informed, from a number of private persons, Merchants of New York, stating their opinion, that several restraints in the Acts of Trade laid on the Commerce of the Colonies, are not only prejudicial to the Colonies, but to the Mother Country. They give their reasons for this opinion. Those reasons are to be judg'd of here. If they are found to be good and well supported by facts, one would think that instead of censure those Merchants might deserve thanks. If otherwise, the petition may be laid aside. Petitioning is not rebellion. The very nature of a petition acknowledges the power it petitions to, and the subjection of the petitioner.

But, in party views, molehills are often magnify'd to mountains. And when the wolf is determined on a quarrel with the lamb, up stream or down stream 'tis all one; pretences are easily found or made, reason and justice are out of the question.

A Friend to both Countries.

The London Chronicle, April 9, 1767

Right, Wrong, and Reasonable

To the PRINTER of the GAZETTEER.

The East India contest, that necessarily took up so much of your paper, being now abated, I hope you will find room for the following answer to the paper intitled, *Right, Wrong,* and *Reasonable, according to American Ideas,* inserted in the Gazetteers of March 5, and 9. I flatter myself that the impartiality of your readers will concur with yours, in liking to see something on the *other side* of the question, in every attack made upon the Colonies.

N. N.

RIGHT, WRONG, and REASONABLE, with regard to America, according to the ideas of the Gentle Shepherd, and the genuine meaning of the papers and pamphlets lately published by him and his associates.

RIGHT.

It is *right*, O ye Americans, when we discourage the importation of those raw materials from foreign countries that we can have from you, and do it for this *sole reason*, that foreigners drain us of our money for those articles, while you take only our manufactures, yet we should charge this upon you as a *favour*, for which you are under the *greatest obligations.*

Secondly, It is *right*, O ye Americans! that when knowing the dearness of labour in your country, we do, to enable you to furnish us with those commodities, and take our manufactures in return, give you a better price than we did use to give to foreigners, which we can well afford, considering the saving of money to our nation, the profit on our manufactures, and the encreased demand for them: We are, nevertheless, to call this by the name of *Bounty*, the better to express our *Goodness* to you, and the more clearly to intimate the *great obligation* you are under for such Goodness; and also to make manifest the *ungratefulness* of your tempers, if you do not, in return for such Bounty, take upon yourselves some *burden* ten hundred times greater than the Bounty amounts to.

Thirdly, It is *right*, O ye Americans! that we, having called all these regulations in commerce by the name of "Indulgences and Favours," and considered them as "Privileges" granted to you, do also, whenever you point out to us the regulations of the same nature, that may be equally advantageous to us, call the advice you give, "Clamour for more and greater Indulgences, Favours and Privileges." And it is farther *right*, O ye Americans! though it is well known you clubbed man for man with us in the American war, and fought side by side with us in extending by conquest the whale, and other fisheries, that you should not conceive yourselves equally intitled to the use of them with other British subjects; but the share allowed you is to be considered as flowing from the mere Grace and Favour of the Gentle Shepherd. And tho' the permitting you to carry rice to foreign markets, directly without the burthensome, useless expence, and loss of time occasioned by coming out of your way to land and re-ship it here, has enabled you to make greater remittances to Britain, and purchase greater quantities of our manufactures, yet if experience in this case prompts you to hint the advantage it would be to us to extend the permission to some other articles, it is *right* in us to charge you with Ingratitude, and to tell you that you would never have been so unreasonable, if we had not repealed the "cooly deliberated, well digested," and wonderfully useful measure of the Gentle Shepherd, called his Stamp-act.

Fourthly, Though it is a certain truth that we went to war with the French in America, merely on a dispute between the two Crowns, concerning the bounds of wilderness lands, belonging to no American, and to secure the Indian trade carried on there with our manufactures, and therefore solely an interest of ours; and though you yourselves told us "you were in no danger from the French, for that you were near twenty to one," yet it is *right*, O ye Americans! for us to declare we went there for *your defence*, at *your request*, and charge you with all the millions spent in that war, giving you no credit for the millions you spent in maintaining a number of troops equal to ours, and yet our taking the whole territory conquered, which is now daily granting in large tracts, to the gentlemen of this country, while we allow, in a case precisely the same, that the acquisitions made by the East India Company, with our assistance, are their own indubitable property.

Fifthly, It is *right*, O ye Americans! for us to charge you with *dreaming* that you have it in your power to make us a bankrupt nation, by engaging us in new wars; with *dreaming* that you may thereby encrease your own strength and prosperity; with *dreaming* that the seat of government will then be transported to America, and Britain dwindle to one of its provinces. And, because Joseph's brethren hated him for a dream he *really* dreamed, we, for a dream you never *dreamed*, and which we only *dream* you *dreamed*, are to hate you most cordially.

WRONG.

First, From the above state of the case, It is *wrong*, O ye Americans! for you to expect hereafter, any protection or countenance from us, in return for the loyalty and zeal you manifested, and the blood and treasure you have expended in our cause during that war; or that we will make any acts of parliament relating to you, from the time we, the Gentle Shepherd, and his flock, get into power, "but such as are calculated for impoverishing you and enriching us."

Secondly, It is *wrong*, O ye Americans! for you to imagine, that we will henceforth give you a preference to foreigners, in purchasing raw materials from you, because "forsooth, you stupidly give the preference to all the modes and manufactures" of Britain, and consume all your labour in the superfluities of this country. And, when you have foolishly run in our debt for them, it is *wrong* in you to hint to us any new regulation of trade, by which you may be better enabled to pay us. And though you have not, and never had any mines of gold and silver in your country, yet it is *wrong* in you to complain when we restrain your trade with foreign money-countries, by which you used to procure cash for us, when we even hinder your using paper-money among yourselves, that enabled you to spare your cash to us, and when dry, as we have drawn you, we want to squeeze blood out of you by new taxes, in the laying of which you have no participation.

Thirdly, It is *wrong*, O ye Americans, "to expect a reciprocation of good offices between us and you; for our standing maxim is, that you exist only for our sakes. We know no other end of colonization but this; nor will we acknowledge any other connection or relation between us and you," than those between a master and his slaves. Your lords we are, and slaves we deem ye, or intend to make ye. "But the dear ties of that relation we will acknowledge and maintain" as long as we can, and, if possible, after you "are tired of them."

Thus much as to the Gentle Shepherdian Ideas of *Right* and *Wrong*. We shall now shew their notions of what is *Reasonable*.

BRITISH IDEAS of what is REASONABLE in American affairs, according to the genuine meaning of some late pamphlets, &c.

These principles of *right* and *wrong* being established, It is *reasonable*, O ye Americans! that we should oblige you to bring your coarse sugars to England to be refined, and carry them back again when refined, that so you may pay two freights and two insurances, to no other purpose than wasting a shilling that we may get a groat. "Otherwise you will grow able to pay your debts."

2. It is *reasonable*, O ye Americans! that when one of your ways of raising money to pay for our manufactures, is by cutting logwood, with immense labour, in the unwholesome swamps of Honduras, and selling to foreigners what the demand here cannot take off, remitting hither the nett proceeds, yet you should be obliged first to bring the same into some British port, land, and re-ship it, at so great an expence, with the loss of time, and hindrance of voyage, as to devour all the profits; "otherwise we cannot keep you so poor, but that you will pay your debts."

3. It is *reasonable*, O ye Americans! that when, for the produce of your lands, you have obtained wines, at Madeira, and have paid the duty on importing them into America, you shall, nevertheless, when you send them to England, by way of remittance, pay the full duty here, without any drawback

of what you have already paid; "otherwise you may, in that way, pay some of your debts."

4. It is *reasonable*, O ye Americans! that though you fought bravely, in conjunction with us, to obtain and secure the fisheries of Newfoundland and Labrador, yet you shall not enjoy a freedom of fishing there in common with other British subjects, or even the freedom allowed by the peace, to our enemies. And though, by your situation, you can carry on the fishery at less expence than the French, and, of course, could undersell them in the Spanish, Portuguese, and Italian markets, and remit the money from thence to Britain, for manufactures, yet we are not to permit this, but chusing rather to fight against nature, will contend with the French ourselves, who are sure, in this article, to outdo us—"otherwise you might pay your debts."

5. It is *reasonable* for us, O ye Americans! to send custom-house officers over to you, of our own chusing, with starving salaries, that lay them under the temptation, and almost under the necessity of conniving at smugglers, or sharing their profit, and then to charge you with their want of conscience or neglect of duty. And though there is scarce a family in Britain honest enough to refuse purchasing smuggled cam-bricks, India goods, French silks, lace, brandies, &c. *if a pennyworth*, we are, nevertheless, to esteem it the greatest of crimes in you, to smuggle even the necessaries of life. For, if you buy any thing you want, cheaper of others than we can sell it to you, "we are afraid you will, by lessening your expences, be enabled to pay your debts."

6. It is *reasonable* for us, O ye Americans! tho' we know the fond preference you give to the manufactures of your mother-country is so great, that a piece of French cloth, or silk, was *never worn* among you, but even when taken in prizes, has been sent away to the French islands, as unsaleable with you, yet, to make you odious here, draw severities upon you, and wean that affection you have for this country, which is so advantageous to our commerce, we are to charge you with a fondness for French manufactures, *without the least foundation of truth*. In fine, It is *reasonable* for us to deprive you even of the common privilege of Englishmen, trials by

Juries: to restrain, by every means, your procuring money from foreigners, to refuse you even the use of paper money, whereby you might better spare your cash to us, and, after all, to "wonder that you do not pay your debts."

The Gazetteer and New Daily Advertiser, April 18, 1767

Of Lightning, and the Method (Now Used in America) of Securing Buildings and Persons from Its Mischievous Effects

Experiments made in electricity first gave philosophers a suspicion that the matter of lightning was the same with the electric matter. Experiments afterwards made on lightning obtained from the clouds by pointed rods, received into bottles, and subjected to every trial, have since proved this suspicion to be perfectly well founded; and that whatever properties we find in electricity, are also the properties of lightning.

This matter of lightning, or of electricity, is an extream subtile fluid, penetrating other bodies, and subsisting in them, equally diffused.

When by any operation of art or nature, there happens to be a greater proportion of this fluid in one body than in another, the body which has most, will communicate to that which has least, till the proportion becomes equal; provided the distance between them be not too great; or, if it is too great, till there be proper conductors to convey it from one to the other.

If the communication be through the air without any conductor, a bright light is seen between the bodies, and a sound is heard. In our small experiments we call this light and sound the electric spark and snap; but in the great operations of nature, the light is what we call *lightning*, and the sound (produced at the same time, tho' generally arriving later at our ears than the light does to our eyes) is, with its echoes, called *thunder*.

If the communication of this fluid is by a conductor, it may be without either light or sound, the subtle fluid passing in the substance of the conductor.

If the conductor be good and of sufficient bigness, the fluid passes through it without hurting it. If otherwise, it is damaged or destroyed.

All metals, and water, are good conductors.—Other bodies may become conductors by having some quantity of water in them, as wood, and other materials used in building, but not having much water in them, they are not good conductors, and therefore are often damaged in the operation.

Glass, wax, silk, wool, hair, feathers, and even wood, perfectly dry are non-conductors: that is, they resist instead of facilitating the passage of this subtle fluid.

When this fluid has an opportunity of passing through two conductors, one good, and sufficient, as of metal, the other not so good, it passes in the best, and will follow it in any direction.

The distance at which a body charged with this fluid will discharge itself suddenly, striking through the air into another body that is not charged, or not so highly charg'd, is different according to the quantity of the fluid, the dimensions and form of the bodies themselves, and the state of the air between them.—This distance, whatever it happens to be between any two bodies, is called their *striking distance*, as till they come within that distance of each other, no stroke will be made.

The clouds have often more of this fluid in proportion than the earth; in which case as soon as they come near enough (that is, within the striking distance) or meet with a conductor, the fluid quits them and strikes into the earth. A cloud fully charged with this fluid, if so high as to be beyond the striking distance from the earth, passes quietly without making noise or giving light; unless it meets with other clouds that have less.

Tall trees, and lofty buildings, as the towers and spires of churches, become sometimes conductors between the clouds and the earth; but not being good ones, that is, not conveying the fluid freely, they are often damaged.

Buildings that have their roofs covered with lead, or other

metal, and spouts of metal continued from the roof into the ground to carry off the water, are never hurt by lightning, as whenever it falls on such a building, it passes in the metals and not in the walls.

When other buildings happen to be within the striking distance from such clouds, the fluid passes in the walls whether of wood, brick or stone, quitting the walls only when it can find better conductors near them, as metal rods, bolts, and hinges of windows or doors, gilding on wainscot, or frames of pictures; the silvering on the backs of looking-glasses; the wires for bells; and the bodies of animals, as containing watry fluids. And in passing thro' the house it follows the direction of these conductors, taking as many in it's way as can assist it in its passage, whether in a strait or crooked line, leaping from one to the other, if not far distant from each other, only rending the wall in the spaces where these partial good conductors are too distant from each other.

An iron rod being placed on the outside of a building, from the highest part continued down into the moist earth, in any direction strait or crooked, following the form of the roof or other parts of the building, will receive the lightning at its upper end, attracting it so as to prevent its striking any other part; and, affording it a good conveyance into the earth, will prevent its damaging any part of the building.

A small quantity of metal is found able to conduct a great quantity of this fluid. A wire no bigger than a goose quill, has been known to conduct (with safety to the building as far as the wire was continued) a quantity of lightning that did prodigious damage both above and below it; and probably larger rods are not necessary, tho' it is common in America, to make them of half an inch, some of three quarters, or an inch diameter.

The rod may be fastened to the wall, chimney, &c. with staples of iron.—The lightning will not leave the rod (a good conductor) to pass into the wall (a bad conductor), through those staples.—It would rather, if any were in the wall, pass out of it into the rod to get more readily by that conductor into the earth.

If the building be very large and extensive, two or more rods may be placed at different parts, for greater security.

Small ragged parts of clouds suspended in the air between the great body of clouds and the earth (like leaf gold in electrical experiments), often serve as partial conductors for the lightning, which proceeds from one of them to another, and by their help comes within the striking distance to the earth or a building. It therefore strikes through those conductors a building that would otherwise be out of the striking distance.

Long sharp points communicating with the earth, and presented to such parts of clouds, drawing silently from them the fluid they are charged with, they are then attracted to the cloud, and may leave the distance so great as to be beyond the reach of striking.

It is therefore that we elevate the upper end of the rod six or eight feet above the highest part of the building, tapering it gradually to a fine sharp point, which is gilt to prevent its rusting.

Thus the pointed rod either prevents a stroke from the cloud, or, if a stroke is made, conducts it to the earth with safety to the building.

The lower end of the rod should enter the earth so deep as to come at the moist part, perhaps two or three feet; and if bent when under the surface so as to go in a horizontal line six or eight feet from the wall, and then bent again downwards three or four feet, it will prevent damage to any of the stones of the foundation.

A person apprehensive of danger from lightning, happening during the time of thunder to be in a house not so secured, will do well to avoid sitting near the chimney, near a looking glass, or any gilt pictures or wainscot; the safest place is in the middle of the room, (so it be not under a metal lustre suspended by a chain) sitting in one chair and laying the feet up in another. It is still safer to bring two or three mattrasses or beds into the middle of the room, and folding them up double, place the chair upon them; for they not being so good conductors as the walls, the lightning will not chuse an interrupted course through the air of the room and the bedding, when it can go thro' a continued better conductor the wall. But where it can be had, a hamock or swinging bed, suspended by silk cords equally distant from the walls on every side, and from the cieling and floor above and below, affords the safest situation a person can have in any room whatever; and what indeed may be deemed quite free from danger of any stroke by lightning.

Paris, Sept. 1767   B. F.

American Longevity

To the PRINTER *of the* LONDON CHRONICLE.

SIR,

I have often heard it remarked, that our Colonies in North America were unhealthy and unfavourable to long life; and more particularly so upon their first settlement. In opposition to this groundless notion, I here send you two paragraphs taken from the Pensylvania Gazette of July 16, and the New-York Gazette of August 27, giving an account of the deaths of the first-born of the city of Philadelphia, and of the province of Pennsylvania:

PHILADELPHIA, July 16.

"At Kennet, in Chester county, the 5th instant, died John Key, in the 85th year of his age, and the next day was interred in the burial place belonging to the people called Quakers, in that township, attended by a large number of reputable people, his neighbours and acquaintance.—He was born in a cave, long afterwards known by the name of Penny-Pot, near Race-street, and William Penn, our first proprietor, gave him a lot of ground, as a compliment on his being the first child born in this city.—In the early part of his life his conversation was very engaging, and his company much sought after by those of his own age; in his decline he was much esteemed for his peaceable disposition. His constitution was very healthy till about 80, when he was seized with the palsy, and continued weakly till his death.—About six years ago he walked on foot from Kennet to Philadelphia in one day, which is near 30 miles.—It has been said that people in this province are short-lived; but when we consider how few children were born here 75 years ago, and observe how many old people there are still alive among us (who were born here) we shall rather think no quarter of the world can shew a greater number of aged persons then this province can, in proportion to the children born."

Philadelphia, Aug. 24. On the 10th instant, at Brandywine Hundred, in New-Castle county, died Emanuel Grubb, in the 86th year of his age, and the next day was interred in St. Martin's church-yard, at Lower-Chichester, in Chester county, attended by a large number of his relations, neighbours, and acquaintance.—He was born in a cave, by the side of Delaware river, not far distant from where he always lived, and died, and was the first child born of English parents in this province. His constitution was remarkably healthy during his whole life, having never been afflicted with any sickness till a few days before his death. His strength and activity were surprizing in a man of his age; he could mount and ride a horse with as much dexterity as a lad of 20.—A few months ago, he rode from his own house to this city, and back again, which is upwards of 40 miles.—His memory was equally surprizing, and not in the least impaired, till his death; he could remember transactions of a late date equally well with those which happened in his younger days. He was exceeding temperate in his living, seldom making use of spirituous liquors; and for his peaceable and friendly disposition, was highly esteemed by all that knew him. This instance, among many, is a proof of the longevity of people born here.

It is worthy of observation also, that Governor Hutchinson, in his valuable History of the Massachusett's Bay, Vol. II. pp. 148 and 216, says,

"July 20, 1704, died at Marshfield, Peregrine White, aged 83 years and eight months, the first-born in Plymouth colony.

"Jan. 14, 1716, died at Salem, Elizabeth Patch, the first-born female in the old colony of Massachusett's Bay, so that she must have lived 86 or 87 years; and April 14, following, died at Newport, in Rhode-Island, Mary Godfrey, aged about 87, being the first child born there.—The longevity of the first-born in each of the three colonies, is worth noting."

As a well-wisher to mankind in general, I thought it worth while to send this to your useful paper, in order to allay the apprehensions of those, whose inclinations, business, or necessities may induce them to settle in that part of the British Empire. I must add at the same time, that I have myself lately travelled over the greater part of that extensive continent; and can with truth say, in spite of all that hath been boldly and positively asserted to the contrary, that I could not discover among that whole people, one grain of disaffection to their brethren in Britain, nor did I meet with a single person who had ever formed the most distant idea of throwing off their allegiance to the mother country. This it is doing them but bare justice to declare; and is all the return I can at present make them for the kindness and hospitality with which, purely on account of my being an *Old England-Man*, I was universally treated.

I am, Sir, your constant reader,

F + S.

The London Chronicle, December 15, 1767

Railing and Reviling

To the PRINTER of the GAZETTEER.

January 6, 1768.

Instead of raving (with your correspondent of yesterday) against the Americans as "diggers of pits for this country," "lunaticks," "sworn enemies," "false," "ungrateful," "cut-throats," &c. which is a treatment of customers that I doubt is not like to bring them back to our shop; I would recommend to all writers on American affairs (however *hard* their *arguments* may be) *soft words*, civility, and good manners. It is only from a redress of grievances and equitable regulations of commerce, with mild and reasonable measures of government, permitting and securing to those people the full enjoyment of their privileges, that we may hope to recover the affection and respect of that great and valuable part of our

fellow-subjects, and restore and confirm the solid union between the two countries, that is so necessary to the strength
and stability of the whole empire. Railing and reviling can
answer no good end; it may make the breach wider; it can
never heal it.

OLD ENGLAND *in its senses.*

The Gazetteer and New Daily Advertiser, January 8, 1768

Causes of the American Discontents Before 1768

To the PRINTER.

The waves never rise but when the winds blow.

SIR,

As the cause of the present ill-humour in America, and of
the Resolutions taken there to purchase less of our manufactures, does not seem to be generally understood, it may afford
some satisfaction to your Readers, if you give them the following short historical state of facts.

From the time that the Colonies were first considered as
capable of granting aids to the Crown, down to the end of
the last war, it is said that the constant mode of obtaining
those aids was by Requisition made from the Crown through
its Governors to the several Assemblies, in circular letters
from the Secretary of State in his Majesty's name, setting
forth the occasion, requiring them to take the matter into
consideration, and expressing a reliance on their prudence,
duty and affection to his Majesty's Government, that they
would grant such sums, or raise such numbers of men, as
were suitable to their respective circumstances.

The Colonies being accustomed to this method, have from
time to time granted money to the Crown, or raised troops
for its service, in proportion to their abilities, and, during all
the last war, beyond their abilities, so that considerable sums
were returned them yearly by Parliament as exceeding their
proportion.

Had this happy method been continued (a method which

left the King's subjects in those remote countries the pleasure
of shewing their zeal and loyalty, and of imagining that they
recommended themselves to their Sovereign by the liberality
of their voluntary grants) there is no doubt but all the money
that could reasonably be expected to be raised from them, in
any manner, might have been obtained from them, without
the least heart-burning, offence, or breach of the harmony of
affections and interests that so long subsisted between the
two countries.

It has been thought wisdom in a Government, exercising
sovereignty over different kinds of people, to have some regard to prevailing and established opinions among the people
to be governed, wherever such opinions might in their effects
promote or obstruct public measures.—If they tend to obstruct public service, they are to be changed before we act
against them, and they can only be changed by reason and
persuasion.—But if public service can be carried on without
thwarting those opinions, if they can be on the contrary made
subservient to it, they are not unnecessarily to be thwarted,
how absurd soever such popular opinions may be in their natures.—This had been the wisdom of our Government with
respect to raising money in the colonies. It was well known
that the Colonists universally were of opinion, that no money
could be levied from English subjects, but by their own consent, given by themselves or their chosen Representatives.
That therefore whatever money was to be raised from the
people in the colonies, must first be granted by their Assemblies; as the money raised in Britain is first to be granted by
the House of Commons. That this right of granting their
own money was essential to English liberty; and that if any
man, or body of men, in which they had no Representative
of their chusing, could tax them at pleasure, they could not
be said to have any property, any thing they could call their
own. But as these opinions did not hinder their granting
money voluntarily and amply, whenever the Crown, by its
servants, came into their Assemblies (as it does into its Parliaments of Britain and Ireland) and demanded aids, therefore
that method was chosen rather than the baneful one of arbitrary taxes.

I do not undertake here to support those opinions; they

have been refuted by a late act of Parliament, declaring its own power; which very Parliament, however, shewed wisely so much tender regard to those inveterate prejudices, as to repeal a tax that had odiously militated against them.—And those prejudices are still so fixed and rooted in the Americans, that it is supposed not a single man among them has been convinced of his error by that act of Parliament.

The Minister, therefore, who first projected to lay aside the accustomed method of requisition, and to raise money on America by Stamps, seems not to have acted wisely in deviating from that method (which the Colonists looked upon as constitutional) and thwarting, unnecessarily, the general fixed prejudices of so great a number of the King's subjects. It was not, however, for want of knowledge that what he was about to do would give them great offence; he appears to have been very sensible of this, and apprehensive that it might occasion some disorders, to prevent or suppress which he projected another Bill, that was brought in the same Session with the Stamp Act, whereby it was to be made lawful for Military Officers in the Colonies to quarter their Soldiers in private houses. This seemed intended to awe the people into a compliance with the other Act. Great opposition, however, being raised here against the Bill, by the Agents from the Colonies, and the Merchants trading thither, the Colonists declaring that, under such a power in the Army, no one could look on his house as his own, or think he had a home, when Soldiers might be thrust into it, and mixed with his family, at the pleasure of an Officer, that part of the Bill was dropt; but there still remained a clause, when it passed into a law, to oblige the several Assemblies to provide quarters for the Soldiers, furnishing them with fire, beds, candles, small beer or rum, and sundry other articles, at the expence of the several Provinces.—And this Act continued in force when the Stamp Act was repealed, though, if obligatory on the Assemblies, it equally militated against the American principle abovementioned, that money is not to be raised on English subjects without their consent.

The Colonies nevertheless, being put into high good humour by the repeal of the Stamp Act, chose to avoid a fresh dispute upon the other, it being temporary, and soon to expire, never (as they hoped) to revive again; and in the mean time they, by various ways, provided for the quartering of the troops, either by Acts of their own Assemblies, without taking notice of the Acts of Parliament, or by some variety or small diminution (as of salt and vinegar) in the supplies required by the Act, that what they did might appear a voluntary act of their own, and not done in obedience to an Act of Parliament, which they thought contrary to right, and therefore void in itself.

It might have been well if the matter had thus passed without notice; but an officious Governor having written home an angry and aggravating letter upon this conduct in the Assembly of his province, the outed projector of the Stamp Act and his adherents, then in the opposition, raised such a clamour against America, as in rebellion, &c. and against those who had been for the repeal of the Stamp Act, as having thereby been encouragers of this supposed rebellion, that it was thought necessary to enforce the Quartering Act by another Act of Parliament, taking away from the Province of New-York, which had been most explicit in its refusal, all the powers of legislation, till it should have complied with that act: The news of which greatly alarmed the people every where in America, as the language of such an act seemed to be—Obey implicitly laws made by the Parliament of Great Britain, to force money from you without your consent, or you shall enjoy no rights or privileges at all.

At the same time the late Chancellor of the Exchequer, desirous of ingratiating himself with the opposition, or driven to it by their clamours, projected the levying more money from America, by new duties on various articles of our own manufacture, as glass, paper, painters colours, &c. appointing a new Board of Customs, and sending over a set of Commissioners (with large salaries) to be established at Boston, who were to have the care of collecting these duties; and which were, by the act, expressly mentioned to be intended for the payment of the salaries of Governors, Judges, and other Officers of the Crown in America, it being a pretty general opinion here, that those Officers ought not to depend on the people there for any part of their support.

It is not my intention to combat this opinion. But perhaps

it may be some satisfaction to the Public to know what ideas the Americans have on the subject. They say then, as to Governors, that they are not like Princes whose posterity have an inheritance in the government of a nation, and therefore an interest in its prosperity; they are generally strangers to the Provinces they are sent to govern; have no estate, natural connection, or relation there, to give them an affection for the country; that they come only to make money as fast as they can, are frequently men of vicious characters and broken fortunes, sent merely to get them off the hands of a Minister somewhere out of the way; that as they intend staying in the country no longer than their government continues, and purpose to leave no family behind them, they are apt to be regardless of the good will of the people, and care not what is said or thought of them after they are gone. Their situation gives them many opportunities of being vexatious, and they are often so, notwithstanding their dependance on the Assemblies for all that part of their support that does not arise from fees established by law, but would probably be much more so if they were to be fully supported by money drawn from the people, without the consent or good will of the people, which is the professed design of this act. That if by means of these forced duties, government is to be supported in America, without the intervention of the Assemblies, their Assemblies will soon be looked upon as useless, and a Governor will not call them, as having nothing to hope from their meeting, and perhaps something to fear from their enquiries into and remonstrances against his mal-administration; that thus the people will be deprived of their most essential rights; that its being, as at present, a Governor's interest to cultivate the good will, by promoting the welfare of the people he governs, can be attended with no prejudice to the Mother Country, since all the laws he may be prevailed to give his assent to, are subject to revision here, and if reported against by the Board of Trade, as hurtful to the interest of this country, may and are immediately repealed by the Crown; nor dare he pass any law contrary to his instructions, as he holds his office during the pleasure of the Crown, and his securities are liable for the penalties of their bonds if he contravenes those instructions.

This is what they say as to Governors.

As to Judges, they alledge, that being appointed from hence by the Crown, and holding their commissions, not during good behaviour, as in Britain, but during pleasure, all the weight of interest would be thrown into one of the scales, (which ought to be held even) if the salaries are also to be paid out of duties forced from the people without their consent, and independent of their Assemblies' approbation or disapprobation of the Judges behaviour; that whenever the Crown will grant commissions to able and honest Judges during good behaviour, the Assemblies will settle permanent and ample salaries on them during their commissions; but at present they have no other means of getting rid of an ignorant, unjust Judge, (and some of scandalous characters have, they say, been sent them) but by starving him out.

I do not suppose these reasonings of the Americans will appear here to have much weight in them. I do not produce them with an expectation of convincing your Readers. I relate them merely in pursuance of the task I have imposed on myself, to be an impartial Historian of American facts and opinions.

                                                            F. B.

To the PRINTER.

The Colonists being greatly alarmed, as I observed in my last, by news of the act for abolishing the legislature of New York, and the imposition of these new duties professedly for such disagreeable and to them appearing dangerous purposes; accompanied by a new set of Revenue Officers, with large appointments, which gave strong suspicion that more business of the same kind was soon to be provided for them, that they might earn those salaries, began seriously to consider their situation, and to revolve afresh in their minds grievances which from their respect and love for this country they had long borne, and seemed almost willing to forget. They reflected how lightly the interests of all America had been esteemed here, when the interest of a few inhabitants of Great Britain happened to have the smallest competition with it. That thus the whole American people were forbidden the advantage of a direct importation of wine, oil, and fruit from

Portugal, but must take them loaded with all the expences of a voyage of one thousand leagues round about, being to be landed first in England to be re-shipped for America; expences amounting, in war time, at least to thirty per cent. more than otherwise they would have been charged with, and all this, merely that a few Portugal Merchants in London might gain a commission on those goods passing through their hands.—Portugal Merchants, by the bye, who can complain loudly of the smallest hardships laid on their trade by foreigners, and yet even the last year could oppose with all their influence the giving ease to their fellow-subjects under so heavy an oppression—That on a frivolous complaint of a few Virginia Merchants, nine Colonies were restrained from making paper money, though become absolutely necessary to their internal commerce, from the constant remittance of their gold and silver to Britain.—But not only the interest of a particular body of Merchants, the interest of any small body of British Tradesmen or Artificers, has been found, they say, to out-weigh that of all the King's subjects in the Colonies.

There cannot be a stronger natural right than that of a man's making the best profit he can of the natural produce of his lands, provided he does not thereby injure the State in general. Iron is to be found every where in America, and beaver furs are the natural produce of that country. Hats, and nails, and steel, are wanted there as well as here. It is of no importance to the common welfare of the Empire, whether a subject gets his living by making hats on this or that side of the water; yet the Hatters of England have prevailed so far as to obtain an act in their own favour, restraining that manufacture in America, in order to oblige the Americans to send their beaver to England to be manufactured, and purchase back the hats loaded with the charges of a double transportation. In the same manner have a few Nail-makers, and still a smaller number of Steel-makers (perhaps there are not half a dozen of these in England) prevailed totally to forbid, by an act of Parliament, the erecting of slitting-mills and steel-furnaces in America, that the Americans may be obliged to take nails for their buildings, and steel for their tools from these artificers under the same disadvantages. Added to these, the Americans remembered the act authorizing the most cruel insult that perhaps was ever offered by one people to another, that of emptying our gaols into their settlements (Scotland too has within these few years obtained the privilege it had not before, of sending its rogues and villains to the Plantations) an insult aggravated by that barbarous ill-placed sarcasm in a report of the Board of Trade, when one of the Provinces complained of the act. "It is necessary that it should be continued for the Better Peopling of your Majesty's Colonies." I say, reflecting on these things, the Americans said to one another, (their news papers are full of such discourses) these people are not content with making a monopoly of us, forbidding us to trade with any other country of Europe, and compelling us to buy every thing of them, though in many articles we could furnish ourselves 10, 20, and even 50 per cent. cheaper elsewhere; but now they have as good as declared they have a right to tax us, *ad libitum*, internally and externally; and that our constitution and liberties shall all be taken away if we do not submit to that claim. They are not content with the high prices at which they sell us their goods, but have now begun to enhance those prices by new duties; and by the expensive apparatus of a new set of Officers, they appear to intend an augmentation and multiplication of those burthens that shall still be more grievous to us. Our people have been foolishly fond of their superfluous modes and manufactures, to the impoverishing our country, carrying off all our cash, and loading us with debt; they will not suffer us to restrain the luxury of our inhabitants as they do that of their own, by laws; they can make laws to discourage or prohibit the importation of French superfluities; but though those of England are as ruinous to us as the French ones are to them; if we make a law of that kind, they immediately repeal it. Thus they get all our money from us by trade, and every profit we can any where make by our fishery, our produce, and our commerce, centers finally with them! but this does not satisfy. It is time then to take care of ourselves by the best means in our power. Let us unite in solemn resolutions and engagements with and to each other, that we will give these new Officers as little trouble as possible by not consuming the British manufactures on which they are to levy the duties. Let us agree to consume no more of their expensive gewgaws; let us live frugally; and let us industriously manufacture what we can for ourselves; thus we shall be able honourably to discharge the debts we already owe them, and after that we may be able to keep some money in our country, not only for the uses of our internal commerce, but for the service of our gracious Sovereign, whenever he shall have occasion for it, and think proper to require it of us in the old constitutional manner. For notwithstanding the reproaches thrown out against us in their public papers and pamphlets; notwithstanding we have been reviled in their Senate as rebels and traitors, we are truly a loyal people. Scotland has had its rebellions, and England its plots, against the present royal family; but America is untainted with those crimes; there is in it scarce a man, there is not a single native of our country who is not firmly attached to his King by principle and by affection. But a new kind of loyalty seems to be required of us, a loyalty to Parliament; a loyalty that is to extend, it seems, to a surrender of all our properties, whenever a House of Commons, in which there is not a single Member of our chusing, shall think fit to grant them away without our consent, and to a patient suffering the loss of our privileges, as Englishmen, if we cannot submit to make such surrender. We were separated too far from Britain by the ocean, but we were united strongly to it by respect and love, so that we could at any time freely have spent our lives and little fortunes in its cause; but this unhappy new system of politics tends to dissolve those bands of union, and to sever us for ever. Woe to the man that first adopted it! Both countries will long have cause to execrate his memory.

These are the wild ravings of the at present half distracted Americans. To be sure no reasonable man in England can approve of such sentiments, and, as I said before, I do not pretend to support or justify them; but I sincerely wish, for the sake of the manufactures and commerce of Great Britain, and for the sake of the strength a firm union with our growing colonies would give us, that those people had never been thus needlessly driven out of their senses.

F. B.

January 7, 1768; reprinted in *The London Chronicle*,
August 30 and September 1, 1774

Subjects of Subjects

Mr. URBAN,

Your anonymous correspondent, (See Vol. xxxvii. p. 620.) has declaimed on a subject, which by an unhappy combination of ignorance and obstinacy has become very like a bone of contention between the young and the old provinces of this great common-wealth.

It seldom happens in disputes of any kind but that one side or the other lay the foundations of their arguments on error; it happens more particularly so with your angry correspondent, for whose information I will beg leave to give a short sketch of the British constitution.

The British state or empire consists of several islands and other distant countries, asunder in different parts of the globe, *but all united in allegiance to one Prince*, and to the *common law* (Scotland excepted) as it existed in the old provinces or mother country, before the colonies or new provinces were formed. The prince, with a select parliament, or assembly, make the legislative power of and for each province within itself. Where vicinity made it convenient, several islands and provinces were at sundry times consolidated, and represented by one parliament, as the Isle of Wight, Cornwall, Wales, Cheshire, Durham, and Scotland; by which means all Great Britain and its contiguous isles, are unitedly represented in one assembly in parliament. It has not as yet been thought proper to unite Ireland to the old provinces, though lying very near; nor any of the provinces of America, which lie at a great distance. But notwithstanding this state of separate assemblies, the allegiance of the distant provinces to the crown will remain for ever unshaken, while they enjoy the rights of Englishmen; that is, with the consent of their sovereign, the right of legislation each for themselves; for this puts them on an exact level, in this respect, with their fellow subjects in the old provinces, and better than this they could not be by any change in their power. But if the old provinces should often exercise the right of making laws for the new, they would probably grow as restless as the Corsicans, when they perceived they were no longer fellow subjects, but the subjects of subjects.

To illustrate this matter by a comparison; Should it happen, through the revolutions of time, that some future king should make choice of Ireland for his seat of government, and that the parliament of that kingdom, with his majesty's concurrence, should assume the right of taxing the people of England, would the people of England quietly acquiesce, or implicitly pay obedience to laws made by virtue of such an assumed right? And yet, as there is no law in being to prevent his majesty from making any part of his dominions the seat of his government, the case is by no means foreign to the present question.

The laws made here to tax the Americans affect them as a distinct body, in which the law makers are in no manner whatever, comprehended; whereas the laws made to tax Great-Britain, affect alike every member who gives his concurrence to such law. And hence arises the essential difference between *real* and *virtual* representations, so much agitated.

Your correspondent observes, 'that we are loaded with 130 millions of debt; great part of which, was contracted by defending the Americans, and therefore that they are bound in gratitude, &c.' Were this argument of weight, and were the right of taxing to follow the obligation of defence, we have expended more than the whole sum on various occasions, in defence of the balance of power on the continent. Will your correspondent for that reason, argue, that Great-Britain has a right of taxing her friends in Germany? Hanover for instance, was formerly said to have cost this nation immense sums for its defence; and Hanover is a district under the obedience of the king of Great-Britain. Will it follow that we have any right to tax Hanover, or that Hanover, in gratitude for the sums we have expended in her behalf, should implicitly give up her ancient rights?

Upon the whole, the point in dispute does not depend on *gratitude* or *defence*, but on the right of Englishmen to give their own money with their own consent. While the Americans were in possession of that right, or thought themselves in possession of it, every requisition for that purpose by the king or his ministers was chearfully complied with; but since that right, by the mistaken *policy of one man*, has been brought in question; murmuring and discontent has succeeded, and every artifice is now practiced to withold sums levied *by a new mode*; which had they been demanded in the *old way*, would have been willingly granted.

I am, Sir, &c.   A. B.

Gentleman's Magazine, January, 1768

On the Candidacy of Barlow Trecothick

To the PRINTER:

I am, Sir, a native of *Boston*, in *New-England*, but I do not concern myself in your *London* election; nor do I believe that any of my countrymen think it of importance to them, whether you choose Alderman *T.* your representative, or reject him. And yet I hear great clamour, as if his nomination were to promote a *Boston* interest. He may be, for ought I know, a man of abilities, and a friend of ours: But, should he get into P——t, what is one man among five or six hundred? A drop in the bucket. He may be well acquainted with the interests of both countries, a moderate prudent man, and so a fit instrument to conciliate jarring interests, and restore harmony between us. But possibly you have men enough as well qualified in those respects, and better in others. Choose whom you please, only never hereafter tell us, as a reason for our submitting to your taxes, *that we are represented in your Parliament*, when even an *Englishman*, having *been in* America, is made an absolute disqualification, a bar to his being chosen at all.

I sit down, Sir, after much patience, merely to take some notice of the invective and abuse, that have, on this occasion, been so liberally bestowed on my country, by your writers who sign themselves *Old England*, *a Londoner*, *a Liveryman of London*, &c. &c. [By the way, Mr. Printer, should I have said liberally or illiberally? Not being now it seems allowed to be an *Englishman*, I ought modestly to doubt my *English*, and submit it as I do to your correction.] The public, however, has been assured by these gentlemen, that "the *Bostonians* have an *evil disposition* towards *Old England*, a rooted *malice* against this country, an *implacable enmity* to it;" they talk of our having "*hostile* intentions," and making "*barbarous* resolutions against it;" they say that "neither *French* nor *Spaniards* have as yet outdone the *Bostonians* in *malicious combinations against its existence;*" that we are "*as inveterate enemies* to *Old England*, as ever the *Carthagenians* appeared to be to *Rome*."—If all this is true, the inference intended is a plain one; it is as proper now to make war on *Boston*, as ever it was to make war against *France* or *Spain*; and it will be as right a thing in *Old-England*, totally to destroy *New-England*, as it was in *Old Rome* to destroy *Carthage*—You should not be contented with cutting the throats of one half of us in the *West*, to make the other half buy your goods whether they will or no, (as some *Londoners say* other *Londoners do* in the *East*) but the word should be, with old *Cato*, DELENDA EST: Don't leave one stone upon another, nor a *Carthagenian* or *Bostonian* alive upon the face of the earth.—Is this what these valiant writers would be at? And shall we again see them, as in the time of the Stamp-Act, exhorting government to pour its armies into the colonies, and deluge the country with blood? But government was, and will be wiser.—And do *these* gentlemen talk of *humanity*? And do *they* complain of *inhumanity*? the *inhumanity* of *Boston* people!—the *horrible inhumanity* of resolving to live within compass, and manufacture what they can for themselves!

O! but this would be "*inhumanity to England*," "it is *Bostonian cruelty*, that wants to starve our poor!"

Supposing it, for a moment, true, give me leave, Sir, on this head, to recriminate a little. I shall do it gently. I will not bring railing accusations of my own making against you *Englishmen*: And [all good friends and fellow citizens as you are] it must be supposed that you touch your own failings tenderly, "*Nought is aggravated, nought set down in anger.*"— I have been a reader then, of your news-papers and pamphlets for these three years past; and I find them filled with complaints, that the country and city swarm with rich *engrossers*, *forestallers*, *monopolizers*, who combine to make an artificial famine, to oppress and starve the poor, in order to make themselves more rich. I find your *farmers* charged in a body, as cruelly withholding the staff of life; your *millers*, *meal-men* and *bakers* represented as thieves and poisoners;

your *merchants* accused of sending away your corn, and starving your own people, to feed foreigners, for the sake of a little profit to themselves, or hoarding it up in magazines till spoilt, rather than let the poor have it at a moderate price.—I find your *landholders*, that great and respectable body, charged with endeavouring by every means in their power to keep up the price of provisions, that the farmers may thereby be enabled to pay them higher rents, for the better support of their excessive luxury. I find even your p——ts, who are chosen chiefly by your *landholders*, charged with entering into their views; and that there have arisen laws to prevent the importation of beef, pork, corn, &c. from your own *Ireland*, as well as from any foreign country, lest the poor in *England* should eat at a less expence; and even laws to tax those poor towards paying a bounty on the exportation of corn, lest too great a plenty at home should lower the price of bread.

Pray, Gentlemen, are these things so?

And are your own people really such tyrants and oppressors of the poor?

I, that am a stranger among ye, cannot be qualified to judge. I can only say, that, as you live together, you have better opportunities of *knowing one another*, than you have of knowing us at 3000 miles distance, and that therefore what you say of *one another* is rather more to be depended on. Not to affront you, therefore, by affecting to doubt these facts of your asserting, I would only submit it to your consideration, whether it might not be at least decent, to cure yourselves of *inhumanity*, before you venture to charge it upon us. Pluck this beam out of your own eyes, before you pretend to spy the mote in ours. We have no malice against your poor, no desire in the least to starve them; but we think we are unable to continue purchasing your manufactures, not only at high prices, but at those prices enhanced by duties; and therefore we resolve to make what we want; not to starve *your* poor, but to prevent becoming poor and starving *ourselves.*—*Charity*, your own proverb says, *begins at home*. Why should you expect us to have more concern for your poor than you have? If you want our help in maintaining them as heretofore, you know how it may be easily had. The means are in your own hands; you know you got all from us, by trade, that we could possibly spare, and kept us besides continually in your debt; what would you, what can you have more? The situation of the colonies seems similar to that of the cows in the fable; forbidden to suckle their own calves, and daily drawn dry, they yet parted with their milk willingly; but when moreover a tax came to be demanded of them, and that too to be paid *in grass* of which they had already too short a provision; it was no wonder they thought their masters unreasonable, and resolved for the future to suck one another.

Boston man as I am, Sir, and inimical, as my country is represented to be, I hate neither *England* nor *Englishmen*, driven (though my ancestors were) by mistaken oppression of former times, out of this happy country, to suffer all the hardships of an *American* wilderness. I retain no resentment on that account. I wish prosperity to the nation; I honour, esteem, and love its people. I only hate calumniators and boutefeus on either side the water, who would for the little dirty purposes of faction, set brother against brother, turn friends into mortal enemies, and ruin an empire by dividing it.—The very injurious treatment *America* has lately received, in so many *London* prints, may have some tendency to alienate still more the affections of that country from this; but as your papers extend thither, I wish our people may by their means be informed, that those abuses do not flow from the general sense of people here; that they are the productions of a few unknown angry writers, heated by an election contest, who rave against *America*, because a candidate they would decry once lived there, and happens to be otherwise unexceptionable: Writers who (as I have shewn) *abuse* their own country as virulently as they do ours; and whose invectives are disapproved by all people of understanding and moderation. Let it be known that there is much good will towards *America* in the generality of this nation; and that however government may sometimes happen to be mistaken or misled, with relation to *American* interests, there is no general intention to oppress us; and that therefore, we may rely upon having every real grievance removed, on proper representations. By spreading these truths in your paper through *America*, Sir, you may come to deserve a share in that blessing which is promised to the peace-makers, when only its reverse can be expected by these unhappy writers.

East-Greenwich, March 8, 1768.   NEW-ENGLAND.

The Pennsylvania Chronicle, December 12, 1768

On the Labouring Poor

SIR,

I have met with much invective in the papers for these two years past, against the hard-heartedness of the rich, and much complaint of the great oppressions suffered in this country by the labouring poor. Will you admit a word or two on the other side of the question? I do not propose to be an advocate for oppression, or oppressors. But when I see that the poor are by such writings exasperated against the rich, and excited to insurrections, by which much mischief is done, and some forfeit their lives, I could wish the true state of things were better understood, the poor not made by these busy writers more uneasy and unhappy than their situation subjects them to be, and the nation not brought into disrepute among foreigners by public groundless accusations of ourselves, as if the rich in England had no compassion for the poor, and Englishmen wanted common humanity.

In justice then to this country, give me leave to remark, that the condition of the poor here is by far the best in Europe, for that, except in England and her American colonies, there is not in any country of the known world, not even in Scotland or Ireland, a provision by law to enforce a support of the poor. Every where else necessity reduces to beggary. This law was not made by the poor. The legislators were men of fortune. By that act they voluntarily subjected their own estates, and the estates of all others, to the payment of a tax for the maintenance of the poor, incumbering those estates with a kind of rent charge for that purpose, whereby the poor are vested with an inheritance, as it were, in all the estates of the rich. I wish they were benefited by this generous provision in any degree equal to the good intention with which it was made, and is continued: But I fear the giving mankind a dependance on any thing for support in age or sickness, besides industry and frugality during youth and health, tends to flatter our natural indolence, to encourage idleness and prodigality, and thereby to promote and increase poverty, the very evil it was intended to cure; thus multiplying beggars, instead of diminishing them.

Besides this tax, which the rich in England have subjected themselves to in behalf of the poor, amounting in some places to five or six shillings in the pound of the annual income, they have, by donations and subscriptions, erected numerous schools in various parts of the kingdom, for educating gratis the children of the poor in reading and writing, and in many of those schools the children are also fed and cloathed. They have erected hospitals, at an immense expence, for the reception and cure of the sick, the lame, the wounded, and the insane poor, for lying-in women, and deserted children. They are also continually contributing towards making up losses occasioned by fire, by storms, or by floods, and to relieve the poor in severe seasons of frost, in times of scarcity, &c. in which benevolent and charitable contributions no nation exceeds us.—Surely there is some gratitude due for so many instances of goodness!

Add to this, all the laws made to discourage foreign manufactures, by laying heavy duties on them, or totally prohibiting them, whereby the rich are obliged to pay much higher prices for what they wear and consume, than if the trade was open: These are so many laws for the support of our labouring poor, made by the rich, and continued at their expence; all the difference of price between our own and foreign commodities, being so much given by our rich to our poor; who would indeed be enabled by it to get by degrees above poverty, if they did not, as too generally they do, consider every increase of wages only as something that enables them to drink more and work less; so that their distress in sickness, age, or times of scarcity, continues to be the same as if such laws had never been made in their favour.

Much malignant censure have some writers bestowed upon the rich for their luxury and expensive living, while the poor are starving, &c. not considering that what the rich expend, the labouring poor receive in payment for their labour. It may seem a paradox if I should assert, that our labouring poor do in every year receive *the whole revenue of the nation*; I mean not only the public revenue, but also the revenue, or clear income, of all private estates, or a sum equivalent to the whole. In support of this position I reason thus. The rich do not work for one another. Their habitations, furniture, cloathing, carriages, food, ornaments, and every thing in short that they, or their families use and consume, is the work or produce of the labouring poor, who are, and must be, continually paid for their labour in producing the same. In these payments the revenues of private estates are expended, for most people live up to their incomes. In cloathing and provision for troops, in arms, ammunition, ships, tents, carriages, &c. &c. (every particular the produce of labour) much of the publick revenue is expended. The pay of officers civil and military, and of the private soldiers and sailors, requires the rest; and they spend that also in paying for what is produced by the labouring poor. I allow that some estates may increase by the owners spending less than their income; but then I conceive that other estates do at the same time diminish, by the owner's spending more than their income, so that when the enriched want to buy more land, they easily find lands in the hands of the impoverished, whose necessities oblige them to sell; and thus this difference is equalled. I allow also, that part of the expence of the rich is in foreign produce or manufactures, for producing which the labouring poor of other nations must be paid; but then I say, that we must first pay our own labouring poor for an equal quantity of our manufactures or produce, to exchange for those foreign productions, or we must pay for them in money, which money, not being the natural produce of our country, must first be purchased from abroad, by sending out its value in the produce or manufactures of this country, for which manufactures our labouring poor are to be paid. And indeed if we did not export more than we import, we could have no money at all. I allow farther, that there are middle men, who make a profit, and even get estates, by purchasing the labour of the poor and selling it at advanced prices to the rich; but then they cannot enjoy that profit or the incomes of estates, but by spending them in employing and paying our labouring poor, in some shape or other, for the products of industry—Even beggars, pensioners, hospitals, and all that are supported by charity, spend their incomes in the same manner. So that finally, as I said at first, *our labouring poor receive annually the whole of the clear revenues of the nation*, and from us they can have no more.

If it be said that their wages are too low, and that they ought to be better paid for their labour, I heartily wish any means could be fallen upon to do it, consistent with their interest and happiness; but as the cheapness of other things is owing to the plenty of those things, so the cheapness of labour is, in most cases, owing to the multitude of labourers, and to their underworking one another in order to obtain employment. How is this to be remedied? A law might be made to raise their wages; but if our manufactures are too dear, they will not vend abroad, and all that part of employment will fail, unless by fighting and conquering we compel other nations to buy our goods, whether they will or no, which some have been mad enough at times to propose. Among ourselves, unless we give our working people less employment, how can we, for what they do, pay them higher than we do? Out of what fund is the additional price of labour to be paid, when all our present incomes are, as it were, mortgaged to them? Should they get higher wages, would that make them less poor, if in consequence they worked fewer days of the week proportionably? I have said a law might be made to raise their wages; but I doubt much whether it could be executed to any purpose, unless another law, now indeed almost obsolete, could at the same time be revived and enforced; a law, I mean, that many have often heard and repeated, but few have ever duly considered. SIX *days shalt thou labour*. This is as positive a part of the commandment as that which says, *the* SEVENTH *day thou shalt rest*; but we remember well to observe the indulgent part, and never think of the other. St Monday is generally as duly kept by our working people as Sunday; the only difference is, that, instead of employing their time, cheaply, at church, they are wasting it expensively at the alehouse.

I am, Sir, &c.
MEDIUS.

Gentleman's Magazine, April, 1768

Phonetic Alphabet

o to huh	It is endeavoured to give the Alphabet a more nat- ural Order, beginning first with the simple Sounds form'd by the Breath, with none or very little Help of Tongue, Teeth and Lips, and produc'd chiefly in the Windpipe.

ish s ing ŋ	Then coming forward to those form'd by the Root of the Tongue next to the Windpipe;	gi ki

r n t d	Then to those form'd more forward by the fore- part of the Tongue against the Roof of the Mouth;

es ez el	Then those form'd still more forward in the Mouth, by the Tip of the Tongue, apply'd first to the Roots of the upper Teeth,

eth, h	Then to the Ends or Edges of the same Teeth;	edh ch

ef ev	Then to those form'd still more forward by the under Lip apply'd to the upper Teeth;

bi pi	Then to those form'd yet more forward by the up- per and under Lip opening to let out the sounding Breath;

m	And lastly ending with the Shutting up of the Mouth or closing the Lips, while any Vowel is sounding.

In this Alphabet c is omitted as unnecessary, k supplying its hard Sound and s the soft.

The Jod j is also omitted, its Sound being supplied by the new Letter ish s, which serves other purposes, assisting in the formation of other Sounds; thus the s with a d before it gives the Sound of the Jod j and soft g, as in James, January, Giant, gentle, *dseems, dsanueri, dsyiant, dsentel*; with a t before it, it gives the Sound of ch soft, as in cherry, chip, *tseri, tsip*; and with an z before it the French sound of the Jod j, as in jamais, *zsame*.

Thus the g has no longer two different Sounds, which occasion'd Confusion, but is as every Letter ought to be, confin'd to one; the same is to be observ'd in all the Letters, Vowels and Consonants, that wherever they are met with, or in whatever Company, their Sound is always the same. It is also intended that there be no superfluous Letters used in Spelling, i.e. no Letter that is not sounded, and this Alphabet by Six new Letters provides that there be no distinct Sounds in the Language without Letters to express them. As to the Difference between short and long Vowels, it is naturally express'd by a single Vowel where short, a double one where long; as, for *mend* write *mend*, but for *remain'd* write *rime en'd*; for *did*, write *did*, but for *deed*, write *diid*, &c.

this to be altered

What in our common Alphabet is suppos'd the third Vowel, i, as we sound it is not a Vowel but a Diphthong, consisting of two of our Vowels join'd, viz. a as sounded in *all* or u as sounded in unto and e: any one will be sensible of this, who sounds those two Vowels ae or ue quick after each other; the Sound begins *aw* or y and ends *ee*. The true Sound of the i is that we now give to e in the words *deed*, *keep*, &c. [   ]

1768?

Phonetic Alphabet

Names of the Letters
express'd in the reform'd
Sounds and Characters

Characters.	Sounded as now in		
o	old	o	the first Vowel naturally, and deepest sound; requires only to open the Mouth, and breathe thro' it.
a[a]	John, Folly	a	the next, requiring the Mouth open'd a little more or hollower.
a	man, can	a	the next, a little more.
e	mane, lane	e	the next, requires the Tongue to be a little more elevated ⎫ tho the Pipe alone will form them, but not so easily.
i	een, seen	i	the next, still a little more, ⎭
u	tool, fool	u	the next, requires the Lips to be gather'd up, leaving a small Opening.
u[ɥ; Yʜ]	um, un, as in umbrage, unto, &c.	ɥ	the next, a very short Vowel, the Sound of which we should express in our present Letters thus, *uh*, a short and not very strong Aspiration.
h	hunter, happy, high	huh	a stronger or more forcible Aspiration.
g	give, gather	gi	the first Consonant, being form'd by the Root of the Tongue, this is the present hard g.
k	keep, kick	ki	a kindred Sound, a little more acute, to be us'd instead of the hard c.
s [s]	sh, ship, wish	ish	a new Letter, wanted in our Language, our sh, separately taken, not being proper Elements of the Sound.

ŋ[y]	ng, ing, reaping, among	ing	a new Letter, wanted for the same Reason; these are form'd back in the Mouth.
n	end	en	form'd more forward in the Mouth, the Tip of the Tongue to the Roof of the Mouth.
r	art	ar	the same, the Tip of the Tongue a little loose or separate from the Roof of the Mouth.
t	teeth	ti	the Tip of the Tongue more forward, touching and then leaving the Roof.
d	deed	di	the same, touching a little fuller.
l	ell, tell	el	the same touching just about the Gums of the upper Teeth.
h[þ]	th, think	eh	the Tongue under and a little behind the upper Teeth, touching them nearly but so as to let the Breath pass between.
ch[dʒ; Ð]	dh, thy	ech	the same a little fuller.
s	essence	es	this Sound is form'd by the Breath passing between the moist End of the Tongue and the upper Teeth.
z	cz, wages	cz	the same a little denser and duller.
f	effect	ef	form'd by the lower Lip against the upper Teeth.
v	ever	ev	the same fuller and duller.
b	bees	bi	the lips put full together and open'd as the Air passes out.
p	peep	pi	the same but a thinner Sound.
m	ember	em	the closing of the Lips, while the e is sounding.

To Mary Stevenson

Diir Pali, Ritsmɥnd, Dsulɥi 20.-68

Ɏi intended to hev sent iu chiz Pepers sunɥr, bɥt biiɡ bizi fargat it.

Mr Kolman hez mended deeli: bɥt iur gud Mɥchɥr hez bin indispoz'd uih e slɥit Fivɥr, atended uih mɥts fiibilnes and uirines. Si uiuld nat allau mi to send iu uɥrd av it at chi tɥim, and iz nau beter.

Ɏi uis iu to kansider chis Alfabet, and giv mi Instanses af sɥts Iɡlis Uɥrds and Saunds az iu mee hink kannat perfektlɥi bi eksprest bɥi it. Ɏi am persueeded it mee bi kamplited bɥi iur help. Ði greeter difikɥlti uil bi to briɡ it into ius. Hauevɥr, if Amendments eer nevɥr atemted, and hiɡs kantinu to gro uɥrs and uɥrs, chee mɥst kɥm to bi in a retsed Kandisɥn at last; sɥts indiid ɥi hink aur Alfabet and Rɥitiɡ alredi in; bɥt if ui go an az ui hev dɥn e fiu Senturiz langer, aur uɥrds uil graduali siis to ekspres Saunds, chee uil onli stand far hiɡs, az chi rittin uɥrds du in chi Tsuiniiz Languads, huits ɥi sɥspekt mɥit oridsinali hev bin e litiral Rɥitiɡ lɥik chat af Iurop, bɥt hru chi Tseendsez in Pronɥsiesɥn braat an bɥi chi Kors af Eedses, and hru chi abstinet Adhirens af chat Pipil to old Kɥstɥms and amɥɡ ɥchɥrs to cheer old manɥr ov Rɥitiɡ, chi oridsinal Saunds af Leters and Uɥrds eer last, and no langɥr kansidered. Ɏi am, mɥi diir Frend, Iurz afeksɥnetli,

From Mary Stevenson

Diir Sɥr,

Ɏi have transkrɥib'd iur Alfabet &c. huits ɥi hink mɥit bi av sɥrvis tu choz hu uis tu akuɥir an akiuret pronɥnsiesɥn if chat kuld bi fiks'd, bɥt ɥi si meni inkanvinienses az uel az difikultis chat uuld atend chi briɡiɡ iur letɥrs & arhagrafi intu kamɥn ius. A Al aur etimalodsis uuld bi last, kansikuentli ui kuld nat asɥrteen chi miiniɡ av meni uɥrds; chi distinksɥn, tu, bituiin uɥrds av difɥrent miiniɡ & similar saund uuld bi chron daun; and aal chi buks alredi riten uuld bi iusles ɥnles *ui* liviɡ rɥitɥrs pɥblis nu idisɥns. In sart ɥi biliiv ui mɥst let

pipil spel an in cheer old ue, and (az ui sal fꭓind it isiiest) du
chi seem aurselvs. With ease & with sincerity I can in the old
way subscribe myself Dear Sir,

Your affectionate humble Servant,

September 26, 1768

To Mary Stevenson

Diir Madam,

Ði abdseksꭓn iu meek to rektifꭓiiŋ aur alfabet, "chat it uil
bi atended uich inkanviniensiz and difikꭓltiz," iz e natural uꭓn;
far it aluaz akꭓrz huen eni refarmesꭓn iz propozed; huechꭓr
in rilidsꭓn, gꭓvernment, laz, and iven daun az lo az rods and
huil karidsiz. Ði tru kuestsꭓn chen, is nat huechꭓr chaer uil bi
no difikꭓltiz ar inkanviniensiz; bꭓt huecher chi difikꭓltiz mê
nat bi sꭓrmaunted; and huechꭓr chi kanviniensiz uil nat, an
chi huol, bi grêtꭓr chanchi inkanviniensiz. Inchis kes, chi difikꭓltiz
er onli in chi biginiŋ av chi praktis: huen chê er uꭓns ovꭓrkꭓm,
chi advantedsez er lastiŋ. To ꭓichꭓr iu ar mi, hu spel uel in chi
prezent mod, ꭓi imadsin chi difikꭓlti av tsendsiŋchat mod far
chi nu, iz nat so grêt, bꭓt chat ui mꭓit pꭓrfektli git ovꭓr it in a
uiiks rꭓitiŋ. Az to choz hu du nat spel uel, if chi tu difikꭓltiz er
kꭓmpêrd, chat av titsiŋchem tru speliŋ in chi prezent mod, and
chat av titsiŋ chem chi nu alfabet and chi nu speliŋ akardiŋ to
it; ꭓi am kanfidentchatchi latꭓr uuld bi bꭓi farchi liist. Ðê natꭓrali
fal into chi nu mehꭓd alredi, az mꭓts az chi imperfeksꭓn av
cher alfabet uil admit av; chêr prezent bad speliŋ iz onli bad,
bikaz kantreri to chi prezent bad ruls: ꭓndꭓr chi nu ruls it uuld
bi gud. Ði difikꭓlti av lꭓrniŋ to spel uel in chi old uê iz so
grêt, chat fiu atên it; hauzands and hauzands rꭓitiŋ an to old
eds, uichaut ever biiŋ ebil to akuꭓir it. 'Tiz, bisꭓidz, e difikꭓlti
kantinuali inkriisiŋ; az chi saund graduali veriz mor and mor
fram chi speliŋ: and to farenꭓrs it mêks chi lꭓrniŋ to pronauns
aur langueds, az riten in aur buks, almost impasibil.

Nau az to "chi inkanviniensiz" iu mensꭓn. Ði fꭓrst iz; chat
"aal aur etimalodsiz uuld bi last, kansikuentli ui kuld nat
asꭓrteen chi miiniŋ av meni uꭓrds." Etimalodsiz er at prezent
veri ꭓensꭓrten; bꭓt sꭓts az chê er, chi old buks uuld stil prizꭓrv

dhem, and etimalod sists uuld dhêr fꭒind dhem. Uꭒrds in dhi kors av tꭒim, tsends dher miiniŋs, az uel az dher speliŋ and pronꭒnsiesꭒn; and ui du nat luk to etimalod si far dher prezent miiniŋs. If ꭒi suld kal e man e Neev and e Vilen, hi uuld hardli bi satisfꭒid uih mꭒi teliŋ him, dhat uꭒn av dhi uꭒrds orid sinali signifꭒid onli e lad ar sꭒrvant; and dhi ꭒdhꭒr, an ꭒndꭒr plauman, ar dhi inhabitant av e vileds. It iz fram prezent iuseds onli, dhi miiniŋ av uꭒrds iz to bi ditꭒrmined.

Iur sekꭒnd inkanviniens iz, dhat "dhi distinksꭒn bituiin uꭒrds av difꭒrent miiniŋ and similar saund uuld bi distraꭒid." Ðat distinksꭒn iz alredi distraꭒid in pronaunsiŋ dhem; and ui rilꭒi an dhi sens alon av dhi sentens to asꭒrteen, huits av dhi several uꭒrds, similar in saund, ui intend. If dhis iz sꭒfisent in dhi rapiditi av diskors, it uil bi muts mor so in riten sentenses; huits mê bi red lez surli; and atended to mor partikularli in kes av difikꭒlti, dhan ui kan atend to e past sentens, huꭒil e spikꭒr iz hꭒrꭒiiŋ ꭒs alaŋ uih nu uꭒns.

Iur hꭒrd inkanviniens iz, dhat "aal dhi buks alredi riten uuld bi iusles." Ðis inkanviniens uuld onli kꭒm an graduali, in e kors av edses. Iu and ꭒi, and ꭒdhꭒr nau liviŋ ridꭒrs, uuld hardli farget dhi ius av dhem. Piipil uuld loŋ lꭒrn to riid dhi old rꭒitiŋ, dho dhê praktist dhi nu. And dhi inkanviniens iz nat greter, dhan huat hes aktuali hapend in a similar kes, in Iteli. Farmerli its inhabitants aal spok and rot Latin: az dhi langueds tsendsd, dhi speliŋ falo'd it. It iz tru dhat at prezent, e miir ꭒnlarn'd Italien kanat riid dhi Latin buks; dho dhe er stil red and ꭒndꭒrstud bꭒi meni. Bꭒt, if dhi speliŋ had nevꭒr bin tsendsed, hi uuld nau hev faund it mꭒts mor difikꭒlt to riid and rꭒit hiz on languads; far riten uꭒrds uuld hev had no rilê sꭒn to saunds, dhe uuld onli hev stud far dhiŋs; so dhat if hi uuld ekspres in rꭒitiŋ dhi ꭒidia hi hez, huen hi saunds dhi uꭒrd *Vescovo*, hi mꭒst iuz dhi leterz *Episcopus*. In sart, huatever dhi difikꭒltiz and inkanviniensiz nau er, dhe uil bi mor iizili sꭒrmaunted nau, dhan hiraftꭒr; and sꭒm tꭒim ar ꭒdhꭒr, it mꭒst bi dꭒn; ar aur rꭒitiŋ uil bikꭒm dhi sêm uidh dhi Tsꭒiniiz, as to dhi difikꭒlti av lꭒrniŋ and iuziŋ it. And it uuld alredi hev bin sꭒts, if ui had kantinud dhi Saksꭒn speliŋ and rꭒitiŋ, iuzed bꭒi our forfadhers. ꭒi am, mꭒi diir frind, iurs afeksꭒnetli,

Lꭒndꭒn, Kreven-striit, Sept. 28, 1768

Queries

For the London Chronicle.

QUERIES *recommended to the Consideration of those Gentlemen who are for* vigorous Measures *with the* AMERICANS.

1. Have the Colonists *refused* to answer any reasonable requisitions made to their *Assemblies* by the Mother Country?

2. If they have *not refused* to grant reasonable aids in the way, which they think consistent with *liberty*, why must they be stripped of their property without their own *consent*, and in a way, which they think *inconsistent* with liberty?

3. What is it for a people to be *enslaved* and *tributary*, if this be not, viz. To be *forced* to give up their property at the arbitrary pleasure of persons, to whose authority they have not *submitted* themselves, nor *chosen* for the purpose of imposing taxes upon them? Wherein consisted the impropriety of King Charles's demanding ship-money by his sole authority, but in its being an exercise of power by the King, which the people had not *given* the King? Have the people of America, as the people of Britain, by sending Representatives, *consented* to a power in the British Parliament to tax them?

4. Has not the British Parliament, by repealing the stamp act, acknowledged that they judged it *improper*? Is there any difference between the stamp act, and the act obliging the Americans to pay *whatever we please*, for articles which they *cannot do without*, as glass and paper? Is there any difference as to justice between our treatment of the Colonists, and the tyranny of the Carthaginians over their conquered Sardinians, when they obliged them to take all their corn from them, and at whatever price they pleased to set upon it?

5. If that be true, which is commonly said, viz. That the Mother Country gains *two millions* a year by the Colonies, would it not have been wiser to have gone on quietly in the *happy way* we were in, till our gains by those rising and flourishing countries should amount to *three, four*, or *five* millions a year, than by these new-fashioned vigorous measures to kill the goose which lays the golden eggs? Would it not have been better policy, instead of *taxing* our Colonists, to have done whatever we could to *enrich* them, and encourage them to take off our articles of *luxury*, on which we may

put our own price, and thus draw them into paying us a *voluntary* tax; than deluge them in blood, thin their countries, empoverish and distress them, interrupt their commerce, force them on bankruptcy, by which our merchants must be ruined, or tempt them to emigrations, or alliances with our enemies?

6. The late war could not have been *carried on* without America, nor without Scotland? Have we treated America and Scotland in such a manner as is likely in future wars to encourage their zeal for the common cause? Or is England alone to be the Drawcansir of the world, and to bully not only her enemies, but her *friends*?

7. Are not the subjects of Britain concerned to check a ministry, who, by this rage of heaping taxes on taxes, are only drawing into their own hands more and more wealth and power, while they are hurting the *commercial* interest of the empire in general, at the same time that, amidst profound *peace*, the national debt and burden on the public continue undiminished?

N.M.C.N.P.C.H.

The London Chronicle, August 18, 1768

On Civil War

To the Printer of the Public Advertiser.

SIR,

Threescore Years did the oppressed United Provinces maintain a War in Defence of their Liberties against the then powerful Kingdom of *Spain*, with all the Wealth of the *Indies* at it's Command; and finally obliged it to acknowledge their Independency in a formal Treaty, sitting down with the Loss of Territory, Treasure and Reputation, and with a broken Strength that has never since been recovered.

Contractors, jobbing mercantile Members of Parliament, Officers starving on Half Pay, and Gunsmiths who *toast*, as the Papers tell us, *a speedy and a perpetual War*, may wish, rather than no War at all, for a *Civil* one in America. These in all Conversations, to encourage us in undertaking it, slight the Strength of those distant People, think nothing of that

Enthusiasm for Liberty, which in other Countries and Ages has supplied all Deficiencies, and enabled a weak People to battle the Efforts of a stronger; but tell us that half a dozen Regiments are sufficient to reduce in less than a Year every Province on the Continent. Half a dozen being once engaged in this blessed Service, it is easy to write and shew the Necessity for more: The more there are, the greater the Profits to those Gentry. And whatever becomes of us poor Devils that live by Manufactures or by Trade, that are to pay Taxes, or that have Money in the Funds, *they* will amass Fortunes, buy our Estates, bribe our Boroughs, and vote in Parliament the Rectitude of the Measure.

I believe our Officers and Soldiers as brave as any in the World; and from that very Opinion of their Bravery I conjecture they would not generally relish the being ordered on this murdering Service against their Countrymen; to shed English Blood, to stifle the British Spirit of Liberty now rising in the Colonies; that LIBERTY which we should rather wish to see nourished and preserved there, as on a loss of it here (which from our vices is perhaps not far distant) we or our Posterity may have Occasion to resort to and participate of; and possibly some of the ablest Officers may chuse, with Sir *Jeffery Amherst*, rather to resign their Commissions. But whatever may be the Bravery and military Prowess of our Troops, and whatever the Zeal with which they would proceed in such a War, there are Reasons that make me suspect it will not be so soon terminated as some Folks would have us believe.

My reasons are drawn chiefly from a Computation founded on *Facts*. It is well known that America is a Country full of Forests, Mountains, &c. That in such a Country a small irregular Force can give Abundance of Trouble to a regular one that is much greater: And that, in the last War, *one* of the *fifteen* Colonies we now have there (and one far short of being the strongest) held out *five Years* against *twenty-five thousand* British regular Troops, joined by *twenty-five thousand* Colonists on their own Pay, and aided by a strong Fleet of Men of War. What the Expence was to this Nation, our Treasury Books and augmented Debt may shew. The Expence to America, as their Pay was higher, could not be much less. The Colony we made War upon was indeed aided by *France*, but

during the whole Contest not with more than five thousand
Men. Now supposing that the twenty-five thousand Colonists
that then joined us should hereafter be against us, and that
this makes no Difference, and considering that instead of *one*
Colony to conquer, we are to have *fifteen*, and that possibly
some of our good Neighbours may think of making a Diversion in their Favour, I apprehend it not out of the Way to
allow *five* Years still to a Colony; and this, by my Computation, will amount to just *seventy-five* Years. I hope Messieurs
the Company of Gunsmiths will for the present be so good
as to be content with a Civil War of *seventy-five* Years, as perhaps we may scarce be able to afford them a *perpetual* one.

And what are we to gain by this War, by which our Trade
and Manufactures are to be ruined, our Strength divided and
diminished, our Debt increased, and our Reputation, as a
generous Nation, and Lovers of Liberty, given up and lost?
Why, we are to convert Millions of the King's loyal Subjects
into Rebels, for the sake of establishing a newly-claimed
power in P—— to tax a distant People, whose Abilities and
Circumstances they cannot be acquainted with, who have a
constitutional Power of taxing themselves; who have never
refused to give us voluntarily more than we can ever expect
to wrest from them by Force; and by our Trade with whom
we gain Millions a Year!

And is there not *one* wise and good Man to be found in
Britain, who can propose some conciliating Measure that
may prevent this terrible Mischief?—I fear not one. For

    Quos Deus vult perdere, dementat prius!

                        N. N.

The Public Advertiser, August 25, 1768

On Sinecures

To the PRINTER of the GAZETTEER
AND *NEW DAILY ADVERTISER*.

Great complaints are every day made, that notwithstanding
Great Britain has involved herself in a very heavy debt, for

the defence of the American colonies in the late war, that now they refuse to pay any part of this debt. On this subject there has been a very smart paper war for some years, which controversy it seems, is like to be decided by the all powerful argument of fire and sword.

This argument, on the side of Great Britain, has much alarmed me, having myself a very considerable interest depending, as well as several near relations on that side the water.

From the epithets of unjust, ungenerous rogues, rebels, &c. which are so lavishly bestowed on the Americans, I have been induced to look into those late acts of parliament, which the colonies refuse to comply with, and to my very great surprize find there is not one single word in those acts for the purpose of raising money to help poor Old England, from which I begin to suspect we are all on a wrong scent. How can we justly accuse them of refusing to assist poor Old England in her distresses, when we neither ask or require it of them?

By those acts the money to be raised is for their own use, not ours. But why in the name of wonder was such an act made? The money to be raised, I find, is for their defence and the support of civil government among themselves. When have they suffered by neglecting to raise money for their own defence? So far were they from neglecting to raise a sufficiency for that purpose during the late war, that I am told the parliament gave them 4 or 500,000l. to reimburse their extra expences. Why then are we to fear, that in a time of profound peace, and when every enemy is driven out of the country, that now they wo'nt raise money for their own defence? This to me is unaccountable; but to send an army to force it for fear it should not be done, is still more unaccountable.

As to their civil government, I have ever understood it is more effectually supported there than in any other part of his Majesty's dominions. My countrymen, we are all by the nose: there is a snake in the grass: give yourselves but the trouble to look at those acts, and reflect one moment as I have done, and you will at once see that we are all set by the ears for we know not what. But by your leave I will venture to hint, for your consideration, a very common custom among pickpockets, i. e. A thief cries catch thief. My reason for this surmise is, from what I have hinted, you at once see we are to have none of this money to ease our taxes: it will be of no use to the Americans, otherwise they would consent to it. Who then is to have the prize we are fighting for? To which I will venture to make answer, Friends and Favourites; for by those acts you will find, that the money raised is put under the direction of the Crown, to pay (or give) to as many or what officers it pleases to appoint in America; all which appointments and salaries, it is well known, are made and concluded upon by the K—g's Ministers.

Whoever therefore will give themselves the trouble to look at these acts, which the Americans refuse to comply with, will at once see the whole is a piece of ministerial policy, designed not for the good of Great Britain or her colonies, but for an American establishment, whereby they may be able to provide for friends and favourites.

The Irish establishment has been much talked of as a sinecure for friends and favourites, and cast-off mistresses; but this American establishment promises a more ample provision for such-like purposes. That this is the truth of the case, every one that will give himself the trouble must see, unless troubled with the present very polite disorder of being short-sighted.

EXPOSITOR.

The Gazetteer and New Daily Advertiser, September 28, 1768

A New Version of the Lord's Prayer

Old Version.	New Version, by BF.
1. Our Father which art in Heaven.	1. Heavenly Father,
2. Hallowed be thy Name.	2. May all revere thee,
3. Thy Kingdom come.	3. And become thy dutiful Children and faithful Subjects.
4. Thy Will be done on Earth as it is in Heaven.	4. May thy Laws be obeyed on Earth as perfectly as they are in Heaven.

5. Give us this Day our daily Bread.	5. Provide for us this Day as thou has hitherto daily done.
6. Forgive us our Debts as we forgive our Debtors.	6. Forgive us our Trespasses, and enable us likewise to forgive those that offend us.
7. And lead us not into Temptation, but deliver us from Evil.	7. Keep us out of Temptation, and deliver us from Evil.

Reasons for the Change of Expression

Old Version. *Our Father which art in Heaven*

New V. *Heavenly Father*, is more concise, equally expressive, and better modern English.

Old. *Hallowed be thy Name.* This seems to relate to an Observance among the Jews not to pronounce the proper or peculiar Name of God, they deeming it a Profanation so to do. We have in our Language no *proper Name* for God; the Word *God* being a common or general Name, expressing all chief Objects of Worship, true or false. The Word *hallowed* is almost obsolete: People now have but an imperfect Conception of the Meaning of the Petition. It is therefore proposed to change the Expression into

New. *May all revere thee.*

Old V. *Thy Kingdom come.* This Petition seems suited to the then Condition of the Jewish Nation. Originally their State was a Theocracy: God was their King. Dissatisfied with that kind of Government, they desired a visible earthly King in the manner of the Nations round them. They had such King's accordingly; but their Happiness was not increas'd by the Change, and they had reason to wish and pray for a Return of the Theocracy, or Government of God. Christians in these Times have other Ideas when they speak of the Kingdom of God, such as are perhaps more adequately express'd by

New V. *And become thy dutiful Children and faithful Subjects.*

Old V. *Thy Will be done on Earth as it is in Heaven.* More explicitly,

New V. *May thy Laws be obeyed on Earth as perfectly as they are in Heaven.*

Old V. *Give us this Day* our *daily Bread.* Give us what is *ours*, seems to put in a Claim of Right, and to contain too little of the grateful Acknowledgment and Sense of Dependance that becomes Creatures who live on the daily Bounty of their Creator. Therefore it is changed to

New V. *Provide for us this Day, as thou hast hitherto daily done.*

Old V. *Forgive us our Debts as we forgive our Debtors.* Matthew. *Forgive us our Sins, for we also forgive every one that is indebted to us.* Luke.

Offerings were *due* to God on many Occasions by the Jewish Law, which when People could not pay, or had forgotten as Debtors are apt to do, it was proper to pray that those Debts might be forgiven. Our Liturgy uses neither the *Debtors* of Matthew, nor the *indebted* of Luke, but instead of them speaks of *those that trespass against us.* Perhaps the Considering it as a Christian Duty to forgive Debtors, was by the Compilers thought an inconvenient Idea in a trading Nation. There seems however something presumptious in this Mode of Expression, which has the Air of proposing ourselves as an Example of Goodness fit for God to imitate. *We hope you will at least be as good as we are*; you see we forgive one another, and therefore we pray that you would forgive us. Some have considered it in another Sense, *Forgive us* as *we forgive others*; i.e. If we do not forgive others we pray that thou wouldst not forgive us. But this being a kind of conditional *Imprecation* against ourselves, seems improper in such a Prayer; and therefore it may be better to say humbly and modestly

New V. *Forgive us our Trespasses, and enable us likewise to forgive those that offend us.* This instead of assuming that we have already in and of ourselves the Grace of Forgiveness, acknowledges our Dependance on God, the Fountain of Mercy, for any Share we may have of it, praying that he would communicate of it to us.

Old V. *And lead us not into Temptation.* The Jews had a Notion, that God sometimes tempted, or directed or permitted the Tempting of People. Thus it was said he tempted Pharaoh; directed Satan to tempt Job; and a false Prophet to tempt Ahab, &c. Under this Persuasion it was natural for them to pray that he would not put them to such severe Trials. We now suppose that Temptation, so far as it is supernatural, comes from the Devil only; and this Petition continued, conveys a Suspicion which in our present Conceptions seems unworthy of God, therefore might be altered to

New V. Keep *us* out of *Temptation*.

B. Franklin's Version of The Lord's Prayer.

Heavenly Father, may all revere thee, and become thy dutiful Children and faithful Subjects; may thy Laws be obeyed on Earth as perfectly as they are in Heaven: Provide for us this Day as thou hast hitherto daily done: Forgive us our Trespasses, and enable us likewise to forgive those that offend us. Keep us out of Temptation, and deliver us from Evil.

1768?

Defense of American Placeholders

To the PRINTER.

Your correspondent *Machiavel* tells us, that "Nothing can be a greater burlesque on Patriotism, than the conduct of the Americans, who affect discontent at being taxed, and therefore not only petition and remonstrate, but are continually writing pamphlets, filling news-papers, and consecrating Trees to Liberty; when, at the same time, many of them are writing to administration how to enforce the collection of such duties as are imposed, &c. &c. with a view to obtain offices and pensions under the Crown, in America."—And then he gives us a list of fifteen Americans, whom he charges with having been successfully guilty of this baseness. The whole apparently with a view of lessening any concern the friends of Liberty here may have for the injured people of that country, and of discountenancing any endeavours for their relief, by thus rendering them both contemptible and odious.

But, methinks it should be considered,

1. That if not only *fifteen*, but fifteen hundred, out of three millions, had been seduced by corruption, to betray the interests of their country, the proportion is not so great as to judge of the rest by them, to conclude that therefore they might be oppressed without injury, stripped of their rights without remorse; their petitions and remonstrances disregarded; their constitution dissolved; their towns insulted and dragooned; their real patriots hanged as traitors, not for any disloyalty to their King, but merely for doubting the power of parliament, in particular cases, or, perhaps, only thwarting the views of a wrong-headed, pertinacious minister.

2. That being loyal subjects to their sovereign, the Americans think they have as good a right to enjoy offices under him in America, as a Scotchman has in Scotland, or an Englishman in England; and that they may equally hold them consistent with honour; since they have never yet been taught to believe that the interests of their King and his subjects are so contrary and incompatible, that an honest man cannot serve the one without betraying the other.

Let me farther add, that, among the gentlemen in his list, I know some, who, far from receiving the offices they hold, as the wages of corruption, rose in them gradually and regularly, in a course of years; others had been conferred as rewards of public service, by sea and land, during war; others enjoyed their offices many years before any dispute arose, or was dreamt of, between the two countries; and have yet, throughout those disputes, been firm to the cause of their country, at all hazards. If there are any of them who are known, or even, on probable grounds, suspected, to have betray'd it, such are in universal odium among their virtuous compatriots; and therefore their country ought not to be censured upon their account. To defend it from such indiscriminate censure, is the chief end of my giving you this trouble.

Your correspondent adds, "Behold how true it is, that *every* man has his price." In a former paper [Dec. 19.] he had told us, (speaking of mankind) "We are honest as long as we thrive by it; but if the Devil himself gives better wages, we change our party." For the honour of my species, as well as of my country, I cannot but suppose these maxims much *too general*. But as this writer has professedly adopted them in their full extent, I must conclude they may be true *so far at least as relates to himself*, since it is plain *he knows of no exception*.

An AMERICAN.

The Gazetteer and New Daily Advertiser, January 17, 1769

Positions To Be Examined

April 4. 1769

1 All Food or Subsistence for Mankind arise from the Earth or Waters.

2 Necessaries of Life that are not Foods, and all other Conveniencies, have their Values estimated by the Proportion of Food consumed while we are employed in procuring them.

3 A small People with a large Territory may subsist on the Productions of Nature, with no other Labour than that of gathering the Vegetables and catching the Animals.

4 A large People with a small Territory finds these insufficient, and, to subsist, must labour the Earth to make it produce greater Quantities of vegetable Food, suitable for the Nourishment of Men, and of the Animals they intend to eat.

5 From the Labour arises a *great Increase* of vegetable and animal Food, and of Materials for Clothing, as Flax, Wool, Silk, &c. The Superfluity of these is Wealth. With this Wealth we pay for the Labour employed in building our Houses, Cities, &c. which are therefore only Subsistence thus metamorphosed.

6 *Manufactures* are only *another Shape* into which so much Provisions and Subsistence are turned as were *equal in Value* to the Manufactures produced. This appears from hence, that the Manufacturer does not in fact, obtain from the Employer, for his Labour, *more* than a mere Subsistence, including Raiment Fuel and Shelter; all which derive their Value from the Provisions consumed in procuring them.

7 The Produce of the Earth, thus converted into Manu-

factures, may be more easily carried to distant Markets than before such Conversion.

8 *Fair* Commerce is where equal Values are exchanged for equal the Expence of Transport included. Thus if it costs A. in England as much Labour and Charge to raise a Bushel of Wheat as it costs B. in France to produce four Gallons of Wine then are four Gallons of Wine the fair Exchange for a Bushel of Wheat. A and B meeting at half Distance with their Commodities to make the Exchange. The Advantage of this fair Commerce is, that each Party increases the Number of his Enjoyments, having, instead of Wheat alone or Wine alone, the Use of both Wheat and Wine.

9 Where the Labour and Expence of producing both Commodities are known to both Parties Bargains will generally be fair and equal. Where they are known to one Party only, Bargains will often be unequal, Knowledge taking its Advantage of Ignorance.

10 Thus he that carries 1000 Bushels of Wheat abroad to sell, may not probably obtain so great a Profit thereon as if he had first turned the Wheat into Manufactures by subsisting therewith the Workmen while producing those Manufactures: since there are many expediting and facilitating Methods of working, not generally known; and Strangers to the Manufactures, though they know pretty well the Expences of raising Wheat, are unacquainted with those short Methods of working, and thence being apt to suppose more Labour employed in the Manufactures than there really is, are more easily imposed on in their Value, and induced to allow more for them than they are honestly worth.

11 Thus the Advantage of having Manufactures in a Country, does not consist as is commonly supposed, in their highly advancing the Value of rough Materials, of which they are formed; since, though sixpenny worth of Flax may be worth twenty shillings when worked into Lace, yet the very Cause of it's being worth twenty shillings is, that besides the Flax, it has cost nineteen shillings and sixpence in Subsistence to the Manufacturer. But the Advantage of Manufactures is, that under their shape Provisions may be more easily carried to a foreign Market; and by their means our Traders may more

easily cheat Strangers. Few, where it is not made are Judges of the Value of Lace. The importer may demand Forty, and perhaps get Thirty shillings for that which cost him but twenty.

12 Finally, there seem to be but three Ways for a Nation to acquire Wealth. The first is by *War* as the Romans did in plundering their conquered Neighbours. This is *Robbery*. The second by *Commerce* which is generally *Cheating*. The third by *Agriculture* the only *honest Way*; wherein Man receives a real Increase of the Seed thrown into the Ground, in a kind of continual Miracle wrought by the Hand of God in his Favour, as a Reward for his innocent Life, and virtuous Industry.

New Fables

For the Public Advertiser.
NEW FABLES, *humbly inscribed to the* S——y
of St——e *for the* American Department.

FABLE I.
A Herd of Cows had long afforded Plenty of Milk, Butter and Cheese to an avaritious Farmer, who grudged them the Grass they subsisted on, and at length mowed it to make Money of the Hay, leaving them to *shift for Food* as they could, and yet still expected to *milk them* as before; but the Cows, offended with his Unreasonableness, resolved for the future *to suckle one another*.

FABLE II.
An Eagle, King of Birds, sailing on his Wings aloft over a Farmer's Yard, saw a Cat there basking in the Sun, *mistook it for a Rabbit*, stoop'd, seized it, and carried it up into the Air, *intending to prey on it*. The Cat turning, set her Claws into the Eagle's Breast; who, finding his Mistake, opened his Talons, and would have let her drop; but Puss, unwilling to fall so far, held faster; and the Eagle, to get rid of the Inconvenience, found it necessary to *set her down where he took her up*.

FABLE III.

A Lion's Whelp was put on board a Guinea Ship bound to America as a Present to a Friend in that Country: It was tame and harmless as a Kitten, and therefore not confined, but suffered to walk about the Ship at Pleasure. A stately, full-grown English Mastiff, belonging to the Captain, despising the Weakness of the young Lion, frequently took it's *Food* by Force, and often turned it out of it's Lodging Box, when he had a Mind to repose therein himself. The young Lion nevertheless grew daily in Size and Strength, and the Voyage being long, he became at last a more equal Match for the Mastiff; who continuing his Insults, received a stunning Blow from the Lion's Paw that fetched his Skin over his Ears, and deterred him from any future Contest with such growing Strength; regretting that he had not rather secured it's Friendship than provoked it's Enmity.

The Public Advertiser, January 2, 1770

A Conversation on Slavery

To the Printer of the Public Advertiser.

SIR,   *Broad-Street Buildings, Jan.* 26, 1770.
Many Reflections being of late thrown out against the Americans, and particularly against our worthy Lord-Mayor, on Account of their keeping Slaves in their Country, I send you the following Conversation on that Subject, which, for Substance, and much of the Expression, is, I assure you, a *real one*; having myself been present when it passed. If you think it suitable for your Paper, you will, by publishing it, oblige
                                                        Your Friend,
                                                        N. N.

A Conversation *between an* ENGLISHMAN, *a* SCOTCHMAN, *and an* AMERICAN, *on the Subject of* SLAVERY.

Englishman. You Americans make a great Clamour upon every little imaginary Infringement of what you take to be your Liberties; and yet there are no People upon Earth such Enemies to Liberty, such absolute Tyrants, where you have the Opportunity, as you yourselves are.

American. How does that appear?

Eng. Read *Granville Sharpe*'s Book upon Slavery: There it appears with a Witness.

Amer. I have read it.

Eng. And pray what do you think of it?

Amer. To speak my Opinion candidly, I think it in the Main a good Book. I applaud the Author's Zeal for Liberty in general. I am pleased with his Humanity. But his *general Reflections* on *all Americans*, as having no real Regard for Liberty; as having so little Dislike of Despotism and Tyranny, that they do not scruple to exercise them with unbounded Rigour over their miserable Slaves, and the like, I cannot approve of; nor of the Conclusion he draws, that therefore our Claim to the Enjoyment of Liberty for ourselves, is unjust. I think, that in all this, he is too severe upon the Americans, and passes over with too partial an Eye the Faults of his own Country. This seems to me not quite fair: and it is particularly *injurious* to us at this Time, to endeavour to render us odious, and to encourage those who would oppress us, by representing us as unworthy of the Liberty we are now contending for.

Eng. What Share has that Author's Country (England I mean) in the Enormities he complains of? And why should not his Reflections on the Americans be general?

Amer. They ought not to be general, because the Foundation for them is not general. New England, the most populous of all the English Possessions in America, has very few Slaves; and those are chiefly in the capital Towns, not employed in the hardest Labour, but as Footmen or Housemaids. The same may be said of the next populous Provinces, New-York, New Jersey, and Pensylvania. Even in Virginia, Maryland, and the Carolinas, where they are employed in Field-work, what Slaves there are belong chiefly to the old rich Inhabitants, near the navigable Waters, who are few compared with the numerous Families of Back-Settlers, that have scarce any Slaves among them. In Truth, there is not, take North-America through, perhaps, one Family in a Hundred

that has a Slave in it. Many Thousands there abhor the Slave
Trade as much as Mr. Sharpe can do, conscientiously avoid
being concerned with it, and do every Thing in their Power
to abolish it. Supposing it then with that Gentleman, a Crime
to keep a Slave, can it be right to stigmatize us all with that
Crime? If one Man of a Hundred in England were dishonest,
would it be right from thence to characterize the Nation, and
say the English are Rogues and Thieves? But farther, of those
who do keep Slaves, all are not Tyrants and Oppressors.
Many treat their Slaves with great Humanity, and provide full
as well for them in Sickness and in Health, as your poor labouring People in England are provided for. Your working
Poor are not indeed absolutely Slaves; but there seems something a little like Slavery, where the Laws oblige them to
work for their Masters so many Hours at such a Rate, and
leave them no Liberty to demand or bargain for more, but
imprison them in a Workhouse if they refuse to work on such
Terms; and even imprison a humane Master if he thinks fit to
pay them better; at the same Time confining the poor ingenious Artificer to this Island, and forbidding him to go
abroad, though offered better Wages in foreign Countries. As
to the Share England has in these Enormities of America, remember, Sir, that she began the Slave Trade; that her Merchants of London, Bristol, Liverpool and Glasgow, send their
Ships to Africa for the Purpose of purchasing Slaves. If any
unjust Methods are used to procure them; if Wars are fomented to obtain Prisoners; if free People are enticed on
board, and then confined and brought away; if petty Princes
are bribed to sell their Subjects, who indeed are already a
Kind of Slaves, is America to have all the Blame of this
Wickedness? You bring the Slaves to us, and tempt us to
purchase them. I do not justify our falling into the Temptation. To be sure, if you have stolen Men to sell to us, and
we buy them, you may urge against us the old and true saying, that *the Receiver is as bad as the Thief*. This Maxim was
probably made for those who needed the Information, as
being perhaps ignorant that *receiving* was in it's Nature as
bad as *stealing*: But the Reverse of the Position was never
thought necessary to be formed into a Maxim, nobody ever
doubted that *the Thief is as bad as the Receiver*. This you have

not only done and continue to do, but several Laws heretofore made in our Colonies, to discourage the Importation of Slaves, by laying a heavy Duty, payable by the Importer, have been disapproved and repealed by your Government here, as being prejudicial, forsooth, to the Interest of the African Company.

Eng. I never heard before of any such Laws made in America. But the severe Laws you have made, on Pretence of their being necessary for the Government of your Slaves (and even of your white Servants) as they stand quoted by Mr. Sharpe, give us no good Opinion of your general Humanity, or of your Respect for Liberty. These are not the Acts of a few private Persons; they are made by your Representatives in your Assemblies, and are therefore the Act of the whole.

Amer. They are so; and possibly some of them made in Colonies where the Slaves greatly out-number the Whites, as in Barbadoes now, and in Virginia formerly, may be more severe than is necessary; being dictated perhaps by Fear and too strong an Opinion, that nothing but extream Severity could keep the Slaves in Obedience, and secure the Lives of their Masters. In other Colonies, where their Numbers are so small as to give no Apprehensions of that Kind, the Laws are milder, and the Slaves in every Respect, except in the Article of Liberty, are under the Protection of those Laws: A white Man is as liable to suffer Death for killing a Slave, though his own, as for any other Homicide. But it should be considered, with regard to these severe Laws, that in Proportion to the greater Ignorance or Wickedness of the People to be governed, Laws must be more severe: Experience every where teaches this. Perhaps you may imagine the Negroes to be a mild tempered, tractable Kind of People. Some of them indeed are so. But the Majority are of a plotting Disposition, dark, sullen, malicious, revengeful and cruel in the highest Degree. Your Merchants and Mariners, who bring them from Guinea, often find this to their Cost in the Insurrections of the Slaves on board the Ships upon the Coast, who kill all when they get the upper Hand. Those Insurrections are not suppressed or prevented but by what your People think a very necessary Severity, the shooting or hanging

Numbers sometimes on the Voyage. Indeed many of them, being mischievous Villains in their own Country, are sold off by their Princes in the Way of Punishment by Exile and Slavery, as you here ship off your Convicts: And since your Government will not suffer a Colony by any Law of it's own to keep Slaves out of the Country, can you blame the making such Laws as are thought necessary to govern them while they are in it.

Eng. But your Laws for the Government of your white Servants are almost as severe as those for the Negroes.

Amer. In some Colonies they are so, those particularly to which you send your Convicts. Honest hired Servants are treated as mildly in America every where as in England: But the Villains you transport and sell to us must be ruled with a Rod of Iron. We have made Laws in several Colonies to prevent their Importation: These have been immediately repealed here, as being contrary to an Act of Parliament. We do not thank you for forcing them upon us. We look upon it as an unexampled Barbarity in your Government to empty your Gaols into our Settlements; and we resent it as the highest of Insults. If mild Laws could govern such People, why don't you keep and govern them by your own mild Laws at home? If you think we treat them with unreasonable Severity, why are you so cruel as to send them to us? And pray let it be remembered, that these very Laws, the cruel Spirit of which you Englishmen are now pleased so to censure, were, when made, sent over hither, and submitted, as all Colony Laws must be, to the King in Council for Approbation, which Approbation they received, I suppose upon thorough Consideration and sage Advice. If they are nevertheless to be blamed, be so just as to take a Share of the Blame to yourselves.

Scotchman. You should not say we force the Convicts upon you. You know you may, if you please, refuse to buy them. If you were not of a tyrannical Disposition; if you did not like to have some under you, on whom you might exercise and gratify that Disposition; if you had really a true Sense of Liberty, about which you make such a Pother, you would purchase neither Slaves nor Convict Servants, you would not endure such a Thing as Slavery among you.

Amer. It is true we may refuse to buy them, and prudent People do so. But there are still a Number of imprudent People, who are tempted by the Lowness of the Price, and the Length of the Time for which your Convicts are sold, to purchase them. We would prevent this Temptation. We would keep your British Man-Merchants, with their detestable Ware, from coming among us: But this you will not allow us to do. And therefore I say you force upon us the Convicts as well as the Slaves. But, Sir, as to your Observation, that if we had a real Love of Liberty, we should not suffer such a Thing as Slavery among us, I am a little surprised to hear this from you, a North Briton, in whose own Country, Scotland, Slavery still subsists, established by Law.

Scotchman. I suppose you mean the heretable Jurisdictions. There was not properly any Slavery in them: And, besides, they are now all taken away by Act of Parliament.

Amer. No, Sir, I mean the Slavery in your Mines. All the Wretches that dig Coal for you, in those dark Caverns under Ground, unblessed by Sunshine, are absolute Slaves by your Law, and their Children after them, from the Time they first carry a Basket to the End of their Days. They are bought and sold with the Colliery, and have no more Liberty to leave it than our Negroes have to leave their Master's Plantation. If having black Faces, indeed, subjected Men to the Condition of Slavery, you might have some small Pretence for keeping the poor Colliers in that Condition: But remember, that under the Smut their Skin *is white*, that they are *honest good People*, and at the same Time are *your own Countrymen*!

Eng. I am glad you cannot reproach England with this; our Colliers are as free as any other Labourers.

Amer. And do you therefore pretend that you have no such Thing as Slavery in England?

Eng. No such Thing most certainly.

Amer. I fancy I could make it appear to you that you have, if we could first agree upon the Definition of a Slave. And if your Author's Position is true, that those who keep Slaves have therefore no Right to Liberty themselves, you Englishmen will be found as destitute of such Rights as we Americans I imagine.

Eng. What is then your Definition of a Slave? Pray let us hear it, that we may see whether or no we can agree in it.

Amer. A Slave, according to my Notion, is a human Creature, stolen, taken by Force, or bought of another or of himself, with Money; and who being so taken or bought, is compelled to serve the Taker, or Purchaser, during Pleasure or during Life. He may be sold again, or let for Hire, by his Master to another, and is then obliged to serve that other; he is one who is bound to obey, not only the Commands of his Master, but also the Commands of the lowest Servant of that Master, when set over him; who must come when he is called, go when he is bid, and stay where he is ordered, though to the farthest Part of the World, and in the most unwholesome Climate; who must wear such Cloaths as his Master thinks fit to give him, and no other, though different from the common Fashion, and contrived to be a distinguishing Badge of Servitude; and must be content with such Food or Subsistence as his Master thinks fit to order for him, or with such small Allowance in Money as shall be given him in Lieu of Victuals or Cloathing; who must never absent himself from his Master's Service without Leave; who is subject to severe Punishments for small Offences, to enormous Whippings, and even Death, for absconding from his Service, or for Disobedience to Orders. I imagine such a Man is a Slave to all Intents and Purposes.

Eng. I agree to your Definition. But surely, surely, you will not say there are any such Slaves in England?

Amer. Yes, many Thousands, if an English Sailor or Soldier is well described in that Definition. The Sailor is often *forced* into Service, torn from all his natural Connections. The Soldier is generally bought in the first Place for a Guinea and a Crown at the Drum-Head: His Master may sell his Service, if he pleases, to any Foreign Prince, or barter it for any Consideration by Treaty, and send him to shoot or be shot at in Germany or Portugal, in Guinea or the Indies. He is engaged for Life; and every other Circumstance of my Definition agrees with his Situation. In one Particular, indeed, English Slavery goes beyond that exercised in America.

Eng. What is that?

Amer. We cannot command a Slave of ours to do an

immoral or a wicked Action. We cannot oblige him, for Instance, to commit MURDER! If we should order it, he may refuse, and our Laws would justify him. But Soldiers must, on Pain of Death, obey the Orders they receive; though, like Herod's Troops, they should be commanded to slay all your Children under two Years old, cut the Throats of your Children in the Colonies, or shoot your Women and Children in St. G——e's F——ds.

The Public Advertiser, January 30, 1770

The Cravenstreet Gazette

No 113

Saturday, Sept. 22. 1770

This Morning Queen Margaret, accompanied by her first Maid of Honour, Miss Franklin, set out for Rochester. Immediately on their Departure, the whole Street was in Tears— from a heavy Shower of Rain.

It is whispered that the new Family Administration which took place on her Majesty's Departure, promises, like all other new Administrations, to govern much better than the old one.

We hear that the *great* Person (so called from his enormous Size) of a certain Family in a certain Street, is grievously affected at the late Changes, and could hardly be comforted this Morning, tho' the new Ministry promised him a roasted Shoulder of Mutton, and Potatoes, for his Dinner.

It is said, that the same *great* Person intended to pay his Respects to another great Personage this Day, at St. James's, it being Coronation-Day; hoping thereby a little to amuse his Grief; but was prevented by an Accident, Queen Margaret, or her Maid of Honour having carried off the Key of the Drawers, so that the Lady of the Bedchamber could not come at a laced Shirt for his Highness. Great Clamours were made on this Occasion against her Majesty.

Other Accounts say, that the Shirts were afterwards found,

tho' too late, in another Place. And some suspect, that the Wanting a Shirt from those Drawers was only a ministerial Pretence to excuse Picking the Locks, that the new Administration might have every thing at Command.

We hear that the Lady Chamberlain of the Household went to Market this Morning by her own self, gave the Butcher whatever he ask'd for the Mutton, and had no Dispute with the Potatoe Woman—to their great Amazement—at the Change of Times!

It is confidently asserted, that this Afternoon, the Weather being wet, the great *Person* a little chilly, and no body at home to find fault with the Expence of Fuel, he was indulg'd with a Fire in his Chamber. It seems the Design is, to make him contented, by Degrees, with the Absence of the Queen.

A Project has been under Consideration of Government, to take the Opportunity of her Majesty's Absence, for doing a Thing she was always averse to, viz. Fixing a new Lock on the Street Door, or getting a Key made to the old one; it being found extreamly inconvenient, that one or other of the Great Officers of State, should, whenever the Maid goes out for a Ha'pworth of Sand or a Pint of Porter, be obliged to attend the Door to let her in again. But Opinion, being divided, which of the two Expedients to adopt, the Project is for the present laid aside.

We have good Authority to assure our Readers, that a Cabinet Council was held this Afternoon at Tea; the Subject of which was a Proposal for the Reformation of Manners, and a more strict Observation of the Lord's Day. The Result was, an unanimous Resolution that no Meat should be dress'd tomorrow; whereby the Cook and the first Minister will both be at Liberty to go to Church, the one having nothing to do, and the other no Roast to rule. It seems the cold Shoulder of Mutton, and the Applepye, were thought sufficient for Sunday's Dinner. All pious People applaud this Measure, and 'tis thought the new Ministry will soon become popular.

We hear that Mr. Wilkes was at a certain House in Craven Street this Day, and enquired after the absent Queen. His good Lady and the Children were well.

The Report that Mr. Wilkes the Patriot made the above

Visit, is without Foundation, it being his Brother the Courtier.

Sunday, Sept. 23.

It is now found by sad Experience, that good Resolutions are easier made than executed. Notwithstanding yesterday's solemn Order of Council, no body went to Church to day. It seems the *great* Person's broad-built-bulk lay so long abed, that Breakfast was not over 'till it was too late to dress. At least this is the Excuse. In fine, it seems a vain thing to hope Reformation from the Example of our great Folks. The Cook and the Minister, however, both took Advantage of the Order so far, as to save themselves all Trouble, and the Clause of *cold Dinner* was enforc'd, tho' the *going to Church* was dispens'd with; just as the common working People observe the Commandment; *the seventh Day thou shalt rest*, they think a sacred Injunction; but the other *Six Days shalt thou labour* is deem'd a mere Piece of Advice which they may practice when they want Bread and are out of Credit at the Alehouse, and may neglect whenever they have Money in their Pockets. It must nevertheless be said in justice to our Court, that whatever Inclination they had to Gaming, no Cards were brought out to Day. Lord and Lady Hewson walk'd after Dinner to Kensington to pay their Duty to the Dowager, and Dr. Fatsides made 469 Turns in his Dining Room as the exact Distance of a Visit to the lovely Lady Barwell, whom he did not find at home, so there was no Struggle for and against a Kiss, and he sat down to dream in the Easy Chair that he had it without any Trouble.

Monday, Sept. 24.

We are credibly informed, that the *great* Person dined this Day with the Club at the Cat-and-Bagpipes in the City, on cold Round of boil'd Beef. This, it seems, he was under some Necessity of Doing (tho' he rather dislikes Beef) because truly the Ministers were to be all abroad somewhere to dine on hot roast Venison. It is thought that if the Queen had been at home, he would not have been so slighted. And tho' he shows outwardly no Marks of Dissatisfaction, it is suspected that he begins to wish for her Majesty's Return.

It is currently reported, that poor Nanny had nothing for Dinner in the Kitchen, for herself and Puss, but the Scrapings of the Bones of Saturday's Mutton.

This Evening there was high Play at the Groom Porter's in Cravenstreet House. The Great Person lost Money. It is supposed the Ministers, as is usually supposed of all Ministers, shared the Emoluments among them.

Tuesday, Sept. 25.

This Morning the good Lord Hutton call'd at Cravenstreet House, and enquired very respectfully and affectionately concerning the Welfare of the absent Queen. He then imparted to the big Man a Piece of Intelligence important to them both, which he had just received from Lady Hawkesworth, viz. That the amiable and excellent Companion Miss Dorothea Blount had made a Vow to marry absolutely him of the two, whose Wife should first depart this Life. It is impossible to express with Words the various Agitations of Mind appearing in both their Faces on this Occasion. *Vanity* at the Preference given them to the rest of Mankind; *Affection* to their present Wives; *Fear* of losing them; *Hope*, (if they must lose them) to obtain the propos'd Comfort; *Jealousy* of each other, in case both Wives should die together; &c. &c. &c. all working at the same time, jumbled their Features into inexplicable Confusion. They parted at length with Professions and outward Appearances indeed of ever-during Friendship; but it was shrewdly suspected that each of them sincerely wished Health and long Life to the other's Wife; and that however long either of those Friends might like to live himself, the other would be very well pleas'd to survive him.

It is remark'd that the Skies have wept every Day in Cravenstreet the Absence of the Queen.

The Publick may be assured, that this Morning a certain *great Person* was ask'd very complaisantly by the Mistress of the Houshold, if he would chuse to have the Blade Bone of Saturday's Mutton that had been kept for his Dinner to Day, *broil'd* or *cold*? He answer'd gravely, *If there is any Flesh on it, it may be broil'd; if not, it may as well be cold.* Orders were accordingly given for broiling it. But when it came to Table, there was indeed so very little Flesh, or rather none at all (Puss having din'd on it yesterday after Nanny) that if our new Administration had been as good Oeconomists as they would be thought, the Expence of Broiling might well have been sav'd to the Publick, and carried to the Sinking Fund. It is assured the great Person bears all with infinite Patience. But the Nation is astonish'd at the insolent Presumption that dares treat so much Mildness in so cruel a manner.

A terrible Accident had *like to have happened* this Afternoon at Tea. The Boiler was set too near the End of the little square Table. The first Ministress was sitting at one End of the Table to administer the Tea; the great Person was about to sit down at the other End where the Boiler stood. By a sudden Motion, the Lady gave the Table a Tilt. Had it gone over, the great *Person* must have been scalded; perhaps to Death. Various are the Surmises and Observations on this Occasion. The Godly say, it would have been a just Judgment on him, for preventing by his Laziness, the Family's going to Church last Sunday. The Opposition do not stick to insinuate that there was a Design to scald him, prevented only by his quick Catching the Table. The Friends of the Ministry give out, that he carelessly jogg'd the Table himself, and would have been inevitably scalded had not the Ministress sav'd him. It is hard for the Publick to come at the Truth in these Cases.

At six o'Clock this Afternoon News came by the Post, that her Majesty arrived safely at Rochester on Saturday Night. The Bells immediately rang—for Candles, to illuminate the Parlour; the Court went into Cribbidge, and the Evening concluded with every other Demonstration of Joy.

It is reported that all the principal Officers of the State, have received an Invitation from the Dutchess Dowager of Rochester to go down thither on Saturday next. But it is not yet known whether the great Affairs they have on their Hands will permit them to make this Excursion.

We hear that from the Time of her Majesty's leaving Craven Street House to this Day, no Care is taken to file the Newspapers; but they lie about in every Room, in every Window, and on every Chair, just where the Doctor lays them when he has read them. It is impossible Government can long go on in such Hands.

To the Publisher of the Craven Street Gazette.

Sir,

I make no doubt of the Truth of what the Papers tell us, that a certain great *Person* has been half-starved on the bare Blade-bone, *of a Sheep* (I cannot call it *of Mutton* because none was on it) by a Set of the most careless, thoughtless, inconsiderate, corrupt, ignorant, blundering, foolish, crafty, and Knavish Ministers, that ever got into a House and pretended to govern a Family and provide a Dinner. Alas, for the poor Old England of Craven Street! If these nefarious Wretches continue in Power another Week, the Nation will be ruined—Undone!—totally undone, if the Queen does not return; or (which is better) turn them all out and appoint me and my Friends to succeed them. I am a great Admirer of your useful and impartial Paper; and therefore request you will insert this without fail; from Your humble Servant

INDIGNATION.

To the Publisher of the Craven Street Gazette.

Sir,

Your Correspondent *Indignation* has made a fine Story in your Paper against our excellent Cravenstreet Ministry, as if they meant to starve his Highness, giving him only a bare Blade Bone for his Dinner, while they riot upon roast Venison, &c. The Wickedness of Writers in this Age is truly amazing! I believe we never had since the Foundation of our State, a more faithful, upright, worthy, careful, considerate, incorrupt, discreet, wise, prudent and beneficent Ministry than the present. But if even the Angel Gabriel would condescend to be our Minister and provide our Dinners, he could scarcely escape Newspaper Defamation from a Gang of hungry everrestless, discontented and malicious Scribblers. It is, Sir, a piece of Justice you owe our righteous Administration to undeceive the Publick on this Occasion, by assuring them of the Fact, which is, that there was provided, and actually smoking on the Table under his Royal Nose at the same Instant, as fine a Piece of Ribbs of Beef, roasted, as ever Knife was put into; with Potatoes, Horse radish, pickled Walnuts, &c. which Beef his Highness might have eaten of, if so he had pleased to do; and which he forbore to do, merely from a whimsical

Opinion (with Respect be it spoken) that Beef doth not with him perspire well, but makes his Back itch, to his no small Vexation, now that he hath lost the little Chinese Ivory Hand at the End of a Stick, commonly called a *Scratchback*, presented to him by her Majesty. This is the Truth; and if your boasted Impartiality is real, you will not hesitate a Moment to insert this Letter in your very next Paper. I am, tho' a little angry with you at present. Yours as you behave

A HATER OF SCANDAL.

JUNIUS and CINNA *came to Hand too late for this Days Paper, but shall have Place in our next.*

Marriages.	None since our last; but Puss begins to go a Courting.
Deaths.	In the back Closet, and elsewhere, many poor Mice.
Stocks.	Biscuit very low.
	Buckwheat and Indian meal, both sour.
	Tea, lowering daily in the Canister.

Postscript. Wednesday Sept. 26.

Those in the Secret of Affairs do not scruple to assert soundly, that our present First Ministress is very notable, having this day been at Market, bought excellent Mutton Chops, and Apples 4 a penny, made a very fine Applepye with her own Hands, and mended two pair of Breeches.

The Rise and Present State of Our Misunderstanding

To the PRINTER *of the* LONDON CHRONICLE.

SIR,

Much abuse has lately been thrown out against the Colonies, by the Writers for the American part of our Administration. Our Fellow Subjects there are continually represented as Rebels to their Sovereign, and inimical to the British nation;

in order to create a dislike of them here, that the harsh measures which have been taken, and are intended against them, may not be blamed by the People of England. Therefore to prevent our being led into mistakes in so important a business, it is fit that a full and particular account of the rise and present state of our misunderstanding with the Colonies should be laid before the Public. This, from the opportunities I have had, and the pains I have taken to inform myself, I think I am enabled to do, and I hope I shall do it with truth and candor.

The fact then is, that there is not nor has been any rebellion in America. If the rescue of a seizure by Smugglers, or the drubbing an Informer or low Custom-house Officer, were rebellion, England, Scotland, and Ireland, might be said to be in rebellion almost every week in the year; and instances of that kind are much fewer in America than here. The Americans were ever attached to the House of Hanover, and honour their present gracious Sovereign sincerely. This is therefore a groundless calumny. Nor have they any enmity to Britain: they love and honour the name of Englishman; they were fond of English manners, fashions, and manufactures; they had no desire of breaking the connection between the two countries, but wished a perpetual intercourse of good offices, commerce, and friendship. They are always willing to give aids to the Crown in proportion to their abilities: They think, however, and have always thought, that they themselves have alone the right of granting their own money, by their own Representatives in Assembly met, and that the Parliament of Britain hath no right to raise a revenue from them without their consent.

The Parliament hath, nevertheless, of late made several attempts to raise such a revenue among them.

Heretofore, whenever the Colonies thought themselves aggrieved by British government, they applied for redress by humble petition; and it was usual to receive and consider their petitions, and give them a reasonable answer.

They proceeded in the same manner on the late occasions. They sent over petitions after petitions to the House of Commons, and some to the House of Lords. These were scarce any of them received. Some (offered while the acts were under consideration) were refused on this reason, that it was against an order of the House to receive petitions against money bills; others, because they contained expressions that called the right of Parliament in question; and therefore, it was said, no Member dared to present them. Finding the petitions of separate Colonies were not attended to, they thought to give them more weight by petitioning jointly. To this end a congress of Committees from all the Assemblies was held at New York, when petitions to the King and both Houses of Parliament were agreed to and sent hither. But these could not be received, or were rejected, on the pretence that the congress was an illegal assembly which had no right to petition. Lastly, on occasion of the Duty Act, the Assemblies proposed by a correspondence with each other to obtain attention, by sending at the same time similar petitions. These were intended to the King their Sovereign, requesting his gracious influence with his Parliament to procure them redress. But this they were told by the American Minister was a FLAGITIOUS * attempt! All the Governors were by him directed to prevent it, or to dissolve the Assemblies that persisted in it; and several of them were accordingly dissolved. And of those petitions that nevertheless came hither and were presented, it is said that no notice was ever taken, or any answer given to them.

By this management the ancient well contrived channel of communication between the head and members of this great Empire, thro' which the notice of grievances could be received that remedies might be applied, hath been cut off. How wisely, the Publick will judge. History of a similar conduct in the Ministry of Spain with regard to the Low Countries, makes one doubt a little the prudence (in any Government how great soever) of discouraging Petitions, and treating Petitioners (how mean soever) with contempt.

Instead of *preventing* complaints by removing the causes, it has been thought best that Soldiers should be sent to *silence* them.

The Soldiers have behaved in such a manner as to occasion more complaints.

*See Lord H.'s Letters to the Governors.

They took possession of the publick building in which the Assembly or Parliament of New England usually convenes, obliged the Members to pass through lanes of men in arms to get to their Chamber, disturbing them in their debates by drumming and piping in and round the House, and pointed the cannon against the doors, treating the Province and People with every indignity and insult, proper to provoke their resentment, and produce some rash action that might justify making a massacre among them. And they have fired upon and murdered several of the inhabitants.

The Americans, upon the treatment their Petitions had repeatedly received, determined to petition no more: But said to one another, "We are too remote from Britain to have our complaints regarded by the Parliament there, especially as we have no share in their Election, nor any Representatives among them. They will not hear *us*, but perhaps they will hear *their own people*, their Merchants and Manufacturers, who are maintained and enriched in some degree by the commerce with our country. Let us agree to with-hold that commerce till our grievances are redressed. This will afford those people a foundation for petitioning, and they will be attended to as they were on a former occasion, and meet with success." This reasoning and expectation were the sole foundation of the Non-Importation agreements in America, and *not any enmity to Britain*.

In this expectation it seems they were mistaken. The Merchants trading to North America not well liking the Ministry, unwilling to solicit or be obliged to them for any thing, and hoping soon to see a change for others more to their mind, were backward in petitioning the Parliament. And when they did petition, the City being out of favour at Court, their Petition was very little attended to, and produced no effect. To prevent the Manufacturers from taking any part in the affair, they have been artfully amused with assurances that the Colonies could not long subsist without the trade, that manufactures among themselves were impossible, that they might depend there would be an extraordinary demand for goods as soon as the total want of conveniencies should compel the Americans to resume the commerce; and therefore they would do well to be quiet, mind their business, and get a great stock of goods beforehand to be ready for that demand, when the advanced price would make them ample amends for the delay.

In the mean time the Merchants in America have reaped great advantages. They have sold off most of the old goods that lay upon their hands; they have got in most of their debts from the people, and have in a great measure discharged their debt to England, that bore a heavy interest; this they have done at an advantage of near 20 per cent. in most of the Colonies, by the lowness of exchange, occasioned by the non-importation; and this nation has lost near that proportion (if I am rightly informed) on all the money drawn for these by British Agents, to pay and provide for the troops and ships of war, and to discharge other expences of contingent service. This loss must amount to a very great sum, besides the loss in commerce.

Many of these Merchants in America, however, having nearly compleated these points, and seeing the main end of their agreement, (the total abolition of the duties) not likely to be so soon obtained as they expected, begin to grow uneasy under the delay, and are rather desirous of altering the agreement made against general importation, and reducing it to the exclusion of those commercial articles only, on which the duties are, or shall be imposed. But the generality of the people in America, the artizans in the towns, and the farmers throughout the country, finding the non-importation advantageous to them all; to the artisans, as it occasions fuller employment, and encourages the beginners that introduce new arts; and to the farmers, as it prevents much useless expence in their families, and thereby enables them more expeditiously to improve their plantations to the raising a greater produce, at the same time that it is a spur to domestic industry, in such manufactures as though not fine, are now become fashionable and reputable, and from their superior strength are much more serviceable than the flimsy fineries that used to be made for them in Britain; and all feeling the advantage of having had money returned into the country for its produce, from Spain, Portugal, Italy, (and even from England since the balance of trade has turned against her) instead of those British superfluities for which all that cash was formerly remitted, or

ordered into England. I say, the generality of the people in
America, pleased with this situation of things, and relishing
the sweets of it, have now taken the lead, in a great degree,
out of the hands of the Merchants, and in town and county
meetings are entering into solemn resolutions not to purchase
or consume British commodities, if they are imported, till the
acts they esteem injurious to their privileges are repealed; and
that if any Merchants do import before that time, they will
mark them as enemies to their country, and never deal with
them when the trade shall be opened. This is now become a
restraint upon the Merchants. A party, however, of those at
New-York, have broken through the agreement, and ordered
goods; and the Merchants here, who had long lain idle, being
rejoiced at this opening, have sent them over immense quantities, expecting a quick sale and speedy returns. But the event
is yet very uncertain. The trade of New-York was chiefly with
East New Jersey and Connecticut, their two neighbouring
Colonies, and these have resolved to have no farther dealings
with that city. Several counties, too, of the Province of New-
York, and the greatest part of the inhabitants of the city itself,
have protested against the infraction of the agreement, and
determined not to buy or use the goods when they arrive. So
that the exporters begin now to apprehend that their sanguine hopes will be disappointed. And as Rhode Island has
returned to the agreement, some think it not unlikely that
New-York may do the same.

What remedy, if any, the wisdom of Parliament shall think
fit to apply to these disorders, a little time will shew. Mean
while, I cannot but think that those writers, who busily employ their talents in endeavouring to exasperate this nation
against the Colonies, are doing it a very ill office: For their
virulent writings being dispersed among the inhabitants of
the Plantations (who read all our papers and pamphlets, and
imagine them of greater estimation here than they really are)
do in some degree irritate the Colonists against a country
which treats them, as they imagine, so injuriously:—And on
our side, as nothing is likely to be well done that is done in
anger; as customers are not naturally brought back to a shop
by unkind usage; as the Americans are growing, and soon
will be, a great people, and their friendship or enmity be-

come daily of more and more consequence; as their fisheries, their coasting trade, their West-Indian and European trades, greatly increase the numbers of English seamen, and thereby augment our naval power; as their joint operations with our's in time of war must make the whole national effort more weighty and more effectual; as enmities between countries, fostered and promoted till they have taken root, are scarce ever to be eradicated; and, when those countries are under the same Prince, such enmities are of the most mischievous consequence, encouraging foreign enemies, weakening the whole empire, and tending to its dissolution; therefore I cannot but wish, that no steps may be taken against the Colonists, tending to abridge their privileges, alter their charters, or inflict punishments on them, at the instance of *angry Governors, discarded Agents, or rash indiscreet Officers of the Customs*, who, having quarrelled with them, are their enemies, and are daily irritating Government here against them, by misrepresentations of their actions, and aggravations of their faults, with much malice: I hope the great principle of common justice, that *no man should be condemned unheard*, will not by us be violated in the case of a whole people; and that lenient measures will be adopted, as most likely to heal the wound effectually: For harsh treatment may increase the inflammation, make the cure less practicable, and in time bring on the necessity of an amputation; death indeed to the severed limb, weakness and lameness to the mutilated body.

N. N.

The London Chronicle, November 8, 1770

Account of an Audience with Hillsborough

Wednesday, Jan. 16. '71

I went this Morning to wait on Lord Hillsborough. The Porter at first deny'd his Lordship, on which I left my Name, and drove off. But before the Coach got out of the

Square, the Coachman heard a Call, turn'd, and went back
to the Door, when the Porter came and said, His Lordship
will see you, Sir. I was shown into the Levee Room, where
I found Governor Barnard, who I understand attends there
constantly. Several other Gentlemen were there attending,
with whom I sat down a few Minutes. When Secretary
Pownall came out to us, and said his Lordship desired I
would come in.

I was pleas'd with this ready Admission, and Preference,
(having sometimes waited 3 or 4 Hours for my Turn) and
being pleas'd, I could more easily put on the open chearful
Countenance that my Friends advis'd me to wear. His Lordship came towards me, and said "I was dressing in order to
go to Court; but hearing that you were at the Door, who are
a Man of Business, I determin'd to see you immediately." I
thank'd his Lordship and said that my Business at present was
not much, it was only to pay my Respects to his Lordship
and to acquaint him with my Appointment by the House of
Representatives of the Province of Massachusetts Bay, to be
their Agent here, in which Station if I could be of any Service—I was going on to say, to the Publick I should be very
happy; but his Lordship whose Countenance chang'd at my
naming that Province cut me short, by saying, with something between a Smile and a Sneer,

L H.   I must set you right there, Mr. Franklin, you are not
         Agent.

B F.   Why; my Lord?

L.H.   You are not appointed.

B.F   I do not understand your Lordship. I have the Ap-
         pointment in my Pocket.

L.H.   You are mistaken. I have later and better Advices.
         I have a Letter from Governor Hutchinson. He
         would not give his Assent to the Bill.

B.F.   There was no Bill, my Lord; it is a Vote of the
         House.

L.H.   There was a Bill presented to the Governor, for the
         Purpose of appointing you, and another, one Dr.
         Lee, I think he is call'd, to which the Governor re-
         fus'd his Assent.

B.F.   I cannot understand this, my Lord. I think There

	must be some Mistake in it. Is your Lordship quite sure that you have such a Letter?
L H.	I will convince you of it directly. *Rings the Bell*. Mr. Pownall will come in and satisfy you.
B.F.	It is not necessary that I should now detain your Lordship from Dressing. You are going to Court. I will wait on your Lordship another time.
L.H.	No, stay, He will come in immediately. *To the Servant*. Tell Mr. Pownall I want him. *Mr. Pownall comes in.*
L.H.	Have not you at hand Govr. Hutchinson's Letter mentioning his Refusing his Assent to the Bill for appointing Dr. Franklin Agent?
SEC. P.	My Lord?
L H.	Is there not such a Letter?
SEC. P.	No, my Lord. There is a Letter relating to some Bill for payment of Salary to Mr. DeBerdt and I think to some other Agent, to which the Governor had refus'd his Assent.
L H.	And is there nothing in that Letter to the purpose I mention?
SEC. P.	No, my Lord.
B F.	I thought it could not well be, my Lord, as my Letters are by the last Ships and mention no such Thing. Here is an authentic Copy of the Vote of the House appointing me, in which there is no Mention of any Act intended. Will your Lordship please to look at it? (*With some seeming Unwillingness he takes it, but does not look into it*).
L H.	An Information of this kind is not properly brought to me as Secretary of State. The Board of Trade is the proper Place.
B.F.	I will leave the Paper then with Mr. Pownall, to be—
L.H.	(*Hastily*) To what End would you leave it with him?
B F.	To be entred on the Minutes of that Board, as usual.
L.H.	(*Angrily*) It shall not be entred there. No such Paper shall be entred there while I have any thing to do with the Business of that Board. The House of Representatives has no Right to appoint an Agent. We

shall take no Notice of any Agents but such as are appointed by Acts of Assembly to which the Governor gives his Assent. We have had Confusion enough already. Here is one Agent appointed by the Council, another by the House of Representatives; Which of these is Agent for the Province? Who are we to hear on Provincial Affairs? An Agent appointed by Act of Assembly we can understand. No other will be attended to for the future, I can assure you.

B.F. I cannot conceive, my Lord, why the Consent of the *Governor* should be thought necessary to the Appointment of an Agent for the *People*. It seems to me, that—

L H. (*With a mix'd Look of Anger and Contempt*) I shall not enter into a Dispute with YOU, Sir, upon this Subject.

B F. I beg your Lordship's Pardon. I do not presume to dispute with your Lordship: I would only say, that it seems to me, that every Body of Men, who cannot appear in Person where Business relating to them may be transacted, should have a Right to appear by an Agent; The Concurrence of the Governor does not seem to me necessary. It is the Business of the People that is to be done, he is not one of them, he is himself an Agent.

L H. Whose Agent is he? (*Hastily*).

B F. The King's, my Lord.

L H. No such Matter. He is one of the Corporation, by the Province Charter. No Agent can be appointed but by an Act, nor any Act pass without his Assent. Besides, This Proceeding is directly contrary to express Instructions.

B.F. I did not know there had been such Instructions, I am not concern'd in any Offence against them, and—

L H. Yes, your Offering such a Paper to be entred is an Offence against them. (*Folding it up again, without having read a Word of it.*) No such Appointment shall be entred. When I came into the Administration of American Affairs, I found them in great Disorder; By *my Firmness* they are now something mended; and while I have the Honour to hold the Seals, I shall continue the same Conduct, the same *Firmness*. I think My Duty to the Master I serve and to the Government of this Nation require it of me. If that Conduct is not approved, They may take my Office from me when they please. I shall make 'em a Bow, and thank 'em. I shall resign with Pleasure. That Gentleman knows it. (*Pointing to Mr. Pownall.*) But while I continue in it, I shall resolutely persevere in the same FIRMNESS. (*Spoken with great Warmth, and turning pale in his Discourse, as if he was angry at something or somebody besides the Agent; and of more Consequence to himself.*)

B.F.   (*Reaching out his Hand for the Paper, which his Lordship returned to him*) I beg your Lordship's Pardon for taking up so much of your time. It is I believe of no great Importance whether the Appointment is acknowledged or not, for I have not the least Conception that an Agent can *at present* be of any Use, to any of the Colonies. I shall therefore give your Lordship no farther Trouble. *Withdrew.*

TO THE MASSACHUSETTS HOUSE OF REPRESENTATIVES:

"The Seeds Sown of a Total Disunion of the Two Countries"

GENTLEMEN,   London, 15 May, 1771.

I have received your favor of the 27th of February, with the Journal of the House of Representatives, and copies of the late oppressive prosecutions in the Admiralty Court, which I shall, as you direct, communicate to Mr. Bollan, and consult with him on the most advantageous use to be made of them for the interest of the province.

I think one may clearly see, in the system of customs to be exacted in America by act of Parliament, the seeds sown of a total disunion of the two countries, though, as yet, that event may be at a considerable distance. The course and natural progress seems to be, first, the appointment of needy men as officers, for others do not care to leave England; then, their necessities make them rapacious, their office makes them proud and insolent, their insolence and rapacity make them odious, and, being conscious that they are hated, they become malicious; their malice urges them to a continual abuse of the inhabitants in their letters to administration, representing them as disaffected and rebellious, and (to encourage the use of severity) as weak, divided, timid, and cowardly. Government believes all; thinks it necessary to support and countenance its officers; their quarrelling with the people is deemed a mark and consequence of their fidelity; they are therefore more highly rewarded, and this makes their conduct still more insolent and provoking.

The resentment of the people will, at times and on particular incidents, burst into outrages and violence upon such officers, and this naturally draws down severity and acts of further oppression from hence. The more the people are dissatisfied, the more rigor will be thought necessary; severe punishments will be inflicted to terrify; rights and privileges will be abolished; greater force will then be required to secure execution and submission; the expense will become enormous; it will then be thought proper, by fresh exactions, to make the people defray it; thence, the British nation and government will become odious, the subjection to it will be deemed no longer tolerable; war ensues, and the bloody struggle will end in absolute slavery to America, or ruin to Britain by the loss of her colonies; the latter most probable, from America's growing strength and magnitude.

But, as the whole empire must, in either case, be greatly weakened, I cannot but wish to see much patience and the utmost discretion in our general conduct, that the fatal period may be postponed, and that, whenever this catastrophe shall happen, it may appear to all mankind, that the fault has not been ours. And, since the collection of these duties has already cost Britain infinitely more, in the loss of commerce, than they amount to, and that loss is likely to continue and increase by the encouragement given to our manufactures through resentment; and since the best pretence for establishing and enforcing the duties is the regulation of trade for the general advantage, it seems to me, that it would be much better for Britain to give them up, on condition of the colonies undertaking to enforce and collect such, as are thought fit to be continued, by laws of their own, and officers of their own appointment, for the public uses of their respective governments. This would alone destroy those seeds of disunion, and both countries might thence much longer continue to grow great together, more secure by their united strength, and more formidable to their common enemies. But the power of appointing friends and dependents to profitable offices is too pleasing to most administrations, to be easily parted with or lessened; and therefore such a proposition, if it were made, is not very likely to meet with attention.

I do not pretend to the gift of prophecy. History shows, that, by these steps, great empires have crumbled heretofore; and the late transactions we have so much cause to complain of show, that we are in the same train, and that, without a greater share of prudence and wisdom, than we have seen both sides to be possessed of, we shall probably come to the same conclusion.

The Parliament, however, is prorogued, without having taken any of the steps we had been threatened with, relating to our charter. Their attention has been engrossed by other affairs, and we have therefore longer time to operate in making such impressions, as may prevent a renewal of this particular attempt by our adversaries. With great esteem and respect, I have the honor to be, &c.

Introduction to a Plan for Benefiting the New Zealanders

Britain is said to have produced originally nothing but *Sloes*. What vast advantages have been communicated to her by the Fruits, Seeds, Roots, Herbage, Animals, and Arts of other Countries! We are by their means become a wealthy and a mighty Nation, abounding in all good Things. Does not some *Duty* hence arise from us towards other Countries still remaining in our former State?

Britain is now the first Maritime Power in the world. Her Ships are innumerable, capable by their Form, Size, and Strength, of sailing all Seas. Her Seamen are equally bold, skilful, and hardy; dextrous in exploring the remotest regions, and ready to engage in Voyages to unknown Countries, tho' attended with the greatest dangers. The Inhabitants of those Countries, our *Fellow-Men*, have Canoes only; not knowing Iron, they cannot build Ships: They have little Astronomy, and no knowledge of the Compass to guide them; they cannot therefore come to us, or obtain any of our advantages. From these circumstances, does not some duty seem to arise from us to them? Does not Providence, by these distinguishing Favours, seem to call on us, to do something ourselves for the common Interests of Humanity?

Those who think it their Duty to ask Bread and other Blessings daily from Heaven, should they not think it equally a duty to communicate of those blessings when they have received them; and show their Gratitude to their Great Benefactor, by the only means in their power, promoting the happiness of his other Children?

Ceres is said to have made a Journey thro' many Countries, to teach the use of Corn, and the art of raising it. For this single benefit, the grateful Nations deified her. How much more may Englishmen deserve such Honour, by communicating the knowledge and use, not of Corn only, but of all the other enjoyments Earth can produce, and which they are now in possession of. *Communiter bona profundere, Deum est.*

Many Voyages have been undertaken with views of profit or of plunder, or to gratify resentment; to procure some advantage to ourselves, or do some mischief to others: but a voyage is now proposed, to visit a distant people on the other side the Globe; not to cheat them, not to rob them, not to seize their lands, or enslave their persons; but merely to do them good, and enable them as far as in our power lies, to live as comfortably as ourselves.

It seems a laudable wish, that all the Nations of the Earth were connected by a knowledge of each other, and a mutual exchange of benefits: But a Commercial Nation particularly should wish for a general Civilization of Mankind, since Trade is always carried on to much greater extent with People who have the Arts and Conveniencies of Life, than it can be with naked Savages. We may therefore hope, in this undertaking, to be of some service to our Country, as well as to those poor people, who, however distant from us, are in truth related to us, and whose Interests do, in some degree, concern every one who can say, *Homo sum, &c.*

August 29, 1771

Toleration in Old and New England

To the PRINTER of the LONDON PACKET.

SIR,

I understand from the public papers, that in the debates on the bill for relieving the Dissenters in the point of subscription to the Church Articles, sundry reflections were thrown out against that people, importing, "that they themselves are of a persecuting intolerant spirit, for that when they had here the superiority they persecuted the church, and still persecute it in America, where they compel its members to pay taxes for maintaining the Presbyterian or independent worship, and at the same time refuse them a toleration in the full exercise of their religion by the administrations of a bishop."

If we look back into history for the character of present sects in Christianity, we shall find few that have not in their turns been persecutors, and complainers of persecution. The primitive Christians thought persecution extremely wrong in the Pagans, but practised it on one another. The first Protestants of the Church of England, blamed persecution in the Roman church, but practised it against the Puritans: these found it wrong in the Bishops, but fell into the same practice themselves both here and in New England. To account for this we should remember, that the doctrine of *toleration* was not then known, or had not prevailed in the world. Persecution was therefore not so much the fault of the sect as of the times. It was not in those days deemed wrong *in itself.* The

general opinion was only, that those *who are in error* ought
not to persecute *the truth*: But the *possessors of truth* were in
the right to persecute *error*, in order to destroy it. Thus every
sect believing itself possessed of *all truth*, and that every tenet
differing from theirs was *error*, conceived that when the
power was in their hands, persecution was a duty required of
them by that God whom they supposed to be offended with
heresy.—By degrees more moderate *and more modest* sentiments have taken place in the Christian world; and among
Protestants particularly all disclaim persecution, none vindicate it, and few practise it. We should then cease to reproach
each other with what was done by our ancestors, but judge
of the present character of sects or churches by their *present
conduct* only.

Now to determine on the justice of this charge against the
present dissenters, particularly those in America, let us consider the following facts. They went from England to establish a new country for themselves, *at their own expence*, where
they might enjoy the free exercise of religion in their own
way. When they had purchased the territory of the natives,
they granted the lands out in townships, requiring for it neither purchase-money nor quit-rent, but this condition only to
be complied with, that the freeholders should for ever support a gospel minister (meaning probably one of the then
governing sects) and a free-school within the township. Thus,
what is commonly called Presbyterianism became the *established religion* of that country. All went on well in this way
while the same religious opinions were general, the support
of minister and school being raised by a proportionate tax on
the lands. But in process of time, some becoming Quakers,
some Baptists, and, of late years some returning to the
Church of England (through the laudable endeavours and a
proper application of their funds by the society for propagating
the gospel) objections were made to the payment of a tax
appropriated to the support of a church they disapproved and
had forsaken. The civil magistrates, however, continued for a
time to collect and apply the tax according to the original
laws which remained in force; and they did it the more freely,
as thinking it just and equitable that the holders of lands
should pay what was contracted to be paid when they were

granted, as the only consideration for the grant, and what had been considered by all subsequent purchasers as a perpetual incumbrance on the estate, bought therefore at a proportion-ably cheaper rate; a payment which it was thought no honest man ought to avoid under the pretence of his having changed his religious persuasion. And this I suppose is one of the best grounds of demanding tythes of dissenters now in England. But the practice being clamoured against by the episcopalians as persecution, the legislature of the Province of the Massa-chusets-Bay, near thirty years since, passed an act for their relief, requiring indeed the tax to be paid as usual, but direct-ing that the several sums levied from members of the Church of England, should be paid over to the Minister of that Church, with whom such members usually attended divine worship, which Minister had power given him to receive and on occasion *to recover the same by law.*

It seems that legislature considered the *end* of the tax was, to secure and improve the morals of the people, and promote their happiness, by supporting among them the public wor-ship of God and the preaching of the gospel; that where par-ticular people fancied a particular mode, that mode might prob-ably therefore be of most use to those people; and that if the good was done, it was not so material in what mode or by whom it was done. The consideration that their brethren the dissenters in England were still compelled to pay tythes to the clergy of the Church, had not weight enough with the leg-islature to prevent this moderate act, which still continues in full force, and I hope no uncharitable conduct of the church toward the dissenters will ever provoke them to repeal it.

With regard to a bishop, I know not upon what ground the dissenters, either here or in America, are charged with refusing the benefit of such an officer to the church in that country. *Here* they seem to have naturally no concern in the affair. *There* they have no power to prevent it, if government should think fit to send one. They would probably *dislike*, indeed, to see an order of men established among them, from whose persecutions their fathers fled into that wilderness, and whose future domination they may possibly fear, *not knowing that their natures are changed.* But the non-appointment of bishops for America seems to arise from another quarter.

The same wisdom of government, probably, that prevents the sitting of convocations, and forbids, by *noli prosequi*'s, the persecution of Dissenters for non-subscription, avoids establishing bishops where the minds of people are not yet prepared to receive them cordially, lest the public peace should be endangered.

And now let us see how this *persecution-account* stands between the parties.

In New-England, where the legislative bodies are almost to a man Dissenters from the Church of England,

1. There is no test to prevent Churchmen holding offices.

2. The sons of Churchmen have the full benefit of the Universities.

3. The taxes for support of public worship, when paid by Churchmen, are given to the Episcopal minister.

In Old England,

1. Dissenters are excluded from all offices of profit and honour.

2. The benefits of education in the Universities are appropriated to the sons of Churchmen.

3. The clergy of the Dissenters receive none of the tythes paid by their people, who must be at the additional charge of maintaining their own separate worship. —

But it is said, the Dissenters of America *oppose* the introduction of a Bishop.

In fact, it is not alone the Dissenters there that give the opposition (if *not encouraging* must be termed *opposing*) but the laity in general dislike the project, and some even of the clergy. The inhabitants of Virginia are almost all Episcopalians. The Church is fully established there, and the Council and General Assembly are perhaps to a man its members, yet when lately at a meeting of the clergy, a resolution was taken to apply for a Bishop, against which several however protested; the assembly of the province at their next meeting, expressed their disapprobation of the thing in the strongest manner, by unanimously ordering the thanks of the house to the protesters: for many of the American laity of the church think it some advantage, whether their own young men come to England for ordination, and improve themselves at the same time by conversation with the learned here, or the congregations are supplied by Englishmen, who have had the benefit of education in English universities, and are ordained before they come abroad. They do not therefore see the necessity of a Bishop merely for ordination, and confirmation is among them deemed a ceremony of no very great importance, since few seek it in England where Bishops are in plenty. These sentiments prevail with many churchmen there, not to promote a design, which they think must sooner or later saddle them with great expences to support it. As to the Dissenters, their minds might probably be more conciliated to the measure, if the Bishops here should, in their wisdom and goodness, think fit to set their sacred character in a more friendly light, by dropping their opposition to the Dissenters application for relief in subscription, and declaring their willingness that Dissenters should be capable of offices, enjoy the benefit of education in the universities, and the privilege of appropriating their tythes to the support of their own clergy. In all these points of toleration, they appear far behind the present Dissenters of New-England, and it may seem to some a step below the dignity of Bishops, to follow the example of such inferiors. I do not, however, despair of their doing it some time or other, since nothing of the kind is too hard for *true christian humility*.

I am, Sir, your's, &c.
A New-England-Man.

The London Packet, June 3, 1772

The Sommersett Case and the Slave Trade

It is said that some generous humane persons subscribed to the expence of obtaining liberty by law for Somerset the Negro.—It is to be wished that the same humanity may extend itself among numbers; if not to the procuring liberty for those that remain in our Colonies, at least to obtain a law for abolishing the African commerce in Slaves, and declaring the children of present Slaves free after they become of age.

By a late computation made in America, it appears that

there are now eight hundred and fifty thousand Negroes in the English Islands and Colonies; and that the yearly importation is about one hundred thousand, of which number about one third perish by the gaol distemper on the passage, and in the sickness called the *seasoning* before they are set to labour. The remnant makes up the deficiencies continually occurring among the main body of those unhappy people, through the distempers occasioned by excessive labour, bad nourishment, uncomfortable accommodation, and broken spirits. Can sweetening our tea, &c. with sugar, be a circumstance of such absolute necessity? Can the petty pleasure thence arising to the taste, compensate for so much misery produced among our fellow creatures, and such a constant butchery of the human species by this pestilential detestable traffic in the bodies and souls of men? — *Pharisaical Britain!* to pride thyself in setting free *a single Slave* that happens to land on thy coasts, while thy Merchants in all thy ports are encouraged by thy laws to continue a commerce whereby so many *hundreds of thousands* are dragged into a slavery that can scarce be said to end with their lives, since it is entailed on their posterity!

The London Chronicle, June 20, 1772

Preface to the Declaration of the Boston Town Meeting

All Accounts of the Discontent so general in our Colonies, have of late Years been industriously smothered, and concealed here; it seeming to suit the Views of the American Minister to have it understood, that by his great Abilities all Faction was subdued, all Opposition suppressed, and the whole Country quieted. — That the true State of Affairs there may be known, and the true Causes of that Discontent well understood, the following Piece (not the Production of a Private Writer, but the unanimous Act of a large American City) lately printed in New-England, is republished here. This Nation, and the other Nations of Europe, may thereby learn with more Certainty the Grounds of a Dissension, that possibly may, sooner or later, have Consequences interesting to them all.

The Colonies had, from their first Settlement, been governed with more Ease, than perhaps can be equalled by any Instance in History, of Dominions so distant. Their Affection and Respect for this Country, while they were treated with Kindness, produced an almost implicit Obedience to the Instructions of the Prince, and even to Acts of the British Parliament, though the Right of binding them by a Legislature in which they were unrepresented, was never clearly understood. That Respect and Affection produced a Partiality in favour of every thing that was English; whence their preference of English Modes and Manufactures; their Submission to Restraints on the Importation of Foreign Goods, which they had but little Desire to use; and the Monopoly we so long enjoyed of their Commerce, to the great enriching of our Merchants and Artificers. The mistaken Policy of the Stamp-Act first disturbed this happy Situation; but the Flame thereby raised was soon extinguished by its Repeal, and the old Harmony restored, with all its concomitant Advantages to our Commerce. The subsequent Act of another Administration, which, not content with an established Exclusion of Foreign Manufactures, began to make our own Merchandize dearer to the Consumers there by heavy Duties, revived it again: And Combinations were entered into throughout the Continent, to stop Trading with Britain till those Duties should be repealed. All were accordingly repealed but One, the Duty on Tea. This was reserved professedly as a standing Claim and Exercise of the Right assumed by Parliament of laying such Duties. The Colonies, on this Repeal, retracted their Agreement, so far as related to all other Goods except that on which the Duty was retained. This was trumpeted *here* by the Minister for the Colonies as a Triumph; *there* it was considered only as a decent and equitable Measure, shewing a Willingness to *meet* the Mother Country in every Advance towards a Reconciliation. And the Disposition to a good Understanding was so prevalent, that possibly they might soon have relaxed in the Article of Tea also. But the System of Commissioners of Customs, Officers without end, with Fleets and Armies for collecting and enforcing those Duties, being continued, and these acting with much Indiscretion and Rashness, giving great and unnecessary Trouble and Obstruction to Business, commencing unjust and vexatious Suits, and harassing Commerce in all its Branches, while that Minister kept the People in a constant State of Irritation by Instructions which appeared to have no other End than the gratifying his Private Resentments *, occasioned a persevering Adherence to their Resolution in that Particular: And the Event should be a Lesson to Ministers, not to risque, through Pique, the obstructing any one Branch of Trade, since the Course and Connection of General Business may be thereby disturbed to a Degree impossible to be foreseen or imagined. For it appears, that the Colonies, finding their Humble Petitions to have this Duty repealed, were rejected and treated with Contempt, and that the Produce of the Duty was applied to the rewarding with undeserved Salaries and Pensions every one of their Enemies, the Duty itself became more odious, and their Resolution to starve it more vigorous and obstinate. The Dutch, the Danes and French, took the Advantage thus offered them by our Imprudence, and began to smuggle their Teas into the Plantations. At first this was somewhat difficult; but at length, as all Business improves by Practice, it became easy. A Coast, 1500 Miles in Length, could not in all Parts be guarded, even by the whole Navy of England, especially where the restraining Authority was by all the Inhabitants deemed unconstitutional, and Smuggling of course considered as Patriotism. The needy Wretches too, who with small Salaries were trusted to watch the Ports Day and Night, in all Weathers, found it easier and more profitable, not only to *wink*, but to sleep in their Beds, the Merchant's Pay being more generous than the King's. Other India Goods also, which by themselves would not have made a Smuggling Voyage sufficiently profitable, accompanied Tea to Advantage; and it is feared the cheap French Silks, formerly rejected as not to the Taste of the Colonists, may have found their way with the Wares of India, and now established themselves in the popular Use and Opinion. It is supposed

*Some of his circular Letters had been criticised and exposed by one or two of the American Assemblies.

that at least a Million of Americans drink Tea twice a Day,
which, at the first Cost here, can scarce be reckoned at less
than Half a Guinea a Head *per Annum*. This Market, that in
the five Years which have run on since the Act passed, would
have paid 2,500,000 Guineas, *for Tea alone*, into the Coffers
of the Company, we have wantonly lost to Foreigners. Meanwhile it is said the Duties have so diminished, that the whole
Remittance of the last Year amounted to no more than the
pitiful Sum of 85 Pounds for the Expence of some Hundred
Thousands in armed Ships and Soldiers to support the Officers. Hence the Tea and other India Goods that might have
been sold in America, remain rotting in the Company's Warehouses, while those of Foreign Ports are known to be cleared
by the American Demand. Hence in some Degree the Company's Inability to pay their Bills; the sinking of their Stock,
by which Millions of Property have been annihilated; the
lowering of their Dividend, whereby so many must be distressed; the Loss to Government of the stipulated 400,000
Pounds a Year, which must make a proportionable Reduction
in our Savings towards the Discharge of our enormous Debt;
and hence in part the severe Blow suffered by Credit in general, to the Ruin of many Families; the Stagnation of Business in Spital-Fields and at Manchester, through want of Vent
for their Goods; with other future Evils, which, as they cannot, from the numerous and secret Connections in General
Commerce, easily be foreseen, can hardly be avoided.

February, 1773

TO THE MASSACHUSETTS HOUSE OF REPRESENTATIVES:
"A Little Time Must Infallibly Bring Us All We Demand or Desire"

Sir,   London, July 7. 1773
    The Parliament is at length prorogu'd without meddling
with the State of America. Their Time was much employ'd
in East India Business: and perhaps it was not thought prudent to lay before them the Advices from New England,

tho' some threatning Intimations had been given of such an
Intention. The King's firm Answer (as it is called) to our
Petitions and Remonstrances, has probably been judged sufficient for the present. I forwarded that Answer to you by
the last Packet, and sent a Copy of it by a Boston Ship the
beginning of last Month. Therein we are told "that his Majesty has well weighed the *Subject matter*, and the *Expressions*
contain'd in those Petitions; and that as he will ever attend
to the *humble* Petitions of his Subjects, and be forward to
redress every *real* Grievance so he is determined to support
the Constitution, and resist with Firmness every Attempt to
derogate from the Authority of the *supreme Legislature*."

By this it seems that, some Exception is taken to the
Expressions of the Petitions as not sufficiently humble; that the
Grievances complain'd of are not thought *real* Grievances;
that Parliament is deem'd the Supreme Legislature, and its
Authority over the Colonies, suppos'd to be *the Constitution*.
Indeed this last Idea is express'd more fully in the next Para-
graph, where the Words of the Act are us'd, declaring the
Right of the Crown with the Advice of Parliament, to make
Laws of *sufficient Force and Validity* to bind its Subjects in
America *in all Cases whatsoever*.

When one considers the King's Situation, surrounded by
Ministers, Councellors, and Judges learned in the Law, who
are all of this Opinion; and reflect how necessary it is for
him to be well with his Parliament, from whose yearly
Grants his Fleets and Armies are to be supported, and the
Deficiencies of his Civil List supplied, it is not to be wondered at that he should be firm in an Opinion establish'd as
far as an Act of Parliament could establish it, by even the
Friends of America at the Time they repeal'd the Stamp-Act;
and which is so generally thought right by his Lords and
Commons, that any Act of his, countenancing the contrary,
would hazard his embroiling himself with those Powerful
Bodies. And from hence it seems hardly to be expected from
him that he should take any Step of that kind. The grievous
Instructions indeed might be withdrawn without their observing it, if his Majesty thought fit so to do; but under the
present Prejudices of all about him, it seems that this is not
yet likely to be advised.

The Question then arises, How are we to obtain Redress? If we look back into the Parliamentary History of this Country, we shall find that in similar Situations of the Subjects here, Redress could seldom be obtained but by withholding Aids when the Sovereign was in Distress, till the Grievances were removed. Hence the rooted Custom of the Commons to keep Money Bills intirely in their own Disposition, not suffering even the Lords to meddle in Grants, either as to Quantity, Manner of raising, or even in the smallest Circumstance. This Country pretends to be collectively our Sovereign. It is now deeply in debt. Its Funds are far short of recovering their Par since the last War: Another would distress it still more. Its People diminish as well as its Credit. Men will be wanted as well as Money. The Colonies are rapidly increasing in Wealth and Numbers. In the last War they maintained an Army of 25000. A Country able to do that is no contemptible Ally. In another War they may do perhaps twice as much with equal Ease. Whenever a War happens, our Aid will be wish'd for, our Friendship desired and cultivated, our Good will courted: Then is the Time to say, *Redress our Grievances*. You take Money from us by Force, and now you ask it of voluntary Grant. You cannot have it both Ways. If you chuse to have it without our Consent, you must go on taking it that way and be content with what little you can so obtain. If you would have our free Gifts, desist from your Compulsive Methods, acknowledge our Rights, and secure our future Enjoyment of them. Our Claims will then be attended to, and our Complaints regarded. By what I perceiv'd not long since when a War was apprehended with Spain, the different Countenance put on by some Great Men here towards those who were thought to have a little Influence in America, and the Language that began to be held with regard to the then Minister for the Colonies, I am confident that if that War had taken place he would have been immediately dismiss'd, all his Measures revers'd, and every step taken to recover our Affection and procure our Assistance. Thence I think it fair to conclude that similar Effects will probably be produced by similar Circumstances.

But as the Strength of an Empire depends not only on the *Union* of its Parts, but on their *Readiness* for United Exertion of their common Force: And as the Discussion of Rights may seem unseasonable in the Commencement of actual War; and the Delay it might occasion be prejudicial to the common Welfare. As likewise the Refusal of one or a few Colonies, would not be so much regarded if the others granted liberally, which perhaps by various Artifices and Motives they might be prevailed on to do; and as this want of Concert would defeat the Expectation of general Redress that otherwise might be justly formed; perhaps it would be best and fairest, for the Colonies in a general Congress now in Peace to be assembled, or by means of the Correspondence lately proposed after a full and solemn Assertion and Declaration of their Rights, to engage firmly with each other that they will never grant aids to the Crown in any General War till those Rights are recogniz'd by the King and both Houses of Parliament; communicating at the same time to the Crown this their Resolution. Such a Step I imagine will bring the Dispute to a Crisis; and whether our Demands are immediately comply'd with, or compulsory Means are thought of to make us Rescind them, our Ends will finally be obtain'd, for even the odium accompanying such compulsory Attempts will contribute to unite and strengthen us, and in the mean time all the World will allow that our Proceeding has been honourable.

No one doubts the Advantage of a strict Union between the Mother Country and the Colonies, if it may be obtain'd and preserv'd on equitable Terms. In every fair Connection each Party should find its own Interest. Britain will find hers in our joining with her in every War she makes to the greater Annoyance and Terror of her Enemies; in our Employment of her Manufacturers, and Enriching of her Merchants by our Commerce; and her Government will feel some additional Strengthening of its Hands, by the Disposition of our profitable Posts and Places. On our side, we have to expect the Protection she can afford us; and the Advantage of a common Umpire in our Disputes thereby preventing Wars we might otherwise have with each other, so that we can without Interruption go on with our Improvements and increase our Numbers. We ask no more of her, and she should not think of forcing more from us. By the Exercise of prudent Moderation on her part, mix'd with a little Kindness; and by a decent Behaviour on ours, excusing where we can excuse from a Consideration of Circumstances, and bearing a little, with the Infirmities of her Government as we would with those of an aged Parent, tho' firmly asserting our Privileges, and declaring that we mean at a proper time to vindicate them, this advantageous Union may still be long continued. We wish it, and we may endeavour it, but God will order it as to his Wisdom shall seem most suitable. The Friends of Liberty here, wish we may long preserve it on our side the Water, that they may find it there if adverse Events should destroy it here. They are therefore anxious and afraid lest we should hazard it by premature Attempts in its favour. They think we may risque much by violent Measures, and that the Risque is unnecessary, since a little Time must infallibly bring us all we demand or desire, and bring it us in Peace and Safety. I do not presume to advise. There are many wiser Men among you, and I hope you will be directed by a still superior Wisdom.

With regard to the Sentiments of People in general here concerning America, I must say that we have among them many Friends and Well-wishers. The Dissenters are all for us, and many of the Merchants and Manufacturers. There seems to be even among the Country Gentlemen a general Sense of our growing Importance, a Disapprobation of the harsh Measures with which we have been treated, and a Wish that some Means may be found of perfect Reconciliation. A few Members of Parliament in both Houses, and perhaps some in high Office have in a Degree the same Ideas, but none of these seem willing as yet to be active in our favour, lest Adversaries should take Advantage and charge it upon them as a Betraying the Interests of this Nation. In this State of things, no Endeavours of mine or our other Friends here "to obtain a Repeal of the Acts so oppressive to the Colonists or the Orders of the Crown so destructive of the Charter rights of our Province in particular," can expect a sudden success. By degrees and a judicious Improvement of Events we may work a Change in Minds and Measures, but otherwise such great Alterations are hardly to be look'd for.

I am thankful to the House for the Mark of their kind Attention in repeating their Grant to me of Six Hundred

Pounds. Whether the Instruction restraining the Governor's Assent is withdrawn or not, or is likely to be I cannot tell, having never solicited or even once mention'd it to Lord Dartmouth, being resolved to owe no Obligation on that Account to the Favour of any Minister. If from a Sense of Right, that Instruction should be recall'd and the general Principle on which it was founded is given up, all will be very well: but you can never think it worth while to employ an Agent here if his being paid or not is to depend on the Breath of a Minister, and I should think it a Situation too suspicious and therefore too dishonourable for me to remain in a single Hour. Living frugally I am under no immediate Necessity; and if I serve my Constituents faithfully tho' it should be unsuccessfully I am confident they will always have it in their Inclination and sometime or other in their Power to make their Grants effectual.

A Gentleman of our Province, Capt. Calef, is come hither as an Agent for some of the Eastern Townships to obtain a Confirmation of their Lands. Sir Francis Bernard seems inclin'd to make Use of this Person's Application for promoting a Separation of that Country from your Province and making it a distinct Government, to which purpose he prepared a Draft of a Memorial for Calef to present setting forth not only the hardship of being without Security in the Property of their Improvements, but also the Distress of the People there for want of Government, that they were at too great a Distance from the Seat of Government in the Massachusetts to be capable of receiving the Benefits of Government from thence, and expressing their Willingness to be separated, and form'd into a new Province, &c. With this Draft Sir Francis and Mr. Calef came to me to have my Opinion. I read it, and observ'd to them that tho' I wish'd the People quieted in their Possessions and would do any thing I could to assist in obtaining the Assurance of their Property, yet as I knew the Province of the Massachusetts had a Right to that Country, of which they were justly tenacious, I must oppose that part of the Memorial if it should be presented. Sir Francis allow'd the Right, but propos'd that a great Tract of Land between Merrimack and Connecticut Rivers which had been allotted to Newhampshire might be restord to our Province by order of the Crown, as a Compensation. This he said would be of more Value to us than that Eastern Country, as being nearer home, &c. I said I would mention it in my Letters, but must in the mean time oppose any Step taken in the Affair before the Sentiments of the General Court should be known as to such an Exchange if it were offer'd. Mr. Calef himself did not seem fond of the Draft, and I have not seen him, or heard any thing farther of it since, but I shall watch it.

Be pleased to present my dutiful Respects to the House, and believe me, with sincere and great Esteem, Sir, Your most obedient and most humble Servant.

On the Hutchinson Letters

A Correspondent observes, that the Discovery of Governor Hutchinson's and Oliver's Letters points out an easy Way of re-establishing Peace and Harmony between Great Britain and her Colonies, and consolating the Confidence of the latter, by producing all the confidential Letters received from America in public Affairs, and from public Men. It is in vain to say, this would be betraying private Correspondence, since if the Truth only was written, no Man need be ashamed or afraid of its being known; and if Falshoods have been maliciously covered under the Cloak of Confidence, 'tis perfectly just the incendiary Writers should be exposed and punished. What a weak, what a wicked Plan of Government is that, which, under the Seal of Secrecy, gives Encouragement to every Species of Malice and Misrepresentation. That Government have been deceived almost to the fatal Issue of declaring War against our Colonies is certain; and it is equally certain, that it is in their Power to make an honourable Sacrifice of the wicked Authors of this dangerous Deception.

The Public Advertiser, August 31, 1773

An Infallible Method To Restore Peace and Harmony

To the Printer *of the* Public Advertiser.

Permit me, Sir, to communicate to the Ministry, thro' the Channel of your Paper, an *infallible Method* (and but one) to silence the Clamours of the Americans; to restore Peace and Harmony between the Colonies and the Mother Country; to regain the Affections of the most loyal, and I will venture to say the most virtuous of his Majesty's Subjects, whose Assistance may one Day be necessary to preserve that Freedom, which is the Glory and Happiness of the English Nation, and without which, from the Luxury and Effeminacy which at present reigns so universally among us, is in imminent Danger of being lost forever. The Method is plain and easy: Place the Americans in the same Individual Situation they were in before that di——cal, unconstitutional, oppressive Revenue Act was formed and endeavoured to be carried into Execution by Mr. Grenville; repeal the odious Tax on Tea; supersede the Board of Commissioners; let the Governors and Judges be appointed by the Crown, and paid by the People as usual; recall the Troops, except what are absolutely necessary for the Preservation of the new-acquired Provinces; in fine, put every Thing on its ancient Footing. The Plea of its being dishonourable to give up a Point once determined upon, is vain and nugatory: The Instances are innumerable of Repeals of Acts of Parliament, which, when passed, were thought wise and necessary.—The Stamp Duty for America is a recent Instance in point—Acts of Prerogative are surely not more sacred than Acts of Parliament. I insist upon it, that nothing would redound so much to the Honour of Administration, nothing would convince Mankind that the Intentions of Government are just and equitable, equal to the little Sacrifice of Vanity and the Pride of Power to the general Welfare of the British Empire. It is asserted, that there are Emissaries from France, who endeavour to foment the Difference between Great Britain and her Colonies. Disappoint this subtle and perfidious Nation. I will venture to prophecy, that notwithstanding this little Breach, the Connexion will be as strong, perhaps stronger than ever.

It was always the Boast of the Americans, that they could claim their Original from the Kingdom of Great Britain, and their Joy upon being re-admitted to all the Privileges of Englishmen will operate as a new Cement to a grateful and generous People, which will for ever ensure their future Loyalty and Obedience.

The above is the sincere Opinion of
A Well-Wisher to
Great Britain and her Colonies.

The Public Advertiser, September 8, 1773

FOR THE PUBLIC ADVERTISER
Rules by Which a Great Empire May Be Reduced to a Small One

[Presented privately to a *late Minister*, when he entered upon his Administration; and now first published.]

An ancient Sage valued himself upon this, that tho' he could not fiddle, he knew how to make a *great City* of a *little one*. The Science that I, a modern Simpleton, am about to communicate is the very reverse.

I address myself to all Ministers who have the Management of extensive Dominions, which from their very Greatness are become troublesome to govern, because the Multiplicity of their Affairs leaves no Time for *fiddling*.

I. In the first Place, Gentlemen, you are to consider, that a great Empire, like a great Cake, is most easily diminished at the Edges. Turn your Attention therefore first to your remotest Provinces; that as you get rid of them, the next may follow in Order.

II. That the Possibility of this Separation may always exist, take special Care the Provinces are never incorporated with the Mother Country, that they do not enjoy the same common Rights, the same Privileges in Commerce, and that they are governed by *severer* Laws, all of *your enacting*, without allowing them any Share in the Choice of the Legislators. By carefully making and preserving such Distinctions, you will (to keep to my Simile of the Cake) act like a wise Gingerbread Baker, who, to facilitate a Division, cuts his Dough half through in those Places, where, when bak'd, he would have it *broken to Pieces*.

III. These remote Provinces have perhaps been acquired, purchas'd, or conquer'd, at the *sole Expence* of the Settlers or their Ancestors, without the Aid of the Mother Country. If this should happen to increase her *Strength* by their growing Numbers ready to join in her Wars, her *Commerce* by their growing Demand for her Manufactures, or her *Naval Power* by greater Employment for her Ships and Seamen, they may probably suppose some Merit in this, and that it entitles them to some Favour; you are therefore to *forget it all*, or resent it as if they had done you Injury. If they happen to be zealous Whigs, Friends of Liberty, nurtur'd in Revolution Principles, *remember all that* to their Prejudice, and contrive to punish it: For such Principles, after a Revolution is thoroughly established, are of *no more Use*, they are even *odious* and *abominable*.

IV. However peaceably your Colonies have submitted to your Government, shewn their Affection to your Interest, and patiently borne their Grievances, you are to *suppose* them always inclined to revolt, and treat them accordingly. Quarter Troops among them, who by their Insolence may *provoke* the rising of Mobs, and by their Bullets and Bayonets *suppress* them. By this Means, like the Husband who uses his Wife ill *from Suspicion*, you may in Time convert your *Suspicions* into *Realities*.

V. Remote Provinces must have *Governors*, and *Judges*, to represent the Royal Person, and execute every where the delegated Parts of his Office and Authority. You Ministers know, that much of the Strength of Government depends on the *Opinion* of the People; and much of that Opinion on the Choice of Rulers placed immediately over them. If you send them wise and good Men for Governors, who study the Interest of the Colonists, and advance their Prosperity, they will think their King wise and good, and that he wishes the Welfare of his Subjects. If you send them learned and upright Men for Judges, they will think him a Lover of Justice. This may attach your Provinces more to his Government. You are therefore to be careful who you recommend for those Offices.—If you can find Prodigals who have ruined their Fortunes, broken Gamesters or Stock-Jobbers, these may do well as *Governors*; for they will probably be rapacious, and provoke the People by their Extortions. Wrangling Proctors and petty-fogging Lawyers too are not amiss, for they will be for ever disputing and quarrelling with their little Parliaments. If withal they should be ignorant, wrong-headed and insolent, so much the better. Attorneys Clerks and Newgate Solicitors will do for *Chief-Justices*, especially if they hold their Places *during your Pleasure*:—And all will contribute to impress those ideas of your Government that are proper for a People *you would wish to renounce it*.

VI. To confirm these Impressions, and strike them deeper, whenever the Injured come to the Capital with Complaints of Mal-administration, Oppression, or Injustice, punish such Suitors with long Delay, enormous Expence, and a final Judgment in Favour of the Oppressor. This will have an admirable Effect every Way. The Trouble of future Complaints will be prevented, and Governors and Judges will be encouraged to farther Acts of Oppression and Injustice; and thence the People may become more disaffected, *and at length desperate*.

VII. When such Governors have crammed their Coffers, and made themselves so odious to the People that they can no longer remain among them with Safety to their Persons, recall and *reward* them with Pensions. You may make them *Baronets* too, if that respectable Order should not think fit to resent it. All will contribute to encourage new Governors in the same Practices, and make the supreme Government *detestable*.

VIII. If when you are engaged in War, your Colonies should vie in liberal Aids of Men and Money against the common Enemy, upon your simple Requisition, and give far beyond their Abilities, reflect, that a Penny taken from them by your Power is more honourable to you than a Pound presented by their Benevolence. Despise therefore their voluntary

Grants, and resolve to harrass them with novel Taxes. They will probably complain to your Parliaments that they are taxed by a Body in which they have no Representative, and that this is contrary to common Right. They will petition for Redress. Let the Parliaments flout their Claims, reject their Petitions, refuse even to suffer the reading of them, and treat the Petitioners with the utmost Contempt. Nothing can have a better Effect, in producing the Alienation proposed; for though many can forgive Injuries, *none ever forgave Contempt*.

IX. In laying these Taxes, never regard the heavy Burthens those remote People already undergo, in defending their own Frontiers, supporting their own provincial Governments, making new Roads, building Bridges, Churches and other public Edifices, which in old Countries have been done to your Hands by your Ancestors, but which occasion constant Calls and Demands on the Purses of a new People. Forget the *Restraints* you lay on their Trade for *your own* Benefit, and the Advantage a *Monopoly* of this Trade gives your exacting Merchants. Think nothing of the Wealth those Merchants and your Manufacturers acquire by the Colony Commerce; their encreased Ability thereby to pay Taxes at home; their accumulating, in the Price of their Commodities, most of those Taxes, and so levying them from their consuming Customers: All this, and the Employment and Support of Thousands of your Poor by the Colonists, you are *intirely to forget*. But remember to make your arbitrary Tax more grievous to your Provinces, by public Declarations importing that your Power of taxing them has *no Limits*, so that when you take from them without their Consent a Shilling in the Pound, you have a clear Right to the other nineteen. This will probably weaken every Idea of *Security in their Property*, and convince them that under such a Government *they have nothing they can call their own*; which can scarce fail of producing *the happiest Consequences*!

X. Possibly indeed some of them might still comfort themselves, and say, 'Though we have no Property, we have yet *something* left that is valuable; we have constitutional *Liberty* both of Person and of Conscience. This King, these Lords, and these Commons, who it seems are too remote from us to know us and feel for us, cannot take from us our *Habeas*

Corpus Right, or our Right of Trial *by a Jury of our Neighbours*: They cannot deprive us of the Exercise of our Religion, alter our ecclesiastical Constitutions, and compel us to be Papists if they please, or Mahometans.' To annihilate this Comfort, begin by Laws to perplex their Commerce with infinite Regulations impossible to be remembered and observed; ordain Seizures of their Property for every Failure; take away the Trial of such Property by Jury, and give it to arbitrary Judges of your own appointing, and of the lowest Characters in the Country, whose Salaries and Emoluments are to arise out of the Duties or Condemnations, and whose Appointments are *during Pleasure*. Then let there be a formal Declaration of both Houses, that Opposition to your Edicts is *Treason*, and that Persons suspected of Treason in the Provinces may, according to some obsolete Law, be seized and sent to the Metropolis of the Empire for Trial; and pass an Act that those there charged with certain other Offences shall be sent away in Chains from their Friends and Country to be tried in the same Manner for Felony. Then erect a new Court of Inquisition among them, accompanied by an armed Force, with Instructions to transport all such suspected Persons, to be ruined by the Expence if they bring over Evidences to prove their Innocence, or be found guilty and hanged if they can't afford it. And lest the People should think you cannot possibly go any farther, pass another solemn declaratory Act, that 'King, Lords, and Commons had, hath, and of Right ought to have, full Power and Authority to make Statutes of sufficient Force and Validity to bind the unrepresented Provinces IN ALL CASES WHATSOEVER.' This will include *spiritual* with temporal; and taken together, must operate wonderfully to your Purpose, by convincing them, that they are at present under a Power something like that spoken of in the Scriptures, which can not only *kill their Bodies*, but *damn their Souls* to all Eternity, by compelling them, if it pleases, *to worship the Devil*.

XI. To make your Taxes more odious, and more likely to procure Resistance, send from the Capital a Board of Officers to superintend the Collection, composed of the most *indiscreet, ill-bred* and *insolent* you can find. Let these have large Salaries out of the extorted Revenue, and live in open grating

Luxury upon the Sweat and Blood of the Industrious, whom they are to worry continually with groundless and expensive Prosecutions before the above-mentioned arbitrary Revenue-Judges, all *at the Cost of the Party prosecuted* tho' acquitted, because *the King is to pay no Costs.*—Let these Men *by your Order* be exempted from all the common Taxes and Burthens of the Province, though they and their Property are protected by its Laws. If any Revenue Officers are *suspected* of the least Tenderness for the People, discard them. If others are justly complained of, protect and reward them. If any of the Under-officers behave so as to provoke the People to drub them, promote those to better Offices: This will encourage others to procure for themselves such profitable Drubbings, by mul-tiplying and enlarging such Provocations, and *all with work towards the End you aim at.*

XII. Another Way to make your Tax odious, is to misapply the Produce of it. If it was originally appropriated for the *Defence* of the Provinces and the better Support of Govern-ment, and the Administration of Justice where it may be *nec-essary*, then apply none of it to that *Defence*, but bestow it where it is *not necessary*, in augmented Salaries or Pensions to every Governor who has distinguished himself by his Enmity to the People, and by calumniating them to their Sovereign. This will make them pay it more unwillingly, and be more apt to quarrel with those that collect it, and those that im-posed it, who will quarrel again with them, and all shall con-tribute to your *main Purpose* of making them *weary of your Government.*

XIII. If the People of any Province have been accustomed to support their own Governors and Judges to Satisfaction, you are to apprehend that such Governors and Judges may be thereby influenced to treat the People kindly, and to do them Justice. This is another Reason for applying Part of that Revenue in larger Salaries to such Governors and Judges, given, as their Commissions are, *during your Pleasure* only, forbidding them to take any Salaries from their Prov-inces; that thus the People may no longer hope any Kind-ness from their Governors, or (in Crown Cases) any Justice from their Judges. And as the Money thus mis-applied in one Province is extorted from all, probably *all will resent the Mis-application*.

XIV. If the Parliaments of your Provinces should dare to claim Rights or complain of your Administration, order them to be harass'd with repeated *Dissolutions*. If the same Men are continually return'd by new Elections, adjourn their Meetings to some Country Village where they cannot be accommodated, and there keep them *during Pleasure*; for this, you know, is your PREROGATIVE; and an excellent one it is, as you may manage it, to promote Discontents among the People, diminish their Respect, and *increase their Disaffection*.

XV. Convert the brave honest Officers of your Navy into pimping Tide-waiters and Colony Officers of the Customs. Let those who in Time of War fought gallantly in Defence of the Commerce of their Countrymen, in Peace be taught to prey upon it. Let them learn to be corrupted by great and real Smugglers, but (to shew their Diligence) scour with armed Boats every Bay, Harbour, River, Creek, Cove or Nook throughout the Coast of your Colonies, stop and detain every Coaster, every Wood-boat, every Fisherman, tumble their Cargoes, and even their Ballast, inside out and upside down; and if a Penn'orth of Pins is found un-entered, let the Whole be seized and confiscated. Thus shall the Trade of your Colonists suffer more from their Friends in Time of Peace, than it did from their Enemies in War. Then let these Boats Crews land upon every Farm in their Way, rob the Orchards, steal the Pigs and Poultry, and insult the Inhabitants. If the injured and exasperated Farmers, unable to procure other Justice, should attack the Agressors, drub them and burn their Boats, you are to call this *High Treason* and *Rebellion*, order Fleets and Armies into their Country, and threaten to carry all the Offenders three thousand Miles to be hang'd, drawn and quartered. *O! this will work admirably!*

XVI. If you are told of Discontents in your Colonies, never believe that they are general, or that you have given Occasion for them; therefore do not think of applying any Remedy, or of changing any offensive Measure. Redress no Grievance, lest they should be encouraged to demand the Redress of some other Grievance. Grant no Request that is just and reasonable, lest they should make another that is unreasonable. Take all your Informations of the State of the Colonies from your Governors and Officers in Enmity with them. Encourage and reward these *Leasing-makers*; secrete their lying Accusations lest they should be confuted; but act upon them as the clearest Evidence, and believe nothing you hear from the Friends of the People. Suppose all *their* Complaints to be invented and promoted by a few factious Demagogues, whom if you could catch and hang, all would be quiet. Catch and hang a few of them accordingly; and the *Blood of the Martyrs* shall *work Miracles* in favour of your Purpose.

XVII. If you see *rival Nations* rejoicing at the Prospect of your Disunion with your Provinces, and endeavouring to promote it: If they translate, publish and applaud all the Complaints of your discontented Colonists, at the same Time privately stimulating you to severer Measures; let not that *alarm* or offend you. Why should it? since you all mean *the same Thing*.

XVIII. If any Colony should at their own Charge erect a Fortress to secure their Port against the Fleets of a foreign Enemy, get your Governor to betray that Fortress into your Hands. Never think of paying what it cost the Country, for that would *look*, at least, like some Regard for Justice; but turn it into a Citadel to awe the Inhabitants and curb their Commerce. If they should have lodged in such Fortress the very Arms they bought and used to aid you in your Conquests, seize them all, 'twill provoke like *Ingratitude* added to *Robbery*. One admirable Effect of these Operations will be, to discourage every other Colony from erecting such Defences, and so their and your Enemies may more easily invade them, to the great Disgrace of your Government, and of course *the Furtherance of your Project*.

XIX. Send Armies into their Country under Pretence of protecting the Inhabitants; but instead of garrisoning the Forts on their Frontiers with those Troops, to prevent Incursions, demolish those Forts, and order the Troops into the Heart of the Country, that the Savages may be encouraged to attack the Frontiers, and that the Troops may be protected by the Inhabitants: This will seem to proceed from your Ill will or your Ignorance, and contribute farther to produce and strengthen an Opinion among them, *that you are no longer fit to govern them.*

XX. Lastly, Invest the General of your Army in the Provinces with great and unconstitutional Powers, and free him from the Controul of even your own Civil Governors. Let him have Troops enow under his Command, with all the Fortresses in his Possession; and who knows but (like some provincial Generals in the Roman Empire, and encouraged by the universal Discontent you have produced) he may take it into his Head to set up for himself. If he should, and you have carefully practised these few *excellent Rules* of mine, take my Word for it, all the Provinces will immediately join him, and you will that Day (if you have not done it sooner) get rid of the Trouble of governing them, and all the *Plagues* attending their *Commerce* and Connection from thenceforth and for ever.

Q. E. D.

The Public Advertiser, September 11, 1773

'Tis Never Too Late To Mend

To the Printer *of the* Public Advertiser.

SIR,

I had the Pleasure to read in your Paper of Saturday last some excellent Rules, by which a GREAT EMPIRE may be reduced to a *small One*. They are drawn up in a fine Vein of *Irony*, which is admirably supported throughout.

If the Ministry have any Sense of Shame remaining, they must blush to see their Conduct with respect to America placed in such a striking Point of Ridicule; and the ingenious Author is intitled to the Thanks both of Great Britain and the Colonies for shewing the Absurdity and bad Policy of such Conduct.

To be sensible of Error is one Step towards Amendment;— no Man is infallible; and MINISTERS are but *Men*;—'tis never too late to mend, nor is it any Impeachment of our Understanding to confess that we have been mistaken; for it implies *that we are wiser To-day than we were the Day before*; and surely *Individuals* need not be ashamed publicly to retract an Error, since the LEGISLATURE itself does it every Time that it repeals one of its own Acts.

But though the Americans have long been oppressed, let them not despair. The Administration of the Colonies is no longer in the Hands of a *Shelburne*, a *Clare*, or a *Hillsborough*;—thank Heaven *that* Department is NOW entrusted to an ENGLISHMAN! Be it *his* Glory to *reverse* those baneful and pernicious Measures which have too long harrassed the Colonies, and have given such a Blow to the *Credit*, the *Commerce*, and the NAVAL POWER of the Mother Country.

I am, SIR,

A sincere Well-wisher to

GREAT BRITAIN

and her COLONIES.

The Public Advertiser, September 14, 1773

An Edict by the King of Prussia

For the Public Advertiser.

The SUBJECT of the following Article of

FOREIGN INTELLIGENCE

being exceeding EXTRAORDINARY, is the Reason of its being separated from the usual Articles of *Foreign News*.

Dantzick, September 5.

WE have long wondered here at the Supineness of the English Nation, under the Prussian Impositions upon its Trade entering our Port. We did not till lately know the *Claims*, antient and modern, that hang over that Nation, and therefore could not suspect that it might submit to those Impositions from a Sense of *Duty*, or from Principles of *Equity*. The following *Edict*, just made public, may, if serious, throw some Light upon this Matter.

'FREDERICK, by the Grace of God, King of *Prussia*, &c.

&c. &c. to all present and to come, * HEALTH. The Peace now enjoyed throughout our Dominions, having afforded us Leisure to apply ourselves to the Regulation of Commerce, the Improvement of our Finances, and at the same Time the easing our *Domestic Subjects* in their Taxes: For these Causes, and other good Considerations us thereunto moving, We hereby make known, that after having deliberated these Affairs in our Council, present our dear Brothers, and other great Officers of the State, Members of the same, WE, of our certain Knowledge, full Power and Authority Royal, have made and issued this present Edict, viz.

'WHEREAS it is well known to all the World, that the first German Settlements made in the Island of *Britain*, were by Colonies of People, Subjects to our renowned Ducal Ancestors, and drawn from *their* Dominions, under the Conduct of *Hengist, Horsa, Hella, Uffa, Cerdicus, Ida*, and others; and that the said Colonies have flourished under the Protection of our august House, for Ages past, have never been *emancipated* therefrom, and yet have hitherto yielded little Profit to the same. And whereas We Ourself have in the last War fought for and defended the said Colonies against the Power of *France*, and thereby enabled them to make Conquests from the said Power in *America*, for which we have not yet received adequate Compensation. And whereas it is just and expedient that a Revenue should be raised from the said Colonies in *Britain* towards our Indemnification; and that those who are Descendants of our antient Subjects, and thence still owe us due Obedience, should contribute to the replenishing of our Royal Coffers, as they must have done had their Ancestors remained in the Territories now to us appertaining: WE do therefore hereby ordain and command, That from and after the Date of these Presents, there shall be levied and paid to our Officers of the Customs, on all Goods, Wares and Merchandizes, and on all Grain and other Produce of the Earth exported from the said Island of *Britain*, and on all Goods of whatever Kind imported into the same, a *Duty* of *Four and an Half* per Cent. *ad Valorem*, for the Use of us and our Successors.—And that the said Duty may more effectually be

**A tous presens & à venir.* Orig.

collected, We do hereby ordain, that all Ships or Vessels bound from *Great Britain* to any other Part of the World, or from any other Part of the World to *Great Britain*, shall in their respective Voyages touch at our Port of KONINGSBERG, there to be unladen, searched, and charged with the said Duties.

'AND WHEREAS there have been from Time to Time discovered in the said Island of *Great Britain* by our Colonists there, many Mines or Beds of Iron Stone; and sundry Subjects of our antient Dominion, skilful in converting the said Stone into Metal, have in Times past transported themselves thither, carrying with them and communicating that Art; and the Inhabitants of the said Island, *presuming* that they had a natural Right to make the best Use they could of the natural Productions of their Country for their own Benefit, have not only built Furnaces for smelting the said Stone into Iron, but have erected Plating Forges, Slitting Mills, and Steel Furnaces, for the more convenient manufacturing of the same, thereby endangering a Diminution of the said Manufacture in our antient Dominion. WE *do therefore* hereby farther ordain, that from and after the Date hereof, no Mill or other Engine for Slitting or Rolling of Iron, or any Plating Forge to work with a Tilt-Hammer, or any Furnace for making Steel, shall be erected or continued in the said Island of *Great Britain*: And the Lord Lieutenant of every County in the said Island is hereby commanded, on Information of any such Erection within his County, to order and by Force to cause the same to be abated and destroyed, as he shall answer the Neglect thereof to Us at his Peril.—But We are nevertheless graciously pleased to permit the Inhabitants of the said Island to transport their Iron into *Prussia*, there to be manufactured, and to them returned, they paying our Prussian Subjects for the Workmanship, with all the Costs of Commission, Freight and Risque coming and returning, any Thing herein contained to the contrary notwithstanding.

'WE do not however think fit to extend this our Indulgence to the Article of *Wool*, but meaning to encourage not only the manufacturing of woollen Cloth, but also the raising of Wool in our antient Dominions, and to prevent *both*, as much as may be, in our said Island, We do hereby absolutely forbid the Transportation of Wool from thence even to the Mother Country *Prussia*; and that those Islanders may be farther and more effectually restrained in making any Advantage of their own Wool in the Way of Manufacture, We command that none shall be carried *out of one County into another*, nor shall any Worsted-Bay, or Woollen-Yarn, Cloth, Says, Bays, Kerseys, Serges, Frizes, Druggets, Cloth-Serges, Shalloons, or any other Drapery Stuffs, or Woollen Manufactures whatsoever, made up or mixt with Wool in any of the said Counties, be carried into any other County, or be Water-borne even across the smallest River or Creek, on Penalty of Forfeiture of the same, together with the Boats, Carriages, Horses, &c. that shall be employed in removing them. *Nevertheless* Our loving Subjects there are hereby permitted, (if they think proper) to use all their Wool as *Manure for the Improvement of their Lands*.

'AND WHEREAS the Art and Mystery of making *Hats* hath arrived at great Perfection in *Prussia*, and the making of Hats by our remote Subjects ought to be as much as possible restrained. And forasmuch as the Islanders before-mentioned, being in Possession of Wool, Beaver, and other Furs, have *presumptuously* conceived they had a Right to make some Advantage thereof, by manufacturing the same into Hats, to the Prejudice of our domestic Manufacture, WE do therefore hereby strictly command and ordain, that no Hats or Felts whatsoever, dyed or undyed, finished or unfinished, shall be loaden or put into or upon any Vessel, Cart, Carriage or Horse, to be transported or conveyed *out of one County* in the said Island *into another County*, or to *any other Place whatsoever*, by any Person or Persons whatsoever, on Pain of forfeiting the same, with a Penalty of *Five Hundred Pounds* Sterling for every Offence. Nor shall any Hat-maker in any of the said Counties employ more than two Apprentices, on Penalty of *Five Pounds* Sterling per Month: We intending hereby that such Hat-makers, being so restrained both in the Production and Sale of their Commodity, may find no Advantage in continuing their Business.—But lest the said Islanders should suffer Inconveniency by the Want of Hats, We are farther graciously pleased to permit them to send their Beaver Furs to

Prussia; and We also permit Hats made thereof to be exported from *Prussia* to *Britain*, the People thus favoured to pay all Costs and Charges of Manufacturing, Interest, Commission to Our Merchants, Insurance and Freight going and returning, as in the Case of Iron.

'And lastly, Being willing farther to favour Our said Colonies in *Britain*, We do hereby also ordain and command, that all the Thieves, Highway and Street-Robbers, Housebreakers, Forgerers, Murderers, So——tes, and Villains of every Denomination, who have forfeited their Lives to the Law in *Prussia*, but whom We, in Our great Clemency, do not think fit here to hang, shall be emptied out of our Gaols into the said Island of *Great Britain for the* BETTER PEOPLING *of that Country*.

'We flatter Ourselves that these Our Royal Regulations and Commands will be thought *just* and *reasonable* by Our much-favoured Colonists in *England*, the said Regulations being copied from their own Statutes of 10 and 11 Will. III. C. 10.— 5 Geo. II. C. 22.—23 Geo. II. C. 29.—4 Geo. I. C. 11. and from other equitable Laws made by their Parliaments, or from Instructions given by their Princes, or from Resolutions of both Houses entered into for the GOOD *Government* of their own Colonies in *Ireland* and *America*.

'And all Persons in the said Island are hereby cautioned not to oppose in any wise the Execution of this Our Edict, or any Part thereof, such Opposition being HIGH TREASON, of which all who are *suspected* shall be transported in Fetters from *Britain* to *Prussia*, there to be tried and executed according to the *Prussian Law*.

'Such is our Pleasure.

  'Given at *Potsdam* this twenty-fifth Day of the Month of August, One Thousand Seven Hundred and Seventy-three, and in the Thirty-third Year of our Reign.

'By the KING in his Council.

'RECHTMÆSSIG, *Secr.*'

Some take this Edict to be merely one of the King's *Jeux d'Esprit*: Others suppose it serious, and that he means a Quarrel with England: But all here think the Assertion it concludes with, "that these Regulations are copied from Acts of the English Parliament respecting their Colonies," a very *injurious* one: it being impossible to believe, that a People distinguished for their *Love of Liberty*, a Nation so *wise*, so *liberal in its Sentiments*, so *just and equitable* towards its *Neighbours*, should, from mean and *injudicious* Views of *petty immediate Profit*, treat *its own Children* in a Manner so *arbitrary* and TYRANNICAL!

The Public Advertiser, September 22, 1773

A Chimney-Sweeper's Logic

To the Printer of the Publick Advertizer

Sir

D.E.Q. that is Sir F. Bernard in his long labour'd, and special dull Answer to Q.E.D. endeavours to persuade the King, that as he was his Majesty's Representative, there was a great Similitude in their Characters and Conduct, and that Sir: F.'s Enemies are *Enemies of his Majesty* and of all Government.

This puts one in mind of the Chimney-sweeper condemn'd to be hang'd for Theft, who being charitably visited by a good Clergyman for whom he had work'd, said, *I hope your Honour will take my part, and get a Reprieve for me, and not let my Enemies have their Will; because it is upon your Account that they have prosecuted and sworn against me.* On my Account! How can that be? *Why, Sir, because as how, ever since they knew I was employ'd by your Honour, they resolv'd upon my Ruin: for they are Enemies to all Religion; and they hate you and me and every body in black.*   Z.Z.

after October 30, 1773

Public Statement on the Hutchinson Letters

To the PRINTER of the LONDON CHRONICLE.

SIR,

Finding that two Gentlemen have been unfortunately engaged in a Duel, about a transaction and its circumstances of which both of them are totally ignorant and innocent, I think it incumbent on me to declare (for the prevention of farther mischief, as far as such a declaration may contribute to prevent it) that I alone am the person who obtained and transmitted to Boston the letters in question.—Mr. W. could not communicate them, because they were never in his possession; and, for the same reason, they could not be taken from him by Mr. T.—They were not of the nature of *"private letters between friends:"* They were written by public officers to persons in public station, on public affairs, and intended to procure public measures; they were therefore handed to other public persons who might be influenced by them to produce those measures: Their tendency was to incense the Mother Country against her Colonies, and, by the steps recommended, to widen the breach, which they effected. The chief Caution expressed with regard to Privacy, was, to keep their contents from the *Colony Agents*, who the writers apprehended might return them, or copies of them, to America. That apprehension was, it seems, well founded; for the first Agent who laid his hands on them, thought it his duty to transmit them to his Constituents.

B. FRANKLIN, *Agent for the House of Representatives of the Massachusetts-Bay.*

Craven-street, Dec. 25, 1773.

The London Chronicle, December 25, 1773

On a Proposed Act To Prevent Emigration

To the Printer of the Publick Advertiser

Sir,

You give us in your Paper of Tuesday, the 16th of November, what is called "the Plan of an Act to be proposed at the next Meeting of Parliament to prevent the Emigration of our People." I know not from what Authority it comes, but as it is very circumstantial, I must suppose some such Plan may be really under Consideration, and that this is thrown out to feel the Pulse of the Publick. I shall therefore, with your leave, give my Sentiments of it in your Paper.

During a Century and half that Englishmen have been at Liberty to remove if they pleased to America, we have heard of no Law to restrain that Liberty, and confine them as Prisoners in this Island. Nor do we perceive any ill Effects produced by their Emigration. Our Estates far from diminishing in Value thro' a Want of Tenants, have been in that Period more than doubled; the Lands in general are better cultivated; their increased Produce finds ready Sale at an advanced Price, and the Complaint has for some time been, not that we want Mouths to consume our Meat, but that we want Meat for our Number of Mouths.

Why then is such a restraining Law *now* thought necessary? A Paragraph in the same Paper from the *Edinburgh Courant* may perhaps throw some Light upon this Question. We are there told "that 1500 People have emigrated to America from the Shire of Sutherland within these two Years, and carried with them £7500 Sterling; which exceeds a Years Rent of the whole County; and that the single Consideration of the *Misery* which most of these People *must suffer* in America, independent of the Loss of Men and Money to the Mother Country, should engage the Attention not only of the *landed Interest, but of Administration.*" The humane Writer of this Paragraph, may, I fancy, console himself, with the Reflection, that perhaps the apprehended future Sufferings of those Emigrants will never exist: for that it was probably the authentic Accounts they had received from Friends already settled there, of the Felicity to be enjoyed in that Country, with a thorough Knowledge of their own Misery at home, which induced their Removal. And, as a Politician, he may be comforted by assuring himself, that if they really meet with greater Misery in America, their future Letters lamenting it, will be more credited than the *Edinburgh Courant*, and effectually without a Law put a Stop to the Emigration. It seems some of the Scottish Chiefs, who delight no longer to live upon their Estates in the honourable Independence they were born to, among their respecting Tenants, but chuse rather a Life of Luxury, tho' among the Dependants of a Court, have lately raised their Rents most grievously to support the Expence. The

Consuming of those Rents in London, tho' equally prejudicial to the poor County of *Sutherland*, no Edinburgh Newspaper complains of; but now that the oppressed Tenants take Flight and carry with them what might have supported the Landlords London Magnificence, he begins to *feel* for the MOTHER-COUNTRY, and its enormous *Loss* of £7500 carried to her Colonies! *Administration* is called upon to remedy the Evil, by another Abridgement of ENGLISH LIBERTY. And surely Administration should do something for these Gentry, as they do any thing for Administration.

But is there not an easier Remedy? Let them return to their Family Seats, live among their People, and instead of fleecing and skinning, patronize and cherish them; promote their Interest, encourage their Industry, and make their Situation comfortable. If the poor Folks are happier at home than they can be abroad, they will not lightly be prevailed with to cross the Ocean. But can their Lord blame them for leaving home in search of better Living, when he first sets them the Example?

I would consider the proposed Law,

1st. As to the NECESSITY of it.

2dly. The PRACTICABILITY.

3dly. The POLICY, if practicable.

and 4thly. The JUSTICE of it.

Pray spare me room for a few Words on each of these Heads.

1ST. As to the *Necessity* of it.

If any Country has more People than can be comfortably subsisted in it, some of those who are incommoded, may be induced to emigrate. As long as the new Situation shall be *far* preferable to the old, the Emigration may possibly continue. But when many of those who at home interfered with others of the same Rank, (in the Competition for Farms, Shops, Business, Offices, and other Means of Subsistence) are gradually withdrawn, the Inconvenience of that Competition ceases; the Number remaining no longer half starve each other, they find they can now subsist comfortably, and tho' perhaps not quite so well as those who have left them, yet the inbred Attachment to a native Country is sufficient to overbalance a moderate Difference, and thus the Emigration ceases naturally. The Waters of the Ocean may move in Currents from one Quarter of the Globe to another, as they happen in some places to be accumulated and in others diminished; but no Law beyond the Law of Gravity, is necessary to prevent their Abandoning any Coast entirely. Thus the different Degrees of Happiness of different Countries and Situations find or rather make their Level by the flowing of People from one to another, and where that Level is once found, the Removals cease. Add to this, that even a real Deficiency of People in any Country occasioned by a wasting War or Pestilence, is speedily supply'd by earlier and of course more prolific Marriages, encouraged by the greater Facility of obtaining the Means of Subsistence. So that a Country half depopulated would soon be repeopled, till the Means of Subsistence were equalled by the Population. All Encrease beyond that Point must perish, or flow off into more favourable Situations. Such Overflowings there have been of Mankind in all Ages, or we should not now have had so many Nations. But to apprehend absolute Depopulation from that Cause, and call for a Law to prevent it, is calling for a Law to stop the Thames, lest its Waters, by what leave it daily at Gravesend, should be quite exhausted. Such a Law therefore I do not conceive to be *Necessary*.

2dly. As to the *Practicability*.

When I consider the Attempts of this kind that have been made, first in the time of Archbishop Laud, by Orders of Council, to stop the Puritans who were flying from his Persecutions, into New-England, and next by Louis XIV, to retain in his Kingdom the persecuted Huguenots; and how ineffectual all the Power of our Crown, with which the Archbishop armed himself, and all the more absolute Power of that great French Monarch, were, to obtain the End for which they were exerted. When I consider too, the extent of Coast to be guarded, and the Multitude of Cruizers necessary effectually to make a Prison of the Island for this confinement of free Englishmen, who naturally love Liberty, and would probably by the very Restraint be more stimulated to break thro' it, I cannot but think such a Law IMPRACTICABLE. The

Offices would not be applied to for Licences, the Ports would
not be used for Embarcation. And yet the People disposed to
leave us would, as the Puritans did, get away by Shipfuls.

3dly. As to the *Policy* of the Law.

Since, as I have shewn, there is no Danger of depopulating
Britain, but that the Places of those who depart will soon be
filled up equal to the Means of obtaining a Livelihood, let us
see whether there are not some general *Advantages* to be expected from the present Emigration. The new Settlers in
America, finding plenty of Subsistence, and Land easily acquired whereon to seat their Children, seldom postpone Marriage thro' fear of Poverty. Their natural Increase is therefore
in a proportion far beyond what it would have been if they
had remained here. New Farms are daily every where forming
in those immense Forests, new Towns and Villages rising;
hence a growing Demand for our Merchandise, to the greater
Employment of our Manufacturers and the enriching of our
Merchants. By this natural Increase of People, the Strength of
the Empire is increased; Men are multiplied out of whom
new Armies may be formed on Occasion, or the old recruited.
The long extended Sea Coast too, of that vast Country, the
great maritime Commerce of its Parts with each other, its
many navigable Rivers and Lakes, and its plentiful Fisheries,
breed multitudes of Seamen, besides those created and supported by its Voyages to Europe; a thriving Nursery this, for
the manning of our Fleets in time of War, and maintaining
our Importance among foreign Nations, by that Navy which
is also our best Security against invasions from our Enemies.
An Extension of Empire by Conquest of inhabited Countries
is not so easily obtained, it is not so easily secured, it alarms
more the neighbouring States, it is more subject to Revolts,
and more apt to occasion new Wars. The Increase of Dominion by Colonies proceeding from yourselves, and by the natural Growth of your own People, cannot be complained of
by your Neighbours as an Injury, none have a right to be
offended with it. Your new Possessions are therefore more
secure, they are more cheaply gained, they are attached to
your Nation by natural Alliance and Affection, and thus they
afford an additional Strength more certainly to be depended

on, than any that can be acquired by a Conquering Power, tho' at an immense Expence of Blood and Treasure. These methinks are national Advantages that more than equiponderate with the Inconveniencies suffered by a few Scotch or Irish Landlords, who perhaps may only find it necessary to abate a little of their present Luxury, or of those advanced Rents they now so unfeelingly demand. From these Considerations, I think I may conclude that the restraining Law proposed, would if practicable be IMPOLITIC.

4thly. As to the *Justice* of it.

I apprehend that every Briton who is made unhappy at home, has a Right to remove from any Part of his King's Dominions into those of any other Prince where he can be happier. If this should be denied me, at least it will be allowed that he has a Right to remove into any other Part of the same Dominions. For by this Right so many Scotchmen remove into England, easing their own Country of its supernumeraries, and benefitting ours by their Industry. And this is the Case with those who go to America. Will not these Scottish Lairds be satisfied unless a Law passes to pin down all Tenants to the Estate they are born on, (*adscriptitii glebae*) to be bought and sold with it? God has given to the Beasts of the Forest and to the Birds of the Air a Right when their Subsistence fails in one Country, to migrate into another, where they can get a more comfortable Living; and shall Man be denyed a Privilege enjoyed by Brutes, merely to gratify a few avaricious Landlords? Must Misery be made *permanent*, and suffered by *many* for the Emolument of One? While the Increase of Human Beings is prevented, and thousands of their Offspring stifled as it were in the Birth, that this petty Pharaoh may enjoy an *Excess* of Opulence? God commands to increase and replenish the Earth: The proposed Law would forbid increasing, and confine Britons to their present Number, keeping half that Number too, in wretchedness. The Common People of Britain and of Ireland, contributed by the Taxes they paid, and by the Blood they lost, to the Success of that War, which brought into our Hands the vast unpeopled Territories of North America; a Country favoured by Heaven with all the Advantages of Soil and Climate;

Germans are now pouring into it, to take Possession of it, and fill it with their Posterity; and shall Britons, and Irelanders, who have a much better Right to it, be forbidden a Share of it, and instead of enjoying there the Plenty and Happiness that might reward their Industry, be compelled to remain here in Poverty and Misery? Considerations such as these persuade me, that the proposed Law would be both UNJUST and INHUMAN.

If then it is *unnecessary*, *impracticable*, *impolitic*, and *unjust*, I hope our Parliament will never receive the Bill, but leave Landlords to their own Remedy, an Abatement of Rents and Frugality of Living; and leave the Liberties of Britons and Irishmen at least as extensive as it found them. I am, Sir, Yours &c.

A Friend to the Poor.

December? 1773

On Franklin's Ingratitude

To the Printer of the Public Advertiser

Sir

Your Correspondent Brittanicus inveighs violently against Dr: Franklin for his Ingratitude to the Ministry of this Nation, who have conferred upon him so many Favours. They gave him the Post Office of America; they made his Son a Governor; and they offer'd him a Post of five hundred a Year in the Salt Office, if he would relinquish the Interests of his Countrey; but he has had the Wickedness to continue true to it, and is as much an American as ever. As it is a settled Point in Government here, that every Man has his Price, 'tis plain they are Bunglers in their Business, and have not given him enough. Their Master has as much reason to be angry with them as Rodrigue in the Play, with his Apothecary for not effectually poisoning Pandolpho, and they must probably make use of the Apothecary's Justification; Viz.

Scene 4th

Rodrigue and *Fell* the Apothecary.

Rodrigue. You promised to have this Pandolpho upon his Bier in less than a Week; 'Tis more than a Month since, and he still walks and stares me in the Face.

Fell. True: and yet I have done my best Endeavours. In various Ways I have given the Miscreant as much Poison as would have kill'd an Elephant. He has swallow'd Dose after Dose; far from hurting him, he seems the better for it. He hath a wonderfully strong Constitution. I find I cannot kill him but by cutting his Throat, and that, as I take it, is not my Business.

Rodrigue. Then it must be mine.

before January 31, 1774

"A War It Will Be"

To the Printer of the Publick Ledger

Sir,

Nothing can equal the present Rage of our Ministerial Writers against our Brethren in America, who have the Misfortune to be *Whigs* in a Reign when *Whiggism* is out of Fashion, who are besides Protestant Dissenters and Lovers of Liberty. One may easily see from what Quarter comes the Abuse of those People in the Papers; their Struggle for their Rights is called REBELLION, and the People REBELS; while those who really rebell'd in Scotland (1745) for the Expulsion of the present reigning Family, and the Establishment of Popery and arbitrary Power on the Ruins of Liberty and Protestantism; who enter'd England, and trampled on its Belly as far as Derby, to the Astonishment of this great City and shaking the publick Credit of the Nation; have now all their Sins forgiven on Account of their modish Principles, and are called not *Rebels*, but by the softer Appellation of *Insurgents*!

These angry Writers use their utmost Efforts to persuade us that this War with the Colonies (for a War it will be) is a *national* Cause when in fact it is merely a *ministerial* one. Administration wants an American Revenue to dissipate in Corruption. The Quarrel is about a paltry threepenny Duty on Tea. There is no real Clashing of Interests between Britain and America. Their Commerce is to their mutual Advantage, or rather most to the Advantage of Britain, which finds a vast Market in America for its Manufactures; and *as good Pay*, I speak from Knowledge, as in any Country she trades to upon the Face of the Globe. But the Fact needs not my Testimony, it speaks for it self; for if we could elsewhere get better Pay and better Prices, we should not send our Goods to America. The gross Calumniators of that People, who want us to imbrue our Hands in Brother's Blood, have the Effrontery to tell the World that the Americans associated in Resolutions not to pay us what they ow'd us unless we re-peal'd the Stamp Act. This is an INFAMOUS FALSHOOD; they know it to be such. I call upon the Incendiaries who have advanc'd it, to produce their Proofs. Let them name any two that enter'd into such an Association, or any one that made such a Declaration. Absurdity marks the very Face of this Lie. Every one acquainted with Trade knows, that a credited Merchant daring to be concern'd in such an Association, could never expect to be trusted again. His Character on the Exchange of London would be ruined forever. The great Credit given them since that time, nay the present Debt due from them, is itself a Proof of the Confidence we have in their Probity.

Another villainous Falshood advanc'd against the Ameri-cans is, that tho' we have been at such Expence in protecting them, they refuse to contribute their Part to the publick gen-eral Expence of the Empire. The Fact is, that *they never did refuse a Requisition of that kind*. A Writer who calls himself *Sagittarius* (I suppose from his flinging about, like Solomon's Fool, Firebrands, *Arrows* and Death) in the Ledger of March 9. asserts that the "Experiment has been tried and that they did not think it expedient to return even an Answer." How does he prove this? Why, "the Colony Agents were told by Mr. Grenville, that a Revenue *would be* required from them to defray the Expences of their Protection." But was the Requisition ever made? Were circular Letters ever sent by his Majesty's Command from the Secretary of State to the several Colony Governments, according to the establish'd Custom, stating the Occasion, and requiring such Supplies as were suitable to their Abilities and Loyalty? And did they then re-fuse not only Compliance but an Answer? No such Matter. Agents are not the Channel thro' which Requisitions are made. If they were told by Mr. Grenville that a "Revenue *would be* required, and yet the Colonies made no Offer, no Grant nor laid any Tax," Does it follow they would not have done it if they had been required? Probably they thought it time enough when the *Requisition* should come, and in fact it never appeared there to this day. In the last War they all gave so liberally, that we thought ourselves bound in honour to return them a Million. But We are disgusted with their Free Gifts; we want to have something that is obtain'd by Force; like a mad Landlord who should refuse the willing Payment of his full Rents, and chuse to take less by way of Robbery.

This shameless Writer, would cajole the People of England, with the Fancy of their being Kings of America, and that their Honour is at Stake by the Americans disputing *their* Government. He thrusts us into the Throne cheek-by-Jole with Majesty, and would have us talk as he writes, of *our* Subjects in America, and *our* Sovereignty over America. Forgetting that the Americans are Subjects of the King, not *our* Subjects, but our *Fellow-Subjects*; and that they have Parliaments of their own, with the Right of granting their own Money by their own Representatives, which we cannot deprive them of but by Violence and Injustice.

Having by a Series of iniquitous and irritating Measures provoked a loyal People almost to Desperation, we now magnify every Act of an American Mob, into REBELLION, tho' the Government there disapprove it and order Prosecution, as is now the Case with regard to the Tea destroyed: And we talk of nothing but Troops and Fleets, and Force, of blocking up Ports, destroying Fisheries, abolishing Charters, &c. &c. Here Mobs of English Sawyers can burn Sawmills; Mobs of English Labourers destroy or plunder Magazines of Corn; Mobs of English Coalheavers attack Houses with Fire Arms; English Smuglers can fight regularly the King's Cruizing Vessels, drive them ashore and burn them, as lately on the Coast of Wales, and on the Coast of Cornwall; but upon these Accounts we hear no Talk of England's being in *Rebellion*; no Threats of taking away its Magna Charta, or repealing its Bill of Rights; For we well know that the Operations of a Mob are often unexpected, sudden, and soon over, so that the Civil

Power can seldom prevent or suppress them, not being able to come in before they have dispers'd themselves: And therefore it is not always accountable for their Mischiefs.

Surely the great Commerce of this Nation with the Americans is of too much Importance to be risk'd in a Quarrel which has no Foundation but ministerial Pique and Obstinacy! To us, in the Way of Trade, comes now, and has long come, all the superlucration arising from their Labour. But Will Our reviling them as Cheats, Hypocrites, Scoundrels, Traitors, Cowards, Tyrants, &c. according to the present Court Mode in all our Papers, make them more our Friends, more fond of our Merchandize? Did ever any Tradesman succeed who attempted to drub Customers into his Shop? And Will honest JOHN BULL the Farmer be long satisfy'd with Servants that before his Face attempt to kill his *Plow-Horses*?

A LONDONER.

after March 9, 1774

An Open Letter to Lord North

For the Public Advertiser.
To Lord NORTH.

My LORD,

All your small Politicians, who are very numerous in the English Nation, from the patriotic Barber to the patriotic Peer, when big with their Schemes for the Good of poor Old England, imagine they have a Right to give Advice to the Minister, and condemn Administration if they do not adopt their Plan. I, my Lord, who have no mean Opinion of my Abilities, which is justified by the Attention that is paid to me when I harangue at the Smyrna and Old Slaughter's, am willing to contribute my Mite to the public Welfare; and have a Proposal to make to your Lordship, which I flatter myself will be approved of by the Ministry, and if carried into Execution, will quiet all the Disturbances in America, procure a decent Revenue from our Colonies, make our royal Master (at least there) a King *de facto*, as well as *de jure*; and finally, as it may be managed, procure a round Sum towards discharging the national Debt.

My Scheme is, without Delay to introduce into North America a Government absolutely and entirely Military. The Opposition which some People suspect would be made by the Colonies, is a mere Bugbear: The Sight of a few Regiments of bold Britons, appearing with Ensigns displayed, and in all the Pomp of War, a Specimen of which may be seen every Summer at the Grand Review on Wimbledon Common, with that great Commander G——l G——e at their Head, accompanied with a Detachment from the Artillery, and Half a Dozen short Sixes, would so intimidate the Americans, that the General might march through the whole Continent of North America, and would have little else to do but to accept of the Submission of the several Towns as he passed. But as the Honour would be too great for one Man to reduce to absolute Subjection so great an Extent of Territory, I would propose that a separate Command be given to L——d G—— G——e, who by his animated Speeches in the House, and coinciding so entirely with your Lordship's Opinion on the proper Methods for humbling America, deserves a Share in the Fame of such a grand Exploit. Let him have one half of the Army under his Direction, and march from New York to South Carolina. No one can object to the Nomination, as his Military Prowess is upon Record. The Regiments that are in America, with those who are about to embark, will be amply sufficient, without being at the Expence of sending more Troops. Those who served in America the last War, know that the Colonists are a dastardly Set of Poltroons; and though they are descended from British Ancestors, they are degenerated to such a Degree, that one born in Britain is equal to twenty Americans. The Yankey Doodles have a Phrase when they are not in a Humour for fighting, which is become proverbial, *I don't feel bould To-day.* When they make this Declaration, there is no prevailing on them to attack the Enemy or defend themselves. If contrary to Expectation they should attempt an Opposition, procure Intelligence when it happens not to be their fighting Day, attack them and they will fly like Sheep pursued by a Wolf. When all North America have thus bent their Neck to the Yoke designed for them, I would propose that the Method made use of by the Planters in the West Indies may be adopted, who appoint what they call a Negro Driver, who is chosen from among the Slaves. It is observed that the little Authority that is given him over his Fellow Slaves, attaches him to his Master's Interest, and his Cruelty would be without Bounds were he not restrained; but the Master is certain, that the utmost Exertion of Strength will be exacted by this cruel Task-master for the Proprietor's Emolument. Let all the Colonists be enrolled in the Militia, subject of course to Martial Law. Appoint a certain Number of Officers from among the conquered People, with good Pay, and other Military Emoluments; they will secure their Obedience in the District where they command. Let no other Courts be allowed through the whole Continent but Courts Martial. An Inhabitant, who disobeys an Order, may by a Court Martial be sentenced to receive from One Hundred to a Thousand Lashes in a frosty Morning, according to the Nature of his Offence. Where Punishment is thus secure, this Advantage will accrue, that there will not be the same Necessity of hanging up so many poor Devils as in this free Country; by which Means the Service of many an able Man is lost to the Community. I humbly propose that the General and Commander in Chief be vested with the Power, and called by the Name of the King's Viceroy of all North America. This will serve to impress the Americans with greater Respect for the first Magistrate, and have a Tendency to secure their Submission. All Orders issuing from this supreme Authority to have the Force of Laws. After this happy Change of Government, how easy to collect what Taxes you please in North America. When the Colonists are drained of their last Shilling, suppose they should be sold to the best Bidder. As they lie convenient for France or Spain, it may be reasonably expected one of those little Powers would be a Purchaser. I think Spain is to be preferred, as their Power hath more of the Ready than France. I will venture a Conjecture, that the Ministry might get at least Two Millions for the Soil, and the People upon it. With such a Sum what glorious Things might he not atchieve! Suppose it should be applied towards the Payment of one hundredth Part of the National Debt, I would give him an Opportunity of drawing down upon him the Blessing of the Poor by making him to take off the Halfpenny Duty on Porter. Considering the probable Stability of the present Ministry, this Honour may be reserved for your Lordship.

My Lord, excuse the Crudity of these indigested Hints, which your Wisdom is so capable of improving; and believe me, with infinite Respect,

Your Lordship's
Most obedient
Humble Servant,
A Friend to Military Government.

Smyrna Coffee-House, April 5.

The Public Advertiser, April 15, 1774

A Method of Humbling Rebellious American Vassals

To the Printer of the Public Advertiser.

SIR,

Permit me, thro' the Channel of your Paper, to convey to the Premier, by him to be laid before his Mercenaries, our Constituents, my own Opinion, and that of many of my Brethren, Freeholders of this imperial Kingdom of the most feasible Method of humbling our rebellious Vassals of North America. As we have declared by our Representatives that we are the supreme Lords of their Persons and Property, and their occupying our Territory at such a remote Distance without a proper Controul from us, except at a very great Expence, encourages a mutinous Disposition, and may, if not timely prevented, dispose them in perhaps less than a Century to deny our Authority, slip their Necks out of the Collar, and from being Slaves set up for Masters, more especially when it is considered that they are a robust, hardy People, encourage early Marriages, and their Women being amazingly prolific, they must of consequence in 100 Years be very numerous, and of course be able to set us at Defiance. Effectually to prevent which, as we have an undoubted Right to do, it is humbly proposed, and we do hereby give it as Part of our Instructions to our Representatives, that a Bill be brought in and passed, and Orders immediately transmitted to G——l G——e, our Commander in Chief in North America, in consequence of it, that all the Males there be c—st—ed. He may make a Progress thro' the several Towns of North America at the Head of five Battalions, which we hear our experienced Generals, who have been consulted, think sufficient to subdue America if they were in open Rebellion; for who can resist the intrepid Sons of Britain, the Terror of France and Spain, and the Conquerors of America in Germany. Let a Company of Sowgelders, consisting of 100 Men, accompany the Army. On their Arrival at any Town or Village, let Orders be given that on the blowing of the Horn all the Males be assembled in the Market Place. If the Corps are Men of Skill and Ability in their Profession, they will make great Dispatch, and retard but very little the Progress of the Army. There may be a Clause in the Bill to be left at the Discretion of the General, whose Powers ought to be very extensive, that the most notorious Offenders, such as Hancock, Adams, &c. who have been the Ringleaders in the Rebellion of our Servants, should be shaved quite close. But that none of the Offenders may escape in the Town of Boston, let all the Males there suffer the latter Operation, as it will be conformable to the modern Maxim that is now generally adopted by our worthy Constituents, that it is better that ten innocent Persons should suffer than that one guilty should escape. It is true, Blood will be shed, but probably not many Lives lost. Bleeding to a certain Degree is salutary. The English, whose Humanity is celebrated by all the World, but particularly by themselves, do not desire the Death of the Delinquent, but his Reformation. The Advantages arising from this Scheme being carried into Execution are obvious. In the Course of fifty Years it is probable we shall not have one rebellious Subject in North America. This will be laying the Axe to the Root of the Tree. In the mean time a considerable Expence may be saved to the Managers of the Opera, and our Nobility and Gentry be entertained at a cheaper Rate by the fine Voices of our own C—st—i, and the Specie remain in the Kingdom, which now, to an enormous Amount, is carried every Year to Italy. It might likewise be of Service to our Levant Trade, as we could supply the Grand Signor's Seraglio, and the Harams of the Grandees of the Turkish Dominions with Cargos of Eunuchs, as also with handsome Women, for which America is as famous as Circassia. I could enumerate many other Advantages. I shall mention but one: It would effectually put a Stop to the Emigrations from this Country now grown so very fashionable.

No Doubt you will esteem it expedient that this useful Project shall have an early Insertion, that no Time may be lost in carrying it into Execution.

I am, Mr. Printer,

> (For myself, and in Behalf of a Number
> of independent Freeholders of Great Britain)
> Your humble Servant,
> A FREEHOLDER OF OLD SARUM.

The Public Advertiser, May 21, 1774

An Act for the More Effectual Keeping of the Colonies Dependent

All the Printers of News Papers in the British Colonies, are requested to publish the following Act of Parliament; which it is said, will be passed the End of the present Session, or the Beginning of the next.

"An Act for the more effectual keeping of his Majesty's American Colonies dependent on the Crown of Great-Britain, and to enforce their Obedience to all such Acts of Parliament as may be necessary for that Purpose."

WHEREAS it is found by experience that Colonies which are planted by Governments, or otherwise dependent on them, do at some time or other, form themselves into unwarrantable and rebellious Associations, and by their perseverance therein, entirely throw off their dependence and subjection to such Parent State: And whereas the British Plantations, in America, have of late, discovered a disposition to follow the same steps, and, in all likelihood, will, if not speedily prevented, form themselves into a separate and independent Government, to the great detriment of the other parts of the British Empire, to the dishonour of his Majesty, and to the prejudice of the trade of this Kingdom in particular: *And whereas the great* ENCREASE *of People, in said Colonies, has an immediate tendency to produce this effect*—To the end therefore that such evil designs may not be carried into execution, and that the said Colonies and Plantations may be, at all times hereafter, kept in due subordination to the authority of the British Parliament, Be it enacted by the King's most excellent Majesty, by, and with the advice and consent of the Lords spiritual and temporal, and Commons in this present Parliament assembled, and by authority of the same.

1. That no person whatever who shall, from and after the passing of this Act, transport him or herself, from the Kingdoms of Great-Britain and Ireland, or the Islands thereunto belonging, to any of his Majesty's Plantations in America, with intent to settle and dwell therein for any *longer* time than the space of seven years, shall presume to depart from the said Kingdoms, until he or she, so transporting him or herself, shall pay, at the Custom-House of the Port, from which such vessel shall take out her clearance, the sum of Fifty Pounds, sterling money of Great-Britain: And be it further enacted that for every child, or servant, which shall be so transported by the parent, or master, the like sum of Fifty Pounds shall be paid in manner aforesaid.—And be it further enacted by the authority aforesaid, that if any person shall transport him, or herself, or procure themselves to be transported, contrary to this Act, every person, so offending, shall be adjudged guilty of felony without benefit of clergy—and that the Captain of the vessel, in which such person shall be so transported, contrary to this Act, shall forfeit and pay, for any such person, the sum of £.500 sterling money aforesaid.

2. And be it further enacted by the authority aforesaid, that if any person, who shall transport him, or herself, from the Kingdoms aforesaid, to any of his Majesty's Plantations, in America, with intent to stay and dwell therein, for any space of time *less* than seven years, shall nevertheless stay, dwell, and abide therein, beyond the said space of seven years, such person so staying, dwelling, and abiding, in any of his Majesty's

Plantations, in America, shall be adjudged guilty of felony without benefit of clergy.

3. Provided always, and be it further enacted, that nothing in this Act shall extend, or be construed to extend to his Majesty's Governors of the said Plantations, or to any other person, or persons, in the actual service and employ of his Majesty, as aforesaid.

4. And be it further enacted by the authority aforesaid, that all Marriages in his Majesty's said Plantations shall be performed in consequence of a Licence from the Governor where such Marriage shall be celebrated, for which Licence the sum of Twenty Pounds shall be paid, and no more, and that all Marriages had without such Licence, shall be void in law to every intent and purpose whatever.

5. And be it further enacted, that on the birth of every male child, the sum of Fifteen Pounds, and on the birth of every female child, the sum of Ten Pounds sterling money shall be paid to the Governor of the Colony or Plantation in which such children shall be born.

6. And be it further enacted by the authority aforesaid, that on the birth of every bastard child in any of his Majesty's said Plantations, the sum of Fifty Pounds sterling money shall be paid by the *Mother* of such bastard child, to the Governor where such bastard child shall happen to be born, and that in case any person, shall hereafter, either with malice prepense, or otherwise kill or destroy any child or children; such killing or destroying shall not henceforth be deemed or adjudged to be murder in any Court or Courts, nor shall such killing be punished in any way or manner whatever.

7. Provided always, and it is hereby further enacted, that nothing in this Act shall extend to make any such killing legal, or justifiable, if the child, so killed or destroyed, be above the age of twelve months, but that every such killing and destroying shall be punished as heretofore, any thing in this Act to the contrary in any wise notwithstanding.

8. And be it further enacted by the authority aforesaid, that from and after the   Day of   in the year   upon the exportation of each and every barrel of FLOUR from any of his Majesty's said Plantations to any port or place beyond the sea, a duty of *Five Shillings* sterling shall be paid to the

Custom-House of the respective Colony, from which such FLOUR shall be so shipped or exported.

9. And be it further enacted, that on the exportation of any WHEAT from his Majesty's said Plantations to any port or place beyond the sea, a duty of *Two Shillings* sterling per *bushel* shall be paid as aforesaid, for every quantity which shall be so shipped or exported. And that if any person, shall export any wheat or flour contrary to the directions of this Act, all such wheat or flour, together with the ship in which it is exported as aforesaid, shall be seized and forfeited to the use of his Majesty, and condemned in any of his Majesty's Courts of Admiralty where such vessel shall happen to be seized as aforesaid.

10. Provided always, and be it further enacted, that if any such flour or wheat, which shall be exported from any of his Majesty's said Plantations, and carried to any port of Great-Britain, with design to re-ship the same to any other port or place beyond the sea, there shall be allowed upon every barrel of flour so re-shipped, a bounty of Two Shillings and Six Pence sterling, and for every bushel of wheat, a bounty of One Shilling sterling.

11. And be it further enacted by the authority aforesaid, that the duties imposed by this Act, shall be applied towards RAISING A REVENUE the better to ENABLE his MAJESTY to BUILD FORTS and to GARRISON the same, and to support and maintain such a REGULAR and STANDING ARMY in the said PLANTATIONS, as shall be sufficient to enforce the EXECUTION of all such Acts of the BRITISH PARLIAMENT, as are already passed, or may hereafter be passed, relative to the said AMERICAN COLONIES.

The Pennsylvania Journal, June 29, 1774, supplement

An Imaginary Speech

To the Printer of the Public Advertiser.

SIR,

In a late Debate, a certain North British Colonel thought proper to recommend himself to the Court, by grossly abusing the Americans. I send you the Answer I should have made to him had I been present when he uttered his Invective, and I rely upon it, that you will shew that Candour and Justice to America which is refused in certain great Assemblies, and not condemn them without a Hearing.

Mr. Sp——r, Sir,

I am an American: In that Character I trust this House will shew some little Indulgence to the Feelings which are excited by what fell this Moment from an honourable and military Gentleman under the Gallery. According to him, Sir, the Americans are unequal to the People of this Country in Devotion to Women, and in Courage, and in what, in his Sight seems worse than all, they are religious.

No one, Sir, feels the Odiousness of Comparisons more than myself. But I am necessitated to pursue, in some measure, the Path which the honourable Gentleman has marked out. Sir, let the rapid Increase and Population of America, compared with the Decrease of England and of Scotland, shew which of the two People are most effectually devoted to the Fair Sex. The Americans are content to leave with that honourable Gentleman and his Companions the Boast, while the Fact is evidently with them. They are sensible, that upon this Subject to talk much, and to do little, are inseparable.

Sir, I am at a Loss to conceive upon what Facts the Gentleman grounds his Impeachment of American Courage. Is it upon the Capture of Louisbourg, and the Conquest of Nova Scotia in the War before the last? Is it upon their having alone taken Crown Point from the French Regulars, and made their General Prisoner, or from their having covered the Retreat of the British Regulars, and saved them from utter Destruction in the Expeditions under Braddock, and to Fort Pitt?

Sir, it happens very unfortunately that the Regulars have impressed the Provincials with a very indifferent Opinion of their Courage. I will tell you why. They saw General Braddock at the Head of a regular Army march with a Thousand Boastings of their Courage and Superiority, and expressing the most sovereign Contempt of the Virginian Provincials who accompanied him. But in a little Time these vain Boasters were totally routed by a very unequal Number of French and Indians, and the Provincials rendered them the unthanked Service of saving them from being cut off to a Man. In the same Manner a Detachment of Highlanders, under a Major Grant, accompanied by the Virginians under Major Lewis, being attacked by the Indians, the Highlanders fled immediately, and left the Provincials to retreat and cover them. They saw several Campaigns of shameful Defeats, or as shameful Inactivity: Till at length the all-pervading Spirit of one great Officer, and the cautious Abilities of another, redeemed the British Name, and led her Sons to Conquest. The Expedition under Colonel Bouquet, assisted by a large Body of Provincials, owed its Success chiefly to those Provincials. I speak it from that brave Officer's own Letters. It was Wolfe, Amherst and Bouquet who roused the Spirit of the Regulars, and led them to Glory and Success; and I am proud to say, Sir, these are not the Men who traduce the Americans, or speak slightly of their Services; nay more, Sir, the Men who disgraced the Regulars are those only who defame the Provincials. But why should any Gentleman talk in general Terms of their wanting Spirit? Indiscriminate Accusations against the Absent are cowardly Calumnies. Will the Gentleman come to Particulars? Will he name the American he has insulted with Impunity? Who is the provincial Officer who turned his Back in the Day of Battle? There is hardly a Day or an Hour, in which the Honourable Gentleman does not meet with an American. Does he insult any one of them with Impunity? Has he, or will he put their Spirit to the Proof? Till he has done that, Silence, I am sure, will do more Honour to his own.

The Honourable Gentleman says, the Regulars treated the Provincials *as Beasts of Burthen*. There are many of the Provincial Officers in this Town: I have the Honour of knowing them; and I can assure this House, that no Man living would say as much to their Face with Impunity. The Americans, Sir, are well satisfied, that the Ministry intend to make Beasts of Burthen of them. They tell you, however, they will not be Hewers of Wood and Drawers of Water for any Men upon Earth: The Object of this Motion is to compel them. It is my Duty to say, they will and ought to resist such an Attempt; and that if I were there, I should do it without a Moment's Hesitation.

I had almost forgot the Honourable Gentleman's Charge

of their being too religious. Sir, they were such Religionists, that vindicated this Country from the Tyranny of the Stuarts. Perhaps the Honourable Gentleman may have some compassionate Feelings for that unhappy Family: Does that sharpen his Resentment against the Americans; who inherit from those Ancestors, not only the same Religion, but the same Love of Liberty and Spirit to defend it?

The Public Advertiser, February 7, 1775

A Dialogue Between Britain, France, Spain, Holland, Saxony, and America

Britain   Sister of *Spain*, I have a Favour to ask of you. My Subjects in *America* are disobedient, and I am about to chastize them. I beg you will not furnish them with any Arms or Ammunition.

Spain   Have you forgotten, then, that when my Subjects in the Low Countries rebelled against me, you not only furnished them with military Stores, but join'd them with an Army and a Fleet? I wonder how you can have the Impudence to ask such a Favour of me, or the Folly to expect it!

Britain   You my dear Sister of France will surely not refuse me this Favour.

France   Did you not assist my Rebel Hugenots with a Fleet and an Army at *Rochelle*? And have you not lately aided privately and sneakingly my Rebel Subjects in *Corsica*? And do you not at this Instant keep their Chief pension'd, and ready to head a fresh Revolt there, whenever you can find or make an Opportunity? Dear Sister you must be a little silly!

Britain   *Honest Holland!* You see it is remembered that I was once your Friend, You will therefore be mine on this Occasion. I know indeed you are accustom'd to smuggle with these Rebels of mine. I will wink at that, Sell 'em as much Tea as you please to enervate the Rascals; since they will not take it of me; but for Gods sake dont supply them with any Arms.

Holland   'Tis true you assisted me against *Philip*, my Tyrant of *Spain* but have I not since assisted you against one of your Tyrants,* and enabled you to expell him? Surely that Accompt, as we Merchants say, is *Ballanc'd*, and I am nothing in your Debt. I have indeed some Complaints against *you*, for endeavouring to starve me by your *Navigation Acts*: But being peaceably dispos'd I do not quarrel with you for that. I shall only go on quietly with my own Business. Trade is my Profession, 'tis all I have to subsist on. And let me tell you, I should make no scruple, (on the prospect of a good Market for that Commodity,) even to send my Ships to Hell and supply the Devil with Brimstone. For you must know I can insure in London against the Burning of my Sails.

America   Why you old blood thirsty Bully! you who have
to   been everywhere vaunting your own Prowess, and
Britain.   defaming the Americans as Poltroons! you who have boasted of being able to march over all their Bellies with a single Regiment! You who by Fraud have possess'd yourself of their strongest Fortress, and all the Arms they had stor'd up in it! You who have a disciplin'd Army in their Country intrench'd to the Teeth and provided with every thing! Do *you* run about begging all Europe not to supply those poor People with a little Powder and Shot? Do you mean, then, to fall upon them naked and unarm'd, and butcher them in cold Blood? Is this your Courage? Is this your Magnanimity?

Britain.   O! you wicked-Whig-Presbyterian-Serpent! Have you the Impudence to appear before me after all your Disobedience? Surrender immediatly all your Liberties and Properties into my Hands, or I will cut you to Pieces. Was it for this that I planted

*James 2nd.

your Country at so great an Expence? that I protected you in your Infancy, and defended you
against all your Enemies?

America. I shall not surrender my Liberty and Property but
with my Life. It is not true that my Country was
planted at your Expence. Your own Records* refute that Falshood to your Face. Nor did you ever
afford me a Man or a shilling to defend me against
the Indians, the only Enemies I had upon my own
Account. But when you have quarrell'd with all
Europe, and drawn me with you into all your
Broils, then you value yourself upon protecting
me from the Enemies you have made for me. I
have no natural Cause of Difference with Spain,
France, or Holland; and yet by turns I have join'd
with you in Wars against them all. You would not
suffer me to make or keep a seperate Peace with
any of them, 'tho I might easily have done it, to
great Advantage. Does your protecting me in
those Wars give you a Right to fleece me? If so, as
I fought for you, as well as you for me, it gives
me a proportionable Right to fleece you. What
think you of an American Law to make a Monopoly of You and your Commerce, as you have done

*See the Journals of the House of Commons 1640. Viz, Die Veneris Martii
10. 1642. Whereas the Plantations in New England have, by the Blessing of
Almighty God, had good and prosperous Success, *without any Publick Charge
to this State*; and are now likely to prove very happy for the Propagation of
the Gospel in those Parts, and very beneficial and commodious to this Kingdom and Nation, the Commons now assembled in Parliament do, for the
better Advancement of those Plantations and the Encouragement of the
Planters to proceed in their Undertaking, Ordain that all Merchandizes and
Goods that by any Merchant or other Person or Persons whatsoever, shall be
exported out of this Kingdom of England into New England, to be spent,
used or employ'd there, or being of the Growth of that *Kingdom*, shall be
from thence imported hither; or shall be laden or put on board in any Ship
or Vessel for Necessaries in passing or returning to and fro; and all and every
the Owner or Owners thereof, shall be freed and discharg'd of and from
paying and yielding any Custom, Subsidy, Taxation, Imposition, or other
Duty for the same, either Inward or Outward, either in this Kingdom or
New England, or in any Port, Haven, Creek, or other place whatsoever, untill
the House of Commons shall take further order therein to the Contrary. And
all and singular Customers, &c. are to Observe this Order.

by your Laws of me and mine? Content yourself
with that Monopoly if you are Wise, and learn
Justice if you would be respected!

Britain   You impudent B—h! am not I your Mother
Country? Is not that a sufficient Title to your Respect and Obedience?

Saxony.   *Mother Country!* Hah, hah, he! What Respect have
you the front to claim as a Mother Country? You
know that *I* am *your* Mother Country, and yet
you pay me none. Nay, it is but the other Day,
since you hired Ruffians* to rob me on the Highway,† and burn my House!‡ For shame! Hide
your Face and hold your Tongue. If you continue
this Conduct you will make yourself the Contempt
of all Europe!

Britain   O Lord! where are my Friends!

France   Friends! Believe us you have none, nor ever will
Spain   have any 'till you mend your Manners. How can
Holland   we who are your Neighbours have any Regard for
and   You, or expect any Equity from You, should your
Saxony all Power increase, when we see how basely and un-
together   justly you have us'd both your *own Mother* and
your *own Children*?

*Prussians.
†They enter'd and rais'd Contributions in Saxony.
‡And they burnt the fine Suburbs of Dresden the Capital of Saxony.

February? 1775

A Proposed Memorial to Lord Dartmouth

No 23

To the Right honourable the Earl of Dartmouth One of his
Majesty's principal Secretaries of State
A Memorial from Benjamin Franklin Agent of the Province
of Massachusetts Bay.
          Given in London, this 16th Day of March, 1775.
Whereas an Injury done, can only give the Party injured a

Right to full Reparation; or, in case that be refused, a Right to return an equal Injury. And whereas the Blockade of Boston, now continued nine Months, hath every Week of its Continuance done Damage to that Town equal to what was suffered there by the India Company; it follows that such *exceeding* Damage is an *Injury* done by this Government, for which Reparation ought to be made. And whereas Reparation of Injuries ought always (agreable to the Custom of all Nations, savage as well as civilized) to be first required, before Satisfaction is taken by a Return of Damage to the Aggressors; which was not done by Great Britain in the Instance above mentioned. I the underwritten, do therefore, as their Agent, in the Behalf of my Country and the said Town of Boston, protest against the Continuance of the said Blockade: And I do hereby solemnly demand Satisfaction for the accumulated Injury done them beyond the Value of the India Company's Tea destroyed.

And whereas the Conquest of the Gulph of St. Lawrence, the Coasts of Labrador and Nova Scotia, and the Fisheries possess'd by the French there and on the Banks of Newfoundland, so far as they were more extended than at present, was made by the *joint Forces* of Britain and the Colonies, the latter having nearly an equal Number of Men in that Service with the former; it follows that the Colonies have an equitable and just Right to participate in the Advantage of those Fisheries. I do therefore in the Behalf of the Colony of the Massachusetts Bay, protest against the Act now under Consideration in Parliament, for depriving that Province, with others, of that Fishery (on pretence of their refusing to purchase British Commodities) as an Act highly unjust and injurious: And I give Notice, that Satisfaction will probably one day be demanded for all the Injury that may be done and suffered in the Execution of such Act: And that the Injustice of the Proceeding is likely to give such Umbrage to *all the Colonies*, that in no future War, wherein other Conquests may be meditated, either a Man or a Shilling will be obtained from any of them to aid such Conquests, till full Satisfaction be made as aforesaid.

March 16, 1775

Proposed Articles of Confederation

Articles of Confederation and perpetual Union, entred into by the Delegates of the several Colonies of New Hampshire &c. in general Congress met at Philadelphia, May 10. 1775.

Art. I. The Name of the Confederacy shall henceforth be *The United Colonies of North America.*

Art. II. The said United Colonies hereby severally enter into a firm League of Friendship with each other, binding on themselves and their Posterity, for their common Defence against their Enemies, for the Security of their Liberties and Propertys, the Safety of their Persons and Families, and their mutual and general welfare.

Art. III. That each Colony shall enjoy and retain as much as it may think fit of its own present Laws, Customs, Rights, Privileges, and peculiar Jurisdictions within its own Limits; and may amend its own Constitution as shall seem best to its own Assembly or Convention.

Art. IV. That for the more convenient Management of general Interests, Delegates shall be annually elected in each Colony to meet in General Congress at such Time and Place as shall be agreed on in the next preceding Congress. Only where particular Circumstances do not make a Deviation necessary, it is understood to be a Rule, that each succeeding Congress be held in a different Colony till the whole Number be gone through, and so in perpetual Rotation; and that accordingly the next Congress after the present shall be held at Annapolis in Maryland.

Art. V. That the Power and Duty of the Congress shall extend to the Determining on War and Peace, to sending and receiving Ambassadors, and entring into Alliances, [the Reconciliation with Great Britain;] the Settling all Disputes and Differences between Colony and Colony about Limits or any other cause if such should arise; and the Planting of new Colonies when proper. The Congress shall also make such general Ordinances as tho' necessary to the General Welfare, particular Assemblies cannot be competent to; viz. those that may relate to our general Commerce or general Currency; to the Establishment of Posts; and the Regulation of our common Forces. The Congress shall also have the Appointment of all Officers civil and military, appertaining to the general Confederacy, such as General Treasurer Secretary, &c.

Art. VI. All Charges of Wars, and all other general Expences to be incurr'd for the common Welfare, shall be defray'd out of a common Treasury, which is to be supply'd by each Colony in proportion to its Number of Male Polls between 16 and 60 Years of Age; the Taxes for paying that proportion are to be laid and levied by the Laws of each Colony.

Art. VII. The Number of Delegates to be elected and sent to the Congress by each Colony, shall be regulated from time to time by the Number of such Polls return'd, so as that one Delegate be allow'd for every [5000] Polls. And the Delegates are to bring with them to every Congress an authenticated Return of the number of Polls in their respective Provinces, which is to be annually taken, for the Purposes abovementioned.

Art. VIII. At every Meeting of the Congress One half of the Members return'd exclusive of Proxies be necessary to make a Quorum, and Each Delegate at the Congress, shall have a Vote in all Cases; and if necessarily absent, shall be allowed to appoint any other Delegate from the same Colony to be his Proxy, who may vote for him.

Art. IX. An executive Council shall be appointed by the Congress out of their own Body, consisting of [12] Persons; of whom in the first Appointment one Third, viz. [4], shall be for one Year, [4] for two Years, and [4] for three Years; and as the said Terms expire, the vacancies shall be filled by Appointments for three Years, whereby One Third of [the] Members will be changed annually. And each Person who has served the said Term of three Years as Counsellor, shall have a Respite of three Years, before he can be elected again. This Council (of whom two thirds shall be a Quorum) in the Recess of the Congress is to execute what shall have been enjoin'd thereby; to manage the general continental Business and Interests to receive Applications from foreign Countries; to prepare Matters for the Consideration of the Congress; to fill up (*pro tempore*) continental Offices that fall vacant; and to draw on the General Treasurer for [such] Monies as may be necessary for general Services, and appropriated by the Congress to such Services.

Art. X. No Colony shall engage in an offensive War with any Nation of Indians without the Consent of the Congress, or great Council above-mentioned, who are first to consider the Justice and Necessity of such War.

Art. XI. A perpetual Alliance offensive and defensive, is to be entered into as soon as may be with the Six Nations; their Limits to be ascertain'd and secur'd to them; their Land not to be encroach'd on, nor any private or Colony Purchases made of them hereafter to be held good; nor any Contract for Lands to be made but between the Great Council of the Indians at Onondaga and the General Congress. The Boundaries and Lands of all the other Indians shall also be ascertain'd and secur'd to them in the same manner; and Persons appointed to reside among them in proper Districts, who shall take care to prevent Injustice in the Trade with them, and be enabled at our General Expence by occasional small Supplies, to relieve their personal Wants and Distresses. And all Purchases from them shall be by the Congress for the General Advantage and Benefit of the United Colonies.

Art. XII. As all new Institutions may have Imperfections which only Time and Experience can discover, it is agreed, that the General Congress from time to time shall propose such Amendment of this Constitution as may be found necessary; which being approv'd by a Majority of the Colony Assemblies, shall be equally binding with the rest of the Articles of this Confederation.

Art. XIII. Any and every Colony from Great Britain upon the Continent of North America not at present engag'd in our Association, may upon Application and joining the said Association, be receiv'd into this Confederation, viz. [Ireland] the West India Islands, Quebec, St. Johns, Nova Scotia, Bermudas, and the East and West Floridas: and shall thereupon be entitled to all the Advantages of our Union, mutual Assistance and Commerce.

These Articles shall be propos'd to the several Provincial Conventions or Assemblies, to be by them consider'd, and if approv'd they are advis'd to impower their Delegates to agree to and ratify the same in the ensuing Congress. After which the *Union* thereby establish'd is to continue firm till the Terms of Reconciliation proposed in the Petition of the last Congress to the King are agreed to; till the Acts since made restraining the American Commerce and Fisheries are repeal'd; till Reparation is made for the Injury done to Boston by shutting up its Port; for the Burning of Charlestown; and for the Expence of this unjust War; and till all the British Troops are withdrawn from America. On the Arrival of these Events the Colonies are to return to their former Connection and Friendship with Britain: But on Failure thereof this Confederation is to be perpetual.

Philadelphia, July 21, 1775

Resolutions on Trade Submitted to Congress

Resolved, That from and after the 20th of July 1776 being one full Year after the Day appointed by a late Act of the Parliament of Great Britain for restraining the Trade of the Confederate Colonies, all the Custom-Houses therein (if the said Act be not first repealed) shall be shut up, and all the Officers of the same discharged from the Execution of their several Functions; and all the Ports of the said Colonies are hereby declared to be thenceforth open to the Ships of every State in Europe that will admit our Commerce and protect it; who may bring in and expose to Sale free of all Duties their respective Produce and Manufactures, and every kind of Merchandise, excepting Teas, and the Merchandize of Great Britain, Ireland, and the British West India Islands.

Resolved, That we will to the utmost of our Power maintain and support this Freedom of Commerce for two Years certain after its Commencement, any Reconciliation between us and Britain notwithstanding; and as much longer beyond that Term, as the late Acts of Parliament for Restraining the Commerce and Fisheries, and altering the Laws and Charters of any of the Colonies, shall continue unrepealed.

Philadelphia, July 21, 1775

Account of the Devices on the Continental Bills of Credit

To the Printers of the PENNSYLVANIA GAZETTE.
GENTLEMEN,
No Explanation of the Devices on the Continental Bills of Credit having yet appeared, I send you the following Account of them, with my Conjectures of their Meaning.

CLERICUS.

An emblematical device, when rightly formed, is said to consist of two parts, a *body* and a *mind*, neither of which is compleat or intelligible, without the aid of the other. The figure is called the *body*, the motto the *mind*. These that I am about to consider appear formed on that rule, and seem to relate to the present struggle between the colonies and the tyrant state, for liberty, property and safety on the one hand, for absolute power and plunder on the other.

On one denomination of the bills there is the figure of a *harp*, with this motto, MAJORA MINORIBUS CONSONANT; literally, *The greater and smaller ones sound together*. As the *harp* is an instrument composed of *great* and *small* strings, included in a *strong frame*, and all so tuned as to agree in concord with each other, I conceive that the *frame* may be intended to represent our new government by a Continental Congress; and the *strings* of different lengths and substance, either the several colonies of different weight and force, or the various ranks of people in all of them, who are now united by that government in the most perfect *harmony*.

On another bill is impressed, a *wild boar of the forest* rushing on the spear of the hunter; with this motto, AUT MORS, AUT VITA DECORA, which may be translated— *Death or liberty*. The wild boar is an animal of great strength and courage, armed with long and sharp tusks, which he well knows how to use in his defence. He is inoffensive while suffered to enjoy his freedom, but when roused and wounded by the hunter, often turns and makes him pay dearly for his injustice and temerity.

On another is drawn an *eagle* on the wing, pouncing upon a *crane*, who turns upon his back, and receives the eagle on the point of his long bill, which pierces the eagle's breast; with this motto, EXITUS IN DUBIO EST; — *The event is uncertain*. The eagle, I suppose, represents Great-Britain, the crane America. This device offers an admonition to each of the contending parties. To the crane, not to depend too much on the success of its *endeavours to avoid* the contest (by petition, negotiation, &c.) but prepare for using the means of defence God and nature hath given it; and to the eagle, not to presume on its superior strength, since a weaker bird may wound it mortally.

> *Sunt dubii eventus, incertaque prælia mortis:*
> *Vincitur, haud raro, qui prope victor erat.*

On another bill we have a *thorny bush*, which a *hand* seems attempting to eradicate. The hand appears to bleed, as pricked by the spines. The motto is, SUSTINE VEL ABSTINE; which may be rendered, *Bear with me, or let me alone*; or thus, *Either support or leave me*. The bush I suppose to mean *America*, and the bleeding hand *Britain*. Would to God that bleeding were stopt, the wounds of that hand healed, and its future operations directed by wisdom and equity; so shall the hawthorn flourish, and form an hedge around it, annoying with her thorns only its invading enemies.

Another had the figure of a *beaver* gnawing a large tree, with this motto, PERSEVERANDO; *By perseverance*. I apprehend the *great tree* may be intended to represent the enormous power Britain has assumed over us, and endeavours to enforce by arms, of taxing us at pleasure, *and binding us in all cases whatsoever*; or the exorbitant profits she makes by monopolizing our commerce. Then the *beaver*, which is known to be able, by assiduous and steady working, to fell large trees, may signify *America*, which, by perseverance in her present measures, will probably reduce that power within proper bounds, and, by establishing the most necessary manufactures among ourselves, abolish the British monopoly.

On another bill we have the plant *acanthus*, sprouting on all sides under a weight placed upon it, with the motto, DE-PRESSA RESURGIT; *Tho' oppressed it rises*. The ancients tell us, that the sight of such an accidental circumstance gave the first

hint to an architect, in forming the beautiful capital of the
Corinthian Column. This, perhaps, was intended to encourage us, by representing, that our present oppressions will not
destroy us, but that they may, by increasing our industry, and
forcing it into new courses, increase the prosperity of our
country, and establish that prosperity on the *base* of liberty,
and the well-proportioned *pillar* of property, elevated for a
pleasing spectacle to all *connoisseurs*, who can *taste* and delight
in the architecture of human happiness.

The figure of a *hand and flail* over *sheaves of wheat*, with
the motto, TRIBULATIO DITAT, *Threshing improves it* (which
we find printed on another of the bills) may perhaps be intended to admonish us, that tho' at present we are under
the *flail*, its blows, how hard soever, will be rather advantageous than hurtful to us: for they will bring forth every
grain of genius and merit in arts, manufactures, war and
council, that are now concealed in the husk, and then the
breath of a breeze will be sufficient to separate from us all
the chaff of Toryism. *Tribulation* too, in our English sense
of the word, improves the mind, it makes us humbler, and
tends to make us wiser. And *threshing*, in one of its senses,
that of beating, often improves those that are threshed.
Many an unwarlike nation have been beaten into heroes by
troublesome warlike neighbours; and the continuance of a
war, tho' it lessen the numbers of a people, often increases
its strength, by the increased discipline and consequent
courage of the number remaining. Thus England, after her
civil war, in which her people threshed one another, became
more formidable to her neighbours. The public distress too
that arises from war, by increasing frugality and industry,
often gives habits that remain after the distress is over, and
thereby naturally *enriches* those on whom it has enforced
those *enriching virtues*.

Another of the bills has for its device, a *storm* descending
from a *black heavy cloud*, with the motto, SERENABIT; *It
will clear up*. This seems designed to encourage the dejected,
who may be too sensible of present inconveniences, and fear
their continuance. It reminds them, agreeable to the adage,
that *after a storm comes a calm*; or as Horace more elegantly
has it—

> *Informes hyemes reducit, Jupiter: idem summovet.*
> *Non si male nunc, et olim*
> *Sic erit.*—*Neque semper arcum tendit Apollo.*

On another bill there is stamped the representation of a
tempestuous sea; a face, with swollen cheeks, wrapt up in a
black cloud, appearing to blow violently on the waters, *the
waves high*, and *all rolling one way*: The motto VI CON-
CITATÆ; which may be rendered, *raised by force*. From the remotest antiquity, in figurative language, great waters have
signified *the people*, and waves an insurrection. The people of
themselves are supposed as naturally inclined to be still, as
the waters to remain level and quiet. Their rising here appears not to be from any internal cause, but from an external
power, expressed by the head of *Æolus*, God of the winds
(or *Boreas*, the *North* wind, as usually the most violent) acting furiously upon them. The black cloud perhaps designs
the British Parliament, and the waves the colonies. Their
rolling all in one direction shews, that the very force used
against them has produced their unanimity. On the reverse
of this bill, we have a smooth sea; the sails of ships on that
sea hanging loose shew a perfect calm; the sun shining fully
denotes a clear sky. The motto is, CESSANTE VENTO, CON-
QUIESCEMUS; *The wind ceasing, we shall be quiet.* Supposing
my explanation of the preceding device to be right, this will
probably import, that when those violent acts of power,
which have roused the colonies, are repealed, they will return to their former tranquility. Britain seems thus charged
with being the sole cause of the present civil war, at the
same time that the only mode of putting an end to it is thus
plainly pointed out to her.

The last is a *wreath of laurel* on a *marble monument*, or
altar. The motto, SI RECTE FACIES; *If you act rightly.* This
seems intended as an encouragement to a brave and steady
conduct in defence of our liberties, as it promises to crown
with honour, by the laurel wreath, those who persevere to the
end in *well-doing*; and with a long duration of that honour,
expressed by the *monument of marble*.

A learned friend of mine thinks this device more particularly addressed to the CONGRESS. He says the ancients

composed for their heroes a wreath of laurel, oak and olive twigs, interwoven; agreeable to the distich,

> *E lauro, quercu, atque olea, duce digna corona.*
> *Prudentem, fortem, pacificumque decet.*

Of *laurel*, as that tree was dedicated to *Apollo*, and understood to signify *knowledge and prudence*; of *oak*, as pertaining to *Jupiter*, and expressing *fortitude*; of *olive*, as the tree of *Pallas*, and as a symbol of *peace*. The whole to show, that those who are intrusted to conduct the great affairs of mankind should act prudently and firmly, retaining, above all, a pacific disposition. This wreath was first placed on an *altar*, to admonish the hero who was to be crowned with it, that true glory is founded on and proceeds from *piety*. My friend therefore thinks, the present device might intend a wreath of that composite kind, though, from the smallness of the work, the engraver could not mark distinctly the differing leaves: And he is rather confirmed in his opinion that this is designed as an admonition to the Congress, when he considers the passage in *Horace* from whence the motto is taken,——*Rex eris, aiunt,*

> *Si recte facies.*

To which also *Ausonius* alludes,

> *Qui recte faciet, non qui dominatur, erit Rex.*

Not the King's Parliament, who act wrong, but the People's Congress, *if it acts right*, shall govern America.

The Pennsylvania Gazette, September 20, 1775

The King's Own Regulars

To the PRINTER of the PENNSYLVANIA EVENING POST.
SIR,

The Ministry have boasted much of their *regular*, their *disciplined* troops, which they fancied capable of beating all the *irregulars* in the world.

One would wonder how men of any attention to what has passed, could deceive themselves into such an opinion, when so many FACTS, within the memory of men not very old, evince the contrary.

The following *Yanky* song gives us a pretty little collection of those facts. I wish to see it printed for the encouragement of our militia. For though it is not safe for men too much to despise their enemies, it is of use that they should have a good opinion (if it is a just opinion) of themselves, when compared to those they are to fight with.

There are three other instances of regulars beaten by irregulars in our time; but these being of foreign troops, were probably not thought fit for the song writer's present purpose. It may not however be amiss to mention them here.

The first was at Genoa, in the war before last. Twenty battalions of Imperialists were in possession of that place, and exasperating the inhabitants by their insolence, particularly by caning some who refused to assist the soldiery in removing the cannon; a mob rose suddenly upon them, drove them out of the gates, and defended the place against them with such spirit, that they never were able to get in again.

The second was at Madrid about ten years since, when the King of Spain offended the people by a too rigorous execution of some trifling edicts relative to cloaks and hats. They demanded the dismission of his Minister, Count de Squilache. The King refused, and assembled the guards with all the regulars near the city, to defend the Count. The people rose, attacked the troops, cut them to pieces, and drove the Minister out of the kingdom.

The third happened this last summer, when a fine regular army of Spaniards, well appointed, attempted to invade Africa. The militia of that country beat them out of it almost as soon as they entered it, and with a prodigious slaughter.

If we search for the cause of this superior bravery in the *people* of a country, compared with what are called regular troops, it may perhaps be found in these particulars; that the men who compose an European regular army, are generally such as have neither property or families to fight for, and who have no principle either of honor, religion, public spirit, regard for liberty, or love of country, to animate them. They are therefore only pressed on to fight by their officers, and had rather be any where else than in a battle. Discipline only gives the officers the power of actuating them; and superior discipline may make them superior to other troops of the same kind not so well disciplined. Thus discipline serves to supply in some degree the defect of principle. But men equally armed, and animated by principle, tho' without discipline, are always superior to them when only equal in numbers; and when principle and discipline are united on the same side, as in our present militia, treble the number of mere unprincipled mercenaries, such as the regular armies commonly consist of, are in my opinion no match for such a militia.

Let us however not be presumptuously careless in our military operations, but mix caution with our courage, and take every prudent measure to guard against the attempts of our enemies; it being as advantageous to defeat their designs as their forces.

The KING'S own REGULARS, and their TRIUMPH over the IRREGULARS. A new SONG.

To the tune of *An old Courtier of the Queen's, and the Queen's old Courtier*. Which is a kind of recitativo, like the chaunting of the prose psalms in cathedrals.

Since you all will have singing, and won't be said nay,
I cannot refuse, when you so beg and pray;
So, I'll sing you a song,—as a body may say,
'Tis of the King's Regulars, who ne'er run away.

O the old Soldiers of the King, and the King's own Regulars.

At Prestonpans we met with some Rebels one day,
We marshall'd our selves all in comely array;
Our hearts were all stout, and bid our legs stay,
But our feet were wrong-headed, and took us away.

O the old Soldiers, &c.

At Falkirk we resolv'd to be braver,
And recover some credit by better behaviour:
We would not acknowledge feet had done us any favour,
So feet swore they would stand, but——legs ran however.

O the old Soldiers, &c.

No troops perform better than we at reviews,
We march and we wheel, and whatever you chuse,
George would see how we fight, and we never refuse,
There we all fight with courage—you may see't in the news.

O the old Soldiers, &c.

To Mohongahela with fifes and with drums,
We march'd in fine order, with cannon and bombs,
That great expedition cost infinite sums;
But a few irregulars cut us all into crumbs.

O the old Soldiers, &c.

It was not fair to shoot at us from behind trees,
If they had stood open, as they ought, before our great
    guns, we should have beat 'em with ease,
They may fight with one another that way if they please,
But it is not *regular* to stand, and fight with such rascals as
    these.

O the old Soldiers, &c.

At Fort George and Oswego, to our great reputation,
We shew'd our vast skill in fortification;
The French fir'd three guns; of the fourth they had no
    occasion;
For we gave up those forts—not thro' fear, but—mere
    persuasion.

O the old Soldiers, &c.

To Ticonderoga we went in a passion,
Swearing to be revenged on the whole French nation;
But we soon turn'd tail, without hesitation,
Because they fought behind trees,—which is not the *regular*
    fashion.

O the old Soldiers, &c.

Lord *Loudun*, he was a regular General, they say;
With a great regular army he went his way,
Against Louisburgh, to make it his prey,
But return'd—without seeing it,—for he did not *feel bold*
    that day.

O the old Soldiers, &c.

Grown proud at reviews, great George had no rest,
Each Grandsire, he had heard, a rebellion supprest.
He wish'd a rebellion, look'd round and saw none,
So resolv'd a rebellion to make—of his own,

With the old Soldiers, &c.

The Yankees he bravely pitch'd on, because he thought
    they wou'd'n't fight,
And so he sent us over to take away their right;
But lest they should spoil our review-clothes, he cry'd braver
    and louder;
For God's sake, brother Kings, don't sell the cowards—any
    powder!

O the old Soldiers, &c.

Our General with his council of war did advise
How at Lexington we might the Yankees surprise;
We march'd—and remarch'd—all surpris'd—at being beat;
And so our wise General's plan of *surprise*—was complete.

O the old Soldiers, &c.

For fifteen miles they follow'd and pelted us, we scarce
    had time to pull a trigger.
But did you ever know a retreat perform'd with more
    vigour?
For we did it in two hours, which sav'd us from perdition;
'Twas not in *going out,* but in *returning,* consisted our
    EXPEDITION.

O the old Soldiers, &c.

Says our General, "We were forc'd to take to our *arms* in
    our own defence,"
(For *arms* read *legs,* and it will be both truth and sense)

Lord Percy (says he) I must say something of him in civility,
And that is—"I can never enough praise him for his great—
    agility."

O the old Soldiers, &c.

Of their firing from behind fences he makes a great
    pother,
Every fence has two sides, they made use of one, and we
    only forgot to use the other;
That we turn'd our backs and ran away so fast, don't let that
    disgrace us;
'Twas only to make good what Sandwich said, that the
    Yankees—could not face us.

O the old Soldiers, &c.

As they could not get before us, how could they look us
    in the face?
We took care they shouldn't, by scampering away apace.
That they had not much to brag of, is a very plain case;
For if they beat us in the fight, we beat them—in the race.

O the old Soldiers of the King, and the King's own Regulars.

November 27, 1775; *Pennsylvania Evening Post*, March 30, 1776

Bradshaw's Epitaph

The following inscription was made out three years ago on
the cannon near which the ashes of President Bradshaw were
lodged, on the top of a high hill near Martha Bray in Jamaica,
to avoid the rage against the Regicides exhibited at the
Restoration:

STRANGER,
Ere thou pass, contemplate this CANNON,
Nor regardless be told
That near its base lies deposited the dust of
JOHN BRADSHAW,
Who, nobly superior to all selfish regards,

Despising alike the pageantry of courtly splendor,
The blast of calumny, and the terrors of royal vengeance,
Presided in the illustrious band of heroes and patriots,
Who fairly and openly adjudged
CHARLES STUART,
Tyrant of England,
To a public and exemplary death,
Thereby presenting to the amazed world,
And transmitting down, through applauding ages,
The most glorious example
Of unshaken virtue, love of freedom, and impartial justice,
Ever exhibited on the blood-stained theatre of human actions.
O, reader,
Pass not on till thou hast blessed his memory,
And never——never forget
THAT REBELLION TO TYRANTS IS OBEDIENCE
TO GOD.

The Pennsylvania Evening Post, December 14, 1775

The Rattle-Snake as a Symbol of America

Messrs. PRINTERS,

I observed on one of the drums belonging to the marines
now raising, there was painted a Rattle-Snake, with this modest motto under it, "Don't tread on me." As I know it is the
custom to have some device on the arms of every country, I
supposed this may have been intended for the arms of America; and as I have nothing to do with public affairs, and as
my time is perfectly my own, in order to divert an idle hour,
I sat down to guess what could have been intended by this
uncommon device—I took care, however, to consult on this
occasion a person who is acquainted with heraldry, from
whom I learned, that it is a rule among the learned in that
science "That the worthy properties of the animal, in the
crest-born, shall be considered," and, "That the base ones
cannot have been intended;" he likewise informed me that the
antients considered the serpent as an emblem of wisdom, and
in a certain attitude of endless duration—both which circum-

stances I suppose may have been had in view.—Having gained this intelligence, and recollecting that countries are sometimes represented by animals peculiar to them, it occured to me that the Rattle-Snake is found in no other quarter of the world besides America, and may therefore have been chosen, on that account, to represent her.

But then "the worthy properties" of a Snake I judged would be hard to point out—This rather raised than suppressed my curiosity, and having frequently seen the Rattle-Snake, I ran over in my mind every property by which she was distinguished, not only from other animals, but from those of the same genus or class of animals, endeavouring to fix some meaning to each, not wholly inconsistent with common sense.

I recollected that her eye excelled in brightness, that of any other animal, and that she has no eye-lids—She may therefore be esteemed an emblem of vigilance.—She never begins an attack, nor, when once engaged, ever surrenders: She is therefore an emblem of magnanimity and true courage.—As if anxious to prevent all pretentions of quarrelling with her, the weapons with which nature has furnished her, she conceals in the roof of her mouth, so that, to those who are unacquainted with her, she appears to be a most defenceless animal; and even when those weapons are shewn and extended for her defence, they appear weak and contemptible; but their wounds however small, are decisive and fatal:— Conscious of this, she never wounds till she has generously given notice, even to her enemy, and cautioned him against the danger of treading on her.—Was I wrong, Sir, in thinking this a strong picture of the temper and conduct of America? The poison of her teeth is the necessary means of digesting her food, and at the same time is certain destruction to her enemies—This may be understood to intimate that those things which are destructive to our enemies, may be to us not only harmless, but absolutely necessary to our existence.—I confess I was wholly at a loss what to make of the rattles, 'till I went back and counted them and found them just thirteen, exactly the number of the Colonies united in America; and I recollected too that this was the only part of the Snake which increased in numbers—Perhaps it might be only fancy, but, I conceited the painter had shewn a half formed additional rattle, which, I suppose, may have been intended to represent the province of Canada.—'Tis curious and amazing to observe how distinct and independant of each other the rattles of this animal are, and yet how firmly they are united together, so as never to be separated but by breaking them to pieces.—One of those rattles singly, is incapable of producing sound, but the ringing of thirteen together, is sufficient to alarm the boldest man living. The Rattle-Snake is solitary, and associates with her kind only when it is necessary for their preservation—In winter, the warmth of a number together will preserve their lives, while singly, they would probably perish—The power of fascination attributed to her, by a generous construction, may be understood to mean, that those who consider the liberty and blessings which America affords, and once come over to her, never afterwards leave her, but spend their lives with her.—She strongly resembles America in this, that she is beautiful in youth and her beauty increaseth with her age, "her tongue also is blue and forked as the lightning, and her abode is among impenetrable rocks."

Having pleased myself with reflections of this kind, I communicated my sentiments to a neighbour of mine, who has a surprizing readiness at guessing at every thing which relates to publick affairs, and indeed I should be jealous of his reputation, in that way, was it not that the event constantly shews that he has guessed wrong—He instantly declared it as his sentiments, that the Congress meant to allude to Lord North's declaration in the House of Commons, that he never would relax his measures until he had brought America to his feet, and to intimate to his Lordship, that were she brought to his feet, it would be dangerous treading on her.—But, I am positive he has guessed wrong, for I am sure the Congress would not condescend, at this time of day, to take the least notice of his Lordship in that or any other way.—In which opinion, I am determined to remain your humble servant,

AN AMERICAN GUESSER.

The Pennsylvania Journal, December 27, 1775

What Would Satisfy the Americans?

Doctor Franklin, being in England in the Year 1775 was asked by a Nobleman, what would satisfy the Americans? Answered, That it might easily be comprised in a few Re's
  Which he immediately wrote on a piece of Paper Thus,

Re
- call your Forces,
- store Castle William,
- pair the Damage done to Boston,
- peal your unconstitutional Acts,
- nounce your pretentions to Tax us,
- fund the duties you have extorted; after this
- quire, and
- ceive payment for the destroyed Tea, with the voluntary grants of the Colonies, And then
- joice in a happy
- conciliation.

1775

LETTERS

To ————

Dear Sir

I have read your Manuscrit with some Attention. By the Arguments it contains against the Doctrine of a particular Providence, tho' you allow a general Providence, you strike at the Foundation of all Religion: For without the Belief of a Providence that takes Cognizance of, guards and guides and may favour particular Persons, there is no Motive to Worship a Deity, to fear its Displeasure, or to pray for its Protection. I will not enter into any Discussion of your Principles, tho' you seem to desire it; At present I shall only give you my Opinion that tho' your Reasonings are subtle, and may prevail with some Readers, you will not succeed so as to change the general Sentiments of Mankind on that Subject, and the Consequence of printing this Piece will be a great deal of Odium drawn upon your self, Mischief to you and no Benefit to others. He that spits against the Wind, spits in his own Face. But were you to succeed, do you imagine any Good would be done by it? You yourself may find it easy to live a virtuous Life without the Assistance afforded by Religion; you having a clear Perception of the Advantages of Virtue and the Disadvantages of Vice, and possessing a Strength of Resolution sufficient to enable you to resist common Temptations. But think how great a Proportion of Mankind consists of weak and ignorant Men and Women, and of inexperienc'd and inconsiderate Youth of both Sexes, who have need of the Motives of Religion to restrain them from Vice, to support their Virtue, and retain them in the Practice of it till it becomes *habitual*, which is the great Point for its Security; And perhaps you are indebted to her originally that is to your Religious Education, for the Habits of Virtue upon which you now justly value yourself. You might easily display your excellent Talents of reasoning on a less hazardous Subject, and thereby obtain Rank with our most distinguish'd Authors. For among us, it is not necessary, as among the Hottentots that a Youth to be receiv'd into the Company of

Men, should prove his Manhood by beating his Mother. I would advise you therefore not to attempt unchaining the Tyger, but to burn this Piece before it is seen by any other Person, whereby you will save yourself a great deal of Mortification from the Enemies it may raise against you, and perhaps a good deal of Regret and Repentance. If Men are so wicked as we now see them *with Religion* what would they be if *without it*? I intend this Letter itself as a *Proof* of my Friendship and therefore add no *Professions* of it, but subscribe simply Yours

December 13, 1757

ELECTRIC SHOCKS IN PARALYTIC CASES

To John Pringle

Sir   Dec. 21. 1757

The following is what I can at present recollect, relating to the Effects of Electricity in Paralytic Cases, which have fallen under my Observation.

Some Years since, when the News papers made Mention of great Cures perform'd in Italy or Germany by means of Electricity, a Number of Paralytics were brought to me from different Parts of Pensilvania and the neighbouring Provinces, to be electris'd, which I did for them, at their Request. My Method was, to place the Patient first in a Chair on an electric Stool, and draw a Number of large strong Sparks from all Parts of the affected Limb or Side. Then I fully charg'd two 6 Gallon Glass Jarrs, each of which had about 3 square feet of Surface coated and I sent the united Shock of these thro' the affected Limb or Limbs, repeating the Stroke commonly three Times each Day. The first Thing observ'd was an immediate greater sensible Warmth in the lame Limbs that had receiv'd the Stroke than in the others; and the next Morning the Patients usually related that they had in the Night felt a pricking Sensation in the Flesh of the paralytic Limbs, and would sometimes shew a Number of small red Spots which they suppos'd were occasion'd by those Prickings: The Limbs too were found more capable of voluntary Motion, and seem'd to receive Strength; a Man, for Instance, who could not, the first Day, lift the lame Hand from off his Knee, would the next Day raise it four or five Inches, the third Day higher, and on the fifth Day was able, but with a feeble languid Motion, to take off his Hat. These Appearances gave great Spirits to the Patients, and made them hope a perfect Cure; but I do not remember that I ever saw any Amendment after the fifth Day: Which the Patients perceiving, and finding the Shocks pretty severe, they became discourag'd, went home and in a short time relapsed; so that I never knew any Advantage from Electricity in Palsies that was permanent. And how far the apparent temporary Advantage might arise from the Exercise in the Patients Journey and coming daily to my House, or from the Spirits given by the Hope of Success, enabling them to exert more Strength in moving their Limbs, I will not pretend to say.

Perhaps some permanent Advantage might have been obtained, if the Electric Shocks had been accompanied with proper Medicine and Regimen, under the Direction of a skilful Physician. It may be, too, that a few great Strokes, as given in my Method, may not be so proper as many small ones; since by the Account from Scotland of the Case in which 200 Shocks from a Phial were given daily, seems that a perfect Cure has been made. As to any uncommon Strength supposed to be in the Machine used in that Case, I imagine it could have no Share in the Effect produced; since the Strength of the Shock from charg'd Glass, is in proportion to the Quantity of Surface of the Glass coated; so that my Shocks from those large Jarrs must have been much greater than any that could be received from a Phial held in the hand.

I am, with great Respect, Sir, Your most obedient Servant

"STRATA OF THE EARTH"

To John Pringle

SIR,   *Craven-street, Jan.* 6, 1758.

I return Mr. *Mitchell's* paper on the strata of the earth*
with thanks. The reading of it, and perusal of the draft that

*See this Paper afterwards printed in the *Philosophical Transactions.*

accompanies it, have reconciled me to those convulsions which all naturalists agree this globe has suffered. Had the different strata of clay, gravel, marble, coals, lime-stone, sand, minerals, &c. continued to lie level, one under the other, as they may be supposed to have done before those convulsions, we should have had the use only of a few of the uppermost of the strata, the others lying too deep and too difficult to be come at; but the shell of the earth being broke, and the fragments thrown into this oblique position, the disjointed ends of a great number of strata of different kinds are brought up to day, and a great variety of useful materials put into our power, which would otherwise have remained eternally concealed from us. So that what has been usually looked upon as a *ruin* suffered by this part of the universe, was, in reality, only a preparation, or means of rendering the earth more fit for use, more capable of being to mankind a convenient and comfortable habitation.

I am, Sir, with great esteem, yours, &c.

COOLING BY EVAPORATION

To John Lining

Dear Sir,   *London, June* 17, 1758.

In a former letter I mentioned the experiment for cooling bodies by evaporation, and that I had, by repeatedly wetting the thermometer with common spirits, brought the mercury down five or six degrees. Being lately at *Cambridge*, and mentioning this in conversation with Dr. *Hadley*, professor of chemistry there, he proposed repeating the experiments with ether, instead of common spirits, as the ether is much quicker in evaporation. We accordingly went to his chamber, where he had both ether and a thermometer. By dipping first the ball of the thermometer into the ether, it appeared that the ether was precisely of the same temperament with the thermometer, which stood then at 65; for it made no alteration in the height of the little column of mercury. But when the thermometer was taken out of the ether, and the ether with which the ball was wet, began to evaporate, the mercury sunk several degrees. The wetting was then repeated by a feather that had been dipped into the ether, when the mercury sunk still lower. We continued this operation, one of us wetting the ball, and another of the company blowing on it with the bellows, to quicken the evaporation, the mercury sinking all the time, till it came down to 7, which is 25 degrees below the freezing point, when we left off.—Soon after it passed the freezing point, a thin coat of ice began to cover the ball. Whether this was water collected and condensed by the coldness of the ball, from the moisture in the air, or from our breath; or whether the feather, when dipped into the ether, might not sometimes go through it, and bring up some of the water that was under it, I am not certain; perhaps all might contribute. The ice continued increasing till we ended the experiment, when it appeared near a quarter of an inch thick all over the ball, with a number of small spicula, pointing outwards. From this experiment one may see the possibility of freezing a man to death on a warm summer's day, if he were to stand in a passage thro' which the wind blew briskly, and to be wet frequently with ether, a spirit that is more inflammable than brandy, or common spirits of wine.

It is but within these few years, that the *European* philosophers seem to have known this power in nature, of cooling bodies by evaporation. But in the east they have long been acquainted with it. A friend tells me, there is a passage in *Bernier's* travels through *Indostan*, written near one hundred years ago, that mentions it as a practice (in travelling over dry desarts in that hot climate) to carry water in flasks wrapt in wet woollen cloths, and hung on the shady side of the camel, or carriage, but in the free air; whereby, as the cloths gradually grow drier, the water contained in the flasks is made cool. They have likewise a kind of earthen pots, unglaz'd, which let the water gradually and slowly ooze through their pores, so as to keep the outside a little wet, notwithstanding the continual evaporation, which gives great coldness to the vessel, and the water contained in it. Even our common sailors seem to have had some notion of this property; for I remember, that being at sea, when I was a youth, I observed one of the sailors, during a calm in the night, often wetting his finger in his mouth, and then hold-ing it up in the air, to discover, as he said, if the air had any motion, and from which side it came; and this he expected to do, by finding one side of his finger grow suddenly cold, and from that side he should look for the next wind; which I then laughed at as a fancy.

May not several phænomena, hitherto unconsidered, or un-accounted for, be explained by this property? During the hot *Sunday* at *Philadelphia*, in *June* 1750, when the thermometer was up at 100 in the shade, I sat in my chamber without exercise, only reading or writing, with no other cloaths on than a shirt, and a pair of long linen drawers, the windows all open, and a brisk wind blowing through the house, the sweat ran off the backs of my hands, and my shirt was often so wet, as to induce me to call for dry ones to put on; in this situa-tion, one might have expected, that the natural heat of the body 96, added to the heat of the air 100, should jointly have created or produced a much greater degree of heat in the body; but the fact was, that my body never grew so hot as the air that surrounded it, or the inanimate bodies immers'd in the same air. For I remember well, that the desk, when I laid my arm upon it; a chair, when I sat down in it; and a dry shirt out of the drawer, when I put it on, all felt exceed-ing warm to me, as if they had been warmed before a fire. And I suppose a dead body would have acquired the temper-ature of the air, though a living one, by continual sweating, and by the evaporation of that sweat, was kept cold.—May not this be a reason why our reapers in *Pensylvania*, working in the open field, in the clear hot sunshine common in our harvest-time *, find themselves well able to go through that labour, without being much incommoded by the heat, while they continue to sweat, and while they supply matter for keeping up that sweat, by drinking frequently of a thin evap-orable liquor, water mixed with rum; but if the sweat stops, they drop, and sometimes die suddenly, if a sweating is not again brought on by drinking that liquor, or, as some rather chuse in that case, a kind of hot punch, made with water,

* *Pensylvania* is in about lat. 40, and the sun, of course, about 12 degrees higher, and therefore much hotter than in *England*. Their harvest is about the end of *June*, or beginning of *July*, when the sun is nearly at the highest.

mixed with honey, and a considerable proportion of vinegar?—May there not be in negroes a quicker evaporation of
the perspirable matter from their skins and lungs, which, by
cooling them more, enables them to bear the sun's heat better
than whites do? (if that is a fact, as it is said to be; for the
alledg'd necessity of having negroes rather than whites, to
work in the *West-India* fields, is founded upon it) though the
colour of their skins would otherwise make them more sensible of the sun's heat, since black cloth heats much sooner, and
more, in the sun, than white cloth. I am persuaded, from several instances happening within my knowledge, that they do
not bear cold weather so well as the whites; they will perish
when exposed to a less degree of it, and are more apt to have
their limbs frost-bitten; and may not this be from the same
cause? Would not the earth grow much hotter under the summer sun, if a constant evaporation from its surface, greater as
the sun shines stronger, did not, by tending to cool it, balance, in some degree, the warmer effects of the sun's rays?—
Is it not owing to the constant evaporation from the surface
of every leaf, that trees, though shone on by the sun, are always, even the leaves themselves, cool to our sense? at least
much cooler than they would otherwise be?—May it not be
owing to this, that fanning ourselves when warm, does really
cool us, though the air is itself warm that we drive with the
fan upon our faces; for the atmosphere round, and next to
our bodies, having imbibed as much of the perspired vapour
as it can well contain, receives no more, and the evaporation
is therefore check'd and retarded, till we drive away that atmosphere, and bring dryer air in its place, that will receive
the vapour, and thereby facilitate and increase the evaporation? Certain it is, that mere blowing of air on a dry body
does not cool it, as any one may satisfy himself, by blowing
with a bellows on the dry ball of a thermometer; the mercury
will not fall; if it moves at all, it rather rises, as being warmed
by the friction of the air on its surface?—To these queries of
imagination, I will only add one practical observation; that
wherever it is thought proper to give ease, in cases of painful
inflammation in the flesh, (as from burnings, or the like) by
cooling the part; linen cloths, wet with spirit, and applied to
the part inflamed, will produce the coolness required, better

than if wet with water, and will continue it longer. For water, though cold when first applied, will soon acquire warmth from the flesh, as it does not evaporate fast enough; but the cloths wet with spirit, will continue cold as long as any spirit is left to keep up the evaporation, the parts warmed escaping as soon as they are warmed, and carrying off the heat with them.

I am, Sir, &c.

FAITH, HOPE, AND CHARITY

To Jane Mecom

Dear Sister   London Sept 16 1758

I received your Favour of June 17. I wonder you have had no Letter from me since my being in England. I have wrote you at least two and I think a third before this; And, what was next to waiting on you in Person, sent you my Picture. In June last I sent Benny a Trunk of Books and wrote to him. I hope they are come to hand, and that he meets with Incouragement in his Business. I congratulate you on the Conquest of Cape Breton, and hope as your People took it by Praying the first Time, you will now pray that it may never be given up again, which you then forgot. Billy is well but in the Country. I left him at Tunbridge Wells, where we spent a fortnight, and he is now gone with some Company to see Portsmouth.

We have been together over a great part of England this Summer; and among other places visited the Town our Father was born in and found some Relations in that part of the Country Still living. Our Cousin Jane Franklin, daughter of our Unkle John, died but about a Year ago. We saw her Husband Robert Page, who gave us some old Letters to his Wife from unkle Benjamin. In one of them, dated Boston July 4. 1723 he writes "Your Unkle Josiah has a Daughter Jane about 12 years Old, a good humour'd Child" So Jenny keep up your Character, and don't be angry when you have no Letters.

In a little Book he sent her, call'd *None but Christ*, he wrote an Acrostick on her Name, which for Namesakes' Sake, as well as the good Advice it contains, I transcribe and send you

> Illuminated from on High,
> And shining brightly in your Sphere
> Nere faint, but keep a steady Eye
> Expecting endless Pleasures there
> Flee Vice, as you'd a Serpent flee,
> Raise Faith and Hope three Stories higher
> And let Christ's endless Love to thee
> N-ere cease to make thy Love Aspire.
> Kindness of Heart by Words express
> Let your Obedience be sincere,
> In Prayer and Praise your God Address
> Nere cease 'till he can cease to hear.

After professing truly that I have a great Esteem and Veneration for the pious Author, permit me a little to play the Commentator and Critic on these Lines. The Meaning of *Three Stories* higher seems somewhat obscure, you are to understand, then, that *Faith, Hope* and *Charity* have been called the three Steps of Jacob's Ladder, reaching from Earth to Heaven. Our Author calls them *Stories*, likening Religion to a Building, and those the three Stories of the Christian Edifice; Thus Improvement in Religion, is called *Building Up*, and *Edification*. *Faith* is then the Ground-floor, *Hope* is up one Pair of Stairs. My dearly beloved Jenny, don't delight so much to dwell in these lower Rooms, but get as fast as you can into the Garret; for in truth the best Room in the House is *Charity*. For my part, I wish the House was turn'd upside down; 'tis so difficult (when one is fat) to get up Stairs; and not only so, but I imagine *Hope* and *Faith* may be more firmly built on *Charity*, than *Charity* upon *Faith* and *Hope*. However that be, I think it a better reading to say

Raise Faith and Hope *one Story* higher

correct it boldly and I'll support the Alteration. For when you are up two Stories already, if you raise your Building three Stories higher, you will make five in all, which is two more than there should be, you expose your upper Rooms more to the Winds and Storms, and besides I am afraid the Foundation will hardly bear them, unless indeed you build with such light Stuff as Straw and Stubble, and that you know won't stand Fire.

Again where the Author Says

> Kindness of Heart by Words express,

Stricke out *Words* and put in *Deeds*. The world is too full of Compliments already; they are the rank Growth of every Soil, and Choak the good Plants of Benevolence and Benificence, Nor do I pretend to be the first in this comparison of Words and Actions to Plants; you may remember an Ancient Poet whose Words we have all Studied and Copy'd at School, said long ago,

> A Man of Words and not of Deeds,
> Is like a Garden full of Weeds.

'Tis pity that *Good Works* among some sorts of People are so little Valued, and *Good Words* admired in their Stead; I mean seemingly *pious Discourses* instead of *Humane Benevolent Actions*. These they almost put out of countenance, by calling Morality *rotten Morality*, Righteousness, *ragged Righteousness* and even *filthy Rags*; and when you mention *Virtue*, they pucker up their Noses as if they smelt a Stink; at the same time that they eagerly snuff up an empty canting Harangue, as if it was a Posie of the Choicest Flowers. So they have inverted the good old Verse, and say now

> A Man of Deeds and not of Words
> Is like a Garden full of ——

I have forgot the Rhime, but remember 'tis something the very Reverse of a Perfume. So much by Way of Commentary.

My Wife will let you see my Letter containing an Account of our Travels, which I would have you read to Sister Douse, and give my Love to her. I have no thoughts of returning 'till next year, and then may possibly have the Pleasure of seeing you and yours, take Boston in my Way home. My Love to Brother and all your Children, concludes at this time from Dear Jenny your affectionate Brother

"HAPPINESS IN THIS LIFE"

To Hugh Roberts

Dear Friend,   London, Sept. 16. 1758

Your kind Letter of June 1. gave me great Pleasure. I thank you for the Concern you express about my Health, which at present seems tolerably confirm'd by my late Journeys into different Parts of the Kingdom, that have been highly entertaining as well as useful to me. Your Visits to my little Family in my Absence are very obliging, and I hope you will be so good as to continue them. Your Remark on the Thistle and the Scotch Motto, made us very merry, as well as your String of Puns. You will allow me to claim a little Merit or Demerit in the last, as having had some hand in making you a Punster; but the Wit of the first is keen, and all your own.

Two of the former Members of the Junto you tell me are departed this Life, Potts and Parsons. Odd Characters, both of them. Parsons, a wise Man, that often acted foolishly. Potts, a Wit, that seldom acted wisely. If *Enough* were the Means to make a Man happy, One had always the *Means* of Happiness without ever enjoying the *Thing*; the other had always the *Thing* without ever possessing the Means. Parsons, even in his Prosperity, always fretting! Potts, in the midst of his Poverty, ever laughing! It seems, then, that Happiness in this Life rather depends on Internals than Externals; and that, besides the natural Effects of Wisdom and Virtue, Vice and Folly, there is such a Thing as being of a happy or an unhappy Constitution. They were both our Friends, and lov'd us. So, Peace to their Shades. They had their Virtues as well as their Foibles; they were both honest Men, and that alone, as the World goes, is one of the greatest of Characters. They were old Acquaintance, in whose Company I formerly enjoy'd a great deal of Pleasure, and I cannot think of losing them, without Concern and Regret.

Let me know in your next, to what Purposes Parsons will'd his Estate from his Family; you hint at something which you have not explain'd.

I shall, as you suppose, look on every Opportunity you give

me of doing you Service, as a Favour, because it will afford me Pleasure. Therefore send your Orders for buying Books as soon as you please. I know how to make you ample Returns for such Favours, by giving you the Pleasure of Building me a House. You may do it without losing any of your own Time; it will only take some Part of that you now spend in other Folks Business. 'Tis only jumping out of their Waters into mine.

I am grieved for our Friend Syng's Loss. You and I, who esteem him, and have valuable Sons ourselves, can sympathise with him sincerely. I hope yours is perfectly recovered, for your sake as well as for his own. I wish he may be in every Respect as good and as useful a Man as his Father. I need not wish him more; and can now only add that I am, with great Esteem, Dear Friend, Yours affectionately

P.S. I rejoice to hear of the Prosperity of the Hospital, and send the Wafers.

I do not quite like your absenting yourself from that good old Club the Junto: Your more frequent PRE SENCE might be a means of keeping them from being ALL ENgag'd in Measures not the best for the Publick Welfare. I exhort you therefore to return to your Duty; and, as the Indians say, to confirm my Words, I send you a Birmingham Tile.

I thought the neatness of the Figures would please you.

Pray send me a good Impression of the Hospital Seal in Wax. 2 or three would not be amiss, I may make a good Use of them.

"CONVERSATION WARMS THE MIND"

To Lord Kames

My dear Lord,   London, Jany. 3. 1760

I ought long before this time to have acknowledg'd the Receipt of your Favour of Nov. 2. Your Lordship was pleas'd kindly to desire to have all my Publications. I had daily Expectations of procuring some of them from a Friend to whom I formerly sent them when I was in America, and postpon'd Writing till I should obtain them; but at length he tells me he cannot find them. Very mortifying, this, to an Author, that his Works should so soon be lost! So I can now only send you my *Observations on the Peopling of Countries*, which happens to have been reprinted here; The *Description of the Pennsylvanian Fireplace*, a Machine of my contriving; and some little Sketches that have been printed in the Grand Magazine; which I should hardly own, did not I flatter myself that your friendly Partiality would make them seem at least tolerable.

How unfortunate I was, that I did not press you and Lady Kames more strongly, to favour us with your Company farther! How much more agreable would our Journey have been, if we could have enjoy'd you as far as York! Mr. Blake, who we hop'd would have handed us along from Friend to Friend, was not at home, and so we knew nobody and convers'd with nobody on all that long Road, till we came thither. The being a Means of contributing in the least Degree to the restoring that good Lady's Health, would have contributed greatly to our Pleasures, and we could have beguil'd the Way by Discoursing 1000 Things that now we may never have an Opportunity of considering together; for Conversation warms the Mind, enlivens the Imagination, and is continually starting fresh Game that is immediately pursu'd and taken and which would never have occur'd in the duller Intercourse of Epistolary Correspondence. So that whenever I reflect on the great Pleasure and Advantage I receiv'd from the free Communication of Sentiments in the Conversation your Lordship honour'd me with at Kaims, and in the little agreable Rides to the Tweedside, I shall forever regret that unlucky premature Parting.

No one can rejoice more sincerely than I do on the Reduction of Canada; and this, not merely as I am a Colonist, but as I am a Briton. I have long been of Opinion, that the Foundations of the future Grandeur and Stability of the British Empire, lie in America; and tho', like other Foundations, they are low and little seen, they are nevertheless, broad and Strong enough to support the greatest Political Structure Human Wisdom ever yet erected. I am therefore by no means for restoring Canada. If we keep it, all the Country from St. Laurence to Missisipi, will in another Century be fill'd with British People; Britain itself will become vastly more populous by the immense Increase of its Commerce; the Atlantic Sea will be cover'd with your Trading Ships; and your naval Power thence continually increasing, will extend your Influence round the whole Globe, and awe the World! If the French remain in Canada, they will continually harass our Colonies by the Indians, impede if not prevent their Growth; your Progress to Greatness will at best be slow, and give room for many Accidents that may for ever prevent it. But I refrain, for I see you begin to think my Notions extravagant, and look upon them as the Ravings of a mad Prophet.

Your Lordship's kind Offer of Penn's Picture is extreamly obliging. But were it certainly his Picture, it would be too valuable a Curiosity for me to think of accepting it. I should only desire the Favour of Leave to take a Copy of it. I could wish to know the History of the Picture before it came into your Hands, and the Grounds for supposing it his. I have at present some Doubts about it; first, because the primitive Quakers us'd to declare against Pictures as a vain Expence; a Man's suffering his Portrait to be taken was condemn'd as Pride; and I think to this day it is very little practis'd among them. Then it is on a Board, and I imagine the Practice of painting Portraits on Boards did not come down so low as Penn's Time; but of this I am not certain. My other Reason is an Anecdote I have heard, viz. That when old Lord Cobham was adorning his Gardens at Stowe with the Busts of famous Men, he made Enquiry of the Family for a Picture of Wm. Penn, in order to get a Bust form'd from it, but could find none. That Sylvanus Bevan, an old Quaker Apothecary, remarkable for the Notice he takes of Countenances, and a Knack he has of cutting in Ivory strong Likenesses of Persons he has once seen, hearing of Lord Cobham's Desire, set himself to recollect Penn's Face, with which he had been well acquainted; and cut a little Bust of him in Ivory which he sent to Lord Cobham, without any Letter of Notice that it was Penn's. But my Lord who had personally known Penn, on seeing it, immediately cry'd out,

Whence came this? It is William Penn himself! And from this little Bust, they say, the large one in the Gardens was formed. I doubt, too, whether the Whisker was not quite out of Use at the time when Penn must have been of the Age appearing in the Face of that Picture. And yet notwithstanding these Reasons, I am not without some Hope that it may be his; because I know some eminent Quakers have had their Pictures privately drawn, and deposited with trusty Friends; and I know also that there is extant at Philadelphia a very good Picture of Mrs. Penn, his last Wife. After all, I own I have a strong Desire to be satisfy'd concerning this Picture; and as Bevan is yet living here, and some other old Quakers that remember William Penn, who died but in 1718, I could wish to have it sent me carefully pack'd in a Box by the Waggon (for I would not trust it by Sea) that I may obtain their Opinion, The Charges I shall very chearfully pay; and if it proves to be Penn's Picture, I shall be greatly oblig'd to your Lordship for Leave to take a Copy of it, and will carefully return the Original.

My Son joins with me in the most respectful Compliments to you, to Lady Kaims, and your promising and amiable Son and Daughter. He had the Pleasure of conversing more particularly with the latter than I did, and told me, when we were by our selves, that he was greatly surprized to find so much sensible Observation and solid Understanding in so young a Person; and suppos'd you must have us'd with your Children some uncommonly good Method of Education, to produce such Fruits so early. Our Conversation till we came to York was chiefly a Recollection and Recapitulation of what we had seen and heard, the Pleasure we had enjoy'd and the Kindnesses we had receiv'd in Scotland, and how far that Country had exceeded our Expectations. On the whole, I must say, I think the Time we spent there, was Six Weeks of the *densest* Happiness I have met with in any Part of my Life. And the agreable and instructive Society we found there in such Plenty, has left so pleasing an Impression on my Memory, that did not strong Connections draw me elsewhere, I believe Scotland would be the Country I should chuse to spend the Remainder of my Days in.

I have the Honour to be, with the sincerest Esteem and

Affection, My Lord, Your Lordship's most obedient and most humble Servant

PS. My Son puts me in mind that a Book published here last Winter, contains a number of Pieces wrote by me as a Member of the Assembly, in our late Controversies with the Proprietary Governors; so I shall leave one of them at Millar's to be sent to you, it being too bulky to be sent per Post.

"THE MORE THEY ARE RESPECTED"

To Jane Mecom

Dear Sister,   London, Jan. 9. 1760

I received a Letter or two from you, in which I perceive you have misunderstood and taken unkindly something I said to you in a former jocular one of mine concerning CHARITY. I forget what it was exactly, but I am sure I neither express nor meant any personal Censure on you or any body. If anything, it was a general Reflection on our Sect; we zealous Presbyterians being too apt to think ourselves alone in the right, and that besides all the Heathens, Mahometans and Papists, whom we give to Satan in a Lump, other Sects of Christian Protestants that do not agree with us, will hardly escape Perdition. And I might recommend it to you to be more charitable in that respect than many others are; not aiming at any Reproof, as you term it; for if I were dispos'd to reprove you, it should be for your only Fault, that of supposing and spying Affronts, and catching at them where they are not. But as you seem sensible of this yourself, I need not mention it; and as it is a Fault that carries with it its own sufficient Punishment, by the Uneasiness and Fretting it produces, I shall not add Weight to it. Besides, I am sure your own good Sense, join'd to your natural good Humour will in time get the better of it.

I am glad that Cousin Benny could advance you the Legacy, since it suited you best to receive it immediately. Your

Resolution to forbear buying the Cloak you wanted, was a prudent one; but when I read it, I concluded you should not however be without one, and so desired a Friend to buy one for you. The Cloth ones, it seems, are quite out of Fashion here, and so will probably soon be out with you; I have therefore got you a very decent one of another kind, which I shall send you by the next convenient Opportunity.

It is remarkable that so many Breaches should be made by Death in our Family in so short a Space. Out of Seventeen Children that our Father had, thirteen liv'd to grow up and settle in the World. I remember these thirteen (some of us then very young) all at one Table, when an Entertainment was made in our House on Occasion of the Return of our Brother Josiah, who had been absent in the East-Indies, and unheard of for nine Years. Of these thirteen, there now remains but three. As our Number diminishes, let our Affection to each other rather increase: for besides its being our Duty, tis our Interest, since the more affectionate Relations are to one another, the more they are respected by the rest of the World.

My Love to Brother Mecom and your Children. I shall hardly have time to write to Benny by this Conveyance. Acquaint him that I received his Letter of Sept. 10, and am glad to hear he is in so prosperous a Way, as not to regret his leaving Antigua. I am, my dear Sister, Your ever affectionate Brother

March 26. The above was wrote at the time it is dated; but on reading it over, I apprehended that something I had said in it about Presbyterians, and Affronts, might possibly give more Offence; and so I threw it by, concluding not to send it. However, Mr. Bailey calling on me, and having no other Letter ready nor time at present to write one, I venture to send it, and beg you will excuse what you find amiss in it. I send also by Mr. Bailey the Cloak mention'd in it, and also a Piece of Linnen, which I beg you to accept of from Your loving Brother

I received your Letter, and Benny's and Peter's by Mr. Baily, which I shall answer per next Opportunity.

To Lord Kames

My dear Lord,   London, May 3. 1760.

Your obliging Favour of January 24th. found me greatly indispos'd with an obstinate Cold and Cough accompany'd with Feverish Complaints and Headachs, that lasted long and harass'd me greatly, not being subdu'd at length but by the whole Round of Cupping, Bleeding, Blistering, &c. When I had any Intervals of Ease and Clearness, I endeavour'd to comply with your Request, in writing something on the present Situation of our Affairs in America, in order to give more correct Notions of the British Interest with regard to the Colonies, than those I found many sensible Men possess'd of. Inclos'd you have the Production, such as it is. I wish it may in any Degree be of Service to the Publick. I shall at least hope this from it for my own Part, that you will consider it as a Letter from me to you, and accept its Length as some Excuse for its being so long acoming.

I am now reading, with great Pleasure and Improvement, your excellent Work, the Principles of Equity. It will be of the greatest Advantage to the Judges in our Colonies, not only in those which have Courts of Chancery, but also in those which having no such Courts are obliged to mix Equity with the Common Law. It will be of the more Service to the Colony Judges, as few of them have been bred to the Law. I have sent a Book to a particular Friend, one of the Judges of the Supreme Court in Pensilvania.

I will shortly send you a Copy of the Chapter you are pleas'd to mention in so obliging a Manner; and shall be extreamly oblig'd in receiving a Copy of the Collection of Maxims for the Conduct of Life, which you are preparing for the Use of your Children. I purpose, likewise, a little Work for the Benefit of Youth, to be call'd *The Art of Virtue*. From the Title I think you will hardly conjecture what the Nature of such a Book may be. I must therefore explain it a little. Many People lead bad Lives that would gladly lead good ones, but know not *how* to make the Change. They have frequently *resolv'd* and *endeavour'd* it; but in vain, because their Endeavours have not been properly conducted. To exhort People to be good, to be just, to be temperate, &c. without *shewing* them *how* they shall *become* so, seems like the ineffectual Charity mention'd by the Apostle, which consisted in saying to the Hungry, the Cold, and the Naked, *be ye fed, be ye warmed, be ye clothed*, without shewing them how they should get Food, Fire or Clothing. Most People have naturally *some* Virtues, but none have naturally *all* the Virtues. To *acquire* those that are wanting, and *secure* what we acquire as well as those we have naturally, is the Subject of *an Art*. It is as properly an Art, as Painting, Navigation, or Architecture. If a Man would become a Painter, Navigator, or Architect, it is not enough that he is *advised* to be one, that he is *convinc'd* by the Arguments of his Adviser that it would be for his Advantage to be one, and that he *resolves* to be one, but he must also be taught the Principles of the Art, be shewn all the Methods of Working, and how to acquire the *Habits* of using properly all the Instruments; and thus regularly and gradually he arrives by Practice at some Perfection in the Art. If he does not proceed thus, he is apt to meet with Difficulties that discourage him, and make him drop the Pursuit. My *Art of Virtue* has also its Instruments, and teaches the Manner of Using them. Christians are directed to have *Faith in Christ*, as the effectual Means of obtaining the Change they desire. It may, when sufficiently strong, be effectual with many. A full Opinion that a Teacher is infinitely wise, good, and powerful, and that he will certainly reward and punish the Obedient and Disobedient, must give great Weight to his Precepts, and make them much more attended to by his Disciples. But all Men cannot have Faith in Christ; and many have it in so weak a Degree, that it does not produce the Effect. Our *Art of Virtue* may therefore be of great Service to those who have not Faith, and come in Aid of the weak Faith of others. Such as are naturally well-disposed, and have been carefully educated, so that good Habits have been early established, and bad ones prevented, have less Need of this Art; but all may be more or less benefited by it. It is, in short, to be adapted for universal Use. I imagine what I have now been writing will seem to savour of great Presumption; I must therefore speedily finish my little Piece, and communicate the Manuscript to you, that you may judge whether it is possible to make good such Pretensions. I shall at the same time hope for the Benefit of your Corrections.

My respectful Compliments to Lady Kaims and your amiable Children, in which my Son joins. With the sincerest Esteem and Attachment, I am, My Lord, Your Lordship's most obedient and most humble Servant

P.S. While I remain in London I shall continue in Craven Street, Strand: if you favour me with your Correspondence when I return to America, please to direct for me in Philadelphia, and your Letters will readily find me tho' sent to any other Part of North America.

SALT DEPOSITS

To Peter Franklin

SIR,   *London, May* 7, 1760.
* * * * * * It has, indeed, as you observe, been the opinion of some very great naturalists, that the sea is salt only from the dissolution of mineral or rock salt, which its waters happened to meet with. But this opinion takes it for granted that all water was originally fresh, of which we can have no proof. I own I am inclined to a different opinion, and rather think all the water on this globe was originally salt, and that the fresh water we find in springs and rivers, is the produce of distillation. The sun raises the vapours from the sea, which form clouds, and fall in rain upon the land, and springs and rivers are formed of that rain.—As to the rock-salt found in mines, I conceive, that instead of communicating its saltness to the sea, it is itself drawn from the sea, and that of course the sea is now fresher than it was originally. This is only another effect of nature's distillery, and might be performed various ways.

It is evident from the quantities of sea-shells, and the bones and teeth of fishes found in high lands, that the sea has formerly covered them. Then, either the sea has been higher than it now is, and has fallen away from those high lands; or they have been lower than they are, and were lifted up out of the water to their present height, by some internal mighty force, such as we still feel some remains of, when whole continents are moved by earthquakes. In either case it may be supposed that large hollows, or valleys among hills, might be left filled with sea-water, which evaporating, and the fluid part drying away in a course of years, would leave the salt covering the bottom; and that salt coming afterwards to be covered with earth, from the neighbouring hills, could only be found by digging through that earth. Or, as we know from their effects, that there are deep fiery caverns under the earth, and even under the sea, if at any time the sea leaks into any of them, the fluid parts of the water must evaporate from that heat, and pass off through some vulcano, while the salt remains, and by degrees, and continual accretion, becomes a great mass. Thus the cavern may at length be filled, and the volcano connected with it cease burning, as many it is said have done; and future miners penetrating such cavern, find what we call a salt mine.—This is a fancy I had on visiting the salt-mines at *Northwich*, with my son. I send you a piece of the rock-salt which he brought up with him out of the mine. * * * * * *

I am, Sir, &c.

"THE KNOWLEDGE OF NATURE"

To Mary Stevenson

Dear Polly,   Cravenstreet, June 11. 1760

'Tis a very sensible Question you ask, how the Air can affect the Barometer, when its Opening appears covered with Wood? If indeed it was so closely covered as to admit of no Communication of the outward Air to the Surface of the Mercury, the Change of Weight in the Air could not possibly affect it. But the least Crevice is sufficient for the Purpose; a Pinhole will do the Business. And if you could look behind the Frame to which your Barometer is fixed, you would certainly find some small Opening.

There are indeed some Barometers in which the Body of Mercury at the lower End is contain'd in a close Leather Bag, and so the Air cannot come into immediate Contact with the Mercury: Yet the same Effect is produc'd. For the Leather being flexible, when the Bag is press'd by any additional Weight of Air, it contracts, and the Mercury is forc'd up into the Tube; when the Air becomes lighter, and its Pressure less, the Weight of the Mercury prevails, and it descends again into the Bag.

Your Observation on what you have lately read concerning Insects, is very just and solid. Superficial Minds are apt to despise those who make that Part of Creation their Study, as mere Triflers; but certainly the World has been much oblig'd to them. Under the Care and Management of Man, the Labours of the little Silkworm afford Employment and Subsistence to Thousands of Families, and become an immense Article of Commerce. The Bee, too, yields us its delicious Honey, and its Wax useful to a multitude of Purposes. Another Insect, it is said, produces the Cochineal, from whence we have our rich Scarlet Dye. The Usefulness of the Cantharides, or Spanish Flies, in Medicine, is known to all, and Thousands owe their Lives to that Knowledge. By human Industry and Observation, other Properties of other Insects may possibly be hereafter discovered, and of equal Utility. A thorough Acquaintance with the Nature of these little Creatures, may also enable Mankind to prevent the Increase of such as are noxious or secure us against the Mischiefs they occasion. These Things doubtless your Books make mention of: I can only add a particular late Instance which I had from a Swedish Gentleman of good Credit. In the green Timber intended for Ship-building at the King's Yards in that Country, a kind of Worms were found, which every Year became more numerous and more pernicious, so that the Ships were greatly damag'd before they came into Use. The King sent Linnaeus, the great Naturalist, from Stockholm, to enquire into the Affair, and see if the Mischief was capable of any Remedy. He found on Examination, that the Worm was produc'd from a small Egg deposited in the little Roughnesses on the Surface of the Wood, by a particular kind of Fly or Beetle; from whence the Worm, as soon as it was hatch'd, began to eat into the Substance of the Wood, and after some time came out again a Fly of the Parent kind, and so the Species increas'd. The Season in which this Fly laid its Eggs, Linnaeus knew to be about a Fortnight (I think) in the Month of May, and at no other time of the Year. He therefore advis'd, that some Days before that Season, all the green Timber should be thrown into the Water, and kept under Water till the Season was over. Which being done by the King's Order, the Flies missing their usual Nests, could not increase; and the Species was either destroy'd or went elsewhere; and the Wood was effectually preserved, for after the first Year, it became too dry and hard for their purpose.

There is, however, a prudent Moderation to be used in Studies of this kind. The Knowledge of Nature may be ornamental, and it may be useful, but if to attain an Eminence in that, we neglect the Knowledge and Practice of essential Duties, we deserve Reprehension. For there is no Rank in Natural Knowledge of equal Dignity and Importance with that of being a good Parent, a good Child, a good Husband, or Wife, a good Neighbour or Friend, a good Subject or Citizen, that is, in short, a good Christian. Nicholas Gimcrack, therefore, who neglected the Care of his Family, to pursue Butterflies, was a just Object of Ridicule, and we must give him up as fair Game to the Satyrist.

Adieu, my dear Friend, and believe me ever Yours affectionately

Your good Mother is well, and gives her Love and Blessing to you. My Compliments to your Aunts, Miss Pitt, &c.

TIDES IN RIVERS

To Mary Stevenson

My dear Friend,   London, Sept. 13. 1760

I have your agreable Letter from Bristol, which I take this first Leisure Hour to answer, having for some time been much engag'd in Business.

Your first Question, *What is the Reason the Water at this Place, tho' cold at the Spring, becomes warm by Pumping?* it will be most prudent in me to forbear attempting to answer, till, by a more circumstantial Account, you assure me of the Fact. I own I should expect that Operation to warm, not so much the Water pump'd as the Person pumping. The Rubbing of dry Solids together, has been long observ'd to produce Heat; but the like Effect has never yet, that I have heard, been produc'd by the mere Agitation of Fluids, or Friction of Fluids with Solids. Water in a Bottle shook for Hours by a Mill Hopper, it is said, discover'd no sensible Addition of Heat. The Production of Animal Heat by Exercise, is therefore to be accounted for in another manner, which I may hereafter endeavour to make you acquainted with.

This Prudence of not attempting to give Reasons before one is sure of Facts, I learnt from one of your Sex, who, as Selden tells us, being in company with some Gentlemen that were viewing and considering something which they call'd a Chinese Shoe, and disputing earnestly about the manner of wearing it, and how it could possibly be put on; put in her Word, and said modestly, *Gentlemen, are you sure it is a Shoe? Should not that be settled first?*

But I shall now endeavour to explain what I said to you about the Tide in Rivers, and to that End shall make a Figure, which tho' not very like a River, may serve to convey my Meaning. Suppose a Canal 140 Miles long communicating at one End with the Sea, and fill'd therefore with Sea Water. I chuse a Canal at first, rather than a River, to throw out of Consideration the Effects produc'd by the Streams of Fresh Water from the Land, the Inequality in Breadth, and the

Crookedness of Courses. Let A, C, be the Head of the Canal, C D the Bottom of it; D F the open Mouth of it next the Sea. Let the strait prick'd Line B G represent Low Water Mark the whole Length of the Canal, A F High Water Mark: Now if a Person standing at E, and observing at the time of

High water there that the Canal is quite full at that Place up
to the Line E, should conclude that the Canal is equally full
to the same Height from End to End, and therefore there was
as much more Water come into the Canal since it was down
at the Low Water Mark, as could be included in the oblong
Space A. B. G. F. he would be greatly mistaken. For the Tide
is *a Wave*, and the Top of the Wave, which makes High Water, as well as every other lower Part, is progressive; and it is
High Water successively, but not at the same time, in all the
several Points between G, F. and A, B.—and in such a
Length as I have mention'd it is Low Water at F G and also
at A B, at or near the same time with its being High Water
at E; so that the Surface of the Water in the Canal, during
that Situation, is properly represented by the Curve prick'd
Line B E G. And on the other hand, when it is Low Water
at E H, it is High Water both at F G and at A B at or near
the same time; and the Surface would then be describ'd by
the inverted Curve Line A H F.

In this View of the Case, you will easily see, that there
must be very little more Water in the Canal at what we call
High Water than there is at Low Water, those Terms not relating to the whole Canal at the same time, but successively
to its Parts. And if you suppose the Canal six times as long,
the Case would not vary as to the Quantity of Water at different times of the Tide; there would only be six Waves in the
Canal at the same time, instead of one, and the Hollows in
the Water would be equal to the Hills.

That this is not mere Theory, but comformable to Fact, we
know by our long Rivers in America. The Delaware, on
which Philadelphia stands, is in this particular similar to the
Canal I have supposed of one Wave: For when it is High
Water at the Capes or Mouth of the River, it is also High
Water at Philadelphia, which stands about 140 Miles from the
Sea; and there is at the same time a Low Water in the Middle
between the two High Waters; where, when it comes to be
High Water, it is at the same time Low Water at the Capes
and at Philadelphia. And the longer Rivers have, some a Wave
and Half, some two, three, or four Waves, according to their
Length. In the shorter Rivers of this Island, one may see the
same thing in Part: for Instance; it is High Water at Graves-

end an Hour before it is High Water at London Bridge; and 20 Miles below Gravesend an Hour before it is High Water at Gravesend. Therefore at the Time of High Water at Gravesend the Top of the Wave is there, and the Water is then not so high by some feet where the Top of the Wave was an Hour before, or where it will be an Hour after, as it is just then at Gravesend.

Now we are not to suppose, that because the Swell or Top of the Wave runs at the Rate of 20 Miles an Hour, that therefore the Current or Water itself of which the Wave is compos'd, runs at that rate. Far from it. To conceive this Motion of a Wave, make a small Experiment or two. Fasten one End of a Cord in a Window near the Top of a House, and let the other End come down to the Ground; take this End in your Hand, and you may, by a sudden Motion occasion a Wave in the Cord that will run quite up to the Window; but tho' the Wave is progressive from your Hand to the Window, the Parts of the Rope do not proceed with the Wave, but remain where they were, except only that kind of Motion that produces the Wave. So if you throw a Stone into a Pond of Water when the Surface is still and smooth, you will see a circular Wave proceed from the Stone as its Center, quite to the Sides of the Pond; but the Water does not proceed with the Wave, it only rises and falls to form it in the different Parts of its Course; and the Waves that follow the first, all make use of the same Water with their Predecessors.

But a Wave in Water is not indeed in all Circumstances exactly like that in a Cord; for Water being a Fluid, and gravitating to the Earth, it naturally runs from a higher Place to a lower; therefore the Parts of the Wave in Water do actually run a little both ways from its Top towards its lower Sides, which the Parts of the Wave in the Cord cannot do. Thus when it is high and standing Water at Gravesend, the Water 20 Miles below has been running Ebb, or towards the Sea for an Hour, or ever since it was High Water there; but the Water at London Bridge will run Flood, or from the Sea yet another Hour, till it is High Water or the Top of the Wave arrives at that Bridge, and then it will have run Ebb an Hour at Gravesend, &c. &c. Now this Motion of the Water, occasion'd only by its Gravity, or Tendency to run from a higher Place to a lower, is by no means so swift as the Motion of the Wave. It scarce exceeds perhaps two Miles in an Hour. If it went as the Wave does 20 Miles an Hour, no Ships could ride at Anchor in such a Stream, nor Boats row against it.

In common Speech, indeed, this Current of the Water both Ways from the Top of the Wave is call'd *the Tide*; thus we say, *the Tide runs strong, the Tide runs at the rate of* 1, 2, *or* 3 *Miles an hour,* &c. and when we are at a Part of the River behind the Top of the Wave, and find the Water lower than Highwater Mark, and running towards the Sea, we say, *the Tide runs Ebb*; and when we are before the Top of the Wave, and find the Water higher than Low-water Mark, and running from the Sea, we say, the *Tide runs Flood*: But these Expressions are only locally proper; for a Tide strictly speaking is *one whole Wave*, including all its Parts higher and lower, and these Waves succeed one another about twice in twenty four Hours.

This Motion of the Water, occasion'd by its Gravity, will explain to you why the Water near the Mouths of Rivers may be salter at Highwater than at Low. Some of the Salt Water, as the Tide Wave enters the River, runs from its Top and fore Side, and mixes with the fresh, and also pushes it back up the River.

Supposing that the Water commonly runs during the Flood at the Rate of two Miles in an Hour, and that the Flood runs 5 Hours, you see that it can bring at most into our Canal only a Quantity of Water equal to the Space included in the Breadth of the Canal, ten Miles of its Length, and the Depth between Low and Highwater Mark. Which is but a fourteenth Part of what would be necessary to fill all the Space between Low and Highwater Mark, for 140 Miles, the whole Length of the Canal.

And indeed such a Quantity of Water as would fill that whole Space, to run in and out every Tide, must create so outrageous a Current, as would do infinite Damage to the Shores, Shipping, &c. and make the Navigation of a River almost impracticable.

I have made this Letter longer than I intended, and therefore reserve for another what I have farther to say on the Subject of Tides and Rivers. I shall now only add, that I have not been exact in the Numbers, because I would avoid perplexing you with minute Calculations, my Design at present being chiefly to give you distinct and clear Ideas of the first Principles.

After writing 6 Folio Pages of Philosophy to a young Girl, is it necessary to finish such a Letter with a Compliment? Is not such a Letter of itself a Compliment? Does it not say, she has a Mind thirsty after Knowledge, and capable of receiving it; and that the most agreable Things one can write to her are those that tend to the Improvement of her Understanding? It does indeed say all this, but then it is still no Compliment; it is no more than plain honest Truth, which is not the Character of a Compliment. So if I would finish my Letter in the Mode, I should yet add something that means nothing, and is *merely* civil and polite. But being naturally awkward at every Circumstance of Ceremony, I shall not attempt it. I had rather conclude abruptly with what pleases me more than any Compliment can please you, that I am allow'd to subscribe my self Your affectionate Friend

"THE BEST ENGLISH"

To David Hume

Dear Sir,   Coventry, Sept. 27. 1760
I have too long postpon'd answering your obliging Letter, a Fault I will not attempt to excuse, but rather rely on your Goodness to forgive it if I am more punctual for the future.

I am oblig'd to you for the favourable Sentiments you express of the Pieces sent you; tho' the Volume relating to our Pensilvania Affairs, was not written by me, nor any Part of it, except the Remarks on the Proprietor's Estimate of his Estate, and some of the inserted Messages and Reports of the Assembly which I wrote when at home, as a Member of Committees appointed by the House for that Service; the rest was by another Hand. But tho' I am satisfy'd by what you say, that the Duke of Bedford was hearty in the Scheme of the Expedition, I am not so clear that others in the Adminis-

tration were equally in earnest in that matter. It is certain that
after the Duke of Newcastle's first Orders to raise Troops in
the Colonies, and Promise to send over Commissions to the
Officers, with Arms, Clothing, &c. for the Men, we never had
another Syllable from him for 18 Months; during all which
time the Army lay idle at Albany for want of Orders and
Necessaries; and it began to be thought at least that if an
Expedition had ever been intended, the first Design and the
Orders given, must, thro' the Multiplicity of Business here at
home, have been quite forgotten.

I am not a little pleas'd to hear of your Change of Sentiments in some particulars relating to America; because I think
it of Importance to our general Welfare that the People of this
Nation should have right Notions of us, and I know no one
that has it more in his Power to rectify their Notions, than
Mr. Hume. I have lately read with great Pleasure, as I do
every thing of yours, the excellent Essay on the *Jealousy of
Commerce*: I think it cannot but have a good Effect in promoting a certain Interest too little thought of by selfish Man,
and scarce ever mention'd, so that we hardly have a Name for
it; I mean the *Interest of Humanity*, or common Good of
Mankind: But I hope particularly from that Essay, an Abatement of the Jealousy that reigns here of the Commerce of the
Colonies, at least so far as such Abatement may be reasonable.

I thank you for your friendly Admonition relating to some
unusual Words in the Pamphlet. It will be of Service to me.
The *pejorate*, and the *colonize*, since they are not in common
use here, I give up as bad; for certainly in Writings intended
for Persuasion and for general Information, one cannot be
too clear, and every Expression in the least obscure is a Fault.
The *unshakeable* too, tho' clear, I give up as rather low. The
introducing new Words where we are already possess'd of
old ones sufficiently expressive, I confess must be generally
wrong, as it tends to change the Language; yet at the same
time I cannot but wish the Usage of our Tongue permitted
making new Words when we want them, by Composition of
old ones whose Meanings are already well understood. The
German allows of it, and it is a common Practice with their
Writers. Many of our present English Words were originally
so made; and many of the Latin Words. In point of Clearness

such compound Words would have the Advantage of any we can borrow from the ancient or from foreign Languages. For instance, the Word *inaccessible*, tho' long in use among us, is not yet, I dare say, so universally understood by our People as the Word *uncomeatable* would immediately be, which we are not allow'd to write. But I hope with you, that we shall always in America make the best English of this Island our Standard, and I believe it will be so. I assure you, it often gives me Pleasure to reflect how greatly the *Audience* (if I may so term it) of a good English Writer will in another Century or two be encreas'd, by the Increase of English People in our Colonies.

My Son presents his Respects with mine to you and Dr. Monro. We receiv'd your printed circular Letter to the Members of the Society, and purpose some time next Winter to send each of us a little Philosophical Essay. With the greatest Esteem I am, Dear Sir, Your most obedient and most humble Servant

COLOR AND HEAT

To Mary Stevenson

My dear Friend

It is, as you observed in our late Conversation, a very general Opinion, that *all Rivers run into the Sea*, or deposite their Waters there. 'Tis a kind of Audacity to call such general Opinions in question, and may subject one to Censure: But we must hazard something in what we think the Cause of Truth: And if we propose our Objections modestly, we shall, tho' mistaken, deserve a Censure less severe, than when we are both mistaken and insolent.

That some Rivers run into the Sea is beyond a doubt: Such, for Instance, are the Amazones, and I think the Oranoko and the Missisipi. The Proof is, that their Waters are fresh quite to the Sea, and out to some Distance from the Land. Our Question is, whether the fresh Waters of those Rivers whose Beds are filled with Salt Water to a considerable

Distance up from the Sea (as the Thames, the Delaware, and the Rivers that communicate with Chesapeak Bay in Virginia) do ever arrive at the Sea? and as I suspect they do not, I am now to acquaint you with my Reasons; or, if they are not allow'd to be Reasons, my Conceptions, at least of this Matter.

The common Supply of Rivers is from Springs, which draw their Origin from Rain that has soak'd into the Earth. The Union of a Number of Springs forms a River. The Waters as they run, expos'd to the Sun, Air and Wind, are continually evaporating. Hence in Travelling one may often see where a River runs, by a long blueish Mist over it, tho' we are at such a Distance as not to see the River itself. The Quantity of this Evaporation is greater or less in proportion to the Surface exposed by the same Quantity of Water to those Causes of Evaporation. While the River runs in a narrow confined Channel in the upper hilly Country, only a small Surface is exposed; a greater as the River widens. Now if a River ends in a Lake, as some do, whereby its Waters are spread so wide as that the Evaporation is equal to the Sum of all its Springs, that Lake will never overflow: And if instead of ending in a Lake, it was drawn into greater Length as a River, so as to expose a Surface equal, in the whole to that Lake, the Evaporation would be equal, and such River would end as a Canal; when the Ignorant might suppose, as they actually do in such cases, that the River loses itself by running under ground, whereas in truth it has run up into the Air.

Now many Rivers that are open to the Sea, widen much before they arrive at it, not merely by the additional Waters they receive, but by having their Course stopt by the opposing Flood Tide; by being turned back twice in twenty-four Hours, and by finding broader Beds in the low flat Countries to dilate themselves in; hence the Evaporation of the fresh Water is proportionably increas'd, so that in some Rivers it may equal the Springs of Supply. In such cases, the Salt Water comes up the River, and meets the fresh in that part where, if there were a Wall or Bank of Earth across from Side to Side, the River would form a Lake, fuller indeed at some times than at others according to the Seasons, but whose

Evaporation would, one time with another, be equal to its Supply.

When the Communication between the two kinds of Water is open, this supposed Wall of Separation may be conceived as a moveable one, which is not only pushed some Miles higher up the River by every Flood Tide from the Sea, and carried down again as far by every Tide of Ebb, but which has even this Space of Vibration removed nearer to the Sea in wet Seasons, when the Springs and Brooks in the upper Country are augmented by the falling Rains so as to swell the River, and farther from the Sea in dry Seasons.

Within a few Miles above and below this moveable Line of Separation, the different Waters mix a little, partly by their Motion to and fro, and partly from the greater specific Gravity of the Salt Water, which inclines it to run under the Fresh, while the fresh Water being lighter runs over the Salt.

Cast your Eye on the Map of North America, and observe the Bay of Chesapeak in Virginia, mentioned above; you will see, communicating with it by their Mouths, the great Rivers Sasquehanah, Potowmack, Rappahanock, York and James, besides a Number of smaller Streams each as big as the Thames. It has been propos'd by philosophical Writers, that to compute how much Water any River discharges into the Sea, in a given time, we should measure its Depth and Swiftness at any Part above the Tide, as, for the Thames, at Kingston or Windsor. But can one imagine, that if all the Water of those vast Rivers went to the Sea, it would not first have pushed the Salt Water out of that narrow-mouthed Bay, and filled it with fresh? The Sasquehanah alone would seem to be sufficient for this, if it were not for the Loss by Evaporation. And yet that Bay is salt quite up to Annapolis.

As to our other Subject, the different Degrees of Heat imbibed from the Sun's Rays by Cloths of different Colours, since I cannot find the Notes of my Experiment to send you, I must give it as well as I can from Memory.

But first let me mention an Experiment you may easily make your self. Walk but a quarter of an Hour in your Garden when the Sun shines, with a Part of your Dress white, and a Part black; then apply your Hand to them alternately, and you will find a very great Difference in their Warmth.

The Black will be quite hot to the Touch, the White still cool.

Another. Try to fire Paper with a burning Glass. If it is White, you will not easily burn it; but if you bring the Focus to a black Spot or upon Letters written or printed, the Paper will immediately be on fire under the Letters.

Thus Fullers and Dyers find black Cloths, of equal Thickness with white ones, and hung out equally wet, dry in the Sun much sooner than the white, being more readily heated by the Sun's Rays. It is the same before a Fire; the Heat of which sooner penetrates black Stockings than white ones, and so is apt sooner to burn a Man's Shins. Also Beer much sooner warms in a black Mug set before the Fire, than in a white one, or in a bright Silver Tankard.

My Experiment was this. I took a number of little Square Pieces of Broad Cloth from a Taylor's Pattern Card, of various Colours. There were Black, deep Blue, lighter Blue, Green, Purple, Red, Yellow, White, and other Colours or Shades of Colours. I laid them all out upon the Snow in a bright Sunshiny Morning. In a few Hours (I cannot now be exact as to the Time) the Black being warm'd most by the Sun was sunk so low as to be below the Stroke of the Sun's Rays; the dark Blue almost as low, the lighter Blue not quite so much as the dark, the other Colours less as they were lighter; and the quite White remain'd on the Surface of the Snow, not having entred it at all. What signifies Philosophy that does not apply to some Use? May we not learn from hence, that black Cloaths are not so fit to wear in a hot Sunny Climate or Season as white ones; because in such Cloaths the Body is more heated by the Sun when we walk abroad and are at the same time heated by the Exercise, which double Heat is apt to bring on putrid dangerous Fevers? That Soldiers and Seamen who must march and labour in the Sun, should in the East or West Indies have an Uniform of white? That Summer Hats for Men or Women, should be white, as repelling that Heat which gives the Headachs to many, and to some the fatal Stroke that the French call the *Coup de Soleil*? That the Ladies Summer Hats, however should be lined with Black, as not reverberating on their Faces those Rays which are reflected upwards from the Earth or Water? That

the putting a white Cap of Paper or Linnen *within* the Crown
of a black Hat, as some do, will not keep out the Heat, tho'
it would if plac'd *without*? That Fruit Walls being black'd may
receive so much Heat from the Sun in the Daytime, as to
continue warm in some degree thro' the Night, and thereby
preserve the Fruit from Frosts, or forward its Growth?—with
sundry other particulars of less or greater Importance, that
will occur from time to time to attentive Minds? I am, Yours
affectionately,

November? 1760

"PREJUDICE . . . AGAINST YOUR WORK"

To John Baskerville

Dear Sir,   Craven-Street, London.
    Let me give you a pleasant Instance of the Prejudice some
have entertained against your Work. Soon after I returned,
discoursing with a Gentleman concerning the Artists of Birmingham, he said you would be a Means of blinding all the
Readers in the Nation, for the Strokes of your Letters being
too thin and narrow, hurt the Eye, and he could never read a
Line of them without Pain. I thought, said I, you were going
to complain of the Gloss on the Paper, some object to: No,
no, says he, I have heard that mentioned, but it is not that;
'tis in the Form and Cut of the Letters themselves; they have
not that natural and easy Proportion between the Height and
Thickness of the Stroke, which makes the common Printing
so much more comfortable to the Eye.—You see this Gentleman was a Connoisseur. In vain I endeavoured to support
your *Character* against the Charge; he knew what he felt, he
could see the Reason of it, and several other Gentlemen
among his Friends had made the same Observation, &c.—
Yesterday he called to visit me, when, mischievously bent to
try his Judgment, I stept into my Closet, tore off the Top of
Mr. Caslon's Specimen, and produced it to him as yours
brought with me from Birmingham, saying, I had been examining it since he spoke to me, and could not for my Life
perceive the Disproportion he mentioned, desiring him to

point it out to me. He readily undertook it, and went over
the several Founts, shewing me every-where what he thought
Instances of that Disproportion; and declared, that he could
not then read the Specimen without feeling very strongly the
Pain he had mentioned to me. I spared him that Time the
Confusion of being told, that these were the Types he had
been reading all his Life with so much Ease to his Eyes; the
Types his adored Newton is printed with, on which he has
pored not a little; nay, the very Types his own Book is
printed with, for he is himself an Author; and yet never discovered this painful Disproportion in them, till he thought
they were yours.

I am, &c.

1760?

FAULTS IN SONGS

To Peter Franklin

Dear Brother,

 * * * * I like your ballad, and think it well adapted for your
purpose of discountenancing expensive foppery, and encouraging industry and frugality. If you can get it generally sung
in your country, it may probably have a good deal of the
effect you hope and expect from it. But as you aimed at making it general, I wonder you chose so uncommon a measure
in poetry, that none of the tunes in common use will suit it.
Had you fitted it to an old one, well known, it must have
spread much faster than I doubt it will do from the best new
tune we can get compos'd for it. I think too, that if you had
given it to some country girl in the heart of the *Massachusets*,
who has never heard any other than psalm tunes, or *Chevy
Chace*, the *Children in the Wood*, the *Spanish Lady*, and such
old simple ditties, but has naturally a good ear, she might
more probably have made a pleasing popular tune for you,
than any of our masters here, and more proper for your purpose, which would best be answered, if every word could as
it is sung be understood by all that hear it, and if the emphasis you intend for particular words could be given by the

singer as well as by the reader; much of the force and impression of the song depending on those circumstances. I will however get it as well done for you as I can.

Do not imagine that I mean to depreciate the skill of our composers of music here; they are admirable at pleasing *practised* ears, and know how to delight *one another*; but, in composing for songs, the reigning taste seems to be quite out of nature, or rather the reverse of nature, and yet like a torrent, hurries them all away with it; one or two perhaps only excepted.

You, in the spirit of some ancient legislators, would influence the manners of your country by the united powers of poetry and music. By what I can learn of *their* songs, the music was simple, conformed itself to the usual pronunciation of words, as to measure, cadence or emphasis, *&c.* never disguised and confounded the language by making a long syllable short, or a short one long when sung; their singing was only a more pleasing, because a melodious manner of speaking; it was capable of all the graces of prose oratory, while it added the pleasure of harmony. A modern song, on the contrary, neglects all the proprieties and beauties of common speech, and in their place introduces its *defects* and *absurdities* as so many graces. I am afraid you will hardly take my word for this, and therefore I must endeavour to support it by proof. Here is the first song I lay my hand on. It happens to be a composition of one of our greatest masters, the ever famous *Handel*. It is not one of his juvenile performances, before his taste could be improved and formed: It appeared when his reputation was at the highest, is greatly admired by all his admirers, and is really excellent in its kind. It is called, *The additional* FAVOURITE *Song in* Judas Maccabeus. Now I reckon among the defects and improprieties of common speech, the following, viz.

1. *Wrong placing the accent or emphasis*, by laying it on words of no importance, or on wrong syllables.

2. *Drawling*; or extending the sound of words or syllables beyond their natural length.

3. *Stuttering*; or making many syllables of one.

4. *Unintelligibleness*; the result of the three foregoing united.

5. *Tautology*; and

6. *Screaming*, without cause.

For the *wrong placing of the accent, or emphasis*, see it on the word *their* instead of being on the word *vain*.

with   *their*   vain   My - ste - rious   Art

And on the word *from*, and the wrong syllable *like*.

God-*like*   Wisdom   *from*   a — bove

For the *Drawling*, see the last syllable of the word *wounded*.

Nor   can   heal   the   wound*ed*   Heart

And in the syllable *wis*, and the word *from*, and syllable *bove*

God-like   *Wis*dom   *from*   a -   *bove*

For the *Stuttering*, see the words *ne'er relieve*, in

Ma - gick   Charms can   *ne'er*   re - *lieve*   you

Here are four syllables made of one, and eight of three; but this is moderate. I have seen in another song that I cannot now find, seventeen syllables made of three, and sixteen of one; the latter I remember was the word *charms*; viz. *Cha, a, a, a, a, a, a, a, a, a, a, a, a, a, a, arms.* Stammering with a witness!

For the *Unintelligibleness*; give this whole song to any

taught singer, and let her sing it to any company that have never heard it; you shall find they will not understand three words in ten. It is therefore that at the oratorio's and operas one sees with books in their hands all those who desire to understand what they hear sung by even our best performers.

For the *Tautology*; you have, *with their vain mysterious art*, twice repeated; *Magic charms can ne'er relieve you*, three times. *Nor can heal the wounded heart*, three times. *Godlike wisdom from above*, twice; and, *this alone can ne'er deceive you*, two or three times. But this is reasonable when compared with *the Monster Polypheme, the Monster Polypheme*, a hundred times over and over, in his admired *Acis and Galatea*.

As to the *screaming*; perhaps I cannot find a fair instance in this song; but whoever has frequented our operas will remember many. And yet here methinks the words *no* and *e'er*, when sung to these notes, have a little of the air of *screaming*, and would actually be scream'd by some singers.

No magic charms can *e'er* re—lieve you.

I send you inclosed the song with its music at length. Read the words without the repetitions. Observe how few they are, and what a shower of notes attend them. You will then perhaps be inclined to think with me, that though the words might be the principal part of an ancient song, they are of small importance in a modern one; they are in short only *a pretence for singing*.

> *I am, as ever,*
> *Your affectionate brother,*

P. S. I might have mentioned *Inarticulation* among the defects in common speech that are assumed as beauties in modern singing. But as that seems more the fault of the singer than of the composer, I omitted it in what related merely to the composition. The fine singer in the present mode, stifles all the hard consonants, and polishes away all the rougher parts of words that serve to distinguish them one from another; so that you hear nothing but an admirable pipe, and understand no more of the song, than you would from its tune played on any other instrument. If ever it was the ambition of musicians to make instruments that should imitate the human voice, that ambition seems now reversed, the voice aiming to be like an instrument. Thus wigs were first made to imitate a good natural head of hair;—but when they became fashionable, though in unnatural forms, we have seen natural hair dressed to look like wigs.

c. 1761

"A CASE IN POINT"

To David Hume

Dear Sir,   London, May 19. 1762.

It is no small Pleasure to me to hear from you that my Paper on the means of preserving Buildings from Damage by Lightning, was acceptable to the Philosophical Society. Mr. Russel's Proposals of Improvement are very sensible and just. A Leaden Spout or Pipe is undoubtedly a good Conductor so far as it goes. If the Conductor enters the Ground just at the Foundation, and from thence is carried horizontally to some Well, or to a distant Rod driven downright into the Earth; I would then propose that the Part under Ground should be Lead, as less liable to consume with Rust than Iron. Because if the Conductor near the Foot of the Wall should be wasted, the Lightning might act on the Moisture of the Earth, and by suddenly rarifying it occasion an Explosion that may damage the Foundation. In the Experiment of discharging my large Case of Electrical Bottles thro' a Piece of small Glass Tube fill'd with Water, the suddenly rarify'd Water has exploded with a Force equal, I think, to that of so much Gunpowder; bursting the Tube into many Pieces, and driving them with Violence in all Directions and to all Parts of the Room. The Shivering of Trees into small Splinters like a Broom, is probably owing to this Rarefaction of the Sap in the longitudinal Pores or capillary Pipes in the Substance of the Wood. And the Blowing-up of Bricks or Stones in a Hearth, Rending Stones out of a Foundation, and Splitting of Walls, is also probably an Effect sometimes of rarify'd Moisture in the Earth, under the Hearth, or in the Walls. We should therefore have a durable Conductor under Ground, or convey the Lightning to the Earth at some Distance.

It must afford Lord Mareschall a good deal of Diversion to preside in a Dispute so ridiculous as that you mention. Judges in their Decisions often use Precedents. I have somewhere met with one that is what the Lawyers call *a Case in Point*. The Church People and the Puritans in a Country Town, had once a bitter Contention concerning the Erecting of a Maypole, which the former desir'd and the latter oppos'd. Each Party endeavour'd to strengthen itself by obtaining the Authority of the Mayor, directing or forbidding a Maypole. He heard their Altercation with great Patience, and then gravely determin'd thus; You that are for having no Maypole shall have no Maypole; and you that are for having a Maypole shall have a Maypole. Get about your Business and let me hear no more of this Quarrel. So methinks Lord Mareschal might say; You that are for no more Damnation than is proportion'd to your Offences, have my Consent that it may be so: And you that are for being damn'd eternally, G–d eternally d—n you all, and let me hear no more of your Disputes.

Your Compliment of *Gold* and *Wisdom* is very obliging to me, but a little injurious to your Country. The various Value of every thing in every Part of this World, arises you know from the various Proportions of the Quantity to the Demand. We are told that Gold and Silver in Solomon's Time were so plenty as to be of no more Value in his Country than the Stones in the Street. You have here at present just such a Plenty of Wisdom. Your People are therefore not to be censur'd for desiring no more among them than they have; and if I have *any*, I should certainly carry it where from its Scarcity it may probably come to a better Market.

I nevertheless regret extreamly the leaving a Country in which I have receiv'd so much Friendship, and Friends whose Conversation has been so agreable and so improving to me; and that I am henceforth to reside at so great a Distance from them is no small Mortification, to My dear Friend, Yours most affectionately

My respectful Compliments if you please to Sir Alexr. Dick, Lord Kaims, Mr. Alexander, Mr. Russel, and any other enquiring Friends. I shall write to them before I leave the Island.

THE GLASS ARMONICA

To Giambatista Beccaria

Rev. SIR,   *London, July* 13, 1762.

I once promised myself the pleasure of seeing you at *Turin*, but as that is not now likely to happen, being just about returning to my native country, *America*, I sit down to take leave of you (among others of my *European* friends that I cannot see) by writing.

I thank you for the honourable mention you have so frequently made of me in your letters to Mr. *Collinson* and others, for the generous defence you undertook and executed with so much success, of my electrical opinions; and for the valuable present you have made me of your new work, from which I have received great information and pleasure. I wish I could in return entertain you with any thing new of mine on that subject; but I have not lately pursued it. Nor do I know of any one here that is at present much engaged in it.

Perhaps, however, it may be agreeable to you, as you live in a musical country, to have an account of the new instrument lately added here to the great number that charming science was before possessed of:—As it is an instrument that seems peculiarly adapted to *Italian* music, especially that of the soft and plaintive kind, I will endeavour to give you such a description of it, and of the manner of constructing it, that you, or any of your friends, may be enabled to imitate it, if you incline so to do, without being at the expence and trouble of the many experiments I have made in endeavouring to bring it to its present perfection.

You have doubtless heard the sweet tone that is drawn from a drinking glass, by passing a wet finger round its brim. One Mr. *Puckeridge*, a gentleman from *Ireland*, was the first who thought of playing tunes, formed of these tones. He collected a number of glasses of different sizes, fixed them near each other on a table, and tuned them by putting into them water, more or less, as each note required. The tones were brought out by passing his fingers round their brims.—He was un-fortunately burnt here, with his instrument, in a fire which consumed the house he lived in. Mr. *E. Delaval*, a most ingenious member of our Royal Society, made one in imita-tion of it, with a better choice and form of glasses, which was the first I saw or heard. Being charmed with the sweetness of its tones, and the music he produced from it, I wished only to see the glasses disposed in a more convenient form, and brought together in a narrower compass, so as to admit of a greater number of tones, and all within reach of hand to a person sitting before the instrument, which I accomplished, after various intermediate trials, and less commodious forms, both of glasses and construction, in the following manner.

The glasses are blown as near as possible in the form of hemispheres, having each an open neck or socket in the middle. The thickness of the glass near the brim about a tenth of an inch, or hardly quite so much, but thicker as it comes nearer the neck, which in the largest glasses is about an inch deep, and an inch and half wide within, these dimensions less-ening as the glasses themselves diminish in size, except that the neck of the smallest ought not to be shorter than half an inch.—The largest glass is nine inches diameter, and the smallest three inches. Between these there are twenty-three different sizes, differing from each other a quarter of an inch in diameter.—To make a single instrument there should be at least six glasses blown of each size; and out of this number one may probably pick 37 glasses, (which are sufficient for 3 octaves with all the semitones) that will be each either the note one wants or a little sharper than that note, and all fit-ting so well into each other as to taper pretty regularly from the largest to the smallest. It is true there are not 37 sizes, but it often happens that two of the same size differ a note or half note in tone, by reason of a difference in thickness, and these may be placed one in the other without sensibly hurting the regularity of the taper form.

The glasses being chosen and every one marked with a diamond the note you intend it for, they are to be tuned by diminishing the thickness of those that are too sharp. This is done by grinding them round from the neck towards the brim, the breadth of one or two inches as may be required; often trying the glass by a well tuned harpsichord, comparing the tone drawn from the glass by your finger, with the note you want, as sounded by that string of the harpsichord. When you come near the matter, be careful to wipe the glass clean and dry before each trial, because the tone is something flatter when the glass is wet, than it will be when dry;—and grinding a very little between each trial, you will thereby tune to great exactness. The more care is necessary in this, because if you go below your required tone, there is no sharpening it again but by grinding somewhat off the brim, which will afterwards require polishing, and thus encrease the trouble.

The glasses being thus tuned, you are to be provided with a case for them, and a spindle on which they are to be fixed. My case is about three feet long, eleven inches every way wide within at the biggest end, and five inches at the smallest end; for it tapers all the way, to adapt it better to the conical figure of the set of glasses. This case opens in the middle of its height, and the upper part turns up by hinges fixed behind. The spindle which is of hard iron, lies horizontally from end to end of the box within, exactly in the middle, and is made to turn on brass gudgeons at each end. It is round, an inch diameter at the thickest end, and tapering to a quarter of an inch at the smallest.—A square shank comes from its thickest end through the box, on which shank a wheel is fixed by a screw. This wheel serves as a fly to make the motion equable, when the spindle, with the glasses, is turned by the foot like a spinning wheel. My wheel is of mahogany, 18 inches diameter, and pretty thick, so as to conceal near its circumference about 25lb of lead.—An ivory pin is fixed in the face of this wheel and about 4 inches from the axis. Over the neck of this pin is put the loop of the string that comes up from the moveable step to give it motion. The case stands on a neat frame with four legs.

To fix the glasses on the spindle, a cork is first to be fitted in each neck pretty tight, and projecting a little without the neck, that the neck of one may not touch the inside of another when put together, for that would make a jarring.— These corks are to be perforated with holes of different diameters, so as to suit that part of the spindle on which they are to be fixed. When a glass is put on, by holding it stiffly between both hands, while another turns the spindle, it may be gradually brought to its place. But care must be taken that the hole be not too small, lest in forcing it up the neck should split; nor too large, lest the glass not being firmly fixed, should turn or move on the spindle, so as to touch and jar against its neighbouring glass. The glasses thus are placed one in another, the largest on the biggest end of the spindle which is to the left hand; the neck of this glass is towards the wheel, and the next goes into it in the same position, only about an inch of its brim appearing beyond the brim of the first; thus proceeding, every glass when fixed shows about an inch of its brim, (or three quarters of an inch, or half an inch, as they grow smaller) beyond the brim of the glass that contains it; and it is from these exposed parts of each glass that the tone is drawn, by laying a finger upon one of them as the spindle and glasses turn round.

My largest glass is G a little below the reach of a common voice, and my highest G, including three compleat octaves.— To distinguish the glasses the more readily to the eye, I have painted the apparent parts of the glasses within side, every semitone white, and the other notes of the octave with the seven prismatic colours, *viz.* C, red; D, orange; E, yellow; F, green; G, blue; A, Indigo; B, purple; and C, red again;—so that glasses of the same colour (the white excepted) are always octaves to each other.

This instrument is played upon, by sitting before the middle of the set of glasses as before the keys of a harpsichord, turning them with the foot, and wetting them now and then with a spunge and clean water. The fingers should be first a little soaked in water and quite free from all greasiness; a little fine chalk upon them is sometimes useful, to make them catch the glass and bring out the tone more readily. Both hands are used, by which means different parts are played together.—Observe, that the tones are best drawn out when the glasses turn *from* the ends of the fingers, not when they turn *to* them.

The advantages of this instrument are, that its tones are incomparably sweet beyond those of any other; that they may be swelled and softened at pleasure by stronger or weaker pressures of the finger, and continued to any length; and that the instrument, being once well tuned, never again wants tuning.

In honour of your musical language, I have borrowed from it the name of this instrument, calling it the *Armonica*.

With great esteem and respect, I am, &c.

SOUND

To Oliver Neave

Dear SIR,   *July* 20, 1762.

I have perused your paper on sound, and would freely mention to you, as you desire it, every thing that appeared to me to need correction:—But nothing of that kind occurs to me, unless it be, where you speak of the air as "the *best* medium for conveying sound." Perhaps this is speaking rather too positively, if there be, as I think there are, some other mediums that will convey it farther and more readily.—It is a well-known experiment, that the scratching of a pin at one end of a long piece of timber, may be heard by an ear applied near the other end, though it could not be heard at the same distance through the air.—And two stones being struck smartly together under water, the stroke may be heard at a greater distance by an ear also placed under water in the same river, than it can be heard through the air. I think I have heard it near a mile; how much farther it may be heard, I know not; but suppose a great deal farther, because the sound did not seem faint, as if at a distance, like distant sounds through air, but smart and strong, and as if present just at the ear.—I wish you would repeat these experiments now

you are upon the subject, and add your own observations.—
And if you were to repeat, with your naturally exact attention
and observation, the common experiment of the bell in the
exhausted receiver, possibly something new may occur to
you, in considering,

1. Whether the experiment is not ambiguous; *i. e.* whether
the gradual exhausting of the air, as it creates an increasing
difference of pressure on the outside, may not occasion in the
glass a difficulty of vibrating, that renders it less fit to communicate to the air without, the vibrations that strike it from
within; and the diminution of the sound arise from this cause,
rather than from the diminution of the air?

2. Whether as the particles of air themselves are at a distance from each other, there must not be some medium between them, proper for conveying sound, since otherwise it
would stop at the first particle?

3. Whether the great difference we experience in hearing
sounds at a distance, when the wind blows towards us from
the sonorous body, or towards that from us, can be well accounted for by adding to or substracting from the swiftness
of sound, the degree of swiftness that is in the wind at the
time? The latter is so small in proportion, that it seems as if
it could scarce produce any sensible effect, and yet the difference is very great. Does not this give some hint, as if there
might be a subtile fluid, the conductor of sound, which
moves at different times in different directions over the surface of the earth, and whose motion may perhaps be much
swifter than that of the air in our strongest winds; and that
in passing through air, it may communicate that motion to
the air which we call wind, though a motion in no degree so
swift as its own?

4. It is somewhere related, that a pistol fired on the top of
an exceeding high mountain, made a noise like thunder in the
valleys below. Perhaps this fact is not exactly related: but if it
is, would not one imagine from it, that the rarer the air, the
greater sound might be produced in it from the same cause?

5. Those balls of fire which are sometimes seen passing over
a country, computed by philosophers to be often 30 miles
high at least, sometimes burst at that height; the air must be
exceeding rare there, and yet the explosion produces a sound

that is heard at that distance, and for 70 miles round on the surface of the earth, so violent too as to shake buildings, and give an apprehension of an earthquake. Does not this look as if a rare atmosphere, almost a vacuum, was no bad conductor of sound?

I have not made up my own mind on these points, and only mention them for your consideration, knowing that every subject is the better for your handling it.

With the greatest esteem, I am, &c.

OIL AND WATER

To John Pringle

SIR,   *Philadelphia, Dec.* 1, 1762.

During our passage to Madeira, the weather being warm, and the cabbin windows constantly open for the benefit of the air, the candles at night flared and run very much, which was an inconvenience. At Madeira we got oil to burn, and with a common glass tumbler or beaker, slung in wire, and suspended to the cieling of the cabbin, and a little wire hoop for the wick, furnish'd with corks to float on the oil, I made an Italian lamp, that gave us very good light all over the table. —The glass at bottom contained water to about one third of its height; another third was taken up with oil; the rest was left empty that the sides of the glass might protect the flame from the wind. There is nothing remarkable in all this; but what follows is particular. At supper, looking on the lamp, I remarked that tho' the surface of the oil was perfectly tranquil, and duly preserved its position and distance with regard to the brim of the glass, the water under the oil was in great commotion, rising and falling in irregular waves, which continued during the whole evening. The lamp was kept burning as a watch light all night, till the oil was spent, and the water only remain'd. In the morning I observed, that though the motion of the ship continued the same, the water was now quiet, and its surface as tranquil as that of the oil had been the evening before. At night again, when oil was put upon it, the water resum'd its irregular motions, rising in high waves almost to the surface of the oil, but without disturbing the smooth level of that surface. And this was repeated every day during the voyage.

Since my arrival in America, I have repeated the experiment frequently thus. I have put a pack-thread round a tumbler, with strings of the same, from each side, meeting above it in a knot at about a foot distance from the top of the tumbler. Then putting in as much water as would fill about one third part of the tumbler, I lifted it up by the knot, and swung it to and fro in the air; when the water appeared to keep its place in the tumbler as steadily as if it had been ice.—But pouring gently in upon the water about as much oil, and then again swinging it in the air as before, the tranquility before possessed by the water, was transferred to the surface of the oil, and the water under it was agitated with the same commotions as at sea.

I have shewn this experiment to a number of ingenious persons. Those who are but slightly acquainted with the principles of hydrostatics, &c. are apt to fancy immediately that they understand it, and readily attempt to explain it; but their explanations have been different, and to me not very intelligible.—Others more deeply skill'd in those principles, seem to wonder at it, and promise to consider it. And I think it is worth considering: For a new appearance, if it cannot be explain'd by our old principles, may afford us new ones, of use perhaps in explaining some other obscure parts of natural knowledge.

I am, &c.

"I LOOK'D ROUND FOR GOD'S JUDGMENTS"

To Jared Ingersoll

Dear Sir   Philada. Dec. 11. 1762

I thank you for your kind Congratulations. It gives me Pleasure to hear from an old Friend, it will give me much more to see him. I hope therefore nothing will prevent the Journey you propose for next Summer, and the Favour you intend me of a Visit. I believe I must make a Journey early in the Spring, to Virginia, but purpose being back again before the hot Weather. You will be kind enough to let me know beforehand what time you expect to be here, that I may not be out of the way; for that would mortify me exceedingly.

I should be glad to know what it is that distinguishes Connecticut Religion from common Religion: Communicate, if you please, some of those particulars that you think will amuse me as a Virtuoso. When I travelled in Flanders I thought of your excessively strict Observation of Sunday; and that a Man could hardly travel on that day among you upon his lawful Occasions, without Hazard of Punishment; while where I was, every one travell'd, if he pleas'd, or diverted himself any other way; and in the Afternoon both high and low went to the Play or the Opera, where there was plenty of Singing, Fiddling and Dancing. I look'd round for God's Judgments but saw no Signs of them. The Cities were well built and full of Inhabitants, the Markets fill'd with Plenty, the People well favour'd and well clothed; the Fields well till'd; the Cattle fat and strong; the Fences, Houses and Windows all in Repair; and *no Old Tenor* anywhere in the Country; which would almost make one suspect, that the Deity is not so angry at that Offence as a New England Justice.

I left our Friend Mr. Jackson well. And I had the great Happiness of finding my little Family well when I came home; and my Friends as cordial and more numerous than ever. May every Prosperity attend you and yours. I am Dear Friend, Yours affectionately

"THE ARTS DELIGHT TO TRAVEL WESTWARD"

To Mary Stevenson

My dear Polley   Philada. March 25. 1763
Your pleasing Favour of Nov. 11 is now before me. It found me as you suppos'd it would, happy with my American Friends and Family about me; and it made me more happy in

showing me that I am not yet forgotten by the dear Friends I left in England. And indeed why should I fear they will ever forget me, when I feel so strongly that I shall ever remember them!

I sympathise with you sincerely in your Grief at the Separation from your old Friend, Miss Pitt. The Reflection that she is going to be more happy when she leaves you, might comfort you, if the Case was likely to be so circumstanc'd; but when the Country and Company she has been educated in, and those she is removing to, are compared, one cannot possibly expect it.

I sympathize with you no less in your Joys. But it is not merely on your Account that I rejoice at the Recovery of your dear Dolly's Health. I love that dear good Girl myself, and I love her other Friends. I am therefore made happy by what must contribute so much to the Happiness of them all. Remember me to her, and to every one of that worthy and amiable Family most affectionately.

Remember me in the same manner to your and my good Doctor and Mrs. Hawkesworth. You have lately, you tell me, had the Pleasure of spending three Days with them at Mr. Stanley's. It was a sweet Society! (Remember me also to Mr. and Mrs. Stanley, and to Miss Arlond)—I too, once partook of that same Pleasure, and can therefore feel what you must have felt. Of all the enviable Things England has, I envy it most its People. Why should that petty Island, which compar'd to America is but like a stepping Stone in a Brook, scarce enough of it above Water to keep one's Shoes dry; why, I say, should that little Island, enjoy in almost every Neighbourhood, more sensible, virtuous and elegant Minds, than we can collect in ranging 100 Leagues of our vast Forests. But, 'tis said, the Arts delight to travel Westward. You have effectually defended us in this glorious War, and in time you will improve us. After the first Cares for the Necessaries of Life are over, we shall come to think of the Embellishments. Already some of our young Geniuses begin to lisp Attempts at Painting, Poetry and Musick. We have a young Painter now studying at Rome: Some Specimens of our Poetry I send you, which if Dr. Hawkesworth's fine Taste cannot approve, his good Heart will at least excuse. The Manuscript

Piece is by a young Friend of mine, and was occasion'd by
the Loss of one of his Friends, who lately made a Voyage to
Antigua to settle some Affairs previous to an intended Marriage with an amiable young Lady here; but unfortunately
died there. I send it you, because the Author is a great
Admirer of Mr. Stanley's musical Compositions, and has
adapted this Piece to an Air in the 6th Concerto of that Gentleman, the sweetly solemn Movement of which he is quite in
Raptures with. He has attempted to compose a Recitativo for
it; but not being able to satisfy himself in the Bass, wishes I
could get it supply'd. If Mr. Stanley would condescend to do
that for him, thro' your Intercession, he would esteem it as
one of the highest Honours, and it would make him excessively happy. You will say that a Recitativo can be but a poor
Specimen of our Music. 'Tis the best and all I have at present;
but you may see better hereafter.

I hope Mr. Ralph's Affairs are mended since you wrote. I
know he had some Expectations when I came away, from a
Hand that could help him. He has Merit, and one would
think ought not to be so unfortunate.

I do not wonder at the Behaviour you mention of Dr.
Smith towards me, for I have long since known him thoroughly. I made that Man my Enemy by doing him too much
Kindness. Tis the honestest Way of acquiring an Enemy. And
since 'tis convenient to have at least one Enemy, who by his
Readiness to revile one on all Occasions may make one careful of one's Conduct, I shall keep him an Enemy for that
purpose; and shall observe your good Mother's Advice, never
again to receive him as a Friend. She once admir'd the benevolent Spirit breath'd in his Sermons. She will now see the
Justness of the Lines your Laureat Whitehead addresses to his
Poets, and which I now address to her,

> Full many a *peevish, envious, slanderous* Elf,
> Is,—in his Works,—Benevolence itself.
> For all Mankind—unknown—his Bosom heaves;
> He only injures those with whom he lives.
> Read then the Man:—does *Truth* his Actions guide,
> Exempt from *Petulance*, exempt from *Pride*?
> To social Duties does his Heart attend,

As Son, as Father, Husband, Brother, *Friend*?
Do those who know him love him?—If they do,
You've *my* Permission: you may love him too.

Nothing can please me more than to see your philosophical Improvements when you have Leisure to communicate them to me. I still owe you a long Letter on that Subject, which I shall pay.

I am vex'd with Mr. James that he has been so dilatory in Mr. Maddison's Armonica. I was unlucky in both the Workmen that I permitted to undertake making those Instruments. The first was fanciful, and never could work to the purpose, because he was ever conceiving some new Improvement that answer'd no End: the other, I doubt, is absolutely idle. I have recommended a Number to him from hence, but must stop my hand.

Adieu, my dear Polly, and believe me as ever, with the sincerest Esteem and Regard, Your truly affectionate Friend, and humble Servant

My Love to Mrs. Tickell and Mrs. Rooke, and to Pitty when you write to her. Mrs. Franklin and Sally desire to be affectionately remembr'd to you.

P.S. I find the printed Poetry I intended to enclose will be too bulky to send per the Packet: I shall send it by a Ship that goes shortly from hence.

"THE NATURAL CAPACITIES OF THE BLACK RACE"

To John Waring

Reverend and dear Sir,   Philada. Dec. 17. 1763

Being but just return'd home from a Tour thro' the northern Colonies, that has employ'd the whole Summer, my Time at present is so taken up that I cannot now write fully in answer to the Letters I have receiv'd from you, but purpose to do it shortly. This is chiefly to acquaint you, that I have visited the Negro School here in Company with the Revd. Mr. Sturgeon and some others; and had the Children thoroughly examin'd. They appear'd all to have made considerable Progress in Reading for the Time they had respectively been in the School, and most of them answer'd readily and well the Questions of the Catechism; they behav'd very orderly, showd a proper Respect and ready Obedience to the Mistress, and seem'd very attentive to, and a good deal affected by, a serious Exhortation with which Mr. Sturgeon concluded our Visit. I was on the whole much pleas'd, and from what I then saw, have conceiv'd a higher Opinion of the natural Capacities of the black Race, than I had ever before entertained. Their Apprehension seems as quick, their Memory as strong, and their Docility in every Respect equal to that of white Children. You will wonder perhaps that I should ever doubt it, and I will not undertake to justify all my Prejudices, nor to account for them. I immediately advanc'd the two Guineas you mention'd, for the Mistress, and Mr. Sturgeon will therefore draw on you for £7 18s. only, which makes up the half Year's Salary of Ten Pounds. Be pleased to present my best Respects to the Associates, and believe me, with sincere Esteem Dear Sir, Your most obedient Servant

"LIKE A MORNING FOG BEFORE THE RISING SUN"

To William Strahan

Dear Straney   Philada. Dec. 19. 1763.

I have before me your Favours of July 16, and Augt. 18. which is the latest. It vexes me excessively to see that Parker and Mecom are so much in Arrear with you. What is due from Parker is safe, and will be paid, I think with Interest; for he is a Man as honest as he is industrious and frugal, and has withal some Estate: his Backwardness has been owing to his bad Partners only, of whom he is now nearly quit. But as to Mecom, he seems so dejected and spiritless, that I fear little will be got of him. He has dropt his Paper, on which he built his last Hopes. I doubt I shall lose £200 by him myself, but am taking Steps to save what I can for you; of which more fully in my next.

Now I am return'd from my long Journeys which have consum'd the whole Summer, I shall apply myself to such a Settlement of all my Affairs, as will enable me to do what your Friendship so warmly urges. I have a great Opinion of your Wisdom (Madeira apart;) and am apt enough to think that what you seem so clear in, and are so earnest about, must be right. Tho' I own, that I sometimes suspect, my Love to England and my Friends there seduces me a little, and makes *my own* middling Reasons for going over; appear very good ones. We shall see in a little Time how Things will turn out.

Blessings on your Heart for the Feast of Politicks you gave me in your last. I could by no other means have obtain'd so clear a View of the present State of your public Affairs as by your Letter. Most of your Observations appear to me ex- treamly judicious, strikingly clear and true. I only differ from you in some of the melancholly Apprehensions you express concerning Consequences; and to comfort you (at the same time flattering my own Vanity,) let me remind you, that I have sometimes been in the right in such Cases, when you happen'd to be in the wrong; as I can prove upon you out of this very Letter of yours. Call to mind your former Fears for the King of Prussia, and remember my telling you that the Man's Abilities were more than equal to all the Force of his Enemies, and that he would finally extricate himself, and triumph. This, by the Account you give me from Major Beck- with, is fully verified. You now fear for our virtuous young King, that the Faction forming will overpower him, and ren- der his Reign uncomfortable. On the contrary, I am of Opin- ion, that his Virtue, and the Consciousness of his sincere Intentions to make his People happy, will give him Firmness and Steadiness in his Measures, and in the Support of the honest Friends he has chosen to serve him; and when that Firmness is fully perceiv'd, Faction will dissolve and be dissi- pated like a Morning Fog before the rising Sun, leaving the rest of the Day clear, with a Sky serene and cloudless. Such, after a few of the first Years, will be the future Course of his Majesty's Reign, which I predict will be happy and truly glorious. Your Fears for the Nation too, appear to me as little founded. A new War I cannot yet see Reason to apprehend. The Peace I think will long continue, and your Nation be as happy as they deserve to be, that is, as happy as their moderate Share of Virtue will allow them to be: Happier than that, no outward Circumstances can make a Nation any more than a private Man. And as to their Quantity of Virtue, I think it bids fair for Increasing; if the old Saying be true, as it certainly is,

Ad Exemplum Regis, &c.

My Love to Mrs. Strahan and your Children in which my Wife and Daughter join with Your ever affectionate Friend

P.S. The western Indians about Fort Detroit now sue for Peace, having lost a great Number of their best Warriors in their vain Attempt to reduce that Fortress; and being at length assur'd by a Belt from the French Commander in the Ilinois Country, that a Peace is concluded between England and France, that he must evacuate the Country and deliver up his Forts, and can no longer supply or support them. It is thought this will draw on a general Peace. I am only afraid it will be concluded before these Barbarians have sufficiently smarted for their perfidious breaking the last.

The Governor of Detroit, Major Gladwin, has granted them a Cessation of Arms, till the General's Pleasure is known.

"AN AMBASSADOR TO THE COUNTRY MOB"

To John Fothergill

Dear Doctor,   Philada. March 14. 1764.

I received your Favour of the 10th. of Decemr. It was a great deal for one to write, whose Time is so little his own. By the way, *When do you intend to live?* i.e. to enjoy Life. When will you retire to your Villa, give your self Repose, delight in Viewing the Operations of Nature in the vegetable Creation, assist her in her Works, get your ingenious Friends at times about you, make them happy with your Conversation, and enjoy theirs; or, if alone, amuse yourself with your Books and elegant Collections? To be hurried about perpetually from one sick Chamber to another, is not Living. Do you please yourself with the Fancy that you are doing Good? You are mistaken. Half the Lives you save are not worth saving, as being useless; and almost the other Half ought not to be sav'd, as being mischievous. Does your Conscience never hint to you the Impiety of being in constant Warfare against the Plans of Providence? Disease was intended as the Punishment of Intemperance, Sloth, and other Vices; and the Example of that Punishment was intended to promote and strengthen the opposite Virtues. But here you step in officiously with your Art, disappoint those wise Intentions of Nature, and make Men safe in their Excesses. Whereby you seem to me to be of just the same Service to Society as some favourite first Minister, who out of the great Benevolence of his Heart should procure Pardons for all Criminals that apply'd to him. Only think of the Consequences!

You tell me the Quakers are charged on your side the Water with being by their Aggressions the Cause of this War. Would you believe it, that they are charg'd here, not with offending the Indians, and thereby provoking the War, but with gaining their Friendship by Presents, supplying them privately with Arms and Ammunition, and engaging them to fall upon and murder the poor white People on the Frontiers? Would you think it possible that Thousands even here should be made to believe this, and many Hundreds of them be raised in Arms, not only to kill some converted Indians supposed to be under the Quakers Protection, but to punish the Quakers who were supposed to give that Protection? Would you think these People audacious enough to avow such Designs in a public Declaration sent to the Governor? Would you imagine that innocent Quakers, Men of Fortune and Character, should think it necessary to fly for Safety out of Philadelphia into the Jersies, fearing the Violence of such armed Mobs, and confiding little in the Power *or Inclination* of the Government to protect them? And would you imagine that strong Suspicions now prevail, that those Mobs, after committing 20 barbarous Murders, hitherto unpunish'd, are privately tamper'd with to be made Instruments of Government, to awe the Assembly into Proprietary Measures? And yet all this has happen'd within a few Weeks past!

More Wonders! You know I don't love the Proprietary, and that he does not love me. Our totally different Tempers forbid it. You might therefore expect, that the late new Appointment of one of his Family, would find me ready for Opposition. And yet when his Nephew arriv'd our Governor, I consider'd Government as Government, paid him all Respect, gave him on all Occasions my best Advice, promoted in the Assembly a ready Compliance with everything he propos'd or recommended; and when those daring Rioters, encourag'd by the general Approbation of the Populace, treated his Proclamations with Contempt, I drew my Pen in the Cause, wrote a Pamphlet (that I have sent you) to render the Rioters unpopular; promoted an Association to support the Authority of the Government and defend the Governor by taking Arms, sign'd it first myself, and was followed by several Hundreds, who took Arms accordingly; the Governor offer'd me the Command of them, but I chose to carry a Musket, and strengthen his Authority by setting an Example of Obedience to his Orders. And, would you think it, this Proprietary Governor did me the Honour, on an Alarm, to run to my House at Midnight, with his Counsellors at his Heels, for Advice, and made it his Head Quarters for some time: And within four and twenty Hours, your old Friend was a common Soldier, a Counsellor, a kind of Dictator, an Ambassador to the Country Mob, and on their Returning home, *Nobody*, again. All this has happened in a few Weeks!

More Wonders! The Assembly receiv'd a Governor of the Proprietary Family with open Arms, address'd him with sincere Expressions of Kindness and Respect, open'd their Purses to him, and presented him with Six Hundred Pounds; made a Riot Act and prepar'd a Militia Bill immediately at his Instance; granted Supplies and did every thing that he requested, and promis'd themselves great Happiness under his Administration. But suddenly, his dropping all Enquiry after the Murderers, and his answering the Deputies of the Rioters privately and refusing the Presence of the Assembly who were equally concern'd in the Matters contain'd in their

Remonstrance, brings him under Suspicion; his Insulting the Assembly without the least Provocation, by charging them with Disloyalty and with making *an Infringement on the King's Prerogatives*, only because they had presumed to name in a Bill offered for his Assent, a trifling Officer (somewhat like one of your Toll-Gatherers at a Turn pike) without consulting him; and his refusing several of their Bills, or proposing Amendments needlessly disgusting; these Things bring him and his Government into sudden Contempt; all Regard for him in the Assembly is lost; all Hopes of Happiness under a Proprietary Government are at an End; it has now scarce Authority enough left to keep the common Peace; and was another Mob to come against him, I question whether, tho' a Dozen Men were sufficient, one could find so many in Philadelphia, willing to rescue him or his Attorney-General, I won't say from Hanging, but from any common Insult. All this, too, has happened in a few Weeks!

In fine, every thing seems in this Country, once the Land of Peace and Order, to be running fast into Anarchy and Confusion. Our only Hopes are, that the Crown will see the Necessity of taking the Government into its own Hands, without which we shall soon have no Government at all.

Your civil Dissensions at home give us here great Concern. But we hope there is Virtue enough in your great Nation to support a good Prince in the Execution of Good Government, and the Exercise of his just Prerogatives, against all the Attempts of Unreasonable Faction.

I have been already too long. Adieu, my dear Friend, and believe me ever Yours affectionately

"SO SELFISH IS THE HUMAN MIND!"

To Peter Collinson

Dear Friend,   Philada. April 30. 1764

I have before me your kind Notices of Feb. 3. and Feb. 10. Those you enclos'd for our Friend Bartram, were carefully deliver'd.

I have not yet seen the Squib you mention against your People, in the Supplement to the Magazine; but I think it impossible they should be worse us'd there than they have lately been here; where sundry inflammatory Pamphlets are printed and spread about to excite a mad armed Mob to massacre them. And it is my Opinion they are still in some Danger, more than they themselves seem to apprehend, as our Government has neither Goodwill nor Authority enough to protect them.

By the enclos'd Papers you will see that we are all to pieces again; and the general Wish seems to be a King's Government. If that is not to be obtain'd, many talk of quitting the Province, and among them your old Friend, who is tired of these Contentions, and longs for philosophic Ease and Leisure.

I suppose by this Time the Wisdom of your Parliament has determin'd in the Points you mention, of Trade, Duties, Troops and Fortifications in America. Our Opinions or Inclinations, if they had been known, would perhaps have weigh'd but little among you. We are in your Hands as Clay in the Hands of the Potter; and so in one more Particular than is generally consider'd: for as the Potter cannot waste or spoil his Clay without injuring himself; so I think there is scarce anything you can do that may be hurtful to us, but what will be as much or more so to you. This must be our chief Security; for Interest with you we have but little: The West Indians vastly outweigh us of the Northern Colonies. What we get above a Subsistence, we lay out with you for your Manufactures. Therefore what you get from us in Taxes you must lose in Trade. The Cat can yield but her Skin. And as you must have the whole Hide, if you first cut Thongs out of it, 'tis at your own Expence. The same in regard to our Trade with the foreign West India Islands: If you restrain it in any Degree, you restrain in the same Proportion our Power of making Remittances to you, and of course our Demand for your Goods; for you will not clothe us out of Charity, tho' to receive 100 per Cent for it, in Heaven. In time perhaps Mankind may be wise enough to let Trade take its own Course, find its own Channels, and regulate its own Proportions, &c. At present, most of the Edicts of Princes,

Placaerts, Laws and Ordinances of Kingdoms and States, for that purpose, prove political Blunders. The Advantages they produce not being *general* for the Commonwealth; but *particular*, to private Persons or Bodies in the State who procur'd them, and *at the Expence of the rest of the People*. Does no body see, that if you confine us in America to your own Sugar Islands for that Commodity, it must raise the Price of it upon you in England? Just so much as the Price advances, so much is every Englishman tax'd to the West Indians. Apropos. Now we are on the Subject of Trade and Manufactures, let me tell you a Piece of News, that though it might displease a very respectable Body among you, the Button-makers, will be agreable to yourself as a Virtuoso: It is, that we have discover'd a Beach in a Bay several Miles round, the Pebbles of which are all in the Form of Buttons, whence it is called *Button-mold Bay*; where thousands of Tons may be had for fetching; and as the Sea washes down the slaty Cliff, more are continually manufacturing out of the Fragments by the Surge. I send you a Specimen of Coat, Wastecoat and Sleeve Buttons; just as Nature has turn'd them. But I think I must not mention the Place, lest some Englishman get a Patent for this *Button-mine*, as one did for the *Coal mine* at Louisburgh, and by neither suffering others to work it, nor working it himself, deprive us of the Advantage God and Nature seem to have intended us. As we have now got Buttons, 'tis something towards our Cloathing; and who knows but in time we may find out where to get Cloth? for as to our being always supply'd by you, 'tis a Folly to expect it. Only consider *the Rate of our Increase*, and tell me if you can increase your Wooll in that Proportion, and where, in your little Island you can feed the Sheep. Nature has put Bounds to your Abilities, tho' none to your Desires. Britain would, if she could, manufacture and trade for all the World; England for all Britain; London for all England; and every Londoner for all London. So selfish is the human Mind! But 'tis well there is One above that rules these Matters with a more equal Hand. He that is pleas'd to feed the Ravens, will undoubtedly take care to prevent a Monopoly of the Carrion. Adieu, my dear Friend, and believe me ever Yours most affectionately

"GO CONSTANTLY TO CHURCH
WHOEVER PREACHES"

To Sarah Franklin

Reedy Island Nov. 8. 1764

My dear Sally,   7 at Night.

We got down here just at Sunset, having taken in more live
Stock at Newcastle with some other things we wanted. Our
good Friends Mr. Galloway, Mr. Wharton, and Mr. James
came with me in the Ship from Chester to Newcastle, and
went ashore there. It was kind to favour me with their good
Company as far as they could. The affectionate Leave taken
of me by so many Friends at Chester was very endearing. God
bless them, and all Pennsylvania.

My dear Child, the natural Prudence and goodness of heart
that God has blessed you with, make it less necessary for me
to be particular in giving you Advice; I shall therefore only
say, that the more attentively dutiful and tender you are towards your good Mama, the more you will recommend your
self to me; But why shou'd I mention *me*, when you have so
much higher a Promise in the Commandment, that such a
conduct will recommend you to the favour of God. You know
I have many Enemies (all indeed on the Public Account, for
I cannot recollect that I have in a private Capacity given just
cause of offence to any one whatever) yet they are Enemies
and very bitter ones, and you must expect their Enmity will
extend in some degree to you, so that your slightest Indiscre-
tions will be magnified into crimes, in order the more sensibly
to wound and afflict me. It is therefore the more necessary
for you to be extreamly circumspect in all your Behaviour that
no Advantage may be given to their Malevolence. Go constantly to Church whoever preaches. The Acts of Devotion in
the common Prayer Book, are your principal Business there;
and if properly attended to, will do more towards mending
the Heart than Sermons generally can do. For they were composed by Men of much greater Piety and Wisdom, than our
common Composers of Sermons can pretend to be. And
therefore I wish you wou'd never miss the Prayer Days. Yet I
do not mean that you shou'd despise Sermons even of the

Colony belonging to Portugal, where we were kindly receiv'd
and entertain'd, our Nation being then in high Honour with
them, on Account of the Protection it was at that time affording their Mother Country from the united Invasions of
France and Spain. 'Tis a fertile Island, and the different
Heights and Situations among its Mountains, afford such different Temperaments of Air, that all the Fruits of Northern
and Southern Countries are produc'd there, Corn, Grapes,
Apples, Peaches, Oranges, Lemons, Plantains, Bananas, &c.
Here we furnish'd ourselves with fresh Provisions and Re-
freshments of all kinds, and after a few Days proceeded on
our Voyage, running Southward till we got into the Trade
Winds, and then with them Westward till we drew near the
Coast of America. The Weather was so favourable, that there
were few Days in which we could not visit from Ship to Ship,
dining with each other and on board the Man of War, which
made the time pass agreably, much more so than when one
goes in a single Ship, for this was like travelling in a moving
Village, with all one's Neighbours about one. On the first of
November, I arriv'd safe and well at my own House, after an
Absence of near Six Years, found my Wife and Daughter well,
the latter grown quite a Woman, with many amiable Accomplishments acquir'd in my Absence, and my Friends as hearty
and affectionate as ever, with whom my House was fill'd for
many Days, to congratulate me on my Return. I had been
chosen yearly during my Absence to represent the City of
Philadelphia in our Provincial Assembly, and on my Appearance in the House they voted me £3000 Sterling for my Services in England and their Thanks delivered by the Speaker.
In February following my Son arriv'd, with my new Daughter, for, with my Consent and Approbation he married soon
after I left England, a very agreable West India Lady, with
whom he is very happy. I accompanied him into his Government, where he met with the kindest Reception from the People of all Ranks, and has lived with them ever since in the
greatest Harmony. A River only parts that Province and ours,
and his Residence is within 17 Miles of me, so that we frequently see each other. In the Spring of 1763 I set out on a
Tour thro' all the Northern Colonies, to inspect and regulate
the Post Offices in the several Provinces. In this Journey I

spent the Summer, travelled about 1600 Miles, and did not get home 'till the Beginning of November. The Assembly sitting thro' the following Winter, and warm Disputes arising between them and the Governor I became wholly engag'd in public Affairs: For besides my Duty as an Assemblyman, I had another Trust to execute, that of being one of the Commissioners appointed by Law to dispose of the publick Money appropriated to the Raising and Paying an Army to act against the Indians and defend the Frontiers. And then in December we had two Insurrections of the back Inhabitants of our Province, by whom 20 poor Indians were murdered that had from the first Settlement of the Province lived among us and under the Protection of our Government. This gave me a good deal of Employment, for as the Rioters threatned farther Mischief, and their Actions seem'd to be approv'd by an encreasing Party, I wrote a Pamphlet entitled a *Narrative*, &c. (which I think I sent you,) to strengthen the Hands of our weak Government, by rendring the Proceedings of the Rioters unpopular and odious. This had a good Effect; and afterwards when a great Body of them with Arms march'd towards the Capital in Defiance of the Government, with an avowed Resolution to put to death 140 Indian Converts then under its Protection, I form'd an Association at the Governor's Request, for his and their Defence, we having no Militia. Near 1000 of the Citizens accordingly took Arms; Governor Penn made my House for some time his Head Quarters, and did every thing by my Advice, so that for about 48 Hours I was a very great Man, as I had been once some Years before in a time of publick Danger; but the fighting Face we put on, and the Reasonings we us'd with the Insurgents (for I went at the Request of the Governor and Council with three others to meet and discourse them) having turn'd them back, and restor'd Quiet to the City, I became a less Man than ever: for I had by these Transactions made myself many Enemies among the Populace; and the Governor (with whose Family our publick Disputes had long plac'd me in an unfriendly Light, and the Services I had lately render'd him not being of the kind that make a Man acceptable) thinking it a favourable Opportunity, join'd the whole Weight of the Proprietary Interest to get me out of the Assembly, which was accordingly effected at the last Election, by a Majority of about 25 in 4000 Voters. The House however, when they met in October, approv'd of the Resolutions taken while I was Speaker, of petitioning the Crown for a Change of Government, and requested me to return to England to prosecute that Petition; which Service I accordingly undertook, and embark'd the Beginning of November last, being accompany'd to the Ship, 16 Miles, by a Cavalcade of three Hundred of my Friends, who fill'd our Sails with their good Wishes, and I arrived in 30 Days at London. Here I have been ever since engag'd in that and other Public Affairs relating to America, which are like to continue some time longer upon my hands; but I promise you, that when I am quit of these, I will engage in no other; and that as soon as I have recover'd the Ease and Leisure I hope for, the Task you require of me, of finishing my *Art of Virtue* shall be perform'd: In the mean time I must request you would excuse me on this Consideration, that the Powers of the Mind are posess'd by different Men in different Degrees, and that every one cannot, like Lord Kaims, intermix literary Pursuits and important Business, without Prejudice to either.

I send you herewith two or three other Pamphlets of my Writing on our political Affairs during my short Residence in America; but I do not insist on your reading them, for I know you employ all your time to some useful Purpose.

In my Passage to America, I read your excellent Work, the Elements of Criticism, in which I found great Entertainment, much to admire, and nothing to reprove. I only wish'd you had examin'd more fully the Subject of Music, and demonstrated that the Pleasure Artists feel in hearing much of that compos'd in the modern Taste, is not the natural Pleasure arising from Melody or Harmony of Sounds, but of the same kind with the Pleasure we feel on seeing the surprizing Feats of Tumblers and Rope Dancers, who execute difficult Things. For my part, I take this to be really the Case and suppose it the Reason why those who being unpractis'd in Music, and therefore unacquainted with those Difficulties, have little or no Pleasure in hearing this Music. Many Pieces of it are mere Compositions of Tricks. I have sometimes at a Concert attended by a common Audience plac'd myself so as to see all their Faces, and observ'd no Signs of Pleasure in them during the Performance of much that was admir'd by the Performers themselves; while a plain old Scottish Tune, which they disdain'd and could scarcely be prevail'd on to play, gave manifest and general Delight. Give me leave on this Occasion to extend a little the Sense of your Position, That "Melody and Harmony are separately agreable, and in Union delightful;" and to give it as my Opinion, that the Reason why the Scotch Tunes have liv'd so long, and will probably live forever (if they escape being stifled in modern affected Ornament) is merely this, that they are really Compositions of Melody and Harmony united, or rather that their Melody is Harmony. I mean the simple Tunes sung by a single Voice. As this will appear paradoxical I must explain my Meaning. In common Acceptation indeed, only an agreable *Succession* of Sounds is called *Melody*, and only the *Co-existence* of agreeing Sounds, *Harmony*. But since the Memory is capable of retaining for some Moments a perfect Idea of the Pitch of a past Sound, so as to compare with it the Pitch of a succeeding Sound, and judge truly of their Agreement or Disagreement, there may and does arise from thence a Sense of Harmony between present and past Sounds, equally pleasing with that between two present Sounds. Now the Construction of the old Scotch Tunes is this, that almost every succeeding *emphatical* Note, is a Third, a Fifth, an Octave, or in short some Note that is in Concord with the preceding Note. Thirds are chiefly used, which are very pleasing Concords. I use the Word *emphatical*, to distinguish those Notes which have a Stress laid on them in Singing the Tune, from the lighter connecting Notes, that serve merely, like Grammar Articles, to tack the others together. That we have a most perfect Idea of a Sound just past, I might appeal to all acquainted with Music, who know how easy it is to repeat a Sound in the same Pitch with one just heard. In Tuning an Instrument, a good Ear can as easily determine that two Strings are in Unison, by sounding them separately, as by sounding them together; their Disagreement is also as easily, I believe I may say more easily and better distinguish'd, when sounded separately; for when sounded together, tho' you know by the Beating that one is higher than the other, you cannot tell which it is. Farther, when we consider by whom these ancient Tunes were composed, and how they were first performed, we shall see that such harmonical Succession of Sounds was natural and even necessary in their Construction. They were compos'd by the Minstrels of those days, to be plaid on the Harp accompany'd by the Voice. The Harp was strung with Wire, and had no Contrivance like that in the modern Harpsichord, by which the Sound of a preceding Note could be stopt the Moment a succeeding Note began. To avoid *actual* Discord it was therefore necessary that the succeeding emphatic Note should be a Chord with the preceding, as their Sounds must exist at the same time. Hence arose that Beauty in those Tunes that has so long pleas'd, and will please for ever, tho' Men scarce know why. That they were originally compos'd for the Harp, and of the most simple kind, I mean a Harp without any Half Notes but those in the natural Scale, and with no more than two Octaves of Strings from C. to C. I conjecture from another Circumstance, which is, that not one of those Tunes really ancient has a single artificial Half Note in it; and that in Tunes where it was most convenient for the Voice, to use the middle Notes of the Harp, and place the Key in F. there the B. which if used should be a B flat, is always omitted by passing over it with a Third. The Connoisseurs in modern Music will say I have no Taste, but I cannot help adding, that I believe our Ancestors in hearing a good Song, distinctly articulated, sung to one of those Tunes and accompanied by the Harp, felt more real Pleasure than is communicated by the generality of modern Operas, exclusive of that arising from the Scenery and Dancing. Most Tunes of late Composition, not having the natural Harmony united with their Melody, have recourse to the artificial Harmony of a Bass and other accompanying Parts. This Support, in my Opinion, the old Tunes do not need, and are rather confus'd than aided by it. Whoever has heard James Oswald play them on his Violoncello, will be less inclin'd to dispute this with me. I have more than once seen Tears of Pleasure in the Eyes of his Auditors; and yet I think even his Playing those Tunes would please more, if he gave them less modern Ornament.

My Son, when we parted, desired me to present his affectionate Respects to you, Lady Kaims, and your amiable

Children; be so good with those to accept mine, and believe me, with sincerest Esteem, My dear Lord, Your Lordship's most obedient and most humble Servant

P.S. I do promise myself the Pleasure of seeing you and my other Friends in Scotland before I return to America.

"WE MIGHT AS WELL HAVE HINDER'D THE SUNS SETTING"

To Charles Thomson

Dear Friend   London July 11th: 1765
   I am extreemly obliged by your kind Letters of Aprill 12th. and 14th. and thank you for the Intelligence they Contain.

The Outrages continueally commited by those misguided people, will doubtless tend to Convince all the Considerate on your side of the Water of the Weakness of our present Government and the Necessity of a Change. I am sure it will contribute towards hastening that Change here so that upon the whole, Good will be brought out of Evil: but yet I Greive to hear of such horrid Disorders.

The Letters and Accounts boasted of from the Proprietor of his being Sure of retaining the Government, as well as those of the Sums offered for it which the People will be obliged to pay, &c. are all idle Tales, fit only for Knaves to propagate and Fools to believe.

A Little Time will dissipate all the smoke they can raise to conceal the real State of Things. The unsettled State of the Ministry ever since the Parliament rose, has stop'd all Proceeding in Publick Affairs and ours amongst the Rest; but Change being now made we shall immidiately proceed, and with the Greater Chearfulness as some we had reason to Doubt of are removed, and some perticular Friends are put in Place.

What you mention of the Lower Counties is undoubtedly right. Had they ever sent their Laws home as they ought to have done, that iniquitous one of priority of Payment to Reseidents would undoubtedly have been Repeald. But the End of all these things is neigh, at Least it seems to be so.

The spicking of the Guns was an audacious Peice of Vil-
lainy, by whomsoever done, it Shows the Necessity of a regular enclos'd Place of Defence, with a Constant Guard to take
Care of what belongs to it, which, when the Country can
afford it, will I hope be provided.

Depend upon it my good Neighbour, I took every Step in
my Power, to prevent the Passing of the Stamp Act; no body
could be more concern'd in Interest than my self to oppose
it, sincerely and Heartily. But the Tide was, too strong
against us. The Nation was provok'd by American Claims of
Independance, and all Parties join'd in resolveing by this Act
to Settle the Point.

We might as well have hinder'd the Suns setting. That we
could not do. But since 'tis down, my Friend, and it may be
long before it rises again, Let us make as good a Night of it
as we can. We may still Light Candles. Frugallity and Industry
will go a great way towards indemnifying us. Idleness and
Pride Tax with a heavier Hand then Kings and Parliaments;
If we can get rid of the former we may easily bear the Latter.

My best Respects to Mrs. Thompson. Adieu my Dear
Friend and beleive me ever Yours affectionately

Excuse my Man John's miserable Clerkship.

"A PRETTY GOOD SORT OF A WORLD"

To Jane Mecom

Dear Sister   London, March 1. 1766

I acknowledge the Receipt of your kind Letters of Nov. 12.
and Dec. 20. the latter per Mr. Williams. I condole with you
on the Death of your Husband, who was I believe a truly
affectionate one to you, and fully sensible of your Merit. It is
not true that I have bought any Estate here. I have indeed
had some thoughts of re-purchasing the little one in Northamptonshire that was our Grandfather's, and had been many
Generations in the Family, but was sold by our Uncle
Thomas's only Child Mrs. Fisher, the same that left you the

Legacy. However I shall not do it unless I determine to remain in England, which I have not yet done.

As to the Reports you mention that are spread to my Disadvantage, I give myself as little Concern about them as possible. I have often met with such Treatment from People that I was all the while endeavouring to serve. At other times I have been extoll'd extravagantly when I have had little or no Merit. These are the Operations of Nature. It sometimes is cloudy, it rains, it hails; again 'tis clear and pleasant, and the Sun shines on us. Take one thing with another, and the World is a pretty good sort of a World; and 'tis our Duty to make the best of it and be thankful. One's true Happiness depends more upon one's own Judgement of one's self, on a Consciousness of Rectitude in Action and Intention, and in the Approbation of those few who judge impartially, than upon the Applause of the unthinking undiscerning Multitude, who are apt to cry Hosanna today, and tomorrow, Crucify him. I see in the Papers that your Governor, Mr. Barnard, has been hardly thought of, and a little unkindly treated, as if he was a favourer of the Stamp Act: Yet it appears by his Letters to Government here, which have been read in Parliament, that he has wrote warmly in favour of the Province and against that Act, both before it pass'd and since; and so did your Lieutenant Governor to my certain Knowledge, tho' the Mob have pull'd down his House. Surely the N. England People, when they are rightly inform'd, will do Justice to those Gentlemen, and think of them as they deserve.

Pray remember me kindly to Cousin Williams, and let him know that I am very sensible of his Kindness to you, and that I am not forgetful of any thing that may concern his Interest or his Pleasure, tho' I have not yet wrote to him. I shall endeavour to make that Omission up to him as soon as possible.

I sent you some things by your Friend Capt. Freeman, which I shall be glad to hear came safe to hand, and that they were acceptable from Your affectionate Brother

My Love to your Children.

P.S. I congratulate you and my Countrymen on the Repeal of the Stamp Act. I send you a few of the Cards on which I wrote my Messages during the Time, it was debated here

whether it might not be proper to reduce the Colonies to
Obedience by Force of Arms: The Moral is, that the Colonies
might be ruined, but that Britain would thereby be maimed.

"I NEVER WAS PROUDER OF ANY DRESS IN MY LIFE"

To Deborah Franklin

My dear Child,   London, April 6. 1766.
   As the Stamp Act is at length repeal'd, I am willing you
should have a new Gown, which you may suppose I did not
send sooner, as I knew you would not like to be finer than
your Neighbours, unless in a Gown of your own Spinning.
Had the Trade between the two Countries totally ceas'd, it
was a Comfort to me to recollect that I had once been cloth'd
from Head to Foot in Woollen and Linnen of my Wife's
Manufacture, that I never was prouder of any Dress in my
Life, and that she and her Daughter might do it again if it
was necessary. I told the Parliament that it was my Opinion,

before the old Cloaths of the Americans were worn out, they might have new ones of their own making. And indeed if they had all as many old Clothes as your old Man has, that would not be very unlikely; for I think you and George reckon'd when I was last at home, at least 20 pair of old Breeches. Joking apart, I have sent you a fine Piece of Pompador Sattin, 14 Yards cost 11s. per Yard. A Silk Negligee and Petticoat of brocaded Lutestring for my dear Sally, with 2 Doz. Gloves, 4 Bottles of Lavender Water, and two little Reels. The Reels are to screw on the Edge of a Table, when she would wind Silk or Thread, the Skein is to be put over them, and winds better than if held in two Hands. There is also an Ivory Knob to each, to which she may with a Bit of Silk Cord hang a Pinhook to fasten her plain Work to like the Hooks on her Weight. I send you also Lace for two Lappet Caps, 3 Ells of Cambrick (the Cambrick by Mr. Yates) 3 Damask Table Cloths, a Piece of Crimson Morin for Curtains, with Tassels, Line and Binding. A large true Turky Carpet cost 10 Guineas, for the Dining Parlour. Some oil'd Silk; and a Gimcrack Corkscrew which you must get some Brother Gimcrack to show you the Use of. In the Chest is a Parcel of Books for my Friend Mr. Coleman, and another for Cousin Colbert. Pray did he receive those I sent him before? I send you also a Box with three fine Cheeses. Perhaps a Bit of them may be left when I come home. Mrs. Stevenson has been very diligent and serviceable in getting these things together for you, and presents her best Respects, as does her Daughter, to both you and Sally. There are too Boxes included in your Bill of Lading for Billy.

I received your kind Letter of Feb. 20. It gives me great Pleasure to hear that our good old Friend Mrs. Smith is on the Recovery. I hope she has yet many happy Years to live. My Love to her.

I fear, from the Account you give of Brother Peter that he cannot hold it long. If it should please God that he leaves us before my Return; I would have the Post Office remain under the Management of their Son, till Mr. Foxcroft and I agree how to settle it.

There are some Droll Prints in the Box, which were given me by the Painter; and being sent when I was not at home, were pack'd up without my Knowledge. I think he was wrong to put in Lord Bute, who had nothing to do with the Stamp Act. But it is the Fashion here to abuse that Nobleman as the Author of all Mischief. I send you a few Bush Beans, a new Sort for your Garden. I shall write to my Friends per Packet, that goes next Saturday. I am very well, and hope this will find you and Sally so with all our Relations and Friends, to whom my Love. I am, as ever, Your affectionate Husband,

P.S. A Young Man, by name Joseph Wharton, came to me the other day, said he had been sick and was in distress for Money, and beg'd me to take a Draft on his Brother at Philadelphia for Twelve Guineas. I did not remember or know him, but could refuse nothing to the Name of my Friend. So I let him have the Money, and enclose his Bill. You will present it for Payment.

"A BRAZEN WALL ROUND ENGLAND
FOR ITS ETERNAL SECURITY"

To Cadwalader Evans

LONDON, May 9, 1766.
Dear Sir:—I received your kind letter of March 3, and thank you for the Intelligence and Hints it contained. I wonder at the Complaint you mentioned. I always considered writing to the Speaker as writing to the Committee. But if it is more to their Satisfaction that I should write to them jointly, it shall be done for the future.

My private Opinion concerning a union in Parliament between the two Countries, is, that it would be best for the Whole. But I think it will never be done. For tho' I believe that if we had no more Representatives than Scotland has, we should be sufficiently strong in the House to prevent, as they do for Scotland, any thing ever passing to our disadvantage; yet we are not able at present to furnish and maintain such a Number, and when we are more able we shall be less willing than we are now. The Parliament here do at present think too highly of themselves to admit Representatives from us if we should ask it; and when they will be desirous of granting it, we shall think too highly of ourselves to accept of it. It would certainly contribute to the strength of the whole, if Ireland and all the Dominions were united and consolidated under one Common Council for general Purposes, each retaining its particular Council or Parliament for its domestic Concerns. But this should have been more early provided for.—In the Infancy of our foreign Establishments, it was neglected, or was not thought of. And now, the Affair is nearly in the Situation of Friar Bacon's Project of making a brazen Wall round England for its eternal Security. His Servant Friar Bungey slept while the brazen Head, which was to dictate how it might be done, said *Time is*, and *Time was*. He only wak'd to hear it say, *Time is past*. An explosion followed that tumbled their House about the Conjuror's Ears.

I hope with you, that my being here at this Juncture has been of some Service to the Colonies. I am sure I have spared no Pains. And as to our particular Affair, I am not in the least doubtful of obtaining what we so justly desire if we continue to desire it: tho' the late confus'd State of Affairs on both sides the Water, have delay'd our Proceeding. With great esteem, I am,

> Dear Friend,
> Yours affectionately,

"DIRT . . . WILL NOT LONG ADHERE TO POLISH'D MARBLE"

To Joseph Galloway

Dear Friend,   London, Nov. 8: 1766

I received your kind Letter of Sept. the 22d. and from another Friend a Copy of that lying Essay in which I am represented as the Author of the Stamp Act, and you as concern'd in it. The Answer you mention is not yet come to hand. Your Consolation, my Friend, and mine, under these Abuses, must be, *that we do not deserve them*. But what can console the Writers and Promoters of such infamously false Accusations, if they should ever come themselves to a Sense of that Malice of their Hearts, and that Stupidity of their Heads, which by these Papers they have manifested and exposed to all the World. Dunces often write Satyrs on themselves, when they think all the while that they are mocking their Neighbours. Let us, as we ever have done, uniformly endeavour the Service of our Country, according to the best of our Judgment and Abilities, and Time will do us Justice. Dirt thrown on a Mud-Wall may stick and incorporate; but it will not long adhere to polish'd Marble. I can now only add that I am, with Sincerest Esteem and Affection, Yours,

The Town begins to fill, and the Parliament sits down next week.

"TRAVELLING IS ONE WAY OF LENGTHENING LIFE"

To Mary Stevenson

Dear Polly   Paris, Sept. 14. 1767

I am always pleas'd with a Letter from you, and I flatter myself you may be sometimes pleas'd in receiving one from me, tho' it should be of little Importance, such as this, which is to consist of a few occasional Remarks made here and in my Journey hither.

Soon after I left you in that agreable Society at Bromley, I took the Resolution of making a Trip with Sir John Pringle into France. We set out the 28th past. All the way to Dover we were furnished with Post Chaises hung so as to lean forward, the Top coming down over one's Eyes, like a Hood, as if to prevent one's seeing the Country, which being one of my great Pleasures, I was engag'd in perpetual Disputes with the Innkeepers, Hostlers and Postillions about getting the Straps taken up a Hole or two before, and let down as much behind, they insisting that the Chaise leaning forward was an Ease to the Horses, and that the contrary would kill them. I suppose the Chaise leaning forward looks to them like a Willingness to go forward; and that its hanging back shows a Reluctance. They added other Reasons that were no Reasons at all, and made me, as upon a 100 other Occasions, almost wish that Mankind had never been endow'd with a reasoning Faculty, since they know so little how to make use of it, and so often mislead themselves by it; and that they had been furnish'd with a good sensible Instinct instead of it.

At Dover the next Morning we embark'd for Calais with a Number of Passengers who had never been before at Sea. They would previously make a hearty Breakfast, because if the Wind should fail, we might not get over till Supper-time. Doubtless they thought that when they had paid for their Breakfast they had a Right to it, and that when they had swallowed it they were sure of it. But they had scarce been out half an Hour before the Sea laid Claim to it, and they were oblig'd to deliver it up. So it seems there are Uncertainties even beyond those between the Cup and the Lip. If ever you go to sea, take my Advice, and live sparingly a Day or two before hand. The Sickness, if any, will be the lighter and sooner over. We got to Calais that Evening.

Various Impositions we suffer'd from Boat-men, Porters, &c. on both Sides the Water. I know not which are most rapacious, the English or French; but the latter have, with their Knavery the most Politeness.

The Roads we found equally good with ours in England, in some Places pav'd with smooth Stone like our new Streets for many Miles together, and Rows of Trees on each Side and yet there are no Turnpikes. But then the poor Peasants complain'd to us grievously, that they were oblig'd to work upon the Roads full two Months in the Year without being paid for their Labour: Whether this is Truth, or whether, like Englishmen, they grumble Cause or no Cause, I have not yet been able fully to inform myself.

The Women we saw at Calais, on the Road, at Bouloigne and in the Inns and Villages, were generally of dark Complexions; but arriving at Abbeville we found a sudden Change, a Multitude both of Women and Men in that Place appearing remarkably fair. Whether this is owing to a small Colony of Spinners, Woolcombers and Weavers, &c. brought hither from Holland with the Woollen Manufacture about 60 Years ago; or to their being less expos'd to the Sun than in other Places, their Business keeping them much within Doors, I know not. Perhaps as in some other Cases, different Causes may club in producing the Effect, but the Effect itself is certain. Never was I in a Place of greater Industry, Wheels and Looms going in every House. As soon as we left Abbeville the Swarthiness return'd. I speak generally, for here are some fair Women at Paris, who I think are not whiten'd by Art. As to Rouge, they don't pretend to imitate Nature in laying it on. There is no gradual Diminution of the Colour from the full Bloom in the Middle of the Cheek to the faint Tint near the Sides, nor does it show itself differently in different Faces. I have not had the Honour of being at any Lady's Toylette to see how it is laid on, but I fancy I can tell you how it is or may be done: Cut a Hole of 3 Inches Diameter in a Piece of Paper, place it on the Side of your Face in such a Manner as that the Top of the Hole may be just under your Eye; then with a Brush dipt in the Colour paint Face and Paper together; so when the Paper is taken off there will remain a round Patch of Red exactly the Form of the Hole. This is the Mode, from the Actresses on the Stage upwards thro' all Ranks of Ladies to the Princesses of the Blood, but it stops there, the Queen not using it, having in the Serenity, Complacence and Benignity that shine so eminently in or rather through her Countenance, sufficient Beauty, tho' now an old Woman, to do extreamly well without it.

You see I speak of the Queen as if I had seen her, and so I have; for you must know I have been at Court. We went to Versailles last Sunday, and had the Honour of being presented to the King, he spoke to both of us very graciously and chearfully, is a handsome Man, has a very lively Look, and appears younger than he is. In the Evening we were at the *Grand Couvert*, where the Family sup in Publick. The Form of their sitting at the Table was this:

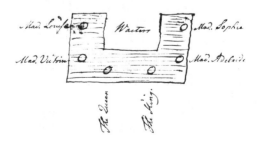

The Table as you see was half a Hollow Square, the Service Gold. When either made a Sign for Drink, the Word was given by one of the Waiters, *A boire pour le Roy*, or *A boire pour la Reine*, &c. then two Persons within the Square approach'd, one with Wine the other with Water in Caraffes, each drank a little Glass of what they brought, and then put both the Caraffes with a Glass on a Salver and presented it. Their Distance from each other was such as that other Chairs might have been plac'd between any two of them. An Officer of the Court brought us up thro' the Croud of Spectators, and plac'd Sir John so as to stand between the King and Madame Adelaide, and me between the Queen and Madame Victoire. The King talk'd a good deal to Sir John, asking many Questions about our Royal Family; and did me too the Honour of taking some Notice of me; that's saying enough, for I would not have you think me so much pleas'd with this King and Queen as to have a Whit less Regard than I us'd to have for ours. No Frenchman shall go beyond me in thinking my own King and Queen the very best in the World and the most amiable.

Versailles has had infinite Sums laid out in Building it and Supplying it with Water: Some say the Expence exceeded 80 Millions Sterling. The Range of Building is immense, the Garden Front most magnificent all of hewn Stone, the Number of Statues, Figures, Urns, &c in Marble and Bronze of exquisite Workmanship is beyond Conception. But the Waterworks are out of Repair, and so is great Part of the Front next the Town, looking with its shabby half Brick Walls and broken Windows not much better than the Houses in Durham Yard. There is, in short, both at Versailles and Paris, a prodigious Mixture of Magnificence and Negligence, with every kind of Elegance except that of Cleanliness, and what we call *Tidyness*. Tho' I must do Paris the Justice to say, that in two Points of Cleanliness they exceed us. The Water they drink, tho' from the River, they render as pure as that of the best Spring, by filtring it thro' Cisterns fill'd with Sand; and the Streets by constant Sweeping are fit to walk in tho' there is no pav'd foot Path. Accordingly many well dress'd People are constantly seen walking in them. The Crouds of Coaches and Chairs for that Reason is not so great; Men as well as

Women carry Umbrellas in their Hands, which they extend in case of Rain or two much Sun; and a Man with an Umbrella not taking up more than 3 foot square or 9 square feet of the Street, when if in a Coach he would take up 240 square feet, you can easily conceive that tho' the Streets here are narrower they may be much less encumber'd. They are extreamly well pav'd, and the Stones being generally Cubes, when worn on one Side may be turn'd and become new.

The Civilities we every where receive give us the strongest Impressions of the French Politeness. It seems to be a Point settled here universally that Strangers are to be treated with Respect, and one has just the same Deference shewn one here by being a Stranger as in England by being a Lady. The Custom House Officers at Port St. Denis, as we enter'd Paris, were about to seize 2 Doz. of excellent Bourdeaux Wine given us at Boulogne, and which we brought with us; but as soon as they found we were Strangers, it was immediately remitted on that Account. At the Church of Notre Dame, when we went to see a magnificent Illumination with Figures &c. for the deceas'd Dauphiness, we found an immense Croud who were kept out by Guards; but the Officer being told that we were Strangers from England, he immediately admitted us, accompanied and show'd us every thing. Why don't we practise this Urbanity to Frenchmen? Why should they be allow'd to out-do us in any thing?

Here is an Exhibition of Paintings, &c. like ours in London, to which Multitudes flock daily. I am not Connoisseur enough to judge which has most Merit. Every Night, Sundays not excepted here are Plays or Operas; and tho' the Weather has been hot, and the Houses full, one is not incommoded by the Heat so much as with us in Winter. They must have some Way of changing the Air that we are not acquainted with. I shall enquire into it.

Travelling is one Way of lengthening Life, at least in Appearance. It is but a Fortnight since we left London; but the Variety of Scenes we have gone through makes it seem equal to Six Months living in one Place. Perhaps I have suffered a greater Change too in my own Person than I could have done in Six Years at home. I had not been here Six Days before my Taylor and Peruquier had transform'd me into a Frenchman.

Only think what a Figure I make in a little Bag Wig and naked Ears! They told me I was become 20 Years younger, and look'd very galante; so being in Paris where the Mode is to be sacredly follow'd, I was once very near making Love to my Friend's Wife.

This Letter shall cost you a Shilling, and you may think it cheap when you consider that it has cost me at least 50 Guineas to get into the Situation that enables me to write it. Besides, I might, if I had staid at home, have won perhaps two shillings of you at Cribbidge. By the Way, now I mention Cards, let me tell you that Quadrille is quite out of Fashion here, and English Whisk all the Mode, at Paris and the Court.

And pray look upon it as no small Matter, that surrounded as I am by the Glories of this World and Amusements of all Sorts, I remember you and Dolly and all the dear good Folks at Bromley. 'Tis true I can't help it, but must and ever shall remember you all with Pleasure. Need I add that I am particularly, my dear good Friend Yours most affectionately

"CONDEMN'D TO LIVE TOGETHER AND TEASE ONE ANOTHER"

To Margaret Stevenson

Dear Madam   Tuesday, Nov. 3 at Noon
  I breakfasted abroad this Morning and Nanny tells me that Mr. West call'd while I was out, and left word that you did not intend to come home till Sunday next, and that you expected me then, to come and fetch you; that Mr. West also desired I would dine at his House that Day: I know not whether Nanny is right in all this, as she has but an indifferent Memory But it seems strange to me that you should think of staying so long. People must have great Confidence in their own Agreableness that can suppose themselves not to become tiresome Guests at the End of Three Days at farthest. I did not imagine you had been so conceited. My Advice to you is, to return with the Stage to-morrow. And if it is proposed that we dine there on Sunday, I shall wait on Mr. and Mrs.

West with Pleasure on that day, taking you with me. But however I pray you not to understand that I so want you at home as not to do very well without you. Every thing goes on smoothly, and the House very quiet; and very clean too, without my saying a Word about it. I am willing to allow that the Arrangements you made before you went may have contributed something towards the good Order and Comfort in which we go on; but yet you are really mistaken in your Fancy that I should, by your Absence, become more sensible of your Usefulness to me, and the Necessity of having you always near me; for in Truth I find such a Satisfaction in being a little more my own Master, going any where and doing any thing just when and how I please without the Advice or Controul of any body's Wisdom but my own small as it is, that I value my own Liberty above all the Advantage of others Services, and begin to think I should be still happier if Nanny and the Cat would follow their Mistress, and leave me to the Enjoyment of an empty House, in which I should never be disturb'd by Questions of Whether I intend to dine at home, and what I would have for Dinner; or by a Mewing Request to be let in or let out. This Happiness however is perhaps too great to be conferr'd on any but Saints and holy Hermits. Sinners like me I might have said US, are condemn'd to live together and tease one another, so concluding you will be sentenc'd to come home tomorrow, I add no more but that I am as ever Your affectionate Friend and humble Servant

My best Compliments to Mr. and Mrs. West.

1767

"A COLLECTION FOR YOU OF ALL THE PAST PARINGS OF MY NAILS"

To Jane Mecom

Dear Sister   London, Dec. 24. 1767

I have received yours of Oct. 23. and condole with you most affectionately in the Affliction you must have suffered by the Loss of so valuable and so amiable a Child. The longer we live we are expos'd to more of these Strokes of Providence: but tho' we consider them as such, and know it is our Duty to submit to the Divine Will, yet when it comes to our Turn to bear what so many Millions before us have borne, and so many Millions after us must bear, we are apt to think our Case particularly hard, Consolations however kindly administred seldom afford us any Relief, Natural Affections will have their Course, and Time proves our best Comforter. This I have experienc'd myself. And as I know your good Sense has suggested to you long before this time, every Argument, Motive and Circumstance that can tend in any degree to relieve your Grief, I will not by repeating them renew it. I am pleas'd to find that in your Troubles you do not overlook the Mercies of God, and that you consider as such the Children that are still spar'd to you. This is a right Temper of Mind, and must be acceptable to that beneficent Being, who is in various Ways continually showring down his Blessings upon many, that receive them as things of course, and feel no grateful Sentiments arising in their Hearts on the Enjoyment of them.

You desire me to send you all the political Pieces I have been the Author of. I have never kept them. They were most of them written occasionally for transient Purposes, and having done their Business, they die and are forgotten. I could as easily make a Collection for you of all the past Parings of my Nails. But I will send you what I write hereafter; and I now enclose you the last Piece of mine that is printed. I wrote it at a Friend's House in the Country who is of the Treasury, if possible to do some Service to the Treasury, by putting a little out of Countenance the Practice of encouraging Smugglers in buying their Commodities. But I suppose it did very little.

Probably the Gentleman has called on you with the small Sum I mention'd; if not, I would not that you should call upon him for it; and therefore do not give you his Name.

Mrs. Stevenson is glad to learn that the Things she sent you were suitable and pleas'd. You mention that you should write for more per Capt. Freeman. We suppose you did not then know, that your People would resolve to wear no more

Millenery. He is not yet arriv'd. Pray are those Resolutions like to be steadily stuck to?

My Love to Jenny, and all our Relations and Friends, and believe me ever Your affectionate Brother

"I AM TOO MUCH OF AN AMERICAN"

To William Franklin

DEAR SON,   *London, Jan. 9, 1768.*

We have had so many alarms of changes which did not take place, that just when I wrote it was thought the ministry would stand their ground. However immediately after the talk was renewed, and it soon appeared the Sunday changes were actually settled. Mr. Conway resigns and Lord Weymouth takes his place. Lord Gower is made president of the council in the room of Lord Northington. Lord Shelburne is stript of the America business which is given to Lord Hillsborough as Secretary of State for America, a new distinct department. Lord Sandwich 'tis said comes into the Post Office in his place. Several of the Bedford party are now to come in. How these changes may affect us a little time will show. Little at present is thought of but elections which gives me hopes that nothing will be done against America this session, though the Boston gazette had occasioned some heats and the Boston resolutions a prodigious clamour. I have endeavoured to palliate matters for them as well as I can: I send you my manuscript of one paper, though I think you take the Chronicle. The editor of that paper one Jones seems a Grenvillian, or is very cautious as you will see, by his corrections and omissions. He has drawn the teeth and pared the nails of my paper, so that it can neither scratch nor bite. It seems only to paw and mumble. I send you also two other late pieces of mine. There is another which I cannot find.

I am told there has been a talk of getting me appointed under secretary to Lord Hillsborough; but with little likelihood as it is a settled point here that I am too much of an American.

I am in very good health, thanks to God: your affectionate father,

FOSSILS

To Jean Chappe d'Auteroche

Sir

London, Jan. 31. 1768

I sent you sometime since, directed to the Care of M. Molini, a Bookseller near the Quây des Augustins a Tooth that I mention'd to you when I had the Pleasure of meeting with you at the Marquis de Courtanvaux's. It was found near the River Ohio in America, about 200 Leagues below Fort du Quesne, at what is called the Great Licking Place, where the Earth has a Saltish Taste that is agreable to the Buffaloes and Deer, who come there at certain Seasons in great Numbers to lick the same. At this place have been found the Skeletons of near 30 large Animals suppos'd to be Elephants, several Tusks like those of Elephants, being found with those Grinder Teeth. Four of these Grinders were sent me by the Gentleman who brought them from the Ohio to New York, together with 4 Tusks, one of which is 6 Feet long and in the thickest Part near 6 Inches Diameter, and also one of the Vertebrae. My Lord Shelbourn receiv'd at the same time 3 or four others with a Jaw Bone and one or two Grinders remaining in it. Some of Our Naturalists here, however, contend, that these are not the Grinders of Elephants but of some carnivorous Animal unknown, because such Knobs or Prominances on the Face of the Tooth are not to be found on those of Elephants, and only, as they say, on those of carnivorous Animals. But it appears to me that Animals capable of carrying such large and heavy Tusks, must themselves be large Creatures, too bulky to have the Activity necessary for pursuing and taking Prey; and therefore I am enclin'd to think those Knobs are only a small Variety, Animals of the same kind and Name often differing more materially, and that those Knobs might be as useful to grind the small Branches of Trees, as to chaw Flesh. However I should be glad to have your Opinion, and to know from you whether any of the kind have been found in Siberia. With great Esteem and Respect, I am Sir, Your most obedient humble Servant

CANAL DEPTHS AND SHIP MOVEMENT

To John Pringle

SIR,   *Craven-street, May* 10, 1768.

You may remember that when we were travelling together in *Holland*, you remarked that the track-schuyt in one of the stages went slower than usual, and enquired of the boatman, what might be the reason; who answered, that it had been a dry season, and the water in the canal was low. On being again asked if it was so low as that the boat touch'd the muddy bottom; he said, no, not so low as that, but so low as to make it harder for the horse to draw the boat. We neither of us at first could conceive that if there was water enough for the boat to swim clear of the bottom, its being deeper would make any difference; but as the man affirmed it seriously as a thing well known among them; and as the punctuality required in their stages, was likely to make such difference, if any there were, more readily observed by them, than by other watermen who did not pass so regularly and constantly backwards and forwards in the same track; I began to apprehend there might be something in it, and attempted to account for it from this consideration, that the boat in proceeding along along the canal, must in every boat's length of her course, move out of her way a body of water, equal in bulk to the room her bottom took up in the water; that the water so moved, must pass on each side of her and under her bottom to get behind her; that if the passage under her bottom was straitened by the shallows, more of that water must pass by her sides, and with a swifter motion, which would retard her, as moving the contrary way; or that the water becoming lower behind the boat than before, she was pressed back by the weight of its difference in height, and her motion retarded by having that weight constantly to overcome. But as it is often lost time to attempt accounting for uncertain facts, I determined to make an experiment of this when I should have convenient time and opportunity.

After our return to *England*, as often as I happened to be on the *Thames*, I enquired of our watermen whether they were sensible of any difference in rowing over shallow or deep water. I found them all agreeing in the fact, that there was a very great difference, but they differed widely in expressing the quantity of the difference; some supposing it was equal to a mile in six, others to a mile in three, &c. As I did not recollect to have met with any mention of this matter in our philosophical books, and conceiving that if the difference should really be great, it might be an object of consideration in the many projects now on foot for digging new navigable canals in this island, I lately put my design of making the experiment in execution, in the following manner.

I provided a trough of plained boards fourteen feet long, six inches wide and six inches deep, in the clear, filled with water within half an inch of the edge, to represent a canal. I had a loose board of nearly the same length and breadth, that being put into the water might be sunk to any depth, and fixed by little wedges where I would chuse to have it stay, in order to make different depths of water, leaving the surface at the same height with regard to the sides of the trough. I had a little boat in form of a lighter or boat of burthen, six inches long, two inches and a quarter wide, and one inch and a quarter deep. When swimming, it drew one inch water. To give motion to the boat, I fixed one end of a long silk thread to its bow, just even with the water's edge, the other end passed over a well-made brass pully, of about an inch diameter, turning freely on a small axis; and a shilling was the weight. Then placing the boat at one end of the trough, the weight would draw it through the water to the other.

Not having a watch that shows seconds, in order to measure the time taken up by the boat in passing from end to end, I counted as fast as I could count to ten repeatedly, keeping an account of the number of tens on my fingers. And as much as possible to correct any little inequalities in my counting, I repeated the experiment a number of times at each

Youth on both sides I should not have thought any Objection. Indeed from the Matches that have fallen under my Observation, I am rather inclined to think that early ones stand the best Chance for Happiness. The Tempers and Habits of young People are not yet become so stiff and uncomplying as when more advanced in Life, they form more easily to each other, and thence many Occasions of Disgust are removed. And if Youth has less of that Prudence that is necessary to manage a Family, yet the Parents and elder Friends of young married Persons are generally at hand to afford their Advice, which amply supplies that Defect; and by early Marriage, Youth is sooner form'd to regular and useful Life, and possibly some of those Accidents Habits or Connections that might have injured either the Constitution or the Reputation, or both, are thereby happily prevented. Particular Circumstances of particular Persons may possibly sometimes make it prudent to delay entering into that State, but in general when Nature has render'd our Bodies fit for it, the Presumption is in Nature's Favour, that she has not judg'd amiss in making us desire it. Late Marriages are often attended too with this farther Inconvenience, that there is not the same Chance the Parents shall live to see their offspring educated. *Late Children*, says the Spanish Proverb, *are early Orphans*: A melancholly Reflection to those whose Case it may be! With us in N. America, Marriages are generally in the Morning of Life, our Children are therefore educated and settled in the World by Noon, and thus our Business being done, we have an Afternoon and Evening of chearful Leisure to our selves, such as your Friend at present enjoys. By these early Marriages we are blest with more Children, and from the Mode among us founded in Nature of every Mother suckling and nursing her own Child, more of them are raised. Thence the swift Progress of Population among us unparallel'd in Europe. In fine, I am glad you are married, and congratulate you cordially upon it. You are now more in the way of becoming a useful Citizen; and you have escap'd the unnatural State of *Celibacy for Life*, the Fate of many here who never intended it, but who having too long postpon'd the Change of their Condition, find at length that 'tis too late to think of it, and So live all their Lives in a

you if you do not follow such Advice. I shall only think that
from a better Acquaintance with Circumstances you form a
better Judgment of what is fit for you to do.

Now I conceive with you that your Aunt, both from her
Affection to you and from the long Habit of having you with
her, would really be miserable without you. Her Temper perhaps was never of the best, and when that is the Case, Age
seldom mends it. Much of her Unhappiness must arise from
thence. And since wrong Turns of the Mind when confirm'd
by Time, are almost as little in our Power to cure, as those of
the Body, I think with you that her Case is a compassionable
one. If she had, though by her own Imprudence, brought on
herself any grievous Sickness, I know you would think it your
Duty to attend and nurse her with filial Tenderness, even were
your own Health to be endangered by it: Your Apprehension
therefore is right, that it may be your Duty to live with her,
tho' inconsistent with your Happiness and your Interest; but
this can only mean present Interest and present Happiness;
for I think your future, greater and more lasting Interest and
Happiness will arise from the Reflection that you have done
your Duty, and from the high Rank you will ever hold in the
Esteem of all that know you, for having persevered in doing
that Duty under so many and great Discouragements. My
Advice then must be, that you return to her as soon as the
Time you propos'd for your Visit is expir'd; and that you
continue by every means in your Power to make the Remainder of her Days as comfortable to her as possible. Invent
Amusements for her; be pleas'd when she accepts of them,
and patient when she perhaps peevishly rejects them. I know
this is hard, but I think you are equal to it; not from any
Servility in your Temper, but from abundant Goodness. In
the mean time all your Friends, sensible of your present uncomfortable Situation, should endeavour to ease your Burthen, by acting in Concert with you, to give her as many
Opportunities as possible of enjoying the Pleasures of Society, for your sake: Nothing is more apt to sour the Temper
of aged People than the Apprehension that they are neglected,
and they are extremely apt to entertain such Suspicions. It
was therefore that I did propose asking her to be of our late
Party: but your Mother disliking it, the Motion was dropt, as

some others have been by my too great Easiness, contrary to my Judgment. Not but that I was sensible her being with us might have lessen'd our Pleasure, but I hoped it might have prevented you some Pain. In fine, nothing can contribute to true Happiness that is inconsistent with Duty; nor can a Course of Action conformable to it, be finally without an ample Reward. For, God governs; and he is *good*. I pray him to direct you: And indeed you will never be without his Direction, if you humbly ask it, and show yourself always ready to obey it. Farewell, *my* dear Friend, and believe me ever sincerely and affectionately *yours*

My Love to Dolly, Miss Blount, Dr. and Mrs. Hawkesworth, Miss Henckell &c. &c. I much commend Dolly for inviting your Aunt into the Country; you see how perfectly that agrees with my Notions. The next Day after you went, she sent the Servant for Nancy, ordering him to take a Place for her in the Stage; and Nancy has been there ever since.

"AT PRESENT I ALMOST DESPAIR"

To ——————

DEAR SIR,   *London, Nov.* 28, 1768.

I received your obliging favour of the 12th instant. Your sentiments of the importance of the present dispute between Great Britain and the colonies, appear to me extremely just. There is nothing I wish for more than to see it amicably and equitably settled.

But Providence will bring about its own ends by its own means; and if it intends the downfal of a nation, that nation will be so blinded by its pride, and other passions, as not to see its danger, or how its fall may be prevented.

Being born and bred in one of the countries, and having lived long and made many agreeable connexions of friendship in the other, I wish all prosperity to both; but I have talked, and written so much and so long on the subject, that my acquaintance are weary of hearing, and the public of reading any more of it, which begins to make me weary of talking and writing; especially as I do not find that I have gained any point, in either country, except that of rendering myself suspected, by my impartiality; in England, of being too much an American, and in America of being too much an Englishman. Your opinion, however, weighs with me, and encourages me to try one effort more, in a full, though concise statement of facts, accompanied with arguments drawn from those facts; to be published about the meeting of parliament, after the holidays.

If any good may be done I shall rejoice; but at present I almost despair.

Have you ever seen the barometer so low as of late? The 22d instant mine was at 28, 41, and yet the weather fine and fair. With sincere esteem, I am, dear friend, yours affectionately,

LEARNING TO SWIM

To Oliver Neave

Dear SIR,

I cannot be of opinion with you that 'tis too late in life for you to learn to swim. The river near the bottom of your garden affords you a most convenient place for the purpose. And as your new employment requires your being often on the water, of which you have such a dread, I think you would do well to make the trial; nothing being so likely to remove those apprehensions as the consciousness of an ability to swim to the shore, in case of an accident, or of supporting yourself in the water till a boat could come to take you up.

I do not know how far corks or bladders may be useful in learning to swim, having never seen much trial of them. Possibly they may be of service in supporting the body while you are learning what is called the stroke, or that manner of drawing in and striking out the hands and feet that is necessary to produce progressive motion. But you will be no swimmer till you can place some confidence in the power of the water to support you; I would therefore advise the acquiring that confidence in the first place; especially as I have known several who by a little of the practice necessary for that purpose, have insensibly acquired the stroke, taught as it were by nature.

The practice I mean is this. Chusing a place where the water deepens gradually, walk coolly into it till it is up to your breast, then turn round, your face to the shore, and throw an egg into the water between you and the shore. It will sink to the bottom, and be easily seen there, as your water is clear. It must lie in water so deep as that you cannot reach it to take it up but by diving for it. To encourage yourself in undertaking to do this, reflect that your progress will be from deeper to shallower water, and that at any time you may by bringing your legs under you and standing on the bottom, raise your head far above the water. Then plunge under it with your eyes open, throwing yourself towards the egg, and endeavouring by the action of your hands and feet against the water to get forward till within reach of it. In this attempt you will find, that the water buoys you up against your inclination; that it is not so easy a thing to sink as you imagined; that you cannot, but by active force, get down to the egg. Thus you feel the power of the water to support you, and learn to confide in that power; while your endeavours to overcome it and to reach the egg, teach you the manner of acting on the water with your feet and hands, which action is afterwards used in swimming to support your head higher above water, or to go forward through it.

I would the more earnestly press you to the trial of this method, because, though I think I satisfyed you that your body is lighter than water, and that you might float in it a long time with your mouth free for breathing, if you would put yourself in a proper posture, and would be still and forbear struggling; yet till you have obtained this experimental confidence in the water, I cannot depend on your having the necessary presence of mind to recollect that posture and the directions I gave you relating to it. The surprize may put all out of your mind. For though we value ourselves on being reasonable knowing creatures, reason and knowledge seem on such occasions to be of little use to us; and the brutes to whom we allow scarce a glimmering of either, appear to have the advantage of us.

I will, however, take this opportunity of repeating those particulars to you, which I mentioned in our last conversation, as by perusing them at your leisure, you may possibly imprint them so in your memory as on occasion to be of some use to you.

1. That though the legs, arms and head, of a human body, being solid parts, are specifically something heavier than fresh water, yet the trunk, particularly the upper part from its hollowness, is so much lighter than water, as that the whole of the body taken together is too light to sink wholly under water, but some part will remain above, untill the lungs become filled with water, which happens from drawing water into them instead of air, when a person in the fright attempts breathing while the mouth and nostrils are under water.

2. That the legs and arms are specifically lighter than salt-water, and will be supported by it, so that a human body would not sink in salt-water, though the lungs were filled as above, but from the greater specific gravity of the head.

3. That therefore a person throwing himself on his back in salt-water, and extending his arms, may easily lie so as to keep his mouth and nostrils free for breathing; and by a small motion of his hands may prevent turning, if he should perceive any tendency to it.

4. That in fresh water, if a man throws himself on his back, near the surface, he cannot long continue in that situation but by proper action of his hands on the water. If he uses no such action, the legs and lower part of the body will gradually sink till he comes into an upright position, in which he will continue suspended, the hollow of the breast keeping the head uppermost.

5. But if in this erect position, the head is kept upright above the shoulders, as when we stand on the ground, the immersion will, by the weight of that part of the head that is out of water, reach above the mouth and nostrils, perhaps a little above the eyes, so that a man cannot long remain suspended in water with his head in that position.

6. The body continuing suspended as before, and upright, if the head be leaned quite back, so that the face looks up-

wards, all the back part of the head being then under water, and its weight consequently in a great measure supported by it, the face will remain above water quite free for breathing, will rise an inch higher every inspiration, and sink as much every expiration, but never so low as that the water may come over the mouth.

7. If therefore a person unacquainted with swimming, and falling accidentally into the water, could have presence of mind sufficient to avoid struggling and plunging, and to let the body take this natural position, he might continue long safe from drowning till perhaps help would come. For as to the cloathes, their additional weight while immersed is very inconsiderable, the water supporting it; though when he comes out of the water, he would find them very heavy indeed.

But, as I said before, I would not advise you or any one to depend on having this presence of mind on such an occasion, but learn fairly to swim; as I wish all men were taught to do in their youth; they would, on many occurrences, be the safer for having that skill, and on many more the happier, as freer from painful apprehensions of danger, to say nothing of the enjoyment in so delightful and wholesome an exercise. Soldiers particularly should, methinks, all be taught to swim; it might be of frequent use either in surprising an enemy, or saving themselves. And if I had now boys to educate, I should prefer those schools (other things being equal) where an opportunity was afforded for acquiring so advantageous an art, which once learnt is never forgotten.

I am, Sir, &c.

before 1769

"A RECEIPT FOR MAKING PARMESAN CHEESE"

To John Bartram

Dear Friend,   London July 9, 1769

It is with great Pleasure I understand by your Favour of April 10. that you continue to enjoy so good a Share of Health. I hope it will long continue. And altho' it may not now be suitable for you to make such wide Excursions as heretofore, you may yet be very useful to your Country and to Mankind, if you sit down quietly at home, digest the Knowledge you have acquired, compile and publish the many Observations you have made, and point out the Advantages that may be drawn from the whole, in publick Undertakings or particular private Practice. It is true many People are fond of Accounts of old Buildings, Monuments, &c. but there is a Number who would be much better pleas'd with such Accounts as you could afford them: And for one I confess that if I could find in any Italian Travels a Receipt for making Parmesan Cheese, it would give me more Satisfaction than a Transcript of any Inscription from any old Stone whatever.

I suppose Mr. Michael Collinson, or Dr. Fothergill have written to you what may be necessary for your Information relating to your Affairs here. I imagine there is no doubt but the King's Bounty to you will be continued; and that it will be proper for you to continue sending now and then a few such curious Seeds as you can procure to keep up your Claim. And now I mention Seeds, I wish you would send me a few of such as are least common, to the Value of a Guinea, which Mr. Foxcroft will pay you for me. They are for a particular Friend who is very curious. If in any thing I can serve you here, command freely Your affectionate Friend

P.S. Pray let me know whether you have had sent you any of the Seeds of the Rhubarb describ'd in the enclos'd Prints. It is said to be of the true kind. If you have it not, I can procure some Seeds for you.

"AFFAIRS ARE PERHAPS BELOW NOTICE"

To George Whitefield

I am under continued apprehensions that we may have bad news from America. The sending soldiers to Boston always appeared to me a dangerous step; they could do no good, they might occasion mischief. When I consider the warm resentment of a people who think themselves injured and oppressed, and the common insolence of the soldiery, who are taught to consider that people as in rebellion, I cannot but fear the consequences of bringing them together. It seems like setting up a smith's forge in a magazine of gunpowder. I *see* with you that our affairs are not well managed by our rulers here below; I wish I could *believe* with you, that they are well attended to by those above: I rather suspect, from certain circumstances, that though the general government of the universe is well administered, our particular little affairs are perhaps below notice, and left to take the chance of human prudence or imprudence, as either may happen to be uppermost. It is, however, an uncomfortable thought, and I leave it.

before September 2, 1769

"WHOEVER SCRUPLES CHEATING THE KING
WILL CERTAINLY NOT WRONG HIS NEIGHBOUR"

To Mary Stevenson

Saturday Evening, Sept 2. 1769
Just come home from a Venison Feast, where I have drank more than a Philosopher ought, I find my dear Polly's chearful chatty Letter that exhilarates me more than all the Wine.

Your good Mother says there is no Occasion for any Intercession of mine in your behalf. She is sensible that she is more in fault than her Daughter. She received an affectionate tender Letter from you, and she has not answered it, tho' she intended to do it; but her Head, not her Heart, has been bad, and unfitted her for Writing. She owns that she is not so good a Subject as you are, and that she is more unwilling to pay Tribute to Cesar, and has less Objection to Smuggling; but 'tis not, she says, mere Selfishness or Avarice; 'tis rather an honest Resentment at the Waste of those Taxes in Pensions, Salaries, Perquisites, Contracts and other Emoluments for the Benefit of People she does not love, and who do not deserve such Advantages, because—I suppose because they are not of her Party. Present my Respects to your good Landlord and his Family: I honour them for their consciencious

Aversion to illicit Trading. There are those in the World who would not wrong a Neighbour, but make no Scruple of cheating the King. The Reverse however does not hold; for whoever scruples cheating the King will certainly not wrong his Neighbour. You ought not to wish yourself an Enthusiast: They have indeed their imaginary Satisfactions and Pleasures; but those are often ballanc'd by imaginary Pains and Mortifications. You can continue to be a good Girl, and thereby lay a solid Foundation for expected future Happiness, without the Enthusiasm that may perhaps be necessary to some others. As those Beings who have a good sensible Instinct, have no need of Reason; so those who have Reason to regulate their Actions, have no Occasion for Enthusiasm. However there are certain Circumstances in Life sometimes, wherein 'tis perhaps best not to hearken to Reason. For instance; Possibly, if the Truth were known, I have Reason to be jealous of this same insinuating handsome young Physician: But as it flatters more my Vanity, and therefore gives me more Pleasure to suppose you were in Spirits on Account of my safe Return, I shall turn a deaf Ear to Reason in this Case, as I have done with Success in twenty others. But I am sure you will always give me Reason enough to continue ever Your affectionate Friend

Our Love to Mrs. Tickell. We all long for your Return: Your Dolly was well last Tuesday, the Girls were there on a Visit to her: I mean at Bromley. Adieu.

No Time now to give you any Account of my French Journey.

"THE TRUE SOURCES OF WEALTH AND PLENTY"

To Timothy Folger

Loving Kinsman,   London, Sept. 29. 1769

Since my Return from abroad, where I spent part of the Summer, I have received your Favours of June 10 and July 26. The Treasury Board is still under Adjournment, the Lords and Secretaries chiefly in the Country; but as soon as they meet again, you may depend on my making the Application you desire.

I shall enquire concerning the Affair of your two Townships settled under Massachusetts Grants, and let you know my Sentiments as soon as I can get proper Information. I should imagine that whatever may be determin'd here of the Massachusetts Rights to the Jurisdiction, the private Property of Settlers must remain secure. In general I have no great Opinion of Applications to be made here in such Cases. It is so much the Practice to draw Matters into Length, put the Parties to immense Charge, and tire them out with Delays, that I would never come from America hither with any Affair I could possibly settle there.

Mrs. Stevenson sends her Love, and thanks you for remembring her. She is vex'd to hear that the Box of Spermaceti Candles is seiz'd; and says, if ever she sees you again, she will put you in a way of making Reprisals. You know she is a Smuggler upon Principle; and she does not consider how averse you are to every thing of the kind. I thank you for your kind Intention. Your Son grows a fine Youth; he is so obliging as to be with us a little when he has Holidays; and Temple is not the only one of the Family that is fond of his Company.

It gives me great Pleasure to hear that our People are steady in their Resolutions of Non Importation, and in the Promoting of Industry among themselves. They will soon be sensible of the Benefit of such Conduct, tho' the Acts should never be repeal'd to their full Satisfaction. For their Earth and their Sea, the true Sources of Wealth and Plenty, will go on producing; and if they receive the annual Increase, and do not waste it as heretofore in the Gewgaws of this Country, but employ their spare time in manufacturing Necessaries for themselves, they must soon be out of debt, they must soon be easy and comfortable in their circumstances, and even wealthy. I have been told, that in some of our County Courts heretofore, there were every quarter several hundred actions of debt, in which the people were sued by Shopkeepers for money due for British *goods* (as they are called, but in fact *evils*). What a loss of time this must occasion to the people, besides the expense. And how can Freeman bear the thought

of subjecting themselves to the hazard of being deprived of
their personal liberty at the caprice of every petty trader, for
the paltry vanity of tricking out himself and family in the
flimsy manufactures of Britain, when they might by their own
industry and ingenuity, appear in *good substantial honourable
homespun*! Could our folks but see what numbers of Merchants, and even Shopkeepers here, make great estates by
American folly; how many shops of A, B, C and Co. with
wares for *exportation to the Colonies*, maintain, each shop three
or four partners and their families, every one with his country-house and equipage, where they live like Princes on the
sweat of our brows; pretending indeed, *sometimes*, to wish
well to our Privileges, but on the present important occasion
few of them affording us any assistance: I am persuaded that
indignation would supply our want of prudence, we should
disdain the thraldom we have so long been held in by this
mischievous commerce, reject it for ever, and seek our resources where God and Nature have placed them WITHIN
OUR SELVES.

Your Merchants, on the other hand, have shown a noble
disinterestedness and *love to their country*, unexampled among
Traders in any other age or nation, and which does them infinite honour all over Europe. The corrupted part indeed of
this people *here* can scarce believe such virtue possible. But
perseverance will convince them, that there is still in the
world such a thing as public spirit. I hope that, if the oppressive Acts are not repealed this winter, your Stocks, that us'd
to be employed in the British Trade, will be turned to the
employment of Manufactures among yourselves: For notwithstanding the former general opinion that manufactures
were impracticable in America, on account of the dearness of
labour, experience shows, in the success of the manufactures
of paper and stockings in Pennsylvania, and of womens shoes
at Lynn in your province, that labour is only dear *from the
want of* CONSTANT *employment*; (he who is often out of work
requiring necessarily as much for the time he does work, as
will maintain him when he does not work:) and that where
we do not *interrupt that employment* by importations, *the
cheapness of our provisions* gives us such advantage over the
Manufacturers in Britain, that (especially in bulky goods,

whose freight would be considerable) *we may always* UNDER-
WORK THEM.

"I HOPE HOWEVER THAT THIS MAY ALL
PROVE FALSE PROPHECY"

To William Strahan

Dear Sir,   Craven Street, Nov. 29. 69
   Being just return'd to Town from a little Excursion I find
yours of the 22d, containing a Number of Queries that would
require a Pamphlet to answer them fully. You however desire
only brief Answers, which I shall endeavour to give you. Previous to your Queries, You tell me, that "you apprehend his
Majesty's Servants have now in Contemplation; 1st. to releive
the Colonists from the Taxes complained of: and 2dly to preserve the Honour, the Dignity, and the Supremacy of the
British Legislature over all his Majesty's Dominions." I hope
your Information is good, and that what you suppose to be
in Contemplation will be carried into Execution, by repealing
all the Laws that have been made for raising a Revenue in
America by Authority of Parliament, without the consent of
the People there. The *Honour* and *Dignity* of the British Legislature will not be hurt by such an Act of Justice and Wisdom: The wisest Councils are liable to be misled, especially
in Matters remote from their Inspection. It is the persisting
in an Error, not the Correcting it that lessens the Honour of
any Man or body of Men. The *Supremacy* of that Legislature,
I believe will be best preserv'd by making a very sparing use
of it, never but for the Evident Good of the Colonies themselves, or of the whole British Empire; never for the Partial
Advantage of Britain to their Prejudice; by such Prudent
Conduct I imagine that Supremacy may be gradually
strengthened and in time fully Established; but otherwise I
apprehend it will be disputed, and lost in the Dispute. At
present the Colonies consent and Submit to it for the regulation of General Commerce: But a Submission to Acts of
Parliament was no part of their original Constitution. Our

former Kings Governed their Colonies, as they Governed
their Dominions in France, without the Participation of British Parliaments. The Parliament of England never presum'd
to interfere with that prerogative till the Time of the Great
Rebellion, when they usurp'd the Government of all the
King's other Dominions, Ireland, Scotland &c. The Colonies
that held for the King, they conquered by Force of Arms, and
Governed afterward as Conquered Countries. But New England having not oppos'd the Parliament, was considered and
treated as a Sister Kingdom in Amity with England; as appears by the Journals, Mar. 10. 1642.

Your first Question is,

1. "Will not a Repeal of all the Duties (that on Tea excepted, which was before paid here on Exportation, and of
Course no new Imposition) fully satisfy the Colonists?"

I think not.

"2 Your Reasons for that Opinion?"

Because it is not *the Sum* paid in that Duty on Tea that is
Complain'd of as a Burthen, but the Principle of the Act express'd in the Preamble, viz. that those Duties were laid for
the Better Support of Government and the Administration of
Justice in the Colonies. This the Colonists think *unnecessary,
unjust*, and *dangerous* to their Most Important Rights. *Unnecessary*, because in all the Colonies (two or three new ones
excepted) Government and the Administration of Justice were
and always had been well supported without any Charge to
Britain; *Unjust* as it made such Colonies liable to pay such
Charge for other Colonies, in which they had no Concern or
Interest; *dangerous*, as such a Mode of raising Money for
these Purposes, tended to render their Assemblies useless: For
if a Revenue could be rais'd in the Colonies for all the purposes of Government, by Act of Parliament, without Grants
from the People there, Governors, who do not generally love
Assemblies, would never call them, they would be laid aside;
and when nothing Should depend upon the People's good
will to Government, their Rights would be trampled on, they
would be treated with Contempt. Another Reason why I
think they would not be satisfy'd with such a partial repeal,
is, that their Agreements not to import till the Repeal takes
place, include the whole, which shows that they object to the

whole; and those Agreements will continue binding on them if the whole is not repealed.

"3. Do you think the only effectual Way of composing the present Differences, is, to put the Americans precisely in the Situation they were in before the passing of the late Stamp Act?"

I think so.

"4. Your Reasons for that Opinion?"

Other Methods have been tryed. They have been rebuked in angry Letters. Their Petitions have been refused or rejected by Parliament. They have been threatened with the Punishments of Treason by Resolves of both Houses. Their Assemblies have been dissolv'd, and Troops have been sent among them; but all these Ways have only exasperated their Minds and widen'd the Breach; their Agreements to use no more British Manufactures have been Strengthen'd, and these Measures instead of composing Differences and promoting a good Correspondence, have almost annihilated your Commerce with those Countries, and greatly endanger'd the National Peace and general Welfare.

"5. If this last Method is deemed by the Legislature and his Majisty's Ministers to be repugnant to their Duty as Guardians of the just Rights of the Crown, and of their Fellow Subjects, can you suggest any other Way of terminating these Disputes, consistent with the Ideas of Justice and propriety conceived by the Kings Subjects on both Sides the Atlantick?"

A. I do not see how that method can be deemed repugnant *to the Rights of the Crown.* If the Americans are put into their former Situation, it must be by an Act of Parliament, in the Passing of which by the King the Rights of the Crown are exercised not infringed. It is indifferent to the Crown whether the Aids received from America are Granted by Parliament here, or by the Assemblies there, provided the Quantum be the same; and it is my Opinion more will generally be Granted there Voluntarily than can ever be exacted and collected from thence by Authority of parliament. As to the rights of *Fellow Subjects* (I suppose you mean the People of Britain) I cannot conceive how they will be infringed by that method. They will still enjoy the Right of Granting their own money; and may still, if it pleases them, keep up their Claim to the Right of granting ours; a Right they can never exercise properly, for want of a sufficient Knowledge of us, our Circumstances and Abilities (to say nothing of the little likelihood there is that we should ever submit to it) therefore a Right that can be of no good use to them. And we shall continue to enjoy, *in fact*, the Right of granting our own Money; with the Opinion now universally prevailing among us that we are free Subjects of the King, and that *Fellow Subjects* of one Part of his Dominions are not Sovereign over *Fellow Subjects* in any other Part. If the Subjects on the different Sides of the Atlantic, have different and opposite Ideas of Justice or Propriety, no one Method can possibly be consistent with both. The best will be to let each enjoy their own Opinions, without disturbing them when they do not interfere with the common Good.

"6. And if this Method were actually followed do you not think it would encourage the Violent and Factious Part of the Colonists to aim at still farther Concessions from the Mother Country?"

A. I do not think it would. There may be a few among them that deserve the Name of factious and Violent, as there are in all Countries, but these would have little influence if the great Majority of Sober reasonable People were satisfy'd. If any Colony should happen to think that some of your regulations of Trade are inconvenient to the general Interest of the Empire, or prejudicial to them without being beneficial to you, they will state these Matters to the Parliament in Petitions as heretofore, but will, I believe, take no violent steps to obtain, what they may hope for in time from the Wisdom of Government here. I know of nothing else they can have in View. The Notion that prevails here of their being desirous of setting up a Kingdom or Common Wealth of their own, is to my certain Knowledge entirely groundless. I therefore think that on a total Repeal of all Duties laid expressly for the purpose of raising a Revenue on the People of America, without their Consent, the present Uneasiness would subside; the Agreements not to import would be dissolved, and the Commerce flourish as heretofore. And I am confirm'd in this Sentiment by all the Letters I have received from America, and by the Opinion of all the Sensible People who have lately come from thence, Crown Officers excepted. I know indeed that the people of Boston are grievously offended by the Quartering of Troops among them, as they think, contrary to Law; and are very angry with the Board of Commissioners to have calumniated them to Government; but as I suppose withdrawing of those Troops may be a Consequence of Reconciliating Measures taking Place; and that the Commission also will either be dissolv'd if found useless, or fill'd with more temporate and prudent Men if still deemed useful and necessary, I do not imagine these Particulars will prevent a return of the Harmony so much to be wished.

"7. If they are relieved in Part only, what do you, as a reasonable and dispassionate Man, and an equal Friend to both sides, imagine will be the probable Consequence?"

A. I imagine that repealing the offensive Duties in part will answer no End to this Country; the Commerce will remain obstructed, and the Americans go on with their Schemes of Frugality, Industry and Manufactures, to their own great Advantage. How much that may tend to the prejudice of Britain I cannot say; perhaps not so much as some apprehend, since she may in time find New Markets. But I think (if the Union of the two Countries continues to subsist) it will not hurt the *general* interest; for whatever Wealth Britain loses by the Failure of its Trade with the Colonies, America will gain; and the Crown will receive equal Aids from its Subjects upon the whole, if not greater.

And now I have answered your Questions as to what *may be* in my Opinion the Consequences of this or that *supposed* Measure, I will go a little farther, and tell you what I fear is more likely to come to pass *in Reality.*

I apprehend, that the Ministry, at least the American part of it, being fully persuaded of the Right of Parliament, think it ought to be enforc'd whatever may be the Consequences; and at the same time do not believe there is even now any Abatement of the Trade between the two Countries on account of these Disputes; or that if there is, it is small and cannot long Continue; they are assured by the Crown officers in America that Manufactures are impossible there; that the Discontented are few, and Persons of little Consequence; that almost all the People of Property and Importance are satisfyd, and disposed to submit quietly to the Taxing-Power of Parliament; and that if the Revenue Acts are continued, those Duties only that are called anti-commercial being repealed, and others perhaps laid in their stead, that Power will ere long be patiently submitted to, and the Agreements not to import be broken when they are found to produce no Change of Measures here. From these and similar Misinformations, which seem to be credited, I think it likely that no thorough redress of Grievances will be afforded to America this Session. This may inflame Matters still more in that Country; farther rash Measures there may create more Resentment here, that may Produce not merely ill-advis'd and useless Dissolutions of their Assemblies, as last Year; but Attempts to Dissolve their Constitutions; more Troops may be sent over, which will create more Uneasiness; to justify the Measures of Government your Ministerial Writers will revile the Americans in your Newspapers, as they have already began to do, treating them as Miscreants, Rogues, Dastards, Rebels, &c. which will tend farther to alienate the Minds of the People here from them, and diminish their Affections to this Country. Possibly too, some of their warm patriots may be distracted enough to expose themselves by some mad Action, to be sent for Hither, and Government here be indiscreet enough to Hang them on the Act of H. 8. Mutual Provocations will thus go on to complete the Separation; and instead of that cordial Affection that once and so long existed, and that Harmony so suitable to the Circumstances, and so Necessary to the Happiness, Strength Safety and Welfare of both Countries; an implacable Malice and Mutual Hatred, (such as we now see subsisting between the Spaniards and Portuguese, the Genoese and Corsicans, from the same Original Misconduct in the Superior Government) will take place; the Sameness of Nation, the Similarity of Religion, Manners and Language not in the least Preventing in our Case, more than it did in theirs. I hope however that this may all prove false Prophecy: And that you and I may live to see as sincere and Perfect a friendship establish'd between our respective Countries as has so many years Subsisted between Mr. Strahan and his truly affectionate Friend

"IF WE ARE STEADY AND PERSEVERE
IN OUR RESOLUTIONS"

To [Charles Thomson]

Dear Sir   London March 18th. 1770

Your very judicious Letter of Novemr. 26th. being communicated by me to some Member of Parliament, was handed about among them, so that it was sometime before I got it again into my Hands. It had due Weight with several, and was of considerable Use. You will see that I printed it at length in the London Chronicle with the Merchants' Letter. When the American Affairs came to be debated in the House of Commons, the Majority, notwithstanding all the Weight of ministerial Influence, was only 62 for continuing the whole last Act; and would not have been so large, nay, I think the Repeal would have been carried, but that the Ministry were persuaded by Governor Bernard and some lying Letters said to be from Boston, that the Associations not to import were all breaking to Pieces, that America was in the greatest Distress for Want of the Goods, that we could not possibly subsist any longer without them, and must of course submit to any Terms Parliament should think fit to impose upon us. This with the idle Notion of the Dignity and Sovereignty of Parliament, which they are so fond of, and imagine will be endanger'd by any farther Concessions, prevailed I know with many to vote with the Ministry, who otherwise, on Account of the Commerce, wish to see the Difference accommodated. But though both the Duke of Grafton and Lord North were and are in my Opinion rather inclined to satisfy us, yet the Bedford Party are so violent against us, and so prevalent in the Council, that more moderate Measures could not take Place. This Party never speak of us but with evident Malice; Rebels and Traitors are the best Names they can afford us, and I believe they only wish for a colourable Pretence and Occasion of ordering the Souldiers to make a Massacre among us.

On the other Hand the Rockingham and Shelburne People, with Lord Chatham's Friends, are disposed to favour us if they were again in Power, which at present they are not like

to be; tho' they, too, would be for keeping up the Claim of
parliamentary Sovereignty, but without exercising it in any
Mode of Taxation. Besides these, we have for sincere Friends
and Wellwishers the Body of Dissenters, generally, throughout England, with many others, not to mention Ireland and
all the rest of Europe, who from various Motives join in applauding the Spirit of Liberty, with which we have claimed
and insisted on our Privileges, and wish us Success, but
whose Suffrage cannot have much Weight in our Affairs.

The Merchants here were at length prevailed on to present
a Petition, but they moved slowly, and some of them I
thought reluctantly; perhaps from a Despair of Success, the
City not being much in favour with the Court at present. The
manufacturing Towns absolutely refused to move at all; some
pretending to be offended with our attempting to manufacture for ourselves; others saying that they had Employment
enough, and that our Trade was of little Importance to them,
whether we continued or refused it. Those who began a little
to feel the Effects of our forbearing to purchase, were persuaded to be quiet by the ministerial People; who gave out
that certain Advices were receiv'd of our beginning to break
our Agreements; of our Attempts to manufacture proving all
abortive and ruining the Undertakers; of our Distress for
Want of Goods, and Dissentions among ourselves, which
promised the total Defeat of all such Kind of Combinations,
and the Prevention of them for the future, if the Government
were not urged imprudently to repeal the Duties. But now
that it appears from late and authentic Accounts, that Agreements continue in full Force, that a Ship is actually return'd
from Boston to Bristol with Nails and Glass, (Articles that
were thought of the utmost Necessity,) and that the Ships
that were waiting here for the Determination of Parliament,
are actually returning to North America in thier Ballast; the
Tone of the Manufacturers begins to change, and there is no
doubt, that if we are steady and persevere in our Resolutions,
these People will soon begin a Clamor that much Pains has
hitherto been used to stifle.

In short, it appears to me, that if we do not now persist in
this Measure till it has had its full Effect, it can never again
be used on any future Occasion with the least prospect of

Success, and that if we do persist another year, we shall never afterwards have occasion to use it. With sincere regards I am, Dear Sir, Your obedient Servant,

"I SHOULD THINK YOU A FORTUNE SUFFICIENT FOR ME WITHOUT A SHILLING"

To Mary Stevenson

Dear Polly   Thursday May 31. 70

I receiv'd your Letter early this Morning, and as I am so engag'd that I cannot see you when you come to-day, I write this Line just to say, That I am sure you are a much better Judge in this Affair of your own than I can possibly be; in that Confidence it was that I forbore giving my Advice when you mention'd it to me, and not from any Disapprobation. My Concern (equal to any Father's) for your Happiness, makes me write this, lest having more Regard for my Opinion than you ought, and imagining it against the Proposal because I did not immediately advise accepting it, you should let that weigh any thing in your Deliberations. I assure you that no Objection has occur'd to me; his Person you see, his Temper and his Understanding you can judge of, his Character for any thing I have ever heard is unblemished; his Profession, with that Skill in it he is suppos'd to have, will be sufficient to support a Family; and therefore considering the Fortune you have in your Hands, (tho' any future Expectation from your Aunt should be disappointed) I do not see but that the Agreement may be a rational one on both sides. I see your Delicacy; and your Humility too; for you fancy that if you do not prove a great Fortune you will not be belov'd; but I am sure that were I in his Situation in every respect, knowing you so well as I do, and esteeming you so highly, I should think you a Fortune sufficient for me without a Shilling. Having thus more explicitly than before, given my Opinion, I leave the rest to your sound Judgment, of which no one has a greater Share; and shall not be too inquisitive after your particular Reasons, your Doubts, your Fears, &c.

For I shall be confident whether you accept or refuse, that
you do right. I only wish you may do what will most contribute to your Happiness, and of course to mine; being ever, my
dear Friend, Yours most affectionately

Don't be angry with me for supposing your Determination
not quite so fix'd as you fancy it.

"THE SOLE LEGISLATOR OF HIS AMERICAN SUBJECTS"

To Samuel Cooper

Dear Sir,   London, June 8. 1770
    I received duly your Favour of March 28. With this I send
you two Speeches in Parliament on our Affairs by a Member
that you know. The Repeal of the whole late Act would undoubtedly have been a prudent Measure, and I have reason
to believe that Lord North was for it, but some of the other
Ministers could not be brought to agree to it. So the Duty
on Tea, with that obnoxious Preamble, remains to continue
the Dispute. But I think the next Session will hardly pass
over without repealing them; for the Parliament must finally
comply with the Sense of the Nation. As to the Standing
Army kept up among us in time of Peace, without the Consent of our Assemblies, I am clearly of Opinion that it is not
agreable to the Constitution. Should the King by the Aid of
his Parliaments in Ireland and the Colonies, raise an Army
and bring it into England, quartering it here in time of
Peace without the Consent of the Parliament of Great Britain, I am persuaded he would soon be told that he had no
Right so to do, and the Nation would ring with Clamours
against it. I own that I see no Difference in the Cases. And
while we continue so many distinct and separate States, our
having the same Head or Sovereign, the King, will not justify such an Invasion of the separate Right of each State to
be consulted on the Establishment of whatever Force is proposed to be kept up within its Limits, and to give or refuse

its Consent as shall appear most for the Public Good of that State. That the Colonies originally were constituted distinct States, and intended to be continued such, is clear to me from a thorough Consideration of their original Charters, and the whole Conduct of the Crown and Nation towards them until the Restoration. Since that Period, the Parliament here has usurp'd an Authority of making Laws for them, which before it had not. We have for some time submitted to that Usurpation, partly thro' Ignorance and Inattention, and partly from our Weakness and Inability to contend. I hope when our Rights are better understood here, we shall, by a prudent and proper Conduct be able to obtain from the Equity of this Nation a Restoration of them. And in the mean time I could wish that such Expressions as, *The supreme Authority of Parliament*; *The Subordinacy of our Assemblies to the Parliament* and the like (which in Reality mean nothing if our Assemblies with the King have a true Legislative Authority) I say, I could wish that such Expressions were no more seen in our publick Pieces. They are too strong for Compliment, and tend to confirm a Claim of Subjects in one Part of the King's Dominions to be Sovereigns over their Fellow-Subjects in another Part of his Dominions; when in truth they have no such Right, and their Claim is founded only on Usurpation, the several States having equal Rights and Liberties, and being only connected, as England and Scotland were before the Union, by having one common Sovereign, the King. This kind of Doctrine the Lords and Commons here would deem little less than Treason against what they think their Share of the Sovereignty over the Colonies. To me those Bodies seem to have been long encroaching on the Rights of their and our Sovereign, assuming too much of his Authority, and betraying his Interests. By our Constitutions he is, with his Plantation Parliaments, the sole Legislator of his American Subjects, and in that Capacity is and ought to be free to exercise his own Judgment unrestrain'd and unlimited by his Parliament here. And our Parliaments have Right to grant him Aids without the Consent of this Parliament, a Circumstance which, by the way begins to give it some Jealousy. Let us therefore hold fast our Loyalty to our King (who has the best Dis-

position towards us, and has a Family-Interest in our Prosperity) as that steady Loyalty is the most probable Means of
securing us from the arbitrary Power of a corrupt Parliament, that does not like us, and conceives itself to have an
Interest in keeping us down and fleecing us. If they should
urge the *Inconvenience* of an Empire's being divided into so
many separate States, and from thence conclude that we are
not so divided; I would answer, that an Inconvenience
proves nothing but itself. England and Scotland were once
separate States, under the same King. The Inconvenience
found in their being separate States, did not prove that the
Parliament of England had a Right to govern Scotland. A
formal Union was thought necessary, and England was an
hundred Years soliciting it, before she could bring it about.
If Great Britain now thinks such an Union necessary with
us, let her propose her Terms, and we may consider of them.
Were the general Sentiments of this Nation to be consulted
in the Case, I should hope the Terms, whether practicable or
not, would at least be equitable: for I think that except
among those with whom the Spirit of Toryism prevails, the
popular Inclination here is, to wish us well, and that we may
preserve our Liberties.

I unbosom my self thus to you in Confidence of your Prudence, and wishing to have your Sentiments on the Subject
in Return.

Mr. Pownall, I suppose, will acquaint you with the Event
of his Motions, and therefore I say nothing more of them,
than that he appears very sincere in his Endeavours to serve
us; on which Account I some time since republish'd with
Pleasure the parting Addresses to him of your Assembly, with
some previous Remarks, to his Honour as well as in Justification of our People.

I hope that before this time those detestable Murderers
have quitted your Province, and that the Spirit of Industry
and Frugality continues and increases. With sincerest Esteem
and Affection, I am, Dear Sir, Your most obedient and most
humble Servant

P.S. Just before the last Session of Parliament commenced a
Friend of mine, who had Connections with some of the

Ministry, wrote me a Letter purposely to draw from me my Sentiments in Writing on the then State of Affairs. I wrote a pretty free Answer, which I know was immediately communicated and a good deal handed about among them. For your *private Amusement* I send you Copies. I wish you may be able to read them, as they are very badly written by a very blundering Clerk.

"HITHERTO MADE NO ATTEMPT UPON MY VIRTUE"

To Mary Stevenson Hewson

Dear Polly,   London, July 18. 1770
   Yours of the 15th. informing me of your agreable Journey and safe Arrival at Hexham gave me great Pleasure, and would make your good Mother happy if I knew how to convey it to her; but 'tis such an out-of-the-way Place she is gone to, and the Name so out of my Head, that the Good News must wait her Return. Enclos'd I send you a Letter which came before she went, and, supposing it from my Daughter Bache, she would have me open and read it to her, so you see if there had been any Intrigue between the Gentleman and you, how all would have been discovered. Your Mother went away on Friday last, taking with her Sally and Temple, trusting me alone with Nanny, who indeed has hitherto made no Attempt upon my Virtue. Neither Dolly nor Barwell, nor any other good Female Soul of your Friends or mine have been nigh me, nor offered me the least Consolation by Letter in my present lonesome State. I hear the Post-man's Bell, so can only add my affectionate Respects to Mr. Hewson, and best Wishes of perpetual Happiness for you both. I am, as ever, my dear good Girl, Your affectionate Friend

"HAVE YOU THEN GOT NE'ER A GRANDMOTHER?"

To Deborah Franklin

My dear Child,   London, Oct. 3. 1770
   I received your kind Letter of Aug. 16. which gave me a

great deal of Satisfaction. I am glad your little Grandson recovered so soon of his Illness, as I see you are quite in Love with him, and your Happiness wrapt up in his; since your whole long Letter is made up of the History of his pretty Actions. It was very prudently done of you not to interfere when his Mother thought fit to correct him; which pleases me the more, as I feared, from your Fondness of him, that he would be too much humoured, and perhaps spoiled. There is a Story of two little Boys in the Street; one was crying bitterly; the other came to him to ask what was the Matter? I have been, says he, for a pennyworth of Vinegar, and I have broke the Glass and spilt the Vinegar, and my Mother will whip me. *No, she won't whip you* says the other. Indeed she will, says he. *What,* says the other*, have you then got ne'er a Grandmother?*

I am sorry I did not send one of my Books to Mr. Rhodes, since he was desirous of seeing it. My Love to him, and to all enquiring Friends. Mrs. West was here to day, and desired me to mention her Love to you. Mr. Strahan and Family are all well, always enquire how you all do, and send their Love. Mrs Stevenson is at present in the Country. But Polly sends her Love to you and Mrs Bache and the young Gentleman. My Love to all. I am, as ever, Your affectionate Husband

"THIS WORLD IS THE TRUE HELL"

To Jane Mecom

Dear Sister   London Dec. 30. 1770

This Ship staying longer than was expected, gives me an Opportunity of writing to you which I thought I must have miss'd when I desir'd Cousin Williams to excuse me to you. I received your kind Letter of Sept. 25 by the young Gentlemen, who, by their discreet Behaviour have recommended themselves very much to me and many of my Acquaintance. Josiah has attained his Heart's Desire of being under the Tuition of Mr. Stanley, who, tho, he had long left off Teaching, kindly undertook at my Request to instruct him, and is much pleased with his Quickness of Apprehension and the Progress he makes; and Jonathan appears a very valuable young Man, sober, regular, and inclin'd to Industry and Frugality, which are promising Signs of Success in Business: I am very happy in their Company.

As to the Rumour you mention (which was, as Josiah tells me, that I had been depriv'd of my Place in the Post Office on Account of a letter I wrote to Philadelphia) it might have this Foundation, that some of the Ministry had been displeas'd at my Writing such Letters, and there were really some Thoughts among them of shewing that Displeasure in that manner. But I had some Friends too, who unrequested by me advis'd the contrary. And my Enemies were forc'd to content themselves with abusing me plentifully in the Newspapers, and endeavouring to provoke me to resign. In this they are not likely to succeed, I being deficient in that Christian Virtue of Resignation. If they would have my Office, they must take it—I have heard of some great Man, whose Rule it was with regard to Offices, *Never to ask for them*, and *never to refuse them*: To which I have always added in my own Practice, *Never to resign them*. As I told my Friends, I rose to that office thro' a long Course of Service in the inferior Degrees of it: Before my time, thro' bad Management, it never produced the Salary annex'd to it; and when I receiv'd it, no Salary was to be allow'd if the office did not produce it. During the first four Years it was so far from defraying itself, that it became £950 Sterling in debt to me and my Collegue. I had been chiefly instrumental in bringing it to its present flourishing State, and therefore thought I had some kind of Right to it. I had hitherto executed the Duties of it faithfully, and to the perfect Satisfaction of my Superiors, which I thought was all that should be expected of me on that Account. As to the Letters complain'd of, it was true I did write them, and they were written in Compliance with another Duty, that to my Country. A Duty quite Distinct from that of Postmaster. My Conduct in this respect was exactly similar with that I held on a similar Occasion but a few Years ago, when the then Ministry were ready to hug me for the Assistance I afforded them in repealing a former Revenue Act. My Sentiments were still the same, that no such

Acts should be made here for America; or, if made should as
soon as possible be repealed; and I thought it should not be
expected of me, to change my Political Opinions every time
his Majesty thought fit to change his Ministers. This was my
Language on the Occasion; and I have lately heard, that tho
I was thought much to blame, it being understood that
every Man who holds an Office should act with the Ministry
whether agreable or not to his own Judgment, yet in consideration of the goodness of my private Character (as they are
pleas'd to compliment me) the office was not to be taken
from me. Possibly they may still change their Minds, and remove me; but no Apprehension of that sort, will, I trust,
make the least Alteration in my Political Conduct. My rule
in which I have always found Satisfaction, is, Never to turn
asside in Publick Affairs thro' Views of private Interest; but
to go strait forward in doing what appears to me right at
the time, leaving the Consequences with Providence. What
in my younger Days enabled me more easily to walk upright, was, that I had a Trade; and that I could live upon a
little; and thence (never having had views of making a Fortune) I was free from Avarice, and contented with the plentiful Supplies my business afforded me. And now it is still
more easy for me to preserve my Freedom and Integrity,
when I consider, that I am almost at the End of my Journey,
and therefore need less to complete the Expence of it; and
that what I now possess thro' the Blessing of God may with
tolerable Oeconomy, be sufficient for me (great Misfortunes
excepted) tho' I should add nothing more to it by any Office
or Employment whatsoever.

I send you by this Opportunity the 2 Books you wrote
for. They cost 3s. a piece. When I was first in London,
about 45 Years since, I knew a person who had an Opinion
something like your Author's—Her Name was *Ilive*, a
Printer's Widow. She dy'd soon after I left England, and by
her Will oblig'd her son to deliver publickly in Salter's Hall
a Solemn Discourse, the purport of which was to prove, that
this World is the true Hell or Place of Punishment for the
Spirits who had transgress'd in a better State, and were sent
here to suffer for their sins in Animals of all Sorts. It is long
since I saw the Discourse, which was printed. I think a good

deal of Scripture was cited in it, and that the Supposition was, that tho' we now remember'd nothing of such pre-existent State; yet after Death we might recollect it, and remember the Punishments we had suffer'd, so as to be the better for them; and others who had not yet offended, might now behold and be warn'd by our Sufferings. In fact we see here that every lower Animal has its Enemy with proper Inclinations, Faculties and Weapons, to terrify, wound and destroy it; and that Men, who are uppermost, are Devils to one another; So that on the establish'd Doctrine of the Goodness and Justice of the great Creator, this apparent State of general and systematical Mischief, seem'd to demand some such Supposition as Mrs. Ilives, to account for it consistent with the Honour of the Diety. But our reasoning Powers when employ'd about what may have been before our Existence here, or shall be after it, cannot go far for want of History and Facts: Revelation only can give us the necessary Information, and that (in the first of these Points especially) has been very sparingly afforded us.

I hope you continue to correspond with your Friends at Philadelphia, or else I shall think there has been some Miff between you; which indeed, to confess the Truth, I was a little afraid, from some Instances of others, might possibly happen, and that prevented my ever urging you to make such a visit especially as I think there is rather an overquantity of Touchwood in your Constitution. My Love to your Children, and believe me ever, Your affectionate Brother

Let none of my Letters go out of your Hands.

HOW RAINDROPS GROW

To Thomas Percival

On my return to London I found your favour, of the sixteenth of May (1771). I wish I could, as you desire, give you a better explanation of the phænomenon in question, since you seem not quite satisfied with your own; but I think we want more and a greater variety of experiments in different circumstances, to enable us to form a thoroughly satisfactory hypothesis. Not that I make the least doubt of the facts already related, as I know both Lord Charles Cavendish, and Dr. Heberden to be very accurate experimenters: but I wish to know the event of the trials proposed in your six queries; and also, whether in the same place where the lower vessel receives nearly twice the quantity of water that is received by the upper, a third vessel placed at half the height will receive a quantity proportionable. I will however endeavour to explain to you what occurred to me, when I first heard of the fact.

I suppose, it will be generally allowed, on a little consideration of the subject, that scarce any drop of water was, when it began to fall from the clouds, of a magnitude equal to that it has acquired, when it arrives at the earth; the same of the several pieces of hail; because they are often so large and weighty, that we cannot conceive a possibility of their being suspended in the air, and remaining at rest there, for any time, how small soever; nor do we conceive any means of forming them so large, before they set out to fall. It seems then, that each beginning drop, and particle of hail, receives continual addition in its progress downwards. This may be several ways: by the union of numbers in their course, so that what was at first only a descending mist, becomes a shower; or by each particle in its descent through air that contains a great quantity of dissolved water, striking against, attaching to itself, and carrying down with it, such particles of that dissolved water, as happen to be in its way; or attracting to itself such as do not lie directly in its course, by its different state with regard either to common or electric fire; or by all these causes united.

In the first case, by the uniting of numbers, larger drops might be made, but the quantity falling in the same space would be the same at all heights; unless, as you mention, the whole should be contracted in falling, the lines described by all the drops converging, so that what set out to fall from a cloud of many thousand acres, should reach the earth in perhaps a third of that extent, of which I somewhat doubt. In the other cases we have two experiments.

1. A dry glass bottle, filled with very cold water, in a warm day, will presently collect from the seemingly dry air that surrounds it, a quantity of water that shall cover its surface and run down its sides, which perhaps is done by the power wherewith the cold water attracts the fluid, common fire that had been united with the dissolved water in the air, and drawing that fire through the glass into itself, leaves the water on the outside.

2. An electrified body left in a room for some time, will be more covered with dust than other bodies in the same room not electrified, which dust seems to be attracted from the circumambient air.

Now we know that the rain, even in our hottest days, comes from a very cold region. Its falling sometimes in the form of ice, shews this clearly; and perhaps even the rain is snow or ice when it first moves downwards, though thawed in falling: And we know that the drops of rain are often electrified: But those causes of addition to each drop of water, or piece of hail, one would think could not long continue to produce the same effect; since the air, through which the drops fall, must soon be stript of its previously dissolved water, so as to be no longer capable of augmenting them. Indeed very heavy showers, of either, are never of long continuance; but moderate rains often continue so long as to puzzle this hypothesis: So that upon the whole I think, as I intimated before, that we are yet hardly ripe for making one.

June? 1771

"AN ADVENTURE TO GAIN FORBIDDEN KNOWLEDGE"

To Jane Mecom

Dear Sister, London, July 17. 1771

I have received your kind Letter of May 10. You seem so sensible of your Error in so hastily suspecting me, that I am now in my turn sorry I took Notice of it. Let us then suppose that Accompt ballanced and settled, and think no more of it.

In some former Letter I believe I mention'd the Price of the Books, which I have now forgotten: But I think it was 3s. each. To be sure there are Objections to the Doctrine of Pre-existence: But it seems to have been invented with a good Intention, to save the Honour of the Deity, which was thought to be injured by the Supposition of his bringing Creatures into the World to be miserable, without any previous misbehaviour of theirs to deserve it. This, however, is perhaps an officious Supporting of the Ark, without being call'd to such Service. Where he has thought fit to draw a Veil, our Attempting to remove it may be deem'd at least an offensive Impertinence. And we shall probably succeed little better in such an Adventure to gain forbidden Knowledge, than our first Parents did when they ate the Apple.

I meant no more by saying Mankind were Devils to one another than that being in general superior to the Malice of the other Creatures, they were not so much tormented by them as by themselves. Upon the whole I am much disposed to like the World as I find it, and to doubt my own Judgment as to what would mend it. I see so much Wisdom in what I understand of its Creation and Government, that I suspect equal Wisdom may be in what I do not understand. And thence have perhaps as much Trust in God as the most pious Christian.

I am very happy that a good Understanding continues between you and the Philadelphia Folks. Our Father, who was a very wise man, us'd to say, nothing was more common than for those who lov'd one another at a distance, to find many Causes of Dislike when they came together; and therefore he did not approve of Visits to Relations in distant Places, which could not well be short enough for them to part good Friends. I saw a Proof of it, in the Disgusts between him and his Brother Benjamin; and tho' I was a Child I still remember how affectionate their Correspondence was while they were separated, and the Disputes and Misunderstandings they had when they came to live some time together in the same House. But you have been more prudent, and restrain'd that "Aptness" you say you have "to interfere in other People's oeconomical Affairs by putting in a Word now and then unasked." And so all's well that ends well.

I thought you had mentioned in one of your Letters a Desire to have Spectacles of some sort sent you; but I cannot now find such a Letter. However I send you a Pair of every Size of Glasses from 1 to 13. To suit yourself, take out a Pair at a time, and hold one of the Glasses first against one Eye, and then against the other, looking on some small Print. If the first Pair suits neither Eye, put them up again before you open a second. Thus you will keep them from mixing. By trying and comparing at your Leisure, you may find those that are best for you, which you cannot well do in a Shop, where for want of Time and Care, People often take such as strain their Eyes and hurt them. I advise your trying each of your Eyes separately, because few Peoples Eyes are Fellows, and almost every body in reading or working uses one Eye principally, the other being dimmer or perhaps fitter for distant Objects; and thence it happens that the Spectacles whose Glasses are Fellows suit sometimes that Eye which before was not used tho' they do not suit the other. When you have suited your self, keep the higher Numbers for future Use as your Eyes may grow older; and oblige your Friends with the others.

I was lately at Sheffield and Birmingham, where I bought a few plated Things which I send you as Tokens, viz. A Pair of Sauceboats, a Pair of flat Candlesticks, and a Saucepan, lined with Silver. Please to accept of them. I have had one of the latter in constant Use 12 Years, and the Silver still holds. But Tinning is soon gone.

Mrs. Stevenson and Mrs. Hewson present their Compliments, the latter has a fine Son. Sally Franklin sends her Duty to you. I wonder you have not heard of her till lately. She has lived with me these 5 Years, a very good Girl, now near 16. She is Great Grandaughter of our Father's Brother John, who was a Dyer at Banbury in Oxfordshire, where our Father learnt that Trade of him, and where our Grandfather Thomas lies buried: I saw his Gravestone. Sally's Father, John's Grandson, is now living at Lutterworth in Leicestershire, where he follows the same Business, his Father too being bred a Dyer, as was our Uncle Benjamin. He is a Widower, and Sally his only Child. These two are the only Descendants of our Grandfather Thomas now remaining in England that

retain that Name of *Franklin*. The Walkers are descended of
John by a Daughter that I have seen, lately deceased. Sally
and Cousin Williams's Children, and Henry Walker who now
attends Josiah are Relations in the same degree to one another
and to your and my Grandchildren, viz

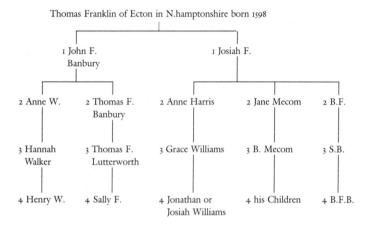

Thomas Franklin of Ecton in N.hamptonshire born 1598

1 John F. Banbury		1 Josiah F.		
2 Anne W.	2 Thomas F. Banbury	2 Anne Harris	2 Jane Mecom	2 B.F.
3 Hannah Walker	3 Thomas F. Lutterworth	3 Grace Williams	3 B. Mecom	3 S.B.
4 Henry W.	4 Sally F.	4 Jonathan or Josiah Williams	4 his Children	4 B.F.B.

What is this Relation called? Is it third Cousins? Having
mentioned so many Dyers in our Family, I will now it's in
my Mind request of you a full and particular Receipt for
Dying Worsted of that beautiful Red, which you learnt of our
Mother. And also a Receipt for making Crown Soap. Let it
be very exact in the smallest Particulars. Enclos'd I send you
a Receipt for making soft Soap in the Sun.

I have never seen any young Men from America that acquir'd by their Behaviour here more general Esteem than
those you recommended to me. Josiah has stuck close to his
musical Studies, and still continues them. Jonathan has been
diligent in Business for his Friends as well as himself, obliging
to every body, tender of his Brother, not fond of the expensive Amusements of the Place, regular in his Hours, and
spending what Leisure Hours he had in the Study of Mathematics. He goes home to settle in Business, and I think there
is great Probability of his doing well. With best Wishes for
you and all yours, I am ever, Your affectionate Brother

I have mislaid the Soap Receipt but will send it when I find it.

"WHAT SORT OF HUSBANDS WOULD BE FITTEST"

To Anna Mordaunt Shipley

Dear Madam, London, Aug. 13. 1771

This is just to let you know that we arriv'd safe and well in Marlborough Street about Six, where I deliver'd up my Charge.

The above seems too short for a Letter; so I will lengthen it by a little Account of our Journey. The first Stage we were rather pensive. I tried several Topics of Conversation, but none of them would hold. But after Breakfast, we began to recover Spirits, and had a good deal of Chat. Will you hear some of it? We talk'd of her Brother, and she wish'd he was married. And don't you wish your Sisters married too? Yes. All but Emily; I would not have her married. Why? Because I can't spare her, I can't part with her. The rest may marry as soon as they please, so they do but get good Husbands. We then took upon us to consider for 'em what sort of Husbands would be fittest for every one of them. We began with Georgiana. She thought a Country Gentleman, that lov'd Travelling and would take her with him, that lov'd Books and would hear her read to him; I added, that had a good Estate and was a Member of Parliament and lov'd to see an Experiment now and then. This she agreed to; so we set him down for Georgiana, and went on to Betsy. Betsy, says I, seems of a sweet mild Temper, and if we should give her a Country Squire, and he should happen to be of a rough, passionate Turn, and be angry now and then, it might break her Heart. O, none of 'em must be so; for then they would not be good Husbands. To make sure of this Point, however, for Betsey, shall we give her a Bishop? O no, that won't do. They all declare against the Church, and against the Army; not one of them will marry either a Clergyman or an Officer; that they

are resolv'd upon. What can be their reason for that? Why
you know, that when a Clergyman or an Officer dies, the
Income goes with 'em; and then what is there to maintain the
Family? there's the Point. Then suppose we give her a good,
honest, sensible City Merchant, who will love her dearly and
is very rich? I don't know but that may do. We proceeded to
Emily, her dear Emily, I was afraid we should hardly find any
thing good enough for Emily; but at last, after first settling
that, if she did marry, Kitty was to live a good deal with her;
we agreed that as Emily was very handsome we might expect
an Earl for her: So having fix'd her, as I thought, a Countess,
we went on to Anna-Maria. She, says Kitty, should have a
rich Man that has a large Family and a great many things to
take care of; for she is very good at managing, helps my
Mama very much, can look over Bills, and order all sorts of
Family Business. Very well; and as there is a Grace and Dignity in her Manner that would become the Station, what do
you think of giving her a Duke? O no! I'll have the Duke for
Emily. You may give the Earl to Anna-Maria if you please:
But Emily shall have the Duke. I contested this Matter some
time; but at length was forc'd to give up the point, leave Emily in Possession of the Duke, and content myself with the
Earl for Anna Maria. And now what shall we do for Kitty?
We have forgot her, all this Time. Well, and what will you do
for her? I suppose that tho' the rest have resolv'd against the
Army, she may not yet have made so rash a Resolution. Yes,
but she has: Unless, now, an old one, an old General that has
done fighting, and is rich, such a one as General Rufane; I
like him a good deal; You must know I like an old Man,
indeed I do: And some how or other all the old Men take to
me, all that come to our House like me better than my other
Sisters: I go to 'em and ask 'em how they do, and they like it
mightily; and the Maids take notice of it, and say when they
see an old Man come, there's a Friend of yours, Miss Kitty.
But then as you like an old General, hadn't you better take
him while he's a young Officer, and let him grow old upon
your Hands, because then, you'll like him better and better
every Year as he grows older and older. No, that won't do.
He must be an old Man of 70 or 80, and take me when I am
about 30: And then you know I may be a rich young Widow.

We din'd at Staines, she was Mrs. Shipley, cut up the Chicken pretty handily (with a little Direction) and help'd me in a very womanly Manner. Now, says she, when I commended her, my Father never likes to see me or Georgiana carve, because we do it, he says, so badly: But how should we learn if we never try? We drank good Papa and Mama's Health, and the Health's of the Dutchess, the Countess, the Merchant's Lady, the Country Gentlewoman, and our Welsh Brother. This brought their Affairs again under Consideration. I doubt, says she, we have not done right for Betsey. I don't think a Merchant will do for her. She is much inclin'd to be a fine Gentlewoman; and is indeed already more of the fine Gentlewoman, I think, than any of my other Sisters; and therefore she shall be a Vice Countess.

Thus we chatted on, and she was very entertaining quite to Town.

I have now made my Letter as much too long as it was at first too short. The Bishop would think it too trifling, therefore don't show it him. I am afraid too that you will think it so, and have a good mind not to send it. Only it tells you Kitty is well at School, and for that I let it go. My Love to the whole amiable Family, best Respects to the Bishop, and 1000 Thanks for all your Kindnesses, and for the happy Days I enjoy'd at Twyford. With the greatest Esteem and Respect, I am, Madam, Your most obedient humble Servant

"COMPAR'D TO THESE PEOPLE
EVERY INDIAN IS A GENTLEMAN"

To Joshua Babcock

Dear Sir,   London, Jan. 13. 1772

It was with great Pleasure I learnt by Mr. Marchant, that you and Mrs. Babcock and all your good Family continue well and happy. I hope I shall find you all in the same State when I next come your Way, and take Shelter as often heretofore under your hospitable Roof. The Colonel, I am told,

continues an active and able Farmer, the most honourable of
all Employments, in my Opinion as being the most useful in
itself, and rendring the Man most independent. My Name-
sake, his Son, will soon I hope be able to drive the Plough
for him.

I have lately made a Tour thro' Ireland and Scotland. In
these Countries a small Part of the Society are Landlords,
great Noblemen and Gentlemen, extreamly opulent, living in
the highest Affluence and Magnificence: The Bulk of the
People Tenants, extreamly poor, living in the most sordid
Wretchedness in dirty Hovels of Mud and Straw, and
cloathed only in Rags. I thought often of the Happiness of
New England, where every Man is a Freeholder, has a Vote
in publick Affairs, lives in a tidy warm House, has plenty of
good Food and Fewel, with whole Cloaths from Head to
Foot, the Manufactury perhaps of his own Family. Long
may they continue in this Situation! But if they should ever
envy the *Trade* of these Countries, I can put them in a Way
to obtain a Share of it. Let them with three fourths of the
People of Ireland, live the Year round on Potatoes and Butter milk, without Shirts, then may their Merchants export
Beef, Butter and Linnen. Let them with the Generality of
the Common People of Scotland go Barefoot, then may they
make large Exports in Shoes and Stockings: And if they will
be content to wear Rags like the Spinners and Weavers of
England, they may make Cloths and Stuffs for all Parts of
the World. Farther, if my Countrymen should ever wish for
the Honour of having among them a Gentry enormously
wealthy, let them sell their Farms and pay rack'd Rents; the
Scale of the Landlords will rise as that of the Tenants is depress'd who will soon become poor, tattered, dirty, and abject in Spirit. Had I never been in the American Colonies,
but was to form my Judgment of Civil Society by what I
have lately seen, I should never advise a Nation of Savages
to admit of Civilisation: For I assure you, that in the Possession and Enjoyment of the various Comforts of Life, compar'd to these People every Indian is a Gentleman: And the
Effect of this kind of Civil Society seems only to be, the de-
pressing Multitudes below the Savage State that a few may
be rais'd above it. My best Wishes attend you and yours,

being ever with great Esteem, Dear Sir, Your most obedient and most humble Servant

ON THE WRITINGS OF ZOROASTER

To Ezra Stiles

Dear Sir,   London, Jany. 13. 1772

I receiv'd your Favour by Mr. Marchant, who appears a very worthy Gentleman, and I shall not fail to render him every Service in my Power.

There is lately published in Paris, a Work intitled *Zend-avesta*, or the Writings of *Zoroaster*, containing the Theological, Philosophical and Moral Ideas of that Legislator, and the Ceremonies of Religious Worship that he establish'd. Translated from the original Zend. In two Vols. 4to. Near half the Work is an Account of the Translator's Travels in India, and his Residence among the Parses during several Years to learn their Languages. I have cast my Eye over the Religious Part; it seems to contain a nice Morality, mix'd with abundance of Prayers, Ceremonies, and Observations. If you desire to have it, I will procure it for you. They say there is no doubt of its being a genuine Translation of the Books at present deem'd sacred as the Writings of Zoroaster by his Followers; but perhaps some of them are of later Date tho' ascrib'd to him: For to me there seems too great a Quantity and Variety of Ceremonies and Prayers to be directed at once by one Man. In the Romish Church they have increas'd gradually in a Course of Ages to their present Bulk. Those who added new Ones from time to time found it necessary to give them Authority by Pretences of their Antiquity. The Books of Moses, indeed, if all written by him, which some doubt, are an Exception to this Observation. With great Esteem, I am ever, Dear Sir, Your affectionate Friend and humble Servant

p s. Since writing the above, Mr. Marchant, understanding you are curious on the Subject of the Eastern ancient Religions, concludes to send you the Book.

To Anthony Benezet

Dear Friend,   London, Augt 22. 1772

   I made a little Extract from yours of April 27. of the Number of Slaves imported and perishing, with some close Remarks on the Hypocrisy of this Country which encourages such a detestable Commerce by Laws, for promoting the Guinea Trade, while it piqu'd itself on its Virtue Love of Liberty, and the Equity of its Courts in setting free a single Negro. This was inserted in the London Chronicle of the 20th of June last. I thank you for the Virginia Address, which I shall also publish with some Remarks. I am glad to hear that the Disposition against keeping Negroes grows more general in North America. Several Pieces have been lately printed here against the Practice, and I hope in time it will be taken into Consideration and suppress'd by the Legislature. Your Labours have already been attended with great Effects. I hope therefore you and your Friends will be encouraged to proceed. My hearty Wishes of Success attend you, being ever, my dear Friend, Yours most affectionately

To Samuel Rhoads

Dear Friend,   London, Augt. 22. 1772

   I think I before acknowledg'd your Favour of Feb. 29. I have since received that of May 30. I am glad my Canal Papers were agreable to you. If any Work of that kind is set on foot in America, I think it would be saving Money to engage by a handsome Salary an Engineer from hence who has been accustomed to such Business. The many Canals on foot here under different great Masters, are daily raising a number of Pupils in the Art, some of whom may want Employ hereafter; and a single Mistake thro' Inexperience, in such important Works, may cost much more than the Expence of Salary to an ingenious young Man already well acquainted with both Principles and Practice. This the Irish have learnt at a dear Rate in the first Attempt of their great Canal, and now are endeavouring to get Smeaton to come and rectify their Errors. With regard to your Question, whether it is best to make the Skuylkill a part of the Navigation to the back Country, or whether the Difficulty, of that River, subject to all the Inconveniencies of Floods, Ice, &c will not be greater than the Expence of Digging, Locks, &c. I can only say, that here they look on the *constant Practicability* of a Navigation, allowing Boats to pass and repass at all Times and Seasons, without Hindrance, to be a Point of the greatest Importance, and therefore they seldom or ever use a River where it can be avoided. Locks in Rivers are subject to many more Accidents than those in still-water Canals; and the Carrying-away a few Locks by Freshes or Ice, not only creates a great Expence, but interrupts Business for a long time till Repairs are made; which may soon be destroyed again; and thus the Carrying-on a Course of Business by such a Navigation be discouraged, as subject to frequent Interruptions: The Toll too must be higher to pay for such Repairs. Rivers are ungovernable Things, especially in Hilly Countries: Canals are quiet and very manageable: Therefore they are often carried on here by the Sides of Rivers, only on Ground above the Reach of Floods, no other Use being made of the Rivers than to supply occasionally the Waste of Water in the Canals. I warmly wish Success to every Attempt for Improvement of our dear Country; and am with sincere Esteem, Yours most affectionately

I congratulate you on the Change of our American Minister. The present has more favourable Dispositions towards us than his Predecessor.

"MORAL OR PRUDENTIAL ALGEBRA"

To Joseph Priestley

Dear Sir,   London Sept. 19. 1772
In the Affair of so much Importance to you, wherein you ask my Advice, I cannot for want of sufficient Premises,

advise you *what* to determine, but if you please I will tell you *how*. When these difficult Cases occur, they are difficult chiefly because while we have them under Consideration all the Reasons *pro* and *con* are not present to the Mind at the same time; but sometimes one Set present themselves, and at other times another, the first being out of Sight. Hence the various Purposes or Inclinations that alternately prevail, and the Uncertainty that perplexes us. To get over this, my Way is, to divide half a Sheet of Paper by a Line into two Columns, writing over the one *Pro*, and over the other *Con*. Then during three or four Days Consideration I put down under the different Heads short Hints of the different Motives that at different Times occur to me for or against the Measure. When I have thus got them all together in one View, I endeavour to estimate their respective Weights; and where I find two, one on each side, that seem equal, I strike them both out: If I find a Reason *pro* equal to some two Reasons *con*, I strike out the three. If I judge some two Reasons *con* equal to some three Reasons *pro*, I strike out the five; and thus proceeding I find at length where the Ballance lies; and if after a Day or two of farther Consideration nothing new that is of Importance occurs on either side, I come to a Determination accordingly. And tho' the Weight of Reasons cannot be taken with the Precision of Algebraic Quantities, yet when each is thus considered separately and comparatively, and the whole lies before me, I think I can judge better, and am less likely to make a rash Step; and in fact I have found great Advantage from this kind of Equation, in what may be called *Moral* or *Prudential Algebra*. Wishing sincerely that you may determine for the best, I am ever, my dear Friend, Yours most affectionately

"ALAS! POOR MUNGO!"

To Georgiana Shipley

Dear Miss,   London, Sept. 26. 1772

I lament with you most sincerely the unfortunate End of poor *Mungo*: Few Squirrels were better accomplish'd; for he had had a good Education, had travell'd far, and seen much of the World. As he had the Honour of being for his Virtues your Favourite, he should not go like common Skuggs without an Elegy or an Epitaph. Let us give him one in the monumental Stile and Measure, which being neither Prose nor Verse, is perhaps the properest for Grief; since to use common Language would look as if we were not affected, and to make Rhimes would seem Trifling in Sorrow.

Alas! poor *Mungo*!
Happy wert thou, hadst thou known
Thy own Felicity!
Remote from the fierce Bald-Eagle,
Tyrant of thy native Woods,
Thou hadst nought to fear from his piercing Talons;
Nor from the murdering Gun
Of the thoughtless Sportsman.
Safe in thy wired Castle,
Grimalkin never could annoy thee.
Daily wert thou fed with the choicest Viands
By the fair Hand
Of an indulgent Mistress.
But, discontented, thou wouldst have more Freedom.
Too soon, alas! didst thou obtain it,
And, wandering,
Fell by the merciless Fangs,
Of wanton, cruel Ranger.
Learn hence, ye who blindly wish more Liberty,
Whether Subjects, Sons, Squirrels or Daughters,
That apparent *Restraint* may be real *Protection*,
Yielding Peace, Plenty, and Security.

You see how much more decent and proper this broken Stile, interrupted as it were with Sighs, is for the Occasion, than if one were to say, by way of Epitaph,

Here Skugg
Lies snug
As a Bug
In a Rug.

And yet perhaps there are People in the World of so little Feeling as to think, *that* would be a good-enough Epitaph for our poor Mungo!

If you wish it, I shall procure another to succeed him. But perhaps you will now chuse some other Amusement. Remember me respectfully to all the [   ] good Family; and believe me ever, Your affectionate Friend

September 26, 1772

"THE INCREASE OF RELIGIOUS AS WELL AS CIVIL LIBERTY"

To William Marshall

Reverend Sir,   London, Feb. 14. 1773
I duly received your respected Letter of Oct. 30. and am very sensible of the Propriety and Equity of the Act passed to indulge your Friends in their Scruples relating to the Mode of Taking an Oath which you plead for so ably by numerous Reasons. That Act with others has now been some time laid before his Majesty in Council. I have not yet heard of any Objection to it; but if such should arise, I shall do my utmost to remove them, and obtain the Royal Assent. Believe me, Reverend Sir, to have the warmest Wishes for the Increase of Religious as well as Civil Liberty thro'out the World; and that I am, with great Regard, Your most obedient humble Servant

"STOOP! STOOP!"

To Samuel Mather

Reverend Sir,   London, July 7. 1773.
By a Line of the 4th. past, I acknowledged the Receipt of your Favour of March 18. and sent you with it two Pamphlets.

I now add another, a spirited Address to the Bishops who opposed the Dissenter's Petition. It is written by a Dissenting Minister at York. There is preserv'd at the End of it a little fugitive Piece of mine, written on the same Occasion.

I perused your Tracts with Pleasure. I see you inherit all the various Learning of your famous Ancestors Cotton and Increase Mather both of whom I remember. The Father, Increase, I once when a Boy, heard preach at the Old South, for Mr. Pemberton, and remember his mentioning the Death of "that wicked old Persecutor of God's People Lewis the XIV." of which News had just been received, but which proved premature. I was some years afterwards at his House at the Northend, on some Errand to him, and remember him sitting in an easy Chair apparently very old and feeble. But Cotton I remember in the Vigour of his Preaching and Usefulness. And particularly in the Year 1723, now half a Century since, I had reason to remember, as I still do a Piece of Advice he gave me. I had been some time with him in his Study, where he condescended to entertain me, a very Youth, with some pleasant and instructive Conversation. As I was taking my Leave he accompany'd me thro' a narrow Passage at which I did not enter, and which had a Beam across it lower than my Head. He continued Talking which occasion'd me to keep my Face partly towards him as I retired, when he suddenly cry'd out, Stoop! Stoop! Not immediately understanding what he meant, I hit my Head hard against the Beam. He then added, *Let this be a Caution to you not always to hold your Head so high; Stoop, young Man, stoop—as you go through the World—and you'll miss many hard Thumps.* This was a way of hammering Instruction into one's Head: And it was so far effectual, that I have ever since remember'd it, tho' I have not always been able to practise it. By the way, permit me to ask if you are the Son or Nephew of that Gentleman? for having lived so many Years far from New England, I have lost the Knowledge of some Family Connections.

You have made the most of your Argument to prove that America might be known to the Ancients. The Inhabitants being totally ignorant of the use of Iron, looks, however, as if the Intercourse could never have been very considerable; and that if they are Descendants of our Adam, they left the

Family before the time of Tubalcain. There is another Discovery of it claimed by the Norwegians, which you have not mentioned, unless it be under the Words "of old viewed and observed" Page 7. About 25 Years since, Professor Kalm, a learned Swede, was with us in Pensilvania. He contended that America was discovered by their Northern People long before the Time of Columbus, which I doubting, he drew up and gave me sometime after a Note of those Discoveries which I send you enclos'd. It is his own Hand writing, and his own English very intelligible for the time he had been among us. The Circumstances give the Account great Appearance of Authenticity. And if one may judge by the Description of the Winter, the Country they visited should be southward of New England, supposing no Change since that time of the Climate. But if it be true as Krantz and I think other Historians tell us, that old Greenland once inhabited and populous, is now render'd uninhabitable by Ice, it should seem that the almost perpetual northern Winter has gained ground to the Southward, and if so, perhaps more northern Countries might anciently have had Vines than can bear them in these Days. The Remarks you have added, on the late Proceedings against America, are very just and judicious: and I cannot at all see any Impropriety in your making them tho' a Minister of the Gospel. This Kingdom is a good deal indebted for its Liberties to the Publick Spirit of its ancient Clergy, who join'd with the Barons in obtaining Magna Charta, and join'd heartily in forming Curses of Excommunication against the Infringers of it. There is no doubt but the Claim of Parliament of Authority to make Laws *binding on the Colonists in all Cases whatsoever*, includes an Authority to change our Religious Constitution, and establish Popery or Mahometanism if they please in its Stead: but, as you intimate *Power* does not infer *Right*; and as the Right is nothing and the *Power* (by our Increase) continually diminishing, the one will soon be as insignificant as the other. You seem only to have made a small Mistake in supposing they modestly avoided to declare they had a Right, the words of the Act being that they have, and of *right* ought to have full Power, &c.

Your Suspicion that "sundry others, besides Govr Bernard

had written hither their Opinions and Counsels, encouraging the late Measures, to the Prejudice of our Country, which have been too much heeded and follow'd" is I apprehend but too well founded. You call them "*traitorous* Individuals" whence I collect, that you suppose them of our own country. There was among the twelve Apostles one Traitor who betrayed with a Kiss. It should be no Wonder therefore if among so many Thousand true Patriots as New England contains there should be found even Twelve Judases, ready to betray their Country for a few paltry Pieces of Silver. Their *Ends*, as well as their *Views*, ought to be similar. But all these Oppressions evidently work for our Good. Providence seems by every Means intent on making us a great People. May our Virtues publick and private grow with us, and be durable, that Liberty Civil and Religious, may be secur'd to our Posterity, and to all from every Part of the old World that take Refuge among us.

I have distributed the Copies of your Piece as you desired. I cannot apprehend they can give just Cause of Offence.

Your Theological Tracts in which you discover your great Reading, are rather more out of my Walk, and therefore I shall say little of them. That on the Lord's Prayer I read with most Attention, having once myself considered a little the same Subject, and attempted a Version of the Prayer which I thought less exceptionable. I have found it among my old Papers, and send it you only to show an Instance of the same Frankness in laying myself open to you, which you say you have used with regard to me. With great Esteem and my best Wishes for a long Continuance of your Usefulness, I am, Reverend Sir, Your most obedient humble Servant

CAUSES OF COLDS

To Benjamin Rush

Dear Sir,   London, July 14. 1773.
    I received your Favour of May 1. with the Pamphlet for which I am obliged to you. It is well written. I hope in time

that the Friends to Liberty and Humanity will get the better
of a Practice that has so long disgrac'd our Nation and
Religion.

A few Days after I receiv'd your Packet for M. Dubourg, I
had an Opportunity of forwarding it to him by M. Poisson-
nier, a Physician of Paris, who kindly undertook to deliver
it. M. Dubourg has been translating my Book into French.
It is nearly printed, and he tells me he purposes a Copy for
you.

I shall communicate your judicious Remark relating to Air
transpir'd by Patients in putrid Diseases to my Friend Dr.
Priestly. I hope that after having discover'd the Benefit of
fresh and cool Air apply'd to the *Sick*, People will begin to
suspect that possibly it may do no Harm to the *Well*. I have
not seen Dr. Cullen's Book: But am glad to hear that he
speaks of Catarrhs or Colds *by Contagion*. I have long been
satisfy'd from Observation, that besides the general Colds
now termed *Influenza's*, which may possibly spread by Contagion as well as by a particular Quality of the Air, People
often catch Cold from one another when shut up together in
small close Rooms, Coaches, &c. and when sitting near and
conversing so as to breathe in each others Transpiration, the
Disorder being in a certain State. I think too that it is the
frowzy corrupt Air from animal Substances, and the perspired Matter from our Bodies, which, being long confin'd
in Beds not lately used, and Clothes not lately worne, and
Books long shut up in close Rooms, obtains that kind of
Putridity which infects us, and occasions the Colds observed
upon sleeping in, wearing, or turning over, such Beds,
Clothes or Books, and not their Coldness or Dampness.
From these Causes, but more from *too full Living* with too
little Exercise, proceed in my Opinion most of the Disorders
which for 100 Years past the English have called *Colds*. As to
Dr. Cullen's Cold or Catarrh *à frigore*, I question whether
such an one ever existed. Travelling in our severe Winters, I
have suffered Cold sometimes to an Extremity only short of
Freezing, but this did not make me *catch Cold*. And for
Moisture, I have been in the River every Evening two or
three Hours for a Fortnight together, when one would suppose I might imbibe enough of it to *take Cold* if Humidity

could give it; but no such Effect followed: Boys never get Cold by Swimming. Nor are People at Sea, or who live at Bermudas, or St. Helena, where the Air must be ever moist, from the Dashing and Breaking of Waves against their Rocks on all sides, more subject to Colds than those who inhabit Parts of a Continent where the Air is dryest. Dampness may indeed assist in producing Putridity, and those Miasms which infect us with the Disorder we call a Cold, but of itself can never by a little Addition of Moisture hurt a Body filled with watry Fluids from Head to foot.

I hope our Friend's Marriage will prove a happy one. Mr. and Mrs. West complain that they never hear from him. Perhaps I have as much reason to complain of him. But I forgive him because I often need the same kind of Forgiveness. With great Esteem and sincere Wishes for your Welfare, I am, Sir, Your most obedient humble Servant

"I 'LL BE HANGED IF THIS IS NOT SOME OF YOUR AMERICAN JOKES UPON US"

To William Franklin

DEAR SON,   *London, October* 6, 1773.

I wrote to you on the 1st of last month, since which I have received yours of July 29, from New York.

I know not what letters of mine governor H. could mean, as advising the people to insist on their independency. But whatever they were, I suppose he has sent copies of them hither, having heard some whisperings about them. I shall however, be able at any time, to justify every thing I have written; the purport being uniformly this, that they should carefully avoid all tumults and every violent measure, and content themselves with verbally keeping up their claims, and holding forth their rights whenever occasion requires; secure, that from the growing importance of America, those claims will ere long be attended to, and acknowledged. From a long and thorough consideration of the subject, I am indeed of opinion, that the parliament has no right to make any law whatever, binding on the colonies. That the king, and not the king, lords, and commons collectively, is their sovereign; and that the king with their respective parliaments, is their only legislator. I know your sentiments differ from mine on these subjects. You are a thorough government man, which I do not wonder at, nor do I aim at converting you. I only wish you to act uprightly and steadily, avoiding that duplicity, which in Hutchinson, adds contempt to indignation. If you can promote the prosperity of your people, and leave them happier than you found them, whatever your political principles are, your memory will be honored.

I have written two pieces here lately for the Public Advertiser, on American affairs, designed to expose the conduct of this country towards the colonies, in a short, comprehensive, and striking view, and stated therefore in out-of-the-way forms, as most likely to take the general attention. The first was called, *Rules by which a great empire may be reduced to a small one*; the second, *An Edict of the king of Prussia*. I sent you one of the first, but could not get enough of the second to spare you one, though my clerk went the next morning to the printer's, and wherever they were sold. They were all gone but two. In my own mind I preferred the first, as a composition for the quantity and variety of the matter contained, and a kind of spirited ending of each paragraph. But I find that others here generally prefer the second. I am not suspected as the author, except by one or two friends; and have heard the latter spoken of in the highest terms as the keenest and severest piece that has appeared here a long time. Lord Mansfield I hear said of it, that it *was very* ABLE *and very* ARTFUL indeed; and would do mischief by giving here a bad impression of the measures of government; and in the colonies, by encouraging them in their contumacy. It is reprinted in the Chronicle, where you will see it, but stripped of all the capitalling and italicing, that intimate the allusions and marks the emphasis of written discourses, to bring them as near as possible to those spoken: printing such a piece all in one even small character, seems to me like repeating one of Whitfield's sermons in the monotony of a school-boy. What made it the more noticed here was, that people in reading it, were, as the phrase is, *taken in*, till they had got half through it, and imagined it a real edict, to which mistake I suppose the king of Prussia's *character* must have contributed. I was down at lord Le Despencer's when the post brought that day's papers. Mr. Whitehead was there too (Paul Whitehead, the author of Manners) who runs early through all the papers, and tells the company what he finds remarkable. He had them in another room, and we were chatting in the breakfast parlour, when he came running into us, out of breath, with the paper in his hand. Here! says he, here's news for ye! *Here's the king of Prussia, claiming a right to this kingdom!* All stared, and I as much as any body; and he went on to read it. When he had read two or three paragraphs, a gentleman present said, *Damn his impudence, I dare say, we shall hear by next post that he is upon his march with one hundred thousand men to back this.* Whitehead, who is very shrewd, soon after began to smoke it, and looking in my face said, *I'll be hanged if this is not some of your American jokes upon us.* The reading went on, and ended with abundance of laughing, and a general verdict that it was a fair hit: and the piece was cut out of the paper and preserved in my lord's collection.

I don't wonder that Hutchinson should be dejected. It must be an uncomfortable thing to live among people who he is conscious universally detest him. Yet I fancy he will not have leave to come home, both because they know not well what to do with him, and because they do not very well like his conduct.

I am ever your affectionate father,

TRANSFER PRINTS ON TILES

To Peter P. Burdett

Sir,   London, Nov. 3, 1773.

I was much pleased with the Specimens you so kindly sent me, of your new Art of Engraving. That on the China is admirable. No one would suppose it any thing but Painting.

I hope you meet with all the Encouragement you merit, and that the Invention will be, (what Inventions seldom are) profitable to the Inventor.

I know not who (now we speak of Inventions) pretends to that of Copper-Plate Engravings for Earthen-Ware, and am not disposed to contest the Honor of it with any body, as the Improvement in taking Impressions not directly from the Plate but from printed Paper, applicable by that means to other than flat Forms, is far beyond my first Idea. But I have reason to apprehend I might have given the Hint on which that Improvement was made. For more than twenty years since, I wrote to Dr. Mitchell from America, proposing to him the printing of square Tiles for ornamenting Chimnies, from Copper Plates, describing the Manner in which I thought it might be done, and advising the Borrowing from the Bookseller, the Plates that had been used in a thin Folio, called *Moral Virtue delineated*, for the Purpose. As the Dutch Delphware Tiles were much used in America, which are only or chiefly Scripture Histories, wretchedly scrawled, I wished to have those moral Prints, (which were originally taken from Horace's poetical Figures) introduced on Tiles, which being about our Chimneys, and constantly in the Eyes of Children when by the Fire-side, might give Parents an Opportunity, in explaining them, to impress moral Sentiments; and I gave Expectations of great Demand for them if executed. Dr. Mitchell wrote to me in Answer, that he had communicated my Scheme to several of the principal Artists in the Earthen Way about London, who rejected it as impracticable: And it was not till some years after that I first saw an enamelled snuff-Box which I was sure was a Copper-plate, tho' the Curvature of the Form made me wonder how the Impression was taken.

I understand the China Work in Philadelphia is declined by the first Owners. Whether any others will take it up and continue it, I know not.

Mr. Banks is at present engaged in preparing to publish the Botanical Discoveries of his Voyage. He employs 10 Engravers for the Plates, in which he is very curious, so as not to be quite satisfied in some Cases with the Expression given by either the Graver, Etching, or Metzotinto, particularly where

there is a Wooliness or a Multitude of small Points or a Leaf.
I sent him the largest of the Specimens you sent containing a
Number of Sprigs. I have not seen him since, to know
whether your Manner would not suit some of his Plants, better than the more common Methods. With great Esteem, I
am, Sir, Your most obedient humble Servant,

OIL ON WATER

To William Brownrigg

Dear Sir,   London, Nov. 7, 1773.
   Our Correspondence might be carried on for a Century
with very few Letters, if you were as apt to procrastinate as
myself. Tho' an habitual Sinner, I am now quite ashamed to
observe, that this is to be an Answer to your Favour of January last.
   I suppose Mrs. Brownrigg did not succeed in making the
Parmesan Cheese, since we have heard nothing of it. But as a
Philosophess, she will not be discouraged by one or two Fail-
ures. Perhaps some Circumstance is omitted in the Receipt,
which by a little more Experience she may discover. The foreign Gentleman, who had learnt in England to like boiled
Plumbpudding, and carried home a Receipt for making it,
wondered to see it brought to his Table in the Form of a
Soup. The Cook declar'd he had exactly followed the Receipt.
And when that came to be examined, a small, but important
Circumstance appeared to have been omitted. There was no
Mention of the Bag.
   I am concerned that you had not, and I fear you have not
yet found time to prepare your excellent Papers for Publication. By omitting it so long, you are wanting to the World,
and to your own Honour.
   I thank you for the Remarks of your learned Friend at Car-
lisle. I had when a Youth, read and smiled at Pliny's Account
of a Practice among the Seamen of his Time, to still the
Waves in a Storm by pouring Oil into the Sea: which he mentions, as well as the Use of Oil by the Divers. But the stilling

a Tempest by throwing Vinegar into the Air had escaped me.
I think with your Friend, that it has been of late too much
the Mode to slight the Learning of the Ancients. The Learned
too, are apt to slight too much the Knowledge of the Vulgar.
The cooling by Evaporation was long an Instance of the
latter. This Art of smoothing the Waves with Oil, is an Instance
of both.

Perhaps you may not dislike to have an Account of all I
have heard, and learnt and done in this Way. Take it, if you
please, as follows.

In 1757 being at Sea in a Fleet of 96 Sail bound against
Louisbourg, I observed the Wakes of two of the Ships to be
remarkably smooth, while all the others were ruffled by the
Wind, which blew fresh. Being puzzled with this differing
Appearance I at last pointed it out to our Captain, and asked
him the meaning of it? "The Cooks, says he, have I suppose,
been just emptying their greasy Water thro' the Scuppers,
which has greased the Sides of those Ships a little;" and this
Answer he gave me with an Air of some little Contempt, as
to a Person ignorant of what every Body else knew. In my
own Mind I at first slighted his Solution, tho' I was not able
to think of another. But recollecting what I had formerly read
in Pliny, I resolved to make some Experiment of the Effect of
Oil on Water when I should have Opportunity.

Afterwards being again at Sea in 1762, I first observed the
wonderful Quietness of Oil on agitated Water in the swinging
Glass Lamp I made to hang up in the Cabin, as described in
my printed Papers, page 438 of the fourth Edition. This I was
continually looking at and considering, as an Appearance to
me inexplicable. An old Sea Captain, then a Passenger with
me, thought little of it, supposing it an Effect of the same
kind with that of Oil put on Water to smooth it, which he
said was a Practice of the Bermudians when they would strike
Fish which they could not see if the surface of the Water was
ruffled by the Wind. This Practice I had never before heard
of, and was obliged to him for the Information, though I
thought him mistaken as to the sameness of the Experiment,
the Operations being different; as well as the Effects. In one
Case, the Water is smooth till the Oil is put on, and then
becomes agitated. In the other it is agitated before the Oil is

applied, and then becomes smooth. The same Gentleman told me he had heard it was a Practice with the Fishermen of Lisbon when about to return into the River, (if they saw before them too great a Surff upon the Bar, which they apprehended might fill their Boats in passing) to empty a Bottle or two of oil into the Sea, which would suppress the Breakers and allow them to pass safely: a Confirmation of this I have not since had an Opportunity of obtaining. But discoursing of it with another Person, who had often been in the Mediterranean, I was informed that the Divers there, who when under Water in their Business, need Light, which the curling of the Surface interrupts, by the Refractions of so many little Waves, they let a small Quantity of Oil now and then out of their Mouths, which rising to the Surface smooths it, and permits the Light to come down to them. All these Informations I at times revolved in my Mind, and wondered to find no mention of them in our Books of Experimental Philosophy.

At length being at Clapham, where there is, on the Common, a large Pond, which I observed to be one Day very rough with the Wind, I fetched out a Cruet of Oil, and dropt a little of it on the Water. I saw it spread itself with surprising Swiftness upon the Surface, but the Effect of smoothing the Waves was not produced; for I had applied it first on the Leeward Side of the Pond where the Waves were largest, and the Wind drove my Oil back upon the Shore. I then went to the Windward Side, where they began to form; and there the Oil tho' not more than a Tea Spoonful produced an instant Calm, over a Space several yards square, which spread amazingly, and extended itself gradually till it reached the Lee Side, making all that Quarter of the Pond, perhaps half an Acre, as smooth as a Looking Glass.

After this, I contrived to take with me, whenever I went into the Country, a little Oil in the upper hollow joint of my bamboo Cane, with which I might repeat the Experiment as Opportunity should offer; and I found it constantly to succeed.

In these Experiments, one Circumstance struck me with particular Surprize. This was the sudden, wide and forcible Spreading of a Drop of Oil on the Face of the Water, which I do not know that any body has hitherto considered. If a

Drop of Oil is put on a polished Marble Table, or on a Looking Glass that lies horizontally; the Drop remains in its Place,
spreading very little. But when put on Water it spreads instantly many feet round, becoming so thin as to produce the
prismatic Colours, for a considerable Space, and beyond them
so much thinner as to be invisible except in its Effect of
smoothing the Waves at a much greater Distance. It seems as
if a mutual Repulsion between its Particles took Place as soon
as it touched the Water, and a Repulsion so strong as to act
on other Bodies swimming on the Surface, as Straws, Leaves,
Chips, &c. forcing them to recede every way from the Drop,
as from a Center, leaving a large clear Space. The Quantity of
this Force, and the Distance to which it will operate, I have
not yet ascertained, but I think it a curious Enquiry, and I
wish to understand whence it arises.

In our Journey to the North when we had the Pleasure of
seeing you at Ormathwaite, we visited Mr. Smeaton near
Leeds. Being about to shew him the smoothing Experiment
on a little Pond near his House, an ingenious Pupil of his,
Mr. Jessop, then present, told us of an odd Appearance on
that Pond, which had lately occurred to him. He was about
to clean a little Cup in which he kept Oil, and he threw upon
the Water some Flies that had been drowned in the Oil. These
Flies presently began to move, and turned round on the
Water very rapidly, as if they were vigorously alive, tho' on
Examination he found they were not so. I immediately
concluded that the Motion was occasioned by the Power of
the Repulsion abovementioned, and that the Oil issuing gradually from the spungy Body of the Fly continued the Motion.
He found some more Flies drowned in Oil, with which the
Experiment was repeated before us; and to show that it was
not any Effect of Life recovered by the Flies, I imitated it by
little bits of oiled Chip, and Paper cut in the form of a
Comma, of this size 𝄬 when the Stream of repelling Particles issuing from the Point, made the Comma turn round the
contrary way. This is not a Chamber Experiment; for it cannot well be repeated in a Bowl or Dish of Water on a Table.
A considerable Surface of Water is necessary to give Room
for the Expansion of a small Quantity of Oil. In a Dish of
Water if the smallest Drop of Oil be let fall in the Middle, the

whole Surface is presently covered with a thin greasy Film proceeding from the Drop; but as soon as that Film has reached the Sides of the Dish, no more will issue from the Drop, but it remains in the Form of Oil, the Sides of the Dish putting a Stop to its Dissipation by prohibiting the farther Expansion of the Film.

Our Friend Sir J. Pringle being soon after in Scotland, learnt there that those employed in the Herring Fishery, could at a Distance see where the Shoals of Herrings were, by the smoothness of the Water over them, which might be occasioned possibly, he thought, by some Oiliness proceeding from their Bodies.

A Gentleman from Rhode-island told me, it had been re-marked that the Harbour of Newport was ever smooth while any Whaling Vessels were in it; which probably arose from hence, that the Blubber which they sometimes bring loose in the Hold, or the Leakage of their Barrels, might afford some Oil to mix with that Water which from time to time they pump out to keep the Vessel free, and that same Oil might spread over the surface of the Water in the Harbour, and pre-vent the forming of any Waves.

This Prevention I would thus endeavour to explain.

There seems to be no natural Repulsion between Water and Air, such as to keep them from coming into Contact with each other. Hence we find a Quantity of Air in Water, and if we extract it by means of the Air-pump; the same Water again exposed to the Air, will soon imbibe an equal Quantity.

Therefore Air in Motion, which is Wind, in passing over the smooth Surface of Water, may rub, as it were, upon that Surface, and raise it into Wrinkles, which if the Wind con-tinues are the elements of future Waves.

The smallest Wave once raised does not immediately sub-side and leave the neighbouring Water quiet; but in subsiding raises nearly as much of the Water next to it, the Friction of its Parts making little Difference. Thus a Stone dropt in a Pool raises first a single Wave round itself, and leaves it by sinking to the Bottom; but that first Wave subsiding raises a second, the second a third, and so on in Circles to a great Extent.

A small Power continually operating will produce a great

Action. A Finger applied to a weighty suspended Bell, can at first move it but little; if repeatedly applied, tho' with no greater Strength, the Motion increases till the Bell swings to its utmost Height and with a Force that cannot be resisted by the whole Strength of the Arm and Body. Thus the small first-raised Waves, being continually acted upon by the Wind are, (tho' the Wind does not increase in Strength) continually increased in Magnitude, rising higher and extending their Bases, so as to include a vast Mass of Water in each Wave, which in its Motion acts with great Violence.

But if there be a mutual Repulsion between the Particles of Oil, and no Attraction between Oil and Water, Oil dropt on Water will not be held together by Adhesion to the Spot whereon it falls, it will not be imbibed by the Water, it will be at Liberty to expand itself, and it will spread on a Surface that besides being smooth to the most perfect degree of Polish, prevents, perhaps by repelling the Oil, all immediate Contact, keeping it at a minute Distance from itself; and the Expansion will continue, till the mutual Repulsion between the Particles of the Oil, is weakened and reduced to nothing by their Distance.

Now I imagine that the Wind blowing over Water thus covered with a Film of Oil, cannot easily catch upon it so as to raise the first Wrinkles, but slides over it, and leaves it smooth as it finds it. It moves a little the Oil, indeed, which being between it and the water serves it to slide with, and prevents Friction as Oil does between those Parts of a Machine that would otherwise rub hard together. Hence the Oil dropt on the Windward Side of a Pond proceeds gradually to Leeward, as may be seen by the smoothness it carries with it, quite to the opposite Side. For the Wind being thus prevented from raising the first Wrinkles that I call the Elements of Waves, cannot produce Waves, which are to be made by continually acting upon and enlarging those Elements, and thus the whole Pond is calmed.

Totally therefore we might supress the Waves in any required Place, if we could come at the Windward Place where they take their Rise. This in the Ocean can seldom if ever be done. But perhaps something may be done on particular Occasions, to moderate the Violence of the Waves, when we are in the midst of them, and prevent their Breaking where that would be inconvenient.

For when the Wind blows fresh, there are continually rising on the Back of every great Wave, a number of small ones, which roughen its Surface, and give the Wind Hold, as it were, to push it with greater Force. This Hold is diminished by preventing the Generation of those small ones. And possibly too, when a Wave's Surface is oiled, the Wind in passing over it, may rather in some degree press it down, and contribute to prevent its rising again, instead of promoting it.

This as a mere Conjecture would have little weight, if the apparent Effects of pouring Oil into the Midst of Waves, were not considerable, and as yet not otherwise accounted for.

When the Wind blows so fresh, as that the Waves are not sufficiently quick in obeying its Impulse, their Tops being thinner and lighter are pushed forward, broken and turned over in a white Foam. Common Waves lift a Vessel without entring it, but these when large sometimes break above and pour over it, doing great Damage.

That this Effect might in any degree be prevented, or the height and violence of Waves in the Sea moderated, we had no certain Account, Pliny's Authority for the Practice of Seamen in his time being slighted. But discoursing lately on this Subject with his Excellency Count Bentinck of Holland, his Son the Honble. Capt. Bentinck, and the learned Professor Allemand, (to all whom I showed the Experiment of smoothing in a Windy Day the large Piece of Water at the Head of the Green Park) a Letter was mentioned which had been received by the Count from Batavia, relating to the saving of a Dutch Ship in a Storm, by pouring Oil into the Sea. I much desired to see that Letter, and a Copy of it was promised me, which I afterwards received. It is as follows.

Extrait d'une Lettre de Mr. Tengnagel à Mr. le Comte de Bentinck, écrite de Batavia le 15 Janvier 1770. Près des Isles Paulus et Amsterdam nous essuiames un orage, qui n'eut rien d'assez particulier pour vous être marqué, si non que notre Capitaine se trouva obligé en *tournant sous le vent,** de verser de l'huile contre la haute mer, pour empecher les vagues de

*Suppos'd to mean, *In wearing the Ship.*

se briser contre le navire, ce qui réussit à nous conserver et a été d'un très bon effet: comme il n'en versa qu'une petite quantité à la fois, la Compagnie doit peut-être son vaisseau à six demi-ahmes d'huile d'olive: j'ai été présent quand cela s'est fait, et je ne vous aurois pas entretenu de cette circonstance, si ce n'étoit que nous avons trouvé les gens ici si prévenus contre l'expérience, que les officiers du bord ni moi n'avons fait aucune difficulté de donner un certificat de la verité sur ce chapitre.

On this Occasion I mentioned to Capt. Bentinck, a thought which had occurred to me in reading the Voyages of our late Circumnavigators, particularly where Accounts are given of pleasant and fertile Islands which they much desired to land upon, when Sickness made it more necessary, but could not effect a Landing thro' a violent Surff breaking on the Shore, which rendered it impracticable. My Idea was, that possibly by sailing to and fro at some Distance from such Lee Shore, continually pouring Oil into the Sea, the Waves might be so much depressed and lessened before they reached the Shore, as to abate the Height and Violence of the Surff and permit a Landing, which in such Circumstances was a Point of sufficient Importance to justify the Expence of Oil that might be requisite for the purpose. That Gentleman, who is ever ready to promote what may be of publick Utility, (tho' his own ingenious Inventions have not always met with the Countenance they merited) was so obliging as to invite me to Portsmouth, where an Opportunity would probably offer, in the course of a few Days, of making the Experiment on some of the Shores about Spithead, in which he kindly proposed to accompany me, and to give Assistance with such Boats as might be necessary. Accordingly, about the middle of October last, I went with some Friends, to Portsmouth; and a Day of Wind happening, which made a Lee-Shore between Haslar Hospital and the Point near Jillkecker; we went from the Centaur with the Longboat and Barge towards that Shore. Our Disposition was this; the Longboat anchored about a ¼ of a Mile from the Shore, part of the Company were landed behind the Point, (a Place more sheltered from the Sea) who came round and placed themselves opposite to the Longboat, where they might observe the Surff, and note if any Change occurred in it upon using the Oil: Another Party in the Barge plied to Windward of the Longboat, as far from her as she was from the Shore, making Trips of about half a Mile each, pouring Oil continually out of a large Stone Bottle, thro' a Hole in the Cork somewhat bigger than a Goose Quill. The Experiment had not in the main Point the Success we wished; for no material Difference was observed in the Height or Force of the Surff upon the Shore: But those who were in the Longboat could observe a Tract of smoothed Water the whole Length of the Distance in which the Barge poured the Oil, and gradually spreading in Breadth towards the Longboat; I call it smoothed, not that it was laid level, but because tho' the Swell continued, its Surface was not roughened by the Wrinkles or smaller Waves before-mentioned, and none, or very few White-caps (or Waves whose Tops turn over in Foam) appeared in that whole Space, tho' to windward and leeward of it there were plenty; and a Wherry that came round the Point under Sail in her way to Portsmouth, seemed to turn into that Tract of choice, and to use it from End to End as a Piece of Turnpike Road.

It may be of Use to relate the Circumstances even of an Experiment that does not succeed, since they may give Hints of Amendment in future Trials: It is therefore I have been thus particular. I shall only add what I apprehend may have been the Reason of our Disappointment.

I conceive that the Operation of Oil on Water, is first to prevent the raising new Waves by the Wind, and secondly, to prevent its pushing those before raised with such Force, and consequently their Continuance of the same repeated Height, as they would have done, if their Surface were not oiled. But Oil will not prevent Waves being raised by another Power, by a Stone, for Instance, falling into a still Pool; for they then rise by the mechanical Impulse of the Stone, which the Greasiness on the surrounding Water cannot lessen or prevent, as it can prevent the Winds catching the Surface and raising it into Waves. Now Waves once raised, whether by the Wind or any other Power, have the same mechanical Operation, by which they continue to rise and fall, as a Pendulum will continue to swing, a long Time after the Force ceases to act by which the

Motion was first produced. That Motion will however cease in time, but time is necessary. Therefore tho' Oil spread on an agitated Sea, may weaken the Push of the Wind on those Waves whose Surfaces are covered by it, and so by receiving less fresh Impulse, they may gradually subside; yet a considerable Time, or a Distance thro' which they will take time to move may be necessary to make the Effect sensible on any Shore in a Diminution of the Surff. For we know that when Wind ceases suddenly, the Waves it has raised do not as suddenly subside, but settle gradually and are not quite down till long after the Wind has ceased. So tho' we should by oiling them take off the Effect of Wind on Waves already raised, it is not to be expected that those Waves should be instantly levelled. The Motion they have received will for some time continue: and if the Shore is not far distant, they arrive there so soon that their Effect upon it will not be visibly diminished. Possibly therefore, if we had began our Operations at a greater Distance, the Effect might have been more sensible. And perhaps we did not pour Oil in sufficient Quantity. Future Experiments may determine this.

After my Thanks to Capt. Bentinck, for the chearful and ready Aids he gave me, I ought not to omit mentioning Mr. Banks, Dr. Solander, General Carnac, and Dr. Blagdon, who all assisted at the Experiment, during that blustring unpleasant Day, with a Patience and Activity that could only be inspired by a Zeal for the Improvement of Knowledge, such especially as might possibly be of use to Men in Situations of Distress.

I would wish you to communicate this to your ingenious Friend Mr. Farish, with my Respects; and believe me to be, with sincere Esteem, Dear Sir, Your most obedient humble Servant.

"NOTHING CAN BE FARTHER FROM THE TRUTH"

To Josiah Tucker

Reverend Sir,   London, Feb. 12, 1774.
    Being informed by a Friend that some severe Strictures on

my Conduct and Character had appeared in a new Book published under your respectable Name, I purchased and read it. After thanking you sincerely for those Parts of it that are so instructive on Points of great Importance to the common Interests of mankind, permit me to complain, that if by the description you give in Page 180, 181, of a certain American Patriot, whom you say you need not name, you do, as is supposed, mean myself, nothing can be farther from the truth than your assertion, that I applied or used any interest directly or indirectly to be appointed one of the Stamp Officers for America; I certainly never expressed a Wish of the kind to any person whatever, much less was I, as you say, "more than ordinary assiduous on this Head." I have heretofore seen in the Newspapers, Insinuations of the same Import, naming me expressly; but being without the name of the Writer, I took no Notice of them. I know not whether they were yours, or were only your Authority for your present charge. But now that they have the Weight of your Name and dignified Character, I am more sensible of the injury. And I beg leave to request that you would reconsider the Grounds on which you have ventured to publish an Accusation that, if believed, must prejudice me extremely in the opinion of good Men, especially in my own country, whence I was sent expressly to oppose the imposition of that Tax. If on such reconsideration and Enquiry you find as I am persuaded you will, that you have been imposed upon by false Reports, or have too lightly given credit to Hearsays in a matter that concerns another's Reputation, I flatter myself that your Equity will induce you to do me Justice, by retracting that Accusation. In Confidence of this, I am with great Esteem, Reverend Sir, Your most obedient and most humble Servant,

"MY SUPPOSED APPLICATION TO MR. GRENVILLE"

To Josiah Tucker

Reverend Sir,   London, Feb. 26, 1774.
  I thank you for the Frankness with which you have com-

municated to me the Particulars of the Information you had received relating to my supposed Application to Mr. Grenville for a Place in the American Stamp-Office. As I deny that either your former or later Informations are true, it seems incumbent on me for your Satisfaction to relate all the Circumstances fairly to you that could possibly give rise to such Mistakes.

Some Days after the Stamp-Act was passed, to which I had given all the Opposition I could with Mr. Grenville, I received a Note from Mr. Wheatly, his Secretary, desiring to see me the next morning. I waited upon him accordingly, and found with him several other Colony Agents. He acquainted us that Mr. Grenville was desirous to make the Execution of the Act as little inconvenient and disagreeable to the Americans as possible, and therefore did not think of sending Stamp Officers from hence, but wished to have discreet and reputable Persons appointed in each Province from among the Inhabitants, such as would be acceptable to them, for as they were to pay the Tax, he thought Strangers should not have the Emoluments. Mr. Wheatly therefore wished us to name for our respective Colonies, informing us that Mr. Grenville would be obliged to us for pointing out to him honest and responsible Men, and would pay great regard to our Nominations. By this plausible and apparently candid Declaration, we were drawn in to nominate, and I named for our Province Mr. Hughes, saying at the same time that I knew not whether he would accept of it, but if he did I was sure he would execute the Office faithfully. I soon after had notice of his appointment. We none of us, I believe, foresaw or imagined, that this Compliance with the request of the Minister, would or could have been called an *Application* of ours, and adduced as a Proof of our *Approbation* of the Act we had been opposing; otherwise I think few of us would have named at all, I am sure I should not. This I assure you and can prove to you by living Evidence, is a true account of the Transaction in question, which if you compare with that you have been induced to give of it in your Book, I am persuaded you will see a *Difference* that is far from being "a Distinction above your Comprehension."

Permit me farther to remark, that your Expression of there

being "no *positive Proofs* of my having solicited to obtain such a place *for myself*," implies that there are nevertheless some *circumstantial* Proofs sufficient at least to support a Suspicion; the latter Part however of the same Sentence, which says, "there are sufficient Evidence still existing of my having *applied for it* in favour of another Person," must I apprehend, if credited, destroy that Suspicion, and be considered as *positive* Proof of the contrary; for if I had Interest enough with Mr. Grenville to obtain that Place for another, is it likely that it would have been refused me had I asked it for myself?

There is another Circumstance which I would offer to your candid Consideration. You describe me as "changing Sides, and appearing at the Bar of the House of Commons to cry down the very Measure I had espoused, and direct the Storm that was falling upon that Minister." As this must have been after my supposed solicitation of the Favour for myself or my Friend; and as Mr. Grenville and Mr. Wheatly were both in the House at the Time, and both asked me Questions, can it be conceived that offended as they must have been with such a Conduct in me, neither of them should put me in mind of this my sudden Changing of Sides, or remark it to the House, or reproach me with it, or require my Reasons for it? and yet all the Members then present know that not a Syllable of the kind fell from either of them, or from any of their Party.

I persuade myself that by this time you begin to suspect you may have been misled by your Informers. I do not ask who they are, because I do not wish to have particular Motives for disliking People, who in general may deserve my Respect. They, too, may have drawn *Consequences* beyond the Information they received from others, and hearing the Office had been *given* to a Person of my Nomination, might as naturally suppose I *had sollicited it*; as Dr. Tucker, hearing I had *sollicited it*, might *"conclude"* it was for myself.

I desire you to believe that I take kindly, as I ought, your freely mentioning to me "that it has long appeared to you that I much exceeded the Bounds of Morality in the Methods I pursued for the Advancement of the supposed Interests of America." I am sensible there is a good deal of Truth in the Adage, that *our Sins and our Debts are always more than we take them to be*; and tho' I cannot at present on Examination of my Conscience charge myself with any Immorality of that kind, it becomes me to suspect that what has *long appeared* to you may have some Foundation. You are so good as to add, that "if it can be proved you have unjustly suspected me, you shall have a Satisfaction in acknowledging the Error." It is often a hard thing to *prove* that Suspicions are unjust, even when we know what they are; and harder when we are unacquainted with them. I must presume therefore that in mentioning them, you had an Intention of communicating the Grounds of them to me, if I should request it, which I now do, and, I assure you, with a sincere Desire and Design of amending what you may show me to have been wrong in my conduct, and to thank you for the Admonition. In your Writings I *appear* a bad Man; but if I am such, and you can thus help me to become *in reality* a good one, I shall esteem it more than a sufficient Reparation, to Reverend Sir, Your most obedient humble Servant

FLAME ON NEW JERSEY RIVERS

To Joseph Priestley

Dear Sir,   Craven Street, April 10, 1774.

In compliance with your request, I have endeavoured to recollect the circumstances of the American experiments I formerly mentioned to you, of raising a flame on the surface of some waters there.

When I passed through New Jersey in 1764, I heard it several times mentioned, that by applying a lighted candle near the surface of some of their rivers, a sudden flame would catch and spread on the water, continuing to burn for near half a minute. But the accounts I received were so imperfect that I could form no guess at the cause of such an effect, and rather doubted the truth of it. I had no opportunity of seeing the experiment; but calling to see a friend who happened to be just returned home from making it himself, I learned from him the manner of it; which was to choose a shallow place, where the bottom could be reached by a walking-stick, and was muddy; the mud was first to be stirred with the stick, and when a number of small bubbles began to arise from it, the candle was applied. The flame was so sudden and so strong, that it catched his ruffle and spoiled it, as I saw. New-Jersey having many pine-trees in different parts of it, I then imagined that something like a volatile oil of turpentine might be mixed with the waters from a pine-swamp, but this supposition did not quite satisfy me. I mentioned the fact to some philosophical friends on my return to England, but it was not much attended to. I suppose I was thought a little too credulous.

In 1765, the Reverend Dr. Chandler received a letter from Dr. Finley, President of the College in that province, relating the same experiment. It was read at the Royal Society, Nov. 21. of that year, but not printed in the Transactions; perhaps because it was thought too strange to be true, and some ridicule might be apprehended if any member should attempt to repeat it in order to ascertain or refute it. The following is a copy of that account.

"A worthy gentleman, who lives at a few miles distance, informed me that in a certain small cove of a mill-pond, near his house, he was surprized to see the surface of the water blaze like inflamed spirits. I soon after went to the place, and made the experiment with the same success. The bottom of the creek was muddy, and when stirred up, so as to cause a considerable curl on the surface, and a lighted candle held within two or three inches of it, the whole surface was in a blaze, as instantly as the vapour of warm inflammable spirits, and continued, when strongly agitated, for the space of several seconds. It was at first imagined to be peculiar to that place; but upon trial it was soon found, that such a bottom in other places exhibited the same phenomenon. The discovery was accidentally made by one belonging to the mill."

I have tried the experiment twice here in England, but without success. The first was in a slow running water with a muddy bottom. The second in a stagnant water at the bottom a deep ditch. Being some time employed in stirring this water, I ascribed an intermitting fever, which seized me a few days after, to my breathing too much of that foul air which I stirred up from the bottom, and which I could not avoid while I stooped in endeavouring to kindle it.—The discoveries you have lately made of the manner in which inflammable air is in some cases produced, may throw light on this experiment, and explain its succeeding in some cases, and not in others. With the highest esteem and respect,

I am, Dear Sir,

Your most obedient humble servant,

"YOU ARE NOW MY ENEMY"

To William Strahan

Mr. Strahan,   Philada. July 5. 1775

You are a Member of Parliament, and one of that Majority which has doomed my Country to Destruction. You have begun to burn our Towns, and murder our People. Look upon your Hands! They are stained with the Blood of your Relations! You and I were long Friends: You are now my Enemy, and I am, Yours,

"THIS IS A HARDER NUT TO CRACK
THAN THEY IMAGINED"

To [Joseph Priestley]

Dear Friend,   *Philadelphia, 7th July, 1775.*

*   *   *   *   *

The Congress met at a time when all minds were so exasperated by the perfidy of General Gage, and his attack on the country people, that propositions of attempting an accommodation were not much relished; and it has been with difficulty that we have carried another humble petition to the crown, to give Britain one more chance, one opportunity more of recovering the friendship of the colonies; which however I think she has not sense enough to embrace, and so I conclude she has lost them for ever.

She has begun to burn our seaport towns; secure, I suppose, that we shall never be able to return the outrage in kind. She may doubtless destroy them all; but if she wishes to recover our commerce, are these the probable means? She must certainly be distracted; for no tradesman out of Bedlam ever thought of encreasing the number of his customers by knocking them on the head; or of enabling them to pay their debts by burning their houses.

If she wishes to have us subjects and that we should submit to her as our compound sovereign, she is now giving us such miserable specimens of her government, that we shall ever detest and avoid it, as a complication of robbery, murder, famine, fire and pestilence.

You will have heard before this reaches you, of the treacherous conduct * * * to the remaining people in Boston, in detaining their *goods*, after stipulating to let them go out with their *effects*; on pretence that merchants goods were not effects; —the defeat of a great body of his troops by the country people at Lexington; some other small advantages gained in skirmishes with their troops; and the action at Bunker's-hill, in which they were twice repulsed, and the third time gained a dear victory. Enough has happened, one would think, to convince your ministers that the Americans will fight, and that this is a harder nut to crack than they imagined.

We have not yet applied to any foreign power for assistance; nor offered our commerce for their friendship. Perhaps we never may: Yet it is natural to think of it if we are pressed.

We have now an army on our establishment which still holds yours besieged.

My time was never more fully employed. In the morning at 6, I am at the committee of safety, appointed by the assembly to put the province in a state of defence; which committee holds till near 9, when I am at the congress, and that sits till after 4 in the afternoon. Both these bodies proceed with the greatest unanimity, and their meetings are well attended. It will scarce be credited in Britain that men can be as diligent with us from zeal for the public good, as with you for thousands per annum. —Such is the difference between uncorrupted new states, and corrupted old ones.

Great frugality and great industry are now become fashionable here: Gentlemen who used to entertain with two or three courses, pride themselves now in treating with simple beef and pudding. By these means, and the stoppage of our consumptive trade with Britain, we shall be better able to pay our voluntary taxes for the support of our troops. Our savings in the article of trade amount to near five million sterling per annum.

I shall communicate your letter to Mr. Winthrop, but the camp is at Cambridge, and he has as little leisure for philosophy as myself. * * * Believe me ever, with sincere esteem, my dear friend,

Yours most affectionately.

"THERE IS NO LITTLE ENEMY"

To David Hartley

Philadelphia, Oct. 3, 1775.

I wish as ardently as you can do for peace, and should rejoice exceedingly in co-operating with you to that end. But every ship from Britain brings some intelligence of new measures that tend more and more to exasperate; and it seems to me that until you have found by dear experience the reducing us by force impracticable, you will think of nothing fair and reasonable.—We have as yet resolved only on defensive measures. If you would recall your forces and stay at home, we should meditate nothing to injure you. A little time so given for cooling on both sides would have excellent effects. But you will goad and provoke us. You despise us too much; and you are insensible of the Italian adage, that *there is no little enemy.*—I am persuaded the body of the British people are our friends; but they are changeable, and by your lying Gazettes may soon be made our enemies. Our respect for them will proportionally diminish; and I see clearly we are on the high road to mutual enmity, hatred, and detestation. A separation will of course be inevitable.—'Tis a million of pities so fair a plan as we have hitherto been engaged in for increasing strength and empire with *public felicity*, should be destroyed by the mangling hands of a few blundering ministers. It will not be destroyed: God will protect and prosper it: You will only exclude yourselves from any share in it.—We hear that more ships and troops are coming out. We know you may do us a great deal of mischief, but we are determined to bear it patiently as long as we can; but if you flatter yourselves with beating us into submission, you know neither the people nor the *country*.

The congress is still sitting, and will wait the result of their *last* petition.

PARIS
1776 – 1785

Contents

The Sale of the Hessians

FROM THE COUNT DE SCHAUMBERGH TO THE BARON
HOHENDORF, COMMANDING THE HESSIAN TROOPS
IN AMERICA

Rome, February 18, 1777.

MONSIEUR LE BARON:—On my return from Naples, I received at Rome your letter of the 27th December of last year. I have learned with unspeakable pleasure the courage our troops exhibited at Trenton, and you cannot imagine my joy on being told that of the 1,950 Hessians engaged in the fight, but 345 escaped. There were just 1,605 men killed, and I cannot sufficiently commend your prudence in sending an exact list of the dead to my minister in London. This precaution was the more necessary, as the report sent to the English ministry does not give but 1,455 dead. This would make 483,450 florins instead of 643,500 which I am entitled to demand under our convention. You will comprehend the prejudice which such an error would work in my finances, and I do not doubt you will take the necessary pains to prove that Lord North's list is false and yours correct.

The court of London objects that there were a hundred wounded who ought not to be included in the list, nor paid for as dead; but I trust you will not overlook my instructions to you on quitting Cassel, and that you will not have tried by human succor to recall the life of the unfortunates whose days could not be lengthened but by the loss of a leg or an arm. That would be making them a pernicious present, and I am sure they would rather die than live in a condition no longer fit for my service. I do not mean by this that you should assassinate them; we should be humane, my dear Baron, but you may insinuate to the surgeons with entire propriety that a crippled man is a reproach to their profession, and that there is no wiser course than to let every one of them die when he ceases to be fit to fight.

I am about to send to you some new recruits. Don't economize them. Remember glory before all things. Glory is true

917

wealth. There is nothing degrades the soldier like the love of money. He must care only for honour and reputation, but this reputation must be acquired in the midst of dangers. A battle gained without costing the conqueror any blood is an inglorious success, while the conquered cover themselves with glory by perishing with their arms in their hands. Do you remember that of the 300 Lacedæmonians who defended the defile of Thermopylæ, not one returned? How happy should I be could I say the same of my brave Hessians!

It is true that their king, Leonidas, perished with them: but things have changed, and it is no longer the custom for princes of the empire to go and fight in America for a cause with which they have no concern. And besides, to whom should they pay the thirty guineas per man if I did not stay in Europe to receive them? Then, it is necessary also that I be ready to send recruits to replace the men you lose. For this purpose I must return to Hesse. It is true, grown men are becoming scarce there, but I will send you boys. Besides, the scarcer the commodity the higher the price. I am assured that the women and little girls have begun to till our lands, and they get on not badly. You did right to send back to Europe that Dr. Crumerus who was so successful in curing dysentery. Don't bother with a man who is subject to looseness of the bowels. That disease makes bad soldiers. One coward will do more mischief in an engagement than ten brave men will do good. Better that they burst in their barracks than fly in a battle, and tarnish the glory of our arms. Besides, you know that they pay me as killed for all who die from disease, and I don't get a farthing for runaways. My trip to Italy, which has cost me enormously, makes it desirable that there should be a great mortality among them. You will therefore promise promotion to all who expose themselves; you will exhort them to seek glory in the midst of dangers; you will say to Major Maundorff that I am not at all content with his saving the 345 men who escaped the massacre of Trenton. Through the whole campaign he has not had ten men killed in consequence of his orders. Finally, let it be your principal object to prolong the war and avoid a decisive engagement on either side, for I have made arrangements for a grand Italian opera, and I do not wish to be obliged to give it up. Meantime I pray God, my dear Baron de Hohendorf, to have you in his holy and gracious keeping.

Model of a Letter of Recommendation

Sir   Paris April 2, 1777

The Bearer of this who is going to America, presses me to give him a Letter of Recommendation, tho' I know nothing of him, not even his Name. This may seem extraordinary, but I assure you it is not uncommon here. Sometimes indeed one unknown Person brings me another equally unknown, to recommend him; and sometimes they recommend one another! As to this Gentleman, I must refer you to himself for his Character and Merits, with which he is certainly better acquainted than I can possibly be; I recommend him however to those Civilities which every Stranger, of whom one knows no Harm, has a Right to, and I request you will do him all the good Offices and show him all the Favour that on further Acquaintance you shall find him to deserve. I have the honour to be, &c.

The Twelve Commandments

TO MADAME BRILLON

Passy March 10.

I am charm'd with the goodness of my spiritual guide, and resign myself implicitly to her Conduct, as she promises to lead me to heaven in so delicious a Road when I could be content to travel thither even in the roughest of all ways with the pleasure of her Company.

How kindly partial to her Penitent in finding him, on examining his conscience, guilty of only one capital sin and to call that by the gentle name of Foible!

I lay fast hold of your promise to absolve me of all Sins past, present, & future, on the easy & pleasing Condition of loving God, America and my guide above all things. I am in Rapture when I think of being absolv'd of the future.

People commonly speak of Ten Commandments.—I have been taught that there are twelve. The first was increase & multiply & replenish the earth. The twelfth is, A new Commandment I give unto you, *that you love one another*. It seems to me that they are a little misplaced, And that the last should have been the first. However I never made any difficulty about that, but was always willing to obey them both whenever I had an opportunity. Pray tell me my dear Casuist, whether my keeping religiously these two commandments tho' not in the Decalogue, may not be accepted in Compensation for my breaking so often one of the ten I mean that which forbids Coveting my neighbour's wife, and which I confess I break constantly God forgive me, as often as I see or think of my lovely Confessor, and I am afraid I should never be able to repent of the Sin even if I had the full Possession of her.

And now I am Consulting you upon a Case of Conscience I will mention the Opinion of a certain Father of the church which I find myself willing to adopt though I am not sure it is orthodox. It is this, that the most effectual way to get rid of a certain Temptation is, as often as it returns, to comply with and satisfy it.

Pray instruct me how far I may venture to practice upon this Principle?

But why should I be so scrupulous when you have promised to absolve me of the future?

Adieu my charming Conductress and believe me ever with the sincerest Esteem & affection.

Your most obed't hum. Serv.

1778

Petition of the Letter Z

FROM THE TATLER N 1778

TO THE WORSHIPFUL ISAAC BICKERSTAFF, ESQ;
CENSOR-GENERAL
THE PETITION OF THE LETTER Z COMMONLY CALLED
EZZARD, ZED, OR IZARD, MOST HUMBLY SHEWETH,

He was always talking of his Family and of his being a Man of Fortune.

That your Petitioner is of as high extraction, and has as good an Estate as any other Letter of the Alphabet.

And complaining of his being treated, not with due Respect

That there is therefore no reason why he should be treated as he is with Disrespect and Indignity.

At the tail of the Commission, of Ministers

That he is not only plac'd at the Tail of the Alphabet, when he had as much Right as any other to be at the Head; but is, by the Injustice of his enemies totally excluded from the Word WISE, and his Place injuriously filled by a little, hissing, crooked, serpentine, venemous Letter called s, when it must be evident to your Worship, and to all the World, that Double U, I, S. E do not spell or sound *Wize*, but *Wice*.

He was not of the Commission for France, A Lee being preferr'd to him, which made him very angry; and the Character here given of S, is just what he in his Passion gave Lee.

Your Petitioner therefore prays that the Alphabet may by your Censorial Authority be reformed, and that in Consideration of his *Long-Suffering* & *Patience* he may be placed at the Head of it; that S may be turned out of the Word Wise, and the Petitioner employ'd instead of him;

The most impatient Man alive

And your Petitioner (as in Duty bound) shall ever pray, &c.

Z

Mr. Bickerstaff having examined the Allegations of the
above Petition, judges and determines, that Z be admonished
to be content with his Station, forbear Reflections upon his
Brother Letters, & remember his own small Usefulness, and
the little Occasion there is for him in the Republick of Letters, since S, whom he so despises, can so well serve instead
of him.

c. August, 1778

The Ephemera

Passy Sept 20, 1778

You may remember, my dear Friend, that when we lately
spent that happy Day in the delightful Garden and sweet Society of the Moulin Joli, I stopt a little in one of our Walks,
and staid some time behind the Company. We had been
shewn numberless Skeletons of a kind of little Fly, called an
Ephemere all whose successive Generations we were told
were bred and expired within the Day. I happen'd to see a
living Company of them on a Leaf, who appear'd to be engag'd in Conversation. — You know I understand all the inferior Animal Tongues: my too great Application to the Study
of them is the best Excuse I can give for the little Progress I
have made in your charming Language. I listened thro' Curiosity to the Discourse of these little Creatures, but as they in
their national Vivacity spoke three or four together, I could
make but little of their Discourse. I found, however, by some
broken Expressions that I caught now & then, they were disputing warmly the Merit of two foreign Musicians, one a
Cousin, the other a *Musketo*; in which Dispute they spent
their time seemingly as regardless of the Shortness of Life, as
if they had been Sure of living a Month. Happy People!
thought I, you live certainly under a wise, just and mild Government; since you have no public Grievances to complain of,
nor any Subject of Contention but the Perfection or Imperfection of foreign Music. I turned from them to an old grey-
headed one, who was single on another Leaf, & talking to

himself. Being amus'd with his Soliloquy, I have put it down in writing in hopes it will likewise amuse her to whom I am So much indebted for the most pleasing of all Amusements, her delicious Company and her heavenly Harmony.

"It was, says he, the Opinion of learned Philosophers of our Race, who lived and flourished long before my time, that this vast World, the *Moulin Joli*, could not itself subsist more than 18 Hours; and I think there was some Foundation for that Opinion, since by the apparent Motion of the great Luminary that gives Life to all Nature, and which in my time has evidently declin'd considerably towards the Ocean at the End of our Earth, it must then finish its Course, be extinguish'd in the Waters that surround us, and leave the World in Cold and Darkness, necessarily producing universal Death and Destruction. I have lived seven of these Hours; a great Age; being no less than 420 minutes of Time. How very few of us continue So long.—I have seen Generations born, flourish and expire. My present Friends are the Children and Grandchildren of the Friends of my Youth, who are now, alas, no more! And I must soon follow them; for by the Course of Nature, tho' still in Health, I cannot expect to live above 7 or 8 Minutes longer. What now avails all my Toil and Labour in amassing Honey-Dew on this Leaf, which I cannot live to enjoy! What the political Struggles I have been engag'd in for the Good of my Compatriotes, Inhabitants of this Bush, or my philosophical Studies for the Benefit of our Race in general! For in Politics *what can Laws do without Morals.** Our present Race of Ephemeres will in a Course of Minutes, become corrupt like those of other and older Bushes, and consequently as wretched. And in Philosophy how small our Progress! Alas, *Art is long and Life is short!*†—My Friends would comfort me with the Idea of a Name they Say I shall leave behind me; and they tell me I have *lived long enough, to Nature and to Glory*;‡—But what will Fame be to an Ephemere who no longer exists? And what will become of all History in the 18th Hour, when the World itself, even the whole *Moulin Joli* shall come to its End, and be buried in

* Quid leges sine moribus. Hor.
†Hippocrates.
‡Cæsar.

universal Ruin?—To me, after all my eager Pursuits, no solid Pleasures now remain, but the Reflection of a long Life spent in meaning well, the sensible Conversation of a few good Lady-Ephemeres, and now and then a kind Smile and a Tune from the ever-amiable BRILLANTE."

The Elysian Fields

M. FRANKLIN TO MADAME HELVÉTIUS

Vexed by your barbarous resolution, announced so positively last evening, to remain single all your life in respect to your dear husband, I went home, fell on my bed, and, believing myself dead, found myself in the Elysian Fields.

I was asked if I desired to see anybody in particular. Lead me to the home of the philosophers.—There are two who live nearby in the garden: they are very good neighbors, and close friends of each other.—Who are they?—Socrates and H——.—I esteem them both prodigiously; but let me see first H——, because I understand a little French, but not one word of Greek. He received me with great courtesy, having known me for some time, he said, by the reputation I had there. He asked me a thousand things about the war, and about the present state of religion, liberty, and the government in France.—You ask nothing then of your dear friend Madame H——; nevertheless she still loves you excessively and I was at her place but an hour ago. Ah! said he, you make me remember my former felicity.—But it is necessary to forget it in order to be happy here. During several of the early years, I thought only of her. Finally I am consoled. I have taken another wife. The most like her that I could find. She is not, it is true, so completely beautiful, but she has as much good sense, a little more of Spirit, and she loves me infinitely. Her continual study is to please me; and she has actually gone to hunt the best Nectar and the best Ambrosia in order to regale me this evening; remain with me and you will see her. I perceive, I said, that your old friend is more faithful than you: for several good offers have been made her, all of which she has refused. I confess to you that I myself have loved her to the point of distraction; but she was hard-hearted to my regard, and has absolutely rejected me for love of you. I pity you, he said, for your bad fortune; for truly she is a good and beautiful woman and very loveable. But the Abbé de la R——, and the Abbé M——, are they not still sometimes at her home? Yes, assuredly, for she has not lost a single one of your friends. If you had won over the Abbé M—— (with coffee and cream) to speak for you, perhaps you would have succeeded; for he is a subtle logician like Duns Scotus or St. Thomas; he places his arguments in such good order that they become nearly irresistible. Also, if the Abbé de la R—— had been bribed (by some beautiful edition of an old classic) to speak against you, that would have been better: for I have always observed, that when he advises something, she has a very strong penchant to do the reverse.—At these words the new Madame H—— entered with the Nectar: at which instant I recognized her to be Madame F——, my old American friend. I reclaimed to her. But she told me coldly, "I have been your good wife forty-nine years and four months, nearly a half century; be content with that. Here I have formed a new connection, which will endure to eternity."

Offended by this refusal of my Eurydice, I suddenly decided to leave these ungrateful spirits, to return to the good earth, to see again the sunshine and you. Here I am! Let us revenge ourselves.

December 7, 1778

Bilked for Breakfast

MR. FRANKLIN TO MADAME LA FRETÉ

Upon my word, you did well, Madam, not to come so far, at so inclement a Season, only to find so wretched a Breakfast. My Son & I were not so wise. I will tell you the Story.

As the Invitation was for eleven O'clock, & you were of the Party, I imagined I should find a substantial Breakfast; that there would be a large Company; that we should have not only Tea, but Coffee, Chocolate, perhaps a Ham, & several other good Things. I resolved to go on Foot; my Shoes were a little too tight; I arrived almost lamed. On entering the Courtyard, I was a little surprised to find it so empty of Carriages, & to see that we were the first to arrive. We go up the Stairs. Not a Sound. We enter the Breakfast Room. No one except the Abbé & Monsieur Cabanis. Breakfast over, & eaten! Nothing on the Table except a few Scraps of Bread & a little Butter. General astonishment; a Servant sent running to tell Madame Helvétius that we have come for Breakfast. She leaves her toilet Table; she enters with her Hair half dressed. It is declared surprising that I have come, when you wrote me that you would not come. I Deny it. To prove it, they show me your Letter, which they have received and kept.

Finally another Breakfast is ordered. One Servant runs for fresh Water, another for Coals. The Bellows are plied with a will. I was very Hungry; it was so late; "a watched pot is slow to boil," as Poor Richard says. Madame sets out for Paris & leaves us. We begin to eat. The Butter is soon finished. The Abbé asks if we want more. Yes, of course. He rings. No one comes. We talk; he forgets the Butter. I began scraping the Dish; at that he seizes it & runs to the Kitchen for some. After a while he comes slowly back, saying mournfully that there is no more of it in the House. To entertain me the Abbé proposes a Walk; my feet refuse. And so we give up Breakfast; & we go upstairs to his apartment to let his good Books furnish the end of our Repast—.

I am left utterly disconsolate, having, instead of half a Dozen of your sweet, affectionate, substantial, & heartily applied Kisses, which I expected from your Charity, having received only the Shadow of one given by Madame Helvétius, willingly enough, it is true, but the lightest & most superficial kiss that can possibly be imagined.

c. 1778

Passport for Captain Cook

To all Captains and Commanders of armed Ships acting by Commission from the Congress of the United States of America, now in war with Great Britain.

Gentlemen,

A Ship having been fitted out from England before the Commencement of this War, to make Discoveries of new Countries in Unknown Seas, under the Conduct of that most celebrated Navigator and Discoverer Captain Cook; an Undertaking truly laudable in itself, as the Increase of Geographical Knowledge facilitates the Communication between distant Nations, in the Exchange of useful Products and Manufactures, and the Extension of Arts, whereby the common Enjoyments of human Life are multiply'd and augmented, and Science of other kinds increased to the benefit of Mankind in general; this is, therefore, most earnestly to recommend to every one of you, that, in case the said Ship, which is now expected to be soon in the European Seas on her Return, should happen to fall into your Hands, you would not consider her as an Enemy, nor suffer any Plunder to be made of the Effects contain'd in her, nor obstruct her immediate Return to England, by detaining her or sending her into any other Part of Europe or to America, but that you would treat the said Captain Cook and his People with all Civility and Kindness, affording them, as common Friends to Mankind, all the Assistance in your Power, which they may happen to stand in need of. In so doing you will not only gratify the Generosity of your own Dispositions, but there is no doubt of your obtaining the Approbation of the Congress, and your other American Owners. I have the honour to be, Gentlemen, your most obedient humble Servant.

Given at Passy, near Paris, this 10th day of March, 1779.

*Plenipotentiary from the Congress of the
United States to the Court of France.*

The Morals of Chess

[Playing at chess is the most ancient and most universal game known among men; for its original is beyond the memory of history, and it has, for numberless ages, been the amusement of all the civilised nations of Asia, the Persians, the Indians, and the Chinese. Europe has had it above a thousand years;

the Spaniards have spread it over their part of America; and it has lately begun to make its appearance in the United States. It is so interesting in itself, as not to need the view of gain to induce engaging in it; and thence it is seldom played for money. Those therefore who have leisure for such diversions, cannot find one that is more innocent: and the following piece, written with a view to correct (among a few young friends) some little improprieties in the practice of it, shows at the same time that it may, in its effects on the mind, be not merely innocent, but advantageous, to the vanquished as well as the victor.]

The Game of Chess is not merely an idle Amusement. Several very valuable qualities of the Mind, useful in the course of human Life, are to be acquir'd or strengthened by it, so as to become habits, ready on all occasions. For Life is a kind of Chess, in which we often have Points to gain, & Competitors or Adversaries to contend with; and in which there is a vast variety of good and ill Events, that are in some degree the Effects of Prudence or the want of it. By playing at Chess, then, we may learn,

I. *Foresight*, which looks a little into futurity, and considers the Consequences that may attend an action; for it is continually occurring to the Player, "If I move this piece, what will be the advantages or disadvantages of my new situation? What Use can my Adversary make of it to annoy me? What other moves can I make to support it, and to defend myself from his attacks?"

II. *Circumspection*, which surveys the whole Chessboard, or scene of action; the relations of the several pieces and situations, the Dangers they are respectively exposed to, the several possibilities of their aiding each other, the probabilities that the Adversary may make this or that move, and attack this or the other Piece, and what different Means can be used to avoid his stroke, or turn its consequences against him.

III. *Caution*, not to make our moves too hastily. This habit is best acquired, by observing strictly the laws of the Game; such as, *If you touch a Piece, you must move it somewhere; if you set it down, you must let it stand.* And it is therefore best that these rules should be observed, as the Game becomes thereby more the image of human Life, and particularly of War; in which, if you have incautiously put yourself into a bad and dangerous position, you cannot obtain your Enemy's Leave to withdraw your Troops, and place them more securely, but you must abide all the consequences of your rashness.

And *lastly*, we learn by Chess the habit of not being discouraged by present appearances in the state of our affairs, the habit of hoping for a favourable Change, and that of persevering in the search of resources. The Game is so full of Events, there is such a variety of turns in it, the Fortune of it is so subject to sudden Vicissitudes, and one so frequently, after long contemplation, discovers the means of extricating one's self from a supposed insurmountable Difficulty, that one is encouraged to continue the Contest to the last, in hopes of Victory from our own skill, or at least of getting a stale mate, from the Negligence of our Adversary. And whoever considers, what in Chess he often sees instances of, that particular pieces of success are apt to produce Presumption, & its consequent Inattention, by which more is afterwards lost than was gain'd by the preceding Advantage, while misfortunes produce more care and attention, by which the loss may be recovered, will learn not to be too much discouraged by any present success of his Adversary, nor to despair of final good fortune upon every little Check he receives in the pursuit of it.

That we may therefore be induced more frequently to chuse this beneficial amusement, in preference to others which are not attended with the same advantages, every Circumstance that may increase the pleasure of it should be regarded; and every action or word that is unfair, disrespectful, or that in any way may give uneasiness, should be avoided, as contrary to the immediate intention of both the Players, which is to pass the Time agreably.

Therefore, first, if it is agreed to play according to the strict rules, then those rules are to be exactly observed by both parties, and should not be insisted on for one side, while deviated from by the other—for this is not equitable.

Secondly, if it is agreed not to observe the rules exactly, but one party demands indulgencies, he should then be as willing to allow them to the other.

Thirdly, no false move should ever be made to extricate yourself out of difficulty, or to gain an advantage. There can be no pleasure in playing with a person once detected in such unfair practice.

Fourthly, if your adversary is long in playing, you ought not to hurry him, or express any uneasiness at his delay. You should not sing, nor whistle, nor look at your watch, nor take up a book to read, nor make a tapping with your feet on the floor, or with your fingers on the table, nor do any thing that may disturb his attention. For all these things displease; and they do not show your skill in playing, but your craftiness or your rudeness.

Fifthly, you ought not to endeavour to amuse and deceive your adversary, by pretending to have made bad moves, and saying that you have now lost the game, in order to make him secure and careless, and inattentive to your schemes: for this is fraud and deceit, not skill in the game.

Sixthly, you must not, when you have gained a victory, use any triumphing or insulting expression, nor show too much pleasure; but endeavour to console your adversary, and make him less dissatisfied with himself, by every kind of civil expression that may be used with truth, such as, "you understand the game better than I, but you are a little inattentive;" or, "you play too fast;" or, "you had the best of the game, but something happened to divert your thoughts, and that turned it in my favour."

Seventhly, if you are a spectator while others play, observe the most perfect silence. For, if you give advice, you offend both parties, him against whom you give it, because it may cause the loss of his game, him in whose favour you give it, because, though it be good, and he follows it, he loses the pleasure he might have had, if you had permitted him to think until it had occurred to himself. Even after a move or moves, you must not, by replacing the pieces, show how they might have been placed better; for that displeases, and may occasion disputes and doubts about their true situation. All talking to the players lessens or diverts their attention, and is therefore unpleasing. Nor should you give the least hint to either party, by any kind of noise or motion. If you do, you are unworthy to be a spectator. If you have a mind to exercise or show your judgment, do it in playing your own game, when you have an opportunity, not in criticizing, or meddling with, or counselling the play of others.

Lastly, if the game is not to be played rigorously, according to the rules above mentioned, then moderate your desire of victory over your adversary, and be pleased with one over yourself. Snatch not eagerly at every advantage offered by his unskilfulness or inattention; but point out to him kindly, that by such a move he places or leaves a piece in danger and unsupported; that by another he will put his king in a perilous situation, &c. By this generous civility (so opposite to the unfairness above forbidden) you may, indeed, happen to lose the game to your opponent; but you will win what is better, his esteem, his respect, and his affection, together with the silent approbation and good-will of impartial spectators.

June, 1779

The Whistle

Passy, November 10 1779.

I received my dear Friend's two Letters, one for Wednesday & one for Saturday. This is again Wednesday. I do not deserve one for to day, because I have not answered the former. But indolent as I am, and averse to Writing, the Fear of having no more of your pleasing Epistles, if I do not contribute to the Correspondance, obliges me to take up my Pen: And as M. B. has kindly sent me Word, that he sets out to-morrow to see you; instead of spending this Wednesday Evening as I have long done its Name-sakes, in your delightful Company, I sit down to spend it in thinking of you, in writing to you, & in reading over & over again your Letters.

I am charm'd with your Description of Paradise, & with your Plan of living there. And I approve much of your Conclusion, that in the mean time we should draw all the Good

we can from this World. In my Opinion we might all draw
more Good, from it than we do, & suffer less Evil, if we
would but take care *not to give too much for our Whistles*. For
to me it seems that most of the unhappy People we meet
with, are become so by Neglect of that Caution.

You ask what I mean?—You love Stories, and will excuse
my telling you one of my self. When I was a Child of seven
Years old, my Friends on a Holiday fill'd my little Pocket with
Halfpence. I went directly to a Shop where they sold Toys for
Children; and being charm'd with the Sound of a Whistle
that I met by the way, in the hands of another Boy, I voluntarily offer'd and gave all my Money for it. When I came
home, whistling all over the House, much pleas'd with my
Whistle, but disturbing all the Family, my Brothers, Sisters &
Cousins, understanding the Bargain I had made, told me I
had given four times as much for it as it was worth, put me
in mind what good Things I might have bought with the rest
of the Money, & laught at me so much for my Folly that I
cry'd with Vexation; and the Reflection gave me more Chagrin than the Whistle gave me Pleasure.

This however was afterwards of use to me, the Impression
continuing on my Mind; so that often when I was tempted
to buy some unnecessary thing, I said to my self, *Do not give
too much for the Whistle*; and I sav'd my Money.

As I grew up, came into the World, and observed the Actions of Men, I thought I met many *who gave too much for the
Whistle.*—When I saw one ambitious of Court Favour, sacrificing his Time in Attendance at Levees, his Repose, his Liberty, his Virtue and perhaps his Friend, to obtain it; I have
said to my self, *This Man gives too much for his Whistle.*—
When I saw another fond of Popularity, constantly employing
himself in political Bustles, neglecting his own Affairs, and
ruining them by that Neglect, *He pays*, says I, *too much for his
Whistle.*—If I knew a Miser, who gave up every kind of
comfortable Living, all the Pleasure of doing Good to
others, all the Esteem of his Fellow Citizens, & the Joys of
benevolent Friendship, for the sake of Accumulating Wealth,
Poor Man, says I, *you pay too much for your Whistle.*—When
I met with a Man of Pleasure, sacrificing every laudable
Improvement of his Mind or of his Fortune, to mere cor-

poreal Satisfactions, & ruining his Health in their Pursuit, *Mistaken Man*, says I, *you are providing Pain for your self instead of Pleasure, you pay too much for your Whistle.*—If I see one fond of Appearance, of fine Cloaths, fine Houses, fine Furniture, fine Equipages, all above his Fortune, for which he contracts Debts, and ends his Career in a Prison; *Alas*, says I, *he has paid too much for his Whistle.*—When I saw a beautiful sweet-temper'd Girl, marry'd to an ill-natured Brute of a Husband; *What a Pity*, says I, *that she should pay so much for a Whistle!*—In short, I conceiv'd that great Part of the Miseries of Mankind, were brought upon them by the false Estimates they had made of the Value of Things, and by their *giving too much for the Whistle.*

Yet I ought to have Charity for these unhappy People, when I consider that with all this Wisdom of which I am boasting, there are certain things in the World so tempting; for Example the Apples of King John, which happily are not to be bought, for if they were put to sale by Auction, I might very easily be led to ruin my self in the Purchase, and find that I had once more *given too much for the Whistle.*

Adieu, my dearest Friend, and believe me ever yours very sincerely and with unalterable Affection.

Passy, 1779

The Levée

In the first chapter of Job we have an account of a transaction said to have arisen in the court, or at the *levée*, of the best of all possible princes, or of governments by a single person, viz. that of God himself.

At this *levée*, in which the sons of God were assembled, Satan also appeared.

It is probable the writer of that ancient book took his idea of this *levée* from those of the eastern monarchs of the age he lived in.

It is to this day usual at the *levées* of princes, to have persons assembled who are enemies to each other, who seek to obtain favor by whispering calumny and detraction, and thereby ruining those that distinguish themselves by their virtue and merit. And kings frequently ask a familiar question or two, of every one in the circle, merely to show their benignity. These circumstances are particularly exemplified in this relation.

If a modern king, for instance, finds a person in the circle who has not lately been there, he naturally asks him how he has passed his time since he last had the pleasure of seeing him? the gentleman perhaps replies that he has been in the country to view his estates, and visit some friends. Thus Satan being asked whence he cometh? answers, "From going to and fro in the earth, and walking up and down in it." And being further asked, whether he had considered the uprightness and fidelity of the prince's servant Job, he immediately displays all the malignance of the designing courtier, by answering with another question: "Doth Job serve God for naught? Hast thou not given him immense wealth, and protected him in the possession of it? Deprive him of that, and he will curse thee to thy face." In modern phrase, Take away his places and his pensions, and your Majesty will soon find him in the opposition.

This whisper against Job had its effect. He was delivered into the power of his adversary, who deprived him of his fortune, destroyed his family, and completely ruined him.

The book of Job is called by divines a sacred poem, and, with the rest of the Holy Scriptures, is understood to be written for our instruction.

What then is the instruction to be gathered from this supposed transaction?

Trust not a single person with the government of your state. For if the Deity himself, being the monarch may for a time give way to calumny, and suffer it to operate the destruction of the best of subjects; what mischief may you not expect from such power in a mere man, though the best of men, from whom the truth is often industriously hidden, and to whom falsehood is often presented in its place, by artful, interested, and malicious courtiers?

And be cautious in trusting him even with limited powers, lest sooner or later he sap and destroy those limits, and render himself absolute.

For by the disposal of places, he attaches to himself all the placeholders, with their numerous connexions, and also all the expecters and hopers of places, which will form a strong party in promoting his views. By various political engagements for the interest of neighbouring states or princes, he procures their aid in establishing his own personal power. So that, through the hopes of emolument in one part of his subjects, and the fear of his resentment in the other, all opposition falls before him.

1779?

Proposed New Version of the Bible

TO THE PRINTER OF ***

SIR,

It is now more than one hundred and seventy years since the translation of our common English Bible. The language in that time is much changed, and the style, being obsolete, and thence less agreeable, is perhaps one reason why the reading of that excellent book is of late so much neglected. I have therefore thought it would be well to procure a new version, in which, preserving the sense, the turn of phrase and manner of expression should be modern. I do not pretend to have the necessary abilities for such a work myself; I throw out the hint for the consideration of the learned; and only venture to send you a few verses of the first chapter of Job, which may serve as a sample of the kind of version I would recommend.

A. B.

PART OF THE FIRST CHAPTER OF JOB MODERNIZED

OLD TEXT	NEW VERSION
Verse 6. Now there was a day when the sons of God came to present themselves before the Lord, and Satan came also amongst them.	Verse 6. And it being *levée* day in heaven, all God's nobility came to court, to present themselves before him; and Satan also appeared in the circle, as one of the ministry.

7. And the Lord said unto Satan, Whence comest thou? Then Satan answered the Lord, and said, From going to and fro in the earth, and from walking up and down in it.

8. And the Lord said unto Satan, Hast thou considered my servant Job, that there is none like him in the earth, a perfect and an upright man, one that feareth God, and escheweth evil?

9. Then Satan answered the Lord, and said, Doth Job fear God for naught?

10. Hast thou not made an hedge about his house, and about all that he hath on every side? Thou hast blessed the work of his hands, and his substance is increased in the land.

11. But put forth thine hand now, and touch all that he hath, and he will curse thee to thy face.

7. And God said to Satan, You have been some time absent; where were you? And Satan answered I have been at my country-seat, and in different places visiting my friends.

8. And God said, Well, what think you of Lord Job? You see he is my best friend, a perfectly honest man, full of respect for me, and avoiding every thing that might offend me.

9. And Satan answered, Does your Majesty imagine that his good conduct is the effect of mere personal attachment and affection?

10. Have you not protected him, and heaped your benefits upon him, till he is grown enormously rich?

11. Try him;—only withdraw your favor, turn him out of his places, and withhold his pensions, and you will soon find him in the opposition.

1779?

Drinking Song

TO THE ABBÉ DE LA ROCHE, AT AUTEUIL

I have run over, my dear friend, the little book of poetry by M. Helvetius, with which you presented me. The poem on *Happiness* pleased me much, and brought to my recollection a little drinking song which I wrote forty years ago upon the same subject, and which is nearly on the same plan, with many of the same thoughts, but very concisely expressed. It is as follows:—

Singer.
Fair Venus calls, her voice obey,
In beauty's arms spend night and day.
The joys of love, all joys excel,
And loving's certainly doing well.

Chorus.

Oh! no!
Not so!
For honest souls know,
Friends and a bottle still bear the bell.

Singer.

Then let us get money, like bees lay up honey;
We'll build us new hives, and store each cell.
The sight of our treasure shall yield us great pleasure;
We'll count it, and chink it, and jingle it well.

Chorus.

Oh! no!
Not so!
For honest souls know,
Friends and a bottle still bear the bell.

Singer.

If this does not fit ye, let's govern the city,
In power is pleasure no tongue can tell;
By crowds tho' you're teas'd, your pride shall be pleas'd,
And this can make Lucifer happy in hell!

Chorus.

Oh! no!
Not so!
For honest souls know,
Friends and a bottle still bear the bell.

Singer.

Then toss off your glasses, and scorn the dull asses,
Who, missing the kernel, still gnaw the shell;
What's love, rule, or riches? wise Solomon teaches,
They're vanity, vanity, vanity, still.

Chorus.

That's true;
He knew;
He'd tried them all through;
Friends and a bottle still bore the bell.

'Tis a singer, my dear Abbé, who exhorts his companions

to seek *happiness* in *love*, in *riches*, and in *power*. They reply, singing together, that happiness is not to be found in any of these things; that it is only to be found in *friends* and *wine*. To this proposition the singer at last assents. The phrase *"bear the bell,"* answers to the French expression, *"obtain the prize."*

I have often remarked, in reading the works of M. Helvetius, that although we were born and educated in two countries so remote from each other, we have often been inspired with the same thoughts; and it is a reflection very flattering to me, that we have not only loved the same studies, but, as far as we have mutually known them, the same friends, and *the same woman*.

Adieu! my dear friend, &c.

1779?

A Tale

There was once an Officer, a worthy man, named Montrésor, who was very ill. His parish Priest, thinking he would die, advised him to make his Peace with God, so that he would be received into Paradise. "I don't feel much Uneasiness on that Score," said Montrésor; "for last Night I had a Vision which set me entirely at rest." "What Vision did you have?" asked the good Priest. "I was," he said, "at the Gate of Paradise with a Crowd of People who wanted to enter. And St. Peter asked each of them what Religion he belonged to. One answered, 'I am a Roman Catholic.' 'Very well,' said St. Peter; 'come in, & take your Place over there among the Catholics.' Another said he belonged to the Anglican Church. 'Very well,' said St. Peter; 'come in, & take your Place over there among the Anglicans.' Another said he was a Quaker. 'Very well,' said St. Peter; 'come in, & take a Place among the Quakers.' Finally he asked me what my Religion was. 'Alas!' I replied, 'unfortunately, poor Jacques Montrésor belongs to none at all.' 'That's a pity,' said the Saint. 'I don't know where to put you but come in anyway; just find a Place for yourself wherever you can.' "

1779?

On Wine

FROM THE ABBÉ FRANKLIN
TO THE ABBÉ MORELLET

You have often enlivened me, my dear friend, by your excellent drinking-songs; in return, I beg to edify you by some Christian, moral, and philosophical reflections upon the same subject.

In vino veritas, says the wise man,—*Truth is in wine*. Before the days of Noah, then, men, having nothing but water to drink, could not discover the truth. Thus they went astray, became abominably wicked, and were justly exterminated by *water*, which they loved to drink.

The good man Noah, seeing that through this pernicious beverage all his contemporaries had perished, took it in aversion; and to quench his thirst God created the vine, and revealed to him the means of converting its fruit into wine. By means of this liquor he discovered numberless important truths; so that ever since his time the word to *divine* has been in common use, signifying originally, *to discover by means of* WINE. (VIN) Thus the patriarch Joseph took upon himself to *divine* by means of a cup or glass of wine, a liquor which obtained this name to show that it was not of human but *divine* invention (another proof of the *antiquity* of the French language, in opposition to M. Gébelin); nay, since that time, all things of peculiar excellence, even the Deities themselves, have been called *Divine* or Di*vin*ities.

We hear of the conversion of water into wine at the marriage in Cana as of a miracle. But this conversion is, through the goodness of God, made every day before our eyes. Behold the rain which descends from heaven upon our vineyards; there it enters the roots of the vines, to be changed into wine; a constant proof that God loves us, and loves to see us happy. The miracle in question was only performed to hasten the operation, under circumstances of present necessity, which required it.

It is true that God has also instructed man to reduce wine into water. But into what sort of water?—*Water of Life*. (*Eau de Vie*.) And this, that man may be able upon occasion to perform the miracle of Cana, and convert common water into that excellent species of wine which we call *punch*. My Christian brother, be kind and benevolent like God, and do not spoil his good drink.

He made wine to gladden the heart of man; do not, therefore when at table you see your neighbor pour wine into his glass, be eager to mingle water with it. Why would you drown *truth*? It is probable that your neighbor knows better than you what suits him. Perhaps he does not like water; perhaps he would only put in a few drops for fashion's sake; perhaps he does not wish any one to observe how little he puts in his glass. Do not, then, offer water, except to children; 't is a mistaken piece of politeness, and often very inconvenient. I give you this hint as a man of the world; and I will finish as I began, like a good Christian, in making a religious observation of high importance, taken from the Holy Scriptures. I mean that the apostle Paul counselled Timothy very seriously to put wine into his water for the sake of his health; but that not one of the apostles or holy fathers ever recommended *putting water to wine*.

P.S. To confirm still more your piety and gratitude to Divine Providence, reflect upon the situation which it has given to the *elbow*. You see (Figures 1 and 2) in animals, who are intended to drink the waters that flow upon the earth, that if they have long legs, they have also a long neck, so that they can get at their drink without kneeling down. But man, who was destined to drink wine, must be able to raise the glass to his mouth. If the elbow had been placed nearer the hand (as in Figure 3), the part in advance would have been too short to bring the glass up to the mouth; and if it had been placed nearer the shoulder, (as in Figure 4) that part would have been so long that it would have carried the wine far beyond the mouth. But by the actual situation, (represented in Figure 5), we are enabled to drink at our ease, the glass going exactly to the mouth. Let us, then, with glass in hand, adore this benevolent wisdom;—let us adore and drink!

1779?

Fig. I.

Fig. 2.

D'après le dessin original envoyé par Franklin .

Fig. 3.

Fig. 4.

Fig. 5.

Dialogue Between the Gout and Mr. Franklin

MIDNIGHT, OCTOBER 22, 1780

MR. F.

Eh! oh! eh! What have I done to merit these cruel sufferings?

THE GOUT

Many things; you have ate and drank too freely, and too much indulged those legs of yours in their indolence.

MR. F.

Who is it that accuses me?

THE GOUT

It is I, even I, the Gout.

MR. F.

What! my enemy in person?

THE GOUT

No, not your enemy.

MR. F.

I repeat it, my enemy; for you would not only torment my body to death, but ruin my good name; you reproach me as a glutton and a tippler; now all the world, that knows me, will allow that I am neither the one nor the other.

THE GOUT

The world may think as it pleases; it is always very complaisant to itself, and sometimes to its friends; but I very well know that the quantity of meat and drink proper for a man who takes a reasonable degree of exercise, would be too much for another who never takes any.

MR. F.

I take—eh! oh!—as much exercise—eh!—as I can, Madam Gout. You know my sedentary state, and on that account, it would seem, Madam Gout, as if you might spare me a little, seeing it is not altogether my own fault.

THE GOUT

Not a jot; your rhetoric and your politeness are thrown away;

your apology avails nothing. If your situation in life is a sedentary one, your amusements, your recreation, at least, should be active. You ought to walk or ride; or, if the weather prevents that, play at billiards. But let us examine your course of life. While the mornings are long, and you have leisure to go abroad, what do you do? Why, instead of gaining an appetite for breakfast by salutary exercise, you amuse yourself with books, pamphlets, or newspapers, which commonly are not worth the reading. Yet you eat an inordinate breakfast, four dishes of tea with cream, and one or two buttered toasts, with slices of hung beef, which I fancy are not things the most easily digested. Immediately afterwards you sit down to write at your desk, or converse with persons who apply to you on business. Thus the time passes till one, without any kind of bodily exercise. But all this I could pardon, in regard, as you say, to your sedentary condition. But what is your practice after dinner? Walking in the beautiful gardens of those friends with whom you have dined would be the choice of men of sense; yours is to be fixed down to chess, where you are found engaged for two or three hours! This is your perpetual recreation, which is the least eligible of any for a sedentary man, because, instead of accelerating the motion of the fluids, the rigid attention it requires helps to retard the circulation and obstruct internal secretions. Wrapt in the speculations of this wretched game, you destroy your constitution. What can be expected from such a course of living but a body replete with stagnant humours, ready to fall a prey to all kinds of dangerous maladies, if I, the Gout, did not occasionally bring you relief by agitating those humours, and so purifying or dissipating them? If it was in some nook or alley in Paris, deprived of walks, that you played a while at chess after dinner, this might be excusable; but the same taste prevails with you in Passy, Auteuil, Montmartre, or Sanoy, places where there are the finest gardens and walks, a pure air, beautiful women, and most agreeable and instructive conversation: all which you might enjoy by frequenting the walks. But these are rejected for this abominable game of chess. Fie, then, Mr. Franklin! But amidst my instructions, I had almost forgot to administer my wholesome corrections; so take that twinge— and that.

Mr. F.

Oh! eh! oh! ohhh! As much instruction as you please, Madam Gout, and as many reproaches; but pray, Madam, a truce with your corrections!

The Gout

No, Sir, no, I will not abate a particle of what is so much for your good—therefore——

Mr. F.

Oh! ehhh!—It is not fair to say I take no exercise, when I do very often, going out to dine and returning in my carriage.

The Gout

That, of all imaginable exercises, is the most slight and insignificant, if you allude to the motion of a carriage suspended on springs. By observing the degree of heat obtained by different kinds of motion, we may form an estimate of the quantity of exercise given by each. Thus, for example, if you turn out to walk in winter with cold feet, in an hour's time you will be in a glow all over; ride on horseback, the same effect will scarcely be perceived by four hours' round trotting; but if you loll in a carriage, such as you have mentioned, you may travel all day and gladly enter the last inn to warm your feet by a fire. Flatter yourself then no longer that half an hour's airing in your carriage deserves the name of exercise. Providence has appointed few to roll in carriages, while he has given to all a pair of legs, which are machines infinitely more commodious and serviceable. Be grateful, then, and make a proper use of yours. Would you know how they forward the circulation of your fluids in the very action of transporting you from place to place, observe when you walk that all your weight is alternately thrown from one leg to the other; this occasions a great pressure on the vessels of the foot, and repels their contents; when relieved, by the weight being thrown on the other foot, the vessels of the first are allowed to replenish, and by a return of this weight, this repulsion again succeeds; thus accelerating the circulation of the blood. The heat produced in any given time depends on the degree of this acceleration; the fluids are shaken, the humours attenuated, the secretions facilitated, and all goes well; the cheeks are ruddy, and health is established. Behold your fair friend at Auteuil; a lady who received from bounteous nature more really useful science than half a dozen such pretenders to philosophy as you have been able to extract from all your books. When she honours you with a visit, it is on foot. She walks all hours of the day, and leaves indolence, and its concomitant maladies, to be endured by her horses. In this, see at once the preservative of her health and personal charms. But when you go to Auteuil, you must have your carriage, though it is no farther from Passy to Auteuil than from Auteuil to Passy.

Mr. F.

Your reasonings grow very tiresome.

The Gout

I stand corrected. I will be silent and continue my office; take that, and that.

Mr. F.

Oh! Ohh! Talk on, I pray you.

The Gout

No, no; I have a good number of twinges for you tonight, and you may be sure of some more tomorrow.

Mr. F.

What, with such a fever! I shall go distracted. Oh! eh! Can no one bear it for me?

The Gout

Ask that of your horses; they have served you faithfully.

Mr. F.

How can you so cruelly sport with my torments?

The Gout

Sport! I am very serious. I have here a list of offences against your own health distinctly written, and can justify every stroke inflicted on you.

Mr. F.

Read it then.

THE GOUT

It is too long a detail; but I will briefly mention some particulars.

MR. F.

Proceed. I am all attention.

THE GOUT

Do you remember how often you have promised yourself, the following morning, a walk in the grove of Boulogne, in the garden de La Muette, or in your own garden, and have violated your promise, alleging, at one time, it was too cold, at another too warm, too windy, too moist, or what else you pleased; when in truth it was too nothing but your insuperable love of ease?

MR. F.

That I confess may have happened occasionally, probably ten times in a year.

THE GOUT

Your confession is very far short of the truth; the gross amount is one hundred and ninety-nine times.

MR. F.

Is it possible?

THE GOUT

So possible that it is fact; you may rely on the accuracy of my statement. You know M. Brillon's gardens, and what fine walks they contain; you know the handsome flight of an hundred steps which lead from the terrace above to the lawn below. You have been in the practice of visiting this amiable family twice a week, after dinner, and it is a maxim of your own, that "a man may take as much exercise in walking a mile up and down stairs, as in ten on level ground." What an opportunity was here for you to have had exercise in both these ways! Did you embrace it, and how often?

MR. F.

I cannot immediately answer that question.

THE GOUT

I will do it for you; not once.

MR. F.

Not once?

THE GOUT

Even so. During the summer you went there at six o'clock. You found the charming lady, with her lovely children and friends, eager to walk with you, and entertain you with their agreeable conversation; and what has been your choice? Why, to sit on the terrace, satisfying yourself with the fine prospect, and passing your eye over the beauties of the garden below, without taking one step to descend and walk about in them. On the contrary, you call for tea and the chess-board; and lo! you are occupied in your seat till nine o'clock, and that besides two hours' play after dinner; and then, instead of walking home, which would have bestirred you a little, you step into your carriage. How absurd to suppose that all this carelessness can be reconcilable with health, without my interposition!

MR. F.

I am convinced now of the justness of Poor Richard's remark, that "Our debts and our sins are always greater than we think for."

THE GOUT

So it is. You philosophers are sages in your maxims, and fools in your conduct.

MR. F.

But do you charge among my crimes that I return in a carriage from M. Brillon's?

THE GOUT

Certainly; for having been seated all the while, you cannot object the fatigue of the day, and cannot want therefore the relief of a carriage.

MR. F.

What then would you have me do with my carriage?

THE GOUT

Burn it if you choose; you would at least get heat out of it once in this way; or if you dislike that proposal, here's another for you; observe the poor peasants who work in the vineyards and grounds about the villages of Passy, Auteuil, Chaillot, etc.; you may find every day among these deserving creatures four or five old men and women, bent and perhaps crippled by weight of years, and too long and too great labour. After a most fatiguing day these people have to trudge a mile or two to their smoky huts. Order your coachman to set them down. This is an act that will be good for your soul; and, at the same time, after your visit to the Brillons, if you return on foot, that will be good for your body.

MR. F.

Ah! how tiresome you are!

THE GOUT

Well, then, to my office; it should not be forgotten that I am your physician. There.

MR. F.

Ohhh! what a devil of a physician!

THE GOUT

How ungrateful you are to say so! Is it not I who, in the character of your physician, have saved you from the palsy, dropsy, and apoplexy? One or other of which would have done for you long ago but for me.

MR. F.

I submit, and thank you for the past, but entreat the discontinuance of your visits for the future; for in my mind, one had better die than be cured so dolefully. Permit me just to hint that I have also not been unfriendly to *you*. I never feed physician or quack of any kind, to enter the list against you; if then you do not leave me to my repose, it may be said you are ungrateful too.

THE GOUT

I can scarcely acknowledge that as any objection. As to quacks, I despise them; they may kill you indeed, but cannot injure me. And as to regular physicians, they are at last convinced that the gout, in such a subject as you are, is no disease, but a remedy; and wherefore cure a remedy?—but to our business—there.

MR. F.

Oh! oh!—for Heaven's sake leave me! and I promise faithfully never more to play at chess, but to take exercise daily, and live temperately.

THE GOUT

I know you too well. You promise fair; but, after a few months of good health, you will return to your old habits; your fine promises will be forgotten like the forms of the last year's clouds. Let us then finish the account, and I will go. But I leave you with an assurance of visiting you again at a proper time and place; for my object is your good, and you are sensible now that I am your *real friend*.

The Handsome and the Deformed Leg

There are two Sorts of People in the World, who with equal Degrees of Health & Wealth and the other Comforts of Life, become, the one happy, the other unhappy. This arises very much from the different Views in which they consider Things, Persons, and Events; and the Effect of those different Views upon their own Minds.

In whatever Situation Men can be plac'd, they may find Conveniencies and Inconveniencies: In whatever Company, they may find Persons & Conversations more or less pleasing: At whatever Table they may meet with Meats and Drinks of better and worse Taste, Dishes better and worse dress'd: In whatever Climate they will find good and bad Weather: Under whatever Government, they may find good and bad Laws, and good and bad Administration of those Laws: In every Poem or Work of Genius, they may see Faults and Beauties: In almost every Face & every Person, they may discover fine Features and Defects, good & bad Qualities. Under these Circumstances, the two Sorts of People above-mention'd fix their Attention, those who are to be happy, on the Conveniencies of Things, the pleasant Parts of Conversation, the well-dress'd & well-tasted Dishes, the Goodness of the Wines, the Fine Weather, &c. &c. &c. and enjoy all with Chearfulness: Those who are to be unhappy think and speak only of the contraries. Hence they are continually discontented themselves, and by their Remarks sour the Pleasures of Society, offend personally many People, and make themselves every where disagreable.

If this Turn of Mind was founded in Nature, such unhappy Persons would be the more to be pitied. But as the Disposition to criticise and be disgusted is perhaps taken up originally by Imitation, and unawares grown into a Habit, which tho at present strong, may nevertheless be cured, when those who have it are convinc'd of its bad Effects on their Felicity, I hope this little Admonition may be of Service to them, and put them on changing a Habit, which tho in the Exercise is chiefly an Act of Imagination, yet it has serious Consequences in Life, as it brings on real Griefs and Misfortunes: For, as many are offended by, and nobody well loves this sort of People, no one shows them more than the most common Civility & Respect, and scarcely that; and this frequently puts them out of humour, and draws them into Disputes and Contentions. If they aim at obtaining some Advantage in Rank or Fortune, nobody wishes them Success, or will stir a Step, or speak a Word to favour their Pretensions. If they incur public Censure or Disgrace, no one will defend or excuse, and many join to aggravate their Misconduct, and render them compleatly odious. —

If these People will not change this bad Habit, and condescend to be pleas'd with what is pleasing, without fretting themselves and others about the Contraries, it is good for others to avoid an Acquaintance with them, which is always disagreable, and sometimes very inconvenient, particularly when one finds one's self entangled in their Quarrels. An old philosophical Friend of mine was grown from Experience very cautious in this particular and carefully shun'd any intimacy with such People. He had, like other Philosophers, a Thermometer to show him the Heat of the Weather, & a Barometer to mark when it was likely to prove good or bad; but there being no Instrument yet invented to discover at first Sight this unpleasing Disposition in a Person, he for that purpose made use of his Legs; one of which was remarkably handsome, the other by some Accident crooked and deform'd. If a Stranger, at the first Interview, regarded his ugly

Leg more than his handsome one, he doubted him. If he spoke of it, and took no Notice of the handsome Leg, that was sufficient to determine my Philosopher to have no farther Acquaintance with him.

Everybody has not this two-legged Instrument, but everyone with a little Attention may observe Signs of that carping fault-finding Disposition; and take the same Resolution of avoiding the Acquaintance of those infected with it.

I therefore advise these critical, querulous, discontented unhappy People, that if they wish to be loved & respected by others and happy in themselves, they should *leave off looking at the ugly Leg*.

November, 1780

To the Royal Academy of * * * * *

GENTLEMEN,

I have perused your late mathematical Prize Question, proposed in lieu of one in Natural Philosophy, for the ensuing year, viz. *"Une figure quelconque donnée, on demande d'y inscrire le plus grand nombre de fois possible une autre figure pluspetite quelconque, qui est aussi donnée"*. I was glad to find by these following Words, *"l'Académie a jugé que cette découverte, en étendant les bornes de nos connoissances, ne seroit pas sans UTILITÉ"*, that you esteem *Utility* an essential Point in your Enquiries, which has not always been the case with all Academies; and I conclude therefore that you have given this Question instead of a philosophical, or as the Learned express it, a physical one, because you could not at the time think of a physical one that promis'd greater *Utility*.

Permit me then humbly to propose one of that sort for your consideration, and through you, if you approve it, for the serious Enquiry of learned Physicians, Chemists, &c. of this enlightened Age.

It is universally well known, That in digesting our common Food, there is created or produced in the Bowels of human Creatures, a great Quantity of Wind.

That the permitting this Air to escape and mix with the Atmosphere, is usually offensive to the Company, from the fetid Smell that accompanies it.

That all well-bred People therefore, to avoid giving such Offence, forcibly restrain the Efforts of Nature to discharge that Wind.

That so retain'd contrary to Nature, it not only gives frequently great present Pain, but occasions future Diseases, such as habitual Cholics, Ruptures, Tympanies, &c. often destructive of the Constitution, & sometimes of Life itself.

Were it not for the odiously offensive Smell accompanying such Escapes, polite People would probably be under no more Restraint in discharging such Wind in Company, than they are in spitting, or in blowing their Noses.

My Prize Question therefore should be, *To discover some Drug wholesome & not disagreable, to be mix'd with our common Food, or Sauces, that shall render the natural Discharges of Wind from our Bodies, not only inoffensive, but agreable as Perfumes.*

That this is not a chimerical Project, and altogether impossible, may appear from these Considerations. That we already have some Knowledge of Means capable of *Varying* that Smell. He that dines on stale Flesh, especially with much Addition of Onions, shall be able to afford a Stink that no Company can tolerate; while he that has lived for some Time on Vegetables only, shall have that Breath so pure as to be insensible to the most delicate Noses; and if he can manage so as to avoid the Report, he may any where give Vent to his Griefs, unnoticed. But as there are many to whom an entire Vegetable Diet would be inconvenient, and as a little Quick-Lime thrown into a Jakes will correct the amazing Quantity of fetid Air arising from the vast Mass of putrid Matter contain'd in such Places, and render it rather pleasing to the Smell, who knows but that a little Powder of Lime (or some other thing equivalent) taken in our Food, or perhaps a Glass of Limewater drank at Dinner, may have the same Effect on the Air produc'd in and issuing from our Bowels? This is worth the Experiment. Certain it is also that we have the Power of changing by slight Means the Smell of another Discharge, that of our Water. A few Stems of Asparagus eaten, shall give our Urine a disagreable Odour; and a Pill of

Turpentine no bigger than a Pea, shall bestow on it the pleasing Smell of Violets. And why should it be thought more impossible in Nature, to find Means of making a Perfume of our *Wind* than of our *Water*?

For the Encouragement of this Enquiry, (from the immortal Honour to be reasonably expected by the Inventor) let it be considered of how small Importance to Mankind, or to how small a Part of Mankind have been useful those Discoveries in Science that have heretofore made Philosophers famous. Are there twenty Men in Europe at this Day, the happier, or even the easier, for any Knowledge they have pick'd out of Aristotle? What Comfort can the Vortices of Descartes give to a Man who has Whirlwinds in his Bowels! The Knowledge of Newton's mutual *Attraction* of the Particles of Matter, can it afford Ease to him who is rack'd by their mutual *Repulsion*, and the cruel Distensions it occasions? The Pleasure arising to a few Philosophers, from seeing, a few Times in their Life, the Threads of Light untwisted, and separated by the Newtonian Prism into seven Colours, can it be compared with the Ease and Comfort every Man living might feel seven times a Day, by discharging freely the Wind from his Bowels? Especially if it be converted into a Perfume: For the Pleasures of one Sense being little inferior to those of another, instead of pleasing the *Sight* he might delight the *Smell* of those about him, & make Numbers happy, which to a benevolent Mind must afford infinite Satisfaction. The generous Soul, who now endeavours to find out whether the Friends he entertains like best Claret or Burgundy, Champagne or Madeira, would then enquire also whether they chose Musk or Lilly, Rose or Bergamot, and provide accordingly. And surely such a Liberty of *Ex-pressing* one's *Scent-iments*, and *pleasing one another*, is of infinitely more Importance to human Happiness than that Liberty of the *Press*, or of *abusing one another*, which the English are so ready to fight & die for.—In short, this Invention, if compleated, would be, as *Bacon* expresses it, *bringing Philosophy home to Mens Business and Bosoms*. And I cannot but conclude, that in Comparison therewith, for *universal* and *continual UTILITY*, the Science of the Philosophers abovementioned, even with the Addition, Gentlemen, of your

"Figure quelconque" and the Figures inscrib'd in it, are, all together, scarcely worth a

FART-HING.

Passy, c. 1781

Notes for Conversation

To make a Peace durable, what may give Occasion for future Wars should if practicable be removed.

The Territory of the United States and that of Canada, by long extended Frontiers, touch each other.

The Settlers on the Frontiers of the American Provinces are generally the most disorderly of the People, who, being far removed from the Eye and Controll of their respective Governments, are more bold in committing Offences against Neighbours, and are for ever occasioning Complaints and furnishing Matter for fresh Differences between their States.

By the late Debates in Parliament, and publick Writings, it appears, that Britain desires a *Reconciliation* with the Americans. It is a sweet Word. It means much more than a mere Peace, and what is heartily to be wish'd for. Nations make a Peace whenever they are both weary of making War. But, if one of them has made War upon the other unjustly, and has wantonly and unnecessarily done it great Injuries, and refuses Reparation, though there may, for the present, be Peace, the Resentment of those Injuries will remain, and will break out again in Vengence when Occasions offer. These Occasions will be watch'd for by one side, fear'd by the other, and the Peace will never be secure; nor can any Cordiality subsist between them.

Many Houses and Villages have been burnt in America by the English and their Allies, the Indians. I do not know that the Americans will insist on reparation; perhaps they may. But would it not be better for England to offer it? Nothing could have a greater Tendency to conciliate, and much of the future Commerce and returning Intercourse between the two Countries may depend on the Reconciliation. Would not the advantage of Reconciliation by such means be greater than the Expence?

If then a Way can be proposed, which may tend to efface

the Memory of Injuries, at the same time that it takes away the Occasions of fresh Quarrel and Mischief, will it not be worth considering, especially if it can be done, not only without Expence, but be a means of saving?

Britain possesses Canada. Her chief Advantage from that Possession consists in the Trade for Peltry. Her Expences in governing and defending that Settlement must be considerable. It might be humiliating to her to give it up on the Demand of America. Perhaps America will not demand it; some of her political Rulers may consider the fear of such a Neighbour, as a means of keeping 13 States more united among themselves, and more attentive to Military Discipline. But on the Minds of the People in general would it not have an excellent Effect, if Britain should voluntarily offer to give up this Province; tho' on these Conditions, that she shall in all times coming have and enjoy the Right of Free Trade thither, unincumbred with any Duties whatsoever; that so much of the vacant Lands there shall be sold, as will raise a Sum sufficient to pay for the Houses burnt by the British Troops and their Indians; and also to indemnify the Royalists for the Confiscation of their Estates?

This is mere Conversation matter between Mr. O. and Mr. F., as the former is not impower'd to make Propositions, and the latter cannot make any without the Concurrence of his Colleagues.

April 18, 1782

Numb. 705.

Supplement to the Boston Independent Chronicle

BOSTON, March 12.

Extract of a Letter from Capt. Gerrish, *of the* New-England *Militia, dated* Albany, March 7.

——The Peltry taken in the Expedition [*See the Account of the Expedition to* Oswegatchie *on the River St.* Laurence, *in our Paper of the 1st Instant.*] will as you see amount to a good deal of Money. The Possession of this Booty at first gave us Pleasure; but we were struck with Horror to find among the Packages, 8 large ones containing SCALPS of our unhappy Country-folks, taken in the three last Years by the Senneka Indians from the Inhabitants of the Frontiers of New-York, New-Jersey, Pennsylvania, and Virginia, and sent by them as a Present to Col. Haldimand, Governor of Canada, in order to be by him transmitted to England. They were accompanied by the following curious Letter to that Gentleman.

May it please your Excellency,   *Teoga, Jan.* 3*d,* 1782.
    "At the Request of the Senneka Chiefs I send herewith to your Excellency, under the Care of James Boyd, eight Packs of Scalps, cured, dried, hooped and painted, with all the Indian triumphal Marks, of which the following is Invoice and Explanation.

No. 1. Containing 43 Scalps of Congress Soldiers killed in different Skirmishes; these are stretched on black Hoops, 4 Inches diameter; the inside of the Skin painted red, with a small black Spot to note their being killed with Bullets. Also 62 of Farmers, killed in their Houses; the Hoops red; the Skin painted brown, and marked with a Hoe; a black Circle all round, to denote their being surprised in the Night; and a black Hatchet in the Middle, signifying their being killed with that Weapon.

No. 2. Containing 98 of Farmers killed in their Houses; Hoops red; Figure of a Hoe, to mark their Profession; great white Circle and Sun, to shew they were surprised in the Day-time; a little red Foot, to shew they stood upon their Defence, and died fighting for their Lives and Families.

No. 3. Containing 97 of Farmers; Hoops green, to shew they were killed in their Fields; a large white Circle with a little round Mark on it for the Sun, to shew that it was in the Day-time; black Bullet-mark on some, Hatchet on others.

No. 4. Containing 102 of Farmers, mixed of the several Marks above; only 18 marked with a little yellow Flame, to denote their being of Prisoners burnt alive, after being scalped, their Nails pulled out by the Roots, and other

Torments: one of these latter supposed to be of a rebel Clergyman, his Band being fixed to the Hoop of his Scalp. Most of the Farmers appear by the Hair to have been young or middle-aged Men; there being but 67 very grey Heads among them all; which makes the Service more essential.

No. 5. Containing 88 Scalps of Women; Hair long, braided in the Indian Fashion, to shew they were Mothers; Hoops blue; Skin yellow Ground, with little red Tadpoles to represent, by way of Triumph, the Tears or Grief occasioned to their Relations; a black scalping Knife or Hatchet at the Bottom, to mark their being killed with those Instruments. 17 others, Hair very grey; black Hoops; plain brown Colour; no Mark but the short Club or Cassetete, to shew they were knocked down dead, or had their Brains beat out.

No. 6. Containing 193 Boys' Scalps, of various Ages; small green Hoops; whitish Ground on the Skin, with red Tears in the Middle, and black Bullet-marks, Knife, Hatchet, or Club, as their Deaths happened.

No. 7. 211 Girls' Scalps, big and little; small yellow Hoops; white Ground; Tears; Hatchet, Club, scalping Knife, &c.

No. 8. This Package is a Mixture of all the Varieties abovemention'd, to the Number of 122; with a Box of Birch Bark, containing 29 little Infants' Scalps of various Sizes; small white Hoops; white Ground; no Tears; and only a little black Knife in the Middle, to shew they were ript out of their Mothers' Bellies.

With these Packs, the Chiefs send to your Excellency the following Speech, delivered by Conejogatchie in Council, interpreted by the elder Moore, the Trader, and taken down by me in Writing.

Father,

We send you herewith many Scalps, that you may see we are not idle Friends.

A blue Belt.

Father,

We wish you to send these Scalps over the Water to the great King, that he may regard them and be refreshed; and that he may see our faithfulness in destroying his Enemies, and be convinced that his Presents have not been made to ungrateful people.

A blue and white Belt with red Tassels.

Father,

Attend to what I am now going to say: it is a Matter of much Weight. The great King's Enemies are many, and they grow fast in Number. They were formerly like young Panthers: they could neither bite nor scratch: we could play with them safely: we feared nothing they could do to us. But now their Bodies are become big as the Elk, and strong as the Buffalo: they have also got great and sharp Claws. They have driven us out of our Country for taking Part in your Quarrel. We expect the great King will give us another Country, that our Children may live after us, and be his Friends and Children, as we are. Say this for us to the great King. To enforce it we give this Belt.

A great white Belt with blue Tassels.

Father,

We have only to say farther that your Traders exact more than ever for their Goods: and our Hunting is lessened by the War, so that we have fewer Skins to give for them. This ruins us. Think of some Remedy. We are poor: and you have Plenty of every Thing. We know you will send us Powder and Guns, and Knives and Hatchets: but we also want Shirts and Blankets.

A little white Belt.

I do not doubt but that your Excellency will think it proper to give some farther Encouragement to those honest People. The high Prices they complain of, are the necessary Effect of the War. Whatever Presents may be sent for them through my Hands, shall be distributed with Prudence and Fidelity. I have the Honour of being

> Your Excellency's most obedient
> And most humble Servant,
> JAMES CRAUFURD."

It was at first proposed to bury these Scalps: but Lieutenant Fitzgerald, who you know has got Leave of Absence to go for Ireland on his private Affairs, said he thought it better they should proceed to their Destination; and if they were given to him, he would undertake to carry them to England, and hang them all up in some dark Night on the Trees in St. James's Park, where they could be seen from the King and Queen's Palaces in the Morning; for that the Sight of them might perhaps strike Muley Ishmael (as he called him) with some Compunction of Conscience. They were accordingly delivered to Fitz, and he has brought them safe hither. To-morrow they go with his Baggage in a Waggon for Boston, and will probably be there in a few Days after this Letter.

I am, &c.
SAMUEL GERRISH.

BOSTON, March 20.

Monday last arrived here Lieutenant Fitzgerald abovementioned, and Yesterday the Waggon with the Scalps. Thousands of People are flocking to see them this Morning, and all Mouths are full of Execrations. Fixing them to the Trees is not approved. It is now proposed to make them up in decent little Packets, seal and direct them; one to the King, containing a Sample of every Sort for his Museum; one to the Queen, with some of Women and little Children: the Rest to be distributed among both Houses of Parliament; a double Quantity to the Bishops.

Mr. Willis,

Please to insert in your useful Paper the following Copy of a Letter, from Commodore Jones, directed

To Sir Joseph York, Ambassador from the King of England to the States-general of the United Provinces.

Ipswich, New-England,
Sir,   *March* 7, 1781.

I have lately seen a memorial, said to have been presented by your Excellency to their High Mightinesses the States-general, in which you are pleased to qualify me with the title of *pirate*.

A pirate is defined to be *hostis humani generis*, [an enemy to all mankind]. It happens, Sir, that I am an enemy to no part of mankind, except your nation, the English; which nation at the same time comes much more within the definition; being actually an enemy to, and at war with, one whole quarter of the world, America, considerable parts of Asia and Africa, a great part of Europe, and in a fair way of being at war with the rest.

A pirate makes war for the sake of *rapine*. This is not the kind of war I am engaged in against England. Our's is a war in defence of *liberty* . . . . the most just of all wars; and of our *properties*, which your nation would have taken from us, without our consent, in violation of our rights, and by an armed force. Your's, therefore, is a war of *rapine*; of course, a piratical war: and those who approve of it, and are engaged in it, more justly deserve the name of pirates, which you bestow on me. It is, indeed, a war that coincides with the general spirit of your nation. Your common people in their ale-houses sing the twenty-four songs of Robin Hood, and applaud his deer-stealing and his robberies on the highway: those who have just learning enough to read, are delighted with your histories of the pirates and of the buccaniers: and even your scholars, in the universities, study Quintus Curtius; and are taught to admire Alexander, for what they call "his conquests in the Indies." Severe laws and the hangmen keep down the effects of this spirit somewhat among yourselves, (though in your little island you have, nevertheless, more highway robberies than there are in all the rest of Europe put together): but a foreign war gives it full scope. It is then that, with infinite pleasure, it lets itself loose to strip of their property honest merchants, employed in the innocent and useful occupation of supplying the mutual wants of mankind. Hence, having lately no war with your ancient enemies, rather than be without a war, you chose to make one upon your friends. In this your piratical war with America, the mariners of your fleets, and the owners of your privateers were animated against us by the act of your parliament, which repealed the law of God—"Thou shalt not steal,"—by declaring it lawful for them to rob us of all our property that they could meet with on the Ocean. This act too had a retrospect, and, going beyond bulls of pardon, declared that all the robberies you *had committed*, previous to the act, should be *deemed just and lawful*. Your soldiers too were promised the plunder of our cities: and your officers were flattered with the division of our lands. You had even the baseness to corrupt

our servants, the sailors employed by us, and encourage them
to rob their masters, and bring to you the ships and goods
they were entrusted with. Is there any society of pirates on
the sea or land, who, in declaring wrong to be right, and
right wrong, have less authority than your parliament? Do
any of them more justly than your parliament deserve the *title*
you bestow on me?

You will tell me that we forfeited all our estates by our
refusal to pay the taxes your nation would have imposed on
us, without the consent of our colony parliaments. Have you
then forgot the incontestible principle, which was the foundation of Hambden's glorious lawsuit with Charles the first,
that " what an English king has no right to demand, an English subject has a right to refuse?" But you cannot so soon
have forgotten the instructions of your late honourable father,
who, being himself a sound Whig, taught you certainly the
principles of the Revolution, and that, "if subjects might in
some cases forfeit their property, kings also might forfeit their
title, and all claim to the allegiance of their subjects." I must
then suppose you well acquainted with those Whig principles,
on which permit me, Sir, to ask a few questions.

Is not protection as justly due from a king to his people, as
obedience from the people to their king?

If then a king declares his people to be out of his protection:

If he violates and deprives them of their constitutional rights:

If he wages war against them:

If he plunders their merchants, ravages their coasts, burns
their towns, and destroys their lives:

If he hires foreign mercenaries to help him in their destruction:

If he engages savages to murder their defenceless farmers,
women, and children:

If he cruelly forces such of his subjects as fall into his hands,
to bear arms against their country, and become executioners
of their friends and brethren:

If he sells others of them into bondage, in Africa and the
East Indies:

If he excites domestic insurrections among their servants,
and encourages servants to murder their masters:——

Does not so atrocious a conduct towards his subjects, dissolve their allegiance?

If not,—please to say how or by what means it can possibly be dissolved?

All this horrible wickedness and barbarity has been and daily is practised by the king *your master* (as you call him in your memorial) upon the Americans, whom he is still pleased to claim as his subjects.

During these six years past, he has destroyed not less than forty thousand of those subjects, by battles on land or sea, or by starving them, or poisoning them to death, in the unwholesome air, with the unwholesome food of his prisons. And he has wasted the lives of at least an equal number of his own soldiers and sailors: many of whom have been *forced* into this odious service, and *dragged* from their families and friends, by the outrageous violence of his illegal press-gangs. You are a gentleman of letters, and have read history: do you recollect any instance of any tyrant, since the beginning of the world, who, in the course of so few years, had done so much mischief, by murdering so many of his own people? Let us view one of the worst and blackest of them, Nero. He put to death a few of his courtiers, placemen, and pensioners, and among the rest his *tutor*. Had George the third done the same, and no more, his crime, though detestable, as an act of lawless power, might have been as useful to his nation, as that of Nero was hurtful to Rome; considering the different characters and merits of the sufferers. Nero indeed wished that the people of Rome had but one neck, that he might behead them all by one stroke: but this was a simple wish. George is carrying the wish as fast as he can into execution; and, by continuing in his present course a few years longer, will have destroyed more of the British people than Nero could have found inhabitants in Rome. Hence, the expression of Milton, in speaking of Charles the first, that he was *"Nerone Neronior,"* is still more applicable to George the third. Like Nero and all other tyrants, while they lived, he indeed has his flatterers, his addressers, his applauders. Pensions, places, and hopes of preferment, can bribe even bishops to approve his conduct: but, when those fulsome, purchased addresses and panegyrics are sunk and lost in oblivion or contempt, impartial history will step forth, speak honest truth, and rank him among public calamities. The only difference will be, that plagues, pestilences, and famines are of this world, and arise from the nature of things: but voluntary malice, mischief, and murder are all from Hell: and this King will, therefore, stand foremost in the list of diabolical, bloody, and execrable tyrants. His base-bought parliaments too, who sell him their souls, and extort from the people the money with which they aid his destructive purposes, as they share his guilt, will share his infamy,—parliaments, who to please him, have repeatedly, by different votes year after year, dipped their hands in human blood, insomuch that methinks I see it dried and caked so thick upon them, that if they could wash it off in the Thames which flows under their windows, the whole river would run red to the Ocean.

One is provoked by enormous wickedness: but one is ashamed and humiliated at the view of human baseness. It afflicts me, therefore, to see a gentleman of Sir Joseph York's education and talents, for the sake of a red riband and a paltry stipend, mean enough to stile such a monster *his master*, wear his livery, and hold himself ready at his command even to cut the throats of fellow-subjects. This makes it impossible for me to end my letter with the civility of a compliment, and obliges me to subscribe myself simply,

JOHN PAUL JONES,
whom you are pleased to stile a *Pirate*.

Passy, April, 1782

Articles for a Treaty of Peace with Madame Brillon

Passy, July 27.

What a difference, my dear Friend, between you and me!— You find my Faults so many as to be innumerable, while I can see but one in you; and perhaps that is the Fault of my Spectacles.—The Fault I mean is that kind of Covetousness, by which you would engross all my Affection, and permit me none for the other amiable Ladies of your Country. You seem to imagine that it cannot be divided without being diminish'd: In which you mistake the nature of the Thing and forget the Situation in which you have plac'd and hold me. You renounce and exclude arbitrarily every thing corporal from our Amour, except such a merely civil Embrace now and then as you would permit to a country Cousin,— what is there then remaining that I may not afford to others without a Diminution of what belongs to you? The Operations of the Mind, Esteem, Admiration, Respect, & even Affection for one Object, may be multiply'd as more Objects that merit them present themselves, and yet remain the same to the first, which therefore has no room to complain of Injury. They are in their Nature as divisible as the sweet Sounds of the Forte Piano produc'd by your exquisite Skill: Twenty People may receive the same Pleasure from them, without lessening that which you kindly intend for me; and I might as reasonably require of your Friendship, that they should reach and delight no Ears but mine.

You see by this time how unjust you are in your Demands, and in the open War you declare against me if I do not comply with them. Indeed it is I that have the most Reason to complain. My poor little Boy, whom you ought methinks to have cherish'd, instead of being fat and Jolly like those in your elegant Drawings, is meagre and starv'd almost to death for want of the substantial Nourishment which you his Mother inhumanly deny him, and yet would now clip his little Wings to prevent his seeking it elsewhere!—

I fancy we shall neither of us get any thing by this War, and therefore as feeling my self the Weakest, I will do what indeed ought always to be done by the Wisest, be first in making the Propositions for Peace. That a Peace may be lasting, the Articles of the Treaty should be regulated upon the Principles of the most perfect Equity & Reciprocity. In this View I have drawn up & offer the following, viz.—

Article i.

There shall be eternal Peace, Friendship & Love, between Madame B. and Mr F.

ARTICLE 2.

In order to maintain the same inviolably, Made B. on her Part stipulates and agrees, that Mr F. shall come to her whenever she sends for him.

ART. 3.

That he shall stay with her as long as she pleases.

ART. 4.

That when he is with her, he shall be oblig'd to drink Tea, play Chess, hear Musick; or do any other thing that she requires of him.

ART. 5.

And that he shall love no other Woman but herself.

ART. 6.

And the said Mr F. on his part stipulates and agrees, that he will go away from M. B.'s whenever he pleases.

ART. 7.

That he will stay away as long as he pleases.

ART. 8.

That when he is with her, he will do what he pleases.

ART. 9.

And that he will love any other Woman as far as he finds her amiable.

Let me know what you think of these Preliminaries. To me they seem to express the true Meaning and Intention of each Party more plainly than most Treaties.—I shall insist pretty strongly on the eighth Article, tho' without much Hope of your Consent to it; and on the ninth also, tho I despair of ever finding any other Woman that I could love with equal Tenderness: being ever, my dear dear Friend,

                                        Yours most sincerely

Apologue

Lion, king of a certain forest, had among his subjects a body of faithful dogs, in principle and affection strongly attached to his person and government, but through whose assistance he had extended his dominions, and had become the terror of his enemies.

Lion, however, influenced by evil counsellors, took an aversion to the dogs, condemned them unheard, and ordered his tigers, leopards, and panthers to attack and destroy them.

The dogs petitioned humbly, but their petitions were rejected haughtily; and they were forced to defend themselves, which they did with bravery.

A few among them, of a mongrel race, derived from a mixture with wolves and foxes, corrupted by royal promises of great rewards, deserted the honest dogs and joined their enemies.

The dogs were finally victorious: a treaty of peace was made, in which Lion acknowledged them to be free, and disclaimed all future authority over them.

The mongrels not being permitted to return among them, claimed of the royalists the reward that had been promised.

A council of the beasts was held to consider their demand.

The wolves and the foxes agreed unanimously that the demand was just, that royal promises ought to be kept, and that every loyal subject should contribute freely to enable his majesty to fulfil them.

The horse alone, with a boldness and freedom that became the nobleness of his nature, delivered a contrary opinion.

"The King," said he, "has been misled, by bad ministers, to war unjustly upon his faithful subjects. Royal promises, when made to encourage us to act for the public good, should indeed be honourably acquitted; but if to encourage us to betray and destroy each other, they are wicked and void from the beginning. The advisers of such promises, and those who murdered in consequence of them, instead of being recompensed, should be severely punished. Consider how greatly our common strength is already diminished by our loss of the dogs. If you enable the King to reward those fratricides, you will establish a precedent that may justify a future tyrant to make like promises; and every example of such an unnatural brute rewarded will give them additional weight. Horses and bulls, as well as dogs, may thus be divided against their own kind, and civil wars produced at pleasure, till we are so weakened that neither liberty nor safety is any longer to be found in the forest, and nothing remains but abject submission to the will of a despot, who may devour us as he pleases."

The council had sense enough to resolve—that the demand be rejected.

c. November, 1782

Remarks Concerning the Savages
of North-America

Savages we call them, because their manners differ from ours, which we think the Perfection of Civility; they think the same of theirs.

Perhaps if we could examine the manners of different Nations with Impartiality, we should find no People so rude as to be without any Rules of Politeness; nor any so polite as not to have some remains of Rudeness.

The Indian Men, when young, are Hunters and Warriors; when old, Counsellors; for all their Government is by the Counsel or Advice of the Sages; there is no Force, there are no Prisons, no Officers to compel Obedience, or inflict Punishment. Hence they generally study Oratory; the best Speaker having the most Influence. The Indian Women till the Ground, dress the Food, nurse and bring up the Children, and preserve and hand down to Posterity the Memory of Public Transactions. These Employments of Men and Women are accounted natural and honorable. Having few Artificial Wants, they have abundance of Leisure for Improvement by Conversation. Our laborious manner of Life compared with theirs, they esteem slavish and base; and the Learning on which we value ourselves; they regard as frivolous and useless. An Instance of this occurred at the Treaty of Lancaster in Pennsylvania, Anno 1744, between the Government of Virginia & the Six Nations. After the principal Business was settled, the Commissioners from Virginia acquainted the Indians by a Speech, that there was at Williamsburg a College with a Fund for Educating Indian Youth, and that if the Chiefs of the Six-Nations would send down half a dozen of their Sons to that College, the Government would take Care that they should be well provided for, and instructed in all the Learning of the white People. It is one of the Indian Rules of Politeness not to answer a public Proposition the same day that it is made; they think it would be treating it as a light Matter; and that they show it Respect by taking time to consider it, as of a Matter important. They therefore deferred their Answer till the day following; when their Speaker began by

expressing their deep Sense of the Kindness of the Virginia
Government, in making them that Offer; for we know, says
he, that you highly esteem the kind of Learning taught in
those Colleges, and that the Maintenance of our Young Men
while with you, would be very expensive to you. We are convinced therefore that you mean to do us good by your Proposal, and we thank you heartily. But you who are wise must
know, that different Nations have different Conceptions of
things; and you will therefore not take it amiss, if our Ideas
of this Kind of Education happen not to be the same with
yours. We have had some Experience of it: Several of our
Young People were formerly brought up at the Colleges of
the Northern Provinces; they were instructed in all your Sciences; but when they came back to us, they were bad Run-
ners, ignorant of every means of living in the Woods, unable
to bear either Cold or Hunger, knew neither how to build a
Cabin, take a Deer, or kill an Enemy, spoke our Language
imperfectly; were therefore neither fit for Hunters, Warriors,
or Counsellors; they were totally good for nothing. We are
however not the less obliged by your kind Offer, tho' we decline accepting it; and to show our grateful Sense of it, if the
Gentlemen of Virginia will send us a dozen of their Sons, we
will take great Care of their Education, instruct them in all
we know, and make *Men* of them.

Having frequent Occasions to hold public Councils, they
have acquired great Order and Decency in conducting them.
The old Men sit in the foremost Ranks, the Warriors in the
next, and the Women and Children in the hindmost. The
Business of the Women is to take exact notice of what passes,
imprint it in their Memories, for they have no Writing, and
communicate it to their Children. They are the Records of
the Council, and they preserve Tradition of the Stipulations
in Treaties a hundred Years back, which when we compare
with our Writings we always find exact. He that would speak,
rises. The rest observe a profound Silence. When he has finished and sits down, they leave him five or six Minutes to
recollect, that if he has omitted any thing he intended to say,
or has any thing to add, he may rise again and deliver it. To
interrupt another, even in common Conversation, is reckoned
highly indecent. How different this is from the Conduct of a

polite British House of Commons, where scarce a Day passes without some Confusion that makes the Speaker hoarse in calling *to order*; and how different from the mode of Conversation in many polite Companies of Europe, where if you do not deliver your Sentence with great Rapidity, you are cut off in the middle of it by the impatient Loquacity of those you converse with, & never suffer'd to finish it.

The Politeness of these Savages in Conversation is indeed carried to excess, since it does not permit them to contradict, or deny the Truth of what is asserted in their Presence. By this means they indeed avoid Disputes, but then it becomes difficult to know their Minds, or what Impression you make upon them. The Missionaries who have attempted to convert them to Christianity, all complain of this as one of the great Difficulties of their Mission. The Indians hear with Patience the Truths of the Gospel explained to them, and give their usual Tokens of Assent and Approbation: you would think they were convinced. No such Matter. It is mere Civility.

A Suedish Minister having assembled the Chiefs of the Sasquehanah Indians, made a Sermon to them, acquainting them with the principal historical Facts on which our Religion is founded, such as the Fall of our first Parents by Eating an Apple, the Coming of Christ to repair the Mischief, his Miracles and Suffering, &c. When he had finished, an Indian Orator stood up to thank him. What you have told us, says he, is all very good. It is indeed bad to eat Apples. It is better to make them all into Cyder. We are much obliged by your Kindness in coming so far to tell us those things which you have heard from your Mothers. In Return I will tell you some of those we have heard from ours.

In the Beginning our Fathers had only the Flesh of Animals to subsist on, and if their Hunting was unsuccessful, they were starving. Two of our young Hunters having killed a Deer, made a Fire in the Woods to broil some Parts of it. When they were about to satisfy their Hunger, they beheld a beautiful young Woman descend from the Clouds, and seat herself on that Hill which you see yonder among the blue Mountains. They said to each other, it is a Spirit that perhaps has smelt our broiling Venison, & wishes to eat of it: let us offer some to her. They presented her with the Tongue: She was pleased with the Taste of it, & said, your Kindness shall be rewarded. Come to this Place after thirteen Moons, and you shall find something that will be of great Benefit in nourishing you and your Children to the latest Generations. They did so, and to their Surprise found Plants they had never seen before, but which from that ancient time have been constantly cultivated among us to our great Advantage. Where her right Hand had touch'd the Ground, they found Maize; where her left Hand had touch'd it, they found Kidney-beans; and where her Backside had sat on it, they found Tobacco. The good Missionary, disgusted with this idle Tale, said, what I delivered to you were sacred Truths; but what you tell me is mere Fable, Fiction & Falsehood. The Indian offended, reply'd, my Brother, it seems your Friends have not done you Justice in your Education; they have not well instructed you in the Rules of common Civility. You saw that we who understand and practise those Rules, believed all your Stories; why do you refuse to believe ours?

When any of them come into our Towns, our People are apt to croud round them, gaze upon them, and incommode them where they desire to be private; this they esteem great Rudeness, and the Effect of want of Instruction in the Rules of Civility and good Manners. We have, say they, as much Curiosity as you, and when you come into our Towns we wish for Opportunities of looking at you; but for this purpose we hide ourselves behind Bushes where you are to pass, and never intrude ourselves into your Company.

Their Manner of entring one anothers Villages has likewise its Rules. It is reckon'd uncivil in travelling Strangers to enter a Village abruptly, without giving Notice of their Approach. Therefore as soon as they arrive within hearing, they stop and hollow, remaining there till invited to enter. Two old Men usually come out to them, and lead them in. There is in every Village a vacant Dwelling, called the Strangers House. Here they are placed, while the old Men go round from Hut to Hut acquainting the Inhabitants that Strangers are arrived, who are probably hungry and weary; and every one sends them what he can spare of Victuals and Skins to repose on. When the Strangers are refresh'd, Pipes & Tobacco are brought; and then, but not before, Conversation begins, with

Enquiries who they are, whither bound, what News, &c. and it usually ends with Offers of Service, if the Strangers have Occasion of Guides or any Necessaries for continuing their Journey; and nothing is exacted for the Entertainment.

The same Hospitality, esteemed among them as a principal Virtue, is practised by private Persons; of which *Conrad Weiser*, our Interpreter, gave me the following Instance. He had been naturaliz'd among the Six-Nations, and spoke well the Mohock Language. In going thro' the Indian Country, to carry a Message from our Governor to the Council at *Onondaga*, he called at the Habitation of *Canassetego*, an old Acquaintance, who embraced him, spread Furs for him to sit on, placed before him some boiled Beans and Venison, and mixed some Rum and Water for his Drink. When he was well refresh'd, and had lit his Pipe, Canassetego began to converse with him, ask'd how he had fared the many Years since they had seen each other, whence he then came, what occasioned the Journey, &c. &c. Conrad answered all his Questions; and when the Discourse began to flag, the Indian, to continue it, said, Conrad, you have liv'd long among the white People, and know something of their Customs; I have been sometimes at Albany, and have observed that once in seven Days, they shut up their Shops and assemble all in the great House; tell me, what it is for? what do they do there? They meet there, says Conrad, to hear & learn *good things*. I do not doubt, says the Indian, that they tell you so; they have told me the same; but I doubt the Truth of what they say, & I will tell you my Reasons. I went lately to Albany to sell my Skins, & buy Blankets, Knives, Powder, Rum, &c. You know I used generally to deal with Hans Hanson; but I was a little inclined this time to try some other Merchants. However I called first upon Hans, and ask'd him what he would give for Beaver; He said he could not give more than four Shillings a Pound; but, says he, I cannot talk on Business now; this is the Day when we meet together to learn *good things*, and I am going to the Meeting. So I thought to myself since I cannot do any Business to day, I may as well go to the Meeting too; and I went with him. There stood up a Man in black, and began to talk to the People very angrily. I did not understand what he said; but perceiving that he looked much at me, & at Hanson, I imagined he was angry at seeing me there; so I went out, sat down near the House, struck Fire & lit my Pipe; waiting till the Meeting should break up. I thought too, that the Man had mentioned something of Beaver, and I suspected it might be the Subject of their Meeting. So when they came out I accosted any Merchant; well Hans, says I, I hope you have agreed to give more than four Shillings a Pound. No, says he, I cannot give so much. I cannot give more than three Shillings and six Pence. I then spoke to several other Dealers, but they all sung the same Song, three & six Pence, three & six Pence. This made it clear to me that my Suspicion was right; and that whatever they pretended of Meeting to learn *good things*, the real Purpose was to consult, how to cheat Indians in the Price of Beaver. Consider but a little, Conrad, and you must be of my Opinion. If they met so often to learn *good things*, they would certainly have learnt some before this time. But they are still ignorant. You know our Practice. If a white Man in travelling thro' our Country, enters one of our Cabins, we all treat him as I treat you; we dry him if he is wet, we warm him if he is cold, and give him Meat & Drink that he may allay his Thirst and Hunger, & we spread soft Furs for him to rest & sleep on: We demand nothing in return *. But if I go into a white Man's House at Albany, and ask for Victuals & Drink, they say, where is your Money? and if I have none, they say, get out, you Indian Dog. You see they have not yet learnt those little *good things*, that we need no Meetings to be instructed in, because our Mothers taught them to us when we were Children. And therefore it is impossible their Meetings should be as they say for any such purpose, or have any such Effect; they are only to contrive *the Cheating of Indians in the Price of Beaver.*

* *It is remarkable that in all Ages and Countries, Hospitality has been allowed as the Virtue of those, whom the civiliz'd were pleased to call Barbarians; the Greeks celebrated the Scythians for it. The Saracens possess'd it eminently; and it is to this day the reigning Virtue of the wild Arabs. S. Paul too, in the Relation of his Voyage & Shipwreck, on the Island of Melita, says,* The Barbarous People shew'd us no little Kindness; for they kindled a Fire, and received us every one, because of the present Rain & because of the Cold.

Passy, 1783

Information to Those Who Would Remove to America

Many Persons in Europe having directly or by Letters, express'd to the Writer of this, who is well acquainted with North-America, their Desire of transporting and establishing themselves in that Country; but who appear to him to have formed thro' Ignorance, mistaken Ideas & Expectations of what is to be obtained there; he thinks it may be useful, and prevent inconvenient, expensive & fruitless Removals and Voyages of improper Persons, if he gives some clearer & truer Notions of that Part of the World than appear to have hitherto prevailed.

He finds it is imagined by Numbers that the Inhabitants of North-America are rich, capable of rewarding, and dispos'd to reward all sorts of Ingenuity; that they are at the same time ignorant of all the Sciences; & consequently that strangers possessing Talents in the Belles-Letters, fine Arts, &c. must be highly esteemed, and so well paid as to become easily rich themselves; that there are also abundance of profitable Offices to be disposed of, which the Natives are not qualified to fill; and that having few Persons of Family among them, Strangers of Birth must be greatly respected, and of course easily obtain the best of those Offices, which will make all their Fortunes: that the Goverments too, to encourage Emigrations from Europe, not only pay the expence of personal Transportation, but give Lands gratis to Strangers, with Negroes to work for them, Utensils of Husbandry, & Stocks of Cattle. These are all wild Imaginations; and those who go to America with Expectations founded upon them, will surely find themselves disappointed.

The Truth is, that tho' there are in that Country few People so miserable as the Poor of Europe, there are also very few that in Europe would be called rich: it is rather a general happy Mediocrity that prevails. There are few great Proprietors of the Soil, and few Tenants; most People cultivate their own Lands, or follow some Handicraft or Merchandise; very few rich enough to live idly upon their Rents or Incomes; or to pay the high Prices given in Europe, for Paintings, Statues,

Architecture and the other Works of Art that are more curious than useful. Hence the natural Geniuses that have arisen
in America, with such Talents, have uniformly quitted that
Country for Europe, where they can be more suitably rewarded. It is true that Letters and mathematical Knowledge
are in Esteem there, but they are at the same time more common than is apprehended; there being already existing nine
Colleges or Universities, viz. four in New-England, and one
in each of the Provinces of New-York, New-Jersey, Pensilvania, Maryland and Virginia, all furnish'd with learned
Professors; besides a number of smaller Academies: These
educate many of their Youth in the Languages and those Sciences that qualify Men for the Professions of Divinity, Law
or Physick. Strangers indeed are by no means excluded from
exercising those Professions, and the quick Increase of Inhabitants every where gives them a Chance of Employ, which
they have in common with the Natives. Of civil Offices or
Employments there are few; no superfluous Ones as in Europe; and it is a Rule establish'd in some of the States, that
no Office should be so profitable as to make it desirable. The
36 Article of the Constitution of Pensilvania, runs expresly in
these Words: *As every Freeman, to preserve his Independance, (if
he has not a sufficient Estate) ought to have some Profession, Calling, Trade or Farm, whereby he may honestly subsist, there can be
no Necessity for, nor Use in, establishing Offices of Profit; the usual
Effects of which are Dependance and Servility, unbecoming Freemen, in the Possessors and Expectants; Faction, Contention, Corruption, and Disorder among the People. Wherefore whenever an
Office, thro' Increase of Fees or otherwise, becomes so profitable as
to occasion many to apply for it, the Profits ought to be lessened by
the Legislature.*

These Ideas prevailing more or less in all the United States,
it cannot be worth any Man's while, who has a means of Living at home, to expatriate himself in hopes of obtaining a
profitable civil Office in America; and as to military Offices,
they are at an End with the War; the Armies being disbanded.
Much less is it adviseable for a Person to go thither who has
no other Quality to recommend him but his Birth. In Europe
it has indeed its Value, but it is a Commodity that cannot be
carried to a worse Market than to that of America, where

People do not enquire concerning a Stranger, *What is he?* but *What can he do?* If he has any useful Art, he is welcome; and if he exercises it and behaves well, he will be respected by all that know him; but a mere Man of Quality, who on that Account wants to live upon the Public, by some Office or Salary, will be despis'd and disregarded. The Husbandman is in honor there, & even the Mechanic, because their Employments are useful. The People have a Saying, that God Almighty is himself a Mechanic, the greatest in the Universe; and he is respected and admired more for the Variety, Ingenuity and Utility of his Handiworks, than for the Antiquity of his Family. They are pleas'd with the Observation of a Negro, and frequently mention it, that *Boccarorra* (meaning the Whiteman) make de Blackman workee, make de Horse workee, make de Ox workee, make ebery ting workee; only de Hog. He de Hog, no workee; he eat, he drink, he walk about, he go to sleep when he please, *he libb like a Gentleman.* According to these Opinions of the Americans, one of them would think himself more oblig'd to a Genealogist, who could prove for him that his Ancestors & Relations for ten Generations had been Ploughmen, Smiths, Carpenters, Turners, Weavers, Tanners, or even Shoemakers, & consequently that they were useful Members of Society; than if he could only prove that they were Gentlemen, doing nothing of Value, but living idly on the Labour of others, mere *fruges consumere nati**, and otherwise *good* for *nothing*, till by their Death, their Estates like the Carcase of the Negro's Gentleman-Hog, come to be *cut up*.

With Regard to Encouragements for Strangers from Government, they are really only what are derived from good Laws & Liberty. Strangers are welcome because there is room enough for them all, and therefore the old Inhabitants are not jealous of them; the Laws protect them sufficiently, so that they have no need of the Patronage of great Men; and every one will enjoy securely the Profits of his Industry. But if he does not bring a Fortune with him, he must work and be industrious to live. One or two Years Residence give him all the Rights of a Citizen; but the Government does not at

* There are a Number of us born
    Merely to eat up the Corn. WATTS.

present, whatever it may have done in former times, hire People to become Settlers, by Paying their Passages, giving Land, Negroes, Utensils, Stock, or any other kind of Emolument whatsoever. In short America is the Land of Labour, and by no means what the English call *Lubberland*, and the French *Pays de Cocagne*, where the Streets are said to be pav'd with half-peck Loaves, the Houses til'd with Pancakes, and where the Fowls fly about ready roasted, crying, *Come eat me!*

Who then are the kind of Persons to whom an Emigration to America may be advantageous? and what are the Advantages they may reasonably expect?

Land being cheap in that Country, from the vast Forests still void of Inhabitants, and not likely to be occupied in an Age to come, insomuch that the Propriety of an hundred Acres of fertile Soil full of Wood may be obtained near the Frontiers in many Places for eight or ten Guineas, hearty young Labouring Men, who understand the Husbandry of Corn and Cattle, which is nearly the same in that Country as in Europe, may easily establish themselves there. A little Money sav'd of the good Wages they receive there while they work for others, enables them to buy the Land and begin their Plantation, in which they are assisted by the Good Will of their Neighbours and some Credit. Multitudes of poor People from England, Ireland, Scotland and Germany, have by this means in a few Years become wealthy Farmers, who in their own Countries, where all the Lands are fully occupied, and the Wages of Labour low, could never have emerged from the mean Condition wherein they were born.

From the Salubrity of the Air, the Healthiness of the Climate, the Plenty of good Provisions, and the Encouragement to early Marriages, by the certainty of Subsistance in cultivating the Earth, the Increase of Inhabitants by natural Generation is very rapid in America, and becomes still more so by the Accession of Strangers; hence there is a continual Demand for more Artisans of all the necessary and useful kinds, to supply those Cultivators of the Earth with Houses, and with Furniture & Utensils of the grosser Sorts which cannot so well be brought from Europe. Tolerably good Workmen in any of those mechanic Arts, are sure to find Employ, and to be well paid for their Work, there being no Restraints preventing Strangers from exercising any Art they understand, nor any Permission necessary. If they are poor, they begin first as Servants or Journeymen; and if they are sober, industrious & frugal, they soon become Masters, establish themselves in Business, marry, raise Families, and become respectable Citizens.

Also, Persons of moderate Fortunes and Capitals, who having a Number of Children to provide for, are desirous of bringing them up to Industry, and to secure Estates for their Posterity, have Opportunities of doing it in America, which Europe does not afford. There they may be taught & practice profitable mechanic Arts, without incurring Disgrace on that Account; but on the contrary acquiring Respect by such Abilities. There small Capitals laid out in Lands, which daily become more valuable by the Increase of People, afford a solid Prospect of ample Fortunes thereafter for those Children. The Writer of this has known several Instances of large Tracts of Land, bought on what was then the Frontier of Pensilvania, for ten Pounds per hundred Acres, which, after twenty Years, when the Settlements had been extended far beyond them, sold readily, without any Improvement made upon them, for three Pounds per Acre. The Acre in America is the same with the English Acre or the Acre of Normandy.

Those who desire to understand the State of Government in America, would do well to read the Constitutions of the several States, and the Articles of Confederation that bind the whole together for general Purposes under the Direction of one Assembly called the Congress. These Constitutions have been printed by Order of Congress in America; two Editions of them have also been printed in London, and a good Translation of them into French has lately been published at Paris.

Several of the Princes of Europe having of late Years, from an Opinion of Advantage to arise by producing all Commodities & Manufactures within their own Dominions, so as to diminish or render useless their Importations, have endeavoured to entice Workmen from other Countries, by high Salaries, Privileges, &c. Many Persons pretending to be skilled in various great Manufactures, imagining that America must be in Want of them, and that the Congress would probably be dispos'd to imitate the Princes above mentioned, have proposed to go over, on Condition of having their Passages paid, Lands given, Salaries appointed, exclusive Privileges for Terms of Years, &c. Such Persons on reading the Articles of Confederation will find that the Congress have no Power committed to them, or Money put into their Hands, for such purposes; and that if any such Encouragement is given, it must be by the Government of some separate State. This however has rarely been done in America; and when it has been done it has rarely succeeded, so as to establish a Manufacture which the Country was not yet so ripe for as to encourage private Persons to set it up; Labour being generally too dear there, & Hands difficult to be kept together, every one desiring to be a Master, and the Cheapness of Land enclining many to leave Trades for Agriculture. Some indeed have met with Success, and are carried on to Advantage; but they are generally such as require only a few Hands, or wherein great Part of the Work is perform'd by Machines. Goods that are bulky, & of so small Value as not well to bear the Expence of Freight, may often be made cheaper in the Country than they can be imported; and the Manufacture of such Goods will be profitable wherever there is a sufficient Demand. The Farmers in America produce indeed a good deal of Wool & Flax; and none is exported, it is all work'd up; but it is in the Way of Domestic Manufacture for the Use of the Family. The buying up Quantities of Wool & Flax with the Design to employ Spinners, Weavers, &c. and form great Establishments, producing Quantities of Linen and Woollen Goods for Sale, has been several times attempted in different Provinces; but those Projects have generally failed, Goods of equal Value being imported cheaper. And when the Governments have been solicited to support such Schemes by Encouragements, in Money, or by imposing Duties on Importation of such Goods, it has been generally refused, on this Principle, that if the Country is ripe for the Manufacture, it may be carried on by private Persons to Advantage; and if not, it is a Folly to think of forceing Nature. Great Establishments of Manufacture, require great Numbers of Poor to do the Work for small Wages; these Poor are to be found in Europe, but will not be found in America, till the Lands are all taken up and cultivated, and the excess of People who cannot get Land, want Employment. The Manufacture of Silk, they say, is natural in France, as that of Cloth in England, because each Country produces in Plenty the first Material: But if England will have a Manufacture of Silk as well as that of Cloth, and France one of Cloth as well as that of Silk, these unnatural Operations must be supported by mutual Prohibitions or high Duties on the Importation of each others Goods, by which means the Workmen are enabled to tax the home-Consumer by greater Prices, while the higher Wages they receive makes them neither happier nor richer, since they only drink more and work less. Therefore the Governments in America do nothing to encourage such Projects. The People by this Means are not impos'd on, either by the Merchant or Mechanic; if the Merchant demands too much Profit on imported Shoes, they buy of the Shoemaker: and if he asks too high a Price, they take them of the Merchant: thus the two Professions are Checks on each other. The Shoemaker however has on the whole a considerable Profit upon his Labour in America, beyond what he had in Europe, as he can add to his Price a Sum nearly equal to all the Expences of Freight & Commission, Risque or Insurance, &c. necessarily charged by the Merchant. And the Case is the same with the Workmen in every other Mechanic Art. Hence it is that Artisans generally live better and more easily in America than in Europe, and such as are good Œconomists make a comfortable Provision for Age, & for their Children. Such may therefore remove with Advantage to America.

In the old longsettled Countries of Europe, all Arts, Trades, Professions, Farms, &c. are so full that it is difficult for a poor Man who has Children, to place them where they may gain, or learn to gain a decent Livelihood. The Artisans, who fear creating future Rivals in Business, refuse to take Apprentices, but upon Conditions of Money, Maintenance or the like, which the Parents are unable to comply with. Hence the Youth are dragg'd up in Ignorance of every gainful Art, and oblig'd to become Soldiers or Servants or Thieves, for a Subsistence. In America the rapid Increase of Inhabitants takes away that Fear of Rivalship, & Artisans willingly receive Apprentices from the hope of Profit by their Labour during the Remainder of the Time stipulated after they shall be instructed. Hence it is easy for poor Families to get their Children instructed; for the Artisans are so desirous of Apprentices, that many of them will even give Money to the Parents to have Boys from ten to fifteen Years of Age bound Apprentices to them till the Age of twenty one; and many poor Parents have by that means, on their Arrival in the Country, raised Money enough to buy Land sufficient to establish themselves, and to subsist the rest of their Family by Agriculture. These Contracts for Apprentices are made before a Magistrate, who regulates the Agreement according to Reason and Justice; and having in view the Formation of a future useful Citizen, obliges the Master to engage by a written Indenture, not only that during the time of Service stipulated, the Apprentice shall be duly provided with Meat, Drink, Apparel, washing & Lodging, and at its Expiration with a compleat new suit of Clothes, but also that he shall be taught to read, write & cast Accompts, & that he shall be well instructed in the Art or Profession of his Master, or some other, by which he may afterwards gain a Livelihood, and be able in his turn to raise a Family. A Copy of this Indenture is given to the Apprentice or his Friends, & the Magistrate keeps a Record of it, to which Recourse may be had, in case of Failure by the Master in any Point of Performance. This Desire among the Masters to have more Hands employ'd in working for them, induces them to pay the Passages of young Persons, of both Sexes, who on their Arrival agree to serve them one, two, three or four Years; those who have already learnt a Trade agreeing for a shorter Term in Proportion to their Skill and the consequent immediate Value of their Service; and those who have none, agreeing for a longer Term, in Consideration of being taught an Art their Poverty would not permit them to acquire in their own Country.

The almost general Mediocrity of Fortune that prevails in America, obliging its People to follow some Business for Subsistance, those Vices that arise usually from Idleness are in a great Measure prevented. Industry and constant Employment are great Preservatives of the Morals and Virtue of a Nation. Hence bad Examples to Youth are more rare in America, which must be a comfortable Consideration to Parents. To this may be truly added, that serious Religion under its various Denominations, is not only tolerated but respected and practised. Atheism is unknown there, Infidelity rare & secret, so that Persons may live to a great Age in that Country without having their Piety shock'd by meeting with either an Atheist or an Infidel. And the Divine Being seems to have manifested his Approbation of the mutual Forbearance and Kindness with which the different Sects treat each other, by the remarkable Prosperity with which he has been pleased to favour the whole Country.

Passy, February, 1784

An Economical Project

TO THE AUTHORS OF THE JOURNAL OF PARIS

MESSIEURS,

You often entertain us with accounts of new discoveries. Permit me to communicate to the public, through your paper, one that has lately been made by myself, and which I conceive may be of great utility.

I was the other evening in a grand company, where the new lamp of Messrs. Quinquet and Lange was introduced, and much admired for its splendour; but a general inquiry was made, whether the oil it consumed was not in proportion to the light it afforded, in which case there would be no saving in the use of it. No one present could satisfy us in that point, which all agreed ought to be known, it being a very desirable thing to lessen, if possible, the expense of lighting our apartments, when every other article of family expense was so much augmented.

I was pleased to see this general concern for economy, for I love economy exceedingly.

I went home, and to bed, three or four hours after midnight, with my head full of the subject. An accidental sudden noise waked me about six in the morning, when I was surprised to find my room filled with light; and I imagined at first, that a number of those lamps had been brought into it; but, rubbing my eyes, I perceived the light came in at the windows. I got up and looked out to see what might be the occasion of it, when I saw the sun just rising above the horizon, from whence he poured his rays plentifully into my chamber, my domestic having negligently omitted, the preceding evening, to close the shutters.

I looked at my watch, which goes very well, and found that it was but six o'clock; and still thinking it something extraordinary that the sun should rise so early, I looked into the almanac, where I found it to be the hour given for his rising on that day. I looked forward, too, and found he was to rise still earlier every day till towards the end of June; and that at no time in the year he retarded his rising so long as till eight o'clock. Your readers, who with me have never seen any signs of sunshine before noon, and seldom regard the astronomical part of the almanac, will be as much astonished as I was, when they hear of his rising so early; and especially when I assure them, *that he gives light as soon as he rises.* I am convinced of this. I am certain of my fact. One cannot be more certain of any fact. I saw it with my own eyes. And, having repeated this observation the three following mornings, I found always precisely the same result.

Yet it so happens, that when I speak of this discovery to others, I can easily perceive by their countenances, though they forbear expressing it in words, that they do not quite believe me. One, indeed, who is a learned natural philosopher, has assured me that I must certainly be mistaken as to the circumstance of the light coming into my room; for it being well known, as he says, that there could be no light abroad at that hour, it follows that none could enter from without; and that of consequence, my windows being accidentally left open, instead of letting in the light, had only served to let out the darkness; and he used many ingenious arguments to show me how I might, by that means, have been deceived. I owned that he puzzled me a little, but he did not satisfy me; and the subsequent observations I made, as above mentioned, confirmed me in my first opinion.

This event has given rise in my mind to several serious and important reflections. I considered that, if I had not been awakened so early in the morning, I should have slept six hours longer by the light of the sun, and in exchange have lived six hours the following night by candle-light; and, the latter being a much more expensive light than the former, my love of economy induced me to muster up what little arithmetic I was master of, and to make some calculations, which I shall give you, after observing that utility is, in my opinion the test of value in matters of invention, and that a discovery which can be applied to no use, or is not good for something, is good for nothing.

I took for the basis of my calculation the supposition that there are one hundred thousand families in Paris, and that these families consume in the night half a pound of bougies, or candles, per hour. I think this is a moderate allowance, taking one family with another; for though I believe some consume less, I know that many consume a great deal more. Then estimating seven hours per day as the medium quantity between the time of the sun's rising and ours, he rising during the six following months from six to eight hours before noon, and there being seven hours of course per night in which we burn candles, the account will stand thus;—

In the six months between the 20th of March and the 20th of September, there are

Nights   183

Hours of each night in which we burn candles   7

Multiplication gives for the total number of _____
hours.   1,281

These 1,281 hours multiplied by 100,000, the number of inhabitants, give 128,100,000

One hundred twenty-eight millions and one hundred thousand hours, spent at Paris by candle-light, which, at half a pound of wax and tallow per hour, gives the weight of. 64,050,000

Sixty-four millions and fifty thousand of pounds, which, estimating the whole at the medium price of thirty sols the pound, makes the sum of ninety-six millions and seventy-five thousand livres tournois. 96,075,000

An immense sum! that the city of Paris might save every year, by the economy of using sunshine instead of candles.

If it should be said, that people are apt to be obstinately attached to old customs, and that it will be difficult to induce them to rise before noon, consequently my discovery can be of little use; I answer, *Nil desperandum.* I believe all who have common sense, as soon as they have learnt from this paper that it is daylight when the sun rises, will contrive to rise with him; and, to compel the rest, I would propose the following regulations;

First. Let a tax be laid of a louis per window, on every window that is provided with shutters to keep out the light of the sun.

Second. Let the same salutary operation of police be made use of, to prevent our burning candles, that inclined us last winter to be more economical in burning wood; that is, let guards be placed in the shops of the wax and tallow chandlers, and no family be permitted to be supplied with more than one pound of candles per week.

Third. Let guards also be posted to stop all the coaches, &c. that would pass the streets after sun-set, except those of physicians, surgeons, and midwives.

Fourth. Every morning, as soon as the sun rises, let all the bells in every church be set ringing; and if that is not sufficient, let cannon be fired in every street, to wake the sluggards effectually, and make them open their eyes to see their true interest.

All the difficulty will be in the first two or three days; after which the reformation will be as natural and easy as the present irregularity; for, *ce n'est que le premier pas qui coûte*. Oblige a man to rise at four in the morning, and it is more than probable he will go willingly to bed at eight in the evening; and, having had eight hours sleep, he will rise more willingly at four in the morning following. But this sum of ninety-six millions and seventy-five thousand livres is not the whole of what may be saved by my economical project. You may observe, that I have calculated upon only one half of the year, and much may be saved in the other, though the days are shorter. Besides, the immense stock of wax and tallow left unconsumed during the summer, will probably make candles much cheaper for the ensuing winter, and continue them cheaper as long as the proposed reformation shall be supported.

For the great benefit of this discovery, thus freely communicated and bestowed by me on the public, I demand neither place, pension, exclusive privilege, nor any other reward whatever. I expect only to have the honour of it. And yet I know there are little, envious minds, who will, as usual, deny me this, and say, that my invention was known to the ancients, and perhaps they may bring passages out of the old books in proof of it. I will not dispute with these people, that the ancients knew not the sun would rise at certain hours; they possibly had, as we have, almanacs that predicted it; but it does not follow thence, that they knew *he gave light as soon as he rose*. This is what I claim as my discovery. If the ancients knew it, it might have been long since forgotten; for it certainly was unknown to the moderns, at least to the Parisians, which to prove, I need use but one plain simple argument. They are as well instructed, judicious, and prudent a people as exist anywhere in the world, all professing, like myself, to be lovers of economy; and, from the many heavy taxes required from them by the necessities of the state, have surely an abundant reason to be economical. I say it is impossible that so sensible a people, under such circumstances, should have lived so long by the smoky, unwholesome, and enormously expensive light of candles, if they had really known, that they might have had as much pure light of the sun for nothing. I am, &c.

A Subscriber.

Journal de Paris, April 26, 1784

Loose Thoughts on a Universal Fluid

Passy, June 25, 1784.

Universal Space, as far as we know of it, seems to be filled with a subtil Fluid, whose Motion, or Vibration, is called Light.

This Fluid may possibly be the same with that, which, being attracted by, and entring into other more solid Matter, dilates the Substance, by separating the constituent Particles, and so rendering some Solids fluid, and maintaining the Fluidity of others; of which Fluid when our Bodies are totally deprived, they are said to be frozen; when they have a proper Quantity, they are in Health, and fit to perform all their Functions; it is then called natural Heat; when too much, it is called Fever; and, when forced into the Body in too great a Quantity from without, it gives Pain by separating and destroying the Flesh, and is then called Burning; and the Fluid so entring and acting is called Fire.

While organized Bodies, animal or vegetable, are augmenting in Growth, or are supplying their continual Waste, is not this done by attracting and consolidating this Fluid called Fire, so as to form of it a Part of their Substance; and is it not a Separation of the Parts of such Substance, which, dissolving its solid State, sets that subtil Fluid at Liberty, when it again makes its appearance as Fire?

For the Power of Man relative to Matter seems limited to the dividing it, or mixing the various kinds of it, or changing its Form and Appearance by different Compositions of it; but does not extend to the making or creating of new Matter, or annihilating the old. Thus, if Fire be an original Element, or kind of Matter, its Quantity is fixed and permanent in the Universe. We cannot destroy any Part of it, or make addition to it; we can only separate it from that which confines it, and so set it at Liberty, as when we put Wood in a Situation to be burnt; or transfer it from one Solid to another, as when we make Lime by burning Stone, a Part of the Fire dislodg'd from the Wood being left in the Stone. May not this Fluid, when at Liberty, be capable of penetrating and entring into all Bodies organiz'd or not, quitting easily in totality those not organiz'd; and quitting easily in part those which are; the part assum'd and fix'd remaining till the Body is dissolved?

Is it not this Fluid which keeps asunder the Particles of Air, permitting them to approach, or separating them more, in proportion as its Quantity is diminish'd or augmented? Is it not the greater Gravity of the Particles of Air, which forces the Particles of this Fluid to mount with the Matters to which it is attach'd, as Smoke or Vapour?

Does it not seem to have a great Affinity with Water, since it will quit a Solid to unite with that Fluid, and go off with it in Vapour, leaving the Solid cold to the Touch, and the Degree measurable by the Thermometer?

The Vapour rises attach'd to this Fluid, but at a certain height they separate, and the Vapour descends in Rain, retaining but little of it, in Snow or Hail less. What becomes of that Fluid? Does it rise above our Atmosphere, and mix with the universal Mass of the same kind? Or does a spherical Stratum of it, denser, or less mix'd with Air, attracted by this Globe, and repell'd or push'd up only to a certain height from its Surface, by the greater Weight of Air, remain there, surrounding the Globe, and proceeding with it round the Sun?

In such case, as there may be a Continuity or Communication of this Fluid thro' the Air quite down to the Earth, is it not by the Vibrations given to it by the Sun that Light appears to us; and may it not be, that every one of the infinitely small Vibrations, striking common Matter with a certain Force, enters its Substance, is held there by Attraction, and augmented by succeeding Vibrations, till the Matter has receiv'd as much as their Force can drive into it?

Is it not thus, that the Surface of this Globe is continually heated by such repeated Vibrations in the Day, and cooled by the Escape of the Heat, when those Vibrations are discontinu'd in the Night, or intercepted and reflected by Clouds?

Is it not thus that Fire is amass'd, and makes the greatest Part of the Substance of combustible Bodies?

Perhaps, when this Globe was first form'd, and its original Particles took their Place at certain Distances from the Centre, in proportion to their greater or less Gravity, the fluid Fire, attracted towards that Centre, might in great part be oblig'd, as lightest, to take place above the rest, and thus form the Sphere of Fire above suppos'd, which would afterwards be continually diminishing by the Substance it afforded to organiz'd Bodies, and the Quantity restor'd to it again by the Burning or other Separating of the Parts of those Bodies.

Is not the natural Heat of Animals thus produc'd, by separating in Digestion the Parts of Food, and setting their Fire at Liberty?

Is it not this Sphere of Fire, which kindles the wandring Globes that sometimes pass thro' it in our Course round the Sun, have their Surface kindled by it, and burst when their included Air is greatly rarified by the Heat on their burning Surfaces? May it not have been from such Considerations that the ancient Philosophers supposed a Sphere of Fire to exist above the Air of our Atmosphere?

The Flies

TO MADAME HELVÉTIUS

The Flies of the Apartments of Mr. Franklin request Permission to present their Respects to Madame Helvétius, & to express in their best Language their Gratitude for the Protection which she has been kind enough to give them,

Bizz izzzz ouizz a ouizzzz izzzzzzzz, &c.

We have long lived under the hospitable Roof of the said Good Man Franklin. He has given us free Lodgings; we have also eaten & drunk the whole Year at his Expense without its having cost us anything. Often, when his Friends & he have emptied a Bowl of Punch, he has left us a sufficient Quantity to intoxicate a hundred of us Flies. We have drunk freely of it, & after that we have made our Sallies, our Circles & our Cotillions very prettily in the Air of his Room, & have gaily consummated our little Loves under his Nose. In short, we should have been the happiest People in the World, if he had not permitted a Number of our declared Enemies to remain at the top of his Wainscoting, where they spread their Nets to catch us, & tore us pitilessly to pieces. People of a Disposition both subtle & ferocious, abominable Combination! You, most excellent Woman, had the goodness to order that all these Assassins with their Habitations & their Snares should be swept away; & your Orders (as they always ought to be) were carried out immediately. Since that Time we live happily, & we enjoy the Beneficence of the said Good Man Franklin without fear.

One Thing alone remains for us to wish in order to assure the Permanence of our Good Fortune; permit us to say it,

Bizz izzzz ouizz a ouizzzz izzzzzzzz, &c.

It is to see the two of you henceforth forming a single Household.

1784?

LETTERS

To Lord Howe

My Lord,   Philada. July 20th. 1776.

I received safe the Letters your Lordship so kindly forwarded to me, and beg you to accept my Thanks.

The Official Dispatches to which you refer me, contain nothing more than what we had seen in the Act of Parliament, viz. Offers of Pardon upon Submission; which I was sorry to find, as it must give your Lordship Pain to be sent so far on so hopeless a Business.

Directing Pardons to be offered the Colonies, who are the very Parties injured, expresses indeed that Opinion of our Ignorance, Baseness, and Insensibility which your uninform'd and proud Nation has long been pleased to entertain of us; but it can have no other Effect than that of increasing our Resentment. It is impossible we should think of Submission to a Government, that has with the most wanton Barbarity and Cruelty, burnt our defenceless Towns in the midst of Winter, excited the Savages to massacre our Farmers, and our Slaves to murder their Masters, and is even now bringing foreign Mercenaries to deluge our Settlements with Blood. These atrocious Injuries have extinguished every remaining Spark of Affection for that Parent Country we once held so dear: But were it possible for *us* to forget and forgive them, it is not possible for *you* (I mean the British Nation) to forgive the People you have so heavily injured; you can never confide again in those as Fellow Subjects, and permit them to enjoy equal Freedom, to whom you know you have given such just Cause of lasting Enmity. And this must impel you, were we again under your Government, to endeavour the breaking our Sprit by the severest Tyranny, and obstructing by every means in your Power our growing Strength and Prosperity.

But your Lordship mentions "the Kings paternal Solicitude for promoting the Establishment of lasting *Peace* and Union with the Colonies." If by *Peace* is here meant, a Peace to be entered into between Britain and America as distinct States now at War, and his Majesty has given your Lordship Powers to treat with us of such a Peace, I may venture to say, tho' without Authority, that I think a Treaty for that purpose not yet quite impracticable, before we enter into Foreign Alliances. But I am persuaded you have no such Powers. Your Nation, tho' by punishing those American Governors who have created and fomented the Discord, rebuilding our burnt Towns, and repairing as far as possible the Mischiefs done us, She might yet recover a great Share of our Regard and the greatest part of our growing Commerce, with all the Advantage of that additional Strength to be derived from a Friendship with us; I know too well her abounding Pride and deficient Wisdom, to believe she will ever take such Salutary Measures. Her Fondness for Conquest as a Warlike Nation, her Lust of Dominion as an Ambitious one, and her Thirst for a gainful Monopoly as a Commercial one, (none of them legitimate Causes of War) will all join to hide from her Eyes every View of her true Interests; and continually goad her on in these ruinous distant Expeditions, so destructive both of Lives and Treasure, that must prove as perrnicious to her in the End as the Croisades formerly were to most of the Nations of Europe.

I have not the Vanity, my Lord, to think of intimidating by thus predicting the Effects of this War; for I know it will in England have the Fate of all my former Predictions, not to be believed till the Event shall verify it.

Long did I endeavour with unfeigned and unwearied Zeal, to preserve from breaking, that fine and noble China Vase the British Empire: for I knew that being once broken, the separate Parts could not retain even their Share of the Strength or Value that existed in the Whole, and that a perfect Re-Union of those Parts could scarce even be hoped for. Your Lordship may possibly remember the Tears of Joy that wet my Cheek, when, at your good Sister's in London, you once gave me Expectations that a Reconciliation might soon take place. I had the Misfortune to find those Expectations disappointed, and to be treated as the Cause of the Mischief I was labouring to prevent. My Consolation under that groundless and malevolent Treatment was, that I retained the Friendship of many

Wise and Good Men in that Country, and among the rest some Share in the Regard of Lord Howe.

The well founded Esteem, and permit me to say Affection, which I shall always have for your Lordship, makes it painful to me to see you engag'd in conducting a War, the great Ground of which, as expressed in your Letter, is, "the Necessity of preventing the American Trade from passing into foreign Channels." To me it seems that neither the obtaining or retaining of any Trade, how valuable soever, is an Object for which Men may justly Spill each others Blood; that the true and sure means of extending and securing Commerce is the goodness and cheapness of Commodities; and that the profits of no Trade can ever be equal to the Expence of compelling it, and of holding it, by Fleets and Armies. I consider this War against us therefore, as both unjust, and unwise; and I am persuaded cool dispassionate Posterity will condemn to Infamy those who advised it; and that even Success will not save from some degree of Dishonour, those who voluntarily engag'd to conduct it. I know your great Motive in coming hither was the Hope of being instrumental in a Reconciliation; and I believe when you find *that* impossible on any Terms given you to propose, you will relinquish so odious a Command, and return to a more honourable private Station. With the greatest and most sincere Respect I have the honour to be, My Lord your Lordships most obedient humble Servant

"WOMEN . . . OUGHT TO BE FIX'D IN
REVOLUTION PRINCIPLES"

To Emma Thompson

Paris, Feb. 8. 1777

You are too early, Hussy, (as well as too saucy) in calling me Rebel; you should wait for the Event, which will determine whether it is a Rebellion or only a Revolution. Here the Ladies are more civil; they call us *les Insurgens*, a Character that usually pleases them: And methinks you, with all other Women who smart or have smarted under the Tyranny of a bad Husband, ought to be fix'd in *Revolution* Principles, and act accordingly.

In my way to Canada last Spring, I saw dear Mrs. Barrow at New York. Mr. Barrow had been from her two or three Months, to keep Gov. Tryon and other Tories Company, on board the Asia one of the King's Ships which lay in the Harbour; and in all that time, naughty Man, had not ventur'd once on shore to see her. Our Troops were then pouring into the Town, and she was packing up to leave it; fearing as she had a large House they would incommode her by quartering Officers in it. As she appear'd in great Perplexity, scarce knowing where to go I persuaded her to stay, and I went to the General Officers then commanding there, and recommended her to their Protection, which they promis'd, and perform'd. On my Return from Canada, (where I was a Piece of a Governor, and I think a very good one, for a Fortnight; and might have been so till this time if your wicked Army, Enemies to all good Government, had not come and driven me out) I found her still in quiet Possession of her House. I enquired how our People had behav'd to her; she spoke in high Terms of the respectful Attention they had paid her, and the Quiet and Security they had procur'd her. I said I was glad of it; and that if they had us'd her ill, I would have turn'd Tory. *Then*, says she, (with that pleasing Gaiety so natural to her) *I wish they had.* For you must know she is a Toryess as well as you and can as flippantly call Rebel. I drank Tea with her; we talk'd affectionately of you and our other Friends the Wilkes's, of whom she had receiv'd no late Intelligence. What became of her since, I have not heard. The Street she then liv'd in was some Months after chiefly burnt down; but as the Town was then, and ever since has been in Possession of the King's Troops, I have had no Opportunity of knowing whether she suffer'd any Loss in the Conflagration. I hope she did not, as if she did, I should wish I had not persuaded her to stay there. I am glad to learn from you that that unhappy tho' deserving Family the W's are getting into some Business that may afford them Subsistence. I pray that God will bless them, and that they may see happier Days. Mr. Cheap's and Dr. Huck's good Fortunes please me. Pray learn, (if you have not already learnt) like me, to be pleas'd with other People's Pleasures, and happy with their Happinesses; when none occur of your own; then perhaps you will not so soon be weary of the Place you chance to be in, and so fond of Rambling to get rid of your *Ennui*. I fancy You have hit upon the right Reason of your being weary of St. Omer, viz. that you are out of Temper which is the effect of full living and idleness. A month in Bridewell, beating Hemp upon Bread and Water, would give you Health and Spirits, and subsequent Chearfulness, and Contentment with every other Situation. I prescribe that Regimen for you my Dear, in pure good Will, without a Fee. And, if you do not get into Temper, neither Brussels nor Lisle will suit you. I know nothing of the Price of Living in either of those Places; but I am sure that a single Woman, as you are, might with Oeconomy, upon two hundred Pounds a year, maintain herself comfortably any where, and me into the Bargain. Don't invite me in earnest, however, to come and live with you; for being posted here I ought not to comply, and I am not sure I should be able to refuse. Present my Respects to Mrs. Payne and Mrs. Heathcoat, for tho' I have not the Honour of knowing them, yet as you say they are Friends to the American Cause, I am sure they must be Women of good Understanding. I know you wish you could see me, but as you can't, I will describe my self to you. Figure me in your mind as jolly as formerly, and as strong and hearty, only a few Years older, very plainly dress'd, wearing my thin grey strait Hair, that peeps out under my only Coiffure, a fine Fur Cap, which comes down my Forehead almost to my Spectacles. Think how this must appear among the Powder'd Heads of Paris. I wish every Gentleman and Lady in France would only be so obliging as to follow my Fashion, comb their own Heads as I do mine, dismiss their Friseurs, and pay me half the Money they paid to them. You see the Gentry might well afford this; and I could then inlist those Friseurs, who are at least 100,000; and with the Money I would maintain them, make a Visit with them to England, and dress the Heads of your Ministers and Privy Counsellors, which I conceive to be at present *un peu dérangées*. Adieu, Madcap, and believe me ever Your affectionate Friend and humble Servant

PS. Don't be proud of this long Letter. A Fit of the Gout which has confin'd me 5 Days, and made me refuse to see any Company, has given me a little time to trifle. Otherwise it would have been very short. Visitors and Business would have interrupted. And perhaps, with Mrs. Barrow, *you wish they had.*

"WHOEVER WRITES TO A STRANGER SHOULD OBSERVE 3 POINTS"

To ——— *Lith*

Sir,   Passy near Paris, April 6. 1777

I have just been honoured with a Letter from you, dated the 26th past, in which you express your self as astonished, and appear to be angry that you have no Answer to a Letter you wrote me of the 11th of December, which you are sure was delivered to me.

In Exculpation of my self, I assure you that I never receiv'd any Letter from you of that date. And indeed being then but 4 Days landed at Nantes, I think you could scarce have heard so soon of my being in Europe.

But I receiv'd one from you of the 8th of January, which I own I did not answer. It may displease you if I give you the Reason; but as it may be of use to you in your future Correspondences, I will hazard that for a Gentleman to whom I feel myself oblig'd, as an American, on Account of his Good Will to our Cause.

Whoever writes to a Stranger should observe 3 Points; 1. That what he proposes be practicable. 2. His Propositions should be made in explicit Terms so as to be easily understood. 3. What he desires should be in itself reasonable. Hereby he will give a favourable Impression of his Understanding, and create a Desire of further Acquaintance. Now it happen'd that you were negligent in *all* these Points: for first you desired to have Means procur'd for you of taking a Voyage to America *"avec Sureté"*; which is not possible, as the Dangers of the Sea subsist always, and at present there is the additional Danger of being taken by the English. Then you desire that this may be *"sans trop grandes Dépenses,"* which is not intelligible enough to be answer'd, because not knowing your Ability of bearing Expences, one cannot judge what may be *trop grandes*. Lastly you desire Letters of Address to the Congress and to General Washington; which it is not reasonable to ask of *one* who knows no more of you than that your Name is LITH, and that you live at BAYREUTH.

In your last, you also express yourself in vague Terms when you desire to be inform'd whether you may expect *"d'etre recu d'une maniere convenable"* in our Troops? As it is impossible to know what your Ideas are of the *maniere convenable*, how can one answer this? And then you demand whether I will support you by my Authority in giving you Letters of Recommendation? I doubt not your being a Man of Merit; and knowing it yourself, you may forget that it is not known to every body; but reflect a Moment, Sir, and you will be convinc'd, that if I were to practice giving Letters of Recommendation to Persons of whose Character I knew no more than I do of yours, my Recommendations would soon be of no Authority at all.

I thank you however for your kind Desire of being Serviceable to my Countrymen: And I wish in return that I could be of Service to you in the Scheme you have form'd of going to America. But Numbers of experienc'd Officers here have offer'd to go over and join our Army, and I could give them no Encouragement, because I have no Orders for that purpose, and I know it extremely difficult to place them when they come there. I cannot but think therefore, that it is best for you not to make so long, so expensive, and so hazardous a Voyage, but to take the Advice of your Friends, and *stay in Franconia*. I have the honour to be Sir, &c.

"DISPUTES ARE APT TO SOUR ONES TEMPER"

To [Lebègue de Presle]

Sir   Passy, Oct. 4 1777

I am much oblig'd by your Communication of the Letter from England. I am of your Opinion that a Translation of it will not be proper for Publication here. Our Friend's Expressions concerning Mr. Wilson will be thought too angry to be made use of by one Philosopher when speaking of another; and on a philosophical Question. He seems as much heated about this one Point, as the Jansenists and Molinists were about the Five. As to my writing any thing on the Subject, which you seem to desire, I think it not necessary; especially as I have nothing to add to what I have already said upon it in a Paper read to the Committee who ordered the Conductors at Purfleet, which Paper is printed in the last French Edition of my Writings. I have never entered into any Controversy in defence of my philosophical Opinions; I leave them to take their Chance in the World. If they are right, Truth and Experience will support them. If wrong, they ought to be refuted and rejected. Disputes are apt to sour ones Temper and disturb one's Quiet. I have no private Interest in the Reception of my Inventions by the World, having never made nor proposed to make the least Profit by any of them. The King's changing his pointed Conductors for blunt ones is therefore a Matter of small Importance to me. If I had a Wish about it, it would be that he had rejected them altogether as ineffectual, For it is only since he thought himself and Family safe from the Thunder of Heaven, that he dared to use his own Thunder in destroying his innocent Subjects.

Be pleased when you write to present my respectful Compliments and Thanks to Mr. Magellans. I have forwarded your Letter to your Brother, and am with great Esteem, Sir Your most obedient humble Servant

"YOUR MAGISTERIAL SNUBBINGS AND REBUKES"

To Arthur Lee

SIR   Passy, April 3, 1778
It is true I have omitted answering some of your Letters. I do not like to answer angry Letters. I hate Disputes. I am old, cannot have long to live, have much to do and no time for Altercation. If I have often receiv'd and borne your Magisterial Snubbings and Rebukes without Reply, ascribe it to

the right Causes, my Concern for the Honour & Success of our Mission, which would be hurt by our Quarrelling, my Love of Peace, my Respect for your good Qualities, and my Pity of your Sick Mind, which is forever tormenting itself, with its Jealousies, Suspicions & Fancies that others mean you ill, wrong you, or fail in Respect for you.—If you do not cure your self of this Temper it will end in Insanity, of which it is the Symptomatick Forerunner, as I have seen in several Instances. God preserve you from so terrible an Evil: and for his sake pray suffer me to live in quiet. I have the honour to be very respectfully,

> Sir, etc,

"A SORT OF TAR-AND-FEATHER HONOUR"

To Charles de Weissenstein

SIR,   Passy, July 1, 1778.

I received your letter, dated at Brussels the 16th past. My vanity might possibly be flattered by your expressions of compliment to my understanding, if your *proposals* did not more clearly manifest a mean opinion of it.

You conjure me, in the name of the omniscient and just God, before whom I must appear, and by my hopes of future fame, to consider if some expedient cannot be found to put a stop to the desolation of America, and prevent the miseries of a general war. As I am conscious of having taken every step in my power to prevent the breach, and no one to widen it, I can appear cheerfully before that God, fearing nothing from his justice in this particular, though I have much occasion for his mercy in many others. As to my future fame, I am content to rest it on my past and present conduct, without seeking an addition to it in the crooked, dark paths, you propose to me, where I should most certainly lose it. This your solemn address would therefore have been more properly made to your sovereign and his venal Parliament. He and they, who wickedly began, and madly continue, a war for the desolation of America, are alone accountable for the consequences.

You endeavour to impress me with a bad opinion of French

faith; but the instances of their friendly endeavours to serve a race of weak princes, who, by their own imprudence, defeated every attempt to promote their interest, weigh but little with me, when I consider the steady friendship of France to the Thirteen United States of Switzerland, which has now continued inviolate two hundred years. You tell me, that she will certainly cheat us, and that she despises us already. I do not believe that she will cheat us, and I am not certain that she despises us; but I see clearly that you are endeavouring to cheat us by your conciliatory bills; that you actually despised our understandings, when you flattered yourselves those artifices would succeed; and that not only France, but all Europe, yourselves included, most certainly and for ever would despise us, if we were weak enough to accept your insidious propositions.

Our expectations of the future grandeur of America are not so magnificent, and therefore not so vain or visionary, as you represent them to be. The body of our people are not merchants, but humble husbandmen, who delight in the cultivation of their lands, which, from their fertility and the variety of our climates, are capable of furnishing all the necessaries and conveniences of life without external commerce; and we have too much land to have the least temptation to extend our territory by conquest from peaceable neighbours, as well as too much justice to think of it. Our militia, you find by experience, are sufficient to defend our lands from invasion; and the commerce with us will be defended by all the nations who find an advantage in it. We, therefore, have not the occasion you imagine, of fleets or standing armies, but may leave those expensive machines to be maintained for the pomp of princes, and the wealth of ancient states. We propose, if possible, to live in peace with all mankind; and after you have been convinced, to your cost, that there is nothing to be got by attacking us, we have reason to hope, that no other power will judge it prudent to quarrel with us, lest they divert us from our own quiet industry, and turn us into corsairs preying upon theirs. The weight therefore of an independent empire, which you seem certain of our inability to bear, will not be so great as you imagine. The expense of our civil government we have always borne, and can easily bear, because it is small. A virtuous and laborious people may be cheaply governed. Determining, as we do, to have no offices of profit, nor any sinecures or useless appointments, so common in ancient or corrupted states, we can govern ourselves a year, for the sum you pay in a single department, or for what one jobbing contractor, by the favour of a minister, can cheat you out of in a single article.

You think we flatter ourselves, and are deceived into an opinion that England *must* acknowledge our independency. We, on the other hand, think you flatter yourselves in imagining such an acknowledgment a vast boon, which we strongly desire, and which you may gain some great advantage by granting or withholding. We have never asked it of you; we only tell you, that you can have no treaty with us but as an independent state; and you may please yourselves and your children with the rattle of your right to govern us, as long as you have done with that of your King's being King of France, without giving us the least concern, if you do not attempt to exercise it. That this pretended right is indisputable, as you say, we utterly deny. Your Parliament never had a right to govern us, and your King has forfeited it by his bloody tyranny. But I thank you for letting me know a little of your mind, that, even if the Parliament should acknowledge our independency, the act would not be binding to posterity, and that your nation would resume and prosecute the claim as soon as they found it convenient from the influence of your passions, and your present malice against us. We suspected before, that you would not be actually bound by your conciliatory acts, longer than till they had served their purpose of inducing us to disband our forces; but we were not certain, that you were knaves by principle, and that we ought not to have the least confidence in your offers, promises, or treaties, though confirmed by Parliament.

I now indeed recollect my being informed, long since, when in England, that a certain very great personage, then young, studied much a certain book, called *Arcana Imperii*. I had the curiosity to procure the book and read it. There are sensible and good things in it, but some bad ones; for, if I remember rightly, a particular king is applauded for his politically exciting a rebellion among his subjects, at a time when they had not strength to support it, that he might, in subduing them, take away their privileges, which were troublesome to him; and a question is formally stated and discussed, *Whether a prince, who, to appease a revolt, makes promises of indemnity to the revolters, is obliged to fulfil those promises.* Honest and good men would say, Ay; but this politician says, as you say, No. And he gives this pretty reason, that, though it was right to make the promises, because otherwise the revolt would not be suppressed, yet it would be wrong to keep them, because revolters ought to be punished to deter from future revolts.

If these are the principles of your nation, no confidence can be placed in you; it is in vain to treat with you; and the wars can only end in being reduced to an utter inability of continuing them.

One main drift of your letter seems to be, to impress me with an idea of your own impartiality, by just censures of your ministers and measures, and to draw from me propositions of peace, or approbations of those you have enclosed to me which you intimate may by your means be conveyed to the King directly, without the intervention of those ministers. You would have me give them to, or drop them for, a stranger, whom I may find next Monday in the church of Notre Dame, to be known by a rose in his hat. You yourself, Sir, are quite unknown to me; you have not trusted me with your true name. Our taking the least step towards a treaty with England through you, might, if you are an enemy, be made use of to ruin us with our new and good friends. I may be indiscreet enough in many things; but certainly, if I were disposed to make propositions (which I cannot do, having none committed to me to make), I should never think of delivering them to the Lord knows who, to be carried to the Lord knows where, to serve no one knows what purposes. Being at this time one of the most remarkable figures in Paris, even my appearance in the church of Notre Dame, where I cannot have any conceivable business, and especially being seen to leave or drop any letter to any person there, would be a matter of some speculation, and might, from the suspicions it must naturally give, have very mischievous consequences to our credit here.

The very proposing of a correspondence so to be managed, in a manner not necessary where fair dealing is intended, gives just reason to suppose you intend the contrary. Besides, as your court has sent Commissioners to treat with the Congress, with all the powers that could be given them by the crown under the act of Parliament, what good purpose can be served by privately obtaining propositions from us? Before those Commissioners went, we might have treated in virtue of our general powers, (with the knowledge, advice, and approbation of our friends), upon any propositions made to us. But, under the present circumstances, for us to make propositions, while a treaty is supposed to be actually on foot with the Congress, would be extremely improper, highly presumptuous with regard to our constituents, and answer no good end whatever.

I write this letter to you, notwithstanding; (which I think I can convey in a less mysterious manner, and guess it may come to your hands;) I write it because I would let you know our sense of your procedure, which appears as insidious as that of your conciliatory bills. Your true way to obtain peace, if your ministers desire it, is, to propose openly to the Congress fair and equal terms, and you may possibly come sooner to such a resolution, when you find, that personal flatteries, general cajolings, and panegyrics on our *virtue* and *wisdom* are not likely to have the effect you seem to expect; the persuading us to act basely and foolishly, in betraying our country and posterity into the hands of our most bitter enemies, giving up or selling our arms and warlike stores, dismissing our ships of war and troops, and putting those enemies in possession of our forts and ports.

This proposition of delivering ourselves, bound and gagged, ready for hanging, without even a right to complain, and without a friend to be found afterwards among all mankind, you would have us embrace upon the faith of an act of Parliament! Good God! an act of your Parliament! This demonstrates that you do not yet know us, and that you fancy we do not know you; but it is not merely this flimsy faith, that we are to act upon; you offer us *hope*, the hope of PLACES, PENSIONS, and PEERAGES. These, judging from yourselves, you think are motives irresistible. This offer to corrupt us, Sir, is with me your credential, and convinces me that you are not a private volunteer in your application. It bears the stamp of British court character. It is even the signature of your King. But think for a moment in what light it must be viewed in America. By PLACES, you mean places among us, for you take care by a special article to secure your own to yourselves. We must then pay the salaries in order to enrich ourselves with these places. But you will give us PENSIONS, probably to be paid too out of your expected American revenue, and which none of us can accept without deserving, and perhaps obtaining, a SUS-*pension*. PEERAGES! alas! Sir, our long observation of the vast servile majority of your peers, voting constantly for every measure proposed by a minister, however weak or wicked, leaves us small respect for that title. We consider it as a sort of *tar-and-feather* honour, or a mixture of foulness and folly, which every man among us, who should accept it from your King, would be obliged to renounce, or exchange for that conferred by the mobs of their own country, or wear it with everlasting infamy. I am, Sir, your humble servant,

"GOD-SEND OR THE WRECKERS"

To David Hartley

DEAR SIR,   Passy, Feb. 3, 1779.

I have just received your favour of the 23d past, in which you mention, "that the alliance between France and America is the great StumblingBlock in the way of Making Peace;" and you go on to observe, that "whatever Engagements America may have entred into, they may, (at least by consent of Parties) *be relinquished*, for the purpose of removing so material an Obstacle to any general Treaty of free and unengaged Parties" adding, that "if the parties could meet for the sake of Peace upon *free* and *open* Ground, you should think *that* a very fair Proposition to be offered to the People of England, and an equitable Proposition in itself."

The long, steady, & kind regard you have shown for the Welfare of America, by the whole Tenour of your Conduct in Parliament, satisfies me, that this Proposition never took its

Rise with you, but has been suggested from some other quarter; and that your Excess of Humanity, your Love of Peace, & your fears for us, that the Destruction we are threatened with will certainly be effected, have thrown a Mist before your Eyes, which hindred you from seeing the Malignity and Mischief of it. We know that your King hates Whigs and Presbyterians; that he thirsts for our Blood, of which he has already drunk large Draughts; that his servile unprincipled Ministers are ready to execute the wickedest of his Orders, and his venal Parliament equally ready to vote them just. Not the Smallest Appearance of a Reason can be imagined capable of inducing us to think of relinquishing a Solid Alliance with one of the most amiable, as well as most powerful Princes of Europe, for the Expectation of unknown Terms of Peace, to be afterwards offer'd to us by *such a government*; a Government, that has already shamefully broke all the Compacts it ever made with us! This is worse than advising us to drop the Substance for the Shadow. The Dog after he found his Mistake, might possibly have recover'd his Mutton; but we could never hope to be trusted again by France, or indeed by any other Nation under heaven. Nor does there appear any more Necessity for dissolving an Alliance with France before you can treat with us, than there would of dissolving your alliance with Holland, or your Union with Scotland, before we could treat with you. Ours is therefore no *material Obstacle* to a Treaty as you suppose it to be. Had Lord North been the Author of such a Proposition, all the World would have said it was insidious, and meant only to deceive & divide us from our Friends, and then to ruin us; supposing our Fears might be strong enough to procure an Acceptance of it; but thanks to God, that is not the Case! We have long since settled all the Account in our own Minds. We know the worst you can do to us, if you have your Wish, is to confiscate our Estates & take our Lives, to rob & murder us; and this you have seen we are ready to hazard, rather than come again under your detested Government.

You must observe, my dear Friend, that I am a little warm.—Excuse me.—'Tis over.—Only let me counsel you not to think of being sent hither on so fruitless an Errand, as that of making such a Proposition.

It puts me in mind of the comick Farce intitled, *God-send or The Wreckers.* You may have forgotten it; but I will endeavour to amuse you by recollecting a little of it.

SCENE. *Mount's Bay.*

[*A Ship riding at anchor in a great Storm. A Lee Shore full of Rocks, and lin'd with people, furnish'd with Axes & Carriages to cut up Wrecks, knock the Sailors on the Head, and carry off the Plunder; according to Custom.*]

1*st. Wrecker.* This Ship rides it out longer than I expected. She must have good Ground Tackle.

2 *Wrecker.* We had better send off a Boat to her, and persuade her to take a Pilot, who can afterwards run her ashore, where we can best come at her.

3 *Wrecker.* I doubt whether the boat can live in this Sea; but if there are any brave Fellows willing to hazard themselves for the good of the Public, & a double Share, let them say aye.

Several Wreckers. I, I, I, I.

[*The Boat goes off, and comes under the Ship's Stern.*]

Spokesman. So ho, the Ship, ahoa!

Captain. Hulloa.

Sp. Wou'd you have a Pilot?

Capt. No, no!

Sp. It blows hard, & you are in Danger.

Capt. I know it.

Sp. Will you buy a better Cable? We have one in the boat here.

Capt. What do you ask for it?

Sp. Cut that you have, & then we'll talk about the price of this.

Capt. I shall not do such a foolish Thing. I have liv'd in your Parish formerly, & know the Heads of ye too well to trust ye; keep off from my Cable there; I see you have a mind to cut it yourselves. If you go any nearer to it, I'll fire into you and sink you.

Sp. It is a damn'd rotten French Cable, and will part of itself in half an hour. Where will you be then, Captain? You had better take our offer.

Capt. You offer nothing, you Rogues, but Treachery and Mischief. My cable is good & strong, and will hold long enough to baulk all your Projects.

Sp. You talk unkindly, Captain, to People who came here only for your Good.

Capt. I know you come for all our *Goods*, but, by God's help, you shall have none of them; you shall not serve us as you did the Indiaman.

Sp. Come, my Lads, let's be gone. This Fellow is not so great a Fool as we—took him to be.

"I-DOLL-IZED IN THIS COUNTRY"

To Sarah Bache

DEAR SALLY,   Passy, June 3, 1779.

I have before me your letters of October 22d and January 17th. They are the only ones I received from you in the course of eighteen months. If you knew how happy your letters make me, and considered how many miscarry, I think you would write oftener.

I am much obliged to the Miss Cliftons for the kind care they took of my house and furniture. Present my thankful acknowledgments to them, and tell them I wish them all sorts of happiness.

The clay medallion of me you say you gave to Mr. Hopkinson was the first of the kind made in France. A variety of others have been made since of different sizes; some to be set in the lids of snuffboxes, and some so small as to be worn in rings; and the numbers sold are incredible. These, with the pictures, busts, and prints, (of which copies upon copies are spread everywhere,) have made your father's face as well known as that of the moon, so that he durst not do any thing that would oblige him to run away, as his phiz would discover him wherever he should venture to show it. It is said by learned etymologists, that the name *doll*, for the images children play with, is derived from the word IDOL. From the number of *dolls* now made of him, he may be truly said, *in that sense*, to be *i-doll-ized* in this country.

I think you did right to stay out of town till the summer was over, for the sake of your child's health. I hope you will get out again this summer, during the hot months; for I begin to love the dear little creature from your description of her.

I was charmed with the account you gave me of your industry, the tablecloths of your own spinning, &c.; but the latter part of the paragraph, that you had sent for linen from France, because weaving and flax were grown dear, alas, that dissolved the charm; and your sending for long black pins, and lace, and *feathers!* disgusted me as much as if you had put salt into my strawberries. The spinning, I see, is laid aside, and you are to be dressed for the ball! You seem not to know, my dear daughter, that, of all the dear things in this world, idleness is the dearest, except mischief.

The project you mention, of removing Temple from me was an unkind one. To deprive an old man, sent to serve his country in a foreign one, of the comfort of a child to attend him, to assist him in health and take care of him in sickness, would be cruel, if it was practicable. In this case it could not be done; for, as the pretended suspicions of him are groundless, and his behaviour in every respect unexceptionable, I should not part with the child, but with the employment. But I am confident, that, whatever may be proposed by weak or malicious people, the Congress is too wise and too good to think of treating me in that manner.

Ben, if I should live long enough to want it, is like to be another comfort to me. As I intend him for a Presbyterian as well as a republican, I have sent him to finish his education at Geneva. He is much grown, in very good health, draws a little, as you will see by the enclosed, learns Latin, writing, arithmetic, and dancing, and speaks French better than English. He made a translation of your last letter to him, so that some of your works may now appear in a foreign language. He has not been long from me. I send the accounts I have of him, and I shall put him in mind of writing to you. I cannot propose to you to part with your own dear Will. I must one of these days go back to see him; happy to be once more all together! but futurities are uncertain. Teach him, however, in the mean time, to direct his worship more properly, for the deity of Hercules is now quite out of fashion.

The present you mention as sent by me was rather that of a merchant at Bordeaux; for he would never give me any account of it, and neither Temple nor I know any thing of the particulars.

When I began to read your account of the high prices of goods, "a pair of gloves, $7; a yard of common gauze, $24, and that it now required a fortune to maintain a family in a very plain way," I expected you would conclude with telling me, that everybody as well as yourself was grown frugal and industrious; and I could scarce believe my eyes in reading forward, that "there never was so much pleasure and dressing going on;" and that you yourself wanted black pins and feathers from France to appear, I suppose, in the mode! This leads me to imagine, that perhaps it is not so much that the goods are grown dear, as that the money is grown cheap, as every thing else will do when excessively plenty; and that people are still as easy nearly in their circumstances, as when a pair of gloves might be had for half a crown. The war indeed may in some degree raise the prices of goods, and the high taxes which are necessary to support the war may make our frugality necessary; and, as I am always preaching that doctrine, I cannot in conscience or in decency encourage the contrary, by my example, in furnishing my children with foolish modes and luxuries. I therefore send all the articles you desire, that are useful and necessary, and omit the rest; for, as you say you should "have great pride in wearing any thing I send, and showing it as your father's taste," I must avoid giving you an opportunity of doing that with either lace or feathers. If you wear your cambric ruffles as I do, and take care not to mend the holes, they will come in time to be lace; and feathers, my dear girl, may be had in America from every cock's tail.

If you happen again to see General Washington, assure him of my very great and sincere respect, and tell him, that all the old Generals here amuse themselves in studying the accounts of his operations, and approve highly of his conduct.

Present my affectionate regards to all friends that inquire

after me, particularly Mr. Duffield and family, and write oftener, my dear child, to your loving father,

DESIGNS AND MOTTOES FOR COINS

To Edward Bridgen

DEAR SIR,   Passy, Octo^r 2^d 1779.
I received your Favor of the 17th past, and the two Samples
of Copper are since come to hand. The Metal seems to be
very good, and the price reasonable; but I have not yet received the Orders necessary to justify my making the Purchase
proposed. There has indeed been an intention to strike Copper Coin, that may not only be useful as small Change, but
serve other purposes.

Instead of repeating continually upon every halfpenny the
dull story that everybody knows, (and what it would have
been no loss to mankind if nobody had ever known,) that
Geo. III is King of Great Britain, France, and Ireland, &c.
&c., to put on one side, some important Proverb of Solomon, some pious moral, prudential or economical Precept,
the frequent Inculcation of which, by seeing it every time
one receives a piece of Money, might make an impression
upon the mind, especially of young Persons, and tend to
regulate the Conduct; such as, on some, *The fear of the Lord
is the beginning of Wisdom*; on others, *Honesty is the best Policy*; on others, *He that by the Plow would thrive, himself must
either hold or drive*; on others, *Keep thy Shop, and thy Shop will
keep thee*; on others, *A penny saved is a penny got*; on others,
*He that buys what he has no need of, will soon be forced to sell
his necessaries*; on others, *Early to bed and early to rise, will
make a man healthy, wealthy, and wise*; and so on, to a great
variety.

The other side it was proposed to fill with good Designs,
drawn and engraved by the best artists in France, of all the
different Species of Barbarity with which the English have
carried on the War in America, expressing every abominable
circumstance of their Cruelty and Inhumanity, that figures

can express, to make an Impression on the minds of Posterity as strong and durable as that on the Copper. This Resolution has been a long time forborne; but the late burning of defenceless Towns in Connecticut, on the flimsy pretence that the people fired from behind their Houses, when it is known to have been premeditated and ordered from England, will probably give the finishing provocation, and may occasion a vast demand for your Metal.

I thank you for your kind wishes respecting my Health. I return them most cordially fourfold into your own bosom. Adieu.

"SOMEBODY . . . GAVE IT OUT THAT
I LOV'D LADIES"

To Elizabeth Partridge

MRS. PARTRIDGE   Passy, Oct. 11. 1779.

Your kind Letter, my dear Friend, was long in coming; but it gave me the Pleasure of knowing that you had been well in October and January last. The Difficulty, Delay & Interruption of Correspondence with those I love, is one of the great Inconveniencies I find in living so far from home: but we must bear these & more, with Patience, if we can; if not, we must bear them as I do with Impatience.

You mention the Kindness of the French Ladies to me. I must explain that matter. This is the civilest nation upon Earth. Your first Acquaintances endeavour to find out what you like, and they tell others. If 'tis understood that you like Mutton, dine where you will you find Mutton. Somebody, it seems, gave it out that I lov'd Ladies; and then every body presented me their Ladies (or the Ladies presented themselves) to be *embrac'd*, that is to have their Necks kiss'd. For as to kissing of Lips or Cheeks it is not the Mode here, the first, is reckon'd rude, & the other may rub off the Paint. The French Ladies have however 1000 other ways of rendering themselves agreable; by their various Attentions and Civilities, & their sensible Conversation. 'Tis a delightful People to live with.

I thank you for the Boston Newspapers, tho' I see nothing so clearly in them as that your Printers do indeed want new Letters. They perfectly blind me in endeavouring to read them. If you should ever have any Secrets that you wish to be well kept, get them printed in those Papers. You enquire if Printers Types may be had here? Of all Sorts, very good, cheaper than in England, and of harder Metal.—I will see any Orders executed in that way that any of your Friends may think fit to send. They will doubtless send Money with their Orders. Very good Printing Ink is likewise to be had here. I cannot by this opportunity send the miniature you desire, but I send you a little Head in China, more like, perhaps, than the Painting would be. It may be set in a Locket, if you like it, cover'd with Glass, and may serve for the present. When Peace comes we may afford to be more extravagant. I send with it a Couple of Fatherly Kisses for you & your amiable Daughter, the whole wrapt up together in Cotton to be kept warm.

Present my respectful Compliments to Mr Partridge.

Adieu, my dear Child, & believe me ever

Your affectionate Papah

"YOUR COOL CONDUCT AND PERSEVERING BRAVERY"

To John Paul Jones

DEAR SIR, Passy, Oct. 15, 1779.

I received the Account of your Cruize and Engagement with the *Serapis*, which you did me the honour to send me from the Texel. I have since received your Favor of the 8th, from Amsterdam. For some Days after the Arrival of your Express, scarce any thing was talked of at Paris and Versailles, but your cool Conduct and persevering Bravery during that terrible Conflict. You may believe, that the Impression on my Mind was not less strong than on that of others; but I do not chuse to say in a letter to yourself all I think on such an Occasion.

The Ministry are much dissatisfied with Captain Landais, and M. de Sartine has signified to me in writing that it is expected that I should send for him to Paris, and call him to Account for his Conduct particularly for deferring so long his coming to your Assistance, by which Means, it is supposed, the States lost some of their valuable Citizens, and the King lost many of his Subjects, Volunteers in your Ship, together with the Ship itself.

I have, accordingly, written to him this Day, acquainting him that he is charged with Disobedience of Orders in the Cruize, and Neglect of his Duty in the Engagement; that, a Court-Martial being at this Time inconvenient, if not impracticable, I would give him an earlier Opportunity of offering what he has to say in his Justification, and for that Purpose direct him to render himself immediately here, bringing with him such Papers or Testimonies, as he may think useful in his Defence. I know not whether he will obey my orders, nor what the Ministry will do with him, if he comes; but I suspect that they may by some of their concise Operations save the Trouble of a Court-Martial. It will be well, however, for you to furnish me with what you may judge proper to support the Charges against him, that I may be able to give a just and clear Account of the Affair to Congress. In the mean time it will be necessary, if he should refuse to come, that you should put him under an Arrest, and in that Case, as well as if he comes, that you should either appoint some Person to command his Ship or take it upon yourself; for I know of no Person to recommend to you as fit for that Station.

I am uneasy about your Prisoners; I wish they were safe in France. You will then have compleated the glorious work of giving Liberty to all the Americans that have so long languished for it in the British Prisons; for there are not so many there, as you have now taken.

I have the Pleasure to inform you, that the two Prizes sent to Norway are safely arrived at Berghen. With the highest Esteem, I am, &c.

P.S. I am sorry for your Misunderstanding with M. de Chaumont, who has a great Regard for you.

To Benjamin Vaughan

DEAR SIR, Passy, Nov. 9. 1779.

I have received several kind Letters from you, which I have not regularly answered. They gave me however great Pleasure, as they acquainted me with your Welfare, and that of your Family and other Friends; and I hope you will continue writing to me as often as you can do it conveniently.

I thank you much for the great Care and Pains you have taken in regulating and correcting the Edition of those Papers. Your Friendship for me appears in almost every Page; and if the Preservation of any of them should prove of Use to the Publick, it is to you that the Publick will owe the Obligation. In looking them over, I have noted some Faults of Impression that hurt the Sense, and some other little Matters, which you will find all in a Sheet under the title of *Errata*. You can best judge whether it may be worth while to add any of them to the Errata already printed, or whether it may not be as well to reserve the whole for Correction in another Edition, if such should ever be. Inclos'd I send a more perfect copy of the *Chapter*.

If I should ever recover the Pieces that were in the Hands of my Son, and those I left among my Papers in America, I think there may be enough to make three more such Volumes, of which a great part would be more interesting.

As to the *Time* of publishing, of which you ask my Opinion I am not furnish'd with any Reasons, or Ideas of Reasons, on which to form any Opinion. Naturally I should suppose the Bookseller to be from Experience the best Judge, and I should be for leaving it to him.

I did not write the Pamphlet you mention. I know nothing of it. I suppose it is the same, concerning which Dr. Priestley formerly asked me the same Question. That for which he took it was intitled, *A Dissertation on Liberty and Necessity, Pleasure and Pain*, with these Lines in the TitlePage.

> "Whatever is, is right. But purblind Man
> Sees but a part o' the Chain, the nearest Link;

His eye not carrying to that equal Beam,
That poises all above." DRYDEN.

London, Printed M.D.C.C.X.X.V.

It was addressed to Mr. J. R., that is, James Ralph, then a youth of about my age, and my intimate friend; afterwards a political writer and historian. The purport of it was to prove the doctrine of fate, from the supposed attributes of God; in some such manner as this: that in erecting and governing the world, as he was infinitely wise, he knew what would be best; infinitely good, he must be disposed, and infinitely powerful, he must be able to execute it: consequently all is right. There were only an hundred copies printed, of which I gave a few to friends, and afterwards disliking the piece, as conceiving it might have an ill tendency, I burnt the rest, except one copy, the margin of which was filled with manuscript notes by Lyons, author of the Infallibility of Human Judgment, who was at that time another of my acquaintance in London. I was not nineteen years of age when it was written. In 1730, I wrote a piece on the other side of the question, which began with laying for its foundation this fact: "That almost all men in all ages and countries, have at times made use of prayer." Thence I reasoned, that if all things are ordained, prayer must among the rest be ordained. But as prayer can produce no change in things that are ordained, praying must then be useless and an absurdity. God would therefore not ordain praying if everything else was ordained. But praying exists, therefore all things are not ordained, etc. This pamphlet was never printed, and the manuscript has been long lost. The great uncertainty I found in metaphysical reasonings disgusted me, and I quitted that kind of reading and study for others more satisfactory.

I return the Manuscripts you were so obliging as to send me; I am concern'd at your having no other copys, I hope these will get safe to your hands. I do not remember the Duke de Chaulnes showing me the Letter you mention. I have received Dr. Crawford's book, but not your Abstract, which I wait for as you desire.

I send you also M. Dupont's *Table Economique*, which I think an excellent Thing, as it contains in a clear Method all the principles of that new sect, called here *les Economistes*.

Poor Henley's dying in that manner is inconceivable to me. Is any Reason given to account for it, besides insanity?

Remember me affectionately to all your good Family, and believe me, with great Esteem, my dear Friend, yours, most sincerely,

"THAT MEN WOULD CEASE TO BE WOLVES"

To Joseph Priestley

DEAR SIR,   Passy, Feb. 8. 1780.

Your kind Letter of September 27 came to hand but very lately, the Bearer having staied long in Holland. I always rejoice to hear of your being still employ'd in experimental Researches into Nature, and of the Success you meet with. The rapid Progress *true* Science now makes, occasions my regretting sometimes that I was born so soon. It is impossible to imagine the Height to which may be carried, in a thousand years, the Power of Man over Matter. We may perhaps learn to deprive large Masses of their Gravity, and give them absolute Levity, for the sake of easy Transport. Agriculture may diminish its Labour and double its Produce; all Diseases may by sure means be prevented or cured, not excepting even that of Old Age, and our Lives lengthened at pleasure even beyond the antediluvian Standard. O that moral Science were in as fair a way of Improvement, that Men would cease to be Wolves to one another, and that human Beings would at length learn what they now improperly call Humanity!

I am glad my little Paper on the *Aurora Borealis* pleased. If it should occasion further Enquiry, and so produce a better Hypothesis, it will not be wholly useless. I am ever, with the greatest and most sincere Esteem, dear Sir, yours very affectionately

I have consider'd the Situation of that Person very attentively. I think that, with a little help from the *Moral Algebra*, he might form a better judgment than any other Person can form for him. But, since my Opinion seems to be desired, I give it for continuing to the End of the Term, under all the present disagreeable Circumstances. The connection will then die a natural Death. No Reason will be expected to be given for the Separation, and of course no Offence taken at Reasons given; the Friendship may still subsist, and in some other way be useful. The Time diminishes daily, and is usefully employ'd. All human Situations have their Inconveniencies; we *feel* those that we find in the present, and we neither *feel* nor *see* those that exist in another. Hence we make frequent and troublesome Changes without Amendment, and often for the worse.

In my Youth, I was Passenger in a little Sloop, descending the River Delaware. There being no Wind, we were obliged, when the Ebb was spent, to cast anchor, and wait for the next. The Heat of the Sun on the Vessel was excessive, the Company Strangers to me, and not very agreable. Near the river Side I saw what I took to be a pleasant green Meadow, in the middle of which was a large shady Tree, where it struck my Fancy I could sit and read, (having a Book in my Pocket,) and pass the time agreably till the tide turned. I therefore prevail'd with the Captain to put me ashore. Being landed, I found the greatest part of my Meadow was really a Marsh, in crossing which, to come at my Tree, I was up to my Knees in Mire; and I had not placed myself under its Shade five Minutes, before the Muskitoes in Swarms found me out, attack'd my Legs, Hands, and Face, and made my Reading and my Rest impossible; so that I return'd to the Beach, and call'd for the Boat to come and take me aboard again, where I was oblig'd to bear the Heat I had strove to quit, and also the Laugh of the Company. Similar Cases in the Affairs of Life have since frequently fallen under my Observation.

I have had Thoughts of a College for him in America. I know no one who might be more useful to the Publick in the Instruction of Youth. But there are possible Unpleasantnesses in that Situation; it cannot be obtain'd but by a too hazardous Voyage at this time for a Family; and the Time for Experiments would be all otherwise engaged.

To George Washington

SIR,   Passy, March 5 1780.

I have received but lately the Letter your Excellency did me the honour of writing to me in Recommendation of the Marquis de la Fayette. His modesty detained it long in his own Hands. We became acquainted, however, from the time of his Arrival at Paris; and his Zeal for the Honour of our Country, his Activity in our Affairs here, and his firm Attachment to our Cause and to you, impress'd me with the same Regard and Esteem for him that your Excellency's Letter would have done, had it been immediately delivered to me.

Should peace arrive after another Campaign or two, and afford us a little Leisure, I should be happy to see your Excellency in Europe, and to accompany you, if my Age and Strength would permit, in visiting some of its ancient and most famous Kingdoms. You would, on this side of the Sea, enjoy the great Reputation you have acquir'd, pure and free from those little Shades that the Jealousy and Envy of a Man's Countrymen and Cotemporaries are ever endeavouring to cast over living Merit. Here you would know, and enjoy, what Posterity will say of Washington. For 1000 Leagues have nearly the same Effect with 1000 Years. The feeble Voice of those grovelling Passions cannot extend so far either in Time or Distance. At present I enjoy that Pleasure for you, as I frequently hear the old Generals of this martial Country, (who study the Maps of America, and mark upon them all your Operations,) speak with sincere Approbation and great Applause of your conduct; and join in giving you the Character of one of the greatest Captains of the Age.

I must soon quit the Scene, but you may live to see our Country flourish, as it will amazingly and rapidly after the War is over. Like a Field of young Indian Corn, which long Fair weather and Sunshine had enfeebled and discolored, and which in that weak State, by a Thunder Gust, of violent Wind, Hail, and Rain, seem'd to be threaten'd with absolute Destruction; yet the Storm being past, it recovers fresh

Verdure, shoots up with double Vigour, and delights the Eye, not of its Owner only, but of every observing Traveller.

The best Wishes that can be form'd for your Health, Honour, and Happiness, ever attend you from your Excellency's most obedient and most humble servant

"THAN IF YOU HAD SWALLOWED A HANDSPIKE"

To Thomas Bond

DEAR SIR,   Passy, March 16, 1780.

I received your kind letter of September the 22d, and I thank you for the pleasing account you give me of the health and welfare of my old friends, Hugh Roberts, Luke Morris, Philip Syng, Samuel Rhoads, &c., with the same of yourself and family. Shake the old ones by the hand for me, and give the young ones my blessing. For my own part, I do not find that I grow any older. Being arrived at seventy, and considering that by travelling further in the same road I should probably be led to the grave, I stopped short, turned about, and walked back again; which having done these four years, you may now call me sixty-six. Advise those old friends of ours to follow my example; keep up your spirits, and that will keep up your bodies; you will no more stoop under the weight of age, than if you had swallowed a handspike.

I am glad the Philosophical Society made that compliment to M. Gérard. I wish they would do the same to M. Feutry, a worthy gentleman here; and to Dr. Ingenhousz, who has made some great discoveries lately respecting the leaves of trees in improving air for the use of animals. He will send you his book. He is physician to the Empress Queen. I have not yet seen your piece on inoculation. Remember me respectfully and affectionately to Mrs. Bond, your children, and all friends. I am ever, &c.

P.S. I have bought some valuable books, which I intend to present to the Society; but shall not send them till safer times.

"THE MOULIN JOLI IS A LITTLE ISLAND
IN THE SEINE"

To William Carmichael

DEAR SIR,   Passy, June 17, 1780.

Your favours of the 22d past came duly to hand. Sir John
Dalrymple has been here some time, but I hear nothing of his
political operations. The learned talk of the discovery he has
made in the Escurial Library, of forty Epistles of Brutus, a
missing part of Tacitus, and a piece of Seneca, that have never
yet been printed, which excite much curiosity. He has not
been with me, and I am told, by one of his friends, that,
though he wished to see me, he did not think it prudent. So
I suppose I shall have no communication with him; for I shall
not seek it. As Count de Vergennes has mentioned nothing
to me of any memorial from him, I suppose he has not presented it; perhaps discouraged by the reception it met with in
Spain. So I wish, for curiosity's sake, you would send me a
copy of it.

The Marquis de Lafayette arrived safely at Boston on the
28th of April, and, it is said, gave expectations of the coming
of a squadron and troops. The vessel that brings this left New
London the 2d of May; her captain reports, that the siege of
Charleston was raised, the troops attacked in their retreat, and
Clinton killed; but this wants confirmation. London has been
in the utmost confusion for seven or eight days. The beginning of this month, a mob of fanatics, joined by a mob of
rogues, burnt and destroyed property to the amount, it is
said, of a million sterling. Chapels of foreign ambassadors,
houses of members of Parliament that had promoted the act
for favouring Catholics, and the houses of many private persons of that religion, were pillaged and consumed, or pulled
down, to the number of fifty; among the rest, Lord Mansfield's is burnt, with all his furniture, pictures, books, and
papers. Thus he, who approved the burning of American
houses, has had fire brought home to him. He himself was
horribly scared, and Governor Hutchinson, it is said, died
outright of the fright. The mob, tired with roaring and rioting seven days and nights, were at length suppressed, and

quiet restored on the 9th, in the evening. Next day Lord George Gordon was committed to the tower.

Enclosed I send you the little piece you desire. To understand it rightly you should be acquainted with some few circumstances. The person to whom it was addressed is Madame Brillon, a lady of most respectable character and pleasing conversation; mistress of an amiable family in this neighbourhood, with which I spend an evening twice in every week. She has, among other elegant accomplishments, that of an excellent musician; and, with her daughters, who sing prettily, and some friends who play, she kindly entertains me and my grandson with little concerts, a cup of tea, and a game of chess. I call this *my Opera*, for I rarely go to the Opera at Paris.

The Moulin Joli is a little island in the Seine about two leagues hence, part of the country-seat of another friend, where we visit every summer, and spend a day in the pleasing society of the ingenious, learned, and very polite persons who inhabit it. At the time when the letter was written, all conversations at Paris were filled with disputes about the music of Gluck and Picini, a German and Italian musician, who divided the town into violent parties. A friend of this lady having obtained a copy of it, under a promise not to give another, did not observe that promise; so that many have been taken, and it is become as public as such a thing can well be, that is not printed; but I could not dream of its being heard of at Madrid! The thought was partly taken from a little piece of some unknown writer, which I met with fifty years since in a newspaper, and which the sight of the Ephemera brought to my recollection. Adieu, my dear friend, and believe me ever yours most affectionately,

"MR. ADAMS HAS GIVEN OFFENCE TO THE COURT HERE"

To Samuel Huntington

SIR,   Passy, August 9, 1780.

With this your Excellency will receive a Copy of my last, dated May 31st, the Original of which, with Copies of preceding Letters, went by the *Alliance*, Capt. Landais, who sailed the Beginning of last Month, and who I wish may arrive safe in America, being apprehensive, that by her long Delay in Port, from the Mutiny of the People, who after she was ready to sail refused to weigh Anchor till paid Wages, she may fall in the Way of the English Fleet now out; or that her Crew, who have ever been infected with Disorder and Mutiny, may carry her into England. She had, on her first coming out, a Conspiracy for that purpose; besides which her Officers and Captain quarrell'd with each other, the Captain with Comm^e Jones, and there have been so many Embroils among them, that it was impossible to get the Business forward while she staied, and she is at length gone, without taking the Quantity of Stores she was capable of taking, and was ordered to take.

I suppose the Conduct of that Captain will be enquired into by a Court-Martial. Capt. Jones goes home in the *Ariel*, a Ship we have borrowed of Government here, and carries 146 Chests of Arms, and 400 Barrels of Powder. To take the rest of the Stores, and Cloathing I have been obliged to freight a Ship, which, being well arm'd and well mann'd, will, I hope, get safe. The cloathes for 10,000 Men are, I think, all made up; there are also Arms for 15,000, new and good, with 2,000 Barrels of Powder. Besides this, there is a great Quantity of Cloth I have bought, of which you will have the Invoices, sent by Mr. Williams; another large Quantity purchas'd by Mr. Ross; all going in the same Ship.

The little Authority we have here to govern our armed Ships, and the Inconvenience of Distance from the Ports, occasion abundance of Irregularities in the Conduct of both Men and Officers. I hope, therefore, that no more of those Vessels will be sent hither, till our Code of Laws is perfected respecting Ships abroad, and proper Persons appointed to manage such Affairs in the SeaPorts. They give me infinite Trouble; and, tho' I endeavour to act for the best, it is without Satisfaction to myself, being unacquainted with that kind of Business. I have often mention'd the Appointment of a Consul or Consuls. The Congress have, perhaps, not yet had time to consider that Matter.

Having already sent you, by different Conveyances, Copies

of my Proceedings with the Court of Denmark, relative to the three Prizes delivered up to the English, and requested the Instructions of Congress, I hope soon to receive them. I mention'd a Letter from the Congress to that Court, as what I thought might have a good Effect. I have since had more Reasons to be of that Opinion.

The unexpected Delay of Mr. Dean's Arrival has retarded the Settlement of the joint Accounts of the Commission, he having had the chief Management of the commercial Part, and being therefore best able to explain Difficulties. I have just now the Pleasure to hear that the *Fier Rodrique*, with her Convoy from Virginia, arrived at Bordeaux, all safe except one Tobacco Ship, that foundered at Sea, the Men saved; and I have a letter from Mr. Deane that he is at Rochelle, proposes to stop a few Days at Nantes, and then proceed to Paris, when I shall endeavour to see that Business completed with all possible Expedition.

Mr. Adams has given Offence to the Court here, by some Sentiments and Expressions contained in several of his Letters written to the Count de Vergennes. I mention this with Reluctance, tho' perhaps it would have been my Duty to acquaint you with such a Circumstance, even were it not required of me by the Minister himself. He has sent me Copies of the Correspondence, desiring I would communicate them to Congress; and I send them herewith. Mr. Adams did not show me his Letters before he sent them. I have, in a former Letter to Mr. Lovell, mentioned some of the Inconveniencies, that attend the having more than one Minister at the same Court; one of which Inconveniencies is, that they do not always hold the same Language, and that the Impressions made by one, and intended for the Service of his Constituents, may be effaced by the Discourse of the other. It is true, that Mr. Adams's proper Business is elsewhere; but, the Time not being come for that Business, and having nothing else here wherewith to employ himself, he seems to have endeavoured to supply what he may suppose my Negociations defective in. He thinks, as he tells me himself, that America has been too free in Expressions of Gratitude to France; for that she is more oblig'd to us than we to her; and that we should show Spirit in our Applications. I apprehend, that he mistakes his Ground, and that this Court is to be treated with Decency and Delicacy. The King, a young and virtuous Prince, has, I am persuaded, a Pleasure in reflecting on the generous Benevolence of the Action in assisting an oppressed People, and proposes it as a Part of the Glory of his Reign. I think it right to encrease this Pleasure by our thankful Acknowledgments, and that such an Expression of Gratitude is not only our Duty, but our Interest. A different Conduct seems to me what is not only improper and unbecoming, but what may be hurtful to us. Mr. Adams, on the other hand, who, at the same time means our Welfare and Interest as much as I, or any man, can do, seems to think a little apparent Stoutness, and greater air of Independence and Boldness in our Demands, will procure us more ample Assistance. It is for Congress to judge and regulate their Affairs accordingly.

M. Vergennes, who appears much offended, told me, yesterday, that he would enter into no further Discussions with Mr. Adams, nor answer any more of his Letters. He is gone to Holland to try, as he told me, whether something might not be done to render us less dependent on France. He says, the Ideas of this Court and those of the People in America are so totally different, that it is impossible for any Minister to please both. He ought to know America better than I do, having been there lately, and he may chuse to do what he thinks will best please the People of America. But, when I consider the Expressions of Congress in many of their public Acts, and particularly in their Letter to the Chev. de la Luzerne, of the 24th of May last, I cannot but imagine, that he mistakes the Sentiments of a few for a general Opinion. It is my Intention, while I stay here, to procure what Advantages I can for our Country, by endeavouring to please this Court; and I wish I could prevent any thing being said by any of our Countrymen here, that may have a contrary Effect, and increase an Opinion lately showing itself in Paris, that we seek a Difference, and with a view of reconciling ourselves to England. Some of them have of late been very indiscreet in their Conversations.

I received, eight months after their Date, the Instructions of Congress relating to a new Article for guaranteeing the Fisheries. The expected Negociations for a Peace appearing of late more remote, and being too much occupied with other Affairs, I have not hitherto proposed that Article. But I purpose doing it next Week. It appears so reasonable and equitable, that I do not foresee any Difficulty. In my next, I shall give you an Account of what passes on the Occasion.

The Silver Medal ordered for the Chev^r de Fleury, has been delivered to his Order here, he being gone to America. The others, for Brigadier-General Wayne and Colonel Stuart, I shall send by the next good Opportunity.

The Two Thousand Pounds I furnished to Messrs. Adams and Jay, agreable to an Order of Congress, for themselves and Secretaries, being nearly expended, and no Supplies to them arriving, I have thought it my Duty to furnish them with further Sums, hoping the Supplies promised will soon arrive to reimburse me, and enable me to pay the Bills drawn on Mr. Laurens in Holland, which I have engaged for, to save the public Credit, the Holders of those Bills threatening otherwise to protest them. Messrs. de Neufville of Amsterdam had accepted some of them. I have promised those Gentlemen to provide for the Payment before they become due, and to accept such others as shall be presented to me. I hear, and hope it is true, that the Drawing of such Bills is stopped, and that their Number and Value is not very great.

The Bills drawn in favour of M. de Beaumarchais for the Interest of his Debt are paid.

The German Prince, who gave me a Proposal some Months since for furnishing Troops to the Congress, has lately desired an Answer. I gave no Expectation, that it was likely you would agree to such a Proposal; but, being pressed to send it you, it went with some of my former Letters.

M. Fouquet, who was employ'd by Congress to instruct People in making Gunpowder, is arriv'd here, after a long Passage; he has requested me to transmit a Memorial to Congress, which I do, enclos'd.

The great public Event in Europe of this Year is the Proposal, by Russia, of an armed Neutrality for protecting the Liberty of Commerce. The proposition is accepted now by most of the maritime Powers. As it is likely to become the Law of Nations, *that free Ships should make free Goods*, I wish the Congress to consider, whether it may not be proper to give Orders to their Cruizers not to molest Foreign Ships, but conform to the Spirit of that Treaty of Neutrality.

The English have been much elated with their Success at Charlestown. The late News of the Junction of the French and Spanish Fleets, has a little abated their Spirits; and I hope that Junction, and the Arrival of the French Troops and Ships in N. America, will soon produce News, that may afford us also in our Turn some Satisfaction.

Application has been made to me here, requesting that I would solicit Congress to permit the Exchange of William John Mawhood, a Lieutenant in the 17th Regiment, taken Prisoner at Stony Point, July 15th, 1779, and confin'd near Philadelphia; or, if the exchange cannot conveniently be made, that he may be permitted to return to England on his Parole. By doing this at my Request, the Congress will enable me to oblige several Friends of ours, who are Persons of Merit and Distinction in this country.

Be pleased, Sir, to present my Duty to Congress, and believe me to be, with great Respect, &c.

P.S. A similar Application has been made to me in favour of Richard Croft, Lieutenant in the 20th Regiment, a Prisoner at Charlottesville. I shall be much obliged by any Kindness shown to that young Gentleman, and so will some Friends of ours in England, who respect his Father.

"A NEIGHBOUR MIGHT AS WELL ASK ME TO SELL
MY STREET DOOR"

To John Jay

DEAR SIR,   Passy, October 2d, 1780.

I received duly and in good order the several letters you have written to me of August 16th, 19th, September 8th, and 22d. The papers that accompanied them of your writing gave me the pleasure of seeing the affairs of our country in such good hands, and the prospect, from your youth, of its having the service of so able a minister for a great number of years.

But the little success that has attended your late applications for money mortified me exceedingly; and the storm of bills which I found coming upon us both, has terrified and vexed me to such a degree that I have been deprived of sleep, and so much indisposed by continual anxiety, as to be rendered almost incapable of writing.

At length I got over a reluctance that was almost invincible, and made another application to the government here for more money. I drew up and presented a state of debts and newly-expected demands, and requested its aid to extricate me. Judging from your letters that you were not likely to obtain any thing considerable from your court, I put down in my estimate the 25,000 dollars drawn upon you, with the same sum drawn upon me, as what would probably come to me for payment. I have now the pleasure to acquaint you that my memorial was received in the kindest and most friendly manner, and though the court here is not without its embarrassments on account of money, I was told to make myself easy, for that I should be assisted with what was necessary. Mr. Searle arriving about this time, and assuring me there had been a plentiful harvest, and great crops of all kinds; that the Congress had demanded of the several States contributions in produce, which would be cheerfully given; that they would therefore have plenty of provisions to dispose of; and I being much pleased with the generous behaviour just experienced, I presented another paper, proposing, in order to ease the government here, which had been so willing to ease us, that the Congress might furnish their army in America with provisions in part of payment for the services lent us. This proposition, I was told, was well taken; but it being considered that the States having the enemy in their country, and obliged to make great expenses for the present campaign, the furnishing so much provisions as the French army might need, might straiten and be inconvenient to the Congress, his majesty did not at this time think it right to accept the offer. You will not wonder at my loving this good prince: he will win the hearts of all America.

If you are not so fortunate in Spain, continue however the even good temper you have hitherto manifested. Spain owes us nothing; therefore, whatever friendship she shows us in lending money or furnishing clothes, &c. though not equal to our wants and wishes, is however *tant de gagne*; those who have begun to assist us, are more likely to continue than to decline, and we are still so much obliged as their aids amount to. But I hope and am confident, that court will be wiser than to take advantage of our distress, and insist on our making sacrifices by an agreement, which the circumstances of such distress would hereafter weaken, and the very proposition can only give disgust at present. Poor as we are, yet as I know we shall be rich, I would rather agree with them to buy at a great price the whole of their right on the Mississippi, than sell a drop of its waters. A neighbour might as well ask me to sell my street door.

I wish you could obtain an account of what they have supplied us with already in money and goods.

Mr. Grand, informing me that one of the bills drawn on you having been sent from hence to Madrid, was come back unaccepted, I have directed him to pay it; and he has, at my request, undertaken to write to the Marquis D'Yranda, to assist you with money to answer such bills as you are not otherwise enabled to pay, and to draw on him for the amount, which drafts I shall answer here as far as 25,000 dollars. If you expect more, acquaint me. But pray write to Congress as I do, to forbear this practice, which is so extremely hazardous, and may, some time or other, prove very mischievous to their credit and affairs. I have undertaken, too, for all the bills drawn on Mr. Laurens, that have yet appeared. He was to have sailed three days after Mr. Searle, that is, the 18th July. Mr. Searle begins to be in pain for him, having no good opinion of the little vessel he was to embark in.

We have letters from America to the 7th August. The spirit of our people was never higher. Vast exertions making preparatory for some important action. Great harmony and affection between the troops of the two nations. The new money in good credit, &c.

I will write to you again shortly, and to Mr. Carmichael. I shall now be able to pay up your salaries complete for the year; but as demands unforeseen are continually coming upon me, I still retain the expectations you have given me of being reimbursed out of the first remittances you receive.

If you find any inclination to hug me for the good news of this letter, I constitute and appoint Mrs. Jay my attorney, to receive in my behalf your embraces. With great and sincere esteem,

> I have the honour to be, dear sir,
> Your most obedient and most humble servant,

RELIGIOUS TESTS

To Richard Price

DEAR SIR,   Passy, Oct. 9, 1780.

Besides the Pleasure of their Company, I had the great Satisfaction of hearing by your two valuable Friends, and learning from your Letter, that you enjoy a good State of Health. May God continue it, as well for the Good of Mankind as for your Comfort. I thank you much for the second Edition of your excellent Pamphlet. I forwarded that you sent to Mr. Dana, he being in Holland. I wish also to see the Piece you have written (as Mr. Jones tells me) on Toleration. I do not expect that your new Parliament will be either wiser or honester than the last. All Projects to procure an honest one, by Place Bills, &c., appear to me vain and Impracticable. The true Cure, I imagine, is to be found only in rendring all Places unprofitable, and the King too poor to give Bribes and Pensions. Till this is done, which can only be by a Revolution (and I think you have not Virtue enough left to procure one), your Nation will always be plundered, and obliged to pay by Taxes the Plunderers for Plundering and Ruining. Liberty and Virtue therefore join in the call, COME OUT OF HER, MY PEOPLE!

I am fully of your Opinion respecting religious Tests; but, tho' the People of Massachusetts have not in their new Constitution kept quite clear of them, yet, if we consider what that People were 100 Years ago, we must allow they have gone great Lengths in Liberality of Sentiment on religious Subjects; and we may hope for greater Degrees of Perfection, when their Constitution, some years hence, shall be revised.

If Christian Preachers had continued to teach as Christ and his Apostles did, without Salaries, and as the Quakers now do, I imagine Tests would never have existed; for I think they were invented, not so much to secure Religion itself, as the Emoluments of it. When a Religion is good, I conceive that it will support itself; and, when it cannot support itself, and God does not take care to support, so that its Professors are oblig'd to call for the help of the Civil Power, it is a sign, I apprehend, of its being a bad one. But I shall be out of my Depth, if I wade any deeper in Theology, and I will not trouble you with Politicks, nor with News which are almost as uncertain; but conclude with a heartfelt Wish to embrace you once more, and enjoy your sweet Society in Peace, among our honest, worthy, ingenious Friends at the *London*. Adieu,

"I THINK A WORTHIER MAN NEVER LIVED"

To Benjamin Waterhouse

SIR,   Passy, Jan. 18. 1781.

I received your obliging Letter of the 16th past, enclosing one from my dear Friend, Dr. Fothergill. I was happy to hear from him, that he was quite free of the Disorder that had like to have remov'd him last summer. But I had soon after a Letter from another Friend, acquainting me, that he was again dangerously ill of the same Malady; and the newspapers have since announced his Death! I condole with you most sincerely on this Occasion. I think a worthier Man never lived. For besides his constant Readiness to serve his Friends, he was always studying and projecting something for the Good of his Country and of Mankind in general, and putting others, who had it in their Power, on executing what was out of his own reach; but whatever was within it he took care to do himself; and his incredible Industry and unwearied Activity enabled him to do much more than can now be ever known, his Modesty being equal to his other Virtues.

I shall take care to forward his Letter to Mr. Pemberton. Enclos'd is one I have just received under Cover from that

Gentleman. You will take care to convey it by some safe Opportunity to London.

With hearty Wishes for your Prosperity and Success in your Profession, and that you may be a good Copy of your deceas'd Relation, I am, Sir, etc.,

"I SHALL BE READY TO BREAK, RUN AWAY, OR GO TO PRISON WITH YOU"

To John Adams

SIR,   Passy, Feb. 22. 1781

I received the Letter your Excell^y did me honour of writing to me the 15th Inst. respecting Bills, presented to you for Acceptance drawn by Congress in favour of N. Tracey for 10,000£ Sterling payable 90 Days Sight; and desiring to know if I can furnish Funds for the Payment.

I have lately made a fresh & strong Application for more Money. I have not yet received a positive Answer. I have however two of the Christian Graces, Faith & Hope. But my Faith is only that of which the Apostle Speaks, the Evidence of things not seen. For in Truth I do not see at present how so many Bills drawn at random on our Ministers in France, Spain & Holland, are to be paid. Nor that anything but omnipotent Necessity can excuse the Imprudence of it. Yet I think Bills drawn upon us by the Congress ought at all Risques to be accepted. I shall accordingly use my best Endeavours to procure Money for their honourable Discharge against they become due, if you should not in the meantime be provided; and if those Endeavours fail, I shall be ready to break, run away, or go to prison with you, as it shall please God.

Sir G. Grand has returned to me the remainder of the Book of Promises, sign'd by us, which his House had not an Opportunity of issuing. Perhaps the late Charge of Affairs in that Country may open a way for them. If on consulting him you should be of that Opinion, I will send them to you.—With great Respect, I have the honour to be

                                                      Sir,

P. S.   Late Advices from Congress mention that Col. Laurens is coming over as Envoy extraordinary to this Court & Col. Palfray as Consul General. They may be expected every day.

"AS THE INDIANS HAD NO LETTERS,
THEY HAD NO ORTHOGRAPHY"

To Court de Gebelin

DEAR SIR,   Passy, May 7, 1781.
    I am glad the little Book prov'd acceptable. It does not appear to me intended for a Grammar to teach the Language. It is rather what we call in English a *Spelling Book*, in which the only Method observ'd is, to arrange the Words according to their Number of Syllables, placing those of one Syllable together, then those of two Syllables, and so on. And it is to be observ'd, that *Sa ki ma*, for Instance, is not three Words, but one Word of three Syllables; and the reason that *Hyphens* are not plac'd between the Syllables is, that the Printer had not enough of them.
    As the Indians had no Letters, they had no Orthography. The Delaware Language being differently spelt from the Virginian may not always arise from a Difference in the Languages; for Strangers who learn the Language of an Indian Nation, finding no Orthography, are at Liberty in writing the Language to use such Compositions of Letters as they think will best produce the Sounds of the Words. I have observ'd, that our Europeans of different Nations, who learn the same Indian Language, form each his own Orthography according to the usual Sounds given to the Letters in his own Language. Thus the same Words of the Mohawk Language written by an English, a French, and a German Interpreter, often differ very much in the Spelling; and, without knowing the usual Powers of the Letters in the Language of the Interpreter, one cannot come at the Pronunciation of the Indian Words. The Spelling Book in question was, I think, written by a German.
    You mention a Virginian Bible. Is it not the Bible of the

Massachusetts Language, translated by Elliot, and printed in New England, about the middle of the last Century? I know this Bible, but have never heard of one in the Virginian Language. Your Observations of the Similitude between many of the Words, and those of the ancient World, are indeed very curious.

This Inscription, which you find to be Phenician, is, I think, near *Taunton* (not *Jannston*, as you write it). There is some Account of it in the old *Philosophical Transactions*. I have never been at the Place, but shall be glad to see your Remarks on it.

The Compass appears to have been long known in China, before it was known in Europe; unless we suppose it known to Homer, who makes the Prince, that lent Ships to Ulysses, boast that they had a *spirit* in them, by whose Directions they could find their way in a cloudy Day, or the darkest Night. If any Phenicians arriv'd in America, I should rather think it was not by the Accident of a Storm, but in the Course of their long and adventurous Voyages; and that they coasted from Denmark and Norway, over to Greenland, and down Southward by Newfoundland, Nova Scotia, &c., to New England; as the Danes themselves certainly did some ages before Columbus.

Our new American Society will be happy in the Correspondence you mention, and when it is possible for me, I shall be glad to attend the Meetings of your Society, which I am sure must be very instructive. With great and sincere esteem, I have the honour to be, &c.

"I HAVE ACTED IMPRUDENTLY"

To Comte de Vergennes

SIR,   Passy. June 10th 1781
     I received the letter your Excellency did me the honour of writing to me on the 8th Inst. in answer to mine of the 4th.
     The state of Mr. Laurens's transaction in Holland, as I understood it, is this. Capt. Gillon represented to him, that he

had bought clothing &c. for the troops of South Carolina, to the value of 10,000£ sterling, which were actually shipp'd in the *Indienne*; that he now wanted money to get his ship out, and therefore proposed to M.ʳ Laurens to take those goods of him for the United States. M.ʳ Laurens agreed to take such as would suit their wants, and to pay for the same by Bills upon me at six months' sight; and proposed to send in her some other articles that could be bought in Holland. His motives were that this fine ship, if she could be got out, would be a safe conveyance; and that she would afterwards be useful to the Congress on our Coasts. He informed me that he had mentioned to your Excellency Capt. Gillon's proposal, and that you seem'd to approve of it. I accordingly consented to his ordering those drafts upon me; but this will not be any great addition to my difficulty, since in the term of 6 months, I can probably receive from Congress the Power which you judge necessary for applying any part of the loan opened in Holland, to the discharge of those Bills.

With regard to the drafts made by Congress on M.ʳ Jay, in expectation of a friendly loan from the Court of Spain, on M.ʳ Laurens and M.ʳ Adams in Holland, from assurances given by some People of that Country that a loan might be easily by them obtained there; and large drafts upon myself, exclusive of the Loan Office Interest Bills; these all together occasion an embarrassment, which it is my duty to lay before your Excellency, and to acquaint you with the consequences I apprehend may attend their not being duly discharged. Those Bills were occasioned first by the sums necessary last year to assemble our army and put it in a condition to act vigorously with the King's Sea and Land Forces arrived and expected to arrive from France against New York, and to defend the Southern Colonies. Our main Army was accordingly put into such a condition as to face M.ʳ Clinton before New York all summer; but the additional forces expected from France not arriving, the project was not pursued, and the advantage hoped for from that exertion and expence was not obtained, tho' the funds of Congress were thereby equally exhausted. A second necessity for drawing those Bills, arose from the delay of five months in the sailing of M.ʳ de Chaumont's ship, occasioned by the distraction of his affairs, whereby the clothing for the army not arriving in time before winter, the Congress were obliged to purchase the cloths taken by Privateers from the Quebec Fleet; and this could only be done by payment for the same in Bills. All these Bills were drawn by solemn resolutions of Congress; and it seems to me evident, that if no part of the aids lately resolved on by his Majesty can be applied to their discharge, with out an express order from Congress for that purpose, the Public Credit of the United States instead of being "re-animated" as his Majesty graciously intended, will be destroy'd; for the Bills unpaid, must, according to the usual Course be returned under protest, long before such order can be obtained, which protest will by our laws, entitle the Holders to a Damage of 20 p^r cent, whereby the public will incur a net loss of one fifth of the whole sum drawn for; an effect, that will be made use of by their Enemies to discredit their Government among the People, and must weaken their hands much more in that respect, than by the mere loss of so much money. On these considerations, and also from an opinion that a bill already drawn by order of Congress, was as good and clear a declaration of their will with regard to the disposition of so much of any funds they might have at their disposal in Europe, as any future order of theirs could be, I ventured to accept and to promise payment of all the Bills above mention'd. What I have requested of your Excellency in my late letter, and what I now beg leave to repeat, is only that so much of the intended aid may be retained, as shall be necessary to pay those acceptances as they become due. I had not the least apprehension that this could meet with any difficulty; and I hope on reconsideration, your Excellency may still judge, that it will be for the advantage of the common cause if this request is granted.

I have already paid most of the Bills drawn on M. Jay, which the Money furnish'd to him by the Court of Spain did not suffice to pay: I have also paid a part of those drawn on Mr Laurens, Mr Adams and myself: To do this I have been obliged to anticipate our funds, so that, as our Banker informs me, I shall by the end of this month owe him about 400,000 Livres, tho' he has already rec^d from M. D'Harvelay for the quarter of August. I have acted imprudently in making these acceptances and entering into these engagements without first consulting your Excellency and obtaining your explicit approbation; but I acted as I thought for the best; I imagined it a case of absolute necessity, and relying on assistance from the new aids intended us, and considering the fatal consequence of protests, I thought at the time that I acted prudently and safely.

The supplies I shall want for the payment of these Bills will be gradual: If I cannot obtain them but by an order from Congress, I must not only stop payment of those not yet become due, but I apprehend that I shall be obliged to refuse acceptance of some of the interest Bills, having disabled myself from paying them, by paying so many others.

I therefore beg your Excellency would reconsider this important affair. I am sorry to find myself under a necessity of giving you so much trouble. I wish rather to diminish your cares than to increase them; being with the most perfect Respect, Sir,   Your Excellency's most

                    obedient and most humble servant

"THESE SUPERIOR AIRS YOU GIVE YOURSELF,
YOUNG GENTLEMAN, OF REPROOF TO ME"

To William Jackson

SIR,   Passy, July 10, 1781.

Last Night I received your 4th Letter on the Same Subject. You are anxious to carry the Money with you, because it will reanimate the Credit of America. My Situation and long Acquaintance with affairs relating to the public Credit enables me, I think, to judge better than you can do, who are a Novice in them, what Employment of it will most conduce to that End; and I imagine the retaining it to pay the Congress Drafts has infinitely the Advantage. You repeat that the Ship is detain'd by my Refusal. You forget your having written to me expressly that she waited for Convoy. You remind me of the great Expence the Detention of the Ship occasions. Who has given Orders to stop her? It was not me. I had no Authority to do it. Have you? And do you imagine, if you had taken such Authority upon you, that the Congress ought to

bear the Expence occasion'd by your Imprudence? and that
the Blame of detaining the necessary Stores the Ship contains
will be excus'd by your fond Desire of carrying the Money?
The Noise you have rashly made about this Matter, contrary
to the Advice of Mr. Adams, which you ask'd and receiv'd,
and which was to comply with my Requisition, has already
done great Mischief to our Credit in Holland. Messrs. Fizeaux have declar'd they will advance to him no more Money
on his Bills upon me to assist in paying the Congress Drafts
on him. Your Commodore, too, complains, in a Letter I have
seen, that he finds it difficult to get Money for my Acceptances of your Drafts in order to clear his Ship, tho' before
this Proceeding of yours Bills on me were, as Mr. Adams assures me, in as good Credit on the Exchange of Amsterdam
as those of any Banker in Europe. I suppose the Difficulty
mention'd by the Commodore is the true Reason of the ship's
Stay, if in fact the Convoy is gone without her. Credit is a
delicate thing, capable of being blasted with a Breath. The
public Talk you have occasion'd about my Stopping the
Money, and the Conjectures of the Reasons or Necessity of
doing it, have created Doubts and Suspicions of most pernicious Consequence. It is a Matter that should have pass'd in
Silence. You repeat as a Reason for your Conduct, that the
Money was obtain'd by the great Exertions of Col. Laurens.
Who obtain'd the Grant is of no Importance, tho' the Use I
propose to make of it is of the greatest. But the Fact is not as
you state it. I obtain'd it before he came. And if he were here
I am sure I could convince him of the Necessity of leaving it.
Especially after I should have inform'd him that you had
made in Holland the enormous Purchase of £40,000 Sterling's worth of Goods over and above the £10,000 worth,
which I had agreed should be purchased by him on my
Credit, and that you had induc'd me to engage for the Payment of your Purchase by showing me a Paper said to contain
his Orders to you for making it, which I then took to be his
Handwriting, tho' I afterwards found it to be yours, and not
sign'd by him. It would be an additional Reason with him,
when I should remind him that he himself, to induce me to
come into the Proposal of Commodore Gillon and the rest of
the Holland Transaction, to which I was averse, assur'd me

that he had mention'd it to the Minister, and that it was approv'd of: That on the contrary I find the Minister remembers nothing of it, very much dislikes it, and absolutely refuses to furnish any Money to discharge that Account. You finish your Letter by telling me that, "the daily Enhancement of Expence to the United States from these Difficulties is worthy the Attention of those whose *Duty* is to œconomize the Public Money, and to whom the commonWeal is intrusted without deranging the special Department of another." The Ship's lying there with 5 or 600 Men on board is undoubtedly a great daily Expence, but it is you that occasion it; and these Superior Airs you give yourself, young Gentleman, of Reproof to me, and Reminding me of my Duty do not become you, whose special Department and Employ in public Affairs, of which you are so vain, is but of yesterday, and would never have existed but by my Concurrence, and would have ended in the Disgrace if I had not supported your enormous Purchases by accepting your Drafts. The charging me with want of œconomy is particularly improper in *you*, when the only Instance you know of it is my having indiscreetly comply'd with your Demand in advancing you 120 Louis for the Expence of your Journey to Paris and when the only Instance I know of your œconomizing Money is your sending me three Expresses, one after another, on the same Day, all the way from Holland to Paris, each with a Letter saying the same thing to the same purpose. This Dispute is as useless as it is unpleasant. It can only create ill Blood. Pray let us end it. I have the honour to be, etc.,

"ASSISTING WITH AN EQUAL SUM A STRANGER
WHO HAS EQUAL NEED OF IT"

To William Nixon

REV^D SIR,   Passy, Sept. 5, 1781.

I duly received the Letter you did me the Honour of writing to me the 25th past, together with the valuable little Book, of which you are the Author. There can be no doubt, but that a Gentleman of your Learning and Abilities might make a very useful Member of Society in our new Country, and meet with Encouragement there, either as an Instructor in one of our Universities, or as a Clergyman of the Church of Ireland. But I am not impowered to engage any Person to go over thither, and my Abilities to assist the Distressed are very limited. I suppose you will soon be set at Liberty in England by the Cartel for the Exchange of Prisoners. In the mean time, if Five *Louis-d'ors* may be of present Service to you, please to draw on me for that Sum, and your Bill shall be paid on Sight. Some time or other you may have an Opportunity of assisting with an equal Sum a stranger who has equal need of it. Do so. By that means you will discharge any Obligation you may suppose yourself under to me. Enjoin him to do the same on Occasion. By pursuing such a Practice, much Good may be done with little money. Let kind Offices go round. Mankind are all of a Family. I have the honour to be, Revd Sir, &c.

ON FINE PRINTING

To William Strahan

DEAR SIR,   Passy, December 4, 1781.

Not remembering precisely the address of Mrs. Strange, I beg leave to request you would forward the Enclosed to her, which I received under my Cover from America.

I formerly sent you from Philadelphia part of an Edition of "Tully on Old Age," to be sold in London; and you put the Books, if I remember right, into the Hands of Mr. Becket for that Purpose. Probably he may have some of them still in his Warehouse, as I never had an account of their being sold. I shall be much oblig'd by your procuring and sending me one of them.

A strong Emulation exists at present between Paris and Madrid, with regard to beautiful Printing. Here a M. Didot *le jeune* has a Passion for the Art, and besides having procured the best Types, he has much improv'd the Press. The utmost Care is taken of his Presswork; his Ink is black, and his Paper fine and white. He has executed several charming Editions.

But the "Salust" and the "Don Quixote" of Madrid are thought to excel them. Didot however, improves every day, and by his zeal and indefatigable application bids fair to carry the Art to a high Pitch of Perfection. I will send you a Sample of his Work when I have an opportunity.

I am glad to hear that you have married your Daughter happily, and that your Prosperity continues. I hope it may never meet with any Interruption having still, tho' at present divided by public Circumstances, a Remembrance of our ancient private Friendship. Please to present my affectionate Respects to Mrs. Strahan, and my Love to your Children. With great Esteem and Regard, I am, dear Sir,

Your most humble and most obedient Servant,

"NOR A SYLLABLE OF APPROBATION"

To John Adams

SIR   Passy, Dec. 17, 1781

I have received the Packet containing the correspondence relating to the Goods. I suppose that Mr Barclay is there before this time, and the Affair in a way of Accommodation. Young Mr Neufville is here; but I have thought it best not to give him as yet any Hopes of my paying the Bills unless the Goods are delivered. I shall write fully by next Post. This serves chiefly to acquaint you that I will endeavour to pay the Bills that have been presented to you drawn on Mr Laurens. But you terrify me, by acquainting me that there are yet a great number behind. It is hard that I never had any information sent me of the Sums drawn, a Line of Order to pay, nor a Syllable of Approbation for having paid any of the Bills drawn on Mr Laurens, Mr Jay or yourself. As yet I do not see that I can go any further, and therefore can engage for no more than you have mention'd.

With great Esteem, I have the honour to be Sir
Your Excellency's
most obedient and most
humble Servant

ON THE LIBERTAS MEDAL

To Robert R. Livingston

SIR,   Passy, March 4, 1782.

Since I wrote the two short letters, of which I herewith send you copies, I have been honoured with yours, dated the 16th of December.

Enclosed I send two letters from Count de Vergennes, relating to certain complaints from Ostend and Copenhagen against our cruisers. I formerly forwarded a similar complaint from Portugal, to which I have yet received no answer. The ambassador of that kingdom frequently teazes me for it. I hope now, that by your means this kind of affairs will be more immediately attended to; ill blood and mischief may be thereby sometimes prevented.

The Marquis de Lafayette was at his return hither received by all ranks with all possible distinction. He daily gains in the general esteem and affection, and promises to be a great man here. He is warmly attached to our cause; we are on the most friendly and confidential footing with each other, and he is really very serviceable to me in my applications for additional assistance.

I have done what I could in recommending Messieurs Duportail and Gouvion, as you desired. I did it with pleasure, as I have much esteem for them.

I will endeavour to procure a sketch of an emblem for the purpose you mention. This puts me in mind of a medal I have had a mind to strike, since the late great event you gave me an account of, representing the United States by the figure of an infant Hercules in his cradle, strangling the two serpents; and France by that of Minerva, sitting by as his nurse, with her spear and helmet, and her robe specked with a few *fleurs de lis*. The extinguishing of two entire armies in one war is what has rarely happened, and it gives a presage of the future force of our growing empire.

I thank you much for the newspapers you have been so kind as to send me. I send also to you, by every opportunity, packets of the French, Dutch, and English papers. Enclosed is the last *Courier of Europe*, wherein you will find a late curious debate on continuing the war with America, which the minister carried in the affirmative only by his own vote. It seems the nation is sick of it, but the King is obstinate. *There is a change made of the American Secretary*, and another is talked of in the room of Lord Sandwich. But I suppose we have no reason to desire such changes. If the King will have a war with us, his old servants are as well for us as any he is likely to put in their places. The ministry, you will see, declare, that the war in America is for the future to be only *defensive*. I hope we shall be too prudent to have the least dependence on this declaration. It is only thrown out to lull us; for, depend upon it, the King hates us cordially, and will be content with nothing short of our extirpation.

I shall be glad to receive the account you are preparing of the wanton damages done our possessions. I wish you could also furnish me with one, of the barbarities committed on our people. They may both be of excellent use on certain occasions. I received the duplicate of yours in cipher. Hereafter, I wish you would use that in which those instructions were written, that relate to the future peace. I am accustomed to that, and I think it very good and more convenient in the practice.

The friendly disposition of this court towards us continues. We have sometimes pressed a little too hard, expecting and demanding, perhaps, more than we ought, and have used improper arguments, which may have occasioned a little dissatisfaction, but it has not been lasting. In my opinion, the surest way to obtain liberal aid from others is vigorously to help ourselves. People fear assisting the negligent, the indolent, and the careless, lest the aids they afford should be lost. I know we have done a great deal; but it is said, we are apt to be supine after a little success, and too backward in furnishing our contingents. This is really a generous nation, fond of glory, and particularly that of protecting the oppressed. Trade is not the admiration of their noblesse, who always govern here. Telling them, their *commerce* will be advantaged by our success, and that it is their *interest* to help us, seems as much as to say, "Help us, and we shall not be obliged to you." Such indiscreet and improper language has been sometimes held here by some of our people, and produced no good effects.

The constant harmony, subsisting between the armies of the two nations in America, is a circumstance, that has afforded me infinite pleasure. It should be carefully cultivated. I hope nothing will happen to disturb it. The French officers, who have returned to France this winter, speak of our people in the handsomest and kindest manner; and there is a strong desire in many of the young noblemen to go over to fight for us; there is no restraining some of them; and several changes among the officers of their army have lately taken place in consequence.

You must be so sensible of the utility of maintaining a perfect good understanding with the Chevalier de la Luzerne, that I need say nothing on that head. The affairs of a distant people in any court of Europe will always be much affected by the representations of the minister of that court residing among them.

We have here great quantities of supplies, of all kinds, ready to be sent over, and which would have been on their way before this time, if the unlucky loss of the transports, that were under M. de Guichen, and other demands for more ships, had not created a difficulty to find freight for them. I hope however, that you will receive them with the next convoy.

The accounts we have of the economy introduced by Mr. Morris begin to be of service to us here, and will by degrees obviate the inconvenience, that an opinion of our disorders and mismanagements had occasioned. I inform him by this conveyance of the money aids we shall have this year. The sum is not so great as we could wish; and we must so much the more exert ourselves. A small increase of industry in every American, male and female, with a small diminution of luxury, would produce a sum far superior to all we can hope to beg or borrow from all our friends in Europe.

There are now near a thousand of our brave fellows prisoners in England, many of whom have patiently endured the hardships of that confinement several years, resisting every temptation to serve our enemies. Will not your late great advantages put it in your power to do something for their relief? The slender supply I have been able to afford, of a shilling a week to each, for their greater comfort during the winter, amounts weekly to fifty pounds sterling. An exchange would make so many of our countrymen happy, add to our strength, and diminish our expense. But our privateers, who cruise in Europe, will not be at the trouble of bringing in their prisoners, and I have none to exchange for them.

Generals Cornwallis and Arnold are both arrived in England. It is reported, that the former, in all his conversations, discourages the prosecution of the war in America; if so, he will of course be out of favour. We hear much of audiences given to the latter, and of his being present at councils.

You desire to know, whether any intercepted letters of Mr. Deane have been published in Europe? I have seen but one in the English papers, that to Mr. Wadsworth, and none in any of the French and Dutch papers, but some may have been printed that have not fallen in my way. There is no doubt of their being all genuine. His conversation, since his return from America, has, as I have been informed, gone gradually more and more into that style, and at length come to an open vindication of Arnold's conduct; and, within these few days, he has sent me a letter of twenty full pages, recapitulating those letters, and threatening to write and publish an account of the treatment he has received from Congress, &c. He resides at Ghent, is distressed both in mind and circumstances, raves and writes abundance, and I imagine it will end in his going over to join his friend Arnold in England. I had an exceeding good opinion of him when he acted with me, and I believe he was then sincere and hearty in our cause. But he is changed, and his character ruined in his own country and in this, so that I see no other but England to which he can now retire. He says, that we owe him about twelve thousand pounds sterling; and his great complaint is, that we do not settle his accounts and pay him. Mr. Johnston having declined the service, I proposed engaging Mr. Searle to undertake it; but Mr. Deane objected to him, as being his enemy. In my opinion he was, for that reason, even fitter for the service of Mr. Deane; since accounts are of a mathematical nature, and cannot be changed by an enemy, while that enemy's testimony, that he had found them well supported by authentic vouchers, would have weighed more than the same testimony from a friend.

With regard to negotiations for a peace, I see but little probability of their being entered upon seriously this year, unless the English minister has failed in raising his funds, which it is said he has secured; so that we must provide for another campaign, in which I hope God will continue to favour us, and humble our cruel and haughty enemies; a circumstance which, whatever Mr. Deane may say to the contrary, will give pleasure to all Europe.

This year opens well, by the reduction of Port Mahon, and the garrison prisoners of war, and we are not without hopes, that Gibraltar may soon follow. A few more signal successes in America will do much towards reducing our enemies to reason. Your expressions of good opinion with regard to me, and wishes of my continuance in this employment, are very obliging. As long as the Congress think I can be useful to our affairs, it is my duty to obey their orders; but I should be happy to see them better executed by another, and myself at liberty, enjoying, before I quit the stage of life, some small degree of leisure and tranquillity. With great esteem, &c.

"A HAPPY NAME FOR A PRINCE
AS OBSTINANT AS A MULE"

To John Adams

SIR   Passy, April 22, 1782

Mess.rs Fizeaux and Grand have lately sent me two accounts of which they desire my approbation. As they relate to Payments made by those Gentlemen of your Acceptances of Bills of Exchange, your Approbation must be of more importance than mine, you having more certain knowledge of the Affair. I therefore send them enclos'd to you and request you would be pleas'd to compare them with your List of Acceptations, and return them to me with your opinion, as they will be my Justification for advancing the Money.

I am very happy to hear of the rapid progress of your affairs. They fear in England that the States will make with us an alliance offensive and defensive, and the public Funds which they had puff'd up four or five per cent by the hope of a Separate Peace with Holland are falling again. They fill their papers continually with lies to raise and fall the Stocks. It is not amiss that they should thus be left to ruin one another, for they have been very—mischievous to the rest of mankind. I send enclosed a paper, of the Veracity of which I have some doubt, as to the Form, but none as to the Substance, for I believe the Number of People actually scalp'd in this murdering war by the Indians to exceed what is mentioned in invoice, and that Muley Istmael (a happy name for a prince as obstinant as a mule) is full as black a Tyrant as he is represented in Paul Jones' pretended letter. These being *substantial* Truths the Form is to be considered as Paper and Packthread. If it were republish'd in England it might make them a little asham'd of themselves.

I am very respectfully

Your Excellency's

most obedient and most

humble Servant

"MEN I FIND TO BE A SORT OF BEINGS VERY BADLY CONSTRUCTED"

To Joseph Priestley

DEAR SIR,   Passy near Paris, June 7, 1782.

I received your kind Letter of the 7th of April, also one of the 3d of May. I have always great Pleasure in hearing from you, in learning that you are well, and that you continue your Experiments. I should rejoice much, if I could once more recover the Leisure to search with you into the Works of Nature; I mean the *inanimate*, not the *animate* or moral part of them, the more I discover'd of the former, the more I admir'd them; the more I know of the latter, the more I am disgusted with them. Men I find to be a Sort of Beings very badly constructed, as they are generally more easily provok'd than reconcil'd, more disposed to do Mischief to each other than to make Reparation, much more easily deceiv'd than undeceiv'd, and having more Pride and even Pleasure in killing than in begetting one another; for without a Blush they assemble in great armies at NoonDay to destroy, and when they have kill'd as many as they can, they exaggerate the Number to augment the fancied Glory; but they creep into Corners, or cover themselves with the Darkness of night, when they mean to beget, as being asham'd of a virtuous Action. A virtuous Action it would be, and a vicious one the killing of them, if the Species were really worth producing or preserving; but of this I begin to doubt.

I know you have no such Doubts, because, in your zeal for their welfare, you are taking a great deal of pains to save their Souls. Perhaps as you grow older, you may look upon this as a hopeless Project, or an idle Amusement, repent of having murdered in mephitic air so many honest, harmless mice, and wish that to prevent mischief, you had used Boys and Girls instead of them. In what Light we are viewed by superior Beings, may be gathered from a Piece of late West India News, which possibly has not yet reached you. A young Angel of Distinction being sent down to this world on some Business, for the first time, had an old courier-spirit assigned him as a Guide. They arriv'd over the Seas of Martinico, in the middle of the long Day of obstinate Fight between the Fleets of Rodney and De Grasse. When, thro' the Clouds of smoke, he saw the Fire of the Guns, the Decks covered with mangled Limbs, and Bodies dead or dying; the ships sinking, burning, or blown into the Air; and the Quantity of Pain, Misery, and Destruction, the Crews yet alive were thus with so much Eagerness dealing round to one another; he turn'd angrily to his Guide, and said, "You blundering Blockhead, you are ignorant of your Business; you undertook to conduct me to the Earth, and you have brought me into Hell!" "No, Sir," says the Guide, "I have made no mistake; this is really the Earth, and these are men. Devils never treat one another in this cruel manner; they have more Sense, and more of what Men (vainly) call *Humanity*."

But to be serious, my dear old Friend, I love you as much as ever, and I love all the honest Souls that meet at the London Coffee-House. I only wonder how it happen'd, that they and my other Friends in England came to be such good Creatures in the midst of so perverse a Generation. I long to see them and you once more, and I labour for Peace with more Earnestness, that I may again be happy in your sweet society.

I show'd your letter to the Duke de Larochefoucault, who thinks with me, the new Experiments you have made are extremely curious; and he has given me thereupon a Note, which I inclose, and I request you would furnish me with the answer desired.

Yesterday the Count du Nord was at the Academy of Sciences, when sundry Experiments were exhibited for his Entertainment; among them, one by M. Lavoisier, to show that the strongest Fire we yet know, is made in a Charcoal blown upon with dephlogisticated air. In a Heat so produced, he melted Platina presently, the Fire being much more powerful than that of the strongest burning mirror. Adieu, and believe me ever, yours most affectionately,

"BY THE PRESS WE CAN SPEAK TO NATIONS"

To Richard Price

DEAR SIR,   Passy, June 13, 1782.

I congratulate you on the late revolution in your public affairs. Much good may arise from it, though possibly not all, that good men and even the new ministers themselves may have wished or expected. The change, however, in the sentiments of the nation, in which I see evident effects of your writings, with those of our deceased friend Mr. Burgh, and others of our valuable Club, should encourage you to proceed.

The ancient Roman and Greek orators could only speak to the number of citizens capable of being assembled within the reach of their voice. Their *writings* had little effect, because the bulk of the people could not read. Now by the press we can speak to nations; and good books and well written pamphlets have great and general influence. The facility, with which the same truths may be repeatedly enforced by placing them daily in different lights in *newspapers*, which are everywhere read, gives a great chance of establishing them. And we now find, that it is not only right to strike while the iron is hot, but that it may be very practicable to heat it by continually striking.

I suppose all may now correspond with more freedom, and I shall be glad to hear from you as often as may be convenient to you. Please to present my best respects to our good old friends of the London Coffee-House. I often figure to myself the pleasure I should have in being once more seated among them. With the greatest and most sincere esteem and affection, I am, my dear friend, yours ever,

"I AM COVETOUS, AND LOVE GOOD BARGAINS"

To Miss Alexander

Passy, June 24, 1782.

—I am not at all displeas'd, that the Thesis and Dedication, with which we were threatned, are blown over, for I dislike much all sorts of Mummery. The Republic of Letters has gained no Reputation, whatever else it may have gain'd, by the Commerce of Dedications; I never made one, and I never desir'd, that one should be made to me. When I submitted to receive this, it was from the bad Habit I have long had of doing every thing that Ladies desire me to do; there is no refusing any thing to Madame la Marck, nor to you. I have been to pay my Respects to that amiable lady, not merely because it was a Compliment due to her, but because I love her; which induces me to excuse her not letting me in; the same Reason I should have for excusing your faults, if you had any.

I have not seen your Papa since the Receipt of your pleasing Letter, so could arrange nothing with him respecting the Carriage. During seven or eight days, I shall be very busy; after that you shall hear from me, and the Carriage shall be at your Service. How could you think of writing to me about Chimneys and Fires, in such Weather as this! Now is the time for the frugal Lady you mention to save her Wood, obtain *plus de Chaleur*, and lay it up against Winter, as people do Ice against Summer. Frugality is an enriching Virtue; a Virtue I never could acquire in myself; but I was once lucky enough to find it in a Wife, who thereby became a Fortune to me. Do you possess it? If you do, and I were 20 Years younger, I would give your Father 1,000 Guineas for you. I know you would be worth more to me as a *Ménagère*, but I am covetous, and love good Bargains. Adieu, my dear Friend, and believe me ever yours most affectionately,

"THE MORE I AM CONVINC'D OF A FUTURE STATE"

To James Hutton

MY OLD AND DEAR FRIEND,   Passy, July 7, 1782.

A Letter written by you to M. Bertin, *Ministre d'Etat*, containing an Account of the abominable Murders committed by some of the frontier People on the poor Moravian Indians, has given me infinite Pain and Vexation. The Dispensations of Providence in this World puzzle my weak Reason. I cannot comprehend why cruel Men should have been permitted thus to destroy their Fellow Creatures. Some of the Indians may be suppos'd to have committed Sins, but one cannot think the little Children had committed any worthy of Death. Why has a single Man in England, who happens to love Blood and to hate Americans, been permitted to gratify that bad Temper by hiring German Murderers, and joining them with his own, to destroy in a continued Course of bloody Years near 100,000 human Creatures, many of them possessed of useful Talents, Virtues and Abilities to which he has no Pretension! It is he who has furnished the Savages with Hatchets and Scalping Knives, and engages them to fall upon our defenceless Farmers, and murder them with their Wives and Children, paying for their Scalps, of which the account kept in America already amounts, as I have heard, to near *two Thousand*!

Perhaps the people of the frontiers, exasperated by the Cruelties of the Indians, have been induced to kill all Indians that fall into their Hands without Distinction; so that even these horrid Murders of our poor Moravians may be laid to his Charge. And yet this Man lives, enjoys all the good Things this World can afford, and is surrounded by Flatterers, who keep even his Conscience quiet by telling him he is the best of Princes! I wonder at this, but I cannot therefore part with the comfortable Belief of a Divine Providence; and the more I see the Impossibility, from the number & extent of his Crimes, of giving equivalent Punishment to a wicked Man in this Life, the more I am convinc'd of a future State, in which all that here appears to be wrong shall be set right, all that is crooked made straight. In this Faith let you & I, my dear Friend, comfort ourselves; it is the only Comfort, in the present dark Scene of Things, that is allow'd us.

I shall not fail to write to the Government of America, urging that effectual Care may be taken to protect & save the Remainder of those unhappy People.

Since writing the above, I have received a Philadelphia Paper, containing some Account of the same horrid Transaction, a little different, and some Circumstances alledged as Excuses or Palliations, but extreamly weak & insufficient. I send it to you inclos'd. With great and sincere Esteem, I am ever, my dear Friend, yours most affectionately,

"TO COOP US UP WITHIN
THE ALLEGANY MOUNTAINS"

To Robert R. Livingston

SIR,   Passy, August 12, 1782.

I have lately been honoured with your several letters, of March 9th, and May 22d, and 30th. The paper, containing a state of the commerce in North America, and explaining the necessity and utility of convoys for its protection, I have laid before the minister, accompanied by a letter, pressing that it be taken into immediate consideration; and I hope it may be attended with success.

The order of Congress, for liquidating the accounts between this court and the United States, was executed before it arrived. All the accounts against us for money lent, and stores, arms, ammunition, clothing, &c., furnished by government, were brought in and examined, and a balance received, which made the debt amount to the even sum of eighteen millions, exclusive of the Holland loan, for which the King is guarantee. I send a copy of the instrument to Mr. Morris. In reading it, you will discover several fresh marks of the King's goodness towards us, amounting to the value of near two millions. These, added to the free gifts before made to us at different times, form an object of at least twelve millions, for which no returns but that of gratitude and friendship are expected. These, I hope, may be everlasting. The constant good understanding between France and the Swiss Cantons, and the steady benevolence of this crown towards them, afford us a well grounded hope that our alliance may be as durable and as happy for both nations; there being strong reasons for our union, and no crossing interests between us. I write fully to Mr. Morris on money affairs, who will doubtless communicate to you my letter, so that I need say the less to you on that subject.

The letter to the King was well received; the accounts of your rejoicings on the news of the Dauphin's birth gave pleasure here; as do the firm conduct of Congress in refusing to treat with General Carleton, and the unanimous resolutions of the Assemblies of different States on the same subject. All ranks of this nation appear to be in good humour with us, and our reputation rises throughout Europe. I understand from the Swedish ambassador, that their treaty with us will go on as soon as ours with Holland is finished; our treaty with France, with such improvements as that with Holland may suggest, being intended as the basis.

There have been various misunderstandings and mismanagements among the parties concerned in the expedition of the *Bon Homme Richard*, which have occasioned delay in dividing the prize money. M. de Chaumont, who was chosen by the captains of all the vessels in the expedition as their agent, has long been in a state little short of bankruptcy, and some of the delays have possibly been occasioned by the distress of his affairs. He now informs me, that the money is in the hands of the minister of the marine. I shall in a few days present the memorial you propose, with one relating to the prisoners, and will acquaint you with the answer. Mr. Barclay is still in Holland; when he returns he may take into his hands what money can be obtained on that account.

I think your observations respecting the Danish complaints through the minister of France perfectly just. I will receive no more of them by that channel, and will give your reasons to justify my refusal.

Your approbation of my idea of a medal, to perpetuate the memory of York and Saratoga victories, gives me great pleasure, and encourages me to have it struck. I wish you would acquaint me with what kind of a monument at York the emblems required are to be fixed on; whether an obelisk or a column; its dimensions; whether any part of it is to be marble, and the emblems carved on it, and whether the work is to be executed by the excellent artists in that way which Paris affords; and, if so, to what expense they are to be limited. This puts me in mind of a monument I got made here and sent to America, by order of Congress, five years since. I have heard of its arrival, and nothing more. It was admired here for its elegant antique simplicity of design, and the various beautiful marbles used in its composition. It was intended to be fixed against a wall in the State House of Philadelphia. I know not why it has been so long neglected; it would, methinks, be well to inquire after it, and get it put up somewhere. Directions for fixing it were sent with it. I enclose a print of it. The inscription in the engraving is not on the monument; it was merely the fancy of the engraver. There is a white plate of marble left smooth to receive such inscription as the Congress should think proper.

Our countrymen, who have been prisoners in England, are sent home, a few excepted, who were sick, and who will be forwarded as soon as recovered. This eases us of a very considerable charge.

I communicated to the Marquis de Lafayette the paragraph of your letter which related to him. He is still here, and, as there seems not so much likelihood of an active campaign in America, he is probably more useful where he is. His departure, however, though delayed, is not absolutely laid aside.

The second changes in the ministry of England have occasioned, or have afforded, pretences for various delays in the negotiation for peace. Mr. Grenville had two successive imperfect commissions. He was at length recalled, and Mr. Fitzherbert is now arrived to replace him, with a commission in due form to treat with France, Spain, and Holland. Mr. Oswald, who is here, is informed by a letter from the new Secretary of State, that a commission, empowering him to treat with the Commissioners of Congress, will pass the seals, and be sent him in a few days; till he arrives, this court will not proceed in its own negotiation. I send the *Enabling Act*, as it is called. Mr. Jay will acquaint you with what passes between him and the Spanish ambassador, respecting the proposed treaty with Spain. I will only mention, that my conjecture of that court's design to coop us up within the Allegany Mountains is now manifested. I hope Congress will insist on the Mississippi as the boundary, and the free navigation of the river, from which they could entirely exclude us.

An account of a terrible massacre of the Moravian Indians has been put into my hands. I send you the papers, that you may see how the fact is represented in Europe. I hope measures will be taken to secure what is left of those unfortunate people.

Mr. Laurens is at Nantes, waiting for a passage with his family to America. His state of health is unfortunately very bad. Perhaps the sea air may recover him, and restore him well to his country. I heartily wish it. He has suffered much by his confinement. Be pleased, Sir, to present my duty to the Congress, and assure them of my most faithful services. With great esteem, I have the honour to be, &c.

"TOO HARSH EVEN FOR THE BOYS"

To the Marquis de Lafayette

DEAR SIR   Passy, Sept. 17. 1782.
I continue to suffer from this cruel Gout: But in the midst of my Pain the News of Mad^m de la Fayette's safe Delivery, and your Acquisition of a Daughter gives me Pleasure.

In naming your Children I think you do well to begin with

the most antient State. And as we cannot have too many of so good a Race I hope you & Mme. de la Fayette will go thro the Thirteen. But as that may be in the common Way too severe a Task for her delicate Frame, and Children of Seven Months may become as Strong as those of Nine, I consent to the Abridgement of Two Months for each; and I wish her to spend the Twenty-six Months so gained, in perfect Ease, Health & Pleasure.

While you are proceeding, I hope our States will some of them new-name themselves. Miss Virginia, Miss Carolina, & Miss Georgiana will sound prettily enough for the Girls; but Massachusetts & Connecticut, are too harsh even for the Boys, unless they were to be Savages.

That God may bless you in the Event of this Day as in every other, prays

Your affectionate Friend & Servant

"HOW SUCH A GLOBE WAS FORMED"

To the Abbé Soulavie

SIR,   Passey, September 22, 1782.

I return the papers with some corrections. I did not find coal mines under the Calcareous rock in Derby Shire. I only remarked that at the lowest part of that rocky mountain which was in sight, there were oyster shells mixed in the stone; and part of the high county of Derby being probably as much above the level of the sea, as the coal mines of White-haven were below it, seemed a proof that there had been a great bouleversement in the surface of that Island, some part of it having been depressed under the sea, and other parts which had been under it being raised above it. Such changes in the superficial part of the globe seemed to me unlikely to happen if the earth were solid to the centre. I therefore imag-ined that the internal part might be a fluid more dense, and of greater specific gravity than any of the solids we are ac-quainted with; which therefore might swim in or upon that fluid. Thus the surface of the globe would be a shell, capable of being broken and disordered by the violent movements of the fluid on which it rested. And as air has been compressed by art so as to be twice as dense as water, in which case if such air and water could be contained in a strong glass vessel, the air would be seen to take the lowest place, and the water to float above and upon it; and as we know not yet the degree of density to which air may be compressed; and M. Amontons calculated, that its density increasing as it approached the centre in the same proportion as above the surface, it would at the depth of —— leagues be heavier than gold, possibly the dense fluid occupying the internal parts of the globe might be air compressed. And as the force of expansion in dense air when heated is in proportion to its density; this central air might afford another agent to move the surface, as well as be of use in keeping alive the subterraneous fires: Though as you observe, the sudden rarefaction of water coming into contact with those fires, may also be an agent sufficiently strong for that purpose, when acting between the incumbent earth and the fluid on which it rests.

If one might indulge imagination in supposing how such a globe was formed, I should conceive, that all the elements in separate particles being originally mixed in confusion and occupying a great space, they would as soon as the almighty fiat ordained gravity or the mutual attraction of certain parts, and the mutual repulsion of other parts to exist, all move towards their common centre: That the air being a fluid whose parts repel each other, though drawn to the common centre by their gravity, would be densest towards the centre, and rarer as more remote; consequently all matters lighter than the central part of that air and immersed in it, would recede from the centre and rise till they arrived at that region of the air which was of the same specific gravity with themselves, where they would rest; while other matter, mixed with the lighter air would descend, and the two meeting would form the shell of the first earth, leaving the upper atmosphere nearly clear. The original movement of the parts towards their common centre, would naturally form a whirl there; which would continue in the turning of the new formed globe upon its axis, and the greatest diameter of the shell would be in its equator.

If by any accident afterwards the axis should be changed, the
dense internal fluid by altering its form must burst the shell
and throw all its substance into the confusion in which we
find it.

I will not trouble you at present with my fancies concerning the manner of forming the rest of our system. Superior
beings smile at our theories, and at our presumption in making them. I will just mention that your observation of the
ferruginous nature of the lava which is thrown out from the
depths of our valcanos, gave me great pleasure. It has long
been a supposition of mine that the iron contained in the
substance of this globe, has made it capable of becoming as it
is a great magnet. That the fluid of magnetism exists perhaps
in all space; so that there is a magnetical North and South of
the universe as well as of this globe, and that if it were possible for a man to fly from star to star, he might govern his
course by the compass. That it was by the power of this general magnetism this globe became a particular magnet. In soft
or hot iron the fluid of magnetism is naturally diffused
equally; when within the influence of a magnet, it is drawn
to one end of the iron, made denser there, and rarer at the
other, while the iron continues soft and hot, it is only a temporary magnet: If it cools or grows hard in that situation, it
becomes a permanent one, the magnetic fluid not easily re-
suming its equilibrium. Perhaps it may be owing to the permanent magnetism of this globe, which it had not at first,
that its axis is at present kept parallel to itself, and not liable
to the changes it formerly suffered, which occasioned the rupture of its shell, the submersions and emersions of its lands
and the confusion of its seasons. The present polar and equatorial diameters differing from each other near ten leagues; it
is easy to conceive in case some power should shift the axis
gradually, and place it in the present equator, and make the
new equator pass through the present poles, what a sinking
of the water would happen in the present equatorial regions,
and what a rising in the present polar regions; so that vast
tracts would be discovered that now are under water, and
others covered that now are dry, the water rising and sinking
in the different extremes near five leagues.—Such an operation as this, possibly, occasioned much of Europe, and among

the rest, this mountain of Passy, on which I live, and which is composed of lime stone, rock and sea shells, to be abandoned by the sea, and to change its ancient climate, which seems to have been a hot one. The globe being now become a permanent magnet, we are perhaps safe from any future change of its axis. But we are still subject to the accidents on the surface which are occasioned by a wave in the internal ponderous fluid; and such a wave is producible by the sudden violent explosion you mention, happening from the junction of water and fire under the earth, which not only lifts the incumbent earth that is over the explosion, but impressing with the same force the fluid under it, creates a wave that may run a thousand leagues lifting and thereby shaking successively all the countries under which it passes. I know not whether I have expressed myself so clearly, as not to get out of your sight in these reveries. If they occasion any new enquiries and produce a better hypothesis, they will not be quite useless. You see I have given a loose to imagination; but I approve much more your method of philosophizing, which proceeds upon actual observation, makes a collection of facts, and concludes no farther than those facts will warrant. In my present circumstances, that mode of studying the nature of this globe is out of my power, and therefore I have permitted myself to wander a little in the wilds of fancy. With great esteem I have the honour to be, &c.

P. S. I have heard that chemists can by their art decompose stone and wood, extracting a considerable quantity of water from the one, and air from the other. It seems natural to conclude from this, that water and air were ingredients in their original composition. For men cannot make new matter of any kind. In the same manner may we not suppose, that when we consume combustibles of all kinds, and produce heat or light, we do not create that heat or light; but only decompose a substance which received it originally as a part of its composition? Heat may thus be considered as originally in a fluid state, but, attracted by organized bodies in their growth, becomes a part of the solid. Besides this, I can conceive that in the first assemblage of the particles of which this earth is composed each brought its portion of the loose heat that had been connected with it, and the whole when pressed together produced the internal fire that still subsists.

"A SINGLE INDISCRETION OF OURS"

To Comte de Vergennes

SIR,   Passy, December 17, 1782.

I received the letter your Excellency did me the honour of writing to me on the 15th instant. The proposal of having a passport from England was agreed to by me the more willingly, as I at that time had hopes of obtaining some money to send in the *Washington*, and the passport would have made its transportation safer, with that of our despatches, and of yours also, if you had thought fit to make use of the occasion. Your Excellency objected, as I understood it, that the English ministers, by their letters sent in the same ship, might convey inconvenient expectations into America. It was therefore I proposed not to press for the passport till your preliminaries were also agreed to. They have sent the passport without being pressed to do it, and they have sent no letters to go under it, and ours will prevent the inconvenience apprehended. In a subsequent conversation, your Excellency mentioned your intention of sending some of the King's cutters, whence I imagined, that detaining the *Washington* was no longer necessary; and it was certainly incumbent on us to give Congress as early an account as possible of our proceedings, who will think it extremely strange to hear of them by other means, without a line from us. I acquainted your Excellency, however, with our intention of despatching that ship, supposing you might possibly have something to send by her.

Nothing has been agreed in the preliminaries contrary to the interests of France; and no peace is to take place between us and England, till you have concluded yours. Your observation is, however, apparently just, that, in not consulting you before they were signed, we have been guilty of neglecting a point of *bienséance*. But, as this was not from want of respect for the King, whom we all love and honour, we hope it will be excused, and that the great work, which has hitherto been so happily conducted, is so nearly brought to perfection, and is so glorious to his reign, will not be ruined by a single indiscretion of ours. And certainly the whole edifice sinks to the ground immediately, if you refuse on that account to give us any further assistance.

We have not yet despatched the ship, and I beg leave to wait upon you on Friday for your answer.

It is not possible for any one to be more sensible than I am, of what I and every American owe to the King, for the many and great benefits and favours he has bestowed upon us. All my letters to America are proofs of this; all tending to make the same impressions on the minds of my countrymen, that I felt in my own. And I believe, that no Prince was ever more beloved and respected by his own subjects, than the King is by the people of the United States. *The English, I just now learn, flatter themselves they have already divided us.* I hope this little misunderstanding will therefore be kept a secret, and that they will find themselves totally mistaken. With great and sincere respect, I am, Sir, &c.

"ALL WARS ARE FOLLIES"

To Mary Hewson

Passy, Jan. 27. 1783.

—The Departure of my dearest Friend, which I learn from your last Letter, greatly affects me. To meet with her once more in this Life was one of the principal Motives of my proposing to visit England again, before my Return to America. The last Year carried off my Friends Dr. Pringle, and Dr. Fothergill, Lord Kaims, and Lord le Despencer. This has begun to take away the rest, and strikes the hardest. Thus the Ties I had to that Country, and indeed to the World in general, are loosened one by one, and I shall soon have no Attachment left to make me unwilling to follow.

I intended writing when I sent the 11 Books, but I lost the Time in looking for the 12th. I wrote with that; and hope it came to hand. I therein ask'd your Counsel about my coming to England. On Reflection, I think I can, from my Knowledge of your Prudence, foresee what it will be, viz. not to come too soon, lest it should seem braving and insulting some who ought to be respected. I shall, therefore, omit that Journey till I am near going to America, and then just step over to take Leave of my Friends, and spend a few days with you. I purpose bringing Ben with me, and perhaps may leave him under your Care.

At length we are in Peace, God be praised, and long, very long, may it continue. All Wars are Follies, very expensive, and very mischievous ones. When will Mankind be convinced of this, and agree to settle their Differences by Arbitration? Were they to do it, even by the Cast of a Dye, it would be better than by Fighting and destroying each other.

Spring is coming on, when Travelling will be delightful. Can you not, when your children are all at School, make a little Party, and take a Trip hither? I have now a large House, delightfully situated, in which I could accommodate you and two or three Friends, and I am but half an Hour's Drive from Paris.

In looking forward, Twenty-five Years seems a long Period, but, in looking back, how short! Could you imagine, that 'tis now full a Quarter of a Century since we were first acquainted? It was in 1757. During the greatest Part of the Time, I lived in the same House with my dear deceased Friend, your Mother; of course you and I saw and convers'd with each other much and often. It is to all our Honours, that in all that time we never had among us the smallest Misunderstanding. Our Friendship has been all clear Sunshine, without the least Cloud in its Hemisphere. Let me conclude by saying to you, what I have had too frequent Occasions to say to my other remaining old Friends, "The fewer we become, the more let us love one another." Adieu, and believe me ever yours most affectionately,

"IN SOME THINGS, ABSOLUTELY OUT OF HIS SENSES"

To Robert R. Livingston

SIR,   Passy, July 22, 1783.
    You have complain'd, sometimes with reason, of not

hearing from your foreign Ministers; we have had cause to make the same Complaint, six full Months having interven'd between the latest date of your preceding Letters and the receipt of those by Captain Barney. During all this time we were ignorant of the Reception of the Provisional Treaty, and the Sentiments of Congress upon it, which, if we had received sooner, might have forwarded the Proceedings on the Definitive Treaty, and, perhaps, brought them to a Conclusion at a time more favourable than the present. But these occasional Interruptions of Correspondence are the inevitable Consequences of a State of War, and of such remote Situations. Barney had a short Passage, and arrived some Days before Colonel Ogden, who also brought Dispatches from you, all of which are come safe to hand. We, the Commissioners, have in our joint Capacity written a Letter to you, which you will receive with this.

I shall now answer yours of March 26, May 9, and May 31. It gave me great Pleasure to learn by the first, that the News of the Peace diffused general Satisfaction. I will not now take upon me to justify the apparent Reserve, respecting this Court, at the Signature, which you disapprove. We have touch'd upon it in our general Letter. I do not see, however, that they have much reason to complain of that Transaction. Nothing was stipulated to their Prejudice, and none of the Stipulations were to have Force, but by a subsequent Act of their own. I suppose, indeed, that they have not complain'd of it, or you would have sent us a Copy of the Complaint, that we might have answer'd it. I long since satisfi'd Comte de V. about it here. We did what appear'd to all of us best at the Time, and, if we have done wrong, the Congress will do right, after hearing us, to censure us. Their Nomination of Five Persons to the Service seems to mark, that they had some Dependence on our joint Judgment, since one alone could have made a Treaty by Direction of the French Ministry as well as twenty.

I will only add, that, with respect to myself, neither the Letter from M. Marbois, handed us thro' the British Negociators (a suspicious Channel), nor the Conversations respecting the Fishery, the Boundaries, the Royalists, &c., recommending Moderation in our Demands, are of Weight sufficient in my Mind to fix an Opinion, that this Court wish'd to restrain us in obtaining any Degree of Advantage we could prevail on our Enemies to accord; since those Discourses are fairly resolvable, by supposing a very natural Apprehension, that we, relying too much on the Ability of France to continue the War in our favour, and supply us constantly with Money, might insist on more Advantages than the English would be willing to grant, and thereby lose the Opportunity of making Peace, so necessary to all our Friends.

I ought not, however, to conceal from you, that one of my Colleagues is of a very different Opinion from me in these Matters. He thinks the French Minister one of the greatest Enemies of our Country, that he would have straitned our Boundaries, to prevent the Growth of our People; contracted our Fishery, to obstruct the Increase of our Seamen; and retained the Royalists among us, to keep us divided; that he privately opposes all our Negociations with foreign Courts, and afforded us, during the War, the Assistance we receiv'd, only to keep it alive, that we might be so much the more weaken'd by it; that to think of Gratitude to France is the greatest of Follies, and that to be influenc'd by it would ruin us. He makes no Secret of his having these Opinions, expresses them publicly, sometimes in presence of the English Ministers, and speaks of hundreds of Instances which he could produce in Proof of them. None of which however, have yet appear'd to me, unless the Conversations and Letter above-mentioned are reckoned such.

If I were not convinc'd of the real Inability of this Court to furnish the further Supplys we ask'd, I should suspect these Discourses of a Person in his Station might have influenced the Refusal; but I think they have gone no farther than to occasion a Suspicion, that we have a considerable Party of Antigallicans in America, who are not Tories, and consequently to produce some doubts of the Continuance of our Friendship. As such Doubts may hereafter have a bad Effect, I think we cannot take too much care to remove them; and it is, therefore, I write this, to put you on your guard, (believing it my duty, tho' I know that I hazard by it a mortal Enmity), and to caution you respecting the Insinuations of this Gentleman against this Court, and the Instances he supposes of their ill will to us, which I take to be as imaginary as I know his Fancies to be, that Count de V. and myself are continually plotting against him, and employing the News-Writers of Europe to depreciate his Character, &c. But as Shakespear says, "Trifles light as Air," &c. I am persuaded, however, that he means well for his Country, is always an honest Man, often a wise one, but sometimes, and in some things, absolutely out of his senses.

When the Commercial Article, mentioned in yours of the 26th was struck out of our propos'd Preliminaries by the then British Ministry, the reason given was, that sundry Acts of Parliament still in force were against it, and must be first repeal'd, which I believe was really their Intention, and sundry Bills were accordingly bro't in for that purpose; but, new Ministers with different Principles succeeding, a commercial Proclamation totally different from those Bills has lately appeared. I send enclos'd a Copy of it. We shall try what can be done in the Definitive Treaty towards setting aside that Proclamation; but, if it should be persisted in, it will then be a Matter worthy the attentive Discussion of Congress, whether it will be most prudent to retort with a similar Regulation in order to force its Repeal (which may possibly tend to bring on another Quarrel), or to let it pass without notice, and leave it to its own Inconvenience, or rather Impracticability, in the Execution, and to the Complaints of the West India Planters, who must all pay much dearer for our Produce, under those Restrictions.

I am not enough Master of the Course of our Commerce to give an Opinion on this particular Question, and it does not behove me to do it; yet I have seen so much Embarrassment and so little Advantage in all the Restraining and Compulsive Systems, that I feel myself strongly inclin'd to believe, that a State, which leaves all her Ports open to all the World upon equal Terms, will, by that means, have foreign Commodities cheaper, sell its own Productions dearer, and be on the whole the most prosperous. I have heard some Merchants say, that there is 10 per cent Difference between *Will you buy?* and *Will you sell?* When Foreigners bring us their Goods, they want to part with them speedily, that they may purchase their Cargoes and despatch their Ships, which are at constant

Charges in our Ports; we have then the Advantage of their *Will you buy?* And when they demand our Produce, we have the Advantage of their *Will you sell?* And the concurring Demands of a Number also contribute to raise our Prices. Thus both those Questions are in our favour at home, against us abroad.

The employing, however, of our own Ships and raising a Breed of Seamen among us, tho' it should not be a matter of so much private Profit as some imagine, is nevertheless of political Importance, and must have weight in considering this Subject.

The Judgment you make of the Conduct of France in the Peace, and the greater Glory acquired by her Moderation than even by her Arms, appears to me perfectly just. The Character of this Court and Nation seems, of late years, to be considerably changed. The Ideas of Aggrandizement by Conquest are out of fashion, and those of Commerce are more enlightened and more generous than heretofore. We shall soon, I believe, feel something of this in our being admitted to a greater Freedom of Trade with their Islands. The Wise here think France great enough; and its Ambition at present seems to be only that of Justice and Magnanimity towards other Nations, Fidelity and Utility to its Allies.

The Ambassador of Portugal was much pleas'd with the Proceedings relating to their Vessel, which you sent me, and assures me they will have a good Effect at his Court. He appears extremely desirous of a Treaty with our States; I have accordingly propos'd to him the Plan of one (nearly the same with that sent me for Sweden), and, after my agreeing to some Alterations, he has sent it to his Court for Approbation. He told me at Versailles, last Tuesday, that he expected its Return to him on Saturday next, and anxiously desired that I would not despatch our Pacquet without it, that Congress might consider it, and, if approv'd, send a Commission to me or some other Minister to sign it.

I venture to go thus far in treating, on the Authority only of a kind of general Power, given formerly by a Resolution of Congress to Messrs. Franklin, Deane, and Lee; but a special Commission seems more proper to compleat a Treaty, and more agreable to the usual Forms of such Business.

I am in just the same Situation with Denmark; that Court, by its Minister here, has desired a Treaty with us. I have propos'd a Plan formed on that sent me for Sweden; it had been under Consideration some time at Copenhagen, and is expected here this Week, so that I may possibly send that also by this Conveyance. You will have seen by my Letter to the Danish Prime Minister, that I did not forget the Affair of the Prizes. What I then wrote, produc'd a verbal Offer made me here, of £10,000 Sterling, propos'd to be given by his Majesty to the Captors, if I would accept it as a full Discharge of our Demand. I could not do this, I said, because it was not more than a fifth Part of the Estimated Value. In answer, I was told, that the Estimation was probably extravagant, that it would be difficult to come at the Knowledge of their true Value, and that, whatever they might be worth in themselves, they should not be estimated as of such Value to us when at Bergen, since the English probably watched them, and might have retaken them in their Way to America; at least, they were at the common Risques of the Seas and Enemies, and the Insurance was a considerable Drawback; that this Sum might be consider'd as so much sav'd for us by the King's Interference; for that, if the English Claimants had been suffered to carry the Cause into the common Courts, they must have recovered the Prizes by the Laws of Denmark; it was added, that the King's Honour was concern'd, that he sincerely desir'd our Friendship, but he would avoid, by giving this Sum in the Form of a Present to the Captors, the Appearance of its being exacted from him as the Reparation of an Injury, when it was really intended rather as a Proof of his strong Disposition to cultivate a good Understanding with us.

I reply'd, that the Value might possibly be exaggerated; but that we did not desire more than should be found just upon Enquiry, and that it was not difficult to learn from London what Sums were insur'd upon the Ships and Cargoes, which would be some Guide; and that a reasonable Abatement might be made for the risque; but that the Congress could not, in justice to their Mariners, deprive them of any Part that was truly due to those brave Men, whatever Abatement they might think fit to make (as a Mark of their Regard for the

King's Friendship) of the Part belonging to the publick; that I had, however, no Instructions or Authority to make any Abatement of any kind, and could, therefore, only acquaint Congress with the Offer, and the Reasons that accompanied it, which I promised to state fully and candidly (as I have now done), and attend their Orders; desiring only that it might be observ'd, we had presented our Complaint with Decency, that we had charg'd no Fault on the Danish Government, but what might arise from Inattention or Precipitancy, and that we had intimated no Resentment, but had waited, with Patience and Respect, the King's Determination, confiding, that he would follow the equitable Disposition of his own Breast, by doing us Justice as soon as he could do it with Conveniency; that the best and wisest Princes sometimes erred, that it belong'd to the Condition of Man, and was, therefore, inevitable, and that the true Honour in such Cases consisted, not in disowning or hiding the Error, but in making ample Reparation; that, tho' I could not accept what was offered on the Terms proposed, our Treaty might go on, and its Articles be prepared and considered, and, in the mean time, I hoped his Danish Majesty would reconsider the Offer, and make it more adequate to the Loss we had sustained. Thus that matter rests; but I hourly expect to hear farther, and perhaps may have more to say on it before the Ship's Departure.

I shall be glad to have the Proceedings you mention respecting the Brig *Providentia.* I hope the Equity and Justice of our Admiralty Courts respecting the Property of Strangers will always maintain their Reputation; and I wish particularly to cultivate the Disposition of Friendship towards us, apparent in the late Proceedings of Denmark, as the Danish Islands may be of use to our West India Commerce, while the English impolitic Restraints continue.

The Elector of Saxony, as I understand from his Minister here, has thoughts of sending one to Congress, and proposing a Treaty of Commerce and Amity with us. Prussia has likewise an Inclination to share in a Trade with America, and the Minister of that Court, tho' he has not directly propos'd a Treaty, has given me a Pacquet of Lists of the several Sorts of Merchandise they can furnish us with, which he requests me to send to America for the Information of our Merchants.

I have received no Answer yet from Congress to my Request of being dismiss'd from their Service. They should, methinks, reflect, that if they continue me here, the Faults I may henceforth commit, thro' the Infirmities of Age, will be rather theirs than mine. I am glad my Journal afforded you any Pleasure. I will, as you desire, endeavour to continue it. I thank you for the Pamphlet; it contains a great deal of Information respecting our Finances. We shall, as you advise, avoid publishing it. But I see they are publishing it in the English Papers. I was glad I had a copy authenticated by the Signature of Secr^y Thomson, by which I could assure M. de Vergennes, that the Money Contract I had made with him was ratified by Congress, he having just before express'd some uneasiness to me at its being so long neglected. I find it was ratified soon after it was receiv'd, but the Ratification, except in that Pamphlet, has not yet come to hand. I have done my best to procure the farther Loan directed by the Resolution of Congress. It was not possible. I have written on that Matter to Mr. Morris. I wish the rest of the Estimates of Losses and Mischiefs were come to hand; they would still be of Use.

Mr. Barclay has in his Hands the Affair of the *Alliance* and *Bon Homme Richard*. I will afford him all the Assistance in my Power, but it is a very perplex'd Business. That Expedition, tho' for particular Reasons under American Commissions and Colours, was carry'd on at the King's expence, and under his Orders. M. de Chaumont was the Agent appointed by the Minister of the Marine to make the Outfit. He was also chosen by all the Captains of the Squadron, as appears by an Instrument under their Hands, to be their Agent, receive, sell, and divide Prizes, &c. The Crown bought two of them at public Sale, and the Money, I understand, is lodg'd in the Hands of a responsible Person at L'Orient. M. de Chaumont says he has given in his Accounts to the Marine, and that he has no more to do with the Affair, except to receive a Ballance due to him. That Account, however, is I believe unsettled, and the Absence of some of the Captains is said to make another Difficulty, which retards the Completion of the

Business. I never paid or receiv'd any thing relating to that Expedition, nor had any other Concern in it, than barely ordering the *Alliance* to join the Squadron, at M. de Sartine's Request. I know not whether the other Captains will not claim a Share in what we may obtain from Denmark, tho' the Prizes were made by the *Alliance*, when separate from the Squadron. If so, that is another Difficulty in the way of making Abatement in our Demand, without their Consent.

I am sorry to find, that you have Thoughts of quitting the Service. I do not think your Place can be easily well supply'd. You mention, that an entire new Arrangement, with respect to foreign Affairs, is under Consideration. I wish to know whether any Notice is likely to be taken in it of my Grandson. He has now gone through an Apprenticeship of near seven Years in the ministerial Business, and is very capable of serving the States in that Line, as possessing all the Requisites of Knowledge, Zeal, Activity, Language, and Address. He is well lik'd here, and Count de Vergennes has express'd to me in warm Terms his very good Opinion of him. The late Swedish Ambassador, Count de Creutz, who has gone home to be Prime Minister, desir'd I would endeavour to procure his being sent to Sweden, with a public Character, assuring me, that he should be glad to receive him there as our Minister, and that he knew it would be pleasing to the King. The present Swedish Ambassador has also propos'd the same thing to me, as you will see by a Letter of his, which I enclose. One of the Danish Ministers, M. Walterstorff, who will probably be sent in a public Character to Congress, has also express'd his Wish, that my Grandson may be sent to Denmark. But it is not my Custom to solicit Employments for myself, or any of my Family, and I shall not do it in this Case. I only hope, that if he is not to be employ'd in your new Arrangement, I may be inform'd of it as soon as possible, that, while I have Strength left for it, I may accompany him in a Tour to Italy, returning thro' Germany, which I think he may make to more Advantage with me than alone, and which I have long promis'd to afford him, as a Reward for his faithful Service, and his tender filial Attachment to me.

July 25. While I was writing the above, M. Walterstorff came in, and deliver'd me a Pacquet from M. de Rosencrone, the Danish Prime Minister, containing the Project of the Treaty with some proposed Alterations, and a Paper of Reasons in support of them. Fearing that we should not have time to copy them, I send herewith the Originals, relying on his Promise to furnish me with Copies in a few Days. He seemed to think, that the Interest of the Merchants is concern'd in the immediate Conclusion of the Treaty, that they may form their Plans of Commerce, and wish'd to know whether I did not think my general Power, above mentioned, sufficient for that purpose. I told him, I thought a particular Commission more agreable to the Forms; but, if his Danish Majesty would be content for the present with the general Authority, formerly given me, I believ'd I might venture to act upon it, reserving, by a separate Article, to Congress a Power of shortning the Term, in Case any Part of the Treaty should not be to their mind, unless the Alteration of such Part should hereafter be agreed on.

The Prince de Deux-Ponts was lately at Paris, and apply'd to me for Information respecting a Commerce which is desired between the Electorate of Bavaria and America. I have it also from a good Hand at the Court of Vienna, that the Emperor is desirous of establishing a Commerce with us from Trieste as well as Flanders, and would make a Treaty with us, if propos'd to him. Since our Trade is laid open, and no longer a Monopoly to England, all Europe seems desirous of sharing in it, and for that purpose to cultivate our Friendship. That it may be better known everywhere, what sort of People, and what kind of Government they will have to treat with, I prevailed with a Friend, the Duc de Rochefoucauld, to translate our Book of Constitutions into French, and I presented Copies to all the foreign Ministers. I send you one herewith. They are much admired by the Politicians here, and it is thought will induce considerable Emigrations of substantial People from different Parts of Europe to America. It is particularly a Matter of Wonder, that, in the Midst of a cruel War raging in the Bowels of our Country, our Sages should have the Firmness of Mind to sit down calmly and form such compleat Plans of Government. They add considerably to the Reputation of the United States.

I have mentioned above the Port of Trieste, with which we

may possibly have a Commerce, and I am told that many useful Productions and Manufactures of Hungary may be had extreamly cheap there. But it becomes necessary first to consider how our Mediterranean Trade is to be protected from the Corsaires of Barbary. You will see by the enclos'd Copy of a Letter I receiv'd from Algiers, the Danger two of our Ships escap'd last Winter. I think it not improbable that those Rovers may be privately encouraged by the English to fall upon us, to prevent our Interference in the Carrying Trade; for I have in London heard it is a Maxim among the Merchants, that, if *there were no Algiers, it would be worth England's while to build one*. I wonder, however, that the rest of Europe do not combine to destroy those Nests, and secure Commerce from their future Piracies.

I made the Grand Master of Malta a Present of one of our Medals in Silver, writing him a Letter, of which I enclose a Copy; and I believe our People will be kindly receiv'd in his Ports; but that is not sufficient; and perhaps, now we have Peace, it will be proper to send Ministers, with suitable Presents, to establish a Friendship with the Emperor of Morocco, and the other Barbary States, if possible. Mr. Jay will inform you of some Steps, that have been taken by a Person at Alicant, without Authority, towards a Treaty with that Emperor. I send you herewith a few more of the above-mentioned Medals, which have given great Satisfaction to this Court and Nation. I should be glad to know how they are lik'd with you.

Our People, who were Prisoners in England, are now all discharg'd. During the whole War, those who were in Forton prison, near Portsmouth, were much befriended by the constant charitable Care of Mr. Wren, a Presbyterian Minister there, who spared no Pains to assist them in their Sickness and Distress, by procuring and distributing among them the Contributions of good Christians, and prudently dispensing the Allowance I made them, which gave him a great deal of trouble, but he went through it chearfully. I think some public Notice should be taken of this good Man. I wish the Congress would enable me to make him a Present, and that some of our Universities would confer upon him the Degree of Doctor.

The Duke of Manchester, who has always been our Friend in the House of Lords, is now here as Ambassador from England. I dine with him to-day, (26th,) and, if any thing of Importance occurs, I will add it in a Postcript. Be pleased to present my dutiful Respects to the Congress, assure them of my most faithful Services, and believe me to be, with great and sincere Esteem, Sir, &c.

"THERE NEVER WAS A GOOD WAR,
OR A BAD PEACE"

To Sir Joseph Banks

DEAR SIR,   Passy, July 27, 1783.

I received your very kind letter by Dr. Blagden, and esteem myself much honoured by your friendly Remembrance. I have been too much and too closely engaged in public Affairs, since his being here, to enjoy all the Benefit of his Conversation you were so good as to intend me. I hope soon to have more Leisure, and to spend a part of it in those Studies, that are much more agreable to me than political Operations.

I join with you most cordially in rejoicing at the return of Peace. I hope it will be lasting, and that Mankind will at length, as they call themselves reasonable Creatures, have Reason and Sense enough to settle their Differences without cutting Throats; for, in my opinion, *there never was a good War, or a bad Peace.* What vast additions to the Conveniences and Comforts of Living might Mankind have acquired, if the Money spent in Wars had been employed in Works of public utility! What an extension of Agriculture, even to the Tops of our Mountains: what Rivers rendered navigable, or joined by Canals: what Bridges, Aqueducts, new Roads, and other public Works, Edifices, and Improvements, rendering England a compleat Paradise, might have been obtained by spending those Millions in doing good, which in the last War have been spent in doing Mischief; in bringing Misery into thousands of Families, and destroying the Lives of so many thousands of working people, who might have performed the useful labour!

I am pleased with the late astronomical Discoveries made by our Society. Furnished as all Europe now is with Academies of Science, with nice Instruments and the Spirit of Experiment, the progress of human knowledge will be rapid, and discoveries made, of which we have at present no Conception. I begin to be almost sorry I was born so soon, since I cannot have the happiness of knowing what will be known 100 years hence.

I wish continued success to the Labours of the Royal Society, and that you may long adorn their chair; being, with the highest esteem, dear Sir, &c.

P. S. Dr. Blagden will acquaint you with the experiment of a vast Globe sent up into the Air, much talked of here, and which, if prosecuted, may furnish means of new knowledge.

FIRST BALLOON EXPERIMENTS

To Sir Joseph Banks

SIR,   Passy, Aug. 30. 1783.
On Wednesday the 27th Instant, the new aerostatic Experiment, invented by Messrs Mongolfier of Annonay was repeated by M[r]. Charles; Professor of Experimental Philosophy at Paris.

A hollow Globe 12 feet diameter was formed of what is called in England Oiled Silk, here Taffetas *gommée*, the Silk being impregnated with a Solution of Gum-elastic in Lintseed Oil, as is said. The Parts were sewed together while wet with the Gum, and some of it was afterwards passed over the Seams, to render it as tight as possible.

It was afterwards filled with the inflammable Air that is produced by pouring Oil of Vitriol upon Filings of Iron, when it was found to have a Tendency upwards so strong as to be capable of lifting a Weight of 39 Pounds, exclusive of its own weight which was 25 lb, and the Weight of the Air contain'd.

It was brought early in the Morning to the *Champ de Mars*, a Field in which Reviews are sometimes made, lying between the Military School and the River. There it was held down by a Cord, till 5 in the Afternoon, when it was to be let loose. Care was taken before the Hour to replace what Portion had been lost of the inflammable Air, or of its Force, by injecting more.

It is supposed that not less than 50,000 People were assembled to see the Experiment. The Champ de Mars being surrounded by Multitudes, and vast Numbers on the opposite Side of the River.

At 5 o Clock Notice was given to the Spectators by the Firing of two Cannon, that the Cord was about to be cut. And presently the Globe was seen to rise, and that as fast as a Body of 12 feet diameter with a force only of 39 pounds, could be suppos'd to move the resisting Air out of its way. There was some Wind, but not very strong. A little Rain had wet it, so that it shone, and made an agreable Appearance. It diminish'd in Apparent Magnitude as it rose, till it enter'd the Clouds, when it seem'd to me scarce bigger than an Orange, and soon after became invisible, the Clouds concealing it.

The Multitude separated, all well satisfied & much delighted with the Success of the Experiment, and amusing one another with Discourses of the various Uses it may possibly be apply'd to, among which many were very extravagant. But possibly it may pave the Way to some Discoveries in Natural Philosophy of which at present we have no Conception.

A Note secur'd from the Weather had been affix'd to the Globe, signifying the Time & Place of its Departure, and praying those who might happen to find it, to send an Account of its State to certain Persons at Paris. No News was heard of it till the next Day, when Information was receiv'd, that it fell a little after 6 oClock at Gonesse, a Place about 4 Leagues distance; and that it was rent open, and some say had Ice in it. It is suppos'd to have burst by the Elasticity of the contain'd Air when no longer compress'd by so heavy an Atmosphere.

One of 38 feet Diameter is preparing by M. Mongolfier himself at the Expence of the Academy, which is to go up in a few Days. I am told it is constructed of Linen & Paper, and is to be filled with a different Air, not yet made public, but cheaper than that produc'd by the Oil of Vitriol of which 200 Paris Pints were consum'd in filling the other.

It is said that for some Days after its being fill'd, the Ball was found to lose an eighth Part of its Force of Levity in 24 Hours: Whether this was from Imperfection in the Tightness of the Ball, or a Change in the Nature of the Air, Experiments may easily discover.

I thought it my Duty, Sir, to send an early Account of this extraordinary Fact, to the Society which does me the honour to reckon me among its Members; and I will endeavour to make it more perfect, as I receive farther Information.

With great Respect, I am, Sir,

P. S. Since writing the above, I am favour'd with your kind Letter of the 25.th I am much oblig'd to you for the Care you have taken to forward the Transactions, as well as to the Council for so readily ordering them on Application.—Please to accept and present my Thanks.

I just now learn, that some Observers say, the Ball was 150 seconds in rising, from the Cutting of the Cord till hid in the Clouds; that its height was then about 500 Toises, but, mov'd out of the Perpendicular by the Wind, it had made a Slant so as to form a Triangle, whose base on the Earth was about 200 Toises. It is said the Country people who saw it fall were frightened, conceiv'd from its bounding a little when it touch'd the Ground, that there was some living Animal in it, and attack'd it with Stones and Knives, so that it was much mangled; but it is now brought to Town & will be repaired.—

The great one of M. Mongolfier, is to go up as is said, from Versailles, in about 8 or 10 Days. It is not a Globe but of a different form, more convenient for penetrating the Air. It contains 50,000 cubic Feet, and is supposed to have a Force of Levity equal to 1500 pounds weight. A Philosopher here, M. Pilatre de Rozier, has seriously apply'd to the Academy for Leave to go up with it, in order to make some

Experiments. He was complimented on his Zeal and Courage for the Promotion of Science, but advis'd to wait till the Management of these Balls was made by Experience more certain & safe. They say the filling of it in M. Mongolfier's Way will not cost more than half a Crown. One is talk'd of to be 110 feet Diameter. Several Gentlemen have ordered small ones to be made for their Amusement; one has ordered four of 15 feet diameter each; I know not with what Purpose; but such is the present Enthusiasm for promoting & improving this Discovery, that probably we shall soon make considerable Progress in the Art of constructing and Using the Machines. —

Among the Pleasantries Conversation produces on this Subject, some suppose Flying to be now invented, and that since Men may be supported in the Air, nothing is wanted but some light handy Instruments to give and direct Motion. Some think Progressive Motion on the Earth may be advanc'd by it, and that a Running Footman or a Horse slung & suspended under such a Globe so as to leave no more of Weight pressing the Earth with their Feet, than perhaps 8 or 10 Pounds, might with a fair Wind run in a straight Line across Countries as fast as that Wind, and over Hedges, Ditches, & even Waters. It has been even fancied that in time People will keep such Globes anchored in the Air, to which by Pullies they may draw up Game to be preserved in the Cool, & Water to be frozen when Ice is wanted. And that to get Money, it will be contrived to give People an extensive view of the Country, by running them upon an Elbow Chair a Mile high for a Guinea, &c. &c.

A Pamphlet is printing in which we are to have a full and perfect Account of the Experiments hitherto made, & I will send it to you. M. Mongolfier's Air to fill the Globe has hitherto been kept secret. Some suppose it to be only common Air heated by passing thro' the Flame of burning Straw, & thereby extreamly rarified. If so its Levity will soon be diminished by Condensation when it comes into the cooler Regions above.

Sept. 2d. — I add this paper just now given me, B. F. The print contains a view of Champ de Mars, and the ball in the air with this subscription:

Experience de la machine aérostatique de M^{essrs.} de Mont-
golfier, d'Anonai en Vivarais, réepétée à Paris le 27 Août. 1783
au Champ de Mars, avec un ballon de taffetas enduit de
gomme elastique, de 36 pieds 6 onces de circonference. Le
ballon plein d'air inflammable a été executé par Mons. Robert, en vertu d'une souscription nationale, sous la direction
de Mr. Faujas de Saint Fond (et M. Charles).

N. B.—M. Charles' name is wrote with pen, not engraved.

Calculas du Ballon do 12 pieds de diametre enlevé le Mer-
credy 27 Août 1783.

Circonference du grand cercle. . . .	37	pieds
Diametre	12	
	74	
	37	
Surface	444	
Tiers du rayon	2	
Solidite	888	pieds cubes
Air atm. à 12 gros le pied	12	
	1776	
	888	
Pesanteur de l'air atm.	10,656	gros

$$26 \begin{cases} 8 \\ \overline{} \\ 1332 \end{cases} \text{ounces} \dfrac{/16}{/83} \text{ lb., 4 ounces.}$$

25,

6   52

L'air atmospherique dont le ballon occupait la place, pesant
83 lb. 4 onces et sa force pour s'elever etant de 40 lb. il falloit
que son enveloppe et l'air inflammable qu'elle contenoit ne
pesassent que 42 lb. 4 onces. L'enveloppe en pesoit 25, reste
pour l'air inflammable 18 lb. 4 onces.

En supposant le ballon de 6 pieds de diametre, son volume
etant le 8me, du ier le poids de l'air dont il occupoit la place
seroit le 8me, de 83 lb., 4 onces = 10 lb., 6 onces, 4 gros.
L'air inflammable ⅛ de 18 lb., 4 onces = 2 lb., 4 onces, 4
gros. L'enveloppe ¼ de 25 lb., = 6 lb., 4 onces. Les dernières
valeurs reunies sont 8 lb., 8 onces, 4 gros, qui otès de 10 lb.,
6 onces, 4 gros pesanteur de l'air atmospherique dont le ballon occupoit la place, laisse pour sa force d'elevation 1 lb., 14
onces.

"FALLS LITTLE SHORT OF TREASON"

To John Jay

Sir,   Passy, September 10, 1783.

I have received a letter from a very respectable person in America, containing the following words, viz.

"It is confidently reported, propagated, and believed by some among us, that the Court of France was at the bottom against our obtaining the fishery and territory in that great extent, in which both are secured to us by the treaty; that our Minister at that Court favored, or did not oppose this design against us; and that it was entirely owing to the firmness, sagacity, and disinterestedness of Mr Adams, with whom Mr Jay united, that we have obtained these important advantages."

It is not my purpose to dispute any share of the honor of that treaty, which the friends of my colleagues may be disposed to give them, but having now spent fifty years of my life in public offices and trusts, and having still one ambition left, that of carrying the character of fidelity at least to the grave with me, I cannot allow that I was behind any of them in zeal and faithfulness. I therefore think, that I ought not to suffer an accusation, which falls little short of treason to my country, to pass without notice, when the means of effectual vindication are at hand. You, Sir, were a witness of my conduct in that affair. To you and my other colleagues I appeal, by sending to each a similar letter with this, and I have no doubt of your readiness to do a brother Commissioner justice, by certificates, that will entirely destroy the effect of that accusation.

I have the honor to be, with much esteem, &c.

"ALL PROPERTY . . . SEEMS TO ME TO BE
THE CREATURE OF PUBLIC CONVENTION"

To Robert Morris

Sir,   Passy, Dec. 25, 1783.

I have received your Favour of the 30th of September, for

which I thank you. My Apprehension, that the Union between France and our States might be diminished by Accounts from hence, was occasioned by the extravagant and violent Language held here by a Public Person, in public Company, which had that Tendency; and it was natural for me to think his Letters might hold the same Language, in which I was right; for I have since had Letters from Boston informing me of it. Luckily here, and I hope there, it is imputed to the true Cause, a Disorder in the Brain, which, tho' not constant, has its Fits too frequent. I will not fill my Letter with an Account of those Discourses. Mr. Laurens, when you see him, can give it to you; I mean such as he heard in Company with other Persons, for I would not have him relate private Conversations. They distress'd me much at the time, being then at your earnest Instances soliciting for more aids of Money; the Success of which Solicitation such ungrateful and provoking Language might, I feared, have had a Tendency to prevent. Enough of this at present.

I have been exceedingly hurt and afflicted by the Difficulty some of your late Bills met with in Holland. As soon as I receiv'd the Letter from Messrs. Willinck & Co., which I inclose, I sent for Mr. Grand, who brought me a Sketch of his Account with you, by which it appear'd that the Demands upon us, existing and expected, would more than absorb the Funds in his Hands. We could not indulge the smallest Hope of obtaining further Assistance here, the Public Finances being in a state of Embarrassment, private Persons full of Distrust occasioned by the late Stoppage of Payment at the *Caisse d'Escompte*, and money in general extreamly scarce. But he agreed to do what I propos'd, lend his Credit in the Way of Drawing and Redrawing between Holland and Paris, to gain Time till you could furnish Funds to reimburse Messrs. Willenck & Co. I believe he made this Proposition to them by the Return of the Express. I know not why it was not accepted. Mr. Grand, I suppose, will himself give you an Account of all the Transaction, and of his Application to Messrs. Couteulx & Co.; therefore, I need not add more upon this disagreable Subject.

I have found Difficulties in settling the Account of Salaries with the other Ministers, that have made it impracticable for me to do it. I have, therefore, after keeping the Bills that were to have been proportioned among us long in my hands, given them up to Mr. Grand, who, finding the same Difficulties, will, I suppose, return them to you. None has come to hand for the two or three last Quarters, and we are indebted to his Kindness for advancing us Money, or we must have run in Debt for our Subsistence. He risques in doing this, since he has not for it your Orders.

There arise frequently contingent Expences, for which no provision has yet been made. In a former letter to the Secretary for Foreign Affairs, I gave a List of them, and desired to know the Pleasure of Congress concerning them. I have only had for Answer, that they were under Consideration, and that he believed House-Rent would not be allowed; but I am still in Uncertainty as to that and the Rest. I wish some resolutions were taken on this Point of Contingencies, that I may know how to settle my Accounts with Mr. Barclay. American Ministers in Europe are too remote from their Constituents to consult them, and take their Orders on every Occasion, as the Ministers here of European Courts can easily do. There seems, therefore, a Necessity of allowing more to their Discretion, and of giving them a Credit to a certain Amount on some Banker, who may answer their Orders; for which, however, they should be accountable. I mention this for the sake of other Ministers, hoping and expecting soon to be discharg'd myself, and also for the Good of the Service.

The Remissness of our People in Paying Taxes is highly blameable; the Unwillingness to pay them is still more so. I see, in some Resolutions of Town Meetings, a Remonstrance against giving Congress a Power to take, as they call it, the People's Money out of their Pockets, tho' only to pay the Interest and Principal of Debts duly contracted. They seem to mistake the Point. Money, justly due from the People, is their Creditors' Money, and no longer the Money of the People, who, if they withold it, should be compell'd to pay by some Law.

All Property, indeed, except the Savage's temporary Cabin, his Bow, his Matchcoat, and other little Acquisitions, absolutely necessary for his Subsistence, seems to me to be the

Creature of public Convention. Hence the Public has the Right of Regulating Descents, and all other Conveyances of Property, and even of limiting the Quantity and the Uses of it. All the Property that is necessary to a Man, for the Conservation of the Individual and the Propagation of the Species, is his natural Right, which none can justly deprive him of: But all Property superfluous to such purposes is the Property of the Publick, who, by their Laws, have created it, and who may therefore by other Laws dispose of it, whenever the Welfare of the Publick shall demand such Disposition. He that does not like civil Society on these Terms, let him retire and live among Savages. He can have no right to the benefits of Society, who will not pay his Club towards the Support of it.

The Marquis de la F., who loves to be employ'd in our Affairs, and is often very useful, has lately had several Conversations with the Ministers and Persons concern'd in forming new Regulations, respecting the Commerce between our two Countries, which are not yet concluded. I therefore thought it well to communicate to him a Copy of your Letter, which contains so many sensible and just Observations on that Subject. He will make a proper Use of them, and perhaps they may have more Weight, as appearing to come from a Frenchman, than they would have if it were known that they were the Observations of an American. I perfectly agree with you in all the Sentiments you have express'd on this Occasion.

You have made no Answer to the Proposition I sent of furnishing Tobacco to the Farmers General. They have since made a Contract with Mess.rs Alexander & Williams for the same Purpose but it is such a one as does not prevent their making another with you if hereafter it should suit you.

I am sorry for the Publick's sake, that you are about to quit your Office, but on personal Considerations I shall congratulate you; for I cannot conceive of a more happy Man, than he, who having been long loaded with public Cares, finds himself reliev'd from them, and enjoying private repose in the Bosom of his Friends and Family.

The Government here has set on foot a new Loan of an Hundred Millions. I enclose the Plan.

It is thought very advantageous for the Lenders. You may judge by that how much the Money is wanted, and how seasonable the Peace was for all concerned.

If Mr. Alexander, who is gone to Virginia, should happen to come to Philadelphia, I beg leave to recommend him to your Civilities as an old Friend of mine whom I very much esteem.

With sincere Regard & Attachment, I am ever, Dear Sir,
Your most etc.

"A GOOD PEOPLE TO LIVE AMONG"

To ———

Your Queries concerning the Value of Land in different Circumstances & Situations, Modes of Settlement, &c. &c. are quite out of my Power to answer; having while I lived in America been always an Inhabitant of Capital Cities, and not in the way of learning any thing correctly of Country Affairs. There is a Book lately published in London, written by Mr. Hector St. John, its Title, Letters from an American Farmer, which contains a good deal of Information on those Subjects; and as I know the Author to be an observing intelligent Man, I suppose the Information to be good as far as it goes, and I recommend the Book to your perusal.

There is no doubt but great Tracts may be purchased on the Frontiers of Virginia, & the Carolinas, at moderate Rates. In Virginia it used to be at 5£ Sterling the 100 Acres. I know not the present Price, but do not see why it should be higher.

Emigrants arriving pay no Fine or Premium for being admitted to all the Privileges of Citizens. Those are acquired by two Years Residence.

No Rewards are given to encourage new Settlers to come among us, whatever degree of Property they may bring with them, nor any Exemptions from common Duties. Our Country offers to Strangers nothing but a good Climate, fertile Soil, wholesome Air, Free Governments, wise Laws, Liberty, a good People to live among, and a hearty Welcome. Those

Europeans who have these or greater Advantages at home, would do well to stay where they are.

January, 1784?

"THE TURK'Y IS IN COMPARISON A MUCH MORE RESPECTABLE BIRD"

To Sarah Bache

MY DEAR CHILD,   Passy, Jan. 26, 1784.

Your Care in sending me the Newspapers is very agreable to me. I received by Capt. Barney those relating to the *Cincinnati*. My Opinion of the Institution cannot be of much Importance; I only wonder that, when the united Wisdom of our Nation had, in the Articles of Confederation, manifested their Dislike of establishing Ranks of Nobility, by Authority either of the Congress or of any particular State, a Number of private Persons should think proper to distinguish themselves and their Posterity, from their fellow Citizens, and form an Order of *hereditary Knights*, in direct Opposition to the solemnly declared Sense of their Country! I imagine it must be likewise contrary to the Good Sense of most of those drawn into it by the Persuasion of its Projectors, who have been too much struck with the Ribbands and Crosses they have seen among them hanging to the Buttonholes of Foreign Officers. And I suppose those, who disapprove of it, have not hitherto given it much Opposition, from a Principle somewhat like that of your good Mother, relating to punctilious Persons, who are always exacting little Observances of Respect; that, *"if People can be pleased with small Matters, it is a pity but they should have them."*

In this View, perhaps, I should not myself, if my Advice had been ask'd, have objected to their wearing their Ribband and Badge according to their Fancy, tho' I certainly should to the entailing it as an Honour on their Posterity. For Honour, worthily obtain'd (as for Example that of our Officers), is in its Nature a *personal* Thing, and incommunicable to any but those who had some Share in obtaining it. Thus among the Chinese, the most ancient, and from long Experience the wisest of

Nations, honour does not *descend*, but *ascends*. If a man from his Learning, his Wisdom, or his Valour, is promoted by the Emperor to the Rank of Mandarin, his Parents are immediately entitled to all the same Ceremonies of Respect from the People, that are establish'd as due to the Mandarin himself; on the supposition that it must have been owing to the Education, Instruction, and good Example afforded him by his Parents, that he was rendered capable of serving the Publick.

This *ascending* Honour is therefore useful to the State, as it encourages Parents to give their Children a good and virtuous Education. But the *descending Honour*, to Posterity who could have no Share in obtaining it, is not only groundless and absurd, but often hurtful to that Posterity, since it is apt to make them proud, disdaining to be employ'd in useful Arts, and thence falling into Poverty, and all the Meannesses, Servility, and Wretchedness attending it; which is the present case with much of what is called the *Noblesse* in Europe. Or if, to keep up the Dignity of the Family, Estates are entailed entire on the Eldest male heir, another Pest to Industry and Improvement of the Country is introduc'd, which will be followed by all the odious mixture of pride and Beggary, and idleness, that have half depopulated and *decultivated* Spain; occasioning continual Extinction of Families by the Discouragements of Marriage and neglect in the improvement of estates.

I wish, therefore, that the Cincinnati, if they must go on with their Project, would direct the Badges of their Order to be worn by their Parents, instead of handing them down to their Children. It would be a good Precedent, and might have good Effects. It would also be a kind of Obedience to the Fourth Commandment, in which God enjoins us to *honour* our Father and Mother, but has nowhere directed us to honour our Children. And certainly no mode of honouring those immediate Authors of our Being can be more effectual, than that of doing praiseworthy Actions, which reflect Honour on those who gave us our Education; or more becoming, than that of manifesting, by some public Expression or Token, that it is to their Instruction and Example we ascribe the Merit of those Actions.

But the Absurdity of *descending Honours* is not a mere Matter of philosophical Opinion; it is capable of mathematical Demonstration. A Man's Son, for instance, is but half of his Family, the other half belonging to the Family of his Wife. His Son, too, marrying into another Family, his Share in the Grandson is but a fourth; in the Great Grandson, by the same Process, it is but an Eighth; in the next Generation a Sixteenth; the next a Thirty-second; the next a Sixty-fourth; the next an Hundred and twenty-eighth; the next a Two hundred and Fifty-sixth; and the next a Five hundred and twelfth; thus in nine Generations, which will not require more than 300 years (no very great Antiquity for a Family), our present Chevalier of the Order of Cincinnatus's Share in the then existing Knight, will be but a 512th part; which, allowing the present certain Fidelity of American Wives to be insur'd down through all those Nine Generations, is so small a Consideration, that methinks no reasonable Man would hazard for the sake of it the disagreable Consequences of the Jealousy, Envy, and Ill will of his Countrymen.

Let us go back with our Calculation from this young Noble, the 512th part of the present Knight, thro' his nine Generations, till we return to the year of the Institution. He must have had a Father and Mother, they are two. Each of them had a father and Mother, they are four. Those of the next preceding Generation will be eight, the next Sixteen, the next thirty-two, the next sixty-four, the next one hundred and Twenty-eight, the next Two hundred and fifty-six, and the ninth in this Retrocession Five hundred and twelve, who must be now existing, and all contribute their Proportion of this future *Chevalier de Cincinnatus*. These, with the rest, make together as follows:

$$
\begin{array}{r}
2 \\
4 \\
8 \\
16 \\
32 \\
64 \\
128 \\
256 \\
\underline{512} \\
\end{array}
$$

Total   1022

One Thousand and Twenty-two Men and Women, contributors to the formation of one Knight. And, if we are to have a Thousand of these future knights, there must be now and hereafter existing One million and Twenty-two Thousand Fathers and Mothers, who are to contribute to their Production, unless a Part of the Number are employ'd in making more Knights than One. Let us strike off then the 22,000, on the Supposition of this double Employ, and then consider whether, after a reasonable Estimation of the Number of Rogues, and Fools, and Royalists and Scoundrels and Prostitutes, that are mix'd with, and help to make up necessarily their Million of Predecessors, Posterity will have much reason to boast of the noble Blood of the then existing Set of Chevaliers de Cincinnatus. The future genealogists, too, of these Chevaliers, in proving the lineal descent of their honour through so many generations (even supposing honour capable in its nature of descending), will only prove the small share of this honour, which can be justly claimed by any one of them; since the above simple process in arithmetic makes it quite plain and clear that, in proportion as the antiquity of the family shall augment, the right to the honour of the ancestor will diminish; and a few generations more would reduce it to something so small as to be very near an absolute nullity. I hope, therefore, that the Order will drop this part of their project, and content themselves, as the Knights of the Garter, Bath, Thistle, St. Louis, and other Orders of Europe do, with a Life Enjoyment of their little Badge and Ribband, and let the Distinction die with those who have merited it. This I imagine will give no offence. For my own part, I shall think it a Convenience, when I go into a Company where there may be Faces unknown to me, if I discover, by this Badge, the Persons who merit some particular Expression of my Respect; and it will save modest Virtue the Trouble of calling for our Regard, by awkward roundabout Intimations of having been heretofore employ'd in the Continental Service.

The Gentleman, who made the Voyage to France to provide the Ribands and Medals, has executed his Commission. To me they seem tolerably done; but all such Things are criticis'd. Some find Fault with the Latin, as wanting classic

Elegance and Correctness; and, since our Nine Universities were not able to furnish better Latin, it was pity, they say, that the Mottos had not been in English. Others object to the Title, as not properly assumable by any but Gen. Washington, and a few others who serv'd without Pay. Others object to the *Bald Eagle* as looking too much like a *Dindon*, or Turkey. For my own part, I wish the Bald Eagle had not been chosen as the Representative of our Country; he is a Bird of bad moral Character; he does not get his living honestly; you may have seen him perch'd on some dead Tree, near the River where, too lazy to fish for himself, he watches the Labour of the Fishing-Hawk; and, when that diligent Bird has at length taken a Fish, and is bearing it to his Nest for the support of his Mate and young ones, the Bald Eagle pursues him, and takes it from him. With all this Injustice he is never in good Case; but, like those among Men who live by Sharping and Robbing, he is generally poor, and often very lousy. Besides, he is a rank Coward; the little *KingBird*, not bigger than a Sparrow, attacks him boldly and drives him out of the District. He is therefore by no means a proper emblem for the brave and honest Cincinnati of America, who have driven all the *Kingbirds* from our Country; though exactly fit for that Order of Knights, which the French call *Chevaliers d'Industrie*.

I am, on this account, not displeas'd that the Figure is not known as a Bald Eagle, but looks more like a Turk'y. For in Truth, the Turk'y is in comparison a much more respectable Bird, and withal a true original Native of America. Eagles have been found in all Countries, but the Turk'y was peculiar to ours; the first of the Species seen in Europe being brought to France by the Jesuits from Canada, and serv'd up at the Wedding Table of Charles the Ninth. He is, though a little vain and silly, it is true, but not the worse emblem for that, a Bird of Courage, and would not hesitate to attack a Grenadier of the British Guards, who should presume to invade his FarmYard with a *red* Coat on.

I shall not enter into the Criticisms made upon their Latin. The gallant officers of America may not have the merit of being great scholars, but they undoubtedly merit much, as brave soldiers, from their Country, which should therefore not leave them merely to *Fame* for their *"Virtutis Premium,"* which is one of their Latin Mottos. Their *"Esto perpetua,"* another, is an excellent Wish, if they meant it for their Country; bad, if intended for their Order. The States should not only restore to them the *Omnia* of their first Motto, which many of them have left and lost, but pay them justly, and reward them generously. They should not be suffered to remain, with all their new-created Chivalry, *entirely* in the Situation of the Gentleman in the Story, which their *omnia reliquit* reminds me of. You know every thing makes me recollect some Story. He had built a very fine House, and thereby much impair'd his Fortune. He had a Pride, however, in showing it to his Acquaintance. One of them, after viewing it all, remark'd a Motto over the Door, "ŌIA VANITAS." "What," says he, "is the Meaning of this ŌIA? it is a word I don't understand." "I will tell you," said the Gentleman; "I had a mind to have the Motto cut on a Piece of smooth Marble, but there was not room for it between the Ornaments, to be put in Characters large enough to be read. I therefore made use of a Contraction antiently very common in Latin Manuscripts, by which the *m*'s and *n*'s in Words are omitted, and the Omission noted by a little Dash above, which you may see there; so that the Word is *omnia*, OMNIA VANITAS." "O," says his Friend, "I now comprehend the Meaning of your motto, it relates to your Edifice; and signifies, that, if you have abridged your *Omnia*, you have, nevertheless, left your VANITAS legible at full length." I am, as ever, your affectionate father,

"MY ADVICE 'SMELLS OF MADEIRA'"

To William Strahan

DEAR SIR,   Passy, Feb. 16, 1784.
    I receiv'd and read with Pleasure your kind Letter of the first Inst, as it inform'd me of the Welfare of you and yours. I am glad the Accounts you have from your Kinswoman at Philadelphia are agreable, and I shall be happy if any Recommendations from me can be serviceable to Dr. Ross, or any other friend of yours, going to America.

Your arguments, persuading me to come once more to England, are very powerful. To be sure, I long to see again my Friends there, whom I love abundantly; but there are difficulties and Objections of several kinds, which at present I do not see how to get over.

I lament with you the political Disorders England at present labours under. Your Papers are full of strange Accounts of Anarchy and Confusion in America, of which we know nothing, while your own Affairs are really in a Situation deplorable. In my humble Opinion, the Root of the Evil lies not so much in too long, or too unequally chosen Parliaments, as in the enormous Salaries, Emoluments, and Patronage of your great Offices; and that you will never be at rest till they are all abolish'd, and every place of Honour made at the same time, instead of a Place of Profit, a place of Expence and burthen.

Ambition and avarice are each of them strong Passions, and when they are united in the same Persons, and have the same Objects in view for their Gratification, they are too strong for Public Spirit and Love of Country, and are apt to produce the most violent Factions and Contentions. They should therefore be separated, and made to act one against the other. Those Places, to speak in our old stile (Brother Type), may be for the good of the *Chapel*, but they are bad for the Master, as they create constant Quarrels that hinder the Business. For example, here are near two Months that your Government has been employed in *getting its form to press*; which is not yet fit to *work on*, every Page of it being *squabbled*, and the whole ready to fall into *pye*. The Founts too must be very scanty, or strangely *out of sorts*, since your *Compositors* cannot find either *upper* or *lower case Letters* sufficient to set the word ADMINISTRATION, but are forc'd to be continually *turning for them*. However, to return to common (tho' perhaps too saucy) Language, don't despair; you have still one resource left, and that not a bad one, since it may reunite the Empire. We have some Remains of Affection for you, and shall always be ready to receive and take care of you in Case of Distress. So if you have not Sense and Virtue enough to govern yourselves, e'en dissolve your present old crazy Constitution, and *send members to Congress*.

You will say my *Advice* "smells of *Madeira.*" You are right. This foolish Letter is mere chitchat *between ourselves* over the *second bottle.* If, therefore, you show it to anybody, (except our indulgent Friends, Dagge and Lady Strahan) I will positively *Solless* you. Yours ever most affectionately,

METHODS OF TREATING DISEASES

To La Sabliere de la Condamine

SIR,   Passy, March 19, 1784

I receiv'd the very obliging Letter you did me honour of writing to me the 8th Inst. with the epigram &c. for which please to accept my Thanks.

You desire my Sentiments concerning the Cures perform'd by Comus & Mesmer. I think that in general, Maladies caus'd by Obstructions may be treated by Electricity with Advantage. As to the Animal Magnetism, so much talk'd of, I am totally unacquainted with it, and must doubt its Existence till I can see or feel some Effect of it. None of the Cures said to be perform'd by it, have fallen under my Observation; and there being so many Disorders which cure themselves and such a Disposition in Mankind to deceive themselves and one another on these Occasions; and living long having given me frequent Opportunities of seeing certain Remedies cry'd up as curing everything, and yet soon after totally laid aside as useless, I cannot but fear that the Expectation of great Advantage from the new Method of treating Diseases, will prove a Delusion. That Delusion may however in some cases be of use while it lasts. There are in every great rich City a Number of Persons who are never in health, because they are fond of Medicines and always taking them, whereby they derange the natural Functions, and hurt their Constitutions. If these People can be persuaded to forbear their Drugs in Expectation of being cured by only the Physician's Finger or an Iron Rod pointing at them, they may possibly find good Effects tho' they mistake the Cause. I have the honour to be, Sir, &c.

"STOOP, STOOP!"

To Samuel Mather

REV^d SIR,   Passy, May 12, 1784.

I received your kind letter, with your excellent advice to the people of the United States, which I read with great pleasure, and hope it will be duly regarded. Such writings, though they may be lightly passed over by many readers, yet, if they make a deep impression on one active mind in a hundred, the effects may be considerable. Permit me to mention one little instance, which, though it relates to myself, will not be quite uninteresting to you. When I was a boy, I met with a book, entitled *"Essays to do Good,"* which I think was written by your father. It had been so little regarded by a former possessor, that several leaves of it were torn out; but the remainder gave me such a turn of thinking, as to have an influence on my conduct through life; for I have always set a greater value on the character of a *doer of good*, than on any other kind of reputation; and if I have been, as you seem to think, a useful citizen, the public owes the advantage of it to that book.

You mention your being in your 78th year; I am in my 79th; we are grown old together. It is now more than 60 years since I left Boston, but I remember well both your father and grandfather, having heard them both in the pulpit, and seen them in their houses. The last time I saw your father was in the beginning of 1724, when I visited him after my first trip to Pennsylvania. He received me in his library, and on my taking leave showed me a shorter way out of the house through a narrow passage, which was crossed by a beam over head. We were still talking as I withdrew, he accompanying me behind, and I turning partly towards him, when he said hastily, *"Stoop, stoop!"* I did not understand him, till I felt my head hit against the beam. He was a man that never missed any occasion of giving instruction, and upon this he said to me, *"You are young, and have the world before you;* STOOP *as you go through it, and you will miss many hard thumps."* This advice, thus beat into my head, has frequently been of use to me; and I often think of it, when I see pride mortified, and misfortunes brought upon people by their carrying their heads too high.

I long much to see again my native place, and to lay my bones there. I left it in 1723; I visited it in 1733, 1743, 1753, and 1763. In 1773 I was in England; in 1775 I had a sight of it, but could not enter, it being in possession of the enemy. I did hope to have been there in 1783, but could not obtain my dismission from this employment here; and now I fear I shall never have that happiness. My best wishes however attend my dear country. *Esto perpetua.* It is now blest with an excellent constitution; may it last for ever!

This powerful monarchy continues its friendship for the United States. It is a friendship of the utmost importance to our security, and should be carefully cultivated. Britain has not yet well digested the loss of its dominion over us, and has still at times some flattering hopes of recovering it. Accidents may increase those hopes, and encourage dangerous attempts. A breach between us and France would infallibly bring the English again upon our backs; and yet we have some wild heads among our countrymen, who are endeavouring to weaken that connexion! Let us preserve our reputation by performing our engagements; our credit by fulfilling our con-tracts; and friends by gratitude and kindness; for we know not how soon we may again have occasion for all of them. With great and sincere esteem, I have the honour to be, &c.

"BEWARE OF BEING LULLED INTO A
DANGEROUS SECURITY"

To Charles Thomson

DEAR SIR,   Passy, May 13, 1784.

Yesterday evening Mr. Hartley met with Mr. Jay and myself when the ratifications of the Definitive Treaty were exchanged. I send a copy of the English Ratification to the President.

Thus the great and hazardous enterprize we have been en-gaged in is, God be praised, happily compleated; an event I hardly expected I should live to see. A few years of Peace, will improve, will restore and encrease our strength; but our fu-ture safety will depend on our union and our virtue. Britain will be long watching for advantages, to recover what she has lost. If we do not convince the world, that we are a Nation to be depended on for fidelity in Treaties; if we appear negligent in paying our Debts, and ungrateful to those who have served and befriended us; our reputation, and all the strength it is capable of procuring, will be lost, and fresh attacks upon us will be encouraged and promoted by better prospects of success. Let us therefore beware of being lulled into a dangerous security; and of being both enervated and impoverished by luxury; of being weakened by internal contentions and divisions; of being shamefully extravagant in contracting private debts, while we are backward in discharging honorably those of the public; of neglect in military exercises and discipline, and in providing stores of arms and munitions of war, to be ready on occasion; for all these are circumstances that give confidence to enemies, and diffidence to friends; and the expenses required to prevent a war are much lighter than those that will, if not prevented, be absolutely necessary to maintain it.

I am long kept in suspense without being able to learn the purpose of Congress respecting my request of recall, and that of some employment for my secretary, William Temple Franklin. If I am kept here another winter, and as much weakened by it as by the last, I may as well resolve to spend the remainder of my days here; for I shall be hardly able to bear the fatigues of the voyage in returning. During my long absence from America, my friends are continually diminishing by death, and my inducements to return in proportion. But I can make no preparations either for going conveniently, or staying comfortably here, nor take any steps towards making some other provision for my grandson, till I know what I am to expect. Be so good, my dear friend, as to send me a little private information. With great esteem, I am ever yours, most affectionately

" 'DAMN YOUR SOULS. MAKE TOBACCO!' "

To Mason Locke Weems and Edward Gant

GENTLEMEN,   Passy, July 18, 1784.

On receipt of your Letter, acquainting me that the Archbishop of Canterbury would not permit you to be ordain'd, unless you took the Oath of Allegiance, I apply'd to a Clergyman of my Acquaintance for Information on the Subject of your obtaining Ordination here. His Opinion was, that it could not be done; and that, if it were done, you would be requir'd to vow Obedience to the Archbishop of Paris. I next inquired of the Pope's Nuncio, whether you might not be ordain'd by their Bishop in America, Powers being sent him for that purpose, if he has them not already. The answer was, "The Thing is impossible, unless the Gentlemen become Catholics."

This is an Affair of which I know very little, and therefore I may ask Questions and propose means that are improper or impracticable. But what is the necessity of your being connected with the Church of England? Would it not be as well, if you were of the Church of Ireland? The Religion is the same, tho' there is a different set of Bishops and Archbishops. Perhaps if you were to apply to the Bishop of Derry, who is a man of liberal Sentiments, he might give you Orders as of that Church. If both Britain and Ireland refuse you, (and I am not sure that the Bishops of Denmark or Sweden would ordain you, unless you become Lutherans,) what is to be done? Next to becoming Presbyterians, the Episcopalian clergy of America, in my humble Opinion, cannot do better than to follow the Example of the first Clergy of Scotland, soon after the Conversion of that Country to Christianity, who when their King had built the Cathedral of St. Andrew's, and requested the King of Northumberland to lend his Bishops to ordain one for them, that their Clergy might not as heretofore be obliged to go to Northumberland for Orders, and their Request was refused; they assembled in the Cathedral; and, the Mitre, Crosier, and Robes of a Bishop being laid upon the Altar, they, after earnest Prayers for Direction in their Choice, elected one of their own Number; when the King said to him, *"Arise, go to the Altar, and receive your Office at the Hand of God."* His brethren led him to the Altar, robed him, put the Crozier in his Hand, and the Mitre on his Head, and he became the first Bishop of Scotland.

If the British Isles were sunk in the Sea (and the Surface of this Globe has suffered greater Changes), you would probably take some such Method as this; and, if they persist in denying you Ordination, 'tis the same thing. An hundred years hence, when People are more enlightened, it will be wondered at, that Men in America, qualified by their Learning and Piety to pray for and instruct their Neighbors, should not be permitted to do it till they had made a Voyage of six thousand Miles out and home, to ask leave of a cross old Gentleman at Canterbury; who seems, by your Account, to have as little Regard for the Souls of the People of Maryland, as King William's Attorney-General, Seymour, had for those of Virginia. The Reverend Commissary Blair, who projected the College of that Province, and was in England to solicit Benefactions and a Charter, relates, that the Queen, in the King's Absence, having ordered Seymour to draw up the Charter, which was to be given, with £2000 in Money, he oppos'd the Grant; saying that the Nation was engag'd in an expensive War, that the Money was wanted for better purposes, and he did not see the least Occasion for a College in Virginia. Blair represented to him, that its Intention was to educate and qualify young Men to be Ministers of the Gospel, much wanted there; and begged Mr. Attorney would consider, that the People of Virginia had souls to be saved, as well as the People of England. *"Souls!"* says he, *"damn your Souls. Make Tobacco!"* I have the honour to be, Gentlemen, &c.

"OUR OPINIONS ARE NOT IN OUR OWN POWER"

To William Franklin

DEAR SON,   Passy, Aug. 16, 1784.

I received your Letter of the 22d past, and am glad to find that you desire to revive the affectionate Intercourse, that formerly existed between us. It will be very agreable to me; indeed nothing has ever hurt me so much and affected me with such keen Sensations, as to find myself deserted in my old Age by my only Son; and not only deserted, but to find him taking up Arms against me, in a Cause, wherein my good Fame, Fortune and Life were all at Stake. You conceived, you say, that your Duty to your King and Regard for your Country requir'd this. I ought not to blame you for differing in Sentiment with me in Public Affairs. We are Men, all subject to Errors. Our Opinions are not in our own Power; they are form'd and govern'd much by Circumstances, that are often as inexplicable as they are irresistible. Your Situation was such that few would have censured your remaining Neuter, *tho' there are Natural Duties which precede political ones, and cannot be extinguish'd by them.*

This is a disagreable Subject. I drop it. And we will endeavour, as you propose mutually to forget what has happened relating to it, as well as we can. I send your Son over to pay his Duty to you. You will find him much improv'd. He is greatly esteem'd and belov'd in this Country, and will make his Way anywhere. It is my Desire, that he should study the Law, as a necessary Part of Knowledge for a public Man, and profitable if he should have occasion to practise it. I would have you therefore put into his hands those Law-books you have, viz. Blackstone, Coke, Bacon, Viner, &c. He will inform you, that he received the Letter sent him by Mr. Galloway, and the Paper it enclosed, safe.

On my leaving America, I deposited with that Friend for you, a Chest of Papers, among which was a Manuscript of nine or ten Volumes, relating to Manufactures, Agriculture, Commerce, Finance, etc., which cost me in England about 70 Guineas; eight Quire Books, containing the Rough Drafts of all my Letters while I liv'd in London. These are missing. I hope you have got them, if not, they are lost. Mr. Vaughan has publish'd in London a Volume of what he calls my Political Works. He proposes a second Edition; but, as the first was very incompleat, and you had many Things that were omitted, (for I used to send you sometimes the Rough Drafts, and sometimes the printed Pieces I wrote in London,) I have directed him to apply to you for what may be in your Power to furnish him with, or to delay his Publication till I can be at home again, if that may ever happen.

I did intend returning this year; but the Congress, instead of giving me Leave to do so, have sent me another Commission, which will keep me here at least a Year longer; and perhaps I may then be too old and feeble to bear the Voyage. I am here among a People that love and respect me, a most amiable Nation to live with; and perhaps I may conclude to die among them; for my Friends in America are dying off, one after another, and I have been so long abroad, that I should now be almost a Stranger in my own Country.

I shall be glad to see you when convenient, but would not have you come here at present. You may confide to your son the Family Affairs you wished to confer upon with me, for he is discreet. And I trust, that you will prudently avoid introducing him to Company, that it may be improper for him to be seen with. I shall hear from you by him and any letters to me afterwards, will come safe under Cover directed to Mr. Ferdinand Grand, Banker at Paris. Wishing you Health, and more Happiness than it seems you have lately experienced, I remain your affectionate father,

"THE YANKEYS NEVER FELT BOLD"

To William Strahan

DEAR FRIEND,   Passy, Augt 19.th 1784.

I received your kind Letter of Ap^l 17th. You will have the goodness to place my delay in answering to the Account of Indisposition and Business, and excuse it. I have now that letter before me; and my Grandson, whom you may formerly remember a little Scholar of Mr. Elphinston's, purposing to set out in a day or two on a visit to his Father in London, I set down to scribble a little to you, first recommending him as a worthy young Man to your Civilities and Counsels.

You press me much to come to England. I am not without strong Inducements to do so; the Fund of Knowledge you promise to Communicate to me is an Addition to them, and no small one. At present it is impracticable. But, when my Grandson returns, come with him. We will then talk the matter over, and perhaps you may take me back with you. I have a Bed at your service, and will try to make your Residence, while you can stay with us, as agreable to you, if possible, as I am sure it will be to me.

You do not "approve the annihilation of profitable Places; for you do not see why a Statesman, who does his Business well, should not be paid for his Labour as well as any other Workman." Agreed. But why more than any other Workman? The less the Salary the greater the Honor. In so great a Nation, there are many rich enough to afford giving their time to the Public; and there are, I make no doubt, many wise and able Men, who would take as much Pleasure in governing for nothing, as they do in playing Chess for nothing. It would be one of the noblest of Amusements. That this Opinion is not Chimerical, the Country I now live in affords a Proof; its whole Civil and Criminal Law Administration being done for nothing, or in some sense for less than nothing; since the Members of its Judiciary Parliaments buy their Places, and do not make more than *three per cent* for their Money by their Fees and Emoluments, while the legal Interest is *five*; so that in Fact they give two per cent to be allow'd to govern, and all their time and trouble into the Bargain. Thus *Profit*, one Motive for desiring Place, being abolish'd, there remains only *Ambition*; and that being in some degree ballanced by *Loss*, you may easily conceive, that there will not be very violent Factions and Contentions for such Places, nor much of the Mischief to the Country, that attends your Factions, which have often occasioned Wars, and overloaded you with Debts impayable.

I allow you all the Force of your Joke upon the Vagrancy of our Congress. They have a right to sit *where* they please, of which perhaps they have made too much Use by shifting too often. But they have two other Rights; those of sitting *when* they please, and as *long* as they please, in which methinks they have the advantage of your Parliament; for they cannot be dissolved by the Breath of a Minister, or sent packing as you were the other day, when it was your earnest desire to have remained longer together.

You "fairly acknowledge, that the late War terminated quite contrary to your Expectation." Your expectation was ill founded; for you would not believe your old Friend, who told you repeatedly, that by those Measures England would lose her Colonies, as Epictetus warned in vain his Master that he would break his Leg. You believ'd rather the Tales you

heard of our Poltroonery and Impotence of Body and Mind.
Do you not remember the Story you told me of the Scotch
sergeant, who met with a Party of Forty American Soldiers,
and, tho' alone, disarm'd them all, and brought them in Prisoners? A Story almost as Improbable as that of the Irishman,
who pretended to have alone taken and brought in Five of
the enemy by *surrounding* them. And yet, my Friend, sensible
and Judicious as you are, but partaking of the general Infatuation, you seemed to believe it.

The Word *general* puts me in mind of a General, your General Clarke, who had the Folly to say in my hearing at Sir
John Pringle's, that, with a Thousand British grenadiers, he
would undertake to go from one end of America to the other,
and geld all the Males, partly by force and partly by a little
Coaxing. It is plain he took us for a species of Animals very
little superior to Brutes. The Parliament too believ'd the stories of another foolish General, I forget his Name, that the
Yankeys never *felt bold*. Yankey was understood to be a sort of
Yahoo, and the Parliament did not think the Petitions of such
Creatures were fit to be received and read in so wise an Assembly. What was the consequence of this monstrous Pride
and Insolence? You first sent small Armies to subdue us, believing them more than sufficient, but soon found yourselves
obliged to send greater; these, whenever they ventured to
penetrate our Country beyond the Protection of their Ships,
were either repulsed and obliged to scamper out, or were surrounded, beaten, and taken Prisoners. An American Planter,
who had never seen Europe, was chosen by us to Command
our Troops, and continued during the whole War. This Man
sent home to you, one after another, five of your best Generals baffled, their Heads bare of Laurels, disgraced even in
the Opinion of their Employers.

Your contempt of our Understandings, in Comparison with
your own, appeared to be not much better founded than that
of our Courage, if we may judge by this Circumstance, that,
in whatever Court of Europe a Yankey negociator appeared,
the wise British Minister was routed, put in a passion, pick'd
a quarrel with your Friends, and was sent home with a Flea
in his Ear.

But after all, my dear Friend, do not imagine that I am vain enough to ascribe our Success to any superiority in any of those Points. I am too well acquainted with all the Springs and Levers of our Machine, not to see, that our human means were unequal to our undertaking, and that, if it had not been for the Justice of our Cause, and the consequent Interposition of Providence, in which we had Faith, we must have been ruined. If I had ever before been an Atheist, I should now have been convinced of the Being and Government of a Deity! It is he who abases the Proud and favours the Humble. May we never forget his Goodness to us, and may our future Conduct manifest our Gratitude.

But let us leave these serious Reflections and converse with our usual Pleasantry. I remember your observing once to me as we sat together in the House of Commons, that no two Journeymen Printers, within your Knowledge, had met with such Success in the World as ourselves. You were then at the head of your Profession, and soon afterwards became a Member of Parliament. I was an Agent for a few Provinces, and now act for them all. But we have risen by different Modes. I, as a Republican Printer, always liked a Form well *plain'd down*; being averse to those *overbearing* Letters that hold their Heads so *high*, as to hinder their Neighbours from appearing. You, as a Monarchist, chose to work upon *Crown* Paper, and found it profitable; while I work'd upon *pro patria* (often indeed call'd *Fools Cap*) with no less advantage. Both our *Heaps hold out* very well, and we seem likely to make a pretty good day's Work of it. With regard to Public Affairs (to continue in the same stile), it seems to me that the Compositors in your Chapel do not *cast off their Copy* well, nor perfectly understand *Imposing*; their *Forms*, too, are continually pester'd by the *Outs* and *Doubles*, that are not easy to be corrected. And I think they were wrong in laying aside some *Faces*, and particularly certain *Head-pieces*, that would have been both useful and ornamental. But, Courage! The Business may still flourish with good Management; and the Master become as rich as any of the Company.

By the way, the rapid Growth and extension of the English language in America, must become greatly Advantageous to the booksellers, and holders of Copy-Rights in England. A vast audience is assembling there for English Authors, ancient, present, and future, our People doubling every twenty Years; and this will demand large and of course profitable Impressions of your most valuable Books. I would, therefore, if I possessed such rights, entail them, if such a thing be practicable, upon my Posterity; for their Worth will be continually augmenting. This may look a little like Advice, and yet I have drank no *Madeira* these Ten Months.

The Subject, however, leads me to another Thought, which is, that you do wrong to discourage the Emigration of Englishmen to America. In my piece on Population, I have proved, I think, that Emigration does not diminish but multiplies a Nation. You will not have fewer at home for those that go Abroad; and as every Man who comes among us, and takes up a piece of Land, becomes a Citizen, and by our Constitution has a Voice in Elections, and a share in the Government of the Country, why should you be against acquiring by this fair Means a Repossession of it, and leave it to be taken by Foreigners of all Nations and Languages, who by their Numbers may drown and stifle the English, which otherwise would probably become in the course of two Centuries the most extensive Language in the World, the Spanish only excepted? It is a Fact, that the Irish emigrants and their children are now in Possession of the Government of Pennsylvania, by their Majority in the Assembly, as well as of a great Part of the Territory; and I remember well the first Ship that brought any of them over. I am ever, my dear Friend, yours most affectionately,

ON DIVINE INSPIRATION

To Joseph Priestley

DEAR SIR,   Passy, Aug* 21, 1784.
Understanding that my Letter intended for you by General Melvill, was lost at the Hôtel d'Espagne, I take this Opportunity by my Grandson to give you the purport of it, as well as I can recollect. I thank'd you for the Pleasure you had pro-

cured me of the General's Conversation, whom I found a judicious, sensible, and amiable Man. I was glad to hear that you possess'd a comfortable Retirement, and more so that you had Thoughts of removing to Philadelphia, for that it would make me very happy to have you there. Your *Companions* would be very acceptable to the Library, but I hoped you would long live to enjoy their Company yourself. I agreed with you in Sentiments concerning the Old Testament, and thought the Clause in our Constitution, which required the Members of Assembly to declare their belief, *that the whole of it was given by divine Inspiration*, had better have been omitted. That I had opposed the Clause; but, being overpower'd by Numbers, and fearing more might in future Times be grafted on it, I prevailed to have the additional Clause, "that *no further or more extended Profession of Faith should ever be exacted.*" I observ'd to you too, that the Evil of it was the less, as *no Inhabitant*, nor any Officer of Government, except the Members of Assembly, were oblig'd to make that Declaration.

So much for that Letter; to which I may now add, that there are several Things in the Old Testament, impossible to be given by *divine* Inspiration; such as the Approbation ascribed to the Angel of the Lord, of that abominably wicked and detestable Action of Jael, the wife of Heber, the Kenite.* If the rest of the Book were like that, I should rather suppose it given by Inspiration from another Quarter, and renounce the whole.

By the way, how goes on the Unitarian Church in Essex Street? And the honest Minister of it, is he comfortably supported? Your old Colleague, Mr. Radcliff, is he living? And what became of Mr. Denham?

My Grandson, who will have the honour of delivering this to you, may bring me a Line from you; and I hope will bring me an Account of your continuing well and happy.

I jog on still, with as much Health, and as few of the Infirmities of old Age, as I have any Reason to expect. But whatever is impair'd in my Constitution, my Regard for my old Friends remains firm and entire. You will always have a good Share of it, for I am ever with great and sincere esteem, dear Sir, &c.

*Judges, chap. iv.

To Richard Price

DEAR FRIEND,   Passy, March 18, 1785.

My nephew, Mr. Williams, will have the honour of delivering you this line. It is to request from you a List of a few good Books, to the Value of about Twenty-five Pounds, such as are most proper to inculcate Principles of sound Religion and just Government. A New Town in the State of Massachusetts having done me the honour of naming itself after me, and proposing to build a Steeple to their meeting-house if I would give them a Bell, I have advis'd the sparing themselves the Expence of a Steeple, for the present, and that they would accept of Books instead of a Bell, Sense being preferable to Sound. These are therefore intended as the Commencement of a little Parochial Library for the Use of a Society of intelligent, respectable Farmers, such as our Country People generally consist of. Besides your own Works, I would only mention, on the Recommendation of my sister, "Stennet's *Discourses on Personal Religion*," which may be one Book of the Number, if you know and approve of it.

With the highest Esteem and Respect, I am ever, my dear Friend, yours most affectionately,

To George Whatley

DEAR OLD FRIEND,   Passy, May 23, 1785.

I sent you a few Lines the other Day, with the Medallion, when I should have written more, but was prevented by the coming in of a *Bavard*, who worried me till Evening. I bore with him, and now you are to bear with me; for I shall probably *bavarder* in answering your Letter.

I am not acquainted with the Saying of Alphonsus, which you allude to as a Sanctification of your Rigidity, in refusing to allow me the Plea of Old Age, as an Excuse for my Want of Exactness in Correspondence. What was that Saying? You do not, it seems, feel any occasion for such an Excuse, though you are, as you say, rising 75. But I am rising (perhaps more properly falling) 80, and I leave the Excuse with you till you arrive at that Age; perhaps you may then be more sensible of its Validity, and see fit to use it for yourself.

I must agree with you, that the Gout is bad, and that the Stone is worse. I am happy in not having them both together, and I join in your Prayer, that you may live till you die without either. But I doubt the Author of the Epitaph you send me was a little mistaken, when he, speaking of the World, says, that

> "he ne'er car'd a pin
> What they said or may say of the Mortal within."

It is so natural to wish to be well spoken of, whether alive or dead, that I imagine he could not be quite exempt from that Desire; and that at least he wish'd to be thought a Wit, or he would not have given himself the Trouble of writing so good an Epitaph to leave behind him. Was it not as worthy of his Care, that the World should say he was an honest and a good Man? I like better the concluding Sentiment in the old Song, call'd *The Old Man's Wish*, wherein, after wishing for a warm House in a country Town, an easy Horse, some good old authors, ingenious and cheerful Companions, a Pudding on Sundays, with stout Ale, and a bottle of Burgundy, &c. &c., in separate Stanzas, each ending with this burthen,

> "May I govern my Passions with an absolute sway,
> Grow wiser and better as my Strength wears away,
> Without Gout or Stone, by a gentle Decay;"

he adds,

> "With a Courage undaunted may I face my last day,
> And, when I am gone, may the better Sort say,
> 'In the Morning when sober, in the Evening when mellow,
> He's gone, and has not left behind him his Fellow;
> For he governed his Passions, &c.'"

But what signifies our Wishing? Things happen, after all, as they will happen. I have sung that *wishing Song* a thousand times, when I was young, and now find, at Fourscore, that the three Contraries have befallen me, being subject to the Gout and the Stone, and not being yet Master of all my Passions. Like the proud Girl in my Country, who wished and resolv'd not to marry a Parson, nor a Presbyterian, nor an Irishman; and at length found herself married to an Irish Presbyterian Parson.

You see I have some reason to wish, that, in a future State, I may not only be *as well as I was*, but a little better. And I hope it; for I, too, with your Poet, *trust in God.* And when I observe, that there is great Frugality, as well as Wisdom, in his Works, since he has been evidently sparing both of Labour and Materials; for by the various wonderful Inventions of Propagation, he has provided for the continual peopling his World with Plants and Animals, without being at the Trouble of repeated new Creations; and by the natural Reduction of compound Substances to their original Elements, capable of being employ'd in new Compositions, he has prevented the Necessity of creating new Matter; so that the Earth, Water, Air, and perhaps Fire, which being compounded form Wood, do, when the Wood is dissolved, return, and again become Air, Earth, Fire, and Water; I say, that, when I see nothing annihilated, and not even a Drop of Water wasted, I cannot suspect the Annihilation of Souls, or believe, that he will suffer the daily Waste of Millions of Minds ready made that now exist, and put himself to the continual Trouble of making new ones. Thus finding myself to exist in the World, I believe I shall, in some Shape or other, always exist; and, with all the inconveniencies human Life is liable to, I shall not object to a new Edition of mine; hoping, however, that the *Errata* of the last may be corrected.

I return your Note of Children receiv'd in the Foundling Hospital at Paris, from 1741 to 1755, inclusive; and I have added the Years preceding as far back as 1710 together with the general Christnings of the City, and the Years succeeding down to 1770. Those since that Period I have not been able to obtain. I have noted in the Margin the gradual Increase, viz. from every tenth Child so thrown upon the Public, till it comes to every third! Fifteen Years have passed since the last Account, and probably it may now amount to one half. Is it right to encourage this monstrous Deficiency of natural Affection? A Surgeon I met with here excused the Women of Paris, by saying, seriously, that they *could not* give suck; *"Car,"* dit il, *"elles n'ont point de tetons."* He assur'd me it was a Fact, and bade me look at them, and observe how flat they were on the Breast; "they have nothing more there," said he, "than I have upon the Back of my hand." I have since thought that there might be some Truth in his Observation, and that, possibly, Nature, finding they made no use of Bubbies, has left off giving them any. Yet, since Rousseau, with admirable Eloquence, pleaded for the Rights of Children to their Mother's Milk, the Mode has changed a little; and some Ladies of Quality now suckle their Infants and find Milk enough. May the Mode descend to the lower Ranks, till it becomes no longer the Custom to pack their Infants away, as soon as born, to the *Enfans Trouvés*, with the careless Observation, that the King is better able to maintain them.

I am credibly inform'd, that nine-tenths of them die there pretty soon, which is said to be a great Relief to the Institution, whose Funds would not otherwise be sufficient to bring up the Remainder. Except the few Persons of Quality above mentioned, and the Multitude who send to the Hospital, the Practice is to hire Nurses in the Country to carry out the Children, and take care of them there. There is an Office for examining the Health of Nurses, and giving them Licenses. They come to Town on certain Days of the Week in Companies to receive the Children, and we often meet Trains of them on the Road returning to the neighbouring Villages, with each a Child in her Arms. But those, who are good enough to try this way of raising their Children, are often not able to pay the Expence; so that the Prisons of Paris are crowded with wretched Fathers and Mothers confined *pour Mois de Nourrice*, tho' it is laudably a favorite Charity to pay for them, and set such Prisoners at Liberty. I wish Success to the new Project of assisting the Poor to keep their Children at home, because I think there is no Nurse like a Mother (or not many), and that, if Parents did not immediately send their Infants out of their Sight, they would in a few days begin to love them, and thence be spurr'd to greater Industry for their Maintenance. This is a Subject you understand better than I, and, therefore, having perhaps said too much, I drop it. I only add to the Notes a Remark, from the *History of the Academy of Sciences*, much in favour of the Foundling Institution.

The Philadelphia Bank goes on, as I hear, very well. What you call the Cincinnati Institution is no Institution of our Government, but a private Convention among the Officers of our late Army, and so universally dislik'd by the People, that it is supposed it will be dropt. It was considered as an Attempt to establish something like an hereditary Rank or Nobility. I hold with you, that it was wrong; may I add, that all *descending* Honours are wrong and absurd; that the Honour of virtuous Actions appertains only to him that performs them, and is in its nature incommunicable. If it were communicable by Descent, it must also be divisible among the Descendants; and the more ancient the Family, the less would be found existing in any one Branch of it; to say nothing of the greater Chance of unlucky Interruptions.

Our Constitution seems not to be well understood with you. If the Congress were a permanent Body, there would be more Reason in being jealous of giving it Powers. But its Members are chosen annually, cannot be chosen more than three Years successively, nor more than three Years in seven; and any of them may be recall'd at any time, whenever their Constituents shall be dissatisfied with their Conduct. They are of the People, and return again to mix with the People, having no more durable preëminence than the different Grains of Sand in an Hourglass. Such an Assembly cannot easily become dangerous to Liberty. They are the Servants of the People, sent together to do the People's Business, and promote the public Welfare; their Powers must be sufficient, or their Duties cannot be performed. They have no profitable Appointments, but a mere Payment of daily Wages, such as are scarcely equivalent to their Expences; so that, having no Chance for great Places, and enormous Salaries or Pensions, as in some Countries, there is no triguing or bribing for Elections.

I wish Old England were as happy in its Government, but I do not see it. Your People, however, think their Constitution the best in the World, and affect to despise ours. It is comfortable to have a good Opinion of one's self, and of every thing that belongs to us; to think one's own Religion, King, and Wife, the best of all possible Wives, Kings, or Religions. I remember three Greenlanders, who had travell'd two Years in Europe under the care of some Moravian Missionaries, and had visited Germany, Denmark, Holland, and England. When I asked them at Philadelphia, where they were in their Way home, whether, now they had seen how much more commodiously the white People lived by the help of the Arts, they would not choose to remain among us; their Answer was, that they were pleased with having had an Opportunity of seeing so many fine things, *but they chose to* LIVE *in their own Country*. Which Country, by the way, consisted of rock only, for the Moravians were obliged to carry Earth in their Ship from New York, for the purpose of making there a Cabbage Garden.

By Mr. Dollond's Saying, that my double Spectacles can only serve particular Eyes, I doubt he has not been rightly informed of their Construction. I imagine it will be found pretty generally true, that the same Convexity of Glass, through which a Man sees clearest and best at the Distance proper for Reading, is not the best for greater Distances. I therefore had formerly two Pair of Spectacles, which I shifted occasionally, as in travelling I sometimes read, and often wanted to regard the Prospects. Finding this Change troublesome, and not always sufficiently ready, I had the Glasses cut, and half of each kind associated in the same Circle, thus,

By this means, as I wear my Spectacles constantly, I have only to move my Eyes up or down, as I want to see distinctly far

or near, the proper Glasses being always ready. This I find more particularly convenient since my being in France, the Glasses that serve me best at Table to see what I eat, not being the best to see the Faces of those on the other Side of the Table who speak to me; and when one's Ears are not well accustomed to the Sounds of a Language, a Sight of the Movements in the Features of him that speaks helps to explain; so that I understand French better by the help of my Spectacles.

My intended translator of your Piece, the only one I know who understands the *Subject*, as well as the two Languages, (which a translator ought to do, or he cannot make so good a Translation,) is at present occupied in an Affair that prevents his undertaking it; but that will soon be over. I thank you for the Notes. I should be glad to have another of the printed Pamphlets.

We shall always be ready to take your Children, if you send them to us. I only wonder, that, since London draws to itself, and consumes such Numbers of your Country People, the Country should not, to supply their Places, want and willingly receive the Children you have to dispose of. That Circumstance, together with the Multitude who voluntarily part with their Freedom as Men, to serve for a time as Lackeys, or for Life as Soldiers, in consideration of small Wages, seems to me a Proof that your Island is over-peopled. And yet it is afraid of Emigrations! Adieu, my dear Friend, and believe me ever yours very affectionately,

PHILADELPHIA
1785–1790

Contents

THE CONSTITUTIONAL CONVENTION

LETTERS

A Petition of the Left Hand

I address myself to all the friends of youth, and conjure them to direct their compassionate regards to my unhappy fate, in order to remove the prejudices of which I am the victim. There are twin sisters of us; and the two eyes of man do not more resemble, nor are capable of being upon better terms with each other, than my sister and myself, were it not for the partiality of our parents, who make the most injurious distinctions between us. From my infancy, I have been led to consider my sister as a being of a more elevated rank. I was suffered to grow up without the least instruction, while nothing was spared in her education. She had masters to teach her writing, drawing, music, and other accomplishments; but if by chance I touched a pencil, a pen, or a needle, I was bitterly rebuked; and more than once I have been beaten for being awkward, and wanting a graceful manner. It is true, my sister associated me with her upon some occasions; but she always made a point of taking the lead, calling upon me only from necessity, or to figure by her side.

But conceive not, Sirs, that my complaints are instigated merely by vanity. No; my uneasiness is occasioned by an object much more serious. It is the practice in our family, that the whole business of providing for its subsistence falls upon my sister and myself. If any indisposition should attack my sister,—and I mention it in confidence upon this occasion, that she is subject to the gout, the rheumatism, and cramp, without making mention of other accidents,—what would be the fate of our poor family? Must not the regret of our parents be excessive, at having placed so great a difference between sisters who are so perfectly equal? Alas! we must perish from distress; for it would not be in my power even to scrawl a suppliant petition for relief, having been obliged to employ the hand of another in transcribing the request which I have now the honour to prefer to you.

Condescend, Sirs, to make my parents sensible of the injustice of an exclusive tenderness, and of the necessity of distributing their care and affection among all their children equally. I am, with a profound respect, Sirs, your obedient servant,

THE LEFT HAND.

1785

Description of an Instrument for Taking Down Books from High Shelves

January, 1786.

Old men find it inconvenient to mount a ladder or steps for that purpose, their heads being sometimes subject to giddinesses, and their activity, with the steadiness of their joints, being abated by age; besides the trouble of removing the steps every time a book is wanted from a different part of their library.

For a remedy, I have lately made the following simple machine, which I call the *Long Arm*.

A B, the *Arm*, is a stick of pine, an inch square and 8 feet long. *C, D*, the *Thumb* and *Finger*, are two pieces of ash lath, an inch and half wide, and a quarter of an inch thick. These are fixed by wood screws on opposite sides of the end *A* of the arm *A B*; the finger *D* being longer and standing out an inch and half farther than the thumb *C*. The outside of the ends of these laths are pared off sloping and thin, that they may more easily enter between books that stand together on a shelf. Two small holes are bored through them at *i, k*. *E F*, the sinew, is a cord of the size of a small goosequill, with a loop at one end. When applied to the machine it passes through the two laths, and is stopped by a knot in its other end behind the longest at *k*. The hole at *i* is nearer the end of the arm than that at *k*, about an inch. A number of knots are also on the cord, distant three or four inches from each other.

To use this instrument; put one hand into the loop, and draw the sinew straight down the side of the arm; then enter the end of the finger between the book you would take down and that which is next to it. The laths being flexible, you may

easily by a slight pressure sideways open them wider if the
book is thick, or close them if it is thin by pulling the string,
so as to enter the shorter lath or thumb between your book

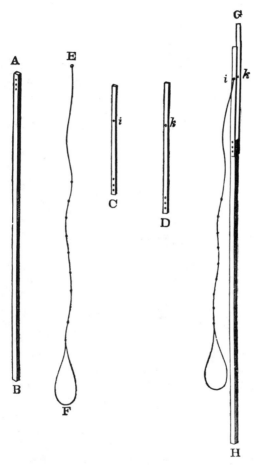

and that which is next to its other side, then push till the back
of your book comes to touch the string. Then draw the string
or sinew tight, which will cause the thumb and finger to
pinch the book strongly, so that you may draw it out. As it
leaves the other books, turn the instrument a *quarter* round,
so that the book may lie flat and rest on its side upon the

under lath or finger. The knots on the sinew will help you to keep it tight and close to the side of the arm as you take it down hand over hand, till the book comes to you; which would drop from between the thumb and finger if the sinew was let loose.

All new tools require some practice before we can become expert in the use of them. This requires very little.

Made in the proportions above given, it serves well for books in duodecimo or octavo. Quartos and folios are too heavy for it; but those are usually placed on the lower shelves within reach of hand.

The book taken down, may, when done with, be put up again into its place by the same machine.

The Art of Procuring Pleasant Dreams

INSCRIBED TO MISS SHIPLEY,
BEING WRITTEN AT HER REQUEST

As a great part of our life is spent in sleep during which we have sometimes pleasant and sometimes painful dreams, it becomes of some consequence to obtain the one kind and avoid the other; for whether real or imaginary, pain is pain and pleasure is pleasure. If we can sleep without dreaming, it is well that painful dreams are avoided. If while we sleep we can have any pleasing dream, it is, as the French say, *autant de gagné*, so much added to the pleasure of life.

To this end it is, in the first place, necessary to be careful in preserving health, by due exercise and great temperance; for, in sickness, the imagination is disturbed, and disagreeable, sometimes terrible, ideas are apt to present themselves. Exercise should precede meals, not immediately follow them; the first promotes, the latter, unless moderate, obstructs digestion. If, after exercise, we feed sparingly, the digestion will be easy and good, the body lightsome, the temper cheerful, and all the animal functions performed agreeably. Sleep, when it follows, will be natural and undisturbed; while indolence, with full feeding, occasions nightmares and horrors inexpressible; we fall from precipices, are assaulted by wild beasts, murderers, and demons, and experience every variety of distress. Observe, however, that the quantities of food and exercise are relative things; those who move much may, and indeed ought to eat more; those who use little exercise should eat little. In general, mankind, since the improvement of cookery, eat about twice as much as nature requires. Suppers are not bad, if we have not dined; but restless nights naturally follow hearty suppers after full dinners. Indeed, as there is a difference in constitutions, some rest well after these meals; it costs them only a frightful dream and an apoplexy, after which they sleep till doomsday. Nothing is more common in the newspapers, than instances of people who, after eating a hearty supper, are found dead abed in the morning.

Another means of preserving health, to be attended to, is the having a constant supply of fresh air in your bed-chamber. It has been a great mistake, the sleeping in rooms exactly closed, and in beds surrounded by curtains. No outward air that may come in to you is so unwholesome as the unchanged air, often breathed, of a close chamber. As boiling water does not grow hotter by longer boiling, if the particles that receive greater heat can escape; so living bodies do not putrefy, if the particles, so fast as they become putrid, can be thrown off. Nature expels them by the pores of the skin and the lungs, and in a free, open air they are carried off; but in a close room we receive them again and again, though they become more and more corrupt. A number of persons crowded into a small room thus spoil the air in a few minutes, and even render it mortal, as in the Black Hole at Calcutta. A single person is said to spoil only a gallon of air per minute, and therefore requires a longer time to spoil a chamber-full; but it is done, however, in proportion, and many putrid disorders hence have their origin. It is recorded of Methusalem, who, being the longest liver, may be supposed to have best preserved his health, that he slept always in the open air; for, when he had lived five hundred years, an angel said to him; "Arise, Methusalem, and build thee an house, for thou shalt live yet five hundred years longer." But Methusalem answered, and said, "If I am to live but five hundred years longer, it is not worth while to build me an house; I will sleep in the air, as I have been used to do." Physicians, after having for ages contended that the sick should not be indulged with fresh air, have at length discovered that it may do them good. It is therefore to be hoped, that they may in time discover likewise, that it is not hurtful to those who are in health, and that we may be then cured of the *aërophobia*, that at present distresses weak minds, and makes them choose to be stifled and poisoned, rather than leave open the window of a bed-chamber, or put down the glass of a coach.

Confined air, when saturated with perspirable matter, will not receive more; and that matter must remain in our bodies, and occasion diseases; but it gives some previous notice of its being about to be hurtful, by producing certain uneasiness, slight indeed at first, which as with regard to the lungs is a trifling sensation, and to the pores of the skin a kind of rest-lessness, which is difficult to describe, and few that feel it know the cause of it. But we may recollect, that sometimes on waking in the night, we have, if warmly covered, found it difficult to get asleep again. We turn often without finding repose in any position. This fidgettiness (to use a vulgar expression for want of a better) is occasioned wholly by an uneasiness in the skin, owing to the retention of the perspir-able matter—the bed-clothes having received their quantity, and, being saturated, refusing to take any more. To become sensible of this by an experiment, let a person keep his posi-tion in the bed, but throw off the bed-clothes, and suffer fresh air to approach the part uncovered of his body; he will then feel that part suddenly refreshed; for the air will imme-diately relieve the skin, by receiving, licking up, and carrying off, the load of perspirable matter that incommoded it. For every portion of cool air that approaches the warm skin, in receiving its part of that vapour, receives therewith a degree of heat that rarefies and renders it lighter, when it will be pushed away with its burthen, by cooler and therefore heavier fresh air, which for a moment supplies its place, and then, being likewise changed and warmed, gives way to a succeed-ing quantity. This is the order of nature, to prevent animals being infected by their own perspiration. He will now be sen-sible of the difference between the part exposed to the air and that which, remaining sunk in the bed, denies the air access: for this part now manifests its uneasiness more distinctly by the comparison, and the seat of the uneasiness is more plainly perceived than when the whole surface of the body was affected by it.

Here, then, is one great and general cause of unpleasing dreams. For when the body is uneasy, the mind will be disturbed by it, and disagreeable ideas of various kinds will in sleep be the natural consequences. The remedies, preventive and curative, follow:

1. By eating moderately (as before advised for health's sake) less perspirable matter is produced in a given time; hence the bed-clothes receive it longer before they are saturated, and we may therefore sleep longer before we are made uneasy by their refusing to receive any more.

2. By using thinner and more porous bed-clothes, which will suffer the perspirable matter more easily to pass through them, we are less incommoded, such being longer tolerable.

3. When you are awakened by this uneasiness, and find you cannot easily sleep again, get out of bed, beat up and turn your pillow, shake the bed-clothes well, with at least twenty shakes, then throw the bed open and leave it to cool; in the meanwhile, continuing undrest, walk about your chamber till your skin has had time to discharge its load, which it will do sooner as the air may be dried and colder. When you begin to feel the cold air unpleasant, then return to your bed, and you will soon fall asleep, and your sleep will be sweet and pleasant. All the scenes presented to your fancy will be too of the pleasing kind. I am often as agreeably entertained with them, as by the scenery of an opera. If you happen to be too indolent to get out of bed, you may, instead of it, lift up your bed-clothes with one arm and leg, so as to draw in a good deal of fresh air, and by letting them fall force it out again. This, repeated twenty times, will so clear them of the perspirable matter they have imbibed, as to permit your sleeping well for some time afterwards. But this latter method is not equal to the former.

Those who do not love trouble, and can afford to have two beds, will find great luxury in rising, when they wake in a hot bed, and going into the cool one. Such shifting of beds would also be of great service to persons ill of a fever, as it refreshes and frequently procures sleep. A very large bed, that will admit a removal so distant from the first situation as to be cool and sweet, may in a degree answer the same end.

One or two observations more will conclude this little piece. Care must be taken, when you lie down, to dispose your pillow so as to suit your manner of placing your head, and to be perfectly easy; then place your limbs so as not to bear inconveniently hard upon one another, as, for instance, the joints of your ankles; for, though a bad position may at first give but little pain and be hardly noticed, yet a continuance will render it less tolerable, and the uneasiness may come on while you are asleep, and disturb your imagination. These are the rules of the art. But, though they will generally prove effectual in producing the end intended, there is a case in which the most punctual observance of them will be totally fruitless. I need not mention the case to you, my dear friend, but my account of the art would be imperfect without it. The case is, when the person who desires to have pleasant dreams has not taken care to preserve, what is necessary above all things,

A GOOD CONSCIENCE.

May 2, 1786

The Retort Courteous

"John Oxly, Pawnbroker of Bethnal Green, was indicted for assaulting Jonathan Boldsworth on the Highway, putting him in fear, and taking from him one Silver Watch, value 5*l.* 5*s.* The Prisoner pleaded, that, having sold the Watch to the Prosecutor, and being immediately after informed by a Person who knew him, that he was not likely to pay for the same, he had only followed him and taken the Watch back again. But it appearing on the Trial, that, presuming he had not been known when he committed the Robbery, he had afterwards sued the Prosecutor for the Debt, on his Note of Hand, he was found Guilty, DEATH." — *Old Bailey Sessions Paper*, 1747.

I chose the above Extract from the Proceedings at the Old Bailey in the Trial of Criminals, as a Motto or Text, on which to amplify in my ensuing Discourse. But on second Thoughts, having given it forth, I shall, after the Example of some other Preachers, quit it for the present, and leave to my

Readers, if I should happen to have any, the Task of discovering what Relation there may possibly be between my Text and my Sermon.

During some Years past, the British Newspapers have been filled with Reflections on the Inhabitants of America, for *not paying their old Debts to English Merchants.* And from these Papers the same Reflections have been translated into Foreign Prints, and circulated throughout Europe; whereby the American Character, respecting Honour, Probity, and Justice in commercial Transactions, is made to suffer in the Opinion of Strangers, which may be attended with pernicious Consequences.

At length we are told that the British Court has taken up the Complaint, and seriously offer'd it as a reason for refusing to evacuate the Frontier Posts according to Treaty. This gives a kind of Authenticity to the Charge, and makes it now more necessary to examine the matter thoro'ly; to inquire impartially into the Conduct of both Nations; take Blame to ourselves where we have merited it; and, where it may be fairly done, mitigate the Severity of the Censures that are so liberally bestow'd upon us.

We may begin by observing, that before the War our mercantile Character was good. In Proof of this (and a stronger Proof can hardly be desired), the Votes of the House of Commons in 1774–5 have recorded a Petition signed by the Body of the Merchants of London trading to North America, in which they expressly set forth, not only that the Trade was profitable to the Kingdom, but that the Remittances and Payments were as punctually and faithfully made, as in any other Branch of Commerce whatever. These Gentlemen were certainly competent Judges, and as to that Point could have no Interest in deceiving the Government.

The making of these punctual Remittances was however a Difficulty. Britain, acting on the selfish and perhaps mistaken Principle of receiving nothing from abroad that could be produced at home, would take no Articles of our Produce that interfered with any of her own; and what did not interfere, she loaded with heavy Duties. We had no Mines of Gold or Silver. We were therefore oblig'd to run the World over, in search of something that would be receiv'd in England. We sent our Provisions and Lumber to the West Indies, where Exchange was made for Sugars, Cotton, &c. to remit. We brought Mollasses from thence, distill'd it into Rum, with which we traded in Africa, and remitted the Gold Dust to England. We employ'd ourselves in the Fisheries, and sent the Fish we caught, together with Quantities of Wheat Flour, and Rice, to Spain and Portugal, from whence the Amount was remitted to England in Cash or Bills of Exchange. Great Quantities of our Rice, too, went to Holland, Hamburgh &c., and the Value of that was also sent to Britain. Add to this, that contenting ourselves with Paper, all the hard Money we could possibly pick up among the Foreign West India Islands, was continually sent off to Britain, not a Ship going thither from America without some Chests of those precious Metals.

Imagine this great Machine of mutually advantageous Commerce, going roundly on, in full Train; our Ports all busy, receiving and selling British Manufactures, and equipping Ships for the circuitous Trade, that was finally to procure the necessary Remittances; the Seas covered with those Ships, and with several hundred Sail of our Fishermen, all working for Britain; and then let us consider what Effect the Conduct of Britain, in 1774 and 1775 and the following Years, must naturally have on the future Ability of our Merchants to make the Payments in question.

We will not here enter into the Motives of that Conduct; they are well enough known, and not to her Honour. The first Step was shutting up the Port of Boston by an Act of Parliament; the next, to prohibit by another the New England Fishery. An Army and a Fleet were sent to enforce these Acts. Here was a Stop put at once to all the mercantile Operations of one of the greatest trading Cities of America; the Fishing Vessels all laid up, and the usual Remittances, by way of Spain, Portugal, and the Straits, render'd impossible. Yet the Cry was now begun against us, *These New England People do not pay their Debts!*

The Ships of the Fleet employ'd themselves in cruising separately all along the Coast. The marine Gentry are seldom so well contented with their Pay, as not to like a little Plunder. They stopp'd and seiz'd, under slight Pretences, the American

Vessels they met with, belonging to whatever Colony. This checked the Commerce of them all. Ships loaded with Cargoes destin'd either directly or indirectly to make Remittance in England, were not spared. If the Difference between the two Countries had been then accommodated, these unauthoriz'd Plunderers would have been called to account, and many of their Exploits must have been found Piracy. But what cur'd all this, set their Minds at ease, made short Work, and gave full Scope to their Piratical Disposition, was another Act of Parliament, forbidding any Inquisition into those *past* Facts, declaring them all Lawful, and all American Property to be forfeited, whether on Sea or Land, and authorizing the King's British Subjects to take, seize, sink, burn, or destroy, whatever they could find of it. The Property suddenly, and by surprise taken from our Merchants by the Operation of this Act, is incomputable. And yet the Cry did not diminish, *These Americans don't pay their Debts!*

Had the several States of America, on the Publication of this Act seiz'd all British Property in their Power, whether consisting of Lands in their Country, Ships in their Harbours, or Debts in the Hands of their Merchants, by way of Retaliation, it is probable a great Part of the World would have deem'd such Conduct justifiable. They, it seems, thought otherwise, and it was done only in one or two States, and that under particular Circumstances of Provocation. And not having thus abolish'd all Demands, the Cry subsists, that *the Americans should pay their Debts!*

General Gage, being with his Army (before the declaration of open War) in peaceable Possession of Boston, shut its Gates, and plac'd Guards all around to prevent its Communication with the Country. The Inhabitants were on the Point of Starving. The general, though they were evidently at his Mercy, fearing that, while they had any Arms in their Hands, frantic Desperation might possibly do him some Mischief, propos'd to them a Capitulation, in which he stipulated, that if they would deliver up their Arms, they might leave the Town with their Families and *Goods*. In faith of this Agreement, they deliver'd their Arms. But when they began to pack up for their Departure, they were inform'd, that by the word *Goods*, the General understood only Houshold Goods, that is, their Beds, Chairs, and Tables, not *Merchant Goods*; those he was inform'd they were indebted for to the Merchants of England, and he must secure them for the Creditors. They were accordingly all seized, to an immense Value, *what had been paid for not excepted*. It is to be supposed, tho' we have never heard of it, that this very honourable General, when he returned home, made a just Dividend of those Goods, or their Value, among the said Creditors. But the Cry nevertheless continued, *These Boston People do not pay their Debts!*

The Army, having thus ruin'd Boston, proceeded to different Parts of the Continent. They got possession of all the capital trading Towns. The Troops gorg'd themselves with Plunder. They stopp'd all the Trade of Philadelphia for near a year, of Rhode Island longer, of New York near eight Years, of Charlestown in South Carolina and Savanah in Georgia, I forget how long. This continu'd Interruption of their Commerce ruin'd many Merchants. The Army also burnt to the Ground the fine Towns of Falmouth and Charlestown near Boston, New London, Fairfield, Norwalk, Esopus, Norfolk, the chief trading City in Virginia, besides innumerable Country Seats and private Farm-Houses. This wanton Destruction of Property operated doubly to the Disabling of our Merchants, who were importers from Britain, in making their Payments, by the immoderate Loss they sustain'd themselves, and also the Loss suffered by their Country Debtors, who had bought of them the British Goods, and who were now render'd unable to pay. The Debts to Britain of course remained undischarg'd, and the Clamour continu'd, *These knavish Americans will not pay us!*

Many of the British Debts, particularly in Virginia and the Carolinas, arose from the Sales made of Negroes in those Provinces by the British Guinea merchants. These, with all before in the country, were employed when the war came on, in raising tobacco and rice for remittance in payment of British debts. An order arrives from England, advised by one of their most celebrated *moralists*, Dr. Johnson, in his *Taxation no Tyranny*, to excite these slaves to rise, cut the throats of their purchasers, and resort to the British army, where they should be rewarded with freedom. This was done, and the planters were thus deprived of near thirty thousand of their

working people. Yet the demand for those sold and unpaid
still exists; and the cry continues against the Virginians and
Carolinians, that *they do not pay their debts!*

Virginia suffered great loss in this kind of property by another ingenious and humane British invention. Having the
small-pox in their army while in that country, they inoculated
some of the negroes they took as prisoners belonging to a
number of plantations, and then let them escape, or sent
them, covered with the pock, to mix with and spread the distemper among the others of their colour, as well as among
the white country people; which occasioned a great mortality
of both, and certainly did not contribute to the enabling debtors in making payment. The war too having put a stop to the
exportation of tobacco, there was a great accumulation of several years' produce in all the public inspecting warehouses and
private stores of the planters. Arnold, Phillips, and Cornwallis, with British troops, then entered and overran the country,
burnt all the inspecting and other stores of tobacco, to the
amount of some hundred ship-loads; all which might, on the
return of peace, if it had not been thus wantonly destroyed,
have been remitted to British creditors. But *these d—d Virginians, why don't they pay their debts?*

Paper money was in those times our universal currency.
But, it being the instrument with which we combated our
enemies, they resolved to deprive us of its use by depreciating
it; and the most effectual means they could contrive was to
counterfeit it. The artists they employed performed so well,
that immense quantities of these counterfeits, which issued
from the British government in New York, were circulated
among the inhabitants of all the States, before the fraud was
detected. This operated considerably in depreciating the
whole mass, first, by the vast additional quantity, and next by
the uncertainty in distinguishing the true from the false; and
the depreciation was a loss to all and the ruin of many. It is
true our enemies gained a vast deal of our property by the
operation; but it did not go into the hands of our particular
creditors; so their demands still subsisted, and we were still
abused *for not paying our debts!*

By the seventh article of the treaty of peace, it was solemnly
stipulated, that the King's troops, in evacuating their posts in

the United States, should not carry away with them any negroes. In direct violation of this article, General Carleton, in
evacuating New York, carried off all the negroes that were
with his army, to the amount of several hundreds. It is not
doubted that he must have had secret orders to justify him in
this transaction; but the reason given out was, that, as they
had quitted their masters and joined the King's troops on the
faith of proclamations promising them their liberty, the national honour forbade returning them into slavery. The
national honour was, it seemed, pledged to both parts of a
contradiction, and its wisdom, since it could not do it with
both, chose to keep faith rather with its old black, than its
new white friends; a circumstance demonstrating clear as day-
light, that, in making a present peace, they meditated a future
war, and hoped, that, though the promised manumission of
slaves had not been effectual in the *last*, in the *next* it might
be more successful; and that, had the negroes been forsaken,
no aid could be hereafter expected from those of the colour
in a future invasion. The treaty however with us was thus
broken almost as soon as made, and this by the people who
charge us with breaking it by not paying perhaps for some of
the very negroes carried off in defiance of it. Why should England observe treaties, *when these Americans do not pay their
debts?*

Unreasonable, however, as this clamour appears in general,
I do not pretend, by exposing it, to justify those debtors who
are still able to pay, and refuse it on pretence of injuries suffered by the war. Public injuries can never discharge private
obligations. Contracts between merchant and merchant
should be sacredly observed, where the ability remains, whatever may be the madness of ministers. It is therefore to be
hoped the fourth article of the treaty of peace which stipulates, *that no legal obstruction shall be given to the payment of
debts contracted before the war*, will be punctually carried into
execution, and that every law in every State which impedes it,
may be immediately repealed. Those laws were indeed made
with honest intentions, that the half-ruined debtor, not being
too suddenly pressed by *some*, might have time to arrange and
recover his affairs so as to do justice to *all* his creditors. But,
since the intention in making those acts has been misappre-

hended, and the acts wilfully misconstrued into a design of defrauding them, and now made a matter of reproach to us, I think it will be right to repeal them all. Individual Americans may be ruined, but the country will save by the operation; since these unthinking, merciless creditors must be contented with all that is to be had, instead of all that may be due to them, and the accounts will be settled by insolvency. When all have paid that can pay, I think the remaining British creditors, who suffered by the inability of their ruined debtors, have some right to call upon their own government (which by its bad projects has ruined those debtors) for a compensation. A sum given by Parliament for this purpose would be more properly disposed, than in rewarding pretended loyalists, who fomented the war. And, the heavier the sum, the more tendency it might have to discourage such destructive projects hereafter.

Among the merchants of Britain, trading formerly to America, there are to my knowledge many considerate and generous men, who never joined in this clamour, and who, on the return of peace, though by the treaty entitled to an immediate suit for their debts, were kindly disposed to give their debtors reasonable time for restoring their circumstances, so as to be able to make payment conveniently. These deserve the most grateful acknowledgments. And indeed it was in their favour, and perhaps for their sakes in favour of all other British creditors, that the law of Pennsylvania, though since much exclaimed against, was made, restraining the recovery of old debts during a certain time. For this restraint was general, respecting domestic as well as British debts, it being thought unfair, in cases where there was not sufficient for all, that the inhabitants, taking advantage of their nearer situation, should swallow the whole, excluding foreign creditors from any share. And in cases where the favourable part of the foreign creditors were disposed to give time, with the views abovementioned, if others less humane and considerate were allowed to bring immediate suits and ruin the debtor, those views would be defeated. When this law expired in September, 1784, a new one was made, continuing for some time longer the restraint with respect to domestic debts, but expressly taking it away where the debt was due from citizens of the State to any of the subjects of Great Britain;* which shows clearly the disposition of the Assembly, and that the fair intentions above ascribed to them in making the former act, are not merely the imagination of the writer.

Indeed, the clamour has been much augmented by numbers joining it, who really had no claim on our country. Every debtor in Britain, engaged in whatever trade, when he had no better excuse to give for delay of payment, accused the want of returns from America. And the indignation, thus excited against us, now appears so general among the English, that one would imagine their nation, which is so exact in expecting punctual payment from all the rest of the world, must be at home the model of justice, the very pattern of punctuality. Yet, if one were disposed to recriminate, it would not be difficult to find sufficient Matter in several Parts of their Conduct. But this I forbear. The two separate Nations are now at Peace, and there can be no use in mutual Provocations to fresh Enmity. If I have shown clearly that the present Inability of many American Merchants to discharge their Debts, contracted before the War, is not so much their Fault, as the Fault of the crediting Nation, who, by making an unjust War on them, obstructing their Commerce, plundering and devastating their Country, were the Cause of that Inability, I have answered the Purpose of writing this Paper. How far the Refusal of the British Court to execute the Treaty in delivering up the Frontier Posts may on account of this Deficiency of Payment, be justifiable, is chearfully submitted to the World's impartial Judgment.

*Extract from an Act of the General Assembly of Pennsylvania, entitled, "An Act for directing the Mode of recovering Debts contracted before the first Day of January, in the Year of our Lord one thousand seven hundred and seventy-seven."

Exception in Favour of British Creditors.

"Sect. 7. And provided also, and be it further enacted by the authority aforesaid, that this Act, nor any thing therein contained, shall not extend, or be construed to extend, to any debt or debts which were due before the fourth day of July, one thousand seven hundred and seventy-six, by any of the citizens of the State, to any of the subjects of Great Britain."

1786

THE CONSTITUTIONAL CONVENTION

Speech in the Convention
on the Subject of Salaries

SIR,

It is with Reluctance that I rise to express a Disapprobation of any one Article of the Plan, for which we are so much obliged to the honourable Gentleman who laid it before us. From its first Reading, I have borne a good Will to it, and, in general, wish'd it Success. In this Particular of Salaries to the Executive Branch, I happen to differ; and, as my Opinion may appear new and chimerical, it is only from a Persuasion that it is right, and from a Sense of Duty, that I hazard it. The Committee will judge of my Reasons when they have heard them, and their judgment may possibly change mine. I think I see Inconveniences in the Appointment of Salaries; I see none in refusing them, but on the contrary great Advantages.

Sir, there are two Passions which have a powerful Influence in the Affairs of Men. These are *Ambition* and *Avarice*; the Love of Power and the Love of Money. Separately, each of these has great Force in prompting Men to Action; but when united in View of the same Object, they have in many Minds the most violent Effects. Place before the Eyes of such Men a Post of *Honour*, that shall at the same time be a Place of *Profit*, and they will move Heaven and Earth to obtain it. The vast Number of such Places it is that renders the British Government so tempestuous. The Struggles for them are the true Source of all those Factions which are perpetually dividing the Nation, distracting its Councils, hurrying it sometimes into fruitless and mischievous Wars, and often compelling a Submission to dishonourable Terms of Peace.

And of what kind are the men that will strive for this profitable Preëminence, thro' all the Bustle of Cabal, the Heat of Contention, the infinite mutual Abuse of Parties, tearing to Pieces the best of Characters? It will not be the wise and moderate, the Lovers of Peace and good Order, the men fittest for the Trust. It will be the Bold and the Violent, the men of strong Passions and indefatigable Activity in their selfish Pursuits. These will thrust themselves into your Government, and be your Rulers. And these, too, will be mistaken in the expected Happiness of their Situation; for their vanquish'd competitors, of the same Spirit, and from the same Motives, will perpetually be endeavouring to distress their Administration, thwart their Measures, and render them odious to the People.

Besides these Evils, Sir, tho' we may set out in the Beginning with moderate Salaries, we shall find, that such will not be of long Continuance. Reasons will never be wanting for propos'd Augmentations; and there will always be a Party for giving more to the Rulers, that the Rulers may be able in Return to give more to them. Hence, as all History informs us, there has been in every State and Kingdom a constant kind of Warfare between the Governing and the Governed; the one striving to obtain more for its Support, and the other to pay less. And this has alone occasion'd great Convulsions, actual civil Wars, ending either in dethroning of the Princes or enslaving of the People. Generally, indeed, the Ruling Power carries its Point, and we see the Revenues of Princes constantly increasing, and we see that they are never satisfied, but always in want of more. The more the People are discontented with the Oppression of Taxes, the greater Need the Prince has of Money to distribute among his Partisans, and pay the Troops that are to suppress all Resistance, and enable him to plunder at Pleasure. There is scarce a King in a hundred, who would not, if he could, follow the Example of Pharaoh,—get first all the People's Money, then all their Lands, and then make them and their Children Servants for ever. It will be said, that we do not propose to establish Kings. I know it. But there is a natural Inclination in Mankind to kingly Government. It sometimes relieves them from Aristocratic Domination. They had rather have one Tyrant than 500. It gives more of the Appearance of Equality among Citizens; and that they like. I am apprehensive, therefore,— perhaps too apprehensive,—that the Government of these States may in future times end in a Monarchy. But this Catastrophe, I think, may be long delay'd, if in our propos'd System we do not sow the Seeds of Contention, Faction, and Tumult, by making our Posts of Honour Places of Profit. If we do, I fear, that, tho' we employ at first a Number and not a single Person, the Number will in time be set aside; it will only nourish the Fœtus of a King (as the honourable Gentleman from Virg[a] very aptly express'd it), and a King will the sooner be set over us.

It may be imagined by some, that this is an Utopian Idea, and that we can never find Men to serve us in the Executive Department, without paying them well for their Services. I conceive this to be a Mistake. Some existing Facts present themselves to me, which incline me to a contrary Opinion. The High Sheriff of a County in England is an honourable Office, but it is not a profitable one. It is rather expensive, and therefore not sought for. But yet it is executed, and well executed, and usually by some of the principal Gentlemen of the County. In France, the Office of Counsellor, or Member of their judiciary Parliaments, is more honourable. It is therefore purchas'd at a high Price; there are indeed Fees on the Law Proceedings, which are divided among them, but these Fees do not amount to more than three per cent on the Sum paid for the Place. Therefore, as legal Interest is there at five per cent, they in fact pay two per cent for being allow'd to do the Judiciary Business of the Nation, which is at the same time entirely exempt from the Burthen of paying them any Salaries for their Services. I do not, however, mean to recommend this as an eligible Mode for our judiciary Department. I only bring the Instance to show, that the Pleasure of doing Good and serving their Country, and the Respect such Conduct entitles them to, are sufficient Motives with some Minds, to give up a great Portion of their Time to the Public, without the mean Inducement of pecuniary Satisfaction.

Another Instance is that of a respectable Society, who have made the Experiment, and practis'd it with Success, now more than a hundred years. I mean the Quakers. It is an establish'd Rule with them that they are not to go to law, but in their Controversies they must apply to their Monthly, Quarterly, and Yearly Meetings. Committees of these sit with Patience to hear the Parties, and spend much time in composing their Differences. In doing this, they are supported by a Sense of Duty, and the Respect paid to Usefulness. It is honourable to be so employ'd, but it was never made profitable by Salaries, Fees, or Perquisites. And indeed, in all Cases of public Service, the less the Profit the greater the Honour.

To bring the Matter nearer home, have we not seen the greatest and most important of our Offices, that of General of our Armies, executed for Eight Years together, without the smallest Salary, by a patriot whom I will not now offend by any other Praise; and this, thro' Fatigues and Distresses, in common with the other brave Men, his military Friends and Companions, and the constant Anxieties peculiar to his Station? And shall we doubt finding three or four Men in all the United States, with public Spirit enough to bear sitting in peaceful Council, for perhaps an equal Term, merely to preside over our civil Concerns, and see that our Laws are duly executed? Sir, I have a better opinion of our Country. I think we shall never be without a sufficient Number of wise and good Men to undertake, and execute well and faithfully, the Office in question.

Sir, the Saving of the Salaries, that may at first be propos'd, is not an object with me. The subsequent Mischiefs of proposing them are what I apprehend. And therefore it is that I move the Amendment. If it is not seconded or accepted, I must be contented with the Satisfaction of having delivered my Opinion frankly, and done my Duty.

June 2, 1787

Speech in a Committee of the Convention on the Proportion of Representation and Votes

MR. CHAIRMAN,

It has given me great Pleasure to observe, that, till this Point, *the Proportion of Representation*, came before us, our Debates were carry'd on with great Coolness and Temper. If any thing of a contrary kind has, on this Occasion, appeared, I hope it will not be repeated; for we are sent hither to *consult*, not to *contend*, with each other; and Declaration of a fix'd Opinion, and of determined Resolutions never to change it, neither enlighten nor convince us. Positiveness and

Warmth on one side naturally beget their like on the other; and tend to create and augment Discord and Division in a great Concern, wherein Harmony and Union are extremely necessary, to give Weight to our Counsels, and render them effectual in promoting and securing the common Good.

I must own, that I was originally of Opinion it would be better if every Member of Congress, or our national Council, were to consider himself rather as a Representative of the whole, than as an Agent for the Interests of a particular State; in which Case the Proportion of Members for each State would be of less Consequence, and it would not be very material whether they voted by States or individually. But as I find this is not to be expected, I now think the Number of Representatives should bear some Proportion to the Number of the Represented, and that the Decisions should be by the Majority of Members, not by the Majority of States. This is objected to, from an Apprehension that the greater States would then swallow up the Smaller. I do not at present clearly see what Advantage the greater States could propose to themselves by swallowing the smaller, and therefore do not apprehend they would attempt it. I recollect, that in the Beginning of this Century, when the Union was propos'd of the two Kingdoms, England and Scotland, the Scotch patriots were full of Fears, that, unless they had an equal Number of Representatives in Parliament, they should be ruined by the Superiority of the English. They finally agreed, however, that the different Proportions of Importance in the Union of the two Nations should be attended to; whereby they were to have only Forty Members in the House of Commons, and only Sixteen of their Peers were to sit in the House of Lords; a very great Inferiority of Numbers! And yet, to this Day, I do not recollect that any thing has been done in the Parliament of Great Britain to the Prejudice of Scotland; and whoever looks over the Lists of publick Officers, Civil and Military, of that Nation, will find, I believe, that the North Britons enjoy at least their full proportion of Emolument.

But, Sir, in the present Mode of Voting by States, it is equally in the Power of the lesser States to swallow up the greater; and this is mathematically demonstrable. Suppose, for example, that 7 smaller States had each 3 members in the

House, and the Six larger to have, one with another, 6 Members; and that, upon a Question, two Members of each smaller State should be in the Affirmative, and one in the Negative; they will make

Affirmatives,   14   Negatives 7
And that all the large States should
    be unanimously in the negative;
    they would make   Negatives 36
                                                              —
                                                    In all 43

It is then apparent, that the 14 carry the question against the 43, and the Minority overpowers the Majority, contrary to the common Practice of Assemblies in all Countries and Ages.

The greater States, Sir, are naturally as unwilling to have their Property left in the Disposition of the smaller, as the smaller are to leave theirs in the Disposition of the greater. An honourable Gentleman has, to avoid this difficulty, hinted a Proposition of equalizing the States. It appears to me an equitable one; and I should, for my own Part, not be against such a Measure, if it might be found practicable. Formerly, indeed, when almost every Province had a different Constitution, some with greater, others with fewer Privileges, it was of Importance to the Borderers, when their Boundaries were contested, whether, by running the Division Lines, they were placed on one Side or the other. At present, when such Differences are done away, it is less material. The Interest of a State is made up of the Interests of its individual Members. If they are not injured, the State is not injured. Small States are more easily, well, and happily governed, than large ones. If, therefore, in such an equal Division, it should be found necessary to diminish Pennsylvania, I should not be averse to the giving a part of it to N. Jersey, and another to Delaware: But as there would probably be considerable Difficulties in adjusting such a Division; and, however equally made at first, it would be continually varying by the Augmentation of Inhabitants in some States, and their more fixed proportion in others, and thence frequent Occasion for new Divisions; I beg leave to propose for the Consideration of the Committee another Mode, which appears to me to be as equitable, more easily carry'd into Practice, and more permanent in its Nature.

Let the weakest State say what Proportion of Money or Force it is able and willing to furnish for the general Purposes of the Union.

Let all the others oblige themselves to furnish each an equal Proportion.

The whole of these joint Supplies to be absolutely in the Disposition of Congress.

The Congress in this Case to be compos'd of an equal Number of Delegates from each State;

And their Decisions to be by the Majority of individual Members voting.

If these joint and equal Supplies should, on particular Occasions, not be sufficient, let Congress make Requisitions on the richer and more powerful States for further Aids, to be voluntarily afforded; so leaving each State the Right of considering the Necessity and Utility of the Aid desired, and of giving more or less, as it should be found proper.

This Mode is not new; it was formerly practic'd with Success by the British Government, with respect to Ireland and the Colonies. We sometimes gave even more than they expected, or thought just to accept; and in the last War, carried on while we were united, they gave us back in 5 Years a Million Sterling. We should probably have continu'd such voluntary Contributions, whenever the Occasions appear'd to require them for the common Good of the Empire. It was not till they chose to force us, and to deprive us of the Merit and Pleasure of voluntary Contributions, that we refus'd and resisted. Those Contributions, however, were to be dispos'd of at the Pleasure of a Government in which we had no Representative. I am therefore persuaded, that they will not be refus'd to one in which the Representation shall be equal.

My learned Colleague has already mentioned that the present method of voting by States, was submitted to originally by Congress, under a Conviction of its Impropriety, Inequality, and Injustice. This appears in the Words of their Resolution. It is of Sept. 6, 1774. The words are,

"Resolved, That, in determining Questions in this Congress, each Colony or Province shall have one vote; the

Congress not being possessed of, or at present able to procure, Materials for ascertaining the Importance of each Colony."

June 11, 1787

Motion for Prayers in the Convention

MR. PRESIDENT,

The small Progress we have made, after 4 or 5 Weeks' close Attendance and continual Reasonings with each other, our different Sentiments on almost every Question, several of the last producing as many *Noes* as *Ayes*, is, methinks, a melancholy Proof of the Imperfection of the Human Understanding. We indeed seem to *feel* our own want of political Wisdom, since we have been running all about in Search of it. We have gone back to ancient History for Models of Government, and examin'd the different Forms of those Republics, which, having been originally form'd with the Seeds of their own Dissolution, now no longer exist; and we have view'd modern States all round Europe, but find none of their Constitutions suitable to our Circumstances.

In this Situation of this Assembly, groping, as it were, in the dark to find Political Truth, and scarce able to distinguish it when presented to us, how has it happened, Sir, that we have not hitherto once thought of humbly applying to the Father of Lights to illuminate our Understandings? In the Beginning of the Contest with Britain, when we were sensible of Danger, we had daily Prayers in this Room for the Divine Protection. Our Prayers, Sir, were heard;—and they were graciously answered. All of us, who were engag'd in the Struggle, must have observed frequent Instances of a superintending Providence in our Favour. To that kind Providence we owe this happy Opportunity of Consulting in Peace on the Means of establishing our future national Felicity. And have we now forgotten that powerful Friend? or do we imagine we no longer need its assistance? I have lived, Sir, a long time; and the longer I live, the more convincing proofs I see of this Truth, *that* GOD *governs in the Affairs of Men.* And if a Sparrow cannot fall to the Ground without his Notice, is it probable that an Empire can rise without his Aid? We have been assured, Sir, in the Sacred Writings, that "except the Lord build the House, they labour in vain that build it." I firmly believe this; and I also believe, that, without his concurring Aid, we shall succeed in this political Building no better than the Builders of Babel; we shall be divided by our little, partial, local Interests, our Projects will be confounded, and we ourselves shall become a Reproach and a Bye-word down to future Ages. And, what is worse, Mankind may hereafter, from this unfortunate Instance, despair of establishing Government by human Wisdom, and leave it to Chance, War, and Conquest.

I therefore beg leave to move,

That henceforth Prayers, imploring the Assistance of Heaven and its Blessing on our Deliberations, be held in this Assembly every morning before we proceed to Business; and that one or more of the Clergy of this city be requested to officiate in that Service.*

*The convention, except three or four persons, thought prayers unnecessary!

June 28, 1787

Speech in the Convention at the Conclusion of its Deliberations

I confess that I do not entirely approve of this Constitution at present, but Sir, I am not sure I shall never approve it: For having lived long, I have experienced many Instances of being oblig'd, by better Information or fuller Consideration, to change Opinions even on important Subjects, which I once thought right, but found to be otherwise. It is therefore that the older I grow the more apt I am to doubt my own Judgment and to pay more Respect to the Judgment of others. Most Men indeed as well as most Sects in Religion, think themselves in Possession of all Truth, and that wherever others differ from them it is so far Error. Steele, a Protestant, in a Dedication tells the Pope, that the only Difference between our two Churches in their Opinions of the Certainty of their Doctrine, is, the Romish Church is infallible, and the Church of England is never in the Wrong. But tho' many private Persons think almost as highly of their own Infallibility, as that of their Sect, few express it so naturally as a certain French lady, who in a little Dispute with her Sister, said, I don't know how it happens, Sister, but I meet with no body but myself that's *always* in the right. *Il n'y a que moi qui a toujours raison.*

In these Sentiments, Sir, I agree to this Constitution, with all its Faults, if they are such: because I think a General Government necessary for us, and there is no *Form* of Government but what may be a Blessing to the People if well administred; and I believe farther that this is likely to be well administred for a Course of Years, and can only end in Despotism as other Forms have done before it, when the People shall become so corrupted as to need Despotic Government, being incapable of any other. I doubt too whether any other Convention we can obtain, may be able to make a better Constitution: For when you assemble a Number of Men to have the Advantage of their joint Wisdom, you inevitably assemble with those Men all their Prejudices, their Passions, their Errors of Opinion, their local Interests, and their selfish Views. From such an Assembly can a perfect Production be expected? It therefore astonishes me, Sir, to find this System approaching so near to Perfection as it does; and I think it will astonish our Enemies, who are waiting with Confidence to hear that our Councils are confounded, like those of the Builders of Babel, and that our States are on the Point of Separation, only to meet hereafter for the Purpose of cutting one another's Throats. Thus I consent, Sir, to this Constitution because I expect no better, and because I am not sure that it is not the best. The Opinions I have had of its Errors, I sacrifice to the Public Good. I have never whisper'd a Syllable of them abroad. Within these Walls they were born, & here they shall die. If every one of us in returning to our Constituents were to report the Objections he has had to it, and endeavour to gain Partizans in support of them, we might prevent its being generally received, and thereby lose all the salutary Effects & great Advantages resulting naturally in our favour among foreign Nations, as well as among ourselves, from our real or apparent Unanimity. Much of the Strength and Efficiency of any Government, in procuring & securing Happiness to the People depends on Opinion, on the general Opinion of the Goodness of that Government as well as of the Wisdom & Integrity of its Governors. I hope therefore that for our own Sakes, as a Part of the People, and for the Sake of our Posterity, we shall act heartily & unanimously in recommending this Constitution, wherever our Influence may extend, and turn our future Thoughts and Endeavours to the Means of having it well administred. —

On the whole, Sir, I cannot help expressing a Wish, that every Member of the Convention, who may still have Objections to it, would with me on this Occasion doubt a little of his own Infallibility, and to make *manifest* our *Unanimity*, put his Name to this Instrument. —

Then the Motion was made for adding the last Formula, viz Done in Convention by the unanimous Consent &c— which was agreed to and added—accordingly.

September 17, 1787

On Sending Felons to America

FOR THE PENNSYLVANIA GAZETTE

SIR,

We may all remember the Time when our Mother Country, as a Mark of her parental Tenderness, emptied her Jails into our Habitations, *"for the* BETTER *Peopling,"* as she express'd it, *"of the Colonies."* It is certain that no due Returns have yet been made for these valuable Consignments. We are therefore much in her Debt on that Account; and, as she is of late clamorous for the Payment of all we owe her, and some of our Debts are of a kind not so easily discharg'd, I am for doing however what is in our Power. It will show our good-will as to the rest. The Felons she planted among us have produc'd such an amazing Increase, that we are now enabled to make ample Remittance in the same Commodity. And since the Wheelbarrow Law is not found effectually to reform them, and many of our Vessels are idle through her Restraints on our Trade, why should we not employ those Vessels in transporting the Felons to Britain?

I was led into this Thought by perusing the Copy of a Petition to Parliament, which fell lately by Accident into my Hands. It has no Date, but I conjecture from some Circumstances, that it must have been about the year 1767 or 68. (It seems, if presented, it had no Effect, since the Act passed.) I imagine it may not be unacceptable to your Readers, and therefore transcribe it for your paper; viz.

To the Honourable the Knights, Citizens, and Burgesses of Great Britain, in Parliament assembled,

The PETITION of B. F., Agent for the Province of Pensilvania;

Most humbly sheweth;

That the Transporting of Felons from England to the Plantations in America, is, and hath long been, a great Grievance to the said Plantations in general.

That the said Felons, being landed in America, not only continue their evil Practices to the Annoyance of his Majesty's good Subjects there, but contribute greatly to corrupt the

Morals of the Servants and poorer People among whom they are mixed.

That many of the said Felons escape from the Servitude to which they were destined, into other Colonies, where their Condition is not known; and, wandering at large from one populous Town to another, commit many Burglaries, Robberies, and Murders, to the great Terror of the People; and occasioning heavy Charges for apprehending and securing such Felons, and bringing them to Justice.

That your Petitioner humbly conceives the Easing one Part of the British Dominions of their Felons, by burthening another Part with the same Felons, cannot increase the common Happiness of his Majesty's Subjects, and that therefore the Trouble and Expence of transporting them is upon the whole altogether useless.

That your petitioner, nevertheless, observes with extream Concern in the Votes of Friday last, that leave is given to bring in a Bill for extending to Scotland, the Act made in the 4th Year of the Reign of King George the First, whereby the aforesaid Grievances are, as he understands, to be greatly increased by allowing Scotland also to transport its Felons to America.

Your petitioner therefore humbly prays, in behalf of Pensilvania, and the other Plantations in America, that the House would take the Premises into Consideration, and in their great Wisdom and Goodness repeal all Acts, and Clauses of Acts, for transporting of Felons; or, if this may not at present be done, that they would at least reject the propos'd Bill for extending the said Acts to Scotland; or, if it be thought fit to allow of such Extension, that then the said Extension may be carried further, and the Plantations be also, by an equitable Clause in the same bill, permitted to transport their Felons to Scotland.

And your Petitioner, as in Duty bound, shall pray, &c.

This Petition, as I am informed, was not receiv'd by the House, and the Act passed.

On second Thoughts, I am of Opinion, that besides employing our own Vessels, as above propos'd, every English Ship arriving in our Ports with Goods for sale, should be obliged to give Bond, before she is permitted to Trade, engaging that she will carry back to Britain at least one Felon for every Fifty Tons of her Burthen. Thus we shall not only discharge sooner our Debts, but furnish our old Friends with the means of *"better Peopling,"* and with more Expedition, their promising new Colony of Botany Bay.

                              I am yours, &c.

                                              A. Z.

1787

TO THE EDITOR OF THE FEDERAL GAZETTE:

A Comparison of the Conduct of the Ancient Jews and of the Anti-Federalists in the United States of America

A zealous Advocate for the propos'd Federal Constitution, in a certain public Assembly, said, that "the Repugnance of a great part of Mankind to good Government was such, that he believed, that, if an angel from Heaven was to bring down a Constitution form'd there for our Use, it would nevertheless meet with violent Opposition." He was reprov'd for the suppos'd Extravagance of the Sentiment; and he did not justify it. Probably it might not have immediately occur'd to him, that the Experiment had been try'd, and that the Event was recorded in the most faithful of all Histories, the Holy Bible; otherwise he might, as it seems to me, have supported his Opinion by that unexceptionable Authority.

The Supreme Being had been pleased to nourish up a single Family, by continued Acts of his attentive Providence, till it became a great People; and, having rescued them from Bondage by many Miracles, performed by his Servant Moses, he personally deliver'd to that chosen Servant, in the presence of the whole Nation, a Constitution and Code of Laws for their Observance; accompanied and sanction'd with Promises of great Rewards, and Threats of severe Punishments, as the Consequence of their Obedience or Disobedience.

This Constitution, tho' the Deity himself was to be at its Head (and it is therefore call'd by Political Writers a *Theocracy*), could not be carried into Execution but by the Means

of his Ministers; Aaron and his Sons were therefore commission'd to be, with Moses, the first establish'd Ministry of the
new Government.

One would have thought, that this Appointment of Men,
who had distinguish'd themselves in procuring the Liberty of
their Nation, and had hazarded their Lives in openly opposing the Will of a powerful Monarch, who would have retain'd
that Nation in Slavery, might have been an Appointment acceptable to a grateful People; and that a Constitution fram'd
for them by the Deity himself might, on that Account, have
been secure of a universal welcome Reception. Yet there were
in every one of the *thirteen Tribes* some discontented, restless
Spirits, who were continually exciting them to reject the propos'd new Government, and this from various Motives.

Many still retained an Affection for Egypt, the Land of
their Nativity; and these, whenever they felt any Inconvenience or Hardship, tho' the natural and unavoidable Effect of
their Change of Situation, exclaim'd against their Leaders as
the Authors of their Trouble; and were not only for returning
into Egypt, but for stoning their deliverers.* Those inclin'd
to idolatry were displeas'd that their *Golden Calf* was destroy'd. Many of the Chiefs thought the new Constitution
might be injurious to their particular Interests, that the *profitable Places* would be *engrossed by the Families and Friends of
Moses and Aaron*, and others equally well-born excluded.† In
Josephus and the Talmud, we learn some Particulars, not so
fully narrated in the Scripture. We are there told, "That Corah
was ambitious of the Priesthood, and offended that it was
conferred on Aaron; and this, as he said, by the Authority of
Moses only, *without the Consent of the People.* He accus'd
Moses of having, by various Artifices, fraudulently obtain'd
the Government, and depriv'd the People of their Liberties;
and of *conspiring* with Aaron to perpetuate the Tyranny in
their Family. Thus, tho' Corah's real Motive was the Sup-
planting of Aaron, he persuaded the People that he meant

*Numbers, ch. xiv.

†Numbers, ch. xiv, verse 3. "And they gathered themselves together against
Moses and Aaron, and said unto them, 'Ye take too much upon you, seeing
all the congregation are holy, *every one of them*; wherefore, then, lift ye up
yourselves above the congregation?' "

only the *Public Good*; and they, moved by his Insinuations, began to cry out, 'Let us maintain the Common Liberty of our *respective Tribes*; we have freed ourselves from the Slavery impos'd on us by the Egyptians, and shall we now suffer ourselves to be made Slaves by Moses? If we must have a Master, it were better to return to Pharaoh, who at least fed us with Bread and Onions, than to serve this new Tyrant, who by his Operations has brought us into Danger of Famine.' Then they called in question the *Reality of his Conference* with God; and objected the *Privacy of the Meetings*, and the *preventing any of the People from being present* at the Colloquies, or even approaching the Place, as Grounds of great Suspicion. They accused Moses also of *Peculation*; as embezzling part of the Golden Spoons and the Silver Chargers, that the Princes had offer'd at the Dedication of the Altar,* and the Offerings of Gold by the common People,† as well as most of the Poll-Tax;‡ and Aaron they accus'd of pocketing much of the Gold of which he pretended to have made a molten Calf. Besides *Peculation*, they charg'd Moses with *Ambition*; to gratify which Passion he had, they said, deceiv'd the People, by promising to bring them *to* a land flowing with Milk and Honey; instead of doing which, he had brought them *from* such a Land; and that he thought light of all this mischief, provided he could make himself an *absolute Prince*.§ That, to support the new Dignity with Splendor in his Family, the partial Poll-Tax already levied and given to Aaron‖ was to be follow'd by a general one,¶ which would probably be augmented from time to time, if he were suffered to go on promulgating new Laws, on pretence of new occasional Revelations of the divine Will, till their whole Fortunes were devour'd by that Aristocracy."

Moses deny'd the Charge of Peculation; and his Accusers were destitute of Proofs to support it; tho' *Facts*, if real, are in their Nature capable of Proof. "I have not," said he (with

*Numbers, ch. vii.

†Exodus, ch. xxxv, verse 22.

‡Numbers, ch. iii, and Exodus, ch. xxx.

§Numbers, ch. xvi, verse 13. "Is it a small thing that thou hast brought us up out of a land that floweth with milk and honey, to kill us in the wilderness, except thou make thyself altogether a prince over us?"

‖ Numbers, ch. iii

¶Exodus, ch. xxx.

holy Confidence in the Presence of his God), "I have not taken from this People the value of an Ass, nor done them any other Injury." But his Enemies had made the Charge, and with some Success among the Populace; for no kind of Accusation is so readily made, or easily believ'd, by Knaves as the Accusation of Knavery.

In fine, no less than two hundred and fifty of the principal Men, "famous in the Congregation, Men of Renown,"* heading and exciting the Mob, worked them up to such a pitch of Frenzy, that they called out, "Stone 'em, stone 'em, and thereby *secure our Liberties*; and let us chuse other Captains, that may lead us back into Egypt, in case we do not succeed in reducing the Canaanites!"

On the whole, it appears, that the Israelites were a People jealous of their newly-acquired Liberty, which Jealousy was in itself no Fault; but, when they suffer'd it to be work'd upon by artful Men, pretending Public Good, with nothing really in view but private Interest, they were led to oppose the Establishment of the *New Constitution*, whereby they brought upon themselves much Inconvenience and Misfortune. It appears further, from the same inestimable History, that, when after many Ages that Constitution was become old and much abus'd, and an Amendment of it was propos'd, the populace, as they had accus'd Moses of the Ambition of making himself a *Prince*, and cried out, "Stone him, stone him;" so, excited by their High Priests and SCRIBES, they exclaim'd against the Messiah, that he aim'd at becoming King of the Jews, and cry'd out, *"Crucify him, Crucify him."* From all which we may gather, that popular Opposition to a public Measure is no Proof of its Impropriety, even tho' the Opposition be excited and headed by Men of Distinction.

To conclude, I beg I may not be understood to infer, that our General Convention was divinely inspired, when it form'd the new federal Constitution, merely because that Constitution has been unreasonably and vehemently opposed; yet I must own I have so much Faith in the general Government of the world by *Providence*, that I can hardly conceive a Transaction of such momentous Importance to the Welfare of

*Numbers, ch. xvi.

Millions now existing, and to exist in the Posterity of a great Nation, should be suffered to pass without being in some degree influenc'd, guided, and governed by that omnipotent, omnipresent, and beneficent Ruler, in whom all inferior Spirits live, and move, and have their Being.

The Federal Gazette, April 8, 1788

TO THE EDITORS OF THE PENNSYLVANIA GAZETTE:

On the Abuse of the Press

MESSRS. HALL AND SELLERS,

I lately heard a remark, that on examination of *The Penn-sylvania Gazette* for fifty years, from its commencement, it appeared, that, during that long period, scarce one libellous piece had ever appeared in it. This generally chaste conduct of your paper is much to its reputation; for it has long been the opinion of sober, judicious people, that nothing is more likely to endanger the liberty of the press, than the abuse of that liberty, by employing it in personal accusation, detraction, and calumny. The excesses some of our papers have been guilty of in this particular, have set this State in a bad light abroad, as appears by the following letter, which I wish you to publish, not merely to show your own disapprobation of the practice, but as a caution to others of the profession throughout the United States. For I have seen a European newspaper, in which the editor, who had been charged with frequently calumniating the Americans, justifies himself by saying, "that he had published nothing disgraceful to us, which he had not taken from our own printed papers." I am, &c.

A. B.

"DEAR FRIEND,   New York, March 30, 1788.

"My Gout has at length left me, after five Months' painful Confinement. It afforded me, however, the Leisure to read, or hear read, all the Packets of your various Newspapers, which you so kindly sent for my Amusement.

"Mrs. W. has partaken of it; she likes to read the Advertisements; but she remarks some kind of Inconsistency in the announcing so many Diversions for almost every Evening of the Week, and such Quantities to be sold of expensive Superfluities, Fineries, and Luxuries *just imported*, in a Country, that at the same time fills its Papers with Complaints of *Hard Times*, and Want of Money. I tell her, that such Complaints are common to all Times and all Countries, and were made even in Solomon's Time; when, as we are told, Silver was as plenty in Jerusalem as the Stones in the Street; and yet, even then, there were People who grumbled, so as to incur this Censure from that knowing Prince. *'Say not thou that the former Times were better than these; for thou dost not enquire rightly concerning that matter.'*

"But the Inconsistence that strikes me the most is, that between the Name of your City, Philadelphia, (*Brotherly Love,*) and the Spirit of Rancour, Malice, and *Hatred* that breathes in its NewsPapers. For I learn from those Papers, that your State is divided into Parties, that each Party ascribes all the public Operations of the other to vicious Motives; that they do not even suspect one another of the smallest Degree of Honesty; that the antifederalists are such, merely from the Fear of losing Power, Places, or Emoluments, which they have in Possession or in Expectation; that the Federalists are a set of *Conspirators*, who aim at establishing a Tyranny over the Persons and Property of their Countrymen, and to live in Splendor on the Plunder of the People. I learn, too, that your Justices of the Peace, tho' chosen by their Neighbours, make a villainous Trade of their Office, and promote Discord to augment Fees, and fleece their Electors; and that this would not be mended by placing the Choice in the Executive Council, who, with interested or party Views, are continually making as improper Appointments; witness a *'petty Fidler, Sycophant, and Scoundrel,'* appointed Judge of the Admiralty; *'an old Woman and Fomenter of Sedition'* to be another of the Judges, and *'a Jeffries'* Chief Justice, &c. &c.; with *'two Harpies'* the Comptroller and Naval Officers, to prey upon the Merchants and deprive them of their Property by Force of Arms, &c.

"I am inform'd also by these Papers, that your General Assembly, tho' the annual choice of the People, shows no Regard to their Rights, but from sinister Views or Ignorance makes Laws in direct Violation of the Constitution, to divest the Inhabitants of their Property and give it to Strangers and Intruders; and that the Council, either fearing the Resentment of their Constituents, or plotting to enslave them, had projected to disarm them, and given Orders for that purpose; and finally, that your President, the unanimous joint choice of the Council and Assembly, is 'an old Rogue,' who gave his Assent to the federal Constitution merely to avoid refunding Money he had purloin'd from the United States.

"There is, indeed, a good deal of manifest *Inconsistency* in all this, and yet a Stranger, seeing it in your own Prints, tho' he does not believe it all, may probably believe enough of it to conclude, that Pennsylvania is peopled by a Set of the most unprincipled, wicked, rascally, and quarrelsome Scoundrels upon the Face of the Globe. I have sometimes, indeed, suspected, that those Papers are the Manufacture of foreign Enemies among you, who write with a view of disgracing your Country, and making you appear contemptible and detestable all the World over; but then I wonder at the Indiscretion of your Printers in publishing such Writings! There is, however, one of your *Inconsistencies* that consoles me a little, which is, that tho' *living*, you give one another the characters of Devils; *dead*, you are all Angels! It is delightful, when any of you die, to read what good Husbands, good Fathers, good Friends, good Citizens, and good Christians you were, concluding with a Scrap of Poetry that places you, with certainty, every one in Heaven. So that I think Pennsylvania a good country *to dye in*, though a very bad one to *live in*."

after March 30, 1788

FOR THE FEDERAL GAZETTE.

An Account of the Supremest Court of Judicature in Pennsylvania, viz. The Court of the Press

POWER OF THIS COURT.

It may receive and promulgate accusations of all kinds against all persons and characters among the citizens of the state, and even against all inferior courts, and may judge, sentence and condemn to infamy, not only private individuals, but public bodies, &c. with or without enquiry or hearing, *at the court's discretion*.

In whose favor or for whose emolument this court is established.

In favor of about one citizen in 500, who by education, or practice in scribbling, has acquired a tolerable stile as to grammar and construction so as to bear printing; or who is possessed of a press and a few types. This 500th part of the citizens have the privilege of accusing and abusing the other 499 parts, at their pleasure; or they may hire out their pens and press to others for that purpose.

Practice of the Court.

It is not governed by any of the rules of common courts of law. The accused is allowed no grand jury to judge of the truth of the accusation before it is publicly made; nor is the name of the accuser made known to him; nor has he an opportunity of confronting the witnesses against him; for they are kept in the dark, as in the Spanish Court of Inquisition.— Nor is there any petty jury of his peers sworn to try the truth of the charges. The proceedings are also sometimes so rapid, that an honest good citizen may find himself suddenly and unexpectedly accused, and in the same morning judged and condemned, and sentence pronounced against him, That he is a *rogue* and a *villain*. Yet if an officer of this court receives the slightest check for misconduct in this his office, he claims immediately the rights of a free citizen by the constitution, and demands to know his accuser, to confront the witnesses, and to have a fair trial by a jury of his peers.

The foundation of its authority.

It is said to be founded on an article in the state-constitution, which establishes *the liberty of the press*. A liberty which every Pennsylvanian would fight and die for: Though few of us, I believe, have distinct ideas of its nature and extent. It seems indeed somewhat like the *liberty* of the *press* that felons have by the common law of England before conviction, that is, to be either *pressed* to death or hanged. If by the *liberty of the press* were understood merely the liberty of discussing the propriety of public measures and political opinions, let us have as much of it as you please: But if it means the liberty of affronting, calumniating and defaming one another, I, for my part, own myself willing to part with my share of it, whenever our legislators shall please so to alter the law and shall chearfully consent to exchange my *liberty* of abusing others for the *privilege* of not being abused myself.

By whom this court is commissioned or constituted.

It is not by any commission from the Supreme Executive Council, who might previously judge of the abilities, integrity, knowledge, &c. of the persons to be appointed to this great trust, of deciding upon the characters and good fame of the citizens; for this court is above that council, and may *accuse, judge,* and *condemn* it, at pleasure. Nor is it hereditary, as is the court of *dernier resort* in the peerage of England. But any man who can procure pen, ink, and paper, with a press, a few types, and a huge pair of BLACKING balls, may commissionate himself: And his court is immediately established in the plenary possession and exercise of its rights. For if you make the least complaint of the *judge's* conduct, he daubs his blacking balls in your face wherever he meets you; and besides tearing your private character to slitters, marks you out for the odium of the public, as an *enemy to the liberty of the press.*

Of the natural support of these courts.

Their support is founded in the depravity of such minds as have not been mended by religion, nor improved by good education;

> "*There is a lust in man no charm can tame,*
> *Of loudly publishing his neighbour's shame.*"
> Hence,
> "*On eagle's wings immortal scandals fly,*
> *While virtuous actions are but born and die.*"
> Dryden.

Whoever feels pain in hearing a good character of his neighbour, will feel a pleasure in the reverse. And of those, who, despairing to rise into distinction by their virtues, and are happy if others can be depressed on a level with themselves, there are a number sufficient in every great town to maintain one of these courts by their subscriptions.—A shrewd observer once said that in walking the streets in a slippery morning, one might see where the good natured people lived by the ashes thrown on the ice before their doors: probably he would have formed a different conjecture of the temper of those whom he might find engaged in such subscriptions.

Of the checks proper to be established against the abuse of power in those courts.

Hitherto there are none. But since so much has been written and published on the federal constitution, and the necessity of checks in all other parts of good government has been so clearly and learnedly explained, I find myself so far enlightened as to suspect some check may be proper in this part also; but I have been at a loss to imagine any that may not be construed an infringement of the sacred *liberty of the Press.* At length however I think I have found one, that instead of diminishing general liberty, shall augment it; which is, by restoring to the people a species of liberty of which they have been deprived by our laws, I mean the *liberty of the Cudgel.*— In the rude state of society, prior to the existence of laws, if one man gave another ill language, the affronted person might return it by a box on the ear; and if repeated, by a good drubbing; and this without offending against any law; but now the right of making such returns is denied, and they are punished as breaches of the peace; while the right of abusing seems to remain in full force: the laws made against it being rendered ineffectual by the *liberty of the Press.*

My proposal then is, to leave the liberty of the Press untouched, to be exercised in its full extent, force and vigour, but to permit the *liberty of the Cudgel* to go with it *pari passu.* Thus my fellow-citizens, if an impudent writer attacks your reputation, dearer to you perhaps than your life, and puts his name to the charge, you may go to him as openly and break his head. If he conceals himself behind the printer, and you can nevertheless discover who he is, you may in a like manner way-lay him in the night, attack him behind, and give him a good drubbing. If your adversary hire better writers than himself to abuse you the more effectually, you may hire brawny porters, stronger than yourself, to assist you in giving him a more effectual drubbing.—Thus far goes my project, as to *private* resentment and retribution. But if the public should ever happen to be affronted, *as it ought to be* with the conduct of such writers, I would not advise proceeding immediately to these extremities; but that we should in moderation content ourselves with tarring and feathering, and tossing them in a blanket.

If, however, it should be thought that this proposal of mine may disturb the public peace, I would then humbly recommend to our legislators to take up the consideration of both liberties, that of the Press, and that of the Cudgel, and by an explicit law mark their extent and limits; and at the same time that they secure the person of a citizen from assaults, they would likewise provide for the security of his reputation.

The Federal Gazette, September 12, 1789

An Address to the Public
FROM THE PENNSYLVANIA SOCIETY FOR PROMOTING THE ABOLITION OF SLAVERY, AND THE RELIEF OF FREE NEGROES UNLAWFULLY HELD IN BONDAGE

It is with peculiar satisfaction we assure the friends of humanity, that, in prosecuting the design of our association, our endeavours have proved successful, far beyond our most sanguine expectations.

Encouraged by this success, and by the daily progress of that luminous and benign spirit of liberty, which is diffusing itself throughout the world, and humbly hoping for the continuance of the divine blessing on our labours, we have ventured to make an important addition to our original plan, and do therefore earnestly solicit the support and assistance of all who can feel the tender emotions of sympathy and compassion, or relish the exalted pleasure of beneficence.

Slavery is such an atrocious debasement of human nature, that its very extirpation, if not performed with solicitous care, may sometimes open a source of serious evils.

The unhappy man, who has long been treated as a brute animal, too frequently sinks beneath the common standard of the human species. The galling chains, that bind his body, do also fetter his intellectual faculties, and impair the social affections of his heart. Accustomed to move like a mere machine, by the will of a master, reflection is suspended; he has not the power of choice; and reason and conscience have but little influence over his conduct, because he is chiefly governed by the passion of fear. He is poor and friendless; perhaps worn out by extreme labour, age, and disease.

Under such circumstances, freedom may often prove a misfortune to himself, and prejudicial to society.

Attention to emancipated black people, it is therefore to be hoped, will become a branch of our national policy; but, as far as we contribute to promote this emancipation, so far that attention is evidently a serious duty incumbent on us, and which we mean to discharge to the best of our judgment and abilities.

To instruct, to advise, to qualify those, who have been restored to freedom, for the exercise and enjoyment of civil liberty, to promote in them habits of industry, to furnish them with employments suited to their age, sex, talents, and other circumstances, and to procure their children an education calculated for their future situation in life; these are the great outlines of the annexed plan, which we have adopted, and which we conceive will essentially promote the public good, and the happiness of these our hitherto too much neglected fellow-creatures.

A plan so extensive cannot be carried into execution without considerable pecuniary resources, beyond the present ordinary funds of the Society. We hope much from the generosity of enlightened and benevolent freemen, and will gratefully receive any donations or subscriptions for this purpose, which may be made to our treasurer, James Starr, or to James Pemberton, chairman of our committee of correspondence.

Signed, by order of the Society,

B. FRANKLIN, *President*.

Philadelphia, 9th of
November, 1789.

Plan for Improving the Condition of the Free Blacks

The business relative to free blacks shall be transacted by a committee of twenty-four persons, annually elected by ballot, at the meeting of this Society, in the month called April; and, in order to perform the different services with expedition, regularity, and energy, this committee shall resolve itself into the following sub-committees, viz.

I. A Committee of Inspection, who shall superintend the morals, general conduct, and ordinary situation of the free negroes, and afford them advice and instruction, protection from wrongs, and other friendly offices.

II. A Committee of Guardians, who shall place out children and young people with suitable persons, that they may (during a moderate time of apprenticeship or servitude) learn some trade or other business of subsistence. The committee may effect this partly by a persuasive influence on parents and the persons concerned, and partly by coöperating with the laws, which are, or may be, enacted for this and similar purposes. In forming contracts on these occasions, the committee shall secure to the Society, as far as may be practicable, the right of guardianship over the persons so bound.

III. A Committee of Education, who shall superintend the school instruction of the children and youth of the free blacks. They may either influence them to attend regularly the schools already established in this city, or form others with this view; they shall, in either case, provide, that the pupils may receive such learning as is necessary for their future situation in life, and especially a deep impression of the most important and generally acknowledged moral and religious principles. They shall also procure and preserve a regular record of the marriages, births, and manumissions of all free blacks.

IV. A Committee of Employ, who shall endeavour to procure constant employment for those free negroes who are able to work; as the want of this would occasion poverty, idleness, and many vicious habits. This committee will, by sedulous inquiry, be enabled to find common labour for a great number; they will also provide, that such as indicate proper talents may learn various trades, which may be done by prevailing upon them to bind themselves for such a term of years as shall compensate their masters for the expense and trouble of instruction and maintenance. The committee may attempt the institution of some useful and simple manufactures, which require but little skill, and also may assist, in commencing business, such as appear to be qualified for it.

Whenever the committee of inspection shall find persons of any particular description requiring attention, they shall immediately direct them to the committee of whose care they are the proper objects.

In matters of a mixed nature, the committees shall confer, and, if necessary, act in concert. Affairs of great importance shall be referred to the whole committee.

The expense, incurred by the prosecution of this plan, shall be defrayed by a fund, to be formed by donations or subscriptions for these particular purposes, and to be kept separate from the other funds of this Society.

The committee shall make a report of their proceedings, and of the state of their stock, to the Society, at their quarterly meetings, in the months called April and October.

1789?

Sidi Mehemet Ibrahim on the Slave Trade

TO THE EDITOR OF THE FEDERAL GAZETTE

SIR,   March 23d, 1790.

Reading last night in your excellent Paper the speech of Mr. Jackson in Congress against their meddling with the Affair of Slavery, or attempting to mend the Condition of the Slaves, it put me in mind of a similar One made about 100 Years since by Sidi Mehemet Ibrahim, a member of the Divan of Algiers, which may be seen in Martin's Account of his Consulship, anno 1687. It was against granting the Petition of the Sect called *Erika*, or Purists, who pray'd for the Abolition of Piracy and Slavery as being unjust. Mr. Jackson does not quote it; perhaps he has not seen it. If, therefore, some of its Reasonings are to be found in his eloquent Speech, it may only show that men's Interests and Intellects operate and are operated on with surprising similarity in all Countries and Climates, when under similar Circumstances. The African's Speech, as translated, is as follows.

"Allah Bismillah, &c.
God is great, and Mahomet is his Prophet.

"Have these *Erika* considered the Consequences of granting their Petition? If we cease our Cruises against the Christians, how shall we be furnished with the Commodities their Countries produce, and which are so necessary for us? If we forbear to make Slaves of their People, who in this hot Climate are to cultivate our Lands? Who are to perform the common Labours of our City, and in our Families? Must we not then be our own Slaves? And is there not more Compassion and more Favour due to us as Mussulmen, than to these Christian Dogs? We have now above 50,000 Slaves in and near Algiers. This Number, if not kept up by fresh Supplies, will soon diminish, and be gradually annihilated. If we then cease taking and plundering the Infidel Ships, and making Slaves of the Seamen and Passengers, our Lands will become of no Value for want of Cultivation; the Rents of Houses in the City will sink one half; and the Revenues of Government arising from its Share of Prizes be totally destroy'd! And for what? To gratify the whims of a whimsical Sect, who would have us, not only forbear making more Slaves, but even to manumit those we have.

"But who is to indemnify their Masters for the Loss? Will the State do it? Is our Treasury sufficient? Will the *Erika* do it? Can they do it? Or would they, to do what they think Justice to the Slaves, do a greater Injustice to the Owners? And if we set our Slaves free, what is to be done with them? Few of them will return to their Countries; they know too well the greater Hardships they must there be subject to; they will not embrace our holy Religion; they will not adopt our Manners; our People will not pollute themselves by intermarrying with them. Must we maintain them as Beggars in our Streets, or suffer our Properties to be the Prey of their Pillage? For Men long accustom'd to Slavery will not work for a Livelihood when not compell'd. And what is there so piti-able in their present Condition? Were they not Slaves in their own Countries?

"Are not Spain, Portugal, France, and the Italian states govern'd by Despots, who hold all their Subjects in Slavery, without Exception? Even England treats its Sailors as Slaves; for they are, whenever the Government pleases, seiz'd, and confin'd in Ships of War, condemn'd not only to work, but to fight, for small Wages, or a mere Subsistence, not better than our Slaves are allow'd by us. Is their Condition then made worse by their falling into our Hands? No; they have only exchanged one Slavery for another, and I may say a bet-ter; for here they are brought into a Land where the Sun of Islamism gives forth its Light, and shines in full Splendor, and they have an Opportunity of making themselves ac-quainted with the true Doctrine, and thereby saving their im-mortal Souls. Those who remain at home have not that Happiness. Sending the Slaves home then would be sending them out of Light into Darkness.

"I repeat the Question, What is to be done with them? I have heard it suggested, that they may be planted in the Wil-derness, where there is plenty of Land for them to subsist on, and where they may flourish as a free State; but they are, I doubt, too little dispos'd to labour without Compulsion, as well as too ignorant to establish a good government, and the wild Arabs would soon molest and destroy or again enslave them. While serving us, we take care to provide them with every thing, and they are treated with Humanity. The La-bourers in their own Country are, as I am well informed, worse fed, lodged, and cloathed. The Condition of most of them is therefore already mended, and requires no further Im-provement. Here their Lives are in Safety. They are not liable to be impress'd for Soldiers, and forc'd to cut one another's Christian Throats, as in the Wars of their own Countries. If some of the religious mad Bigots, who now teaze us with their silly Petitions, have in a Fit of blind Zeal freed their Slaves, it was not Generosity, it was not Humanity, that mov'd them to the Action; it was from the conscious Burthen of a Load of Sins, and Hope, from the supposed Merits of so good a Work, to be excus'd Damnation.

"How grossly are they mistaken in imagining Slavery to be disallow'd by the Alcoran! Are not the two Precepts, to quote no more, *'Masters, treat your Slaves with kindness; Slaves, serve your Masters with Cheerfulness and Fidelity,'* clear Proofs to the contrary? Nor can the Plundering of Infidels be in that sacred Book forbidden, since it is well known from it, that God has given the World, and all that it contains, to his faithful Mussulmen, who are to enjoy it of Right as fast as they conquer it. Let us then hear no more of this detestable Proposition, the Manumission of Christian Slaves, the Adoption of which would, by depreciating our Lands and Houses, and thereby depriving so many good Citizens of their Properties, create universal Discontent, and provoke Insurrections, to the endangering of Government and producing general Confusion. I have therefore no doubt, but this wise Council will prefer the Comfort and Happiness of a whole Nation of true Believers to the Whim of a few *Erika*, and dismiss their Petition."

The Result was, as Martin tells us, that the Divan came to this Resolution; "The Doctrine, that Plundering and Enslaving the Christians is unjust, is at best *problematical*; but that it is the Interest of this State to continue the Practice, is clear; therefore let the Petition be rejected."

And it was rejected accordingly.

And since like Motives are apt to produce in the Minds of Men like Opinions and Resolutions, may we not, Mr. Brown, venture to predict, from this Account, that the Petitions to the Parliament of England for abolishing the Slave-Trade, to say nothing of other Legislatures, and the Debates upon them, will have a similar Conclusion? I am, Sir, your constant Reader and humble Servant,

HISTORICUS.

The Federal Gazette, March 25, 1790

LETTERS

"WHEN WE LAUNCH OUR LITTLE FLEET
OF BARQUES"

To Jonathan Shipley

DEAR FRIEND,   Philadelphia, Feb. 24th, 1786.

I received lately your kind letter of Nov. 27th. My Reception here was, as you have heard, very honourable indeed; but I was betray'd by it, and by some Remains of Ambition, from which I had imagined myself free, to accept of the Chair of Government for the State of Pennsylvania, when the proper thing for me was Repose and a private Life. I hope, however, to be able to bear the Fatigue for one Year, and then to retire.

I have much regretted our having so little Opportunity for Conversation when we last met. You could have given me Informations and Counsels that I wanted, but we were scarce a Minute together without being broke in upon. I am to thank you, however, for the Pleasure I had after our Parting, in reading the new Book you gave me, which I think generally well written and likely to do good; tho' the Reading Time of most People is of late so taken up with News Papers and little periodical Pamphlets, that few now-a-days venture to attempt reading a Quarto Volume. I have admir'd to see, that, in the last Century, a Folio, *Burton on Melancholly*, went through Six Editions in about Twenty Years. We have, I believe, more Readers now, but not of such large Books.

You seem desirous of knowing what Progress we make here in improving our Governments. We are, I think, in the right Road of Improvement, for we are making Experiments. I do not oppose all that seem wrong, for the Multitude are more effectually set right by Experience, than kept from going wrong by Reasoning with them. And I think we are daily more and more enlightened; so that I have no doubt of our obtaining in a few Years as much public Felicity, as good Government is capable of affording.

Your NewsPapers are fill'd with fictitious Accounts of Anarchy, Confusion, Distresses, and Miseries, we are suppos'd to be involv'd in, as Consequences of the Revolution; and the few remaining Friends of the old Government among us take pains to magnify every little Inconvenience a Change in the Course of Commerce may have occasion'd. To obviate the Complaints they endeavour to excite, was written the enclos'd little Piece, from which you may form a truer Idea of our Situation, than your own public Prints would give you. And I can assure you, that the great Body of our Nation find themselves happy in the Change, and have not the smallest Inclination to return to the Domination of Britain. There could not be a stronger Proof of the general Approbation of the Measures, that promoted the Change, and of the Change itself, than has been given by the Assembly and Council of this State, in the nearly unanimous Choice for their Governor, of one who had been so much concern'd in those Measures; the Assembly being themselves the unbrib'd Choice of the People, and therefore may be truly suppos'd of the same Sentiments. I say nearly unanimous, because, of between 70 and 80 Votes, there were only my own and one other in the negative.

As to my Domestic Circumstances, of which you kindly desire to hear something, they are at present as happy as I could wish them. I am surrounded by my Offspring, a Dutiful and Affectionate Daughter in my House, with Six Grandchildren, the eldest of which you have seen, who is now at a College in the next Street, finishing the learned Part of his Education; the others promising, both for Parts and good Dispositions. What their Conduct may be, when they grow up and enter the important Scenes of Life, I shall not live to *see*, and I cannot *foresee*. I therefore enjoy among them the present Hour, and leave the future to Providence.

He that raises a large Family does, indeed, while he lives to observe them, *stand*, as Watts says, *a broader Mark for Sorrow*; but then he stands a broader Mark for Pleasure too. When we launch our little Fleet of Barques into the Ocean, bound to different Ports, we hope for each a prosperous Voyage; but contrary Winds, hidden Shoals, Storms, and Enemies come in for a Share in the Disposition of Events; and though these occasion a Mixture of Disappointment, yet, considering the Risque where we can make no Insurance, we should think ourselves happy if some return with Success. My Son's Son, Temple Franklin, whom you have also seen, having had a fine

Farm of 600 Acres convey'd to him by his Father when we were at Southampton, has drop'd for the present his Views of acting in the political Line, and applies himself ardently to the Study and Practice of Agriculture. This is much more agreable to me, who esteem it the most useful, the most independent, and therefore the noblest of Employments. His Lands are on navigable water, communicating with the Delaware, and but about 16 Miles from this City. He has associated to himself a very skillful English Farmer lately arrived here, who is to instruct him in the Business, and partakes for a Term of the Profits; so that there is a great apparent Probability of their Success.

You will kindly expect a Word or two concerning myself. My Health and Spirits continue, Thanks to God, as when you saw me. The only complaint I then had, does not grow worse, and is tolerable. I still have Enjoyment in the Company of my Friends; and, being easy in my Circumstances, have many Reasons to like Living. But the Course of Nature must soon put a period to my present Mode of Existence. This I shall submit to with less Regret, as, having seen during a long Life a good deal of this World, I feel a growing Curiosity to be acquainted with some other; and can chearfully, with filial Confidence, resign my Spirit to the conduct of that great and good Parent of Mankind, who created it, and who has so graciously protected and prospered me from my Birth to the present Hour. Wherever I am, I hope always to retain the pleasing remembrance of your Friendship, being with sincere and great Esteem, my dear Friend, yours most affectionately,

P. S. We all join in Respects to Mrs. Shipley, and best wishes for the whole amiable Family.

LEAD POISONING

To Benjamin Vaughan

DEAR FRIEND, Philad[a], July 31, 1786.

I recollect, that, when I had the great Pleasure of seeing you at Southampton, now a 12month since, we had some

Conversation on the bad Effects of Lead taken inwardly; and that at your Request I promis'd to send you in writing a particular Account of several Facts I then mention'd to you, of which you thought some good use might be made. I now sit down to fulfil that Promise.

The first Thing I remember of this kind was a general Discourse in Boston, when I was a Boy, of a Complaint from North Carolina against New England Rum, that it poison'd their People, giving them the Dry Bellyach, with a Loss of the Use of their Limbs. The Distilleries being examin'd on the Occasion, it was found that several of them used leaden Still-heads and Worms, and the Physicians were of Opinion, that the Mischief was occasioned by that Use of Lead. The Legislature of the Massachusetts thereupon pass'd an Act, prohibiting under severe Penalties the Use of such Still-heads and Worms thereafter. Inclos'd I send you a Copy of the Acc^t, taken from my printed Law-book.

In 1724, being in London, I went to work in the Printing-House of Mr. Palmer, Bartholomew Close, as a Compositor. I there found a Practice, I had never seen before, of drying a Case of Types (which are wet in Distribution) by placing it sloping before the Fire. I found this had the additional Advantage, when the Types were not only dry'd but heated, of being comfortable to the Hands working over them in cold weather. I therefore sometimes heated my Case when the Types did not want drying. But an old Workman, observing it, advis'd me not to do so, telling me I might lose the Use of my Hands by it, as two of our Companions had nearly done, one of whom that us'd to earn his Guinea a Week, could not then make more than ten Shillings, and the other, who had the Dangles, but seven and sixpence. This, with a kind of obscure Pain, that I had sometimes felt, as it were in the Bones of my Hand when working over the Types made very hot, induced me to omit the Practice. But talking afterwards with Mr. James, a Letter-founder in the same Close, and asking him if his People, who work'd over the little Furnaces of melted Metal, were not subject to that Disorder; he made light of any danger from the effluvia, but ascribed it to Particles of the Metal swallow'd with their Food by slovenly Workmen, who went to their Meals after handling the Metal, without well washing their Fingers, so that some of the metalline Particles were taken off by their Bread and eaten with it. This appeared to have some Reason in it. But the Pain I had experienc'd made me still afraid of those Effluvia.

Being in Derbishire at some of the Furnaces for Smelting of Lead Ore, I was told, that the Smoke of those Furnaces was pernicious to the neighbouring Grass and other Vegetables; but I do not recollect to have heard any thing of the Effect of such Vegetables eaten by Animals. It may be well to make the Enquiry.

In America I have often observ'd, that on the Roofs of our shingled Houses, where Moss is apt to grow in northern Exposures, if there be any thing on the Roof painted with white Lead, such as Balusters, or Frames of dormant Windows, &c., there is constantly a Streak on the Shingles from such Paint down to the Eaves, on which no Moss will grow, but the wood remains constantly clean and free from it. We seldom drink RainWater that falls on our Houses; and if we did, perhaps the small Quantity of Lead, descending from such Paint, might not be sufficient to produce any sensible ill Effect on our Bodies. But I have been told of a Case in Europe, I forgot the Place, where a whole Family was afflicted with what we call the Dry Bellyach, or *Colica Pictonum*, by drinking RainWater. It was at a Country-Seat, which, being situated too high to have the Advantage of a Well, was supply'd with Water from a Tank, which received the Water from the leaded Roofs. This had been drunk several Years without Mischief; but some young Trees planted near the House growing up above the Roof, and shedding their Leaves upon it, it was suppos'd that an Acid in those Leaves had corroded the Lead they cover'd, and furnish'd the Water of that Year with its baneful Particles and Qualities.

When I was in Paris with Sir John Pringle in 1767, he visited *La Charité*, a Hospital particularly famous for the Cure of that Malady, and brought from thence a Pamphlet containing a List of the Names of Persons, specifying their Professions or Trades, who had been cured there. I had the Curiosity to examine that List, and found that all the Patients were of Trades, that, some way or other, use or work in Lead; such as Plumbers, Glaziers, Painters, &c., excepting only two kinds, Stonecutters and Soldiers. These I could not reconcile to my Notion, that Lead was the cause of that Disorder. But on my mentioning this Difficulty to a Physician of that Hospital, he inform'd me that the Stonecutters are continually using melted Lead to fix the Ends of Iron Balustrades in Stone; and that the Soldiers had been employ'd by Painters, as Labourers, in Grinding of Colours.

This, my dear Friend, is all I can at present recollect on the Subject. You will see by it, that the Opinion of this mischievous Effect from Lead is at least above Sixty Years old; and you will observe with Concern how long a useful Truth may be known and exist, before it is generally receiv'd and practis'd on.

I am, ever, yours most affectionately,

"INVENTION AND IMPROVEMENT ARE PROLIFIC"

To Rev. John Lathrop

REVEREND SIR,   Philadᵃ, May 31, 1788.

I received your obliging Favour of the 6th Inst by Mr. Hilliard, with whose Conversation I was much pleased, and would have been glad to have had more of it, if he could have spar'd it to me; but the short time of his stay has prevented. You need make no apology for introducing any of your friends to me. I consider it as doing me Honour, as well as giving me Pleasure.

I thank you for the pamphlet of the Humane Society. In return please to accept one of the same kind, which was published while I resided in France. If your Society have not hitherto seen it, it may possibly afford them useful Hints.

It would certainly, as you observe, be a very great Pleasure to me, if I could once again visit my Native Town, and walk over the Grounds I used to frequent when a Boy, and where I enjoyed many of the innocent Pleasures of Youth, which would be so brought to my Remembrance, and where I might find some of my old Acquaintance to converse with. But when I consider how well I am situated here, with every thing about me, that I can call either necessary or convenient; the fatigues and bad accommodations to be met with and suffered in a land journey, and the unpleasantness of sea voyages, to one, who, although he has crossed the Atlantic eight times, and made many smaller trips, does not recollect his having ever been at sea without taking a firm resolution never to go to sea again; and that, if I were arrived in Boston, I should see but little of it, as I could neither bear walking nor riding in a carriage over its pebbled streets; and, above all, that I should find very few indeed of my old friends living, it being now sixty-five years since I left it to settle here;—all this considered, I say, it seems probable, though not certain, that I shall hardly again visit that beloved place. But I enjoy the company and conversation of its inhabitants, when any of them are so good as to visit me; for, besides their general good sense, which I value, the Boston manner, turn of phrase, and even tone of voice, and accent in pronunciation, all please, and seem to refresh and revive me.

I have been long impressed with the same sentiments you so well express, of the growing felicity of mankind, from the improvements in philosophy, morals, politics, and even the conveniences of common living, by the invention and acquisition of new and useful utensils and instruments, that I have sometimes almost wished it had been my destiny to be born two or three centuries hence. For invention and improvement are prolific, and beget more of their kind. The present progress is rapid. Many of great importance, now unthought of, will before that period be produced; and then I might not only enjoy their advantages, but have my curiosity gratified in knowing what they are to be. I see a little absurdity in what I have just written, but it is to a friend, who will wink and let it pass, while I mention one reason more for such a wish, which is, that, if the art of physic shall be improved in proportion with other arts, we may then be able to avoid diseases, and live as long as the patriarchs in Genesis; to which I suppose we should make little objection.

I am glad my dear sister has so good and kind a neighbour. I sometimes suspect she may be backward in acquainting me with circumstances in which I might be more useful to her. If any such should occur to your observation, your mentioning them to me will be a favour I shall be thankful for. With great esteem, I have the honour to be, Reverend Sir, &c.

HONEST HERETICS

To Benjamin Vaughan

October 24, 1788.

——Having now finished my term in the Presidentship, and resolving to engage no more in public affairs, I hope to be a better correspondent for the little time I have to live. I am recovering from a long continued gout, and am diligently employed in writing the History of my Life, to the doing of which the persuasions contained in your letter of January 31, 1783, have not a little contributed. I am now in the year 1756 just before I was sent to England. To shorten the work, as well as for other reasons, I omit all facts and transactions that may not have a tendency to benefit the young reader, by showing him from my example, and my success in emerging from poverty, and acquiring some degree of wealth, power, and reputation, the advantages of certain modes of conduct which I observed, and of avoiding the errors which were prejudicial to me. If a writer can judge properly of his own work, I fancy on reading over what is already done, that the book may be found entertaining, interesting, and useful, more so than I expected when I began it. If my present state of health continues, I hope to finish it this winter: when done you shall have a manuscript copy of it, that I may obtain from your judgment and friendship, such remarks as may contribute to its improvement.

The violence of our party debates about the new constitution seems much abated, indeed almost extinct, and we are getting fast into good order. I kept out of those disputes pretty well, having wrote only one little piece, which I send you inclosed.

I regret the immense quantity of misery brought upon mankind by this Turkish war; and I am afraid the King of Sweden may burn his fingers by attacking Russia. When will princes learn arithmetick enough to calculate if they want pieces of one another's territory, how much cheaper it would be to buy them, than to make war for them, even though they were to give an hundred years purchase? But if glory cannot be valued, and therefore the wars for it cannot be subject to arithmetical calculation so as to show their advantage or disadvantage, at least wars for trade, which have gain for their object, may be proper subjects for such computation; and a trading nation as well as a single trader ought to calculate the probabilities of profit and loss, before engaging in any considerable adventure. This however nations seldom do, and we have had frequent instances of their spending more money in wars for acquiring or securing branches of commerce, that an hundred years' profit or the full enjoyment of them can compensate.

Remember me affectionately to good Dr. Price and to the honest heretic Dr. Priestly. I do not call him *honest* by way of distinction; for I think all the heretics I have known have been virtuous men. They have the virtue of fortitude or they would not venture to own their heresy; and they cannot afford to be deficient in any of the other virtues, as that would give advantage to their many enemies; and they have not like orthodox sinners, such a number of friends to excuse or justify them. Do not, however mistake me. It is not to my good friend's heresy that I impute his honesty. On the contrary, 'tis his honesty that has brought upon him the character of heretic. I am ever, my dear friend, yours sincerely,

"THE DISPLEASURE OF THE GREAT AND IMPARTIAL
RULER OF THE UNIVERSE"

To John Langdon

Sir:

The Pennsylvania Society for promoting the abolition of slavery, and the relief of free Negroes unlawfully held in bondage, have taken the liberty to ask your Excellency's acceptance of a few copies of their Constitution and the laws of

Pennsylvania, which relate to one of the objects of their Institution; also, of a copy of Thomas Clarkson's excellent Essay upon the Commerce and Slavery of the Africans.

The Society have heard, with great regret, that a considerable part of the slaves, who have been sold in the Southern States since the establishment of peace, have been imported in vessels fitted out in the state, over which, your Excellency presides. From your Excellency's station, they hope your influence will be exerted, hereafter, to prevent a practice which is so evidently repugnant to the political principles and form of government lately adopted by citizens of the United States, and which cannot fail of delaying the enjoyment of the blessings of peace and liberty, by drawing down, the displeasure of the great and impartial Ruler of the Universe upon our country.

I am, in behalf of the Society,

    Sir, your most obedient servant,

1788

"BEING A LITTLE MIFFY"

To Jane Mecom

DEAR SISTER,   Philada Aug 3. 1789

I have receiv'd your kind Letter of the 23d past, and am glad to learn that you have at length got some of those I so long since wrote to you. I think your Post Office is very badly managed. I expect your Bill, & shall pay it when it appears. —I would have you put the Books into Cousin Jonathan's Hands who will dispose of them for you if he can, or return them hither. I am very much pleas'd to hear that you have had no Misunderstanding with his good Father. Indeed if there had been any such, I should have concluded that it was your Fault: for I think our Family were always subject to being a little Miffy.—By the way, is our Relationship in Nantucket quite worn out?—I have met with none from thence of late Years who were dispos'd to be acquainted with me, except Capt. Timothy Fulger. They are wonderfully shy. But

I admire their honest plainness of Speech. About a Year ago
I invited two of them to dine with me. Their Answer was
that they would—if they could not do better. I suppose they
did better, for I never saw them afterwards; and so had no
Opportunity of showing my Miff, if I had one.—Give my
Love to Cousin Williams's and thank them from me for all
the Kindnesses to you, which I have always been acquainted
with by you, and take as if done to myself. I am sorry to learn
from his Son, that his Health is not so firm as formerly. A
Journey hither by Land might do him good, and I should be
happy to see him.—I shall make the Addition you desire to
my Superscriptions, desiring in Return that you would make
a Substraction from yours. The Word Excellency does not belong to me, and Dr will be sufficient to distinguish me from
my Grandson. This Family joins in Love to you and yours,
with

Your affectionate Brother

"A GOOD MOTION NEVER DIES"

To John Wright

DEAR FRIEND,   Philadelphia, November 4, 1789.
    I received your kind letter of July the 31st, which gave me
great pleasure, as it informed me of the welfare both of yourself and your good lady, to whom please to present my respects. I thank you for the epistle of your yearly meeting, and
for the card, a specimen of printing, which was enclosed.
    We have now had one session of Congress, which was con-
ducted under our new Constitution, and with as much general satisfaction as could reasonably be expected. I wish the
struggle in France may end as happily for that nation. We are
now in the full enjoyment of our new government for *eleven*
of the States, and it is generally thought that North Carolina
is about to join it. Rhode Island will probably take longer
time for consideration.
    We have had a most plentiful year for the fruits of the
earth, and our people seem to be recovering fast from the

extravagance and idle habits, which the war had introduced; and to engage seriously in the country habits of temperance, frugality, and industry, which give the most pleasing prospect of future national felicity. Your merchants, however, are, I think, imprudent in crowding in upon us such quantities of goods for sale here, which are not written for by ours, and are beyond the faculties of this country to consume in any reasonable time. This surplus of goods is, therefore, to raise present money, sent to the vendues, or auction-houses, of which we have six or seven in and near this city; where they are sold frequently for less than prime cost, to the great loss of the indiscreet adventurers. Our newspapers are doubtless to be seen at your coffee-houses near the Exchange. In their advertisements you may observe the constancy and quantity of this kind of sales; as well as the quantity of goods imported by our regular traders. I see in your English newspapers frequent mention of our being out of credit with you; to us it appears, that we have abundantly too much, and that your exporting merchants are rather out of their senses.

I wish success to your endeavours for obtaining an abolition of the Slave Trade. The epistle from your Yearly Meeting, for the year 1758, was not the *first sowing* of the good seed you mention; for I find by an old pamphlet in my possession, that George Keith, near a hundred years since, wrote a paper against the practice, said to be "given forth by the appointment of the meeting held by him, at Philip James's house, in the city of Philadelphia, about the year 1693;" wherein a strict charge was given to Friends, "that they should set their negroes at liberty, after some reasonable time of service, &c. &c." And about the year 1728, or 1729, I myself printed a book for Ralph Sandyford, another of your Friends in this city, against keeping negroes in slavery; two editions of which he distributed gratis. And about the year 1736, I printed another book on the same subject for Benjamin Lay, who also professed being one of your Friends, and he distributed the books chiefly among them. By these instances it appears, that the seed was indeed sown in the good ground of your profession, though much earlier than the time you mention, and its springing up to effect at last, though so late, is some confirmation of Lord Bacon's observation, that *a good motion never dies*; and it may encourage us in making such, though hopeless of their taking immediate effect.

I doubt whether I shall be able to finish my Memoirs, and, if I finish them, whether they will be proper for publication. You seem to have too high an opinion of them, and to expect too much from them.

I think you are right in preferring a mixed form of government for your country, under its present circumstances; and if it were possible for you to reduce the enormous salaries and emoluments of great officers, which are at bottom the source of all your violent factions, that form might be conducted more quietly and happily; but I am afraid, that none of your factions, when they get uppermost, will ever have virtue enough to reduce those salaries and emoluments, but will rather choose to enjoy them.

I enclose a bill for twenty-five pounds, for which, when received, please to credit my account, and out of it pay Mr. Benjamin Vaughan, of Jeffries Square, and Mr. William Vaughan, his brother, of Mincing Lane, such accounts against me as they shall present to you for that purpose. I am, my dear friend, yours very affectionately,

"ALL THESE IMPROVEMENTS BACKWARDS"

To Noah Webster

DEAR SIR,   Philadª, Decʳ 26, 1789.

I received some Time since your *Dissertations on the English Language*. The Book was not accompanied by any Letter or Message, informing me to whom I am obliged for it, but I suppose it is to yourself. It is an excellent Work, and will be greatly useful in turning the Thoughts of our Countrymen to correct Writing. Please to accept my Thanks for it as well as for the great honour you have done me in its Dedication. I ought to have made this Acknowledgment sooner, but much Indisposition prevented me.

I cannot but applaud your Zeal for preserving the Purity of

our Language, both in its Expressions and Pronunciation, and in correcting the popular Errors several of our States are continually falling into with respect to both. Give me leave to mention some of them, though possibly they may have already occurred to you. I wish, however, in some future Publication of yours, you would set a discountenancing Mark upon them. The first I remember is the word *improved*. When I left New England, in the year 23, this Word had never been used among us, as far as I know, but in the sense of *ameliorated* or *made better*, except once in a very old Book of Dr. Mather's, entitled *Remarkable Providences*. As that eminent Man wrote a very obscure Hand, I remember that when I read that Word in his Book, used instead of the Word *imployed*, I conjectured that it was an Error of the Printer, who had mistaken a too short *l* in the Writing for an *r*, and a *y* with too short a Tail for a *v*; whereby *imployed* was converted into *improved*.

But when I returned to Boston, in 1733, I found this Change had obtained Favour, and was then become common; for I met with it often in perusing the Newspapers, where it frequently made an Appearance rather ridiculous. Such, for Instance, as the Advertisement of a Country-House to be sold, which had been many years *improved* as a Tavern; and, in the Character of a deceased Country Gentleman, that he had been for more than 30 Years *improved* as a Justice-of-Peace. This Use of the Word *improved* is peculiar to New England, and not to be met with among any other Speakers of English, either on this or the other Side of the Water.

During my late Absence in France, I find that several other new Words have been introduced into our parliamentary Language; for Example, I find a Verb formed from the Substantive *Notice*; *I should not have* NOTICED *this, were it not that the Gentleman,* &c. Also another Verb from the Substantive *Advocate*; *The Gentleman who* ADVOCATES *or has* ADVOCATED *that Motion,* &c. Another from the Substantive *Progress*, the most awkward and abominable of the three; *The committee, having* PROGRESSED, *resolved to adjourn*. The Word *opposed*, tho' not a new Word, I find used in a new Manner, as, *The Gentlemen who are* OPPOSED *to this Measure; to which I have also myself always been* OPPOSED. If you should happen to be of my Opinion with respect to these Innovations, you will use your Authority in reprobating them.

The Latin Language, long the Vehicle used in distributing Knowledge among the different Nations of Europe, is daily more and more neglected; and one of the modern Tongues, viz. the French, seems in point of Universality to have supplied its place. It is spoken in all the Courts of Europe; and most of the Literati, those even who do not speak it, have acquired Knowledge enough of it to enable them easily to read the Books that are written in it. This gives a considerable Advantage to that Nation; it enables its Authors to inculcate and spread through other Nations such Sentiments and Opinions on important Points, as are most conducive to its Interests, or which may contribute to its Reputation by promoting the common Interests of Mankind. It is perhaps owing to its being written in French, that Voltaire's Treatise on *Toleration* has had so sudden and so great an Effect on the Bigotry of Europe, as almost entirely to disarm it. The general Use of the French Language has likewise a very advantageous Effect on the Profits of the Bookselling Branch of Commerce, it being well known, that the more Copies can be sold that are struck off from one Composition of Types, the Profits increase in a much greater Proportion than they do in making a great Number of Pieces in any other Kind of Manufacture. And at present there is no Capital Town in Europe without a French Bookseller's Shop corresponding with Paris.

Our English bids fair to obtain the second Place. The great Body of excellent printed Sermons in our Language, and the Freedom of our Writings on political Subjects, have induced a Number of Divines of different Sects and Nations, as well as Gentlemen concerned in public Affairs, to study it; so far at least as to read it. And if we were to endeavour the Facilitating its Progress, the Study of our Tongue might become much more general. Those, who have employed some Part of their Time in learning a new Language, must have frequently observed, that, while their Acquaintance with it was imperfect, Difficulties small in themselves operated as great ones in obstructing their Progress. A Book, for Example, ill printed, or a Pronunciation in speaking, not well articulated, would render a Sentence unintelligible; which, from a clear Print or a distinct Speaker, would have been immediately comprehended. If therefore we would have the Benefit of seeing our Language more generally known among Mankind, we should endeavour to remove all the Difficulties, however small, that discourage the learning it.

But I am sorry to observe, that, of late Years, those Difficulties, instead of being diminished, have been augmented. In examining the English Books, that were printed between the Restoration and the Accession of George the 2^d, we may observe, that all *Substantives* were begun with a capital, in which we imitated our Mother Tongue, the German. This was more particularly useful to those, who were not well acquainted with the English; there being such a prodigious Number of our Words, that are both *Verbs* and *Substantives*, and spelt in the same manner, tho' often accented differently in Pronunciation.

This Method has, by the Fancy of Printers, of late Years been laid aside, from an Idea, that suppressing the Capitals shows the Character to greater Advantage; those Letters prominent above the line disturbing its even regular Appearance. The Effect of this Change is so considerable, that a learned Man of France, who used to read our Books, tho' not perfectly acquainted with our Language, in Conversation with me on the Subject of our Authors, attributed the greater Obscurity he found in our modern Books, compared with those of the Period above mentioned, to a Change of Style for the worse in our Writers, of which Mistake I convinced him, by marking for him each *Substantive* with a Capital in a Paragraph, which he then easily understood, tho' before he could not comprehend it. This shows the Inconvenience of that pretended Improvement.

From the same Fondness for an even and uniform Appearance of Characters in the Line, the Printers have of late banished also the Italic Types, in which Words of Importance to be attended to in the Sense of the Sentence, and Words on which an Emphasis should be put in Reading, used to be printed. And lately another Fancy has induced some Printers to use the short round *s*, instead of the long one, which formerly served well to distinguish a word readily by its varied appearance. Certainly the omitting this prominent Letter

makes the Line appear more even; but renders it less immediately legible; as the paring all Men's Noses might smooth
and level their Faces, but would render their Physiognomies
less distinguishable.

Add to all these Improvements *backwards*, another modern
Fancy, that grey Printing is more beautiful than black; hence
the English new Books are printed in so dim a Character, as
to be read with difficulty by old Eyes, unless in a very strong
Light and with good Glasses. Whoever compares a Volume
of the *Gentleman's Magazine*, printed between the Years 1731
and 1740, with one of those printed in the last ten Years, will
be convinced of the much greater Degree of Perspicuity given
by black Ink than by grey. Lord Chesterfield pleasantly remarked this Difference to Faulkener, the Printer of the Dublin *Journal*, who was vainly making Encomiums on his own
Paper, as the most complete of any in the World; "But, Mr.
Faulkener," said my Lord, "don't you think it might be still
farther improved by using Paper and Ink not quite so near of
a Colour?" For all these Reasons I cannot but wish, that our
American Printers would in their Editions avoid these fancied
Improvements, and thereby render their Works more agreable
to Foreigners in Europe, to the great advantage of our Bookselling Commerce.

Farther, to be more sensible of the Advantage of clear and
distinct Printing, let us consider the Assistance it affords in
Reading well aloud to an Auditory. In so doing the Eye generally slides forward three or four Words before the Voice. If
the Sight clearly distinguishes what the coming Words are, it
gives time to order the Modulation of the Voice to express
them properly. But, if they are obscurely printed, or disguis'd
by omitting the Capitals and long *s's* or otherwise, the Reader
is apt to modulate wrong; and, finding he has done so, he is
oblig'd to go back and begin the Sentence again, which lessens the Pleasure of the Hearers.

This leads me to mention an old Error in our Mode of
Printing. We are sensible, that, when a Question is met with
in Reading, there is a proper Variation to be used in the Management of the Voice. We have therefore a Point called an
Interrogation, affix'd to the Question in order to distinguish
it. But this is absurdly placed at its End; so that the Reader

does not discover it, till he finds he has wrongly modulated his Voice, and is therefore obliged to begin again the Sentence. To prevent this, the Spanish Printers, more sensibly, place an Interrogation at the Beginning as well as at the End of a Question. We have another Error of the same kind in printing Plays, where something often occurs that is mark'd as spoken *aside*. But the Word *aside* is placed at the End of the Speech, when it ought to precede it, as a Direction to the Reader, that he may govern his Voice accordingly. The Practice of our Ladies in meeting five or six together to form a little busy Party, where each is employ'd in some useful Work while one reads to them, is so commendable in itself, that it deserves the Attention of Authors and Printers to make it as pleasing as possible, both to the Reader and Hearers.

After these general Observations, permit me to make one that I imagine may regard your Interest. It is that *your Spelling Book* is miserably printed here, so as in many Places to be scarcely legible, and on wretched Paper. If this is not attended to, and the new one lately advertis'd as coming out should be preferable in these Respects, it may hurt the future Sale of yours.

I congratulate you on your Marriage, of which the Newspapers inform me. My best wishes attend you, being with sincere esteem, Sir, &c.

"AS TO JESUS OF NAZARETH"

To Ezra Stiles

REVEREND AND DEAR SIR,   Philadᵃ, March 9. 1790.

I received your kind Letter of Jan'y 28, and am glad you have at length received the portrait of Gov'r Yale from his Family, and deposited it in the College Library. He was a great and good Man, and had the Merit of doing infinite Service to your Country by his Munificence to that Institution. The Honour you propose doing me by placing mine in the same Room with his, is much too great for my Deserts; but you always had a Partiality for me, and to that it must be ascribed. I am however too much obliged to Yale College, the first learned Society that took Notice of me and adorned me with its Honours, to refuse a Request that comes from it thro' so esteemed a Friend. But I do not think any one of the Portraits you mention, as in my Possession, worthy of the Place and Company you propose to place it in. You have an excellent Artist lately arrived. If he will undertake to make one for you, I shall cheerfully pay the Expence; but he must not delay setting about it, or I may slip thro' his fingers, for I am now in my eighty-fifth year, and very infirm.

I send with this a very learned Work, as it seems to me, on the antient Samaritan Coins, lately printed in Spain, and at least curious for the Beauty of the Impression. Please to accept it for your College Library. I have subscribed for the Encyclopædia now printing here, with the Intention of presenting it to the College. I shall probably depart before the Work is finished, but shall leave Directions for its Continuance to the End. With this you will receive some of the first numbers.

You desire to know something of my Religion. It is the first time I have been questioned upon it. But I cannot take your Curiosity amiss, and shall endeavour in a few Words to gratify it. Here is my Creed. I believe in one God, Creator of the Universe. That he governs it by his Providence. That he ought to be worshipped. That the most acceptable Service we render to him is doing good to his other Children. That the soul of Man is immortal, and will be treated with Justice in another Life respecting its Conduct in this. These I take to be the fundamental Principles of all sound Religion, and I regard them as you do in whatever Sect I meet with them.

As to Jesus of Nazareth, my Opinion of whom you particularly desire, I think the System of Morals and his Religion, as he left them to us, the best the World ever saw or is likely to see; but I apprehend it has received various corrupting Changes, and I have, with most of the present Dissenters in England, some Doubts as to his Divinity; tho' it is a question I do not dogmatize upon, having never studied it, and think it needless to busy myself with it now, when I expect soon an Opportunity of knowing the Truth with less Trouble. I see no harm, however, in its being believed, if that Belief has the good Consequence, as probably it has, of making his Doctrines more respected and better observed; especially as I do not perceive, that the Supreme takes it amiss, by distinguishing the Unbelievers in his Government of the World with any peculiar Marks of his Displeasure.

I shall only add, respecting myself, that, having experienced the Goodness of that Being in conducting me prosperously thro' a long life, I have no doubt of its Continuance in the next, though without the smallest Conceit of meriting such Goodness. My Sentiments on this Head you will see in the Copy of an old Letter enclosed, which I wrote in answer to one from a zealous Religionist, whom I had relieved in a paralytic case by electricity, and who, being afraid I should grow proud upon it, sent me his serious though rather impertinent Caution. I send you also the Copy of another Letter, which will shew something of my Disposition relating to Religion. With great and sincere Esteem and Affection, I am, Your obliged old Friend and most obedient humble Servant

P. S. Had not your College some Present of Books from the King of France? Please to let me know, if you had an Expectation given you of more, and the Nature of that Expectation? I have a Reason for the Enquiry.

I confide, that you will not expose me to Criticism and censure by publishing any part of this Communication to you. I have ever let others enjoy their religious Sentiments, without reflecting on them for those that appeared to me unsupportable and even absurd. All Sects here, and we have a great Variety, have experienced my good will in assisting them with Subscriptions for building their new Places of Worship; and, as I have never opposed any of their Doctrines, I hope to go out of the World in Peace with them all.

POOR RICHARD'S
ALMANACK
1733–1758

Contents

Poor Richard, 1733

Courteous Reader,

I might in this place attempt to gain thy Favour, by declaring that I write Almanacks with no other View than that of the publick Good; but in this I should not be sincere; and Men are now a-days too wise to be deceiv'd by Pretences how specious soever. The plain Truth of the Matter is, I am excessive poor, and my Wife, good Woman, is, I tell her, excessive proud; she cannot bear, she says, to sit spinning in her Shift of Tow, while I do nothing but gaze at the Stars; and has threatned more than once to burn all my Books and Rattling-Traps (as she calls my Instruments) if I do not make some profitable Use of them for the good of my Family. The Printer has offer'd me some considerable share of the Profits, and I have thus begun to comply with my Dame's desire.

Indeed this Motive would have had Force enough to have made me publish an Almanack many Years since, had it not been overpower'd by my Regard for my good Friend and Fellow-Student, Mr. *Titan Leeds*, whose Interest I was extreamly unwilling to hurt: But this Obstacle (I am far from speaking it with Pleasure) is soon to be removed, since inexorable Death, who was never known to respect Merit, has already prepared the mortal Dart, the fatal Sister has already extended her destroying Shears, and that ingenious Man must soon be taken from us. He dies, by my Calculation made at his Request, on *Oct.* 17. 1733. 3 ho. 29 m. *P.M.* at the very instant of the ☌ of ☉ and ☿: By his own Calculation he will survive till the 26th of the same Month. This small difference between us we have disputed whenever we have met these 9 Years past; but at length he is inclinable to agree with my Judgment; Which of us is most exact, a little Time will now determine. As therefore these Provinces may not longer expect to see any of his Performances after this Year, I think my self free to take up the Task, and request a share of the publick Encouragement; which I am the more apt to hope for on this Account, that the Buyer of my Almanack may consider himself, not only as purchasing an useful Utensil, but as performing an Act of Charity, to his poor   *Friend and Servant*   *R. SAUNDERS.*

———

Never spare the Parson's wine, nor the Baker's pudding.

> Visits should be short, like a winters day,
> Lest you're too troublesom hasten away.

A house without woman & Fire-light, is like a body without soul or sprite.

Kings & Bears often worry their keepers.

Light purse, heavy heart.

He's a Fool that makes his Doctor his Heir.

Ne'er take a wife till thou hast a house (& a fire) to put her in.

He's gone, and forgot nothing but to say *Farewel*—to his creditors.

Love well, whip well.

> Let my respected friend *J. G.*
> Accept this humble verse of me. *viz.*
> Ingenious, learned, envy'd Youth,
> Go on as thou'st began;
> Even thy enemies take pride
> That thou'rt their countryman.

Hunger never saw bad bread.

Beware of meat twice boil'd, & an old foe reconcil'd.

Great Talkers, little Doers.

A rich rogue, is like a fat hog, who never does good til as dead as a log.

Relation without friendship, friendship without power, power without will, will witho. effect, effect without profit, & profit without vertue, are not worth a farto.

Eat to live, and not live to eat.

> March windy, and April rainy,
> makes *May* the pleasantest month of any.

The favour of the Great is no inheritance.

Fools make feasts and wise men eat 'em.

Beware of the young Doctor & the old Barber.

He has chang'd his one ey'd horse for a blind one.

The poor have little, beggars none, the rich too much, *enough* not one.

After 3 days men grow weary, of a wench, a guest, & weather rainy.

To lengthen thy Life, lessen thy Meals.

The proof of gold is fire, the proof of woman, gold; the proof of man, a woman.

After feasts made, the maker scratches his head.

Neither Shame nor Grace yet *Bob.*

> Many estates are spent in the getting,
> Since women for tea forsook spinning & knitting.

He that lies down with Dogs, shall rise up with fleas.

A fat kitchin, a lean Will.

Distrust & caution are the parents of security.

Tongue double, brings trouble.

Take counsel in wine, but resolve afterwards in water.

He that drinks fast, pays slow.

Great famine when wolves eat wolves.

A good Wife lost is God's gift lost.

A taught horse, and a woman to teach, and teachers practising what they preach.

He is ill cloth'd, who is bare of Virtue.

The heart of a fool is in his mouth, but the mouth of a wise man is in his heart.

Men & Melons are hard to know.

He's the best physician that knows the worthlessness of the most medicines.

Beware of meat twice boil'd, and an old Foe reconcil'd.

A fine genius in his own country, is like gold in the mine.

There is no little enemy.

He has lost his Boots but sav'd his spurs.

The old Man has given all to his Son: O fool! to undress thy self before thou art going to bed.

Cheese and salt meat, should be sparingly eat.

Doors and walls are fools paper.

Anoint a villain and he'll stab you, stab him & he'l anoint you.

Keep your mouth wet, feet dry.

Where bread is wanting, all's to be sold.

There is neither honour nor gain, got in dealing with a vil-lain.

>   The fool hath made a vow, I guess,
>   Never to let the Fire have peace.

Snowy winter, a plentiful harvest.

Nothing more like a Fool, than a drunken Man.

>   God works wonders now & then;
>   Behold! a Lawyer, an honest Man!

He that lives carnally, won't live eternally.

Innocence is its own Defence.

>   Time *eateth* all things, could old Poets say;
>   The Times are chang'd, our times *drink* all away.

Never mind it, she'l be sober after the Holidays.

Poor Richard, 1734

Courteous Readers,

Your kind and charitable Assistance last Year, in purchasing so large an Impression of my Almanacks, has made my Circumstances much more easy in the World, and requires my grateful Acknowledgment. My Wife has been enabled to get a Pot of her own, and is no longer oblig'd to borrow one from a Neighbour; nor have we ever since been without something of our own to put in it. She has also got a pair of Shoes, two new Shifts, and a new warm Petticoat; and for my part, I have bought a second-hand Coat, so good, that I am now not asham'd to go to Town or be seen there. These Things have render'd her Temper so much more pacifick than it us'd to be, that I may say, I have slept more, and more quietly within this last Year, than in the three foregoing Years put together. Accept my hearty Thanks therefor, and my sincere Wishes for your Health and Prosperity.

In the Preface to my last Almanack, I foretold the Death of my dear old Friend and Fellow-Student, the learned and ingenious Mr. *Titan Leeds*, which was to be on the 17th of *October*, 1733, 3 h. 29 m. *P. M.* at the very Instant of the ☌ of ☉ and ☿. By his own Calculation he was to survive till the 26th of the same Month, and expire in the Time of the Eclipse, near 11 a clock, *A. M.* At which of these Times he died, or whether he be really yet dead, I cannot at this present Writing positively assure my Readers; forasmuch as a Disorder in my own Family demanded my Presence, and would not permit me as I had intended, to be with him in his last Moments, to receive his last Embrace, to close his Eyes, and do the Duty of a Friend in performing the last Offices to the Departed. Therefore it is that I cannot positively affirm whether he be dead or not; for the Stars only show to the Skilful, what will happen in the natural and universal Chain of Causes and Effects; but 'tis well known, that the Events which would otherwise certainly happen at certain Times in the Course of Nature, are sometimes set aside or postpon'd for wise and good Reasons, by the immediate particular Dispositions of Providence; which particular Dispositions the Stars can by no Means discover or foreshow. There is however, (and I cannot speak it without Sorrow) there is the strongest Probability that my dear Friend is *no more*; for there appears in his Name, as I am assured, an Almanack for the Year 1734, in which I am treated in a very gross and unhandsome Manner; in which I am called *a false Predicter, an Ignorant, a conceited Scribler, a Fool, and a Lyar*. Mr. *Leeds* was too well bred to use any Man so indecently and so scurrilously, and moreover his Esteem and Affection for me was extraordinary: So that it is to be feared, that Pamphlet may be only a Contrivance of somebody or other, who hopes perhaps to sell two or three Year's Almanacks still, by the sole Force and Virtue of Mr. *Leeds*'s Name; but certainly, to put Words into the Mouth of a Gentleman and a Man of Letters, against his Friend, which the meanest and most scandalous of the People might be asham'd to utter even in a drunken Quarrel, is an unpardonable Injury to his Memory, and an Imposition upon the Publick.

Mr. *Leeds* was not only profoundly skilful in the useful Science he profess'd, but he was a Man of *exemplary Sobriety*, a most *sincere Friend*, and an *exact Performer of his Word*. These valuable Qualifications, with many others, so much endear'd him to me, that although it should be so, that, contrary to all Probability, contrary to my Prediction and his own, he might possibly be yet alive, yet my Loss of Honour as a Prognosticator, cannot afford me so much Mortification, as his Life, Health and Safety would give me Joy and Satisfaction. I am,

Courteous and kind Reader,

Your poor Friend and Servant,

Octob. 30. 1733.   *R. SAUNDERS.*

———

Would you live with ease,
Do what you ought, and not what you please.

Principiis obsta.

Better slip with foot than tongue.

You cannot pluck roses without fear of thorns,
Nor enjoy a fair wife without danger of horns.

Without justice, courage is weak.

Many dishes many diseases,
Many medicines few cures.

Where carcasses are, eagles will gather,
And where good laws are, much people flock thither.

Hot things, sharp things, sweet things, cold things
All rot the teeth, and make them look like old things.

Blame-all and *Praise-all* are two blockheads.

Be temperate in wine, in eating, girls, & sloth;
Or the Gout will seize you and plague you both.

No man e'er was glorious, who was not laborious.

What pains our Justice takes his faults to hide,
With half that pains sure he might cure 'em quite.

In success be moderate.

Take this remark from *Richard* poor and lame,
Whate'er's begun in anger ends in shame.

What one relishes, nourishes.

Fools multiply folly.

Beauty & folly are old companions.

Hope of gain
Lessens pain.

All things are easy to Industry,
All things difficult to *Sloth*.

If you ride a Horse, sit close and tight,
If you ride a Man, sit easy and light.

A new truth is a truth, an old error is an error,
Tho' *Clodpate* wont allow either.

Don't think to hunt two hares with one dog.

Astrologers say,
This is a good Day,
To make Love in May.

Who pleasure gives,
Shall joy receive.

Be not sick too late, nor well too soon.

Where there's Marriage without Love, there will be Love without Marriage.

Lawyers, Preachers, and Tomtits Eggs, there are more of them hatch'd than come to perfection.

Be neither silly, nor cunning, but wise.

Neither a Fortress nor a Maidenhead will hold out long after they begin to parly.

Jack *Little* sow'd little, & little he'll reap.

All things are cheap to the saving, dear to the wasteful.

Would you persuade, speak of Interest, not of Reason.

> Some men grow mad by studying much to know,
> But who grows mad by studying good to grow.

Happy's the Woing, that's not long a doing.

Don't value a man for the Quality he is of, but for the Qualities he possesses.

Bucephalus the Horse of *Alexand.* hath as lasting fame as his Master.

> Rain or Snow,
> To *Chili* go,
> You'll find it so,
> For ought we know.
> Time will show.

There have been as great Souls unknown to fame as any of the most famous.

Do good to thy Friend to keep him, to thy enemy to gain him.

A good Man is seldom uneasy, an ill one never easie.

Teach your child to hold his tongue, he'l learn fast enough to speak.

He that cannot obey, cannot command.

An innocent *Plowman* is more worthy than a vicious *Prince*.

Sam's Religion is like a *Chedder Cheese*, 'tis made of the *milk* of one & twenty Parishes.

> Grief for a dead Wife, & a troublesome Guest,
> Continues to the *threshold*, and there is at rest;
> But I mean such wives as are none of the best.

As Charms are nonsence, Nonsence is a Charm.

An Egg to day is better than a Hen to-morrow.

Drink Water, Put the Money in your Pocket, and leave the *Dry-bellyach* in the *Punchbowl*.

He that is rich need not live sparingly, and he that can live sparingly need not be rich.

If you wou'd be reveng'd of your enemy, govern your self.

A wicked Hero will turn his back to an innocent coward.

> *Laws* like to *Cobwebs* catch small Flies,
> Great ones break thro' before your eyes.

Strange, that he who lives by Shifts, can seldom shift himself.

As sore places meet most rubs, proud folks meet most affronts.

The magistrate should obey the Laws, the People should obey the magistrate.

When 'tis fair be sure take your Great coat with you.

He does not possess Wealth, it possesses him.

Necessity has no Law; I know some Attorneys of the name.

Onions can make ev'n Heirs and Widows weep.

Avarice and Happiness never saw each other, how then shou'd they become acquainted.

> The thrifty maxim of the wary *Dutch*,
> Is to save all the Money they can touch.

He that waits upon Fortune, is never sure of a Dinner.

A learned blockhead is a greater blockhead than an ignorant one.

Marry your Son when you will, but your Daughter when you can.

———

By Mrs. *Bridget Saunders*, my Dutchess, in Answer to the *December* Verses of last Year.
> He that for sake of Drink neglects his Trade,
> And spends each Night in Taverns till 'tis late,
> And rises when the Sun is four hours high,
> And ne'er regards his starving Family;
> God in his Mercy may do much to save him.
> But, woe to the poor Wife, whose Lot it is to have him.

———

He that knows nothing of it, may by chance be a Prophet; while the wisest that is may happen to miss.

> If you wou'd have Guests merry with your cheer,
> Be so your self, or so at least appear.

> Famine, Plague, War, and an unnumber'd throng
> Of Guilt-avenging Ills, to Man belong;
> Is't not enough Plagues, Wars, and Famines rise
> To lash our crimes, but must our Wives be wise?

> Reader, farewel, all Happiness attend thee:
> May each *New-Year* better and richer find thee.

Poor Richard, 1735

Courteous Reader,
  This is the third Time of my appearing in print, hitherto very much to my own Satisfaction, and, I have reason to hope, to the Satisfaction of the Publick also; for the Publick is generous, and has been very charitable and good to me. I should be ungrateful then, if I did not take every Opportunity of expressing my Gratitude; for *ingratum si dixeris, omnia dixeris*: I therefore return the Publick my most humble and hearty Thanks.

Whatever may be the Musick of the Spheres, how great soever the Harmony of the Stars, 'tis certain there is no Harmony among the Stargazers; but they are perpetually growling and snarling at one another like strange Curs, or like some Men at their Wives: I had resolved to keep the Peace on my own part, and affront none of them; and I shall persist in that Resolution: But having receiv'd much Abuse from *Titan Leeds* deceas'd, (*Titan Leeds* when living would not have us'd me so!) I say, having receiv'd much Abuse from the Ghost of *Titan Leeds*, who pretends to be still living, and to write Almanacks in spight of me and my Predictions, I cannot help saying, that tho' I take it patiently, I take it very unkindly. And whatever he may pretend, 'tis undoubtedly true that he is really defunct and dead. First because the Stars are seldom disappointed, never but in the Case of wise Men, *Sapiens dominabitur astris*, and they foreshow'd his Death at the Time I predicted it. Secondly, 'Twas requisite and necessary he should die punctually at that Time, for the Honour of Astrology, the Art professed both by him and his Father before him. Thirdly, 'Tis plain to every one that reads his two last Almanacks (for 1734 and 35) that they are not written with that *Life* his Performances use to be written with; the Wit is low and flat, the little Hints dull and spiritless, nothing smart in them but *Hudibras's* Verses against Astrology at the Heads of the Months in the last, which no Astrologer but a *dead one* would have inserted, and no Man *living* would or could write such Stuff as the rest. But lastly, I shall convince him from his own Words, that he is dead, (*ex ore suo condemnatus est*) for in his Preface to his Almanack for 1734, he says, *"Saunders adds another* GROSS FALSHOOD *in his Almanack,* viz. *that by my own Calculation I shall* survive *until the* 26th *of the said Month October* 1733, *which is as* untrue *as the former."* Now if it be, as *Leeds* says, *untrue* and a *gross Falshood* that he surviv'd till the 26th of October 1733, then it is certainly *true* that he died *before* that Time: And if he died before that Time, he is dead now, to all Intents and Purposes, any thing he may say to the contrary notwithstanding. And at what Time before the 26th is it so likely he should die, as at the Time by me predicted, viz. the 17th of October aforesaid? But if some People will walk and be troublesome after Death, it may

Necessity never made a good bargain.

If Pride leads the Van, Beggary brings up the Rear.

There's many witty men whose brains can't fill their bellies.

Weighty Questions ask for deliberate Answers.

> When ♂ and ♀ in ♂ lie,
> Then, Maids, whate'er is ask'd of you, deny.

Be slow in chusing a Friend, slower in changing.

> Old *Hob* was lately married in the Night,
> What needed Day, his fair young Wife is light.

Pain wastes the Body, Pleasures the Understanding.

The cunning man steals a horse, the wise man lets him alone.

> Nothing but Money,
> Is sweeter than Honey.

Humility makes great men twice honourable.

> A Ship under sail and a big-bellied Woman,
> Are the handsomest two things that can be seen common.

Keep thy shop, & thy shop will keep thee.

The King's cheese is half wasted in parings: But no matter, 'tis made of the peoples milk.

> What's given shines,
> What's receiv'd is rusty.

Sloth and Silence are a Fool's Virtues.

> Of learned Fools I have seen ten times ten,
> Of unlearned wise men I have seen a hundred.

Three may keep a Secret, if two of them are dead.

Poverty wants some things, Luxury many things, Avarice all things.

A Lie stands on 1 leg, Truth on 2.

There's small Revenge in Words, but Words may be greatly revenged.

Great wits jump (says the Poet) and hit his Head against the Post.

A man is never so ridiculous by those Qualities that are his own as by those that he affects to have.

Deny Self for Self's sake.

> *Tim* moderate fare and abstinence much prizes,
> In publick, but in private gormandizes.

Ever since Follies have pleas'd, Fools have been able to divert.

It is better to take many Injuries than to give one.

Opportunity is the great Bawd.

Early to bed and early to rise, makes a man healthy wealthy and wise.

To be humble to Superiors is Duty, to Equals Courtesy, to Inferiors Nobleness.

Here comes the Orator! with his Flood of Words, and his Drop of Reason.

An old young man, will be a young old man.

Sal laughs at every thing you say. Why? Because she has fine Teeth.

> If what most men admire, they would despise,
> 'Twould look as if mankind were growing wise.

The Sun never repents of the good he does, nor does he ever demand a recompence.

Are you angry that others disappoint you? remember you cannot depend upon yourself.

One Mend-fault is worth two Findfaults, but one Findfault is better than two Makefaults.

> *Reader*, I wish thee Health, Wealth, Happiness,
> And may kind Heaven thy Year's Industry bless.

Poor Richard, 1736

Loving Readers,

Your kind Acceptance of my former Labours, has encouraged me to continue writing, tho' the general Approbation you have been so good as to favour me with, has excited the Envy of some, and drawn upon me the Malice of others. These Ill-willers of mine, despited at the great Reputation I gain'd by exactly predicting another Man's Death, have endeavour'd to deprive me of it all at once in the most effectual Manner, by reporting that I my self was never alive. They say in short, *That there is no such a Man as I am*; and have spread this Notion so thoroughly in the Country, that I have been frequently told it to my Face by those that don't know me. This is not civil Treatment, to endeavour to deprive me of my very Being, and reduce me to a Non-entity in the Opinion of the publick. But so long as I know my self to walk about, eat, drink and sleep, I am satisfied that *there is really such a Man as I am*, whatever they may say to the contrary: And the World may be satisfied likewise; for if there were no such Man as I am, how is it possible I should appear publickly to hundreds of People, as I have done for several Years past, in print? I need not, indeed, have taken any Notice of so idle a Report, if it had not been for the sake of my Printer, to whom my Enemies are pleased to ascribe my Productions; and who it seems is as unwilling to father my Offspring, as I am to lose the Credit of it: Therefore to clear him entirely, as well as to vindicate my own Honour, I make this publick and serious Declaration, which I desire may be believed, to wit, *That what I have written heretofore, and do now write, neither was nor is written by any other Man or Men, Person or Persons whatsoever.* Those who are not satisfied with this, must needs be very unreasonable.

My Performance for this Year follows; it submits itself, kind Reader, to thy Censure, but hopes for thy Candor, to forgive its Faults. It devotes itself entirely to thy Service, and will serve thee faithfully: And if it has the good Fortune to please its Master, 'tis Gratification enough for the Labour of

Poor

R. SAUNDERS.

He is no clown that drives the plow, but he that doth clownish things.

If you know how to spend less than you get, you have the Philosophers-Stone.

The good Paymaster is Lord of another man's Purse.

Fish & Visitors stink in 3 days.

He that has neither fools, whores nor beggars among his kindred, is the son of a thunder-gust.

Diligence is the Mother of Good-Luck.

He that lives upon Hope, dies farting.

Do not do that which you would not have known.

Never praise your Cyder, Horse, or Bedfellow.

Wealth is not his that has it, but his that enjoys it.

Tis easy to see, hard to foresee.

In a discreet man's mouth, a publick thing is private.

Let thy maidservant be faithful, strong, and homely.

Keep flax from fire, youth from gaming.

Bargaining has neither friends nor relations.

Admiration is the Daughter of Ignorance.

There's more old Drunkards than old Doctors.

She that paints her Face, thinks of her Tail.

Here comes Courage! that seiz'd the lion absent, and run away from the present mouse.

He that takes a wife, takes care.

Nor Eye in a letter, nor Hand in a purse, nor Ear in the secret of another.

He that buys by the penny, maintains not only himself, but other people.

He that can have Patience, can have what he will.

Now I've a sheep and a cow, every body bids me good morrow.

God helps them that help themselves.

Why does the blind man's wife paint herself.

None preaches better than the ant, and she says nothing.

The absent are never without fault, nor the present without excuse.

Gifts burst rocks.

> If wind blows on you thro' a hole,
> Make your will and take care of your soul.

The rotten Apple spoils his Companion.

He that sells upon trust, loses many friends, and always wants money.

Don't throw stones at your neighbours, if your own windows are glass.

The excellency of hogs is fatness, of men virtue.

Good wives and good plantations are made by good husbands.

Pox take you, is no curse to some people.

Force shites upon Reason's Back.

Lovers, Travellers, and Poets, will give money to be heard.

He that speaks much, is much mistaken.

Creditors have better memories than debtors.

Forwarn'd, forearm'd, unless in the case of Cuckolds, who are often forearm'd before warn'd.

Three things are men most liable to be cheated in, a Horse, a Wig, and a Wife.

He that lives well, is learned enough.

Poverty, Poetry, and new Titles of Honour, make Men ridiculous.

He that scatters Thorns, let him not go barefoot.

There's none deceived but he that trusts.

God heals, and the Doctor takes the Fees.

If you desire many things, many things will seem but a few.

Mary's mouth costs her nothing, for she never opens it but at others expence.

Receive before you write, but write before you pay.

I saw few die of Hunger, of Eating 100000.

Maids of *America*, who gave you bad teeth?
Answ. Hot Soupings & frozen Apples.

Marry your Daughter and eat fresh Fish betimes.

If God blesses a Man, his Bitch brings forth Pigs.

> He that would live in peace & at ease,
> Must not speak all he knows, nor judge all he sees.

Poor Richard, 1737

Courteous and kind Reader,

This is the fifth Time I have appear'd in Publick, chalking out the future Year for my honest Countrymen, and foretelling what shall, and what may, and what may not come to pass; in which I have the Pleasure to find that I have given general Satisfaction. Indeed, among the Multitude of our astrological Predictions, 'tis no wonder if some few fail; for, without any Defect in the Art itself, 'tis well known that a small Error, a single wrong Figure overseen in a Calculation, may occasion great Mistakes: But however we Almanack-makers may *miss it* in other Things, I believe it will be generally allow'd *That we always hit the Day of the Month*, and that I suppose is esteem'd one of the most useful Things in an Almanack.

As to the Weather, if I were to fall into the Method my Brother *J——n* sometimes uses, and tell you, *Snow here or in New England, —Rain here or in South-Carolina, —Cold to the Northward, —Warm to the Southward*, and the like, whatever Errors I might commit, I should be something more secure of not being detected in them: But I consider, it will be of no Service to any body to know what Weather it is 1000 miles off, and therefore I always set down positively what Weather my Reader will have, be he where he will at the time. We modestly desire only the favourable Allowance of *a day or two before* and *a day or two after* the precise Day against which the Weather is set; and if it does not come to pass accordingly, let the Fault be laid upon the Printer, who, 'tis very like, may have transpos'd or misplac'd it, perhaps for the Conveniency of putting in his Holidays: And since, in spight of all I can say, People will give him great part of the Credit of making my Almanacks, 'tis but reasonable he should take some share of the Blame.

I must not omit here to thank the Publick for the gracious and kind Encouragement they have hitherto given me: But if the generous Purchaser of my Labours could see how often his *Fi'-pence* helps to light up the comfortable Fire, line the Pot, fill the Cup and make glad the Heart of a poor Man and an honest good old Woman, he would not think his Money ill laid out, tho' the Almanack of his

                    Friend and Servant   R. SAUNDERS
were one half blank Paper.

———

HINTS for those that would be Rich.

The Use of Money is all the Advantage there is in having Money.

For 6 *l.* a Year, you may have the Use of 100 *l.* if you are a Man of known Prudence and Honesty.

He that spends a Groat a day idly, spends idly above 6 *l.* a year, which is the Price of using 100 *l.*

He that wastes idly a Groat's worth of his Time per Day, one Day with another, wastes the Privilege of using 100 *l.* each Day.

He that idly loses 5 *s.* worth of time, loses 5 *s.* & might as prudently throw 5 *s.* in the River.

He that loses 5 *s.* not only loses that Sum, but all the Advantage that might be made by turning it in Dealing, which by the time that a young Man becomes old, amounts to a comfortable Bag of Mony.

Again, He that sells upon Credit, asks a Price for what he sells, equivalent to the Principal and Interest of his Money for the Time he is like to be kept out of it: therefore

He that buys upon Credit, pays Interest for what he buys.

And he that pays ready Money, might let that Money out to Use: so that

He that possesses any Thing he has bought, pays Interest for the Use of it.

Consider then, when you are tempted to buy any unnecessary Housholdstuff, or any superfluous thing, whether you will be willing to pay *Interest, and Interest upon Interest* for it as long as you live; and more if it grows worse by using.

Yet, in buying Goods, 'tis best to pay ready Money, because,

He that sells upon Credit, expects to lose 5 *per Cent.* by bad Debts; therefore he charges, on all he sells upon Credit, an Advance that shall make up that Deficiency.

Those who pay for what they buy upon Credit, pay their Share of this Advance.

He that pays ready Money, escapes or may escape that Charge.

A Penny sav'd is Twopence clear, A Pin a day is a Groat a Year. Save & have. Every little makes a mickle.

———

The greatest monarch on the proudest throne, is oblig'd to sit upon his own arse.

The Master-piece of Man, is to live to the purpose.

He that steals the old man's supper, do's him no wrong.

A countryman between 2 Lawyers, is like a fish between two cats.

He that can take rest is greater than he that can take cities.

The misers cheese is wholesomest.

Felix quem, *&c.*

Love & lordship hate companions.

The nearest way to come at glory, is to do that for
conscience which we do for glory.

There is much money given to be laught at, though the
purchasers don't know it; witness *A's* fine horse, & *B's*
fine house.

He that can compose himself, is wiser than he that composes
books.

Poor Dick, eats like a well man, and drinks like a sick.

After crosses and losses men grow humbler & wiser.

Love, Cough, & a Smoke, can't well be hid.

Well done is better than well said.

> Fine linnen, girls and gold so bright,
> Chuse not to take by candle-light.

He that can travel well afoot, keeps a good horse.

There are no ugly Loves, nor handsome Prisons.

No better relation than a prudent & faithful Friend.

A Traveller should have a hog's nose, deer's legs, and an
ass's back.

At the working man's house hunger looks in but dares not
enter.

A good Lawyer a bad Neighbour.

> Certainlie these things agree,
> The Priest, the Lawyer, & Death all three:
> Death takes both the weak and the strong.
> The lawyer takes from both right and wrong,
> And the priest from living and dead has his Fee.

The worst wheel of the cart makes the most noise.

Don't misinform your Doctor nor your Lawyer.

> I never saw an oft-transplanted tree,
> Nor yet an oft-removed family,
> That throve so well as those that settled be.

Let the Letter stay for the Post, and not the Post for the Letter.

Three good meals a day is bad living.

Tis better leave for an enemy at one's death, than beg of a friend in one's life.

> To whom thy secret thou dost tell,
> To him thy freedom thou dost sell.

If you'd have a Servant that you like, serve your self.

He that pursues two Hares at once, does not catch one and lets t'other go.

If you want a neat wife, chuse her on a Saturday.

If you have time dont wait for time.

Tell a miser he's rich, and a woman she's old, you'll get no money of one, nor kindness of t'other.

Don't go to the doctor with every distemper, nor to the lawyer with every quarrel, nor to the pot for every thirst.

The Creditors are a superstitious sect, great observers of set days and times.

The noblest question in the world is *What Good may I do in it?*

Nec sibi, sed toto, genitum se credere mundo.

Nothing so popular as GOODNESS.

Poor Richard, 1738

PREFACE by Mistress SAUNDERS

Dear Readers,

My good Man set out last Week for *Potowmack*, to visit an old Stargazer of his Acquaintance, and see about a little Place for us to settle and end our Days on. He left the Copy of his Almanack seal'd up, and bid me send it to the Press. I suspected something, and therefore as soon as he was gone, I open'd it, to see if he had not been flinging some of his old Skitts at me. Just as I thought, so it was. And truly, (for want of somewhat else to say, I suppose) he had put into his Preface, that his Wife *Bridget*—was this, and that, and t'other.— What a peasecods! cannot I have a little Fault or two, but all the Country must see it in print! They have already been told, at one time that I am proud, another time that I am loud, and that I have got a new Petticoat, and abundance of such kind of stuff; and now, forsooth! all the World must know, that *Poor Dick's* Wife has lately taken a fancy to drink a little Tea now and then. A mighty matter, truly, to make a Song of! 'Tis true; I had a little Tea of a Present from the Printer last Year; and what, must a body throw it away? In short, I thought the Preface was not worth a printing, and so I fairly scratch'd it all out, and I believe you'll like our Almanack never the worse for it.

Upon looking over the Months, I see he has put in abundance of foul Weather this Year; and therefore I have scatter'd here and there, where I could find room, some *fair, pleasant, sunshiny*, &c. for the Good-Women to dry their Clothes in. If it does not come to pass according to my Desire, I have shown my Good-will, however; and I hope they'll take it in good part.

I had a Design to make some other Corrections; and particularly to change some of the Verses that I don't very well like; but I have just now unluckily broke my Spectacles; which obliges me to give it you as it is, and conclude

Your loving Friend,
BRIDGET SAUNDERS.

————

There are three faithful friends, an old wife, an old dog, and ready money.

Great talkers should be cropt, for they've no need of ears.

If you'd have your shoes last, put no nails in 'em.

Who has deceiv'd thee so oft as thy self?

Is there any thing Men take more pains about than to render themselves unhappy?

Nothing brings more pain than too much pleasure; nothing more bondage than too much liberty, (or libertinism.)

Read much, but not many Books.

He that would have a short Lent, let him borrow Money to be repaid at Easter.

Write with the learned, pronounce with the vulgar.

Fly Pleasures, and they'll follow you.

Squirrel-like she covers her back with her tail.

Cæsar did not merit the triumphal Car, more than he that conquers himself.

Hast thou virtue? acquire also the graces & beauties of virtue.

Buy what thou hast no need of; and e'er long thou shalt sell thy necessaries.

If thou hast wit & learning, add to it Wisdom and Modesty.

You may be more happy than Princes, if you will be more virtuous.

> If you wou'd not be forgotten
> As soon as you are dead and rotten,
> Either write things worth reading,
> or do things worth the writing.

Sell not virtue to purchase wealth, nor Liberty to purchase power.

God bless the King, and grant him long to Reign.

Let thy vices die before thee.

Keep your eyes wide open before marriage, half shut afterwards.

The ancients tell us what is best; but we must learn of the moderns what is fittest.

Since I cannot govern my own tongue, tho' within my own teeth, how can I hope to govern the tongues of others?

'Tis less discredit to abridge petty charges, than to stoop to petty Gettings.

Since thou art not sure of a minute, throw not away an hour.

If you do what you should not, you must hear what you would not.

Defer not thy well-doing; be not like St. *George*, who is always a horseback, and never rides on.

Wish not so much to live long as to live well.

As we must account for every idle word, so we must for every idle silence.

I have never seen the Philosopher's Stone that turns lead into Gold, but I have known the pursuit of it turn a Man's Gold into Lead.

Never intreat a servant to dwell with thee.

Time is an herb that cures all Diseases.

Reading makes a full Man, Meditation a profound Man, discourse a clear Man.

If any man flatters me, I'll flatter him again; tho' he were my best Friend.

Wish a miser long life, and you wish him no good.

None but the well-bred man knows how to confess a fault, or acknowledge himself in an error.

Drive thy business; let not that drive thee.

There is much difference between imitating a good man, and counterfeiting him.

Wink at small faults; remember thou hast great ones.

Eat to please thyself, but dress to please others.

Search others for their virtues, thy self for thy vices.

Never spare the Parson's wine, nor Baker's Pudding.

> Each year one vicious habit rooted out,
> In time might make the worst Man good throughout.

Poor Richard, 1739

Kind Reader,

Encouraged by thy former Generosity, I once more present thee with an Almanack, which is the 7th of my Publication.— While thou art putting Pence in my Pocket, and furnishing my Cottage with Necessaries, *Poor Dick* is not unmindful to do something for thy Benefit. The Stars are watch'd as narrowly as old *Bess* watch'd her Daughter, that thou mayst be acquainted with their Motions, and told a Tale of their Influences and Effects, which may do thee more good than a Dream of last Year's Snow.

Ignorant Men wonder how we Astrologers foretell the Weather so exactly, unless we deal with the old black Devil. Alas! 'tis as easy as pissing abed. For Instance; The Stargazer peeps at the Heavens thro' a long Glass: He sees perhaps *TAURUS*, or the great Bull, in a mighty Chase, stamping on the Floor of his House, swinging his Tail about, stretching out his Neck, and opening wide his Mouth. 'Tis natural from these Appearances to judge that this furious Bull is puffing, blowing, and roaring. Distance being consider'd, and Time allow'd for all this to come down, there you have Wind and Thunder. He spies perhaps *VIRGO* (or the Virgin;) she turns her Head round as it were to see if any body observ'd her; then crouching down gently, with her Hands on her Knees, she looks wistfully for a while right forward. He judges rightly what she's about: And having calculated the Distance and allow'd Time for it's Falling, finds that next Spring we shall have a fine *April* shower. What can be more natural and easy than this? I might instance the like in many other particulars; but this may be sufficient to prevent our being taken for Conjurers. O the wonderful Knowledge to be found in the Stars! Even the smallest Things are written there, if you had but Skill to read. When my Brother *J—m–n* erected a Scheme to know which was best for his sick Horse, to sup a new-laid Egg, or a little Broth, he found that the Stars plainly gave their Verdict for Broth, and the Horse having sup'd his Broth;—Now, what do you think became of that Horse? You shall know in my next.

Besides the usual Things expected in an Almanack, I hope the profess'd Teachers of Mankind will excuse my scattering here and there some instructive Hints in Matters of Morality and Religion. And be not thou disturbed, O grave and sober Reader, if among the many serious Sentences in my Book, thou findest me trifling now and then, and talking idly. In all the Dishes I have hitherto cook'd for thee, there is solid Meat enough for thy Money. There are Scraps from the Table of Wisdom, that will if well digested, yield strong Nourishment to thy Mind. But squeamish Stomachs cannot eat without Pickles; which, 'tis true are good for nothing else, but they provoke an Appetite. The Vain Youth that reads my Almanack for the sake of an idle Joke, will perhaps meet with a serious Reflection, that he may ever after be the better for.

Some People observing the great Yearly Demand for my Almanack, imagine I must by this Time have become rich, and consequently ought to call myself *Poor Dick* no longer. But, the Case is this, When I first begun to publish, the Printer made a fair Agreement with me for my Copies, by Virtue of which he runs away with the greatest Part of the Profit.—However, much good may't do him; I do not grudge it him; he is a Man I have a great Regard for, and I wish his Profit ten times greater than it is. For I am, dear Reader, his, as well as thy   *Affectionate Friend*,

R. SAUNDERS.

———

When Death puts out our Flame, the Snuff will tell,
If we were Wax, or Tallow by the Smell.

At a great Pennyworth, pause a while.

As to his Wife, *John* minds St. *Paul*, He's one
That hath a Wife, and is as if he'd none.

Kings and Bears often worry their Keepers.

If thou wouldst live long, live well; for Folly and Wickedness shorten Life.

> Prythee isn't Miss *Cloe's* a comical Case?
> She lends out her Tail, and she borrows her Face.

Trust thy self, and another shall not betray thee.

He that pays for Work before it's done, has but a pennyworth for twopence.

Historians relate, not so much what is done, as what they would have believed.

> O Maltster! break that cheating Peck; 'tis plain,
> When e'er you use it, you're a Knave in Grain.

> Doll learning *propria quæ maribus* without book,
> Like *Nomen crescentis genitivo* doth look.

Grace thou thy House, and let not that grace thee.

Thou canst not joke an Enemy into a Friend; but thou may'st a Friend into an Enemy.

> Eyes & Priests
> Bear no Jests.

He that falls in love with himself, will have no Rivals.

Let thy Child's first Lesson be Obedience, and the second may be what thou wilt.

Blessed is he that expects nothing, for he shall never be disappointed.

Rather go to bed supperless, than run in debt for a Breakfast.

Let thy Discontents be Secrets.

An infallible Remedy for the *Tooth-ach*, viz Wash the Root of an aching Tooth, in *Elder Vinegar*, and let it dry half an hour in the Sun; after which it will never ach more; *Probatum est.*

> A Man of Knowledge like a rich Soil, feeds
> If not a world of Corn, a world of Weeds.

A modern Wit is one of *David's* Fools.

No Resolution of Repenting hereafter, can be sincere.

> *Pollio*, who values nothing that's within,
> Buys Books as men hunt Beavers,—for their Skin.

Honour thy Father and Mother, *i. e.* Live so as to be an Honour to them tho' they are dead.

If thou injurest Conscience, it will have its Revenge on thee.

Hear no ill of a Friend, nor speak any of an Enemy.

Pay what you owe, and you'll know what's your own.

Be not niggardly of what costs thee nothing, as courtesy, counsel, & countenance.

Thirst after Desert, not Reward.

Beware of him that is slow to anger: He is angry for something, and will not be pleased for nothing.

No longer virtuous no longer free; is a Maxim as true with regard to a private Person as a Common-wealth.

> When Man and Woman die, as Poets sung,
> His Heart's the last part moves, her last, the tongue.

Proclaim not all thou knowest, all thou owest, all thou hast, nor all thou canst.

Let our Fathers and Grandfathers be valued for *their* Goodness, ourselves for our own.

Industry need not wish.

Sin is not hurtful because it is forbidden but it is forbidden because it's hurtful. Nor is a Duty beneficial because it is commanded, but it is commanded, because it's beneficial.

> *A*—, they say, has Wit; for what?
> For writing?—No; For writing not.

> *George* came to the Crown without striking a Blow.
> Ah! quoth the Pretender, would I could do so.

Love, and be lov'd.

O Lazy-Bones! Dost thou think God would have given thee Arms and Legs, if he had not design'd thou should'st use them.

A Cure for Poetry,
Seven wealthy Towns contend for *Homer*, dead,
Thro' which the living *Homer* beg'd his Bread.

Great Beauty, great strength, & great Riches, are really & truly of no great Use; a right Heart exceeds all.

Poor Richard, *1740*

Courteous Reader,   OCTOBER 7. 1739.
     You may remember that in my first Almanack, published for the Year 1733, I predicted the Death of my dear Friend *Titan Leeds*, Philomat. to happen that Year on the 17th Day of *October*, 3 h. 29 m. *P. M.* The good Man, it seems, died accordingly: But *W. B.* and *A. B.* have continued to publish Almanacks in his Name ever since; asserting for some Years that he was still living; At length when the Truth could no longer be conceal'd from the World, they confess his Death in their Almanack for 1739, but pretend that he died not till last Year, and that before his Departure he had furnished them with Calculations for 7 Years to come. Ah, *My Friends*, these are poor Shifts and thin Disguises; of which indeed I should have taken little or no Notice, if you had not at the same time accus'd me as a false Predictor; an Aspersion that the more affects me, as my whole Livelyhood depends on a contrary Character.
     But to put this Matter beyond Dispute, I shall acquaint the World with a Fact, as strange and surprizing as it is true; being as follows, *viz.*
     On the 4th Instant, towards midnight, as I sat in my little Study writing this Preface, I fell fast asleep; and continued in that Condition for some time, without dreaming any thing,

to my Knowledge. On awaking, I found lying before me the following Letter, *viz*.

Dear Friend SAUNDERS,

My Respect for you continues even in this separate State, and I am griev'd to see the Aspersions thrown on you by the Malevolence of avaricious Publishers of Almanacks, who envy your Success. They say your Prediction of my Death in 1733 was false, and they pretend that I remained alive many Years after. But I do hereby certify, that I did actually die at that time, precisely at the Hour you mention'd, with a Variation only of 5 *min*. 53 *sec*. which must be allow'd to be no great matter in such Cases. And I do farther declare that I furnish'd them with no Calculations of the Planets Motions, *&c*. seven Years after my Death, as they are pleased to give out: so that the Stuff they publish as an Almanack in my Name is no more mine than 'tis yours.

You will wonder perhaps, how this Paper comes written on your Table. You must know that no separate Spirits are under any Confinement till after the final Settlement of all Accounts. In the mean time we wander where we please, visit our old Friends, observe their Actions, enter sometimes into their Imaginations, and give them Hints waking or sleeping that may be of Advantage to them. Finding you asleep, I entred your left Nostril, ascended into your Brain, found out where the Ends of those Nerves were fastned that move your right Hand and Fingers, by the Help of which I am now writing unknown to you; but when you open your Eyes, you will see that the Hand written is mine, tho' wrote with yours.

The People of this Infidel Age, perhaps, will hardly believe this Story. But you may give them these three Signs by which they shall be convinc'd of the Truth of it. About the middle of *June* next, *J. J*——*n*, Philomat, shall be openly reconciled to the *Church of Rome*, and give all his Goods and Chattles to the Chappel, being perverted by a certain *Country School-master*. On the 7*th* of *September* following my old Friend *W. B*——*t* shall be sober 9 Hours, to the Astonishment of all his Neighbours: And about the same time *W. B.* and *A. B.*

will publish another Almanack in my Name, in spight of Truth and Common-Sense.

As I can see much clearer into Futurity, since I got free from the dark Prison of Flesh, in which I was continually molested and almost blinded with Fogs arising from Tiff, and the Smoke of burnt Drams; I shall in kindness to you, frequently give you Informations of things to come, for the Improvement of your Almanack: Being Dear *Dick*,

Your affectionate Friend,   T. *Leeds.*

For my own part I am convinc'd that the above Letter is genuine. If the Reader doubts of it, let him carefully observe the three Signs; and if they do not actually come to pass, believe as he pleases.

I am his humble Friend,
R. *SAUNDERS.*

––––––

To bear other Peoples Afflictions, every one has Courage enough, and to spare.

> No wonder *Tom* grows fat, th' unwieldy Sinner,
> Makes his whole Life but one continual Dinner.

An empty Bag cannot stand upright.

Happy that nation, fortunate that age, whose history is not diverting.

> What is a butterfly? At best
> He's but a caterpiller drest.
> The gaudy Fop's his picture just.

None are deceived but they that confide.

> An open Foe may prove a curse;
> But a pretended friend is worse.

> A wolf eats sheep but now and then,
> Ten Thousands are devour'd by Men.

> Man's tongue is soft, and bone doth lack;
> Yet a stroke therewith may break a man's back.

Many a Meal is lost for want of meat.

To all apparent Beauties blind
Each Blemish strikes an envious Mind.

The Poor have little, Beggars none;
the Rich too much, enough not one.

There are lazy Minds as well as lazy Bodies.

Tricks and Treachery are the Practice of Fools, that have not
Wit enough to be honest.

Who says Jack is not generous? he is always fond of giving,
and cares not for receiving.—What? Why; Advice.

The Man who with undaunted toils,
sails unknown seas to unknown soils,
With various wonders feasts his Sight:
What stranger wonders does he write?

Fear not Death; for the sooner we die, the longer shall we
be immortal.

Those who in quarrels interpose,
Must often wipe a bloody nose.

Promises may get thee Friends, but Nonperformance will
turn them into Enemies.

In other men we faults can spy,
And blame the mote that dims their eye;
Each little speck and blemish find;
To our own stronger errors blind.

When you speak to a man, look on his eyes; when he speaks
to thee, look on his mouth.

Jane, why those tears? why droops your head?
Is then your other husband dead?
Or doth a worse disgrace betide?
Hath no one since his death apply'd?

Observe all men; thy self most.

Thou hadst better eat salt with the Philosophers of *Greece*,
than sugar with the Courtiers of *Italy*.

Seek Virtue, and, of that possest,
To Providence, resign the rest.

Marry above thy match, and thou'lt get a Master.

Fear to do ill, and you need fear nought else.

He makes a Foe who makes a jest.

Can grave and formal pass for wise,
When Men the solemn Owl despise?

Some are justly laught at for keeping their Money foolishly,
others for spending it idly: He is the greatest fool that
lays it out in a purchase of repentance.

Who knows a fool, must know his brother;
For one will recommend another.

Avoid dishonest Gain: No price;
Can recompence the Pangs of Vice.

When befriended, remember it:
When you befriend, forget it.

Great souls with gen'rous pity melt;
Which coward tyrants never felt.

Employ thy time well, if thou meanest to gain leisure.

A Flatterer never seems absurd:
The Flatter'd always take his Word.

Lend Money to an Enemy, and thou'lt gain him, to a Friend
and thou'lt lose him.

Neither praise nor dispraise, till seven Christmasses be over.

Poor Richard, 1741

Enjoy the present hour, be mindful of the past;
And neither fear nor wish the Approaches of the last.

Learn of the skilful: He that teaches himself, hath a fool for
his master.

Best is the Tongue that feels the rein;—
He that talks much, must talk in vain;
We from the wordy Torrent fly:
Who listens to the chattering Pye?

Think *Cato* sees thee.

No Wood without Bark.

Monkeys warm with envious spite,
Their most obliging FRIENDS will bite;—
And, fond to copy human Ways,
Practise new Mischiefs all their days.

Joke went out, and brought home his fellow, and they two
began a quarrel.

Let thy discontents be thy Secrets;—if the world knows
them, 'twill despise *thee* and increase *them*.

E'er you remark another's Sin,
Bid your own Conscience look within.

Anger and Folly walk cheek-by-jole; Repentance treads on
both their Heels.

Turn Turk *Tim*, and renounce thy Faith in Words as well as
Actions: Is it worse to follow *Mahomet* than the Devil?

Don't overload Gratitude; if you do, she'll kick.

Be always asham'd to catch thy self idle.

Where yet was ever found the Mother,
Who'd change her booby for another?

At 20 years of age the Will reigns; at 30 the Wit; at 40 the
Judgment.

Christianity commands us to pass by Injuries; Policy, to let
them pass by us.

Lying rides upon Debt's back.

They who have nothing to be troubled at, will be troubled at
nothing.

Wife from thy Spouse each blemish hide
More than from all the World beside:
Let DECENCY be all thy Pride.

Nick's Passions grow fat and hearty; his Understanding looks consumptive!

If evils come not, then our fears are vain:
And if they do, Fear but augments the pain.

If you would keep your Secret from an enemy, tell it not to a friend.

Rob not for burnt offerings.

Bess brags she 'as *Beauty*, and can prove the same;
As how? why thus, Sir, 'tis her *puppy's* name.

Up, Sluggard, and waste not life; in the grave will be sleeping enough.

Well done, is twice done.

Clearly spoken, Mr. Fog! You explain English by Greek.

Formio bewails his Sins with the same heart,
As Friends do Friends when they're about to part.
Believe it *Formio* will not entertain,
One chearful Thought till they do meet again.

Honours change Manners.

Jack eating rotten cheese, did say,
Like *Sampson* I my thousands slay;
I vow, quoth *Roger*, so you do,
And with the self-same weapon too.

There are no fools so troublesome as those that have wit.

Quarrels never could last long,
If on one side only lay the wrong.

Let no Pleasure tempt thee, no Profit allure thee, no Ambition corrupt thee, no Example sway thee, no Persuasion move thee, to do any thing which thou knowest to be Evil; So shalt thou always live jollily: for a good Conscience is a continual Christmass.

Poor Richard, 1742

Courteous READER,

This is the ninth Year of my Endeavours to serve thee in the Capacity of a Calendar-Writer. The Encouragement I have met with must be ascrib'd, in a great Measure, to your Charity, excited by the open honest Declaration I made of my Poverty at my first Appearance. This my Brother *Philomaths* could, without being Conjurers, discover; and *Poor Richard's* Success, has produced ye a *Poor Will*, and a *Poor Robin*; and no doubt *Poor John*, &c. will follow, and we shall all be *in Name* what some Folks say we are already *in Fact*, A Parcel of *poor Almanack Makers*. During the Course of these nine Years, what Buffetings have I not sustained! The Fraternity have been all in Arms. Honest *Titan*, deceas'd, was rais'd, and made to abuse his old Friend. Both Authors and Printers were angry. Hard Names, and many, were bestow'd on me. They deny'd me to be the Author of my own Works; declar'd there never was any such Person; asserted that I was dead 60 Years ago; prognosticated my Death to happen within a Twelvemonth: with many other malicious Inconsistences, the Effects of blind Passion, Envy at my Success; and a vain Hope of depriving me (dear Reader) of thy wonted Countenance and Favour.— *Who knows him?* they cry: *Where does he live?*—But what is that to them? If I delight in a private Life, have they any Right to drag me out of my Retirement? I have good Reasons for concealing the Place of my Abode. 'Tis time for an old Man, as I am, to think of preparing for his great Remove. The perpetual Teasing of both Neighbours and Strangers, to calculate Nativities, give Judgments on Schemes, erect Figures, discover Thieves, detect Horse-Stealers, describe the Route of Runaways and stray'd Cattle; The Croud of Visitors with a 1000 trifling Questions; *Will my Ship return safe? Will my Mare win the Race? Will her next Colt be a Pacer? When will my Wife die? Who shall be my Husband, and HOW LONG first?*

When is the best time to cut Hair, trim Cocks, or sow Sallad? These and the like Impertinences I have now neither Taste nor Leisure for. I have had enough of 'em. All that these angry Folks can say, will never provoke me to tell them where I live. I would eat my Nails first.

My last Adversary is *J. J——n*, Philomat. who *declares and protests* (in his Preface, 1741) that the *false Prophecy put in my Almanack, concerning him, the Year before, is altogether* false and untrue: *and that I am one of Baal's false Prophets.* This *false, false Prophecy* he speaks of, related to his Reconciliation with the Church of *Rome*; which, notwithstanding his Declaring and Protesting, is, I fear, too true. Two Things in his elegiac Verses confirm me in this Suspicion. He calls the First of *November* by the Name of *All Hallows Day.* Reader; does not this smell of Popery? Does it in the least savour of the pure Language of Friends? But the plainest Thing is; his Adoration of Saints, which he confesses to be his Practice, in these Words, page 4.

> *When any Trouble did me befal,*
> *To my dear* Mary *then I would call:*

Did he think the whole World were so stupid as not to take Notice of this? So ignorant as not to know, that all Catholicks pay the highest Regard to the *Virgin-Mary*? Ah! Friend *John*, We must allow you to be a Poet, but you are certainly no Protestant. I could heartily wish your Religion were as good as your Verses.

RICHARD SAUNDERS.

———

Strange! that a Man who has wit enough to write a Satyr; should have folly enough to publish it.

He that hath a Trade, hath an Estate.

Have you somewhat to do to-morrow; do it to-day.

> No workman without tools,
> Nor Lawyer without Fools,
> Can live by their Rules.

> The painful Preacher, like a candle bright,
> Consumes himself in giving others Light.

Speak and speed: the close mouth catches no flies.

Visit your Aunt, but not every Day; and call at your Brother's, but not every night.

Bis dat, qui cito dat.

Money and good Manners make the Gentleman.

Late Children, early Orphans.

> *Ben* beats his Pate, and fancys wit will come;
> But he may knock, there's no body at home.

The good Spinner hath a large Shift.

> *Tom*, vain's your Pains; They all will fail:
> Ne'er was good Arrow made of a Sow's Tail.

> Empty Free-booters, cover'd with Scorn:
> They went out for Wealth, & come ragged and torn,
> As the Ram went for Wool, and was sent back shorn.

Ill Customs & bad Advice are seldom forgotten.

He that sows thorns, should not go barefoot.

Reniego de grillos, aunque sean d'oro.

Men meet, mountains never.

When Knaves fall out, honest Men get their goods: When Priests dispute, we come at the Truth.

> *Kate* would have *Thomas*, no one blame her can:
> *Tom* won't have *Kate*, and who can blame the Man?

A large train makes a light Purse.

Death takes no bribes.

One good Husband is worth two good Wives; for the scarcer things are the more they're valued.

He that riseth late, must trot all day, and shall scarce overtake his business at night.

He that speaks ill of the Mare, will buy her.

You may drive a gift without a gimblet.

Eat few Suppers, and you'll need few Medicines.

> You will be careful, if you are wise;
> How you touch Men's Religion, or Credit, or Eyes.

> After Fish,
> Milk do not wish.

Heb Dduw heb ddim, a Duw a digon.

They who have nothing to trouble them, will be troubled at nothing.

> Against Diseases here, the strongest Fence,
> Is the defensive Virtue, Abstinence.

> Fient de chien, & marc d'argent,
> Seront tout un au jour du jugement.

> If thou dost ill, the joy fades, not the pains;
> If well, the pain doth fade, the joy remains.

To err is human, to repent divine, to persist devilish.

> Money & Man a mutual Friendship show:
> Man makes *false* Money, Money makes Man so.

Industry pays Debts, Despair encreases them.

> Bright as the day and as the morning fair,
> Such *Cloe* is, & common as the air.

Here comes *Glib-tongue*: who can out-flatter a Dedication; and lie, like ten Epitaphs.

Hope and a Red-Rag, are Baits for Men and Mackrel.

> With the old Almanack and the old Year,
> Leave thy old Vices, tho' ever so dear.

Rules of Health and long Life, and to preserve from Malignant Fevers, and Sickness in general.

Eat and drink such an exact Quantity as the Constitution of thy Body allows of, in reference to the Services of the Mind.

They that study much, ought not to eat so much as those that work hard, their Digestion being not so good.

The exact Quantity and Quality being found out, is to be kept to constantly.

Excess in all other Things whatever, as well as in Meat and Drink, is also to be avoided.

Youth, Age, and Sick require a different Quantity.

And so do those of contrary Complexions; for that which is too much for a flegmatick Man, is not sufficient for a Cholerick.

The Measure of Food ought to be (as much as possibly may be) exactly proportionable to the Quality and Condition of the Stomach, because the Stomach digests it.

That Quantity that is sufficient, the Stomach can perfectly concoct and digest, and it sufficeth the due Nourishment of the Body.

A greater Quantity of some things may be eaten than of others, some being of lighter Digestion than others.

The Difficulty lies, in finding out an exact Measure; but eat for Necessity, not Pleasure, for Lust knows not where Necessity ends.

Wouldst thou enjoy a long Life, a healthy Body, and a vigorous Mind, and be acquainted also with the wonderful Works of God? labour in the first place to bring thy Appetite into Subjection to Reason.

Rules to find out a fit Measure of Meat and Drink.

If thou eatest so much as makes thee unfit for Study, or other Business, thou exceedest the due Measure.

If thou art dull and heavy after Meat, it's a sign thou hast exceeded the due Measure; for Meat and Drink ought to refresh the Body, and make it chearful, and not to dull and oppress it.

If thou findest these ill Symptoms, consider whether too much Meat, or too much Drink occasions it, or both, and abate by little and little, till thou findest the Inconveniency removed.

Keep out of the Sight of Feasts and Banquets as much as may be; for 'tis more difficult to refrain good Cheer, when it's present, than from the Desire of it when it is away;

the like you may observe in the Objects of all the other Senses.

If a Man casually exceeds, let him fast the next Meal, and all may be well again, provided it be not too often done; as if he exceed at Dinner, let him refrain a Supper, *&c.*

A temperate Diet frees from Diseases; such are seldom ill, but if they are surprised with Sickness, they bear it better, and recover sooner; for most Distempers have their Original from Repletion.

Use now and then a little Exercise a quarter of an Hour before Meals, as to swing a Weight, or swing your Arms about with a small Weight in each Hand; to leap, or the like, for that stirs the Muscles of the Breast.

A temperate Diet arms the Body against all external Accidents; so that they are not so easily hurt by Heat, Cold or Labour; if they at any time should be prejudiced, they are more easily cured, either of Wounds, Dislocations or Bruises.

But when malignant Fevers are rife in the Country or City where thou dwelst, 'tis adviseable to eat and drink more freely, by Way of Prevention; for those are Diseases that are not caused by Repletion, and seldom attack Full-feeders.

A sober Diet makes a Man die without Pain; it maintains the Senses in Vigour; it mitigates the Violence of Passions and Affections.

It preserves the Memory, it helps the Understanding, it allays the Heat of Lust; it brings a Man to a Consideration of his latter End; it makes the Body a fit Tabernacle for the Lord to dwell in; which makes us happy in this World, and eternally happy in the World to come, through Jesus Christ our Lord and Saviour.

Poor Richard, 1743

Friendly READER,

Because I would have every Man make Advantage of the Blessings of Providence, and few are acquainted with the Method of making Wine of the Grapes which grow wild in our Woods, I do here present them with a few easy Directions, drawn from some Years Experience, which, if they will follow, they may furnish themselves with a wholesome sprightly Claret, which will keep for several Years, and is not inferior to that which passeth for *French* Claret.

Begin to gather Grapes from the 10th of *September* (the ripest first) to the last of *October*, and having clear'd them of Spider webs, and dead Leaves, put them into a large Molosses- or Rum-Hogshead; after having washed it well, and knock'd one Head out, fix it upon the other Head, on a Stand, or Blocks in the Cellar, if you have any, if not, in the warmest Part of the House, about 2 Feet from the Ground; as the Grapes sink, put up more, for 3 or 4 Days; after which, get into the Hogshead bare-leg'd, and tread them down until the Juice works up about your Legs, which will be in less than half an Hour; then get out, and turn the Bottom ones up, and tread them again, a Quarter of an Hour; this will be sufficient to get out the good Juice; more pressing wou'd burst the unripe Fruit, and give it an ill Taste: This done, cover the Hogshead close with a thick Blanket, and if you have no Cellar, and the Weather proves Cold, with two.

In this Manner you must let it take its first Ferment, for 4 or 5 Days it will work furiously; when the Ferment abates, which you will know by its making less Noise, make a Spilehole within six Inches of the Bottom, and twice a Day draw some in a Glass. When it looks as clear as Rock-water, draw it off into a clean, rather than new Cask, proportioning it to the Contents of the Hogshead or Wine * Vat; that is, if the Hogshead holds twenty Bushels of Grapes, Stems and all, the Cask must at least, hold 20 Gallons, for they will yield a Gallon per Bushel. Your Juice or † Must thus drawn from the Vat, proceed to the second Ferment.

You must reserve in Jugs or Bottles, 1 Gallon or 5 Quarts of the Must to every 20 Gallons you have to work; which you will use according to the following Directions.

*Vat *or* Fatt, *a Name for the Vessel, in which you tread the Grapes, and in which the* Must *takes its first Ferment.*

†Must *is a Name for the Juice of the Vine before it is fermented, afterwards 'tis called Wine.*

Place your Cask, which must be chock full, with the Bung up, and open twice every Day, Morning and Night; feed your Cask with the reserved Must; two Spoonfuls at a time will suffice, clearing the Bung after you feed it, with your Finger or a Spoon, of the Grape-Stones and other Filth which the Ferment will throw up; you must continue feeding it thus until *Christmas*, when you may bung it up, and it will be fit for Use or to be rack'd into clean Casks or Bottles, by *February*.

N. B. Gather the Grapes after the Dew is off, and in all dry Seasons. Let not the Children come at the Must, it will scour them severely. If you make Wine for Sale, or to go beyond Sea, one quarter Part must be distill'd, and the Brandy put into the three Quarters remaining. One Bushel of Grapes, heap Measure, as you gather them from the Vine, will make at least a Gallon of Wine, if good, five Quarts.

These Directions are not design'd for those who are skill'd in making Wine, but for those who have hitherto had no Acquaintance with that Art.

———

How few there are who have courage enough to own their
    Faults, or resolution enough to mend them!

Men differ daily, about things which are subject to Sense,
    is it likely then they should agree about things
    invisible.

    Mark with what insolence and pride,
    Blown *Bufo* takes his haughty stride;
    As if no toad was toad beside.

Ill Company is like a dog who dirts those most, that he
    loves best.

    In prosperous fortunes be modest and wise,
    The greatest may fall, and the lowest may rise:
    But insolent People that fall in disgrace,
    Are wretched and no-body pities their Case.

Le sage entend á demi mot.

Sorrow is dry.

The World is full of fools and faint hearts; and yet every one has courage enough to bear the misfortunes, and wisdom enough to manage the Affairs of his neighbour.

Beware, beware! he'll cheat 'ithout scruple, who can without fear.

The D—l wipes his B—ch with poor Folks Pride.

> Content and Riches seldom meet together,
> Riches take thou, contentment I had rather.

> Speak with contempt of none, from slave to king,
> The meanest Bee hath, and will use, a sting.

The church the state, and the poor, are 3 daughters which we should maintain, but not portion off.

A achwyno heb achos; gwneler achos iddo.

> A little well-gotten will do us more good,
> Than lordships and scepters by Rapine and Blood.

Borgen macht sorgen.

Let all Men know thee, but no man know thee thoroughly: Men freely ford that see the shallows.

> 'Tis easy to frame a good bold resolution;
> but hard is the Task that concerns execution.

> Cold & cunning come from the north:
> But cunning sans wisdom is nothing worth.

> 'Tis vain to repine,
> Tho' a learned Divine
> Will die *this day* at nine.

A noddo duw, ry noddir.

Ah simple Man! when a boy two precious jewels were given thee, Time, and good Advice; one thou hast lost, and the other thrown away.

> Na funno i hûn.
> Na wnaid i ûn.

> *Dick* told his spouse, he durst be bold to swear,
> Whate'er she pray'd for, Heav'n would thwart her
>   pray'r:
> Indeed! says *Nell*, 'tis what I'm pleas'd to hear;
> For now I'll pray for your long life, my dear.

The sleeping Fox catches no poultry. Up! up!

If you'd be wealthy, think of saving, more than of getting:
The *Indies* have not made *Spain* rich, because her Outgoes
equal her Incomes.

Tugend bestehet wen alles vergehet.

> Came you from Court? for in your Mien,
> A self-important air is seen.

> Hear what *Jack Spaniard* says,
> Con todo el Mundo Guerra,
> Y Paz con Ingalatierra.

If you'd have it done, Go: If not, send.

Many a long dispute among Divines may be thus abridg'd,
It is so: It is not so. It is so; It is not so.

Experience keeps a dear school, yet Fools will learn in no
other.

Felix quem faciunt aliena pericula cautum.

How many observe Christ's Birth-day! How few, his
Precepts! O! 'tis easier to keep Holidays than
Commandments.

Poor Richard, 1744

Courteous Reader,

This is the Twelfth Year that I have in this Way laboured
for the Benefit—of Whom?—of the Publick, if you'll be so
good-natured as to believe it; if not, e'en take the naked
Truth, 'twas for the Benefit of my own dear self; not forgetting in the mean time, our gracious Consort and Dutchess the

peaceful, quiet, silent Lady *Bridget*. But whether my Labours have been of any Service to the Publick or not, the Publick I must acknowledge has been of Service to me; I have lived Comfortably by its Benevolent Encouragement; and I hope I shall always bear a grateful Sense of its continued Favour.

My Adversary *J—n J——n* has indeed made an Attempt to *out-shine* me, by pretending to penetrate *a Year deeper* into Futurity; and giving his Readers *gratis* in his Almanack for 1743 an Eclipse of the Year 1744, to be beforehand with me: His Words are, "The first Day of *April* next Year 1744, there will be a GREAT ECLIPSE of the Sun; it begins about an Hour before Sunset. It being in the Sign Aries, the House of Mars, and in the 7th, shows Heat, Difference and Animosities between Persons of the highest Rank and Quality," *&c.* I am very glad, for the Sake of these Persons of Rank and Quality, that there is *no manner of Truth* in this Prediction: They may, if they please, live in Love and Peace. And I caution his Readers (they are but few, indeed, and so the Matter's the less) not to give themselves any Trouble about observing this imaginary Great Eclipse; for they may stare till they're blind without seeing the least Sign of it. I might, on this Occasion, return Mr. *J——n* the Name of *Baal's false Prophet* he gave me some Years ago in his Wrath, on Account of my Predicting his Reconciliation with the *Church of Rome*, (tho' he seems now to have given up that Point) but I think such Language between old Men and Scholars unbecoming; and I leave him to settle the Affair with the Buyers of his Almanack as well as he can, who perhaps will not take it very kindly, that he has done what in him lay (by sending them out to gaze at an invisible Eclipse on the first of *April*) to make *April Fools* of them all. His old thread-bare Excuse which he repeats Year after Year about the *Weather*, "That no Man can be infallible therein, by Reason of the many contrary Causes happening at or near the same time, and the Unconstancy of the Summer Showers and gusts," *&c.* will hardly serve him in the Affair of *Eclipses*; and I know not where he'll get another.

I have made no Alteration in my usual Method, except adding the Rising and Setting of the Planets, and the Lunar Conjunctions. Those who are so disposed, may thereby very

Where there's no Law, there's no Bread.

As Pride increases, Fortune declines.

Drive thy Business, or it will drive thee.

A full Belly is the Mother of all Evil.

The same man cannot be both Friend and Flatterer.

He who multiplies Riches multiplies Cares.

An old Man in a House is a good Sign.

Those who are fear'd, are hated.

The Things which hurt, instruct.

The Eye of a Master, will do more Work than his Hand.

A soft Tongue may strike hard.

If you'd be belov'd, make yourself amiable.

A true Friend is the best Possession.

Fear God, and your Enemies will fear you.

> *Epitaph on a Scolding Wife by her Husband.*
> Here my poor *Bridget*'s Corps doth lie,
> she is at rest,—and so am I.

Poor Richard, 1745

Courteous Reader,

For the Benefit of the Publick, and my own Profit, I have performed this my thirteenth annual Labour, which I hope will be as acceptable as the former.

The rising and setting of the Planets, and their Conjunctions with the Moon, I have continued; whereby those who are unacquainted with those heavenly Bodies, may soon learn to distinguish them from the fixed Stars, by observing the following Directions.

All those glittering Stars (except five) which we see in the

Firmament of Heaven, are called fixed Stars, because they keep the same Distance from one another, and from the Ecliptic; they rise and set on the same Points of the Horizon, and appear like so many lucid Points fixed to the celestial Firmament. The other five have a particular and different Motion, for which Reason they have not always the same Distance from one another; and therefore they have been called wandering Stars or Planets, *viz.* *Saturn* ♄, *Jupiter* ♃, *Mars* ♂, *Venus* ♀, and *Mercury* ☿, and these may be distinguished from the fixed Stars by their not twinkling. The brightest of the five is *Venus*, which appears the biggest; and when this glorious Star appears, and goes before the Sun, it is called *Phosphorus*, or the Morning-Star, and *Hesperus*, or the Evening-Star, when it follows the Sun. *Jupiter* appears almost as big as *Venus*, but not so bright. *Mars* may be easily known from the rest of the Planets, because it appears red like a hot Iron or burning Coal, and twinkles a little. *Saturn*, in Appearance, is less than *Mars*, and of a pale Colour, *Mercury* is so near the Sun, that it is seldom seen.

Against the 6th Day of *January* you may see ♂ rise 10 35, which signifies the Planet *Mars* rises 35 Minutes after 10 o' Clock at Night, when that Planet may be seen to appear in the East. Also against the 10th Day of *January* you will find ♀ sets 7 13, which shows *Venus* sets 13 Minutes after 7 o' Clock at Night. If you look towards the West that Evening, you may see that beautiful Star till the Time of its setting. Again, on the 18th Day of the same Month, you will find ♄ rise 9 18, which shews that *Saturn* rises 18 Minutes after 9 at Night.

Or the Planets may be known by observing them at the Time of their Conjunctions with the Moon, *viz.* against the 14 Day of *January* are inserted these Characters, ♂ ☽ ♄, which shews there will be a Conjunction of the Moon and *Saturn* on that Day. If you look out about 5 o' Clock in the Morning, you will see *Saturn* very near the Moon. The like is to be observed at any other time by the rising and setting of the Planets, and their Conjunctions with the Moon; by which Method they may be distinctly known from the fixed Stars.

I have nothing further to add at present, but my hearty

Wishes for your Welfare, both temporal and spiritual, and Thanks for all your past Favours, being,

Dear Reader,

Thy obliged Friend,

R. SAUNDERS.

———

Beware of little Expences, a small Leak will sink a great Ship.

Wars bring scars.

A light purse is a heavy Curse.

As often as we do good, we sacrifice.

Help, Hands;
For I have no Lands.

It's common for Men to give 6 pretended Reasons instead of one real one.

Vanity backbites more than *Malice.*

He's a Fool that cannot conceal his Wisdom.

Great spenders are bad lenders.

All blood is alike ancient.

You may talk too much on the best of subjects.

A Man without ceremony has need of great merit in its place.

No gains without pains.

Had I revenged wrong, I had not worn my skirts so long.

Graft good Fruit all, or graft not at all.

Idleness is the greatest Prodigality.

Old young and old long.

Punch-coal, cut-candle, and set brand on end,
is neither good house wife, nor good house-wife's friend.

He who buys had need have 100 Eyes,
but one's enough for him that sells the Stuff.

There are no fools so troublesome as those that have wit.

Many complain of their Memory, few of their Judgment.

One Man may be more cunning than another, but not more cunning than every body else.

To God we owe fear and love; to our neighbours justice and charity; to our selves prudence and sobriety.

Fools make feasts and wise men eat them.

Light-heel'd mothers make leaden-heel'd daughters.

> The good or ill hap of a good or ill life,
> is the good or ill choice of a good or ill wife.

'Tis easier to prevent bad habits than to break them.

Every Man has Assurance enough to boast of his honesty, few of their Understanding.

Interest which blinds some People, enlightens others.

> An ounce of wit that is bought,
> Is worth a pound that is taught.

He that resolves to mend hereafter, resolves not to mend now.

Poor Richard, 1746

PREFACE.

Who is *Poor Richard*? People oft enquire,
Where lives? What is he?—never yet the nigher.
Somewhat to ease your Curiositie,
Take these slight Sketches of my Dame and me.
   Thanks to kind Readers and a careful Wife,
With Plenty bless'd, I lead an easy Life;
My Business Writing; hers to drain the Mead,
Or crown the barren Hill with useful Shade;
In the smooth Glebe to see the Plowshare worn,
And fill the Granary with needful Corn.
Press nectarous Cyder from my loaded Trees,

Print the sweet Butter, turn the drying Cheese.
Some Books we read, tho' few there are that hit
The happy Point where Wisdom joins with Wit;
That set fair Virtue naked to our View,
And teach us what is *decent*, what is *true*.
The Friend sincere, and honest Man, with Joy
Treating or treated oft our Time employ.
Our Table neat, Meals temperate; and our Door
Op'ning spontaneous to the bashful Poor.
Free from the bitter Rage of Party Zeal,
All those we love who seek the publick Weal.
Nor blindly follow Superstition's Lore,
Which cheats deluded Mankind o'er and o'er.
Not over righteous, quite beyond the Rule,
Conscience perplext by every canting Tool.
Nor yet when Folly hides the dubious Line,
Where Good and Bad their blended Colours join;
Rush indiscreetly down the dangerous Steep,
And plunge uncertain in the darksome Deep.
Cautious, if right; if wrong resolv'd to part
The Inmate Snake that folds about the Heart.
Observe the *Mean*, the *Motive* and the *End*;
Mending our selves, or striving still to mend.
Our Souls sincere, our Purpose fair and free,
Without Vain Glory or Hypocrisy:
Thankful if well; if ill, we kiss the Rod;
Resign with Hope, and put our Trust in GOD.

———

When the Well's dry, we know the Worth of Water.

He that whines for Glass without G
Take away L and that's he.

A good Wife & Health,
is a Man's best Wealth.

A quarrelsome Man has no good Neighbours.

Wide will wear,
but Narrow will tear.

Silks and Sattins put out the Kitchen Fire.

Vice knows she's ugly, so puts on her Mask.

It's the easiest Thing in the World for a Man to deceive himself.

> Women & Wine, Game & Deceit,
> Make the Wealth small and the Wants great.

All Mankind are beholden to him that is kind to the Good.

A Plowman on his Legs is higher than a Gentleman on his Knees.

Virtue and Happiness are Mother and Daughter.

The generous Mind least regards money, and yet most feels the Want of it.

For one poor Man there are an hundred indigent.

Dost thou love Life? then do not squander Time; for that's the Stuff Life is made of.

Good Sense is a Thing all need, few have, and none think they want.

What's proper, is becoming: See the Blacksmith with his white Silk Apron!

The Tongue is ever turning to the aching Tooth.

Want of Care does us more Damage than Want of Knowledge.

Take Courage, Mortal; Death can't banish thee out of the Universe.

The Sting of a Reproach, is the Truth of it.

Do me the Favour to deny me at once.

The most exquisite Folly is made of Wisdom spun too fine.

A life of leisure, and a life of laziness, are two things.

Mad Kings and mad Bulls, are not to be held by treaties & packthread.

Changing Countries or Beds, cures neither a bad Manager, nor a Fever.

A true great Man will neither trample on a Worm, nor sneak to an Emperor.

Ni ffyddra llaw dyn, er gwneithr da idd ei hûn.

> *Tim* and his Handsaw are good in their Place,
> Tho' not fit for preaching or shaving a face.

Half-Hospitality opens his Doors and shuts up his Countenance.

Poor Richard, 1747

Courteous Reader,

This is the 15th Time I have entertain'd thee with my annual Productions; I hope to thy Profit as well as mine. For besides the astronomical Calculations, and other Things usually contain'd in Almanacks, which have their daily Use indeed while the Year continues, but then become of no Value, I have constantly interspers'd *moral* Sentences, *prudent* Maxims, and *wise* Sayings, many of them containing *much good Sense* in *very few* Words, and therefore apt to leave *strong* and *lasting* Impressions on the Memory of young Persons, whereby they may receive Benefit as long as they live, when both Almanack and Almanack-maker have been long thrown by and forgotten. If I now and then insert a Joke or two, that seem to have little in them, my Apology is, that such may have their Use, since perhaps for their Sake light airy Minds peruse the rest, and so are struck by somewhat of more Weight and Moment. The Verses on the Heads of the Months are also generally design'd to have the same Tendency. I need not tell thee that not many of them are of my own Making. If thou hast any Judgment in Poetry, thou wilt easily discern the Workman from the Bungler. I know as well as thee, that I am no *Poet born*; and it is a Trade I never learnt, nor indeed could learn. *If I make Verses, 'tis in Spight—Of Nature and my Stars, I write.* Why then should I give my Readers *bad Lines* of my own, when *good Ones* of other People's are so plenty? 'Tis methinks a poor Excuse for the bad Entertainment of Guests, that the Food we set before them, tho' coarse and ordinary, is *of one's own Raising, off one's own Plantation,* &c. when there is Plenty of what is ten times better, to be had in the Market.—On the contrary, I assure ye, my Friends, that I have procur'd the best I could for ye, and *much Good may't do ye.*

I cannot omit this Opportunity of making honourable Mention of the late deceased Ornament and Head of our Profession, Mr. JACOB TAYLOR, who for upwards of 40 Years (with some few Intermissions only) supply'd the good People of this and the neighbouring Colonies, with the most compleat Ephemeris and most accurate Calculations that have hitherto appear'd in *America.*—He was an ingenious Mathematician, as well as an expert and skilful Astronomer; and moreover, no mean Philosopher, but what is more than all, He was a PIOUS and an HONEST Man. *Requiescat in pace.*

I am thy poor Friend, to serve thee,

R. SAUNDERS.

———

Strive to be the *greatest* Man in your Country, and you may be disappointed; Strive to be the *best*, and you may succeed: He may well win the race that runs by himself.

'Tis a strange Forest that has no rotten Wood in't.
And a strange Kindred that all are good in't.

None know the unfortunate, and the fortunate do not know themselves.

There's a time to wink as well as to see.

Honest *Tom!* you may trust him with a house-full of untold Milstones.

There is no Man so bad, but he secretly respects the Good.

When there's more Malice shown than Matter:
On the Writer falls the satyr.

Courage would fight, but *Discretion* won't let him.

Delicate *Dick!* whisper'd the Proclamation.

Cornelius ought to be *Tacitus*.

> *Pride* and the *Gout*,
> are seldom cur'd throughout.

We are not so sensible of the greatest Health as of the least Sickness.

A good Example is the best sermon.

A Father's a Treasure; a Brother's a Comfort; a Friend is both.

Despair ruins some, Presumption many.

> A quiet Conscience sleeps in Thunder,
> but Rest and Guilt live far asunder.

He that won't be counsell'd, can't be help'd.

Craft must be at charge for clothes, but *Truth* can go naked.

Write Injuries in Dust, Benefits in Marble.

What is Serving God? 'Tis doing Good to Man.

What maintains one Vice would bring up two Children.

Many have been ruin'd by buying good pennyworths.

Better is a little with content than much with contention.

> A Slip of the Foot you may soon recover:
> But a Slip of the Tongue you may never get over.

What signifies your Patience, if you can't find it when you want it.

d. wise, l. foolish.

Time enough, always proves *little enough*.

It is wise not to seek a Secret, and Honest not to reveal it.

A Mob's a Monster; Heads enough, but no Brains.

The Devil sweetens Poison with Honey.

He that cannot bear with other People's Passions, cannot govern his own.

He that by the Plow would thrive,
himself must either hold or drive.

Poor Richard Improved, 1748

Kind Reader,

The favourable Reception my annual Labours have met with from the Publick these 15 Years past, has engaged me in Gratitude to endeavour some Improvement of my Almanack. And since my Friend *Taylor* is no more, whose *Ephemerides* so long and so agreeably serv'd and entertain'd these Provinces, I have taken the Liberty to imitate his well-known Method, and give two Pages for each Month; which affords me Room for several valuable Additions, as will best appear on Inspection and Comparison with former Almanacks. Yet I have not so far follow'd his Method, as not to continue my own where I thought it preferable; and thus my Book is increas'd to a Size beyond his, and contains much more Matter.

Hail Night serene! thro' Thee where'er we turn
Our wond'ring Eyes, Heav'n's Lamps profusely burn;
And Stars unnumber'd all the Sky adorn.
But lo!—what's that I see appear?
It seems far off a pointed flame;
From Earthwards too the shining Meteor came:
How swift it climbs th' etherial Space!
And now it traverses each Sphere,
And seems some knowing Mind, familiar to the Place.
Dame, hand my Glass, the longest, strait prepare;—
'Tis He—'tis TAYLOR's Soul, that travels there.
O stay! thou happy Spirit, stay,
And lead me on thro' all th' unbeaten Wilds of Day;
Where Planets in pure Streams of Ether driven,
Swim thro' the blue Expanse of Heav'n.
There let me, thy Companion, stray
From Orb to Orb, and now behold
Unnumber'd Suns, all Seas of molten Gold,
And trace each Comet's wandring Way.——

Souse down into Prose again, my Muse; for Poetry's no more thy Element, than Air is that of the Flying-Fish; whose Flights, like thine, are therefore always short and heavy.——

We complain sometimes of hard Winters in this Country; but our Winters will appear as Summers, when compar'd with those that some of our Countrymen undergo in the most Northern *British* Colony on this Continent, which is that upon *Churchill* River, in *Hudson's Bay*, Lat. 58d. 56m. Long. from *London* 94d. 50m. West. Captain *Middleton*, a Member of the *Royal Society*, who had made many Voyages thither, and winter'd there 1741–2, when he was in Search of the *North-West* Passage to the *South-Sea*, gives an Account of it to that Society, from which I have extracted these Particulars, *viz.*

The Hares, Rabbits, Foxes, and Partridges, in *September* and the Beginning of *October*, change their Colour to a snowy White, and continue white till the following Spring.

The Lakes and standing Waters, which are not above 10 or 12 Feet deep, are frozen to the Ground in Winter, and the Fishes therein all perish. Yet in Rivers near the Sea, and Lakes of a greater Depth than 10 or 12 Feet, Fishes are caught all the Winter, by cutting Holes thro' the Ice, and therein putting Lines and Hooks. As soon as the Fish are brought into the open Air, they instantly freeze stiff.

Beef, Pork, Mutton, and Venison, kill'd in the Beginning of the Winter, are preserved by the Frost for 6 or 7 Months, entirely free from Putrefaction. Likewise Geese, Partridges, and other Fowls, kill'd at the same Time, and kept with their Feathers on and Guts in, are preserv'd by the Frost, and prove good Eating. All Kinds of Fish are preserv'd in the same Manner.

In large Lakes and Rivers, the Ice is sometimes broken by imprison'd Vapours; and the Rocks, Trees, Joists, and Rafters of our Buildings, are burst with a Noise not less terrible than the firing of many Guns together. The Rocks which are split by the Frost, are heaved up in great Heaps, leaving large Cavities behind. If Beer or Water be left even in Copper Pots by the Bed-side, the Pots will be split before Morning. Bottles of strong Beer, Brandy, strong Brine, Spirits of Wine, set out in the open Air for 3 or 4 Hours, freeze to solid Ice. The Frost is never out of the Ground, how deep is not certain; but on digging 10 or 12 Feet down in the two Summer Months, it has been found hard frozen.

All the Water they use for Cooking, Brewing, *&c.* is melted Snow and Ice; no Spring is yet found free from freezing, tho' dug ever so deep down.—All Waters inland, are frozen fast by the Beginning of *October*, and continue so to the Middle of *May*.

The Walls of the Houses are of Stone, two Feet thick; the Windows very small, with thick wooden Shutters, which are close shut 18 Hours every Day in Winter. In the Cellars they put their Wines, Brandies, *&c.* Four large Fires are made every Day, in great Stoves to warm the Rooms: As soon as the Wood is burnt down to a Coal, the Tops of the Chimnies are close stopped, with an Iron Cover; this keeps the Heat in, but almost stifles the People. And notwithstanding this, in 4 or 5 Hours after the Fire is out, the Inside of the Walls and Bed-places will be 2 or 3 Inches thick with Ice, which is every Morning cut away with a Hatchet. Three or four Times a Day, Iron Shot, of 24 Pounds Weight, are made red hot, and hung up in the Windows of their Apartments, to moderate the Air that comes in at Crevices; yet this, with a Fire kept burning the greatest Part of 24 Hours, will not prevent Beer, Wine, Ink, *&c.* from Freezing.

For their Winter Dress, a Man makes use of three Pair of Socks, of coarse Blanketting, or Duffeld, for the Feet, with a Pair of Deerskin Shoes over them; two Pair of thick *English* Stockings, and a Pair of Cloth Stockings upon them; Breeches lined with Flannel; two or three *English* Jackets, and a Fur, or Leather Gown over them; a large Beaver Cap, double, to come over the Face and Shoulders, and a Cloth of Blanketting under the Chin; with Yarn Gloves, and a large Pair of Beaver Mittins, hanging down from the Shoulders before, to put the Hands in, reaching up as high as the Elbows. Yet notwithstanding this warm Clothing, those that stir Abroad when any Wind blows from the Northward, are sometimes dreadfully frozen; some have their Hands, Arms, and Face blistered and froze in a terrible Manner, the Skin coming off soon after they enter a warm House, and some lose their Toes. And keeping House, or lying-in for the Cure of these

Disorders, brings on the Scurvy, which many die of, and few are free from; nothing preventing it but Exercise and stirring Abroad.

The Fogs and Mists, brought by northerly Winds in Winter, appear visible to the naked Eye to be Icicles innumerable, as small as fine Hairs, and pointed as sharp as Needles. These Icicles lodge in their Clothes, and if their Faces and Hands are uncover'd, presently raise Blisters as white as a Linnen Cloth, and as hard as Horn. Yet if they immediately turn their Back to the Weather, and can bear a Hand out of the Mitten, and with it rub the blister'd Part for a small Time, they sometimes bring the Skin to its former State; if not, they make the best of their Way to a Fire, bathe the Part in hot Water, and thereby dissipate the Humours raised by the frozen Air; otherwise the Skin wou'd be off in a short Time, with much hot, serous, watry Matter, coming from under along with the Skin; and this happens to some almost every Time they go Abroad, for 5 or 6 Months in the Winter, so extreme cold is the Air, when the Wind blows any Thing strong.—Thus far Captain *Middleton*. And now, my tender Reader, thou that shudderest when the Wind blows a little at N-West, and criest, *'Tis extrrrrrream cohohold! 'Tis terrrrrrible cohold!* what dost thou think of removing to that delightful Country? Or dost thou not rather chuse to stay in *Pennsylvania*, thanking God that *He has caused thy Lines to fall in pleasant Places.*

I am,
Thy Friend to serve thee,
R. SAUNDERS.

———

Robbers must exalted be,
Small ones on the Gallow-Tree,
While greater ones ascend to Thrones,
But what is that to thee or me?

Lost Time is never found again.

———

On the 19th of this Month, *Anno* 1493, was born the famous Astronomer *Copernicus*, to whom we owe the Invention, or rather the Revival (it being taught by *Pythagoras* near 2000 Years before) of that now generally receiv'd System of the World which bears his Name, and supposes the Sun in the Center, this Earth a Planet revolving round it in 365 Days, 6 Hours, *&c.* and that Day and Night are caused by the Turning of the Earth on its own Axis once round in 24 h. *&c.* The *Ptolomean* System, which prevail'd before *Copernicus*, suppos'd the Earth to be fix'd, and that the Sun went round it daily. Mr. *Whiston*, a modern Astronomer, says, the Sun is 230,000 times bigger than the Earth, and 81 Millions of Miles distant from it: That vast Body must then have mov'd more than 480 Millions of Miles in 24 h. A prodigious Journey round this little Spot! How much more natural is *Copernicus*'s Scheme!—*Ptolomy* is compar'd to a whimsical Cook, who, instead of Turning his Meat in Roasting, should fix That, and contrive to have his whole Fire, Kitchen and all, whirling continually round it.

———

> To lead a virtuous Life, my Friends, and get to Heaven in Season,
> You've just so much more Need of *Faith*, as you have less of *Reason*.

To avoid Pleurisies, *&c.* in cool Weather; Fevers, Fluxes, *&c.* in hot; beware of *Over-Eating* and *Over-Heating*.

The Heathens when they dy'd, went to Bed without a Candle.

> Knaves & Nettles are akin;
> stroak 'em kindly, yet they'll sting.

———

On the 20th of this month, 1727, died the prince of astronomers and philosophers, sir *Isaac Newton*, aged 85 years: Who, as *Thomson* expresses it, *Trac'd the boundless works of God, from laws sublimely simple.*

> What were his raptures then! how pure! how strong!
> And what the triumphs of old *Greece* and *Rome*,
> By his diminish'd, but the pride of boys
> In some small fray victorious! when instead
> Of shatter'd parcels of this earth usurp'd
> By violence unmanly, and sore deeds

Of cruelty and blood; *Nature* herself
Stood all-subdu'd by him, and open laid
Her every latent glory to his view.

Mr. *Pope's* epitaph on sir *Isaac Newton*, is justly admired for
its conciseness, strength, boldness, and sublimity:

Nature and nature's laws lay hid in night;
God said, *Let* NEWTON *be*, and all was light.

Life with Fools consists in Drinking;
With the wise Man Living's Thinking.

Eilen thut selten gut.

On the 25th of this month, *Anno* 1599, was OLIVER CROM-
WELL born, the son of a private gentleman, but became the
conqueror and protector (some say the tyrant) of three great
kingdoms. His son *Richard* succeeded him, but being of an
easy peaceable disposition, he soon descended from that lofty
station, and became a private man, living, unmolested, to a
good old age; for he died not till about the latter end of
queen *Anne's* reign, at his lodgings in *Lombard-street*, where
he had lived many years unknown, and seen great changes in
government, and violent struggles for that, which, by experience, he knew could afford no solid happiness.

Oliver was once about to remove to *New-England*, his
goods being on shipboard; but somewhat alter'd his mind.
There he would doubtless have risen to be a *Select Man*, perhaps a *Governor*; and then might have had 100 bushels of *Indian* corn *per Annum*, the salary of a governor of that then
small colony in those days.

Sell-cheap kept Shop on *Goodwin Sands*, and yet had Store of
Custom.

Liberality is not giving much but giving wisely.

Finikin *Dick*, curs'd with nice Taste,
Ne'er meets with good dinner, half starv'd at a feast.

Alas! that Heroes ever were made!
The *Plague*, and the *Hero*, are both of a Trade!
Yet the Plague spares our Goods which the Heroe does not;
So a Plague take such Heroes and let their Fames rot. *Q. P. D.*

The 19th of this month, 1719, died the celebrated *Joseph Addison*, Esq; aged 47, whose writings have contributed more to the improvement of the minds of the *British* nation, and polishing their manners, than those of any other *English* pen whatever.

To Friend, Lawyer, Doctor, tell plain your whole Case;
Nor think on bad Matters to put a good Face:
How can they advise, if they see but a Part?
'Tis very ill driving black Hogs in the dark.

Suspicion may be no Fault, but shewing it may be a great one.

He that's secure is not safe.

The second Vice is Lying; the first is Running in Debt.

The Muses love the Morning.

Muschitoes, or *Musketoes*, a little venomous fly, so light, that perhaps 50 of them, before they've fill'd their bellies, scarce weigh a grain, yet each has all the parts necessary to life, motion, digestion, generation, *&c.* as veins, arteries, muscles, *&c.* each has in his little body room for the five senses of seeing, hearing, feeling, smelling, tasting: How inconceivably small must their organs be! How inexpressibly fine the workmanship! And yet there are little animals discovered by the microscope, to whom a *Musketo* is an *Elephant*!—In a scarce summer any citizen may provide Musketoes sufficient for his own family, by leaving tubs of rain-water uncover'd in his yard; for in such water they lay their eggs, which when hatch'd, become first little fish, afterwards put forth legs and wings, leave the water, and fly into your windows. *Probatum est.*

Two Faults of one a Fool will make;
He half repairs, that owns & does forsake.

Harry Smatter,
has a Mouth for every Matter.

When you're good to others, you are best to yourself.

Half Wits talk much but say little.

If *Jack's* in love, he's no judge of *Jill*'s Beauty.

Most Fools think they are only ignorant.

On the 14th of this month, *Anno* 1644, was born WILLIAM PENN, the great founder of this Province; who prudently and benevolently sought success to himself by no other means, than securing the *liberty*, and endeavouring the *happiness* of his people. Let no envious mind grudge his posterity those advantages which arise to them from the wisdom and goodness of their ancestor; and to which their own merit, as well as the laws, give them an additional title.

On the 28th, *Anno* 1704, died the famous *John Locke*, Esq; the *Newton* of the *Microcosm*: For, as *Thomson* says,

He made the whole internal world *his own.*

His book on the *Human Understanding*, shows it. *Microcosm*, honest reader, is a hard word, and, they say, signifies the *little world*, man being so called, as containing within himself the four elements of the *greater*, &c. &c. I here explain *Greek* to thee by *English*, which, I think, is rather a more intelligible way, than explaining *English* by *Greek*, as a certain writer does, who gravely tells us, *Man is rightly called* a little world, *because he is a* Microcosm.

On the 29th, *Anno* 1618, was the famous sir *Walter Rawleigh* beheaded; to the eternal shame of the attorney-general, who first prosecuted him, and of the king, who ratify'd the sentence.

How happy is he, who can satisfy his hunger with any

food, quench his thirst with any drink, please his ear with any musick, delight his eye with any painting, any sculpture, any architecture, and divert his mind with any book or any company! How many mortifications must he suffer, that cannot bear any thing but beauty, order, elegance & perfection! *Your man of* taste, *is nothing but a man of* distaste.

———

Pardoning the Bad, is injuring the Good.

He is not well-bred, that cannot bear Ill-Breeding in others.

> In Christmas feasting pray take care;
> Let not your table be a Snare;
> but with the Poor God's Bounty share.

Poor Richard Improved, 1749

Wealth and Content are not always Bed-fellows.

Wise Men learn by others harms; Fools by their own.

———

On the 7th of this month 1692 died *Robert Boyle*, Esq; one of the greatest philosophers the last age produced. He first brought the machine called an *Airpump*, into use; by which many of the surprizing properties of that wonderful element were discovered and demonstrated. His knowledge of natural history, and skill in chymistry, were very great and extensive; and his piety inferior to neither.

> ——BOYLE, *whose pious search*
> *Amid the dark recesses of his works*
> *The great* CREATOR *sought:*——Thomson.

is therefore an instance, that tho' *Ignorance* may in some be the *Mother of Devotion*, yet true learning and exalted piety are by no means inconsistent.

———

When we read in antient history of the speeches made by generals to very numerous armies, we sometimes wonder how they could be well heard; but supposing the men got together so close, that each took up no more ground than two foot in breadth, and one in depth, 45000 might stand in a space that was but 100 yards square, and 21780 on a single acre of ground. There are many voices that may be heard at 100 yards distance.

The end of Passion is the beginning of Repentance.

Words may shew a man's Wit, but *Actions* his Meaning.

On the 18th of this month, *anno* 1546 died that famous reformer, LUTHER: who struck the great blow to papal tyranny in *Europe*. He was remarkably *temperate* in meat and drink, sometimes fasting four days together; and at other times, for many days eating only a little bread and a herring. *Cicero* says, *There was never any* great *man who was not an* industrious *man*; to which may, perhaps, be added, *There was never any* industrious *man who was not a* temperate *man*: For intemperance in diet, abates the vigour and dulls the action both of mind and body.

Of SOUND.

Mr. *Flamstead*, Dr. *Halley* and Mr. *Derham*, agree that sound moves 1142 feet in a second, which is one *English* mile in 4 seconds and 5 8ths; that it moves in the same time in every different state of the atmosphere; that winds hardly make any difference in its velocity; that a languid or loud sound moves with the same velocity; and that different kinds of sounds, as of bells, guns, &c. have the same velocity, and are equally swift in the beginning as end of their motion.

'Tis a well spent penny that saves a groat.

Many Foxes grow grey, but few grow good.

Presumption first blinds a Man, then sets him a running.

The nose of a lady here, is not delighted with perfumes that she understands are in *Arabia*. Fine musick in *China* gives no pleasure to the nicest ear in *Pennsilvania*. Nor does the most exquisite dish serv'd up in *Japan*, regale a luxurious palate in any other country. But the benevolent mind of a virtuous man, is pleas'd, when it is inform'd of good and generous actions, in what part of the world soever they are done.

————

A cold April,
The Barn will fill.

Content makes poor men rich; Discontent makes rich Men poor.

Too much plenty makes Mouth dainty.

————

On the 7th of this month, 1626, died that *great little* man, Sir FRANCIS BACON; *great* in his prodigious genius, parts and learning; and *little*, in his servile compliances with a *little* court, and submissive flattery of a *little* prince. *Pope* characterises him thus, in one strong line;

> *If Parts allure thee, think how* BACON *shin'd,*
> *The wisest, brightest, meanest of mankind.*

He is justly esteem'd the father of the modern experimental philosophy. And another poet treats him more favourably, ascribing his blemishes to a wrong unfortunate choice of his way of Life;

> ——— BACON, hapless in his choice,
> Unfit to stand the civil storm of state,
> And thro' the smooth barbarity of courts,
> With firm, but pliant virtue, forward still
> To urge his course. Him for the studious shade
> Kind nature form'd, deep, comprehensive, clear,
> Exact, and elegant; in one rich soul,
> PLATO, the STAGYRITE, and TULLY join'd.
> The great deliverer he! who from the gloom
> Of cloister'd monks, and jargon-teaching schools,
> Led forth the true Philosophy, there long
> Held in the magic chain of words and forms,
> And definitions void: He led her forth,
> Daughter of HEAV'N! that slow ascending still,
> Investigating sure the chain of things,
> With radiant finger points to HEAV'N again.

If *Passion* drives, let *Reason* hold the Reins.

> Neither trust, nor contend, nor lay wagers, nor lend;
> And you'll have peace to your Lives end.

Drink does not drown *Care*, but waters it, and makes it grow faster.

Who dainties love, shall Beggars prove.

———

On the 27th, anno 1564, died at *Geneva* that famous reformer, Mr. *John Calvin*, A man of equal *temperance* and *sobriety* with *Luther*, and perhaps yet greater *industry*. His lectures were yearly 186, his sermons yearly 286; he published besides every year some great volume in folio; to which add his constant employments, in governing the church, answering letters from all parts of the reformed world, from pastors, concerning doubts, or asking counsel, *&c. &c.* He ate little meat, and slept but very little; and as his whole time was filled up with useful action, he may be said to have *lived* long, tho' he died at 55 years of age; since *sleep* and *sloth* can hardly be called *living*.

———

A Man has no more *Goods* than he gets Good by.

Welcome, Mischief, if thou comest alone.

Different Sects like different clocks, may be all near the matter, 'tho they don't quite agree.

———

On the 15th of this month, anno 1215, was *Magna Charta* sign'd by King *John*, for declaring and establishing *English Liberty*.

———

It was wise counsel given to a young man, *Pitch upon that course of life which is most excellent, and* CUSTOM *will make it the most delightful*. But many pitch on no course of life at all, nor form any scheme of living, by which to attain any valuable end; but wander perpetually from one thing to another.

> Hast thou not yet propos'd some certain end,
> To which thy life, thy every act may tend?

Hast thou no mark at which to bend thy bow?
Or like a boy pursu'st the carrion crow
With pellets and with stones, from tree to tree,
A fruitless toil, and liv'st *extempore*?
Watch the disease in time: For when, within
The dropsy rages, and extends the skin,
In vain for helebore the patient cries,
And sees the doctor, but too late is wise:
Too late for cure, he proffers half his wealth;
Ten thousand doctors cannot give him health.
    Learn, wretches, learn the motions of the mind,
Why you were mad, for what you were design'd,
And the great *moral end* of human kind.
Study thy self; what rank or what degree,
The wise creator has ordain'd for thee:
And all the offices of that estate,
Perform, and with thy prudence guide thy fate.

If your head is wax, don't walk in the Sun.

> *Pretty* & *Witty*,
> will wound if they hit ye.

Having been poor is no shame, but being ashamed of it, is.

'Tis a laudable Ambition, that aims at being better than his Neighbours.

The wise Man draws more Advantage from his Enemies, than the Fool from his Friends.

PRIDE is said to be the *last* vice the good man gets clear of. 'Tis a meer *Proteus*, and disguises itself under all manner of appearances, putting on sometimes even the mask of *humility*. If some are proud of neatness and propriety of dress; others are equally so of despising it, and acting the perpetual sloven.

All would live long, but none would be old.

Declaiming against Pride, is not always a Sign of Humility.

Neglect kills Injuries, Revenge increases them.

9 Men in 10 are suicides.

Doing an Injury puts you below your Enemy; *Revenging* one makes you but *even* with him; *Forgiving* it sets you *above* him.

Most of the Learning in use, is of no great Use.

Great Good-nature, without Prudence, is a great Misfortune.

> Keep Conscience clear,
> Then never fear.

A Man in a Passion rides a mad Horse.

> Reader farewel, all Happiness attend thee;
> May each New-Year, better and richer find thee.

————

On the 25th of this month, *anno* 1642, was born the great Sir Isaac Newton, prince of the modern astronomers and philosophers. But what is all our little boasted knowledge, compar'd with that of the angels? If they see our actions, and are acquainted with our affairs, our whole body of science must appear to them as little better than ignorance; and the common herd of our learned men, scarce worth their notice. Now and then one of our very great philosophers, an *Aristotle*, or a *Newton*, may, perhaps, by his most refined speculations, afford them a little entertainment, as it seems a mimicking of their own sublime amusements. Hence *Pope* says of the latter,

> *Superior beings, when of late they saw*
> *A mortal man unfold all nature's law,*
> *Admir'd such wisdom in a human shape,*
> *And shew'd a* Newton, *as we shew an ape.*

————

How to get RICHES.

The Art of getting Riches consists very much in Thrift. All Men are not equally qualified for getting Money, but it is in the Power of every one alike to practise this Virtue.

He that would be beforehand in the World, must be beforehand with his Business: It is not only ill Management, but discovers a slothful Disposition, to do that in the Afternoon, which should have been done in the Morning.

Useful Attainments in your Minority will procure Riches in Maturity, of which Writing and Accounts are not the meanest.

Learning, whether Speculative or Practical, is, in Popular or Mixt Governments, the Natural Source of Wealth and Honour.

PRECEPT I.

In Things of moment, on thy self depend,
Nor trust too far thy Servant or thy Friend:
With private Views, thy Friend may promise fair,
And Servants very seldom prove sincere.

PRECEPT II.

What can be done, with Care perform to Day,
Dangers unthought-of will attend Delay;
Your distant Prospects all precarious are,
And Fortune is as fickle as she's fair.

PRECEPT III.

Nor trivial Loss, nor trivial Gain despise;
Molehills, if often heap'd, to Mountains rise:
Weigh every small Expence, and nothing waste,
Farthings long sav'd, amount to Pounds at last.

Poor Richard Improved, 1750

To the READER.

The Hope of acquiring lasting FAME, is, with many Authors, a most powerful Motive to Writing. Some, tho' few, have succeeded; and others, tho' perhaps fewer, may succeed here-after, and be as well known to Posterity by their Works, as the Antients are to us. We *Philomaths,* as ambitious of Fame as any other Writers whatever, after all our painful Watchings and laborious Calculations, have the constant Mortification to see our Works thrown by at the End of the Year, and treated as mere waste Paper. Our only Consolation is, that short-lived as they are, they out-live those of most of our Cotemporaries.

Yet, condemned to renew the *Sisyphean* Toil, we every Year heave another heavy Mass up the Muses Hill, which never can the Summit reach, and soon comes tumbling down again.

This, kind Reader, is my seventeenth Labour of the Kind. Thro' thy continued Good-will, they have procur'd me, if no *Bays*, at least *Pence*; and the latter is perhaps the better of the two; since 'tis not improbable that a Man may receive more solid Satisfaction from *Pudding*, while he is *living*, than from *Praise*, after he is *dead*.

In my last, a few Faults escap'd; some belong to the Author, but most to the Printer: Let each take his Share of the Blame, confess, and amend for the future. In the second Page of *August*, I mention'd 120 as the next perfect Number to 28; it was wrong, 120 being no perfect Number; the next to 28 I find to be 496. The first is 6; let the curious Reader, fond of mathematical Questions, find the fourth. In the 2d Page of *March*, in some Copies, the Earth's Circumference was said to be nigh 4000, instead of 24000 Miles, the Figure 2 being omitted at the Beginning. This was Mr. Printer's Fault; who being also somewhat niggardly of his Vowels, as well as profuse of his Consonants, put in one Place, among the Poetry, *mad*, instead of *made*, and in another *wrapp'd*, instead of *warp'd*; to the utter demolishing of all Sense in those Lines, leaving nothing standing but the Rhime. These, and some others, of the like kind, let the Readers forgive, or rebuke him for, as to their Wisdom and Goodness shall seem meet: For in such Cases the Loss and Damage is chiefly to the Reader, who, if he does not take my Sense at first Reading, 'tis odds he never gets it; for ten to one he does not read my Works a second Time.

Printers indeed should be very careful how they omit a Figure or a Letter: For by such Means sometimes a terrible Alteration is made in the Sense. I have heard, that once, in a new Edition of the *Common Prayer*, the following Sentence, *We shall all be changed in a Moment, in the Twinkling of an Eye*; by the Omission of a single Letter, became, *We shall all be hanged in a Moment*, &c. to the no small Surprize of the first Congregation it was read to.

May this Year prove a happy One to Thee and Thine, is the hearty Wish of, Kind Reader,

Thy obliged Friend,
R. SAUNDERS.

————

There are three Things extreamly hard, Steel, a Diamond and to know one's self.

Hunger is the best Pickle.

He is a Governor that governs his Passions, and he a Servant that serves them.

A Cypher and Humility make the other Figures & Virtues of ten-fold Value.

If it were not for the Belly, the Back might wear Gold.

Wouldst thou confound thine Enemy, be good thy self.

Pride is as loud a Beggar as *Want*, and a great deal more saucy.

Pay what you owe, and what you're worth you'll know.

Sorrow is good for nothing but Sin.

Many a Man thinks he is buying Pleasure, when he is really selling himself a Slave to it.

> Graft good Fruit all,
> Or graft not at all.

Tis hard (but glorious) to be poor and honest: An empty Sack can hardly stand upright; but if it does, 'tis a stout one!

He that can bear a Reproof, and mend by it, if he is not wise, is in a fair way of being so.

Beatus esse sine Virtute, nemo potest.

Sound, & sound Doctrine, may pass through a Ram's Horn, and a Preacher, without straitening the one, or amending the other.

Clean your Finger, before you point at my Spots.

He that spills the Rum, loses that only; He that drinks it, often loses both that and himself.

> That Ignorance makes devout, if right the Notion,
> 'Troth, *Rufus*, thou'rt a Man of great Devotion.

What an admirable Invention is Writing, by which a Man may communicate his Mind without opening his Mouth, and at 1000 Leagues Distance, and even to future Ages, only by the Help of 22 Letters, which may be joined 5852616738497664000 Ways, and will express all Things in a very narrow Compass. 'Tis a Pity this excellent Art has not preserved the Name and Memory of its Inventor.

Those that have much Business must have much Pardon.

Discontented Minds, and Fevers of the Body are not to be cured by changing Beds or Businesses.

> Little Strokes,
> Fell great Oaks.

You may be too cunning for One, but not for All.

Genius without Education is like Silver in the Mine.

Many would live by their Wits, but break for want of Stock.

Poor *Plain dealing*! dead without Issue!

You can bear your own Faults, and why not a Fault in your Wife.

Tho' Modesty is a Virtue, Bashfulness is a Vice.

> Hide not your Talents, they for Use were made.
> What's a Sun-Dial in the Shade!

What signifies knowing the Names, if you know not the Natures of Things.

Tim was so learned, that he could name a Horse in nine Languages; So ignorant, that he bought a Cow to ride on.

The Golden Age never was the present Age.

'Tis a Shame that your Family is an Honour to you! You ought to be an Honour to your Family.

Glass, China, and Reputation, are easily crack'd, and never well mended.

Poor Richard Improved, 1751

COURTEOUS READER,

Astrology is one of the most ancient Sciences, had in high Esteem of old, by the Wise and Great. Formerly, no Prince would make War or Peace, nor any General fight a Battle, in short, no important Affair was undertaken without first consulting an *Astrologer*, who examined the Aspects and Configurations of the heavenly Bodies, and mark'd the *lucky Hour*. Now the noble Art (more Shame to the Age we live in!) is dwindled into Contempt; the Great neglect us, Empires make Leagues, and Parliaments Laws, without advising with us; and scarce any other Use is made of our learned Labours, than to find the best Time of cutting Corns, or gelding Pigs.—This Mischief we owe in a great Measure to ourselves: The Ignorant Herd of Mankind, had they not been encourag'd to it by some of us, would never have dared to depreciate our sacred Dictates; but *Urania* has been betray'd by her own Sons; those whom she had favour'd with the greatest Skill in her divine Art, the most eminent Astronomers among the Moderns, the *Newtons*, *Halleys*, and *Whistons*, have wantonly contemn'd and abus'd her, contrary to the Light of their own Consciences. Of these, only the last nam'd, *Whiston*, has liv'd to repent, and speak his Mind honestly. In his former Works he had treated *Judiciary Astrology* as a Chimera, and asserted, That not only the fixed Stars, but the Planets (Sun and Moon excepted) were at so immense a Distance, as to be incapable of any Influence on this Earth, and consequently nothing could be foretold from their Positions: but now in the Memoirs of his Life, publish'd 1749, in the 82d Year of his Age, he foretels, Page 607, the sudden Destruction of the *Turkish* Empire, and of the House of *Austria*, *German* Emperors, *&c.* and *Popes* of *Rome*; the Restoration of the *Jews*, and Commencement of the *Millennium*; all by the Year 1766; and this not only from Scripture Prophecies; but (take his own Words)—"From the remarkable *astronomical* Signals that are to alarm Mankind of what is coming, *viz.* The *Northern Lights* since 1715; the six Comets at the Protestant Reformation in four Years, 1530, 1531, 1533, 1534, compar'd with the seven Comets already seen in these last eleven Years 1737, 1739, 1742, 1743, 1744, 1746, and 1748.—From the great Annular Eclipse of the Sun, *July* 14, 1748, whose Center pass'd through all the four Monarchies, from *Scotland* to the *East-Indies.*—From the Occultation of the *Pleiades* by the Moon each periodical Month, after the Eclipse last *July*, for above three Years, visible to the whole *Roman* Empire; as there was a like Occultation of the *Hyades* from *A.* 590, to *A.* 595, for six Years foretold by *Isaiah.*—From the Transit of *Mercury* over the *Sun*, *April* 25, 1753, which will be visible thro' that Empire.—From the Comet of *A. D.* 1456, 1531, 1607, and 1682, which will appear again about 1757 ending, or 1758 beginning, and will also be visible thro' that Empire.—From the Transit of *Venus* over the *Sun*, *May* 26, 1761, which will be visible over the same Empire: And lastly, from the annular Eclipse of the *Sun*, *March* 11, 1764, which will be visible over the same Empire."—From these *Astronomical Signs*, he foretels those great Events, That within 16 Years from this Time, "the *Millennium* or 1000 Years Reign of Christ shall begin, there shall be a *new Heavens*, and a *new Earth*; there shall be no more an Infidel in *Christendom*, Page 398, nor a Gaming-Table at *Tunbridge!*"—When these Predictions are accomplished, what glorious Proofs they will be of the Truth of our Art?—And if they happen to fail, there is no doubt but so profound an Astronomer as Mr. *Whiston*, will be able to see *other* Signs in the Heavens, foreshowing that the Conversion of Infidels was to be postponed, and the *Millennium* adjourn'd.—After these great Things can any Man doubt our being capable of predicting a little Rain or Sun-shine?—Reader, Farewell, and make the best Use of your Years and your Almanacks, for you see, that according to *Whiston*, you may have at most, but sixteen more of them.

R. SAUNDERS.

Patowmack, July 30, 1750.

Pray don't burn my House to roast your Eggs.

> Some *Worth* it argues, a Friend's *Worth* to know;
> *Virtue* to own the Virtue of a Foe.

Prosperity discovers Vice, Adversity Virtue.

The *Romans* were 477 Years, without so much as a Sun-dial to show the Time of Day: The first they had was brought from *Sicily*, by *Valerius Messala*: One hundred and eighteen Years afterwards, *Scipio Nasica*, produced to them an Invention for measuring the Hours in cloudy Weather, it was by the Dropping of Water out of one Vessel into another, somewhat like our Sand-Glasses. Clocks and Watches, to shew the Hour, are very modern Inventions. The Sub-dividing Hours into Minutes, and Minutes into Seconds, by those curious Machines, is not older than the Days of our Fathers, but now brought to a surprising Nicety.

Since our Time is reduced to a Standard, and the Bullion of the Day minted out into Hours, the Industrious know how to employ every Piece of Time to a real Advantage in their different Professions: And he that is prodigal of his Hours, is, in Effect, a Squanderer of Money. I remember a notable Woman, who was fully sensible of the intrinsic Value of *Time*. Her Husband was a Shoemaker, and an excellent Craftsman, but never minded how the Minutes passed. In vain did she inculcate to him, That *Time is Money*. He had too much Wit to apprehend her, and it prov'd his Ruin. When at the Ale-house among his idle Companions, if one remark'd that the Clock struck Eleven, *What is that, says he, among us all?* If she sent him Word by the Boy, that it had struck Twelve; *Tell her to be easy, it can never be more.* If, that it had struck One, *Bid her be comforted, for it can never be less.*

If we lose our Money, it gives us some Concern. If we are cheated or robb'd of it, we are angry: But Money lost may be found; what we are robb'd of may be restored: The Treasure of Time once lost, can never be recovered; yet we squander it as tho' 'twere nothing worth, or we had no Use for it.

> The Bell strikes *One*: We take no Note of Time,
> But from its Loss. To give it then a Tongue
> Is wise in Man. If heard aright

It is the Knell of our departed Hours;
Where are they? With the Years beyond the Flood:
It is the Signal that demands Dispatch;
How much is to be done?——
    Be wise To-day, 'tis Madness to defer;
Next day the fatal Precedent will plead;
Thus on, till Wisdom is push'd out of Life:
Procrastination is the Thief of Time,
Year after Year it steals till all are fled,
And to the Mercies of a Moment leaves
The vast Concerns of an eternal Scene.
If not so frequent, would not this be strange?
That 'tis so frequent, *This* is stranger still.

———

Many a Man would have been worse, if his Estate had been better.

We may give Advice, but we cannot give Conduct.

He that is conscious of a Stink in his Breeches, is jealous of every Wrinkle in another's Nose.

Love and *Tooth-ach* have many Cures, but none infallible, except *Possession* and *Dispossession.*

There are lazy Minds as well as lazy Bodies.

Most People return small Favours, acknowledge middling ones, and repay great ones with Ingratitude.

———

That admirable Instrument the MICROSCOPE has opened to us of these latter Ages, a World utterly unknown to the Ancients. There are very few Substances, in which it does not shew something curious and unexpected; but for the Sake of such Readers as are unacquainted with that Instrument, I shall set down some of the most remarkably entertaining Objects, upon which actual Observations have been made.

1. The Globules of the Blood, which are computed to be almost a two thousandth Part of an Inch in Diameter, each consisting of six small Globules, each of which again probably consists of six smaller, and so on. The Circulation of the Blood is to be seen very distinctly in the Tail of a small Fish,

the Web of the Foot of a Frog, &c. and the Globules to split and divide, before they can enter the smallest Vessels.

2. The Bones of all Creatures, sliced extremely thin, afford an entertaining Object for the Microscope, consisting of innumerable Perforations, and Ramifications, disposed in an endless Variety of Forms.

3. The Flesh of all Land and Sea Animals dried, and cut into very thin Slices, gives a beautiful View of the various Fibres, and their Convolutions. The Brain, the spinal Marrow, and even the Hairs of Animals, exhibit different Curiosities.

4. The human Skin, by the Help of the Microscope, is found to be covered over with an infinite Number of Scales lying over one another, as in fishes; and it is probably the same in other Animals. It has been computed that a Grain of Sand will cover two hundred of these Scales.

5. All Sorts of Feathers, especially those of the Peacock, afford a surprizing View in the Microscope. It is supposed that a single Feather contains no less than a Million of different Parts.

6. Flies are found by the Microscope to be produced from Eggs laid by the Mothers, from whence they are hatched in the Form of Maggots, or small Worms, which are afterwards transformed into Aurelias, and these into perfect Flies. This is the Process most of the winged Insects go through in their Production. They have a great Number of Eyes fixed to their Heads, so that they see on all Sides around them, without turning their Heads or Eyes. A common Fly is supposed to have eight thousand, and a great Drone Fly no less than fourteen thousand Eyes, with a distinct optic Nerve to each; and each Eye appears through the Microscope, tho' magnified many hundred thousand Times, more exactly shaped, and more curiously polished, than human Art could finish an Object as large as the whole Cluster, containing seven thousand distinct ones. The Wings of Flies, especially of the Moth and Butterfly Kind, are found to be contrived with admirable Art, to answer their Use, and with inimitable Beauty and Ornament. The Dust, which sticks to the Fingers, when we handle them, is found to be Feathers; each of which has its Quill and vane Parts as compleat as that of a Fowl or a Goose, and are

inserted in the Film of the Wing, with the utmost Regularity of Arrangement. With the Microscope, the Stings of Moths and Bees appear to be Instruments finished to the highest Perfection; their Points, and saw-like Teeth, being perfectly polished and sharp; whereas the Edge of a Razor appears like that of a Butcher's Cleaver, and the Point of a Lancet like an iron Spike just come from the Anvil.

7. By the Help of the Microscope the innumerable and inconceivably minute Animalcules in various Fluids are discovered, of the Existence of which we have no Reason to suppose any Mortal had the least Suspicion, till last Century. In the Melt of a single Cod-fish ten Times more living Creatures are contained, than the Inhabitants of *Europe*, *Asia*, *Africa*, and *America*, taking it for granted, that all Parts of the World are as well peopled as *Holland*, which is very far from being the Case. Of a certain Species some are discovered so extremely minute, that it has been computed, three Millions of them, or three Times the Number of the Inhabitants of *London* and *Westminster*, would not equal the Bulk of a Grain of Sand. Of Animalcules, some Species resemble Tadpoles, Serpents or Eels, others are of a roundish or oval Form, others of very curiously turned and various Shapes; but in general they are extremely vigorous and lively, and almost constantly in Motion. Animalcules are to be found (besides those in the Bodies of Animals) in the Infusions of Pepper, Senna, Pinks, Roses, Jessamin, Tea, Rasberry Stalks, Fennel, Sage, Melons, sour Grapes, Wheat, Hay, Straw, and almost all vegetable Substances; in the Water, that is in the Shells of Oysters, Cockles, and other Shell-fish, in the Foulness upon our Teeth, and those of other Animals, in our Skins when affected with certain Diseases; in Vinegar, and Paste, and so on infinitely. In each of these Substances, when exposed to the Air some Time, Multitudes of living Creatures, beyond the Reach of Numbers, are discovered, of which many Hundreds of Species are already known, as different from one another as those of the largest Animals, and very probably there are many more yet unknown. As it is certain, that in the above mentioned Fluids few or no Animalcules are to be found, when covered from the Air, but when open to the Access of the Air, their Numbers are

beyond reckoning; it is hardly to be doubted, but that either the Air is replete with infinite Multitudes of living Creatures too small for Sight, which come and deposite their Eggs in Places proper for the Nutrition of the Young, or that their Eggs are floating every where in the Air, and falling promiscuously every where, only those are hatched, or come to Perfection, which fall upon Places fitted for them, and the others perish. However it is, the countless Numbers of those living Creatures, the Profusion of Life every where to be observed, is above Measure astonishing, and shews the Maker to be an infinite Being.

8. By the Help of the Microscope, we find that the Scales of almost every different Fish are different from those of others, in internal Texture; and that all of them are wrought with surprising Art and Beauty.

9. By Means of this noble Instrument we find, that the Seeds of almost all Manner of Vegetables contain in them the Stamina of the future Plant or Tree, and that their Production from the Seed, and their Growth to Maturity is only the Swelling and Enlarging of the Stamina by the Addition of nutritious Juices. It is probable the Manner of Production and Growth of Animals is analogous to this. The Fertility of some Plants is almost beyond Belief. One particularly is said by Naturalists to produce annually a Million of Seeds from one. The Farina of Flowers is found by the Help of the Microscope to be a regular organized Body, and not a meer Dust, as it appears to the naked Eye, and is reasonably supposed to be necessary to Fertility in Plants and Trees.

10. By the Microscope have been discovered many singular Properties of that most unaccountable of all Creatures the Polype, which is found at the Bottom of Ditches, and standing Waters; whose Manner of Production, Feeding and Digestion, are different from those of all other Animals. The young ones come out of the Sides of the old, like Buds and Branches from Trees, and at length drop off perfect Polypes. They do not seem to be of different Sexes. They take in Worms, and other Sustenance, by Means of a Sett of long Arms or *Antennæ*, which surround their Mouths, and after keeping them some Time in their Stomachs, throw them out again the same Way. The Animal's Body consists of a single

Cavity, like a Tube or Gut, and what is wonderful, and almost beyond Belief, is, that it will live and feed after it is turned inside out, and even when cut into a great many Pieces, each several Piece becomes a compleat Polype. They are infested with a Kind of Vermin, as are almost all Animals from the largest down to Bees and other Insects. These Vermin sometimes in a long Time will eat up the Head and Part of the Body of a Polype, after which, if it be cleared of them, it shall have the devoured Parts grow up again, and become as compleat as ever. Some Polypes have around their Mouths a Sort of Plume, which they whirl round, and making with it an Eddy in the Water, draw in their Prey, and devour it.

11. By the Microscope it is found, that neither the Wood, the Bark, the Root, the Leaves, the Fruit, nor even the Pith of the meanest Vegetable is a Mass of crude or indigested Matter; but that every different Species is different in its internal Structure, and all curiously and delicately wrought. A Bit of Cork, cut extremely thin, a Slice of Oak or Fir, or a Bit of Elder Pith, in the Microscope, are so many curious Pieces of *Mosaic* Work. Even a Bit of Charcoal or burnt Wood appears with the Microscope an admirable Object.

12. By this Instrument it is found, that what we call Mouldiness upon Flesh, Leather, or other Substances, is no other than a great Number of extremely small, but perfect Plants, having Stalks and Tops like Mushrooms, and sometimes an Appearance of Leaves. The Seeds of these minute Plants must, in all Probability, be diffused universally through the Air, and falling upon Substances fit for their Growth, spring up in astonishing Profusion. There is, in short, no End of microscopic Objects. A Sprig of Moss, with the Help of that Instrument, is found to be a regular Plant, consisting of a Root, a Stock, Branches, Leaves, *&c.* and Naturalists tell us, there are some Hundreds of different Species of it. A Bit of Spunge before the Microscope is a curious Piece of Net-work. Every different chymical Salt has its Parts differently figured. A Leaf of a common stinging Nettle, the Beard of a wild Oat, the Surfaces of some Pebble-stones, a Flake of Snow, a few Grains of Sand, or almost any natural Thing, with this Instrument, exhibit exquisite Beauties; while, on the contrary, the

Nice Eaters seldom meet with a good Dinner.

Not to oversee Workmen, is to leave them your Purse open.

The Wise and Brave dares own that he was wrong.

Cunning proceeds from Want of Capacity.

———

It is an amusing Speculation to look back, and compute what Numbers of Men and Women among the Ancients, clubb'd their Endeavours to the Production of a single Modern. As you reckon backwards the Number encreases in the same Proportion as the Price of the Coat which was sold for a Half-penny a Button, continually doubled.

Thus, a present Nobleman (for Instance) is			1
His Father and Mother were			2
His Grandfathers and Grandmothers			4
His Great Grandfathers and Great Grandmothers,			8
And, supposing no Intermarriages among Relations,			
the next Predecessors will be			16
The next Ditto,	32	The next Ditto,	8192
The next Ditto,	64	The next Ditto,	16384
The next Ditto,	128	The next Ditto,	32768
The next Ditto,	256	The next Ditto,	65536
The next Ditto,	512	The next Ditto,	131072
The next Ditto,	1024	The next Ditto,	262144
The next Ditto,	2048	The next Ditto,	524288
The next Ditto,	4096	The next Do.	1048576

Here are only computed 21 Generations, which, allowing 3 Generations to 100 Years, carry us back no farther than the *Norman* Conquest, at which Time each present Nobleman, to exclude all ignoble Blood from his Veins, ought to have had One Million, Forty-eight Thousand, Five Hundred and Seventy-six noble Ancestors. Carry the Reckoning back 300 Years farther, and the Number amounts to above 500 Millions; which are more than exist at any one Time upon Earth, and shews the Impossibility of preserving Blood free from such Mixtures, and that the Pretension of such Purity of Blood in ancient Families is a mere Joke. Hence we see how it happens that every Nation has a kind of general Cast of Feature, by which it may be distinguished; continual Intermarriages for a

Course of Ages rendring all the People related by Blood, and, as it were, of one Family.

———

The Proud hate Pride—in others.

Who judges best of a Man, his Enemies or himself?

Drunkenness, that worst of Evils, makes some Men Fools, some Beasts, some Devils.

'Tis not a Holiday that's not kept holy.

Poor Richard Improved, 1752

KIND READER,

Since the King and Parliament have thought fit to alter our Year, by taking eleven Days out of *September*, 1752, and directing us to begin our Account for the future on the First of *January*, some Account of the Changes the Year hath heretofore undergone, and the Reasons of them, may a little gratify thy Curiosity.

The Vicissitude of *Seasons* seems to have given Occasion to the first Institution of the *Year*. Man naturally curious to know the Cause of that Diversity, soon found it was the Nearness and Distance of the Sun; and upon this, gave the Name *Year* to the Space of Time wherein that Luminary, performing his whole Course, returned to the same Point of his Orbit.

And hence, as it was on Account of the Seasons, in a great Measure, that the *Year* was instituted, their chief Regard and Attention was, that the same Parts of the *Year* should always correspond to the same Seasons; *i. e.* that the Beginning of the Year should always be when the Sun was in the same Point of his Orbit; and that they should keep Pace, come round, and end together.

This, different Nations aimed to attain by different Ways; making the *Year* to commence from different Points of the Zodiac; and even the Time of his Progress different. So that some of their Years were much more perfect than others, but none of them quite just; *i. e.* none of them but whose Parts shifted with Regard to the Parts of the Sun's Course.

It was the *Egyptians*, if we may credit *Herodotus*, that first formed the *Year*, making it to contain 360 Days, which they subdivided into twelve Months, of thirty Days each.

Mercury Trismegistus added five Days more to the Account.—And on this Footing *Thales* is said to have instituted the Year among the *Greeks.* Tho' that Form of the Year did not hold throughout all *Greece.* Add that the *Jewish, Syrian, Roman, Persian, Ethiopic, Arabic,* &c. Years, are all different.

In effect, considering the poor State of Astronomy in those Ages, it is no Wonder different People should disagree in the Calculus of the Sun's Course. We are even assured by *Diodorus Siculus, Plutarch,* and *Pliny,* that the *Egyptian Year* itself was at first very different from what it became afterwards.

According to our Account, the *Solar Year,* or the Interval of Time in which the Sun finishes his Course thro' the Zodiac, and returns to the same Point thereof from which he had departed, is 365 Days, 5 Hours, 49 Minutes; tho' some Astronomers make it a few Seconds, and some a whole Minute less; as *Kepler,* for Instance, who makes it 365 Days, 5 Hours, 48 Minutes, 57 Seconds, 39 Thirds. *Ricciolus,* 365 Days, 5 Hours, 48 Minutes. *Tycho Brahe,* 365 Days, 5 Hours, 48 Minutes.

The *Civil Year* is that Form of the *Year* which each Nation has contrived to compute Time by; or the *Civil* is the *Tropical Year,* considered as only consisting of a certain Number of whole Days; the odd Hours and Minutes being set aside, to render the Computation of Time in the common Occasions of Life more easy.

Hence as the *Tropical Year* is 365 Days, 5 Hours, 49 Minutes; the *Civil Year* is 365 Days. And hence also, as it is necessary to keep Pace with the Heavens, it is required that every fourth Year consist of 366 Days, which would for ever keep the Year exactly right, if the odd Hours of each Year were precisely 6.

The ancient *Roman Year,* as first settled by *Romulus,* consisted of ten Months only; *viz.* I. *March,* containing 31 Days. II. *April,* 30. III. *May,* 31. IV. *June* 30. V. *Quintilis,* 31. VI. *Sextilis,* 30. VII. *September,* 30. VIII. *October,* 31. IX. *November,*

30. X. *December*, 30; in all 304 Days; which came short of the *Solar Year*, by 61 Days.

Hence the Beginning of *Romulus*'s Year was vague, and unfixed to any precise Season; which Inconvenience to remove, that Prince ordered so many Days to be added yearly, as would make the State of the Heavens correspond to the first Month, without incorporating these additional Days, or calling them by the Name of any Month.

Numa Pompilius corrected this irregular Constitution of the Year, and composed two new Months, *January* and *February*, of the Days that were used to be added to the former Year. Thus, *Numa*'s *Year* consisted of twelve Months; *viz.* I. *January*, containing 29 Days. II. *February*, 28. III. *March*, 31. IV. *April*, 29. V. *May*, 31. VI. *June*, 29. VII. *Quintilis*, 31. VIII. *Sextilis*, 29. IX. *September*, 29. X. *October*, 31. XI. *November*, 29. XII. *December*, 29; in all 355 Days, which came short of the common Solar Year by ten Days; so that its Beginning was vague and unfixed.

Numa, however, desiring to have it fixed to the Winter Solstice, ordered 22 Days to be intercalated in *February* every second Year, 23 every fourth, 22 every sixth, and 23 every eighth Year.

But this Rule failing to keep Matters even, Recourse was had to a new Way of Intercalating; and instead of 23 Days every eighth Year, only 15 were added; and the Care of the whole committed to the *Pontifex Maximus*, or High Priest; who, neglecting the Trust, let Things run to the utmost Confusion. And thus the *Roman* Year stood till *Julius Cæsar* made a Reformation.

The *Julian Year*, is a Solar Year, containing commonly 365 Days; tho' every fourth Year, called *Bissextile*, contains 366.— The Names and Order of the Months of the *Julian Year*, and the Number of Days in each, are well known to us, having been long in Use.

The astronomical Quantity, therefore, of the *Julian Year*, is 365 Days, 6 Hours, which exceeds the true Solar Year by 11 Minutes; which Excess in 131 Years amounts to a whole Day.—And thus the *Roman Year* stood, till the Reformation made therein by Pope *Gregory*.

Julius Cæsar, in the Contrivance of his Form of the Year,

was assisted by *Sosigenes*, a famous Mathematician, called over from *Egypt* for this very Purpose; who, to supply the Defect of 67 Days which had been lost thro' the Fault of the High Priests, and to fix the Beginning of the Year to the Winter Solstice, made that Year to consist of 15 Months, or 445 Days; which for that Reason is used to be called *Annus Confusionis*, the *Year of Confusion*.

This Form of the Year was used by all Christian Nations, till the Middle of the 16th Century; and still continues to be so by several Nations; among the Rest, by the *Swedes*, *Danes*, &c. and by the *English* till the second of *September* next, when they are to assume the Use of the *Gregorian Year*.

The GREGORIAN YEAR is the *Julian Year* corrected by this Rule; that whereas on the common Footing, every Secular or Hundredth Year, is *Bissextile*; on the new Footing, three of them are common Years, and only the fourth *Bissextile*.

The Error of eleven Minutes in the *Julian Year*, little as it was, yet, by being repeated over and over, at length became considerable; and from the Time when *Cæsar* made his Correction, was grown into 13 Days, by which the Equinoxes were greatly disturbed. To remedy this Irregularity, which was still a growing, Pope *Gregory* the XIII. called together the chief Astronomers of his Time, and concerted this Correction; and to restore the Equinoxes to their Place threw out the ten Days that had been got from the Council of *Nice*, and which had shifted the fifth of *October* to the 15th.

In the Year 1700, the Error of ten Days was grown to eleven; upon which the Protestant States of *Germany*, to prevent further Confusion, accepted the *Gregorian* Correction. And now in 1752, the *English* follow their Example.

Yet is the *Gregorian Year* far from being perfect, for we have shewn, that, in four Centuries, the *Julian Year* gains three Days, one Hour, twenty Minutes: But it is only the three Days are kept out in the *Gregorian Year*; so that here is still an Excess of one Hour, twenty Minutes, in four Centuries; which in 72 Centuries will amount to a whole Day.

As to the Commencement of the Year, the *legal Year* in *England* used to begin on the Day of the *Annunciation*; *i. e.* on the 25th of *March*; tho' the historical Year began on the Day of the *Circumcision*; *i. e.* the first of *January*, on which

Day the *Italian* and *German* Year also begins; and on which Day ours is to begin from this Time forward, the first Day of *January* being now by Act of Parliament declared the first Day of the Year 1752.

At the Yearly Meeting of the People called *Quakers*, held in *London*, since the Passing of this Act, it was agreed to recommend to their Friends a Conformity thereto, both in omitting the eleven Days of *September* thereby directed to be omitted, and beginning the Year hereafter on the first Day of the Month called *January*, which is henceforth to be by them called and written, *The First Month*, and the rest likewise in their Order, so that *September* will now be the *Ninth Month*, *December* the *Twelfth*.

This *Act of Parliament*, as it contains many Matters of Importance, and extends expresly to all the *British Colonies*, I shall for the Satisfaction of the Publick, give at full length: Wishing withal, according to ancient Custom, that this *New Year* (which is indeed a New Year, such an one as we never saw before, and shall never see again) may be a happy Year to all my kind Readers.

> I am, Your faithful Servant,
> R. SAUNDERS.

––––––

Observe old *Vellum*; he praises former Times, as if he'd a mind to sell 'em.

Kings have long Arms, but Misfortune longer: Let none think themselves out of her Reach.

For want of a Nail the Shoe is lost; for want of a Shoe, the Horse is lost; for want of a Horse the Rider is lost.

The busy Man has few idle Visitors; to the boiling Pot the Flies come not.

Calamity and Prosperity are the Touchstones of Integrity.

The Prodigal generally does more Injustice than the Covetous.

Generous Minds are all of kin.

'Tis more noble to forgive, and more manly to despise, than to revenge an Injury.

A Brother may not be a Friend, but a Friend will always be a Brother.

Meanness is the Parent of Insolence.

Mankind are very odd Creatures: One Half censure what they practise, the other half practise what they censure; the rest always say and do as they ought.

Severity is often Clemency; Clemency Severity.

Bis dat qui cito dat: He gives twice that gives soon; *i. e.* he will soon be called upon to give again.

A Temper to bear much, will have much to bear.

Pride dines upon Vanity, sups on Contempt.

Great Merit is coy, as well as great Pride.

An undutiful Daughter, will prove an unmanageable Wife.

Old Boys have their Playthings as well as young Ones; the Difference is only in the Price.

The too obliging Temper is evermore disobliging itself.

Hold your Council before Dinner; the full Belly hates Thinking as well as Acting.

The Brave and the Wise can both pity and excuse; when Cowards and Fools shew no Mercy.

Ceremony is not Civility; nor Civility Ceremony.

If Man could have Half his Wishes, he would double his Troubles.

It is ill Jesting with the Joiner's Tools, worse with the Doctor's.

Children and Princes will quarrel for Trifles.

Praise to the undeserving, is severe Satyr.

Success has ruin'd many a Man.

> Great Pride and Meanness sure are near ally'd;
> Or thin Partitions do their Bounds divide.

Poor Richard Improved, 1753

COURTEOUS READER,

This is the twentieth Time of my addressing thee in this Manner, and I have reason to flatter myself my Labours have not been unacceptable to the Publick. I am particularly pleas'd to understand that my *Predictions of the Weather* give such general Satisfaction; and indeed, such Care is taken in the Calculations, on which those Predictions are founded, that I could almost venture to say, there's not a single One of them, promising *Snow*, *Rain*, *Hail*, *Heat*, *Frost*, *Fogs*, *Wind*, or *Thunder*, but what comes to pass *punctually* and *precisely* on the very Day, in some Place or other on this little *diminutive* Globe of ours; (and when you consider the vast Distance of the Stars from whence we take our Aim, you must allow it no small Degree of Exactness to hit any Part of it) I say on this Globe; for tho' in other Matters I confine the Usefulness of my *Ephemeris* to the *Northern Colonies*, yet in that important Matter of the Weather, which is of such *general Concern*, I would have it more extensively useful, and therefore take in both Hemispheres, and all Latitudes from *Hudson's Bay* to *Cape Horn*.

You will find this Almanack in my former Method, only conformable to the *New-Stile* established by the Act of Parliament, which I gave you in my last at length; the new Act since made for Amendment of that first Act, not affecting us in the least, being intended only to regulate some Corporation Matters in *England*, before unprovided for. I have only added a Column in the second Page of each Month, containing the Days of the *Old Stile* opposite to their corresponding Days in the *New*, which may, in many Cases, be of Use; and so conclude (believing you will excuse a short Preface, when it is to make Room for something better)

Thy Friend and Servant,
R. SAUNDERS.

———

'Tis against some Mens Principle to pay Interest, and seems against others Interest to pay the Principal.

Philosophy as well as Foppery often changes Fashion.

Setting too good an Example is a Kind of Slander seldom forgiven; 'tis *Scandalum Magnatum.*

A great Talker may be no Fool, but he is one that relies on him.

When Reason preaches, if you won't hear her she'll box your Ears.

It is not Leisure that is not used.

The Good-will of the Governed will be starv'd, if not fed by the good Deeds of the Governors.

Paintings and Fightings are best seen at a distance.

> If you would reap Praise you must sow the Seeds, Gentle Words and useful Deeds.

Ignorance leads Men into a Party, and *Shame* keeps them from getting out again.

Haste makes Waste.

Many have quarrel'd about Religion, that never practis'd it.

Sudden Power is apt to be insolent, *Sudden Liberty* saucy; that behaves best which has grown gradually.

He that best understands the World, least likes it.

Anger is never without a Reason, but seldom with a good One.

He that is of Opinion Money will do every Thing, may well be suspected of doing every Thing for Money.

An ill Wound, but not an ill Name, may be healed.

When out of Favour, none know thee; when in, thou dost not know thyself.

A lean Award is better than a fat Judgment.

God, *Parents*, and *Instructors*, can never be requited.

He that builds before he counts the Cost, acts foolishly; and he that counts before he builds, finds he did not count wisely.

Patience in Market, is worth Pounds in a Year.

Danger is Sauce for Prayers.

If you have no Honey in your Pot, have some in your Mouth.

A Pair of good Ears will drain dry an hundred Tongues.

Serving God is Doing Good to Man, but Praying is thought an easier Service, and therefore more generally chosen.

Nothing humbler than *Ambition*, when it is about to climb.

The discontented Man finds no easy Chair.

Virtue and a Trade, are a Child's best Portion.

Gifts much expected, are *paid*, not *given*.

————

How to secure Houses, &c. from LIGHTNING.

It has pleased God in his Goodness to Mankind, at length to discover to them the Means of securing their Habitations and other Buildings from Mischief by Thunder and Lightning. The Method is this: Provide a small Iron Rod (it may be made of the Rod-iron used by the Nailers) but of such a Length, that one End being three or four Feet in the moist Ground, the other may be six or eight Feet above the highest Part of the Building. To the upper End of the Rod fasten about a Foot of Brass Wire, the Size of a common Knitting-needle, sharpened to a fine Point; the Rod may be secured to the House by a few small Staples. If the House or Barn be long, there may be a Rod and Point at each End, and a middling Wire along the Ridge from one to the other. A House thus furnished will not be damaged by Lightning, it being attracted by the Points, and passing thro the Metal into the Ground without hurting any Thing. Vessels also, having a sharp pointed Rod fix'd on the Top of their Masts, with a Wire from the Foot of the Rod reaching down, round one of the Shrouds, to the Water, will not be hurt by Lightning.

Poor Richard Improved, 1754

Kind READER,

I have now serv'd you three Apprenticeships, yet, old as I am, I have no Inclination to quit your Service, but should be glad to be able to continue in it three times three Apprenticeships longer.

The first *Astrologers* I think, were honest Husbandmen; and so it seems are the last; for my Brethren *Jerman* and *Moore,* and myself, the only remaining Almanack-makers of this Country, are all of that Class: Tho' in intermediate Times our Art has been cultivated in great Cities, and even in the Courts of Princes; witness History, from the Days of King NEBUCHADNEZZAR I. of *Babylon,* to those of Queen JAMES I. of *England.*—But you will ask, perhaps, how I prove that the first Astrologers were Countrymen?—I own this is a Matter beyond the Memory of History, for Astrology was before Letters; but I prove it from the Book of the Heavens, from the Names of the twelve Signs, which were mostly given to remark some Circumstance relative to rural Affairs, in the several successive Months of the Year, and by that Means to supply the Want of Almanacks.—Thus, as the Year of the Ancients began most naturally with the Spring, *Aries* and *Taurus,* that is, the Ram and the Bull, represented the successive Addition to their Flocks of Sheep and Kine, by their Produce in that Season, Lambs and Calves.—*Gemini* were originally the Kids, but called the Twins, as Goats more commonly bring forth two than one: These follow'd the Calves.—*Cancer,* the Crab, came next, when that Kind of Fish were in Season.—Then follow'd *Leo,* the Lion, and *Virgo,* the Wench, to mark the Summer Months, and Dog-days, when those Creatures were most mischievous. In Autumn comes first *Libra,* the Ballance, to point out the Time for weighing and selling the Summer's Produce; or rather, a Time of Leisure for holding Courts of Justice in which they might plague themselves and Neighbours; I know some suppose this Sign to signify the equal Poise, at that Time, of Day and Night; but the other Signification is the truer, as plainly appears by the following Sign *Scorpio,* or the Scorpion, with the Sting in his Tail, which certainly denotes the Paying of Costs.—Then follows *Sagittary*, the Archer, to show the Season of Hunting; for now the Leaves being off the Trees and Bushes, the Game might be more easily seen and struck with their Arrows.—The *Goat* accompanies the short Days and long Nights of Winter, to shew the Season of Mirth, Feasting and Jollity; for what can *Capricorn* mean, but Dancing or Cutting of *Capers*?—At length comes *Aquarius*, or the Water-bearer, to show the Season of Snows, Rains and Floods; and lastly *Pisces*, or the two Shads, to denote the approaching Return of those Fish up the Rivers: Make your Wears, hawl your Seins; Catch 'em and pickle 'em, my Friends; they are excellent Relishers of old Cyder.—But if you can't get Shad, Mackrell may do better.

I know, gentle Readers, that many of you always expect a Preface, and think yourselves slighted if that's omitted. So here you have it, and much good may't do ye. As little as it is to the Purpose, there are many less so, now-a-days.—I have left out, you see, all the usual Stuff about the *Importunity of Friends*, and the like, or I might have made it much bigger. You think, however, that 'tis big enough o'Conscience, for any Matter of Good that's in it;—I think so too, if it fills the Page, which is the Needful at present, from

Your loving Friend to serve,

R. SAUNDERS.

The first Degree of Folly, is to conceit one's self wise; the second to profess it; the third to despise Counsel.

Take heed of the Vinegar of sweet Wine, and the Anger of Good-nature.

The Bell calls others to Church, but itself never minds the Sermon.

Cut the Wings of your Hens and Hopes, lest they lead you a weary Dance after them.

In Rivers & bad Governments, the lightest Things swim at top.

The Cat in Gloves catches no Mice.

If you'd know the Value of Money, go and borrow some.

The Horse thinks one thing, and he that saddles him another.

Love your Neighbour; yet don't pull down your Hedge.

When *Prosperity* was well mounted, she let go the Bridle, and soon came tumbling out of the Saddle.

Some make Conscience of wearing a Hat in the Church, who make none of robbing the Altar.

In the Affairs of this World Men are saved, not by Faith, but by the Want of it.

Friendship cannot live with *Ceremony*, nor without *Civility*.

Praise little, dispraise less.

The learned Fool writes his Nonsense in better Language than the unlearned; but still 'tis Nonsense.

A Child thinks 20 *Shillings* and 20 Years can scarce ever be spent.

Don't think so much of your own Cunning, as to forget other Mens: A cunning Man is overmatch'd by a cunning Man and a Half.

Willows are weak, but they bind the Faggot.

You may give a Man an Office, but you cannot give him Discretion.

He that doth what he should not, shall feel what he would not.

To be intimate with a foolish Friend, is like going to bed to a Razor.

Little Rogues easily become great Ones.

You may sometimes be much in the wrong, in owning your being in the right.

Friends are the true Sceptres of Princes.

Where Sense is wanting, every thing is wanting.

Many Princes sin with *David*, but few repent with him.

He that hath no *ill* Fortune will be troubled with *good*.

For Age and Want save while you may;
No Morning Sun lasts a whole Day.

Learning to the Studious; Riches to the Careful; Power to
the Bold; Heaven to the Virtuous.

Now glad the Poor with *Christmas* Cheer;
Thank God you're able so to end the Year.

Poor Richard Improved, *1755*

Courteous READER,

It is a common Saying, that *One Half of the World does not
know how the other Half lives.* To add somewhat to your
Knowledge in that Particular, I gave you in a former Almanack, an Account of the Manner of living at *Hudson's-Bay*,
and the Effects produced by the excessive Cold of that Climate, which seem'd so strange to some of you, that it was
taken for a Romance, tho' really authentick.—In this, I shall
give you some Idea of a Country under the Torrid Zone,
which for the Variety of its Weather (where one would naturally expect the greatest Uniformity) is extreamly remarkable.
The Account is extracted from the Journal of Monsieur *Bouguer*, one of the *French* Academicians, sent by their King to
measure a Degree of Latitude under the Equinoctial, in order
to settle a Dispute between the *English* and *French* Philosophers concerning the Shape of the Earth, others being at the
same Time sent for the same Purpose to *Lapland*, under the
Polar Circle.—The Mountains in that Country are so lofty,
that the highest we have, being compared to them, are mere
Mole-hills. This Extract relates chiefly to the Country among
those Mountains.

The Method of this Almanack is the same I have observed
for some Years past; only in the third Column the Names of
some of the principal fixed Stars are put down against those
Days on which they come to the Meridian at nine a Clock in
the Evening, whereby those unacquainted, may learn to know
them. I am,

Your obliged Friend and Servant,
R. SAUNDERS.

A Man without a Wife, is but half a Man.

Speak little, do much.

He that would travel much, should eat little.

When the Wine enters, out goes the Truth.

If you would be loved, love and be loveable.

Ask and have, is sometimes dear buying.

The hasty Bitch brings forth blind Puppies.

Where there is Hunger, Law is not regarded; and where
Law is not regarded, there will be Hunger.

Two dry Sticks will burn a green One.

The honest Man takes Pains, and then enjoys Pleasures; the
Knave takes Pleasure, and then suffers Pains.

Think of three Things, whence you came, where you are
going, and to whom you must account.

Necessity has no Law; Why? Because 'tis not to be had
without Money.

There was never a good Knife made of bad Steel.

The Wolf sheds his Coat once a Year, his Disposition never.

> *Who is wise?* He that learns from every One.
> *Who is powerful?* He that governs his Passions.
> *Who is rich?* He that is content.
> *Who is that?* Nobody.

A full Belly brings forth every Evil.

The Day is short, the Work great, the Workmen lazy, the
Wages high, the Master urgeth; Up, then, and be doing.

The Doors of Wisdom are never shut.

Much Virtue in Herbs, little in Men.

The Master's Eye will do more Work than both his Hands.

When you taste Honey, remember Gall.

Being ignorant is not so much a Shame, as being unwilling to learn.

God gives all Things to Industry.

An hundred Thieves cannot strip one naked Man, especially if his Skin's off.

Diligence overcomes Difficulties, Sloth makes them.

Neglect mending a small Fault, and 'twill soon be a great One.

Bad Gains are truly Losses.

A long Life may not be good enough, but a good Life is long enough.

Be at War with your Vices, at Peace with your Neighbours, and let every New-Year find you a better Man.

Poor Richard Improved, 1756

COURTEOUS READER,

I suppose my Almanack may be worth the Money thou hast paid for it, hadst thou no other Advantage from it, than to find the *Day of the Month*, the *remarkable Days*, the *Changes of the Moon*, the *Sun and Moon's Rising and Setting*, and to foreknow the *Tides* and the *Weather*; these, with other Astronomical Curiosities, I have yearly and constantly prepared for thy Use and Entertainment, during now near two Revolutions of the Planet *Jupiter*. But I hope this is not all the Advantage thou hast reaped; for with a View to the Improvement of thy *Mind* and thy *Estate*, I have constantly interspers'd in every little Vacancy, *Moral Hints*, *Wise Sayings*, and *Maxims of Thrift*, tending to impress the Benefits arising from *Honesty*, *Sobriety*, *Industry* and *Frugality*; which if thou hast duly observed, it is highly probable thou art *wiser* and *richer* many fold more than the Pence my Labours have cost thee. Howbeit, I shall not therefore raise my Price because thou art better able to pay; but being thankful for past Favours, shall endeavour to make my little Book more worthy thy Regard, by adding to those *Recipes* which were intended for the *Cure* of the *Mind*, some valuable Ones regarding the *Health* of the *Body*. They are recommended by the Skilful, and by successful Practice. I wish a Blessing may attend the Use of them, and to thee all Happiness, being

Thy obliged Friend,
R. SAUNDERS.

A Change of *Fortune* hurts a wise Man no more than a Change of the *Moon*.

> Does Mischief, Misconduct, & Warrings displease ye;
> Think there's a Providence, 'twill make ye easy.

Mine is better than *Ours*.

Love your Enemies, for they tell you your Faults.

He that has a Trade, has an Office of Profit and Honour.

Be civil to *all*; serviceable to *many*; familiar with *few*; Friend to *one*; Enemy to *none*.

Vain-Glory flowereth, but beareth no Fruit.

As I spent some Weeks last Winter, in visiting my old Acquaintance in the *Jerseys*, great Complaints I heard for Want of Money, and that Leave to make more Paper Bills could not be obtained. *Friends and Countrymen*, my Advice on this Head shall cost you nothing, and if you will not be angry with me for giving it, I promise you not to be offended if you do not take it.

You spend yearly at least *Two Hundred Thousand Pounds*, 'tis said, in *European*, *East-Indian*, and *West-Indian* Commodities: Supposing one Half of this Expence to be in *Things absolutely necessary*, the other Half may be call'd *Superfluities*, or at best, Conveniences, which however you might live without for one little Year, and not suffer exceedingly. Now to save this Half, observe these few Directions.

1. When you incline to have new Cloaths, look first well over the old Ones, and see if you cannot shift with them another Year, either by Scouring, Mending, or even Patching if necessary. Remember a Patch on your Coat, and Money in your Pocket, is better and more creditable than a Writ on your Back, and no Money to take it off.

2. When you incline to buy China Ware, Chinces, *India* Silks, or any other of their flimsey slight Manufactures; I would not be so hard with you, as to insist on your absolutely *resolving against it*; all I advise, is, to *put it off* (as you do your Repentance) *till another Year*; and this, in some Respects, may prevent an Occasion of Repentance.

3. If you are now a Drinker of Punch, Wine or Tea, twice a Day; for the ensuing Year drink them but *once* a Day. If you now drink them but once a Day, do it but every other Day. If you do it now but once a Week, reduce the Practice to once a Fortnight. And if you do not exceed in Quantity as you lessen the Times, half your Expence in these Articles will be saved.

4thly and lastly, When you incline to drink Rum, fill the Glass *half* with Water.

Thus at the Year's End, there will be *An Hundred Thousand Pounds* more Money in your Country.

If Paper Money in ever so great a Quantity could be made, no Man could get any of it without giving something for it. But all he saves in this Way, will be *his own for nothing*; and his Country actually so much richer. Then the Merchants old and doubtful Debts may be honestly paid off, and Trading become surer thereafter, if not so extensive.

————

Laws *too gentle* are seldom *obeyed*; *too severe*, seldom *executed*.

Trouble springs from *Idleness*; *Toil* from *Ease*.

Love, and be *loved*.

A wise Man will desire no more, than what he may get justly, use soberly, distribute chearfully, and leave contentedly.

The diligent Spinner has a large Shift.

A false Friend and a Shadow, attend only while the Sun shines.

To-morrow, every Fault is to be amended; but that *To-morrow* never comes.

> Plough deep, while Sluggards sleep;
> And you shall have Corn, to sell and to keep.

He that sows Thorns, should never go barefoot.

Laziness travels so slowly, that *Poverty* soon overtakes him.

Sampson with his *strong Body*, had a *weak Head*, or he would not have laid it in a Harlot's Lap.

> When a Friend deals with a Friend
> Let the Bargain be clear and well penn'd,
> That they may continue Friends to the End.

He that never eats too much, will never be lazy.

To be *proud* of *Knowledge*, is to be *blind* with *Light*; to be *proud* of *Virtue*, is to *poison* yourself with the *Antidote*.

> Get what you can, and what you get, hold;
> 'Tis the *Stone* that will turn all your Lead into Gold.

An honest Man will receive neither *Money* nor *Praise*, that is not his Due.

————

Well, my Friend, thou art now just entering the last Month of another Year. If thou art a Man of Business, and of prudent Care, belike thou wilt now settle thy Accounts, to satisfy thyself whether thou hast gain'd or lost in the Year past, and how much of either, the better to regulate thy future Industry or thy common Expences. This is commendable.—But it is not all.—Wilt thou not examine also thy *moral* Accompts, and see what Improvements thou hast made in the Conduct of Life, what Vice subdued, what Virtue acquired; how much *better*, and how much *wiser*, as well as how much *richer* thou art grown? What shall it *profit* a Man, if he *gain* the whole World, and *lose* his own Soul? Without some Care in this Matter, tho' thou may'st come to count thy Thousands, thou wilt possibly still appear poor in the Eyes of the Discerning, even *here*, and be really so for ever *hereafter*.

Saying and *Doing*, have quarrel'd and parted.

Tell me my Faults, and mend your own.

Poor Richard Improved, 1757

COURTEOUS READER,

As no temporal Concern is of more Importance to us than *Health*, and that depends so much on the Air we every Moment breathe, the Choice of a good wholesome Situation to fix a Dwelling in, is a very serious Affair to every Countryman about to begin the World, and well worth his Consideration, especially as not only the *Comfort* of Living, but even the *Necessaries of Life*, depend in a great Measure upon it; since a Family frequently sick can rarely if ever thrive.—The following Extracts therefore from a late Medical Writer, Dr. *Pringle*, on that Subject, will, I hope, be acceptable and useful to some of my Readers.

I hear that some have already, to their great Advantage, put in Practice the Use of Oxen recommended in my last.—'Tis a Pleasure to me to be any way serviceable in communicating useful Hints to the Publick; and I shall be obliged to others for affording me the Opportunity of enjoying that Pleasure more frequently, by sending me from time to time such of their own Observations, as may be advantageous if published in the Almanack.

I am thy obliged Friend,
RICHARD SAUNDERS.

———

How to make a STRIKING SUNDIAL, *by which not only a Man's own Family, but all his Neighbours for ten Miles round, may know what o Clock it is, when the Sun shines, without seeing the Dial.*

Chuse an open Place in your Yard or Garden, on which the Sun may shine all Day without any Impediment from Trees or Buildings. On the Ground mark out your Hour Lines, as for a horizontal Dial, according to Art, taking Room enough for the Guns. On the Line for One o' Clock, place one Gun;

on the Two o' Clock Line two Guns, and so of the rest. The Guns must all be charged with Powder, but Ball is unnecessary. Your Gnomon or Style must have twelve burning Glasses annex'd to it, and be so placed as that the Sun shining through the Glasses, one after the other, shall cause the Focus or burning Spot to fall on the Hour Line of One, for Example, at one a Clock, and there kindle a Train of Gunpowder that shall fire one Gun. At Two a Clock, a Focus shall fall on the Hour Line of Two, and kindle another Train that shall discharge two Guns successively; and so of the rest.

Note, There must be 78 Guns in all. Thirty-two Pounders will be best for this Use; but 18 Pounders may do, and will cost less, as well as use less Powder, for nine Pounds of Powder will do for one Charge of each eighteen Pounder, whereas the Thirty-two Pounders would require for each Gun 16 Pounds.

Note also, That the chief Expence will be the Powder, for the Cannon once bought, will, with Care, last 100 Years.

Note moreover, That there will be a great Saving of Powder in cloudy Days.

Kind Reader, Methinks I hear thee say, *That it is indeed a good Thing to know how the Time passes, but this Kind of Dial, notwithstanding the mentioned Savings, would be very expensive; and the Cost greater than the Advantage.* Thou art wise, my Friend, to be so considerate beforehand; some Fools would not have found out so much, till they had made the Dial and try'd it.—Let all such learn that many a private and many a publick Project, are like this *Striking Dial*, great Cost for little Profit.

————

He that would rise at Court, must begin by Creeping.

Many a Man's own Tongue gives Evidence against his Understanding.

Nothing dries sooner than a Tear.

'Tis easier to build two Chimneys, than maintain one in Fuel.

Anger warms the Invention, but overheats the Oven.

It is Ill-Manners to silence a Fool, and Cruelty to let him go on.

Scarlet, Silk and Velvet, have put out the Kitchen Fire.

He that would catch Fish, must venture his Bait.

Men take more pains to mask than mend.

One *To-day* is worth two *To-morrows*.

Since Man is but of a very limited Power in his own Person, and consequently can effect no great Matter merely by his own personal Strength, but as he acts in Society and Conjunction with others; and since no Man can engage the active Assistance of others, without first engaging their Trust; And moreover, since Men will trust no further than they judge one, for his *Sincerity*, fit to be trusted; it follows, that a discovered Dissembler can atchieve nothing great or considerable. For not being able to gain Mens Trust, he cannot gain their Concurrence; and so is left alone to act singly and upon his own Bottom; and while that is the Sphere of his Activity, all that he can do must needs be contemptible.

> Sincerity has such resistless Charms,
> She oft the fiercest of our Foes disarms:
> No Art she knows, in native Whiteness dress'd,
> Her Thoughts all pure, and therefore all express'd:
> She takes from Error its Deformity;
> And without her all other Virtues die.
> Bright Source of Goodness! to my Aid descend,
> Watch o'er my Heart, and all my Words attend.

The way to be safe, is never to be secure.

Dally not with other Folks Women or Money.

Work as if you were to live 100 Years, Pray as if you were to die To-morrow.

It is generally agreed to be Folly, *to hazard the Loss of a Friend, rather than lose a Jest*. But few consider how easily a Friend may be thus lost. Depending on the known Regard their Friends have for them, Jesters take more Freedom with Friends than they would dare to do with others, little thinking how much deeper we are wounded by an Affront from

one we love. But the strictest Intimacy can never warrant
Freedoms of this Sort; and it is indeed preposterous to think
they should; unless we can suppose Injuries are less Evils
when they are done us by Friends, than when they come from
other Hands.

    Excess of Wit may oftentimes beguile:
Jests are not always pardon'd—by a Smile.
Men may disguise their Malice at the Heart,
And seem at Ease—tho' pain'd with inward Smart.
Mistaken, we—think all such Wounds of course
Reflection cures;—alas! it makes them worse.
Like Scratches they with double Anguish seize,
Rankle in time, and fester by Degrees.

But sarcastical Jests on a Man's Person or his Manners, tho'
hard to bear, are perhaps more easily borne than those that
touch his Religion. Men are generally warm in what regards
their religious Tenets, either from Tenderness of Conscience,
or a high Sense of their own Judgments. People of plain Parts
and honest Dispositions, look on Salvation as too serious a
Thing to be jested with; and Men of speculative Religion,
who profess from the Conviction rather of their Heads than
Hearts, are not a bit less vehement than the real Devotees.
He who says a slight or a severe Thing of their Faith, seems
to them to have thereby undervalued their Understandings,
and will consequently incur their Aversion, which no Man of
common Sense would hazard for a lively Expression; much
less a Person of good Breeding, who should make it his chief
Aim to be well with all.

    Like some grave Matron of a noble Line,
With awful Beauty does Religion shine.
Just Sense should teach us to revere the Dame,
Nor, by imprudent Jests, to spot her Fame.
In common Life you'll own this Reas'ning right,
That none but Fools in gross Abuse delight:
Then use it here—nor think the Caution vain;
To be *polite*, Men need not be profane.

———

Pride breakfasted with *Plenty*, dined with *Poverty*, supped
with *Infamy*.

Retirement does not always secure Virtue; *Lot* was upright in the City, wicked in the Mountain.

Idleness is the Dead Sea, that swallows all Virtues: Be active in Business, that *Temptation* may miss her Aim: The Bird that sits, is easily shot.

Shame and the *Dry-belly-ach* were Diseases of the last Age; this seems to be cured of them.

In studying Law or Physick, or any other Art or Science, by which you propose to get your Livelihood, though you find it at first hard, difficult and unpleasing, use *Diligence, Patience* and *Perseverance*; the Irksomness of your Task will thus diminish daily, and your Labour shall finally be crowned with Success. You shall go beyond all your Competitors who are careless, idle or superficial in their Acquisitions, and be at the Head of your Profession. —*Ability* will command *Business, Business Wealth*; and *Wealth* an easy and honourable *Retirement* when Age shall require it.

> Near to the wide extended Coasts of *Spain*,
> Some Islands triumph o'er the raging Main;
> Where dwelt of old, as tuneful Poets say,
> *Slingers*, who bore from all the Prize away.
> While Infants yet, their feeble Nerves they try'd;
> Nor needful Food, till won by Art, supply'd.
> Fix'd was the Mark, the Youngster oft in vain,
> Whirl'd the misguided Stone with fruitless Pain:
> 'Till, by long Practice, to Perfection brought,
> With easy Sleight their former Task they wrought.
> Swift from their Arm th' unerring Pebble flew,
> And high in Air, the flutt'ring Victim slew.
> So in each Art Men rise but by Degrees,
> And Months of Labour lead to Years of Ease.

Tho' the Mastiff be gentle, yet bite him not by the Lip.

Great-Alms-giving, lessens no Man's Living.

The royal Crown cures not the Head-ach.

Act uprightly, and despise Calumny; Dirt may stick to a Mud Wall, but not to polish'd Marble.

PARADOXES.

I. The *Christians* observe the *first* Day of the Week for their *Sunday*, the *Jews* the *Seventh* for their Sabbath, the *Turks* the *sixth* Day of the Week for the Time of their Worship; but there is a particular Place of the Globe, to which if a *Christian*, *Jew*, and *Turk* sail in one and the same Ship, they shall keep the Time for their Worship on different Days, as above, all the Time they are sailing to that particular Place; but when they arrive at that Place, and during the Time they remain at it, they shall all keep their Sabbath on one and the same Day; but when they depart from that Place, they shall all differ as before.

II. There is a certain Port, from which if three Ships depart at one and the same time, and sail on three particular different Courses, till they return to the Port they departed from; and if in one of these Ships be *Christians*, in the second *Jews*, and in the third *Turks*, when they return to the Port they departed from, they shall differ so with respect to real and apparent Time, that they all shall keep their Sabbath on one and the same Day of the Week, and yet each of them separately shall believe that he keeps his Sabbath on the Day of the Week his Religion requires.

The *Borrower* is a Slave to the *Lender*; the *Security* to *both*.

Singularity in the right, hath ruined many: Happy those who are convinced of the general Opinion.

Proportion your Charity to the Strength of your Estate, or God will proportion your Estate to the Weakness of your Charity.

The Tongue offends, and the Ears get the Cuffing.

Some antient Philosophers have said, that Happiness depends more on the inward Disposition of Mind than on outward Circumstances; and that he who cannot be happy in any State, can be so in no State. To be happy, they tell us we must be content. Right. But they do not teach how we may become content. *Poor Richard* shall give you a short good Rule for that. *To be content, look backward on those who possess less than yourself, not forward on those who possess more*. If this does not make you *content*, you don't deserve to be *happy*.

———

Sleep without Supping, and you'll rise without owing for it.

> When other Sins grow old by Time,
> Then Avarice is in its prime,
> Yet feed the Poor at *Christmas* time.

———

Learning is a valuable Thing in the Affairs of this Life, but of infinitely more Importance is *Godliness*, as it tends not only to make us happy here but hereafter. At the Day of Judgment, we shall not be asked, what Proficiency we have made in Languages or Philosophy; but whether we have liv'd virtuously and piously, as Men endued with Reason, guided by the Dictates of Religion. In that Hour it will more avail us, that we have thrown a Handful of Flour or Chaff in Charity to a Nest of contemptible Pismires, than that we could muster all the Hosts of Heaven, and call every Star by its proper Name. For then the Constellations themselves shall disappear, the Sun and Moon shall give no more Light, and all the Frame of Nature shall vanish. But our good or bad Works shall remain for ever, recorded in the Archives of Eternity.

> Unmov'd alone the *Virtuous* now appear,
> And in their Looks a calm Assurance wear.
> From East, from West, from North and South they come,
> To take from the most righteous Judge their Doom;
> Who thus, to them, with a serene Regard;
> (The Books of Life before him laid,
> And all the secret Records wide display'd)
> "According to your Works be your Reward:
> Possess immortal Kingdoms as your Due,
> Prepar'd from an eternal Date for you."

Poor Richard Improved, 1758

COURTEOUS READER,

I have heard that nothing gives an Author so great Pleasure, as to find his Works respectfully quoted by other learned

Authors. This Pleasure I have seldom enjoyed; for tho' I have been, if I may say it without Vanity, an *eminent Author* of Almanacks annually now a full Quarter of a Century, my Brother Authors in the same Way, for what Reason I know not, have ever been very sparing in their Applauses; and no other Author has taken the least Notice of me, so that did not my Writings produce me some solid *Pudding*, the great Deficiency of *Praise* would have quite discouraged me.

I concluded at length, that the People were the best Judges of my Merit; for they buy my Works; and besides, in my Rambles, where I am not personally known, I have frequently heard one or other of my Adages repeated, with, *as Poor Richard says*, at the End on't; this gave me some Satisfaction, as it showed not only that my Instructions were regarded, but discovered likewise some Respect for my Authority; and I own, that to encourage the Practice of remembering and repeating those wise Sentences, I have sometimes *quoted myself* with great Gravity.

Judge then how much I must have been gratified by an Incident I am going to relate to you. I stopt my Horse lately where a great Number of People were collected at a Vendue of Merchant Goods. The Hour of Sale not being come, they were conversing on the Badness of the Times, and one of the Company call'd to a plain clean old Man, with white Locks, *Pray, Father* Abraham, *what think you of the Times? Won't these heavy Taxes quite ruin the Country? How shall we be ever able to pay them? What would you advise us to?* —Father *Abraham* stood up, and reply'd, If you'd have my Advice, I'll give it you in short, for a *Word to the Wise is enough*, and *many Words won't fill a Bushel*, as *Poor Richard says*. They join'd in desiring him to speak his Mind, and gathering round him, he proceeded as follows;

"Friends, says he, and Neighbours, the Taxes are indeed very heavy, and if those laid on by the Government were the only Ones we had to pay, we might more easily discharge them; but we have many others, and much more grievous to some of us. We are taxed twice as much by our *Idleness*, three times as much by our *Pride*, and four times as much by our *Folly*, and from these Taxes the Commissioners cannot ease or deliver us by allowing an Abatement. However let us hearken to good Advice, and something may be done for us; *God helps them that help themselves*, as *Poor Richard* says, in his Almanack of 1733.

It would be thought a hard Government that should tax its People one tenth Part of their *Time*, to be employed in its Service. But *Idleness* taxes many of us much more, if we reckon all that is spent in absolute *Sloth*, or doing of nothing, with that which is spent in idle Employments or Amusements, that amount to nothing. *Sloth*, by bringing on Diseases, absolutely shortens Life. *Sloth, like Rust, consumes faster than Labour wears, while the used Key is always bright*, as *Poor Richard* says. But *dost thou love Life, then do not squander Time, for that's the Stuff Life is made of*, as *Poor Richard* says.—How much more than is necessary do we spend in Sleep! forgetting that *The sleeping Fox catches no Poultry*, and that *there will be sleeping enough in the Grave*, as *Poor Richard* says. If Time be of all Things the most precious, *wasting Time* must be, as *Poor Richard* says, *the greatest Prodigality*, since, as he elsewhere tells us, *Lost Time is never found again*; and what we call *Time-enough, always proves little enough*: Let us then up and be doing, and doing to the Purpose; so by Diligence shall we do more with less Perplexity. *Sloth makes all Things difficult, but Industry all easy*, as *Poor Richard* says; and *He that riseth late, must trot all Day, and shall scarce overtake his Business at Night*. While *Laziness travels so slowly, that Poverty soon overtakes him*, as we read in *Poor Richard*, who adds, *Drive thy Business, let not that drive thee*; and *Early to Bed, and early to rise, makes a Man healthy, wealthy and wise*.

So what signifies *wishing* and *hoping* for better Times. We may make these Times better if we bestir ourselves. *Industry need not wish*, as *Poor Richard* says, and *He that lives upon Hope will die fasting. There are no Gains, without Pains*; then *Help Hands, for I have no Lands*, or if I have, they are smartly taxed. And, as *Poor Richard* likewise observes, *He that hath a Trade hath an Estate*, and *He that hath a Calling hath an Office of Profit and Honour*; but then the *Trade* must be worked at, and the *Calling* well followed, or neither the *Estate*, nor the *Office*, will enable us to pay our Taxes.—If we are industrious we shall never starve; for, as *Poor Richard* says, *At the working Man's House* Hunger *looks in, but dares not enter*. Nor will the

Bailiff or the Constable enter, for *Industry pays Debts, while Despair encreaseth them*, says *Poor Richard.*—What though you have found no Treasure, nor has any rich Relation left you a Legacy, *Diligence is the Mother of Good-luck*, as *Poor Richard* says, *and God gives all Things to Industry*. Then *plough deep, while Sluggards sleep, and you shall have Corn to sell and to keep*, says *Poor Dick*. Work while it is called To-day, for you know not how much you may be hindered To-morrow, which makes *Poor Richard* say, *One To-day is worth two To-morrows*; and farther, *Have you somewhat to do To-morrow, do it To-day*. If you were a Servant, would you not be ashamed that a good Master should catch you idle? Are you then your own Master, *be ashamed to catch yourself idle*, as *Poor Dick* says. When there is so much to be done for yourself, your Family, your Country, and your gracious King, be up by Peep of Day; *Let not the Sun look down and say, Inglorious here he lies*. Handle your Tools without Mittens; remember that *the Cat in Gloves catches no Mice*, as *Poor Richard* says. 'Tis true there is much to be done, and perhaps you are weak handed, but stick to it steadily, and you will see great Effects, for *constant Dropping wears away Stones*, and by *Diligence and Patience the Mouse ate in two the Cable*; and *little Strokes fell great Oaks*, as *Poor Richard* says in his Almanack, the Year I cannot just now remember.

Methinks I hear some of you say, *Must a Man afford himself no Leisure?*—I will tell thee, my Friend, what *Poor Richard* says, *Employ thy Time well if thou meanest to gain Leisure*; and, *since thou art not sure of a Minute, throw not away an Hour.* Leisure, is Time for doing something useful; this Leisure the diligent Man will obtain, but the lazy Man never; so that, as *Poor Richard* says, a *Life of Leisure and a Life of Laziness are two Things*. Do you imagine that Sloth will afford you more Comfort than Labour? No, for as *Poor Richard* says, *Trouble springs from Idleness, and grievous Toil from needless Ease. Many without Labour, would live by their* WITS *only, but they break for want of Stock*. Whereas Industry gives Comfort, and Plenty, and Respect: *Fly Pleasures, and they'll follow you. The diligent Spinner has a large Shift*; and *now I have a Sheep and a Cow, every Body bids me Good morrow*; all which is well said by *Poor Richard*.

But with our Industry, we must likewise be *steady*, *settled* and *careful*, and oversee our own Affairs *with our own Eyes*, and not trust too much to others; for, as *Poor Richard* says,

> *I never saw an oft removed Tree,*
> *Nor yet an oft removed Family,*
> *That throve so well as those that settled be.*

And again, *Three Removes is as bad as a Fire*; and again, *Keep thy Shop, and thy Shop will keep thee*; and again, *If you would have your Business done, go; If not, send*. And again,

> *He that by the Plough would thrive,*
> *Himself must either hold or drive.*

And again, *The Eye of a Master will do more Work than both his Hands*; and again, *Want of Care does us more Damage than Want of Knowledge*; and again, *Not to oversee Workmen, is to leave them your Purse open*. Trusting too much to others Care is the Ruin of many; for, as the *Almanack* says, *In the Affairs of this World, Men are saved, not by Faith, but by the Want of it*; but a Man's own Care is profitable; for, saith *Poor Dick*, *Learning is to the Studious*, and *Riches to the Careful*, as well as *Power to the Bold*, and *Heaven to the Virtuous*. And farther, *If you would have a faithful Servant, and one that you like, serve yourself*. And again, he adviseth to Circumspection and Care, even in the smallest Matters, because sometimes *a little Neglect may breed great Mischief*; adding, *For want of a Nail the Shoe was lost; for want of a Shoe the Horse was lost; and for want of a Horse the Rider was lost*, being overtaken and slain by the Enemy, all for want of Care about a Horse-shoe Nail.

So much for Industry, my Friends, and Attention to one's own Business; but to these we must add *Frugality*, if we would make our *Industry* more certainly successful. A Man may, if he knows not how to save as he gets, *keep his Nose all his Life to the Grindstone*, and die not worth a *Groat* at last. *A fat Kitchen makes a lean Will*, as *Poor Richard* says; and,

> *Many Estates are spent in the Getting,*
> *Since Women for Tea forsook Spinning and Knitting,*
> *And Men for Punch forsook Hewing and Splitting.*

If you would be wealthy, says he, in another Almanack, *think of Saving as well as of Getting: The* Indies *have not made* Spain *rich, because her* Outgoes *are greater than her* Incomes. Away then with your expensive Follies, and you will not have so much Cause to complain of hard Times, heavy Taxes, and chargeable Families; for, as *Poor Dick* says,

Women and Wine, Game and Deceit,
Make the Wealth small, and the Wants great.

And farther, *What maintains one Vice, would bring up two Children.* You may think perhaps, That a *little* Tea, or a *little* Punch now and then, Diet a *little* more costly, Clothes a *little* finer, and a *little* Entertainment now and then, can be no *great* Matter; but remember what *Poor Richard* says, *Many* a Little *makes a Mickle*; and farther, *Beware of* little *Expences*; *a small Leak will sink a great Ship*; and again, *Who Dainties love, shall Beggars prove*; and moreover, *Fools make Feasts, and wise Men eat them.*

Here you are all got together at this Vendue of *Fineries* and *Knicknacks.* You call them *Goods*, but if you do not take Care, they will prove *Evils* to some of you. You expect they will be sold *cheap*, and perhaps they may for less than they cost; but if you have no Occasion for them, they must be *dear* to you. Remember what *Poor Richard* says, *Buy what thou hast no Need of, and ere long thou shalt sell thy Necessaries.* And again, *At a great Pennyworth pause a while*: He means, that perhaps the Cheapness is *apparent* only, and not *real*; or the Bargain, by straitning thee in thy Business, may do thee more Harm than Good. For in another Place he says, *Many have been ruined by buying good Pennyworths.* Again, *Poor Richard* says, *'Tis foolish to lay out Money in a Purchase of Repentance*; and yet this Folly is practised every Day at Vendues, for want of minding the Almanack. *Wise Men*, as *Poor Dick* says, *learn by others Harms, Fools scarcely by their own*; but, *Felix quem faciunt aliena Pericula cautum.* Many a one, for the Sake of Finery on the Back, have gone with a hungry Belly, and half starved their Families; *Silks and Sattins, Scarlet and Velvets*, as *Poor Richard* says, *put out the Kitchen Fire.* These are not the *Necessaries* of Life; they can scarcely be called the *Conveniencies*, and yet only because they look pretty, how many *want* to *have* them. The *artificial* Wants of Mankind thus become more numerous than the *natural*; and, as *Poor Dick* says, *For one* poor *Person, there are an hundred* indigent. By these, and other Extravagancies, the Genteel are reduced to Poverty, and forced to borrow of those whom they formerly despised, but who through *Industry* and *Frugality* have maintained their Standing; in which Case it appears plainly, that a *Ploughman on his Legs is higher than a Gentleman on his Knees*, as *Poor Richard* says. Perhaps they have had a small Estate left them, which they knew not the Getting of; they think *'tis Day, and will never be Night*; that a little to be spent out of *so much*, is not worth minding; (*a Child and a Fool*, as *Poor Richard* says, *imagine* Twenty Shillings *and Twenty Years can never be spent*) but, *always taking out of the Meal-tub, and never putting in, soon comes to the Bottom*; then, as *Poor Dick* says, *When the Well's dry, they know the Worth of Water*. But this they might have known before, if they had taken his Advice; *If you would know the Value of Money, go and try to borrow some*; for, *he that goes a borrowing goes a sorrowing*; and indeed so does he that lends to such People, when he goes *to get it in again.* — *Poor Dick* farther advises, and says,

> *Fond* Pride of Dress*, is sure a very Curse;*
> *E'er* Fancy *you consult, consult your Purse.*

And again, *Pride is as loud a Beggar as Want, and a great deal more saucy*. When you have bought one fine Thing you must buy ten more, that your Appearance may be all of a Piece; but *Poor Dick* says, *'Tis easier to* suppress *the first Desire, than to* satisfy *all that follow it*. And 'tis as truly Folly for the Poor to ape the Rich, as for the Frog to swell, in order to equal the Ox.

> *Great Estates may venture more,*
> *But little Boats should keep near Shore.*

'Tis however a Folly soon punished; for *Pride that dines on Vanity sups on Contempt*, as *Poor Richard* says. And in another Place, *Pride breakfasted with Plenty, dined with Poverty, and supped with Infamy*. And after all, of what Use is this *Pride of Appearance*, for which so much is risked, so much is suffered? It cannot promote Health, or ease Pain; it makes no Increase of Merit in the Person, it creates Envy, it hastens Misfortune.

> *What is a Butterfly? At best*
> *He's but a Caterpillar drest.*
> *The gaudy Fop's his Picture just,*

as *Poor Richard* says.

But what Madness must it be to *run in Debt* for these

Superfluities! We are offered, by the Terms of this Vendue, *Six Months Credit*; and that perhaps has induced some of us to attend it, because we cannot spare the ready Money, and hope now to be fine without it. But, ah, think what you do when you run in Debt; *You give to another Power over your Liberty*. If you cannot pay at the Time, you will be ashamed to see your Creditor; you will be in Fear when you speak to him; you will make poor pitiful sneaking Excuses, and by Degrees come to lose your Veracity, and sink into base down-right lying; for, as *Poor Richard* says, *The second Vice is Lying, the first is running in Debt.* And again, to the same Purpose, *Lying rides upon Debt's Back.* Whereas a freeborn *Englishman* ought not to be ashamed or afraid to see or speak to any Man living. But Poverty often deprives a Man of all Spirit and Virtue: *'Tis hard for an empty Bag to stand upright*, as *Poor Richard* truly says. What would you think of that Prince, or that Government, who should issue an Edict forbidding you to dress like a Gentleman or a Gentlewoman, on Pain of Imprisonment or Servitude? Would you not say, that you are free, have a Right to dress as you please, and that such an Edict would be a Breach of your Privileges, and such a Government tyrannical? And yet you are about to put yourself under that Tyranny when you run in Debt for such Dress! Your Creditor has Authority at his Pleasure to deprive you of your Liberty, by confining you in Goal for Life, or to sell you for a Servant, if you should not be able to pay him! When you have got your Bargain, you may, perhaps, think little of Payment; but *Creditors, Poor Richard* tells us, *have better Memories than Debtors*; and in another Place says, *Creditors are a superstitious Sect, great Observers of set Days and Times*. The Day comes round before you are aware, and the Demand is made before you are prepared to satisfy it. Or if you bear your Debt in Mind, the Term which at first seemed so long, will, as it lessens, appear extreamly short. *Time* will seem to have added Wings to his Heels as well as Shoulders. *Those have a short Lent,* saith *Poor Richard, who owe Money to be paid at Easter.* Then since, as he says, *The Borrower is a Slave to the Lender, and the Debtor to the Creditor*, disdain the Chain, preserve your Freedom; and maintain your Independency: Be *indus-*

trious and *free*; be *frugal* and *free*. At present, perhaps, you may think yourself in thriving Circumstances, and that you can bear a little Extravagance without Injury; but,

> *For Age and Want, save while you may;*
> *No Morning Sun lasts a whole Day,*

as *Poor Richard* says.—Gain may be temporary and uncertain, but ever while you live, Expence is constant and certain; and *'tis easier to build two Chimnies than to keep one in Fuel*, as *Poor Richard* says. So *rather go to Bed supperless than rise in Debt.*

> *Get what you can, and what you get hold;*
> *'Tis the Stone that will turn all your Lead into Gold,*

as *Poor Richard* says. And when you have got the Philosopher's Stone, sure you will no longer complain of bad Times, or the Difficulty of paying Taxes.

This Doctrine, my Friends, is *Reason* and *Wisdom*; but after all, do not depend too much upon your own *Industry*, and *Frugality*, and *Prudence*, though excellent Things, for they may all be blasted without the Blessing of Heaven; and therefore ask that Blessing humbly, and be not uncharitable to those that at present seem to want it, but comfort and help them. Remember *Job* suffered, and was afterwards prosperous.

And now to conclude, *Experience keeps a dear School, but Fools will learn in no other, and scarce in that*; for it is true, *we may give Advice, but we cannot give Conduct*, as *Poor Richard* says: However, remember this, *They that won't be counselled, can't be helped*, as *Poor Richard* says: And farther, That *if you will not hear Reason, she'll surely rap your Knuckles*."

Thus the old Gentleman ended his Harangue. The People heard it, and approved the Doctrine, and immediately practised the contrary, just as if it had been a common Sermon; for the Vendue opened, and they began to buy extravagantly, notwithstanding all his Cautions, and their own Fear of Taxes.—I found the good Man had thoroughly studied my Almanacks, and digested all I had dropt on those Topicks during the Course of Five-and-twenty Years. The frequent Mention he made of me must have tired any one else, but my Vanity was wonderfully delighted with it, though I was conscious that not a tenth Part of the Wisdom was my own which he ascribed to me, but rather the *Gleanings* I had made of the Sense of all Ages and Nations. However, I resolved to

be the better for the Echo of it; and though I had at first
determined to buy Stuff for a new Coat, I went away resolved
to wear my old One a little longer. *Reader*, if thou wilt do
the same, thy Profit will be as great as mine.

I am, as ever,

Thine to serve thee,

July 7, 1757.   RICHARD SAUNDERS.

————

One *Nestor* is worth two *Ajaxes*.

> When you're an Anvil, hold you still;
> When you're a Hammer, strike your Fill.

When Knaves betray each other, one can scarce be blamed,
or the other pitied.

He that carries a small Crime easily, will carry it on when it
comes to be an Ox.

Happy *Tom Crump*, ne'er sees his own Hump.

Fools need Advice most, but wise Men only are the better
for it.

Silence is not always a Sign of Wisdom, but Babbling is ever
a Mark of Folly.

Great Modesty often hides great Merit.

You may delay, but *Time* will not.

Virtue may not always make a Face handsome, but *Vice* will
certainly make it ugly.

Prodigality of *Time*, produces Poverty of Mind as well as of
Estate.

Content is the Philosopher's Stone, that turns all it touches
into Gold.

He that's content, hath enough; He that complains, has too
much.

Pride gets into the Coach, and *Shame* mounts behind.

The first Mistake in publick Business, is the going into it.

Half the Truth is often a great Lie.

The Way to see by *Faith*, is to shut the Eye of *Reason*: The Morning Daylight appears plainer when you put out your Candle.

A full Belly makes a dull Brain: The Muses starve in a Cook's Shop.

Spare and have is better than *spend and crave*.

Good-Will, like the Wind, floweth where it listeth.

The Honey is sweet, but the Bee has a Sting.

In a corrupt Age, the putting the World in order would breed Confusion; then e'en mind your own Business.

To serve the Publick faithfully, and at the same time please it entirely, is impracticable.

Proud Modern Learning despises the antient: *School-men* are now laught at by *School-boys*.

Men often *mistake* themselves, seldom *forget* themselves.

The idle Man is the Devil's Hireling; whose Livery is Rags, whose Diet and Wages are Famine and Diseases.

Rob not God, nor the Poor, lest thou ruin thyself; the Eagle snatcht a Coal from the Altar, but it fired her Nest.

> With bounteous Cheer,
> Conclude the Year.

THE AUTOBIOGRAPHY

Part One

Twyford, at the Bishop
of St Asaph's
1771.

Dear Son,

I have ever had a Pleasure in obtaining any little Anecdotes of my Ancestors. You may remember the Enquiries I made among the Remains of my Relations when you were with me in England; and the Journey I took for that purpose. Now imagining it may be equally agreable to you to know the Circumstances of *my* Life, many of which you are yet unacquainted with; and expecting a Weeks uninterrupted Leisure in my present Country Retirement, I sit down to write them for you. To which I have besides some other Inducements. Having emerg'd from the Poverty & Obscurity in which I was born & bred, to a State of Affluence & some Degree of Reputation in the World, and having gone so far thro' Life with a considerable Share of Felicity, the conducing Means I made use of, which, with the Blessing of God, so well succeeded, my Posterity may like to know, as they may find some of them suitable to their own Situations, & therefore fit to be imitated.—That Felicity, when I reflected on it, has induc'd me sometimes to say, that were it offer'd to my Choice, I should have no Objection to a Repetition of the same Life from its Beginning, only asking the Advantage Authors have in a second Edition to correct some Faults of the first. So would I if I might, besides corr^g the Faults, change some sinister Accidents & Events of it for others more favourable, but tho' this were deny'd, I should still accept the Offer. However, since such a Repetition is not to be expected, the Thing most like living one's Life over again, seems to be a *Recollection* of that Life; and to make that Recollection as durable as possible, the putting it down in Writing.—Hereby, too, I shall indulge the Inclination so natural in old Men, to be talking of themselves and their own past Actions, and I shall indulge it, without being troublesome to others who thro' respect to Age might think themselves oblig'd to give me a Hearing, since this may be read or not as any one pleases.

And lastly, (I may as well confess it, since my Denial of it will be believ'd by no body) perhaps I shall a good deal gratify my own *Vanity*. Indeed I scarce ever heard or saw the introductory Words, *Without Vanity I may say*, &c. but some vain thing immediately follow'd. Most People dislike Vanity in others whatever Share they have of it themselves, but I give it fair Quarter wherever I meet with it, being persuaded that it is often productive of Good to the Possessor & to others that are within his Sphere of Action: And therefore in many Cases it would not be quite absurd if a Man were to thank God for his Vanity among the other Comforts of Life.—

And now I speak of thanking God, I desire with all Humility to acknowledge, that I owe the mention'd Happiness of my past Life to his kind Providence, which led me to the Means I us'd & gave them Success.—My Belief of This, induces me to *hope*, tho' I must not *presume*, that the same Goodness will still be exercis'd towards me in continuing that Happiness, or in enabling me to bear a fatal Reverso, which I may experience as others have done, the Complexion of my future Fortune being known to him only: and in whose Power it is to bless to us even our Afflictions.

The Notes one of my Uncles (who had the same kind of Curiosity in collecting Family Anecdotes) once put into my Hands, furnish'd me with several Particulars, relating to our Ancestors. From those Notes I learnt that the Family had liv'd in the same Village, Ecton in Northamptonshire, for 300 Years, & how much longer he knew not, (perhaps from the Time when the Name *Franklin* that before was the Name of an Order of People, was assum'd by them for a Surname, when others took Surnames all over the Kingdom.—*) on a

---

*As a proof that FRANKLIN was anciently the common name of an order or rank in England, see Judge Fortescue, *De laudibus Legum Angliae*, written about the year 1412, in which is the following passage, to show that good juries might easily be formed in any part of England.

"Regio etiam illa, ita respersa refertaque est *possessoribus terrarum* et agrorum, quod in ea, villula tam parva reperiri non poterit, in qua non est *miles*, *armiger*, vel pater-familias, qualis ibidem *Franklin* vulgariter nuncupatur, magnis ditatus possessionibus, nec non libere tenentes et alii *valecti* plurimi, suis patrimoniis sufficientes ad faciendum juratam, in forma praenotata."

"Moreover, the same country is so filled and replenished with landed

Freehold of about 30 Acres, aided by the Smith's Business which had continued in the Family till his Time, the eldest Son being always bred to that Business. A Custom which he & my Father both followed as to their eldest Sons.—When I search'd the Register at Ecton, I found an Account of their Births, Marriages and Burials, from the Year 1555 only, there being no Register kept in that Parish at any time preceding.—By that Register I perceiv'd that I was the youngest Son of the youngest Son for 5 Generations back. My Grandfather Thomas, who was born in 1598, lived at Ecton till he grew too old to follow Business longer, when he went to live with his Son John, a Dyer at Banbury in Oxfordshire, with whom my Father serv'd an Apprenticeship. There my Grandfather died and lies buried. We saw his Gravestone in 1758. His eldest Son Thomas liv'd in the House at Ecton, and left it with the Land to his only Child, a Daughter, who with her Husband, one Fisher of Wellingborough sold it to Mr Isted, now Lord of the Manor there. My Grandfather had 4 Sons that grew up, viz. Thomas, John, Benjamin and Josiah. I will give you what Account I can of them at this distance from my Papers, and if those are not lost in my Absence, you will among them find many more Particulars. Thomas was bred a Smith under his Father, but being ingenious, and encourag'd in Learning (as all his Brothers like wise werre,) by an Esquire Palmer then the principal Gentleman in that Parish, he qualify'd himself for the Business of Scrivener, became a con-

---

menne, that therein so small a Thorpe cannot be found werein dweleth not a knight, an esquire, or such a householder, as is there commonly called a *Franklin*, enriched with great possessions; and also other freeholders and many yeomen able for their livelihoods to make a jury in form aforementioned."—(*Old Translation.*)

Chaucer too calls his Country Gentleman, a *Franklin*, and after describing his good housekeeping thus characterises him:

> "This worthy Franklin bore a purse of silk,
> Fix'd to his girdle, white as morning milk.
> Knight of the Shire, first Justice at th' Assize,
> To help the poor, the doubtful to advise.
> In all employments, generous, just, he proved;
> Renown'd for courtesy, by all beloved."

siderable Man in the County Affairs, was a chief Mover of all
publick Spirited Undertakings, for the County or Town of
Northampton & his own Village, of which many Instances
were told us at Ecton and he was much taken Notice of and
patroniz'd by the then Lord Halifax. He died in 1702 Jan. 6.
old Stile, just 4 Years to a Day before I was born. The Account we receiv'd of his Life & Character from some old
People at Ecton, I remember struck you as something extraordinary from its Similarity to what you knew of mine. Had he
died on the same Day, you said one might have suppos'd a
Transmigration.—John was bred a Dyer, I believe of Wool-
lens. Benjamin, was bred a Silk Dyer, serving an Apprenticeship at London. He was an ingenious Man, I remember him
well, for when I was a Boy he came over to my Father in
Boston, and lived in the House with us some Years. He lived
to a great Age. His Grandson Samuel Franklin now lives in
Boston. He left behind him two Quarto Volumes, M.S. of his
own Poetry, consisting of little occasional Pieces address'd to
his Friends and Relations, of which the following sent to me,
is a Specimen.

Sent to My Name upon a Report
of his Inclination to Martial affaires
7 July 1710

Beleeve me Ben. It is a Dangerous Trade
The Sword has Many Marr'd as well as Made
By it doe many fall Not Many Rise
Makes Many poor few Rich and fewer Wise
Fills Towns with Ruin, fields with blood beside
Tis Sloths Maintainer, And the Shield of pride
Fair Citties Rich to Day, in plenty flow
War fills with want, Tomorrow, & with woe
Ruin'd Estates, The Nurse of Vice, broke limbs & scarss
   Are the Effects of Desolating Warrs

Sent to B. F. in N. E. 15 July 1710

B   e to thy parents an Obedient Son
E   ach Day let Duty constantly be Done
N   ever give Way to sloth or lust or pride

I   f free you'd be from Thousand Ills beside
A   bove all Ills be sure Avoide the shelfe
M   ans Danger lyes in Satan sin and selfe
I   n vertue Learning Wisdome progress Make
N   ere shrink at Suffering for thy saviours sake
F   raud and all Falshood in thy Dealings Flee
R   eligious Always in thy station be
A   dore the Maker of thy Inward part
N   ow's the Accepted time, Give him thy Heart
K   eep a Good Consceince 'tis a constant Frind
L   ike Judge and Witness This Thy Acts Attend
I   n Heart with bended knee Alone Adore
N   one but the Three in One Forevermore.

He had form'd a Shorthand of his own, which he taught me, but never practicing it I have now forgot it. I was nam'd after this Uncle, there being a particular Affection between him and my Father. He was very pious, a great Attender of Sermons of the best Preachers, which he took down in his Shorthand and had with him many Volumes of them. —He was also much of a Politician, too much perhaps for his Station. There fell lately into my Hands in London a Collection he had made of all the principal Pamphlets relating to Publick Affairs from 1641 to 1717. Many of the Volumes are wanting, as appears by the Numbering, but there still remains 8 Vols. Folio, and 24 in 4to & 8vo.—A Dealer in old Books met with them, and knowing me by my sometimes buying of him, he brought them to me. It seems my Uncle must have left them here when he went to America, which was above 50 Years since. There are many of his Notes in the Margins.—

This obscure Family of ours was early in the Reformation, and continu'd Protestants thro' the Reign of Queen Mary, when they were sometimes in Danger of Trouble on Account of their Zeal against Popery. They had got an English Bible, & to conceal & secure it, it was fastned open with Tapes under & within the Frame of a Joint Stool. When my Great Great Grandfather read in it to his Family, he turn'd up the

Joint Stool upon his Knees, turning over the Leaves then under the Tapes. One of the Children stood at the Door to give Notice if he saw the Apparitor coming, who was an Officer of the Spiritual Court. In that Case the Stool was turn'd down again upon its feet, when the Bible remain'd conceal'd under it as before. This Anecdote I had from my Uncle Benjamin.—The Family continu'd all of the Church of England till about the End of Charles the 2^{ds} Reign, when some of the Ministers that had been outed for Nonconformity, holding Conventicles in Northamptonshire, Benjamin & Josiah adher'd to them, and so continu'd all their Lives. The rest of the Family remain'd with the Episcopal Church.

Josiah, my Father, married young, and carried his Wife with three Children unto New England, about 1682. The Conventicles having been forbidden by Law, & frequently disturbed, induced some considerable Men of his Acquaintance to remove to that Country, and he was prevail'd with to accompany them thither, where they expected to enjoy their Mode of Religion with Freedom.—By the same Wife he had 4 Children more born there, and by a second Wife ten more, in all 17, of which I remember 13 sitting at one time at his Table, who all grew up to be Men & Women, and married;— I was the youngest Son and the youngest Child but two, & was born in Boston, N. England.

My Mother the 2^d Wife was Abiah Folger, a Daughter of Peter Folger, one of the first Settlers of New England, of whom honourable mention is made by Cotton Mather, in his Church History of that Country, (entitled Magnalia Christi Americana) as a *godly learned Englishman*, if I remember the Words rightly.—I have heard that he wrote sundry small occasional Pieces, but only one of them was printed which I saw now many Years since. It was written in 1675, in the homespun Verse of that Time & People, and address'd to those then concern'd in the Government there. It was in favour of Liberty of Conscience, & in behalf of the Baptists, Quakers, & other Sectaries, that had been under Persecution; ascribing the Indian Wars & other Distresses, that had befallen the Country to that Persecution, as so many Judgments of God, to punish so heinous an Offence; and exhorting a Repeal of those uncharitable Laws. The whole appear'd to me as

written with a good deal of Decent Plainness & manly Freedom. The six last concluding Lines I remember, tho' I have
forgotten the two first of the Stanza, but the Purport of them
was that his Censures proceeded from *Goodwill*, & therefore
he would be known as the Author,

> because to be a Libeller, (says he)
>   I hate it with my Heart.
> From *Sherburne Town where now I dwell,
>   My Name I do put here,
> Without Offence, your real Friend,
>   It is Peter Folgier.

*In the Island of Nantucket.

My elder Brothers were all put Apprentices to different
Trades. I was put to the Grammar School at Eight Years of
Age, my Father intending to devote me as the Tithe of his
Sons to the Service of the Church. My early Readiness in
learning to read (which must have been very early, as I do
not remember when I could not read) and the Opinion of all
his Friends that I should certainly make a good Scholar, encourag'd him in this Purpose of his. My Uncle Benjamin too
approv'd of it, and propos'd to give me all his Shorthand Volumes of Sermons I suppose as a Stock to set up with, if I
would learn his Character. I continu'd however at the Grammar School not quite one Year, tho' in that time I had risen
gradually from the Middle of the Class of that Year to be the
Head of it, and farther was remov'd into the next Class above
it, in order to go with that into the third at the End of the
Year. But my Father in the mean time, from a View of the
Expence of a College Education which, having so large a
Family, he could not well afford, and the mean Living many
so educated were afterwards able to obtain, Reasons that he
gave to his Friends in my Hearing, altered his first Intention,
took me from the Grammar School, and sent me to a School
for Writing & Arithmetic kept by a then famous Man, Mr
Geo. Brownell, very successful in his Profession generally, and
that by mild encouraging Methods. Under him I acquired fair
Writing pretty soon, but I fail'd in the Arithmetic, & made
no Progress in it.—At Ten Years old, I was taken home to

assist my Father in his Business, which was that of a Tallow Chandler and Sope-Boiler. A Business he was not bred to, but had assumed on his Arrival in New England & on finding his Dying Trade would not maintain his Family, being in little Request. Accordingly I was employed in cutting Wick for the Candles, filling the Dipping Mold, & the Molds for cast Candles, attending the Shop, going of Errands, &c.—I dislik'd the Trade and had a strong Inclination for the Sea; but my Father declar'd against it; however, living near the Water, I was much in and about it, learnt early to swim well, & to manage Boats, and when in a Boat or Canoe with other Boys I was commonly allow'd to govern, especially in any case of Difficulty; and upon other Occasions I was generally a Leader among the Boys, and sometimes led them into Scrapes, of wch I will mention one Instance, as it shows an early projecting public Spirit, tho' not then justly conducted. There was a Salt Marsh that bounded part of the Mill Pond, on the Edge of which at Highwater, we us'd to stand to fish for Minews. By much Trampling, we had made it a mere Quagmire. My Proposal was to build a Wharf there fit for us to stand upon, and I show'd my Comrades a large Heap of Stones which were intended for a new House near the Marsh, and which would very well suit our Purpose. Accordingly in the Evening when the Workmen were gone, I assembled a Number of my Playfellows, and working with them diligently like so many Emmets, sometimes two or three to a Stone, we brought them all away and built our little Wharff.— The next Morning the Workmen were surpriz'd at Missing the Stones; which were found in our Wharff; Enquiry was made after the Removers; we were discovered & complain'd of; several of us were corrected by our Fathers; and tho' I pleaded the Usefulness of the Work, mine convinc'd me that nothing was useful which was not honest.—

I think you may like to know something of his Person & Character. He had an excellent Constitution of Body, was of middle Stature, but well set and very strong. He was ingenious, could draw prettily, was skill'd a little in Music and had a clear pleasing Voice, so that when he play'd Psalm Tunes on his Violin & sung withal as he some times did in an Evening after the Business of the Day was over, it was extreamly agreable to hear. He had a mechanical Genius too, and on occasion was very handy in the Use of other Tradesmen's Tools. But his great Excellence lay in a sound Understanding, and solid Judgment in prudential Matters, both in private & publick Affairs. In the latter indeed he was never employed, the numerous Family he had to educate & the Straitness of his Circumstances, keeping him close to his Trade, but I remember well his being frequently visited by leading People, who consulted him for his Opinion on Affairs of the Town or of the Church he belong'd to & show'd a good deal of Respect for his Judgment and Advice. He was also much consulted by private Persons about their Affairs when any Difficulty occur'd, & frequently chosen an Arbitrator between contending Parties.—At his Table he lik'd to have as often as he could, some sensible Friend or Neighbour, to converse with, and always took care to start some ingenious or useful Topic for Discourse, which might tend to improve the Minds of his Children. By this means he turn'd our Attention to what was good, just, & prudent in the Conduct of Life; and little or no Notice was ever taken of what related to the Victuals on the Table, whether it was well or ill drest, in or out of season, of good or bad flavour, preferable or inferior to this or that other thing of the kind; so that I was bro't up in such a perfect Inattention to those Matters as to be quite Indifferent what kind of Food was set before me; and so unobservant of it, that to this Day, if I am ask'd I can scarce tell, a few Hours after Dinner, what I din'd upon.— This has been a Convenience to me in travelling, where my Companions have been sometimes very unhappy for want of a suitable Gratification of their more delicate because better instructed Tastes and Appetites.—

My Mother had likewise an excellent Constitution. She suckled all her 10 Children. I never knew either my Father or Mother to have any Sickness but that of which they dy'd, he at 89 & she at 85 Years of age. They lie buried together at Boston, where I some Years since plac'd a Marble stone over their Grave with this Inscription

Josiah Franklin
And Abiah his Wife

Lie here interred.
They lived lovingly together in Wedlock
Fifty-five Years.—
Without an Estate or any gainful Employment,
By constant Labour and Industry,
With God's Blessing,
They maintained a large Family
Comfortably;
And brought up thirteen Children,
And seven Grandchildren
Reputably.
From this Instance, Reader,
Be encouraged to Diligence in thy Calling,
And distrust not Providence.
He was a pious & prudent Man,
She a discreet and virtuous Woman.
Their youngest Son,
In filial Regard to their Memory,
Places this Stone.
J. F. born 1655—Died 1744. Ætat 89
A. F. born 1667—died 1752——85

By my rambling Digressions I perceive my self to be grown old. I us'd to write more methodically.—But one does not dress for private Company as for a publick Ball. 'Tis perhaps only Negligence.—

To return. I continu'd thus employ'd in my Father's Business for two Years, that is till I was 12 Years old; and my Brother John, who was bred to that Business having left my Father, married and set up for himself at Rhodeisland, there was all Appearance that I was destin'd to supply his Place and be a Tallow Chandler. But my Dislike to the Trade continuing, my Father was under Apprehensions that if he did not find one for me more agreable, I should break away and get to Sea, as his Son Josiah had done to his great Vexation. He therefore sometimes took me to walk with him, and see Joiners, Bricklayers, Turners, Braziers, &c. at their Work, that he might observe my Inclination, & endeavour to fix it on some Trade or other on Land.—It has ever since been a Pleasure to me to see good Workmen handle their Tools; and it has been useful to me, having learnt so much by it, as to be able to do little Jobs my self in my House, when a Workman could not readily be got; & to construct little Machines for my Experiments while the Intention of making the Experiment was fresh & warm in my Mind. My Father at last fix'd upon the Cutler's Trade, and my Uncle Benjamin's Son Samuel who was bred to that Business in London being about that time establish'd in Boston, I was sent to be with him some time on liking. But his Expectations of a Fee with me displeasing my Father, I was taken home again.—

From a Child I was fond of Reading, and all the little Money that came into my Hands was ever laid out in Books. Pleas'd with the Pilgrim's Progress, my first Collection was of John Bunyan's Works, in separate little Volumes. I afterwards sold them to enable me to buy R. Burton's Historical Collections; they were small Chapmen's Books and cheap, 40 or 50 in all.—My Father's little Library consisted chiefly of Books in polemic Divinity, most of which I read, and have since often regretted, that at a time when I had such a Thirst for Knowledge, more proper Books had not fallen in my Way, since it was now resolv'd I should not be a Clergyman. Plutarch's Lives there was, in which I read abundantly, and I still think that time spent to great Advantage. There was also a Book of Defoe's called an Essay on Projects and another of Dr Mather's call'd Essays to do Good, which perhaps gave me a Turn of Thinking that had an Influence on some of the principal future Events of my Life.

This Bookish Inclination at length determin'd my Father to make me a Printer, tho' he had already one Son, (James) of that Profession. In 1717 my Brother James return'd from England with a Press & Letters to set up his Business in Boston. I lik'd it much better than that of my Father, but still had a Hankering for the Sea.—To prevent the apprehended Effect of such an Inclination, my Father was impatient to have me bound to my Brother. I stood out some time, but at last was persuaded and signed the Indentures, when I was yet but 12 Years old.—I was to serve as an Apprentice till I was 21 Years of Age, only I was to be allow'd Journeyman's Wages during the last Year. In a little time I made great Proficiency in the

Business, and became a useful Hand to my Brother. I now had Access to better Books. An Acquaintance with the Apprentices of Booksellers, enabled me sometimes to borrow a small one, which I was careful to return soon & clean. Often I sat up in my Room reading the greatest Part of the Night, when the Book was borrow'd in the Evening & to be return'd early in the Morning lest it should be miss'd or wanted.—And after some time an ingenious Tradesman* who had a pretty Collection of Books, & who frequented our Printing House, took Notice of me, invited me to his Library, & very kindly lent me such Books as I chose to read. I now took a Fancy to Poetry, and made some little Pieces. My Brother, thinking it might turn to account encourag'd me, & put me on composing two occasional Ballads. One was called the *Light House Tragedy*, & contain'd an Acc.ᵗ of the drowning of Capt. Worthilake with his Two Daughters; the other was a Sailor Song on the Taking of *Teach* or Blackbeard the Pirate. They were wretched Stuff, in the Grubstreet Ballad Stile, and when they were printed he sent me about the Town to sell them. The first sold wonderfully, the Event being recent, having made a great Noise. This flatter'd my Vanity. But my Father discourag'd me, by ridiculing my Performances, and telling me Verse-makers were generally Beggars; so I escap'd being a Poet, most probably a very bad one. But as Prose Writing has been a great Use to me in the Course of my Life, and was a principal Means of my Advancement, I shall tell you how in such a Situation I acquir'd what little Ability I have in that Way.

There was another Bookish Lad in the Town, John Collins by Name, with whom I was intimately acquainted. We sometimes disputed, and very fond we were of Argument, & very desirous of confuting one another. Which disputacious Turn, by the way, is apt to become a very bad Habit, making People often extreamly disagreable in Company, by the Contradiction that is necessary to bring it into Practice, & thence, besides souring & spoiling the Conversation, is productive of Disgusts & perhaps Enmities where you may have occasion for Friendship. I had caught it by reading my Father's Books

*Mr Matthew Adams

of Dispute about Religion. Persons of good Sense, I have since observ'd, seldom fall into it, except Lawyers, University Men, and Men of all Sorts that have been bred at Edinborough. A Question was once some how or other started between Collins & me, of the Propriety of educating the Female Sex in Learning, & their Abilities for Study. He was of Opinion that it was improper; & that they were naturally unequal to it. I took the contrary Side, perhaps a little for Dispute sake. He was naturally more eloquent, had a ready Plenty of Words, and sometimes as I thought bore me down more by his Fluency than by the Strength of his Reasons. As we parted without settling the Point, & were not to see one another again for some time, I sat down to put my Arguments in Writing, which I copied fair & sent to him. He answer'd & I reply'd. Three or four Letters of a Side had pass'd, when my Father happen'd to find my Papers, and read them. Without entring into the Discussion, he took occasion to talk to me about the Manner of my Writing, observ'd that tho' I had the Advantage of my Antagonist in correct Spelling & pointing (which I ow'd to the Printing House) I fell far short in elegance of Expression, in Method and in Perspicuity, of which he convinc'd me by several Instances. I saw the Justice of his Remarks, & thence grew more attentive to the *Manner* in Writing, and determin'd to endeavour at Improvement. —

About this time I met with an odd Volume of the Spectator. I had never before seen any of them. I bought it, read it over and over, and was much delighted with it. I thought the Writing excellent, & wish'd if possible to imitate it. With that View, I took some of the Papers, & making short Hints of the Sentiment in each Sentence, laid them by a few Days, and then without looking at the Book, try'd to compleat the Papers again, by expressing each hinted Sentiment at length & as fully as it had been express'd before, in any suitable Words that should come to hand.

Then I compar'd my Spectator with the Original, discover'd some of my Faults & corrected them. But I found I wanted a Stock of Words or a Readiness in recollecting & using them, which I thought I should have acquir'd before that time, if I had gone on making Verses, since the continual

Occasion for Words of the same Import but of different Length, to suit the Measure, or of different Sound for the Rhyme, would have laid me under a constant Necessity of searching for Variety, and also have tended to fix that Variety in my Mind, & make me Master of it. Therefore I took some of the Tales & turn'd them into Verse: And after a time, when I had pretty well forgotten the Prose, turn'd them back again. I also sometimes jumbled my Collections of Hints into Confusion, and after some Weeks, endeavour'd to reduce them into the best Order, before I began to form the full Sentences & compleat the Paper. This was to teach me Method in the Arrangement of Thoughts. By comparing my Work afterwards with the original, I discover'd many faults and amended them; but I sometimes had the Pleasure of Fancying that in certain Particulars of small Import, I had been lucky enough to improve the Method or the Language and this encourag'd me to think I might possibly in time come to be a tolerable English Writer, of which I was extreamly ambitious.

My Time for these Exercises & for Reading, was at Night after Work, or before Work begun in the Morning; or on Sundays, when I contrived to be in the Printing House alone, evading as much as I could the common Attendance on publick Worship, which my Father used to exact of me when I was under his Care:—And which indeed I still thought a Duty; tho' I could not, as it seemed to me, afford the Time to practise it.

When about 16 Years of Age, I happen'd to meet with a Book written by one Tryon, recommending a Vegetable Diet. I determined to go into it. My Brother being yet unmarried, did not keep House, but boarded himself & his Apprentices in another Family. My refusing to eat Flesh occasioned an Inconveniency, and I was frequently chid for my singularity. I made my self acquainted with Tryon's Manner of preparing some of his Dishes, such as Boiling Potatoes, or Rice, making Hasty Pudding, & a few others, and then propos'd to my Brother, that if he would give me Weekly half the Money he paid for my Board, I would board my self. He instantly agreed to it, and I presently found that I could save half what he paid me. This was an additional Fund for buying Books:

But I had another Advantage in it. My Brother and the rest going from the Printing House to their Meals, I remain'd there alone, and dispatching presently my light Repast, (which often was no more than a Bisket or a Slice of Bread, a Handful of Raisins or a Tart from the Pastry Cook's, and a Glass of Water) had the rest of the Time till their Return, for Study, in which I made the greater Progress from that greater Clearness of Head & quicker Apprehension which usually attend Temperance in Eating & Drinking. And now it was that being on some Occasion made asham'd of my Ignorance in Figures, which I had twice fail'd in learning when at School, I took Cocker's Book of Arithmetick, & went thro' the whole by my self with great Ease.—I also read Seller's & Sturmy's Books of Navigation, & became acquainted with the little Geometry they contain, but never proceeded far in that Science.—And I read about this Time Locke on Human Understanding and the Art of Thinking by Messrs du Port Royal.

While I was intent on improving my Language, I met with an English Grammar (I think it was Greenwood's) at the End of which there were two little Sketches of the Arts of Rhetoric and Logic, the latter finishing with a Specimen of a Dispute in the Socratic Method. And soon after I procur'd Xenophon's Memorable Things of Socrates, wherein there are many Instances of the same Method. I was charm'd with it, adopted it, dropt my abrupt Contradiction, and positive Argumentation, and put on the humble Enquirer & Doubter. And being then, from reading Shaftsbury & Collins, become a real Doubter in many Points of our Religious Doctrine, I found this Method safest for my self & very embarassing to those against whom I used it, therefore I took a Delight in it, practis'd it continually & grew very artful & expert in drawing People even of superior Knowledge into Concessions the Consequences of which they did not foresee, entangling them in Difficulties out of which they could not extricate themselves, and so obtaining Victories that neither my self nor my Cause always deserved.—I continu'd this Method some few Years, but gradually left it, retaining only the Habit of expressing my self in Terms of modest Diffidence, never using when I advance any thing that may possibly be disputed, the

Words, *Certainly*, *undoubtedly*, or any others that give the Air of Positiveness to an Opinion; but rather say, *I conceive*, or *I apprehend* a Thing to be so or so, *It appears to me*, or *I should think it so or so for such & such Reasons*, or *I imagine* it to be so, or *it is so* if *I am not mistaken.*—This Habit I believe has been of great Advantage to me, when I have had occasion to inculcate my Opinions & persuade Men into Measures that I have been from time to time engag'd in promoting.—And as the chief Ends of Conversation are to *inform*, or to be *informed*, to *please* or to *persuade*, I wish well meaning sensible Men would not lessen their Power of doing Good by a Positive assuming Manner that seldom fails to disgust, tends to create Opposition, and to defeat every one of those Purposes for which Speech was given us, to wit, giving or receiving Information, or Pleasure: For If you would *inform*, a positive dogmatical Manner in advancing your Sentiments, may provoke Contradiction & prevent a candid Attention. If you wish Information & Improvement from the Knowledge of others and yet at the same time express your self as firmly fix'd in your present Opinions, modest sensible Men, who do not love Disputation, will probably leave you undisturb'd in the Possession of your Error; and by such a Manner you can seldom hope to recommend your self in *pleasing* your Hearers, or to persuade those whose Concurrence you desire.—Pope says, judiciously,

> *Men should be taught as if you taught them not,*
> *And things unknown propos'd as things forgot,*—

farther recommending it to us,

> *To speak tho' sure, with seeming Diffidence.*

And he might have couple'd with this Line that which he has coupled with another, I think less properly,

> *For want of Modesty is want of Sense.*

If you ask why *less properly*, I must repeat the Lines;

> "Immodest Words admit of *no* Defence;
> "*For* Want of Modesty is Want of Sense."

Now is not *Want of Sense*, (where a Man is so unfortunate as to want it) some Apology for his *Want of Modesty*? and would not the Lines stand more justly thus?

> Immodest Words admit *but this* Defence,
> That Want of Modesty is Want of Sense.

This however I should submit to better Judgments.—

My Brother had in 1720 or 21, begun to print a Newspaper. It was the second that appear'd in America, & was called *The New England Courant*. The only one before it, was *the Boston News Letter*. I remember his being dissuaded by some of his Friends from the Undertaking, as not likely to succeed, one Newspaper being in their Judgment enough for America.— At this time 1771 there are not less than five & twenty.—He went on however with the Undertaking, and after having work'd in composing the Types & printing off the Sheets I was employ'd to carry the Papers thro' the Streets to the Customers.—He had some ingenious Men among his Friends who amus'd themselves by writing little Pieces for this Paper, which gain'd it Credit, & made it more in Demand; and these Gentlemen often visited us.—Hearing their Conversations, and their Accounts of the Approbation their Papers were receiv'd with, I was excited to try my Hand among them. But being still a Boy, & suspecting that my Brother would object to printing any Thing of mine in his Paper if he knew it to be mine, I contriv'd to disguise my Hand, & writing an anonymous Paper I put it in at Night under the Door of the Printing House. It was found in the Morning & communicated to his Writing Friends when they call'd in as Usual. They read it, commented on it in my Hearing, and I had the exquisite Pleasure, of finding it met with their Approbation, and that in their different Guesses at the Author none were named but Men of some Character among us for Learning & Ingenuity.—I suppose now that I was rather lucky in my Judges: And that perhaps they were not really so very good ones as I then esteem'd them. Encourag'd however by this, I wrote and convey'd in the same Way to the Press several more Papers, which were equally approv'd, and I kept my Secret till my small Fund of Sense for such Performances was pretty well exhausted, & then I discovered it; when I began to be considered a little more by my Brother's Acquaintance, and in a manner that did not quite please him, as he thought, probably with reason, that it tended to make me too vain. And perhaps this might be one Occasion of the Differences that we began to have about this Time. Tho' a Brother, he considered himself as my Master, & me as his Apprentice; and accordingly expected the same Services from me as he would from another; while I thought he demean'd me too much in some he requir'd of me, who from a Brother expected more Indulgence. Our Disputes were often brought before our Father, and I fancy I was either generally in the right, or else a better Pleader, because the Judgment was generally in my favour: But my Brother was passionate & had often beaten me, which I took extreamly amiss; * and thinking my Apprenticeship very tedious, I was continually wishing for some Opportunity of shortening it, which at length offered in a manner unexpected.

One of the Pieces in our News-Paper, on some political Point which I have now forgotten, gave Offence to the Assembly. He was taken up, censur'd and imprison'd for a Month by the Speaker's Warrant, I suppose because he would not discover his Author. I too was taken up & examin'd before the Council; but tho' I did not give them any Satisfaction, they contented themselves with admonishing me, and dismiss'd me; considering me perhaps as an Apprentice who was bound to keep his Master's Secrets. During my Brother's Confinement, which I resented a good deal, notwithstanding our private Differences, I had the Management of the Paper, and I made bold to give our Rulers some Rubs in it, which my Brother took very kindly, while others began to consider me in an unfavourable Light, as a young Genius that had a Turn for Libelling & Satyr. My Brother's Discharge was accompany'd with an Order of the House, (a very odd one) *that James Franklin should no longer print the Paper called the New England Courant.* There was a Consultation held in our Printing House among his Friends what he should do in this

---

*I fancy his harsh & tyrannical Treatment of me, might be a means of impressing me with that Aversion to arbitrary Power that has stuck to me thro' my whole Life.

Case. Some propos'd to evade the Order by changing the Name of the Paper; but my Brother seeing Inconveniences in that, it was finally concluded on as a better Way, to let it be printed for the future under the Name of *Benjamin Franklin.* And to avoid the Censure of the Assembly that might fall on him, as still printing it by his Apprentice, the Contrivance was, that my old Indenture should be return'd to me with a full Discharge on the Back of it, to be shown on Occasion; but to secure to him the Benefit of my Service I was to sign new Indentures for the Remainder of the Term, wch were to be kept private. A very flimsy Scheme it was, but however it was immediately executed, and the Paper went on accordingly under my Name for several Months. At length a fresh Difference arising between my Brother and me, I took upon me to assert my Freedom, presuming that he would not venture to produce the new Indentures. It was not fair in me to take this Advantage, and this I therefore reckon one of the first Errata of my Life: But the Unfairness of it weigh'd little with me, when under the Impressions of Resentment, for the Blows his Passion too often urg'd him to bestow upon me. Tho' He was otherwise not an ill-natur'd Man: Perhaps I was too saucy & provoking.—

When he found I would leave him, he took care to prevent my getting Employment in any other Printing-House of the Town, by going round & speaking to every Master, who accordingly refus'd to give me Work. I then thought of going to New York as the nearest Place where there was a Printer: and I was the rather inclin'd to leave Boston, when I reflected that I had already made my self a little obnoxious, to the governing Party; & from the arbitrary Proceedings of the Assembly in my Brother's Case it was likely I might if I stay'd soon bring my self into Scrapes; and farther that my indiscrete Disputations about Religion began to make me pointed at with Horror by good People, as an Infidel or Atheist; I determin'd on the Point: but my Father now siding with my Brother, I was sensible that if I attempted to go openly, Means would be used to prevent me. My Friend Collins therefore undertook to manage a little for me. He agreed with the Captain of a New York Sloop for my Passage, under the Notion of my being a young Acquaintance of his that had got a naughty

Girl with Child, whose Friends would compel me to marry her, and therefore I could not appear or come away publickly. So I sold some of my Books to raise a little Money, Was taken on board privately, and as we had a fair Wind, in three Days I found my self in New York near 300 Miles from home, a Boy of but 17, without the least Recommendation to or Knowledge of any Person in the Place, and with very little Money in my Pocket.—

My Inclinations for the Sea, were by this time worne out, or I might now have gratify'd them.—But having a Trade, & supposing my self a pretty good Workman, I offer'd my Service to the Printer of the Place, old Mr W.ᵐ Bradford.—He could give me no Employment, having little to do, and Help enough already: But, says he, my Son at Philadelphia has lately lost his principal Hand, Aquila Rose, by Death. If you go thither I believe he may employ you.—Philadelphia was 100 Miles farther. I set out, however, in a Boat for Amboy; leaving my Chest and Things to follow me round by Sea. In crossing the Bay we met with a Squall that tore our rotten Sails to pieces, prevented our getting into the Kill, and drove us upon Long Island. In our Way a drunken Dutchman, who was a Passenger too, fell over board; when he was sinking I reach'd thro' the Water to his shock Pate & drew him up so that we got him in again.—His Ducking sober'd him a little, & he went to sleep, taking first out of his Pocket a Book which he desir'd I would dry for him. It prov'd to be my old favourite Author Bunyan's Pilgrim's Progress in Dutch, finely printed on good Paper with copper Cuts, a Dress better than I had ever seen it wear in its own Language. I have since found that it has been translated into most of the Languages of Europe, and suppose it has been more generally read than any other Book except perhaps the Bible.—Honest John was the first that I know of who mix'd Narration & Dialogue, a Method of Writing very engaging to the Reader, who in the most interesting Parts finds himself as it were brought into the Company, & present at the Discourse. De foe in his Cruso, his Moll Flanders, Religious Courtship, Family Instructor, & other Pieces, has imitated it with Success. And Richardson has done the same in his Pamela, &c.—

When we drew near the Island we found it was at a Place

where there could be no Landing, there being a great Surff on the stony Beach. So we dropt Anchor & swung round towards the Shore. Some People came down to the Water Edge & hallow'd to us, as we did to them. But the Wind was so high & the Surff so loud, that we could not hear so as to understand each other. There were Canoes on the Shore, & we made Signs & hallow'd that they should fetch us, but they either did not understand us, or thought it impracticable. So they went away, and Night coming on, we had no Remedy but to wait till the Wind should abate, and in the mean time the Boatman & I concluded to sleep if we could, and so crouded into the Scuttle with the Dutchman who was still wet, and the Spray beating over the Head of our Boat, leak'd thro' to us, so that we were soon almost as wet as he. In this Manner we lay all Night with very little Rest. But the Wind abating the next Day, we made a Shift to reach Amboy before Night, having been 30 Hours on the Water without Victuals, or any Drink but a Bottle of filthy Rum:—The Water we sail'd on being salt.—

In the Evening I found my self very feverish, & went ill to Bed. But having read somewhere that cold Water drank plentifully was good for a Fever, I follow'd the Prescription, sweat plentifully most of the Night, my Fever left me, and in the Morning crossing the Ferry, proceeded on my Journey, on foot, having 50 Miles to Burlington, where I was told I should find Boats that would carry me the rest of the Way to Philadelphia.

It rain'd very hard all the Day, I was thoroughly soak'd, and by Noon a good deal tir'd, so I stopt at a poor Inn, where I staid all Night, beginning now to wish I had never left home. I cut so miserable a Figure too, that I found by the Questions ask'd me I was suspected to be some runaway Servant, and in danger of being taken up on that Suspicion.—However I proceeded the next Day, and got in the Evening to an Inn within 8 or 10 Miles of Burlington, kept by one Dr Brown.—

He entred into Conversation with me while I took some Refreshment, and finding I had read a little, became very sociable and friendly. Our Acquaintance continu'd as long as he liv'd. He had been, I imagine, an itinerant Doctor, for there

was no Town in England, or Country in Europe, of which
he could not give a very particular Account. He had some
Letters, & was ingenious, but much of an Unbeliever, &
wickedly undertook some Years after to travesty the Bible in
doggrel Verse as Cotton had done Virgil.—By this means he
set many of the Facts in a very ridiculous Light, & might have
hurt weak minds if his Work had been publish'd:—but it
never was.—At his House I lay that Night, and the next
Morning reach'd Burlington.—But had the Mortification to
find that the regular Boats were gone, a little before my coming, and no other expected to go till Tuesday, this being Saturday. Wherefore I return'd to an old Woman in the Town of
whom I had bought Gingerbread to eat on the Water, &
ask'd her Advice; she invited me to lodge at her House till a
Passage by Water should offer; & being tired with my foot
Travelling, I accepted the Invitation. She understanding I was
a Printer, would have had me stay at that Town & follow my
Business, being ignorant of the Stock necessary to begin with.
She was very hospitable, gave me a Dinner of Ox Cheek with
great Goodwill, accepting only of a Pot of Ale in return. And
I tho't my self fix'd till Tuesday should come. However walking in the Evening by the Side of the River a Boat came by,
which I found was going towards Philadelphia, with several
People in her. They took me in, and as there was no Wind,
we row'd all the Way; and about Midnight not having yet
seen the City, some of the Company were confident we must
have pass'd it, and would row no farther, the others knew not
where we were, so we put towards the Shore, got into a
Creek, landed near an old Fence with the Rails of which we
made a Fire, the Night being cold, in October, and there we
remain'd till Daylight. Then one of the Company knew the
Place to be Cooper's Creek a little above Philadelphia, which
we saw as soon as we got out of the Creek, and arriv'd there
about 8 or 9 a Clock, on the Sunday morning, and landed at
the Market street Wharff.—

I have been the more particular in this Description of my
Journey, & shall be so of my first Entry into that City, that
you may in your Mind compare such unlikely Beginning with
the Figure I have since made there. I was in my working
Dress, my best Cloaths being to come round by Sea. I was

dirty from my Journey; my Pockets were stuff'd out with Shirts & Stockings; I knew no Soul, nor where to look for Lodging. I was fatigu'd with Travelling, Rowing & Want of Rest. I was very hungry, and my whole Stock of Cash consisted of a Dutch Dollar and about a Shilling in Copper. The latter I gave the People of the Boat for my Passage, who at first refus'd it on Acc^t of my Rowing; but I insisted on their taking it, a Man being sometimes more generous when he has but a little Money than when he has plenty, perhaps thro' Fear of being thought to have but little. Then I walk'd up the Street, gazing about, till near the Market House I met a Boy with Bread. I had made many a Meal on Bread, & inquiring where he got it, I went immediately to the Baker's he directed me to in second Street; and ask'd for Bisket, intending such as we had in Boston, but they it seems were not made in Philadelphia, then I ask'd for a threepenny Loaf, and was told they had none such: so not considering or knowing the Difference of Money & the greater Cheapness nor the Names of his Bread, I bad him give me three pennyworth of any sort. He gave me accordingly three great Puffy Rolls. I was surpriz'd at the Quantity, but took it, and having no Room in my Pockets, walk'd off, with a Roll under each Arm, & eating the other. Thus I went up Market Street as far as fourth Street, passing by the Door of Mr Read, my future Wife's Father, when she standing at the Door saw me, & thought I made as I certainly did a most awkward ridiculous Appearance. Then I turn'd and went down Chestnut Street and part of Walnut Street, eating my Roll all the Way, and coming round found my self again at Market street Wharff, near the Boat I came in, to which I went for a Draught of the River Water, and being fill'd with one of my Rolls, gave the other two to a Woman & her Child that came down the River in the Boat with us and were waiting to go farther. Thus refresh'd I walk'd again up the Street, which by this time had many clean dress'd People in it who were all walking the same Way; I join'd them, and thereby was led into the great Meeting House of the Quakers near the Market. I sat down among them, and after looking round a while & hearing nothing said, being very drowzy thro' Labour & want of Rest the preceding Night, I fell fast asleep, and continu'd so till the

Meeting broke up, when one was kind enough to rouse me. This was therefore the first House I was in or slept in, in Philadelphia.—

Walking again down towards the River, & looking in the Faces of People, I met a young Quaker Man whose Countenance I lik'd, and accosting him requested he would tell me where a Stranger could get Lodging. We were then near the Sign of the Three Mariners. Here, says he, is one Place that entertains Strangers, but it is not a reputable House; if thee wilt walk with me, I'll show thee a better. He brought me to the Crooked Billet in Water-Street. Here I got a Dinner. And while I was eating it, several sly Questions were ask'd me, as it seem'd to be suspected from my youth & Appearance, that I might be some Runaway. After Dinner my Sleepiness return'd: and being shown to a Bed, I lay down without undressing, and slept till Six in the Evening; was call'd to Supper; went to Bed again very early and slept soundly till the next Morning. Then I made my self as tidy as I could, and went to Andrew Bradford the Printer's.—I found in the Shop the old Man his Father, whom I had seen at New York, and who travelling on horse back had got to Philadelphia before me.—He introduc'd me to his Son, who receiv'd me civilly, gave me a Breakfast, but told me he did not at present want a Hand, being lately supply'd with one. But there was another Printer in town lately set up, one Keimer, who perhaps might employ me; if not, I should be welcome to lodge at his House, & he would give me a little Work to do now & then till fuller Business should offer.

The old Gentleman said, he would go with me to the new Printer: And when we found him, Neighbour, says Bradford, I have brought to see you a young Man of your Business, perhaps you may want such a One. He ask'd me a few Questions, put a Composing Stick in my Hand to see how I work'd, and then said he would employ me soon, tho' he had just then nothing for me to do. And taking old Bradford whom he had never seen before, to be one of the Towns People that had a Good Will for him, enter'd into a Conversation on his present Undertaking & Prospects; while Bradford not discovering that he was the other Printer's Father;

on Keimer's Saying he expected soon to get the greatest Part of the Business into his own Hands, drew him on by artful Questions and starting little Doubts, to explain all his Views, what Interest he rely'd on, & in what manner he intended to proceed.—I who stood by & heard all, saw immediately that one of them was a crafty old Sophister, and the other a mere Novice. Bradford left me with Keimer, who was greatly surpriz'd when I told him who the old Man was.

Keimer's Printing House I found, consisted of an old shatter'd Press, and one small worn-out Fount of English, which he was then using himself, composing in it an Elegy on Aquila Rose before-mentioned, an ingenious young Man of excellent Character much respected in the Town, Clerk of the Assembly, & a pretty Poet. Keimer made Verses, too, but very indifferently.—He could not be said to write them, for his Manner was to compose them in the Types directly out of his Head; so there being no Copy, but one Pair of Cases, and the Elegy likely to require all the Letter, no one could help him.—I endeavour'd to put his Press (which he had not yet us'd, & of which he understood nothing) into Order fit to be work'd with; & promising to come & print off his Elegy as soon as he should have got it ready, I return'd to Bradford's who gave me a little Job to do for the present, & there I lodged & dieted. A few Days after Keimer sent for me to print off the Elegy. And now he had got another Pair of Cases, and a Pamphlet to reprint, on which he set me to work.—

These two Printers I found poorly qualified for their Business. Bradford had not been bred to it, & was very illiterate; and Keimer tho' something of a Scholar, was a mere Compositor, knowing nothing of Presswork. He had been one of the French Prophets and could act their enthusiastic Agitations. At this time he did not profess any particular Religion, but something of all on occasion; was very ignorant of the World, & had, as I afterwards found, a good deal of the Knave in his Composition. He did not like my Lodging at Bradford's while I work'd with him. He had a House indeed, but without Furniture, so he could not lodge me: But he got me a Lodging at Mr Read's before-mentioned, who was the Owner of his House. And my Chest & Clothes being come by this time, I made rather a more respectable Appearance in the Eyes of Miss Read, than I had done when she first happen'd to see me eating my Roll in the Street.—

I began now to have some Acquaintance among the young People of the Town, that were Lovers of Reading with whom I spent my Evenings very pleasantly and gaining Money by my Industry & Frugality, I lived very agreably, forgetting Boston as much as I could, and not desiring that any there should know where I resided except my Friend Collins who was in my Secret, & kept it when I wrote to him.—At length an Incident happened that sent me back again much sooner than I had intended.—

I had a Brother-in-law, Robert Holmes, Master of a Sloop, that traded between Boston and Delaware. He being at New Castle 40 Miles below Philadelphia, heard there of me, and wrote me a Letter, mentioning the Concern of my Friends in Boston at my abrupt Departure, assuring me of their Goodwill to me, and that every thing would be accommodated to my Mind if I would return, to which he exhorted me very earnestly.—I wrote an Answer to his Letter, thank'd him for his Advice, but stated my Reasons for quitting Boston fully, & in such a Light as to convince him I was not so wrong as he had apprehended.—Sir William Keith Governor of the Province, was then at New Castle, and Capt. Holmes happening to be in Company with him when my Letter came to hand, spoke to him of me, and show'd him the Letter. The Governor read it, and seem'd surpriz'd when he was told my Age. He said I appear'd a young Man of promising Parts, and therefore should be encouraged: The Printers at Philadelphia were wretched ones, and if I would set up there, he made no doubt I should succeed; for his Part, he would procure me the publick Business, & do me every other Service in his Power. This my Brother-in-Law afterwards told me in Boston. But I knew as yet nothing of it; when one Day Keimer and I being at Work together near the Window, we saw the Governor and another Gentleman (which prov'd to be Col. French, of New Castle) finely dress'd, come directly across the Street to our House, & heard them at the Door. Keimer ran down immediately, thinking it a Visit to him. But the Governor enquir'd for me, came up, & with a Condescension &

Politeness I had been quite unus'd to, made me many Compliments, desired to be acquainted with me, blam'd me kindly for not having made my self known to him when I first came to the Place, and would have me away with him to the Tavern where he was going with Col. French to taste as he said some excellent Madeira. I was not a little surpriz'd, and Keimer star'd like a Pig poison'd. I went however with the Governor & Col. French, to a Tavern the Corner of Third Street, and over the Madeira he propos'd my Setting up my Business, laid beforre me the Probabilities of Success, & both he & Col French, assur'd me I should have their Interest & Influence in procuring the Publick Business of both Governments. On my doubting whether my Father would assist me in it, Sir William said he would give me a Letter to him, in which he would state the Advantages,—and he did not doubt of prevailing with him. So it was concluded I should return to Boston in the first Vessel with the Governor's Letter recommending me to my Father. In the mean time the Intention was to be kept secret, and I went on working with Keimer as usual, the Governor sending for me now & then to dine with him, a very great Honour I thought it, and conversing with me in the most affable, familiar, & friendly manner imaginable. About the End of April 1724. a little Vessel offer'd for Boston. I took Leave of Keimer as going to see my Friends. The Governor gave me an ample Letter, saying many flattering things of me to my Father, and strongly recommending the Project of my setting up at Philadelphia, as a Thing that must make my Fortune.—We struck on a Shoal in going down the Bay & sprung a Leak, we had a blustring time at Sea, and were oblig'd to pump almost continually, at which I took my Turn.—We arriv'd safe however at Boston in about a Fortnight.—I had been absent Seven Months and my Friends had heard nothing of me, for my Br. Holmes was not yet return'd; and had not written about me. My unexpected Appearance surpriz'd the Family; all were however very glad to see me and made me Welcome, except my Brother. I went to see him at his Printing-House: I was better dress'd than ever while in his Service, having a genteel new Suit from Head to foot, a Watch, and my Pockets lin'd with near Five Pounds Sterling in Silver. He receiv'd me not very frankly,

look'd me all over, and turn'd to his Work again. The Jour-
ney-Men were inquisitive where I had been, what sort of a
Country it was, and how I lik'd it? I prais'd it much, & the
happy Life I led in it; expressing strongly my Intention of
returning to it; and one of them asking what kind of Money
we had there, I produc'd a handful of Silver, and spread it
before them, which was a kind of Raree-Show they had not
been us'd to, Paper being the Money of Boston. Then I took
an Opportunity of letting them see my Watch: and lastly, (my
Brother still grum & sullen) I gave them a Piece of Eight to
drink & took my Leave.—This Visit of mine offended him
extreamly. For when my Mother some time after spoke to
him of a Reconciliation, & of her Wishes to see us on good
Terms together, & that we might live for the future as Brothers, he said, I had insulted him in such a Manner before his
People that he could never forget or forgive it.—In this however he was mistaken.—

My Father receiv'd the Governor's Letter with some apparent Surprize; but said little of it to me for some Days; when
Capt. Homes returning, he show'd it to him, ask'd if he knew
Keith, and what kind of a Man he was: Adding his Opinion
that he must be of small Discretion, to think of setting a Boy
up in Business who wanted yet 3 Years of being at Man's
Estate. Homes said what he could in fav^r of the Project; but
my Father was clear in the Impropriety of it; and at last gave
a flat Denial to it. Then he wrote a civil Letter to Sir William
thanking him for the Patronage he had so kindly offered me,
but declining to assist me as yet in Setting up, I being in his
Opinion too young to be trusted with the Management of a
Business so important; & for which the Preparation must be
so expensive.—

My Friend & Companion Collins, who was a Clerk at the
Post-Office, pleas'd with the Account I gave him of my new
Country, determin'd to go thither also:—And while I waited
for my Fathers Determination, he set out before me by Land
to Rhodeisland, leaving his Books which were a pretty Collection of Mathematicks & Natural Philosophy, to come with
mine & me to New York where he propos'd to wait for me.
My Father, tho' he did not approve Sir William's Proposition
was yet pleas'd that I had been able to obtain so advantageous

a Character from a Person of such Note where I had resided,
and that I had been so industrious & careful as to equip my
self so handsomely in so short a time: therefore seeing no
Prospect of an Accommodation between my Brother & me,
he gave his Consent to my Returning again to Philadelphia,
advis'd me to behave respectfully to the People there, endeavour to obtain the general Esteem, & avoid lampooning
& libelling to which he thought I had too much Inclination;— telling me, that by steady Industry and a prudent Par-
simony, I might save enough by the time I was One and
Twenty to set me up, & that if I came near the Matter he
would help me out with the Rest.—This was all I could obtain, except some small Gifts as Tokens of his & my Mother's
Love, when I embark'd again for New-York, now with their
Approbation & their Blessing.—

   The Sloop putting in at Newport, Rhodeisland, I visited
my Brother John, who had been married & settled there some
Years. He received me very affectionately, for he always lov'd
me.—A Friend of his, one Vernon, having some Money due
to him in Pensilvania, about 35 Pounds Currency, desired I
would receive it for him, and keep it till I had his Directions
what to remit it in. Accordingly he gave me an Order.—This
afterwards occasion'd me a good deal of Uneasiness.—At
Newport we took in a Number of Passengers for New York:
Among which were two young Women, Companions, and a
grave, sensible Matron-like Quaker-Woman with her Atten-
dants.—I had shown an obliging Readiness to do her some
little Services which impress'd her I suppose with a degree of
Good-will towards me.—Therefore when she saw a daily
growing Familiarity between me & the two Young Women,
which they appear'd to encourage, she took me aside & said,
Young Man, I am concern'd for thee, as thou has no Friend
with thee, and seems not to know much of the World, or of
the Snares Youth is expos'd to; depend upon it those are very
bad Women, I can see it in all their Actions, and if thee art
not upon thy Guard, they will draw thee into some Danger:
they are Strangers to thee,—and I advise thee in a friendly
Concern for thy Welfare, to have no Acquaintance with
them.—As I seem'd at first not to think so ill of them as she
did, she mention'd some Things she had observ'd & heard

that had escap'd my Notice; but now convinc'd me she was right. I thank'd her for her kind Advice, and promis'd to follow it.—When we arriv'd at New York, they told me where they liv'd, & invited me to come and see them: but I avoided it. And it was well I did: For the next Day, the Captain miss'd a Silver Spoon & some other Things that had been taken out of his Cabbin, and knowing that these were a Couple of Strumpets, he got a Warrant to search their Lodgings, found the stolen Goods, and had the Thieves punish'd.—So tho' we had escap'd a sunken Rock which we scrap'd upon in the Passage, I thought this Escape of rather more Importance to me. At New York I found my Friend Collins, who had arriv'd there some Time before me. We had been intimate from Children, and had read the same Books together. But he had the Advantage of more time for Reading, & Studying and a wonderful Genius for Mathematical Learning in which he far outstript me. While I liv'd in Boston most of my Hours of Leisure for Conversation were spent with him, & he continu'd a sober as well as an industrious Lad; was much respected for his Learning by several of the Clergy & other Gentlemen, & seem'd to promise making a good Figure in Life: but during my Absence he had acquir'd a Habit of Sotting with Brandy; and I found by his own Account & what I heard from others, that he had been drunk every day since his Arrival at New York, & behav'd very oddly. He had gam'd too and lost his Money, so that I was oblig'd to discharge his Lodgings, & defray his Expences to and at Philadelphia: —Which prov'd extreamly inconvenient to me.—The then Governor of N York, Burnet, Son of Bishop Burnet hearing from the Captain that a young Man, one of his Passengers, had a great many Books, desired he would bring me to see him. I waited upon him accordingly, and should have taken Collins with me but that he was not sober. The Gov.r treated me with greet Civility, show'd me his Library, which was a very large one, & we had a good deal of Conversation about Books & Authors. This was the second Governor who had done me the Honour to take Notice of me, which to a poor Boy like me was very pleasing.—We proceeded to Philadelphia. I received on the Way Vernon's Money, without which we could hardly have finish'd our Journey.—Collins wish'd to be employ'd in some Counting House; but whether they discover'd his Dramming by his Breath, or by his Behaviour, tho' he had some Recommendations, he met with no Success in any Application, and continu'd Lodging & Boarding at the same House with me & at my Expence. Knowing I had that Money of Vernon's he was continually borrowing of me, still promising Repayment as soon as he should be in Business. At length he had got so much of it, that I was distress'd to think what I should do, in case of being call'd on to remit it.—His Drinking continu'd, about which we sometimes quarrel'd, for when a little intoxicated he was very fractious. Once in a Boat on the Delaware with some other young Men, he refused to row in his Turn: I will be row'd home, says he. We will not row you, says I. You must says he, or stay all Night on the Water, just as you please. The others said, Let us row; What signifies it? But my Mind being soured with his other Conduct, I continu'd to refuse. So he swore he would make me row, or throw me overboard; and coming along stepping on the Thwarts towards me, when he came up & struck at me, I clapt my Hand under his Crutch, and rising pitch'd him head-foremost into the River. I knew he was a good Swimmer, and so was under little Concern about him; but before he could get round to lay hold of the Boat, we had with a few Strokes pull'd her out of his Reach.—And ever when he drew near the Boat, we ask'd if he would row, striking a few Strokes to slide her away from him.—He was ready to die with Vexation, & obstinately would not promise to row; however seeing him at last beginning to tire, we lifted him in; and brought him home dripping wet in the Evening. We hardly exchang'd a civil Word afterwards; and a West India Captain who had a Commission to procure a Tutor for the Sons of a Gentleman at Barbadoes, happening to meet with him, agreed to carry him thither. He left me then, promising to remit me the first Money he should receive in order to discharge the Debt. But I never heard of him after.—The Breaking into this Money of Vernon's was one of the first great Errata of my Life. And this Affair show'd that my Father was not much out in his Judgment when he suppos'd me too Young to manage Business of Importance. But Sir William, on reading his Letter, said he was too prudent. There was great Difference in Persons, and Discretion did not always accompany Years, nor was Youth always without it. And since he will not set you up, says he, I will do it my self. Give me an Inventory of the Things necessary to be had from England, and I will send for them. You shall repay me when you are able; I am resolv'd to have a good Printer here, and I am sure you must succeed. This was spoken with such an Appearance of Cordiality, that I had not the least doubt of his meaning what he said.—I had hitherto kept the Proposition of my Setting up a Secret in Philadelphia, & I still kept it. Had it been known that I depended on the Governor, probably some Friend that knew him better would have advis'd me not to rely on him, as I afterwards heard it as his known Character to be liberal of Promises which he never meant to keep.—Yet unsolicited as he was by me, how could I think his generous Offers insincere? I believ'd him one of the best Men in the World.—

I presented him an Inventory of a little Print^g House, amounting by my Computation to about 100£ Sterling. He lik'd it, but ask'd me if my being on the Spot in England to chuse the Types & see that every thing was good of the kind, might not be of some Advantage. Then, says he, when there, you may make Acquaintances & establish Correspondencies in the Bookselling, & Stationary Way. I agreed that this might be advantageous. Then says he, get yourself ready to go with Annis; which was the annual Ship, and the only one at that Time usually passing between London and Philadelphia. But it would be some Months before Annis sail'd, so I continu'd working with Keimer, fretting about the Money Collins had got from me, and in daily Apprehensions of being call'd upon by Vernon, which however did not happen for some Years after.—

I believe I have omitted mentioning that in my first Voyage from Boston, being becalm'd off Block Island, our People set about catching Cod & hawl'd up a great many. Hitherto I had stuck to my Resolution of not eating animal Food; and on this Occasion, I consider'd with my Master Tryon, the taking every Fish as a kind of unprovok'd Murder, since none of them had or ever could do us any Injury that might justify the Slaughter.— All this seem'd very reasonable.—But I had formerly been a great Lover of Fish, & when this came hot out of the Frying Pan, it smelt admirably well. I balanc'd some time between Principle & Inclination: till I recollected, that when the Fish were opened, I saw smaller Fish taken out of their Stomachs:—Then, thought I, if you eat one another, I don't see why we mayn't eat you. So I din'd upon Cod very heartily and continu'd to eat with other People, returning only now & then occasionally to a vegetable Diet. So convenient a thing it is to be a *reasonable Creature*, since it enables one to find or make a Reason for every thing one has a mind to do.—

Keimer & I liv'd on a pretty good familiar Footing & agreed tolerably well: for he suspected nothing of my Setting up. He retain'd a great deal of his old Enthusiasms, and lov'd an Argumentation. We therefore had many Disputations. I us'd to work him so with my Socratic Method, and had trapann'd him so often by Questions apparently so distant from any Point we had in hand, and yet by degrees led to the Point, and brought him into Difficulties & Contradictions, that at last he grew ridiculously cautious, and would hardly answer me the most common Question, without asking first, *What do you intend to infer from that?* However it gave him so high an Opinion of my Abilities in the Confuting Way, that he seriously propos'd my being his Colleague in a Project he had of setting up a new Sect. He was to preach the Doctrines, and I was to confound all Opponents. When he came to explain with me upon the Doctrines, I found several Conundrums which I objected to, unless I might have my Way a little too, and introduce some of mine. Keimer wore his Beard at full Length, because somewhere in the Mosaic Law it is said, *thou shalt not mar the Corners of thy Beard.* He likewise kept the seventh day Sabbath; and these two Points were Essentials with him.—I dislik'd both, but agreed to admit them upon Condition of his adopting the Doctrine of using no animal Food. I doubt, says he, my Constitution will not bear that. I assur'd him it would, & that he would be the better for it. He was usually a great Glutton, and I promis'd my self some Diversion in half-starving him. He agreed to try the Practice if I would keep him Company. I did so and we held it for three Months. We had our Victuals dress'd and brought to us regularly by a Woman in the Neighbourhood, who had from me a List of 40 Dishes to be prepar'd for us at different times, in all which there was neither Fish Flesh nor Fowl, and the Whim suited me the better at this time from the Cheapness of it, not costing us above 18^d Sterling each, per Week.—I have since kept several Lents most strictly, Leaving the common Diet for that, and that for the common, abruptly, without the least Inconvenience: So that I think there is little in the Advice of making those Changes by easy Gradations.—I went on pleasantly, but Poor Keimer suffer'd grievously, tir'd of the Project, long'd for the Flesh Pots of Egypt, and order'd a roast Pig; He invited me & two Women Friends to dine with him, but it being brought too soon upon table, he could not resist the Temptation, and ate it all up before we came.—

I had made some Courtship during this time to Miss Read, I had a great Respect & Affection for her, and had some Reason to believe she had the same for me: but as I was about to take a long Voyage, and we were both very young, only a little above 18. it was thought most prudent by her Mother to prevent our going too far at present, as a Marriage if it was to take place would be more convenient after my Return, when I should be as I expected set up in my Business. Perhaps too she thought my Expectations not so well founded as I imagined them to be.—

My chief Acquaintances at this time were, Charles Osborne, Joseph Watson, & James Ralph; All Lovers of Reading. The two first were Clerks to an eminent Scrivener or Conveyancer in the Town, Charles Brogden; the other was Clerk to a Merchant. Watson was a pious sensible young Man, of great Integrity.—The others rather more lax in their Principles of Religion, particularly Ralph, who as well as Collins had been unsettled by me, for which they both made me suffer.—Osborne was sensible, candid, frank, sincere, and affectionate to his Friends; but in litterary Matters too fond of Criticising. Ralph, was ingenious, genteel in his Manners, & extreamly eloquent; I think I never knew a prettier Talker.— Both of them great Admirers of Poetry, and began to try their Hands in little Pieces. Many pleasant Walks we four had together, on Sundays into the Woods near Skuylkill, where we read to one another & conferr'd on what we read. Ralph was inclin'd to pursue the Study of Poetry, not doubting but he might become eminent in it and make his Fortune by it, alledging that the best Poets must when they first began to write, make as many Faults as he did.—Osborne dissuaded him, assur'd him he had no Genius for Poetry, & advis'd him to think of nothing beyond the Business he was bred to; that in the mercantile way tho' he had no Stock, he might by his Diligence & Punctuality recommend himself to Employment as a Factor, and in time acquire wherewith to trade on his own Account. I approv'd the amusing one's Self with Poetry now & then, so far as to improve one's Language, but no farther. On this it was propos'd that we should each of us at our next Meeting produce a Piece of our own Composing, in order to improve by our mutual Observations, Criticisms & Corrections. As Language & Expression was what we had in View, we excluded all Considerations of Invention, by agreeing that the Task should be a Version of the 18th Psalm, which describes the Descent of a Deity. When the Time of our Meeting drew nigh, Ralph call'd on me first, & let me know his Piece was ready. I told him I had been busy, & having little Inclination had done nothing.—He then show'd me his Piece for my Opinion; and I much approv'd it, as it appear'd to me to have great Merit. Now, says he, Osborne never will allow the least Merit in any thing of mine, but makes 1000 Criticisms out of mere Envy. He is not so jealous of you. I wish therefore you would take this Piece, & produce it as yours. I will pretend not to have had time, & so produce nothing: We shall then see what he will say to it.—It was agreed, and I immediately transcrib'd it that it might appear in my own hand. We met. Watson's Performance was read: there were some Beauties in it: but many Defects. Osborne's was read: It was much better. Ralph did it Justice, remark'd some Faults, but applauded the Beauties. He himself had nothing to produce. I was backward, seem'd desirous of being excus'd, had not had sufficient Time to correct; &c. but no Excuse could be admitted, produce I must. It was read and repeated; Watson and Osborne gave up the Contest; and join'd in applauding it immoderately. Ralph only made some Criticisms & propos'd some Amendments, but I defended my

Text. Osborne was against Ralph, & told him he was no better a Critic than Poet; so he dropt the Argument. As they two
went home together, Osborne express'd himself still more
strongly in favour of what he thought my Production, having
restrain'd himself before as he said, lest I should think it Flattery. But who would have imagin'd, says he, that Franklin
had been capable of such a Performance; such Painting, such
Force! such Fire! he has even improv'd the Original! In his
common Conversation, he seems to have no Choice of
Words; he hesitates and blunders; and yet, good God, how
he writes!—When we next met, Ralph discover'd the Trick
we had plaid him, and Osborne was a little laught at. This
Transaction fix'd Ralph in his Resolution of becoming a Poet.
I did all I could to dissuade him from it, but He continu'd
scribbling Verses, till *Pope* cur'd him.—He became however
a pretty good Prose Writer. More of him hereafter. But as I
may not have occasion again to mention the other two, I shall
just remark here, that Watson died in my Arms a few Years
after, much lamented, being the best of our Set. Osborne
went to the West Indies, where he became an eminent Lawyer
& made Money, but died young. He and I had made a serious Agreement, that the one who happen'd first to die,
should if possible make a friendly Visit to the other, and acquaint him how he found things in that separate State. But
he never fulfill'd his Promise.

The Governor, seeming to like my Company, had me
frequently to his House; & his Setting me up was always
mention'd as a fix'd thing. I was to take with me Letters
recommendatory to a Number of his Friends, besides the
Letter of Credit, to furnish me with the necessary Money for
purchasing the Press & Types, Paper, &c. For these Letters I
was appointed to call at different times, when they were to be
ready, but a future time was still named.—Thus we went on
till the Ship whose Departure too had been several times
postponed was on the Point of sailing. Then when I call'd to
take my Leave & receive the Letters, his Secretary, Dr Bard,
came out to me and said the Governor was extreamly busy,
in writing, but would be down at Newcastle before the Ship,
& there the Letters would be delivered to me.

Ralph, tho' married & having one Child, had determined

to accompany me in this Voyage. It was thought he intended to establish a Correspondence, & obtain Goods to sell on Commission. But I found afterwards, that thro' some Discontent with his Wifes Relations, he purposed to leave her on their Hands, & never return again.—Having taken leave of my Friends, & interchang'd some Promises with Miss Read, I left Philadelphia in the Ship, which anchor'd at Newcastle. The Governor was there. But when I went to his Lodging, the Secretary came to me from him with the civillest Message in the World, that he could not then see me being engag'd in Business of the utmost Importance, but should send the Letters to me on board, wish'd me heartily a good Voyage and a speedy Return, &c. I return'd on board, a little puzzled, but still not doubting.—

Mr Andrew Hamilton, a famous Lawyer of Philadelphia, had taken Passage in the same Ship for himself and Son: and with Mr Denham a Quaker Merchant, & Messrs Onion & Russel Masters of an Iron Work in Maryland, had engag'd the Great Cabin; so that Ralph and I were forc'd to take up with a Birth in the Steerage:—And none on board knowing us, were considered as ordinary Persons.—But Mr Hamilton & his Son (it was James, since Governor) return'd from New Castle to Philadelphia, the Father being recall'd by a great Fee to plead for a seized Ship.—And just before we sail'd Col. French coming on board, & showing me great Respect, I was more taken Notice of, and with my Friend Ralph invited by the other Gentlemen to come into the Cabin, there being now Room. Accordingly we remov'd thither.

Understanding that Col. French had brought on board the Governor's Dispatches, I ask'd the Captain for those Letters that were to be under my Care. He said all were put into the Bag together; and he could not then come at them; but before we landed in England, I should have an Opportunity of picking them out. So I was satisfy'd for the present, and we proceeded on our Voyage. We had a sociable Company in the Cabin, and lived uncommonly well, having the Addition of all Mr Hamilton's Stores, who had laid in plentifully. In this Passage Mr Denham contracted a Friendship for me that continued during his Life. The Voyage was otherwise not a pleasant one, as we had a great deal of bad Weather.—

When we came into the Channel, the Captain kept his Word with me, & gave me an Opportunity of examining the Bag for the Governor's Letters. I found none upon which my Name was put, as under my Care; I pick'd out 6 or 7 that by the Handwriting I thought might be the promis'd Letters, especially as one of them was directed to Basket the King's Printer, and another to some Stationer. We arriv'd in London the 24th of December, 1724.—I waited upon the Stationer who came first in my Way, delivering the Letter as from Gov. Keith. I don't know such a Person, says he: but opening the Letter, O, this is from Riddlesden; I have lately found him to be a compleat Rascal, and I will have nothing to do with him, nor receive any Letters from him. So putting the Letter into my Hand, he turn'd on his Heel & left me to serve some Customer.—I was surprized to find these were not the Governor's Letters. And after recollecting and comparing Circumstances, I began to doubt his Sincerity.—I found my Friend Denham, and opened the whole Affair to him. He let me into Keith's Character, told me there was not the least Probability that he had written any Letters for me, that no one who knew him had the smallest Dependance on him, and he laught at the Notion of the Governor's giving me a Letter of Credit, having as he said no Credit to give.—On my expressing some Concern about what I should do: He advis'd me to endeavour getting some Employment in the Way of my Business. Among the Printers here, says he, you will improve yourself; and when you return to America, you will set up to greater Advantage.—

We both of us happen'd to know, as well as the Stationer, that Riddlesden the Attorney, was a very Knave. He had half ruin'd Miss Read's Father by drawing him in to be bound for him. By his Letter it appear'd, there was a secret Scheme on foot to the Prejudice of Hamilton, (Suppos'd to be then coming over with us,) and that Keith was concern'd in it with Riddlesden. Denham, who was a Friend of Hamilton's, thought he ought to be acquainted with it. So when he arriv'd in England, which was soon after, partly from Resentment & Ill-Will to Keith & Riddlesden, & partly from Good Will to him: I waited on him, and gave him the Letter. He thank'd me cordially, the Information being of Importance to him. And from that time he became my Friend, greatly to my Advantage afterwards on many Occasions.

But what shall we think of a Governor's playing such pitiful Tricks, & imposing so grossly on a poor ignorant Boy! It was a Habit he had acquired. He wish'd to please every body; and having little to give, he gave Expectations.—He was otherwise an ingenious sensible Man, a pretty good Writer, & a good Governor for the People, tho' not for his Constituents the Proprietaries, whose Instructions he sometimes disregarded.—Several of our best Laws were of his Planning, and pass'd during his Administration.—

Ralph and I were inseparable Companions. We took Lodgings together in Little Britain at 3/6 per Week, as much as we could then afford.—He found some Relations, but they were poor & unable to assist him. He now let me know his Intentions of remaining in London, and that he never meant to return to Philad.ª—He had brought no Money with him, the whole he could muster having been expended in paying his Passage.—I had 15 Pistoles: So he borrowed occasionally of me, to subsist while he was looking out for Business.—He first endeavoured to get into the Playhouse, believing himself qualify'd for an Actor; but Wilkes, to whom he apply'd, advis'd him candidly not to think of that Employment, as it was impossible he should succeed in it.—Then he propos'd to Roberts, a Publisher in Paternoster Row, to write for him a Weekly Paper like the Spectator, on certain Conditions, which Roberts did not approve. Then he endeavour'd to get Employmt. as a Hackney Writer to copy for the Stationers & Lawyers about the Temple: but could find no Vacancy.—

I immediately got into Work at Palmer's then a famous Printing House in Bartholomew Close; and here I continu'd near a Year. I was pretty diligent; but spent with Ralph a good deal of my Earnings in going to Plays & other Places of Amusement. We had together consum'd all my Pistoles, and now just rubb'd on from hand to mouth. He seem'd quite to forget his Wife & Child, and I by degrees my Engagements wth Miss Read, to whom I never wrote more than one Letter, & that was to let her know I was not likely soon to return. This was another of the great Errata of my Life, which I should wish to correct if I were to live it over again.—In fact, by our Expences, I was constantly kept unable to pay my Passage.

At Palmer's I was employ'd in Composing for the second Edition of Woollaston's Religion of Nature. Some of his Reasonings not appearing to me well-founded, I wrote a little metaphysical Piece, in which I made Remarks on them. It was entitled, *A Dissertation on Liberty & Necessity, Pleasure and Pain.*—I inscrib'd it to my Friend Ralph.—I printed a small Number. It occasion'd my being more consider'd by Mr Palmer, as a young Man of some Ingenuity, tho' he seriously expostulated with me upon the Principles of my Pamphlet which to him appear'd abominable. My printing this Pamphlet was another Erratum.

While I lodg'd in Little Britain I made an Acquaintance with one Wilcox a Bookseller, whose Shop was at the next Door. He had an immense Collection of second-hand Books. Circulating Libraries were not then in Use; but we agreed that on certain reasonable Terms which I have now forgotten, I might take, read & return any of his Books. This I esteem'd a great Advantage, & I made as much Use of it as I could.—

My Pamphlet by some means falling into the Hands of one Lyons, a Surgeon, Author of a Book intituled *The Infallibility of Human Judgment*, it occasioned an Acquaintance between us; he took great Notice of me, call'd on me often, to converse on these Subjects, carried me to the Horns a pale Ale-House in   Lane, Cheapside, and introduc'd me to Dr Mandevile, Author of the Fable of the Bees who had a Club there, of which he was the Soul, being a most facetious entertaining Companion. Lyons too introduc'd me to Dr Pemberton, at Batson's Coffee House, who promis'd to give me an Opportunity some time or other of seeing Sir Isaac Newton, of which I was extreamly desirous; but this never happened.

I had brought over a few Curiosities among which the principal was a Purse made of the Asbestos, which purifies by Fire. Sir Hans Sloane heard of it, came to see me, and invited me to his House in Bloomsbury Square; where he show'd me all his Curiosities, and persuaded me to let him add that to the Number, for which he paid me handsomely.—

In our House there lodg'd a young Woman; a Millener,

who I think had a Shop in the Cloisters. She had been gen-
teelly bred; was sensible & lively, and of most pleasing Conversation.—Ralph read Plays to her in the Evenings, they
grew intimate, she took another Lodging, and he follow'd
her. They liv'd together some time, but he being still out of
Business, & her Income not sufficient to maintain them with
her Child, he took a Resolution of going from London, to
try for a Country School, which he thought himself well qualify'd to undertake, as he wrote an excellent Hand, & was a
Master of Arithmetic & Accounts.—This however he deem'd
a Business below him, & confident of future better Fortune
when he should be unwilling to have it known that he once
was so meanly employ'd, he chang'd his Name, & did me the
Honour to assume mine.—For I soon after had a Letter from
him, acquainting me, that he was settled in a small Village in
Berkshire, I think it was, where he taught reading & writing
to 10 or a dozen Boys at 6 pence each per Week, recommending Mrs T. to my Care, and desiring me to write to him
directing for Mr Franklin Schoolmaster at such a Place. He
continu'd to write frequently, sending me large Specimens of
an Epic Poem, which he was then composing, and desiring
my Remarks & Corrections.—These I gave him from time to
time, but endeavour'd rather to discourage his Proceeding.
One of Young's Satires was then just publish'd. I copy'd &
sent him a great Part of it, which set in a strong Light the
Folly of pursuing the Muses with any Hope of Advancement
by them. All was in vain. Sheets of the Poem continu'd to
come by every Post. In the mean time Mrs T. having on his
Account lost her Friends & Business, was often in Distresses,
& us'd to send for me, and borrow what I could spare to help
her out of them. I grew fond of her Company, and being at
this time under no Religious Restraints, & presuming on my
Importance to her, I attempted Familiarities, (another Erratum) which she repuls'd with a proper Resentment, and
acquainted him with my Behaviour. This made a Breach
between us, & when he return'd again to London, he let me
know he thought I had cancel'd all the Obligations he had
been under to me.—So I found I was never to expect his
Repaying me what I lent to him or advanc'd for him. This
was however not then of much Consequence, as he was

totally unable.—And in the Loss of his Friendship I found my self reliev'd from a Burthen. I now began to think of getting a little Money beforehand; and expecting better Work, I left Palmer's to work at Watts's near Lincoln's Inn Fields, a still greater Printing House. Here I continu'd all the rest of my Stay in London.

At my first Admission into this Printing House, I took to working at Press, imagining I felt a Want of the Bodily Exercise I had been us'd to in America, where Presswork is mix'd with Composing. I drank only Water; the other Workmen, near 50 in Number, were great Guzzlers of Beer. On occasion I carried up & down Stairs a large Form of Types in each hand, when others carried but one in both Hands. They wonder'd to see from this & several Instances that the Water-American as they call'd me was *stronger* than themselves who drunk *strong* Beer. We had an Alehouse Boy who attended always in the House to supply the Workmen. My Companion at the Press, drank every day a Pint before Breakfast, a Pint at Breakfast with his Bread and Cheese; a Pint between Breakfast and Dinner; a Pint at Dinner; a Pint in the Afternoon about Six o'clock, and another when he had done his Day's-Work. I thought it a detestable Custom.—But it was necessary, he suppos'd, to drink *strong* Beer that he might be *strong* to labour. I endeavour'd to convince him that the Bodily Strength afforded by Beer could only be in proportion to the Grain or Flour of the Barley dissolved in the Water of which it was made; that there was more Flour in a Pennyworth of Bread, and therefore if he would eat that with a Pint of Water, it would give him more Strength than a Quart of Beer.—He drank on however, & had 4 or 5 Shillings to pay out of his Wages every Saturday Night for that muddling Liquor; an Expence I was free from.—And thus these poor Devils keep themselves always under.

Watts after some Weeks desiring to have me in the Composing-Room, I left the Pressmen. A new *Bienvenu* or Sum for Drink, being 5/, was demanded of me by the Compostors. I thought it an Imposition, as I had paid below. The Master thought so too, and forbad my Paying it. I stood out two or three Weeks, was accordingly considered as an Excommunicate, and had so many little Pieces of private Mischief done me, by mixing my Sorts, transposing my Pages, breaking my Matter, &c. &c. if I were ever so little out of the Room, & all ascrib'd to the Chapel Ghost, which they said ever haunted those not regularly admitted, that notwithstanding the Master's Protection, I found myself oblig'd to comply and pay the Money; convinc'd of the Folly of being on ill Terms with those one is to live with continually. I was now on a fair Footing with them, and soon acquir'd considerable Influence. I propos'd some reasonable Alterations in their * Chapel Laws, and carried them against all Opposition. From my Example a great Part of them, left their muddling Breakfast of Beer & Bread & Cheese, finding they could with me be supply'd from a neighbouring House with a large Porringer of hot Water-gruel, sprinkled with Pepper, crumb'd with Bread, & a Bit of Butter in it, for the Price of a Pint of Beer, viz, three halfpence. This was a more comfortable as well as cheaper Breakfast, & kept their Heads clearer.—Those who continu'd sotting with Beer all day, were often, by not paying, out of Credit at the Alehouse, and us'd to make Interest with me to get Beer, *their Light*, as they phras'd it, *being out*. I watch'd the Pay table on Saturday Night, & collected what I stood engag'd for them, having to pay some times near Thirty Shillings a Week on their Accounts.—This, and my being esteem'd a pretty good Riggite, that is a jocular verbal Satyrist, supported my Consequence in the Society.—My constant Attendance, (I never making a St. Monday), recommended me to the Master; and my uncommon Quickness at Composing, occasion'd my being put upon all Work of Dispatch which was generally better paid. So I went on now very agreably.—

My Lodging in Little Britain being too remote, I found another in Duke-street opposite to the Romish Chapel. It was two pair of Stairs backwards at an Italian Warehouse. A Widow Lady kept the House; she had a Daughter & a Maid Servant, and a Journey-man who attended the Warehouse, but lodg'd abroad.—After sending to enquire my Character at the House where I last lodg'd, she agreed to take me in at the same Rate 3/6 per Week, cheaper as she said from the Pro-

*A Printing House is always called a Chappel by the Workmen.—

tection she expected in having a Man lodge in the House. She
was a Widow, an elderly Woman, had been bred a Protestant,
being a Clergyman's Daughter, but was converted to the
Catholic Religion by her Husband, whose Memory she much
revered, had lived much among People of Distinction, and
knew a 1000 Anecdotes of them as far back as the Times of
Charles the second. She was lame in her Knees with the
Gout, and therefore seldom stirr'd out of her Room, so
sometimes wanted Company; and hers was so highly amusing
to me; that I was sure to spend an Evening with her whenever she desired it. Our Supper was only half an Anchovy
each, on a very little Strip of Bread & Butter, and half a Pint
of Ale between us.—But the Entertainment was in her Conversation. My always keeping good Hours, and giving little
Trouble in the Family, made her unwilling to part with me;
so that when I talk'd of a Lodging I had heard of, nearer my
Business, for 2/ a Week, which, intent as I now was on saving
Money, made some Difference; she bid me not think of it,
for she would abate me two Shillings a Week for the future,
so I remain'd with her at 1/6 as long as I staid in London.—

   In a Garret of her House there lived a Maiden Lady of 70
in the most retired Manner, of whom my Landlady gave me
this Account, that she was a Roman-Catholic, had been sent
abroad when young & lodg'd in a Nunnery with an Intent of
becoming a Nun: but the Country not agreeing with her, she
return'd to England, where there being no Nunnery, she had
vow'd to lead the Life of a Nun as near as might be done in
those Circumstances: Accordingly She had given all her Estate to charitable Uses, reserving only Twelve Pounds a Year
to live on, and out of this Sum she still gave a great deal in
Charity, living her self on Watergruel only, & using no Fire
but to boil it.—She had lived many Years in that Garret,
being permitted to remain there gratis by successive catholic
Tenants of the House below, as they deem'd it a Blessing to
have her there. A Priest visited her, to confess her every Day.
I have ask'd her, says my Landlady, how she, as she liv'd,
could possibly find so much Employment for a Confessor? O,
says she, it is impossible to avoid *vain Thoughts*. I was permitted once to visit her: She was chearful & polite, & convers'd pleasantly. The Room was clean, but had no other

Furniture than a Matras, a Table with a Crucifix & Book, a Stool, which she gave me to sit on, and a Picture over the Chimney of St. *Veronica*, displaying her Handkerchief with the miraculous Figure of Christ's bleeding Face on it, which she explain'd to me with great Seriousness. She look'd pale, but was never sick, and I give it as another Instance on how small an Income Life & Health may be supported.—

At Watts's Printinghouse I contracted an Acquaintance with an ingenious young Man, one Wygate, who having wealthy Relations, had been better educated than most Printers, was a tolerable Latinist, spoke French, & lov'd Reading. I taught him, & a Friend of his, to swim, at twice going into the River, & they soon became good Swimmers. They introduc'd me to some Gentlemen from the Country who went to Chelsea by Water to see the College and Don Saltero's Curiosities. In our Return, at the Request of the Company, whose Curiosity Wygate had excited, I stript & leapt into the River, & swam from near Chelsea to Blackfryars, performing on the Way many Feats of Activity both upon & under Water, that surpriz'd & pleas'd those to whom they were Novelties.—I had from a Child been ever delighted with this Exercise, had studied & practis'd all Thevenot's Motions & Positions, added some of my own, aiming at the graceful & easy, as well as the Useful.—All these I took this Occasion of exhibiting to the Company, & was much flatter'd by their Admiration.—And Wygate, who was desirous of becoming a Master, grew more & more attach'd to me, on that account, as well as from the Similarity of our Studies. He at length propos'd to me travelling all over Europe together, supporting ourselves every where by working at our Business. I was once inclin'd to it. But mentioning it to my good Friend Mr Denham, with whom I often spent an Hour, when I had Leisure. He dissuaded me from it; advising me to think only of return^g to Pensilvania, which he was now about to do.—

I must record one Trait of this good Man's Character. He had formerly been in Business at Bristol, but fail'd in Debt to a Number of People, compounded and went to America. There, by a close Application to Business as a Merchant, he acquir'd a plentiful Fortune in a few Years. Returning to England in the Ship with me, He invited his old Creditors to an

Entertainment, at which he thank'd them for the easy Composition they had favour'd him with, & when they expected nothing but the Treat, every Man at the first Remove, found under his Plate an Order on a Banker for the full Amount of the unpaid Remainder with Interest.

He now told me he was about to return to Philadelphia, and should carry over a great Quantity of Goods in order to open a Store there: He propos'd to take me over as his Clerk, to keep his Books (in which he would instruct me) copy his Letters, and attend the Store. He added, that as soon as I should be acquainted with mercantile Business he would promote me by sending me with a Cargo of Flour & Bread &c to the West Indies, and procure me Commissions from others; which would be profitable, & if I manag'd well, would establish me handsomely. The Thing pleas'd me, for I was grown tired of London, remember'd with Pleasure the happy Months I had spent in Pennsylvania, and wish'd again to see it. Therefore I immediately agreed, on the Terms of Fifty Pounds a Year Pensylvania Money; less indeed than my then present Gettings as a Compostor, but affording a better Prospect.—

I now took Leave of Printing, as I thought for ever, and was daily employ'd in my new Business; going about with Mr Denham among the Tradesmen, to purchase various Articles, & see them pack'd up, doing Errands, calling upon Workmen to dispatch, &c. and when all was on board, I had a few Days Leisure. On one of these Days I was to my Surprize sent for by a great Man I knew only by Name, a Sir William Wyndham and I waited upon him. He had heard by some means or other of my Swimming from Chelsey to Blackfryars, and of my teaching Wygate and another young Man to swim in a few Hours. He had two Sons about to set out on their Travels; he wish'd to have them first taught Swimming; and propos'd to gratify me handsomely if I would teach them.—They were not yet come to Town and my Stay was uncertain, so I could not undertake it. But from this Incident I thought it likely, that if I were to remain in England and open a Swimming School, I might get a good deal of Money.—And it struck me so strongly, that had the Overture been sooner made me, probably I should not so

soon have returned to America.—After Many Years, you & I
had something of more Importance to do with one of these
Sons of Sir William Wyndham, become Earl of Egremont,
which I shall mention in its Place.—

Thus I spent about 18 Months in London. Most Part of the
Time, I work'd hard at my Business, & spent but little upon
my self except in seeing Plays, & in Books.—My Friend
Ralph had kept me poor. He owed me about 27 Pounds;
which I was now never likely to receive; a great Sum out of
my small Earnings. I lov'd him notwithstanding, for he had
many amiable Qualities.—tho' I had by no means improv'd
my Fortune.—But I had pick'd up some very ingenious Acquaintance whose Conversation was of great Advantage to
me, and I had read considerably.

We sail'd from Gravesend on the 23^d of July 1726.—For The
Incidents of the Voyage, I refer you to my Journal, where you
will find them all minutely related. Perhaps the most important Part of that Journal is the *Plan* to be found in it which I
formed at Sea, for regulating my future Conduct in Life. It is
the more remarkable, as being form'd when I was so young,
and yet being pretty faithfully adhered to quite thro' to old
Age.—We landed in Philadelphia the 11th of October, where
I found sundry Alterations. Keith was no longer Governor,
being superceded by Major Gordon: I met him walking the
Streets as a common Citizen. He seem'd a little asham'd at
seeing me, but pass'd without saying any thing. I should have
been as much asham'd at seeing Miss Read, had not her Fr.^{ds}
despairing with Reason of my Return, after the Receipt of
my Letter, persuaded her to marry another, one Rogers, a
Potter, which was done in my Absence. With him however
she was never happy, and soon parted from him, refusing to
cohabit with him, or bear his Name It being now said that
he had another Wife. He was a worthless Fellow tho' an excellent Workman which was the Temptation to her Friends.
He got into Debt, and ran away in 1727 or 28, went to the
West Indies, and died there. Keimer had got a better House,
a Shop well supply'd with Stationary, plenty of new Types, a
number of Hands tho' none good, and seem'd to have a great
deal of Business.

Mr Denham took a Store in Water Street, where we open'd

our Goods. I attended the Business diligently, studied Accounts, and grew in a little Time expert at selling.—We lodg'd and boarded together, he counsell'd me as a Father, having a sincere Regard for me: I respected & lov'd him: and we might have gone on together very happily: But in the Beginning of Feb.ʸ 172⁶⁄₇ when I had just pass'd my 21ˢᵗ Year, we both were taken ill. My Distemper was a Pleurisy, which very nearly carried me off:—I suffered a good deal, gave up the Point in my own mind, & was rather disappointed when I found my self recovering; regretting in some degree that I must now sometime or other have all that disagreable Work to do over again.—I forget what his Distemper was. It held him a long time, and at length carried him off. He left me a small Legacy in a nuncupative Will, as a Token of his Kindness for me, and he left me once more to the wide World. For the Store was taken into the Care of his Executors, and my Employment under him ended:—My Brother-in-law Homes, being now at Philadelphia, advis'd my Return to my Business. And Keimer tempted me with an Offer of large Wages by the Year to come & take the Management of his Printing-House that he might better attend his Stationer's Shop.—I had heard a bad Character of him in London, from his Wife & her Friends, & was not fond of having any more to do with him. I try'd for farther Employment as a Merchant's Clerk; but not readily meeting with any, I clos'd again with Keimer.—

I found in *his* House these Hands; Hugh Meredith a Welsh-Pensilvanian, 30 Years of Age, bred to Country Work: honest, sensible, had a great deal of solid Observation, was something of a Reader, but given to drink:—Stephen Potts, a young Country Man of full Age, bred to the Same:—of uncommon natural Parts, & great Wit & Humour, but a little idle.—These he had agreed with at extream low Wages, per Week, to be rais'd a Shilling every 3 Months, as they would deserve by improving in their Business, & the Expectation of these high Wages to come on hereafter was what he had drawn them in with.—Meredith was to work at Press, Potts at Bookbinding, which he by Agreement, was to teach them, tho' he knew neither one nor t'other. John ——— a wild Irishman brought up to no Business, whose Service for 4

Years Keimer had purchas'd from the Captain of a Ship. He too was to be made a Pressman. George Webb, an Oxford Scholar, whose Time for 4 Years he had likewise bought, intending him for a Compositor: of whom more presently. And David Harry, a Country Boy, whom he had taken Apprentice. I soon perceiv'd that the Intention of engaging me at Wages so much higher than he had been us'd to give, was to have these raw cheap Hands form'd thro' me, and as soon as I had instructed them, then, they being all articled to him, he should be able to do without me.—I went on however, very chearfully; put his Printing House in Order, which had been in great Confusion, and brought his Hands by degrees to mind their Business and to do it better.

It was an odd Thing to find an Oxford Scholar in the Situation of a bought Servant. He was not more than 18 Years of Age, & gave me this Account of himself; that he was born in Gloucester, educated at a Grammar School there, had been distinguish'd among the Scholars for some apparent Superiority in performing his Part when they exhibited Plays; belong'd to the Witty Club there, and had written some Pieces in Prose & Verse which were printed in the Gloucester Newspapers.—Thence he was sent to Oxford; there he continu'd about a Year, but not well-satisfy'd, wishing of all things to see London & become a Player. At length receiving his Quarterly Allowance of 15 Guineas, instead of discharging his Debts, he walk'd out of Town, hid his Gown in a Furz Bush, and footed it to London, where having no Friend to advise him, he fell into bad Company, soon spent his Guineas, found no means of being introduc'd among the Players, grew necessitous, pawn'd his Cloaths & wanted Bread. Walking the Street very hungry, & not knowing what to do with himself, a Crimp's Bill was put into his Hand, offering immediate Entertainment & Encouragement to such as would bind themselves to serve in America. He went directly, sign'd the Indentures, was put into the Ship & came over; never writing a Line to acquaint his Friends what was become of him. He was lively, witty, good-natur'd and a pleasant Companion; but idle, thoughtless & imprudent to the last Degree.

John the Irishman soon ran away. With the rest I began to live very agreably; for they all respected me, the more as they found Keimer incapable of instructing them, and that from me they learnt something daily. We never work'd on a Saturday, that being Keimer's Sabbath. So I had two Days for Reading. My Acquaintance with ingenious People in the Town, increased. Keimer himself treated me with great Civility & apparent Regard; and nothing now made me uneasy but my Debt to Vernon, which I was yet unable to pay being hitherto but a poor Oeconomist.—He however kindly made no Demand of it.

Our Printing-House often wanted Sorts, and there was no Letter Founder in America. I had seen Types cast at James's in London, but without much Attention to the Manner: However I now contriv'd a Mould, made use of the Letters we had, as Puncheons, struck the Matrices in Lead, and thus supply'd in a pretty tolerable way all Deficiencies. I also engrav'd several Things on occasion. I made the Ink, I was Warehouse-man & every thing, in short quite a Factotum.—

But however serviceable I might be, I found that my Services became every Day of less Importance, as the other Hands improv'd in the Business. And when Keimer paid my second Quarter's Wages, he let me know that he felt them too heavy, and thought I should make an Abatement. He grew by degrees less civil, put on more of the Master, frequently found Fault, was captious and seem'd ready for an Out-breaking. I went on nevertheless with a good deal of Patience, thinking that his incumber'd Circumstances were partly the Cause. At length a Trifle snapt our Connexion. For a great Noise happening near the Courthouse, I put my Head out of the Window to see what was the Matter. Keimer being in the Street look'd up & saw me, call'd out to me in a loud Voice and angry Tone to mind my Business, adding some reproachful Words, that nettled me the more for their Publicity, all the Neighbours who were looking out on the same Occasion being Witnesses how I was treated. He came up immediately into the Printing-House, continu'd the Quarrel, high Words pass'd on both Sides, he gave me the Quarter's Warning we had stipulated, expressing a Wish that he had not been oblig'd to so long a Warning: I told him his Wish was unnecessary for I would leave him that Instant; and so taking my Hat walk'd out of Doors; desiring Meredith whom I saw below to take care of some Things I left, & bring them to my Lodging.—

Meredith came accordingly in the Evening, when we talk'd my Affair over. He had conceiv'd a great Regard for me, & was very unwilling that I should leave the House while he remain'd in it. He dissuaded me from returning to my native Country which I began to think of. He reminded me that Keimer was in debt for all he possess'd, that his Creditors began to be uneasy, that he kept his Shop miserably, sold often without Profit for ready Money, and often trusted without keeping Account. That he must therefore fail; which would make a Vacancy I might profit of.—I objected my Want of Money. He then let me know, that his Father had a high Opinion of me, and from some Discourse that had pass'd between them, he was sure would advance Money to set us up, if I would enter into Partnership with him.—My Time, says he, will be out with Keimer in the Spring. By that time we may have our Press & Types in from London:—I am sensible I am no Workman. If you like it, Your Skill in the Business shall be set against the Stock I furnish; and we will share the Profits equally.—The Proposal was agreable, and I consented. His Father was in Town, and approv'd of it, the more as he saw I had great Influence with his Son, had prevail'd on him to abstain long from Dramdrinking, and he hop'd might break him of that wretched Habit entirely, when we came to be so closely connected. I gave an Inventory to the Father, who carry'd it to a Merchant; the Things were sent for; the Secret was to be kept till they should arrive, and in the mean time I was to get Work if I could at the other Printing House.—But I found no Vacancy there, and so remain'd idle a few Days, when Keimer, on a Prospect of being employ'd to print some Paper-money, in New Jersey, which would require Cuts & various Types that I only could supply, and apprehending Bradford might engage me & get the Jobb from him, sent me a very civil Message, that old Friends should not part for a few Words the Effect of sudden Passion, and wishing me to return. Meredith persuaded me to comply, as it would give more Opportunity for his Improvement under my daily Instructions.—So I return'd, and we went on more smoothly than for some time before.—The New Jersey Jobb was obtain'd. I contriv'd a Copper-Plate Press for it, the first that had been seen in the Country.—I cut several Ornaments and Checks for the Bills. We went together to Burlington, where I executed the Whole to Satisfaction, & he received so large a Sum for the Work, as to be enabled thereby to keep his Head much longer above Water.—

At Burlington I made an Acquaintance with many principal People of the Province. Several of them had been appointed by the Assembly a Committee to attend the Press, and take Care that no more Bills were printed than the Law directed. They were therefore by Turns constantly with us, and generally he who attended brought with him a Friend or two for Company. My Mind having been much more improv'd by Reading than Keimer's, I suppose it was for that Reason my Conversation seem'd to be more valu'd. They had me to their Houses, introduc'd me to their Friends and show'd me much Civility, while he, tho' the Master, was a little neglected. In truth he was an odd Fish, ignorant of common Life, fond of rudely opposing receiv'd Opinions, slovenly to extream dirtiness, enthusiastic in some Points of Religion, and a little Knavish withal. We continu'd there near 3 Months, and by that time I could reckon among my acquired Friends, Judge Allen, Samuel Bustill, the Secretary of the Province, Isaac Pearson, Joseph Cooper & several of the Smiths, Members of Assembly, and Isaac Decow the Surveyor General. The latter was a shrewd sagacious old Man, who told me that he began for himself when young by wheeling Clay for the Brickmakers, learnt to write after he was of Age, carry'd the Chain for Surveyors, who taught him Surveying, and he had now by his Industry acquir'd a good Estate; and says he, I foresee, that you will soon work this Man out of his Business & make a Fortune in it at Philadelphia. He had not then the least Intimation of my Intention to set up there or any where.— These Friends were afterwards of great Use to me, as I occasionally was to some of them.—They all continued their Regard for me as long as they lived.—

Before I enter upon my public Appearance in Business, it may be well to let you know the then State of my Mind, with regard to my Principles and Morals, that you may see how far those influenc'd the future Events of my Life. My Parent's had early given me religious Impressions, and brought me through my Childhood piously in the Dissenting Way. But I was scarce 15 when, after doubting by turns of several Points as I found them disputed in the different Books I read, I began to doubt of Revelation it self. Some Books against Deism fell into my Hands; they were said to be the Substance of Sermons preached at Boyle's Lectures. It happened that they wrought an Effect on me quite contrary to what was intended by them: For the Arguments of the Deists which were quoted to be refuted, appeared to me much Stronger than the Refutations. In short I soon became a thorough Deist. My Arguments perverted some others, particularly Collins & Ralph: but each of them having afterwards wrong'd me greatly without the least Compunction, and recollecting Keith's Conduct towards me, (who was another Freethinker) and my own towards Vernon & Miss Read which at Times gave me great Trouble, I began to suspect that this Doctrine tho' it might be true, was not very useful.—My London Pamphlet, which had for its Motto those Lines of Dryden

> ——Whatever is, is right
> Tho' purblind Man / Sees but a Part of
> The Chain, the nearest Link,
> His Eyes not carrying to the equal Beam,
> That poizes all, above.

And from the Attributes of God, his infinite Wisdom, Goodness & Power concluded that nothing could possibly be wrong in the World, & that Vice & Virtue were empty Distinctions, no such Things existing: appear'd now not so clever a Performance as I once thought it; and I doubted whether some Error had not insinuated itself unperceiv'd, into my Argument, so as to infect all that follow'd, as is common in metaphysical Reasonings.—I grew convinc'd that *Truth, Sincerity* & *Integrity* in Dealings between Man & Man, were of the utmost Importance to the Felicity of Life, and I form'd written Resolutions, (w*ch* still remain in my Journal Book) to practise them ever while I lived. Revelation had indeed no weight with me as such; but I entertain'd an Opinion, that tho' certain Actions might not be bad *because* they were forbidden by it, or good *because* it commanded them; yet probably those Actions might be forbidden *because* they were bad for us, or commanded *because* they were beneficial to us, in their own Natures, all the Circumstances of things considered. And this Persuasion, with the kind hand of Providence, or some guardian Angel, or accidental favourable Circumstances & Situations, or all together, preserved me (thro' this dangerous Time of Youth & the hazardous Situations I was sometimes in among Strangers, remote from the Eye & Advice of my Father,) without any *wilful* gross Immorality or Injustice that might have been expected from my Want of Religion.—I say *wilful*, because the Instances I have mentioned, had something of *Necessity* in them, from my Youth, Inexperience, & the Knavery of others.—I had therefore a tolerable Character to begin the World with, I valued it properly, & determin'd to preserve it.—

We had not been long return'd to Philadelphia, before the New Types arriv'd from London.—We settled with Keimer, & left him by his Consent before he heard of it.—We found a House to hire near the Market, and took it. To lessen the Rent, (which was then but 24£ a Year tho' I have since known it let for 70) We took in Tho⁵ Godfrey a Glazier, & his Family, who were to pay a considerable Part of it to us, and we to board with them. We had scarce opened our Letters & put our Press in Order, before George House, an Acquaintance of mine, brought a Countryman to us; whom he had met in the Street enquiring for a Printer. All our Cash was now expended in the Variety of Particulars we had been obliged to procure, & this Countryman's Five Shillings, being our First Fruits & coming so seasonably, gave me more Pleasure than any Crown I have since earn'd; and from the Gratitude I felt towards House, has made me often more ready than perhaps I should otherwise have been to assist young Beginners.—

There are Croakers in every Country always boding its Ruin. Such a one then lived in Philadelphia, a Person of Note, an elderly Man, with a wise Look and very grave Manner of Speaking. His Name was Samuel Mickle. This Gentleman, a Stranger to me, stopt one Day at my Door, and ask'd me if I was the young Man who had lately opened a new

Printing-house: Being answer'd in the Affirmative; He said he was sorry for me; because it was an expensive Undertaking, & the Expence would be lost, for Philadelphia was a sinking Place, the People already half Bankrupts or near being so; all Appearances of the contrary such as new Buildings & the Rise of Rents, being to his certain Knowledge fallacious, for they were in fact among the Things that would soon ruin us. And he gave me such a Detail of Misfortunes now existing or that were soon to exist, that he left me half-melancholy. Had I known him before I engag'd in this Business, probably I never should have done it.—This Man continu'd to live in this decaying Place, & to declaim in the same Strain, refusing for many Years to buy a House there, because all was going to Destruction, and at last I had the Pleasure of seeing him give five times as much for one as he might have bought it for when he first began his Croaking.—

I should have mention'd before, that in the Autumn of the preceding Year, I had form'd most of my ingenious Acquaintance into a Club, for mutual Improvement, which we call'd the Junto. We met on Friday Evenings. The Rules I drew up, requir'd that every Member in his Turn should produce one or more Queries on any Point of Morals, Politics or Natural Philosophy, to be discuss'd by the Company, and once in three Months produce and read an Essay of his own Writing on any Subject he pleased. Our Debates were to be under the Direction of a President, and to be conducted in the sincere Spirit of Enquiry after Truth, without fondness for Dispute, or Desire of Victory; and to prevent Warmth, all Expressions of Positiveness in Opinion, or of direct Contradiction, were after some time made contraband & prohibited under small pecuniary Penalties. The first Members were, Joseph Brientnal, a Copyer of Deeds for the Scriveners; a good-natur'd friendly middle-ag'd Man, a great Lover of Poetry, reading all he could meet with, & writing some that was tolerable; very ingenious in many little Nicknackeries, & of sensible Conversation. Thomas Godfrey, a self-taught Mathematician, great in his Way, & afterwards Inventor of what is now call'd Hadley's Quadrant. But he knew little out of his way, and was not a pleasing Companion, as like most Great Mathematicians I have met with, he expected unusual Precision in every thing said, or was forever denying or distinguishing upon Trifles, to the Disturbance of all Conversation.—He soon left us.— Nicholas Scull, a Surveyor, afterwards Surveyor-General, Who lov'd Books, & sometimes made a few Verses. William Parsons, bred a Shoemaker, but loving Reading, had acquir'd a considerable Share of Mathematics, which he first studied with a View to Astrology that he afterwards laught at. He also became Surveyor General.—William Maugridge, a Joiner, & a most exquisite Mechanic, & a solid sensible Man. Hugh Meredith, Stephen Potts, & George Webb, I have Characteris'd before. Robert Grace, a young Gentleman of some Fortune, generous, lively & witty, a Lover of Punning and of his Friends. And William Coleman, then a Merchant's Clerk, about my Age, who had the coolest clearest Head, the best Heart, and the exactest Morals, of almost any Man I ever met with. He became afterwards a Merchant of great Note, and one of our Provincial Judges: Our Friendship continued without Interruption to his Death, upwards of 40 Years. And the Club continu'd almost as long and was the best School of Philosophy, Morals & Politics that then existed in the Province; for our Queries which were read the Week preceding their Discussion, put us on reading with Attention upon the several Subjects, that we might speak more to the purpose: and here too we acquired better Habits of Conversation, every thing being studied in our Rules which might prevent our disgusting each other. From hence the long Continuance of the Club, which I shall have frequent Occasion to speak farther of hereafter; But my giving this Account of it here, is to show something of the Interest I had, every one of these exerting themselves in recommending Business to us.— Brientnal particularly procur'd us from the Quakers, the Printing 40 Sheets of their History, the rest being to be done by Keimer: and upon this we work'd exceeding hard, for the Price was low. It was a Folio, Pro Patria Size, in Pica with Long Primer Notes. I compos'd of it a Sheet a Day, and Meredith work'd it off at Press. It was often 11 at Night and sometimes later, before I had finish'd my Distribution for the next days Work: For the little Jobbs sent in by our other Friends now & then put us back. But so determin'd I was to continue doing a Sheet a Day of the Folio, that one Night when having impos'd my Forms, I thought my Days Work over, one of them by accident was broken and two Pages reduc'd to Pie, I immediately distributed & compos'd it over again before I went to bed. And this Industry visible to our Neighbours began to give us Character and Credit; particularly I was told, that mention being made of the new Printing Office at the Merchants Every-night-Club, the general Opinion was that it must fail, there being already two Printers in the Place, Keimer & Bradford; but Doctor Baird (whom you and I saw many Years after at his native Place, St. Andrews in Scotland) gave a contrary Opinion; for the Industry of that Franklin, says he, is superior to any thing I ever saw of the kind: I see him still at work when I go home from Club; and he is at Work again before his Neighbours are out of bed. This struck the rest, and we soon after had Offers from one of them to supply us with Stationary. But as yet we did not chuse to engage in Shop Business.

I mention this Industry the more particularly and the more freely, tho' it seems to be talking in my own Praise, that those of my Posterity who shall read it, may know the Use of that Virtue, when they see its Effects in my Favour throughout this Relation.—

George Webb, who had found a Friend that lent him wherewith to purchase his Time of Keimer, now came to offer himself as a Journeyman to us. We could not then imploy him, but I foolishly let him know, as a Secret, that I soon intended to begin a Newspaper, & might then have Work for him.—My Hopes of Success as I told him were founded on this, that the then only Newspaper, printed by Bradford was a paltry thing, wretchedly manag'd, no way entertaining; and yet was profitable to him.—I therefore thought a good Paper could scarcely fail of good Encouragem.^t I requested Webb not to mention it, but he told it to Keimer, who immediately, to be beforehand with me, published Proposals for Printing one himself,—on which Webb was to be employ'd.—I resented this, and to counteract them, as I could not yet begin our Paper, I wrote several Pieces of Entertainm.^t for Bradford's Paper, under the Title of the Busy Body which Breintnal continu'd some Months. By this means the Attention of the Publick was fix'd on that Paper, & Keimers Proposals which we burlesqu'd & ridicul'd, were disregarded. He began his Paper however, and after carrying it on three Quarters of a Year, with at most only 90 Subscribers, he offer'd it to me for a Trifle, & I having been ready some time to go on with it, took it in hand directly and it prov'd in a few Years extreamly profitable to me. —

I perceive that I am apt to speak in the singular Number, though our Partnership still continu'd. The Reason may be, that in fact the whole Management of the Business lay upon me. Meredith was no Compostor, a poor Pressman, & seldom sober. My Friends lamented my Connection with him, but I was to make the best of it.

Our first Papers made a quite different Appearance from any before in the Province, a better Type & better printed: but some spirited Remarks* of my Writing on the Dispute then going on between Govr Burnet and the Massachusetts Assembly, struck the principal People, occasion'd the Paper &

*"His Excellency Governor *Burnet* died unexpectedly about two Days after the Date of this Reply to his last Message: And it was thought the Dispute would have ended with him, or at least have lain dormant till the Arrival of a new Governor from *England*, who possibly might, or might not be inclin'd to enter too rigorously into the Measures of his Predecessor. But our last Advices by the Post acquaint us, that his Honour the Lieutenant Governour (on whom the Government immediately devolves upon the Death or Absence of the Commander in Chief) has vigorously renew'd the Struggle on his own Account; of which the Particulars will be seen in our Next.

"Perhaps some of our Readers may not fully understand the Original or Ground of this warm Contest between the Governour and Assembly. — It seems, that People have for these Hundred Years past, enjoyed the Privilege of Rewarding the Governour for the Time being, according to *their Sense* of his Merit and Services; and few or none of their Governors have hitherto complain'd, or had Reason to complain, of a too scanty Allowance. But the late Gov. *Burnet* brought with him Instructions to demand a *settled Salary* of 1000 *l. per Annum*, Sterling, on him and all his Successors, and the Assembly were required to fix it immediately. He insisted on it strenuously to the last, and they as constantly refused it. It appears by their Votes and Proceedings, that they thought it an Imposition, contrary to their own Charter, and to *Magna Charta*; and they judg'd that by the Dictates of Reason there should be a mutual Dependence between the *Governor* and the *Governed*, and that to make any Governour independent of his People, would be dangerous, and destructive of their Liberties, and the ready Way to establish Tyranny: They thought likewise, that the Province was not the less dependent on the Crown of *Great-Britain*, by the Governour's depending immediately on them and his own good Conduct for an ample Support, because all Acts and Laws

the Manager of it to be much talk'd of, & in a few Weeks brought them all to be our Subscribers. Their Example was follow'd by many, and our Number went on growing continually.—This was one of the first good Effects of my having learnt a little to scribble.—Another was, that the leading Men, seeing a News Paper now in the hands of one who could also handle a Pen, thought it convenient to oblige & encourage me.—Bradford still printed the Votes & Laws & other Publick Business. He had printed an Address of the House to the Governor in a coarse blundering manner; We reprinted it elegantly & correctly, and sent one to every Member. They were sensible of the Difference, it strengthen'd the Hands of our Friends in the House, and they voted us their Printers for the Year ensuing.

Among my Friends in the House I must not forget Mr Hamilton before mentioned, who was then returned from England & had a Seat in it. He interested himself for me strongly in that Instance, as he did in many others afterwards,

---

which he might be induc'd to pass, must nevertheless be constantly sent Home for Approbation in Order to continue in Force. Many other Reasons were given and Arguments us'd in the Course of the Controversy, needless to particularize here, because all the material Papers relating to it, have been inserted already in our Public News.

"Much deserved Praise has the deceas'd Governour receiv'd, for his steady Integrity in adhering to his Instructions, notwithstanding the great Difficulty and Opposition he met with, and the strong Temptations offer'd from time to time to induce him to give up the Point.—And yet perhaps something is due to the *Assembly* (as the Love and Zeal of that Country for the present Establishment is too well known to suffer any Suspicion of Want of Loyalty) who continue thus resolutely to Abide by what *they Think* their Right, and that of the People they represent, maugre all the Arts and Menaces of a Governour fam'd for his Cunning and Politicks, back'd with Instructions from Home, and powerfully aided by the great Advantage such an Officer always has of engaging the principal Men of a Place in his Party, by conferring where he pleases so many Posts of Profit and Honour. Their happy Mother Country will perhaps observe with Pleasure, that tho' her gallant Cocks and matchless Dogs abate their native Fire and Intrepidity when transported to a Foreign Clime (as the common Notion is) yet her SONS in the remotest Part of the Earth, and even to the third and fourth Descent, still retain that ardent Spirit of Liberty, and that undaunted Courage in the Defence of it, which has in every Age so gloriously distinguished BRITONS and ENGLISHMEN from all the Rest of Mankind."

continuing his Patronage till his Death.* Mr Vernon about this time put me in mind of the Debt I ow'd him:—but did not press me.—I wrote him an ingenuous Letter of Acknowledgments, crav'd his Forbearance a little longer which he allow'd me, & as soon as I was able I paid the Principal with Interest & many Thanks.—So that *Erratum* was in some degree corrected.—

But now another Difficulty came upon me, which I had never the least Reason to expect. Mr. Meredith's Father, who was to have paid for our Printing House according to the Expectations given me, was able to advance only one Hundred Pounds, Currency, which had been paid, & a Hundred more was due to the Merchant; who grew impatient & su'd us all. We gave Bail, but saw that if the Money could not be rais'd in time, the Suit must come to a Judgment & Execution, & our hopeful Prospects must with us be ruined, as the Press & Letters must be sold for Payment, perhaps at half-Price.—In this Distress two true Friends whose Kindness I have never forgotten nor ever shall forget while I can remember any thing, came to me separately unknown to each other, and without any Application from me, offering each of them to advance me all the Money that should be necessary to enable me to take the whole Business upon my self if that should be practicable, but they did not like my continuing the Partnership with Meredith, who as they said was often seen drunk in the Streets, & playing at low Games in Alehouses, much to our Discredit. These two Friends were *William Coleman* & *Robert Grace*. I told them I could not propose a Separation while any Prospect remain'd of the Merediths fulfilling their Part of our Agreement. Because I thought my self under great Obligations to them for what they had done & would do if they could. But if they finally fail'd in their Performance, & our Partnership must be dissolv'd, I should then think myself at Liberty to accept the Assistance of my Friends. Thus the matter rested for some time. When I said to my Partner, perhaps your Father is dissatisfied at the Part you have undertaken in this Affair of ours, and is unwilling to advance for you & me what he

*I got his Son once 500£.

would for you alone: If that is the Case, tell me, and I will resign the whole to you & go about my Business. No—says he, my Father has really been disappointed and is really unable; and I am unwilling to distress him farther. I see this is a Business I am not fit for. I was bred a Farmer, and it was a Folly in me to come to Town & put my self at 30 Years of Age an Apprentice to learn a new Trade. Many of our Welsh People are going to settle in North Carolina where Land is cheap: I am inclin'd to go with them, & follow my old Employment. You may find Friends to assist you. If you will take the Debts of the Company upon you, return to my Father the hundred Pound he has advanc'd, pay my little personal Debts, and give me Thirty Pounds & a new Saddle, I will relinquish the Partnership & leave the whole in your Hands. I agreed to this Proposal. It was drawn up in Writing, sign'd & seal'd immediately. I gave him what he demanded & he went soon after to Carolina; from whence he sent me next Year two long Letters, containing the best Account that had been given of that Country, the Climate, Soil, Husbandry, &c. for in those Matters he was very judicious. I printed them in the Papers, and they gave grate Satisfaction to the Publick.

As soon as he was gone, I recurr'd to my two Friends; and because I would not give an unkind Preference to either, I took half what each had offered & I wanted, of one, & half of the other; paid off the Company Debts, and went on with the Business in my own Name, advertising that the Partnership was dissolved. I think this was in or about the Year 1729.—

About this Time there was a Cry among the People for more Paper-Money, only 15,000£ being extant in the Province & that soon to be sunk. The wealthy Inhabitants oppos'd any Addition, being against all Paper Currency, from an Apprehension that it would depreciate as it had done in New England to the Prejudice of all Creditors.—We had discuss'd this Point in our Junto, where I was on the Side of an Addition, being persuaded that the first small Sum struck in 1723 had done much good, by increasing the Trade Employment, & Number of Inhabitants in the Province, since I now saw all the old Houses inhabited, & many new ones building, where as I remember'd well, that when I first walk'd about the Streets of Philadelphia, eating my Roll, I saw most of the Houses in Walnut street between Second & Front streets with Bills on their Doors, to be let; and many likewise in Chesnut Street, & other Streets; which made me then think the Inhabitants of the City were one after another deserting it.—Our Debates possess'd me so fully of the Subject, that I wrote and printed an anonymous Pamphlet on it, entituled, *The Nature & Necessity of a Paper Currency.* It was well receiv'd by the common People in general; but the Rich Men dislik'd it; for it increas'd and strengthen'd the Clamour for more Money; and they happening to have no Writers among them that were able to answer it, their Opposition slacken'd, & the Point was carried by a Majority in the House. My Friends there, who conceiv'd I had been of some Service, thought fit to reward me, by employing me in printing the Money, a very profitable Jobb, and a great Help to me.—This was another Advantage gain'd by my being able to write. The Utility of this Currency became by Time and Experience so evident, as never afterwards to be much disputed, so that it grew soon to 55000,£ and in 1739 to 80,000£ since which it arose during War to upwards of 350,000£. Trade, Building & Inhabitants all the while increasing. Tho' I now think there are Limits beyond which the Quantity may be hurtful.—

I soon after obtain'd, thro' my Friend Hamilton, the Printing of the NewCastle Paper Money, another profitable Jobb, as I then thought it; small Things appearing great to those in small Circumstances. And these to me were really great Advantages, as they were great Encouragements.—He procured me also the Printing of the Laws and Votes of that Government which continu'd in my Hands as long as I follow'd the Business.—

I now open'd a little Stationer's Shop. I had in it Blanks of all Sorts the correctest that ever appear'd among us, being assisted in that by my Friend Brientnal; I had also Paper, Parchment, Chapmen's Books, &c. One Whitemash a Compositor I had known in London, an excellent Workman now came to me & work'd with me constantly & diligently, and I took an Apprentice the Son of Aquila Rose. I began now gradually to pay off the Debt I was under for the Printing-

House.—In order to secure my Credit and Character as a Tradesmen, I took care not only to be in *Reality* Industrious & frugal, but to avoid all *Appearances* of the Contrary. I drest plainly; I was seen at no Places of idle Diversion; I never went out a-fishing or shooting; a Book, indeed, sometimes debauch'd me from my Work; but that was seldom, snug, & gave no Scandal: and to show that I was not above my Business, I sometimes brought home the Paper I purchas'd at the Stores, thro' the Streets on a Wheelbarrow. Thus being esteem'd an industrious thriving young Man, and paying duly for what I bought, the Merchants who imported Stationary solicited my Custom, others propos'd supplying me with Books, & I went on swimmingly.—In the mean time Keimer's Credit & Business declining daily, he was at last forc'd to sell his Printing-house to satisfy his Creditors. He went to Barbadoes, & there lived some Years, in very poor Circumstances.

His Apprentice David Harry, whom I had instructed while I work'd with him, set up in his Place at Philadelphia having bought his Materials. I was at first apprehensive of a powerful Rival in Harry, as his Friends were very able, & had a good deal of Interest. I therefore propos'd a Partnership to him; which he, fortunately for me, rejected with Scorn. He was very proud, dress'd like a Gentleman, liv'd expensively, took much Diversion & Pleasure abroad, ran in debt, & neglected his Business, upon which all Business left him; and finding nothing to do, he follow'd Keimer to Barbadoes; taking the Printinghouse with him. There this Apprentice employ'd his former Master as a Journeyman. They quarrel'd often. Harry went continually behind-hand, and at length was forc'd to sell his Types, and return to his Country Work in Pensilvania. The Person that bought them, employ'd Keimer to use them, but in a few years he died. There remain'd now no Competitor with me at Philadelphia, but the old one, Bradford, who was rich & easy, did a little Printing now & then by straggling Hands, but was not very anxious about the Business. However, as he kept the Post Office, it was imagined he had better Opportunities of obtaining News, his Paper was thought a better Distributer of Advertisements than mine, & therefore had many more, which was a profitable thing to him & a

Disadvantage to me. For tho' I did indeed receive & send
Papers by the Post, yet the publick Opinion was otherwise;
for what I did send was by Bribing the Riders who took them
privately: Bradford being unkind enough to forbid it: which
occasion'd some Resentment on my Part; and I thought so
meanly of him for it, that when I afterwards came into his
Situation, I took care never to imitate it.

I had hitherto continu'd to board with Godfrey who lived
in Part of my House with his Wife & Children, & had one
Side of the Shop for his Glazier's Business, tho' he work'd
little, being always absorb'd in his Mathematics.—Mrs Godfrey projected a Match for me with a Relation's Daughter,
took Opportunities of bringing us often together, till a serious Courtship on my Part ensu'd the Girl being in herself
very deserving. The old Folks encourag'd me by continual
Invitations to Supper, & by leaving us together, till at length
it was time to explain. Mrs Godfrey manag'd our little Treaty.
I let her know that I expected as much Money with their
Daughter as would pay off my Remaining Debt for the Printing-house, which I believe was not then above a Hundred
Pounds. She brought me Word they had no such Sum to
spare. I said they might mortgage their House in the Loan
Office.—The Answer to this after some Days was, that they
did not approve the Match; that on Enquiry of Bradford they
had been inform'd the Printing Business was not a profitable
one, the Types would soon be worn out & more wanted, that
S. Keimer & D. Harry had fail'd one after the other, and I
should probably soon follow them; and therefore I was forbidden the House, & the Daughter shut up.—Whether this
was a real Change of Sentiment, or only Artifice, on a Supposition of our being too far engag'd in Affection to retract,
& therefore that we should steal a Marriage, which would
leave them at Liberty to give or withold what they pleas'd, I
know not: But I suspected the latter, resented it, and went no
more. Mrs Godfrey brought me afterwards some more favourable Accounts of their Disposition, & would have drawn
me on again: But I declared absolutely my Resolution to have
nothing more to do with that Family. This was resented by
the Godfreys, we differ'd, and they removed, leaving me the
whole House, and I resolved to take no more Inmates. But

this Affair having turn'd my Thoughts to Marriage, I look'd round me, and made Overtures of Acquaintance in other Places; but soon found that the Business of a Printer being generally thought a poor one, I was not to expect Money with a Wife unless with such a one, as I should not otherwise think agreable.—In the mean time, that hard-to-be-govern'd Passion of Youth, had hurried me frequently into Intrigues with low Women that fell in my Way, which were attended with some Expence & great Inconvenience, besides a continual Risque to my Health by a Distemper which of all Things I dreaded, tho' by great good Luck I escaped it.—

A friendly Correspondence as Neighbours & old Acquaintances, had continued between me & Mrs Read's Family who all had a Regard for me from the time of my first Lodging in their House. I was often invited there and consulted in their Affairs, wherein I sometimes was of Service.—I pity'd poor Miss Read's unfortunate Situation, who was generally dejected, seldom chearful, and avoided Company. I consider'd my Giddiness & Inconstancy when in London as in a great degree the Cause of her Unhappiness; tho' the Mother was good enough to think the Fault more her own than mine, as she had prevented our Marrying before I went thither, and persuaded the other Match in my Absence. Our mutual Affection was revived, but there were now great Objections to our Union. That Match was indeed look'd upon as invalid, a preceding Wife being said to be living in England; but this could not easily be prov'd, because of the Distance &c. And tho' there was a Report of his Death, it was not certain. Then, tho' it should be true, he had left many Debts which his Successor might be call'd upon to pay. We ventured however, over all these Difficulties, and I took her to Wife Sept. 1. 1730. None of the Inconveniencies happened that we had apprehended, she prov'd a good & faithful Helpmate, assisted me much by attending the Shop, we throve together, and have ever mutually endeavour'd to make each other happy.— Thus I corrected that great *Erratum* as well as I could.

About this Time our Club meeting, not at a Tavern, but in a little Room of Mr Grace's set apart for that Purpose; a Proposition was made by me, that since our Books were often referr'd to in our Disquisitions upon the Queries, it might be convenient to us to have them all together where we met, that upon Occasion they might be consulted; and By thus clubbing our Books to a common Library, we should, while we lik'd to keep them together, have each of us the Advantage of using the Books of all the other Members, which would be nearly as beneficial as if each owned the whole. It was lik'd and agreed to, & we fill'd one End of the Room with such Books as we could best spare. The Number was not so great as we expected; and tho' they had been of great Use, yet some Inconveniencies occurring for want of due Care of them, the Collection after about a Year was separated, & each took his Books home again.

And now I set on foot my first Project of a public Nature, that for a Subscription Library. I drew up the Proposals, got them put into Form by our great Scrivener Brockden, and by the help of my Friends in the Junto, procur'd Fifty Subscribers of 40/ each to begin with & 10/ a Year for 50 Years, the Term our Company was to continue. We afterwards obtain'd a Charter, the Company being increas'd to 100. This was the Mother of all the N American Subscription Libraries now so numerous. It is become a great thing itself, & continually increasing.—These Libraries have improv'd the general Conversation of the Americans, made the common Tradesmen & Farmers as intelligent as most Gentlemen from other Countries, and perhaps have contributed in some degree to the Stand so generally made throughout the Colonies in Defence of their Privileges.—

Mem?

Thus far was written with the Intention express'd in the Beginning and therefore contains several little family Anecdotes of no Importance to others. What follows was written many Years after in compliance with the Advice contain'd in these Letters, and accordingly intended for the Publick. The Affairs of the Revolution occasion'd the Interruption.

Part Two

Letter from Mr. Abel James, with Notes on my Life, (received in Paris.)

My dear & honored Friend.

I have often been desirous of writing to thee, but could not be reconciled to the Thought that the Letter might fall into the Hands of the British, lest some Printer or busy Body should publish some Part of the Contents & give our Friends Pain & myself Censure.

Some Time since there fell into my Hands to my great Joy about 23 Sheets in thy own hand-writing containing an Account of the Parentage & Life of thyself, directed to thy Son ending in the Year 1730 with which there were Notes likewise in thy writing, a Copy of which I inclose in Hopes it may be a means if thou continuedst it up to a later period, that the first & latter part may be put together; & if it is not yet continued, I hope thou wilt not delay it, Life is uncertain as the Preacher tells us, and what will the World say if kind, humane & benevolent Ben Franklin should leave his Friends & the World deprived of so pleasing & profitable a Work, a Work which would be useful & entertaining not only to a few, but to millions.

The Influence Writings under that Class have on the Minds of Youth is very great, and has no where appeared so plain as in our public Friends' Journals. It almost insensibly leads the Youth into the Resolution of endeavouring to become as good and as eminent as the Journalist. Should thine for Instance when published, and I think it could not fail of it, lead the Youth to equal the Industry & Temperance of thy early Youth, what a Blessing with that Class would such a Work be. I know of no Character living nor many of them put together, who has so much in his Power as Thyself to promote a greater Spirit of Industry & early Attention to Business, Frugality and Temperance with the American Youth. Not that I think the Work would have no other Merit & Use in the World, far from it, but the first is of such vast Importance, that I know nothing that can equal it.

The foregoing letter and the minutes accompanying it being shewn to a friend, I received from him the following:

LETTER FROM MR. BENJAMIN VAUGHAN.

Paris, January 31, 1783.

MY DEAREST SIR,

When I had read over your sheets of minutes of the principal incidents of your life, recovered for you by your Quaker acquaintance; I told you I would send you a letter expressing my reasons why I thought it would be useful to complete and publish it as he desired. Various concerns have for some time past prevented this letter being written, and I do not know whether it was worth any expectation: happening to be at leisure however at present, I shall by writing at least interest and instruct myself; but as the terms I am inclined to use may tend to offend a person of your manners, I shall only tell you how I would address any other person, who was as good and as great as yourself, but less diffident. I would say to him, Sir, I *solicit* the history of your life from the following motives.

Your history is so remarkable, that if you do not give it, somebody else will certainly give it; and perhaps so as nearly to do as much harm, as your own management of the thing might do good.

It will moreover present a table of the internal circumstances of your country, which will very much tend to invite to it settlers of virtuous and manly minds. And considering the eagerness with which such information is sought by them, and the extent of your reputation, I do not know of a more efficacious advertisement than your Biography would give.

All that has happened to you is also connected with the detail of the manners and situation of *a rising* people; and in this respect I do not think that the writings of Caesar and Tacitus can be more interesting to a true judge of human nature and society.

But these, Sir, are small reasons in my opinion, compared with the chance which your life will give for the forming of future great men; and in conjunction with your *Art of Virtue*, (which you design to publish) of improving the features of private character, and consequently of aiding all happiness both public and domestic.

The two works I allude to, Sir, will in particular give a noble rule and example of *self-education*. School and other education constantly proceed upon false principles, and shew a clumsy apparatus pointed at a false mark; but your apparatus is simple, and the mark a true one; and while parents and young persons are left destitute of other just means of estimating and becoming prepared for a reasonable course in life, your discovery that the thing is in many a man's private power, will be invaluable!

Influence upon the private character late in life, is not only an influence late in life, but a weak influence. It is in *youth* that we plant our chief habits and prejudices; it is in youth that we take our party as to profession, pursuits, and matrimony. In youth therefore the turn is given; in youth the education even of the next generation is given; in youth the private and public character is determined; and the term of life extending but from youth to age, life ought to begin well from youth; and more especially *before* we take our party as to our principal objects.

But your Biography will not merely teach self-education, but the education of *a wise man*; and the wisest man will receive lights and improve his progress, by seeing detailed the conduct of another wise man. And why are weaker men to be deprived of such helps, when we see our race has been blundering on in the dark, almost without a guide in this particular, from the farthest trace of time. Shew then, Sir, how much is to be done, *both to sons and fathers*; and invite all wise men to become like yourself; and other men to become wise.

When we see how cruel statesmen and warriors can be to the humble race, and how absurd distinguished men can be to their acquaintance, it will be instructive to observe the instances multiply of pacific acquiescing manners; and to find how compatible it is to be great and *domestic*; enviable and yet *good-humoured*.

The little private incidents which you will also have to relate, will have considerable use, as we want above all things, *rules of prudence in ordinary affairs*; and it will be curious to see how you have acted in these. It will be so far a sort of key to life, and explain many things that all men ought to have once explained to them, to give them a chance of becoming wise by foresight.

The nearest thing to having experience of one's own, is to have other people's affairs brought before us in a shape that is interesting; this is sure to happen from your pen. Your affairs and management will have an air of simplicity or importance that will not fail to strike; and I am convinced you have conducted them with as much originality as if you had been conducting discussions in politics or philosophy; and what more worthy of experiments and system, (its importance and its errors considered) than human life!

Some men have been virtuous blindly, others have speculated fantastically, and others have been shrewd to bad purposes; but you, Sir, I am sure, will give under your hand, nothing but what is at the same moment, wise, practical, and good.

Your account of yourself (for I suppose the parallel I am drawing for Dr. Franklin, will hold not only in point of character but of private history), will shew that you are ashamed of no origin; a thing the more important, as you prove how little necessary all origin is to happiness, virtue, or greatness.

As no end likewise happens without a means, so we shall find, Sir, that even you yourself framed a plan by which you became considerable; but at the same time we may see that though the event is flattering, the means are as simple as wisdom could make them; that is depending upon nature, virtue, thought, and habit.

Another thing demonstrated will be the propriety of every man's waiting for his time for appearing upon the stage of the world. Our sensations being very much fixed to the moment, we are apt to forget that more moments are to follow the first, and consequently that man should arrange his conduct so as to suit the *whole* of a life. Your attribution appears to have been applied to your *life*, and the passing moments of it have been enlivened with content and enjoyment, instead of being tormented with foolish impatience or regrets. Such a conduct is easy for those who make virtue and themselves their standard, and who try to keep themselves in countenance by examples of other truly great men, of whom patience is so often the characteristic.

Your Quaker correspondent, Sir, (for here again I will suppose the subject of my letter resembling Dr. Franklin,) praised your frugality, diligence, and temperance, which he considered as a pattern for all youth: but it is singular that he should have forgotten your modesty, and your disinterestedness, without which you never could have waited for your advancement, or found your situation in the mean time comfortable; which is a strong lesson to shew the poverty of glory, and the importance of regulating our minds.

If this correspondent had known the nature of your reputation as well as I do, he would have said; your former writings and measures would secure attention to your Biography, and Art of Virtue; and your Biography and Art of Virtue, in return, would secure attention to them. This is an advantage attendant upon a various character, and which brings all that belongs to it into greater play; and it is the more useful, as perhaps more persons are at a loss for the *means* of improving their minds and characters, than they are for the time or the inclination to do it.

But there is one concluding reflection, Sir, that will shew the use of your life as a mere piece of biography. This style of writing seems a little gone out of vogue, and yet it is a very useful one; and your specimen of it may be particularly serviceable, as it will make a subject of comparison with the lives of various public cut-throats and intriguers, and with absurd monastic self-tormentors, or vain literary triflers. If it encourages more writings of the same kind with your own, and induces more men to spend lives fit to be written; it will be worth all Plutarch's Lives put together.

But being tired of figuring to myself a character of which every feature suits only one man in the world, without giving him the praise of it; I shall end my letter, my dear Dr. Franklin, with a personal application to your proper self.

I am earnestly desirous then, my dear Sir, that you should let the world into the traits of your genuine character, as civil broils may otherwise tend to disguise or traduce it. Considering your great age, the caution of your character, and your peculiar style of thinking, it is not likely that any one besides yourself can be sufficiently master of the facts of your life, or the intentions of your mind.

Besides all this, the immense revolution of the present period, will necessarily turn our attention towards the author of it; and when virtuous principles have been pretended in it, it will be highly important to shew that such have really influenced; and, as your own character will be the principal one to receive a scrutiny, it is proper (even for its effects upon your vast and rising country, as well as upon England and upon Europe), that it should stand respectable and eternal. For the furtherance of human happiness, I have always maintained that it is necessary to prove that man is not even at present a vicious and detestable animal; and still more to prove that good management may greatly amend him; and it is for much the same reason, that I am anxious to see the opinion established, that there are fair characters existing among the individuals of the race; for the moment that all men, without exception, shall be conceived abandoned, good people will cease efforts deemed to be hopeless, and perhaps think of taking their share in the scramble of life, or at least of making it comfortable principally for themselves.

Take then, my dear Sir, this work most speedily into hand: shew yourself good as you are good, temperate as you are temperate; and above all things, prove yourself as one who from your infancy have loved justice, liberty, and concord, in a way that has made it natural and consistent for you to have acted, as we have seen you act in the last seventeen years of your life. Let Englishmen be made not only to respect, but even to love you. When they think well of individuals in your native country, they will go nearer to thinking well of your country; and when your countrymen see themselves well thought of by Englishmen, they will go nearer to thinking well of England. Extend your views even further; do not stop at those who speak the English tongue, but after having settled so many points in nature and politics, think of bettering the whole race of men.

As I have not read any part of the life in question, but know only the character that lived it, I write somewhat at hazard. I am sure however, that the life, and the treatise I allude to (on the *Art of Virtue*), will necessarily fulfil the chief of my expectations; and still more so if you take up the measure of suiting these performances to the several views above stated. Should they even prove unsuccessful in all that a sanguine admirer of yours hopes from them, you will at least have framed pieces to interest the human mind; and whoever gives a feeling of pleasure that is innocent to man, has added so much to the fair side of a life otherwise too much darkened by anxiety, and too much injured by pain.

In the hope therefore that you will listen to the prayer addressed to you in this letter, I beg to subscribe myself, my dearest Sir, &c. &c.

Signed   BENJ. VAUGHAN.

Continuation of the Account of my Life.
Begun at Passy 1784

It is some time since I receiv'd the above Letters, but I have been too busy till now to think of complying with the Request they contain. It might too be much better done if I were at home among my Papers, which would aid my Memory, & help to ascertain Dates. But my Return being uncertain, and having just now a little Leisure, I will endeavour to recollect & write what I can; If I live to get home, it may there be corrected and improv'd.

Not having any Copy here of what is already written, I know not whether an Account is given of the means I used to establish the Philadelphia publick Library, which from a small Beginning is now become so considerable, though I remember to have come down to near the Time of that Transaction, 1730. I will therefore begin here, with an Account of it, which may be struck out if found to have been already given. —

At the time I establish'd my self in Pensylvania, there was not a good Bookseller's Shop in any of the Colonies to the Southward of Boston. In New-York & Philad[a] the Printers were indeed Stationers, they sold only Paper, &c. Almanacks, Ballads, and a few common School Books. Those who lov'd Reading were oblig'd to send for their Books from England. — The Members of the Junto had each a few. We had left the Alehouse where we first met, and hired a Room to hold our Club in. I propos'd that we should all of us bring our Books to that Room, where they would not only be ready to consult in our Conferences, but become a common

Benefit, each of us being at Liberty to borrow such as he wish'd to read at home. This was accordingly done, and for some time contented us. Finding the Advantage of this little Collection, I propos'd to render the Benefit from Books more common by commencing a Public Subscription Library. I drew a Sketch of the Plan and Rules that would be necessary, and got a skilful Conveyancer Mr Charles Brockden to put the whole in Form of Articles of Agreement to be subscribed, by which each Subscriber engag'd to pay a certain Sum down for the first Purchase of Books and an annual Contribution for encreasing them.—So few were the Readers at that time in Philadelphia, and the Majority of us so poor, that I was not able with great Industry to find more than Fifty Persons, mostly young Tradesmen, willing to pay down for this purpose Forty shillings each, & Ten Shillings per Annum. On this little Fund we began. The Books were imported. The Library was open one Day in the Week for lending them to the Subscribers, on their Promisory Notes to pay Double the Value if not duly returned. The Institution soon manifested its Utility, was imitated by other Towns and in other Provinces, the Librarys were augmented by Donations, Reading became fashionable, and our People having no publick Amusements to divert their Attention from Study became better acquainted with Books, and in a few Years were observ'd by Strangers to be better instructed & more intelligent than People of the same Rank generally are in other Countries.—

When we were about to sign the above-mentioned Articles, which were to be binding on us, our Heirs, &c for fifty Years, Mr Brockden, the Scrivener, said to us, "You are young Men, but it is scarce probable that any of you will live to see the Expiration of the Term fix'd in this Instrument." A Number of us, however, are yet living: But the Instrument was after a few Years rendred null by a Charter that incorporated & gave Perpetuity to the Company.—

The Objections, & Reluctances I met with in Soliciting the Subscriptions, made me soon feel the Impropriety of presenting one's self as the Proposer of any useful Project that might be suppos'd to raise one's Reputation in the smallest degree above that of one's Neighbours, when one has need of their

Assistance to accomplish that Project. I therefore put my self as much as I could out of sight, and stated it as a Scheme of *a Number of Friends*, who had requested me to go about and propose it to such as they thought Lovers of Reading. In this way my Affair went on more smoothly, and I ever after practis'd it on such Occasions; and from my frequent Successes, can heartily recommend it. The present little Sacrifice of your Vanity will afterwards be amply repaid. If it remains a while uncertain to whom the Merit belongs, some one more vain than yourself will be encourag'd to claim it, and then even Envy will be dispos'd to do you Justice, by plucking those assum'd Feathers, & restoring them to their right Owner.

This Library afforded me the Means of Improvement by constant Study, for which I set apart an Hour or two each Day; and thus repair'd in some Degree the Loss of the Learned Education my Father once intended for me. Reading was the only Amusement I allow'd my self. I spent no time in Taverns, Games, or Frolicks of any kind. And my Industry in my Business continu'd as indefatigable as it was necessary. I was in debt for my Printing-house, I had a young Family coming on to be educated, and I had to contend with for Business two Printers who were establish'd in the Place before me. My Circumstances however grew daily easier: my original Habits of Frugality continuing. And My Father having among his Instructions to me when a Boy, frequently repeated a Proverb of Solomon, *"Seest thou a Man diligent in his Calling, he shall stand before Kings, he shall not stand before mean Men."* I from thence consider'd Industry as a Means of obtaining Wealth and Distinction, which encourag'd me; tho' I did not think that I should ever literally stand before Kings, which however has since happened.—for I have stood before five, & even had the honour of sitting down with one, the King of Denmark, to Dinner.

We have an English Proverb that says,

> He that would thrive
> Must ask his Wife;

it was lucky for me that I had one as much dispos'd to Industry & Frugality as my self. She assisted me chearfully in my Business, folding & stitching Pamphlets, tending Shop, purchasing old Linen Rags for the Paper-makers, &c &c. We kept no idle Servants, our Table was plain & simple, our Furniture of the cheapest. For instance my Breakfast was a long time Bread & Milk, (no Tea,) and I ate it out of a twopenny earthen Porringer with a Pewter Spoon. But mark how Luxury will enter Families, and make a Progress, in Spite of Principle. Being Call'd one Morning to Breakfast, I found it in a China Bowl with a Spoon of Silver. They had been bought for me without my Knowledge by my Wife, and had cost her the enormous Sum of three and twenty Shillings, for which she had no other Excuse or Apology to make, but that she thought *her* Husband deserv'd a Silver Spoon & China Bowl as well as any of his Neighbours. This was the first Appearance of Plate & China in our House, which afterwards in a Course of Years as our Wealth encreas'd, augmented gradually to several Hundred Pounds in Value.—

I had been religiously educated as a Presbyterian; and tho' some of the Dogmas of that Persuasion, such as the Eternal Decrees of God, Election, Reprobation, &c. appear'd to me unintelligible, others doubtful, & I early absented myself from the Public Assemblies of the Sect, Sunday being my Studying-Day, I never was without some religious Principles; I never doubted, for instance, the Existance of the Deity, that he made the World, & govern'd it by his Providence; that the most acceptable Service of God was the doing Good to Man; that our Souls are immortal; and that all Crime will be punished & Virtue rewarded either here or hereafter; these I esteem'd the Essentials of every Religion, and being to be found in all the Religions we had in our Country I respected them all, tho' with different degrees of Respect as I found them more or less mix'd with other Articles which without any Tendency to inspire, promote or confirm Morality, serv'd principally to divide us & make us unfriendly to one another.— This Respect to all, with an Opinion that the worst had some good Effects, induc'd me to avoid all Discourse that might tend to lessen the good Opinion another might have of his own Religion; and as our Province increas'd in People and new Places of worship were continually wanted, & generally erected by voluntary Contribution, my Mite for such purpose, whatever might be the Sect, was never refused.—

Tho' I seldom attended any Public Worship, I had still an Opinion of its Propriety, and of its Utility when rightly conducted, and I regularly paid my annual Subscription for the Support of the only Presbyterian Minister or Meeting we had in Philadelphia. He us'd to visit me sometimes as a Friend, and admonish me to attend his Administrations, and I was now and then prevail'd on to do so, once for five Sundays successively. Had he been, *in my Opinion*, a good Preacher perhaps I might have continued, notwithstanding the occasion I had for the Sunday's Leisure in my Course of Study: But his Discourses were chiefly either polemic Arguments, or Explications of the peculiar Doctrines of our Sect, and were all to me very dry, uninteresting and unedifying, since not a single moral Principle was inculcated or enforc'd, their Aim seeming to be rather to make us Presbyterians than good Citizens. At length he took for his Text that Verse of the 4th Chapter of Philippians, *Finally, Brethren, Whatsoever Things are true, honest, just, pure, lovely, or of good report, if there be any virtue, or any praise, think on these Things*; & I imagin'd in a Sermon on such a Text, we could not miss of having some Morality: But he confin'd himself to five Points only as meant by the Apostle, viz. 1. Keeping holy the Sabbath Day. 2. Being diligent in Reading the Holy Scriptures. 3. Attending duly the Publick Worship. 4. Partaking of the Sacrament. 5. Paying a due Respect to God's Ministers.—These might be all good Things, but as they were not the kind of good Things that I expected from that Text, I despaired of ever meeting with them from any other, was disgusted, and attended his Preaching no more.—I had some Years before compos'd a little Liturgy or Form of Prayer for my own private Use, viz, in 1728. entitled, *Articles of Belief & Acts of Religion*. I return'd to the Use of this, and went no more to the public Assemblies.—My Conduct might be blameable, but I leave it without attempting farther to excuse it, my present purpose being to relate Facts, and not to make Apologies for them.—

It was about this time that I conceiv'd the bold and arduous Project of arriving at moral Perfection. I wish'd to live without committing any Fault at any time; I would conquer all that either Natural Inclination, Custom, or Company might lead me into. As I knew, or thought I knew, what was right and wrong, I did not see why I might not *always* do the one and avoid the other. But I soon found I had undertaken a Task of more Difficulty than I had imagined: While my Care was employ'd in guarding against one Fault, I was often surpriz'd by another. Habit took the Advantage of Inattention. Inclination was sometimes too strong for Reason. I concluded at length, that the mere speculative Conviction that it was our Interest to be compleatly virtuous, was not sufficient to prevent our Slipping, and that the contrary Habits must be broken and good Ones acquired and established, before we can have any Dependance on a steady uniform Rectitude of Conduct. For this purpose I therefore contriv'd the following Method.—

In the various Enumerations of the moral Virtues I had met with in my Reading, I found the Catalogue more or less numerous, as different Writers included more or fewer Ideas under the same Name. Temperance, for Example, was by some confin'd to Eating & Drinking, while by others it was extended to mean the moderating every other Pleasure, Appetite, Inclination or Passion, bodily or mental, even to our Avarice & Ambition. I propos'd to myself, for the sake of Clearness, to use rather more Names with fewer Ideas annex'd to each, than a few Names with more Ideas; and I included under Thirteen Names of Virtues all that at that time occurr'd to me as necessary or desirable, and annex'd to each a short Precept, which fully express'd the Extent I gave to its Meaning.—

These Names of Virtues with their Precepts were

    1. TEMPERANCE.

Eat not to Dulness

Drink not to Elevation.

    2. SILENCE.

Speak not but what may benefit others or your self. Avoid trifling Conversation.

    3. ORDER.

Let all your Things have their Places. Let each Part of your Business have its Time.

4. RESOLUTION.

Resolve to perform what you ought. Perform without fail what you resolve.

5. FRUGALITY.

Make no Expence but to do good to others or yourself: i.e. Waste nothing.

6. INDUSTRY.

Lose no Time.—Be always employ'd in something useful.—Cut off all unnecessary Actions.—

7. SINCERITY.

Use no hurtful Deceit.

Think innocently and justly; and, if you speak; speak accordingly.

8. JUSTICE.

Wrong none, by doing Injuries or omitting the Benefits that are your Duty.

9. MODERATION.

Avoid Extreams. Forbear resenting Injuries so much as you think they deserve.

10. CLEANLINESS

Tolerate no Uncleanness in Body, Cloaths or Habitation.—

11. TRANQUILITY

Be not disturbed at Trifles, or at Accidents common or unavoidable.

12. CHASTITY.

Rarely use Venery but for Health or Offspring; Never to Dulness, Weakness, or the Injury of your own or another's Peace or Reputation.—

13. HUMILITY.

Imitate Jesus and Socrates.—

My intention being to acquire the *Habitude* of all these Virtues, I judg'd it would be well not to distract my Attention by attempting the whole at once, but to fix it on one of them at a time, and when I should be Master of that, then to proceed to another, and so on till I should have gone thro' the thirteen. And as the previous Acquisition of some might facilitate the Acquisition of certain others, I arrang'd them with that View as they stand above. *Temperance* first, as it tends to procure that Coolness & Clearness of Head, which is so necessary where constant Vigilance was to be kept up, and Guard maintained, against the unremitting Attraction of ancient Habits, and the Force of perpetual Temptations. This being acquir'd & establish'd, *Silence* would be more easy, and my Desire being to gain Knowledge at the same time that I improv'd in Virtue, and considering that in Conversation it was obtain'd rather by the Use of the Ears than of the Tongue, & therefore wishing to break a Habit I was getting into of Prattling, Punning & Joking, which only made me acceptable to trifling Company, I gave *Silence* the second Place. This, and the next, *Order*, I expected would allow me more Time for attending to my Project and my Studies; RESOLUTION once become habitual, would keep me firm in my Endeavours to obtain all the subsequent Virtues; *Frugality* & *Industry*, by freeing me from my remaining Debt, & producing Affluence & Independance would make more easy the Practice of *Sincerity* and *Justice*, &c. &c.. Conceiving then that agreeable to the Advice of Pythagoras in his Golden Verses,* daily Examination would be necessary, I contriv'd the following Method for conducting that Examination.

I made a little Book in which I allotted a Page for each of the Virtues. I rul'd each Page with red Ink so as to have seven Columns, one for each Day of the Week, marking each Column with a Letter for the Day. I cross'd these Columns with thirteen red Lines, marking the Beginning of each Line with

Let not the stealing God of Sleep surprize,
Nor creep in Slumbers on thy weary Eyes,
Ere ev'ry Action of the former Day,
Strictly *thou dost, and* righteously *survey.*
With Rev'rence at thy own Tribunal stand,
And answer justly to thy own Demand.
Where have I been? In what have I transgrest?
What Good or Ill has this Day's Life exprest?
Where have I fail'd in what I ought to do?
In what to GOD, *to Man, or to myself I owe?*
Inquire severe whate'er from first to last,
From Morning's Dawn till Ev'nings Gloom has past.
If Evil were thy Deeds, repenting mourn,
And let thy Soul with strong Remorse be torn:
If Good, the Good with Peace of Mind repay, ⎫
And to thy secret Self with Pleasure say, ⎬
Rejoice, my Heart, for all went well to Day. ⎭

the first Letter of one of the Virtues, on which Line & in its proper Column I might mark by a little black Spot every Fault I found upon Examination, to have been committed respecting that Virtue upon that Day.

Form of the Pages

	S	M	T	W	T	F	S
TEMPERANCE.							
Eat not to Dulness. Drink not to Elevation.							
T							
S	●●	●		●		●	
O	●	●	●		●	●	●
R			●			●	
F		●			●		
I			●				
S							
J							
M							
Cl.							
T							
Ch							
H							

Not so or/silent aderly (handwritten margin note)

I determined to give a Week's strict Attention to each of the Virtues successively. Thus in the first Week my great Guard was to avoid every the least Offence against Temperance, leaving the other Virtues to their ordinary Chance, only marking every Evening the Faults of the Day. Thus if in the first Week I could keep my first Line marked T clear of Spots, I suppos'd the Habit of that Virtue so much strengthen'd and its opposite weaken'd, that I might venture extending my Attention to include the next, and for the following Week keep both Lines clear of Spots. Proceeding thus to the last, I could go thro' a Course compleat in Thirteen Weeks, and four Courses in a Year.—And like him who having a Garden to weed, does not attempt to eradicate all the bad Herbs at once, which would exceed his Reach and his Strength, but works on one of the Beds at a time, & having accomplish'd the first proceeds to a second; so I should have, (I hoped) the encouraging Pleasure of seeing on my Pages the Progress I made in Virtue, by clearing successively my Lines of their Spots, till in the End by a Number of Courses, I should be happy in viewing a clean Book after a thirteen Weeks daily Examination.

This my little Book had for its Motto these Lines from *Addison's Cato*;

> *Here will I hold: If there is a Pow'r above us,*
> *(And that there is, all Nature cries aloud*
> *Thro' all her Works) he must delight in Virtue,*
> *And that which he delights in must be happy.*

Another from *Cicero*.

> *O Vitæ Philosophia Dux! O Virtutum indagatrix, expultrixque vitiorum! Unus dies bene, & ex preceptis tuis actus, peccanti immortalitati est anteponendus.*

Another from the Proverbs of Solomon speaking of Wisdom or Virtue;

> Length of Days is in her right hand, and in her Left Hand Riches and Honours; Her Ways are Ways of Pleasantness, and all her Paths are Peace.   III, 16, 17.

And conceiving God to be the Fountain of Wisdom, I thought it right and necessary to solicit his Assistance for obtaining it; to this End I form'd the following little Prayer, which was prefix'd to my Tables of Examination; for daily Use.

> *O Powerful Goodness! bountiful Father! merciful Guide! Increase in me that Wisdom which discovers my truest Interests; Strengthen my Resolutions to perform what that Wisdom dictates. Accept my kind Offices to thy other Children, as the only Return in my Power for thy continual Favours to me.*

I us'd also sometimes a little Prayer which I took from *Thomson's* Poems. viz

> *Father of Light and Life, thou Good supreme,*
> *O teach me what is good, teach me thy self!*
> *Save me from Folly, Vanity and Vice,*
> *From every low Pursuit, and fill my Soul*
> *With Knowledge, conscious Peace, & Virtue pure,*
> *Sacred, substantial, neverfading Bliss!*

omitted them entirely, being employ'd in Voyages & Business abroad with a Multiplicity of Affairs, that interfered. But I always carried my little Book with me. My Scheme of ORDER, gave me the most Trouble, and I found, that tho' it might be practicable where a Man's Business was such as to leave him the Disposition of his Time, that of a Journey-man Printer for instance, it was not possible to be exactly observ'd by a Master, who must mix with the World, and often receive People of Business at their own Hours.— *Order* too, with regard to Places for Things, Papers, &c. I found extreamly difficult to acquire. I had not been early accustomed to it, & having an exceeding good Memory, I was not so sensible of the Inconvenience attending Want of Method. This Article therefore cost me so much painful Attention & my Faults in it vex'd me so much, and I made so little Progress in Amendment, & had such frequent Relapses, that I was almost ready to give up the Attempt, and content my self with a faulty Character in that respect. Like the Man who in buying an Ax of a Smith my Neighbour, desired to have the whole of its Surface as bright as the Edge; the Smith consented to grind it bright for him if he would turn the Wheel. He turn'd while the Smith press'd the broad Face of the Ax hard & heavily on the Stone, which made the Turning of it very fatiguing. The Man came every now & then from the Wheel to see how the Work went on; and at length would take his Ax as it was without farther Grinding. No, says the Smith, Turn on, turn on; we shall have it bright by and by; as yet 'tis only speckled. Yes, says the Man; but— *I think I like a speckled Ax best.*— And I believe this may have been the Case with many who having for want of some such Means as I employ'd found the Difficulty of obtaining good, & breaking bad Habits, in other Points of Vice & Virtue, have given up the Struggle, & concluded that *a speckled Ax was best.* For something that pretended to be Reason was every now and then suggesting to me, that such extream Nicety as I exacted of my self might be a kind of Foppery in Morals, which if it were known would make me ridiculous; that a perfect Character might be attended with the Inconvenience of being envied and hated; and that a benevolent Man should allow a few Faults in himself, to keep his Friends in Countenance. In Truth I found myself incorrigible with respect to *Order*; and now I am grown old, and my Memory bad, I feel very sensibly the want of it. But on the whole, tho' I never arrived at the Perfection I had been so ambitious of obtaining, but fell far short of it, yet I was by the Endeavour made a better and a happier Man than I otherwise should have been, if I had not attempted it; As those who aim at perfect Writing by imitating the engraved Copies, tho' they never reach the wish'd for Excellence of those Copies, their Hand is mended by the Endeavour, and is tolerable while it continues fair & legible. —

And it may be well my Posterity should be informed, that to this little Artifice, with the Blessing of God, their Ancestor ow'd the constant Felicity of his Life down to his 79th Year in which this is written. What Reverses may attend the Remainder is in the Hand of Providence: But if they arrive the Reflection on past Happiness enjoy'd ought to help his Bearing them with more Resignation. To *Temperance* he ascribes his long-continu'd Health, & what is still left to him of a good Constitution. To *Industry* and *Frugality* the early Easiness of his Circumstances, & Acquisition of his Fortune, with all that Knowledge which enabled him to be an useful Citizen, and obtain'd for him some Degree of Reputation among the Learned. To *Sincerity* & *Justice* the Confidence of his Country, and the honourable Employs it conferr'd upon him. And to the joint Influence of the whole Mass of the Virtues, even in their imperfect State he was able to acquire them, all that Evenness of Temper, & that Chearfulness in Conversation which makes his Company still sought for, & agreable even to his younger Acquaintance. I hope therefore that some of my Descendants may follow the Example & reap the Benefit. —

It will be remark'd that, tho' my Scheme was not wholly without Religion there was in it no Mark of any of the distinguishing Tenets of any particular Sect. — I had purposely avoided them; for being fully persuaded of the Utility and Excellency of my Method, and that it might be serviceable to People in all Religions, and intending some time or other to publish it, I would not have any thing in it that should prejudice any one of any Sect against it. — I purposed writing a little Comment on each Virtue, in which I would have shown the Advantages of possessing it, & the Mischiefs attending its opposite Vice; and I should have called my Book the ART *of Virtue*, because it would have shown the *Means & Manner* of obtaining Virtue; which would have distinguish'd it from the mere Exhortation to be good, that does not instruct & indicate the Means; but is like the Apostle's Man of verbal Charity, who only, without showing to the Naked & the Hungry *how* or where they might get Cloaths or Victuals, exhorted them to be fed & clothed. *James* II, 15, 16.—

But it so happened that my Intention of writing & publishing this Comment was never fulfilled. I did indeed, from time to time put down short Hints of the Sentiments, Reasonings, &c. to be made use of in it; some of which I have still by me: But the necessary close Attention to private Business in the earlier part of Life, and public Business since, have occasioned my postponing it. For it being connected in my Mind with a *great and extensive Project* that required the whole Man to execute, and which an unforeseen Succession of Employs prevented my attending to, it has hitherto remain'd unfinish'd.—

In this Piece it was my Design to explain and enforce this Doctrine, that vicious Actions are not hurtful because they are forbidden, but forbidden because they are hurtful, the Nature of Man alone consider'd: That it was therefore every ones Interest to be virtuous, who wish'd to be happy even in this World. And I should from this Circumstance, there being always in the World a Number of rich Merchants, Nobility, States and Princes, who have need of honest Instruments for the Management of their Affairs, and such being so rare, have endeavoured to convince young Persons, that no Qualities were so likely to make a poor Man's Fortune as those of Probity & Integrity.

My List of Virtues contain'd at first but twelve: But a Quaker Friend having kindly inform'd me that I was generally thought proud; that my Pride show'd itself frequently in Conversation; that I was not content with being in the right when discussing any Point, but was overbearing & rather insolent; of which he convinc'd me by mentioning several Instances;—I determined endeavouring to cure myself if I could of this Vice or Folly among the rest, and I added

Humility to my List, giving an extensive Meaning to the Word.—I cannot boast of much Success in acquiring the *Reality* of this Virtue; but I had a good deal with regard to the *Appearance* of it.—I made it a Rule to forbear all direct Contradiction to the Sentiments of others, and all positive Assertion of my own. I even forbid myself agreable to the old Laws of our Junto, the Use of every Word or Expression in the Language that imported a fix'd Opinion; such as *certainly*, *undoubtedly*, &c. and I adopted instead of them, *I conceive*, *I apprehend*, or *I imagine* a thing to be so or so, or it so appears to me at present.—When another asserted something that I thought an Error, I deny'd my self the Pleasure of contradicting him abruptly, and of showing immediately some Absurdity in his Proposition; and in answering I began by observing that in certain Cases or Circumstances his Opinion would be right, but that in the present case there *appear'd* or *seem'd* to me some Difference, &c. I soon found the Advantage of this Change in my Manners. The Conversations I engag'd in went on more pleasantly. The modest way in which I propos'd my Opinions, procur'd them a readier Reception and less Contradiction; I had less Mortification when I was found to be in the wrong, and I more easily prevail'd with others to give up their Mistakes & join with me when I happen'd to be in the right. And this Mode, which I at first put on, with some violence to natural Inclination, became at length so easy & so habitual to me, that perhaps for these Fifty Years past no one has ever heard a dogmatical Expression escape me. And to this Habit (after my Character of Integrity) I think it principally owing, that I had early so much Weight with my Fellow Citizens, when I proposed new Institutions, or Alterations in the old; and so much Influence in public Councils when I became a Member. For I was but a bad Speaker, never eloquent, subject to much Hesitation in my choice of Words, hardly correct in Language, and yet I generally carried my Points.—

In reality there is perhaps no one of our natural Passions so hard to subdue as *Pride*. Disguise it, struggle with it, beat it down, stifle it, mortify it as much as one pleases, it is still alive, and will every now and then peep out and show itself.

Part Three

I am now about to write at home, Augt 1788.—but cannot have the help expected from my Papers, many of them being lost in the War. I have however found the following.

Having mentioned *a great & extensive Project* which I had conceiv'd, it seems proper that some Account should be here given of that Project and its Object. Its first Rise in my Mind appears in the following little Paper, accidentally preserv'd, viz.

OBSERVATIONS on my Reading History in Library, May 9. 1731.

"That the great Affairs of the World, the Wars, Revolutions, &c. are carried on and effected by Parties.—

"That the View of these Parties is their present general Interest, or what they take to be such.—

"That the different Views of these different Parties, occasion all Confusion.

"That while a Party is carrying on a general Design, each Man has his particular private Interest in View.

"That as soon as a Party has gain'd its general Point, each Member becomes intent upon his particular Interest, which thwarting others, breaks that Party into Divisions, and occasions more Confusion.

"That few in Public Affairs act from a meer View of the Good of their Country, whatever they may pretend; and tho' their Actings bring real Good to their Country, yet Men primarily consider'd that their own and their Country's Interest was united, and did not act from a Principle of Benevolence.

"That fewer still in public Affairs act with a View to the Good of Mankind.

"There seems to me at present to be great Occasion for raising an united Party for Virtue, by forming the Virtuous and good Men of all Nations into a regular Body, to be govern'd by suitable good and wise Rules, which good and wise Men may probably be more unanimous in their Obedience to, than common People are to common Laws.

"I at present think, that whoever attempts this aright, and is well qualified, cannot fail of pleasing God, & of meeting with Success.— B F."—

Revolving this Project in my Mind, as to be undertaken hereafter when my Circumstances should afford me the necessary Leisure, I put down from time to time on Pieces of Paper such Thoughts as occur'd to me respecting it. Most of these are lost; but I find one purporting to be the Substance of an intended Creed, containing as I thought the Essentials of every known Religion, and being free of every thing that might shock the Professors of any Religion. It is express'd in these Words. viz.

"That there is one God who made all things.

"That he governs the World by his Providence.—

"That he ought to be worshipped by Adoration, Prayer & Thanksgiving.

"But that the most acceptable Service of God is doing Good to Man.

"That the Soul is immortal.

"And that God will certainly reward Virtue and punish Vice either here or hereafter."—

My Ideas at that time were, that the Sect should be begun & spread at first among young and single Men only; that each Person to be initiated should not only declare his Assent to such Creed, but should have exercis'd himself with the Thirteen Weeks Examination and Practice of the Virtues as in the before-mention'd Model; that the Existence of such a Society should be kept a Secret till it was become considerable, to prevent Solicitations for the Admission of improper Persons; but that the Members should each of them search among his Acquaintance for ingenuous well-disposed Youths, to whom with prudent Caution the Scheme should be gradually communicated: That the Members should engage to afford their Advice Assistance and Support to each other in promoting one another's Interest Business and Advancement in Life: That for Distinction we should be call'd the Society of the *Free and Easy*; Free, as being by the general Practice and Habit of the Virtues, free from the Dominion of Vice, and particularly by the Practice of Industry & Frugality, free from Debt, which exposes a Man to Confinement and a Species of Slavery to his Creditors. This is as much as I can now recollect of the Project, except that I communicated it in part to two young Men, who adopted it with some Enthusiasm. But my then narrow Circumstances, and the Necessity I was under of sticking close to my Business, occasion'd my Postponing the farther Prosecution of it at that time, and my multifarious Occupations public & private induc'd me to continue postponing, so that it has been omitted till I have no longer Strength or Activity left sufficient for such an Enterprize: Tho' I am still of Opinion that it was a practicable Scheme, and might have been very useful, by forming a great Number of good Citizens: And I was not discourag'd by the seeming Magnitude of the Undertaking, as I have always thought that one Man of tolerable Abilities may work great Changes, & accomplish great Affairs among Mankind, if he first forms a good Plan, and, cutting off all Amusements or other Employments that would divert his Attention, makes the Execution of that same Plan his sole Study and Business.—

In 1732 I first published my Almanack, under the Name of *Richard Saunders*; it was continu'd by me about 25 Years, commonly call'd *Poor Richard's* Almanack. I endeavour'd to make it both entertaining and useful, and it accordingly came to be in such Demand that I reap'd considerable Profit from it, vending annually near ten Thousand. And observing that it was generally read, scarce any Neighbourhood in the Province being without it, I consider'd it as a proper Vehicle for conveying Instruction among the common People, who bought scarce any other Books. I therefore filled all the little Spaces that occurr'd between the Remarkable Days in the Calendar, with Proverbial Sentences, chiefly such as inculcated Industry and Frugality, as the Means of procuring Wealth and thereby securing Virtue, it being more difficult for a Man in Want to act always honestly, as (to use here one of those Proverbs) *it is hard for an empty Sack to stand upright*. These Proverbs, which contained the Wisdom of many Ages and Nations, I assembled and form'd into a connected Discourse prefix'd to the Almanack of 1757, as the Harangue of a wise old Man to the People attending an Auction. The bringing all these scatter'd Counsels thus into a Focus, enabled them to make greater Impression. The Piece being universally approv'd was copied in all the Newspapers of the Continent, reprinted in Britain on a Broadside to be stuck up in Houses, two Translations were made of it in French, and great Numbers bought by the Clergy & Gentry to distribute gratis among their poor Parishioners and Tenants. In Pennsylvania, as it discouraged useless Expence in foreign Superfluities, some thought it had its share of Influence in producing that growing Plenty of Money which was observable for several Years after its Publication.—

I consider'd my Newspaper also as another Means of communicating Instruction, & in that View frequently reprinted in it Extracts from the Spectator and other moral Writers, and sometimes publish'd little Pieces of my own which had been first compos'd for Reading in our Junto. Of these are a Socratic Dialogue tending to prove, that, whatever might be his Parts and Abilities, a vicious Man could not properly be called a Man of Sense. And a Discourse on Self denial, showing that Virtue was not Secure, till its Practice became a Habitude, & was free from the Opposition of contrary Inclinations.—These may be found in the Papers about the beginning of 1735.—In the Conduct of my Newspaper I carefully excluded all Libelling and Personal Abuse, which is of late Years become so disgraceful to our Country. Whenever I was solicited to insert any thing of that kind, and the Writers pleaded as they generally did, the Liberty of the Press, and that a Newspaper was like a Stage Coach in which any one who would pay had a Right to a Place, my Answer was, that I would print the Piece separately if desired, and the Author might have as many Copies as he pleased to distribute himself, but that I would not take upon me to spread his Detraction, and that having contracted with my Subscribers to furnish them with what might be either useful or entertaining, I could not fill their Papers with private Altercation in which they had no Concern without doing them manifest Injustice. Now many of our Printers make no scruple of gratifying the Malice of Individuals by false Accusations of the fairest Characters among ourselves, augmenting Animosity even to the producing of Duels, and are moreover so indiscreet as to print scurrilous Reflections on the Government of neighbouring States, and even on the Conduct of our best national Allies, which may be attended with the most pernicious Consequences.— These Things I mention as a Caution to young Printers, &

that they may be encouraged not to pollute their Presses and disgrace their Profession by such infamous Practices, but refuse steadily; as they may see by my Example, that such a Course of Conduct will not on the whole be injurious to their Interests.—

In 1733, I sent one of my Journeymen to Charleston South Carolina where a Printer was wanting. I furnish'd him with a Press and Letters, on an Agreement of Partnership, by which I was to receive One Third of the Profits of the Business, paying One Third of the Expence. He was a Man of Learning and honest, but ignorant in Matters of Account; and tho' he sometimes made me Remittances, I could get no Account from him, nor any satisfactory State of our Partnership while he lived. On his Decease, the Business was continued by his Widow, who being born & bred in Holland, where as I have been inform'd the Knowledge of Accompts makes a Part of Female Education, she not only sent me as clear a State as she could find of the Transactions past, but continu'd to account with the greatest Regularity & Exactitude every Quarter afterwards; and manag'd the Business with such Success that she not only brought up reputably a Family of Children, but at the Expiration of the Term was able to purchase of me the Printing-House and establish her Son in it. I mention this Affair chiefly for the Sake of recommending that Branch of Education for our young Females, as likely to be of more Use to them & their Children in Case of Widowhood than either Music or Dancing, by preserving them from Losses by Imposition of crafty Men, and enabling them to continue perhaps a profitable mercantile House with establish'd Correspondence till a Son is grown up fit to undertake and go on with it, to the lasting Advantage and enriching of the Family.—

About the Year 1734. there arrived among us from Ireland, a young Presbyterian Preacher named Hemphill, who delivered with a good Voice, & apparently extempore, most excellent Discourses, which drew together considerable Numbers of different Persuasions, who join'd in admiring them. Among the rest I became one of his constant Hearers, his Sermons pleasing me as they had little of the dogmatical kind, but inculcated strongly the Practice of Virtue, or what in the religious Stile are called Good Works. Those however, of our Congregation, who considered themselves as orthodox Presbyterians, disapprov'd his Doctrine, and were join'd by most of the old Clergy, who arraign'd him of Heterodoxy before the Synod, in order to have him silenc'd. I became his zealous Partisan, and contributed all I could to raise a Party in his Favour; and we combated for him a while with some Hopes of Success. There was much Scribbling pro & con upon the Occasion; and finding that tho' an elegant Preacher he was but a poor Writer, I lent him my Pen and wrote for him two or three Pamphlets, and one Piece in the Gazette of April 1735. Those Pamphlets, as is generally the Case with controversial Writings, tho' eagerly read at the time, were soon out of Vogue, and I question whether a single Copy of them now exists. During the Contest an unlucky Occurrence hurt his Cause exceedingly. One of our Adversaries having heard him preach a Sermon that was much admired, thought he had somewhere read that Sermon before, or at least a part of it. On Search he found that Part quoted at length in one of the British Reviews, from a Discourse of Dr Forster's. This Detection gave many of our Party Disgust, who accordingly abandoned his Cause, and occasion'd our more speedy Discomfiture in the Synod. I stuck by him, however, as I rather approv'd his giving us good Sermons compos'd by others, than bad ones of his own Manufacture; tho' the latter was the Practice of our common Teachers. He afterwards acknowledg'd to me that none of those he preach'd were his own; adding that his Memory was such as enabled him to retain and repeat any Sermon after one Reading only.—On our Defeat he left us, in search elsewhere of better Fortune, and I quitted the Congregation, never joining it after, tho' I continu'd many Years my Subscription for the Support of its Ministers.—

I had begun in 1733 to study Languages. I soon made myself so much a Master of the French as to be able to read the Books with Ease. I then undertook the Italian. An Acquaintance who was also learning it, us'd often to tempt me to play Chess with him. Finding this took up too much of the Time I had to spare for Study, I at length refus'd to play any more, unless on this Condition, that the Victor in every Game,

should have a Right to impose a Task, either in Parts of the
Grammar to be got by heart, or in Translation, &c. which
Tasks the Vanquish'd was to perform upon Honour before
our next Meeting. As we play'd pretty equally we thus beat
one another into that Language.—I afterwards with a little
Pains-taking acquir'd as much of the Spanish as to read their
Books also. I have already mention'd that I had only one
Years Instruction in a Latin School, and that when very
young, after which I neglected that Language entirely.—But
when I had attained an Acquaintance with the French, Italian
and Spanish, I was surpriz'd to find, on looking over a Latin
Testament, that I understood so much more of that Language
than I had imagined; which encouraged me to apply my self
again to the Study of it, & I met with the more Success, as
those preceding Languages had greatly smooth'd my Way.
From these Circumstances I have thought, that there is some
Inconsistency in our common Mode of Teaching Languages.
We are told that it is proper to begin first with the Latin, and
having acquir'd that it will be more easy to attain those modern Languages which are deriv'd from it; and yet we do not
begin with the Greek in order more easily to acquire the
Latin. It is true, that if you can clamber & get to the Top of
a Stair-Case without using the Steps, you will more easily
gain them in descending: but certainly if you begin with the
lowest you will with more Ease ascend to the Top. And I
would therefore offer it to the Consideration of those who
superintend the Educating of our Youth, whether, since many
of those who begin with the Latin, quit the same after spending some Years, without having made any great Proficiency,
and what they have learnt becomes almost useless, so that
their time has been lost, it would not have been better to have
begun them with the French, proceeding to the Italian &c.
for tho' after spending the same time they should quit the
Study of Languages, & never arrive at the Latin, they would
however have acquir'd another Tongue or two that being in
modern Use might be serviceable to them in common Life.

After ten Years Absence from Boston, and having become
more easy in my Circumstances, I made a Journey thither to
visit my Relations, which I could not sooner well afford. In
returning I call'd at Newport, to see my Brother then settled

there with his Printing-House. Our former Differences were forgotten, and our Meeting was very cordial and affectionate. He was fast declining in his Health, and requested of me that in case of his Death which he apprehended not far distant, I would take home his Son, then but 10 Years of Age, and bring him up to the Printing Business. This I accordingly perform'd, sending him a few Years to School before I took him into the Office. His Mother carry'd on the Business till he was grown up, when I assisted him with an Assortment of new Types, those of his Father being in a Manner worn out.—Thus it was that I made my Brother ample Amends for the Service I had depriv'd him of by leaving him so early.—

In 1736 I lost one of my Sons a fine Boy of 4 Years old, by the Small Pox taken in the common way. I long regretted bitterly & still regret that I had not given it to him by Inoculation; This I mention for the Sake of Parents, who omit that Operation on the Supposition that they should never forgive themselves if a Child died under it; my Example showing that the Regret may be the same either way, and that therefore the safer should be chosen.—

Our Club, the Junto, was found so useful, & afforded such Satisfaction to the Members, that several were desirous of introducing their Friends, which could not well be done without exceeding what we had settled as a convenient Number, viz. Twelve. We had from the Beginning made it a Rule to keep our Institution a Secret, which was pretty well observ'd. The Intention was, to avoid Applications of improper Persons for Admittance, some of whom perhaps we might find it difficult to refuse. I was one of those who were against any Addition to our Number, but instead of it made in Writing a Proposal, that every Member separately should endeavour to form a subordinate Club, with the same Rules respecting Queries, &c. and without informing them of the Connexion with the Junto. The Advantages propos'd were the Improvement of so many more young Citizens by the Use of our Institutions; Our better Acquaintance with the general Sentiments of the Inhabitants on any Occasion, as the Junto-Member might propose what Queries we should desire, and was to report to Junto what pass'd in his separate Club; the Promotion of our particular Interests in Business by more extensive Recommendations; and the Increase of our Influence in public Affairs & our Power of doing Good by spreading thro' the several Clubs the Sentiments of the Junto. The Project was approv'd, and every Member undertook to form his Club: but they did not all succeed. Five or six only were compleated, which were call'd by different Names, as the Vine, the Union, the Band, &c. they were useful to themselves, & afforded us a good deal of Amusement, Information & Instruction, besides answering in some considerable Degree our Views of influencing the public Opinion on particular Occasions, of which I shall give some Instances in course of time as they happened.—

My first Promotion was my being chosen in 1736 Clerk of the General Assembly. The Choice was made that Year without Opposition; but the Year following when I was again propos'd (the Choice, like that of the Members being annual) a new Member made a long Speech against me in order to favour some other Candidate. I was however chosen; which was the more agreable to me, as besides the Pay for immediate Service as Clerk, the Place gave me a better Opportunity of keeping up an Interest among the Members, which secur'd to me the Business of Printing the Votes, Laws, Paper Money, and other occasional Jobbs for the Public, that on the whole were very profitable. I therefore did not like the Opposition of this new Member, who was a Gentleman of Fortune, & Education, with Talents that were likely to give him in time great Influence in the House, which indeed afterwards happened. I did not however aim at gaining his Favour by paying any servile Respect to him, but after some time took this other Method. Having heard that he had in his Library a certain very scarce & curious Book, I wrote a Note to him expressing my Desire of perusing that Book, and requesting he would do me the Favour of lending it to me for a few Days. He sent it immediately; and I return'd it in about a Week, with another Note expressing strongly my Sense of the Favour. When we next met in the House he spoke to me, (which he had never done before) and with great Civility. And he ever afterwards manifested a Readiness to serve me on all Occasions, so that we became great Friends, & our Friendship continu'd to his Death. This is another Instance of the Truth of an old Maxim I had learnt, which says, *He that has once done you a Kindness will be more ready to do you another, than he whom you yourself have obliged*. And it shows how much more profitable it is prudently to remove, than to resent, return & continue inimical Proceedings.—

In 1737, Col. Spotswood, late Governor of Virginia, & then Post-master, General, being dissatisfied with the Conduct of his Deputy at Philadelphia, respecting some Negligence in rendering, & Inexactitude of his Accounts, took from him the Commission & offered it to me. I accepted it readily, and found it of great Advantage; for tho' the Salary was small, it facilitated the Correspondence that improv'd my Newspaper, encreas'd the Number demanded, as well as the Advertisements to be inserted, so that it came to afford me a very considerable Income. My old Competitor's Newspaper declin'd proportionably, and I was satisfy'd without retaliating his Refusal, while Postmaster, to permit my Papers being carried by the Riders. Thus He suffer'd greatly from his Neglect in due Accounting; and I mention it as a Lesson to those young Men who may be employ'd in managing Affairs for others that they should always render Accounts & make Remittances, with great Clearness and Punctuality.—The Character of observing Such a Conduct is the most powerful of all Recommendations to new Employments & Increase of Business.

I began now to turn my Thoughts a little to public Affairs, beginning however with small Matters. The City Watch was one of the first Things that I conceiv'd to want Regulation. It was managed by the Constables of the respective Wards in Turn. The Constable warn'd a Number of Housekeepers to attend him for the Night. Those who chose never to attend paid him Six Shillings a Year to be excus'd, which was suppos'd to be for hiring Substitutes; but was in Reality much more than was necessary for that purpose, and made the Constableship a Place of Profit. And the Constable for a little Drink often got such Ragamuffins about him as a Watch, that reputable Housekeepers did not chuse to mix with. Walking the Rounds too was often neglected, and most of the Night spent in Tippling. I thereupon wrote a Paper to be read in Junto, representing these Irregularities, but insisting more particularly on the Inequality of this Six Shilling Tax of the

Constables, respecting the Circumstances of those who paid it, since a poor Widow Housekeeper, all whose Property to be guarded by the Watch did not perhaps exceed the Value of Fifty Pounds, paid as much as the wealthiest Merchant who had Thousands of Pounds-worth of Goods in his Stores. On the whole I proposed as a more effectual Watch, the Hiring of proper Men to serve constantly in that Business; and as a more equitable Way of supporting the Charge, the levying a Tax that should be proportion'd to Property. This Idea being approv'd by the Junto, was communicated to the other Clubs, but as arising in each of them. And tho' the Plan was not immediately carried into Execution, yet by preparing the Minds of People for the Change, it paved the Way for the Law obtain'd a few Years after, when the Members of our Clubs were grown into more Influence.—

About this time I wrote a Paper, (first to be read in Junto but it was afterwards publish'd) on the different Accidents and Carelessnesses by which Houses were set on fire, with Cautions against them, and Means proposed of avoiding them. This was much spoken of as a useful Piece, and gave rise to a Project, which soon followed it, of forming a Company for the more ready Extinguishing of Fires, and mutual Assistance in Removing & Securing of Goods when in Danger. Associates in this Scheme were presently found amounting to Thirty. Our Articles of Agreement oblig'd every Member to keep always in good Order and fit for Use, a certain Number of Leather Buckets, with strong Bags & Baskets (for packing & transporting of Goods), which were to be brought to every Fire; and we agreed to meet once a Month & spend a social Evening together, in discoursing, and communicating such Ideas as occur'd to us upon the Subject of Fires as might be useful in our Conduct on such Occasions. The Utility of this Institution soon appeard, and many more desiring to be admitted than we thought convenient for one Company, they were advised to form another; which was accordingly done. And this went on, one new Company being formed after another, till they became so numerous as to include most of the Inhabitants who were Men of Property; and now at the time of my Writing this, tho' upwards of Fifty Years since its Establishment, that which I first formed, called the Union Fire Company, still subsists and flourishes, tho' the first Members are all deceas'd but myself & one who is older by a Year than I am.—The small Fines that have been paid by Members for Absence at the Monthly Meetings, have been apply'd to the Purchase of Fire Engines, Ladders, Firehooks, and other useful Implements for each Company, so that I question whether there is a City in the World better provided with the Means of putting a Stop to beginning Conflagrations; and in fact since these Institutions, the City has never lost by Fire more than one or two Houses at a time, and the Flames have often been extinguish'd before the House in which they began has been half-consumed.—

In 1739 arriv'd among us from England the Rev. Mr White-fiel, who had made himself remarkable there as an itinerant Preacher. He was at first permitted to preach in some of our Churches; but the Clergy taking a Dislike to him, soon re-fus'd him their Pulpits and he was oblig'd to preach in the Fields. The Multitudes of all Sects and Denominations that attended his Sermons were enormous and it was matter of Speculation to me who was one of the Number, to observe the extraordinary Influence of his Oratory on his Hearers, and how much they admir'd & respected him, notwithstanding his common Abuse of them, by assuring them they were nat-urally *half Beasts and half Devils*. It was wonderful to see the Change soon made in the Manners of our Inhabitants; from being thoughtless or indifferent about Religion, it seem'd as if all the World were growing Religious; so that one could not walk thro' the Town in an Evening without Hearing Psalms sung in different Families of every Street. And it being found inconvenient to assemble in the open Air, subject to its Inclemencies, the Building of a House to meet-in was no sooner propos'd and Persons appointed to receive Contribu-tions, but sufficient Sums were soon receiv'd to procure the Ground and erect the Building which was 100 feet long & 70 broad, about the Size of Westminster-hall; and the Work was carried on with such Spirit as to be finished in a much shorter time than could have been expected. Both House and Ground were vested in Trustees, expressly for the Use of any Preacher of any religious Persuasion who might desire to say some-thing to the People of Philadelphia, the Design in building not being to accommodate any particular Sect, but the Inhabitants in general, so that even if the Mufti of Constantinople were to send a Missionary to preach Mahometanism to us, he would find a Pulpit at his Service.—

Mr Whitfield, in leaving us, went preaching all the Way thro' the Colonies to Georgia. The Settlement of that Province had lately been begun; but instead of being made with hardy industrious Husbandmen accustomed to Labour, the only People fit for such an Enterprise, it was with Families of broken Shopkeepers and other insolvent Debtors, many of indolent & idle habits, taken out of the Goals, who being set down in the Woods, unqualified for clearing Land, & unable to endure the Hardships of a new Settlement, perished in Numbers, leaving many helpless Children unprovided for. The Sight of their miserable Situation inspired the benevolent Heart of Mr Whitefield with the Idea of building an Orphan House there, in which they might be supported and educated. Returning northward he preach'd up this Charity, & made large Collections;—for his Eloquence had a wonderful Power over the Hearts & Purses of his Hearers, of which I myself was an Instance. I did not disapprove of the Design, but as Georgia was then destitute of Materials & Workmen, and it was propos'd to send them from Philadelphia at a great Expence, I thought it would have been better to have built the House here & brought the Children to it. This I advis'd, but he was resolute in his first Project, and rejected my Counsel, and I thereupon refus'd to contribute. I happened soon after to attend one of his Sermons, in the Course of which I perceived he intended to finish with a Collection, & I silently resolved he should get nothing from me. I had in my Pocket a Handful of Copper, Money, three or four silver Dollars, and five Pistoles in Gold. As he proceeded I began to soften, and concluded to give the Coppers. Another Stroke of his Oratory made me asham'd of that, and determin'd me to give the Silver; & he finish'd so admirably, that I empty'd my Pocket wholly into the Collector's Dish, Gold and all. At this Sermon there was also one of our Club, who being of my Sentiments respecting the Building in Georgia, and suspecting a Collection might be intended, had by Precaution emptied his Pockets before he came from home; towards the

Conclusion of the Discourse however, he felt a strong Desire to give, and apply'd to a Neighbour who stood near him to borrow some Money for the Purpose. The Application was unfortunately to perhaps the only Man in the Company who had the firmness not to be affected by the Preacher. His Answer was, *At any other time, Friend Hopkinson, I would lend to thee freely; but not now; for thee seems to be out of thy right Senses.*—

Some of Mr Whitfield's Enemies affected to suppose that he would apply these Collections to his own private Emolument; but I, who was intimately acquainted with him, (being employ'd in printing his Sermons and Journals, &c.) never had the least Suspicion of his Integrity, but am to this day decidedly of Opinion that he was in all his Conduct, a perfectly *honest Man*. And methinks my Testimony in his Favour ought to have the more Weight, as we had no religious Connection. He us'd indeed sometimes to pray for my Conversion, but never had the Satisfaction of believing that his Prayers were heard. Ours was a mere civil Friendship, sincere on both Sides, and lasted to his Death.

The following Instance will show something of the Terms on which we stood. Upon one of his Arrivals from England at Boston, he wrote to me that he should come soon to Philadelphia, but knew not where he could lodge when there, as he understood his old kind Host Mr Benezet was remov'd to Germantown. My Answer was; You know my House, if you can make shift with its scanty Accommodations you will be most heartily welcome. He reply'd, that if I made that kind Offer for Christ's sake, I should not miss of a Reward.—And I return'd, *Don't let me be mistaken; it was not for Christ's sake, but for your sake.* One of our common Acquaintance jocosely remark'd, that knowing it to be the Custom of the Saints, when they receiv'd any favour, to shift the Burthen of the Obligation from off their own Shoulders, and place it in Heaven, I had contriv'd to fix it on Earth.—

The last time I saw Mr Whitefield was in London, when he consulted me about his Orphan House Concern, and his Purpose of appropriating it to the Establishment of a College.

He had a loud and clear Voice, and articulated his Words & Sentences so perfectly that he might be heard and under-

stood at a great Distance, especially as his Auditories, however numerous, observ'd the most exact Silence. He preach'd
one Evening from the Top of the Court House Steps, which
are in the Middle of Market Street, and on the West Side of
Second Street which crosses it at right angles. Both Streets
were fill'd with his Hearers to a considerable Distance. Being
among the hindmost in Market Street, I had the Curiosity to
learn how far he could be heard, by retiring backwards down
the Street towards the River, and I found his Voice distinct
till I came near Front-Street, when some Noise in that Street,
obscur'd it. Imagining then a Semi-Circle, of which my Distance should be the Radius, and that it were fill'd with Auditors, to each of whom I allow'd two square feet, I computed
that he might well be heard by more than Thirty-Thousand.
This reconcil'd me to the Newspaper Accounts of his having
preach'd to 25000 People in the Fields, and to the antient
Histories of Generals haranguing whole Armies, of which I
had sometimes doubted.—

By hearing him often I came to distinguish easily between
Sermons newly compos'd, & those which he had often
preach'd in the Course of his Travels. His Delivery of the
latter was so improv'd by frequent Repetitions, that every
Accent, every Emphasis, every Modulation of Voice, was so
perfectly well turn'd and well plac'd, that without being
interested in the Subject, one could not help being pleas'd
with the Discourse, a Pleasure of much the same kind with
that receiv'd from an excellent Piece of Musick. This is an
Advantage itinerant Preachers have over those who are stationary: as the latter cannot well improve their Delivery of a
Sermon by so many Rehearsals.—

His Writing and Printing from time to time gave great
Advantage to his Enemies. Unguarded Expressions and even
erroneous Opinions del^d in Preaching might have been
afterwards explain'd, or qualify'd by supposing others that
might have accompany'd them; or they might have been
deny'd; But *litera scripta manet*. Critics attack'd his Writings
violently, and with so much Appearance of Reason as to diminish the Number of his Votaries, and prevent their Encrease: So that I am of Opinion, if he had never written any
thing he would have left behind him a much more numerous

and important Sect. And his Reputation might in that case
have been still growing, even after his Death; as there being
nothing of his Writing on which to found a Censure; and
give him a lower Character, his Proselites would be left at
Liberty to feign for him as great a Variety of Excellencies,
as their enthusiastic Admiration might wish him to have
possessed.

My Business was now continually augmenting, and my
Circumstances growing daily easier, my Newspaper having
become very profitable, as being for a time almost the only
one in this and the neighbouring Provinces.—I experienc'd
too the Truth of the Observation, that *after getting the first
hundred Pound, it is more easy to get the second*: Money itself
being of a prolific Nature: The Partnership at Carolina having succeeded, I was encourag'd to engage in others, and to
promote several of my Workmen who had behaved well, by
establishing them with Printing-Houses in different Colonies,
on the same Terms with that in Carolina. Most of them did
well, being enabled at the End of our Term, Six Years, to purchase the Types of me; and go on working for themselves, by
which means several Families were raised. Partnerships often
finish in Quarrels, but I was happy in this, that mine were all
carry'd on and ended amicably; owing I think a good deal to
the Precaution of having very explicitly settled in our Articles
every thing to be done by or expected from each Partner, so
that there was nothing to dispute, which Precaution I would
therefore recommend to all who enter into Partnerships, for
whatever Esteem Partners may have for & Confidence in each
other at the time of the Contract, little Jealousies and Disgusts may arise, with Ideas of Inequality in the Care &
Burthen of the Business, &c. which are attended often with
Breach of Friendship & of the Connection, perhaps with
Lawsuits and other disagreable Consequences.

I had on the whole abundant Reason to be satisfied with
my being established in Pennsylvania. There were however
two things that I regretted: There being no Provision for
Defence, nor for a compleat Education of Youth. No Militia
nor any College. I therefore in 1743, drew up a Proposal for
establishing an Academy; & at that time thinking the Rev^d
Mr Peters, who was out of Employ, a fit Person to superin-

tend such an Institution, I communicated the Project to him.
But he having more profitable Views in the Service of the
Proprietor, which succeeded, declin'd the Undertaking. And
not knowing another at that time suitable for such a Trust, I
let the Scheme lie a while dormant.—I succeeded better the
next Year, 1744, in proposing and establishing a Philosophical
Society. The Paper I wrote for that purpose will be found
among my Writings when collected.—

With respect to Defence, Spain having been several Years
at War against Britain, and being at length join'd by France,
which brought us into greater Danger; and the laboured &
long-continued Endeavours of our Governor Thomas to prevail with our Quaker Assembly to pass a Militia Law, & make
other Provisions for the Security of the Province having
proved abortive, I determined to try what might be done by
a voluntary Association of the People. To promote this I first
wrote & published a Pamphlet, intitled, PLAIN TRUTH, in
which I stated our defenceless Situation in strong Lights,
with the Necessity of Union & Discipline for our Defence,
and promis'd to propose in a few Days an Association to be
generally signed for that purpose. The Pamphlet had a sudden
& surprizing Effect. I was call'd upon for the Instrument of
Association: And having settled the Draft of it with a few
Friends, I appointed a Meeting of the Citizens in the large
Building before mentioned. The House was pretty full. I had
prepared a Number of printed Copies, and provided Pens and
Ink dispers'd all over the Room. I harangu'd them a little on
the Subject, read the Paper & explain'd it, and then distrib-
uted the Copies which were eagerly signed, not the least
Objection being made. When the Company separated, & the
Papers were collected we found above Twelve hundred
Hands; and other Copies being dispers'd in the Country the
Subscribers amounted at length to upwards of Ten Thousand.
These all furnish'd themselves as soon as they could with
Arms; form'd themselves into Companies, and Regiments,
chose their own Officers, & met every Week to be instructed
in the manual Exercise, and other Parts of military Discipline.
The Women, by Subscriptions among themselves, provided
Silk Colours, which they presented to the Companies, painted
with different Devices and Motto's which I supplied. The

Officers of the Companies composing the Philadelphia Regiment, being met, chose me for their Colonel; but conceiving myself unfit, I declin'd that Station, & recommended Mr Lawrence, a fine Person and Man of Influence, who was accordingly appointed. I then propos'd a Lottery to defray the Expence of Building a Battery below the Town, and furnishing it with Cannon. It filled expeditiously and the Battery was soon erected, the Merlons being fram'd of Logs & fill'd with Earth. We bought some old Cannon from Boston, but these not being sufficient, we wrote to England for more, soliciting at the same Time our Proprietaries for some Assistance, tho' without much Expectation of obtaining it. Mean while Colonel Lawrence, William Allen, Abraham Taylor, Esquires, and myself were sent to New York by the Associators, commission'd to borrow some Cannon of Governor Clinton. He at first refus'd us peremptorily: but at a Dinner with his Council where there was great Drinking of Madeira Wine, as the Custom at that Place then was, he soften'd by degrees, and said he would lend us Six. After a few more Bumpers he advanc'd to Ten. And at length he very good-naturedly conceded Eighteen. They were fine Cannon, 18 pounders, with their Carriages, which we soon transported and mounted on our Battery, where the Associators kept a nightly Guard while the War lasted: And among the rest I regularly took my Turn of Duty there as a common Soldier.—

My Activity in these Operations was agreable to the Governor and Council; they took me into Confidence, & I was consulted by them in every Measure wherein their Concurrence was thought useful to the Association. Calling in the Aid of Religion, I propos'd to them the Proclaiming a Fast, to promote Reformation, & implore the Blessing of Heaven on our Undertaking. They embrac'd the Motion, but as it was the first Fast ever thought of in the Province, the Secretary had no Precedent from which to draw the Proclamation. My Education in New England, where a Fast is proclaim'd every Year, was here of some Advantage. I drew it in the accustomed Stile, it was translated into German, printed in both Languages and divulg'd thro' the Province. This gave the Clergy of the different Sects an Opportunity of Influencing their Congregations to join in the Association; and it would probably have been general among all but Quakers if the Peace had not soon interven'd.

It was thought by some of my Friends that by my Activity in these Affairs, I should offend that Sect, and thereby lose my Interest in the Assembly where they were a great Majority. A young Gentleman who had likewise some Friends in the House, and wish'd to succeed me as their Clerk, acquainted me that it was decided to displace me at the next Election, and he therefore in good Will advis'd me to resign, as more consistent with my Honour than being turn'd out. My Answer to him was, that I had read or heard of some Public Man, who made it a Rule never to ask for an Office, and never to refuse one when offer'd to him. I approve, says I, of his Rule, and will practise it with a small Addition; I shall never *ask*, never *refuse*, nor ever *resign* an Office. If they will have my Office of Clerk to dispose of to another, they shall take it from me. I will not by giving it up, lose my Right of some time or other making Reprisals on my Adversaries. I heard however no more of this. I was chosen again, unanimously as usual, at the next Election. Possibly as they dislik'd my late Intimacy with the Members of Council, who had join'd the Governors in all the Disputes about military Preparations with which the House had long been harass'd, they might have been pleas'd if I would voluntarily have left them; but they did not care to displace me on Account merely of my Zeal for the Association; and they could not well give another Reason.—Indeed I had some Cause to believe, that the Defence of the Country was not disagreeable to any of them, provided they were not requir'd to assist in it. And I found that a much greater Number of them than I could have imagined, tho' against offensive War, were clearly for the defensive. Many Pamphlets *pro & con.* were publish'd on the Subject, and some by good Quakers in favour of Defence, which I believe convinc'd most of their younger People. A Transaction in our Fire Company gave me some Insight into their prevailing Sentiments. It had been propos'd that we should encourage the Scheme for building a Battery by laying out the present Stock, then about Sixty Pounds, in Tickets of the Lottery. By our Rules no Money could be dispos'd of but at the next Meeting after the Proposal. The Company consisted of Thirty Members, of which Twenty-two were Quakers, & Eight only of other Persuasions. We eight punctually attended the Meeting; but tho' we thought that some of the Quakers would join us, we were by no means sure of a Majority. Only one Quaker, Mr James Morris, appear'd to oppose the Measure: He express'd much Sorrow that it had ever been propos'd, as he said *Friends* were all against it, and it would create such Discord as might break up the Company. We told him, that we saw no Reason for that; we were the Minority, and if *Friends* were against the Measure and outvoted us, we must and should, agreable to the Usage of all Societies, submit. When the Hour for Business arriv'd, it was mov'd to put the Vote. He allow'd we might then do it by the Rules, but as he could assure us that a Number of Members intended to be present for the purpose of opposing it, it would be but candid to allow a little time for their appearing. While we were disputing this, a Waiter came to tell me two Gentlemen below desir'd to speak with me. I went down, and found they were two of our Quaker Members. They told me there were eight of them assembled at a Tavern just by; that they were determin'd to come and vote with us if there should be occasion, which they hop'd would not be the Case; and desir'd we would not call for their Assistance if we could do without it, as their Voting for such a Measure might embroil them with their Elders & Friends; Being thus secure of a Majority, I went up, and after a little seeming Hesitation, agreed to a Delay of another Hour. This Mr Morris allow'd to be extreamly fair. Not one of his opposing Friends appear'd, at which he express'd great Surprize; and at the Expiration of the Hour, we carry'd the Resolution Eight to one; And as of the 22 Quakers, Eight were ready to vote with us and, Thirteen by their Absence manifested that they were not inclin'd to oppose the Measure, I afterwards estimated the Proportion of Quakers sincerely against Defence as one to twenty one only. For these were all regular Members, of that Society, and in good Reputation among them, and had due Notice of what was propos'd at that Meeting.

The honourable & learned Mr Logan, who had always been of that Sect, was one who wrote an Address to them, declaring his Approbation of defensive War, and supporting his Opinion by many strong Arguments: He put into my Hands Sixty Pounds, to be laid out in Lottery Tickets for the Battery, with Directions to apply what Prizes might be drawn wholly to that Service. He told me the following Anecdote of his old Master Wm Penn respecting Defence. He came over from England, when a young Man, with that Proprietary, and as his Secretary. It was War Time, and their Ship was chas'd by an armed Vessel suppos'd to be an Enemy. Their Captain prepar'd for Defence, but told Wm Penn and his Company of Quakers, that he did not expect their Assistance, and they might retire into the Cabin; which they did, except James Logan, who chose to stay upon Deck, and was quarter'd to a Gun. The suppos'd Enemy prov'd a Friend; so there was no Fighting. But when the Secretary went down to communicate the Intelligence, Wm Penn rebuk'd him severely for staying upon Deck and undertaking to assist in defending the Vessel, contrary to the Principles of *Friends*, especially as it had not been required by the Captain. This Reproof being before all the Company, piqu'd the Secretary, who answer'd, *I being thy Servant, why did thee not order me to come down: but thee was willing enough that I should stay and help to fight the Ship when thee thought there was Danger.*

My being many Years in the Assembly, the Majority of which were constantly Quakers, gave me frequent Opportunities of seeing the Embarassment given them by their Principle against War, whenever Application was made to them by Order of the Crown to grant Aids for military Purposes. They were unwilling to offend Government on the one hand, by a direct Refusal, and their Friends the Body of Quakers on the other, by a Compliance contrary to their Principles. Hence a Variety of Evasions to avoid Complying, and Modes of disguising the Compliance when it became unavoidable. The common Mode at last was to grant Money under the Phrase of its being *for the King's Use*, and never to enquire how it was applied. But if the Demand was not directly from the Crown, that Phrase was found not so proper, and some other was to be invented. As when Powder was wanting, (I think it was for the Garrison at Louisburg,) and the Government of New England solicited a Grant of some from Pensilvania, which was much urg'd on the House by Governor

Thomas, they could not grant Money to buy Powder, because that was an Ingredient of War, but they voted an Aid to New England, of Three Thousand Pounds, to be put into the hands of the Governor, and appropriated it for the Purchasing of Bread, Flour, Wheat, *or other Grain*. Some of the Council desirous of giving the House still farther Embarassment, advis'd the Governor not to accept Provision, as not being the Thing he had demanded. But he reply'd, "I shall take the Money, for I understand very well their Meaning; *Other Grain*, is Gunpowder;" which he accordingly bought; and they never objected to it. It was in Allusion to this Fact, that when in our Fire Company we feared the Success of our Proposal in favour of the Lottery, & I had said to my Friend Mr Syng, one of our Members, if we fail, let us move the Purchase of a Fire Engine with the Money; the Quakers can have no Objection to that: and then if you nominate me, and I you, as a Committee for that purpose, we will buy a great Gun, which is certainly a *Fire-Engine*: I see, says he, you have improv'd by being so long in the Assembly; your equivocal Project would be just a Match for their Wheat *or other Grain*.

These Embarassments that the Quakers suffer'd from having establish'd & published it as one of their Principles, that no kind of War was lawful, and which being once published, they could not afterwards, however they might change their minds, easily get rid of, reminds me of what I think a more prudent Conduct in another Sect among us; that of the Dunkers. I was acquainted with one of its Founders, Michael Welfare, soon after it appear'd.—He complain'd to me that they were grievously calumniated by the Zealots of other Persuasions, and charg'd with abominable Principles and Practices to which they were utter Strangers. I told him this had always been the case with new Sects; and that to put a Stop to such Abuse, I imagin'd it might be well to publish the Articles of their Belief and the Rules of their Discipline. He said that it had been propos'd among them, but not agreed to, for this Reason; "When we were first drawn together as a Society, says he, it had pleased God to inlighten our Minds so far, as to see that some Doctrines which we once esteemed Truths were Errors, & that others which we had esteemed Errors were real Truths. From time to time he has been pleased to afford us farther Light, and our Principles have been improving, & our Errors diminishing. Now we are not sure that we are arriv'd at the End of this Progression, and at the Perfection of Spiritual or Theological Knowledge; and we fear that if we should once print our Confession of Faith, we should feel ourselves as if bound & confin'd by it, and perhaps be unwilling to receive farther Improvement; and our Successors still more so, as conceiving what we their Elders & Founders had done, to be something sacred, never to be departed from."—This Modesty in a Sect is perhaps a singular Instance in the History of Mankind, every other Sect supposing itself in Possession of all Truth, and that those who differ are so far in the Wrong: Like a Man travelling in foggy Weather: Those at some Distance before him on the Road he sees wrapt up in the Fog, as well as those behind him, and also the People in the Fields on each side; but neer him all appears clear.—Tho' in truth he is as much in the Fog as any of them. To avoid this kind of Embarrassment the Quakers have of late Years been gradually declining the public Service in the Assembly & in the Magistracy. Chusing rather to quit their Power than their Principle.

In Order of Time I should have mentioned before, that having in 1742 invented an open Stove, for the better warming of Rooms and at the same time saving Fuel, as the fresh Air admitted was warmed in Entring, I made a Present of the Model to Mr Robert Grace, one of my early Friends, who having an Iron Furnace, found the Casting of the Plates for these Stoves a profitable Thing, as they were growing in Demand. To promote that Demand I wrote and published a Pamphlet Intitled, *An Account of the New-Invented* PENNSYL-VANIA FIRE PLACES: *Wherein their Construction & manner of Operation is particularly explained; their Advantages above every other Method of warming Rooms demonstrated; and all Objections that have been raised against the Use of them answered & obviated, &c.* This Pamphlet had a good Effect, Gov.ʳ Thomas was so pleas'd with the Construction of this Stove, as describ'd in it that he offer'd to give me a Patent for the sole Vending of them for a Term of Years; but I declin'd it from a Principle which has ever weigh'd with me on such Occasions, viz. *That as we enjoy great Advantages from the Inventions of others, we should be glad of an Opportunity to serve others by any Invention of ours, and this we should do freely and generously.* An Ironmonger in London, however, after assuming a good deal of my Pamphlet & working it up into his own, and making some small Changes in the Machine, which rather hurt its Operation, got a Patent for it there, and made as I was told a little Fortune by it.—And this is not the only Instance of Patents taken out for my Inventions by others, tho' not always with the same Success:—which I never contested, as having no Desire of profiting by Patents my self, and hating Disputes.—The Use of these Fireplaces in very many Houses both of this and the neighbouring Colonies, has been and is a great Saving of Wood to the Inhabitants.—

Peace being concluded, and the Association Business therefore at an End, I turn'd my Thoughts again to the Affair of establishing an Academy. The first Step I took was to associate in the Design a Number of active Friends, of whom the Junto furnished a good Part; the next was to write and publish a Pamphlet intitled, *Proposals relating to the Education of Youth in Pennsylvania.*—This I distributed among the principal Inhabitants gratis; and as soon as I could suppose their Minds a little prepared by the Perusal of it, I set on foot a Subscription for Opening and Supporting an Academy; it was to be paid in Quotas yearly for Five Years; by so dividing it I judg'd the Subscription might be larger, and I believe it was so, amounting to no less (if I remember right) than Five thousand Pounds.—In the Introduction to these Proposals, I stated their Publication not as an Act of mine, but of some *publick-spirited Gentlemen;* avoiding as much as I could, according to my usual Rule, the presenting myself to the Publick as the Author of any Scheme for their Benefit.—

The Subscribers, to carry the Project into immediate Execution chose out of their Number Twenty-four Trustees, and appointed Mr Francis, then Attorney General, and myself, to draw up Constitutions for the Government of the Academy, which being done and signed, an House was hired, Masters engag'd and the Schools opened I think in the same Year 1749. The Scholars encreasing fast, the House was soon found too small, and we were looking out for a Piece of Ground properly situated, with Intention to build, when

Providence threw into our way a large House ready built, which with a few Alterations might well serve our purpose, this was the Building before mentioned erected by the Hearers of Mr Whitefield, and was obtain'd for us in the following Manner.

It is to be noted, that the Contributions to this Building being made by People of different Sects, Care was taken in the Nomination of Trustees, in whom the Building & Ground was to be vested, that a Predominancy should not be given to any Sect, lest in time that Predominancy might be a means of appropriating the whole to the Use of such Sect, contrary to the original Intention; it was therefore that one of each Sect was appointed, viz. one Church-of-England-man, one Presbyterian, one Baptist, one Moravian, &c. Those in case of Vacancy by Death were to fill it by Election from among the Contributors. The Moravian happen'd not to please his Colleagues, and on his Death, they resolved to have no other of that Sect. The Difficulty then was, how to avoid having two of some other Sect, by means of the new Choice. Several Persons were named and for that Reason not agreed to. At length one mention'd me, with the Observation that I was merely an honest Man, & of no Sect at all; which prevail'd with them to chuse me. The Enthusiasm which existed when the House was built, had long since abated, and its Trustees had not been able to procure fresh Contributions for paying the Ground Rent, and discharging some other Debts the Building had occasion'd, which embarrass'd them greatly. Being now a Member of both Sets of Trustees, that for the Building & that for the Academy, I had good Opportunity of negociating with both, & brought them finally to an Agreement, by which the Trustees for the Building were to cede it to those of the Academy, the latter undertaking to discharge the Debt, to keep forever open in the Building a large Hall for occasional Preachers according to the original Intention, and maintain a Free School for the Instruction of poor Children. Writings were accordingly drawn, and on paying the Debts the Trustees of the Academy were put in Possession of the Premises, and by dividing the great & lofty Hall into Stories, and different Rooms above & below for the several Schools, and purchasing some additional Ground, the whole was soon made fit for our purpose, and the Scholars remov'd into the Building. The Care and Trouble of agreeing with the Workmen, purchasing Materials, and superintending the Work fell upon me, and I went thro' it the more chearfully, as it did not then interfere with my private Business, having the Year before taken a very able, industrious & honest Partner, Mr David Hall, with whose Character I was well acquainted, as he had work'd for me four Years. He took off my Hands all Care of the Printing-Office, paying me punctually my Share of the Profits. This Partnership continued Eighteen Years, successfully for us both.—

The Trustees of the Academy after a while were incorporated by a Charter from the Governor; their Funds were increas'd by Contributions in Britain, and Grants of Land from the Proprietaries, to which the Assembly has since made considerable Addition, and thus was established the present University of Philadelphia. I have been continued one of its Trustees from the Beginning, now near forty Years, and have had the very great Pleasure of seeing a Number of the Youth who have receiv'd their Education in it, distinguish'd by their improv'd Abilities, serviceable in public Stations, and Ornaments to their Country.

When I disengag'd myself as above mentioned from private Business, I flatter'd myself that, by the sufficient tho' moderate Fortune I had acquir'd, I had secur'd Leisure during the rest of my Life, for Philosophical Studies and Amusements; I purchas'd all Dr Spence's Apparatus, who had come from England to lecture here; and I proceeded in my Electrical Experiments with great Alacrity; but the Publick now considering me as a Man of Leisure, laid hold of me for their Purposes; every Part of our Civil Government, and almost at the same time, imposing some Duty upon me. The Governor put me into the Commission of the Peace; the Corporation of the City chose me of the Common Council, and soon after an Alderman; and the Citizens at large chose me a Burgess to represent them in Assembly. This latter Station was the more agreable to me, as I was at length tired with sitting there to hear Debates in which as Clerk I could take no part, and which were often so unentertaining, that I was induc'd to amuse myself with making magic Squares, or Circles, or any thing to avoid Weariness. And I conceiv'd my becoming a Member would enlarge my Power of doing Good. I would not however insinuate that my Ambition was not flatter'd by all these Promotions. It certainly was. For considering my low Beginning they were great Things to me. And they were still more pleasing, as being so many spontaneous Testimonies of the public's good Opinion, and by me entirely unsolicited.

The Office of Justice of the Peace I try'd a little, by attending a few Courts, and sitting on the Bench to hear Causes. But finding that more Knowledge of the Common Law than I possess'd, was necessary to act in that Station with Credit, I gradually withdrew from it, excusing myself by my being oblig'd to attend the higher Dutys of a Legislator in the Assembly. My Election to this Trust was repeated every Year for Ten Years, without my ever asking any Elector for his Vote, or signifying either directly or indirectly any Desire of being chosen.—On taking my Seat in the House, my Son was appointed their Clerk.

The Year following, a Treaty being to be held with the Indians at Carlisle, the Governor sent a Message to the House, proposing that they should nominate some of their Members to be join'd with some Members of Council as Commissioners for that purpose. The House nam'd the Speaker (Mr Norris) and my self; and being commission'd we went to Carlisle, and met the Indians accordingly.—As those People are extreamly apt to get drunk, and when so are very quarrelsome & disorderly, we strictly forbad the selling any Liquor to them; and when they complain'd of this Restriction, we told them that if they would continue sober during the Treaty, we would give them Plenty of Rum when Business was over. They promis'd this; and they kept their Promise—because they could get no Liquor—and the Treaty was conducted very orderly, and concluded to mutual Satisfaction. They then claim'd and receiv'd the Rum. This was in the Afternoon. They were near 100 Men, Women & Children, and were lodg'd in temporary Cabins built in the Form of a Square just without the Town. In the Evening, hearing a great Noise among them, the Commission.ʳˢ walk'd out to see what was the Matter. We found they had made a great Bonfire in the Middle of the Square. They were all drunk Men and Women, quarrelling and fighting. Their dark-colour'd Bodies, half naked, seen only by the gloomy Light of the Bonfire, running after and beating one another with Firebrands, accompanied by their horrid Yellings, form'd a Scene the most resembling our Ideas of Hell that could well be imagin'd. There was no appeasing the Tumult, and we retired to our Lodging. At Midnight a Number of them came thundering at our Door, demanding more Rum; of which we took no Notice. The next Day, sensible they had misbehav'd in giving us that Disturbance, they sent three of their old Counsellors to make their Apology. The Orator acknowledg'd the Fault, but laid it upon the Rum; and then endeavour'd to excuse the Rum, by saying, *"The great Spirit who made all things made every thing for some Use, and whatever Use he design'd any thing for, that Use it should always be put to; Now, when he made Rum, he said,* LET THIS BE FOR INDIANS TO GET DRUNK WITH. *And it must be so."*—And indeed if it be the Design of Providence to extirpate these Savages in order to make room for Cultivators of the Earth, it seems not improbable that Rum may be the appointed Means. It has already annihilated all the Tribes who formerly inhabited the Seacoast.—

In 1751. Dr Thomas Bond, a particular Friend of mine, conceiv'd the Idea of establishing a Hospital in Philadelphia for the Reception and Cure of poor sick Persons, whether Inhabitants of the Province or Strangers. A very beneficent Design, which has been ascrib'd to me, but was originally his. He was zealous & active in endeavouring to procure Subscriptions for it; but the Proposal being a Novelty in America, and at first not well understood, he met with small Success. At length he came to me, with the Compliment that he found there was no such thing as carrying a public Spirited Project through, without my being concern'd in it; "for, says he, I am often ask'd by those to whom I propose Subscribing, Have you consulted Franklin upon this Business? and what does he think of it?—And when I tell them that I have not, (supposing it rather out of your Line,) they do not subscribe, but say they will consider of it." I enquir'd into the Nature, & probable Utility of his Scheme, and receiving from him a very satisfactory Explanation, I not only subscrib'd to it myself, but engag'd heartily in the Design of Procuring Subscriptions from others. Previous however to the Solicitation, I endeavoured to prepare the Minds of the People by writing on the Subject in the Newspapers, which was my usual Custom in such Cases, but which he had omitted. The Subscriptions afterwards were more free and generous, but beginning to flag, I saw they would be insufficient without some Assistance from the Assembly, and therefore propos'd to petition for it, which was done. The Country Members did not at first relish the Project. They objected that it could only be serviceable to the City, and therefore the Citizens should alone be at the Expence of it; and they doubted whether the Citizens themselves generally approv'd of it: My Allegation on the contrary, that it met with such Approbation as to leave no doubt of our being able to raise 2000£ by voluntary Donations, they considered as a most extravagant Supposition, and utterly impossible. On this I form'd my Plan; and asking Leave to bring in a Bill, for incorporating the Contributors, according to the Prayers of their Petition, and granting them a blank Sum of Money, which Leave was obtain'd chiefly on the Consideration that the House could throw the Bill out if they did not like it, I drew it so as to make the important Clause a conditional One, viz. "And be it enacted by the Authority aforesaid That when the said Contributors shall have met and chosen their Managers and Treasurer, *and shall have raised by their Contributions a Capital Stock of 2000£ Value*, (the yearly Interest of which is to be applied to the Accommodating of the Sick Poor in the said Hospital, free of Charge for Diet, Attendance, Advice and Medicines) and *shall make the same appear to the Satisfaction of the Speaker of the Assembly* for the time being; that *then* it shall and may be lawful for the said Speaker, and he is hereby required to sign an Order on the Provincial Treasurer for the Payment of Two Thousand Pounds in two yearly Payments, to the Treasurer of the said Hospital, to be applied to the Founding, Building and Finishing of the same."—This Condition carried the Bill through; for the Members who had oppos'd the Grant, and now conceiv'd they might have the Credit of being charitable without the Expence, agreed to its Passage; And then in soliciting Subscriptions among the People we urg'd the conditional

Promise of the Law as an additional Motive to give, since every Man's Donation would be doubled. Thus the Clause work'd both ways. The Subscriptions accordingly soon exceeded the requisite Sum, and we claim'd and receiv'd the Public Gift, which enabled us to carry the Design into Execution. A convenient and handsome Building was soon erected, the Institution has by constant Experience been found useful, and flourishes to this Day.—And I do not remember any of my political Maneuvres, the Success of which gave me at the time more Pleasure. Or that in after-thinking of it, I more easily excus'd my-self for having made some Use of Cunning.—

It was about this time that another Projector, the Revd Gilbert Tennent, came to me, with a Request that I would assist him in procuring a Subscription for erecting a new Meeting-house. It was to be for the Use of a Congregation he had gathered among the Presbyterians who were originally Disciples of Mr Whitefield. Unwilling to make myself disagreable to my fellow Citizens, by too frequently soliciting their Contributions, I absolutely refus'd. He then desir'd I would furnish him with a List of the Names of Persons I knew by Experience to be generous and public-spirited. I thought it would be unbecoming in me, after their kind Compliance with my Solicitations, to mark them out to be worried by other Beggars, and therefore refus'd also to give such a List.—He then desir'd I would at least give him my Advice. That I will readily do, said I; and, in the first Place, I advise you to apply to all those whom you know will give something; next to those whom you are uncertain whether they will give any thing or not; and show them the List of those who have given: and lastly, do not neglect those who you are sure will give nothing; for in some of them you may be mistaken.—He laugh'd, and thank'd me, and said he would take my Advice. He did so, for he ask'd of *every body*; and he obtain'd a much larger Sum than he expected, with which he erected the capacious and very elegant Meeting-house that stands in Arch street.—

Our City, tho' laid out with a beautifull Regularity, the Streets large, strait, and crossing each other at right Angles, had the Disgrace of suffering those Streets to remain long unpav'd, and in wet Weather the Wheels of heavy Carriages plough'd them into a Quagmire, so that it was difficult to cross them. And in dry Weather the Dust was offensive. I had liv'd near what was call'd the Jersey Market, and saw with Pain the Inhabitants wading in Mud while purchasing their Provisions. A Strip of Ground down the middle of that Market was at length pav'd with Brick, so that being once in the Market they had firm Footing, but were often over Shoes in Dirt to get there.—By talking and writing on the Subject, I was at length instrumental in getting the Street pav'd with Stone between the Market and the brick'd Foot-Pavement that was on each Side next the Houses. This for some time gave an easy Access to the Market, dry-shod. But the rest of the Street not being pav'd, whenever a Carriage came out of the Mud upon this Pavement, it shook off and left its Dirt on it, and it was soon cover'd with Mire, which was not remov'd, the City as yet having no Scavengers.—After some Enquiry I found a poor industrious Man, who was willing to undertake keeping the Pavement clean, by sweeping it twice a week & carrying off the Dirt from before all the Neighbours Doors, for the Sum of Sixpence per Month, to be paid by each House. I then wrote and printed a Paper, setting forth the Advantages to the Neighbourhood that might be obtain'd by this small Expence; the greater Ease in keeping our Houses clean, so much Dirt not being brought in by People's Feet; the Benefit to the Shops by more Custom, as Buyers could more easily get at them, and by not having in windy Weather the Dust blown in upon their Goods, &c. &c. I sent one of these Papers to each House, and in a Day or two went round to see who would subscribe an Agreement to pay these Sixpences. It was unanimously sign'd, and for a time well executed. All the Inhabitants of the City were delighted with the Cleanliness of the Pavement that surrounded the Market; it being a Convenience to all; and this rais'd a general Desire to have all the Streets paved; & made the People more willing to submit to a Tax for that purpose. After some time I drew a Bill for Paving the City, and brought it into the Assembly. It was just before I went to England in 1757. and did not pass till I was gone, and then with an Alteration in the Mode of Assessment, which I thought not for the better, but with an additional Provision for lighting as well as Paving the Streets, which was a great Improvement.—It was by a private Person, the late Mr John Clifton, his giving a Sample of the Utility of Lamps by placing one at his Door, that the People were first impress'd with the Idea of enlightning all the City. The Honour of this public Benefit has also been ascrib'd to me, but it belongs truly to that Gentleman. I did but follow his Example; and have only some Merit to claim respecting the Form of our Lamps as differing from the Globe Lamps we at first were supply'd with from London. Those we found inconvenient in these respects; they admitted no Air below, the Smoke therefore did not readily go out above, but circulated in the Globe, lodg'd on its Inside, and soon obstructed the Light they were intended to afford; giving, besides, the daily Trouble of wiping them clean: and an accidental Stroke on one of them would demolish it, & render it totally useless. I therefore suggested the composing them of four flat Panes, with a long Funnel above to draw up the Smoke, and Crevices admitting Air below, to facilitate the Ascent of the Smoke. By this means they were kept clean, and did not grow dark in a few Hours as the London Lamps do, but continu'd bright till Morning; and an accidental Stroke would generally break but a single Pane, easily repair'd. I have sometimes wonder'd that the Londoners did not, from the Effect Holes in the Bottom of the Globe Lamps us'd at Vauxhall, have in keeping them clean, learn to have such Holes in their Street Lamps. But those Holes being made for another purpose, viz. to communicate Flame more suddenly to the Wick, by a little Flax hanging down thro' them, the other Use of letting in Air seems not to have been thought of.—And therefore, after the Lamps have been lit a few Hours, the Streets of London are very poorly illuminated.—

The Mention of these Improvements puts me in mind of one I propos'd when in London, to Dr Fothergill, who was among the best Men I have known, and a great Promoter of useful Projects. I had observ'd that the Streets when dry were never swept and the light Dust carried away, but it was suffer'd to accumulate till wet Weather reduc'd it to Mud, and then after lying some Days so deep on the Pavement that there was no Crossing but in Paths kept clean by poor People with Brooms, it was with great Labour rak'd together & thrown up into Carts open above, the Sides of which suffer'd some of the Slush at every jolt on the Pavement to shake out and fall, some times to the Annoyance of Foot-Passengers. The Reason given for not sweeping the dusty Streets was, that the Dust would fly into the Windows of Shops and Houses. An accidental Occurrence had instructed me how much Sweeping might be done in a little Time. I found at my Door in Craven Street one Morning a poor Woman sweeping my Pavement with a birch Broom. She appeared very pale & feeble as just come out of a Fit of Sickness. I ask'd who employ'd her to sweep there. She said, "Nobody; but I am very poor and in Distress, and I sweeps before Gentlefolkeses Doors, and hopes they will give me something." I bid her sweep the whole Street clean and I would give her a Shilling. This was at 9 aClock. At 12 she came for the Shilling. From the Slowness I saw at first in her Working, I could scarce believe that the Work was done so soon, and sent my Servant to examine it, who reported that the whole Street was swept perfectly clean, and all the Dust plac'd in the Gutter which was in the Middle. And the next Rain wash'd it quite away, so that the Pavement & even the Kennel were perfectly clean.— I then judg'd that if that feeble Woman could sweep such a Street in 3 Hours, a strong active Man might have done it in half the time. And here let me remark the Convenience of having but one Gutter in such a narrow Street, running down its Middle, instead of two, one on each Side near the Footway. For Where all the Rain that falls on a Street runs from the Sides and meets in the middle, it forms there a Current strong enough to wash away all the Mud it meets with: But when divided into two Channels, it is often too weak to cleanse either, and only makes the Mud it finds more fluid, so that the Wheels of Carriages and Feet of Horses throw and dash it up on the Foot Pavement which is thereby rendred foul and slippery, and sometimes splash it upon those who are walking.—My Proposal communicated to the good Doctor, was as follows.

"For the more effectual cleaning and keeping clean the Streets of London and Westminster, it is proposed,

"That the several Watchmen be contracted with to have the

Dust swept up in dry Seasons, and the Mud rak'd up at other Times, each in the several Streets & Lanes of his Round.

"That they be furnish'd with Brooms and other proper Instruments for these purposes, to be kept at their respective Stands, ready to furnish the poor People they may employ in the Service.

"That in the dry Summer Months the Dust be all swept up into Heaps at proper Distances, before the Shops and Windows of Houses are usually opened: when the Scavengers with close-covered Carts shall also carry it all away.—

"That the Mud when rak'd up be not left in Heaps to be spread abroad again by the Wheels of Carriages & Trampling of Horses; but that the Scavengers be provided with Bodies of Carts, not plac'd high upon Wheels, but low upon Sliders; with Lattice Bottoms, which being cover'd with Straw, will retain the Mud thrown into them, and permit the Water to drain from it, whereby it will become much lighter, Water making the greatest Part of its Weight. These Bodies of Carts to be plac'd at convenient Distances, and the Mud brought to them in Wheelbarrows, they remaining where plac'd till the Mud is drain'd, and then Horses brought to draw them away."—

I have since had Doubts of the Practicability of the latter Part of this Proposal, on Account of the Narrowness of some Streets, and the Difficulty of placing the Draining Sleds so as not to encumber too much the Passage: But I am still of Opinion that the former, requiring the Dust, to be swept up & carry'd away before the Shops are open, is very practicable in the Summer, when the Days are long. For in walking thro' the Strand and Fleet street one Morning at 7 aClock I observ'd there was not one shop open tho' it had been Day-light & the Sun up above three Hours. The Inhabitants of London chusing voluntarily to live much by Candle Light, and sleep by Sunshine; and yet often complain a little absurdly, of the Duty on Candles and the high Price of Tallow.—

Some may think these trifling Matters not worth minding or relating: But when they consider, that tho' Dust blown into the Eyes of a single Person or into a single Shop on a windy Day, is but of small Importance, yet the great Number of the Instances in a populous City, and its frequent Repetitions give it Weight & Consequence; perhaps they will not censure very severely those who bestow some of Attention to Affairs of this seemingly low Nature. Human Felicity is pro-duc'd not so much by great Pieces of good Fortune that sel-dom happen, as by little Advantages that occur every Day. Thus if you teach a poor young Man to shave himself and keep his Razor in order, you may contribute more to the Happiness of his Life than in giving him a 1000 Guineas. The Money may be soon spent, and the Regret only remaining of having foolishly consum'd it. But in the other Case he escapes the frequent Vexation of waiting for Barbers, & of their sometimes, dirty Fingers, offensive Breaths and dull Razors. He shaves when most convenient to him, and enjoys daily the Pleasure of its being done with a good Instrument.—With these Sentiments I have hazarded the few preceding Pages, hoping they may afford Hints which some time or other may be useful to a City I love, having lived many Years in it very happily; and perhaps to some of our Towns in America.—

Having been for some time employed by the Postmaster General of America, as his Comptroller, in regulating the sev-eral Offices, and bringing the Officers to account, I was upon his Death in 1753 appointed jointly with Mr William Hunter to succeed him by a Commission from the Postmaster Gen-eral in England. The American Office had never hitherto paid any thing to that of Britain. We were to have 600£ a Year between us if we could make that Sum out of the Profits of the Office. To do this, a Variety of Improvements were nec-essary; some of these were inevitably at first expensive; so that in the first four Years the Office became above 900£ in debt to us.—But it soon after began to repay us, and before I was displac'd, by a Freak of the Minister's, of which I shall speak hereafter, we had brought it to yield *three times* as much clear Revenue to the Crown as the Post-Office of Ireland. Since that imprudent Transaction, they have receiv'd from it,—Not one Farthing.—

The Business of the Post-Office occasion'd my taking a Journey this Year to New England, where the College of Cambridge of their own Motion, presented me with the De-gree of Master of Arts. Yale College in Connecticut, had be-fore made me a similar Compliment. Thus without studying in any College I came to partake of their Honours. They were confer'd in Consideration of my Improvements & Discoveries in the electric Branch of Natural Philosophy.—

In 1754, War with France being again apprehended, a Congress of Commissioners from the different Colonies, was by an Order of the Lords of Trade, to be assembled at Albany, there to confer with the Chiefs of the Six Nations, concerning the Means of defending both their Country and ours. Governor Hamilton, having receiv'd this Order, acquainted the House with it, requesting they would furnish proper Presents for the Indians to be given on this Occasion; and naming the Speaker (Mr Norris) and my self, to join Mr Thomas Penn & Mr Secretary Peters, as Commissioners to act for Pennsylvania. The House approv'd the Nomination, and provided the Goods for the Present, tho' they did not much like treating out of the Province, and we met the other Commissioners and met at Albany about the Middle of June. In our Way thither, I projected and drew up a Plan for the Union of all the Colonies, under one Government so far as might be necessary for Defence, and other important general Purposes. As we pass'd thro' New York, I had there shown my Project to Mr James Alexander & Mr Kennedy, two Gentlemen of great Knowledge in public Affairs, and being fortified by their Approbation I ventur'd to lay it before the Congress. It then appear'd that several of the Commissioners had form'd Plans of the same kind. A previous Question was first taken whether a Union should be established, which pass'd in the Affirmative unanimously. A Committee was then appointed. One Member from each Colony, to consider the several Plans and report. Mine happen'd to be prefer'd, and with a few Amendments was accordingly reported. By this Plan, the general Government was to be administred by a President General appointed and supported by the Crown, and a Grand Council to be chosen by the Representatives of the People of the several Colonies met in their respective Assemblies. The Debates upon it in Congress went on daily hand in hand with the Indian Business. Many Objections and Difficulties were started, but at length they were all overcome, and the Plan was unanimously agreed to, and Copies ordered to be transmitted to the Board of Trade and to the Assemblies of the several Provinces. Its Fate was singular. The Assemblies did not adopt it, as they all thought there was too much *Prerogative* in it; and in England it was judg'd to have too much of the *Democratic*: The Board of Trade therefore did not approve of it; nor recommend it for the Approbation of his Majesty; but another Scheme was form'd (suppos'd better to answer the same Purpose) whereby the Governors of the Provinces with some Members of their respective Councils were to meet and order the raising of Troops, building of Forts, &c. &c to draw on the Treasury of Great Britain for the Expence, which was afterwards to be refunded by an Act of Parliament laying a Tax on America. My Plan, with my Reasons in support of it, is to be found among my political Papers that are printed. Being the Winter following in Boston, I had much Conversation with Govr Shirley upon both the Plans. Part of what pass'd between us on the Occasion may also be seen among those Papers.—The different & contrary Reasons of dislike to my Plan, makes me suspect that it was really the true Medium; & I am still of Opinion it would have been happy for both Sides the Water if it had been adopted. The Colonies so united would have been sufficiently strong to have defended themselves; there would then have been no need of Troops from England; of course the subsequent Pretence for Taxing America, and the bloody Contest it occasioned, would have been avoided. But such Mistakes are not new; History is full of the Errors of States & Princes.

> *"Look round the habitable World, how few*
> *Know their own Good, or knowing it pursue."*

Those who govern, having much Business on their hands, do not generally like to take the Trouble of considering and carrying into Execution new Projects. The best public Measures are therefore seldom *adopted from previous Wisdom*, but *forc'd by the Occasion*.

The Governor of Pennsylvania in sending it down to the Assembly, express'd his Approbation of the Plan "as appearing to him to be drawn up with great Clearness & Strength of Judgment, and therefore recommended it as well worthy their closest & most serious Attention." The House however, by the Managem.^t of a certain Member, took it up when I happen'd to be absent, which I thought not very fair, and reprobated it without paying any Attention to it at all, to my no small Mortification.

In my Journey to Boston this Year I met at New York with our new Governor, Mr Morris, just arriv'd there from England, with whom I had been before intimately acquainted. He brought a Commission to supersede Mr Hamilton, who, tir'd with the Disputes his Proprietary Instructions subjected him to, had resigned. Mr Morris ask'd me, if I thought he must expect as uncomfortable an Administration. I said, No; you may on the contrary have a very comfortable one, if you will only take care not to enter into any Dispute with the Assembly; "My dear Friend, says he, pleasantly, how can you advise my avoiding Disputes. You know I love Disputing; it is one of my greatest Pleasures: However, to show the Regard I have for your Counsel, I promise you I will if possible avoid them." He had some Reason for loving to dispute, being eloquent, an acute Sophister, and therefore generally successful in argumentative Conversation. He had been brought up to it from a Boy, his Father (as I have heard) accustoming his Children to dispute with one another for his Diversion while sitting at Table after Dinner. But I think the Practice was not wise, for in the Course of my Observation, these disputing, contradicting & confuting People are generally unfortunate in their Affairs. They get Victory sometimes, but they never get Good Will, which would be of more use to them. We parted, he going to Philadelphia, and I to Boston. In returning, I met at New York with the Votes of the Assembly, by which it appear'd that notwithstanding his Promise to me, he and the House were already in high Contention, and it was a continual Battle between them, as long as he retain'd the Government. I had my Share of it; for as soon as I got back to my Seat in the Assembly, I was put on every Committee for answering his Speeches and Messages, and by the Committees always desired to make the Drafts. Our Answers as well as his Messages were often tart, and sometimes indecently abusive. And as he knew I wrote for the Assembly, one might have imagined that when we met we could hardly avoid cutting Throats. But he was so good-natur'd a Man, that no personal Difference between him and me was occasion'd by the Contest, and we often din'd to-gether. One Afternoon in the height of this public Quarrel, we met in the Street. "Franklin, says he, you must go home with me and spend the Evening. I am to have some Company that you will like;" and taking me by the Arm he led me to his House. In gay Conversation over our Wine after Supper he told us Jokingly that he much admir'd the Idea of Sancho Panza, who when it was propos'd to give him a Government, requested it might be a Government of *Blacks*, as then, if he could not agree with his People he might sell them. One of his Friends who sat next me, says, "Franklin, why do you continue to side with these damn'd Quakers? had not you better sell them? the Proprietor would give you a good Price." The Governor, says I, has not yet *black'd* them enough. He had indeed labour'd hard to blacken the Assembly in all his Messages, but they wip'd off his Colouring as fast as he laid it on, and plac'd it in return thick upon his own Face; so that finding he was likely to be negrify'd himself, he as well as Mr Hamilton, grew tir'd of the Contest, and quitted the Government.

These public Quarrels were all at bottom owing to the Proprietaries, our hereditary Governors; who when any Expence was to be incurr'd for the Defence of their Province, with incredible Meanness instructed their Deputies to pass no Act for levying the necessary Taxes, unless their vast Estates were in the same Act expresly excused; and they had even taken Bonds of those Deputies to observe such Instructions. The Assemblies for three Years held out against this Injustice, Tho' constrain'd to bend at last. At length Capt. Denny, who was Governor Morris's Successor, ventur'd to disobey those Instructions; how that was brought about I shall show hereafter.

But I am got forward too fast with my Story; there are still some Transactions to be mentioned that happened during the Administration of Governor Morris.—

War being, in a manner, commenced with France, the Government of Massachusets Bay projected an Attack upon Crown Point, and sent Mr Quincy to Pennsylvania, and Mr Pownall, afterwards Govr Pownall, to N. York to sollicit Assistance. As I was in the Assembly, knew its Temper, & was Mr Quincy's Countryman, he apply'd to me for my Influence & Assistance. I dictated his Address to them which was well receiv'd. They voted an Aid of Ten Thousand Pounds, to be laid out in Provisions. But the Governor refusing his Assent to their Bill, (which included this with other Sums granted for the Use of the Crown) unless a Clause were inserted exempting the Proprietary Estate from bearing any Part of the Tax that would be necessary, the Assembly, tho' very desirous of making their Grant to New England effectual, were at a Loss how to accomplish it. Mr Quincy laboured hard with the Governor to obtain his Assent, but he was obstinate. I then suggested a Method of doing the Business without the Governor, by Orders on the Trustees of the Loan-Office, which by Law the Assembly had the Right of Drawing. There was indeed little or no Money at that time in the Office, and therefor I propos'd that the Orders should be payable in a Year and to bear an Interest of Five percent. With these Orders I suppos'd the Provisions might easily be purchas'd. The Assembly with very little Hesitation adopted the Proposal. The Orders were immediately printed, and I was one of the Committee directed to sign and dispose of them. The Fund for Paying them was the Interest of all the Paper Currency then extant in the Province upon Loan, together with the Revenue arising from the Excise which being known to be more than sufficient, they obtain'd instant Credit, and were not only receiv'd in Payment for the Provisions, but many money'd People who had Cash lying by them, vested it in those Orders, which they found advantageous, as they bore Interest while upon hand, and might on any Occasion be used as Money: So that they were eagerly all bought up, and in a few Weeks none of them were to be seen. Thus this important Affair was by my means compleated, Mr Quincy return'd Thanks to the Assembly in a handsome Memorial, went home highly pleas'd with the Success of his Embassy, and ever after bore for me the most cordial and affectionate Friendship.—

The British Government not chusing to permit the Union of the Colonies, as propos'd at Albany, and to trust that Union with their Defence, lest they should thereby grow too military, and feel their own Strength, Suspicions & Jealousies

at this time being entertain'd of them; sent over General
Braddock with two Regiments of Regular English Troops for
that purpose. He landed at Alexandria in Virginia, and thence
march'd to Frederic Town in Maryland, where he halted for
Carriages. Our Assembly apprehending, from some Information, that he had conceived violent Prejudices against them,
as averse to the Service, wish'd me to wait upon him, not as
from them, but as Postmaster General, under the guise of
proposing to settle with him the Mode of conducting with
most Celerity and Certainty the Dispatches between him and
the Governors of the several Provinces, with whom he must
necessarily have continual Correspondence, and of which they
propos'd to pay the Expence. My Son accompanied me on
this Journey. We found the General at Frederic Town, waiting
impatiently for the Return of those he had sent thro' the back
Parts of Maryland & Virginia to collect Waggons. I staid with
him several Days, Din'd with him daily, and had full Opportunity of removing all his Prejudices, by the Information of
what the Assembly had before his Arrival actually done and
were still willing to do to facilitate his Operations. When I
was about to depart, the Returns of Waggons to be obtain'd
were brought in, by which it appear'd that they amounted
only to twenty-five, and not all of those were in serviceable
Condition. The General and all the Officers were surpriz'd,
declar'd the Expedition was then at an End, being impossible,
and exclaim'd against the Ministers for ignorantly landing
them in a Country destitute of the Means of conveying their
Stores, Baggage, &c. not less than 150 Waggons being necessary. I happen'd to say, I thought it was pity they had not
been landed rather in Pennsylvania, as in that Country almost
every Farmer had his Waggon. The General eagerly laid hold
of my Words, and said, "Then you, Sir, who are a Man of
Interest there, can probably procure them for us; and I beg
you will undertake it." I ask'd what Terms were to be offer'd
the Owners of the Waggons; and I was desir'd to put on
Paper the Terms that appear'd to me necessary. This I did,
and they were agreed to, and a Commission and Instructions
accordingly prepar'd immediately. What those Terms were
will appear in the Advertisement I publish'd as soon as I arriv'd at Lancaster; which being, from the great and sudden

Effect it produc'd, a Piece of some Curiosity, I shall insert at length, as follows.

ADVERTISEMENT.

Lancaster, April 26, 1755.

WHEREAS 150 Waggons, with 4 Horses to each Waggon, and 1500 Saddle or Pack-Horses are wanted for the Service of his Majesty's Forces now about to rendezvous at *Wills's* Creek; and his Excellency General *Braddock* hath been pleased to impower me to contract for the Hire of the same; I hereby give Notice, that I shall attend for that Purpose at *Lancaster* from this Time till next *Wednesday* Evening; and at *York* from next *Thursday* Morning 'till *Friday* Evening; where I shall be ready to agree for Waggons and Teams, or single Horses, on the following Terms, *viz.*

1st. That there shall be paid for each Waggon with 4 good Horses and a Driver, *Fifteen Shillings* per *Diem*: And for each able Horse with a Pack-Saddle or other Saddle and Furniture, *Two Shillings* per *Diem*. And for each able Horse without a Saddle, *Eighteen Pence* per *Diem*.

2dly, That the Pay commence from the Time of their joining the Forces at *Wills's* Creek (which must be on or before the twentieth of *May* ensuing) and that a reasonable Allowance be made over and above for the Time necessary for their travelling to *Wills's* Creek and home again after their Discharge.

3dly, Each Waggon and Team, and every Saddle or Pack Horse is to be valued by indifferent Persons, chosen between me and the Owner, and in Case of the Loss of any Waggon, Team or other Horse in the Service, the Price according to such Valuation, is to be allowed and paid.

4thly, Seven Days Pay is to be advanced and paid in hand by me to the Owner of each Waggon and Team, or Horse, at the Time of contracting, if required; and the Remainder to be paid by General *Braddock*, or by the Paymaster of the Army, at the Time of their Discharge, or from time to time as it shall be demanded.

5thly, No Drivers of Waggons, or Persons taking care of the hired Horses, are on any Account to be called upon to do the Duty of Soldiers, or be otherwise employ'd than in conducting or taking Care of their Carriages and Horses.

6*thly*, All Oats, Indian Corn or other Forage, that Waggons or Horses bring to the Camp more than is necessary for the Subsistence of the Horses, is to be taken for the Use of the Army, and a reasonable Price paid for it.

Note. My Son *William Franklin*, is impowered to enter into like Contracts with any Person in *Cumberland* County.

B. FRANKLIN.

To the Inhabitants of the Counties of
Lancaster, York, *and* Cumberland.

Friends and Countrymen,

BEING occasionally at the Camp at *Frederic* a few Days since, I found the General and Officers of the Army extreamly exasperated, on Account of their not being supply'd with Horses and Carriages, which had been expected from this Province as most able to furnish them; but thro' the Dissensions between our Governor and Assembly, Money had not been provided nor any Steps taken for that Purpose.

It was proposed to send an armed Force immediately into these Counties, to seize as many of the best Carriages and Horses as should be wanted, and compel as many Persons into the Service as would be necessary to drive and take care of them.

I apprehended that the Progress of a Body of Soldiers thro' these Counties on such an Occasion, especially considering the Temper they are in, and their Resentment against us, would be attended with many and great Inconveniencies to the Inhabitants; and therefore more willingly undertook the Trouble of trying first what might be done by fair and equitable Means.

The People of these back Counties have lately complained to the Assembly that a sufficient Currency was wanting; you have now an Opportunity of receiving and dividing among you a very considerable Sum; for if the Service of this Expedition should continue (as it's more than probable it will) for 120 Days, the Hire of these Waggons and Horses will amount to upwards of *Thirty thousand Pounds*, which will be paid you in Silver and Gold of the King's Money.

The Service will be light and easy, for the Army will scarce march above 12 Miles per Day, and the Waggons and Baggage

Horses, as they carry those Things that are absolutely necessary to the Welfare of the Army, must march with the Army and no faster, and are, for the Army's sake, always plac'd where they can be most secure, whether on a March or in Camp.

If you are really, as I believe you are, good and loyal Subjects to His Majesty, you may now do a most acceptable Service, and make it easy to yourselves; for three or four of such as cannot separately spare from the Business of their Plantations a Waggon and four Horses and a Driver, may do it together, one furnishing the Waggon, another one or two Horses, and another the Driver, and divide the Pay proportionably between you. But if you do not this Service to your King and Country voluntarily, when such good Pay and reasonable Terms are offered you, your Loyalty will be strongly suspected; the King's Business must be done; so many brave Troops, come so far for your Defence, must not stand idle, thro' your backwardness to do what may be reasonably expected from you; Waggons and Horses must be had; violent Measures will probably be used; and you will be to seek for a Recompence where you can find it, and your Case perhaps be little pitied or regarded.

I have no particular Interest in this Affair; as (except the Satisfaction of endeavouring to do Good and prevent Mischief) I shall have only my Labour for my Pains. If this Method of obtaining the Waggons and Horses is not like to succeed, I am oblig'd to send Word to the General in fourteen Days; and I suppose Sir *John St. Clair* the Hussar, with a Body of Soldiers, will immediately enter the Province, for the Purpose aforesaid, of which I shall be sorry to hear, because

I am,   *very sincerely and truly*

your Friend and Well-wisher,

B. FRANKLIN

I receiv'd of the General about 800£ to be disburs'd in Advance-money to the Waggon-Owners &c: but that Sum being insufficient, I advanc'd upwards of 200£ more, and in two Weeks, the 150 Waggons with 259 carrying Horses were on their March for the Camp.—The Advertisement promised Payment according to the Valuation, in case any Waggon or

These 20 Parcels well pack'd were plac'd on as many Horses, each Parcel with the Horse, being intended as a Present for one Officer. They were very thankfully receiv'd, and the Kindness acknowledg'd by Letters to me from the Colonels of both Regiments in the most grateful Terms. The General too was highly satisfied with my Conduct in procuring him the Waggons, &c. and readily paid my Acc^t of Disbursements; thanking me repeatedly and requesting my farther Assistance in sending Provisions after him. I undertook this also, and was busily employ'd in it till we heard of his Defeat, advancing, for the Service, of my own Money, upwards of 1000£ Sterling, of which I sent him an Account. It came to his Hands luckily for me a few Days before the Battle, and he return'd me immediately an Order on the Paymaster for the round Sum of 1000£ leaving the Remainder to the next Account. I consider this Payment as good Luck; having never been able to obtain that Remainder; of which more hereafter.

This General was I think a brave Man, and might probably have made a Figure as a good Officer in some European War. But he had too much self-confidence, too high an Opinion of the Validity of Regular Troops, and too mean a One of both Americans and Indians. George Croghan, our Indian Interpreter, join'd him on his March with 100 of those People, who might have been of great Use to his Army as Guides, Scouts, &c. if he had treated them kindly;—but he slighted & neglected them, and they gradually left him. In Conversation with him one day, he was giving me some Account of his intended Progress. "After taking Fort Du Quesne, says he, I am to proceed to Niagara; and having taken that, to Frontenac, if the Season will allow time; and I suppose it will; for Duquesne can hardly detain me above three or four Days; and then I see nothing that can obstruct my March to Niagara."—Having before revolv'd in my Mind the long Line his Army must make in their March, by a very narrow Road to be cut for them thro' the Woods & Bushes; & also what I had read of a former Defeat of 1500 French who invaded the Iroquois Country, I had conceiv'd some Doubts,— & some Fears for the Event of the Campaign. But I ventur'd only to say, To be sure, Sir, if you arrive well before Duquesne, with these fine Troops so well provided with Artillery, that Place, not yet compleatly fortified, and as we hear with no very strong Garrison, can probably make but a short Resistance. The only Danger I apprehend of Obstruction to your March, is from Ambuscades of Indians, who by constant Practice are dextrous in laying & executing them. And the slender Line near four Miles long, which your Army must make, may expose it to be attack'd by Surprize in its Flanks, and to be cut like a Thread into several Pieces, which from their Distance cannot come up in time to support each other. He smil'd at my Ignorance, & reply'd, "These Savages may indeed be a formidable Enemy to your raw American Militia; but, upon the King's regular & disciplin'd Troops, Sir, it is impossible they should make any Impression." I was conscious of an Impropriety in my Disputing with a military Man in Matters of his Profession, and said no more.—The Enemy however did not take the Advantage of his Army which I apprehended its long Line of March expos'd it to, but let it advance without Interruption till within 9 Miles of the Place; and then when more in a Body, (for it had just pass'd a River, where the Front had halted till all were come over) & in a more open Part of the Woods than any it had pass'd, attack'd its advanc'd Guard, by a heavy Fire from behind Trees & Bushes; which was the first Intelligence the General had of an Enemy's being near him. This Guard being disordered, the General hurried the Troops up to their Assistance, which was done in great Confusion thro' Waggons, Baggage and Cattle; and presently the Fire came upon their Flank; the Officers being on Horseback were more easily distinguish'd, pick'd out as Marks, and fell very fast; and the Soldiers were crowded together in a Huddle, having or hearing no Orders, and standing to be shot at till two thirds of them were killed, and then being seiz'd with a Pannick the whole fled with Precipitation. The Waggoners took each a Horse out of his Team, and scamper'd; their Example was immediately follow'd by others, so that all the Waggons, Provisions, Artillery and Stores were left to the Enemy. The General being wounded was brought off with Difficulty, his Secretary Mr Shirley was killed by his Side, and out of 86 Officers 63 were killed or wounded, and 714 Men killed out of 1100. These 1100 had been picked Men, from the whole Army, the Rest had been left behind with

Col. Dunbar, who was to follow with the heavier Part of the Stores, Provisions and Baggage. The Flyers, not being pursu'd, arriv'd at Dunbar's Camp, and the Pannick they brought with them instantly seiz'd him and all his People. And tho' he had now above 1000 Men, and the Enemy who had beaten Braddock did not at most exceed 400, Indians and French together; instead of Proceeding and endeavouring to recover some of the lost Honour, he order'd all the Stores Ammunition, &c to be destroy'd, that he might have more Horses to assist his Flight towards the Settlements and less Lumber to remove. He was there met with Requests from the Governor's of Virginia, Maryland and Pennsylvania, that he would post his Troops on the Frontiers so as to afford some Protection to the Inhabitants; but he continu'd his hasty March thro' all the Country, not thinking himself safe till he arriv'd at Philadelphia, where the Inhabitants could protect him. This whole Transaction gave us Americans the first Suspicion that our exalted Ideas of the Prowess of British Regulars had not been well founded.—

In their first March too, from their Landing till they got beyond the Settlements, they had plundered and stript the Inhabitants, totally ruining some poor Families, besides insulting, abusing & confining the People if they remonstrated. —This was enough to put us out of Conceit of such Defenders if we had really wanted any. How different was the Conduct of our French Friends in 1781, who during a March thro' the most inhabited Part of our Country, from Rhodeisland to Virginia, near 700 Miles, occasion'd not the smallest Complaint, for the Loss of a Pig, a Chicken, or even an Apple!

Capt. Orme, who was one of the General's Aid de Camps, and being grievously wounded was brought off with him, and continu'd with him to his Death, which happen'd in a few Days, told me, that he was totally silent, all the first Day, and at Night only said, *Who'd have thought it?* that he was silent again the following Days, only saying at last, *We shall better know how to deal with them another time*; and dy'd a few Minutes after.

The Secretary's Papers with all the General's Orders, Instructions and Correspondence falling into the Enemy's Hands, they selected and translated into French a Number of the Articles, which they printed to prove the hostile Intentions of the British Court before the Declaration of War. Among these I saw some Letters of the General to the Ministry speaking highly of the great Service I had rendred the Army, & recommending me to their Notice. David Hume too, who was some Years after Secretary to Lord Harcourt when Minister in France, and afterwards to Gen! Conway when Secretary of State, told me he had seen among the Papers in that Office Letters from Braddock highly recommending me. But the Expedition having been unfortunate, my Service it seems was not thought of much Value, for those Recommendations were never of any Use to me.—

As to Rewards from himself, I ask'd only one, which was, that he would give Orders to his Officers not to enlist any more of our bought Servants, and that he would discharge such as had been already enlisted. This he readily granted, and several were accordingly return'd to their Masters on my Application.—Dunbar, when the Command devolv'd on him, was not so generous. He Being at Philadelphia on his Retreat, or rather Flight, I apply'd to him for the Discharge of the Servants of three poor Farmers of Lancaster County that he had inlisted, reminding him of the late General's Orders on that head. He promis'd me, that if the Masters would come to him at Trenton, where he should be in a few Days on his March to New York, he would there deliver their Men to them. They accordingly were at the Expence & Trouble of going to Trenton,—and there he refus'd to perform his Promise, to their great Loss & Disappointment.—

As soon as the Loss of the Waggons and Horses was generally known, all the Owners came upon me for the Valuation wch I had given Bond to pay. Their Demands gave me a great deal of Trouble, my acquainting them that the Money was ready in the Paymaster's Hands, but that Orders for pay^{g} it must first be obtained from General Shirley, and my assuring them that I had apply'd to that General by Letter, but he being at a Distance an Answer could not soon be receiv'd, and they must have Patience; all this was not sufficient to satisfy, and some began to sue me. General Shirley at length reliev'd me from this terrible Situation, by appointing Commissioners to examine the Claims and ordering Payment.

They amounted to near twenty Thousand Pound, which to pay would have ruined me.

Before we had the News of this Defeat, the two Doctors Bond came to me with a Subscription Paper, for raising Money to defray the Expence of a grand Fire Work, which it was intended to exhibit at a Rejoicing on receipt of the News of our Taking Fort Duquesne. I looked grave and said, "it would, I thought, be time enough to prepare for the Rejoicing when we knew we should have occasion to rejoice."— They seem'd surpriz'd that I did not immediately comply with their Proposal. "Why, the D——l, says one of them, you surely don't suppose that the Fort will not be taken?" "I don't know that it will not be taken; but I know that the Events of War are subject to great Uncertainty."—I gave them the Reasons of my doubting. The Subscription was dropt, and the Projectors thereby miss'd that Mortification they would have undergone if the Firework had been prepared.—Dr Bond on some other Occasions afterwards said, that he did not like Franklin's forebodings.—

Governor Morris who had continually worried the Assembly wth Message after Message before the Defeat of Braddock, to beat them into the making of Acts to raise Money for the Defence of the Province without Taxing among others the Proprietary Estates, and had rejected all their Bills for not having such an exempting Clause, now redoubled his Attacks, with more hope of Success, the Danger & Necessity being greater. The Assembly however continu'd firm, believing they had Justice on their side, and that it would be giving up an essential Right, if they suffered the Governor to amend their Money-Bills. In one of the last, indeed, which was for granting 50,000£ his propos'd Amendment was only of a single Word; the Bill express'd that all Estates real and personal were to be taxed, those of the Proprietaries *not* excepted. His Amendment was; For *not* read *only*. A small but very material Alteration!—However, when the News of this Disaster reach'd England, our Friends there whom we had taken care to furnish with all the Assembly's Answers to the Governor's Messages, rais'd a Clamour against the Proprietaries for their Meanness & Injustice in giving their Governor such Instructions, some going so far as to say that by obstructing the

Defence of their Province, they forfeited their Right to it. They were intimidated by this, and sent Orders to their Receiver General to add 5000£ of their Money to whatever Sum might be given by the Assembly, for such Purpose. This being notified to the House, was accepted in Lieu of their Share of a general Tax, and a new Bill was form'd with an exempting Clause which pass'd accordingly. By this Act I was appointed one of the Commissioners for disposing of the Money, 60,000£. I had been active in modelling it, and procuring its Passage: and had at the same time drawn a Bill for establishing and disciplining a voluntary Militia, which I carried thro' the House without much Difficulty, as Care was taken in it, to leave the Quakers at their Liberty. To promote the Association necessary to form the Militia, I wrote a Dialogue,* stating and answering all the Objections I could think of to such a Militia, which was printed & had as I thought great Effect. While the several Companies in the City & Country were forming and learning their Exercise, the Governor prevail'd with me to take Charge of our Northwestern Frontier, which was infested by the Enemy, and provide for the Defence of the Inhabitants by raising Troops, & building a Line of Forts. I undertook this military Business, tho' I did not conceive myself well-qualified for it. He gave me a Commission with full Powers and a Parcel of blank Commissions for Officers to be given to whom I thought fit. I had but little Difficulty in raising Men, having soon 560 under my Command. My Son who had in the preceding War been an Officer in the Army rais'd against Canada, was my Aid de Camp, and of great Use to me. The Indians had burnt Gnadenhut, a Village settled by the Moravians, and massacred the Inhabitants, but the Place was thought a good Situation for one of the Forts. In order to march thither, I assembled the Companies at Bethlehem, the chief Establishment of those People. I was surprized to find it in so good a Posture of Defence. The Destruction of Gnadenhut had made them apprehend Danger. The principal Buildings were defended by a Stockade: They had purchased a Quantity of Arms & Ammunition from New York, and had even plac'd Quantities of small Paving

*This Dialogue and the Militia Act, are in the Gent Magazine for Feb[y] & March 1756—

Stones between the Windows of their high Stone Houses, for their Women to throw down upon the Heads of any Indians that should attempt to force into them. The armed Bretheren too, kept Watch, and reliev'd as methodically as in any Garrison Town. In Conversation with Bishop Spangenberg, I mention'd this my Surprize; for knowing they had obtain'd an Act of Parliament exempting them from military Duties in the Colonies, I had suppos'd they were conscienciously scrupulous of bearing Arms. He answer'd me, "That it was not one of their establish'd Principles; but that at the time of their obtaining that Act, it was thought to be a Principle with many of their People. On this Occasion, however, they to their Surprize found it adopted by but a few." It seems they were either deceiv'd in themselves, or deceiv'd the Parliament. But Common Sense aided by present Danger, will sometimes be too strong for whimsicall Opinions.

It was the Beginning of January when we set out upon this Business of Building Forts. I sent one Detachment towards the Minisinks, with Instructions to erect one for the Security of that upper Part of the Country; and another to the lower Part, with similar Instructions. And I concluded to go myself with the rest of my Force to Gnadenhut, where a Fort was tho't more immediately necessary. The Moravians procur'd me five Waggons for our Tools, Stores, Baggage, &c. Just before we left Bethlehem, Eleven Farmers who had been driven from their Plantations by the Indians, came to me, requesting a supply of Fire Arms, that they might go back and fetch off their Cattle. I gave them each a Gun with suitable Ammunition. We had not march'd many Miles before it began to rain, and it continu'd raining all Day. There were no Habitations on the Road, to shelter us, till we arriv'd near Night, at the House of a German, where and in his Barn we were all huddled together as wet as Water could make us. It was well we were not attack'd in our March, for Our Arms were of the most ordinary Sort, and our Men could not keep their Gunlocks dry. The Indians are dextrous in Contrivances for that purpose, which we had not. They met that Day the eleven poor Farmers above-mentioned & kill'd Ten of them. The one who escap'd inform'd that his & his Companions Guns would not go off, the Priming being wet with the Rain. The next Day being fair, we continu'd our March and arriv'd at the desolated Gnadenhut. There was a Saw Mill near, round which were left several Piles of Boards, with which we soon hutted ourselves; an Operation the more necessary at that inclement Season, as we had no Tents. Our first Work was to bury more effectually the Dead we found there, who had been half interr'd by the Country People. The next Morning our Fort was plann'd and mark'd out, the Circumference measuring 455 feet, which would require as many Palisades to be made of Trees one with another of a Foot Diameter each. Our Axes, of which we had 70 were immediately set to work, to cut down Trees; and our Men being dextrous in the Use of them, great Dispatch was made. Seeing the Trees fall so fast, I had the Curiosity to look at my Watch when two Men began to cut at a Pine. In 6 Minutes they had it upon the Ground; and I found it of 14 Inches Diameter. Each Pine made three Palisades of 18 Feet long, pointed at one End. While these were preparing, our other Men, dug a Trench all round of three feet deep in which the Palisades were to be planted, and our Waggons, the Body being taken off, and the fore and hind Wheels separated by taking out the Pin which united the two Parts of the Perch, we had 10 Carriages with two Horses each, to bring the Palisades from the Woods to the Spot. When they were set up, our Carpenters built a Stage of Boards all round within, about 6 Feet high, for the Men to stand on when to fire thro' the Loopholes. We had one swivel Gun which we mounted on one of the Angles; and fired it as soon as fix'd, to let the Indians know, if any were within hearing, that we had such Pieces. And thus our Fort, (if such a magnificent Name may be given to so miserable a Stockade) was finished in a Week, tho' it rain'd so hard every other Day that the Men could not work.

This gave me occasion to observe, that when Men are employ'd they are best contented. For on the Days they work'd they were good-natur'd and chearful; and with the consciousness of having done a good Days work they spent the Evenings jollily; but on the idle Days they were mutinous and quarrelsome, finding fault with their Pork, the Bread, &c. and in continual ill-humour: which put me in mind of a Sea-Captain, whose Rule it was to keep his Men constantly at

Work; and when his Mate once told him that they had done every thing, and there was nothing farther to employ them about; O, says he, *make them scour the Anchor.*

This kind of Fort, however contemptible, is a sufficient Defence against Indians who have no Cannon. Finding our selves now posted securely, and having a Place to retreat to on Occasion, we ventur'd out in Parties to scour the adjacent Country. We met with no Indians, but we found the Places on the neighbouring Hills where they had lain to watch our Proceedings. There was an Art in their Contrivance of these Places that seems worth mention. It being Winter, a Fire was necessary for them. But a common Fire on the Surface of the Ground would by its Light have discover'd their Position at a Distance. They had therefore dug Holes in the Ground about three feet Diameter, and some what deeper. We saw where they had with their Hatchets cut off the Charcoal from the Sides of burnt Logs lying in the Woods. With these Coals they had made small Fires in the Bottom of the Holes, and we observ'd among the Weeds & Grass the Prints of their Bodies made by their laying all round with their Legs hanging down in the Holes to keep their Feet warm, which with them is an essential Point. This kind of Fire, so manag'd, could not discover them either by its Light, Flame; Sparks or even Smoke. It appear'd that their Number was not great, and it seems they saw we were too many to be attack'd by them with Prospect of Advantage.

We had for our Chaplain a zealous Presbyterian Minister, Mr Beatty, who complain'd to me that the Men did not generally attend his Prayers & Exhortations. When they enlisted, they were promis'd, besides Pay & Provisions, a Gill of Rum a Day, which was punctually serv'd out to them half in the Morning and the other half in the Evening, and I observ'd they were as punctual in attending to receive it. Upon which I said to Mr. Beatty, "It is perhaps below the Dignity of your Profession to act as Steward of the Rum. But if you were to deal it out, and only just after Prayers, you would have them all about you." He lik'd the Thought, undertook the Office, and with the help of a few hands to measure out the Liquor executed it to Satisfaction; and never were Prayers more generally & more punctually attended. So that I thought this

Method preferable to the Punishments inflicted by some military Laws for Non-Attendance on Divine Service.

I had hardly finish'd this Business, and got my Fort well stor'd with Provisions, when I receiv'd a Letter from the Governor, acquainting me that he had called the Assembly, and wish'd my Attendance there, if the Posture of Affairs on the Frontiers was such that my remaining there was no longer necessary. My Friends too of the Assembly pressing me by their Letters to be if possible at the Meeting, and my three intended Forts being now compleated, and the Inhabitants contented to remain on their Farms under that Protection, I resolved to return. The more willingly as a New England Officer, Col. Clapham, experienc'd in Indian War, being on a Visit to our Establishment, consented to accept the Command. I gave him a Commission, and parading the Garrison had it read before them, and introduc'd him to them as an Officer who from his Skill in Military Affairs, was much more fit to command them than myself; and giving them a little Exhortation took my Leave. I was escorted as far as Bethlehem, where I rested a few Days, to recover from the Fatigue I had undergone. The first Night being in a good Bed, I could hardly sleep, it was so different from my hard Lodging on the Floor of our Hut at Gnaden, wrapt only in a Blanket or two.—

While at Bethlehem, I enquir'd a little into the Practices of the Moravians. Some of them had accompanied me, and all were very kind to me. I found they work'd for a common Stock, eat at common Tables, and slept in common Dormitorys, great Numbers together. In the Dormitories I observ'd Loopholes at certain Distances all along just under the Cieling, which I thought judiciously plac'd for Change of Air. I was at their Church, where I was entertain'd with good Musick, the Organ being accompanied with Violins, Hautboys, Flutes, Clarinets, &c. I understood that their Sermons were not usually preached to mix'd Congregations; of Men Women and Children, as is our common Practice; but that they assembled sometimes the married Men, at other times their Wives, then the Young Men, the young Women, and the little Children, each Division by itself. The Sermon I heard was to the latter, who came in and were plac'd in Rows on Benches, the Boys under the Conduct of a young Man their Tutor, and the Girls conducted by a young Woman. The Discourse seem'd well adapted to their Capacities, and was delivered in a pleasing familiar Manner, coaxing them as it were to be good. They behav'd very orderly, but look'd pale and unhealthy, which made me suspect they were kept too much within-doors, or not allow'd sufficient Exercise. I enquir'd concerning the Moravian Marriages, whether the Report was true that they were by Lot? I was told that Lots were us'd only in particular Cases. That generally when a young Man found himself dispos'd to marry, he inform'd the Elders of his Class, who consulted the Elder Ladies that govern'd the young Women. As these Elders of the different Sexes were well acquainted with the Tempers & Dispositions of their respective Pupils, they could best judge what Matches were suitable, and their Judgments were generally acquiesc'd in. But if for example it should happen that two or three young Women were found to be *equally* proper for the young Man, the Lot was then recurr'd to. I objected, If the Matches are not made by the mutual Choice of the Parties, some of them may chance to be very unhappy. And so they may, answer'd my Informer, if you let the Parties chuse for themselves.— Which indeed I could not deny.

Being return'd to Philadelphia, I found the Association went on swimmingly, the Inhabitants that were not Quakers having pretty generally come into it, form'd themselves into Companies, and chosen their Captains, Lieutenants and Ensigns according to the new Law. Dr B. visited me, and gave me an Account of the Pains he had taken to spread a general good Liking to the Law, and ascrib'd much to those Endeavours. I had had the Vanity to ascribe all to my Dialogue; However, not knowing but that he might be in the right, I let him enjoy his Opinion, which I take to be generally the best way in such Cases.—The Officers meeting chose me to be Colonel of the Regiment;—which I this time accepted. I forget how many Companies we had, but We paraded about 1200 well-looking Men, with a Company of Artillery who had been furnish'd with 6 brass Field Pieces, which they had become so expert in the Use of as to fire twelve times in a Minute. The first Time I review'd my Regiment, they accompanied me to my House, and would salute me with some Rounds fired before my Door, which shook down and broke several Glasses of my Electrical Apparatus. And my new Honour prov'd not much less brittle; for all our Commissions were soon after broke by a Repeal of the Law in England.—

During the short time of my Colonelship, being about to set out on a Journey to Virginia, the Officers of my Regiment took it into their heads that it would be proper for them to escort me out of town as far as the Lower Ferry. Just as I was getting on Horseback, they came to my door, between 30 & 40, mounted, and all in their Uniforms. I had not been previously acquainted with the Project, or I should have prevented it, being naturally averse to the assuming of State on any Occasion, & I was a good deal chagrin'd at their Appearance, as I could not avoid their accompanying me. What made it worse, was, that as soon as we began to move, they drew their Swords, and rode with them naked all the way. Somebody wrote an Account of this to our Proprietor, and it gave him great Offence. No such Honour had been paid him when in the Province; nor to any of his Governors; and he said it was only proper to Princes of the Blood Royal; which may be true for aught I know, who was, and still am, ignorant of the Etiquette, in such Cases. This silly Affair, however greatly increas'd his Rancour against me, which was before considerable, not a little, on account of my Conduct in the Assembly, respecting the Exemption of his Estate from Taxation, which I had always oppos'd very warmly, & not without severe Reflections on his Meanness & Injustice in contending for it. He accus'd me to the Ministry as being the great Obstacle to the King's Service, preventing by my Influence in the House the proper Forming of the Bills for raising Money; and he instanc'd this Parade with my Officers as a Proof of my having an Intention to take the Government of the Province out of his Hands by Force. He also apply'd to Sir Everard Fauckener, then Post Master General, to deprive me of my Office. But this had no other Effect, than to procure from Sir Everard a gentle Admonition.

Notwithstanding the continual Wrangle between the Governor and the House, in which I as a Member had so large a

Share, there still subsisted a civil Intercourse between that Gentleman & myself, and we never had any personal Difference. I have sometimes since thought that his little or no Resentment against me for the Answers it was known I drew up to his Messages, might be the Effect of professional Habit, and that, being bred a Lawyer, he might consider us both as merely Advocates for contending Clients in a Suit, he for the Proprietaries & I for the Assembly, He would therefore sometimes call in a friendly way to advise with me on difficult Points, and sometimes, tho' not often, take my Advice. We acted in Concert to supply Braddock's Army with Provisions, and When the shocking News arriv'd of his Defeat, the Govern.^r sent in haste for me, to consult with him on Measures for preventing the Desertion of the back Counties. I forget now the Advice I gave, but I think it was, that Dunbar should be written to and prevail'd with if possible to post his Troops on the Frontiers for their Protection, till by Reinforcements from the Colonies he might be able to proceed on the Expedition.—And after my Return from the Frontier, he would have had me undertake the Conduct of such an Expedition with Provincial Troops, for the Reduction of Fort Duquesne, Dunbar & his Men being otherwise employ'd; and he propos'd to commission me as General. I had not so good an Opinion of my military Abilities as he profess'd to have; and I believe his Professions must have exceeded his real Sentiments: but probably he might think that my Popularity would facilitate the Raising of the Men, and my Influence in Assembly the Grant of Money to pay them;—and that perhaps without taxing the Proprietary Estate. Finding me not so forward to engage as he expected, the Project was dropt: and he soon after left the Government, being superseded by Capt. Denny.—

Before I proceed in relating the Part I had in public Affairs under this new Governor's Administration, it may not be amiss here to give some Account of the Rise & Progress of my Philosophical Reputation.—

In 1746 being at Boston, I met there with a Dr Spence, who was lately arrived from Scotland, and show'd me some electric Experiments. They were imperfectly perform'd, as he was not very expert; but being on a Subject quite new to me, they equally surpriz'd and pleas'd me. Soon after my Return to Philadelphia, our Library Company receiv'd from Mr Peter Colinson, F.R.S. of London a Present of a Glass Tube, with some Account of the Use of it in making such Experiments. I eagerly seiz'd the Opportunity of repeating what I had seen at Boston, and by much Practice acquir'd great Readiness in performing those also which we had an Account of from England, adding a Number of new Ones.—I say much Practice, for my House was continually full for some time, with People who came to see these new Wonders. To divide a little this Incumbrance among my Friends, I caused a Number of similar Tubes to be blown at our Glass-House, with which they furnish'd themselves, so that we had at length several Performers. Among these the principal was Mr Kinnersley, an ingenious Neighbour, who being out of Business, I encouraged to undertake showing the Experiments for Money, and drew up for him two Lectures, in which the Experiments were rang'd in such Order and accompanied with Explanations, in such Method, as that the foregoing should assist in Comprehending the following. He procur'd an elegant Apparatus for the purpose, in which all the little Machines that I had roughly made for myself, were nicely form'd by Instrument-makers. His Lectures were well attended and gave great Satisfaction; and after some time he went thro' the Colonies exhibiting them in every capital Town, and pick'd up some Money. In the West India Islands indeed it was with Difficulty the Experim.[ts] could be made, from the general Moisture of the Air.

Oblig'd as we were to Mr Colinson for his Present of the Tube, &c. I thought it right he should be inform'd of our Success in using it, and wrote him several Letters containing Accounts of our Experiments. He got them read in the Royal Society, where they were not at first thought worth so much Notice as to be printed in their Transactions. One Paper which I wrote for Mr. Kinnersley, on the Sameness of Lightning with Electricity, I sent to Dr. Mitchel, an Acquaintance of mine, and one of the Members also of that Society; who wrote me word that it had been read but was laught at by the Connoisseurs: The Papers however being shown to Dr Fothergill, he thought them of too much value to be stifled, and advis'd the Printing of them. Mr Collinson then gave them to *Cave* for publication in his Gentleman's Magazine; but he chose to print them separately in a Pamphlet, and Dr Fothergill wrote the Preface. *Cave* it seems judg'd rightly for his Profit; for by the Additions that arriv'd afterwards they swell'd to a Quarto Volume, which has had five Editions, and cost him nothing for Copy-money.

It was however some time before those Papers were much taken Notice of in England. A Copy of them happening to fall into the Hands of the Count de Buffon, a Philosopher deservedly of great Reputation in France, and indeed all over Europe he prevail'd with M. Dalibard to translate them into French; and they were printed at Paris. The Publication offended the Abbé Nollet, Preceptor in Natural Philosophy to the Royal Family, and an able Experimenter, who had form'd and publish'd a Theory of Electricity, which then had the general Vogue. He could not at first believe that such a Work came from America, & said it must have been fabricated by his Enemies at Paris, to decry his System. Afterwards having been assur'd that there really existed such a Person as Franklin of Philadelphia, which he had doubted, he wrote and published a Volume of Letters, chiefly address'd to me, defending his Theory, & denying the Verity of my Experiments and of the Positions deduc'd from them. I once purpos'd answering the Abbé, and actually began the Answer. But on Consideration that my Writings contain'd only a Description of Experiments, which any one might repeat & verify, and if not to be verify'd could not be defended; or of Observations, offer'd as Conjectures, & not deliverd dogmatically, therefore not laying me under any Obligation to defend them; and reflecting that a Dispute between two Persons writing in different Languages might be lengthend greatly by mis-translations, and thence misconceptions of one anothers Meaning, much of one of the Abbe's Letters being founded on an Error in the Translation; I concluded to let my Papers shift for themselves; believing it was better to spend what time I could spare from public Business in making new Experiments, than in Disputing about those already made. I therefore never answer'd M. Nollet; and the Event gave me no Cause to repent my Silence; for my friend M. le Roy of the Royal Academy of Sciences took up my Cause & refuted him, my Book was translated into the Italian, German and Latin Languages, and the Doctrine it contain'd was by degrees universally adopted by the Philosophers of Europe in preference to that of the Abbé, so that he liv'd to see himself the last of his Sect: except Mr B—— his Eleve & immediate Disciple.

What gave my Book the more sudden and general Celebrity, was the Success of one of its propos'd Experiments, made by Messrs Dalibard & Delor, at Marly; for drawing Lightning from the Clouds. This engag'd the public Attention every where. M. Delor, who had an Apparatus for experimental Philosophy, and lectur'd in that Branch of Science, undertook to repeat what he call'd the *Philadelphia Experiments*, and after they were performed before the King & Court, all the Curious of Paris flock'd to see them. I will not swell this Narrative with an Account of that capital Experiment, nor of the infinite Pleasure I receiv'd in the Success of a similar one I made soon after with a Kite at Philadelphia, as both are to be found in the Histories of Electricity.—Dr Wright, an English Physician then at Paris, wrote to a Friend who was of the Royal Society an Account of the high Esteem my Experiments were in among the Learned abroad, and of their Wonder that my Writings had been so little noticed in England. The Society on this resum'd the Consideration of the Letters that had been read to them, and the celebrated Dr Watson drew up a summary Acc^t of them, & of all I had afterwards sent to England on the Subject, which he accompanied with some Praise of the Writer. This Summary was then printed in their Transactions: And some Members of the Society in London, particularly the very ingenious Mr Canton, having verified the Experiment of procuring Lightnin from the Clouds by a Pointed Rod, and acquainting them with the Success, they soon made me more than Amends for the Slight with which they had before treated me. Without my having made any Application for that Honour, they chose me a Member, and voted that I should be excus'd the customary Payments, which would have amounted to twenty-five Guineas, and ever since have given me their Transactions gratis.—They also presented me with the Gold Medal of Sir Godfrey Copley for the Year 1753, the Delivery of which was

accompanied by a very handsome Speech of the President
Lord Macclesfield, wherein I was highly honoured.—

Our new Governor, Capt. Denny, brought over for me the
before mentioned Medal from the Royal Society, which he
presented to me at an Entertainment given him by the City.
He accompanied it with very polite Expressions of his Esteem
for me, having, as he said been long acquainted with my
Character. After Dinner, when the Company as was customary at that time, were engag'd in Drinking, he took me aside
into another Room, and acquainted me that he had been advis'd by his Friends in England to cultivate a Friendship with
me, as one who was capable of giving him the best Advice,
& of contributing most effectually to the making his Administration easy. That he therefore desired of all things to have
a good Understanding with me; and he begg'd me to be assur'd of his Readiness on all Occasions to render me every
Service that might be in his Power. He said much to me also
of the Proprietor's good Dispositions towards the Province,
and of the Advantage it might be to us all, and to me in
particular, if the Opposition that had been so long continu'd
to his Measures, were dropt, and Harmony restor'd between
him and the People, in effecting which it was thought no one
could be more serviceable than my self, and I might depend
on adequate Acknowledgements & Recompences, &c. &c.
The Drinkers finding we did not return immediately to the
Table, sent us a Decanter of Madeira, which the Governor
made liberal Use of, and in proportion became more profuse
of his Solicitations and Promises. My Answers were to this
purpose, that my Circumstances, Thanks to God, were such
as to make Proprietary Favours unnecessary to me; and that
being a Member of the Assembly I could not possibly accept
of any; that however I had no personal Enmity to the Proprietary, and that whenever the public Measures he propos'd
should appear to be for the Good of the People, no one
should espouse and forward them more zealously than myself,
my past Opposition having been founded on this, that the
Measures which had been urg'd were evidently intended to
serve the Proprietary Interest with great Prejudice to that of
the People. That I was much obliged to him (the Governor)
for his Professions of Regard to me, and that he might rely

on every thing in my Power to make his Administration as easy to him as possible, hoping at the same time that he had not brought with him the same unfortunate Instructions his Predecessor had been hamper'd with. On this he did not then explain himself. But when he afterwards came to do Business with the Assembly they appear'd again, the Disputes were renewed, and I was as active as ever in the Opposition, being the Penman first of the Request to have a Communication of the Instructions, and then of the Remarks upon them, which may be found in the Votes of the Time, and in the Historical Review I afterwards publish'd; but between us personally no Enmity arose; we were often together, he was a Man of Letters, had seen much of the World, and was very entertaining & pleasing in Conversation. He gave me the first Information that my old Friend Ja^s Ralph was still alive, that he was esteem'd one of the best political Writers in England, had been employ'd in the Dispute between Prince Frederic and the King, and had obtain'd a Pension of Three Hundred a Year; that his Reputation was indeed small as a Poet, *Pope* having damn'd his Poetry in the Dunciad, but his Prose was thought as good as any Man's.—

The Assembly finally, finding the Proprietaries obstinately persisted in manacling their Deputies with Instructions inconsistent not only with the Privileges of the People, but with the Service of the Crown, resolv'd to petition the King against them, and appointed me their Agent to go over to England to present & support the Petition. The House had sent up a Bill to the Governor granting a Sum of Sixty Thousand Pounds for the King's Use, (10,000£ of which was subjected to the Orders of the then General Lord Loudon,) which the Governor absolutely refus'd to pass in Compliance with his Instructions. I had agreed with Captain Morris of the Packet at New York for my Passage, and my Stores were put on board, when Lord Loudon arriv'd at Philadelphia, expresly, as he told me to endeavour an Accomodation between the Governor and Assembly, that his Majesty's Service might not be obstructed by their Dissensions: Accordingly he desir'd the Governor & myself to meet him, that he might hear what was to be said on both sides. We met and discuss'd the Business. In behalf of the Assembly I urg'd all the Arguments that may be found in the publick Papers of that Time, which were of my Writing, and are printed with the Minutes of the Assembly & the Governor pleaded his Instructions, the Bond he had given to observ them, and his Ruin if he disobey'd: Yet seem'd not unwilling to hazard himself if Lord Loudon would advise it. This his Lordship did not chuse to do, tho' I once thought I had nearly prevail'd with him to do it; but finally he rather chose to urge the Compliance of the Assembly; and he intreated me to use my Endeavours with them for that purpose; declaring he could spare none of the King's Troops for the Defence of our Frontiers, and that if we did not continue to provide for that Defence ourselves they must remain expos'd to the Enemy. I acquainted the House with what had pass'd, and presenting them with a Set of Resolutions I had drawn up, declaring our Rights, & that we did not relinquish our Claim to those Rights but only suspended the Exercise of them on this Occasion thro' *Force*, against which we protested, they at length agreed to drop that Bill and frame another conformable to the Proprietary Instructions. This of course the Governor pass'd, and I was then at Liberty to proceed on my Voyage: but in the meantime the Pacquet had sail'd with my Sea-Stores, which was some Loss to me, and my only Recompence was his Lordship's Thanks for my Service, all the Credit of obtaining the Accommodation falling to his Share.

He set out for New York before me; and as the Time for dispatching the Pacquet Boats, was in his Disposition, and there were two then remaining there, one of which he said was to sail very soon, I requested to know the precise time, that I might not miss her by any Delay of mine. His Answer was, I have given out that she is to sail on Saturday next, but I may let you know *entre nous*, that if you are there by Monday morning you will be in time, but do not delay longer. By some Accidental Hindrance at a Ferry, it was Monday Noon before I arrived, and I was much afraid she might have sailed as the Wind was fair, but I was soon made easy by the Information that she was still in the Harbour, and would not move till the next Day.—

One would imagine that I was now on the very point of Departing for Europe. I thought so; but I was not then so well acquainted with his Lordship's Character, of which *Indecision* was one of the Strongest Features. I shall give some Instances. It was about the Beginning of April that I came to New York, and I think it was near the End of June before we sail'd. There were then two of the Pacquet Boats which had been long in Port, but were detain'd for the General's Letters, which were always to be ready to-morrow. Another Pacquet arriv'd, and she too was detain'd, and before we sail'd a fourth was expected. Ours was the first to be dispatch'd, as having been there longest. Passengers were engag'd in all, & some extreamly impatient to be gone, and the Merchants uneasy about their Letters, & the Orders they had given for Insurance (it being War-time) & for Fall Goods, But their Anxiety avail'd nothing; his Lordships Letters were not ready. And yet whoever waited on him found him always at his Desk, Pen in hand, and concluded he must needs write abundantly. Going my self one Morning to pay my Respects, I found in his Antechamber one Innis, a Messenger of Philadelphia, who had come from thence express, with a Pacquet from Governor Denny for the General. He deliver'd to me some Letters from my Friends there, which occasion'd my enquiring when he was to return & where he lodg'd, that I might send some Letters by him. He told me he was order'd to call to-morrow at nine for the General's Answer to the Governor, and should set off immediately. I put my Letters into his Hands the same Day. A Fortnight after I met him again in the same Place. So you are soon return'd, Innis! *Return'd*; No, I am not *gone* yet.—How so?—I have call'd here by Order every Morning these two Weeks past for his Lordship's Letter, and it is not yet ready.—Is it possible, when he is so great a Writer, for I see him constantly at his Scritore. Yes, says Innis, but he is like St. George on the Signs, *always on horseback, and never rides on.* This Observation of the Messenger was it seems well founded; for when in England, I understood that Mr Pitt gave it as one Reason for Removing this General, and sending Amherst & Wolf, *that the Ministers never heard from him, and could not know what he was doing.*

This daily Expectation of Sailing, and all the three Packets going down Sandy hook, to join the Fleet there the Passengers, thought it best to be on board, lest by a sudden Order

the Ships should sail, and they be left behind. There if I remember right we were about Six Weeks, consuming our Sea
Stores, and oblig'd to procure more. At length the Fleet
sail'd, the General and all his Army on board, bound to
Lewisburg with Intent to besiege and take that Fortress; all
the Packet-Boats in Company, ordered to attend the General's
Ship, ready to receive his Dispatches when those should be
ready. We were out 5 Days before we got a Letter with Leave
to part; and then our Ship quitted the Fleet and steered for
England. The other two Packets he still detain'd, carry'd them
with him to Halifax, where he staid some time to exercise the
Men in sham Attacks upon sham Forts, then alter'd his Mind
as to besieging Louisburg, and return'd to New York with all
his Troops, together with the two Packets abovementioned
and all their Passengers. During his Absence the French and
Savages had taken Fort George on the Frontier of that Province, and the Savages had massacred many of the Garrison
after Capitulation. I saw afterwards in London, Capt. Bon-
nell, who commanded one of those Packets. He told me, that
when he had been detain'd a Month, he acquainted his Lordship that his Ship was grown foul, to a degree that must necessarily hinder her fast Sailing, a Point of consequence for a
Packet Boat, and requested an Allowance of Time to heave
her down and clean her Bottom. He was ask'd how long time
that would require. He answer'd Three Days. The General
reply'd, If you can do it in one Day, I give leave; otherwise
not; for you must certainly sail the Day after to-morrow. So
he never obtain'd leave tho' detain'd afterwards from day to
day during full three Months. I saw also in London one of
Bonell's Passengers, who was so enrag'd against his Lordship
for deceiving and detaining him so long at New-York, and
then carrying him to Halifax, and back again, that he swore
he would sue him for Damages. Whether he did or not I
never heard; but as he represented the Injury to his Affairs it
was very considerable. On the whole I then wonder'd much,
how such a Man came to be entrusted with so important a
Business as the Conduct of a great Army: but having since
seen more of the great World, and the means of obtaining &
Motives for giving Places, & Employments my Wonder is diminished. General Shirley, on whom the Command of the

Army devolved upon the Death of Braddock, would in my Opinion if continued in Place, have made a much better Campaign than that of Loudon in 1757, which was frivolous, expensive and disgraceful to our Nation beyond Conception: For tho' Shirley was not a bred Soldier, he was sensible and sagacious in himself, and attentive to good Advice from others, capable of forming judicious Plans, quick and active in carrying them into Execution. Loudon, instead of defending the Colonies with his great Army, left them totally expos'd while he paraded it idly at Halifax, by which means Fort George was lost;—besides he derang'd all our mercantile Operations, & distress'd our Trade by a long Embargo on the Exportation of Provisions, on pretence of keeping Supplies from being obtain'd by the Enemy, but in Reality for beating down their Price in Favour of the Contractors, in whose Profits it was said, perhaps from Suspicion only, he had a Share. And when at length the Embargo was taken off, by neglecting to send Notice of it to Charlestown, the Carolina Fleet was detain'd near three Months longer, whereby their Bottoms were so much damag'd by the Worm, that a great Part of them founder'd in the Passage home. Shirley was I believe sincerely glad of being reliev'd from so burthensom a Charge as the Conduct of an Army must be to a Man unacquainted with military Business. I was at the Entertainment given by the City of New York, to Lord Loudon on his taking upon him the Command. Shirley, tho' thereby superseded, was present also. There was a great Company of Officers, Citizens and Strangers, and some Chairs having been borrowed in the Neighbourhood, there was one among them very low which fell to the Lot of Mr Shirley. Perceiving it as I sat by him, I said, they have given you, Sir, too low a Seat.—No Matter, says he; Mr Franklin; I find *a low Seat* the easiest!

While I was, as aforemention'd, detain'd at New York, I receiv'd all the Accounts of the Provisions, &c. that I had furnish'd to Braddock, some of which Acc^{ts} could not sooner be obtain'd from the different Persons I had employ'd to assist in the Business. I presented them to Lord Loudon, desiring to be paid the Ballance. He caus'd them to be regularly examin'd by the proper Officer, who, after comparing every Article with its Voucher, certified them to be right, and the

Ballance due, for which his Lordship promis'd to give me an Order on the Paymaster. This, however, was put off from time to time, and tho' I called often for it by Appointment, I did not get it. At length, just before my Departure, he told me he had on better Consideration concluded not to mix his Accounts with those of his Predecessors. And you, says he, when in England, have only to exhibit your Accounts at the Treasury, and you will be paid immediately. I mention'd, but without Effect, the great & unexpected Expence I had been put to by being detain'd so long at N York, as a Reason for my desiring to be presently paid; and On my observing that it was not right I should be put to any farther Trouble or Delay in obtaining the Money I had advanc'd, as I charg'd no Commissions for my Service. O, Sir, says he, you must not think of persuading us that you are no Gainer. We understand better those Affairs, and know that every one concern'd in supplying the Army finds means in the doing it to fill his own Pockets. I assur'd him that was not my Case, and that I had not pocketed a Farthing: but he appear'd clearly not to believe me; and indeed I have since learnt that immense Fortunes are often made in such Employments.—As to my Ballance, I am not paid it to this Day, of which more hereafter.—

Our Captain of the Pacquet had boasted much before we sail'd, of the Swiftness of his Ship. Unfortunately when we came to Sea, she proved the dullest of 96 Sail, to his no small Mortification. After many Conjectures respecting the Cause, when we were near another Ship almost as dull as ours, which however gain'd upon us, the Captain order'd all hands to come aft and stand as near the Ensign Staff as possible. We were, Passengers included, about forty Persons. While we stood there the Ship mended her Pace, and soon left our Neighbour far behind, which prov'd clearly what our Captain suspected, that she was loaded too much by the Head. The Casks of Water it seems had been all plac'd forward. These he therefore order'd to be remov'd farther aft; on which the Ship recover'd her Character, and prov'd the best Sailer in the Fleet. The Captain said she had once gone at the Rate of 13 Knots, which is accounted 13 Miles per hour. We had on board as a Passenger Captain Kennedy of the Navy, who contended that it was impossible, that no Ship ever sailed so fast, and that there must have been some Error in the Division of the Log-Line, or some Mistake in heaving the Log. A Wager ensu'd between the two Captains, to be decided when there should be sufficient Wind. Kennedy thereupon examin'd rigorously the Log-line, and being satisfy'd with that, he determin'd to throw the Log himself. Accordingly some Days after when the Wind blew very fair & fresh, and the Captain of the Packet (Lutwidge) said he believ'd she then went at the Rate of 13 Knots, Kennedy made the Experiment, and own'd his Wager lost. The above Fact I give for the sake of the following Observation. It has been remark'd as an Imperfection in the Art of Ship-building, that it can never be known 'till she is try'd, whether a new Ship will or will not be a good Sailer; for that the Model of a good sailing Ship has been exactly follow'd in a new One, which has prov'd on the contrary remarkably dull. I apprehend this may be partly occasion'd by the different Opinions of Seamen respecting the Modes of lading, rigging & sailing of a Ship. Each has his System. And the same Vessel laden by the Judgment & Orders of one Captain shall sail better or worse than when by the Orders of another. Besides, it scarce ever happens that a Ship is form'd, fitted for the Sea, & sail'd by the same Person. One Man builds the Hull, another riggs her, a third lades and sails her. No one of these has the Advantage of knowing all the Ideas & Experience of the others, & therefore cannot draw just Conclusions from a Combination of the whole. Even in the simple Operation of Sailing when at Sea, I have often observ'd different Judgments in the Officers who commanded the successive Watches, the Wind being the same, One would have the Sails trimm'd sharper or flatter than another, so that they seem'd to have no certain Rule to govern by. Yet I think a Set of Experiments might be instituted, first to determine the most proper Form of the Hull for swift sailing; next the best Dimensions & properest Place for the Masts; then the Form & Quantity of Sail, and their Position as the Winds may be; and lastly the Disposition of her Lading. This is the Age of Experiments; and such a Set accurately made & combin'd would be of great Use. I am therefore persuaded that ere long some ingenious Philosopher will undertake it:—to whom I wish Success—

We were several times chas'd on our Passage, but outsail'd every thing, and in thirty Days had Soundings. We had a good Observation, and the Captain judg'd himself so near our Port, (Falmouth) that if we made a good Run in the Night we might be off the Mouth of that Harbour in the Morning, and by running in the Night might escape the Notice of the Enemy's Privateers, who often cruis'd near the Entrance of the Channel. Accordingly all the Sail was set that we could possibly make, and the Wind being very fresh & fair, we went right before it, & made great Way. The Captain after his Observation, shap'd his Course as he thought so as to pass wide of the Scilly Isles: but it seems there is sometimes a strong Indraught setting up St. George's Channel which deceives Seamen, and caus'd the Loss of Sir Cloudsley Shovel's Squadron. This Indraught was probably the Cause of what happen'd to us. We had a Watchman plac'd in the Bow to whom they often call'd, *Look well out befor'e, there*; and he as often answer'd *Aye, Aye!* But perhaps had his Eyes shut, and was half asleep at the time: they sometimes answering as is said mechanically: For he did not see a Light just before us, which had been hid by the Studding Sails from the Man at Helm & from the rest of the Watch; but by an accidental Yaw of the Ship was discover'd, & occasion'd a great Alarm, we being very near it, the light appearing to me as big as a Cart Wheel. It was Midnight, & Our Captain fast asleep. But Capt. Kennedy jumping upon Deck, & seeing the Danger, ordered the Ship to wear round, all Sails standing. An Operation dangerous to the Masts, but it carried us clear, and we escap'd Shipwreck, for we were running right upon the Rocks on which the Lighthouse was erected. This Deliverance impress'd me strongly with the Utility of Lighthouses, and made me resolve to encourage the building more of them in America, if I should live to return there.—

In the Morning it was found by the Soundings, &c. that we were near our Port, but a thick fog hid the Land from our Sight. About 9 aClock the Fog began to rise, and seem'd to be lifted up from the Water like the Curtain at a Play-house, discovering underneath the Town of Falmouth, the Vessels in its Harbour, & the Fields that surrounded it. A most pleasing Spectacle to those who had been so long without any other

Prospects, than the uniform View of a vacant Ocean!—And it gave us the more Pleasure, as we were now freed from the Anxieties which the State of War occasion'd.—

I set out immediately wth my Son for London, and we only stopt a little by the Way to view Stonehenge on Salisbury Plain, and Lord Pembroke's House and Gardens, with his very curious Antiquities at Wilton.

We arriv'd in London the 27th of July 1757. As soon as I was settled in a Lodging Mr Charles had provided for me, I went to visit Dr Fothergill, to whom I was strongly recommended, and whose Counsel respecting my Proceedings I was advis'd to obtain. He was against an immediate Complaint to Governm^{t}, and thought the Proprietaries should first be personally apply'd to, who might possibly be induc'd by the Interposition & Persuasion of some private Friends to accommodate Matters amicably. I then waited on my old Friend and Correspondent Mr Peter Collinson, who told me that John Hanbury, the great Virginia Merchant, had requested to be informed when I should arrive, that he might carry me to Lord Granville's, who was then President of the Council, and wish'd to see me as soon as possible. I agreed to go with him the next Morning. Accordingly Mr Hanbury called for me and took me in his Carriage to that Nobleman's, who receiv'd me with great Civility; and after some Questions respecting the present State of Affairs in America, & Discourse thereupon, he said to me, "You Americans have wrong Ideas of the Nature of your Constitution; you contend that the King's Instructions to his Governors are not Laws, and think yourselves at Liberty to regard or disregard them at your own Discretion. But those Instructions are not like the Pocket Instructions given to a Minister going abroad, for regulating his Conduct in some trifling Point of Ceremony. They are first drawn up by Judges learned in the Laws; they are then considered, debated & perhaps amended in Council, after which they are signed by the King. They are then so far as relates to you, the *Law of the Land*; for THE KING IS THE LEGISLATOR OF THE COLONIES." I told his Lordship this was new Doctrine to me. I had always understood from our Charters, that our Laws were to be made by our Assemblies, to be presented indeed to the King for his Royal Assent, but that being once given the King could not repeal or alter them. And as the Assemblies could not make permanent Laws without his Assent, so neither could he make a Law for them without theirs. He assur'd me I was totally mistaken. I did not think so however. And his Lordship's Conversation having a little alarm'd me as to what might be the Sentiments of the Court concerning us, I wrote it down as soon as I return'd to my Lodgings.—I recollected that about 20 Years before, a Clause in a Bill brought into Parliament by the Ministry, had propos'd to make the King's Instructions Laws in the Colonies; but the Clause was thrown out by the Commons, for which we ador'd them as our Friends & Friends of Liberty, till by their Conduct towards us in 1765, it seem'd that they had refus'd that Point of Sovereignty to the King, only that they might reserve it for themselves.

After some Days, Dr Fothergill having spoken to the Proprietaries, they agreed to a Meeting with me at Mr J. Penn's House in Spring Garden. The Conversation at first consisted of mutual Declarations of Disposition to reasonable Accommodation; but I suppose each Party had its own Ideas of what should be meant by *reasonable*. We then went into Consideration of our several Points of Complaint which I enumerated. The Proprietaries justify'd their Conduct as well as they could, and I the Assembly's. We now appeared very wide, and so far from each other in our Opinions, as to discourage all Hope of Agreement. However, it was concluded that I should give them the Heads of our Complaints in Writing, and they promis'd then to consider them.—I did so soon after; but they put the Paper into the Hands of their Solicitor Ferdinando John Paris, who manag'd for them all their Law Business in their great Suit with the neighbouring Proprietary of Maryland, Lord Baltimore, which had subsisted 70 Years, and wrote for them all their Papers & Messages in their Dispute with the Assembly. He was a proud angry Man; and as I had occasionally in the Answers of the Assembly treated his Papers with some Severity, they being really weak in point of Argument, and haughty in Expression, he had conceiv'd a mortal Enmity to me, which discovering itself whenever we met, I declin'd the Proprietary's Proposal that he and I should discuss the Heads of Complaint between our two selves, and refus'd treating with any one but them. They then by his Advice put the Paper into the Hands of the Attorney and Solicitor General for their Opinion and Counsel upon it, where it lay unanswered a Year wanting eight Days, during which time I made frequent Demands of an Answer from the Proprietaries but without obtaining any other than that they had not yet receiv'd the Opinion of the Attorney & Solicitor General: What it was when they did receive it I never learnt, for they did not communicate it to me, but sent a long Message to the Assembly drawn & signed by Paris reciting my Paper, complaining of its want of Formality as a Rudeness on my part, and giving a flimsey Justification of their Conduct, adding that they should be willing to accomodate Matters, if the Assembly would send over *some Person of Candour* to treat with them for that purpose, intimating thereby that I was not such. The want of Formality or Rudeness, was probably my not having address'd the Paper to them with their assum'd Titles of true and absolute Proprietaries of the Province of Pensilvania, wch I omitted as not thinking it necessary in a Paper the Intention of which was only to reduce to a Certainty by writing what in Conversation I had delivered *vivâ voce*. But during this Delay, the Assembly having prevail'd with Govr Denny to pass an Act taxing the Proprietary Estate in common with the Estates of the People, which was the grand Point in Dispute, they omitted answering the Message.

When this Act however came over, the Proprietaries counsell'd by Paris determin'd to oppose its receiving the Royal Assent. Accordingly they petition'd the King in Council, and a Hearing was appointed, in which two Lawyers were employ'd by them against the Act, and two by me in Support of it. They alledg'd that the Act was intended to load the Proprietary Estate in order to spare those of the People, and that if it were suffer'd to continue in force, & the Proprietaries who were in Odium with the People, left to their Mercy in proportioning the Taxes, they would inevitably be ruined. We reply'd that the Act had no such Intention and would have no such Effect. That the Assessors were honest & discreet Men, under an Oath to assess fairly & equitably, & that any Advantage each of them might expect in lessening his own

Tax by augmenting that of the Proprietaries was too trifling to induce them to perjure themselves. This is the purport of what I remember as urg'd by both Sides, except that we insisted strongly on the mischievous Consequences that must attend a Repeal; for that the Money, 100,000£, being printed and given to the King's Use, expended in his Service, & now spread among the People, the Repeal would strike it dead in their Hands to the Ruin of many, & the total Discouragement of future Grants, and the Selfishness of the Proprietors in soliciting such a general Catastrophe, merely from a groundless Fear of their Estate being taxed too highly, was insisted on in the strongest Terms. On this Lord Mansfield, one of the Council rose, & beckoning to me, took me into the Clerk's Chamber, while the Lawyers were pleading, and ask'd me if I was really of Opinion that no Injury would be done the Proprietary Estate in the Execution of the Act. I said, Certainly. Then says he, you can have little Objection to enter into an Engagement to assure that Point. I answer'd None, at all. He then call'd in Paris, and after som Discourse his Lordship's Proposition was accepted on both Sides; a Paper to the purpose was drawn up by the Clerk of the Council, which I sign'd with Mr Charles, who was also an Agent of the Province for their ordinary Affairs; when Lord Mansfield return'd to the Council Chamber where finally the Law was allowed to pass. Some Changes were however recommended and we also engag'd they should be made by a subsequent Law; but the Assembly did not think them necessary, For one Year's Tax having been levied by the Act before the Order of Council arrived, they appointed a Committee to examine the Percedings of the Assessors, & On this Committee they put several particular Friends of the Proprietaries. After a full Enquiry they unanimously sign'd a Report that they found the Tax had been assess'd with perfect Equity. The Assembly look'd on my entring into the first Part of the Engagement as an essential Service to the Province, since it secur'd the Credit of the Paper Money then spread over all the Country; and they gave me their Thanks in form when I return'd.—But the Proprietaries were enrag'd at Governor Denny for having pass'd the Act, & turn'd him out, with Threats of suing him for Breach of Instructions which he had given Bond to observe. He however having done it the Instance of the General & for his Majesty's Service, and having some powerful Interest at Court, despis'd the Threats, and they were never put in Execution

Chronology

1706   Born January 17 (Jan. 6, 1705, Old Style) in Milk Street, Boston, opposite Old South Church, where he was baptized Benjamin; youngest son and fifteenth child of Josiah Franklin, tallow chandler and soap boiler who had emigrated from England in 1683 to practice his Puritan faith freely. Eleven brothers and sisters are then living: five of Josiah's seven children by first wife (Elizabeth, b. 1678; Samuel, b. 1681; Hannah, b. 1683; Josiah, b. 1685; Anne, b. 1687) and six of seven so far born to second wife, Abiah Folger Franklin, who came from family of Nantucket Puritans (John, b. 1690; Peter, b. 1692; Mary, b. 1694; James, b. 1697; Sarah, b. 1699; Thomas, b. 1703). Two sisters, Lydia (b. 1708) and Jane (b. 1712) followed.

1714–16   Studies at Boston Grammar School (now Boston Latin) 1714–15, but because of expense, is withdrawn by father at end of school year. Father's widowed brother, Benjamin, comes from England in 1715 and joins household. Attends George Brownell's English school, which follows nonclassical curriculum, for second and final year of formal study (1715–16).

1716–17   Works with father making candles and soap, but dislikes it; tries cutler's trade briefly, but returns to father's shop. Older brother James returns from London, March 1717, and sets up printing business in Boston.

1718–20   Apprenticed to James. Writes broadside ballads "The Lighthouse Tragedy," 1718, and "On the Taking of *Teach* or Blackbeard the Pirate," 1719 (neither extant). December 1719, James hired to print *The Boston Gazette*, second American newspaper; loses contract August 1, 1720. Franklin borrows books to read—among them Bunyan, Defoe, Locke, Xenophon, various histories and religious polemics, as well as such contemporary freethinkers as Shaftesbury and Collins—and improves writing by imitating London *Spectator* essays of Addison and Steele.

1721   Continues working for James when he starts his own newspaper, lively and irreverent *New-England Courant*, August 7, first American newspaper to feature humorous essays and other literary content.

1722   Becomes vegetarian, saving money for books. April to Oc-
            tober, writes fourteen "Silence Dogood" essays for *Cou-
            rant*, submitting them anonymously, believing his brother
            will not print them otherwise. Manages paper while James
            is imprisoned by Massachusetts Assembly (June 12–July 7)
            for suggesting collusion between pirates and local officials.

1723   After *Courant* satirizes ministers and local officials, James
            is forbidden by Massachusetts Assembly to print news-
            paper without prior censorship. James defies order, prints
            Courant, then goes into hiding, leaving Franklin again in
            charge (Jan. 24–Feb. 12). *Courant* hereafter lists Benjamin
            Franklin as editor. Unhappy with James's "harsh & tyran-
            nical" treatment ("Tho' a Brother, he considered himself
            as my Master"), sails secretly September 25 for New York,
            breaking indentures, but fails to find work. Sails for Phil-
            adelphia October 1, encounters squall and spends thirty
            hours on the water; arrives at Perth Amboy, New Jersey,
            next evening with fever. Walks two days across New Jersey
            to Bordentown, then to Burlington; arrives in Philadel-
            phia October 6 with only a Dutch dollar and a few copper
            pence. Finds work the next day with Samuel Keimer as
            journeyman printer. Takes lodging with John Read (father
            of future wife, Deborah) next door to Keimer's shop in
            Market Street.

1724   Encouraged by Pennsylvania Governor William Keith,
            who has sought his acquaintance, to open his own print-
            ing shop; Keith promises to get him public printing. Re-
            turns to Boston near end of April to ask father for money
            to set up business, but Josiah gives him only small pres-
            ents and good wishes. Visits brother James, who takes
            offense at Franklin's display of prosperity. Calls on Cotton
            Mather. Returns to Philadelphia early June, where Keith
            offers to lend money to set up printing shop and suggests
            he go to London to buy materials and arrange for supplies
            from stationers, booksellers, and printers. John Read dies
            July 3. During the fall, Franklin reveals to Deborah Read
            his plan to sail to London; her mother discourages their
            courtship. Sails for London November 5 with friend James
            Ralph and merchant Thomas Denham, relying on letters
            of credit promised by Governor Keith to obtain printing
            equipment. Arrives Christmas Eve and finds that Keith,
            with "no credit to give," had duped him, and sent no

letters; finds employment before January at Samuel Palmer's printing office. Lodges with Ralph in Little Britain section of inner London, next door to bookseller John Wilcox, from whom he borrows books to continue education.

1725   After setting in type William Wollaston's *The Religion of Nature Delineated*, writes and prints rejoinder, *A Dissertation on Liberty and Necessity, Pleasure and Pain*, arguing against free will. William Lyons, surgeon, admires pamphlet and introduces him to Bernard Mandeville and Henry Pemberton, another physician, who promises introduction to Isaac Newton (never fulfilled). Deborah Read marries John Rogers August 5 in Philadelphia; Rogers abandons her in December and is never heard from again. Franklin leaves Palmer's printing shop in fall for larger establishment of John Watts. Moves to Duke Street.

1726   Sails for home July 21 with Thomas Denham, who has hired him as clerk. Keeps journal of voyage July 22–October 11. Following arrival, works for Denham as shopkeeper and bookkeeper.

1727   Denham falls severely ill (dies July 4, 1728); March and April, Franklin critically ill with pleurisy. Returns to printing with Keimer in June. Forms Junto, self-improvement and mutual aid society for ambitious young men of his acquaintance, which meets on Friday evenings; members include three others from Keimer's shop (Hugh Meredith, Stephen Potts, George Webb) along with Joseph Breintnall, Thomas Godfrey, Nicholas Scull, William Parsons, William Maugridge, Robert Grace, Philip Syng, Hugh Roberts, and William Coleman, young men of various occupations and similar interests.

1728   Prints paper currency with Keimer at Burlington, New Jersey, February to May; quits in June and forms printing partnership with friend Hugh Meredith, whose father loans them money to start. Keimer, learning of Franklin's plans for newspaper, hurries into print, October 1, proposal for paper to be called *The Pennsylvania Gazette* (first issue appears Dec. 24). Observing objectionable conduct of freethinkers among his acquaintance, formulates private creed and worship service (*Articles of Belief and Acts of Religion*) November 20, outlining mixture of deistic and polytheistic tenets.

1729 Begins "Busy-Body" essay series February 4 in *The American Weekly Mercury*, Philadelphia newspaper published by Andrew Bradford, hoping to divert readership from Keimer's *Gazette*. Writes *A Modest Enquiry into the Nature and Necessity of a Paper Currency*, published April 10, first of many proposals to stimulate economy by increasing money supply. Buys failing *Pennsylvania Gazette* from Keimer September 25; October 2 issue is first to bear his name. During next decade, it becomes the most widely read newspaper in colonies. About 1729 or 1730, son William is born, out of wedlock, to an unidentified mother.

1730 Named official printer for Pennsylvania January 30. Borrows money from two friends, William Coleman and Robert Grace, to buy out Meredith, who wants to return to farming. Unable to marry Deborah (Read) Rogers in legal ceremony (because Rogers was not known to have died and Franklin, in any case, didn't want to be liable for his debts), forms common-law union with her, September 1; son William is taken into household. Begins to study French and German.

1731 Joins Freemasons in January, beginning lifelong involvement; June, elected junior warden of St. John's Lodge (the first of many Masonic offices he will hold in America and Europe). Drafts "Instrument of Association" for Library Company of Philadelphia, first American subscription library, July 1. Sponsors his journeyman Thomas Whitemarsh as printing partner in South Carolina, advancing necessary equipment and materials in return for one-third of profits, for six-year term (first of several financial sponsorships that will gradually increase his wealth).

1732 Publishes America's first German-language newspaper, *Philadelphische Zeitung*, May 6; it soon fails. Son Francis Folger Franklin born October 20 (baptized in Christ Church, Sept. 16, 1733). Publishes first *Poor Richard's Almanack* December 19 (continued annually by Franklin until he goes to England in 1757). Occasional attendance at Presbyterian services comes to an end.

1733   Conceives "the bold and arduous Project of arriving at moral Perfection"; July 1, begins keeping ledger, systematically recording personal faults. In fall, visits family in Boston and brother James in Newport, Rhode Island. November, sponsors another journeyman, Louis Timothée, as South Carolina printing partner succeeding Whitemarsh. Studies Italian, Spanish, and Latin.

1734   Elected grand master of Masons of Pennsylvania June 24.

1735   Brother James dies February 4 in Newport. Franklin proposes fire protection society in *Pennsylvania Gazette*. Resumes church attendance during winter and spring to hear sermons of Rev. Samuel Hemphill, who emphasizes practical morals. After Hemphill is denounced by ministerial colleagues as unorthodox in April, Franklin writes pamphlets in his defense; when Hemphill is suspended by Presbyterian Synod in September, leaves congregation permanently, but continues to contribute money. Suffers second pleurisy attack in early summer, with left lung suppurating. Proposes system of paid night watchmen for Philadelphia (adopted in 1752).

1736   Prints New Jersey's paper currency in Burlington, July to September; to hinder forgeries, devises new nature-printing technique (reproducing images of tree leaves). Appointed clerk of Pennsylvania Assembly October 15. Son Francis, age four, dies of smallpox November 21 and is buried in Christ Church burial ground. Organizes Union Fire Company, Philadelphia's first, December 7.

1737   Begins duties as postmaster of Philadelphia October 5. Increasingly bored with Assembly proceedings, amuses himself by contriving mathematical puzzles.

1738   Accused in *American Weekly Mercury* (Feb. 14) of participation in mock Masonic initiation in 1737 which resulted in fatal burning of young apprentice. Denies responsibility in trial testimony and in *Gazette* account.

1739   Befriends evangelist George Whitefield, English Methodist preacher, who arrives in Philadelphia November 2 urging religious revival in addresses to large outdoor crowds.

Franklin solicits subscriptions to print Whitefield's journals and sermons.

1740   *American Weekly Mercury* (Feb. 12) criticizes Franklin for favoring the popular anti-Proprietary party in his reporting. (Proprietors were descendants of Pennsylvania's founder, William Penn, who lived in England and were privileged by charter to appoint and instruct governor of the colony.) Becomes official printer for New Jersey (appointment continues to 1744). Announces in *Gazette* (Nov. 13) forthcoming *General Magazine*; accuses Andrew Bradford and John Webbe of stealing his plan for first American magazine; Franklin's price (9 *d.* per issue) undercuts Bradford's proposed magazine (announced at 12 *s.* per year).

1741   Designs Pennsylvania fireplace (Franklin stove) during winter of 1740–41; early version advertised for sale to the public February 5. Publishes first issue of *The General Magazine and Historical Chronicle* February 16; it fails after six issues.

1742   Sponsors employee James Parker as printing partner in New York. Organizes and publicizes, March 17, a project to sponsor Philadelphia botanist John Bartram's collecting trips.

1743   Publishes *A Proposal for Promoting Useful Knowledge* May 14, founding document of American Philosophical Society (first scientific society in America). Journeys to New England in late spring, meeting Cadwallader Colden in New York and attending Archibald Spencer's lectures on electricity in Boston. Begins business correspondence with William Strahan that will develop into lifelong friendship; encourages David Hall, young journeyman printer in Strahan's London shop, to emigrate to America, suggesting that he will sponsor Hall in another colony. Daughter Sarah ("Sally") born August 31; baptized in Christ Church October 27.

1744   David Hall arrives in Philadelphia, June 20, and lodges with Franklin. Publishes *An Account of the New Invented Pennsylvanian Fire-Places.*

1745 Drafts presentment of the Grand Jury against public houses and other nuisances, January 3. Father dies January 16, aged eighty-seven. Peter Collinson, member of Royal Society of London, sends pamphlet about recent German experiments in electricity to Library Company in April, together with glass tube, stimulating Franklin to begin electrical experimentation. Publishes woodcut of the "Plan of the Town and Harbour of Louisburgh" June 6, first illustrated news event in *The Pennsylvania Gazette*.

1746 "Immersed in electrical experiments" during the summer. Visits New England in fall and winter.

1747 Sends, May 25, first account of electrical experiments to Peter Collinson, who shows it to members of the Royal Society. November and December, publishes pamphlet *Plain Truth* warning of Pennsylvania's vulnerability to French and Spanish privateer raids on the Delaware River. Organizes voluntary militia for defense.

1748 Refuses position as colonel in militia, January 1, avowing military inexperience, and serves instead as common soldier. Forms printing partnership with David Hall, January 1, placing shop in Hall's hands in return for half the profits, and retires as printer; hereafter devotes himself mainly to scientific research and civic affairs. (Annual income from printing partnerships, real estate investments, and postmastership will amount to almost two thousand pounds in coming years, as much as the salary of Pennsylvania's governor.) Moves to new house away from shop, and acquires first of several black slaves. April, sponsors Thomas Smith, another of his journeymen, as printing partner in Antigua. Elected to Common Council of Philadelphia October 4.

1749 Writes "new Hypothesis for explaining . . . Thunder-gusts" for Ebenezer Kinnersley, April 29. Kinnersley, lecturing in Annapolis, Maryland, on electricity, first publishes and demonstrates (in miniature) Franklin's lightning rod experiments, May 10. Named Justice of the Peace for Philadelphia, June 30. Appointed provincial grand master of Masons of Pennsylvania, July 10. Writes *Proposals Relating to the Education of Youth in Pensilvania* by October 23, resulting in establishment of Philadelphia

Academy, now University of Pennsylvania (formally opens Jan. 7, 1751). November 7, notes similarities between lightning and electricity in his journal of experiments, and calls for experiment to prove their identity.

1750 Has first attack of gout in February. Proposes use of lightning rods to protect houses in March 2 letter to Collinson. July 29, devises experiment involving sentry-box with pointed rod on its roof, to be erected on hilltop or in church steeple, with rod attached to Leyden jar which would collect the electrical charge, and thus prove lightning to be a form of electricity. Revises lightning rod proposal to include provision for grounding. Severely shocked, December 23, while electrocuting a turkey.

1751 Pennsylvania Assembly passes Franklin's innovative bill, providing public funds to match private contributions, to found Pennsylvania Hospital, February 7. Collection of scientific letters, *Experiments and Observations on Electricity*, edited by Dr. John Fothergill, published in London in April. Elected May 9 and takes seat in Pennsylvania Assembly August 13 (reelected annually until 1764); son William succeeds him as clerk. Initiates proposal to merge city's fire companies into insurance company July 26; representatives of different companies meet on September 7 and organize Philadelphia Contributionship. Elected alderman of Philadelphia, October 1.

1752 Pennsylvania Hospital opens February 6. Mother dies in Boston, May 8, aged eighty-four. June, devises and performs kite experiment proving lightning is electrical. August, sponsors nephew Benjamin Mecom as partner in printing office in West Indies. September, equips his house with lightning rod, connecting it to bells that ring when rod is electrified. *Pennsylvania Gazette* of October 19 explains how to perform kite experiment; writes for *Poor Richard* of 1753 instructions for installing lightning rods. Designs a flexible catheter for brother John, who suffers from bladder stone, December 8.

1753 Abbé Nollet publishes *Lettres sur l'Electricité* in January, disputing Franklin's electrical theories. Second set of electrical experiments (*Supplemental Experiments and Observations*) published in London in March. Sponsors former journeyman Samuel Holland as printing partner in Lancaster, Pennsylvania, June 14. Travels through New England from mid-June to September, receiving honorary Master of Arts degrees from Harvard (July 25) and Yale (Sept. 12). Appointed joint deputy postmaster general of North America August 10, having solicited appointment from England. September 26–October 4, negotiates treaty at Carlisle, Pennsylvania, with Ohio Indians; prints resulting treaty in November. Awarded Copley Medal of Royal Society of London, November 30, for work in electricity.

1754   Disturbed by increasing French pressure along western frontier, devises and prints cartoon of snake cut into sections, over heading "Join or Die," in *Gazette* May 9—America's first political cartoon. Attends Albany Congress as commissioner from Pennsylvania, June–July; meeting brings together representatives from seven colonies to restore alliance with Iroquois and arrange common defense of frontier against French. July 2, conference votes to form colonial union; Franklin proposes plan, which is approved July 10 and sent to colonies for ratification. Pennsylvania Assembly rejects Albany Plan August 17, as do other colonies and British government. Third set of electrical experiments (*New Experiments and Observations on Electricity*) published in September in London, along with second edition of first two parts. Writes series of letters to Massachusetts Governor William Shirley in December protesting taxation without representation and claiming American right to self-government.

1755   Sets up postal communications for Major-General Edward Braddock, commander of British forces in North America; confers with Braddock at Frederick, Maryland, April 22–23, undertaking to supply Braddock's forces with wagons for their march against French at Fort Duquesne. Requisitions wagons at Lancaster and York, Pennsylvania, April 26–May 11. Writes biblical hoaxes "A Parable Against Persecution" and "A Parable on Brotherly Love" by summer. August, joins forces with Quaker party to demand that landholdings of Proprietors be taxed, along with other property, to raise money for defense of frontier. Chosen colonel in October by regiment of foot raised in Philadelphia. Assembly passes Franklin's militia bill, November 25, and approves £60,000 for defense, November 27. Travels to frontier to build forts and organize defenses, December 18 to February 5, with son William as aide.

1756   Unanimously elected to membership in Royal Society of London, April 29, and admitted with waiver of customary fees. Pennsylvania Assembly passes Franklin's bill providing night watchmen and street lighting for Philadelphia on March 9. Meets George Washington, March 21, on way to Virginia on post office business. Receives honorary Master's degree from William and Mary College April 20. Elected corresponding member of Royal Society of Arts, September 1. Undertakes military inspection tour to Carlisle, Harris's Ferry, and New York, October 2–14. Along with other commissioners, confers with Delaware Indians at Easton, Pennsylvania, November 5–18.

1757   Accepts nomination by Pennsylvania Assembly to serve as agent to England, to negotiate long-standing dispute with Proprietors, February 3. Meets with Lord Loudoun, commander-in-chief of British forces in America, March 14–22, presenting Assembly's position favoring bill to raise taxes for military supplies. Loudoun persuades Pennsylvania Governor Denny to waive instructions of Proprietors (who refused to have their estates taxed) and pass bill. Travels to New York with son William April 4 en route to England; delayed until June 23 waiting for Loudoun to give permission to sail. While at sea, completes preface for *Poor Richard* for 1758, "Father Abraham's Speech" (later known as "The Way to Wealth"), the last of series of almanacs written by Franklin. Arrives in London July 26 and stays with Peter Collinson; sees Lord Granville, president of Privy Council, who alarms Franklin with his claim that King is supreme legislator of colonies. Takes lodgings on July 30 at No. 7 Craven Street with Mrs. Margaret Stevenson, widow with whom he thereafter makes his home in England. Meets with Proprietors Richard and Thomas Penn in August, giving them list of grievances. Late September to early November, ill with severe cold, headaches, and dizziness. Resumes conferences with Thomas Penn November 14.

1758   Establishes routine of club attendance that lasts throughout years in England. On Mondays often dines at George and *Vulture* with group of scientists, philanthropists, and explorers, including John Ellicot and, occasionally, Captain James Cook. Thursdays, usually dines with favorite group, Club of Honest Whigs, at St. Paul's Coffeehouse; members include John Canton, Richard Price, Joseph Priestley, James Burgh, William Rose, Andrew Kippis, and, occasionally, James Boswell. Sundays, frequently dines with Sir John Pringle, who gradually displaces printer William Strahan as closest friend in England; Alexander Small and David Hume are often guests. January to May, confers with Penns and defends Pennsylvania at Board of Trade; finally, November 27, Penns concede limited taxation, but they write the next day to Pennsylvania Assembly averring that Franklin lacks candor. Spends week at Cambridge in late May performing evaporation experiments with John Hadley, professor of chemistry. Visits ancestral homes at Ecton and Banbury in July with son William, collecting genealogical information. Invents damper for stoves or chimneys, December 2.

1759   Receives honorary degree of Doctor of Laws in absentia from University of St. Andrews in Scotland, February 12; hereafter referred to as "Dr. Franklin." Reports to Joseph Galloway April 7 that Richard Jackson, Englishman who later served as agent of Pennsylvania Assembly in London and then became friend of America in Parliament, proposed to get him elected to Parliament, "but I am too old to think of changing Countries." Takes extensive tour of northern England and Scotland, August 8–November 2, meeting Adam Smith, William Robertson, and Lord Kames.

1760   Third edition of *Experiments and Observations on Electricity* published (reprinted 1762 and 1764). Writes *The Interest of Great Britain Considered* ("The Canada Pamphlet"), published April 17, arguing economic and strategic importance of Canada to colonies and Britain. Meets Dr. Samuel Johnson on May 1 at the Associates of Dr. Bray, a philanthropic organization (of which Franklin had been elected chairman on March 6) that sponsors charity schools for blacks in Philadelphia, New York, Rhode Island, and Williamsburg, Virginia. Board of Trade rejects seven of nineteen acts passed by Pennsylvania Assembly, including taxes on Penn estates, June 24; August, Franklin appeals to Privy Council, which overrules Board of Trade and allows taxation of Penn estates.

1761   Has emerged as active and influential member of Society of Arts (which mainly sponsors farming methods and introduces new crops), of Royal Society of London (premier scientific society of the day), and of Associates of Dr. Bray. Tours Austrian Netherlands and Dutch Republic with son William and Richard Jackson, August–September. Upon return to England, witnesses coronation of George III September 22.

1762   Receives honorary degree of Doctor of Civil Law from Oxford, April 30. Sends Giambatista Beccaria, Italian scientist who disseminated Franklin's electrical theories, a description on July 13 of recently invented musical instrument, glass armonica, which he had been working on since 1761; Mozart and Beethoven later compose for it. Leaves London in August for Portsmouth to embark for Pennsylvania; arrives in Philadelphia November 1. Son William marries Elizabeth Downes September 4 in London, and is commissioned royal governor of New Jersey September 9.

1763   Tours New Jersey, New York, and New England inspecting post offices June 7 to November 5. Visits charity school sponsored by Associates of Dr. Bray in Philadelphia, and reports December 17 that he has "conceived a higher Opinion of the natural Capacities of the black Race, than I had ever before entertained."

1764   Angered by massacre of friendly Christian Indians in Lancaster County by frontier mob ("Paxton Boys"), drafts bill providing for trial of capital offenses between whites and Indians, January 4; bill arouses intense opposition and Assembly quickly kills it. Publishes *A Narrative of the Late Massacres* January 30, denouncing Paxton Boys; they march on Philadelphia, February 5–8. Franklin organizes defense, then meets with leaders of rioters and persuades them to present grievances and disperse. Writes *Cool Thoughts* (April 12), supporting Assembly's recent resolutions in favor of royal charter. Elected speaker of Assembly, May 26; drafts petition to King for change of government, and signs it as speaker after Assembly adopts it. Massachusetts House of Representatives writes Franklin as speaker urging other colonies to oppose Stamp Act, Parliamentary measure to raise revenue by taxing printed matter in colonies; September 12, Franklin lays proposal before Assembly, which instructs its London agent, Richard Jackson, to oppose passage of proposed Stamp Act, to seek modifications of Sugar Act (enacted April 5), and to argue that only the Pennsylvania legislature has the right to impose taxes in Pennsylvania; Franklin signs instructions. August and September, election campaign for Assembly features vicious attacks on Franklin's character (it is alleged that he favored royal government because he coveted governorship; that he had drawn large income from public monies while Assembly agent in England; that he had been careless with public funds given to his supervision; that William's mother was his maidservant Barbara, and that he had buried her in an unmarked grave; in addition, an old ethnic slur—Franklin had called German immigrants "Palatine Boors" in 1751—was brought up), and he is defeated October 1. His party retains a majority and appoints him October 26 to join Jackson as Assembly's agent in London. Minority members impugn Franklin, who defends his integrity November 5 in *Remarks on a Late Protest*. Leaves Philadelphia November 7; wife, Deborah, again refusing to sail overseas, remains in Philadelphia. Arrives at Isle of Wight December 9; reaches London the next day and takes up residence at old lodgings with Mrs. Stevenson.

1765   With other colonial agents, holds interview February 2 with First Minister George Grenville to protest laying of stamp duties in America. Grenville introduces annual budget in Parliament containing proposal for Stamp Act. Franklin and Thomas Pownall, former colonial governor who favored stronger ties between colonies and Great Britain, meet Grenville February 12 and offer an alternative proposal to raise revenue in America by issuing paper money at interest, but are ignored. Stamp Act passes House of Commons February 27, receives royal assent March 22, and is scheduled to take effect November 1. At Grenville's request, Franklin nominates his friend John Hughes as Pennsylvania stamp distributor, leading to rumors that Franklin actually supports the Stamp Act.

Franklin and Pownall succeed in April in getting Quartering Bill amended to eliminate forcible quartering of British troops in private dwellings in America; amended act passes May 3. Burlesques foolish news reports about America in English newspapers by publishing tall tales, May 3, concluding, "The Grand Leap of the Whale in that Chace up the Fall of Niagara is esteemed by all who have seen it, as one of the finest Spectacles in Nature!" Stamp Act protests spread throughout colonies during summer; in Philadelphia, mobs attack stamp distributors, and Franklin's house is threatened, September 16–17; Deborah arms herself, refusing to flee. Mob is dissuaded by readiness of 800 Franklin supporters to combat them. November 1, Stamp Act fails to go into effect as courts refuse to convene and administration of government in colonies breaks down. Franklin presents Privy Council with Pennsylvania petition for change to royal government, but consideration is postponed. Winter, writes newspaper articles defending the colonies and agitating for repeal of Stamp Act.

1766   Designs anti-Stamp Act cartoon and sends messages during early 1766 on cards bearing design. Partnership with David Hall expires January 21, and Hall buys the shop according to terms of 1748 partnership agreement. Examined by Committee of the Whole of House of Commons February 13 concerning the Stamp Act; Franklin's defense of American position contributes to repeal of act February 22, and establishes him as preeminent representative of American colonies. Travels to Germany with Sir John Pringle, June 15–August 16; elected at Göttingen to Royal Academy of Sciences.

1767   Continues to campaign against Parliamentary taxation of colonies in letters to London newspapers. Charles Townshend, Chancellor of the Exchequer, proposes duties in House of Commons, May 13; passed July 2, they intensify the crisis in the colonies. Franklin and Pringle visit Paris, August 28–October 8, where Horace Walpole calls on them (Sept. 13), and they are presented to Louis XV at Versailles. Daughter Sarah marries Richard Bache, Philadelphia merchant, October 29.

1768 Reviews history of relations between Britain and American colonies in *Causes of the American Discontents before 1768*, January 7. Appointed agent of Georgia Assembly April 11 (serves until May 2, 1774). Writes Mary Stevenson July 20 using phonetic alphabet of his own devising. Fall, has maps printed showing the course of the Gulf Stream.

1769 Supervises publication of corrected and enlarged fourth edition of *Experiments and Observations on Electricity*. Elected president of American Philosophical Society in Philadelphia January 2, and reelected annually until his death. Winter, Deborah Franklin suffers stroke, which impairs her memory and understanding; her health deteriorates thereafter. Joins organizers of land company to seek grants in Ohio Valley from King, hoping to sell parcels to settlers. Grandson Benjamin Franklin Bache born August 12. Appointed agent by New Jersey House of Representatives, November 8 (serves until March 1775). November 29, writes Strahan a major statement of American position intended for private circulation to Cabinet and selected members of Parliament.

1770 Elected agent of Massachusetts House of Representatives October 24 (retaining position until leaving England in March 1775), making him agent for four colonies (Pennsylvania, Georgia, New Jersey, and Massachusetts).

1771 Presents credentials as Massachusetts agent on January 16 to Lord Hillsborough, secretary of state for the colonies, who refuses to accept them because Franklin had been appointed by Assembly without governor's concurrence. Elected to Batavian Society of Experimental Science, Rotterdam, June 11. June 17–24, and again July 30–August 13, visits Bishop Jonathan Shipley at Twyford, where, on latter visit, writes first part of autobiography. Tours Ireland and Scotland with Richard Jackson from August 25 to November 30; attends opening of Irish Parliament, October 8; stays with David Hume in Edinburgh, and with Lord Kames at Blair-Drummond. At end of trip, visits mother and sister of son-in-law Richard Bache at Preston in Lancashire, meets Richard for first time, and returns to London with him.

1772   After Board of Trade rejects land company plans, April 29, appeals to Privy Council on June 5, which approves the grant on July 1, but territory is never officially conveyed. Has come to believe that slavery is inherently evil and unjust (1758 will provided for manumission of two slaves he owned, and he evidently freed them sometime during 1760s); first writes against the institution of slavery in "The Sommersett Case and the Slave Trade," June 20. Elected foreign associate of Académie Royale des Sciences, Paris, August 16. October, Mrs. Stevenson moves to No. 10 Craven Street, and Franklin moves with her. Clandestinely obtains correspondence of Massachusetts Governor Thomas Hutchinson and Lieutenant Governor Andrew Oliver with English authorities, finds that it advocates repressive measures, and sends it to Massachusetts Speaker Thomas Cushing.

1773   Hutchinson letters are laid before Massachusetts House June 2; House resolves that they were intended to subvert constitution and appoints committee to petition crown for Hutchinson's and Oliver's removal. Hutchinson surreptitiously obtains copy of July 7 letter from Franklin to Massachusetts Speaker Cushing and sends it to Lord Dartmouth, colonial secretary, who judges it treasonable and asks General Thomas Gage, commander-in-chief in America, to obtain original so Franklin can be prosecuted; Gage fails to obtain it (Cushing may have destroyed the original after copying to protect Franklin). Franklin forwards to Lord Dartmouth petition for removal of Hutchinson and Oliver. Publishes satires "Rules by Which a Great Empire May Be Reduced to a Small One" and "Edict by the King of Prussia" in September. Experiments with use of oil to calm waters of Spithead in October.

1774   January, attends preliminary hearing on petition to remove Hutchinson and Oliver. News of Boston Tea Party reaches London January 20. Accused of stealing the Hutchinson letters, is excoriated and denounced as thief by Solicitor General Alexander Wedderburn before Privy Council during hearing on petition from Massachusetts House; refuses to respond to Wedderburn's accusations. Dismissed as deputy postmaster general for North America January 31. Unsuccessfully petitions House of Commons against Boston Port Bill; March 31 it becomes law, closing port. Attends opening of Theophilus Lindsey's Essex House Chapel, April 17, first enduring Unitarian congregation in England, contributing five guineas for its construction. Effigies of Wedderburn and Hutchinson carted through Philadelphia May 3, hanged, and burned by electricity. First Continental Congress opens in Philadelphia and adopts Continental Association September 5; petitions King through Franklin and other agents. Franklin becomes involved in two series of negotiations to restore calm between Britain and America: one, evidently authorized by Dartmouth, with merchant David Barclay and physician John Fothergill; the other with Lord Howe, secretly meeting at Howe's sister's, under pretense of playing chess. Drafts "Hints for a Durable Union Between England and America" at request of Barclay and Fothergill; forwarded to Dartmouth's office, it is considered and rejected. December 25, asked by Lord Howe to prepare another set of terms for conciliation; these too are not accepted. Deborah Franklin, who had not seen her husband in ten years, suffers a stroke on December 14 and dies in Philadelphia December 19, aged sixty-six; buried at Christ Church.

1775   Confers several times in late January with William Pitt, Earl of Chatham, on Chatham's unsuccessful conciliatory plan. Address to King, adopted by both Houses of Parliament February 9, declares Massachusetts to be in rebellion. Leaves London for Portsmouth March 20 to embark for America. During voyage, begins writing account of peace negotiations; speculates about why sailing from Europe to America takes longer than reverse crossing; measures temperature of air and water, proving that Gulf Stream is warmer than sea on either side of it. Lands in Philadelphia May 5 and next day is unanimously chosen delegate to Second Continental Congress by Pennsylvania Assembly. Active on various committees of Congress, among them one on paper currency, for which he designs devices and mottoes to be used on Continental money. Drafts Articles of Confederation in July, asserting America's political sovereignty, but Congress is unwilling to take such bold action. Submits resolutions proposing free trade, with no duties whatever; resolution is shelved until April 6, 1776, when it is finally adopted with proviso that individual colonies might impose their own import duties.

August 23, King proclaims colonies in rebellion. Congress reconvenes September 13, and Franklin is again active on various committees. Leaves Philadelphia October 4 with committee to confer with George Washington at his Massachusetts headquarters; returns November 9, bringing sister Jane Mecom, who had fled occupied Boston. Reappointed to several committees and offices of Pennsylvania Assembly, and reappointed delegate to Congress November 4. Congress creates standing committee of secret correspondence November 29 to deal with foreign affairs and appoints Franklin to it; committee meets secretly with agent of French court in December. Writes essays, song, and mock epitaph encouraging American war effort; epitaph, published December 14, concludes with words Jefferson adopts as his personal motto: "Rebellion to Tyrants is Obedience to God."

1776   New Jersey militia, acting on resolution of Congress, deprives William Franklin of official functions as royal governor of New Jersey in January; confined to his home in Perth Amboy, he is arrested in June and sent under guard to Connecticut to be imprisoned. Franklin, in Congress, declines to intercede for his son. Argues for "Instrument of Confederation" January 16 in Congress but is defeated. Urges four New England governments to enter into confederation and invite other colonies then to accede to it, February 19. Congress orders new designs for fractional dollars, and Franklin creates device of thirteen linked circles and "Fugio" design (later used on first United States coin, Fugio cent of 1787). Resigns from Pennsylvania Assembly February 26 to devote himself to Congressional duties. Appointed commissioner to Canada by Congress; March 26–May 30, on mission to Montreal, suffering from large boils, swollen legs, and dizziness. Appointed by Congress to committee to draft declaration of independence, June 1; committee chooses Thomas Jefferson to compose draft of declaration. Votes in favor of Richard Henry Lee's motion for independence, July 2. Congress adopts Declaration of Independence, July 4. Elected delegate from Philadelphia to Pennsylvania state convention, July 8; chosen president of Pennsylvania convention July 16; named by convention as Congressional delegate July 20. Asks for and receives Congress's permission to answer personal letter from Lord Howe; writes, July 20: "Long did I endeavour with unfeigned and unwearied Zeal, to preserve from breaking, that fine and noble China Vase the British Empire." Revises draft of Declaration of Rights before August 15, suggesting radical note (rejected by Pennsylvania convention) that claims the state has the right to discourage large concentrations of property as a danger to the happiness of mankind. During Congressional debates on Articles of Confederation, July 30–August 1, unsuccessfully advocates proportional, rather than equal, representation of states in Congress. Appointed by Congress to meet with Lord Howe, September 11, on Staten Island; they are unable to conciliate English and American differences. September, elected by Congress commissioner to France with Silas Deane and Arthur Lee, and is instructed to negotiate treaty. Drafts "Sketch of Propositions for a peace" in fall, suggesting Britain cede Canada to United States. Leaves Philadelphia and sails for France October 27, taking grandsons William Temple Franklin (William's illegitimate son) and Benjamin Franklin Bache (eldest of Sarah's children). Lands at Auray December 3 and proceeds to Paris; meets secretly on December 28 with Comte de Vergennes, French foreign minister.

1777   Commissioners formally request French aid, January 5; Louis XVI approves response to commissioners January 9, and January 13 they receive verbal promise of two million livres. Moves to Paris suburb of Passy about February 27, where he remains during French mission. Elected to Royal Medical Society of Paris, June 17. Combats reports of British victories spread by English Ambassador Lord Stormont by making his name a laughingstock: asked in August if it was true that six battalions in Washington's army had surrendered, Franklin replies, "No, Monsieur, it is not true; it is only a Stormont." Downplays the significance of Sir William Howe's taking of Philadelphia by commenting "it was not he who had taken Philadelphia, but instead Philadelphia had taken him." August 25, orders fifty pounds of type, evidently intending to set up small printing press at home; quantity of type indicates he was planning to print only small notes, forms, and documents. (Purchases additional type in 1778 and 1779, and occasionally employs printers from 1779 to 1783 to work on larger documents, pamphlets, and books. Probably prints small pieces, including the bagatelles, himself.) News of British defeat at Saratoga in October arrives December 4, and spurs negotiations leading to French alliance. Establishes several circles of friends in Passy area, including Louis Le Veillard, Madame Brillon de Jouy (to whom he writes flirtatious letters and bagatelles), La Comtesse d'Houdetot (Jean Jacques Rousseau's mistress), and especially the widow Madame Helvétius, whose salon includes Anne Robert Jacques Turgot, France's finance minister, and other notable French intellectuals.

1778   Commissioners report to Congress, January 28, French grant of six million livres for year. Treaties of "alliance for mutual defense" and of amity and commerce signed with France February 6; symbolically, Franklin wears to the signing ceremony same brown velvet suit he had worn January 29, 1774, when accused by Wedderburn before Privy Council. American commissioners formally presented to Louis XVI March 20. Assists at initiation of Voltaire in Masonic Lodge of the Nine Sisters, April 7. Embraces Voltaire at request of audience at meeting of French Academy of Sciences, which recognizes them as leading intellectual exemplars of their nations. In London, Boswell quotes Franklin's definition of man as "a toolmaking animal" to Dr. Johnson, April 7. Joined by John Adams, appointed as fellow commissioner to France to replace Silas Deane. France goes to war with Britain, June 17. Replies scornfully July 1 to offer of official rewards in return for aid in scheme of reconciliation proposed by secret English agent. Elected sole minister plenipotentiary to France September 14. Officiates at Masonic funeral services for Voltaire, November 28.

1779   Spain declares war on Britain June 21. Obtains another three million livres from France. December, Benjamin Vaughan publishes *Political, Miscellaneous, and Philsophical Pieces* in London, first general compilation of Franklin's nonscientific writings.

1780   Reports to Congress August 9 that John Adams, now commissioner to negotiate peace with Britain, has given offense to French court by repeated insults in letters to Vergennes, copies of which Franklin sends to Congress at Vergennes's request. Adams is thereafter bitterly hostile to

French and to Franklin. Rejects, October 2, surrendering American claims to the Mississippi as price for Spanish aid: "A Neighbour might as well ask me to sell my Street Door."

1781 Writes Vergennes February 13 of America's financial and military necessities, explaining failure of Spanish mission to date, saying " we can rely on France alone." June 4 and 10, again asks Vergennes for money to pay bills of Congress, as well as those of Adams (who is now in Holland) and John Jay in Spain. Congress appoints Franklin, Jay, Henry Laurens, and Thomas Jefferson to join Adams as commissioners to negotiate peace; new instructions require them to act only with knowledge and concurrence of France. General Charles Cornwallis surrenders to Washington at Yorktown, Virginia, October 19.

1782 Continues to request money from France to pay bills presented by Jay and Adams. Edmund Burke writes him as "the friend of mankind," February 28. Holds informal peace negotiations with British emissaries, March–June; suggests on April 18 to negotiator Richard Oswald that Britain should cede Canada to United States. July 10, Franklin suggests to Oswald "necessary" terms for peace without previously communicating them to Vergennes as his instructions from Congress require. July to October, Jay insists on prior recognition of American independence as condition for formal negotiation; Oswald's new commission from Britain, September 21, effectively recognizes United States. Draft articles for treaty prepared and sent to England without consulting Vergennes. August to October, Franklin has severe attack of gout, succeeded by passing gravel in urine. Adams arrives in Paris October 26 and joins negotiations. Oswald and American commissioners sign preliminary articles of peace November 30; when Vergennes complains in December of American failure to consult French, Franklin diplomatically admits impropriety, expresses gratitude to France, and asks for another loan. Vergennes assures Franklin of further six million livres.

1783 Attends signing of Anglo-French and Anglo-Spanish preliminary articles with Adams at Versailles, January 20; commissioners declare armistice. Requests another six million livres from France January 25, bringing total to twenty million. Crowned with laurel and myrtle March 6 at Musée de Paris celebration of successful conclusion of war. Requests permission from Vergennes to print French translations of American state constitutions together with Articles of Confederation and treaty with France; presents copies, translated by Duc de La Rochefoucauld, to all foreign ministers. Signs treaty of amity and commerce with Sweden April 3. Consulted by papal Nuncio in Paris, July 1783–July 1784, about organizing Roman Catholic Church in United States; suggests John Carroll (who accompanied him on 1776 mission to Canada) as its head (Carroll receives appointment as superior of Catholic clergy in America July 1784, and bishopric shortly thereafter). Fascinated by early experimental balloon ascensions, reports on them to Sir Joseph Banks, president of Royal Society; witnesses two of the first manned flights, November 21 and December 1. When asked by scoffing observer, "What use is it?" replies with defense of pure research: "What use is a new-born baby?" Definitive treaty of peace between Great Britain and United States signed September 3 by David Hartley for the British and by Adams, Franklin, and Jay for United States. Elected honorary fellow of Royal Society of Edinburgh.

1784   Mocks aristocratic pretensions of Society of the Cincinnati (organization of veteran officers of American Revolution) and eagle as symbol of the United States in January 26 letter to daughter Sarah; facetiously proposes native American turkey as better symbol. March, appointed by Louis XVI to investigate F. A. Mesmer's theories of animal magnetism; *Rapport* of August 11 and *Exposé*, read to Academy of Sciences September 4, conclude animal magnetism does not exist. May 12, formal ratification of peace treaty with Great Britain exchanged; Franklin requests on following day to be relieved from post to return home. Writes second part of autobiography, probably during late spring. Congress names Adams, Franklin, and Jefferson joint commissioners to negotiate treaties with European nations and Barbary States; they begin work August 30. Elected member of Royal Academy of History of Madrid.

1785   Receives word May 2 that Congress has given long-awaited permission to come home and has appointed Jefferson his successor as minister plenipotentiary to France. Describes invention of bifocal glasses May 23. Signs treaty with Prussia July 9, embodying idealistic views on neutrality, privateering, and exemption of private property from capture at sea. Leaves Passy July 12; because bladder stone makes coach travel painful, is furnished with one of Queen Marie Antoinette's litters, borne by Spanish mules. Sails from Havre July 22; arrives at Southampton, England, July 24, and is visited by son William (with whom he reconciled the previous year), Bishop and Mrs. Shipley and daughter Catherine, and by other friends. Sails July 28 for Philadelphia. On voyage, writes "Maritime Observations," containing notes on best form of rigging to improve swiftness of vessels; further observations on course, velocity, and temperature of Gulf Stream; and design of sea anchor for holding ship in wind during rough weather. Lands at Philadelphia September 14, met by cannon salutes, pealing bells, and cheering crowds. Elected to Supreme Executive Council of Pennsylvania for three-year term, October 11; elected its president October 18, and unanimously reelected the next two years. Donates salary to charity.

1786   Designs instrument for taking down books from high shelves, January. Finding Market Street house (now occupied by daughter Sarah Bache, her husband, and six children) too cramped, builds addition, including large dining room and library to house more than 4,000 volumes.

1787   February, helps found Society for Political Enquiries, dedicated to improvement of knowledge of government; elected first president. Named president of reorganized Pennsylvania Society for Promoting the Abolition of Slavery, April 23; devotes much of remaining time and energy to abolition. Serves May 28–September 17 as Pennsylvania delegate to Federal Constitutional Convention. Opposes salaries for highest executive positions. Argues June 11 that representation to Congress should be proportional to population. Moves June 28 that sessions of Convention be opened with prayer; motion, proving controversial, is dropped. July 3, proposes "Great Compromise" on representation, making representation proportional to population in House and equal by state in Senate; approved by

Grand Committee, and enacted by Convention July 16. Argues August 7 and 10 for extending right to vote as widely as possible; condemns property qualification for franchise and for officeholding as unnecessary. James Wilson reads Franklin's closing speech at convention September 17, urging every member to "doubt a little of his own Infallibility," put aside specific reservations, and vote unanimously for approval of Constitution.

1788   Writes last will and testament, July 17, leaving bulk of estate to daughter Sarah and her family; makes smaller bequests to grandsons William Temple Franklin and Benjamin Bache; citing "the part he acted against me in the late war," leaves son William almost nothing (adds codicil, June 23, 1789, making bequests to Boston and Philadelphia). Begins writing third part of autobiography in August. Ends service as president of Supreme Executive Council of Pennsylvania October 14, terminating career in public office.

1789   As president of the Pennsylvania Society for Promoting the Abolition of Slavery, writes and signs first remonstrance against slavery addressed to American Congress, February 12; after debate, committee reports March 5 that Congress has no authority to interfere in internal affairs of states. Congratulates Washington on September 16 on the success of new government under his administration and expresses satisfaction that he has lived to see present situation of United States. Sends copies of first three parts of autobiography to friends in England and France November 2 and 13. Observes to Jean Baptiste Le Roy November 13, "In this world, nothing can be said to be certain except death and taxes." Elected member of Russian Imperial Academy of Sciences, St. Petersburg.

1790   Petitions Congress February 3 as president of Pennsylvania Abolition Society against slavery and slave trade. Restates religious beliefs March 9 in letter to Ezra Stiles, expressing faith in benevolent deity. Last public writing, March 23, satirizes a defense of slavery. In last letter and final public service, April 8, replies to Secretary of State Jefferson's query on northeast boundary as settled at Paris by peace commissioners; sends his copy of Mitchell map used there.

Dies quietly at home, the evening of April 17. Although painfully afflicted in last years by bladder stone, dies of pleurisy, accompanied by suppurated lungs. Buried April 21 beside wife, Deborah, and son Francis in Christ Church burial ground, Philadelphia.

Note on the Texts

The present volume contains a broad selection of Benjamin Franklin's writings, both published and private. Included are the complete series of the "Silence Dogood" essays, all of Franklin's "Busy-Body" essays, selections from *The Pennsylvania Gazette*, which Franklin edited and published from 1729 to 1757, letters to English newspapers written during his residence in London from 1757 to 1775, pamphlets and broadsides published separately in Philadelphia and elsewhere, contributions to books and periodicals, a selection of letters, the complete prefaces and maxims from the "Poor Richard" almanacs, and a newly prepared edition of the *Autobiography*.

A number of pieces from *The Pennsylvania Gazette* attributed to Franklin by the editor of this volume have not been included in previous collections of Franklin's writings. These, along with some selections from *The New-England Courant* (also newly attributed to Franklin) and a few newly attributed items from other sources, total fifty-seven pieces. Franklin's authorship of these writings is discussed in J. A. Leo Lemay, *The Canon of Benjamin Franklin 1722–1776: New Attributions and Reconsiderations* (Newark: University of Delaware Press, 1986).

Many of Franklin's writings were published in some form in his lifetime, often under his own supervision as editor, printer, and sometimes typesetter. For these writings, the texts printed here are those of that first publication (newspaper, broadside, pamphlet, or book). The texts of many of the earlier pieces, therefore, are those first printed in *The New-England Courant*, *The Pennsylvania Gazette*, or one of the other American periodicals to which Franklin contributed. For Franklin's published writings while in England, the texts are those of the original newspapers (except in a few cases where the particular issue is not known to be extant). The texts of works published separately, such as *A Dissertation on Liberty and Necessity, Pleasure and Pain* (London, 1725) and *A Modest Enquiry into the Nature and Necessity of a Paper-Currency* (Philadelphia, 1729), are those of the original pamphlet editions.

For many of the remaining pieces (including most of the letters), the texts have been taken from the scholarly edition in progress at Yale University, *The Papers of Benjamin Franklin*, ed. Leonard W. Labaree, William B. Willcox et al. (25 vols. to date, New Haven, 1959–), co-sponsored by Yale and the American Philosophical Society, both major repositories of Franklin materials. This edition is the preferred source for writings edited from manuscript. For manuscript pieces dating from 1778 and later (the *Papers* having so far reached only to that year of Franklin's life), texts have been taken in most cases from *The Writings of Benjamin Franklin*, ed. Albert H. Smyth (10 vols., New York, 1905–07). Where no manuscript of a piece is known to survive, the present volume reprints the text of the best earlier printed source. The order of preference for choosing this source is the following: Franklin's own collection of scientific writings (*Experiments and Observations on Electricity*, London, 1769); the collection of Franklin's writings edited by his friend Benjamin Vaughan (London, 1779); the collection edited by Franklin's grandson William Temple Franklin (London, 1817–18); William Duane's collection (Philadelphia, 1808–18); Jared Sparks's collection (Boston, 1836–40). The few exceptions to this order of preference are detailed in the list of sources below.

Titles of individual pieces in most cases are the customary titles by which the pieces have become known, and are usually derived from the editions that are the sources of the texts. Titles that were given during Franklin's lifetime are indicated by a dagger in the tables of contents of the various sections. Writings are ordered chronologically according to date of composition (if known), or by a date in the text (if given), otherwise by date of publication or by date inferred from external evidence, recorded in datelines added at the end of individual pieces.

In the list of sources below, asterisks indicate items newly attributed to Franklin and discussed in Lemay's *Canon*. The most common sources are indicated by these abbreviations:

Amacher   *Franklin's Wit & Folly: The Bagatelles*. Ed. Richard E. Amacher. New Brunswick, New Jersey: Rutgers University Press. 1953. Copyright 1953 by the Trustees of Rutgers College in New Jersey.

Bagatelles   *The Bagatelles from Passy*. New York: The Eakins Press, 1967. Copyright 1967 The Eakins Press Foundation.

Courant   *The New-England Courant*. Published by James Franklin, Boston.

Duane   *The Works of Dr. Benjamin Franklin, published from the originals by his grandson William Temple Franklin*. 6 vols. Philadelphia: William Duane. 1808–18.

E&O   Benjamin Franklin. *Experiments and Observations on Electricity*. London: David Henry & Francis Newberry, 1769.

Gazette   *The Pennsylvania Gazette*. Published by Benjamin Franklin, Philadelphia.

General Magazine   *The General Magazine, and Historical Chronicle, For all the British Plantations in America*. Published by Benjamin Franklin, Philadelphia.

Papers   *The Papers of Benjamin Franklin*. Ed. Leonard W. Labaree, William B. Willcox et al. 25 vols. to date. New Haven: Yale University Press, 1959–.

Passy   Printed by Franklin on his press at Passy, France.

Smyth   *The Writings of Benjamin Franklin*. Ed. Albert Henry Smyth. 10 vols. New York: The Macmillan Company, 1905–07.

Sparks   *The Works of Benjamin Franklin*. Ed. Jared Sparks. 10 vols. Boston: Hilliard, Gray, and Company, 1836–40.

Vaughan   Benjamin Franklin. *Political, Miscellaneous, and Philosophical Pieces*. Ed. Benjamin Vaughan. London: J. Johnson, 1779.

WTF   *Memoirs of the Life and Writings of Benjamin Franklin*, . . . Ed. William Temple Franklin. 3 vols. London: H. Colburn, 1817–18.

SOURCES

BOSTON AND LONDON, 1722–1726

Silence Dogood
   No. 1. *Courant*, April 2, 1722.
   No. 2. *Courant*, April 16, 1722.
   No. 3. *Courant*, April 30, 1722.
   No. 4. *Courant*, May 14, 1722.

No. 5. *Courant*, May 28, 1722.

No. 6. *Courant*, June 11, 1722.

No. 7, with *accompanying poem. *Courant*, June 25, 1722.

No. 8. *Courant*, July 9, 1722.

No. 9. *Courant*, July 23, 1722.

No. 10. *Courant*, August 13, 1722.

No. 11. *Courant*, August 20, 1722.

No. 12. *Courant*, September 10, 1722.

No. 13. *Courant*, September 24, 1722.

No. 14. *Courant*, October 8, 1722.

*Hugo Grim on Silence Dogood. *Courant*, December 3, 1722.

*Rules for *The New-England Courant*, *Courant*, January 28, 1722/3.

*To "your Honor": Defense of James Franklin to Samuel Sewall. *Courant*, February 4, 1722/3.

On Titles of Honour. *Courant*, February 18, 1722/3.

*High Tide in Boston. *Courant*, March 4, 1722/3.

*Timothy Wagstaff. *Courant*, April 15, 1723.

*Abigail Twitterfield. *Courant*, July 8, 1723.

A Dissertation on Liberty and Necessity, Pleasure and Pain. *A Dissertation on Liberty and Necessity, Pleasure and Pain* (London, 1725).

Plan of Conduct. Robert Walsh, "Life of Benjamin Franklin," *Delaplaine's Repository of the Lives and Portraits of Distinguished Americans* (Philadelphia, 1815–17), II, 51–52.

PHILADELPHIA, 1726–1757

Articles of Belief and Acts of Religion, November 20, 1728. *Papers*, I, 101–09.

Epitaph, 1728. *Papers*, I, 111.

The Busy-Body

No. 1. *The American Weekly Mercury*, February 4, 1728/9.

No. 2. *The American Weekly Mercury*, February 11, 1728/9.

No. 3. *The American Weekly Mercury*, February 18, 1728/9.

No. 4. *The American Weekly Mercury*, February 25, 1728/9.

No. 5. *The American Weekly Mercury*, March 4, 1728/9.

No. 8, with *suppressed addition. *The American Weekly Mercury*, March 27, 1729. The suppressed addition is from the only known copy, in the Library of Congress.

A Modest Enquiry into the Nature and Necessity of a Paper-Currency, April 3, 1729. *A Modest Enquiry into the Nature and Necessity of a Paper-Currency* (Philadelphia: New Printing-Office, 1729).

The Printer to the Reader. *Gazette*, October 2, 1729.

"One Piles a Fidler." *Gazette*, October 16, 1729.

Fire and the Nature of Horses. *Gazette*, December 16, 1729.

*The Trial and Reprieve of Prouse and Mitchel. *Gazette*, December 23, 1729; January 13, 1729/30; January 20, 1729/30.

*A Gallant Duel and an Unhappy Man. *Gazette*, February 10, 1729/30.

Printer's Errors. *Gazette*, March 13, 1729/30.

*Letter of the Drum. *Gazette*, April 23, 1730.

*On that Odd Letter of the Drum. *Gazette*, May 7, 1730.

*An Unlucky She-Wrestler. *Gazette*, July 23, 1730.

*Rules and Maxims for Promoting Matrimonial Happiness. *Gazette*, October 8, 1730.

A Witch Trial at Mount Holly. *Gazette*, October 22, 1730.

*The Aurora Borealis. *Gazette*, October 29, 1730.

*The Earliest New-England Immigrants. *Gazette*, November 5, 1730.

*Lying Shopkeepers. *Gazette*, November 19, 1730.

*Replies by "Betty Diligent" and "Mercator." *Gazette*, December 3, 1730.

On the Providence of God in the Government of the World, 1730. *Papers*, I, 264–69. Dated 1732 in *Papers*.

*Compassion and Regard for the Sick. *Gazette*, March 25, 1731.

*English Officials for America. *Gazette*, May 27, 1731.

Apology for Printers. *Gazette*, June 10, 1731.

"A certain St-n-c-tt-r." *Gazette*, June 17, 1731.

*The Molasses Bill. *Gazette*, June 17, 1731.

"A certain C-n-table." *Gazette*, June 24, 1731.

"George is as good as de best." *Gazette*, July 29, 1731.

Fighting Bucks. *Gazette*, October 14, 1731.

Doctrine to be Preached, 1731. *Papers*, I, 213.

*Death of a Lion. *Gazette*, January 25, 1731/2.

*A Burnt-Offering. *Gazette*, February 15, 1731/2.

Lost Money. *Gazette*, March 30, 1732.

*On Simplicity. *Gazette*, April 13, 1732.

"To melt the Pewter Button." *Gazette*, June 19, 1732.

Anthony Afterwit. *Gazette*, July 10, 1732.

Celia Single. *Gazette*, July 24, 1732.

*Praise for William Penn. *Gazette*, August 12, 1732.

*On Censure or Backbiting. *Gazette*, September 7, 1732.

Alice Addertongue. *Gazette*, September 12, 1732.

*Men are Naturally Benevolent as Well as Selfish. *Gazette*, November 30, 1732.

Death of a Drunk. *Gazette*, December 7, 1732.

Counterfeits. *Gazette*, December 19, 1732; January 11, 1732/3.

Rules for a Club Formerly Established in Philadelphia, 1732. *Vaughan*, 533–36.

Proposals and Queries to be Asked the Junto, 1732. *Papers*, I, 259–64.

*On Drunkenness. *Gazette*, February 1, 1732/3.

*A Meditation on a Quart Mugg. *Gazette*, July 19, 1733.

*Blackamore, on Molatto Gentlemen. *Gazette*, August 30, 1733.

*Brave Men at Fires. *Gazette*, December 20, 1733.

*Queries on a Pennsylvania Militia. *Gazette*, March 6, 1733/4.

*On Constancy. *Gazette*, April 4, 1734.

*The Death of Infants. *Gazette*, June 20, 1734.

*Parody and Reply to a Religious Meditation. *Gazette*, August 8, 1734.

*A Thunderstorm. *Gazette*, September 25, 1734.

*The Murder of a Daughter. *Gazette*, October 24, 1734.

*Variant Accounts of a Battle. *Gazette*, December 19, 1734.

On Protection of Towns from Fire. *Gazette*, February 4, 1734/5.

Self-Denial Not the Essence of Virtue. *Gazette*, February 5, 1734/5.

A Man of Sense. *Gazette*, February 11, 1734/5.

Reply to a Piece of Advice. *Gazette*, March 4, 1734/5.

*On a Pertinacious Obstinacy in Opinion. *Gazette*, March 27, 1735.

Dialogue Between Two Presbyterians. *Gazette*, April 10, 1735.

Women's Court. *Gazette*, April 17, 1735.

Advice to a Pretty Creature and Replies. *Gazette*, November 20, 1735; November 27, 1735.

*A Sea Monster. *Gazette*, April 29, 1736.

The Art of Saying Little in Much. *Gazette*, June 17, 1736.

The Drinker's Dictionary. *Gazette*, January 13, 1736/7.

Captain Farra. *Gazette*, June 2, 1737.

*Upon the Talents Requisite in an Almanack-Writer. *Gazette*, October 20, 1737.

*The Compassion of Captain Croak. *Gazette*, August 10, 1738.

*Octuplets. *Gazette*, November 24, 1738.

*Obadiah Plainman Defends the Meaner Sort. *Gazette*, May 15, 1740.

*Obadiah Plainman to Tom Trueman. *Gazette*, May 29, 1740.

Religious Mood in Philadelphia. *Gazette*, June 12, 1740.

Statement of Editorial Policy. *Gazette*, July 24, 1740.

*Essay on Paper-Currency, Proposing a New Method for Fixing Its Value. *General Magazine*, Vol. I, No. 2 (February, 1741), 117–20.

*Letter from Theophilus, Relating to the Divine Prescience. *General Magazine*, Vol. I, No. 3 (March, 1741), 201–02.

Obituary of Andrew Hamilton. *Gazette*, August 6, 1741.

Obituary of James Merrewether. *Gazette*, April 22, 1742.

I Sing My Plain Country Joan, [c. 1742]. *Father Abraham's Speech To a great Number of People, at a Vendue of Merchant-Goods; Introduced to the Publick by Poor Richard, A famous Pennsylvania Conjurer, and Almanack-Maker,* . . . Boston: Benjamin Mecom, [1758], 24.

A Proposal for Promoting Useful Knowledge Among the British Plantations in America, May 14, 1743. Philadelphia: Broadside.

*Apology for the Young Man in Goal. *The American Weekly Mercury*, September 15, 1743.

An Over-Masted Privateer. *Gazette*, July 5, 1744.

American Privateers. *Gazette*, August 30, 1744.

Account of Louisburgh (with *woodcut). *Gazette*, June 6, 1745. Woodcut reproduced with permission of The Library Company of Philadelphia.

Old Mistresses Apologue, June 25, 1745. *Papers*, III, 30–31.

The Antediluvians Were All Very Sober, [c. 1745]. *Papers*, III, 52.

*Appreciation of George Whitefield. *Gazette*, July 31, 1746.

The Speech of Miss Polly Baker. *The Maryland Gazette*, August 11, 1747.

*Whitefield's Accounts. *Gazette*, April 23, 1747.

Verses on the Virginia Capitol Fire. *The New-York Gazette, revived in the weekly Post-Boy*, June 1, 1747, supplement.

*The Necessity of Self-Defence. *Gazette*, December 29, 1747, supplement.

Devices and Mottoes of the Associators. *Gazette*, January 12, 1747/8; April 16, 1748.

Advice to a Young Tradesman, Written by an Old One, July 21, 1748. George Fisher, *The American Instructor: or Young Man's Best Companion* . . . 9th ed., rev. and corr. (Philadelphia: B. Franklin and D. Hall, 1748), 375–77.

Proposals Relating to the Education of Youth in Pensilvania, October, 1749. *Proposals Relating to the Education of Youth in Pensilvania* (Philadelphia: [B. Franklin and D. Hall], 1749).

*Rules Proper to be Observed in Trade. *Gazette*, February 20, 1749/50.

Rules for Making Oneself a Disagreeable Companion. *Gazette*, November 15, 1750.

Idea of the English School, January, 1751. Richard Peters, *A Sermon on Education. Wherein Some Account is given of the Academy, Established in the City of Philadelphia. Preach'd at the Opening thereof, on the Seventh Day of January, 1750–1* (Philadelphia: [B. Franklin], 1751). Paginated separately and bound with the sermon.

*Course of Experiments. *Gazette*, April 11, 1751.

On Transported Felons. *Gazette*, April 11, 1751.

Rattle-Snakes for Felons. *Gazette*, May 9, 1751.

Appeal for the Hospital. *Gazette*, August 8, 1751; August 15, 1751.

Observations Concerning the Increase of Mankind, Peopling of Countries, &c., 1751. [William Clarke], *Observations On the late and present Conduct of the French, with Regard to their Encroachments upon the British Colonies in North America. . . . To which is added, wrote by another Hand; Observations concerning the Increase of Mankind, Peopling of Countries, &c.* (Boston: S. Kneeland, 1755).

The Kite Experiment. *Gazette*, October 19, 1752.

Join or Die (with Snake Cartoon). *Gazette*, May 9, 1754. Cartoon reproduced with permission of The Library Company of Philadelphia.

The Albany Plan of Union, July 10, 1754. *Papers*, V, 387–92.

Reasons and Motives for the Albany Plan of Union, July, 1754. *Vaughan*, 85–119. "Remark, Feb. 9. 1789" from *Papers*, V, 417.

No Taxation Without Representation: Three Letters of 1754 to Governor William Shirley, with a Preface of 1766. Preface, first letter and letter of December 22: *The London Chronicle*, February 8, 1766. Letter of December 4: *Papers*, V, 443–47.

A Dialogue between X, Y, and Z, Concerning the Present State of Affairs in Pennsylvania. *Gazette*, December 18, 1755.

A Parable Against Persecution, 1755. *Papers*, VI, 122–24.

A Parable on Brotherly Love, 1755. *Papers*, VI, 126–28.

LETTERS

Jane Franklin, January 6, 1726/7. *Duane*, VI, 3.

James Logan [1737?]. *Papers*, II, 184–85.

Josiah and Abiah Franklin, April 13, 1738. *Papers*, II, 202–04.

Jane Mecom, July 28, 1743. *Papers*, II, 384–85.

John Franklin, [May?], 1745. *Sparks*, VII, 16–17.

James Read, August 17, 1745. *The Port Folio* I (1801), 165–66.

Cadwallader Colden, [February, 1746]. *Papers*, III, 67–68.

[Thomas Hopkinson?], [October 16, 1746]. *Papers*, III, 84–89.

Jane Mecom, [June, 1748]. Jared Sparks, ed., *A Collection of the Familiar Letters and Miscellaneous Papers of Benjamin Franklin* (Boston: C. Bowen, 1833), 10–15.

George Whitefield, July 6, 1749. *The Evangelical Magazine* XI (London, 1803), 27–28.

Jared Eliot, February 13, 1749/50. *Papers*, III, 463–66.

James Parker, March 20, 1750/1. Archibald Kennedy, *The Importance of Gaining and Preserving the Friendship of the Indians to the British Interest, Considered* (New York: James Parker, 1751), 27–31.

John Franklin, December 8, 1752. *Papers*, IV, 385–87.

Peter Collinson, [1752?]. *E&O*, 350–54. Magic square reproduced with permission of The Library Company of Philadelphia.

Peter Collinson, [1752?]. *E&O*, 354–56. Magic circle reproduced with permission of The Library Company of Philadelphia.

John Perkins, February 4, 1753. *Papers*, IV, 429–42. Plate (p. 460) and illustration (p. 464) from *E&O* (facing p. 226 and p. 229, respectively) reproduced with permission of The Library Company of Philadelphia.

Cadwallader Colden, February 28, 1753. *Papers*, IV, 446–49.

Peter Collinson, May 9, 1753. *Papers*, IV, 479–86.

Joseph Huey, June 6, 1753. *Papers*, IV, 504–06.

Catharine Ray, March 4, 1755. *Papers*, V, 502–04.

Joshua Babcock, September 1, 1755. *Papers*, VI, 174–75.

Catharine Ray, October 16, 1755. *Papers*, VI, 225.

William Shipley, November 27, 1755. *Papers*, VI, 275–77.

Elizabeth Hubbart, February 22, 1756. *The Massachusetts Magazine, or Monthly Museum of Knowledge and Rational Entertainment*, I (1789), 100.

John Lining, April 14, 1757. *Papers*, VII, 184–90. Drawing from Franklin's manuscript reproduced from *Papers*, VII, 186 (restored).

Jane Mecom, April 19, 1757. *Papers*, VII, 190–91.

Jane Mecom, May 30, 1757. *Duane*, VI, 18–20.

LONDON, 1757–1775

William Franklin to the Printer of the *Citizen*: A Defense of the Quakers and the Pennsylvania Assembly. *Gentleman's Magazine* (September, 1757), 417–18; *The London Chronicle*, September 20, 1757.

A Letter from Father Abraham, to His Beloved Son. *The New-England Magazine*, Vol. I, No. 1 (August, 1758), 20–28.

A New Englandman to the Printer of the *London Chronicle*: A Defense of the Americans. *London Chronicle*, May 12, 1759.

A Description of Those, Who, at Any Rate, Would Have a Peace with France. *London Chronicle*, November 24, 1759.

Humourous Reasons for Restoring Canada. *London Chronicle*, December 27, 1759.

The Jesuit Campanella's Means of Disposing the Enemy to Peace. *London Chronicle*, August 13, 1761.

A Narrative of the Late Massacres. *A Narrative of the Late Massacres* (Philadelphia: Anthony Armbruster, 1764).

The Duke of York's Travels. *Public Advertiser*, May 15, 1765.

The Grand Leap of the Whale. *Public Advertiser*, May 22, 1765.

Invectives Against the Americans. *Gazetteer and New Daily Advertiser*, December 28, 1765.

The Mother Country, [c. 1765]. *Papers*, XII, 431–32.

On the Prospects of War in America. *Public Advertiser*, January 2, 1766.

"Homespun" Celebrates Indian Corn. *Gazetteer and New Daily Advertiser*, January 2, 1766.

On the Paving of Chancery Lane. *Gazetteer and New Daily Advertiser*, January 4, 1766.

On the Tenure of the Manor of East Greenwich. *Gazetteer and New Daily Advertiser*, January 11, 1766.

"Two Taylors." *Gazetteer and New Daily Advertiser*, January 14, 1766.

"Homespun's" Further Defense of Indian Corn. *Gazetteer and New Daily Advertiser*, January 15, 1766.

Pax Quæritur Bello. *Public Advertiser*, January 26, 1766.

On Chastising the Colonies. *London Chronicle*, February 13, 1766.

The Frenchman and the Poker. *Pennsylvania Chronicle*, March 23, 1767.

A Mock Petition to the House of Commons, April 12–15, 1766. *Papers*, XIII, 241–42.

Contempt for the Thames. *Public Advertiser*, August 22, 1766.

On the Price of Corn, and Management of the Poor. *London Chronicle*, November 29, 1766.

The Misrepresentation of America. *London Chronicle*, April 9, 1767.

Reply to Coffee-House Orators. *London Chronicle*, April 9, 1767.

Right, Wrong, and Reasonable. *Gazetteer and New Daily Advertiser*, April 18, 1767.

Of Lightning, and the Method (Now Used in America) of Securing Buildings and Persons from Its Mischievous Effects. *E&O*, 479–85.

American Longevity. *London Chronicle*, December 15, 1767.

Railing and Reviling. *Gazetteer and New Daily Advertiser*, January 6, 1768.

Causes of the American Discontents Before 1768. *London Chronicle*, January 7, 1768.

On a Proposed Act to Prevent Emigration, [December?], 1773. *Papers*, XX, 522–28.

On Franklin's Ingratitude, [before January 31, 1774]. *Papers*, XXI, 72–73.

"A War It Will Be," [after March 9, 1774]. *Papers*, XXI, 134–38.

An Open Letter to Lord North. *Public Advertiser*, April 15, 1774.

A Method of Humbling Rebellious American Vassals. *Public Advertiser*, May 21, 1774.

*An Act for the More Effectual Keeping of the Colonies Dependent. *Pennsylvania Journal*, June 29, 1774.

An Imaginary Speech. *Public Advertiser*, February 7, 1775.

A Dialogue Between Britain, France, Spain, Holland, Saxony, and America, [February?] 1775. *Papers*, XXI, 601–04.

A Proposed Memorial to Lord Dartmouth, March 16, 1775. *Papers*, XXI, 527–28.

Proposed Articles of Confederation, July 21, 1775. *Papers*, XXII, 122–25.

Resolutions on Trade Submitted to Congress, July 21, 1775. *Papers*, XXII, 127–28.

*Account of the Devices on the Continental Bills of Credit. *Pennsylvania Gazette*, September 20, 1775.

The King's Own Regulars. *Pennsylvania Evening Post*, March 30, 1776.

Bradshaw's Epitaph. *Pennsylvania Evening Post*, December 14, 1775.

*The Rattle-Snake as a Symbol of America. *Pennsylvania Journal*, December 27, 1775.

What Would Satisfy the Americans? [1775]. *Papers*, XXI, 599–600.

LETTERS

———, December 13, 1757. *Papers*, VII, 294–95.

John Pringle, December 21, 1757. *Papers*, VII, 298–300.

John Pringle, January 6, 1758. *E&O*, 362.

John Lining, June 17, 1758. *E&O*, 363–68.

Jane Mecom, September 16, 1758. *Papers*, VIII, 152–55.

Hugh Roberts, September 16, 1758. *Papers*, VIII, 159–61.

Lord Kames, January 3, 1760. *Papers*, IX, 5–10.

Jane Mecom, January 9, 1760. *Papers*, IX, 17–19.

Lord Kames, May 3, 1760. *Papers*, IX, 103–06.

Peter Franklin, May 7, 1760. *E&O*, 379–80.

Mary Stevenson, June 11, 1760. *Papers*, IX, 119–22.

Mary Stevenson, September 13, 1760. *Papers*, IX, 212–17. Illustration reproduced with permission of the Library of Congress (restored).

David Hume, September 27, 1760. *Papers*, IX, 227–30.

Mary Stevenson, [November? 1760]. *Papers*, IX, 247–52.

John Baskerville, [1760?]. *General Evening Post*, August 11, 1763.

Peter Franklin, [c. 1761]. *E&O*, 473–78. Music reproduced with permission of The Library Company of Philadelphia.

David Hume, May 19, 1762. *Papers*, X, 82–84.

Giambatista Beccaria, July 13, 1762. *E&O*, 427–33. Illustration reproduced with permission of The Library Company of Philadelphia.

Oliver Neave, July 20, 1762. *E&O*, 435–37.

John Pringle, December 1, 1762. *E&O*, 438–40.

Jared Ingersoll, December 11, 1762. *Papers*, X, 174–76.

Mary Stevenson, March 25, 1763. *Papers*, X, 231–35.

John Waring, December 17, 1763. *Papers*, X, 395–96.

William Strahan, December 19, 1763. *Papers*, X, 406–08.

John Fothergill, March 14, 1764. *Papers*, XI, 101–04.

Peter Collinson, April 30, 1764. *Papers*, XI, 180–83.

Sarah Franklin, November 8, 1764. *Papers*, XI, 448–50.

Lord Kames, June 2, 1765. *Papers*, XII, 158–65.

Charles Thomson, July 11, 1765. *Papers*, XII, 206–08.

Jane Mecom, March 1, 1766. *Papers*, XIII, 187–89. Illustration reproduced with permission of The Library Company of Philadelphia (restored).

Deborah Franklin, April 6, 1766. *Papers*, XIII, 233–34.

Cadwalader Evans, May 9, 1766. *Hazard's Register of Pennsylvania* XVI, 5 (August 1, 1835), 65.

Joseph Galloway, November 8, 1766. *Papers*, XIII, 487–88.

Mary Stevenson, September 14, 1767. *Papers*, XIV, 250–55.

Margaret Stevenson, November 3, [1767]. *Papers*, XIV, 299–300.

Jane Mecom, December 24, 1767. *Papers*, XIV, 344–45.

William Franklin, January 9, 1768. *WTF*, II, 151.

Jean Chappe d'Auteroche, January 31, 1768. *Papers*, XV, 33–34.

John Pringle, May 10, 1768. *E&O*, 492–96.

Jacques Barbeu-Dubourg, July 28, 1768. *The American Museum*, VIII (July, 1790), 120. Misdated July 21 in *American Museum*.

John Alleyne, [August 9, 1768]. *Papers*, XV, 183–85.

Mary Stevenson, October 28, 1768. *Papers*, XV, 244–45.

———, November 28, 1768. *WTF*, II, 169–70.

Oliver Neave, [before 1769]. *E&O*, 463–68.

John Bartram, July 9, 1769. *Papers*, XVI, 172–73.

George Whitefield, [before September 2, 1769]. Joseph Belcher, *George Whitefield* (New York, 1857), 414–15.

Mary Stevenson, September 2, 1769. *Papers*, XVI, 193–94.

Timothy Folger, September 29, 1769. *Papers*, XVI, 207–10.

William Strahan, November 29, 1769. *Papers*, XVI, 243–49.

[Charles Thomson], March 18, 1770. *Papers*, XVII, 111–13.

Mary Stevenson, May 31, 1770. *Papers*, XVII, 152–53.

Samuel Cooper, June 8, 1770. *Papers*, XVII, 161–65.

Mary Stevenson Hewson, July 18, 1770. *Papers*, XVII, 194–95.

Deborah Franklin, October 3, 1770. *Papers*, XVII, 239–40.

Jane Mecom, December 30, 1770. *Papers*, XVII, 313–16.

Thomas Percival, [June? 1771]. *Memoirs of the Literary and Philosophical Society of Manchester*, II (1785), 110–13.

Jane Mecom, July 17, 1771. *Papers*, XVIII, 184–87.

Anna Mordaunt Shipley, August 13, 1771. *Papers*, XVIII, 199–202. Misdated
August 12 in manuscript, according to *Papers*.

Joshua Babcock, January 13, 1772. *Papers*, XIX, 6–7.

Ezra Stiles, January 13, 1772. *Papers*, XIX, 30–31.

Anthony Benezet, August 22, 1772. *Papers*, XIX, 269.

Samuel Rhoads, August 22, 1772. *Papers*, XIX, 278–79.

Joseph Priestley, September 19, 1772. *Papers*, XIX, 299–300.

Georgiana Shipley, September 26, 1772. *Papers*, XIX, 301–03.

William Marshall, February 14, 1773. *Papers*, XX, 71–72.

Samuel Mather, July 7, 1773. *Papers*, XX, 286–89.

Benjamin Rush, July 14, 1773. *Papers*, XX, 314–16.

William Franklin, October 6, 1773. *Duane*, VI, 332–34.

Peter P. Burdett, November 3, 1773. *Papers*, XX, 459–60.

William Brownrigg, November 7, 1773. *Papers*, XX, 463–74.

Josiah Tucker, February 12, 1774. *Papers*, XXI, 83–85.

Josiah Tucker, February 26, 1774. *Papers*, XXI, 125–28.

Joseph Priestley, April 10, 1774. Joseph Priestley, *Experiments and
Observations on Different Kinds of Air*, 3 vols. (London: J. Johnson,
1774–77), I, 321–23.

William Strahan, July 5, 1775. *Papers*, XXII, 85.

[Joseph Priestley], July 7, 1775. *Vaughan*, 552–54.

David Hartley, October 3, 1775. *Vaughan*, 555–56.

PARIS, 1776–1785

The Sale of the Hessians, February 18, 1777. *Smyth*, VII, 27–29.

Model of a Letter of Recommendation, April 2, 1777. *Papers*, XXIII, 549–50.

The Twelve Commandments, March 10, 1778. *Smyth*, X, 437–38.

Petition of the Letter Z, [c. August, 1778]. *The Letters of Benjamin Franklin
& Jane Mecom*, ed. Carl Van Doren (Princeton: Princeton University
Press, 1950), 256–57.

The Ephemera, September 20, 1778. Gilbert Chinard, "Random Notes on
Two 'Bagatelles,'" *Publications of the American Philosophical Society*, 103
(1959), 741, 744.

The Elysian Fields (M. Franklin to Madame Helvétius), December 7, 1778.
Amacher, 54–56. Copyright 1953 by the Trustees of Rutgers College in
New Jersey.

Bilked for Breakfast (Mr. Franklin to Madame la Freté), [c. 1778]. *Bagatelles*,
12–13. Trans. Willard Trask. Copyright 1967 The Eakins Press
Foundation.

Passport for Captain Cook, March 10, 1779. *Smyth*, VII, 242–43.

The Morals of Chess, June, 1779. *Smyth*, VII, 357–62.

The Whistle, November 10, 1779. *Passy*.

The Levée, [1779?]. *Smyth*, VII, 430–32.

Proposed New Version of the Bible, [1779?]. *Smyth*, VII, 432–33.

Drinking Song (To the Abbé de La Roche, at Auteuil), [1779?]. *WTF*, III, 345–47.

A Tale, [1779?]. *Bagatelles*, 27. Trans. Willard Trask. Copyright 1967 The Eakins Press Foundation.

On Wine (From the Abbé Franklin to the Abbé Morellet), [1779?]. *Bagatelles*, 54–59. Trans. Willard Trask. Copyright 1967 The Eakins Press Foundation. Drawings reproduced from the *Mémoires inédits* of the Abbé Morellet with permission of The Library Company of Philadelphia.

Dialogue Between the Gout and Mr. Franklin, October 22, 1780. *Bagatelles*, 34–45. Trans. Willard Trask. Copyright 1967 The Eakins Press Foundation.

The Handsome and the Deformed Leg, November, 1780. *Amacher*, 100–02. Copyright 1953 by the Trustees of Rutgers College in New Jersey.

To the Royal Academy of *****, [c. 1781]. *Passy*.

Notes for Conversation, April 18, 1782. *Smyth*, VIII, 471–72.

Supplement to the Boston Independent Chronicle, April, 1782. *Supplement to the Boston Independent Chronicle*, 2d ed., printed by Franklin on his press at Passy, France.

Articles for a Treaty of Peace with Madame Brillon, July 27, 1782. *Benjamin Franklin's Autobiographical Writings*, ed. Carl Van Doren (New York: Viking Press, 1945), 584–86. Copyright 1945 Carl Van Doren. Reprinted by permission of Viking Penguin Inc.

Apologue, [c. November, 1782]. *Smyth*, VIII, 650–51.

Remarks Concerning the Savages of North-America, 1783. *Passy*.

Information to Those Who Would Remove to America, February, 1784. *Passy*.

An Economical Project, April 26, 1784. *Smyth*, IX, 183–89. Printed in the *Journal de Paris*, April 26, 1784.

Loose Thoughts on a Universal Fluid, June 25, 1784. *Smyth*, IX, 227–30.

The Flies (To Madame Helvétius), [1784?]. *Bagatelles*, 14–15. Trans. Willard Trask. Copyright 1967 The Eakins Press Foundation.

LETTERS

Lord Howe, July 20, 1776. *Papers*, XXII, 519–21.

Emma Thompson, February 8, 1777. *Papers*, XXIII, 297–99.

—— Lith, April 6, 1777. *Papers*, XXIII, 557–59.

[Lebègue de Presle], October 4, 1777. *Papers*, XXV, 25–26.

Arthur Lee, April 3, 1778. *Smyth*, VII, 132.

Charles de Weissenstein, July 1, 1778. *Smyth*, VII, 166–72.

David Hartley, February 3, 1779. *Smyth*, VII, 226–29.

Sarah Bache, June 3, 1779. *Smyth*, VII, 346–50

Edward Bridgen, October 2, 1779. *Smyth*, VII, 381–82.

Elizabeth Partridge, October 11, 1779. *Smyth*, VII, 393–94.

John Paul Jones, October 15, 1779. *Smyth*, VII, 395–96.

Benjamin Vaughan, November 9, 1779. *Smyth*, VII, 410–13.

Joseph Priestley, February 8, 1780. *Smyth*, VIII, 9–12.

George Washington, March 5, 1780. *Smyth*, VIII, 27–79.

Thomas Bond, March 16, 1780. *Smyth*, VIII, 37–38.

William Carmichael, June 17, 1780. *Smyth*, VIII, 98–100.

Samuel Huntington, August 9, 1780. *Smyth*, VIII, 124–30.

John Jay, October 2, 1780. William Jay, *The Life of John Jay: with Selections from his Correspondence and Miscellaneous Papers*, 2 vols. (New York: J. & J. Harper, 1833), II, 62–64.

Richard Price, October 9, 1780. *Smyth*, VIII, 153–54.

Benjamin Waterhouse, January 18, 1781. *Smyth*, VIII, 194–95.

John Adams, February 22, 1781. *Smyth*, VIII, 211–12.

Court de Gebelin, May 7, 1781. *Smyth*, VIII, 246–48.

Comte de Vergennes, June 10, 1781. *Smyth*, VIII, 263–66.

William Jackson, July 10, 1781. *Smyth*, VIII, 281–84.

William Nixon, September 5, 1781. *Smyth*, VIII, 298–99.

William Strahan, December 4, 1781. *Smyth*, VIII, 335–36.

John Adams, December 17, 1781. *Smyth*, VIII, 347–48.

Robert R. Livingston, March 4, 1782. *Smyth*, VIII, 388–94.

John Adams, April 22, 1782. *Smyth*, VIII, 432–33.

Joseph Priestley, June 7, 1782. *Smyth*, VIII, 451–53.

Richard Price, June 13, 1782. *Smyth*, VIII, 457–58.

Miss Alexander, June 24, 1782. *Smyth*, VIII, 458–59.

James Hutton, July 7, 1782. *Smyth*, VIII, 561–63.

Robert R. Livingston, August 12, 1782. *Smyth*, VIII, 576–80.

The Marquis de Lafayette, September 17, 1782. *Smyth*, VIII, 595–96.

The Abbé Soulavie, September 22, 1782. *Transactions of the American Philosophical Society*, III (Philadelphia, 1793), 1–5.

Comte de Vergennes, December 17, 1782. *Smyth*, VIII, 642–43.

Mary Hewson, January 27, 1783. *Smyth*, IX, 11–13.

Robert R. Livingston, July 22, 1783. *Smyth*, IX, 59–73.

Sir Joseph Banks, July 27, 1783. *Smyth*, IX, 73–75.

Sir Joseph Banks, August 30, 1783. *Smyth*, IX, 79–85.

John Jay, September 10, 1783. *The Diplomatic Correspondence of the American Revolution*, ed. Jared Sparks (Boston: N. Hale and Gray & Bowen, 1829–30), IV, 163–64.

Robert Morris, December 25, 1783. *Smyth*, IX, 135–40.

———, [January, 1784?]. *Smyth*, IX, 149–50.

Sarah Bache, January 26, 1784. *Smyth*, IX, 161–68.

William Strahan, February 16, 1784. *Smyth*, IX, 171–73.

La Sabliere de la Condamine, March 19, 1784. *Smyth*, IX, 181–83.

Samuel Mather, May 12, 1784. *Smyth*, IX, 208–10.

Charles Thomson, May 13, 1784. *Smyth*, IX, 212–14.

Mason Locke Weems and Edward Gant, July 18, 1784. *Smyth*, IX, 238–40.

William Franklin, August 16, 1784. *Smyth*, IX, 252–54.

William Strahan, August 19, 1784. *Smyth*, IX, 259–64.

Joseph Priestley, August 21, 1784. *Smyth*, IX, 266–67.

Richard Price, March 18, 1785. *Smyth*, IX, 300–01.

George Whatley, May 23, 1785. *Smyth*, IX, 331–39. Illustration, from Franklin's manuscript, reproduced with permission of the Library of Congress.

PHILADELPHIA, 1785–1790

A Petition of the Left Hand, 1785. *Smyth*, X, 125–26.

Description of an Instrument for Taking Down Books from High Shelves, January, 1786. *Smyth*, VI, 552. Illustration from *Sparks*, VI, 562, reproduced with permission of The Library Company of Philadelphia.

The Art of Procuring Pleasant Dreams, May 2, 1786. *Smyth*, X, 131–37.

The Retort Courteous, 1786. *Smyth*, X, 105–16.

Speech in the Convention on the Subject of Salaries, June 2, 1787. *Smyth*, IX, 590–95.

Speech in a Committee of the Convention on the Proportion of Representation and Votes, June 11, 1787. *Smyth*, IX, 595–99.

Motion for Prayers in the Convention, June 28, 1787. *Smyth*, IX, 600–01.

Speech in the Convention at the Conclusion of its Deliberations, September 17, 1787. *The Documentary History of the Constitution*, ed. John P. Kaminski and Gaspare J. Saladino (Madison: State Historical Society of Wisconsin, 1981), XIII, 213–214.

On Sending Felons to America, 1787. *Smyth*, IX, 628–30.

A Comparison of the Conduct of the Ancient Jews and of the Anti-Federalists in the United States of America, [c. 1788]. *Smyth*, IX, 698–703, from the manuscript in the Library of Congress. Printed in *The Federal Gazette* (Philadelphia), April 8, 1788.

On the Abuse of the Press, [after March 30, 1788]. *Smyth*, IX, 639–42.

An Account of the Supremest Court of Judicature in Pennsylvania, viz. The Court of the Press, September 12, 1789. *The Federal Gazette* (Philadelphia), September 12, 1789.

An Address to the Public from the Pennsylvania Society for Promoting the Abolition of Slavery, and the Relief of Free Negroes Unlawfully Held in Bondage, November 9, 1789. *Smyth*, X, 66–68.

Plan for improving the Condition of the Free Blacks, [1789?]. *Smyth*, X, 127–29.

Sidi Mehemet Ibrahim on the Slave Trade, March 23, 1790. *Smyth*, X, 87–91, from the manuscript in the Library of Congress. Printed in *The Federal Gazette* (Philadelphia), March 25, 1790.

LETTERS

Jonathan Shipley, February 24, 1786. *Smyth*, IX, 488–91.

Benjamin Vaughan, July 31, 1786. *Smyth*, IX, 530–33.

Rev. John Lathrop, May 31, 1788. *Smyth*, IX, 649–52.

Benjamin Vaughan, October 24, 1788. *WTF*, II, 113–14.

John Langdon, 1788. Lewis J. Carey, *Franklin's Economic Views* (Garden City, New York: Doubleday, Doran & Company, 1928), 87–88. Used by permission of Doubleday & Company, Inc.

Jane Mecom, August 3, 1789. *The Letters of Benjamin Franklin & Jane Mecom*, ed. Carl Van Doren (Princeton: Princeton University Press, 1950), 327–28.

John Wright, November 4, 1789. *Smyth*, X, 60–63.
Noah Webster, December 26, 1789. *Smyth*, X, 75–82.
Ezra Stiles, March 9, 1790. *Smyth*, X, 83–86.

The present volume reprints the prefaces, maxims, and a selection of short items thought to have been written by Franklin from the original *Poor Richard's Almanack* printed in Philadelphia by Franklin from 1733 to 1758. The calendars, meteorological data, and other contents have been omitted. The maxims, printed in italics in the originals to distinguish them from the surrounding material in which they were embedded, are printed in roman type here (with styling accordingly reversed).

The text of the *Autobiography* presented here is a newly prepared clear text, derived from the genetic text edited by J. A. Leo Lemay and P. M. Zall, which was prepared from the manuscript in the Huntington Library in San Marino, California (*The Autobiography of Benjamin Franklin: A Genetic Text*. Ed. J. A. Leo Lemay and P. M. Zall. Knoxville: Univ. of Tennessee Press, 1981). The genetic text prints Franklin's cancellations and revisions, using a system of typographical sigla to indicate interlinear interpolations, marginal interpolations, superscriptions, etc. The cancellations are omitted here (along with the related editorial sigla), as are punctuation marks associated with cancellations but left uncanceled themselves. (A few of the more interesting canceled phrases and passages are reproduced in the notes to the present volume.) Franklin's revisions are printed here without the editorial sigla indicating interlinear interpolations, marginal insertions, and canceled words or phrases. Conjectural readings of undecipherable words, printed within square brackets in the genetic text, are accepted here, and printed without brackets.

Some emendations have been necessary in the preparation of this clear text, due to the unfinished nature of Franklin's manuscript. In a number of places, extra punctuation has been omitted. In some cases, the extraneous punctuation occurs where Franklin evidently finished a sentence, then continued it without canceling his previous mark of punctuation. In other cases, punctuation associated with a canceled phrase was left uncanceled itself, or punctuation was rendered superfluous or redundant when Franklin revised a passage, but didn't cancel the superseded punctuation. Where a sentence plainly ends, but Franklin did not punctuate it, a period has been added; no period has been added, however, after the last word of the *Autobiography*. And where Franklin added a word to an italicized passage (or inserted it in a context where parallel words were italicized) but did not italicize the added word, the present text italicizes it. Finally, Franklin's notes, queries, and reminders to himself in the manuscript (e.g., indicating the placement of texts to be added) have been omitted.

Certain other emendations have also been made and are recorded below. In a few places the sense of a passage demanded that a mark of punctuation be added, altered, or omitted for the sake of intelligibility. Spelling, if plainly incorrect (or a slip of the pen), is emended. In six places, Franklin inadvertently repeated a word, and in ten places redundancies indicate that he was considering alternative phrasings but neglected to cancel one of them; the present text emends accordingly (choosing in most cases his second alternative as the more likely), and records the emendation. In the following list, the word or words preceding the bracket are those of the present text, and the words after the bracket are those of the genetic text edition: 1309.39, beloved."] beloved.; 1339.39, if] if if; 1340.30, Watson] Watson Watson; 1341.18, Task] Task Task; 1344.36, ought to] should ought to; 1345.23, that] that,; 1347.39, advanc'd] advan'd; 1350.2, Woman,] Woman; 1350.5, revered,] revered; 1351.9, Wygate,] Wygate.; 1353.26, seeing] seeᵍing; 1353.35, 28,] 28.; 1353.37, Stationary,] Stationary; 1354.28, Work:] Work; 1363.25, Journeyman] Joureyman; 1365.16, then] now then; 1371.17, Situation,] Situation; 1371.25, invalid,] invalid; 1379.24, considerable,] considerable.; 1384.6–7, Care was employ'd] *Attention was taken up* Care was employ'd; 1390.2, But] but; 1390.7, exactly] exastly; 1390.11, it] *Method* it; 1391.17, *Temperance*] *Temperance.*; 1391.40, which] whch; 1392.28, rare,] rare; 1394.3, be] by; 1395.31, the] the the; 1395.33, wise] wiss; 1395.38, BF."—] BF.—; 1397.4, Occupations] Occupapations; 1401.27, Educating] Eduting; 1422.17, so."—] so.—; 1422.28, for] towards for; 1424.26, least] leas; 1426.13, obstructed the] obstructed the the; 1426.17, flat] flatt flat; 1431.28, *pursue.*"] *pursue.*; 1435.22, brought] brought,; 1435.28, Baggage,] Baggage.; 1444.11, you] "you; 1444.12, taken?"] taken?; 1444.14, Uncertainty."—] Uncertainty.—; 1446.16, whimsicall] whimsicll; 1447.29, And] Qu and; 1448.17, the Sides] th Sides; 1448.24, even] evon; 1448.31, punctually] puctually; 1450.33, Opinion,] Opinion.; 1454.19, decry] oppose decry; 1458.14, presenting] presenteding; 1458.19, conformable; agreable conformable; 1459.8, detain'd,] detain'd.; 1459.38, the] thr; 1461.6–7, others,] others.; 1461.24, Business.] Business,; 1465.3, occasion'd] accosion'd; 1466.15, they] the; 1466.39, me,] me.; 1467.18, Paper] Pager.

The genetic text edition inadvertently omits four of the black "Spots" from the illustration of a page of the "Book" in which Franklin recorded his daily offenses against virtue (page 1387 in the present volume). One of the missing spots is on the line corresponding to the second virtue, "Silence," in the column under "Friday"; two are under "Tuesday," on the lines corresponding to the fourth and sixth virtues, "Resolution" and "Industry"; and the fourth is on the line corresponding to the fifth virtue, "Frugality," in the column under "Thursday." In addition, a question mark was omitted and a period substituted after the word "breakfast" in the diagram of the "Scheme of Employment" (page 1389 in the present volume). These have been corrected here.

Franklin never completed his writing and revision of the *Autobiography*, and the text as we have it manifests its unfinished character in various ways. The dashes that appear throughout the manuscript have been retained, even though they may be a manuscript convention that Franklin would not have printed; likewise, manuscript conventions preserved in the genetic text such as ampersands, abbreviations, and superscript characters are printed here as they appeared in the manuscript. Spelling has been neither modernized nor regularized, and original spellings have been retained. Thus the Reverend George Whitefield, for example, appears here variously as *Whitefiel*, *Whitfield*, and *Whitefield*. Ordinary eighteenth-century spellings such as *deny'd*, *publick*, *learnt*, *agreable*, *compleat*, *surpriz'd*, *Cloaths*, *intituled* (or *entituled*), and *chuse*—as well as unusual spellings (some of which are possibly, but not certainly, slips of the pen) such as *werre*, *Sope*, *Wharff*, *Surff*, *beforre*, *Compostors*, *Matras*, *Risque*, *renderd*, *deliverd*, *lenthend*, *Lightnin*, *observ*, *som*, and *Percedings*— have been left unaltered. Some of these spellings have a "phonetic" character and may reflect Franklin's interest in spelling reform (see his phonetic alphabet in the present volume). Italics and large and small capitals indicated by Franklin in the manuscript are followed here. The several supplemental texts that Franklin wished to insert in his manuscript (i.e., the note on the name Franklin, his uncle Benjamin's poems, the *Pennsylvania Gazette* editorial of October 9, 1759, the letters from Abel James and Benjamin Vaughan, the Golden Verses of Pythagoras, and the wagon advertisement) have been printed within the text where Franklin indicated; the texts are from the appendices to the genetic text edition. The title, which is customary ("The Autobiography"), has been added by the editor, although it is not in the manuscript and Franklin usually referred to his manuscript as "Memoirs"; the part titles (e.g., "Part One") are also customary and have been added by the editor.

Throughout this volume, conventional features of eighteenth-century writing (spelling and punctuation) and printing, such as italics for proper names and place names and large and small capitals, have been preserved, since Franklin can be presumed to have authorized them. Only obvious typographical and orthographical errors have been corrected, and these corrections are listed below. The long "s" has been printed as the modern short "s" throughout, and ligatures (except æ and œ digraphs) have been printed as separate letters. Footnote symbols have been reordered to correspond, where necessary, to new pagination. In eighteenth-century printing, quotation marks were placed at the beginning of every line of an extended quotation, but in the present volume only the opening quotation mark has been retained (and a closing quotation mark added where needed).

The *Papers* and *Writings*, as well as the William Temple Franklin, Sparks, and Vaughan editions, modernize and regularize Franklin's orthography in various ways. The *Papers*, for instance, omits some dashes and commas, disregards the italicization of proper nouns, expands contractions, spells out abbreviations, brings superscript letters down to the line, and prints "and" for the ampersand. In pieces reprinted from the *Papers* and other editions, the present volume eliminates editorial comment from the text. For instance, where the editors of the *Papers* print "[illegible]" to indicate that the manuscript they are transcribing cannot be read, the present volume simply indicates an indecipherable word or words by brackets—i.e., "[   ]"—and prints Franklin's interlinear revisions without the word or words canceled in the process (if any) and without brackets. The present volume also accepts the conjectural readings of words (faded or otherwise obscured in the manuscript) that are supplied in a few places by the editors of the *Papers* and the other editions. Usually printed in brackets and sometimes in italics in those editions, they are given without brackets and in roman type here. Editorial comments such as "(*sic*)" have been omitted. Franklin's name at the end of letters has also been omitted. Finally, in a few places, long verse or prose extracts (or other extended passages) printed in italics in the original texts have been printed in roman type in the present volume; styling has accordingly been reversed in these passages, with roman type being set in italics.

This volume is concerned with presenting the texts of the selections included; it does not attempt to reproduce features of their typographic design, such as the display capitalization of chapter and paragraph openings. It does, however, reproduce capital letters for substantives, italic and boldface type, superscript letters, large and small capitals, and other typographical features, where the original texts have preserved them. In a letter to Noah Webster, December 26, 1789 (pp. 1173–78 in the present volume), Franklin decried the disuse of these typographical conventions, and explained what he took to be their functions. To the extent that modern typesetting will allow, therefore, this volume preserves those features. The following is a list of the typographical errors corrected, cited by page and line number: 8.15, good-humoue'd; 16.15, Folly,;; 24.28, Law.; 25.34, *provocatoine*; 26.10, *& quæ*; 27.31, Clery; 28.2, deceas'd,; 28.14, connlude; 32.2, and and; 34.7,

Apperance; 36.18, it it; 37.13–14, Sgnification; 41.9, exempllified; 47.16, Innoeence; 50.12, Aguments; 53.36, the the; 57.4, *Fute*; 62.14, otherwise *e.*; 67.20, throughly; 103.26, The The; 108.23, *Instructor.*; 110.32, mnch; 115.30, perhas; 116.36, Couuntry; 117.22, Admiinstration; 117.22, wrethed; 117.38–39, Vassals;:; 119.29, *at at*; 120.20, a; 130.36, Currency; 135.6, *Arpil*; 136.34, Papers,,; 139.21, People to); 143.27–28, *Pontack's*]; 146.7, *Travellee*; 156.1, Committe; 159.20, uncasiness; 162.3, Falsites; 194.22, able challenge; 195.22, Peple; 196.31, evercise; 197.36, Observatious; 204.20, the; 205.13, surprining; 207.37, Yes.; 218.11, Mug; 222.19, the the; 222.27, more more; 222.31, mrny; 233.22, the these; 235.19, Po); 236.18, Preliminaries.; 241.29, makes; 258.3, Apostle's; 261.31, *which which*; 273.31, Verses.; 274.33, *Stcokdale*; 277.19, Diversion.; 280.15, *"doubtless*; 282.40, Prosceution; 288.37, the e; 291.8, directy; 304.26, WATTTS; 311.29, *Northwest*; 313.23, Mishap.; 320.30-31, industriousMan; 327.24, Editions); 331.7, That; 333.37, I am; 336.32, †Rules; 338.3, Wrirers; 359.18, Colonies."; 367.25, Observaions; 371.21, Chlidren; 373.5, *Guiuea*; 411.7, &c.; 419.8, *enga e*; 428.4, is a; 453.1, 280; 510.29, o her; 520.29, regions; 529.39, proo; 531.16, S me; 532.34, India; 561.34, it ever; 563.37, p per; 564.28, *right.*; 570.38, assemblis; 572.14, question; 572.18, were the; 576.30, become; 577.14, it is; 577.31, box-in-the ear; 594.11, Rebe lion; 595.35, Bovnty; 596.23, unreasonasonable; 597.25, purch sing; 598.11, *Wroug*; 599.15, hebts,"; 599.36, yoe; 601.14, suble; 606.27, lunaticks," sworn; 632.19, Ð is; 675.3, at at; 695.33, thusand; 699.18–19, *amancipated*; 723.29, Regulus; 776.37, who; 792.29, the the; 861.23, any any; 922.34, Music; 923.28, our; 980.31, being; 980.31, oy; 980.32, an; 981.2, sey; 981.4, wil; 981.15, to; 1139.4, it"; 1166.20, if, it; 1168.6, —"Having; 1185.16, desire; 1186.27, effect effect; 1186.30, rainy.; 1187.12, head; 1187.16, fleas; 1187.25, preach; 1188.7, spurs,; 1188.28, afte; 1191.4, things; 1194.4, can; 1194.12, him; 1196.13, behind; 1197.6, deny; 1197.21, milk; 1197.30, 2; 1201.20, people; 1203.38, & and; 1203.39, 5 *s*; 1204.32, cats; 1205.12, said; 1206.17, t'other; 1206.19, for for; 1208.9, you; 1208.12, himself; 1208.20, ou; 1209.5, hour; 1209.9, on; 1209.15, Lead; 1209.24, error; 1210.15, Ingnorant; 1210.21, Mouth; 1211.1, J—m n; 1213.18, tongue; 1217.15, immortal; 1218.24, ti; 1219.17, cheek by-jole; 1220.11, she'as; 1229.4, beware,; 1229.25, nine:; 1230.18, so It is so;;

Notes

In the notes below, the reference numbers denote page and line of the present volume (the line count includes titles). No note is made for material included in a standard desk-reference book. Footnotes in the text are Franklin's own. Translations of classical authors in the notes below are from volumes of the Loeb Classical Library unless otherwise indicated; citations from James Thomson's *The Seasons* are to the line counts in the edition by James Sambrook (Oxford: At the Clarendon Press, 1981). For further biographical information than is provided in the Chronology, see James Parton, *Life and Times of Benjamin Franklin*, 2 vols. (Boston: Ticknor & Fields, 1864), Carl Van Doren, *Benjamin Franklin* (New York: The Viking Press, 1938), Claude-Anne Lopez and Eugenia W. Herbert, *The Private Franklin: The Man and His Family* (New York: W. W. Norton & Company, 1975), and Esmond Wright, *Franklin of Philadelphia* (Cambridge, Massachusetts: The Belknap Press of Harvard Univ. Press, 1986). For historical information on many of the pieces printed in the present volume, see the headnotes and annotations in relevant volumes of *The Papers of Benjamin Franklin*, ed. Leonard W. Labaree, William B. Willcox et al., 25 vols. to date (New Haven: Yale Univ. Press, 1959–). The scholarship of the *Papers* has been an essential aid in preparation of the present volume. See also the annotations, background materials, and bibliography in the Norton Critical Edition of Franklin's *Autobiography*, ed. J. A. Leo Lemay and P. M. Zall (New York: W. W. Norton & Company, 1986).

BOSTON AND LONDON, 1722–1726

5.1   *Silence Dogood*]   The pseudonym mocked Cotton Mather by referring to two of his publications, *Silentarius* (1721) and *Bonifacius or Essays to Do Good* (1710).

5.19–28   At the . . . *Widow.*]   This passage burlesques the inadvertently ludicrous account of the death of John Avery in Cotton Mather's *Magnalia Christi Americana* (1702), Book Three, Second Part, Chapter 1.

10.18   *An . . .* Cicero.]   *De Finibus* 2. 5. "Or do I still require lessons in the use of either Greek or Latin?"

14.2   *Mulier . . .* Ter.]   Terence *Phormio* 4. 5. 14. ("mulier mulieri magis convenit") "A woman is best to deal with a woman."

15.28   ingenious Writer]   Daniel Defoe, *An Essay upon Projects* (1697). The quotation (15.32–16.14, "I have . . . wiser"), from pp. 282–84, is slightly abridged.

17.7–9   *Quem* . . . Seneca.] *Thyestes* 613–14. "Whom the rising sun hath seen high in pride, him the setting sun hath seen laid low."

19.8–12   *Give* . . . Watts.] Isaac Watts, "The Adventurous Muse," in *Horae Lyricae* (2d ed., 1709), ll. 30–33.

20.3–6   *The Muse . . . reigns.*] Isaac Watts, "Two Happy Rivals, Devotion and the Muse," in *Horae Lyricae* (2d ed., 1709), ll. 11–14.

20.25   *GUNSTON . . . Young*] Isaac Watts, "To the Dear Memory of my Honour'd Friend, Thomas Gunston," in *Horae Lyricae* (2d ed., 1709), l. 4.

21.10–11   *Nor* . . . Watts.] Isaac Watts, "The Adventurous Muse," in *Horae Lyricae* (2d ed., 1709), l. 6.

21.28   *A RECEIPT . . . ELEGY.*] An imitation of Alexander Pope's "Receipt to make an Epic Poem," *The Guardian*, No. 78 (June 10, 1713). *The Guardian* was a periodical published by Richard Steele in London in 1713.

21.31   Ætatis Suæ] "Of his (or her) age." The phrase preceded the age of the deceased.

22.17   Mæstus Composuit] "Written in sadness."

22.26–27   *Mater . . . matrem.*] In the June 18 issue of the *Courant*, "Hypercarpus" had argued that pride of heart is the cause of pride of apparel, not its result (as Mrs. Dogood had claimed in No. 6). Her answer to "Hypercarpus" translates roughly as follows: "My mother gave birth to me, and eventually the daughter will give birth to a mother."

23.1   *Doctor* H——k] Dr. John Herrick (fl. 1697–1722) was, like Mrs. Mehitabel Kittel (d. 1718), a resident of Beverly, Massachusetts.

23.16   LAW] Tom Law, of Concord, Massachusetts, wrote popular poetry.

24.4   following Abstract] John Trenchard and Thomas Gordon, "Cato's Letters," No. 15, *London Journal* (Feb. 4, 1720/1).

25.9–10   *Audivit . . . est.*] Tacitus *Annales* 4. 42.

26.2–3   *Queri . . . Odimus*] Pliny *Panegyricus* 68. "We may well complain that it is only the rulers we hate who violate our privacy."

26.9–10   *Rara . . . licet.*] Tacitus *Historiae* 1. 1.

26.27   *Corruptio . . . pessima.*] "The best, when corrupted, are the worst."

26.31–32   hypocritical . . . Religion] Contemporaries would have applied this description to Governor Joseph Dudley (d. 1720) and especially to Chief Justice Samuel Sewall (1652–1730).

28.14 a Paragraph or two] John Trenchard and Thomas Gordon, "Cato's Letters," No. 31, *London Journal* (May 27, 1721).

29.10 *Optimè . . . Cic.*] Cicero *De Officiis* I. 16. ("Optime autem societas hominum coniuntioque servabitur") "The interest of society, however, and its common bonds will be best conserved."

29.14–15 a Book] Daniel Defoe, *An Essay upon Projects* (1697). The quoted passage (29.22–32.37, 'We have . . . Widow') is from pp. 132–41.

31.30–31 *Volenti . . . Injuria*] "Injury is not wished for."

33.22 *Neque . . . visere.*] Plautus *Cistellaria* 227. "I was not allowed to come and see my darling during all that time."

35.23 *Quod . . . ebrii.*] Proverbial. "What is in the hearts of the sober is in the mouths of the drunken."

36.19–26 "It has . . . Rhetorick."] *The Spectator*, No. 247 (Dec. 13, 1711). *The Spectator* was a daily periodical published by Joseph Addison and Richard Steele in London in 1711 and 1712. Franklin mentions its early influence on him in his *Autobiography* (p. 1319 in the present volume).

39.30–31 *Earum . . . Cicero.*] *De Senectute* 5. ("Earum, si placet, causarum quanta quamque sit iusta une quaeque videamus") "Let us, if you please, examine each of these reasons separately and see how much truth they contain."

40.14–15 Clergymen at *Connecticut*] Timothy Cutler (1684–1765) and Daniel Browne (1696–1772), rector and tutor, respectively, at Yale College, and Samuel Johnson, minister at West Haven, Connecticut, abandoned New England Congregationalism in the fall of 1722 and became Anglican ministers.

40.22 *Corah*-like Rebellion] Numbers 16. The spelling *Corah* rather than *Korah*, however, may suggest that Franklin also had John Dryden's characterization of Titus Oates, the fabricator of the Popish Plot, in mind (*Absalom and Achitophel* [1681], I, 632ff).

40.28–29 a Statesman . . . Tale-Bearers.] Another reference to Cotton Mather, whose son Increase was well known as a rake and a beau.

40.34–41.18 'I would . . . former.'] *The Spectator*, No. 185 (Oct. 2, 1711). The quotation (41.12–13, "*Video . . . sequor*") is from Ovid *Metamorphoses* 7. 20. *The Spectator* supplies Nahum Tate's translation: "I see the Right, and I approve it too; / Condemn the Wrong, and yet the Wrong pursue."

41.19–42.4 'I have . . . Church.'] *The Guardian*, No. 80 (June 12, 1713).

44.6 *Vide . . . agas.*] "Behold what you have set in motion."

46.20−21   Lines . . . *Hudibras*]   The "Essay against Hypocrites" in the
Courant, January 14, 1723, was prefaced by a motto from Samuel Butler,
Hudibras (1663, 1664, 1680).

46.37   *Corah-like* Usurpation]   See note 40.22.

47.28−48.14   I humbly . . . ignorant.]   Echoes and mocks the Reverend
Increase Mather's condemnation of James Franklin in *The Boston Gazette*,
January 29, 1721/2.

48.7   *Summum . . . injuria.*]   Cicero *De Officiis* I. 10. 33. "More law, less
justice."

48.33   an Error]   On January 14, 1696/7, Samuel Sewall stood up in the
Old South Church while the minister read aloud before the congregation
Sewall's confession of "Blame and Shame" for his role as a judge in the Salem
witchcraft trials.

49.2   *Mero . . . credit.*]   Petronius *Satyricon* 37. "If she tells him at high
noon it's dark, he'll believe her" (trans. John Sullivan [Penguin, 1965]).

49.26−50.7   'Honour . . . expressed.']   This passage parodies William
Penn, *No Cross, no Crown: Or several Sober Reasons Against Hat-Honour,
Titular-Respects* . . . (1669), pp. 8, 11−12.

51.33−35   Notions . . . *Whiston*, &c.]   Franklin is probably reflecting the
criticisms of the religio-scientific theories of Thomas Burnet, Erasmus Warren, and William Whiston by John Keill, *An Examination of Dr. Burnet's
Theory* (1698).

52.2   *Quô . . . diu.*]   Horace *Epistles* I. 2. 69. "The jar will long keep the
fragrance of what it was once steeped in when new."

52.15   Discourse]   Rev. Thomas Symmes, *Utile Dulci, Or, A Joco-Serious
Dialogue, Concerning Regular Singing* (1723).

54.11−55.3   'Certainly . . . *Heaven*.']   Thomas Pope Blount, *Essays on several Subjects* (Third impression, with very Large Additions, 1697), pp. 244−
46.

55.22   his Discourse]   Franklin may have had in mind a sermon by William Cooper (1692−1743) arguing that "the End and Design of God in the
Institution of Marriage . . . was . . . the Supply and Increase of his Church
with a holy Seed." *God's Concern for a Godly Seed* (1723).

57.3−8   *Whatever . . .* Dryd.]   John Dryden, *Oedipus* (1679), III, i, 244−
48.

57.9   Mr. *J. R.*]   James Ralph (c. 1705−62), Franklin's friend, is character-
ized in the *Autobiography* (p. 1340 in the present volume).

59.34−35   *The Religion of Nature*]   Franklin had just set the type for
the third edition of William Wollaston, *The Religion of Nature Delineated*

(London: Samuel Palmer, 1725), which was advertised for sale at the end of February, 1724/5.

72.1   *Plan of Conduct*]   Composed while Franklin was aboard ship, as part of a journal he kept during his voyage from England to America, the "Plan" survives only in this incomplete form. Mentioned in the *Autobiography* (p. 1353 in the present volume).

PHILADELPHIA, 1726–1757

83.2   IN TWO PARTS.]   Part II is not known to be extant.

83.3–6   Here . . . Cato.]   Joseph Addison, *Cato. A Tragedy* (1713), V, i, 15–18.

84.38   See Junto Paper]   This essay may survive in a revised version, for Franklin's "A Man of Sense" essay (pp. 244–48 in the present volume) also concludes that "the Science of Virtue" is necessary to man's happiness.

85.24   Powerful Goodness, &c.]   The prayer Franklin evidently intended to insert here is included in the *Autobiography* (1388.26–30 in the present volume).

86.25–27   Ray's . . . God]   John Ray, *The Wisdom of God manifested in the Works of the Creation* (1691); Richard Blackmore, *Creation: A Philosophical Poem* (1712); François de Salignac de la Mothe Fénelon, *A Demonstration of the Existence and Attributes of God*, trans. A. Boyer (1713).

86.31   Milton's . . . Creator]   John Milton, *Paradise Lost* (1667), V, 153–55, 160–204.

90.20   End of the First Part.]   See note 83.2.

92.1   *The Busy-Body*]   In the file of *The American Weekly Mercury* in the Library Company of Philadelphia, someone (possibly Franklin) has written in the margin of the February 18 issue: "The Busy Body was begun by B.F. who wrote the first four Numbers, part of N.º 5, part of N.º 8 the rest by J. Brintnal." Further notations in the same hand identify those portions of Nos. 5 and 8 written by each of the two authors. Joseph Breintnall (d. 1746) was one of the first members of the Junto; Franklin describes him in the *Autobiography* (p. 1361 in the present volume). See also notes 108.14 and 111.8 below.

94.15–16   *All Fools . . . Pope.*]   Alexander Pope, *An Essay on Criticism* (1711), ll. 32–33.

96.6–9   *Non vultus . . . Hor.*]   Horace *Odes* 3. 3. 3–6. "Not by the face of a threatening tyrant, not by Auster, stormy master of the restless Adriatic, not by the mighty hand of thundering Jove."

98.1–6   *The Brave . . . Rowe.*]   Nicholas Rowe, *The Fair Penitent* (1703), II, ii, 34–38.

98.35–38   like the . . . thee?] An echo of Thomas Pope Blount, quoted by Timothy Wagstaff above (see note 54.11–55.3).

99.19   *Nequid nimis.*] Terence *Andria* 61. "Moderation in all things."

102.22–24   *Withdraw . . . thee.*] Proverbs 25:17.

104.14   Tiff-Club] A club of Philadelphia tradesmen organized by former Governor William Keith in 1726.

104.23–24   *Vos . . .* Persius.] Persius *Satires* 1. 61–62. "O ye blue-blooded patricians, you who have to live without eyes in the back of your head, turn round and face the gibing in your rear!"

107.20–31   I conceal . . . Morning.] An imitation of *The Spectator*, No. 579 (Aug. 11, 1714).

108.14   *Noli me tangere.*] John 20:17. "Touch me not." The initials "B.F." appear opposite this section of the essay in *The American Weekly Mercury* file in the Library Company of Philadelphia.

111.8   *The Busy-Body, No. 8*] Marginal notations in *The American Weekly Mercury* file in the Library Company of Philadelphia indicate that Franklin wrote the first section (111.9–112.21), Breintnall wrote the letter of Titan Pleiades (112.22–113.15), and Franklin wrote the remainder. Breintnall's pseudonym mocked the New Jersey almanac author Titan Leeds (1699–1738).

111.9–10   *Quid . . .* Virgil.] *Aeneid* 3. 56–57. "To what extremes will you not drive the heart of men, accurst hunger for gold!"

115.9–11   every Cod . . . Eight] Franklin may echo similar statements commonly found in Captain John Smith: "let not the meannesse of the word fish distaste you, for it will afford as good gold as the Mines of *Guiana* or *Potossie.*" *General History of Virginia* (1624), last sentence.

116.1–118.5   *Monday . . .* Virtues.] This late addition to the eighth "Busy-Body" was withdrawn from later printings of this issue of *The American Weekly Mercury*. It is known to survive in only one copy, in the Library of Congress. Franklin's insinuations (at 116.26–27 and 117.36–39) that the Proprietors and their appointed governor were opposed to issuing paper money because of their own greed was controversial, and evidently was the reason for suppressing the addition.

116.13–16   *EXPERIENCE . . .* Country] The paper-currency acts of 1723 stimulated the economy and were generally popular.

116.26–27   *That it . . . Home.*] Franklin suggests that Governor Patrick Gordon (1663–1736) was forbidden by the Proprietors of Pennsylvania to pass another paper-currency act.

119.3–6   *Quid . . .* Pers.] Persius *Satires* 3. 69–71. "What good there is in fresh-minted coin; how much should be spent on country and on your dear kin."

126.37–127.11   By Labour . . . *paribus*.]   Adapted from William Petty, *A Treatise of Taxes and Contributions* (1662), ch. IV, secs. 13–14, and ch. V, sec. 10.

127.11   *cæteris paribus*]   "All other things being equal."

131.26–29; 32–35   we must . . . buy; But if . . . self.]   Adapted from William Petty, *A Treatise of Taxes and Contributions* (1662), chap. V, sec. 3.

135.5   *B. B.*]   The initials suggest that the author is the "Busy-Body."

136.5   Chambers's . . . Dictionaries]   Samuel Keimer (c. 1688–1742), from whom Franklin bought the *Gazette*, had been printing, a page or more at a time, Ephraim Chambers' *Cyclopaedia*, 2 vols. (1728).

136.33   *Religious Courtship*]   Keimer had begun printing Daniel Defoe's *Religious Courtship* (1722) piecemeal in the April 24, 1729, *Gazette*.

137.23   *"One Piles a Fidler"*]   Like other humorous or odd short news notes that follow, this jeu d'esprit was a piece of "filler" Franklin composed to take up space in a column.

139.30   11 o'Clock]   The copies examined of this issue of *The Pennsylvania Gazette* are all defective in this place; it may read "1 o'Clock."

143.22   *Printerum est errare.*]   "To err is [to be a printer]."

144.13   *Spectator*'s Remark]   *The Spectator*, No. 579 (Aug. 11, 1714).

145.12   *Drummer* of *Tedsworth*.]   The Drummer of Tidworth, Wiltshire, who haunted John Mompeson from 1661 to 1663, is the subject of a popular ballad, "A Wonder of Wonders" (1662/3), and also turns up in all the popular witchcraft books of the late seventeenth century. Franklin knew the story from Increase Mather's *An Essay for the Recording of Illustrious Providences* (1684), pp. 156–58, and Joseph Addison's play *The Drummer* (1716). It also figures in William Hogarth's print of *Credulity, Supersition, and Fanaticism.*

147.16–17   *Greutzius . . . Sagarum*]   Evidently Franklin made up the author and title.

151.27–28   *Ver . . . Catul.*]   "The new spring, now harmonious spring, in spring the world is born: In spring loves are in harmony, in spring they marry one another."

152.1–4   *Fælices . . . Horat.*]   Horace *Odes* I. 13. Translated at 155.7–12 (from *The Odes, Satyrs, and Epistles of Horace. Done into English.* Trans. Thomas Creech [1684], p. 21).

157.18–28   In 1716 . . . Certainty.]   Paraphrased from Edmund Halley's account in the *Philosophical Transactions* 29 (1714–16), p. 406.

158.1–8; 11–18   *Our Fathers . . . Rome.; Their Fathers . . . done.*]   The verses are reprinted from *The New-York Gazette* (Nov. 2, 1730), and refer to the quarrel over Governor Jonathan Belcher's salary.

158.28   *Veritas . . . clarior.*]   "Truth is brighter than light."

161.17–18   *As a . . .* Apocrypha.]   Ecclesiasticus 27:2.

163.1–2   *On the Providence . . . World*]   This essay, unpublished by Franklin, was composed for the Junto.

169.2–3   *Mors . . .* Juv.]   Juvenal *Satires* 10. 172–73. "Death alone proclaims how small are our poor human bodies!"

169.4–5   *Post . . . aquis.*]   "After death good deeds remain, eternally; Virtue fears not the Styx and is not carried away by its waters."

174.7–8   *Poets . . . blot*;]   Edmund Waller, "Upon the Earl of Roscommon's Translation of Horace," ll. 41–42, substituting "Were it but" for "Could it be," following *The Spectator*, No. 179 (Sept. 25, 1711).

182.26–31   Cunning . . . Dissemblers.]   Francis Bacon, *Essays* (1625), No. 22, "Of Cunning," and No. 6, "Of Simulation and Dissimulation."

185.7–28   About . . . Management.]   Compare the courtship account in the *Autobiography* (p. 1370 in the present volume). Evidently Thomas Godfrey (1704–49) considered his family insulted by this skit, and so took away the business of printing his almanac from Franklin, who then began *Poor Richard*.

192.9   *Impia . . .* Ovid.]   *Amores* 1. 8. 104. "Wicked poisons have for hiding-place sweet honey."

192.10   *Naturam . . .* Hor.]   Slightly changed from Horace's *Epistles* 1. 10. 24. ("Naturam expelles furca, tamen usque recurret") "You may drive out Nature with a pitchfork, yet she will ever hurry back."

208.3   P S and A N]   Possibly Philip Syng (1703–89) and Anthony Nicholas (d. 1751). Syng, an Irish-born silversmith, was a member of the original Junto; he is mentioned in the *Autobiography* (p. 1416 in the present volume). Anthony Nicholas (or Nichols), a blacksmith, was, with Franklin, a director of the Library Company.

218.33   *Set a . . .* Chesh.]   Proverbial, evidently identified here as a Cheshire saying. "Set a Beggar on Horseback and he'll ride a gallop."

219.31–33   an unnatural . . . Image.]   In Daniel 2:33, the feet are "part of iron and part of clay."

224.38–39   the ancient . . . Mire]   Aesop's fable of Hercules and the Carter.

225.9–11   *Hi mores . . .* Lucan.]   *Pharsalia* 2. 380–82. "Such was the character, such the inflexible rule of austere Cato—to observe moderation and hold fast to the limit, to follow nature, to give his life for his country."

228.5–6   *Ostendunt . . .* Virgil.]   *Aeneid* 6. 869–70. "Him the fates shall but show to earth, nor longer suffer him to stay."

228.19–26   To see . . . Master:] Luke 16:19–21.

230.24   Jesus . . . wept.] John 11:33, 35.

231.6–7   melancholy . . . Subject.] *The Pennsylvania Gazette* for August 1, 1734, reprinted a "Meditation on the Vanity and Brevity of Human Life" from Rev. Joshua Smith's *A Select Manual of Divine Meditations* (2d ed., London, 1733).

232.8–9   *eating . . . Heart.*] Ecclesiastes 9:7.

240.37   Club . . . Engine] The Boston Fire Society was established in 1717.

251.16–17   the Fox . . . Tail] Aesop's fable "The Fox Without a Tail."

251.26–252.3   Our Maker . . . *Milton.*] John Milton, *Paradise Lost* (1667), IV, 748–57, 760–61, 763–67.

252.4–253.13   BUT happy . . . *Thomson.*] James Thomson, *The Seasons*, "Spring," ll. 1113–25, 1135–60, 1166–74.

256.14   *Mr. H.*] Franklin described himself in the *Autobiography* as the "zealous Partisan" of Rev. Samuel Hemphill (fl. 1734–35), a Presbyterian minister from Ireland, against whom the older Presbyterian minister Rev. Jedediah Andrews (1674–1747) brought charges on April 7, 1735. See the *Autobiography* (pp. 1399–1400 in the present volume).

257.7–9   *What doth . . . God.*] Micah 6:8.

257.20   Mr. *Grew*] Theophilus Grew (d. 1759) taught school in Philadelphia before being appointed professor of mathematics in the Academy and College of Philadelphia in 1751.

258.10–11   *He that . . . Infidel.*] A paraphrase of 1 Timothy 5:8.

272.15–16   *Poeta . . . fit*] Proverbial. "A poet is born, not made."

272.16–17   *Almanackorum . . . fit.*] "[An almanac writer] is born, not made."

272.24–28   I have . . . Family.] This reference and succeeding ones are all to Titan Leeds, *American Almanac for . . . 1736.*

272.32–33   Book . . . *England*] Arthur Collins, *The Peerage of England* (1709).

273.26–27   *"But no . . . Poesy."*] Wentworth Dillon, Earl of Roscommon, *Horace: Of the Art of Poetry: A Poem* (1709), ll. 417–18. (*Ars Poetica*: ". . . mediocribus esse poetis non homines, non di, non concessere columnae. . . .")

274.36   violent] A copy of this issue of the *Gazette* in the New York Public Library has "unruly" instead of "violent."

275.31   the Outcry]   In the *Gazette* of May 1, 1740, Franklin printed a brief news item: "Since Mr. *Whitefield*'s Preaching here, the Dancing School, Assembly and Concert Room have been shut up, as inconsistent with the Doctrine of the Gospel: And though the Gentlemen concern'd caus'd the Door to be broke open again, we are inform'd that no Company came the last Assembly Night." The dancing school's leaders objected to the report's claim that Whitefield's opposition had led them to close their doors, and in a letter to the *Gazette* in the May 8 issue they made the distinction between the "BETTER SORT" and the "meaner Sort" that Franklin, as Obadiah Plainman, then heaped scorn upon.

284.18–19   following Piece]   Ebenezer Kinnersley's "A Letter . . . to a Friend in the Country," which appeared as a postscript to this *Gazette*, objected to the emotionalism and enthusiasm accompanying the Great Awakening.

284.19   *Cummings*'s Sermons]   Andrew Bradford had just printed Archibald Cummings' *Faith Absolutely Necessary, but Not Sufficient to Salvation without Good Works* (1740).

286.4–8   It appears . . . Parts]   Franklin echoes the diction used in the House of Commons Resolution of April 25, 1740.

293.9–10   *Servetur . . . constet.*]   Horace *Ars Poetica* 126–27. "Have it kept to the end even as it came forth at the first, and have it self-consistent."

298.1–2   Apology . . . Goal]   In *The Pennsylvania Gazette* for August 25, 1743, there appeared the following news item: "Last Sunday a young Fellow about 20 Years of Age was brought to Town from Whitemarsh and committed to Prison, being charg'd with Ravishing a poor old Woman upwards of Eighty, and injuring her so that her Life is tho't to be in Danger." William Coulter was acquitted of rape but found guilty of assault (*Gazette*, Sept. 29, 1743); the woman was reported, the next year, to be "lately married" (*Gazette*, Dec. 18, 1744).

300.1   PLAN . . . *LOUISBURGH*]   The woodcut was probably executed by Franklin himself. This was the first illustrated news event in the *Gazette*.

310.26   * * * * *]   Franklin was parodying the speech (omitted here) of Virginia Governor Sir William Gooch (1681–1751) to the General Assembly, which he had printed in *The Pennsylvania Gazette* of May 14. The capitol at Williamsburg had burned on January 30, 1747.

313.18   *Carthagena*]   Gooch commanded a force of 400 Virginians at the British attack on Cartagena, 1740. He had been made a baronet on November 4, 1746.

315.1   Chap. xx]   Actually, Chapter 22.

317.7–9   Quid . . . *liceret.*]   Cicero *Pro T. Annio Milone* 10. "What is the meaning of the swords that we carry? We should certainly not be permitted to have them, were we never to be permitted to use them."

318.21   PRO PATRIA]   "For country."

318.24–25   UNITA VIRTUS VALET]   "Virtue united prevails."

318.27   A DEO VICTORIA]   "From God, victory."

318.29–30   INESTIMABILIS]   "Priceless."

318.32   DEUS ADJUVAT FORTES]   "God helps the strong."

318.35   SEMPER PARATUS]   "Always ready."

319.1–2   SALUS . . . LEX]   "The nation's health, the highest law."

319.4   SIC PACEM QUERIMUS]   "Thus we seek peace."

319.7–8   PRO ARIS ET FOCIS]   "For our altars and our hearths."

319.20   Vis Unita Fortior]   "Force is strengthened by union."

319.21–22   Pro Rege & Grege]   "For the king and the people."

319.26   Cavendo Tutus]   "Safe by caution."

319.28   In Nomine Domini]   "In the name of the Lord."

319.30–31   Domine Protege Alimentum]   "Lord, protect our food."

319.34–35   Spero . . . vincere]   "I hope by God to conquer."

319.36–37   Pro Deo . . . Rege]   "For God and King George."

319.38   Pro Libertate Patriæ]   "For the liberty of my country."

323.24–324.16   AUTHORS . . . 1742.]   John Milton, *Paradise Regain'd . . . With a Tractate of Education* (1721); John Locke, *Some Thoughts Concerning Education* (1745); David Fordyce (*not* Francis Hutcheson), *Dialogues on Education*, 2 vols. (1745–48); Obadiah Walker, *Of Education* (1687); Charles Rollin, *The Method of Studying and Teaching the Belles Lettres*, 4 vols. (1749); George Turnbull, *Observations upon Liberal Education, In all its Branches* (1742).

324.38   *Belles Lett. p.* 249]   Vol. 4.

326.14–21   *'Tis Joy . . . Breast.*]   James Thomson, *The Seasons*, "Spring," ll. 1147, 1150–56.

334.33   *Brightland*'s, *Greenwood*'s]   John Brightland, *A Grammar of the English Tongue* (1711); James Greenwood, *An Essay towards a practical English Grammar* (1711).

335.10   *Helvicus*]   Christopherus Helvicus, *The Historical and Chronological Theatre* (1687).

335.37   *Montfaucon*] Bernard de Montfaucon, *L'Antiquité expliquée et representée en figures*, 5 vols. (1719).

340.13–14   *Arbuthnot . . . Foods*] John Arbuthnot, *An Essay Concerning the Effects of Air on Human Bodies* (1733) and *An Essay concerning the Nature of Aliments*, 2 vols. (1731–32); *Medicina Statica: being the Aphorisms of Sanctorius* (1712); and Louis Lémery, *Traité des Aliments* (1702).

340.38–39   *Ray's . . . Nature*] John Ray, *The Wisdom of God manifested in the Works of the Creation* (1691); William Derham, *Physico-Theology* (1713); [Nöel A. Pluche], *Le Spectacle de la Nature*, 8 vols. (1732–51).

348.27   *Croxall's Fables*] Samuel Croxall, *Fables of Aesop and others* (1722).

351.2–3   *Rollin's . . . Histories*] Charles Rollin, *The Ancient History of the Egyptians . . . and Grecians*, 10 vols. (1738–40); *The Roman History . . .* 16 vols. (1739–50).

351.14–15   *Spectacle de la Nature*] [Nöel A. Pluche], *Le Spectacle de la Nature*, vol. 2 (1733).

352.6   *Sir William . . . Pope*] Sir William Temple, *Letters*, 3 vols. (1700–03); *Letters of Mr. Pope and several eminent persons*, 2 vols. (1735).

352.11–12   *Dr. Johnson's . . . Morality*] Samuel Johnson, *Ethices Elementa, Or, The first principles of moral philosophy* (1746).

352.38–353.1   *Dr. Johnson's . . . Knowledge*] Samuel Johnson, *Noetica: Or the first Principles of Human Knowledge* (which Franklin would publish in 1752).

353.12   *Telemachus . . . Cyrus*] François de Salignac de la Mothe Fénelon, *Les aventures de Telemaque, fils d'Ulysse* (1699); Chevalier Andrew Ramsay, *Les Voyages de Cyrus* (1727; English trans. by N. Hooke, 1730).

361.13–14   *Post . . . Aquis*] See note 169.4–5.

362.9   Parable] Luke 10:30–37.

362.18   *Dives*] Luke 16:19–21.

362.25–29   *I was . . . Mankind*] Paraphrasing Matthew 25:34–46.

362.33   Lepers . . . cleansed] Luke 17:11–19.

362.39   *Samaritan*] See note 362.9.

364.14–15   *Homines . . . Orat.*] Cicero *Pro Q. Ligario* 38. "For in nothing do men more nearly approach divinity than in doing good to their fellow-men."

365.13   Extract] Daniel Defoe, *A Tour thro' the Whole Island of Great Britain* (3d ed., 1742), III, 293–94.

374.5   *Palatine Boors*]   See Chronology, 1764.

384.33   do. [   ]]   Benjamin Vaughan, whose edition is the source of the present text, had a row of asterisks here, possibly indicating an abridgement.

386.3   the [   ]]   Here Vaughan, after a row of asterisks, inserted a note: *"The remainder of this article is lost."*

386.4   **III. *Plan* . . .**]   Passages in boldface type, which are articles of the "Plan" that Franklin is explaining, were printed by Vaughan in large type.

401.13   Remark . . . 1789.]   Franklin sent this "Remark" to Matthew Carey (1760–1839) when Carey was preparing to reprint the "Reasons and Motives" in his *American Museum* in 1789. Carey reprinted the document to show that the Constitution, just taking effect, was prefigured in Franklin's plan of colonial union. At Franklin's request the "Remark" was appended by Carey without Franklin's signature.

402.1–3   *No Taxation . . . 1766*]   The prefatory letter was written in 1766 when Franklin republished (in *The London Chronicle*, Feb. 8, 1766) the letters he had written to Shirley in 1754.

408.26–27   Royal Instructions]   In 1744 and 1749 the House of Commons rejected bills to make royal instructions to the governors binding on the colonies.

424.26   Chapter . . . Virtue]   From Logan's ethical treatise, "The Duties of Man Deduced from Nature," never published and now lost.

429.15–16   *in . . . libello*]   Written by Thomas a Kempis in a copy of his *De Imitatione Christi*. "Repose is sought in all things, but is not found, unless in a quiet corner with a little book."

429.18   *in . . . puella*]   "In a corner with a girl."

429.19   in . . . *puellae*]   "In a girl's angle."

431.27–28   ANDREW . . . SOUL"]   Andrew Baxter, *Enquiry into the Nature of the Human Soul* (3d ed., 1745).

439.27   *ad Exemplum Regis*]   "The king's example."

442.32   Manuscript]   By Archibald Kennedy, published as *The Importance of Gaining and Preserving the Friendship of the Indians to the British Interest, Considered* (1751); this letter of Franklin's would be printed as an endorsement on pp. 27–31.

448.17   *difficiles nugæ*]   "Difficult trifles."

449.5–6   *See Plate.*]   This "square of 8" is reproduced in the present volume on p. 460 (Fig. III).

450   *A Magic Square of Squares.*]   There are two typographical errors in the magic square: the box in the upper right-hand corner should read "185" and the tenth box down in the seventh column should read "211."

463.22   Fig. I]   Reproduced on p. 460 in the present volume.

463.23   Fig. II]   Reproduced on p. 460 in the present volume.

467.17–18   your Book]   Colden's *Explications of the First Causes of Action in Matter* (1745), translated into German by Abraham Gotthelf Kästner, who added his objections. Colden's reply to Kästner's criticisms is the text to which Franklin refers at 466.25–27.

468.17   *Magnis . . . ausis.*]   Ovid *Metamorphoses* 2. 328. "Greatly failed, more greatly dared."

474.19–23   sometimes . . . lost.]   John Milton, *Paradise Lost* (1667), XII, 97–101. Franklin substituted "descend" for "decline" in the first line, and reversed "reason" and "virtue" in the second.

478.30–31   A Wit's . . . God.]   Alexander Pope, *An Essay on Man* (1732–34), Epistle IV, ll. 247–48.

480.23   little Paper]   "Observations Concerning the Increase of Mankind" (pp. 367–74 in the present volume).

481.23   relation]   John Franklin (1690–1756), Franklin's brother and Elizabeth Hubbart's stepfather.

488.14   Sister Douse]   Franklin and Jane Mecom's half sister, Elizabeth Douse (1678–1759).

489.6   Cousin Williams]   Jonathan Williams, Jr. (1750–1815), a grandnephew.

LONDON, 1757–1775

505.1–4   *William Franklin . . . Assembly*]   Franklin himself undoubtedly wrote the preface for *The Gentleman's Magazine* as well as the account of the dispute. Although he knew that the Penns were responsible for the newspaper attacks on the Pennsylvania Assembly, he also knew that he would be blamed for vindicating the Assembly (he was then negotiating with the Penns on behalf of the Assembly) if the reply appeared under his name. Therefore he published his account under his son's name.

506.38   *Gentleman's Magazine*]   Founded in 1731, *The Gentleman's Magazine* soon became the most popular English monthly magazine of the eighteenth century.

511.24   *The London Chronicle*]   *The London Chronicle, or Universal Evening*

Post, an evening paper, was printed three times a week by William Strahan, a printer who was one of Franklin's closest English friends.

520.10–12   His . . . *English.*]   Franklin evidently believed the author to be the Scots physician, poet, and playwright Dr. Adam Thomson (1712?–1767), who emigrated to America about 1741 and is best known for his "American method" of inoculation.

527.6–10   'The emptying . . . tables.']   Franklin is paraphrasing himself here. See "On Transported Felons" (pp. 357–59 in the present volume; the paraphrased passage is at 358.37–40.)

533.39   Histoire . . . XII.]   Pierre F. X. de Charlevoix, *Histoire et Description generale de la Nouvelle France*, 3 vols. (1744), I, 559–62.

535.11–12   Of the . . . *Monarchie*]   Franklin himself wrote this imitation of a baroque seventeenth-century prose style and attributed it to the "Jesuit" Campanella (who was actually a Dominican) because both Campanella and the Jesuits had reputations as sinister intriguers.

547.33–548.11   Unhappy . . . *Poor.*]   Homer, *Odyssey*, trans. Alexander Pope (1725–26), XIV, 41–44, 53–54, 57–68.

548.21–26   Doubtless . . . *more.*]   *Odyssey*, trans. Pope, XIV, 443, 445–49.

548.32–549.5   We turn'd . . . *delight.*]   *Odyssey*, trans. Pope, XIV, 299–300, 305–15.

549.11–16   Ah no! . . . *dy'd.*]   *Odyssey*, trans. Pope, XXIII, 63–68.

550.15–25   "The Religion . . . Security."]   John Bell, *Travels from St. Petersburgh*, 2 vols. (1763), II, 465.

550.29   famous Instance]   This anecdote and the following ones were probably created by Franklin.

558.35   Mercy . . . *Brave.*]   *Odyssey*, trans. Pope, XVIII, 107.

559.2   Public Advertiser]   A daily London newspaper published by Henry Sampson Woodfall (1739–1805), who was famous for the opposition essay series signed "Junius."

562.4   A——n]   Athanasian.

562.15   true History]   A reference to Lucian's burlesque of travelers' tales, *Vera Historia*.

565.13   The Gazetteer . . . *Advertiser*]   A daily London newspaper published by Charles Say.

567.5   Act of Parliament]   Franklin refers to American opposition to the Stamp Act.

569.16   On the . . . *Lane*]   Franklin herein satirizes the notorious slowness of legal actions in the Court of Chancery.

578.8   *Pax Quæritur Bello*]   "Peace is sought by war." Franklin's ironic motto may have been inspired by the saying of Cornelius Nepos, "paritur pax bello" ("peace prepares for war"), *Epaminondas* 5.

578.12   Controversy . . . Tuesday]   Measures leading to the repeal of the Stamp Act were then taken up in Parliament.

579.19   G—— G——]   George Grenville, the First Minister from 1763 to 1765, who had proposed the Stamp Act.

579.24–25   C——l . . . Service]   Probably Francis Mclean, an officer "in the P[ortugue]ze Service."

579.34   very proper General]   Probably General James Murray (1721/2–1794), governor of Quebec, whose arbitrary rule had been protested by the British population there in 1765, and who was alleged to favor the French.

581.13   Great Commoner]   William Pitt, an opponent of Grenville.

581.16–17   *Children . . . wrath.*]   Colossians 3:20–21.

582.14–23   Frenchman . . . *Iron.*]   Franklin evidently read this anecdote in Robert Hunter's *Androboros* (1714).

582.26   February–March, 1766]   The original printing of this piece has not been found; hence it is taken here from a later reprinting.

582.28   *A Mock . . . Commons*]   Drawn up when the House of Commons was considering extending to Scotland the system of transportation of felons to the American colonies, it was never presented formally, but only shown to some members by Richard Jackson ("it occasion'd some Laughing," Franklin reported). Franklin later included this piece in his "On Sending Felons to America" (pp. 1142–44 in the present volume).

588.25–26   *letter . . . intentions*]   New York Governor Henry Moore wrote to the Board of Trade on December 10 and 19, 1766, regarding resistance to the Navigation Acts and Quartering Act.

590.21–24   *Cinque . . . PETRARCH.*]   Franklin may have composed this epigraph and attributed it to Petrarch for his supposed authority (the Italian is inexpert). "Five great enemies of peace reside with us; they are avarice, ambition, envy, anger, and pride: if those enemies were sent into exile, perpetual peace would doubtless reign among us."

615.39–40   January . . . 1774]   When this essay was first printed in *The London Chronicle*, January 7, 1768, Franklin complained that the editors had muted its force. In 1774 the *Chronicle* reprinted it, restoring Franklin's original wording. The 1774 version is reprinted here.

616.3   correspondent]   At the end of 1767, a letter signed "S.N." in *The Gentleman's Magazine* had attacked the Boston Town Meeting's nonimportation resolutions of the previous October, and had further objected to the "vain pernicious ideas of independance" that supported such resolutions.

617.39   *one man*] George Grenville.

618.6   *Barlow Trecothick*] Raised in Boston, Trecothick (c. 1718–75) lived some time in Jamaica and returned briefly to New England before settling in London about 1750; he lobbied for repeal of the Stamp Act and as a member of Parliament (1768–74) opposed the government's American policies.

619.14   DELENDA EST] Cato the Elder concluded his speeches in the Roman Senate, "Carthage must be destroyed" (*Delenda est Carthago*).

619.32   *"Nought . . . anger."*] Paraphrase of William Shakespeare, *Othello*, V, ii, 342–43.

621.4   cows . . . fable] Probably written by Franklin. See "New Fables" (p. 645 in the present volume).

621.17–18   boutefeus] "Incendiaries."

634.11   Drawcansir] A blustering braggart, after the burlesque tyrant in "The Rehearsal" (1672) by G. Villiers, Duke of Buckingham.

636.28   *Quos . . . prius!*] A fragment (86) from Euripides: "Those whom God wishes to destroy, he first makes mad."

641.28   list . . . Americans] Franklin, as postmaster general of the colonies, headed the list.

646.22   Lord-Mayor] William Beckford (1709–70) was born in Jamaica.

647.5   *Granville Sharpe*'s Book] *A Representation of the Injustices and Dangerous Tendencies of Tolerating Slavery* (1769).

653.8   St. G——e's F——ds.] St. George's Fields, where supporters of the imprisoned John Wilkes gathered on May 10, 1768; several people were killed when the troops fired upon the crowd.

653.10   *The Cravenstreet Gazette*] Franklin wrote this while his landlady Margaret Stevenson ("Queen Margaret") and his cousin Sarah Franklin ("First Maid of Honor, Miss Franklin") were away, for their amusement. Margaret's daughter, Mary "Polly" Hewson (variously "Lady Chamberlain of the Household," "Cook," "First Ministress," and "Lady of the Bedchamber"), and Polly's husband, Dr. William Hewson ("First Minister"), remained with him at Craven Street. The *"great* Person," "big Man," and "Dr. Fatsides" was of course Franklin.

653.17   new Family Administration] Mary "Polly" (Stevenson) Hewson and her husband, William (1739–74).

655.1–2   Brother the Courtier] Israel Wilkes, brother of John Wilkes, was a friend of Franklin.

655.23   Dowager] Mary (Stevenson) Hewson's aunt, Mrs. Tickell.

655.25   Lady Barwell] Mary Barwell (1733–?), a friend of the Craven

Street circle; member of a wealthy Anglo-Indian family, she handled their business interests in London, and was an influential figure in financial and political affairs.

656.9   Lord Hutton] James Hutton (1715–95), a Moravian and Franklin's friend.

656.13   Lady Hawkesworth] Mrs. John Hawkesworth, a friend of the Craven Street circle.

656.14–15   Dorothea Blount] A close friend of Mary (Stevenson) Hewson.

658.10   Old England] A pseudonym Franklin employed (e.g., see 607.6 in the present volume).

665.33   I went] Franklin originally wrote, "At the earnest Instance and Request of Mr. Strahan I went . . . ," but then deleted the phrase.

666.37–38   Dr. Lee] Arthur Lee (1740–92), Franklin's fellow agent, with whom he was often at odds (see pp. 999–1000 in the present volume).

669.14–15   *the Agent . . . himself.*)] Franklin originally wrote, "the poor Agent; and of more Importance)." The phrase was revised, but in another hand; however, a copy Franklin sent to Samuel Cooper of the Massachusetts House of Representatives showed these revisions.

671.30–31   *Introduction . . . Zealanders*] Foreword to Alexander Dalrymple, *Scheme of a Voyage by Subscription to Convey the Conveniences of Life . . .* (1771).

672.29   *Communiter . . . est.*] "To bring forth good things in common, that is God."

673.8   *Homo sum, &c.*] Terence *Incipit Hearton Timoromenos* 1. 124. ("Homo sum: humani nil a me alienum puto") "I am a man; I hold that what affects another man affects me."

676.2   *noli prosequi*'s] A legal term meaning "to drop prosecution."

677.29–30   Somerset the Negro] James Sommersett, finally freed by Lord Mansfield's decision in the Sommersett case.

678.23–24   *Preface . . . Meeting*] Franklin (identified as the "British Editor" on the first page) wrote this preface to the London reprinting of the official Boston publication of the acts of the town meeting.

691.30–31   make them *Baronets*] After being governor of Massachusetts, Francis Bernard (1712–79) was made a baronet.

693.33–35   *kill . . . Devil*] An allusion to Matthew 10:28.

694.9   discard them] John Temple (1732–98), who was popular with the Americans, was recalled from the Board of Customs Commissioners in 1770.

698.8–10   *Shelburne* . . . ENGLISHMAN!] Shelburne, Clare, and Hillsborough were all members of the Irish peerage; Lord Dartmouth was of the English peerage.

703.12   Sir F. Bernard] See note 691.30–31.

703.31   two Gentlemen] William Whately (d. 1782), who had accused John Temple (see note 694.9) of taking the letters, had fought an inconclusive duel with him on December 11, 1773. Franklin, fearing they might fight again, wrote this notice to prevent another duel.

709.21   *adscriptitii glebae*] "Attached to the soil."

715.10   G——l G——e] General Thomas Gage (1721–87), commander in chief of British forces in the American colonies in 1775.

715.18–19   L——d G—— G——e] Lord George Germain, who would become secretary of state for the American colonies in 1775.

718.2   G——l G——e] General Thomas Gage (see note 715.10).

718.10   Conquerors . . . Germany] An allusion to William Pitt's famous statement in Parliament, December 9, 1762, that "America had been conquered in Germany."

719.15   OLD SARUM] The most notorious of the "rotten boroughs" (so called because their eligible electors were so few as to seriously compromise the system of Parliamentary representation). The town of Old Sarum was no longer populated.

722.35–37   a certain . . . Americans] Col. (later General) James Grant (1720–1806) in Parliament, February 2, 1775.

724.35   Hewers . . . Water] An allusion to Joshua 9:21, 23, 27.

726.24   Fortress] Castle William, in the Boston harbor.

728.29   No 23] In the journal Franklin kept during his negotiations, from which this piece is taken, he added numbers to the documents.

730.1   *Proposed . . . Confederation*] Franklin returned to Philadelphia on May 5, 1775, and soon drew up these articles of colonial union; Congress was as yet unwilling to endorse such a bold step.

734.17   one denomination] The $8 Continental bill. The Third Pennsylvania Regiment, raised in 1777, adopted the device and motto for its flag.

734.28   another bill] The $4 Continental bill. The Sixth Pennsylvania Regiment, raised in 1777, adopted the emblem for its flag.

734.37   another] The $3 Continental bill. The Eighth Pennsylvania Regiment, raised in 1777, adopted the emblem for its flag.

735.11–12   *Sunt . . . erat.*] "The issue of events is doubtful, and the deathly battle uncertain: he is conquered, not seldom, who was nearly victorious." Franklin borrowed the quotation, as well as the device itself, from Joachim Camerarius, *Symbolorum ac Emblematus Ethico-Politicorum*, 4 vols. (1702), III, 64.

735.13   another bill]   The $5 Continental bill. The Fifth Pennsylvania Regiment, raised in 1777, adopted the emblem for its flag.

735.23   Another]   The $6 Continental bill. The Seventh Pennsylvania Regiment, raised in 1777, adopted the emblem for its flag.

735.27–28   *and binding . . . whatsoever*]   The words of the Declaratory Act of March 18, 1766.

735.36   another bill]   The $1 Continental bill. The Twelfth Pennsylvania Regiment, raised in 1777, adopted this device for its flag.

736.10   figure]   The $2 Continental bill.

736.34   Another]   The $7 Continental bill.

737.1–3   *Informes . . . Apollo.*]   Horace *Odes* 2. 10. 15–18, 19–20. "Though Jupiter brings back the unlovely winters, he also takes them away. If we fare ill today, 'twill not be *ever* so. Apollo does not always stretch the bow."

737.4   another bill]   The front of the $20 bill.

737.31   last]   The $30 Continental bill.

738.3–4   *E lauro . . . decet.*]   "From laurel, oak, and olive, is the hero's deserved crown. It is proper to prudence, strength, and peace." Franklin borrowed the quotation, and the device on the $30 bill, from Camerarius (see note 735.11–12), I, 100.

738.19–21   *Rex . . . facies.*]   "You will be king, they affirm, if you do right." Also borrowed from Camerarius, I, 100.

738.23   *Qui recte . . . Rex.*]   "He who does right, not he who domineers, will be king." From Camerarius, I, 100.

738.27   *The King's Own Regulars*]   This song appeared in *The Boston Gazette*, November 27, 1775; the version printed here is a fuller one from *The Pennsylvania Evening Post*, March 30, 1776.

742.4–5   return'd . . . day.]   Franklin here uses an old slur against the Yankees that he had cited earlier in his "Open Letter to Lord North" (p. 715 in the present volume).

743.7–8   Every fence . . . other.]   In his tour of Lexington on November 5, 1789, George Washington, supposedly recalling the British complaint that the Yankees fired at them from behind stone walls, asked "whether there were not two sides to the wall." Washington may have been remembering this stanza.

744.16–17   REBELLION . . . GOD.]   Jefferson adopted this as his personal motto and proposed it as the motto for the great seal of the United States.

744.19   *Rattle-Snake*]   Franklin had used the rattlesnake as a symbol of America in his "Rattle-Snakes for Felons" hoax (pp. 359–61 in the present volume), and in his "Join, or Die" device (p. 377) urging American unity.

747.1   *What . . . Americans?*]   This document, of unknown provenance, records a characteristic Franklinian squib.

750.34   Mr. *Mitchell*'s]   The paper by Rev. John Michell (1724–93) is probably "Conjectures concerning the Cause, and Observations upon the Phaenomena of Earthquakes . . . ," printed in the *Philosophical Transactions* LI, 2 (1760), pp. 566–634.

751.26   Dr. *Hadley*]   Dr. John Hadley (1731–64). See Chronology, 1758.

753.9   *June* 1750]   Actually, June 18, 1749.

756.1   *None but Christ*]   Clement Cotton, *None but Christ* (1723).

758.17   Potts and Parsons]   Stephen Potts (1704–58) and William Parsons (1701–57), the former a Quaker bookbinder (mentioned in the *Autobiography*, pp. 1354, 1362), the latter a shoemaker who became surveyor-general (see *Autobiography*, p. 1362).

759.19–20   PRE SENCE . . . ALL ENgag'd]   Franklin puns on the name of William Allen, leader of the Proprietary party.

763.3   Book]   [Richard Jackson, comp.], *An Historical Review of . . . Pennsylvania* (1759).

764.31   Mr. Bailey]   Rev. Jacob Bailey (1731–1818), who became a Tory, fled to Nova Scotia during the Revolution, and satirized Franklin in his poetry.

765.28   Chapter]   Franklin's "Parable Against Persecution" (pp. 420–21 in the present volume) pretended to be a chapter from Genesis.

765.33   *The Art of Virtue*]   Franklin never published his "Art of Virtue" as a separate work; when Benjamin Vaughan reminded him of his intention to do so in 1783 (see p. 1374 in the present volume), Franklin responded by incorporating the elements of his scheme into Part Two of the *Autobiography* under the guise of his "bold and arduous Project of arriving at moral Perfection" (p. 1383).

770.21–24   Nicholas . . . Satyrist.]   Thomas Shadwell ridiculed Nicholas Gimcrack in his play *The Virtuoso* (1676), and Joseph Addison added to the satire in *The Tatler*, Nos. 216 and 221 (Aug. 26 and Sept. 7, 1710).

771.17   Selden tells us]   John Selden, *Table Talk* (1689), p. 50.

783.31   *The additional . . .* Maccabeus]   "Wise men flatt'ring may deceive us" in Handel's *Judas Maccabeus* (1747), Act 2.

785.10–12   *the Monster . . . Galatea*]   Handel's chorus "Wretched Lovers!" in *Acis and Galatea* (1718), Act 2.

787.11   *a Case in Point*]   Franklin probably created the anecdote.

787.30–32   We are . . . Street.]   2 Chronicles 1:16.

789.3   Mr. *Puckeridge*]   Richard Pockrich, musician (d. 1759).

789.10   Mr. *E. Delaval*]   Franklin had nominated Edward H. Duval (1729–1814) for membership in the Royal Society in 1759.

796.22   *Old Tenor*]   Connecticut money bills infamous for their rapid depreciation.

798.33–799.3   Full . . . too.]   From William Whitehead's *A Charge to the Poets* (1762).

802.10   Ad Exemplum Regis, &c.]   Probably an echo of Claudian *Panegyricus de Quarto Consulatu Honorii Augusti* 299–300: "componitur orbis regis ad exemplum" ("the world shapes itself after its ruler's pattern").

821.10–15   Friar . . . Ears.]   Franklin adapts a legend concerning the theologian Roger Bacon (1214–94?), a heterodox Franciscan; he may have known it from Robert Greene's play, *The Honorable Historie of Frier Bacon, and Frier Bongay* (1594).

824.31   this:]   Franklin's words in the drawing, clockwise from upper right: "Mad. Sophie," "Mad. Adelaide," "The King," "The Queen," "Mad. Victoire," "Mad. Louise," "Waiters."

829.28   last Piece]   Franklin refers to a piece printed in *The London Chronicle*, November 24, 1767, in which he decried the evasion of taxes by smugglers, and insisted that the receiver of smuggled goods was as culpable as the smuggler.

830.25   one paper]   "Causes of the American Discontents Before 1768" (pp. 607–615 in the present volume). See note 615.39–40.

834.30   *July* 28]   Dated July 21 in the copy-text for the present printing, but corrected to July 28, as in its first printing (in French).

863.18–19   great . . . *them.*]   Sir William Temple, *Miscellanea: The Second Part* (1690), "Essay II. Upon the Gardens of Epicurus, or of Gardening in the Year 1685," p. 5.

864.40   Discourse]   Franklin reprinted an advertisement for it, with Samuel Keimer's comments, from Keimer's *Barbadoes Gazette* in *The Pennsylvania Gazette*, February 20, 1733/34.

865.26   Touchwood]   Wood, or another substance easily ignited, used for tinder; hence, a person who is easily incensed.

871.5   13] Franklin wrote "August 12," but since he stayed at the Shipleys' through the 12th, he must have written this letter the next day.

871.7–8   my Charge] Franklin's "Charge" was Catherine (Kitty) Shipley, about eleven years old, the daughter of Bishop Jonathan and Anna Mordaunt Shipley.

876.10   This . . . Chronicle] "The Sommersett Case and the Slave Trade" (pp. 677–78 in the present volume).

877.35   Affair . . . you] Priestley was considering leaving Leeds to become the librarian of Lord Shelburne.

878.34   1772] Franklin wrote "1773" originally, but since he enclosed a draft of this letter to Georgiana Shipley in his letter to Deborah Franklin of February 14, 1773, he must have written it in 1772.

879.3   Skuggs] In a letter to Deborah Franklin (February 14, 1773) Franklin explained, "Skugg, you must know is a common Name by which all Squirrels are called here, as all Cats are called *Puss*."

879.26   Ranger] The dog that killed Georgiana's squirrel.

881.4   fugitive Piece] "Toleration in Old and New England" (pp. 673–77 in the present volume).

881.16   1723] Franklin ran away from Boston in September, 1723.

881.36–37   Argument . . . Ancients] Samuel Mather, *An Attempt to Shew, that America Must be Known to the Ancients* (1773).

882.1   Tubalcain] See Genesis 4:22.

882.4   Professor Kalm] Pehr Kalm (1716–79), the Swedish botanist sent by Linnaeus to America to collect specimens.

882.15   Krantz] David Cranz, *The History of Greenland*, 2 vols. (1767), I, 241–79.

883.24   Version of the Prayer] "A New Version of the Lord's Prayer" (pp. 638–41 in the present volume).

885.11   Friend's] Rev. Thomas Coombe, Jr. (1747–1822), a young friend of Franklin's who at one time lodged in the Craven Street house.

886.18–19   *Rules . . . Prussia*] Pp. 689–97 and 698–703 in the present volume.

888.17   *Moral Virtue delineated*] Marin le Roy de Gomberville, *Moral Virtue Delineated* (1726).

895.33–896.9   Extrait . . . chapitre.] "Extract of a Letter from Mr. Tengnagel to Mr. le Comte de Bentinck, written from Batavia January 15, 1770. Near St. Paul and Amsterdam Islands we endured a storm, which hadn't anything particular about it to be noticed, except that our Captain felt himself obliged in turning leeward, to pour out some oil on the high seas, in order to prevent the waves from breaking against the ship, which succeeded in saving us and had a very good effect: as he had poured only a small quantity altogether, the Company perhaps owes its vessel to six demi-ahms of olive oil: I was present when this happened, and I would not have informed you of that circumstance, if we hadn't found the people here so skeptical of the experience, that neither the officers on shore nor myself raised any objections to giving an assurance of the truth of the matter."

899.1   new Book]   Josiah Tucker, *Four Tracts* (1774).

904.8   *To William Strahan*]   Franklin did not send this angry letter to his friend Strahan.

907.8   *last* petition]   The Olive Branch Petition of July 8, 1775.

PARIS, 1776–1785

919.22   MADAME BRILLON]   Mme. d'Hardancourt Brillon de Jouy (1744–1824), a favorite among Franklin's female friends in France, a talented musician, handsome and lively.

921.1   *Petition of the Letter Z*]   Franklin herein satirizes Ralph Izard (1742–1804), one of his fellow American commissioners in Paris in 1778. His notes in the left column explain the allegory.

921.3   ISAAC BICKERSTAFF]   A character invented by Jonathan Swift, in his parody of an almanac maker's predictions (see note 1185.20); Richard Steele adopted the name for the pretended author of his *Tatler*, of which the present "Petition" pretends to be an issue.

922.11   my dear Friend]   Mme. Brillon.

923.27–28   *what . . . Morals.*]   Horace *Odes* 3. 24. 35.

923.31   *Art . . . short!*]   Hippocrates *Aphorisms* 1. 1.

923.33–34   *lived . . . Glory*]   Cicero *Pro M. Marcello* 25.

924.5   BRILLANTE]   "Diamond." Also a reference to Mme. Brillon.

924.6   *The Elysian Fields*]   This bagatelle, among others, was printed by Franklin only in French; the present text is a translation. The other French bagatelles are "Bilked for Breakfast" (p. 925 in the present volume), "A Tale" (p. 938), "On Wine" (p. 939), "Dialogue Between the Gout and Mr. Franklin" (p. 943), "The Handsome and the Deformed Leg" (p. 950), and "The Flies" (p. 990). The translators are identified in the list of sources in the Note on the Texts.

924.7   MADAME HELVÉTIUS]   Mme. Ligniville de Helvétius, wealthy widow of the Baron Claude Adrian de Helvétius, a writer and philosopher; she conducted a salon that attracted many notable French intellectuals. In her sixties when Franklin met her, she was strong-minded and unconventional. She turned down Franklin's proposal of marriage (perhaps tendered half-seriously), as is evident from the text.

924.16   H——]   Baron Claude Adrian de Helvétius (1715–1771). See note 924.7.

925.5–6   Abbé de la R——]   Martin Lefèbvre de la Roche (d. 1806), a former Benedictine; friend and literary executor of Helvétius, translator of Horace and editor of Montesquieu, and one of Franklin's Passy friends.

925.6   Abbé M——]   Abbé André Morellet (1727–1819), another of Franklin's Passy associates, and a frequent visitor to Mme. Helvétius's salon. He translated Thomas Jefferson's *Notes on the State of Virginia*.

925.29   MADAME LA FRETÉ]   Mme. Martinville de la Freté, another of Franklin's female friends, of whom little is known. Her husband had business dealings with the colonies.

931.22   my dear Friend's]   Mme. Brillon's.

931.28   M. B.]   M. Brillon, the husband of Mme. Brillon (to whom this bagatelle was written); twenty-four years her senior, theirs was a marriage of convenience.

941–42   Drawings]   These drawings, the work of one of Franklin's grandsons, were printed in the *Memoires inédits* (1822) of the Abbé Morellet.

952.14   *****]   "Brusselles" is written after the title in the original manuscript.

952.18–20   *"Une figure . . . donnée"*]   "Given any single figure, one is asked to inscribe therein as many times as possible another smaller figure, also given."

952.21–23   *"l'Académie . . . UTILITÉ"*]   "The Academy has judged that this discovery, by widening the boundaries of our knowledge, will not be without UTILITY."

955.5   *Notes for Conversation*]   Franklin used these notes on April 18, 1782, in discussions with Richard Oswald, at the beginning of the peace negotiations between England and the United States.

956.28–29   *Supplement . . . Chronicle*]   This "Supplement" was printed by Franklin on his press at Passy. The number "705" was the real number of an issue of the *Boston Independent Chronicle* for March.

963.35   *"Nerone Neronior"*]   "More Nero than Nero himself." From John Milton, *Pro Populo Anglicano Defensia* (1651), ch. 1.

977.39–40   *There . . .* WATTS.]   The Latin in the text is from Horace

Epistles I. 2. 27. Watts's paraphrase was: "There are a Number of us creep / Into this World, to eat and sleep; / And know no Reason why they're born, / But merely to consume the Corn." Watts, *Miscellaneous Thoughts* (1734), p. 61.

986.30   *Nil desperandum*]   "Never despair." Horace *Odes* I. 7. 27.

987.14   *ce n'est . . . coûte*]   "It's only the first time that it costs" (i.e., "the first step is the hardest").

996.39   *un peu dérangées*]   "A little deranged."

997.33   *"avec Sureté"*]   "With safety."

997.36   *"sans . . . Dépenses,"*]   "Without too great expenses."

998.8–9   *"d'etre . . . convenable"*]   "To be received in an agreeable manner."

999.29   *To Arthur Lee*]   Franklin did not send this letter; instead, the next day, he wrote again, patiently replying to all of Lee's accusations.

1000.14   *Weissenstein*]   "Weissenstein" was evidently the assumed name of a British secret agent.

1002.36   *Arcana Imperii*]   Mark Zuirius Boxhorn, *Arcana imperii detecta; or, divers select cases in Government* (1701).

1007.1–2   *God-send or The Wreckers*]   Franklin probably created the title and the scene.

1013.27   *Serapis*]   On September 23, 1779, Jones, in his ship the *Bonhomme Richard*, took the English ship the *Serapis*, even though the heavily damaged *Bonhomme Richard* sank the next day.

1015.22   *Chapter*]   "A Parable Against Persecution" (pp. 420–21 in the present volume).

1015.35–36   *A Dissertation . . . Pain*]   Pp. 57–71 in the present volume.

1016.19   piece]   "On the Providence of God in the Government of the World" (pp. 163–68 in the present volume).

1017.33   Situation . . . Person]   Priestley was unhappy in his position as Lord Shelburne's librarian and requested Franklin's advice about leaving the post.

1022.3   little piece]   "The Ephemera" (pp. 922–24 in the present volume).

1022.27–28   little piece]   An essay called "On Human Vanity" reprinted by Franklin in *The Pennsylvania Gazette*, December 4, 1735, from the *Freethinker*, April 24, 1719.

1029.2   *tante de gagne*]   "So much gained."

1030.15   excellent Pamphlet]   *Essay on the Population of England* (2d ed., 1780).

1031.14   the *London*]   The London Coffee House, where Franklin's favorite Club of Honest Whigs had been meeting since March, 1772.

1034.9   Account]   By Cotton Mather. *Philosophical Transactions*, 29 (1714), pp. 70–71, with illustration Fig. 8.

1034.10   Remarks]   Court de Gebelin judged the petroglyphs on Dighton Rock to be Phoenician. *Monde Primitif* (1781), VIII, 561–68.

1039.34   little Book]   *Prosody Made Easy* (1781).

1040.25   "Tully . . . Age,"]   James Logan's translation of Cicero's *Cato Major* (1744). This was among Franklin's finest examples of printing.

1040.32   M. Didot]   François-Ambroise Didot (1730–1804), to whom Franklin's grandson Benjamin Bache was briefly apprenticed.

1041.1   "Salust" . . . Madrid]   The Spanish printer Joachim de Ibarra published his edition of *Don Quixote* in 1771 and Sallust in 1772.

1042.26   a medal]   Franklin later had the medal, *Libertas Americana*, struck by the engraver Augustin Dupré.

1047.5   a paper]   "Supplement to the Boston Independent Chronicle" (pp. 956–64 in the present volume).

1049.25   Club]   Franklin's Club of Honest Whigs met on Thursdays at St. Paul's (later the London) Coffee House.

1050.28   Papa]   William Alexander, Franklin's neighbor in France, a tobacco merchant of Scots birth who later emigrated to Virginia. His daughter Mariamne married Franklin's grandnephew Jonathan Williams, Jr.; this letter is to another daughter.

1050.35   *plus de Chaleur*]   "Much heat."

1051.6   *Ménagère*]   "Manager" (i.e., housekeeper).

1054.17   monument]   The monument in memory of General Richard Montgomery. It was placed in the portico of St. Paul's Church in New York City.

1055.35–1056.1   Children . . . State.]   Lafayette had named his newborn daughter "Virginia."

1060.4   *To Comte de Vergennes*]   As Vergennes complained to Franklin in a letter of December 15, the American peace commissioners had concluded preliminary articles of peace with Britain without communicating with France, despite instructions from Congress "that nothing shall be done without the participation of the King." This letter is Franklin's apology on behalf of the peace commissioners.

1060.34   *bienséance*]   "Propriety" or "decorum."

1061.23   dearest Friend]   Margaret Stevenson died on January 1, 1783.

1064.10−11   one of my Colleagues]   John Adams.

1065.5   Shakespear . . . Air,"]   *Othello,* III, iii, 322−24: "Trifles light as air / Are to the jealous, confirmations strong / As proof is of Holy Writ."

1079.4   respectable person]   Dr. Samuel Cooper (1725−83) of Boston wrote to Franklin warning him of the allegations being made against him in America, presumably by John Adams.

1080.4   Public Person]   John Adams.

1080.29−30   *Caisse d'Escompte*]   According to Franklin, "an institution similar to the Bank of England" (letter to Elias Boudinot, Nov. 1, 1783).

1088.40   *"Virtutis Premium,"*]   "Reward of virtue."

1089.1   *"Esto perpetua"*]   "Let her be eternal."

1089.8   *omnia reliquit*]   "He left all behind."

1089.22   OMNIA VANITAS]   "All is vanity."

1092.12   *"Essays to do Good"*]   Cotton Mather's *Bonifacius* (1710) was also known by its running title, "Essays to Do Good."

1093.10   *Esto perpetua*]   See note 1089.1.

1096.10   Seymour]   Edward Seymour (1633−1708) was one of the Lords of Treasury who opposed James Blair's attempt to secure quitrent money for the salary of Virginia's clergy. John Somers (1651−1716), not Seymour, was attorney general.

1096.11−12   College . . . Province]   The College of William and Mary.

1102.31−32   General Melvill]   Robert Melville (1723−1809).

1103.28   honest Minister]   Theophilus Lindsey (1723−1808). See Chronology, 1774.

1104.30   *bavarder*]   To "chat" or "gossip."

1104.31   Saying of Alphonsus]   King Alphonsus wished to have old friends, old books, old wine, and old wood.

1105.23   *The Old Man's Wish*]   Dr. Walter Pope evidently wrote the song in 1684.

1107.5−6   *"Car . . . tetons."*]   " 'Because,' he said, 'they don't have any breasts at all.' "

1107.18   *Enfans Trouvés*]   "Foundlings" (i.e., orphanage).

1107.34–35   *pour . . . Nourrice*]   "For the nurse's monthly salary" (i.e., for not paying it).

1109.17   Mr. Dollond's]   Peter Dollond (1730–1820), optician.

1109.28   thus,]   Franklin's words in the drawing: top left: "least convex for distant Objects"; bottom left: "most convex for Reading"; top right: "least convex"; bottom right: "most convex."

PHILADELPHIA, 1785–1790

1136.9   43]   Smyth prints this as "41 [sic]" (here and also at 1136.11); in Madison's notes of the debates, the correct sum of 43 is given.

1139.3–4   "except . . . it."]   Psalms 127:1.

1139.35–1140.4   Steele . . . Wrong.]   The mock dedication to Pope Clement XI of Urbano Cerri, *An Account of the state of the Roman Catholic Religion* (1715), though attributed to Richard Steele, was actually by Bishop Benjamin Hoadley. The quotation is: "You are Infallible, and We always in the Right," p. ii.

1140.14–15   if well administred]   Alluding to Alexander Pope, *An Essay on Man* (1733–34), Epistle III, ll. 303–04: "For Forms of Government let fools contest; / Whate'er is best administered is best."

1142.21   Petition to Parliament]   This is Franklin's own "Mock Petition to Parliament" (see pp. 582–83 in the present volume, and note 582.28).

1152.29–34   "There . . . DRYDEN.]   Stephen Hervey's translation of Juvenal's ninth satire, ll. 193–96, published in *The Satires of Decimus Junius Juvenalis. Translated into English Verse. By Mr. Dryden, And several Other Eminent Hands . . .* (1693).

1157.27   Mr. Jackson]   James Jackson (1757–1806), a representative from Georgia in the first Congress, 1789–91.

1160.25   Mr. Brown]   Andrew Brown (c. 1744–1797), publisher of *The Federal Gazette.*

1161.23   *Burton on Melancholly*]   Robert Burton, *The Anatomy of Melancholy* (1621).

1162.4   little Piece]   Probably "The Retort Courteous" (pp. 1122–30 in the present volume).

1168.31   little piece]   Probably "A Comparison of the Conduct of the Ancient Jews and the Anti-Federalists" (pp. 1144–48 in the present volume).

1180.11   Copy . . . enclosed]   To Joseph Huey, June 6, 1753 (pp. 475–77 in the present volume).

1180.15   Copy . . . Letter]   To ———, [Dec. 13, 1757] (pp. 748–49 in the present volume).

POOR RICHARD'S ALMANACK, 1733–1758

1185.20   Mr. *Titan Leeds*]   Titan Leeds (1699–1738) wrote the best-selling almanac of the Middle Colonies—until Poor Richard appeared. Franklin's prediction of Leeds' death echoes Jonathan Swift's Bickerstaff hoax, as well as Thomas Fleet's imitation of Swift in *The New-England Courant*, February 12, 1721/2.

1190.31   Principiis obsta.]   "Meet the first beginnings" (i.e., "Nip it in the bud").

1194.30–31   *ingratum . . . dixeris*]   "If you say he is ungrateful, you say everything."

1195.15–16   *Sapiens . . . astris*]   "The wise man will be governed by the stars."

1195.28   *ex ore . . . est*]   "He is condemned out of his own mouth."

1196.24   Dyrro . . . ddoethach.]   "Give drink to a wise man [and] he will be wiser."

1203.2   *J———n*]   John Jerman (1684–1769), who produced a rival almanac.

1204.35   Felix quem, *&c.*]   See note 1230.21.

1206.23   Nec sibi . . . mundo.]   Cato's rule of life, according to Lucan's *Civil War* 2. 383: "To believe that one is born not for himself, but for the whole world."

1211.1   Brother *J—m-n*]   See note 1203.2.

1212.12–13   Doll . . . look.]   The two Latin phrases were mnemonic tags used in Latin grammars of the time to familiarize students with noun genders and declensions. The whole saying, incorporating the Latin, may be translated as follows: "Doll, learning without book [i.e., from experience] the particular attribute of men, looks like the image of generative increasing [i.e., pregnant]."

1212.29   *Probatum est*]   "It is proved."

1215.33   *J. J———n*]   See note 1203.2.

1215.37   *W. B———t*]   William Birkett, a rival almanac maker.

1218.25   *Poor Richard, 1741*]   "Instead of a trifling Preface that this Page uses to be fill'd with," Franklin wrote, "accept the following Chronological Account of MEMORABLE EVENTS Since the Revolution in 1688," and a list of events followed.

1223.4   Bis . . . dat.] See 1275.8–9.

1223.17   Reniego . . . d'oro.] "Despise chains, though they be of gold."

1224.7   Heb . . . digon.] "Without God, without anything; with God, with enough."

1224.12–13   Fient . . . jugement.] "Dog's dung and silver mark will all be one on Judgment Day."

1228.34   Le sage . . . mot.] "The wise man understands a hint."

1229.13   A achwyno . . . iddo.] "Let him who complains without cause, be given cause to complain."

1229.16   Borgen . . . sorgen.] "He that goes borrowing, goes sorrowing."

1229.26   A noddo . . . noddir.] "What will be protected by God will be protected completely."

1229.30–31   Na funno . . . ûn.] "Let no man do to another what he would not wish for himself."

1230.10   Tugend . . . vergehet.] "Virtue stays when all else goes."

1230.14–15   Con todo . . . Ingalatierra.] "War with all the world, and peace with England."

1230.21   Felix . . . cautum.] "Happy is he whom others' experiences make cautious."

1239.5   Ni ffyddra . . . hûn.] "Man's hand alone, without God's help, cannot do himself good."

1240.11   JACOB TAYLOR] Taylor (1670–1746), formerly surveyor-general of Pennsylvania, was a schoolteacher, poet, and sometime printer.

1240.18   *Requiescat in pace.*] "Rest in peace."

1242.18–36   Hail . . . Way.] Adapted from John Hughes, *The Ecstasy* (1720).

1245.34   this Month] January.

1246.26   this month] March.

1246.28–29   *Thomson . . . simple.*] Adapted from James Thomson, *The Seasons,* "Summer," ll. 1560–62.

1246.30–1247.3   What were . . . view.] James Thomson, *A Poem Sacred to the Memory of Sir Isaac Newton* (1727), ll. 30–38.

1247.6–7   Nature . . . light.] Alexander Pope, Epitaph XII in his collected works.

1247.10   Eilen . . . gut.] "Hurry seldom does well."

1247.11   this month]   April.

1248.7   this month]   June.

1249.9   this month]   October.

1249.17   28th]   Of October.

1249.19   *He made . . . own.*]   James Thomson, *The Seasons*, "Summer,"
l. 1559.

1249.28   29th]   Of October.

1250.12   *Poor Richard Improved, 1749*]   The Preface for 1749, omitted here,
was by John Bartram.

1250.15   this month]   January.

1250.22–24   BOYLE . . . *sought*:]   James Thomson, *The Seasons*, "Summer," ll. 1556–58.

1251.9   this month]   February.

1252.10   this month]   April.

1252.15–16   *If Parts . . . mankind.*]   Alexander Pope, *An Essay on Man*
(1733–34), Epistle IV, ll. 281–82.

1252.21–36   BACON . . . again.]   James Thomson, *The Seasons*, "Summer," ll. 1535–50.

1253.7   27th]   Of May.

1253.23   this month]   June.

1254.12   mad]   As Poor Richard explained in the 1750 almanac, this was a
typographical error (see p. 1257 of the present volume).

1255.12   this month]   December.

1255.24–27   *Superior . . . ape.*]   Alexander Pope, *An Essay on Man* (1733–
34), Epistle II, ll. 31–34.

1257.24–25   *wrapp'd, . . . warp'd*]   This refers to a poem under May in
the 1749 almanac, not reprinted in the present volume.

1258.27   Beatus . . . potest.]   "Beauty without virtue is powerless."

1262.36–1263.13   The Bell . . . still.]   Edward Young, *The Complaint: Or,
Night Thoughts on Life, Death, and Immortality* (1742–45), I, 54–56, 57–61,
389–97.

1277.2   *Scandalum Magnatum*]   "The scandal of the peerage." The name
given to a statute of Richard II by which punishment was to be inflicted for
any scandal or wrong offered to or uttered against a noble personage.

1282.19–20   Journal . . . *Bouguer*]   A translation (not reprinted here) of

Pierre Bouguer, "Relation Abrégée du Voyage Fait au Pérou," *Histoire de L'Académie Royale des Sciences* (1744), pp. 249–73.

1288.13   following Extracts]   The extracts from John Pringle, *Observations on Diseases of the Army* (1752), are not reprinted here.

1288.17   recommended in my last]   The piece called "*Remarks, on the Advantages that may arise from a more general Use of Oxen for Draft in the Province of Pennsylvania*," submitted by a "Correspondent" and printed in the 1756 almanac, is not included in the present volume.

1290.17–24   Sincerity . . . attend.]   Benjamin Stillingfleet, *Essay on Conversation* (1737), ll. 400–07, reprinted in Robert Dodsley, *A Collection of Poems* (1748).

THE AUTOBIOGRAPHY

1307.2   Twyford]   Bishop Jonathan Shipley's country home, fifty miles north of London, where Franklin stayed while writing Part One of the *Autobiography*, between July 30 and August 13, 1771.

1307.5   Son]   William Franklin had been governor of New Jersey since 1762.

1307.17   Reputation]   Franklin's autograph manuscript, in the Huntington Library in San Marino, California, shows that he revised his text extensively. For instance, here Franklin first wrote "Fame," then changed it to "Reputation." Other examples of revisions are given in notes at 1314.9, 1319.8–9, 1319.26–27, 1319.38, 1339.37, 1355.7, 1360.11–12, 1363.23, 1364.7, 1372.30, 1381.11–12, 1384.11, and 1419.1 below.

1310.6   old Stile]   England did not adopt the Gregorian calendar until September 13, 1752. Under the old (Julian) calendar, the new year began on March 25, and the old calendar was, by the eighteenth century, eleven days behind the new. Thus Franklin was born January 6, 1705, "old style," or January 17, 1706, "new style." The Preface to *Poor Richard Improved, 1752,* is an essay on the history of the calendar (pp. 1270–74 in the present volume).

1312.31   one . . . printed]   Peter Folger's *A Looking Glass for the Times*, though written in 1676, was not printed until 1725.

1313.23   his Character]   His shorthand method.

1314.9   against it;]   Franklin first wrote here, "and so it seem'd that I was destin'd for a Tallow Chandler," then canceled the clause.

1316.22   By my rambling Digressions]   It may have been at this point, after writing eight pages of his manuscript, that Franklin felt the need of an outline for his work. Several versions of the outline are extant. The version closest to Franklin's original working outline is a copy in the Pierpont

Morgan Library in New York City, printed in the Lemay–Zall genetic text, and reproduced here with the genetic text's sigla included. These symbols, used throughout the genetic text, are omitted in the clear text of the *Autobiography* in the present volume; they are retained in the following outline as a sample of the genetic text's format.

↑ ↓   single arrows enclose interlinear additions.
< >   angle brackets enclose cancellations.
{ }   braces enclose matter written over by the following matter.
[p. o]   page numbers within brackets indicate the pagination of the original manuscript.

Copie d'un {Autographe} Projet très curieux de Bn. Franklin.—1ere. Esquisse memorandum de ses mémoires. Les additions à l'encre rouge sont de la main de Franklin.

My writing. Mrs.. Dogoods Letters—Differences arise between my Brother and me (his temper and mine) their Cause in general. His News Paper. The Prosecution he suffered. My Examination. Vote of Assembly. His Manner of evading it. Whereby I became free. My Attempt to get employ with other Printers. He prevents me. Our frequent pleadings before our Father. The final Breach. My Inducements to quit Boston. Manner of coming to a Resolution. My leaving him & going to New York. (return to eating Flesh.) thence to Pennsylvania, The Journey, and its Events on the Bay, at Amboy, the Road, meet with Dr. Brown. his Character. his great work. At Burlington. The Good Woman. On the River. My Arrival at Philada... First Meal and first Sleep. Money left. Employment. Lodging. First Acquaintance with my Afterwards Wife. with J. Ralph. with Keimer. their Characters. Osborne. Watson. The Governor takes Notice of me. the Occasion and Manner. his Character. Offers to set me up. My return to Boston. <y> Voyage and Accidents. Reception. My Father dislikes the proposal. I return to New York and Philada... Governor Burnet. J. Collins. the Money for Vernon. The Governors Deceit. Collins not finding Employment goes to Barbados much in my Debt. Ralph and I go to England. Disappointment of Governors Letters. Col. French his Friend. Cornwallis's Letters. Cabbin. Denham. Hamilton, Arrival in England. Get Employment. Ralph not. He is an Expence to me. Adventures in England. Write a Pamphlet and print 100. Schemes. Lyons. Dr Pemberton. My Diligence and yet poor thro Ralph. My Landlady. her Character. Wygate. Wilkes. Cibber. Plays. Books I borrowed. Preachers I heard. Redmayne. At Watts's— Temperance. Ghost,. Conduct and Influence among the Men, persuaded by Mr Denham to return with him to Philada.. & be his Clerk. Our Voyage. and Arrival. My resolutions in Writing. My Sickness. His Death. Found D. R married. Go to work again with Keimer. Terms. His ill Usage of me. My Resentment. Saying of Decow. My Friends at Burlington. Agreement with H Meredith to set up in Partnership. Do so. Success with the Assembly. Hamiltons Friendship. Sewells History. Gazette. Paper Money. Webb. Writing Busy Body. Breintnal. Godfrey. his Character.

Suit against us. Offer of my Friends Coleman and Grace. continue the Business and M. goes to Carolina. Pamphlet on Paper Money. Gazette from Keimer. Junto erected, its plan. Marry. Library erected. Manner of conducting the Project. Its plan and Utility. Children. Almanack. the Use I made of it. Great Industry. Constant Study. Fathers Remark and Advice upon Diligence. Carolina Partnership. Learn French and German. Journey to Boston after 10 years. Affection of my Brother. His Death and leaving me [p. 2] his Son. Art of Virtue. Occasion. City Watch. amended. Post Office. Spotswood. Bradfords Behaviour. Clerk of Assembly. Lose one of my Sons. Project of subordinate Junto's. Write occasionally in the papers. Success in Business. Fire Companys. Engines. Go again to Boston in 1743. See Dr Spence. Whitefield. My Connection with him. His Generosity to me. my returns. Church Differences. My part in them. Propose a College. not then prosecuted. Propose and establish a Philosophical Society. War. Electricity. my first knowledge of it. Partnership with D Hall &c. Dispute in Assembly upon Defence. Project for it. Plain Truth. its Success. 10.000 Men raised and Disciplined. Lotteries. Battery built. New Castle. My Influence in the Council. Colours, Devices and Motto's.— Ladies. Military Watch. Quakers. chosen of the common council. Put in the Commission of the Peace. Logan fond of me. his Library. Appointed post Master General. Chosen Assembly Man. Commissioner to treat with Indians at Carlisle. ↑ and at Easton. ↓ Project and establish Academy. Pamphlet on it. Journey to Boston. At Albany. Plan of Union of the Colonies. Copy of it. Remarks upon it. It fails and how. (Journey to Boston in 1754.) Disputes about it in our Assembly. My part in them. New Governor. Disputes with him. His Character and Sayings to me. Chosen Alderman. Project of Hospital my Share in it. Its Success. Boxes. Made a Commissioner of the treasury My Commission to defend the Frontier Counties. Raise Men & build Forts. Militia Law of my drawing. Made Colonel. Parade of my Officers. Offence to Proprietor. Assistance to Boston Ambassadors— Journey with Shirley &c.. Meet with Braddock. Assistance to him. To the Officers of his Army. Furnish him with Forage. His Concessions to me and Character of me. Success of my Electrical Experiments. Medal sent me per Royal Society and Speech of President. Dennys Arrival & Courtship to me. his Character. My Service to the Army in the Affair of Quarters. Disputes about the Proprietors Taxes continued. Project for paving the City. I am sent to England.] Negociation there. Canada delenda est. My Pamphlet. Its reception and Effect. Projects drawn from me concerning the Conquest. Acquaintance made and their Services to me. Mrs.. S.., Mr Small. Sir John P. Mr. Wood. Sargent Strahan and others. their Characters. Doctorate from Edinburg ↑ St. Andrews ↓ <F——d-> [p. 3] Doctorate from Oxford. Journey to Scotland. Lord Leicester. Mr. Prat.— DeGrey. Jackson. State of Affairs in England. Delays. Event. Journey into Holland and Flanders. Agency from Maryland. Sons Appointment. My Return. Allowance and thanks. Journey to Boston. John Penn Governor. My Conduct towards him. The Paxton Murders. My Pamphlet Rioters march to Philada... Governor retires to my House. My Conduct, <towards him. The Paxton Murders.> Sent out to the Insurgents—Turn them back. Little Thanks. Disputes revived. Resolutions against continuing under Proprietary Government. Another Pamphlet. Cool Thoughts. Sent again to England with Petition. Negociation there. Lord H. his Character. Agencies from New Jersey, Georgia, Massachusets. Journey into Germany 1766. Civilities received there. Gottingen Observations. Ditto into France in 1767. Ditto in 1769. Entertainment there at the Academy. Introduced to the King and the Mesdames. Mad. Victoria and Mrs. Lamagnon. Duc de Chaulnes, M Beaumont. Le Roy. Dali{t}bard. Nollet. See Journals. Holland. Reprint my papers and add many. Books presented to me <by> ↑from↓ many Authors. My Book translated into French. Lightning Kite. various Discoveries. My Manner of prosecuting that Study. King of Denmark invites me to Dinner. Recollect my Fathers Proverb. Stamp Act. My Opposition to it. Recommendation of J. Hughes. Amendment of it. Examination in Parliament. Reputation it gave me. Caress'd by Ministry. Charles Townsends Act. Opposition to it. Stoves and Chimney plates. ↑Armonica.↓ Accquaintance with Ambassadors. Russian Intimation. Writing in Newspapers. Glasses from Germany. Grant of Land in Nova Scotia. Sicknesses. Letters to America returned hither. the Consequences. Insurance Office. My Character. Costs me nothing to be civil to inferiors, a good deal to be submissive to superiors &c &c..

  Farce of perpetl. Motion
  Writing for Jersey Assembly.   verte

[p. 4] Hutchinson's Letters. Temple. Suit in Chancery, Abuse before the Privy Council.—Lord Hillsborough's Character. & Conduct. Lord Dartmouth. Negotiation to prevent the War.—Return to America. Bishop of St Asaph. Congress, Assembly. Committee of Safety. Chevaux de Frize.—Sent to Boston, to the Camp. To Canada. to <Gu> Lord Howe.— To France, Treaty, &c

Source: *The Autobiography of Benjamin Franklin: A Genetic Text*, ed. J. A. Leo Lemay and P. M. Zall (Knoxville: University of Tennessee Press, 1981), pp. 202–05. The headnote in French translates as follows: "Copy of a {Autograph} very curious Project of Bn. Franklin.—1st. Outline memorandum of his memoirs. The additions in red ink are in the hand of Franklin."

1319.8–9   a little . . . sake.]   Franklin first wrote, "because he left me no Choice," then canceled the phrase and substituted this one.

1319.26–27   Spectator.]   A canceled phrase following here indicates that "It was the Third."

1319.38   Stock of Words]   Franklin first wrote "Copia Verborum," then changed to the English phrase.

1322.26–27   *Men . . . forgot*]   Alexander Pope, *An Essay on Criticism* (1711), ll. 574–75, substituting "should" for "must."

1322.29 *To speak . . . Diffidence*] Pope, *An Essay on Criticism*, l. 567, substituting "To" for "And."

1322.30–31 "Immodest . . . Sense."] Wentworth Dillon, Earl of Roscommon, *An Essay on Translated Verse* (1684), ll. 113–14, substituting "Modesty" for "Decency."

1323.9–10 The Boston News Letter] *The Boston News-Letter* began publication in 1704; *The Boston Gazette* in 1719; *The American Weekly Mercury* (Philadelphia) later in 1719; and *The New-England Courant* in 1721.

1323.25–26 anonymous Paper] The first "Silence Dogood" essay (pp. 5–6 in the present volume).

1324.23 Author] James Franklin twice had serious troubles with the authorities. The first time he was imprisoned for nearly a month, June 12 to July 7, 1722; the second time he hid from the sheriff from January 24 to February 12, 1722/3.

1324.35–36 *that . . . Courant*] On January 16, 1722/3, the General Court resolved that James Franklin be forbidden to publish the *Courant* "except it be first supervised by the Secretary of the Province." The *Courant* first appeared under Benjamin Franklin's name on February 12, 1722/3. Franklin gave the "Rulers some Rubs" in his "Rules for *The New-England Courant*" and "To 'your Honour' " (pp. 44–48 in the present volume).

1328.34 Sunday morning] October 6, 1723.

1331.31 French Prophets] The Camisards, Protestant peasants of the Cévennes region of France, famous for their emotionalism.

1334.25 Impropriety of it;] Franklin first continued here, "and said he had advanc'd too much already to my Brother James," then canceled the clause.

1339.37 Glutton] Franklin first called Keimer a "Gormandizer," then changed it to "Glutton."

1342.15 *Pope* cur'd him] Alexander Pope included unfavorable references to Ralph in *The Dunciad* (1728).

1346.4 Woollaston's . . . Nature] See note 59.34–35.

1346.39 handsomely] Franklin offered to sell Sir Hans Sloane the purse in a letter of June 2, 1725.

1347.24 Young's Satires] Probably Edward Young's *The Universal Passion* (1725–28).

1349.1–2 mixing . . . Matter] By mixing his types, putting the manuscript pages in the wrong order, and breaking up the type he had already set.

1351.18 Chelsea to Blackfryars] Over three miles.

1351.22 Thevenot's . . . Positions] Melchisédec Thévenot, *The Art of Swimming* (1699).

1353.18 *Plan*] "Plan of Conduct" (p. 72 in the present volume).

1354.13 carried him off] After a long illness, Denham died on July 4, 1728.

1354.14 small Legacy] In an oral will, Denham forgave Franklin the £10 Franklin owed him for the return from London.

1355.7 Wages] Franklin first wrote "80 Pounds a Year," then canceled the phrase and wrote instead, "Wages so much higher . . ."

1359.8 Boyle's Lectures] The English scientist Robert Boyle (1627–91) endowed a lecture series against "notorious Infidels."

1359.21–25 *Whatever . . . above.*] John Dryden, *Oedipus* (1679), III, i, 244–48, though the first line (quoted accurately on p. 57 in the present volume) is taken from Alexander Pope, *An Essay on Man* (1733–34), Epistle I, l. 294.

1360.11–12 Religion.—] Franklin first continued here, "some foolish Intrigues with low Women excepted, which from the Expence were rather more inconvenient to me than to them." After changing "inconvenient" to "prejudicial," he canceled the clause entirely, but returned to the subject later (see p. 1371 in the present volume).

1361.17–18 Autumn . . . Year] In the fall of 1727.

1362.37 Distribution] Putting the letters back into their cases after the printing had been done.

1363.23 Friend] Franklin added "She Female" before "Friend," then canceled his revision.

1363.38 Busy Body] "The Busy-Body" appeared in Bradford's *American Weekly Mercury* from February 4, 1728, through September 25, 1729 (pp. 92–118 in the present volume).

1364.7 singular Number] Franklin had written "my Paper" at 1363.36–37, then changed it to "our Paper."

1364.15 spirited Remarks*] Franklin's "Remarks" appeared in *The Pennsylvania Gazette*, October 9, 1729, the second issue of the paper after he bought it from Keimer. He did not include the text of this essay in his manuscript. It is reprinted here from the Lemay–Zall *Genetic Text* (pp. 179–81, with the quotation marks added to correspond to Franklin's practice in a similar footnote at 1308.36 in the present volume).

1367.18 two long Letters] In *The Pennsylvania Gazette*, May 6 and 13, 1731.

1367.28–29   the Year 1729.]   The partnership was officially disbanded on July 4, 1730.

1368.8–9   *The Nature . . . Currency.*]   Pp. 119–35 in the present volume.

1372.14   Subscription Library]   The Library Company of Philadelphia was founded on July 1, 1731.

1372.30   Beginning]   Franklin first wrote here, "of gratifying the suppos'd Curiosity of my Son; what follows being . . . " After adding "and others of Posterity" after "Son," he canceled the entire clause.

1373.1   *Part Two*]   Franklin wrote the second section of the *Autobiography* in 1784 at Passy, France (as indicated on pp. 1379 and 1394 of the present volume).

1373.2   *Notes*]   The "Notes" consisted of a copy of the outline of topics that Franklin had made in 1771 for the *Autobiography*. See note 1316.22.

1374.5–1379.10   MY . . . VAUGHAN.]   Quotation marks around this letter, presumably added by William Temple Franklin (it is from his edition that the text of this letter derives), have been omitted.

1374.36   *Art of Virtue*]   See note 765.33.

1381.11–12   plucking . . . Owner.]   Franklin first wrote "returning the Reputation thus assumed to its right owner," then rewrote the clause.

1381.26–28   *"Seest . . . Men."*]   Proverbs 22:29.

1382.17   Presbyterian]   Franklin was raised as a member of Boston's Congregational Old South Church, but Presbyterianism was more similar to Congregationalism than were most religious denominations.

1383.32–33   *Articles . . . Religion*]   Pp. 83–90 in the present volume.

1384.11   our Interest]   Franklin first wrote "my Interest," and, in the next line, "my Slipping."

1387.5   *Form of the Pages.*]   In Franklin's manuscript, the lines of the chart are drawn in red ink; the words, letters, and dots are in black ink.

1388.8–11   *Here . . . happy.*]   Joseph Addison, *Cato* (1713), V, i, 15–18.

1388.13–15   *O Vitæ . . . anteponendus.*]   *Tusculan Disputations* 5. 2. 5 (several lines omitted). "O, Philosophy, guide of life! O teacher of virtue and corrector of vice. One day of virtue is better than an eternity of vice."

1388.33–38   *Father . . . Bliss!*]   James Thomson, *The Seasons*, "Winter," ll. 217–22.

1389   Chart]   In Franklin's manuscript, the lines of the chart are drawn in red ink; the words, numbers, and braces are in black ink.

1395.1   *Part Three*]   Franklin began to write this third part of the *Auto-*

biography in 1788 at home in Philadelphia, and continued it at intervals between then and May, 1789.

1397.34–35   connected Discourse]   "The Way to Wealth" (a title supplied by later editors) is printed in the present volume, pp. 1294–1303.

1398.12–15   Socratic . . . Sense.]   "A Man of Sense" (pp. 244–48 in the present volume).

1398.15   Discourse . . . denial]   "Self-Denial Not the Essence of Virtue" (pp. 242–44 in the present volume).

1405.16   Paper]   "On Protection of Towns from Fire" (pp. 239–42 in the present volume).

1405.25   Articles of Agreement]   Drawn up on December 7, 1736.

1409.36   *litera . . . manet*]   The full proverb is *Vox audita perit, littera scripta manet*. "The spoken word passes away, the written word remains."

1411.7   Paper]   "A Proposal for Promoting Useful Knowledge Among the British Plantations in America" (pp. 295–97 in the present volume).

1416.5   *or other Grain*]   The Assembly so voted on July 25, 1745, although the amount was 4,000 rather than 3,000.

1418.19–20   *Proposals . . . Pennsylvania*]   Pp. 323–44 in the present volume.

1419.1   Providence]   Franklin first wrote "Fortune," then changed it to "Providence."

1420.27   Dr Spence's]   Archibald Spencer.

1420.40   magic . . . circles]   See pp. 450, 452 in the present volume.

1423.3–4   writing . . . Newspapers]   "Appeal for the Hospital" (pp. 361–67 in the present volume.)

1423.23–36   "And be . . . same."]   Franklin presented the bill to the Assembly on January 23, 1750/1.

1429.31   displac'd]   Franklin was fired on January 30, 1774, for his pro-American writings and actions, and especially for surreptitiously obtaining the letters of Massachusetts Governor Thomas Hutchinson and sending them back to America. Since he did not bring the *Autobiography* down to 1774, the topic does not recur.

1429.38–40   Degree . . . Compliment.]   The Harvard degree, July 27, 1753, was first; the Yale degree was September 12; these were the highest degrees Harvard and Yale then awarded.

1430.18   Plan]   "The Albany Plan of Union," pp. 378–82 in the present volume.

1431.27–28 *"Look . . . pursue."*] John Dryden's translation of Juvenal's tenth satire, ll. 1–2, in *The Satires of Decimus Junius Juvenalis. Translated into English Verse. By Mr. Dryden, And several other Eminent Hands . . .* (1693).

1433.7–8 Idea of Sancho Panza] Cervantes, *Don Quixote* (Part 1, chapter 29). Sancho Panza grieves at the idea of governing blacks until he realizes that he can sell them.

1439.24 D°] "Ditto."

1439.29 C.ʷᵗ] "Hundredweight."

1445.14–15 Dialogue] "Dialogue Between X, Y, and Z, Concerning the Present State of Affairs in Philadelphia" (pp. 410–420 in the present volume).

1452.37 Dr Spence] See note 1420.27.

1453.17 two Lectures] "Course of Experiments" (pp. 355–57 in the present volume).

1454.3 print . . . Pamphlet] *Experiments and Observations on Electricity* (1751).

1465.8 1757.] Franklin interrupted his writing at this point and began again sometime after November 13, 1789, with "As soon . . . "

1466.9 Clause in a Bill] The bill containing this clause died when Parliament adjourned in 1744 without passing it.

1466.13–16 Conduct . . . themselves.] The Declaration Act of 1766 asserted Parliament's right to legislate for the colonies.

1469.4 Execution] Franklin stopped writing here, probably shortly before his death on April 17.

Index

Contents of this volume are shown in capitals and small capitals.

CATALOGING INFORMATION

Franklin, Benjamin, 1706–1790.
  Writings.

  (The Library of America ; 37)
Other title information: Boston and London, 1722–1726,
Philadelphia, 1726–1757, London, 1757–1775, Paris, 1776–1785,
Philadelphia, 1785–1790, Poor Richard's almanack, 1733–1758,
The autobiography.
Bibliography, pp. 1498–1512.
Includes index.
1. United States—Politics and government—Colonial period,
ca. 1600–1775. 2. United States—Politics and government—
Revolution, 1775–1783. I. Lemay, J. A. Leo (Joseph A. Leo),
1935–   . II. Title. III. Title: The autobiography of Benjamin
Franklin. IV. Series.
E302.F82   1987   973.2   87–3303
ISBN 0–940450–29–1 (alk. paper)

This book is set in 10 point Linotron Galliard,
a face designed for photocomposition by Matthew Carter
and based on the sixteenth-century face Granjon. The paper
is acid-free Ecusta Nyalite and meets the requirements for perma-
nence of the American National Standards Institute. The binding
material is Brillianta, a 100% woven rayon cloth made by
Van Heek-Scholco Textielfabrieken, Holland. The com-
position is by Haddon Craftsmen, Inc., and The
Clarinda Company. Printing and binding
by R. R. Donnelley & Sons Company.
Designed by Bruce Campbell.